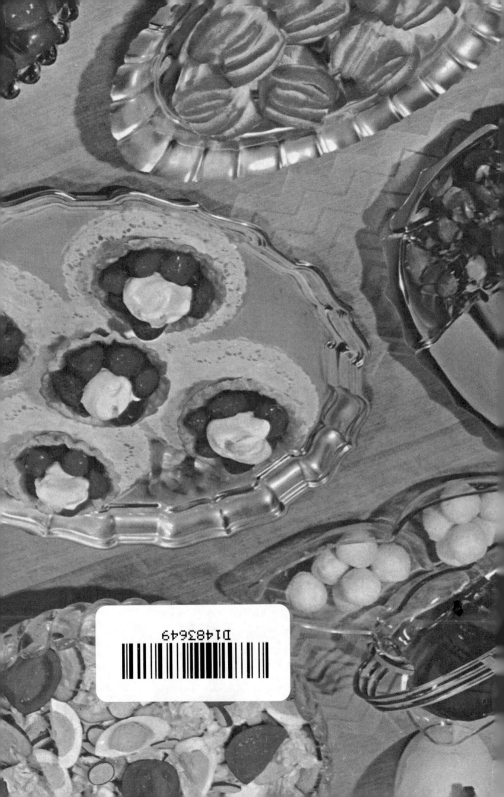

Meta Given's

MODERN ENCYCLOPEDIA OF COOKING

A modern cook book, complete in every detail, brings the latest developments in home economics into your kitchen for a simpler, better and richer life.

REVISED EDITION
VOLUME TWO

J. G. FERGUSON PUBLISHING COMPANY · CHICAGO

Foreign Foods

COOKING ADVENTURES WITH FOREIGN SPECIALTIES

Bread and Cakes

Crusty French Bread, 267
Kolachy, 283
Schnecken, 287
Jule Kake, 291
Kuchens, 291
Streusel Coffee Cake, 293
Swedish Tea Ring, 294
Garlic Bread, 295
Hungarian Poppy Seed Rolls, 296
Swedish Limpa Bread, 300
Bohemian Rye Bread, 301
Brioche, 304
Stollen, 307
Blitz Torte, 375
Dobos Torte, 376
Schaum Torte, 378
Lebkuchen, Dark and Light, 497-8
Mandel Kakas, 499
Pfefferneusse, Dark and Light, 498-9
Springerlie, 500

Cereals

Ravioli, 432
Pizza, 446
Polenta, 446
Lasagne, 449

Desserts and Pastry

Chocolate Pots de Crème, 528, Coffee Pots de Crème, 529
Crème Brûlée, 530
Charlotte Russe, 578
Biscuit Tortoni, 601

Crêpes Suzette, 610
Swedish Rosettes, 612
Strudel, 613
Napoleon Slices, 936
Vol au Vents, 938
French Pies, 987
Rod Grod (Danish Red Pudding), 630

Eggs, Meat and Fish

Soufflés, 678
Gnocchi, 1376
Chinese Egg Rolls, 683
Egg Foo Yeung, 684
Fillet of Sole and Oyster Parmesan, 706
Pheasant in Dough, 770
Pheasant with Chives Dressing, 772
Hasen Pfeffer, 774
Beef Stroganoff, 808
Sauerbraten, 811
Lot-ju-kair-ngow, 816
Swedish Meat Balls, 827
Tamale Pie, 833
Irish Stew, 848
Chinese Pork, 869
Chinese Chop Suey, 870, 882, 897
Blanquette of Veal, 876
Veal Parmigiano, 880
Veal Scallopini, 880
Veal Sub Gum, 881
Lamb and Kidney Kabobs, 900
Steak and Kidney Pie, 901
Italian Style Liver and Macaroni, 905
Liver à la Gourmet, 905

Poultry

Chicken Cacciatore, 1045
Italian Fricassee, 1048
Pollo Con Arros, 1053
Risotto Milanaise, 1054
Chicken Wor Mein, 1056
Moravian Chicken, 1057

Sauces

Allemande, 1250
Béchamel, 1251
Guacamole, 1255
Mornay, 1258
Remoulade, 1260
Velouté, 1261
Vinaigrette, 1262

Soups

Minestra, 1290
Minestrone, 1293
Black Bean Soup, 1271
Liver Dumpling Soup, 1292
Vichyssoise, 1298
Curried Vichyssoise, 1299
Bouillabaisse, 1265
French Onion, 1269

Vegetables

Polish Beets, 1326
Cheese Crusted Celery Root (Celeriac), 1339
Schultzie's Sauerkraut and Dumplings, 1393
Swedish Brown Beans, 1323

737

Frying with Deep Fat

A LARGE number of foods may be fried successfully and almost all are popular because of their crisp, flavorful crust which cannot be duplicated with any other cooking method. The secret of success lies in following a few simple rules. Even an amateur can do beautiful frying if she prepares the food carefully, chooses a fat with a high smoking temp, and uses a frying thermometer.

Deep-fat frying is cooking in hot fat heated to a temp ranging from 325° to 400° F, the exact temp used depending upon the food being cooked. Hydrogenated lard and vegetable fat are most satisfactory for frying because they can be heated to a reasonably high temp without smoking or burning. Regular lard has a fairly low smoking temp. The newer hydrogenated lard, however, has as high a smoking temp as any of the hydrogenated vegetable shortenings, and this lard and the hydrogenated vegetable shortenings are considered the best for all frying purposes.

When fat is heated to the smoking point or beyond, acrolein is developed which gives the fat an acrid flavor and an irritating odor. Once fat is overheated, it should not be used again for frying.

Butter should never be used for deep-fat frying. Ordinarily, it cannot be heated beyond 248° F without burning. Even when thoroughly purified, it cannot be heated beyond 275° F which is lower than a desirable frying temp.

The most reliable check on the temp of the heated fat is a frying thermometer clipped to the kettle throughout the frying process. The well-known bread test was once considered helpful, but now we know it is not a dependable temp check. To make the bread test, a ⅝-inch cube of bread was dropped into the fat. If in 30 seconds it acquired a delicate golden color, it was thought to indicate the approximate temp for good frying. The difficulty with this procedure is that any variation in size or moisture of the cube will affect the browning time. Besides, the test gives only a general indication of the temp of the fat in the beginning; it does not check the temp variations during frying. Fat which is too hot will scorch the food and it will not be cooked throughout. The fat itself will become "smelly" and unsatisfactory for future use. If the fat is not hot enough, the food will become fat-soaked, the fat penetrating before any crust has a chance to form. The kettle used in frying should be big enough and deep enough so that when not quite half-filled with the fat, the quantity will be ample for efficient frying. If it is too full, any excessive bubbling caused by the food or a slight tip of the kettle might cause spilling or overflowing and endanger the cook. A deep kettle with a

738

curved bottom is desirable. Any sediment from the food being fried will sink into this curved bottom.

A wire basket or skimmer to lift food into and out of the kettle is practically a necessity if much deep fat frying is done.

Too much food should never be put into the kettle at any one time because the result will be excessive bubbling, the food will cool the fat too much, and a crust will form too slowly to prevent the food from becoming grease-soaked. When the food is cooked to the desired degree, it should be lifted out of the fat, drained for a moment over the kettle and then placed on absorbent paper for further draining. Salt should be sprinkled immediately over the hot, drained food (salt should never be allowed to get into the fat in the frying kettle). Regular paper toweling is ideal for the draining.

A high quality shortening or lard which is not overheated and which has been strained regularly may be used as many as 6 to 8 times with cooling and re-heatings between. It should be strained through cleansing tissue or a cloth fitted into a funnel or strainer each time it is used to eliminate small particles of food which will influence color and flavor of future fried products and which will also make the fat more liable to burn. Sliced potato does not help to clarify fat but the water in the potatoes increases the free fatty acids. Fat can be readily clarified only by industrial methods. When fatty acids increase, the keeping quality of fat is reduced and the smoking point is lowered.

Many homemakers avoid fried foods because they feel they should be eaten immediately after cooking. However, if properly fried and thoroughly drained on absorbent paper, they may be kept warm for as long as a half hr in a slow oven. Such foods as doughnuts and crullers can be kept for days and reheated in a paper sack just like bread for a product almost as good as when fresh.

GENERAL DIRECTIONS

The way to fry is as follows:

Step 1. Prepare the food for frying and let stand at room temp while the fat is heating. Allowing the food to warm up slightly helps it to fry more successfully.

Step 2. Melt enough fat in the kettle to not quite half fill it. A 3-qt frying kettle and 2 lbs shortening were used in the development of the following recipes.

Step 3. Next *clip the thermometer onto side of kettle,* making sure the bulb is below the surface of the melted fat but does not touch the bottom of the kettle.

Step 4. Lower frying basket into the kettle and begin to heat the fat. Watch to see that the temp does not rise above that required for frying.

Step 5. Bring prepared food to stove on a tray and have an *extra tray spread with paper* toweling also on the stove.

Step 6. Lift up frying basket with one hand and place food in the basket with the other.

Step 7. Lower basket into the fat. If temp drops fast, increase heat; if it shows a tendency to rise above that which is needed, lower heat. Proceed according to directions in each recipe.

Note: For Electric Deep-Fat Fryers use manufacturers' directions.

COOKING ADVENTURES WITH DEEP-FAT FRYING

Appetizers

Fried Cheese Balls, 202

Breads

Banana Doughnuts, 288
Buttermilk Doughnuts, 288
Sour Cream Doughnuts, 289
Crullers, 289
Bismarcks or Jelly Doughnuts, 289
Raised Doughnuts, 290
Crisp Fried Noodles, 431

Croquettes

Hominy Cheese Croquettes, 502
Rice Cheese Croquettes, 503
Swiss Cheese Croquettes, 503
Egg Croquettes, 503
Crabmeat Croquettes, 504
Salmon Croquettes, 504
Lobster Croquettes, 504

Ham Croquettes, 505
Lamb Croquettes, 505
Liver and Bacon Croquettes, 505
Sweetbread Croquettes, 506
Veal Croquettes, 506
Chicken Croquettes, 507
Chickeny Chicken Croquettes, 507
Turkey Croquettes, 508

Fritters

Brain, 893
Corn, 1350
Fruit, 549
Oyster, 723
Parsnip, 1365
Meat and Fish Batter, 1349
Vegetable Batter, 1349
Fruit Batter, 548-549

Fish—Meat—Poultry

Fried Smelts, 708

Cod Fish Balls, 714
French-Fried Fish, 736
French-Fried Soft Shelled Crabs, 716
French-Fried Frogs' Legs, 719
French-Fried Oysters, 724
French-Fried Scallops, 725
French-Fried Shrimp, 727
French-Fried Liver, 904
Deep-Fat-Fried Chicken, 1041-2

Vegetables

French-Fried Cauliflower, 1337
French-Fried Egg Plant, 1348
French-Fried Onions, 1361
French-Fried Parsnips, 1364
French-Fried Potatoes, 1375
French-Fried Hubbard Squash, 1400

FRITTER BATTERS

For fruit or dessert fritters, see pages 549-550.
For meat, fish, or vegetable fritters, see page 1349.
Read also general directions for frying, and hints on these pages.

Game

Too many people let their preconceived notions rather than actual experience influence their opinion of game meat. This unfair prejudice has been responsible for a considerable waste of animals that are killed each year in the hunting seasons. Sometimes the fault is with the hunter; he is either careless in shooting or indifferent about cleaning and dressing carefully and immediately. Other times it is the fault of the cook and either because of a lack of experience or skill, the game is not cooked appropriately. If you fall into the above category, this chapter is "tailor-made" for you. And even if you have eaten and enjoyed game meat all your life, there will be information about hunting, cleaning, dressing and cooking that may be new and helpful. This chapter is dedicated to prove that game can be the PIÈCE DE RÉSISTANCE in even the most elegant company dinner.

★　　★　　★　　★

TOO often the game that is killed each year by hunters all over the country fails to reach the table in its most edible form. Either incompetent handling after killing makes it unappetizing in appearance, odor or flavor, or it is improperly cooked. Those who try to cook these unskillfully prepared animals, or to eat these poorly cooked dishes are led to believe that game can never be as attractive as domestic meat. However, when game is properly bled, cleaned, stored and cooked, it will appeal to those who have previously objected to it, and it will have still greater appeal to those who have always enjoyed it.

A book of this type cannot possibly discuss in detail the handling of all kinds of game, but it can recommend certain basic principles for dressing and cooking that will enable even the inexperienced to prepare clean and attractive meat, and to cook it interestingly and deliciously. The main factors which influence the quality of game meat are: the health of the animal, prompt and adequate bleeding, careful dressing and evisceration, thorough removal of hair or feathers, shot areas, and in some cases fat and scent glands, efficient scrubbing and washing and finally proper storage and cooking methods.

Note: If you haven't a hunter in the family, you can still secure game from various commercial breeders. Much of the game used in the development of recipes in this chapter was obtained from one of these breeders, Mr. Robert Devore of the Chain of Lakes Game Farm, McHenry, Illinois.

THE HEALTH OF THE ANIMAL

The health of any kind of game can be ascertained generally by an observing hunter. Animals or birds with clean, sleek coats that are fleet of foot or wing show dependable signs of being in good health. Most game is hardy and healthy. One exception is the wild rabbit which may have *tularemia* or *rabbit fever*. This wide spread disease is transmitted from the rabbit to man by the bite of a louse or tick that has been infected from a rabbit, or by direct contact in handling, skinning, or disjointing the infected animal. A form of the disease may also occur from eating the inadequately cooked meat of a sick rabbit.

Usually the disease is not fatal to man, but it is serious enough to warrant taking special precautions. However, tularemia is often fatal to rabbits, so an infected animal is a sick one. He *looks* and *acts* sick. Hunters should never shoot slow moving or sick acting rabbits for food. A rabbit slow to react to either hunters or dogs should be viewed with suspicion, and any contact with a suspicious rabbit should be completely avoided. Anyone handling rabbits is strongly advised to wear sound rubber gloves when cleaning, skinning, bleeding, or preparing for cooking even rabbits that have not appeared sickly. The disease is believed to be transmitted to man mainly through the handling of the rabbits, since it usually starts with a lesion on the hands. Therefore rubber gloves provide simple and adequate protection. Once the meat is thoroughly cooked, it is safe to handle and to eat.

PROMPT AND ADEQUATE BLEEDING

Those who are experienced in the dressing of animals know it is good practice to thoroughly bleed them as soon after killing as possible. Animal Husbandry Departments in our colleges and all commercial meat packing plants recommend and practice the thorough bleeding of all animals and poultry, because it not only results in better appearance, but also in better keeping quality. Without exception, the same method of bleeding animals is used—as soon as the animals are stunned (or shot in the case of game), the jugular veins are severed so that the blood may escape quickly. Domestic poultry is killed and bled differently, p 1030 but since game birds are always dead or nearly so, they should be bled the same as animals by cutting the jugular vein. If the animal or bird is then hung up, or in the case of larger animals, placed so the head and shoulders are below the body, the blood drains very rapidly from the carcass. Thorough bleeding can result only when a large blood vessel is opened immediately after killing while the animal is still warm. In a very short time after death, the blood begins to coagulate in the vessels and any attempt to bleed the animal after this change sets in is bound to be slow and incomplete.

This leads to the question of using for food animals that are found dead in traps. In most cases, marsh hare or muskrat which are trapped for their pelts, die in the trap and their pelts are removed before there is any attempt to bleed them. As a rule, when such animals are to be eaten, they are soaked in salt water overnight to remove the blood, and the carcasses improve greatly in appearance. However, muskrat would be much more popular if only the animals found alive in the traps and killed and bled immediately were used for food. The meat is naturally dark, fine-grained and soft, and when it is not bled, these qualities are exaggerated and give many people an unfair opinion of this meat.

The only controversy about the superior quality of thoroughly bled meat over unbled occurs when the use of unbled game birds is discussed. This practice is defended so strongly by some hunters that they go so far as to say that birds that are bled never have as fine a flavor as those that are not bled. However, equally sophisticated people take the opposite view. For all other game, there is no question that thorough bleeding improves the appearance, flavor, and keeping quality.

Since a sharp knife is the only necessary tool, the modern hunter can easily bleed his kill thoroughly. Small game are hung up by the feet; large game can be placed on a slope so that the neck and shoulders are lower than the rest of the body and the jugular vein can be pierced in very little time and with very little trouble.

CAREFUL DRESSING AND EVISCERATION

The necessity for dressing game immediately after it is killed depends on the weather and the type of game. Hunters seem agreed that game birds may be carried safely for a day in cold weather without being eviscerated, but that it is necessary to clean out at once after bleeding the abdominal cavities of large game, such as deer the same day as killed and all small mammals as soon as possible. If the day is warm, all game should be drawn immediately. Washing the inside of the animals or birds should not be done until they can be refrigerated.

Game birds are often aged to develop the "high flavor" that is preferred by many people. The birds are drawn but the feathers left on. A lump of charcoal is put inside the bird, and powdered charcoal thoroughly sifted into the feathers. The bird is then hung in a protected *cool* place until the characteristic flavor is developed (about 5 days). A shorter hanging period is recommended for game birds that are to be eaten by those who do not care for this "high flavor." For this shorter hanging period, the birds should hang in a *cool* protected place with the feathers left on for about 2 days. This recommendation is based on the principle that all meat for human consumption should be allowed to go through the stages of rigor mortis and the subsequent softening. The three important stages are described briefly as follows:

1. *Fresh killed.* The flesh is soft and juicy. As long as it retains animal heat, it should not be eaten. Thorough cooling immediately after killing makes the meat edible but not at its peak of flavor and tenderness.

2. *Rigor mortis.* The meat at this point is hard and tough and is not suitable for cooking.

3. *Aged.* When the effects of rigor mortis begin to disappear, the meat again becomes soft, tender, juicy and is best for cooking. A longer period of hanging is known as "aging" and develops the "high flavor" highly prized by many and strongly disliked by others.

EVISCERATION

The removal of the viscera from any animal or bird needs to be done with such care that no part of the tract or glands is broken open to release any of the contents. This requires some knowledge of the anatomy. In either the bird or the animal, the viscera is attached at one end to the esophagus and the windpipe and at the other end to the body vents. To remove the viscera, the first thing to do is to make an opening in the body large enough to remove the entire viscera intact. In an animal, this means splitting the underside of the body from the neck all the way down. In a bird, it means removing the crop first, then making a slit just below the breastbone through to the cavity and down to and around the vent. See illus. p 1032. The viscera is carefully loosened at any point where it adheres to the lining of the thoracic cavity. This is most efficiently done with bare hands or a rubber gloved hand. When completely loosened, the whole unbroken viscera can be lifted out. When drawn animals cannot be refrigerated for a few hours, the cavity should not be washed, but may be wiped out with a clean cloth, leaves or grass. As soon as refrigeration is possible, the inside cavity should be washed in cold water, then allowed to drain thoroughly.

REMOVAL OF SHOT AREAS

Some hunters insist that game flesh which is permeated with shot has a better flavor than that which has not been shot. However, most authorities on cooking and dressing game will not concur with this opinion. The mangled holes where shot enters the carcass or "blood shot" areas are unsightly in either the raw or cooked meat and these areas deteriorate and develop *off-flavors rapidly.* The presence of shot in the cooked meat also makes it unpleasant and even rather hazardous to eat. Hair and feathers are carried into the flesh with the shot and if not removed, they greatly reduce the appetite appeal of the meat. Whenever possible, therefore, the shot area and any feathers or hair should be removed immediately after bleeding with a sharp pointed knife, and any clotted blood should be squeezed out. With game birds, however, that do not have the feathers removed at once, it is not possible to remove all the shot. As the birds are eviscerated, some of the shot that may have traveled into the body cavity or have broken bones may be discovered and removed. The remaining shot wounds must wait until the feathers or skin are removed. When game is shot up badly, it is usually a waste of time to try to bring it to a state of edibility. It is possible to soak it in salt water long enough to drain out most of the clotted blood, but it also draws out much of the fine flavor.

REMOVAL OF FEATHERS

Game birds may be dressed by dry or wet picking or skinning. Dry picking is very tedious and for most people it is impractical. Wet picking is quick and when done properly, both fine appearance and excellent flavor may be retained. Since birds differ in the tenderness of the skin and coarseness of feathers, it is necessary to use water of different temperatures to obtain satisfactory results. Pheasants, grouse and quail have fairly tender skins and should be dipped in water heated to just 130° F. Mallard ducks require water heated from 150° to 160° F for the feathers to be removed most efficiently. The large Brazilian ducks require still hotter water, from 165° to 170° F. A thermometer is essential in order that the exact temp of the water will be known. The birds are dipped up and down in the hot water until the coarse wing and tail feathers can be pulled out with ease. Then the bird is wrapped immediately in several folds of sacking or muslin and allowed to steam a few minutes. The feathers can then be removed quickly and cleanly by beginning at the tail end and grasping a handful of feathers, then pushing the feathers out and away from you. This motion is in the opposite direction from the lay of the feathers and is less likely to tear the skin than if the pulling is done in the same direction the feathers lay.

Birds that are badly shot up are often skinned to obtain a cleaner and more attractive looking surface. But this skinning removes the fat and the cooked bird does not retain its juice nor have as fine a flavor and appearance as birds with the skin intact.

After ducks or geese are wet picked, the skin will reveal a thick covering of down that must be removed. It helps to first singe the bird (pass it quickly through a blue flame to remove both hairs and down), but the only effective way of completing the job is to sit down with tweezers and a sharp knife and pick and scrape until a clean "downless" and "pin-feather-less" skin is obtained. This takes patience and perseverance but it is absolutely necessary if the cooked duck is to be thoroughly enojyed. Pheasants, quail and grouse are not covered with down, but occasionally they have pin-feathers that must be patiently removed with tweezers and paring knife in the same way.

REMOVAL OF FUR

All fur-bearing animals should be eviscerated at once and skinned as soon as possible. It is said that a good hunter may be judged by the condition of the carcass he brings in: there should be no bits of lung or foreign material clinging to the inside of the carcass and the outer flesh should be free from any hair. In skinning all animals, it is possible to carefully fold back the skin without letting the hair touch the meat. This is important because the hair carries with it odors from the sweat glands, etc., and may give a strong flavor to the meat. The hair also clings to the flesh and is almost impossible to remove by wiping or washing. All shot and blood clots should be cut out at once, and the carcass cooled promptly. The carcass should be chilled for at least 2 or 3 days. At the end of this time, it should be wiped thoroughly with a damp cloth, and washed on the inside with cold water, or water acidulated with lemon juice (1 lemon to each qt of water). Then it should be cut and stored properly or cooked according to the individual recipe.

REMOVAL OF FAT AND GLANDS

Many fur-bearing animals that are used for food will have a strong "gamey" flavor unless the fat just under the skin and the glands that are concealed under this fat are removed. There are four sets of these glands or "kernels" on the legs: two are found under the forelegs and two in each thigh. They are brownish, yellow or red in color and oval or round in shape. Glands of this type are also found along the small of the back. Squirrels, possum, coon, beaver, muskrat, bear and deer have these kernels or glands. The thorough removal of all the fat will also remove the scent glands and will assure a more mild flavor in the cooked game.

SCRUBBING AND WASHING

When the feathers, down and shot are removed, the birds should have a baking soda scrub. Rub the soda well into the skin, and using a damp cloth, give the skin the same kind of a scrubbing you would give a dirty but tender-faced boy. Rinse well in clear water, remove any tiny bits of viscera from the inside, wash inside with clear water, then drain, dry and chill until ready for cooking. After animal carcasses have chilled for at least 2 days, they should be washed thoroughly inside and out with clear water and then wiped carefully with a clean damp cloth to remove any clinging hair. It is never advisable to wash birds or animals after they are cut into smaller pieces.

PROPER STORAGE AND COOKING METHODS

Game for immediate use should be loosely covered in a dish and stored in the refrigerator like any other fresh meat. It should not be allowed to freeze or be left uncovered to dry out on the surface. Game for future use may be stored in a home, low-temp freezing unit, or a commercial freezer locker and kept in perfect condition for several months. Game birds and small animals may be left whole; large animals should be divided into the usual cuts similar to veal or beef, p 801. Freezing of game is done the same as the freezing of meat.

Game is cooked either by dry heat (roasting, broiling, etc.) or by moist heat (braising, stewing, etc.). As a rule, game is less tender and more dry than a corresponding cut or kind of domesticated meat, but like domestic meat, the cut and age of the animal determine the method of cooking that will be most suitable. Since the age and cut is sometimes difficult to determine, it is generally better to overcook a young tender meat than to take a chance on undercooking a tough one. The cuts of the large animals— venison, elk, bear, etc., look very much like the corresponding cuts of beef and can be recognized in this way. Young tender birds and the steaks and chops from young animals may be broiled, fried and roasted. The older birds and the cuts with more connective tissue from the larger animals may be stewed, braised, ground or made into soup. Game meat is usually leaner than domestic and is improved by the addition of lard, suet or other fat. The older method of "roasting" with a cover and with the addition of small amounts of water (now correctly called braising) seems to be more suitable for game than uncovered roasting. Recipes for cooking the various game birds and animals can be found in the following pages. These recipes have been especially developed to appeal to the veteran game gourmet as well as to the uninitiated family who receives their first wild game brought home by the proud hunter.

ANTELOPE

The flesh of antelope is delicious when properly prepared and cooked. The meat is similar to that of deer and elk except that it is leaner. The tender cuts can be used for steaks and roasts but they will either require continued basting with fat or "larding," p 164. When such basting or larding is not practical, braising will produce the most excellent results. Most recipes for the cuts of venison and elk can be used with similar cuts of antelope.

BEAR

The bear carcass resembles that of beef except the fat is exceptionally strong flavored and the lean tissue is not so tender as a beef of similar age. The carcass is divided into cuts much like beef. It is very important to remove the scent glands, see p 746, when the animal is skinned. All the fat should be removed before cooking and butter or other shortening used for browning or for basting the meat as it cooks. Any beef or deer recipe can be followed successfully for the cooking of the different cuts of bear meat if the fat is carefully removed before cooking.

BEAR LOIN STEAKS

2 loin steaks, 2½ lbs, ⅝ to
   ¾-inch thick
1 tbsp butter *or* margarine,
   melted

2 tsp lemon juice
1¼ tsp salt
   Generous dash of pepper
½ cup boiling water

Wipe steaks clean with a damp cloth. Trim off all the fat because it is strong flavored. This leaves about 1½ lbs lean steak. Place steak on a hot, greased broiler rack set 4 inches from heat. Combine butter and lemon juice and brush over top of steaks. Sprinkle with half of the salt and pepper. Broil 7 to 8 min. Turn steaks, brush with remaining lemon-butter and remaining salt and pepper. Broil another 7 or 8 min for well-done steaks. Remove from broiler to platter. Drizzle ½ cup water over rack and scrape down the residue into the drip pan. Remove rack. Stir gravy until well blended; reheat to boiling. Pour over hot steaks and serve immediately. 4 to 5 servings.

Note: If steaks seem tough, the meat may be pounded or diced as in preparation for Cubed Steak.

BEAVER

Beaver meat is much like that of the muskrat. The flesh is dark, fine grained, tender and soft. This animal also has kernels or scent glands that are found between the forelegs, under the thighs and along the spine in the small of the back. They should be removed immediately after the skin has been removed, taking care not to cut into them. Beaver fat has a strong flavor and odor and should be completely stripped off before cooking. One way to make beaver more mild in flavor is to cover it with boiling water and add 1 tbsp each of baking soda and black pepper, then simmer for ten to fifteen min, drain and cook in the usual way.

ROAST BEAVER*

Take pains to remove every speck of fat on the surface, soak in vinegar water overnight (¼ cup vinegar to enough water to cover the meat). Wash in cold water, place in roaster and cut several slits in the lean meat. Sprinkle with salt and pepper and put 4 strips of fresh side pork ½-inch thick over the slits and dust with a little flour. Put about ¼ cup of water in pan and roast with lid on until half done. Add more water if needed to prevent pan from going dry. Cut very fine, equal parts of onion, celery and carrots, enough to fill one cup and sprinkle over the meat. Finish roasting with the lid off until meat is tender. Make gravy by adding water and flour to the juices and vegetables in the pan, p 800. Serve at once. Beaver should be cooked until the meat almost falls off the bones.

Note: Roast beaver in moderate oven (350° F).

*Courtesy of Mrs. Blaine Brannan, Cusino State Game Area, Official Bulletin, Mich. Dept. of Conservation.

ROAST BEAVER À LA MICHIGAN*

1 beaver
    Baking soda
    Salt

Sliced onions
Strips of bacon *or* salt
pork

Remove all surface fat from beaver. Cover meat with a weak solution of soda and water (1 tsp soda to 1 qt of water). Parboil by simmering gently for 10 min. Drain, place meat in roaster, sprinkle with salt, cover with sliced onions, strips of bacon, and roast in moderate oven (350° F) until well done. Serve at once. Beaver should be cooked until the meat almost falls off the bones.

DEER OR VENISON

Deer meat is one of the most delicious of all big game animals. It is much like beef except that the lean is sweeter and the fat is stronger. The scent glands should be removed as soon as the deer is skinned, see p 746. Before the different cuts are cooked, all strong flavored fat should be removed. Any cut corresponding to beef can be cooked by any good beef recipe adapted to the particular cut.

BRAISED VENISON OR ELK CHOPS IN MUSHROOM GRAVY

4 good-sized loin chops,
    about 1½ lb
1¾ tsp salt
1⁄16 tsp pepper
3 tbsp butter *or* margarine

1 cup water
10½ oz can mushroom soup
1 tsp sherry
2 drops tabasco *or* other hot
sauce

Wipe chops clean with a damp cloth and trim off any strong-smelling fat. Sprinkle chops with salt and pepper. Use a skillet with tight-fitting cover. Brown chops slowly (uncovered) on both sides in heated butter. Add ¼ cup of the water, cover and simmer 15 min, then add ¼ cup more water and again cover and simmer 15 min. Next add the rest of the water and the soup. Cover and continue cooking very slowly for half an hr. Last add sherry and tabasco sauce. Serve at once. 4 servings.

*Courtesy of *Good Eating From Woods and Fields*—Michigan State College Extension Division, cooperating with Michigan Dept. of Conservation, Lansing, Mich.

BARBECUED VENISON TENDERLOIN

1 deer tenderloin, 1¼ lb   ½ cup water
2 tbsp butter *or* shortening   2 tsp vinegar
Barbecue Sauce: 1½ tsp salt
  1 cup catchup   ¼ to ½ tsp Worcestershire,
  2 tbsp grated onion   as desired
  ½ cup chopped celery

Cut tenderloin into slices 1¾-inch thick (about 6). Trim off any strong fat or tough membrane. Heat butter in a skillet and brown slices of deer quickly. Meanwhile, combine remaining ingredients and pour over hot meat. Place uncovered in a moderate oven (350° F) for 1 hr. Baste meat occasionally with the barbecue sauce and turn once during the baking. 6 servings.

BROILED TENDERLOIN OF VENISON

2¼ lb deer tenderloin   2 tbsp butter *or* margarine
2¼ tsp salt   ½ to ⅔ cup hot water
Pepper

Wipe tenderloin clean with a damp cloth and cut into 1¾-inch thick slices (about 10). Remove any strong-smelling fat or tough membrane and flatten slightly with a rolling pin. Sprinkle with salt and pepper and place on a hot, greased broiler rack 3 to 4 inches from the heat. Broil for 7 min on each side for medium rare. Remove from broiler, add some of the butter to each slice of deer. To make gravy, drizzle water over broiler rack and scrape any residue through to drip pan. Reheat and boil 2 or 3 min if a more concentrated gravy is desired. Serve immediately. 10 servings.

PAN-BROILED VENISON CHOPS

5 venison loin chops, cut   Dash of pepper
  ½ to ¾-inch thick,   ¼ cup butter *or* margarine
  approximately 1¾ lb   ¼ cup hot water
1¼ tsp salt

Wipe chops clean with a damp cloth. Trim off any strong-smelling fat. Then sprinkle with salt and pepper. Heat butter in skillet. Brown chops slowly on both sides, then lower heat and cook for 5 min on one side. Turn and cook on the other side for 5 min. Remove to a hot platter and cover to keep hot. Add the hot water and thoroughly scrape loose all brown residue from bottom of pan; heat to boiling and pour over the meat or into a separate hot gravy boat. Serve promptly. 4 to 5 servings.

VENISON LOAF

1½ lb shoulder of venison
3 *or* 4 slices day-old white
  bread, 1⅓ cups loosely pkd
  crumbs
3 tbsp finely chopped celery
3 tbsp butter
1 cup water
1 medium bay leaf

Marrow
1¼ tsp salt
Pepper
¼ to ½ tsp marjoram, if
  desired
1½ tsp grated onion
1 egg, slightly beaten

Wipe meat with a clean damp cloth and trim off any tough tissue or strong-smelling fat. Remove bones and grind meat. There should be 1 lb ground. Save marrow. Tear the slices of bread into small crumbs. Sauté celery in butter for 5 min; add water, bay leaf and simmer 3 min. Discard bay leaf. Combine cooled liquid with crumbs; add meat, marrow and remaining ingredients. Mix thoroughly. Turn into a greased loaf pan 3¾ x 7½ x 2½ inches and bake in a moderate oven (350° F) for 1 hr. 5 to 6 servings.

VENISON LOIN ROAST

1 deer loin roast, about 3½ lb
  Salt and pepper
¼ lb suet *or* salt pork

½ cup water
2 *or* 3 medium onions

Wipe roast clean with damp cloth. Trim off any strong-smelling fat. Sprinkle with salt and pepper and place in shallow roasting pan, skin side up. Cut suet or pork in ¼-inch thick slices and lay over top of roast. Place in a moderately slow oven (325° F) and roast uncovered for 2 hr. At the end of the first hr, add ¼ cup hot water and the peeled onions which have been cut in quarters. When deer loin is done, remove crisp suet or pork and discard. Remove onions, skim off extra fat, and add remaining ¼ cup water. Scrape all browned residue from the bottom of the pan to make pan gravy. Return onions, reheat, and serve hot with the roast. 5 to 6 servings.

VENISON PATTIES IN ONION GRAVY

1½ lb shoulder of venison
3 *or* 4 slices day-old bread,
  1½ cups loosely pkd
  crumbs
½ cup finely chopped celery
⅓ cup butter *or* margarine

Marrow, if any
1 egg, slightly beaten
½ cup water
1½ tsp salt
Generous dash of pepper
½ tsp poultry seasoning

Wipe venison with a clean damp cloth, trim off any strong-smelling fat and remove bones. Grind meat twice. Reserve any marrow. Tear slices of bread into small crumbs. Sauté celery in 2 tbsp of the butter for 10 min and add to meat, bread, marrow and remaining ingredients. Mix thoroughly. Shape into small patties or balls about 1 inch in diameter. Brown in the remaining butter quickly; lower heat and cook over medium heat for 10 min. Add onion gravy and simmer 2 min. Makes 3 to 3½ dozen patties. 6 to 8 servings.

Onion Gravy:

1½ tbsp flour
2 tbsp butter
1 cup water
½ tsp salt

1 cup thinly sliced onions, 2 medium
1 cup finely shredded lettuce

Combine flour and melted butter in a skillet and stir over medium heat until mixture is browned (not scorched); add water gradually and cook until mixture is smooth and thickened; stir constantly. Add remaining ingredients, cover and simmer for 15 min.

VENISON POT PIE

2 slices round steak, 2 lb, cut ¾-inch thick
3 tbsp flour
2½ tsp salt
⅛ tsp pepper
⅓ cup shortening
3½ cups water
¼ cup thickly sliced carrots

½ cup coarsely cut celery
¾ lb shelled peas, 2 cups, frozen may be used
2 tbsp chopped onion
¼ tsp sugar
Rich Biscuit Dough, p 234
Butter, melted

Wipe steaks clean with a damp cloth. Trim off any strong-smelling fat. Cut into 1½-inch pieces and dredge thoroughly with the combined flour, salt and pepper. Slowly brown meat and any remaining seasoned flour in the hot shortening. Reduce heat, add 1 cup of the water, cover and simmer for 1½ hr or until meat is nearly tender. Add remaining water gradually as needed, then the vegetables and sugar and continue cooking covered for ½ hr or until vegetables and meat are tender. Pour boiling stew into two casseroles (4½-cup capacity each). Immediately top with biscuit dough rolled to ½-inch thickness. Flute edge and brush with butter. Cut vents in the center. Bake in a hot oven (450° F) for 12 to 15 min or until crust is cooked through and richly browned. Serve immediately. 8 to 10 servings.

VENISON STEW DELUXE

On order of sauerbraten

To make marinade, combine:
  2 cups red wine, Burgundy
    or Claret
  ¼ cup cider vinegar
  *2 juniper berries cut in 4ths
  1 tsp salt
  ¼ tsp whole black peppers
  1 medium bay leaf
  ½ medium onion, sliced
  ½ small carrot, sliced
  2 tbsp sugar

  2 whole cloves
Stew:
  2½ lb shoulder of venison
  3 tbsp shortening
  ⅛ tsp pepper
  1⅛ tsp salt
  1 medium onion, sliced
  ½ cup puréed tomatoes
  ¾ cup water
  1 tbsp flour

Wipe meat clean and trim off any strong-smelling fat; then cut into two-inch cubes. Place in a glass or enamelware pan or bowl, and pour the cold marinade over meat. Cover pan and let stand in refrigerator a day or two. Turn the meat in the marinade twice daily. When ready to cook, lift the meat out to drain on paper toweling to prevent too much sputtering when browning. Heat shortening in an aluminum kettle or skillet (iron may give a dark color) and brown the meat on all sides slowly. Add ¾ cup of the strained marinade, pepper and salt. Cover and simmer gently for 1½ hr. Then add onion, tomatoes and ½ cup water and continue to simmer for 1 hr. Thicken the sauce with flour blended to a smooth paste in remaining ¼ cup of water. Boil two min longer. Serve very hot. 6 servings.

DRESSINGS OR STUFFINGS

BREAD DRESSING

  ¼ cup butter *or* margarine
  ⅓ cup diced onion
  ⅓ cup diced celery
  1 qt cubed 3-day-old white
    bread

  ½ tsp poultry seasoning
  ½ tsp salt
  2 tbsp chopped parsley
  ¾ cup milk

Melt butter in saucepan or skillet. Add onion and celery and sauté until onion is slightly transparent. Add the bread, seasonings and parsley and toss lightly in the butter mixture. Remove from heat. Drizzle the milk over the mixture. Mix and pack lightly into salted cavity of bird. (This amount fills a 2 lb pheasant but must be doubled for a 4 lb chicken.)

*Juniper berries may be obtained from drugstore.

MUSHROOM DRESSING

¼ cup butter	½ tsp salt
½ cup finely cut mushrooms	⅛ tsp pepper
1 tbsp minced onion	½ cup Broth from giblets
2 tbsp finely diced celery	and neck, p 1289
3 cups cubed 3-day-old bread,	1 egg, beaten
4 oz	

Melt butter, add mushrooms and onion. Cover and sauté until onions are soft and yellow and the mushrooms are covered with their own juice, 4 to 5 min. Cool. Add celery, bread, and seasonings. Stir to blend well. Combine broth and egg. Drizzle over bread. Toss thoroughly and pack lightly in cavity of cleaned bird. Makes enough dressing for a 1½ to 2 lb pheasant. Twice this amount of dressing will be required for a roast chicken.

NOODLE DRESSING

3 oz broad noodles	Cooked giblets and neck
¼ cup butter *or* margarine	meat from 1 pheasant *or*
¼ cup chopped onion	duck, cut finely, p 1289
2 tbsp finely chopped celery	¼ tsp salt
1 tbsp chopped green pepper	Dash pepper

Cook noodles in boiling salted water until just tender, p 430. Rinse with hot water and drain well. Melt butter, add onion and sauté lightly. Add the celery, green pepper, meat, seasonings and cooked noodles. Toss well to coat noodles with butter. Pack lightly into salted cavity of cleaned bird. Makes enough dressing for a 2 lb pheasant or duck. Twice this amount of dressing will be required for a roast chicken.

SAGE DRESSING

¼ cup finely chopped onion	½ tsp sage
¼ cup butter *or* margarine	⅛ tsp pepper
2 tbsp finely chopped	¼ tsp salt
celery leaves	½ cup milk
3 cups cubed 3-day-old bread	1 egg, beaten

Add onions to butter that has been melted in a saucepan. Sauté until transparent and yellow. Add the celery leaves, bread and seasonings. Toss to lightly coat with butter. Remove from heat. Combine milk and egg and drizzle over the bread mixture. Stir lightly to blend. Pack loosely into the salted cavity of bird. This will fill a 2 lb dressed pheasant but must be doubled in amount for a 3½ to 4 lb chicken.

WILD DUCK

There are two kinds of duck so far as feeding habits are concerned —those that live off the grain and feed from the fields, and those that live principally from fish and food obtained from the water. The latter have a fishy flavor while the others are much better flavored. Those with fishy flavor may be made palatable by putting a scraped carrot inside the cavity and parboiling in enough water to cover, for 10 min. Then drain and stuff with bread or rice stuffing, or with a spoonful of raw cranberries. If the duck is not fat, lay a slice of salt pork over the breast.

There are two schools of thought about roasting duck—one cooking rare so that the juices run red just like rare beef and the other cooking until thoroughly done. Some sportsmen hold that duck can only be good when it is cooked rare, but equally good hunters like it cooked well done.

BAKED BRAZILIAN DUCK WITH WILD RICE STUFFING

2 cups wild rice	2 tsp salt
1 qt water	¼ tsp pepper
1 dressed duck, 4¾ lb	½ cup water
¼ cup melted butter	

Soak washed rice in 1 qt water overnight. Have the duck cleaned according to directions. Rub 1 tbsp baking soda into skin. Rinse well inside and out with warm water. Drain thoroughly. Drain rice by squeezing or pressing excess water from it. Drizzle with butter and season with salt and pepper. Toss to mix well. Fill rice loosely into salted cavity of duck. Truss, p 1034. Sprinkle with salt and place on rack in roasting pan. Roast in a moderately hot oven (425° F) for 40 min uncovered. Do not prick skin of duck to release excess fat. Add ½ cup water, cover with close fitting lid and continue roasting at moderate (350° F) until tender, 3 to 3½ hr. Remove lid for last 30 min. The giblets and neck may be simmered until tender and used for gravy if desired, p 765. 5 servings.

BAKED WILD DUCK WITH SAUERKRAUT

1 dressed duck, 3¼ lb	1 qt sauerkraut
2 tsp salt	2 apples, diced
¼ cup butter *or* margarine	½ cup celery
¾ cup chopped onions	¾ tsp caraway seed

Remove pinfeathers, singe duck and finish cleaning according to directions. Rub 1 tbsp baking soda into skin and rinse well inside and out with warm water. Drain. Sprinkle inside and out with the salt. Heat butter, add onions and sauté until lightly browned. Drain the sauerkraut, reserve the liquid. Add the sauerkraut and remaining ingredients to onions. Mix well. Fill cavity of duck and truss, p 1034. Place any remaining stuffing in roasting pan around the duck. Bury giblets in this dressing. Cover and bake in a moderate oven (350° F) for 3 hrs. Uncover last hr of cooking to brown the duck. Use the sauerkraut liquid to baste the duck during the roasting. Make gravy from the sauerkraut juice and drippings as desired. 4 servings.

BRAISED DUCK WITH RED CABBAGE

1 dressed wild duck, about 3 lb	½ cup flour
	1 cup water
⅓ cup shortening *or* drippings for frying	1 medium head red cabbage, 3 lb
1½ tsp salt	½ cup vinegar
¼ tsp pepper	2 tbsp sugar

Remove pin feathers and singe according to directions. Rub 1 tbsp of baking soda into skin of duck, then rinse thoroughly in several changes of warm water. Drain. Cut into serving pieces. Heat shortening in an aluminum skillet (do not use iron as the reaction of the vinegar may darken cabbage. An iron skillet may be used to brown the meat, then the meat transferred to a covered saucepan containing the cabbage.) Put salt, pepper and flour in a clean paper bag. Add a few pieces of duck to the bag at a time and shake until each piece is well coated with flour mixture. Brown in hot shortening over medium heat on all sides. Then add ½ cup of the water. Cover tightly and simmer gently until about half done (1 hr). Lift up pieces of duck, lay the coarsely cut cabbage on the bottom of the skillet and replace the duck on top. Add vinegar, sugar and remaining ½ cup water. Cover and continue to cook until cabbage and duck are tender, 45 min to 1 hr. Arrange cabbage and duck on a platter, boil the liquid left in pan vigorously for a few min to obtain a thin, gravy-like consistency. Pour over cabbage and serve at once. 4 or 5 servings.

BRAISED DUCK DINNER

For a braised duck dinner, prepare duck as for preceding "Duck with Red Cabbage." After simmering 1½ hr, add 3 medium, white potatoes, quartered, 6 whole, small carrots and 1 cup cut celery. Cover and continue to cook until vegetables and duck are done. Remove to a hot platter, cover to keep hot. Prepare Milk Gravy from drippings, p 765. 4 to 5 servings.

Note: For directions on removing pin feathers and cleaning see p 745.

BROILED WILD DUCKLING

1 dressed duckling, 2 lb
1 tsp salt
1 tbsp melted butter

2 tbsp hot water
Cooked Giblets and Broth,
p 764

Remove pin feathers, singe, and finish cleaning duckling according to directions. Rub 1 tbsp baking soda into skin and rinse thoroughly in several changes of warm water. Drain well. Remove neck and cook with giblets. Cut duckling in half from neck to tail, being sure to cut exactly in center of back. Kitchen or poultry scissors and a large, sharp knife are ideal for this job. Sprinkle with the salt and brush with butter and hot water mixed together. Place cut side up under preheated broiler, rack placed about 6 inches from heating element. Broil for 30 min, brushing every 10 min with butter mixture. Turn and continue broiling another 30 min, basting as before. Drain excess fat from broiler pan. Add finely cut giblets and broth, concentrated to ½ cup to residue in pan. Stir until residue is dissolved, reheat to boiling and serve with the broiled duckling. 2 servings.

DUCK KING

2 tbsp chopped onion
1 cup coarsely chopped
  mushrooms
2 tbsp duck fat *or* butter
¼ cup flour
1¾ cups milk

½ tsp salt
$\frac{1}{16}$ tsp poultry seasoning
2 tsp lemon juice
1 cup diced, leftover duck
1 large egg, well beaten

Sauté onion and mushrooms in duck fat for 5 min or until onion is yellow and mushrooms are juicy. Add flour and stir until well blended. Gradually add milk and stir over low heat until smooth and thickened. Add salt, poultry seasoning, lemon juice and the duck and stir to blend. Add a little of this hot mixture to the egg and mix thoroughly. Return to double boiler for 2 min, stirring constantly. Serve piping hot on toast. 4 servings.

DUCK SOUP

Carcasses of 4 roast wild
  ducks, leftover
7 cups cold water
1½ tsp salt
Generous dash of pepper
1 cup coarsely cut celery

1 cup sliced carrots
1 medium onion
¼ tsp sugar
1 tsp caraway seed, in cheese-
  cloth bag

Break carcasses into several pieces. There should be 2½ lb bones. Fit bones tightly in kettle. Add water, salt and pepper. Cover and heat to boiling. Reduce heat and simmer 2 hrs. Add remaining ingredients and simmer 25 to 30 min longer. Lift out carcasses. The meat left clinging to the bones may be removed, cut in small pieces, and added to the soup. Reheat and serve. Makes 4 to 5 cups.

QUICK ROAST DUCK

Rare for the Sophisticates

1 wild duck, 2 to 2¼ lbs	3 strips bacon
1 tsp salt	3 tbsp salad oil
Dash of pepper	1 tbsp butter

Remove pin feathers and singe duck according to directions. Rub skin with 1 tbsp baking soda and rinse well inside and out with warm water. Drain thoroughly. Sprinkle inside and out with salt and pepper; lay strips of bacon across the breast. Place breast side up in a small covered roaster. Pour oil into bottom of pan, and place butter inside duck cavity. If duck is cold, allow to stand at room temp for 1 hr. Preheat oven for 10 to 15 min at 500° F to make sure it is very hot. Cover roaster tightly and place in hot oven. After 10 min turn duck and continue to roast 10 more min, covered. Remove cover and continue to roast at 500° F until brown on back side (10 to 15 min). Turn breast side up and continue to roast until breast is an appetizing brown (10 to 15 min). Serve at once with currant gravy, if desired, p 765. Test for doneness by pricking slightly with a fork. If blood runs, duck is not done, if a clear juice oozes out, duck is done. Duck roasted in this way should still be rare near the bones. Total roasting time: 40 to 50 min, allowing about 20 min per lb. 2 to 3 servings.

ROAST BRAZILIAN DUCK WITHOUT DRESSING

1 dressed Brazilian duck,	3 to 3½ tsp salt
4 to 5 lbs	¼ tsp pepper

Remove pin feathers, singe duck and finish cleaning according to directions. Rub 1 tbsp baking soda into skin and rinse well inside and out with warm water. Drain thoroughly. Sprinkle inside and out with salt and pepper. Place breast up on trivet in roaster. Cover and place in a moderate oven (325° F). Roast covered until tender (2 to 2½ hrs). Do not prick skin for fat to ooze out. (See p 1061.) When duck tests tender, remove cover and allow to brown well on all sides (1 hr). The full time required for roasting is from 35 to 40 min per lb. Cook at least ⅔ of time covered. Remove duck to hot platter and cover to keep hot. Skim off excess fat and prepare giblet gravy, p 765. 4 to 6 servings.

Note: For directions on removing pin feathers and cleaning see p 745.

ROAST BRAZILIAN DUCK WITH WILD RICE AND LIVER STUFFING

1 dressed duck, 4¾ to 5 lbs	¼ cup butter *or* margarine
1⅓ cups wild rice, makes 1 qt cooked rice	½ cup finely chopped celery
	¾ tsp salt
½ cup finely chopped onion	⅛ tsp pepper
Duck liver	¼ cup Giblet Broth, p 764

Remove pin feathers, singe and finish cleaning duck according to directions. Rub 1 tbsp soda well into skin and rinse well inside and out with warm water. Drain. Prepare wild rice and liver stuffing as follows: Pour rice slowly into 2 qts boiling water to which 1 tsp salt has been added. Boil for 20 min, lifting the rice from time to time with a fork. Then drain well. Lightly sauté the onions and finely cut liver in the butter. Add the celery, seasoning and broth and pour over the wild rice. Toss to mix well. Sprinkle additional salt (about 1 tsp) into the cavity of duck, then fill lightly with the stuffing. Truss (see p 1034). Place breast up on a trivet in a roasting pan. Cover tightly and roast in a moderate oven (350° F) for 2½ hrs. Then remove cover and continue roasting 1 hr, or until duck is brown on all sides and tender. Place duck in top of roaster, cover and keep hot. Use drippings to make giblet gravy, p 765. 5 servings.

ROAST WILD DUCK WITH MASHED POTATO STUFFING

1 dressed duck, 2½ to 3 lbs	Giblets
2 tsp salt	3 tbsp butter *or* margarine
¼ tsp pepper	¼ cup milk
6 medium potatoes, 1¾ lbs	1 tbsp finely cut parsley
½ cup diced celery	Seasonings to taste
1 tbsp chopped onion	

Remove pin feathers, singe duck, and finish cleaning according to directions. Rub 1 tbsp of baking soda into skin, then rinse well inside and out with warm water. Drain thoroughly. Sprinkle inside and out with salt and pepper. Meanwhile, boil the pared potatoes in barely enough salted water to cover until done. Drain and mash. While potatoes are cooking, sauté celery, onion and the cleaned, cut-up giblets in heated butter until lightly browned. Add milk, cover and simmer 10 min. Add water if necessary to prevent scorching. Mix together mashed potatoes and sautéed giblet mixture thoroughly. Fold in parsley and season with salt and pepper to taste. Pile dressing quite firmly into duck cavity. Truss, p 1034. Place in covered roaster in a moderate oven (325° F). Roast covered until tender, from 1½ to 2½ hrs. Uncover and let brown well on all sides at same temp—about ½ hr. Remove to hot platter and cover to keep hot. Skim off excess fat from drippings.

Enough mashed potato stuffing will ooze into the drippings to thicken the gravy. Stir in 1½ cups of milk, reheat to boiling and season to taste. Serve hot with duck. 2 or 3 servings.

ELK

Elk is very similar to deer except the carcass is larger. Any good recipe for deer can be used with good results for cooking elk.

ELK SANDWICH SPREADS

No. 1
½ cup ground cooked elk, soup meat

3 tbsp mayonnaise
3 tbsp pickled onion, chopped fine

Combine all ingredients.

No. 2
½ cup ground cooked elk

½ tsp prepared horseradish
3 tbsp French dressing

Combine all ingredients.

These spreads may be used for hearty sandwiches or as a spread for crackers to be served with the soup.

ELK SOUP

Knuckle bone and meat, 2½ to 3 lbs
2 qts cold water
1 large onion, quartered
¾ cup diced celery

1 cup diced carrots
4 tsp salt
¼ tsp pepper
⅓ cup rice
2 tsp parsley

Have bone sawed or cracked into several pieces. Wipe pieces clean with a damp cloth. Put into soup kettle and add the water. Heat to boiling. Reduce heat, cover and simmer gently for 2 to 2½ hrs. Remove bone, cut off meat and dice. Return meat and marrow to soup. Then add onion, celery, carrots, seasonings and rice and continue simmering for 20 to 30 min until rice and vegetables are done. Sprinkle parsley over each bowl of soup as it is served. 4 to 6 servings.

ELK STEAK SMOTHERED IN ONIONS

1¼ lbs steak, about ¾-inch thick
1¾ tsp salt
Pepper

2 tbsp butter *or* margarine
1¼ lbs onions, 5 medium
⅓ cup water for less tender steak

Wipe steak clean with a damp cloth, trim off all fat and add to salvaged fat. Season steak with salt and pepper. Brown slowly on both sides in hot butter. Add sliced onions, reduce heat, cook 15 min. Turn steak once and carefully stir onions occasionally. Serve immediately.

This method is satisfactory for tender steak. For less tender steak, add water just after browning meat, and reduce heat to simmering temp. Cover and cook 35 to 40 min or until meat is tender. Add onions during last 15 min of cooking. 2 to 3 servings.

PAN-FRIED ELK STEAK

1½ to 1¾ lbs loin steak	¼ cup shortening
1½ tsp salt	½ cup hot water
Pepper to taste	

Wipe steak clean with a damp cloth and trim off any fat that may have a strong odor. Sprinkle both sides with salt and pepper. Heat shortening in skillet. Brown steak quickly (about 2 min on each side). Lower heat and continue cooking 3 min. Turn and cook for 3 min on other side. Remove to hot platter; scrape loose the brown residue from bottom of pan and add the water; heat to boiling. Serve promptly over meat or in a gravy boat, as desired. 4 servings.

SWISSED ELK OR VENISON ROUND STEAK

2 round steaks, cut about	¼ cup butter *or* margarine
¾-inch thick, about 1½ lbs	1 cup water
¼ cup flour	1 medium onion, chopped
2 tsp salt	1 cup diced celery
¹⁄₁₆ tsp pepper	½ cup sour cream

Wipe steaks clean with a damp cloth. Combine flour, salt and pepper and pound well into the steak, using the back of a heavy butcher knife blade or the edge of a sturdy saucer. Brown both sides of steak and any remaining seasoned flour slowly in the heated butter. Add ¼ cup of the water. Cover and simmer slowly, adding the rest of the water as needed. When the meat is almost tender (1 to 2 hrs), add the onion and celery and cook until thoroughly tender. Stir in the sour cream and cook for 2 min longer. Serve at once. From 1½ to 2½ hrs of cooking will be required, the time depending on age of animal. 5 servings.

GAME BIRDS

GROUSE, PARTRIDGE AND QUAIL

All of these birds are dressed just like pheasants, p 745. Any of the recipes for pheasant can be used to cook grouse, partridge or quail.

Note: For directions on removing pin feathers and cleaning see p 745.

ROAST GROUSE OR PRAIRIE CHICKEN

Roast only young birds that have smooth legs. Cook older birds like Potted Pigeons.

2 dressed, drawn grouse *or* prairie chickens, 3 lbs	2 cups Game Bird Dressing, p 754
2 tsp lemon juice, optional	3 *or* 4 thin strips salt pork
1 tsp salt	6 to 7 inches long
	1 tbsp flour, optional

Start oven 10 min before baking; set to mod. hot (400° F). Dry-pick, singe, wash and eviscerate birds as described under Roast Partridge, p 763. Be sure to probe with crochet hook shot holes for imbedded shot and feathers and rinse these openings out well in cold water. If the area contains much clotted blood, cut out and discard the damaged parts. Drain well after washing. When ready to roast, rub inside with lemon juice, then with salt. Put stuffing into birds, then press legs and wings close to body; wrap pork slices around so as to cover breast and legs well. Wrap twine around bird crisscrossing it and tying to make a compact parcel. Place birds, breast-side down in casserole of a size that fits birds in snugly. Bake 45 min, basting 2 or 3 times with fat that collects in bottom of casserole, then lower heat to mod oven (350° F), turn birds over and continue baking until tender and breast is brown. Roasting requires from 1 to 1¼ hrs. 15 min before birds are done, drain off about half the fat and add ½ cup thin cream to provide pan gravy. Return to oven to finish cooking. Remove twine and transfer birds to hot platter. Garnish with parsley and serve. 4 to 5 servings.

BROILED GROUSE

Clean grouse, cut into halves and broil exactly as described under Broiled Partridge, see below.

BROILED PARTRIDGE

Broiling young partridges 8 to 9 months old is a classic method of preparation

4 partridges, 4 lbs	1 tsp salt
3 tbsp butter, melted	Parsley

Dry-pick, singe, wash and eviscerate birds as described under Roast Partridge. After draining well, use kitchen or poultry scissors to cut birds neatly in half lengthwise, p 1037. Use small slender skewers to pin the halves in shape so wings and legs lie snugly against body. Brush melted butter over top and bottom of halves. Place skin-side down under the hot broiler adjusted to 400° F. See that halves stand level. Use wads of crushed aluminum foil or wet paper toweling to prop them up where needed. Put ½ tsp butter in rib hollow of each half. Broil about 5 min, then sprinkle with salt and brush with melted butter from hollow of each half. Broil 10 min longer, at which time the top should be nicely browned. Now turn over and brush with melted butter and broil to a rich brown, basting 2 or 3 times with rest of butter the last 15 min. Remove skewers. Serve piping hot on hot plate. Garnish with parsley. Pour any juice dripped down into broiler pan over birds. Serves 4 to 6.

ROAST PARTRIDGE

An excellent way to serve partridge which are elegant in form, flavor and texture is roasting

4 partridges, 4 lbs
2 tsp salt

2 cups Game Bird Dressing, p 754
4 to 6 thin slices salt pork

Start oven 10 min before roasting; set to mod hot (400° F). Do not scald these birds to remove feathers. Dry-pick instead as soon as possible after killing while feathers are droopy, due to relaxed muscles. Later on, feathers become set and more difficult to remove. Pluck bunches of the feathers out in the direction in which they lay until bird is nude. Next singe. Wash in cold water to which 1 tbsp baking soda has been added to each quart. Rinse well in clear water, removing any pin feathers with a strawberry huller. Eviscerate, then wash well on inside, being careful to remove the lungs and any clotted blood. Drain well and pat inside dry with a piece of paper toweling or clean cloth. Sprinkle ½ tsp salt on inside of each bird, then fill with stuffing. Push legs and fold wings up close to body. Wrap 1½ slices pork over breast and legs to form a compact parcel and tie into shape with twine. Put birds into a glass casserole. Do not cover. Bake, basting every 10 to 15 min with fat that collects in bottom of casserole. Keep oven door closed while basting. Bake until tender, about 1 hr for young birds 9 to 12 months old. Serves 4 to 6.

BRAISED QUAIL

Dress, singe, wash and eviscerate as described under Roast Partridge, above. Rub ¼ tsp salt on inside of each bird. Tie birds into compact shape by wrapping twine around body and legs. For 3 birds add 3 tbsp butter to saucepan; when bubbling hot, add the quail. Cook over moderate heat, turning often until delicately browned on all sides. Add ½ cup hot water or chicken broth, cover and simmer 10 min, turning once or twice. Serve piping hot on sqs of hot toast. Pour liquid left in saucepan over birds.

BROILED QUAIL

Dress, singe, wash and eviscerate as described under Roast Partridge. Cut apart along back, but do not separate the two halves. Brush with butter and broil like Broiled Partridge, p 762. Broiling requires no more than 5 min to each side. Serve blistering hot.

ROAST QUAIL

Start oven 10 min before roasting; set to mod hot (400° F). Dress, singe, wash and eviscerate quail as described under Roast Partridge, p 763. Rub ¼ tsp salt on inside of each, stuff with ¼ cup of Game Bird Dressing, p 754, or a large oyster. Skewer opening together to hold in dressing. Push legs and wings close to body, lay a short strip of thin salt pork over breast and legs; wrap with twine, crisscrossing and tying it to make a compact parcel. Or omit salt pork, wrap birds with twine to hold in shape and brush with butter. Fit quail snugly, breast-side down, into shallow pan or casserole. Add ¼ cup hot water, chicken or veal broth. Cover. Bake about 20 min. Uncover, turn breast-side up, brush with fat that has collected in bottom of pan, continue baking until breasts are brown, about 15 min longer. A quail weighs about 5 oz dressed. Serve 1 to 2 per person.

GRAVY

COOKING GIBLETS FOR GRAVY

Giblets from 2 pheasants	¾ tsp salt
or 2 ducks	½ small carrot
2 cups water	1 slice onion

After the birds are dressed, singed and washed according to directions, cut the neck off as long as possible very close to the head and close to the body. Clean the gizzard by removing the inside sac containing the food and then cut away both orifices to the gizzard. Remove the bile duct carefully from the liver, being sure not to cut into the sac. Rinse both gizzard and liver well in cold water. Wrap the liver up in waxed paper and place in refrigerator. Put neck and gizzards into saucepan and add the water, salt, carrot and onion. Cover and heat to boiling. Then reduce heat and simmer until both neck and gizzard are very tender and easily pierced with a fork. Add the livers the last half hr of cooking. Use the broth for making gravy. Remove as much meat from the neck as possible and chop it with the gizzard and liver and add to the gravy the last few min of cooking.

CURRANT GRAVY FOR WILD DUCK

Giblets of 1 duck
2 tbsp duck fat *or* butter
3 tbsp finely chopped celery
1 tbsp finely chopped onion
¼ tsp salt

2 tsp flour
Dash of cayenne
½ tsp Worcestershire sauce
Generous dash of tabasco
1 tbsp currant jelly

Before beginning to roast the duck, start giblets, and neck simmering in a covered saucepan in enough water to cover. Add more water only if needed. Simmer until tender. Heat duck fat in skillet, add celery and onion and sauté until yellow and transparent. Mix salt, flour and cayenne and blend into the butter. Add Worcestershire sauce, tabasco and the strained broth from giblets, concentrated to ½ cup. Stir until smooth and slightly thickened. Add jelly and stir until melted. Add finely cut giblets and meat from neck if desired. When "Quick Roast Duck," p 758, is done, remove to hot platter, cover to keep hot. Skim off all but about 1 tbsp fat. Add currant gravy to drippings and fat left in roasting pan, scrape well to loosen any browned residue, season to taste, heat to boiling and serve at once with duck. Makes 1 to 1½ cups gravy.

GIBLET GRAVY

Cooked giblets and broth, above
3 tbsp fat from roast fowl, *or* butter

3 tbsp flour
All meat juice and browned residue
Salt and pepper

Strain the broth from cooked giblets of 2 pheasants or ducks and either boil down or add water (whichever is necessary) to make 2 cups. Cut giblets and neck meat fine. Remove roast fowl to hot platter or roaster lid and cover to keep hot. (Return roast to oven if oven is turned off.) Skim fat from drippings and return 3 tbsp to roasting pan. Blend in flour thoroughly, scraping well to loosen all the browned residue left in pan. Stir constantly to keep very smooth. Add giblet broth gradually, stirring constantly and continue to cook until liquid boils and thickens. Stir in giblets and add seasonings. Reheat to boiling and serve at once in hot gravy boat.

Note: The giblet broth may be concentrated to 1 cup and 1 cup of milk added to make a milk gravy before adding the giblets.

MILK GRAVY FOR ROAST WILD FOWL OR MEAT

The following amount of gravy can be made after roasting two 2 to 2½ lb pheasant or 3 or 4 lbs of deer, venison, etc.

When roast is done, remove to a hot platter or to the cover of roaster and cover to keep hot. Skim off all but 3 tbsp of fat. Allow all browned (not burned) residue and drippings from meat to remain in the pan. Blend in 2 to 3 tbsp of flour thoroughly and brown slightly. Stir constantly and scrape bottom of pan to loosen all the residue. Gradually add 1 cup of milk, stirring constantly until mixture boils and thickens. Add more milk to obtain the desired consistency and flavor. The amount of liquid will vary depending upon the original concentration of flavor in the drippings and the consistency desired. Season to taste. If gravy seems a little bland, a small amount of grated onion (½ tsp) will improve the flavor. The commercial meat extract pastes or chicken bouillon cubes may also be added to advantage if larger amounts of gravy are desired than the roast will provide. The same procedure can be used to make thickened gravy using water instead of milk, or if desired, half water and half milk. Serve gravy in a separate hot gravy boat.

PAN GRAVY

Too often the savory residue from pan-fried or broiled meat is wasted because it adheres tightly to the skillet or the grill. Delicious gravy can be made from this unscorched residue and it should be used as it contains much of the color and flavor that belongs to the meat. To prepare pan gravy, slowly pour ½ cup boiling water over the broiler rack or into the skillet. Meanwhile, use fork or wooden spoon to rub the residue loose from the rack or skillet. Then boil and stir to dissolve residue and concentrate the gravy to the desired strength. Pour gravy over the hot meat or serve separately in a hot gravy boat.

MUSKRATS OR MARSH HARE

This small animal that is reputed for its clean food habits gets its name from its glands which have a musky scent. If these glands are not removed, they give the meat a very strong disagreeable flavor. The musk glands lie on the underside of the body and are light yellow in color with a corrugated surface. There are other scent glands between the forelegs, between the shoulders, on the back, and under the thighs. All of these glands are small and yellow and might easily be mistaken for little lumps of fat. The muskrat has a very unusual skeleton. The bones are flat, fragile, and seem more numerous than in other animals of similar size. The flesh is dark and soft, but when properly prepared makes good eating.

MUSKRAT FRICASSEE

1 dressed muskrat, 1 to	¼ tsp pepper
1½ lbs	¹⁄₁₆ tsp red pepper
1 tbsp salt	¼ cup shortening
1 qt water	Paprika
¼ cup flour	1 large onion, sliced, 1 cup
2 tsp salt	¾ cup water

Wipe muskrat with damp cloth, pick off any hair. Separate hind from fore quarters by cutting across back and just below ribs. Fit into a glass or enamel bowl. Add salt and water to cover. Cover and place in refrigerator overnight. Next day, drain off salt water and rinse muskrat thoroughly in clear water. Drain well. Cut in serving pieces, p 782. Place flour, salt, pepper and red pepper in a clean paper bag. Place a few pieces of muskrat at a time in the bag and shake to coat well. Heat shortening in heavy skillet and brown pieces slowly on all sides over medium heat. Sprinkle the browned surface with paprika. Push the muskrat to one side and add onion. Allow to cook until onion is slightly yellow and transparent. Add ½ cup water, reduce heat, cover and simmer gently until tender, about 20 to 30 min, adding the remaining water as needed. Serve on hot platter with the gravy poured over the top. 2 to 3 servings.

MUSKRAT MARYLAND

1 large dressed muskrat,	½ cup milk
1½ to 2 lbs	¾ cup flour
1 qt water	1 tsp salt
1½ tsp salt	¼ tsp thyme
1 small onion	⅓ cup shortening
½ tsp poultry seasoning	Water
1 egg	

Wipe muskrat with damp cloth, pick off any hair. Separate hind from fore quarters, cutting across the back and just below the ribs. Fit into glass or enamel bowl. Add salt water enough to cover (1 tbsp salt to 1 qt water), cover and place in refrigerator overnight. Next day, drain off salt water and rinse with clear water. Drain well. Place in a kettle and add water, salt, onion and poultry seasoning. Heat to boiling, reduce heat, cover and simmer for 20 min. Lift out parboiled muskrat, drain and cut into serving pieces. Make a batter by beating egg, milk and flour with a rotary beater until smooth. Add salt and thyme. Dip pieces of muskrat in batter and brown slowly in heated shortening until golden on all sides. Add ¼ cup water, cover and simmer for 20 min. Remove cover and cook for 15 to 20 min until crisp again on outside, and tender. Serve with cream gravy if desired. 2 to 4 servings.

POSSUM

The possum carcass resembles that of the coon in shape, but the meat is light in color, the carcass is smaller, and the fat does not have the disagreeable flavor and odor the coon has. However, there are scent glands that must be removed as soon as possible after the animal is skinned. If the fat is objectionable, the carcass should be thoroughly chilled so the fat will be as firm as possible before trying to peel it off. Additional butter or other shortening may be used to brown or baste the meat as it cooks. Roasting or braising is the favorite way to cook this meat.

MRS. DUKE'S BAKED POSSUM AND SWEETS

2 young possums, 2¼ to 2½ lbs each, dressed weight	¾ tsp black pepper
1 baking potato, ½ lb	⅛ tsp red pepper
7 cups cold water	3 tbsp flour
2 lbs sweet potatoes *or* yams	¼ cup cold water
4 tsp salt	2 cups possum broth
	Parsley

Start oven 10 min before baking; set to mod (375° F).

Clean possum carefully and remove scent glands and any clinging hair. Pare potato, wash and cut in quarters lengthwise. Lay potato inside possum. Fit into a 5-qt kettle. Add water, cover kettle but leave open space on one side for steam to escape. Heat to boiling and boil gently 15 to 20 min; then skim froth that collects; pour off about half the broth. Add 3 cups fresh hot water, return to heat, again partially cover and boil gently until meat is tender, but not tender enough to pull away from the bone. Remember possums will not become more tender after they are placed in roasting pan. This requires 1¼ to 1½ hrs of cooking. Lift possum from broth to roasting pan, sprinkle outside well with the seasonings that have been well mixed in a cup. Make gravy by sprinkling flour over cold water, mix to a smooth paste, then blend with 2 cups of broth drained from kettle in which possums were parboiled. Mix and pour around possum. Arrange pared, washed sweet potatoes around possum. Cover pan and bake 16 to 20 min, or until potatoes are about tender. Now uncover and bake until possums and potatoes are tender and beautifully browned or from 35 to 40 min. Baste every 10 min with the gravy in the pan. Remove meat and potatoes to platter and garnish with parsley. Pour gravy into separate dish and serve meat and gravy piping hot. 5 to 6 servings.

CASSEROLE OF POSSUM

1 possum, 1¾ to 2 lbs, dressed weight	1 tbsp salt
5 cups cold water	1 tbsp flour
2 pods dry red pepper, about 1¼-inch long	1½ lb sweet potatoes, cut in half
	Parsley

Start oven 10 min before baking; set to mod (375° F).

Clean possum carefully, removing scent glands and any clinging hair. Wash thoroughly. Place in 3-qt saucepan, add water and salt, and

1 pod of the pepper. Heat to boiling, reduce heat, cover and boil gently until tender but not tender enough to separate from bones, about 1½ hrs. Drain off broth; save 1 cup; discard rest. Put possum into a casserole, sprinkle the flour and the other pod of pepper crushed medium fine over the meat. Put one of the pared, washed sweet potatoes inside the possum and arrange the rest around it. Pour the 1 cup broth around the possum. Bake covered until potatoes and meat are very tender; then remove and bake to an appetizing brown, or about 1 hr. Serve piping hot with a garnish of parsley. 3 to 4 servings.

Note: Hubbard squash or cushaw baked with the possum are equally as good as the potatoes.

PHEASANTS

Young pheasants that have an abundance of food and have grown fast have a layer of fat under the skin and can be cooked successfully in any way that young chicken can—roasted or broiled. If their food is scarce, or if the birds are older, they will need to be cooked much like any other older fowl—by moist heat, either braised or simmered, etc.

BRAISED PHEASANT IN SOUR CREAM

1 dressed pheasant, 1½ lbs
3 tbsp flour
1½ tsp salt
Pepper
3 tbsp butter

1½ cups water
¼ tsp sugar
½ tsp paprika
1 cup sour cream

Remove pin feathers and singe pheasant according to directions. Rinse well inside and out with warm water. Drain well. Cut into serving pieces. Dredge thoroughly with the combined flour, salt and pepper. Brown slowly on all sides in the butter over medium heat (10 to 15 min). Blend any remaining flour into butter in the pan. Add ½ cup of the water and blend until smooth. Lower heat, cover and simmer for 1¾ hrs or until tender, adding remaining water as needed. Add remaining ingredients and blend well. Simmer gently for 15 min. 3 to 4 servings.

BROILED PHEASANT

1 dressed young pheasant,
    1¼ to 1¾ lbs
1 to 1½ tsp salt

1 to 2 tbsp butter
¼ to ⅓ cup water or broth,
    Giblet Broth, p 764

Remove pin feathers and singe pheasant according to directions. Rinse well inside and out with warm water. Drain thoroughly. Cut off neck and combine with cleaned giblets to make broth for basting or gravy. Cut pheasant in half from neck to tail being sure to cut exactly in center of back. Kitchen or poultry scissors and a large sharp knife are ideal for this job. Sprinkle with salt, and brush with butter that is mixed with 2 tbsp of the water or broth. Place skin side down on preheated broiler rack and adjust rack so that it is 4 to 6 inches from the source of heat. Broil for 18 to 25 min depending on the size of bird. Turn once during the broiling to brown well on both sides, and baste with the butter-water or broth mixture 2 or 3 times. Remove to a hot platter, cover to keep hot. Add remaining water or broth to drippings in pan, scrape rack carefully with a wooden spoon to loosen any clinging residue. Remove rack and place pan over direct heat; heat to boiling and boil rapidly to concentrate flavor and dissolve residue. Serve over broiled pheasant or in a separate heated gravy boat. 2 servings.

FRIED PHEASANT

Prepare exactly like Fried Chicken, p 1039.

PHEASANT BAKED IN DOUGH BLANKET

With Vegetable Stuffing

1 dressed pheasant, 2 lbs	¾ tsp salt
Vegetable Stuffing:	⅛ tsp pepper
¾ cup finely chopped onion	*Dough Blanket:*
3 tbsp butter *or* margarine	1½ cups all-purpose flour
¾ cup coarsely grated carrot	1 tsp salt
¾ cup finely diced celery	2 tbsp shortening
2 tbsp chopped parsley	½ cup water

Remove pin feathers and singe pheasant according to directions. Rinse inside and out with several changes of warm water. Drain well. Remove neck and cook with giblets for gravy, p 764. Fill salted cavity with vegetable stuffing made as follows: Lightly sauté onion in heated butter. Add the remaining vegetables and seasonings and toss to mix well. Fill cavity and truss, p 1034. To make dough blanket: Sift together flour and salt; cut in fat with pastry blender or two knives until particles are the size of rice grains. Add water gradually, stirring to make a dough soft enough to roll. Roll out on a lightly floured board from ⅛ to ¼-inch thick into a rectangular sheet about 15 by 10 inches. Wrap dough around pheasant, completely covering it. Moisten edges and pinch together to seal. Place pheasant, breast side up, on a trivet in a shallow roasting pan and roast uncovered in a moderate oven (350° F) for 1½ to 2 hrs. Prepare giblet gravy from drippings. Break away crusty golden brown blanket in pieces and serve with the pheasant and giblet gravy. 4 servings.

Note: For directions on removing pin feathers and cleaning see p 745.

PHEASANT FRICASSEE

1 dressed pheasant, 1½ lbs	¼ cup shortening
⅓ cup flour	1¼ cups water
2 tsp salt	1 tbsp flour
¼ tsp pepper	

Remove pin feathers and singe pheasant according to directions. Rinse well inside and out with several changes of warm water. Drain thoroughly. Cut into serving pieces. Dredge the pieces of pheasant in the combined ⅓ cup of flour, salt and pepper. Heat shortening in a heavy skillet, and brown pheasant slowly on all sides over medium heat, about 15 min. Add ½ cup of the water, reduce heat, cover and simmer gently until tender, about 1 to 1½ hrs. Add another ½ cup of water as needed. Remove pheasant to hot platter and cover to keep hot. Blend the 1 tbsp of flour into the drippings until smooth, gradually add remaining ¼ cup of water and heat until the mixture boils and thickens. Season to taste and serve hot over the pheasant. 3 to 4 servings.

PHEASANT WITH SAUERKRAUT AND APPLES

1 dressed pheasant, 1½ lbs	2 tbsp brown sugar
1½ tsp salt	2 medium tart apples, un-
2 tbsp butter *or* margarine	pared
1 tbsp flour	¼ cup water
No. 2½ can sauerkraut,	4 tsp white wine, opt
3½ cups	¼ to ½ tsp caraway seed

Remove pin feathers and singe pheasant according to directions. Rinse well inside and out with warm water. Drain thoroughly. Cut into serving pieces. Sprinkle with salt. Brown slowly on all sides in the heated butter over medium heat (about 15 min). Remove pheasant from skillet and blend flour into drippings remaining in pan. Add sauerkraut and brown sugar and mix to blend thoroughly. Turn mixture into a 10-cup casserole. Arrange the browned pheasant on top of the kraut. Cut the apples into wedges, remove core, and arrange wedges around the edge of casserole. Add water. Cover and bake in a moderate oven (350° F) for about 1 hr or until pheasant is almost tender. Sprinkle wine and caraway seeds between the pieces of pheasant so that it seeps into the kraut. Cover and return to the oven for 15 min. Serve immediately from casserole. 3 to 4 servings.

ROAST PHEASANT WITH BREAD DRESSING

1 dressed pheasant, 2½ lbs	½ tsp poultry seasoning
¼ cup butter	½ tsp salt
⅓ cup finely chopped onion	2 tbsp chopped parsley
⅓ cup finely chopped celery	¾ cup milk
¼ lb 3 day-old white bread	4 oz salt pork

Remove pin feathers and singe pheasant according to directions. Rinse well inside and out with warm water. Drain thoroughly. Heat butter in a skillet, add onion and celery and sauté until onion is soft and yellow, about 5 min. Pull or tear bread into small crumbs (there should be 3 cups lightly packed). Add bread, seasonings, and parsley to sautéed celery and toss lightly to mix well. Drizzle the milk over the mixture, mix lightly with a fork and pack lightly into the salted cavity of the pheasant. Fill neck cavity as well as body cavity. Truss if desired, p 1034. Place slices of salt pork over breast of bird and place one over each leg. Place breast up on rack in roaster. Cover and roast in a moderate oven (350° F) for 2 hrs. Remove cover the last ½ hr to brown pheasant. Turn off heat, place pheasant in cover of roaster, remove and discard pork; cover and set back into oven to keep hot. Prepare giblet gravy, p 764, and serve with pheasant in a separate heated gravy boat. 4 servings.

ROAST PHEASANT WITH CHIVES DRESSING

1 dressed pheasant, 2½ lbs	¾ cup water
½ lb day-old rye bread	¾ tsp salt
crumbs with *or* without	Generous dash of pepper
caraway	1 egg, slightly beaten
⅓ cup finely cut celery	3 tbsp finely cut chives
Giblets, finely cut *or*	4 slices salt pork, about ¼ lb
ground	1 tbsp flour
2 tbsp butter	⅔ cup milk

Remove pin feathers and singe pheasant according to directions. Rinse well inside and out with warm water. Drain thoroughly. Pull or tear bread into small crumbs (there should be 1 qt of crumbs packed loosely). Sauté celery and giblets in butter for 5 min. Remove from heat, add water, cool and pour over crumbs; add seasoning, egg and chives Toss lightly to mix. Pack into salted cavity of pheasant. Truss, p 1034. Lay pork slices over breast and tops of legs and place, breast up, on rack in roaster. Cover and bake in a moderately slow oven (325° F) for about 2 hrs. Then remove cover and roast ½ hr longer to brown pheasant. Turn off heat, place pheasant in the cover of roaster, cover and set back into oven to keep hot. Skim off all but 2 tbsp of fat. Prepare milk gravy, p 765, from drippings, the 1 tbsp of flour and the milk. 4 servings.

RABBITS

All varieties of rabbits have scent glands that are small, waxy-looking kernels under the forelegs and on either side of the spine, in

Note: For directions on removing pin feathers and cleaning see p 745.

the small of the back and between the shoulders. These should always be removed, taking care not to cut into them. After the rabbit is skinned, very little fat remains and it is not objectionable in flavor or odor. Rabbits may be cooked by any good recipe for chicken, but because there is so little fat on the meat, additional fat will be required for browning or basting, or to add to the gravy or sauce served with the rabbit.

BROILER BARBECUED RABBIT

1 dressed rabbit, 1½ lbs	⅛ tsp pepper
2 cups cold water	1 tsp sugar
2 tsp salt	1 tbsp lemon juice
¼ cup butter, melted	1 tsp Worcestershire sauce
4 tsp grated onion	¼ cup water
1 tsp salt	

Start oven (broiler) 10 min before baking; set to mod hot (350° F). Clean and wash the rabbit thoroughly, p 745. Cut into serving pieces. Place in bowl, cover with cold water and add salt. Soak 1½ hrs. Drain and pat dry with absorbent paper or cloth. Melt butter in saucepan, remove from heat, add remaining ingredients and beat thoroughly. Dip rabbit pieces in sauce and arrange on aluminum-foil-lined shallow pan and place under broiler 3 inches from source of heat. Broil 30 min basting with remaining sauce every 10 min. After top side is well browned, turn rabbit, increase heat to 375° F, and broil another 40 min, basting frequently. Then turn regulator to 400° F and broil 15 min so that meat browns richly. Remove to platter; pour remaining sauce in broiler pan over rabbit. 4 servings.

Note: If larger rabbits are broiled, increase seasonings proportionately to the increase in weight.

FRIED RABBIT

1 dressed rabbit, 1 lb 6 oz	½ tsp salt
1¼ cups cold water	¼ cup bacon fat
¼ cup cider vinegar	1 tbsp flour
1 tsp salt	¼ cup cream
⅛ tsp black pepper	¼ cup milk
1 small clove garlic, cut in half	¼ cup water
¼ cup flour	½ tsp grated onion

Clean rabbit by removing scent glands and removing clinging hair. Use a sharp pointed knife or crochet hook to dig out any shot and tufts of hair. Wash thoroughly inside and out in cold water. Cut into serving pieces. Place rabbit in bowl; combine water, vinegar, salt and pepper; pour over, cover and soak from 2 to 4 hrs. Drain well. Pat dry with cloth or absorbent paper. Toss with flour to coat well. Heat fat in heavy skillet and add rabbit. Cover skillet to steam, and cook tender and brown on one side for about 15 min. Sprinkle with salt, turn, replace cover, lower heat and cook slowly; turn occasionally. A young rabbit requires about 1 to 1¼ hrs. When tender, remove to platter and keep warm. Add 1 tbsp flour to hot fat in skillet, and rub to smooth paste; add cream, milk and water. Cook until thickened; stir continually. Add grated onion. Serve in hot gravy boat. 4 servings.

HASEN PFEFFER

2 cups water	1 dressed, cleaned rabbit,*
½ cup vinegar	cut into serving pieces
3 tbsp sugar	3 tbsp butter *or* shortening
1 tsp salt	1 medium onion, sliced
10 whole cloves	1½ tbsp flour
Half of medium bay leaf	3 tbsp water
10 whole black peppers	½ cup sour cream

Prepare a marinade by combining first 7 ingredients in a saucepan. Heat to boiling quickly; cool. Place rabbit in an enamel or glass bowl and cover with the marinade. Cover bowl and set in refrigerator over night. Lift rabbit from liquid and drain slightly. Brown in the hot butter over medium heat (about 15 min). Reduce heat and add ½ cup of the 2 cups strained marinade. Cover and simmer for 1 hr or until about tender. Add onion and a little more marinade and continue to simmer until rabbit is very tender. Make a paste of flour and water and stir thoroughly into rabbit liquid. Allow to boil 2 min. Stir in the sour cream. Blend thoroughly and heat just to boiling. Serve at once. 3 to 4 servings.

RABBIT FRICASSEE

1 rabbit, 1½ lbs dressed	¼ cup shortening
⅓ cup flour	1 tbsp finely chopped onion
2 tsp salt	¾ cup water (*or* milk if
Dash of pepper	desired)
¼ tsp paprika	

See special precautions for the handling of wild rabbits on p 742. Clean rabbit, then wipe thoroughly with a damp cloth and pick off any hair. Rinse well with water. Dry. Cut into serving pieces, being careful to separate at the joints (never wash after cutting). Mix together the flour, salt, pepper and paprika in a clean paper bag and add a few pieces of rabbit at a time, shaking well until thoroughly dredged. Brown slowly in hot shortening over medium heat (takes about ½ hr). Add

*See special precautions for the handling of wild rabbits on p 742.

any remaining flour mixture from the bag, and the onion. Allow to sauté slightly, then add ½ cup of the water. Cover and simmer gently until done. Add remaining ¼ cup water as needed. Rabbit should be very tender when done (about 1 hr). If more gravy is desired, the amount of liquid and flour may be increased after the rabbit is thoroughly done and removed from the pan. 3 to 4 servings.

RABBIT HASH

A good looking and delicious way to serve leftover rabbit

1½ to 2 cups chopped cooked rabbit
⅓ cup bacon drippings *or* shortening
3 medium baking potatoes, 1¼ lbs

3 medium onions, 6 oz
½ tsp celery salt
¼ tsp salt
Fresh ground black pepper

Remove meat from rabbit bones, and cut into small pieces with kitchen scissors or knife. Put drippings into skillet. Pare potatoes and grate coarsely. Slide potatoes into heated drippings; grate onion and add to potatoes; add rabbit and seasoning. Cover and cook moderately fast until potatoes are beautifully browned on under side. Stir to blend, turn over, cover again, and brown on under side. Cooking requires about 10 min in all. 4 servings.

JUGGED RABBIT

1 dressed rabbit, 1¾ lbs
3 cups cold water
2 tsp salt
¼ cup flour
¼ cup lard
2 egg-size onions
¹⁄₁₆ tsp black pepper
Dash of cayenne

2 slices lemon, ⅛-inch thick
2 chicken bouillon cubes in
2 cups hot water
2 tbsp flour
2½ lbs baking potatoes, pared, cut as for French Fries
½ tsp salt

Start oven 10 min before baking; set to mod (350° F).

Clean rabbit, p 745. Cut in serving pieces and place in bowl. Mix water and salt, pour over rabbit; turn small plate over to weigh down and let stand 20 min. Drain. Place on absorbent paper and pat dry. Roll each piece in flour. Heat lard in heavy skillet, brown rabbit on both sides well and cook slowly about 15 min. Remove to baking dish and add onion and lemon slices with rind removed and potatoes. Drain fat from skillet leaving about 2 tbsp, add flour, stir to keep smooth and slowly add bouillon-water mixture. Cook until gravy is slightly thickened. Pour over rabbit, cover and bake 45 min or until meat and potatoes are tender, 1½ to 2 hrs. 4 servings.

ROAST RABBIT WITH DRESSING

1 dressed rabbit, 1¼ lb	1 tsp poultry seasoning
½ tsp salt	½ tsp salt
Pepper	⅟₁₆ tsp black pepper
⅓ cup diced salt pork, ¼-inch	¼ cup hot water
dice	1 egg, slightly beaten
Rabbit liver and heart	1 tbsp flour
¼ cup chopped onion	5 thin slices salt pork, 5-inch
½ cup fine-cut celery	long
5 slices 3-day old bread	¼ cup water

Start oven 10 min before baking; set to mod (350° F).

Place the rabbit in bowl, cover with cold water to which 2 tsp salt have been added, and let soak 1 to 1¼ hrs. Drain well. Pat dry with absorbent paper or cloth. Sprinkle inside with salt and pepper. Brown the diced salt pork until almost crisp, add onion and celery, and cook until yellow, 3 to 5 min. About 2 min before onions and celery are cooked, add chopped rabbit liver and heart, and sauté. Pull or tear bread into small crumbs, add seasonings and toss; then add onion-celery mixture, and toss again. Add ¼-cup water to skillet, stir and add to slightly beaten egg. Pour over bread mixture and toss lightly with fork. Spoon stuffing lightly into seasoned rabbit, skewer and lace up loosely with string. Place in casserole or roasting pan, sprinkle both sides of rabbit with 1 tbsp flour and place thin slices of salt pork over it. Add water, cover, and bake 2 hrs or until very tender. Remove cover the last ½ hr of baking.

RABBIT SOUP

2 lbs bony pieces of rabbit*	2 slices onion
5 cups cold water	2 tsp salt
¼ cup diced celery	¼ cup rice
1 small carrot	2 tbsp chopped parsley

Use ribs, front legs and bony parts of 2 or 3 rabbits or enough to make 2 lbs. (Use fleshy parts for roasting or frying.) Put rabbit, water, celery, carrot and onion in kettle. Heat to boiling, reduce heat, cover and simmer for 2 hrs. Add salt and simmer another 30 min. Strain. To the boiling broth, add the raw rice slowly and let cook for 20 min. Meanwhile, remove meat from bones, chop and add to the soup. Additional seasoning such as a small amount of sweet basil, marjoram, rosemary or cloves may be added if desired. Add parsley and serve at once. 5 to 6 servings.

*See special precautions for handling wild rabbit on p 742.

RACCOON

Raccoon meat is very dark and when the coon's food is abundant, the body is covered with a thick layer of fat that has an exceptionally strong flavor and odor. This fat also extends in layers between the strong bands of muscle. It should always be removed along with the scent glands. Unless these glands are removed, the meat will have a tainted flavor. The scent glands are located under the forelegs and along the spine in the small of the back. They are usually pea-shaped, have a waxy texture and range from a reddish to a light yellow color. Care should be taken when removing the glands to never cut into them or bring them in contact with the flesh. Those most experienced in the cooking of coon recommend parboiling it first. Some also add a tbsp each of baking soda and black pepper to the parboiling water to remove the strong gamey flavor.

BAKED COON WITH SOUTHERN DRESSING

1 small coon *or* hindquarters and loin of larger young coon, 2 to 2½ lbs dressed weight	3 to 4 cups cold water 1 tbsp salt ⅓ tsp black pepper *or* ½ tsp dry hot red pepper pod

Start oven 10 min before baking; set to mod hot (400° F).

Dress coon carefully so as not to leave any clinging hair. Remove scent glands, kernels under legs. Wrap coon in waxed paper or foil and chill thoroughly or freeze for several hrs. Trim off all but a thin layer of fat and any discolored spots. Wash well in lukewarm water. Cut whole coon or hindquarters and loin into 4 pieces with kitchen scissors or heavy butcher knife. Put into 3-qt kettle, add water, salt and pepper. Heat to boiling, then reduce heat to simmering, cover and cook until tender—from 1 to 2 hrs depending on age of animal. Meanwhile prepare Southern Dressing, p 778. Pour dressing into a casserole. Lay coon over top and press down into dressing. Cover and bake until coon is tender, 45 min to 1 hr. Then uncover and continue baking until coon and dressing are nicely browned or for about 30 min more. Parboiled pared sweet potatoes or winter squash may be baked with this coon instead of the dressing. A tart vegetable such as sauerkraut, sweet sour red cabbage or pickled beets are a good accompaniment. 4 servings.

SOUTHERN DRESSING

6 slices white bread from 1¼   ¾ to 1 tsp poultry seasoning
  lb loaf   or sage
½ cup finely chopped onions,   2 small eggs
  2 small   1 cup coon broth, from par-
1 to 1½ tbsp finely chopped   boiling coon or
  parsley   1 chicken bouillon cube
⅓ cup yellow corn meal   dissolved in 1 cup water
⅛ tsp pepper   1 cup milk

Bread should be 2 or 3 days old, but not stale enough to be dry.
Tear into coarse crumbs and drop into mixing bowl. Add rest of ingredients and stir gently until well blended. 4 cups dressing or enough
for 4 or 5 lb fowl or 2 or 3 lb coon.

MRS. McDANIEL'S BARBECUED COON

1 medium size young coon or   1 dry hot red pepper pod,
  2 small, 4½ to 5 lbs   4 inches long
  dressed weight   ⅓ to ½ cup 5% cider vinegar
1½ qts cold water   ¼ tsp black pepper
2½ tbsp salt   3 to 4 lbs sweet potatoes

Start oven 10 min before baking; set to mod hot (400° F).

Dress coon carefully so as not to leave clinging hair. Be sure to
remove scent glands, kernels under legs. Wrap coon in heavy waxed
paper or aluminum foil and chill thoroughly or freeze for a few hrs.
When ready to cook, pull off and trim off all but a thin layer of the fat
using a sharp paring knife; then trim off any discolored spots with
kitchen scissors. Wash well in lukewarm water. Put coon into a 5-qt
kettle, add cold water, salt and well-crushed red pepper. Heat to boiling,
cover, reduce heat and simmer until coon is about tender, from 1 to
1½ hrs. Remove coon from broth to a roasting pan with a cover. Drizzle
vinegar over outside and inside of coon, sprinkle with black pepper
and more finely crushed red pepper if a peppy barbecued flavor is
desired. Cover and bake 30 min. Meanwhile pare sweet potatoes, boil
gently in enough water or coon broth, if coon flavored potatoes are
desired, to cover for 15 min. Arrange drained sweet potatoes over coon
and bake uncovered until potatoes and coon are attractively brown,
about 45 min. A little more vinegar may be drizzled over coon before
potatoes are added for more pronounced barbecue flavor. A little sugar
may be sifted over potatoes before starting to bake. 8 to 10 servings.

SQUIRRELS

These small fur-bearing animals have scent glands in the small of
the back and under the forelegs and the thighs. These should be re-

moved without cutting into them. The fat on the squirrel is usually very spare and most people do not object to its flavor or odor. Squirrel may be cooked successfully by all good recipes for chicken except that fat should be added to give the necessary rich flavor. Young tender squirrels can be fried, broiled, and roasted; older squirrels need to be simmered, fricasseed, or braised.

SQUIRREL FRICASSEE

2 dressed young squirrels,	½ cup shortening
2 lbs	½ to ¾ cup water
1½ tsp salt	1½ cups milk
Pepper	1 tsp grated onion, if desired
½ cup flour	

Wipe squirrel thoroughly with a damp cloth, pick off any hair. Remove scent glands, p 746. Examine carefully to locate imbedded shot and remove with a sharp pointed knife. Wash thoroughly inside and out in warm water. Drain well and cut into serving pieces, p 782. (Never wash after cutting up.) Combine salt, pepper and flour and dredge squirrel in this mixture to coat well. Heat shortening in a heavy skillet and brown pieces slowly on all sides to a rich brown, about 15 min. Add ¼ cup of the water, cover tightly, reduce the heat and simmer gently until tender (about 30 min). Add remaining water as needed. Squirrel should be very tender when done. Remove squirrel to a hot platter, cover to keep hot. Blend any leftover seasoned flour into the fat remaining in the skillet. Add milk gradually and cook until gravy boils and thickens, stirring constantly. Serve at once with squirrel. Add the grated onion for additional flavor, if desired. 4 servings.

SQUIRREL POT PIE

2 dressed squirrels, 2 to	Dash of black pepper
2½ lbs	2 tbsp butter
2½ cups water	Rolled Dumplings, p 245
1½ tsp salt	Parsley

This is an excellent way to cook old squirrels which are too tough for frying. Wipe thoroughly with a damp cloth and pick off any hair. Remove any shot (see fricasseed squirrel) and scent glands (p 746). Then wash well inside and out with warm water. Cut into serving pieces, p 782. Put squirrel into a kettle, add water and salt, heat to boiling, then reduce heat, cover tightly and simmer until very tender, from 2 to 3 hrs, the time depending on age of animal. The meat should be almost ready to fall from the bones. Add pepper and butter. Increase the heat until liquid boils. Lay the rolled dumplings over the top of squirrel, cover tightly and cook for 12 to 15 min. Do not lift cover during cooking. Remove squirrel to hot plate and arrange dumplings around the edge. Cooking the dumplings in the liquid should thicken the gravy to just the right consistency. Pour gravy over squirrel and dumplings. A little fresh chopped parsley may be sprinkled over the top for garnish. 4 servings.

WOODCHUCK

Like the beaver, woodchuck has dark tender meat, but its flavor is milder. There is a heavy layer of fat on the body just before the animal begins his winter sleep. The excess fat should be removed, but it is not necessary to remove all of it because its flavor is not disagreeable. The meat seems to be improved, however, with the same short parboiling recommended for beaver and coon. This animal also has scent glands that appear as kernels under the forelegs, under the thighs, and between the shoulders, on the back, and along the spine in the small of the back. Care should be used in removing all of these glands for the best flavor in the cooked meat. Woodchuck may be cooked like rabbit or squirrel.

WOODCHUCK PIE

1 woodchuck, 5 to 7 lbs	2 carrots
2 medium onions	2 medium potatoes
2 cloves	1 cup diced celery
1 tbsp whole black peppers	Baking Powder Biscuit
1 branch celery	dough, p 234
1 tbsp salt	

Skin and clean the woodchuck. Be sure to remove the 7 to 9 (depending on age) kernels found under the front legs and along the spine. If these are not removed, the meat will have too strong a flavor. Fit the woodchuck into a large bowl or pan, cover with cold water to which has been added 2 tbsp of salt. Cover and let stand in the refrigerator or in a cool place over night. Next morning drain off the salt water, rinse woodchuck well in cold water. Drain. Cut the woodchuck into serving pieces as you would a rabbit. Fit them compactly into a kettle, add the peeled whole onions stuck with a clove, the whole peppers, branch of celery, and the salt. Barely cover with cold water. Cover kettle, heat to boiling, then reduce heat and simmer until the meat is tender—from 1 to 2 hrs. Remove meat and cool. Boil the broth down to about 5 cups and strain. Add the peeled, sliced carrots and potatoes and the diced celery. Cook until about tender or for about ten min. While vegetables are cooking, remove the meat from the bones and cut meat into dice. Combine with the hot vegetables and taste for seasoning. Add more salt and pepper if desired. Turn into a baking dish large enough that the woodchuck mixture comes within an inch of the top. Cut out biscuits and place on the hot mixture. Bake in a hot oven (450° F) for 15 min, then reduce heat to 400° F and bake until the biscuits are baked well all the way through and the mixture is bubbling hot. 6 to 8 servings.

TURTLE

Although there are more than 50 species of fresh water turtle, only about half a dozen of the species are caught for market in important quantities. Practically all kinds are edible, however, and the main reason for the nonuse of turtles for food is a lack of knowledge of how to dress them.

"The first step in dressing is the removal of the head. This can be easily accomplished in the case of a snapper by causing it to snap at a stick. It grasps the stick with a tenacious hold and the head can be readily pulled forward. Other species can be made to protrude their heads by applying pressure with the foot to the back or upper part of the shell. After the head is well stretched out, the head can be cut off.

"The Fish and Wildlife Service describes the dressing of a turtle as follows: Run a sharp knife around the edges of the skin where it joins the shell. Pull back the skin over the legs to the feet which are then disjointed. The lower part of the shell or plastron is then removed by cutting through the bridges which join the upper and lower shells, cutting close to the lower part of the shell. With snappers and soft-shells, in which the bridges are rather soft and cartilaginous, this can be done with a sharp knife. With the terrapin, the bridge may be cut with a hatchet or saw. Having cut the bridges, the plastron or under shell may be readily removed by inserting a sharp knife just under it and lifting it off. This done, the entrails may be extracted with very little trouble, and the four quarters easily taken out from the carapace or upper shell. If one wishes to save the tenderloin in the upper part or 'ceiling' of the carapace, the ribs may be cut with a hatchet. This may appear to be a lengthy and complicated process, but it is simpler than killing, plucking and drawing a chicken."*

TURTLE SOUP No. 1

1½ qts strained chicken broth	1 medium onion
1 lb turtle meat (without	Salt and pepper to taste
bones or gristle)	1 tbsp chopped parsley
3 tbsp chicken fat	5 to 6 thin slices lemon

Prepare a richly flavored chicken broth seasoned only with salt. Strain. Cut turtle meat into small dice. Brown slowly in the chicken

*From Cooking Wild Game by Frank G. Ashbrook and Edna N. Sater, 1945, published by Orange Judd Publishing Company, New York, N. Y.

fat (or butter). Add chopped onion and sauté slowly over medium heat until onion is soft and yellow. Add turtle, onion, seasoning and any fat to chicken broth, heat to boiling, reduce heat and simmer gently for 10 min. Serve with a sprinkling of parsley on each bowl of soup and a paper-thin slice of lemon floated on top. 5 to 6 servings.

TURTLE SOUP No. 2

3 lbs turtle meat	2 sprigs parsley
3½ qts water	6 cloves
2 medium onions, finely chopped	1 tsp sugar
	1 cup canned tomatoes
1 branch celery, finely chopped	1 tbsp salt
	½ tsp whole black peppers
¼ bay leaf	3 tbsp butter

Wipe meat clean with a damp cloth. Cut meat from bones and add bones and gristle to water in a kettle. Add the remaining ingredients except butter, heat to boiling, reduce heat and simmer covered for 1 hr. Strain and discard vegetables and bones. Meanwhile cut turtle meat in small dice, about ¼-inch, and brown slowly in the butter until cubes are golden brown on all sides. Add browned meat and any remaining drippings to the strained broth, heat to boiling, reduce heat and simmer for 20 to 30 min until a rich flavor is developed in broth and the turtle meat is done. Do not overcook. Add more salt and pepper if needed. Serve piping hot. 8 to 10 servings.

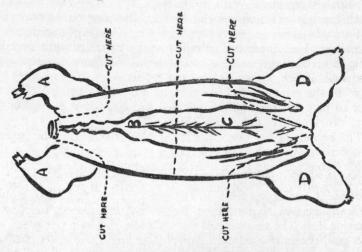

CUTTING FOR SERVING PIECES

The diagram shows where to make the cuts to separate the rabbit, marsh hare or squirrel carcass into serving pieces (a) forelegs, (b) ribs, (c) loin, (d) hind legs.

Garnishing

Garnishes are to foods what lace collars, belt buckles and costume jewelry are to dresses. And just like these ornamental accessories, garnishes must be well-chosen and well-placed to fulfill their function at the dinner table. If your garnishing repertoire is limited to a couple of bunches of parsley on the meat platter and a sprig of mint floating in the orangeade, you'll find that this chapter opens a fascinating new world.

★　　★　　★　　★

JUST as a simple dress may be given distinctive style by the addition of some carefully selected and skillfully placed trimming, so foods can be given added appeal to eye and palate by deft garnishing.

Garnishes for foods are usually devised from other foods, and should preferably be edible. Chefs and caterers sometimes depart from this rule and get beautiful effects, but their results are too elaborate to be practical in the home. Like dresses, which may have self-trimming or contrasting trimming, foods may be garnished with some of their own ingredients, or with other harmonious ingredients.

An example of a self-garnished dish is a Waldorf salad in which the bright red skin is left on the apple pieces, or some of the celery is cut into curls, or a whole nut is perched on top of a thick puff of mayonnaise on each serving. A contrasting garnish would be lemon wedges and parsley served around a baked fish.

HOW TO GARNISH

The keynote of any food garnish should be naturalness and simplicity. This is desirable partly because any food is more attractive when it does not look too "fixed up," and too labored over, and partly because application of an elaborate garnish may result in the food getting cold or losing its freshness before it reaches the table. In any case, it is well to have in mind the desired arrangement of the garnish before the food is even transferred to the serving dish. The amateur will gradually gain skill with practice.

A good system in learning to garnish is to keep in mind the parallel between garnishing food and trimming a dress. Dress trimming is used to make the dress look better—to accent it in line or color, to attract the attention to some special feature or sometimes to distract it from a flaw in the dress or the figure, and always to harmonize with it. It is never desirable to trim clothes so heavily or so profusely that the garments themselves are obscured.

Since garnishing food has the same purpose as trimming a dress, the same rules apply, with the added one that food which is to be eaten must never look handled. It may be possible to try a piece of trimming in several places on a dress without damaging the dress, but any "trying on" of food garnishes should be done in imagination or on paper, not on the food itself. Then when it is time to apply the actual garnish to the actual food, do it quickly with a light touch, and don't be afraid! If a sudden inspiration goes counter to the plan, follow it without hesitation, because that is how the most effective garnishing is often achieved.

WHAT TO GARNISH

There are few foods which are not made more pleasing to the eye, and therefore to the appetite, by a skillfully applied garnish. From the morning glass of orange juice, which is given a festive party-ish appearance by a floating sprig of fresh mint, to dessert at dinner, which may be a handsome layer cake with a garnish of frosting, few items of any menu will fail to respond. However, it is not desirable to garnish too many dishes at any meal, for the same reason that makes it undesirable to wear a much-trimmed hat with an elaborate dress and much jewelry. Let the garnish be applied to the featured dishes, and leave the other foods plain.

On this theory, garnishes are usually applied to roast meats, molded salads, desserts, cakes, pies and pastries, and fancy breads or sandwiches. But vegetables, soups, hot breads, beverages, simple salads, and most other foods may also be garnished if desired.

A FEW EXAMPLES OF GARNISHING

A whole baked ham is imposing enough to deserve the best of attention in garnishing. A form of self-garnishing is almost always done first of all: that is, the fatty surface of the baked ham is scored in squares, diamonds, triangles or other shapes to make the surface more interesting. Cloves are frequently used as an accent on the scored ham, and much variety is possible just in their placing. A clove in the center of each scored shape gives quite a different effect than a clove stuck in each angle, or a cluster of cloves in each center. Instead of cloves, sliced or whole candied cherries, pieces of bright-colored candy, fancy shapes cut from orange peel, pieces of vegetable or fruit, may be "appliquéed" onto the scored ham. Sometimes these are held on by cloves stuck through the pieces, sometimes just by the glaze applied to the ham surface.

The platter on which the ham is served may be garnished too. This is desirable because it helps to fill up the spaces around the ham, making it appear as though it belonged on the platter; and the same is true of poultry and other meats. Usually the platter garnish for ham is some food which is especially pleasing as an accompaniment, such as small whole baked or spiced apples, poached apple rings or wedges, and other fruits. Glazed sweet potatoes, baked sections of Hubbard squash, whole buttered onions, or any suitable vegetable carefully prepared may be used in this way. In general, the color should be bright and attractive and harmonious. Little sprigs or bunches of fresh green parsley often provide a color accent and fill in an empty space on the platter.

Molded salads are most suitably garnished with crisp salad greens. Lacy, curly endive, pale, slender-leaved aristocratic romaine, watercress with its simple form and peppery flavor are some of the widely differing types. Mint leaves may sometimes be used sparingly with molded fruit salads. The molds themselves may also be garnished, and this is usually done by arranging pieces of the ingredients—neatly diced or sliced fruits, vegetables, hard-cooked eggs—in the bottom of the mold and letting them become set in a thin layer of clear gelatin before the rest of the salad mixture is poured in; when unmolded, these pieces of course appear on top of the mold.

Pies are often self-garnished by elaborating the edge of the crust, or by cutting steam vents in the upper crust in a definite decorative pattern. Open-faced pies are garnished with meringue or whipped cream. Ungarnished pies may be served with side garnishes such as wedges or cut-outs of cheese, or grated cheese shaped in tiny fruit or vegetable forms, such as apples, pears, pumpkins and carrots.

Any cake icing is a garnish in itself and when part of the icing is tinted and piped on in fancy designs, it becomes one of the most elaborate of food garnishes. And a simple frosting skillfully applied with quick free swirls producing fresh, spontaneous appearance is much more appealing than one which has the look of having been worked over and smoothed out into a solid plaster-like surface.

WHERE TO PUT THE GARNISH

The best place for the garnish is different for every individual dish and every food. It depends on the shape and size of the food and its relation to the shape and size of the plate. Usually the garnish may be placed wherever there is a vacant place.

Suppose the dish to be garnished is a platter of Swiss steak with sauce poured over the meat. The sauce will flow over and around the meat un-evenly, filling the platter to the rim in some places and leaving it exposed in others. Don't interfere with the natural flow of the sauce to make it more even, for the natural shape is the beautiful shape; but take advantage of the vacant places to place the sprigs of parsley, making them large enough to be in proportion to the size of the platter and of the meat and arranging them so the whole platter is well balanced.

The size of the garnish is of great importance in the whole effect. A big loose bunch of parsley is perfectly suitable to a platter holding a big standing rib roast; a tiny sprig no larger than the tip of the little finger is suitable for the top of a dainty canapé. That same tiny sprig would not only be lost but would look like a joke on the meat platter, and the big bunch would overwhelm all the canapés on the plate. So the garnish, whether of parsley or some other material, should always be in proportion to the size of the dish and the food.

Balance is needed too. A bunch of parsley placed where the sauce left room for it on the Swiss steak platter may make the platter look over-balanced. That would call for another bunch, perhaps a much smaller one, or possibly two more placed elsewhere to bring it into balance again. If one of the additional bunches seems to be needed on top of the steak or right in the flow of the sauce, it is perfectly correct to put it there, since clean fresh parsley is an edible garnish.

Sometimes the garnish belongs on top of the food rather than on the rim or side of the dish. For example, a pat of butter or a dash of paprika may be placed on top of a fluffy mound of mashed potatoes; or slices of hard-cooked egg may top the bowl of potato salad. Sometimes the garnish may be placed to conceal an imperfection in the food, as for instance when the leg meat of a turkey draws far up the bone in roasting. Then the bare bone may be hidden by parsley or sometimes with a paper frill.

Paper frills for turkey or chicken legs, lamb chop bones (Frenched), and rib ends of crown roasts of lamb are one of the few exceptions to the rule that garnishes must be edible. It is possible to make simple paper frills at home. Take a piece of white note paper (ordinary typewriter paper is good) and cut a strip as long as possible and about 2 to 4 inches wide (the wider width for large turkeys, the smaller for chops and small chickens). Fold this strip lengthwise through the center, and with a pair of scissors snip the folded edge into fringe, cutting down each time about ⅔ the width of the folded strip. Then open the strip and fold it back the other way, but do not crease it this time. This strip may be fitted around the bone to be covered, and fastened with Scotch tape, a paper clip, or a common pin at the inside where it will show least. It makes a simple, practical, costless frill as dainty as any that can be bought. The lacy edges from paper doilies may be trimmed off and used for frills of a fancier type.

RULES FOR GARNISHING

With the exception of the general rules of simplicity, naturalness and beauty which were mentioned at the beginning of this chapter, there are no hard and fast rules for garnishing. Every woman makes her own rules and these are dictated by her own experience and her own inclinations.

The beginner should keep in mind the purpose of garnishes which is to make the food more attractive—not to hide them, nor to make them look bizarre, nor even to startle the onlooker.

She should also remember that garnishing is not a matter of life and death, and go ahead without hesitation to follow her own ideas. As she practices, she will develop a "feel" for the right thing and the artistic thing, and may end by surprising herself with her own ingenuity.

It is always good to study garnishes in the food pages of magazines and newspapers of high quality, but very impractical to try to follow them exactly, for it is seldom possible to duplicate exactly the shape and size of the food and platter, and the style of table arrangement in the picture. These illustrations should be regarded simply as idea-provokers.

Food garnishes should be a way of expressing individuality creatively. The important thing is for each woman to work in her own way with her own ideas.

For ideas see illustrations of Canapés in chapter on Appetizers, also pictures on edible garnishes, pp 175–179

Meat

Meat is the hub of the meal for most American families. In this chapter you will learn how to do justice to those occasional de luxe cuts which make a gala meal. Also, what is even more important, you will learn to make the modestly priced pot roasts, stew, braised meats and meat loaves taste so good that the folks will give three cheers for the cuts that keep the budget within bounds.

★　　★　　★　　★

MEAT is the most expensive single item in the food budget. It is also the star performer in most menus . . . certain other foods are just naturally suited to accompany a pork roast, veal chops, leg of lamb, or short ribs. A well-cooked meat will highlight an otherwise plain dinner, but no matter how elegant the trimmings, a poorly cooked meat will result in a disappointing meal. Because a large part of our food dollar is spent for meat, and because this meat plays an important part in the aesthetic and nutritional satisfaction derived from our meals, it is very important that we know how to purchase and cook this food in the best possible way.

Since successful meat cookery for the housewife begins in the meat market, it is essential that she is able to choose the cut of meat most suited to the cooking method. It would be wasteful and unwise to buy a sirloin steak for stew, even if one could afford it; and just as unwise to buy short ribs for broiling. The less tender cuts can be made delicious and tender by the proper cooking, and a tender piece of meat can be ruined by poor cooking. Every cut as well as each grade of meat responds best to a specific method of cooking . . . the only real problem is *learning* the proper method for each. For the same kind of meat (beef, veal, lamb, or pork), there is no difference in nutritive value or digestibility between the tender (and therefore more expensive) and the less tender (and less expensive) cuts when both are properly cooked. The variety meats are an exception to this, since most of them are higher in nutritive value than any of the other cuts. Each grade and cut of meat has an important place in the diet.

The purchasing problem is partly solved by finding a dependable meat market that consistently carries the kind of meat that suits your household in quality and cost. But beyond this, it is essential that every homemaker know certain basic facts about meat for the protection of her family's health and for the wise expenditure of her food money.

The Federal Government provides two services to the consumer in respect to meat. One of these is the inspection of meat by trained veterinarians to prevent the sale of unwholesome or diseased meat, or meat which has been prepared under unsanitary conditions. Under Federal regulations, all meat that is to be shipped in interstate commerce must be federally inspected and stamped. Meat that is not to be shipped from one state to another need not be inspected unless the state laws require it. However, most large meat packers have all their meat inspected regardless of where it is to be sold.

Federally inspected meat bears a stamp placed on all the large, wholesale cuts reading "U. S. Inspected and Passed," which is stamped on the meat with a harmless vegetable coloring as shown in the accompanying sketch. Federal inspection of meat has resulted in the decreased incidence of such animal-borne diseases as trichinosis, tuberculosis, and undulant fever. The housewife should insist that the stores in her community provide government inspected meats of all kinds including sausage and other prepared meats. This is a guarantee of safety to her family, and an assurance that the meat is wholesome and was produced under sanitary conditions. Inspection, however, does not indicate whether the meat is of high or low grade.

This United States Government inspection stamp on wholesale or retail cuts of fresh and cured meats (including sausage) indicates that the meat was federally inspected and passed. The number is the packing house number.

The second service that the Government provides is grading of meat. Grading should not be confused with meat inspection. Grading of meat is optional* while the "inspected and passed" stamp *must* appear on all wholesale meats that pass through interstate commerce. The government is willing to grade meat for a very nominal fee, but so far, this is only done at the packer's or buyer's request. Government grading is highly desirable for it passes on to the retail consumer-buyer the experience of a competent unprejudiced government grader.

Some packers grade their own meat, but these grades are somewhat confusing to the buyer. The packers may be just as expert and thorough in their grading as the government graders, but each packer has his own brand names and there is variation in the names as well as the requirements for each brand. Packer brands may help in selecting the meats of one packer, but give no help in comparing the brands of different packers. Government grades on the other hand, are the same for all packers, and provide a standard for selection of all meats.

Meat carcasses and cuts are assigned to classes and grades indicating their probable flavor and tenderness. The "Classes" refer to the sex and age of the carcass (steers, heifers, cows, bulls, and stags for beef). The "Grades" refer to the shape or build of the carcass (conformation), the amount and

*In order that price ceilings might be maintained during World War II, and during the emergency beginning in 1951, government grading of beef, veal and lamb was made compulsory.

distribution of fat (finish), and the color, texture, and firmness of lean, fat, and bone (quality). The best meat comes from animals that have been bred for generations for meat production, not from dairy cattle or brood sows.

There are seven official U. S. Government grades of beef—U. S. Prime, U. S. Choice, U. S. Good, U. S. Commercial, U. S. Utility, U. S. Cutter, U. S. Canner. The "U. S." is part of the name, and all meat graded by the government carries the full name of the grade down the entire length of the carcass, so that each retail cut plainly carries the grade marking when the carcass is divided for sale. However, only four of these grades are commonly found in retail markets. U. S. Prime is too costly and too rare, and U. S. Cutter, and U. S. Canner cuts are seldom sold in retail stores.

U S D A PRIME—As the name implies, beef of this grade is highly acceptable and palatable. Prime grade beef is produced from young and well-fed beef-type cattle. The youth of the animal and the careful intensive feeding it has had, combine to produce high quality beef. Cuts from such beef have liberal quantities of fat interspersed within the lean (marbling). These characteristics contribute greatly to juiciness, tenderness and flavor of the meat. Rib roasts and loin steaks of this grade are consistently tender, and cuts from the round and chuck also should be highly satisfactory.

U S D A CHOICE—This grade is preferred by most consumers because it is of high quality with less fat than the Prime grade. More of this grade of beef is produced than of any other grade. Choice grade beef is usually available the year round in substantial quantity. Roasts and steaks from the loin and rib are tender and juicy. Cuts from the round or chuck are more suitable for braising or as pot roasts and are tender and have a well-developed flavor.

U S D A GOOD—This grade pleases thrifty homemakers desiring beef with little fat but with other qualities that are acceptable. Although cuts of this grade lack the juiciness associated with a higher degree of fatness, their relative tenderness and high proportion of lean to fat make them the preference of many people.

U S D A COMMERCIAL—Beef that is graded Commercial is produced largely from older animals and usually lacks the tenderness of the three previous grades. Cuts from this grade, when carefully prepared, produce satisfactory and economical meat dishes. Most of these cuts require long, slow cooking with moist heat to make them tender and to develop the rich, full beef flavor characteristic of mature beef. Some young animals produce beef of Commercial grade. Cuts from carcasses of these animals have very thin fat covering and practically no marbling.

U S D A UTILITY—Beef of this grade is produced mostly from cattle somewhat advanced in age. It is usually lacking in natural tenderness and juiciness. The cuts of this grade, as they appear in the retail markets, carry very little fat. However, they provide a palatable, economical source of lean meat for pot roasts, stews or ground-meat dishes. For satisfactory results, long slow cooking by moist heat is essential.

U S CUTTER AND U S CANNER—are the lowest grades of beef used. Boneless cuts from these grades are sometimes found in the lower priced markets. However, they are used mainly in canned meats and in ground sausage products. Bulls and stags may be graded in these two classes, but the name "bull" or "stag" must appear on the carcass along with the grade stamp.

The grading of beef is more important than the grading of other animal meats from the buyer's standpoint, as there is greater variation in quality of beef than there is in lamb, veal or pork. The Government grades for these other meats are as follows:

Veal and Calf. "There are six grades of veal and calf carcasses, each grade being based on the three characteristics used for grading beef carcasses." These grades are U S Prime, U S Choice, U S Good, U S Commercial, U S Utility and U S Cull.

Lamb and Mutton. "There are five Federal grades for lamb and yearling mutton. All are based, as determined for grading, on conformation, finish and quality." (See above.) The grades are: U S Prime, U S Choice, U S Good, U S Utility and U S Cull. There are four grades for Mutton: U S Choice, U S Good, U S Utility and U S Cull.

Pork. "In general, pork produced in the United States is more standardized than any other class of meat, hence there is less need for a greater number of grades. All three groups of pork carcasses, i.e., meat-type, fat-type, and sow (packing) are divided into four grades." U. S. No. 1, U. S. No. 2, U. S. No. 3, and U. S. Cull.

COOKING MEAT

There are only two basic ways of cooking meat; by dry heat and by moist heat. Each of these methods has modifications: under dry heat there is roasting, broiling, pan-broiling and frying; under moist heat, braising and cooking in water. The method to be used depends on the kind and cut of meat to be cooked, and the grade.

In general, dry heat cooking is successful with meats which have comparatively little connective tissue, and which readily become tender when cooked. Moist heat is required by meats with more connective tissue, and which are tenderized only by long, slow cooking. The tender cuts of meat are never at their best when cooked by moist heat; and the less tender meats are never satisfactory when cooked by dry heat.

ROASTING

To roast meat is to cook it by dry heat in the oven. When the method is used correctly, a *roast* is never cooked in a covered roaster, since it would then steam, and therefore be cooked by moist heat. The temp of the oven is probably the most important factor in producing a satisfactory roast. The oven should be pre-heated to a temp of 300–350° F (300° for veal, beef, smoked pork and lamb; 350° for fresk pork) and maintained at this moderately low temp throughout cooking. No water should be added at any time.

Searing, or putting the roast into a very hot oven for a few min and then lowering the temp to finish cooking, was formerly thought to improve a roast by "sealing in the juices," but more modern experimental work has shown that instead of retaining the juices better, searing meat produces greater shrinkage and makes the meat dryer. However, there are still persons who prefer dark brown gravy with their roast meats and continue to sear meat, even at the expense of a loss in weight and juiciness.

Experimental work, repeated time and time again, has provided the basis for the recommendations of low constant temp for meat cookery. As an example, two loin roasts of exactly the same weight are used, and one is the right, the other the left loin of the same carcass; these are called "paired roasts." They are then cooked at two different temps; one is roasted at a constant high temp, 500° F to an internal temp of 185° F (well-done for pork). The other is roasted at 350° F to an internal temp of 185° F. The roast cooked at the high temp was in the oven 1 hr and 15 min, weighed 3 lb 8 oz after cooking, with a weight loss of 1 lb 8 oz or 30%. There were 9 oz of drippings which were burned. The roast cooked at a low temp was in the oven 2 hr and 20 min, weighed 4 lb 4 oz after cooking, with a weight loss of 12 oz or 15%. There were 5 oz of drippings which were not burned. Cooking at low temp actually provided 12 more oz of cooked roast from a five-pound pork roast, and the meat was juicier and of better flavor.

A roast may be salted either before or after cooking; this is the only preparation necessary. The meat is placed in the roaster fat side up, and as the meat cooks, the fat will flow gradually down and make the roast self-basting. Extra basting is not necessary. (Very lean meat such as veal should be larded with fat bacon or salt pork before roasting.)

The use of a meat thermometer is recommended to check the doneness of roast meat even for experienced cooks. During cooking, the roast becomes hot on the outside first, and gradually heats up to the center. When the center of the roast reaches a certain temp, it can be depended upon to have reached a certain doneness. Most modern meat thermometers have a scale marked both in degrees and in doneness; that is, 185° will be marked well done for fresh pork, whereas 170° will be well done for beef (see chart No. 37 and chart No. 28, p 863 and p 804).

In using a meat thermometer, make a hole first by piercing with an ice pick or skewer making certain it is inserted so the bulb will be in the center of the roast, but does not touch any bone or fat. Then insert thermometer before placing the roast in the oven.

BROILING

Broiling is a method of dry heat cookery which is done by direct heat either over hot coals or, as in the modern range, under a gas flame or electric heating unit.

A variation of broiling, called *pan-broiling,* is done in a hot uncovered skillet on top of the stove. Heat is transmitted to the meat by the hot metal. As the meat heats, the fat melts to prevent the meat from sticking. Any excess fat that accumulates in the pan is poured off from time to time, and the meat turned frequently. Both methods are used only for very tender meats, such as fine steaks and lamb chops, and the object is the same, to produce a richly browned surface and plump juicy center which is done just to the desired point. This speedy method results in a product of superior flavor and appearance.

As in roasting, a moderately low temp (350° F) is now being advised for broiling. This temperature is obtained in the following way: If the broiler has a regulator, or if it is regulated by the oven regulator, it should be set for 550° F and pre-heated for 10 min. If there is no temp regulator, the heat may be turned on full. The broiler rack should be placed so the top of the meat is *3 inches* from the source of heat for 2-inch steaks or chops, or 2 inches from the source of heat for 1-inch steaks or chops. This will make the temp at the surface of the meat about 350° F. If the oven is constructed so the broiler tray cannot be placed as far as 3 inches from the heat, one needs to reduce the heat accordingly.

Steaks and chops are the cuts which are usually broiled and pan-broiled. Steaks should be cut at least 1 inch thick, and chops at least ¾ inch thick. Thinner cuts cannot be broiled successfully, because the center will become done before the outside is sufficiently browned and the meat will be dry. Pan-broiled steaks and chops brown more rapidly and may be cut thinner.

Fresh pork and veal should never be broiled. Pork requires thorough cooking to bring out its full flavor and also to make it safe for health; and it cannot be cooked long enough by broiling. Pork chops and steaks may be browned in a skillet without adding fat, but they should be *covered* to finish cooking, and are therefore "braised" rather than "pan-broiled." Veal contains so little fat and so much connective tissue that it requires long, slow cooking with moist heat to make it tender.

The broiling method is extremely simple and very quick. The broiler is preheated, then the surface is quickly rubbed with a piece of suet so it will be lightly greased. Heavy rims of fat on steaks or chops should be trimmed off or the fat should be slashed in several places for excess fat to fry out and to prevent curling. Steaks or chops are then put on the rack and cooked until the upper side is nicely browned. When one side is done, salt is sprinkled over the meat, then it is turned over and broiled on the other side to the desired stage of doneness, then more salt is sprinkled on top. Meat may be broiled rare, medium or well-done, but well-done broiled steaks tend to be dry. Steaks should not be cooked more than medium for the finest flavor and juiciness.

It is difficult to use a thermometer for broiling unless the steak is very large and thick, and even then its use is awkward. The best test for doneness is to make a very small cut into the center of the meat. Experience will soon enable you to judge the proper length of time to broil meats to the doneness preferred by your family.

Pan-broiled meats are cooked in much the same way, except that they are placed in a pre-heated heavy skillet instead of on the broiler rack. The skillet need not be greased with additional fat, but the steaks or chops can be stacked and laid in the pan on the fat rim along the edge and moved about in the skillet long enough to grease it lightly. Then the meat may be separated and laid down flat. This will prevent sticking, and the fat in the meat will immediately begin to cook out. If any additional fat is used, as for lean meat such as lamb patties, it should be just enough to grease the pan. Any excess fat that accumulates in the pan should be drained off during the cooking.

FRYING

The term frying means to cook in a small amount of fat *uncovered*, or to cook in deep-fat (also called "deep-fat frying"). Although the term "frying" is applied to meat, the frying method is rarely used because other methods give better results. Some people brown their meat quickly, then add a small amount of water and cover and continue to cook until the meat is tender; or cover without adding water. This, however, steams the meat and is actually braising, not frying. It is possible to fry thin slices of round steak, veal steak and chops by browning the meat in a small amount of added fat in a skillet. The cooking is continued over low heat, uncovered, turning frequently until the meat is done. Frequently the meat is floured or breaded. This method results in a crisply browned exterior, but the meat is usually less tender than by other methods. Occasionally some cuts are deep-fat fried.

BRAISING

Braising is a method of moist-heat cookery in which a very small amount of liquid is used to complete the cooking after the meat has been very slowly and deeply browned in its own fat or in a small amount of added fat. This deep browning is very necessary to turn out a finished meat dish of a luscious brown color. The long slow cooking in moist heat dissolves out the brown color, and unless it is deep and rich to begin with, the color won't be so attractive when the meat is done. Extra liquid may be added or the braising may be done by the steam from the meat after the pan is tightly covered. Braised meat is always cooked in a tightly covered pan, either on top of the stove or in the oven.

Types of meat dishes which are cooked by braising are pot roasts, Swiss steaks, sauerbraten, fricassees, and meats cooked en casserole, and most cuts of pork and veal.

The liquid used in braising meats may be water, meat stock, vegetable pot liquor, milk, cream or sour cream, tomato juice, diluted vinegar, cider, grape juice, or other fruit juices; or in some cases it may be simply the juice from the meat itself. When an acid, such as vinegar, tomato juice or fruit juice, is the liquid employed, it affects the flavor considerably and may have some tenderizing effect on the connective tissue. In a very tightly covered kettle, such as a Dutch oven with a well-fitting lid, it is often possible to cook a pot roast, for example, without adding any liquid. The steam formed from the meat juices collects as liquid inside the lid and drops back to the bottom of the kettle. When water is used, it should be added in very small portions, as needed, using just enough to prevent the meat from cooking dry and scorching—the secret of attaining attractive, luscious braised meats.

Some of the flavor of the meat is lost to the liquid in braising. Therefore, it is important to use the liquid as gravy to be served with the meat. It may be poured over the meat just as it is, or extended by thickening with flour and adding more liquid (water, milk, cream or stock) after the meat has been removed. The flavor of the liquid or drippings from braised meat is so concentrated that it makes excellent gravy.

Braised meats require more cooking time per lb than roast meats. In fact, the object of braising is to provide longer, slower cooking in moist heat to soften the connective tissue. The cooking temp, whether braising is done in the oven or on top of the stove, should therefore be low, never above simmering.

All the less tender cuts of meat may be cooked by braising with the exception of such cuts as "soup" knuckles, etc. This method not only makes meats more tender but develops their natural rich flavors. Some beef cuts, such as flank and round steaks, are scored or pounded before cooking. This breaks the tough connective tissue and makes a shorter cooking time possible.

COOKING IN WATER

Cooking in water is a method of cooking by moist heat in which considerably more water is used than is required for braising. *Stewing* meat is the cooking of browned or unbrowned small uniform pieces in a small amount of water at a temp slightly below boiling with or without the addition of vegetables.

Stewing meat may be cooked covered either on top of the stove or in the oven; for top-of-stove cooking, a heavy kettle or Dutch oven is desirable; for oven cooking, an aluminum, iron or glass casserole may be used.

Stews may have a brown or light gravy, and may be cooked with potatoes only or with a combination of vegetables, and with any desired assortment of seasonings and spices. If dumplings are cooked with the stew, or if it is to be served with rice, macaroni, noodles or biscuits, the potatoes may be omitted.

The only difference between a brown stew and a light stew is that in brown stew the meat is slowly and deeply browned in a little fat before water is added; in a light stew, the meat is not browned. When meat is well browned, the stew takes on a richer brown color which appeals to most people, although the flavor is not very different from that of light stew.

The kind of meat used will also influence the color of a stew. Beef stews will always have a richer color than stews made with the light meats, veal and lamb.

A large variety of vegetables may be added. Those most frequently used are potatoes, carrots, onions, green beans, turnips, celery, peas and tomatoes. The combination of vegetables for stew should be planned as carefully as though the vegetables were to be served separately. The combinations of flavor, color and texture must all be considered. Vegetables are usually diced or sliced, or otherwise divided to make the pieces about the size of the pieces of meat and also interesting in shape. The vegetables will require less cooking time than the stew meat, and should be added after the meat is partially cooked so that they will not be overcooked when the meat is done. To do this, it is important to know the average time required to cook each vegetable before beginning. (See recipes in chapter on Vegetables and Stew Recipes in this chapter.)

Simmering is the term applied to the cooking of unbrowned large pieces of meat in a larger amount of water than is used in braising. The term "boiling" is often erroneously used when simmering is meant. In a liquid that boils (around 212° F) many bubbles form, rise to the top and break, and in a vigorous boil the top of the liquid rolls and foams. In a simmering liquid (from 185° to 200° F) few bubbles form, they rise to surface only occasionally. The surface of simmering liquid is almost quiet. Meat should never be boiled if the tenderness, shape, flavor and food value of the meat are to be preserved. Ham shanks, picnic shoulders, tongue, and corned beef are most frequently cooked by simmering, though this method is also applied to fresh meat such as veal which is being pre-cooked for veal à la king. When fresh meats are cooked in this way, the cooking water makes an excellent stock or broth which may be used to add flavor to soups and gravies.

Simmering is also the method used to make soup stock. In this particular case, the meat and bones are simmered gently for three or four hrs to extract as much flavor as possible. The meat is usually strained out, and may be chopped and returned to the soup, or used in a well-seasoned hash or croquette mixture. Cracked bones add to both flavor and food value of soup broth; these are of course strained out and discarded after cooking. Soup meat may be put on to cook in either hot or cold water.

Whether meat is being simmered to cook the meat or to obtain broth, the amount of water should be just enough to cover. If an excess is used, the flavor of both the meat and the broth will suffer by dilution.

Table 25 MEAT CUTS FOR MAKING SOUPS*

Beef	Lamb	Veal
Neck	Neck	Neck
Fore shank	Shank	Shank
Knuckle bone	Breast	Breast
Hind shank		

MEAT GRAVY

An important part of the meat course at any meal is the gravy served with it, for good gravy is not only delicious in itself, but enhances the flavor of the meat or the starchy food with which it is served.

A considerable amount of the vitamins and minerals of the meat may be leached out into the gravy, and unless all meat juices are used, much of the nutritive value is wasted.

Gravy usually accompanies roast and braised meats or poultry, some pan-broiled meats, fried chicken, and all meat juices should be used, even the juices that collect from broiled meat.

When we speak of gravy, a thickened or cream gravy is usually meant. But the juices from the meat itself with perhaps a little hot water added to extend the amount and dissolve all the rich-flavored residue in the pan is called pan gravy, preferred by many persons.

Good gravy should have the definite flavor of the meat with which it is served, not of some other meat. Beef gravy is delectable with roast beef, but with roast pork it is out of place. For this reason if it is necessary to "extend" gravy, the correct kind of bouillon cubes or meat extract paste should be used: beef for beef, and chicken for chicken.

Every kind of meat gravy has its own typical flavor; but its color varies, influenced by the method of cooking, the cooking temp, and the kind of liquid used for making the gravy. Most people like a rich brown gravy, except for chicken gravy, which is characteristically a pale tan.

The thickness depends altogether on the preference of the individual family. Some like gravy as thick as thick white sauce, others prefer a minimum of thickening or none at all. In some parts of the United States, a thickened gravy is regarded with contempt; and in other parts unthickened meat juices would be considered an unfinished gravy.

Whenever meat or poultry is roasted, there will be a considerable amount of flavorful juices and fat in the bottom of the roasting pan. Often there is too much fat for good gravy, and the excess should be skimmed off and saved for other cooking uses. Generally, some of the most savory brown residue sticks to the pan. If the gravy is not to be thickened, add a small amount of

*Ten Lessons on Meat for Use in Schools, Sixth Edition, published by National Live Stock and Meat Board, Chicago.

hot water (not more than a few tbsp) and place the pan over the heat, scraping lightly with a wooden spoon until the residue is loosened and dissolved. Cook this solution until it is sufficiently concentrated to have a good rich flavor; or if it should be already too strong in flavor, add more boiling water to dilute it slightly. This juicy pan gravy may be served just as it is with suitable seasoning.

If gravy is to be thickened, the flour is added directly to the fat and brown residue in the roasting pan in the proportion of about 1 tbsp of flour to each tbsp of fat, or enough to make a smooth paste with no free fat. The fat and flour are thoroughly blended together and water or milk added gradually, stirring until the gravy boils and thickens. The thickness can easily be adjusted to suit the family's preference by the amount of liquid added. All the residue will dissolve in the added liquid as the gravy is stirred. When the gravy has thickened, it should be simmered gently with occasional stirring for about 5 min—long enough to cook the flour thoroughly without impairing the flavor of the gravy. Straining will not be necessary if the gravy is kept smooth by stirring as it cooks; it is never desirable to strain, for the flecks give character to the gravy. When fat floats on gravy, too little flour or too much fat is used.

With braised meats or pot roasts that have been dredged with flour before cooking, the gravy may already be thick enough when the meat is done. If a larger quantity of gravy is desired, more liquid and a flour-water paste will be needed to extend the amount. The liquid may be milk, cooking water from vegetables, meat stock, or water flavored with a bouillon cube. But if the meat was not floured, and a considerable amount of unthickened liquid remains in the pan, the gravy may be thickened with a thin paste of flour and water, stirring this into the boiling hot liquid until it reaches the desired thickness; then simmering five min longer to cook the flour.

The gravy from fried or pan-broiled meats like lamb chops, or fried chicken can be made by the same method as with roast meat. Pour off any excess fat and blend the flour with the fat and juices remaining in the pan; then slowly stir in liquid.

Broiled and pan-broiled meats are too often served without gravy, but this is wasteful of flavor and nutritive value. The browned residue from broiler racks and pan should be scraped carefully with a wooden spoon, and a small amount of hot water added. This can be boiled quickly to dissolve the residue, and concentrate the gravy if necessary. This thin gravy should always be served over the meat.

If an unusually large amount of gravy is needed, extra meat broth may be made in advance to be used in place of other liquid to insure a good rich flavor. If a boned roast is being cooked, secure the bones from the butcher and simmer these for several hrs in water to obtain a good-flavored broth. Or if the roast is not boned, buy a soup bone along with the roast and do the same thing. With chicken, extra wing-tips, backs or feet may be bought and cooked along with the neck and giblets to make a concentrated broth.

By using this broth as the liquid, a much larger amount of flavorful gravy may be made than when plain water or milk is used.

Gravy should always go to the table piping hot. The gravy boat should be heated thoroughly before the gravy is poured into it by letting boiling water stand in it for a few min.

Gravy may be served as is, or elaborated by adding mushrooms, grated onion, vegetables, nuts, etc. The recipes for many unusual gravies will be found in this and the game and poultry chapters.

There are a few meat dishes (such as meat loaf) which yield little or no juices for gravy making, and in these cases the place of gravy must be taken by sauces. The Sauce section (p 1250) of this book contains recipes for sauces which are good not only with the meats themselves, but with the vegetables which are served with them.

MILK GRAVY OR THICKENED GRAVY

When roast is done, remove to a hot platter or to cover of roaster and cover to keep hot. When a 3 to 4 lb roast has been cooked, skim off all but 3 tbsp of fat. Allow all browned (not burned) residue and drippings from meat to remain in the pan. Blend in 2 to 3 tbsp of flour thoroughly and stir until smooth and slightly browned. Stir with a wooden spoon and scrape bottom of pan to loosen all the residue. Gradually add 1 cup of milk stirring constantly until mixture boils and thickens. Taste and add seasonings and milk if necessary to obtain the desired flavor and consistency. If gravy is too bland, a small amount of grated onion (½ tsp) will improve the flavor. If flavor is too concentrated and too thick, add more milk or water. Meat extract pastes or bouillon cubes may be used to advantage if a larger amount of gravy is desired than the roast will provide. Cook for 5 min, stirring constantly to cook starch in flour. Serve piping hot in a separate hot gravy boat. This same method can be used to make gravy from braised meats that are not dredged in flour before browning.

BROWN THICKENED GRAVY

Make gravy as directed above but brown the flour slowly to a rich golden color. *Be very careful not to burn.* Add 1 cup of water or meat broth gradually, instead of the milk, and proceed as directed above.

BRAISED MEAT OR POT ROAST GRAVY

To make gravy for braised meat or pot roasts that have a considerable amount of liquid in the pan that is not thickened, make a smooth paste of 2 to 3 tbsp of flour and ¼ cup of cold water. Remove meat from pan to hot platter and cover to keep warm. Heat liquid in pan to boiling, then gradually add the flour-water paste. Stir constantly until gravy boils and thickens and is smooth. Continue to cook for about 2 min to cook flour. Taste and season if necessary, or add more liquid to give the desired consistency. Serve piping hot over meat or in a separate heated gravy boat. If meat has been dredged in flour, the gravy may be thick enough, and only more liquid (water or milk) need be added.

PAN GRAVY

This type of gravy is never thickened. It may be made from the drippings and residue left on the rack and drip pan in the broiler, or from drippings left from roast, fried or pan-broiled meat. All excess grease should be poured or skimmed off. Then a small amount of water is poured over the racks or into the pan with any browned residue, and the pan or rack is carefully but thoroughly scraped with a wooden spoon to loosen the particles. When all this residue is removed, the rack may be taken off the broiler pan. The gravy is then stirred in the broiler pan, or skillet over low heat until all the particles are dissolved. Taste to decide if gravy must be concentrated for best flavor, or if more hot water is needed. Season if necessary. Heat to boiling and pour over the hot meat or serve in a separate heated gravy boat.

BEEF

TABLE 26　　　　TIME TABLE FOR BROILING BEEF

SUITABLE CUTS	WEIGHT	APPROXIMATE COOKING TIME	
		Rare	Medium
BEEF	Pounds	Minutes	Minutes
Chuck steak (U. S. Prime or Choice only)—1 inch	2⅓	24	30
1½ inches	4	40	45
Rib steak (U. S. Prime or Choice only)—1 inch	1½	15	20
1½ inches	2	25	30
2 inches	2¼	35	45
Club or T-bone Steak (U.S. Prime, Choice or Good)—1 inch........	1	15	20
1½ inches	1¼	25	30
2 inches	1½	35	45
Sirloin steak (U. S. Prime, Choice or Good)—1 inch	3	20	25
1½ inches	4¼	30	35
2 inches	5¾	40	45
Porterhouse steak (U. S. Prime, Choice or Good)—1 inch........	2	20	25
1½ inches	2½	30	35
2 inches	3	40	45
Ground beef patties or tenderloin (all grades) 1 inch thick by 3 inches.......	4 ounces	15	25

Note: This time table is based on broiling at a moderate temp. Rare steaks are broiled to an internal temp of 130° F; medium to 160° F. (See p 793.)

*Adapted from *Ten Lessons on Meat for Use in Schools,* Seventh Edition, published by National Live Stock and Meat Board, Chicago.

BEEF*

Chart No. 27

Meat Cuts and How to Cook Them
BEEF CHART

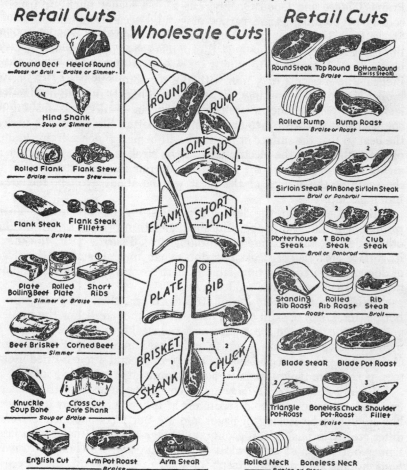

Ten Lessons on Meat for Use in Schools, Sixth Edition, published by National Live Stock and Meat Board, Chicago.

BROILED, FRIED, ROASTED BEEF

See p 800 for Time Table for Broiling

BROILED STEAK

Sirloin, Porterhouse, T-bone, Club and Tenderloin steaks of U. S. Prime, Choice and Good Quality, cut 1 to 2 inches thick are usually cooked by broiling; so are patties of ground meat from these grades. Steaks from beef lower in quality than U. S. Good are best when cut thinner and fried or braised. If the butcher has not trimmed fat off neatly, use a sharp knife to trim it off and make steaks more attractive. Preheat the broiler 4 or 5 min with the regulator set at 550° F, or if broiler has no temp markings, set at "broil." Quickly rub the hot broiler rack with a piece of suet. Place the steak on the broiler rack, shaping it compactly as you wish it to appear on the platter. Slide the rack under the heat so that the surface of the steak will be just 3 inches from the tip of the gas flame or the electric unit, if the steak is 2 inches thick, or 2 inches below if the steak is 1 inch thick. At this distance from the heat, the temp at the surface of the meat will be about 350° F, the ideal broiling temp.

Broil the steak to the desired brownness on the top surface. Then sprinkle with salt and pepper if desired, and turn over to brown on the other side. The time required for broiling steak depends on its thickness, its surface area (larger steaks take somewhat longer), and on the stage of doneness desired. The time table (Chart No. 26, p 800) gives broiling times for steaks and other broiled meats.

When done, sprinkle top of steak with salt, then lift steak onto a hot platter. Drain or skim off the excess fat in the pan below the broiler, and pour the collected meat juice over the steaks, or prepare pan gravy, p 766, to serve with steak. Garnish and serve immediately. French-Fried Onions, p 1361, Sautéed Mushrooms, p 1356, and French-Fried Potatoes, p 1375, are typical, popular accompaniments for broiled steak.

Buying Hints. Tenderloins are often stripped out from the loins of low-grade carcasses and sold separately at a high price; they are tender but are apt to be lacking in flavor and are not recommended. *Sirloins* differ greatly in quality and economy. *Wedge-bone* sirloins are the least tender but the most economical (more meat and less bone). *Round-bone* sirloins are excellent except for a tough narrow end; they are not quite as tender as double-bone and pin-bone sirloins. *Double-bone* is the best of the sirloins from all considerations, tender, flavorsome, and a small amount of waste. *Pin-bone or hip-bone* is excellent but has a large amount of bone (do not pay porterhouse prices for this steak, it is sometimes sold as such . . . look at both sides of a cut when buying steaks).

COUNTRY FRIED STEAK

For frying, have steak sliced from boneless chuck or top round of beef of grades no lower than U. S. Good. If buying lower grades, use sirloin, porterhouse or club steaks. Allow 1½ lbs, cut ½-inch thick for 4 people. Pound with a wooden mallet or edge of heavy saucer until almost paper thin. (Many butchers have special mallets or machines to prepare "cubed" or "minute" steaks.) Dredge in flour mixed with salt, allowing 1 tsp salt for each lb of meat. Heat 2 tbsp of shortening until sizzling hot in a heavy skillet; lay in steak, and brown quickly on both sides. It should then be done. Transfer to hot platter and cover to keep hot. Make gravy from the residue in the pan, pp 799–800. Steaks are best when cut in serving portions before cooking.

PAN-BROILED CUBED STEAK

A method that keeps the juice in

1½ lbs cubed steaks	2 tbsp butter
1½ tsp salt	1 tbsp chopped parsley
Pepper to season	

Use tender round steak, lean marbled with some fat. How to determine when skillet is hot enough for steak: a drop of water dripped into the skillet immediately explodes in steam. At this stage, sprinkle about half the salt into skillet. Lay in steaks which sear quickly. A sure indication that skillet is hot enough is that no juice runs out of steaks. Pan-broil steaks about ½-inch thick until richly browned on both sides— about 2 min to a side. While broiling, enough fat oozes from meat to grease skillet and keep it from sticking. If steaks are ¾-inch thick or more, turn once or twice after both sides are browned, and lower heat so meat will cook through to desired doneness. The state of doneness can be quickly determined by snipping into top of steak with kitchen scissors. When done, remove to hot platter, top each steak with lump of butter. Sprinkle with parsley. Add 1 to 2 tbsp water to hot skillet, scrape up brown residue, and pour over steaks. 4 servings.

Note: Hamburger patties, lamb chops, and pork chops may be prepared in a similar way.

RIB ROAST OF BEEF

When buying a standing rib roast of beef, get one at least 2 ribs thick and ask butcher to cut it "hotel style." When cut this way, the rib ends, which are the short ribs, are still attached. These may be cut off and braised, p 812, for another meal. In the rolled type of rib roast, these short rib ends are wrapped around the rib-eye and so cannot be cooked separately, therefore, it is not desirable to purchase a roast already boned and rolled. Carving of the standing roast is simplified when the butcher separates chine bone by sawing across ribs where they meet the backbone, then tying chine bone in place.

Place the standing rib roast fat-side up (to make it self-basting) in an open roasting pan so it rests on ends of the ribs, lifting roast off the pan. No rack is needed. Sprinkle with salt and pepper and insert the meat thermometer so bulb is in center of the large muscle and touches neither fat nor bone. A meat thermometer is a good investment because it helps one to know when roast is cooked to desired doneness. Roast according to size and at the temp and for time specified in Table 28. Do not cover the roast. Do not add water! When done, clip string and remove chine bone before transferring roast to hot platter. Cover to keep hot. Drain off all clear fat and make gravy from meat juice and residue in pan, p 799. A 2-rib roast weighing 3.6 to 5 lbs serves 5 to 6; a 3-rib roast weighing 8 to 10 lbs serves 10 to 12.

Note: Beef ribs from U. S. Utility Grade should be cooked by moist heat.

TABLE 28   TIME TABLE FOR ROASTING BEEF

Suitable Cuts	Weight	Oven Tempera-ture Constant	Interior Temperature When Removed From Oven	Approxi-mate Time Per Pound
BEEF	*Pounds*	*Degrees F.*	*Degrees F.*	*Minutes*
Standing ribs .... U.S. Commercial or better grades	6-8	300	140 (rare) 160 (medium) 170 (well-done)	18-20 22-25 27-30
Standing ribs (2 ribs).... U.S. Commercial or better grades	3.6	350	140 (rare) 160 (medium) 170 (well-done)	33 45 50
Rolled ribs or Tenderloin.. U.S. Commercial or better grades	6-8	300	140 (rare) 160 (medium) 170 (well-done)	32 38 48
Chuck ribs .... U.S. Good or better grades	5-8	300	150-170	25-30
Rump . . . . U.S. Prime or Choice (well-aged)	5-7	300	150-170	25-30

ROLLED RIB ROAST

With noodle mushrooms mounds

Purchase a large 2-rib standing beef roast, and have butcher remove rib end (which is cooked by braising, p 812), and remove bones and roll meat. Ask for removed bones, and have butcher crack them. The trimmed and rolled roast should weigh about 3 lbs. Rub salt, and pepper if desired, into the surface of the roast. Insert a meat thermometer so that the bulb will be in the center. Place the roast on a rack in an open roasting pan; it should lie on its side in order to have fat on top, making it self-basting. Cook to the desired doneness in a moderately slow oven (300–325° F). Do not cover or add water. The thermometer should read 140° F for rare; 160° F for medium; 170° F for well done. This requires 32 min per lb for rare meat; 38 for medium; or 48 for well done. Make gravy, p 799, from drippings left in pan, and serve with noodle mushroom mounds, made as follows:

Put the beef bones into a saucepan, cover with water, and add a branch of celery and 1 tsp salt. Cover and simmer at least 2 hr while roast is cooking. Remove bones and celery, and add salt to suit taste. Reheat to boiling, add 4 oz noodles and boil until they are tender, about 10 min. The last 2 or 3 min, add a small can of button mushrooms, juice and all, or ¼ lb fresh mushrooms which have been cleaned and sautéed in butter, p 1356. When noodles are done, drain off cooking water and use in making meat gravy. Mold the hot noodles and mushrooms in small custard cups or ½-cup measures and turn out on platter around the roast. Servings of buttered vegetables may be placed on the platter between the noodle mounds. Garnish with parsley. Roast serves 10 to 12.

Buying Hints. A roast cut from the heavy end of the ribs containing the tip of the shoulder blade is called a "Blade Rib Roast." It has less waste but is not as tender and flavorful as the lighter end. It should sell for less per lb and is more economical than the regular rib roast.

DICED MEAT ROAST

¾ lb boned beef chuck *or* shoulder arm	1 egg, beaten
¾ lb boned lean fresh pork	¾ cup cracker crumbs
½ cup hot water	1 tbsp lemon juice
½ tsp salt	¼ lb salt pork
	Parsley

Cut beef and pork in ½-inch dice. Add hot water. Combine all ingredients except salt pork, mixing thoroughly. Pack firmly into a loaf pan size 2½ x 8 x 4½ inches. Slice salt pork thin and lay over top of loaf. Roast in a moderate oven (350° F) for 1 hr. Turn out onto platter, reverse, garnish with parsley, and serve hot. 5 servings.

BRAISED MEAT

General directions

Wipe 2½ lbs of meat with damp cloth. Dredge with flour and brown slowly and richly on both sides in 2 tbsp fat in a heavy skillet or Dutch oven. This browning requires at least half an hr. Sprinkle with 1 tsp salt for each lb meat and a dash of pepper if desired. Add ½ cup water or any desired liquid, such as tomato juice; cover tightly, and simmer over very low heat or in a slow oven (300° F) until meat is tender. Approximate time indicated in following chart. Vegetables (except green vegetables) may be cooked with the meat if desired. Peel or scrape the vegetables and add to the meat during the last 45 min of the cooking period. The following vegetables are suggested: 2 onions, 3 branches celery, 5 carrots, and 5 potatoes. Add small amounts of additional liquid during the cooking period if needed. If gravy is not thick enough, make a paste of flour and water, using 2 tbsp of flour for every cup of liquid and drippings. Add the flour-water paste to the liquid remaining after meat has been removed from skillet (more water may be added to make enough gravy). Stir until gravy boils and thickens.

TABLE 29   TIME TABLE FOR BRAISING BEEF*

SUITABLE CUTS AND GRADES[1]	AVERAGE WEIGHT OR THICKNESS	APPROXIMATE COOKING TIME
Beef Birds (All grades)	½ in. x 2 in. x 4 in.	1½-2½ hours
Brisket (All grades)	3 to 5 lbs.	2-4 hours
Chuck, or Shoulder Arm pot roasts.. (U.S. Good or better grades)	3 to 4 lbs.	1½-2½ hours
Flank (All grades)	2-inch cubes	1½-2 hours
Foreshank (All grades)	2-inch cubes	1½-2½ hours
Fricassee	2-inch cubes	1½-2½ hours
Ground Beef (All grades)	4 oz. patty, 1 in. x 3 inches	15 to 20 minutes
Neck (All grades)	2-inch cubes	1½-2 hours
Oxtails (All grades)	2-inch sections	3 to 4 hours
Plate (All grades)	2-inch cubes	1½-2 hours
Rib (U.S. Utility)	3 to 5 lbs., bone in	2 to 4 hours
Round, pot roast (not including heel of round) (All grades)	3 to 4 lbs.	1½-2½ hours
Round or Chuck Steak (All grades)..	¾-inch thick	45-60 minutes
Rump pot roast (All grades)	3 to 5 lbs.	3-4 hours
Short Ribs (All grades)	Pieces (2 in. x 2 in. x 4 in.)	1½-2½ hours
Stuffed steak (All grades)	½ to ¾ inch thick	1½ hours
Swiss steak (All grades)	1½ to 2½ in. thick	2 to 3 hours

[1] Although theoretically all of the grades (not including Cutter and Canner which are not generally available anyway) can be cooked by braising, the cuts from the two top grades (U.S. Prime and U.S. Choice) contain too much fat to suit the average person. This, in addition to their higher cost as compared to the other grades, makes them impractical cuts for braising. Pot roasts are the only exception.

*Adapted from *Ten Lessons on Meat for Use in Schools,* Seventh Edition, published by National Live Stock and Meat Board, Chicago.

BEEF POT ROAST

A carefully cooked good pot roast is delicious as well as economical

4 lbs beef chuck, shoulder
   arm, round *or* rump
2½ tsp salt
Pepper
1 onion, large egg size

¼ cup water
Gravy:
½ cup water
2 tbsp flour

Wipe meat well with a damp cloth. Trim enough fat from around edge of meat with knife to make a tablespoonful. Then cut it into small pieces with scissors, dropping into heated Dutch oven. Sauté slowly until about 1 tbsp has melted out. Now add meat which has salt rubbed well into both sides. Brown slowly on all sides to a rich color, 25 to 30 min. When meat is brown, drain off fat if there is an excess. Now slip trivet under meat. Sprinkle with pepper. Cover with onion slices. Add water, cover tightly and cook over very low heat until tender, about 2½ hrs. No more water is required if cover is tight and heat is low enough, but if pot goes dry, add ¼ cup more water.

Thirty to 40 min before meat is done, add 4 scraped whole carrots, 4 pared halved potatoes and 2 or 3 peeled, halved onions. When tender, lift meat and vegetables onto platter; cover to keep warm. Skim off excess fat. Measure water and flour into a glass with a cover and shake to a smooth paste. Stir into liquid in Dutch oven and cook until smooth and thickened. Add more water or milk to make 1½ cups gravy. Cold pot roast is good sliced for cold meat platter, sandwiches or hash. 6 servings.

Buying Hints. The *center cut* of rump is recommended, the *7-bone* chuck, or the *top* round. Shoulder arm is also excellent.

Note: When pot roast is cooked in a chicken fryer without a trivet, the water evaporates more quickly, so add ¼ cup cold water as soon as the meat begins to sizzle in the fat.

BEEF POT ROAST SPANISH STYLE

Make Beef Pot Roast, substituting tomato juice for the hot water, and adding it gradually to obtain the best flavored gravy.

BEEF POT ROAST WITH VEGETABLES

When Beef Pot Roast has simmered until nearly tender (1½ to 2 hrs), add 8 small peeled onions, 8 carrots scraped and cut in halves, 8 medium potatoes pared and cut in halves and 3 branches celery cut in inch lengths and cook another ½ hr until meat and vegetables are tender; add a little more water if necessary. Remove meat and vegetables to hot platter and make gravy from liquid, p 799. 8 to 10 servings.

BEEF POT ROAST WITH MACEDOINE OF VEGETABLES

3 lb chuck, round, shoulder arm *or* rump roast	5 small carrots, scraped
3 tbsp bacon fat	1 medium onion, peeled
1 tbsp salt	4 small white turnips, pared
¼ cup water	1½ cups water
3 branches celery, diced	½ tsp salt
5 medium potatoes, pared	1 tsp chopped parsley

Wipe meat with a damp cloth. Heat fat in heavy skillet or Dutch oven and brown meat slowly on all sides—browning takes about 30 min. The deeper the browning is done, the more tempting will be the color of the finished pot roast. Add the tbsp salt and water, cover and *simmer* 1½ hrs, or until almost done, adding a little more water if needed. Meanwhile prepare vegetables: Add celery, whole potatoes and carrots to kettle, cover and cook 15 to 20 min or until tender. Chop onion and turnips and put into a 1-qt saucepan; add water and salt and cook uncovered until tender. When all vegetables are done, combine in the kettle and add only enough of onion-turnip cooking water to make desired amount of gravy. Remove meat and drained vegetables to hot platter. Thicken liquid in kettle with flour-water paste to desired thickness. Sprinkle meat and vegetables with parsley. Serve gravy in a separate dish. 5 servings.

BEEF STROGANOFF

3 tbsp flour	½ lb mushrooms
1 lb top round *or* tenderloin steak cut ½-inch thick	¼ tsp Worcestershire sauce
¼ cup butter *or* margarine	1 cup sour cream
1 small onion chopped fine, ¼ cup	1 tsp salt
	⅛ tsp pepper

Pound flour well into the beef until steak is about ¼-inch thick. Then cut into ¼-inch wide strips. Add beef strips to the butter heated in a heavy skillet and brown on all sides, turning frequently. Remove to bowl and cover to keep hot. Now add onion and cleaned sliced mushrooms; cover and cook slowly 5 min, stirring occasionally. Return meat to skillet, stir in Worcestershire and sour cream, cover and reheat to boiling. Season with salt and pepper, and serve at once with hot, fluffy boiled white, or wild rice. 5 servings.

BEEF SLICES IN ONION SAUCE

1 lb chuck, shoulder arm *or* round cut into ¼-inch slices, crossgrain	1 cup water
	½ lb large onions cut into thick slices
1½ tsp salt	2 tbsp flour
Dash of pepper	1 tsp sugar
3 tbsp shortening	

Season meat with salt and pepper, and brown on both sides in heated shortening in a heavy skillet or Dutch oven. Add ¼ cup of the water, cover tightly and simmer gently from 1 to 1½ hrs or until meat is almost tender. Add remaining water, ¼ cupful at a time as needed to keep pan from going dry. Push meat to one side of pan and carefully place onions in the shortening. Cover and simmer 20 to 30 min longer or until meat is tender and onions are transparent and soft. Carefully transfer meat and onions to a hot platter and cover to keep warm. Stir combined flour and sugar into drippings, adding more water if desired. Heat to boiling and pour over meat and onions. Serve at once. 4 servings.

BRAISED BRISKET WITH SWEET-SOUR GRAVY

3 lb beef brisket	½ cup chopped celery
2 tbsp butter	1 medium onion, sliced
3 tsp salt	¼ cup vinegar
Pepper to suit taste	3 tbsp sugar
1 carrot, scraped and sliced	

Cut brisket across the grain into 2-inch thick slices. Melt butter and brown meat slowly on both sides in a heavy skillet or Dutch oven; add seasonings, vegetables, vinegar and sugar. Cover tightly and simmer for 1½ to 2 hrs, or until very tender. Remove meat to hot platter. If unthickened gravy is desired, skim off excess fat and quickly evaporate liquid remaining in pan by boiling until the required amount remains. For thickened gravy, see p 799. To intensify the sweet-sour flavor, add an additional 1 tbsp vinegar and 1 tsp sugar. 5 to 7 servings.

OVEN BRAISED BRISKET OF BEEF

2¼ lb boned brisket	4 medium size potatoes
1½ tsp salt	½ tsp salt
Dash of pepper	1½ tsp flour mixed with
1 onion, egg size, sliced	2 tbsp water
¼ cup water	

Start oven 10 min before baking; set to moderately slow (325° F). Wipe meat with damp cloth. Place in casserole or roasting pan with tight fitting cover. Sprinkle with salt and pepper. Top with onion slices. Pour water around meat, cover and bake 2½ hrs or until almost tender. No more water is needed. Now pare potatoes, cut in half and place around meat; sprinkle them with salt, cover and continue baking until potatoes and meat are done, about 1 hr longer. Now drain meat juice from casserole into saucepan, add the flour-water paste and cook and stir until gravy thickens. Serve hot. 6 servings.

ROLLED STEAK

1¼ lb round steak, about ½ inch thick	¼ cup celery, finely chopped
¼ cup chopped onion	1¼ cups beef broth or
¼ cup bacon drippings	1 bouillon cube dissolved in 1¼ cups boiling water
1 qt soft bread crumbs pkd firmly	1 egg, beaten
½ tsp sage	Salt and pepper to suit taste

Wipe steak thoroughly with damp cloth. Do not pound all over vigorously with edge of heavy saucer. Sauté onion in drippings until yellow; add to bread crumbs and combine lightly with all remaining ingredients; if crumbs are quite dry, more liquid may be added. Spread dressing over the steak and roll up like a jelly roll; secure by tying at ends and center with string. Brown on all sides in a small amount of fat in a heavy skillet; add ½ cup hot water, cover tightly and place in a moderately slow oven (300° F) for 1 hr, or until meat is very tender. Remove meat roll to hot platter, remove string, cover to keep hot while making gravy from drippings in skillet. 5 servings.

ROULADES—(STUFFED BEEF ROLLS)

For neat Roulades, buy steak that will cut into almost square pieces of right size

1½ lb round steak, ⅓-inch thick	1 tsp salt
	½ tsp paprika
½ cup chopped onion	1½ tbsp flour for gravy
5 lean, thin slices bacon *or* salt pork	1¼ cups water
	½ tsp meat extract paste
2 tbsp flour	

Trim most of fat neatly from steak and render it out in a 10-inch skillet over low heat. Cut meat into 5 even-size pieces, about 5 x 4½-inches. Spread onion over meat. Cut bacon strips in half crosswise and lay 2 pieces over onion in opposite direction to way meat is to be rolled to make rolling easy. Roll up neatly, then wrap string around roll 2 or 3 times crosswise and once lengthwise and tie securely. Roll Roulades in flour blended with salt and paprika to coat well. Now brown the Roulades on all sides in 2 tbsp of the rendered fat. Then add ½ cup of the water, cover and simmer until tender, about 1 hr, turning meat occasionally. When tender, remove Roulades to hot platter. Make gravy by blending flour into fat in skillet until smooth, add remaining ¾ cup water and cook and stir until smooth. Stir in meat extract for richer flavor if desired. Cut strings from roulades and remove carefully. Pour gravy over the meat. 5 servings.

ROUND STEAK BIRDS

1½ lb round steak cut ½-inch thick	1 slice cooked bacon
	3 sprigs parsley, chopped
1 tsp salt	½ medium onion, chopped
1 cup coarse bread crumbs	2 tbsp bacon fat
1 egg, beaten	Hot water *or* beef broth

Cut steak into 5 serving portions. Do not pound steak. Combine crumbs, egg, crumbled bacon, parsley and onion, adding enough hot water or meat broth to bind ingredients together. Place ⅕ of this dressing in center of each piece of meat, and roll up, fastening securely with string. Heat fat in a heavy skillet and brown the meat rolls slowly on all sides. Now add 1 cup hot water or broth, cover and simmer 1 hr or until tender. Add more liquid if necessary. Remove to hot platter, remove string and cover to keep hot while making gravy. Serve gravy poured over the meat rolls. If desired, use meat stock instead of water for cooking birds and making gravy. 5 servings.

SAUERBRATEN No. 1

1½ cups water
½ cup vinegar
½ tsp whole black peppers
4 sq pieces bay leaf, ½ inch
1 tsp salt
1 medium onion, sliced

1½ lb boneless beef chuck *or* rump
2 tbsp butter *or* margarine
2 tbsp flour
½ cup thin *or* sour cream
½ tsp salt
Potato Dumplings

Heat water, vinegar, peppers, bay leaf and salt to *boiling*. Pour over onion and beef placed in an enamel or glass dish and cool. Then cover tightly and store in refrigerator at least 48 hrs, turning meat 2 or 3 times to season it uniformly. Lift out meat and drain; discard 3 pieces of bay leaf and half the peppers. Heat butter in heavy skillet and brown meat slowly on all sides, then sprinkle flour over meat, and again brown lightly on all sides, scraping bottom and sides of skillet with wooden spoon to prevent scorching. Now add all liquid in which beef soaked, stirring until bottom and sides of pan are free from particles of flour and fat. Cover and *simmer* about ½ hr, then remove bay leaf; again cover and *simmer* about 2 hrs longer or until meat is tender, turning meat and stirring gravy occasionally. Stir in cream and salt and simmer 5 min to blend thoroughly. Serve with Potato Dumplings, p 245. 4 servings.

*SAUERBRATEN No. 2

3 to 4 lb pot roast, larded, p 806
Dash of pepper
Dash of nutmeg
2 tsp salt
1 medium onion, sliced
1 bay leaf
2 tbsp parsley, finely chopped
¾ cup vinegar

¾ cup water
¼ cup sugar
2 tbsp butter *or* bacon drippings
2 tbsp flour
¼ cup cream *or* evaporated milk
½ cup seedless raisins

Rub meat with pepper, nutmeg and salt. Place in crock or enamel (not iron) pan. Add onion, bay leaf and parsley. Heat vinegar, water and sugar to *boiling* and pour over meat. Cool, then cover and store in

*Note: Do not cook sauerbraten in an iron kettle or skillet.

refrigerator overnight. Drain meat, brown slowly in butter or drippings in heavy skillet, then add ½ cup of the liquid in which meat soaked and the onion. Cover and simmer very slowly about 3 hrs or until meat is very tender, adding more of the spiced sour liquid as it cooks dry. When done, remove meat and keep hot while making gravy. Blend flour with the cream or evaporated milk and add to strained liquid from meat; add raisins and stir over direct heat until gravy is thickened. Serve over meat. 5 to 7 servings.

Buying Hints: See Beef Pot Roast.

SHORT RIBS AND YORKSHIRE PUDDING

3 lbs short ribs	8 small onions
1½ tsp salt	2 tbsp water

Sprinkle ribs with salt. Place in roasting pan and bake in a moderate oven (350° F) uncovered for 45 min or until ribs are richly browned. Cover and continue baking 1½ hrs, or until tender. After about 1 hr of baking, add whole, peeled onions and water, and 45 min later, add Yorkshire Pudding. 4 servings.

Yorkshire Pudding:

1 cup sifted all-purpose flour	3 eggs, well beaten
¼ tsp salt	1 cup milk

Sift flour, measure and resift with the salt. Beat the eggs, add the milk and flour mixture and continue beating with a rotary beater about 2 min. Increase oven temp to 425° F. Push ribs and onions to one side and pour the thin batter into the hot fat and drippings in other half of pan. Bake uncovered for 15 min, reduce heat to 375° F and continue baking 30 min. Cut into sqs and serve with ribs and onions. (It won't be necessary to serve rolls with the pudding.)

SHORT RIBS POT ROAST

2 lbs beef short ribs	⅛ tsp pepper
¼ cup flour	1 small onion, sliced
2 tbsp shortening	¼ cup water
2 tsp salt	

Choose short ribs of U. S. Good or Commercial grades for most flavor and least amount of waste. Cut ribs into individual servings and dredge in flour. Brown slowly on all sides in the heated shortening in a heavy iron skillet or Dutch oven, allowing 20 or 30 min for browning. Add seasonings, onion and water, cover tightly and simmer gently for 2 hrs or until meat is tender. More water may be added if needed to prevent pan from going dry. The meat may also be browned on top of

Note: See Gravy Recipes, pp 797–800.

the ... until
te ... r if
it ... ngs.
...oked

...erved with

...ES

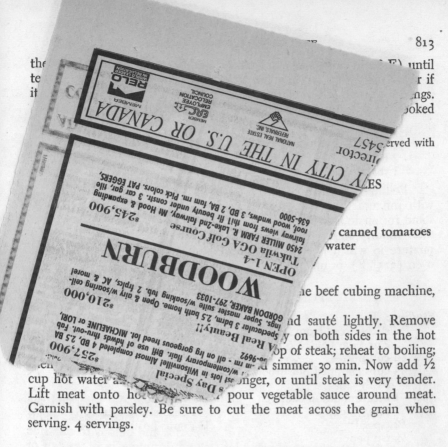

canned tomatoes
water

...he beef cubing machine,

...d sauté lightly. Remove

...y on both sides in the hot

...op of steak; reheat to boiling;

...simmer 30 min. Now add ½ cup hot water a... nger, or until steak is very tender. Lift meat onto ho... pour vegetable sauce around meat. Garnish with parsley. Be sure to cut the meat across the grain when serving. 4 servings.

PEPPER STEAK

Cook meat this savory way and you'll say, "ain't the gravy good?" As good reheated as when freshly cooked

1½ lb inch-thick round steak
¼ cup salad oil
½ clove garlic
3 egg-size onions, sliced
Pinch of thyme *or* basil
⅓ cup tomato sauce *or* purée

½ tsp sugar
1 tsp salt
Dash of pepper
1½ cups cold water *or* bouillon
2½ to 3 medium size green peppers

Cut meat into inch cubes on cutting board. Heat oil in 10-inch heavy skillet, add garlic and meat. Brown slowly, about 20 min, stirring often. Add onion last few min of browning. Now add next 5 ingredients and ½ cup of the water. Cover and *simmer* until meat is tender, from 50 to 60 min, stirring occasionally. Add remaining water in 2 or 3 portions as liquid evaporates. Remove stems, seeds and cores from peppers and cut into inch sqs; add to meat, cover and cook 15 min longer. When done, there should be about ¾ cup rich gravy to serve with the meat. Serve hot with potatoes, rice or noodles. 4 to 5 servings.

STEAK WITH SPANISH SAUCE

1¼ lb round *or* shoulder arm
   steak
1 tbsp vinegar
1 tsp salt
¼ tsp pepper
2 tbsp chopped onion
1 tbsp chopped parsley

2 tbsp chopped celery leaves
½ green pepper, finely
   chopped
2 cups peeled diced tomatoes,
   or canned
2 tbsp meat drippings

Pound steak on both sides with edge of a sturdy saucer. Cover with mixture of the remaining ingredients except drippings and let stand for an hr. Lift meat out and drain. Brown meat slowly on both sides in drippings. Place in a shallow baking dish and add tomato mixture in which meat was soaked. Cover, bake for 2 hrs in a slow oven (325° F), or until meat is tender. Serve at once. 4 servings.

STUFFED FLANK STEAK ROLL

Stuffing:
4 slices bread from 1-lb loaf
   2 *or* 3 days old, 1½ cups
¼ cup butter
1⅓ cups chopped mushrooms,
   ¼ lb
1 medium onion chopped
   fine, ⅓ cup
¼ tsp salt
⅛ tsp pepper

Steak and Gravy:
1 lb flank steak put through
   cubing machine *or* scored
   crisscross
1 tbsp bacon fat
¾ tsp salt
1¼ tbsp flour
1 tbsp shortening
1¼ cups boiling water

Pull bread into coarse crumbs dropping into mixing bowl. Heat butter in skillet, add mushrooms and onion and sauté 4 to 5 min until juicy, stirring constantly. Pour over crumbs, add seasonings and toss lightly but thoroughly.

Flatten steak, pulling evenly into an oblong. Spread with bacon fat and sprinkle with ½ tsp of the salt, then spread with the stuffing. Now start at the wide end and roll up like a jelly roll. Fasten securely with skewers or tie with twine.

Sprinkle with remaining salt and 1 tsp of the flour. Heat shortening in heavy skillet and brown meat roll on all sides. Add ½ cup of the water, cover and simmer 45 min; then add ¼ cup more water and continue simmering 30 min longer or until tender. At this point the water should be evaporated, and in a few min of cooking the roll should be nicely browned. Lift roll to hot platter and remove skewers or twine. Blend rest of flour into fat in skillet until smooth, add remaining water and cook and stir until gravy boils and thickens. Season to taste. Pour hot gravy over roll and serve. 4 servings.

Note: See Gravy Recipes, pp 797–800.

SWISS STEAK No. 1

2 lb round *or* shoulder arm
steak at least 1-inch thick
⅓ cup flour
2 tsp salt

Dash of pepper
3 tbsp shortening
2½ cups water *or* No. 2 can
tomato juice

Wipe steak thoroughly with clean damp cloth. Rub flour, salt and pepper into steak; do not pound with heavy saucer or mallet. Melt shortening in a heavy skillet and brown the steak slowly on both sides. Add ½ cup of the water or tomato juice, cover tightly, and place in a slow oven (300° F) for about 1½ hrs, or until very tender. Add remaining water or juice gradually to prevent skillet from going dry. If preferred, cooking may be finished on top of the stove over low heat, rather than in the oven. Serve meat in its own gravy. 5 or 6 servings.

Variations: Spanish Steak. Instead of the water or tomato juice, add to the browned steak 1 No. 2 can tomatoes, ½ cup sliced celery, 2 tbsp sliced onion, 2 tbsp chopped green pepper. Finish cooking in the same manner as for Swiss Steak.

Chinese Steak: Use water in above recipe and when meat is tender, add 1 cup of bean sprouts or mixed Chinese vegetables. Cook long enough to heat through thoroughly.

SWISS STEAK No. 2

An easy way to serve true beefy flavored beef and gravy. It can wait half an hour or so without detraction. Good for company meals

2¾ lb inch-thick round steak
½ cup flour
1¾ tsp salt
Black pepper
¼ tsp monosodium glutamate

⅓ cup chopped onion
½ cup sliced celery
½ cup potato water
1¾ cup water added in 4
portions

Have ready a heavy 12-inch (✕10) skillet. Wipe meat with damp cloth, then trim fat from rim. Cut enough fat fine and render in skillet to make about 2 tbsp. Stir frequently to prevent scorching. Meanwhile cut meat in 6 serving portions. Pound in flour on both sides with heavy pottery saucer, meat mallet or wooden potato masher. Brown meat slowly in fat on both sides, about 20 min. Now sprinkle with seasonings and the vegetables. Add potato water and cover. Slip an asbestos pad under skillet and *simmer* 2 or 2½ hrs or until meat is fork-tender, adding rest of water as needed. Lift meat with fork from time to time for liquid to run under to prevent sticking. When steak is ready to serve, there should be enough gravy in skillet to come almost to top of steak. Lift meat onto hot platter with pancake turner, arranging around edge of platter, then pour gravy in center. Serve with Company Oven-Browned Mashed Potatoes, p 1379, using the water from these to add to steak. 6 servings.

TOMATO, BEEF, AND GREEN PEPPER
Lot-Ju-Kair-Ngow

1 lb beef round *or* sirloin	½ tsp ground ginger
¼ cup soy sauce	¼ cup salad oil
1 tsp sugar	1 clove garlic, sliced fine
2 large firm tomatoes	2 tsp corn starch
2 large green peppers	1 tbsp soy sauce
2 ginger roots, *or*	Hot boiled rice *or* noodles

Freezing this beef makes it slice thin easier.

Slice beef in strips ½ inch wide and as thin as possible. Pour the ¼ cup of soy sauce and sugar over meat and marinate for ½ hr. In meantime, cut tomatoes and green peppers in 1-inch cubes. Pulverize the ginger roots by hammering between folds of waxed paper to a fine powder, then sift to remove coarse particles and measure 1 tsp. Heat oil in a large skillet and add garlic and ginger. After a minute remove garlic and add green pepper. Sauté for 3 min; stir occasionally during entire remaining cooking period so ingredients will cook evenly. Add beef and its liquid and sauté for 3 min. Add tomatoes and immediately blend cornstarch and remaining soy sauce and gently stir it into the entire mixture. Cook, stirring gently, for another min. Entire cooking period is over medium heat and takes 9 to 10 min. Serve with fluffy rice or crisp noodles. 4 servings.

Note: This is an authentic Cantonese dish and its quality is ruined by overcooking. All of the ingredients must be identifiable and only cooked enough to heat through completely.

COOKING BEEF IN WATER

Simmered

Buying hints: Short plate, short ribs and brisket are good for stew if noodles or dumplings accompany them to utilize the fat. All grades of shank, neck and flank are suitable for cooking in simmering water, and in addition, the heel of round, shoulder arm and chuck ribs from U. S. Commercial and U. S. Utility carcasses should be stewed. Their high percentage of lean meat and low price make them very economical cuts.

BEEF AND VEGETABLE PIE

1½ lbs beef, chuck, round *or*	1 medium onion
shoulder arm (see above)	Salt and pepper to taste
2 tbsp bacon drippings	Plain pastry for single
1½ tsp salt	crust, p 928 *or* Biscuit
4 medium potatoes	dough, p 234
5 medium carrots	

Cut beef in 1-inch dice, brown slowly in bacon drippings and add boiling water to just barely cover meat. Add salt and simmer, covered, for 30 to 60 min, until almost done. (Or have meat ground, brown in bacon drippings, add water and salt and cook 15 to 20 min.) Wash, pare, and dice potatoes; scrape and slice carrots, and peel and slice onion; add to meat (with more boiling water to just cover if needed) and simmer until all are tender, about 20 min longer. To thicken the gravy, stir in flour and water paste, p 163, to give the desired thickness. Add salt and pepper to suit taste. Heat to boiling and pour into an 8-cup buttered casserole. Cover with pastry which has been rolled thin and has a design cut in center for the steam vents, or arrange biscuits over the top. Bake in a moderately hot oven (425° F) about 15 min, or until golden brown. 5 servings.

BEEF STEW

This is a good stew with rich, meaty flavor. See ideas in the 2 variations below for preparing meals the day before for the day after. It's a good trick

1½ lbs boneless beef for stew	4 or 5 six-inch long carrots
3 tbsp bacon fat *or* shortening	4 or 5 medium size potatoes
	Gravy:
1¾ tsp salt	3 tbsp flour
Few dashes of pepper	⅓ cup water
Onion size large egg, peeled	1 tbsp chopped parsley, optional
⅓ cup water, and more as needed	

Wipe meat with damp cloth; cut into 1½-inch cubes. Heat fat until sizzling in a heavy 3-qt saucepan or Dutch oven; add meat, turning it often until a fine rich brown. Add thickly sliced onion to meat last 5 min of browning. When brown, sprinkle with 1 tsp of the salt and pepper. Add water, cover, heat to boiling, then reduce heat and *simmer* until meat is almost done, from 1½ to 2 hrs. After *simmering* 1 hr if more water is needed, stir it in ¼ cup at a time. Half hr before serving time, add scraped washed carrots cut in 2-inch lengths and the pared halved potatoes. Sprinkle with remaining ¾ tsp of salt. Cover and cook until vegetables are just done. There should be enough liquid in kettle to almost cover meat and vegetables.

To make gravy, measure water into a slender glass; sprinkle flour over it, then place hand over top of glass to cover tightly and shake hard until mixture is smooth. Now push meat and vegetables gently to one side; pour flour mixture, *while stirring,* in a thin stream into broth. Cook and stir 2 or 3 min longer until thickened and smooth. To serve, lift meat into center of hot platter; arrange vegetables around it, then pour gravy over all, or serve separately. Sprinkle stew with chopped parsley. Serve immediately. 4 to 5 servings.

Variation No. 1: Double meat and seasonings when making this stew. Next day, reheat leftover stew, then combine with any 2 freshly cooked vegetables, such as Chestnuts, p 122, green beans, celery, tiny onions, etc. Serve over hot rice.

Variation No. 2: Instead of serving the stew over rice, turn mixture into a baking dish to come ¾-inch from top. Cap with small biscuits, p 234. Bake in moderately hot oven (425° F) until biscuits are brown and thoroughly baked, about 20 min.

Variation: Omit potatoes and serve with Drop Dumplings, p 244, or Broad Noodles, p 430.

RICH BROWN BEEF STEW

Stew with rich brown, full-flavored, satin smooth gravy that needs no last minute doctoring

1 lb boneless chuck	¼ cup flour
2 tsp salt	1 qt hot water
⅛ tsp pepper	6 small white onions
2 tbsp shortening	6 medium size carrots
½ tsp sugar	4 large potatoes, 1¼ lbs

Wipe meat with a damp cloth and trim off any fat. Render fat for shortening. Cut meat into 1-inch cubes and place on sheet of waxed paper. Sprinkle with mixture of salt and pepper. Heat shortening in a heavy stewing kettle, add meat, brown slowly and stir constantly. When browned nicely on all sides, sprinkle sugar over meat, and continue browning a second; then add flour and brown it slightly; take care at this point to avoid scorching it. Stir vigorously while browning sugar and flour. Add all the water and stir until the browned particles on sides and bottom of kettle are dissolved. Sift in the salt and pepper left on waxed paper. Cover, simmer 1 hr; stir from time to time. Add onions pricked through several times and simmer 15 min; then add the carrots cut in 2-inch pieces and the potatoes sliced 1-inch thick. Stir occasionally with pancake turner to keep from breaking up vegetables. Cook over low heat until vegetables and meat are done, about 30 min longer. Serve with sprinkling of chopped parsley. 4 servings.

"BOILED" BEEF AND NOODLES

Choose beef plate, ribs, or brisket. Three lbs will be sufficient for 5 servings. Wipe meat thoroughly with damp cloth; cut into large serving portions, barely cover with water, add 3 tsp salt and simmer gently in covered kettle until tender, 1½ to 2½ hrs, depending on quality of meat. Add 4 oz egg noodles about 20 min before serving time; increase heat so liquid boils gently, and continue cooking until noodles are tender. 5 servings.

"BOILED" DINNER WITH CORNED BEEF

2 lbs corned beef	6 small onions
3 carrots	½ medium size head of
6 small parsnips	cabbage
6 medium potatoes	Salt

Barely cover corned beef with cold water and heat to boiling; then reduce heat, cover kettle, and simmer until beef is tender, 2 to 3½ hrs, depending on quality of meat. Scrape carrots and parsnips and split in half lengthwise; pare potatoes and cut in halves, peel onions, and cut cabbage in eighths after removing outer leaves. Add vegetables to kettle, cover and cook 20 to 30 min longer, or until vegetables are tender. Add salt if needed. 5 servings.

CORNED BEEF AND CABBAGE

Barely cover 2 lbs corned beef with cold water; heat to boiling, reduce heat, cover kettle, and simmer about 2½ hrs, or until meat is tender, the time depending on quality of meat. Chop 3 lbs cabbage coarsely and place in a separate kettle; cover with boiling water, add 1 tsp salt, and boil rapidly for 6 to 8 min until just tender in an uncovered kettle. Drain thoroughly. Arrange on platter. Slice corned beef thin across the grain, and arrange slices over the cabbage. 5 servings.

Variation: If preferred, cabbage may be cooked in water drained from the corned beef when it is done. This will impart some flavor to the cabbage and no salt need be added.

GREEN TOMATO STEW

2 tbsp flour	1 cup water
1 tsp salt	¼ tsp sugar
Dash of pepper	1 medium onion, sliced
1¼ lb chuck, round *or* shoulder arm cut into 1½-inch cubes	6 small green tomatoes, 1 lb, washed, cored
2 tbsp shortening	2 large carrots, sliced, 1 cup

Mix flour, salt, and pepper and thoroughly dredge meat. Then brown meat slowly with any remaining flour in hot shortening in heavy skillet or Dutch oven. Reduce heat, add ¼ cup water, cover and simmer for 1 hr. Then add remaining water, sugar, onion and the tomatoes cut into quarters. Cover and simmer for 30 min. Add carrots and continue to simmer for 15 min more. Serve at once. 4 servings.

GROUND BEEF

Buying and Cooking Hints. The most economical and flavorsome cuts for ground beef are: round, chuck or shoulder arm, or heel of round of Good or Choice quality. The chuck and shoulder arm are less expensive than the round, and are just as desirable. The purchase of "ready-ground" meat is not recommended; first because the finely divided particles of ground beef lose moisture and flavor rapidly on standing, and second because it is often ground from meat that could no longer be sold in any other form. "Hamburger" of this kind includes usually too much fat and connective tissue for maximum flavor and tenderness.

Ground hamburger should contain some fat. To obtain the best of ground meat for any purpose, select the cut desired. The butcher will trim off any gristle or tough portions. Then ask him to put the trimmed meat through the grinder with a coarse blade *only once.* Meat that is put through the grinder 2 or 3 times is meat paste, not ground meat, and it never can be used to prepare high quality ground meat foods. Use the ground meat as soon after purchase as possible. In "precooking" or "so-called browning" of loose ground meat, cook it only until the meat turns a grayish white which shows the protein on the outside of the meat particles is cooked. To cook it until it is actually brown in color means that the juices have evaporated and the meat has dried out to a point where it can never be made as juicy as it originally was.

BEEF AND KIDNEY BEAN CASSEROLE

1 tbsp butter *or* drippings
1 lb ground beef
1 tsp salt
No. 2 can tomatoes

No. 2 can red kidney beans, drained, 2½ cups
½ cup buttered bread crumbs

Melt butter in skillet, add meat and stir frequently until grayish in color. Add salt and tomatoes. Arrange in a buttered 8-cup casserole in alternate layers with the beans. Top with bread crumbs and bake in a moderate oven (350° F) for 40 min. Serve at once directly from casserole. 5 servings.

BEEF BEAN POT

½ lb dried kidney beans *or* No. 2 can canned kidney beans, 2½ cups
⅛ lb salt pork, sliced thin
¼ cup chopped onion
½ lb diced *or* ground beef No. 2½ can, 3½ cups, canned tomatoes

3 tsp salt
¼ cup chopped green pepper, if desired
Liquid from beans *plus* water to make 1¼ cups
Crackers *or* toast

If dried kidney beans are used, wash and drain, then simmer in enough boiling salted water to cover, until tender, 1½ to 2½ hrs. Heat pork until some fat accumulates on bottom of skillet or Dutch oven. Add chopped onion and ground beef, and cook until grayish in color. Stir in drained beans, tomatoes, salt, green pepper and liquid. Cover and simmer for ½ hr, or until meat is thoroughly cooked and flavors well-blended. Serve hot on crisp crackers or toast. 5 to 8 servings. If any is left over, it will keep well in a covered jar in the refrigerator.

BEEF TOMATO MACARONI MEDLEY

1½ lb ground beef chuck
2 tbsp butter *or* bacon
    drippings
1 cup water *or* leftover
    vegetable liquid

2½ cups peeled fresh tomatoes,
    or No. 2 can
8 oz Macaroni, cooked, p 430
Salt to taste

Heat the meat slowly in the butter or bacon drippings in a heavy skillet, stirring frequently until the meat is gray in color throughout; or shape meat into patties and brown in the bacon drippings. Add water, cover, and simmer gently about 20 min; then add tomatoes and drained cooked macaroni, season to suit taste, and continue cooking at simmering temp 15 to 20 min longer, or until liquid is reduced to consistency of gravy. 5 servings.

BRAISED BEEF BALLS

1¼ lbs ground beef
1 small onion, grated
1 egg, beaten
1 tsp salt
Few grains of pepper

½ tsp dry mustard
2 tbsp prepared horseradish,
    if desired
2 tbsp bacon drippings

Mix beef with onion, egg, and seasonings. Shape into 5 or 6 balls and brown slowly in a heavy skillet containing hot drippings. Add ¼ cup water, cover, and simmer about 30 min or until flavors are blended and meat is done, add more liquid if needed to prevent pan from going dry. Thicken liquid remaining in skillet after meat is removed, if desired, with 2 tbsp flour blended with ¼ cup cold water. Add enough milk to make 1¼ cups gravy. Serve hot. 5 servings.

CHEESEBURGERS PIQUANT

1¼ lbs ground beef
¼ cup milk
1 tsp salt
Dash of pepper
½ lb American cheese
⅓ cup chili sauce

3 tbsp pickle relish
2 tsp prepared mustard *or*
    prepared horseradish
⅓ cup butter
6 buttered buns, toasted

Mix ground beef with milk, salt and pepper. Form into 6 patties about 3 inches in diameter. Cut 6 slices of cheese to fit buns. Mix the chili sauce, pickle relish and mustard or horseradish thoroughly. Melt butter in skillet and pan-fry the patties slowly for 10 to 15 min, turning several times as they cook. Place on buttered toasted buns, spread with the piquant sauce and top with a slice of cheese. Broil until cheese begins to melt. Serve with other half of hot buttered bun at the side, and with green onions, radishes, celery, olives, or other relishes. 5 servings.

CHILI CON CARNE WITH BEEF

1 lb dried red chili beans	3½ cups puréed canned or
6 cups cold water	fresh cooked tomatoes
1½ tsp salt	1 cup finely chopped celery
2 lbs ground beef	1 tbsp chili powder
¾ cup coarsely chopped onion	1 tbsp salt
⅓ cup chopped suet, if needed	⅛ tsp red pepper
3 tbsp flour	2 tsp cider vinegar
	½ tsp sugar

Wash and drain beans and heat to boiling in the water to which the 1½ tsp salt is added. Reduce heat, cover and simmer for 1½ to 2 hrs until beans are soft but not mushy. Allow beans to cool in their liquid; they seem to absorb liquid while standing. Then measure liquid but do not discard; add water if necessary to make 1 cup. If there is more, concentrate to one cup by boiling rapidly. Brown beef and onion lightly in a heavy skillet or Dutch oven. If meat is very lean, suet may be added. Drain all but 2 tbsp of fat from cooked meat, stir in the flour until smooth. Gradually add tomato purée and stir until mixture boils and thickens. Add remaining ingredients, the beans and liquid. Simmer 10 min, stirring occasionally to mix well. Serve hot with crisp crackers or toast. About 2½ qts.

CHILI CON CARNE WESTERN STYLE

This Chili is good with or without beans

Pinto beans, p 1323	¼ tsp cayenne pepper
2¼ lbs round steak	1 tsp comino, optional
1½ cups chopped onion, 2	2 tbsp chili powder
medium	2 small bay leaves
2 medium cloves garlic	¼ tsp basil, optional
crushed fine	5 cups sieved tomatoes
1 tsp celery salt	1 tbsp salt

When chili with beans is desired, soak beans the night before and put on to cook an hr or so before starting chili.

Trim fat from steak; cut it fine and render out in Dutch oven, then measure and return ¼ cup to kettle. Cut the lean meat into ½-inch cubes. Heat fat hot but not to smoking, add beef cubes and toss around until gray, not brown, on all sides. Add remaining ingredients, heat to boiling, cover and simmer 2½ hrs with occasional stirring. Remove bay leaves, add cooked beans and cook ½ hr longer. Serve very hot with crackers. 8 to 10 servings or 2½ qts.

CHILI MAC

Cook 8 oz macaroni according to directions on package. Drain well and stir into Chili Con Carne and reheat. Serve very hot with crisp crackers.

CHILI SAUCE MERINGUE MEAT LOAF

½ lb ground beef chuck	1 tbsp Worcestershire sauce
½ lb ground pork shoulder	1 cup soft bread crumbs
1 tbsp chopped parsley	2 egg yolks, beaten with
1 small onion, chopped fine	¼ cup water
1½ tsp salt	¼ cup chili sauce
1 tsp horseradish	2 egg whites
1 tsp green pepper, chopped	

Combine all ingredients except chili sauce and egg whites in order given and mix well. Pat into a well-greased loaf pan 8½ x 4½ x 2½ inches. Bake 40 min at 350° F (moderate). Remove from oven, let stand 10 or 15 min for loaf to absorb meat juice in bottom of pan. Turn out on baking sheet and cover with a meringue made by folding the chili sauce into the stiffly beaten egg whites. Return to oven and bake 15 min longer. Transfer to platter very carefully and serve hot. 4 servings.

GROUND BEEF IN GRAVY

1 lb ground beef, round,	2½ cups water
chuck, *or* shoulder arm	1 tsp salt
3 tbsp butter *or* drippings	Dash of pepper
1 tbsp grated onion, if desired	

Cook meat and onion slowly in butter, stir constantly until lightly browned. Add water and seasonings, and simmer covered, for 30 min. Thicken liquid to desired thickness with a flour-water paste, p 163. Serve hot on toast or on Mashed, p 1378, or Baked Potatoes, p 1372. 5 servings.

HAMBURGER BROILED ON A BUN

1 lb ground beef	Dash of pepper
2 tbsp very finely chopped	3 to 4 tbsp butter
onion (omit if using Onion	2 tsp prepared mustard
Gravy)	4 buns, cut in half *or* 8 slices
1 tsp salt	bread

Combine first 4 ingredients and mix well. Soften butter and blend in the mustard. Spread buns with butter mixture then with seasoned meat. Place on preheated broiler rack about two inches from heat, broil 4 to 5 min or until meat cooks to desired doneness. Serve at once with Mushroom Sauce or Onion Gravy. 4 servings.

Mushroom Sauce:

½ lb fresh mushrooms *or*   ¼ cup flour
    3½ oz can   1 to 1½ cups milk
¼ cup butter *or* margarine   ¼ tsp salt

Wash mushrooms and cut in half if large. Melt margarine in top of a double boiler over low direct heat and add mushrooms. Cover, sauté until juicy, about 5 min. Then blend in flour. Add milk gradually, amount depends on thickness desired. Cook over hot water until sauce is smooth and thick. Stir constantly; add salt.

Onion Gravy:

6 thick onion slices, 2   1 cup water
    medium onions   1 tsp meat extract paste, *or*
2 tbsp butter   1 bouillon cube
2 tbsp flour   Dash of salt, if needed

Sauté onions in butter until transparent and soft, about 5 min. Do not brown. Lift out and lay on broiled sandwiches. Blend flour into heated butter, add water gradually and continue to stir until mixture boils and thickens. Add meat extract paste and salt, stir to blend. Reheat and pour over broiled sandwiches and onions.

HAMBURGERS BARBECUED

A teen-ager specialty

½ cup chili sauce   1 tbsp lemon juice
1½ tsp Worcestershire sauce   ¼ tsp chili powder
¼ tsp celery seed   ¼ tsp sugar
½ tsp salt   1 lb ground beef
2 tbsp chopped onion   1 tsp salt
2 tbsp vinegar $\frac{1}{16}$ tsp black pepper
1 tbsp water   ⅛ tsp salt
$\frac{1}{16}$ tsp red pepper   Chopped parsley, optional
½ clove garlic, finely chopped

Place first 12 ingredients in small saucepan over low heat and simmer 5 min. Meanwhile combine next 3 ingredients, shape into 4 patties and broil as for Hamburgers Pan-broiled. Before broiling sprinkle ⅛ tsp salt in hot skillet. When patties are browned, pour in barbecue sauce; reduce the heat, cover tightly and simmer about 10 min. Serve patties with sauce poured over them sprinkled with chopped parsley. 4 servings.

HAMBURGERS "BIG SIZE," "SIZE," AND "HALF-SIZE"

A tempting Arizona style of hamburger

1 lb ground beef, seasoned
Boiled seasoned pinto *or*
kidney beans, p 1323

Chopped onion
Toasted, split buns

Big size, size, and half-size are large, medium or small hamburgers pan-broiled for hungry folk—men, women or adolescents, not so hungry adults and children. Place Hamburgers Pan-broiled (below) on toasted hot buns, pour a corresponding amount of beans with their gravy over hamburgers and top with the desired amount of chopped onions. 4 to 6 servings.

HAMBURGER NOODLE CASSEROLE

2 tbsp butter
¾ lb ground beef
1 medium onion, sliced
1 cup water

1 cup canned tomatoes
1 tsp salt
2½ cups cooked peas
8 oz noodles, cooked

Melt butter in skillet, add meat and stir until lightly browned. Add onion, water, tomatoes and salt; cover, simmer 30 min, stirring occasionally. Add peas with their liquid and noodles, p 430; cook uncovered 10 or 15 min, stirring frequently until liquid cooks down to a gravy. Add more seasonings if desired. Serve hot. 5 servings.

HAMBURGER PATTIES—PAN-BROILED

As good eating as fine steak when properly prepared

1¼ lbs ground beef
2 tbsp minced onion
¾ tsp salt

Pepper, if desired
¼ tsp salt
Parsley

Have meat put through grinder once using medium blade. Add next 3 ingredients. Mix thoroughly but lightly. Measure meat out on waxed paper in ⅓-cup portions. Shape into patties about ½-inch thick. Sprinkle the ¼ tsp salt over bottom of hot, heavy 10-inch skillet. Use no fat. Lay patties in and brown very quickly. No juice oozes out if skillet is hot enough. When under side browns nicely, turn and brown other side quickly. Reduce heat, cover and cook very slowly 2 or 3 min longer to desired doneness. Lift patties to hot platter. Add ¼ cup hot water to skillet, increase heat, scrape with pancake turner until brown residue dissolves and simmers to a rich pan gravy. Pour gravy over patties. Garnish with sprigs of or chopped parsley. 4 servings.

HAMBURGERS WITH VARIED FLAVOR

1. *Savory:* Prepare meat as for Hamburgers Pan-Broiled, except add ¼ cup thin cream, or tomato juice or ¾ tsp prepared mustard.

2. *Company Hamburgers:* Shape seasoned meat into generous ovals or rectangles, then pan-broil as directed above. Serve with Sautéed Mushrooms, p 1356, or French-Fried Onions, p 1361.

HAMBURGER AND CORN PIE

2½ tbsp bacon fat	¾ cup water
¾ lb fresh ground beef chuck	4 tbsp butter
2 tbsp chopped onion	2 cups corn cut from cob
¾ tsp salt	1 tsp salt
⅛ tsp pepper	⅛ tsp pepper
¼ tsp paprika	1 green pepper, medium
2½ tbsp flour	

Start oven 10 min before baking; set to moderately hot (425° F). Heat bacon fat in skillet; add ground beef and onion. Stir and cook until meat is separated and gray in color. Add salt, pepper, paprika; then the flour blended with the water smoothly. Cook 2 or 3 min and stir constantly until thickened. Heat butter in a saucepan, add corn, salt and pepper; stir constantly and cook 2 or 3 min. Pour a little more than half the corn into a well buttered 9 or 10-inch glass pie pan. Place in oven and bake 15 min. Remove quickly from oven and add hot hamburger mixture and rest of corn. Lay quarter rings of green pepper around edge. Return to oven; bake another 15 to 20 min, or until bottom and top are an appetizing brown. 4 to 5 servings.

HAMBURGERS—PICNIC

Divide seasoned hamburger meat into half-cup portions; shape into patties. Lay first patty on a square of waxed paper, cover with a second square, then flatten with palm of hand or pancake turner until patty is ⅛ to ¼-inch thick. Repeat process and stack hamburgers on top of each other. Store in refrigerator. Before placing in picnic basket, wrap in several thicknesses of waxed paper, then in wrapping paper. They can be pan-broiled in a jiffy for hungry folks with the least amount of handling. When cooked, these big hamburgers just fit the buns.

HAMBURGER ROLLS WITH TOMATOES

1½ lbs ground beef	1 tbsp milk
1½ tsp salt	Fine dry bread crumbs
Dash of pepper	3 tbsp shortening
2 tbsp water *or* milk	2½ cups tomatoes
1 egg, beaten	1 medium onion, sliced

Mix meat thoroughly with salt, pepper and water. Form into barrel-shaped rolls. Dip into egg which has been beaten with the 1 tbsp milk, then roll in crumbs. Heat shortening in a heavy skillet and brown rolls on all sides. Rub tomatoes through a sieve and pour over the rolls, add the onion. Cover skillet and simmer 20 to 25 min, turning occasionally. Serve hot with the tomato sauce poured over hamburger rolls. 5 servings.

ITALIAN RICE

¾ cup uncooked rice
2 tbsp bacon drippings
¾ lb ground beef
1 medium onion, chopped
½ green pepper, chopped
⅓ cup chopped celery

2 cups cooked tomatoes
½ cup water
1½ tsp salt
Dash of pepper
2 tsp sugar

Follow directions on pkg for the correct preparation of the rice. Heat drippings in a 10-inch heavy skillet; add rice, ground beef and onion and cook with frequent stirring until meat and rice are brown and onion is soft. Add green pepper and celery, and cook slowly 5 min, stirring frequently. Then add remaining ingredients, cover, and simmer gently for 30 min longer, or until rice is perfectly tender. Stir occasionally. 5 servings.

SWEDISH MEAT BALLS

½ lb round steak
½ lb lean pork
½ cup fine dry bread crumbs
1½ cups milk
1 small egg, beaten
1 tsp salt

Few dashes of pepper
⅛ tsp allspice
¼ cup finely chopped onion
⅓ cup shortening
1¼ tbsp flour
1¼ cups beef *or* veal broth

Have butcher put meat through grinder twice. Soak crumbs in 1 cup of the milk in a 2-qt mixing bowl for 15 min. Now mix in meat very thoroughly. Then stir in egg well, then seasonings and rest of the milk. Add the onion sautéed in 1 tbsp of the shortening. Measure mixture in 2 tbsp-portions onto waxed paper, then shape into balls with fingers dipped frequently in cold water. Heat remaining shortening in skillet, and when bubbling hot, add meat balls and fry until cooked through, shaking pan and turning balls frequently to brown uniformly on all sides. Lift balls out onto hot plate. Now blend flour into fat in skillet until smooth, then stir in broth gradually and cook slowly with constant stirring until gravy is thickened. Add salt and pepper to suit taste, then add meat balls and reheat until hot through. Serve with Swedish Brown Beans. 4 to 5 servings.

ITALIAN SPAGHETTI WITH MEAT BALLS

1 lb mixed ground beef and pork
¼ cup grated sharp cheese
1 tsp caraway seed (fennel may be substituted)
1 tbsp finely chopped parsley
2 tbsp chopped green pepper
Dash of pepper
1 egg, well beaten
2 tsp salt
3 strips of bacon cut in small pieces

¼ cup chopped onion
2 tbsp butter *or* additional bacon fat, if needed
1 qt of canned tomatoes *or* No. 3 can
1 can tomato paste, about ⅓ cup
¼ tsp sugar
1 lb spaghetti, freshly cooked
Parmesan cheese

Combine first 7 ingredients with 1 tsp of the salt, and shape into small balls. Sauté bacon in heavy skillet or large Dutch oven until fat melts out into bottom of pan. Add meat balls and brown slowly on all sides. Add onion and additional butter if pan is dry and sauté onion until soft, about 5 min. Add remaining salt, tomatoes, tomato paste and sugar. (Tomatoes may be sieved if desired to remove seeds, but it is not necessary.) Reduce heat as low as possible and simmer very slowly for 1½ to 2½ hrs, stirring occasionally until sauce is the desired thick consistency. Pour over hot, rinsed, drained spaghetti and serve at once with additional cheese to be sprinkled over top if desired. 4 to 6 generous servings.

Note: A clove of garlic may be cooked with the bacon and then removed before adding meat balls if desired.

JAMBALAYA

¾ cup uncooked rice
3 tbsp bacon drippings
1 clove garlic, cut up
2 green peppers, 1½ cups chopped
1 cup chopped onion
1 lb ground beef
No. 2 can tomatoes, 2½ cups

¼ tsp paprika
¼ tsp chili powder
½ tsp Worcestershire sauce
1½ tsp salt
¼ tsp black pepper
1 small bay leaf
1 tbsp chopped parsley

Follow directions on pkg for cooking rice. Place bacon drippings in Dutch oven or heavy skillet and sauté garlic for 5 min. Remove garlic clove and discard. Sauté peppers and onions until soft. Push to one side of pan and brown meat. Add remaining ingredients, cover and simmer gently for 30 min. Add rice, stir to mix and continue to simmer gently for 15 to 20 min. Serve at once. 4 to 6 servings.

LEMON TANGED MEAT BALLS OR PATTIES

Surprisingly good! You'll like them hot for dinner or sliced cold for sandwiches

1 lb beef, chuck *or* round, put through grinder twice	⅔ cup coarsely grated cheddar cheese
1 cup soft bread crumbs size peas, pressed down lightly	2½ tbsp fine cut green pepper
3½ tbsp lightly spiced catchup	1⅓ tbsp fine cut onion
1 egg, slightly beaten	1⅓ tbsp lemon juice
¾ tsp salt	8 strips lean-streaked bacon

Adjust broiler 3½ inches below source of heat; start heating 10 min before broiling; set to 450° F.

Measure all ingredients in order listed into mixing bowl, except bacon. Mix thoroughly but lightly with a fork. Let stand 5 to 10 min to stiffen. Divide into 8 even portions and shape into patties or balls. Wrap a strip of bacon around each and fasten with a tooth pick. Rub hot broiler quickly with a bit of paper toweling dipped in shortening. Place patties on broiler. Broil 5 min on each side or until bacon is done and meat is cooked through. Crookneck squash, p 1400, is a good accompaniment. 4 servings.

Note: Very flavorful without bacon, but must be handled more carefully to prevent breaking.

MEAT LOAF No. 1

1 lb ground veal	¼ tsp dry mustard
1 lb ground beef	⅛ tsp seasoning salt, if desired
1 lb ground pork	⅛ tsp celery salt
2 eggs	⅛ tsp paprika
⅓ cup chopped onion	¼ tsp pepper
2 tsp salt	

Have meat ground only once in a food chopper with a coarse blade. Combine meats thoroughly in a large mixing bowl. Beat eggs well, add onion and other seasonings and mix well. Add to meat and stir or knead until blended. Pack into an oiled glass bread loaf pan (10 x 5¼ x 3½ inches) and unmold onto a flat baking pan. Bake in a moderate oven (350° F) for 1½ hrs or until well done. 10 servings.

Variation: Upside-Down Meat Loaves: Soak 10 dried apricots for half an hr in just enough lukewarm water to cover. Drain and place one in bottom of each buttered muffin ring. Prepare Meat Loaf No. 1 and pack mixture into muffin rings on top of apricots. Bake in a moderate oven (350° F) for 45 min. Turn out with apricot on top and serve immediately. 10 servings.

MEAT LOAF No. 2

1½ lbs ground beef
1 egg, beaten
1 cup milk
1¼ tsp salt

1 cup coarse soft bread
  crumbs
⅛ tsp pepper
Parsley

Combine all ingredients thoroughly, and pack into a lightly oiled glass bread loaf pan (8¾ x 4¾ x 2¾ inches). Turn out onto a greased shallow baking pan, and bake in a moderate oven (350° F) for about 1 hr, or until done. Serve hot with Tomato Sauce, p 1261, and a parsley garnish. The meat loaf mixture may be baked in custard cups for individual loaves, in which case the baking time should be reduced to 45 min. 5 servings.

MEAT LOAF No. 3

Good meat flavor, slices well hot or cold, but is not too tight textured

2 eggs
½ cup milk
10 2¼-inch sq soda crackers
1 tbsp butter
2 tbsp fine-chopped onion
⅓ cup fine-chopped celery

1¾ lbs ground lean beef
½ lb ground lean pork
1¾ tsp salt
¼ tsp pepper
1 tsp monosodium glutamate
1 tsp baking powder

Start oven 10 min before baking; set to moderate (350° F). Have a shallow 10 x 6¼ x 2¼-inch glass baking pan ready. Beat eggs in a 2-qt mixing bowl. Stir in milk, then crushed crackers and let stand 5 min. Meanwhile melt butter in skillet, add onion and celery and sauté until onion is soft but not browned. Add meat to the milk mixture, then the celery, onions, seasonings and baking powder. Mix thoroughly, using a wooden spoon or the hands. Turn into the baking pan and shape neatly but lightly into a loaf. Bake from 65 to 70 min. Serves 8 to 10.

Note: Unmolding the uncooked loaf and baking it on a flat pan produces more brown crusty surface. However, loaf may be baked in the loaf pan if preferred. In this case, pat two thicknesses of plain paper (cut to fit) down over top of meat to hold in the steam. Remove paper after loaf has cooked 1 hr to brown the top. After removing meat loaf from oven, let it stand on the back of the stove 15 min to absorb the meat juice before slicing.

CHEESE MEAT LOAF

Tasty, moist, sliceable

1 egg
1 lb ground beef
1 cup coarsely crushed saltine
  crackers
¼ cup chopped green pepper,
  optional
¼ cup finely chopped onion

1¼ tsp salt
½ cup grated Cheddar cheese
1½ tsp Worcestershire sauce
1 tsp sugar
1 cup tomato juice
⅛ tsp pepper
Parsley

Nothing stirs the family appetite more than an announcement about a big juicy steak coming up on tonight's dinner menu. Broiled tomato slices not only point up the beauty of the steak, but they taste good with it.

© Kingan and Company.

EDIBLE GARNISHES

Tools required to prepare these garnishes: a very sharp, rigid paring knife with a sharp, slender point, an egg slicer, a pastry jagger, a few sharp-edged cookie cutters.

Row 1: Tomato lily. Select small, perfect, not too ripe tomato. Cut skin and about ⅛-inch of the flesh to form 6 petals. Carefully loosen petals and bend them outward, leaving ball-shaped center intact. Sprinkle this with sieved hard-cooked egg yolk. Place on greens—leaf lettuce or curly endive.

Row 2: Radish roses—three methods of cutting.
Section of peeled cucumber cut into ⅛-inch slices which are left joined at one side; a lengthwise slice of red radish inserted in each gash, and a sprig of parsley at each end for garnish.

Row 3: a. Slice of tomato, slice of hard-cooked egg and half of small pear tomato.
b. Wedges of unpeeled tomato laid together to resemble tulip with lengthwise slices of cooked fresh okra pod for stem and leaves.
c. Slice of tomato, slice of hard-cooked egg, and 3 crosswise slices of cooked fresh okra with seeds removed.
d. Tomato wedges with slice of cooked fresh okra on end of each.

Row 4: a. Half slices of hard-cooked egg laid together for edge garnish.
b. Half slices of egg laid together like butterfly wings; antennae are ends of green onions or chives; "eyes" are rings cut from green onion tips.
c. Hard-cooked egg slice cut and spread like tulip with green onion tip leaves.
d. Slice of hard-cooked egg surrounded by whites from other slices bent to form petals; dash of paprika in center.
e. Three slices of hard-cooked egg laid together, overlapping, with wedges cut from another slice on top, and tiny sprig of parsley in center.
f. Two slices of egg laid together, edges touching; end slice of egg laid over joining, with two tiny egg-yolk wedges and a strip of pimiento topping that.
g. Quarters of hard-cooked egg slices laid in a row with a dot of green pepper to accent points of contact.

Row 5: a. Half-slice of lemon with "bow" made from pimiento strip to resemble old-fashioned party fan.
b. Lemon is cut in deep grooves lengthwise to expose the white, sprinkled with paprika, and rubbed off, leaving paprika only in grooves; then lemon is cut in quarters and 2 quarters laid together with parsley garnish. For fish.
c. Lemon slice with half the pulp cut away, garnished with pimiento strip and parsley.
d. Lemon wedge with pimiento strips laid across it.
e. End of lemon cut in quarters which are left joined at center and spread apart; half a candied cherry in center.
f. Two wedges cut from lemon slice to make a mushroom-like profile; garnished with bits of curly endive or parsley.
g. Slice prepared like *c*, except rind is cut through and ends are curled under to meet at the center.

Row 6: a. Ripe olive, pitted with olive pitter; hole filled with piece cut from carrot to fit hole, with ends slivered and curled by placing in ice water until crisp.
b. Conventional flower cut from carrot slice, with tiny white turnip center; 2 or 3 or more of these may be placed as a bouquet on bed of greens.
c. Cup cut from section of carrot, scooped out with edge scalloped, filled with cooked peas.
d. Same as *a*.

Row 7: Egg lily. White of hard-cooked egg cut in sixths, placed point to point like flower petals; ball of egg-yolk salad dropped in center with spears of chives or green onion tips stuck in it for accent. Lily is flanked by slices of egg topped with tiny sprigs of parsley.

EDIBLE GARNISHES

Row 1: Bunch of black Morocco grapes combined with seedless green grapes.

Row 2: a. Slice of white onion topped with parsley and strips of radish skin.
b. Two onion rings topped with slices of unpeeled cucumber and radish slices.
c. Onion slice topped with 2 pear tomatoes cut in halves.
d. Onion rings topped by pieces cut from green pepper.

Row 3: Bread mosaics—pieces of whole wheat and white bread cut out with different-sized cookie cutters and fitted together to produce color contrast.

Row 4: Several ham garnishes—
a. Blanched almonds around candied cherry, candied peel in center.
b. Poached orange slices with center stuck full of whole cloves.
c. Slice of pineapple topped with candied cherry halves.
d. Quarters of candied cherries arranged as petals, with almond centers.
e. Diamonds of candied peel studded with cloves, candied cherry center.
f. Daisy in profile—blanched almonds, candied cherry center, angelica stem.

Row 5: a. *Nicotiana*—Cut thin slice of white turnip about 2 inches in diameter. Cut into 5 petals, leaving joined in center, and trim each petal to diamond shape. Leave white or tint deep red with food coloring. Cut white centers (small cylinders of turnip) and scoop out slightly. Fasten to flower with green-tinted toothpick. Slip green onion top over end of toothpick.
b. *Aster*—Cut 2 thin slices from white turnip. Make 32 slits in each, leaving just the center of each slice intact. Make each petal round on one slice, coming to point on other. Lay slice with pointed petals on top of other slice; in center place ring cut from carrot slice, and with darker carrot center inside. Fasten together with toothpick; slip green onion top over end.
c. *Daffodil*—Cut thin slice of white turnip about 3 inches in diameter. Cut 6 petals, pointed at outer edge and rounded toward center, roughly diamond-shaped. Cut a 1-inch slice of carrot and hollow out center, nicking the edge. Fasten to center of flower with toothpick; slip green onion top over the end.
d. *Dogwood*—Cut thin slice of white turnip about 3 inches in diameter. Cut into quarters, leaving connected at center. Round off outer edges of petals, keeping them broad; cut small round notch in center of each outside edge; touch notches with green color. Make hole in center with toothpick; for parsley stem insert long stem of parsley with terminal leaves left on.
e. *Cosmos*—Cut thin slice of white turnip about 3 inches in diameter. Make 8 cuts, leaving connected at center, and slightly round off outer edges, leaving corners squarish. Make petal edges jagged, and use pastry jagger to make 2 or 3 lines down each petal. Use small round of carrot for center and dot with chocolate shot. Lay on leaf of curly endive.

Row 6: a. *Calla lily*—Cut thin slice from large white turnip and trim to make slightly pointed on one side. Cut slender cone-shaped stamen from carrot, slightly shorter than diameter of the turnip slice, and place on turnip slice with point toward pointed side of slice. Wrap turnip slice around large end of stamen; fasten with toothpick. Place in ice water until ready to serve.
b. *Water lily*—Choose well-shaped white turnip about 3 inches in diameter. Peel. Cut 3 tiers of petals, starting with lowest tier and making 8 to 10 petals around. Second-tier petals should be cut between first-tier petals, etc. Cut wedge-shaped pieces from solid center portion, then cut out remaining center. Each tier of petals should be cut down as deep as possible so as to open out easily. Cut 5 or 6 large leaves from thick cucumber skin and arrange as base for lily. Set lily on base; sprinkle grated raw carrot in center.
c. *Daisy*—Cut thin slice from white turnip about 2 inches in diameter. Make cuts dividing it into quarters, then cut each quarter into 4 petals, leaving all joined at center. Trim petals to shape of daisy petals. Cut a round from one end of a ripe olive for the center, and fasten on with a toothpick; slip a leaf of curly endive over the toothpick for stem and leaves.

DESIGNS TWO BOTTOM ROWS—*Irene Taylor.*

Spanish Pork Chops, p 857, are really just braised pork chops in a savory tomato sauce, p 1261. Boiled rice decoratively replaces potatoes as their accompaniment.

The loin end of a leg of lamb provides an elegant lamb roast for the small family. This cut of lamb corresponds to the sirloin of beef. It is the broad upper "meaty" end of the leg of lamb and is very tender, juicy and flavorful. It has only a moderate amount of bone, and is cooked just like a whole leg.

The modest liver sausage, when pan-broiled and served with delicate creamed cabbage wedges, becomes a surprisingly aristocratic dish full of vitamins and minerals too. In the center is a hard-cooked egg with a sprinkling of paprika.

This is Heart Sauerbraten, p 897, an excellent way to prepare this firm muscular meat. Gravy and noodles are perfect accompaniments, and thick slices of cinnamon apples, p 559, with a tiny bunch of white grapes on the top make a beautiful and delicious garnish.

You too can arrange a beautiful platter of cold cuts. Of course, you start with quality cuts and slices of uniform thickness. The shape of the slices and their color make it easy to do an attractive arrangement job, as you can see. But let your inner artistic self guide you in making your very own arrangement. Add a little parsley or cress, some slices of hard-cooked egg, olives or radishes for that "finished touch."

Start oven 10 min before baking; set to moderate (350° F). Break egg into mixing bowl. Add remaining ingredients except parsley. Mix lightly but thoroughly. Turn meat into a greased 6½ x 11 x 1½-inch pan. Pat the mixture into a neat loaf shape about 9-inches long and 4-inches wide. Bake to a rich brown, 45 to 50 min, or until no red juice runs out when pricked with a skewer in center. Let stand on back of stove about 10 min. Use pancake turners or 2 spatulas to lift onto a hot platter. Garnish with parsley. Creamed Mushrooms or Parsley Sauce, pp 1306, 1234, make a good accompaniment. Cold slices make delicious sandwiches. 4 to 5 servings.

PAN-FRIED GROUND BEEF PATTIES

1 lb *freshly* ground round steak *or* chuck

¾ tsp salt
Pepper

Place 9-inch (⚹8) heavy skillet over medium heat for 2 or 3 min. Meanwhile make patties. Use the parchment paper which covers meat to hold patties while shaping. Hold paper in left hand against meat, and with spatula or knife, remove about ⅕ of the meat onto paper; then pat and smooth out with spatula to a uniformly thick flat 3-inch patty. Press meat smooth with spatula, *but do not pack*. Sprinkle half the salt over bottom of skillet. Lay patties in hot skillet and cook until underside is well browned, then turn. Sprinkle with salt and pepper and cook until nicely browned on underside, 8 to 10 min in all. Remove to serving plate. Dot with butter if desired. For pan gravy add 2 or 3 tbsp water to skillet, stir and heat to loosen residue, then pour over meat. 3 to 4 servings.

QUICK SPAGHETTI

1½ tbsp butter
1 medium onion *or* 1 clove
  garlic, chopped fine
1 lb ground beef
1¼ tsp salt

No. 2½ can tomatoes,
3½ cups
⅓ cup tomato paste *or* catchup
¾ lb spaghetti
⅛ lb sharp cheese, grated

Heat butter in heavy skillet or Dutch oven; add onion or garlic and brown lightly. Add beef and stir constantly to keep well separated, browning lightly. Add salt, and tomatoes which have been rubbed through a sieve. Cover and simmer 15 to 30 min. About 5 min before serving, add tomato paste and stir until well blended. Meanwhile cook spaghetti in 4 qts boiling salted water (4 tsp salt), dipping ends into boiling water and slowly pushing rest in as ends become softened. Cook until tender, about 20 min; drain, rinse with hot water, and again drain. Heap onto hot platter, pour hot meat sauce over spaghetti, and sprinkle grated cheese on top. 5 servings.

ODDS AND ENDS SPAGHETTI SAUCE

Surprisingly good. Delicious sauce, make this the day you defrost

1 cup finely chopped onions, 3 medium
1 green pepper, medium
1 good sized clove garlic
6 to 7 branches celery
½ medium tart apple
¼ cup parsley leaves, pressed down
¼ cup margarine *or* butter

½ lb ground beef
¼ cup water
1 tsp salt
⅟₁₆ tsp pepper
Few dashes nutmeg
⅛ to ¼ tsp orégano
Freshly grated Parmesan cheese

Clean all vegetables; pare apple and remove core; put all through food chopper with the medium blade. Heat margarine or butter in a 3 qt saucepan; add vegetables and cook slowly 5 min; stir occasionally. Add remaining ingredients. Cover, simmer 1 hr or until vegetables and meat are tender, stirring occasionally. It is important that the cooking be done slowly and that the sauce does not become too dry. It should retain enough liquid to be about the consistency of thick white sauce. A tsp of cornstarch may be blended smoothly with 1 tbsp water and slowly stirred into mixture at the last. Serve over hot, freshly cooked, well drained spaghetti. Serve with grated Parmesan cheese. 5 servings.

SALISBURY STEAK

1½ lbs ground beef
1½ tsp salt
Pepper to taste

2 tsp grated onion
1 egg, beaten
Melted butter

Purchase meat in the piece and have it ground once. Combine all ingredients except butter, mixing thoroughly but lightly. On a buttered shallow baking pan, mold the meat into the shape of an oblong, oval or rectangle to fit platter, making it about 1¼ inches thick and pushing edges up so they will be sq like a steak. Brush top and sides with melted butter and place in a hot oven (450° F). Bake 10 min, then reduce heat to moderately slow (325° F) to finish cooking, which will take about 25 min longer. Brush with butter once or twice during baking. Slide carefully onto hot platter, using pancake turner. Serve with Sautéed Mushrooms, p 1356, French-Fried Onions, p 1361 or Tomato Sauce, p 1261, if desired, or with more melted butter. 5 servings.

STUFFED CABBAGE ROLLS

1 head of cabbage, 3 lbs
1 lb ground beef
2 tsp chopped onion

1 egg, beaten
½ cup milk
1 tsp salt

Trim off soiled leaves of cabbage and remove core. Cover with boiling water and let stand 5 min or until cabbage leaves are limp.

Separate leaves carefully reserving five of the largest leaves for the rolls. Combine meat thoroughly with onion, egg, milk, and salt. Place ⅓ of the meat mixture on each leaf and fold up envelope fashion. Fasten with tooth pick. Lay, flap down, in Dutch oven or saucepan. Add ½ cup water, and cover rolls with rest of cabbage leaves. Simmer covered, for 1 hr. Serve with Tomato Sauce, p 1261. 5 servings.

Variation. The cabbage rolls may be browned delicately in butter or drippings before adding rest of cabbage leaves and the water.

STEAK SHORT CAKE

2 tbsp butter *or* margarine	1 recipe of Baking Powder
½ lb ground beef	Biscuits, p 234
1 medium onion, chopped	Milk
½ cup fine dry bread crumbs	11 oz can cream of mushroom
½ tsp salt	soup
⅓ cup milk	½ cup water *or* milk
¼ cup chopped green pepper	1 tbsp chopped parsley

Melt butter in a skillet, add beef and brown lightly, breaking up with fork. Add onion, crumbs, salt, the ⅓ cup milk and green pepper. Stir well. Meanwhile turn biscuit dough out onto lightly floured board and knead about 8 times, then roll or pat out into rectangle 6 x 12 inches and ¼-inch thick. Cut into eight 3-inch sqs. Divide meat mixture on four of the sqs. Then place remaining sqs on top to form shortcakes. Crease tops with back of knife to form pattern, then brush with milk. Place on greased baking sheet and bake in a hot oven (425° F) for 15 min. Meanwhile place soup in saucepan, add water, stir until blended and heat to boiling. Remove from stove, add parsley. Transfer shortcake to platter, serve immediately with mushroom sauce. 4 servings.

Note: Regular Mushroom Sauce (p 1259), or Creamed Peas (p 1367) could be used in place of mushroom soup.

TAMALE PIE

A Mexican dish that may be prepared today and baked tomorrow

¾ cup corn meal	2½ cups canned tomatoes
3 cups water *and*	1 to 1½ tbsp chili powder
1 tsp salt	½ tsp orégano, optional
1 tbsp fat *or* oil	1¾ tsp salt
1 lb ground beef chuck	⅛ tsp pepper
1 small clove garlic, chopped, optional	2 tbsp seedless raisins
½ cup finely chopped onion	½ cup grated aged American
½ cup chopped ripe olives	cheese

Sift corn meal into boiling salted water in top of double boiler and cook over direct heat with constant stirring until just thick; cover, place over hot water and cook 20 to 30 min, stirring often. Cool slightly, then turn into greased 8-cup casserole or baking dish. When mush is almost cold, pat it out evenly around sides and bottom of dish, extending it a little above top of dish for rim after filling is added. Refrigerate until ready to use. Heat fat in skillet, add beef and cook with frequent stirring until gray in color. Add next 9 ingredients and stirring often, cook about 15 min until liquid is partially evaporated. Turn mixture into prepared casserole and sprinkle with cheese. Carefully curve extending mush over filling to make a rim. Cover and place in refrigerator, or bake immediately in moderate oven (375° F) 45 to 50 min. 5 servings.

DRIED BEEF

CREAMED DRIED BEEF

¼ lb dried beef	2 cups milk
¼ cup butter	¹⁄₁₆ tsp pepper
1 cup fine-diced celery	Baked potatoes
3 tbsp flour	

To freshen beef, separate slices carefully, then pour hot water over it; let stand a min, no more, then drain. Now cut beef in ribbons with scissors. Melt butter in a 9-inch skillet, add beef and celery and sauté about 7 min until beef is lightly browned. Sprinkle flour over beef mixture and stir until flour is blended smoothly with the fat. Add the milk gradually, stirring to keep smooth, then add pepper and cook over low heat until mixture boils and thickens. Serve hot over Baked Potatoes, p 1372, toast or Noodles, p 430. 4 servings.

Note: Celery may be omitted.

CREAMED EGGS AND DRIED BEEF ON TOAST

¼ lb dried beef	2 cups milk
3 tbsp butter	3 Hard-cooked Eggs, p 663
3 tbsp flour	Salt

To freshen beef, separate slices, rinse in hot water, then drain and cut fine with scissors. Melt butter, add beef and heat until beef is frizzled. Then blend in flour, add milk and stir over direct heat until sauce boils and thickens. Add quartered hard-cooked eggs, and place over boiling water until heated thoroughly. Add salt if required. 5 servings.

DRIED BEEF AND NOODLE CASSEROLE

¼ lb dried beef	3 cups milk
7 oz broad noodles	1 cup grated sharp cheese,
1½ qts boiling water	¼ lb
1 tsp salt	2 tbsp fine bread crumbs
3 tbsp butter	mixed with
3 tbsp flour	2 tbsp melted butter

Separate beef slices, rinse in hot water, then drain and cut fine with scissors. Drop noodles into boiling water, add salt, and cook rapidly until noodles are just tender, about 10 min; drain, rinse with hot water, drain again. Meanwhile heat butter, add beef and sauté for about 5 min or until lightly browned. Add flour, blend until smooth, then add milk gradually, stirring constantly until thickened. Add all but 2 tbsp of the cheese and stir until cheese melts. Arrange noodles and sauce in layers in a buttered 6-cup casserole. Mix remaining cheese with bread crumbs and melted butter, and sprinkle over top. Bake in a moderate oven (375° F) for about 20 min, or until topping is nicely toasted. 5 servings.

FRIZZLED DRIED BEEF

Separate ¼ lb dried beef carefully into whole slices, rinse in hot water, then drain. Melt 2 tbsp butter or bacon drippings in skillet, and lay in whole beef slices. Cook slowly until fat is absorbed and beef is curled up and slightly crisped. Serve hot. 5 servings.

BEEF LEFTOVERS

BUBBLE AND SQUEAK

*Cabbage and onions and leftover meat,
when put together make bubble and squeak*

4 to 6 onions, egg size	4 to 6 generous slices left-
1 qt boiling water	over cooked round steak
4 cups coarsely shredded	*or* roast beef, 1 lb
cabbage	Salt
1 tsp salt	Black pepper, freshly
¼ cup margarine *or*	ground
shortening	

Dip onions in hot water to remove skins neatly. Drop cabbage into boiling water, add salt and boil gently uncovered 5 min or until not quite tender. Drain. Meanwhile heat margarine in skillet that has a cover. Brown meat lightly on both sides. Remove to hot platter and cover to keep hot. Brown thick-sliced onions delicately in remaining fat, add cabbage and cook from 3 to 5 min longer or until onions are delicately browned on underside and the cabbage is barely tender. Add more salt if needed and a light sprinkle of pepper. Arrange vegetables neatly around meat. Garnish with parsley. 4 to 5 servings.

BEEF HASH No. 1

1½ cups beef broth *or* 1 bouil-	2½ cups diced, cooked left-
lon cube in 1½ cups water	over beef
2 cups grated raw potato	1 tsp salt
1 medium onion, grated	2 tbsp bacon fat

Use 1 cup broth made from bones left from beef roast, or substitute bouillon. Combine broth, potato, onion, beef and salt, and put into hot fat in a heavy skillet. Cover and simmer for 25 to 30 min, or until potato and onion are well cooked and hash is slightly browned on under side. Remove from heat, fold hash in omelet fashion and slide onto a hot platter, using a wide spatula or turner. 5 servings.

Note: Hash may be served with poached eggs, tartar sauce or chili sauce and garnished with parsley.

BEEF HASH No. 2

2 medium onions, sliced
2 tbsp bacon drippings
4 medium-size potatoes
Milk

2 cups diced, cooked left-over beef roast
Salt and pepper to taste
Parsley

Sauté onions in bacon drippings until soft. Add potatoes, cut in small dice and beef; add just enough milk to cover, and seasonings. Mix well, cover skillet and simmer until under side of hash is well browned. Slide hash onto a hot platter and garnish with parsley. 5 servings.

OLD-FASHIONED HASH

Good materials make good hash which pleases the discriminating

1½ cups lean cooked roast beef *or* pot roast
2¼ cups chopped cold boiled potatoes
⅓ to ½ cup chopped onion
1¼ tsp salt

¾ tsp monosodium glutamate, optional
⅛ tsp pepper
2½ tbsp butter *or* margarine
1¼ cups boiling water

Chop or cut meat into ¼-inch cubes. Combine with potatoes and onion. Potatoes cooked in jackets, cooled and peeled are best. Sprinkle with seasonings, and toss lightly with fork until well mixed. Melt butter in skillet, preferably a heavy iron one, pour in boiling water and heat to boiling; add meat mixture, spread evenly; cover and cook over medium heat until browned on under side. This requires about 15 min. Turn carefully with spatula or pancake turner, and, if necessary add a little more butter, cover and brown but do not cook hash too dry. Entire cooking time requires 20 to 25 min. Serve with broiled tomatoes or chili sauce. 3 servings.

BEEF PINWHEELS WITH MUSHROOM SAUCE

1 recipe Baking Powder Biscuit dough, p 234
¼ cup butter
⅓ cup finely chopped onion
2½ cups ground, leftover cooked beef
½ cup leftover beef gravy

1 tsp prepared horseradish
2 cups medium white sauce
½ lb mushrooms, cleaned, cut
½ tsp chopped onion
¼ tsp salt
¼ cup finely chopped parsley

Prepare standard biscuit recipe using 2 cups flour. Melt ½ of the butter in skillet. Add onions and sauté until slightly transparent, about 5 min. Add the ground meat, gravy, horseradish and ¼ cup of the white sauce. Let stand to cool. Roll biscuit dough into 9" x 12" rectangle. Spread with meat mixture. Roll as for jelly roll. Seal edges. Cut into 8 crosswise slices. Place on greased baking sheet, cut side down. Bake at 425° F (hot) 25 to 30 min. Cover pinwheels first 15 min with plain paper to prevent drying out. Then remove. Meanwhile sauté mushrooms in remaining butter. Add the ½ tsp onion and the salt and the remaining white sauce. Heat to boiling. Add the parsley and serve hot over baked pinwheels. 4 to 6 servings.

BEEF OR CHICKEN TURNOVERS

1½ cups chopped cooked beef or chicken, pkd	1 tsp grated onion
	Salt, pepper to taste
2 tbsp butter	2 tbsp finely chopped celery
2 tbsp flour	1 recipe Baking Powder
⅔ cup milk or broth	Biscuits, p 234

Sauté meat or chicken lightly in heated butter; blend in flour until smooth and gradually add the milk. Stir constantly over medium heat until smooth and thickened. Add remaining ingredients, stir to blend and cool slightly. Make biscuit dough according to directions. Turn out on floured board and roll or pat out into a 6 x 15-inch rectangle and ⅛-inch thick. Cut into 5 pieces 3 x 6 inches. Heap ⅕ of the mixture on half of each piece of dough. Moisten edges and fold other half over meat. Press edges together with tines of fork to seal. Cut design in center top of turnovers for steam vents. Bake on a greased baking sheet in a moderately hot oven (425° F) for 15 to 20 min or until crust is well browned. Serve at once with creamed mushrooms, peas, or other creamed vegetable. 5 servings.

GOULASH

2 cups diced cooked leftover roast beef or pot roast	No. 2 can tomatoes
	1 lb small white onions
1½ lbs potatoes, 3 or 4	Salt to suit taste
1 cup beef broth or water	

Combine meat with potatoes which have been pared and cut into 1-inch dice. Add broth and tomatoes, cover, and cook until potatoes are tender. Meanwhile, peel onions, leave whole and boil in enough water to cover until just tender. Add to meat and vegetable mixture. Season to suit taste and serve piping hot. 5 servings.

PLANKED STEAK

Heat treated plank, see p 1445, in a slow oven (225° F) 1 hr. Brown steak cut 1½ to 2 inches thick for 5 min on both sides either in a skillet or under broiler. While steak browns, beat egg into 1 qt hot mashed potatoes. Transfer steak to hot plank that is brushed with butter. Quickly pipe potatoes around steak leaving spaces for broiled tomatoes, freshly cooked peas, cauliflower and mushrooms. Cut tomatoes in half crosswise, slip into spaces allowed. Brush steak and tomatoes with melted butter, sprinkle with salt and pepper. Return to moderately hot oven (400° F) or to broiler to finish cooking steak and brown potatoes. Add rest of vegetables to spaces left on plank. Garnish with parsley, serve immediately.

MEAT BALLS WITH SAUERKRAUT

4 cups ground, cooked leftover meat, lightly pkd
2 cups cold cooked cereal
3 tbsp chopped onion
1 tsp salt
¼ tsp pepper
½ tsp celery salt
1 egg or 2 yolks, unbeaten

2 tbsp bacon drippings
No. 2½ can sauerkraut,
3½ cups
⅓ cup brown sugar, firmly
pkd, if desired
¼ cup water
2 tbsp vinegar

Combine first 7 ingredients thoroughly, shape in small balls, and brown slowly on all sides in a skillet with the bacon drippings. Pour sauerkraut and juice over meat balls. Add brown sugar, water, and vinegar; cover and simmer about 20 min, or until meat balls are done through. 5 generous servings.

Note: One lb of fresh ground beef may be used in place of the 4 cups leftover meat.

LAMB*

CHART No. 30

Meat Cuts and How to Cook Them
LAMB CHART

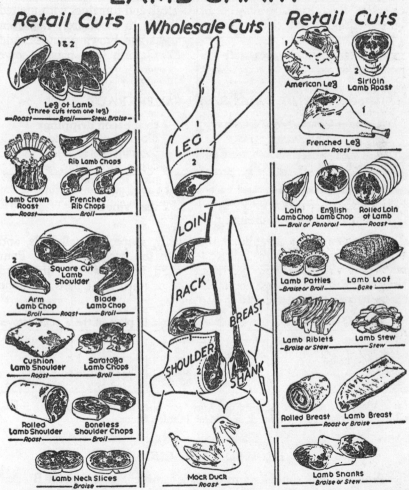

Ten Lessons on Meat for Use in Schools, Sixth Edition, published by National Live Stock and Meat Board, Chicago.

BROILED, PAN-BROILED, ROASTED LAMB

TABLE 31　　　　TIME TABLE FOR BROILING LAMB*

| | | APPROXIMATE COOKING TIME | |
SUITABLE CUTS	WEIGHT Pounds	Rare Minutes	Medium Minutes
LAMB			
Shoulder chops or steaks from legs—1 inch	3 ounces	Lamb chops	12
1½ inches	6 ounces	are not served	18
2 inches	10 ounces	rare	22
Rib chops—1 inch....................	2 ounces		12
1½ inches	4 ounces		18
2 inches	5 ounces		22
Loin chops—1 inch...................	3		12
1½ inches	5		18
2 inches	6		22
Ground lamb patties			
1 inch by 3 inches.................	4 ounces		18

Note: This time table is based on broiling at a moderate temp (350° F). See p 793 for detailed broiling instructions. Lamb chops are broiled to an internal temp of 170° F.

TABLE 32　　　　TIME TABLE FOR ROASTING LAMB*

SUITABLE CUTS	WEIGHT	OVEN TEMPERA-TURE CONSTANT	INTERIOR TEMPERATURE WHEN REMOVED FROM OVEN	APPROXIMATE TIME PER . POUND
LAMB	Pounds	Degrees F.	Degrees F.	Minutes
Leg, loin or crown roasts ..	6½-7½	300	175-180	30-35
Shoulder—Rolled	3-4	300	175-180	40-45
Shoulder	4½-5½	300	175-180	30-35
Cushion	3-4	300	175-180	30-35

*Adapted from Ten Lessons on Meat for Use in Schools, Sixth Edition, published by National Live Stock and Meat Board, Chicago.

BROILED LAMB CHOPS

Broil rib, loin, shoulder arm or blade lamb chops just as for Broiled Steak, p 802. Have chops cut 1 to 2 inches thick and broil from 12 to 22 min depending on thickness as indicated in the table above. Pleasing accompaniments for broiled lamb chops are sautéed pineapple slices or mint jelly. Fresh mint is an attractive garnish in place of parsley.

PAN-BROILED LAMB CHOPS

Have loin, rib, shoulder arm or blade lamb chops cut not more than ½-inch thick for pan-broiling. Stack the chops together and hold them with the fat edges down in a hot skillet, rocking them back and forth until the surface is delicately browned and enough of the fat is fried out to grease the skillet and prevent the lean meat from sticking. Now separate the chops and lay them flat in the moderately hot skillet. Turn every 30 seconds for the first 2 or 3 min; then lower the heat and continue cooking, allowing 12 min altogether for ½-inch chops. Any excess fat accumulating in pan should be drained off during cooking. The last time of turning, sprinkle both sides with salt, and pepper if desired. Remove to a hot platter. The rich brown residue left sticking to the bottom of the skillet makes a flavorful gravy. Add about ⅓ cup water for 7 chops, place over low heat, and loosen residue by stirring with a fork. Heat to boiling, season to suit taste, and pour over chops or potatoes to be served with them. Garnish chops with fresh mint or parsley.

ROAST LAMB SHOULDER

Mint Barbecue Sauce

Have a 3 to 4 lb shoulder of lamb boned and rolled. Cut small gashes or pockets here and there and insert slices of garlic. (Remove garlic before serving.) Rub with 1 tbsp salt and ¼ tsp pepper and place on rack in shallow uncovered roasting pan. Roast (add no water or flour) in a moderately slow oven (300° to 325° F) for approximately 40 to 45 min per lb, or until meat thermometer registers 175° to 180° F (well-done). During the last hr, baste frequently with the following Barbecue Sauce.

Melt 2 tbsp butter, ½ cup mint jelly and 2 tbsp vinegar together with ½ tsp dry mustard. Serve additional Barbecue Sauce with sliced roast. Serves 3 to the lb of boned meat.

ROAST LAMB SHOULDER WITH DRESSING

4 lbs lamb shoulder	1 cup chopped celery
1 tbsp salt	6 cups coarse dry bread
¼ tsp curry powder	crumbs
½ tsp paprika	2 egg yolks
1 tsp salt	1 cup milk
Pinch of dry mustard	2 tbsp melted butter
2 tbsp chopped onion	

Wipe meat thoroughly with a damp cloth. If butcher has not made a pocket, split open and remove bones, cutting so meat can be rolled around the dressing. (Simmer the bones for 1 hr in enough water to cover to make lamb broth for soup or gravy.) Rub meat inside and out with the 1 tbsp salt. Combine the next 6 ingredients and mix thoroughly with the dry crumbs. Beat egg yolks, add the milk and melted butter and mix with the seasoned crumbs. Let stand until all the liquid has been soaked up. Pack dressing lightly into pocket of meat. Shape into a neat roll and fasten with skewers and string. Place in open roasting pan and bake in a slow oven (300° F), allowing 30 to 35 min for each lb of meat. Make gravy, p 799, using broth from bones. 8 to 10 servings.

ROAST LEG OF LAMB

Wipe the leg of lamb clean with a damp cloth; do not remove the fell. Cut a clove of garlic into 4 pieces. Make 4 equally spaced shallow gashes on the fat side of leg, and insert the pieces of garlic in these gashes (garlic may be omitted). Rub the leg all over with salt and pepper. Place on a trivet or small rack in an open roasting pan, fat side up; in lamb, the fat layer is on the inside of the leg rather than on the outside or skin side. Insert meat thermometer in the thickest part of the leg so the bulb is at the center of the roast, touching neither bone nor fat. Place in moderately slow oven (300° to 325° F) and cook 30 to 35 min to the lb, or until thermometer registers 175° to 180° F. Transfer to hot platter and cover to keep hot, remove pieces of garlic. Drain off excess fat from roasting pan and make gravy from savory brown residue, p 799. Lamb should be well-done and should be served very hot. Garnish with parsley or fresh mint and serve with Mint Jelly or Mint Sauce. A 6 to 6½-lb leg of lamb serves 8 to 10.

BRAISED LAMB

BAKED LAMB STEAKS

A tasty, fragrant way to cook lamb

4 small lamb steaks, ¾" thick, 1½ lbs	1½ tsp salt
	⅙ tsp pepper
2 to 3 tbsp flour	2 cups canned tomatoes,
2 medium onions, ½ lb	sieved
1 tbsp parsley, chopped	1 cup water
1 tsp orégano	

Start oven 10 min before baking; set to moderately slow (325° F). Wipe lamb steaks with a damp cloth. Cut through the fat rim in 3 or 4 places. Dredge steaks in flour. Lay them in an 8" x 8" x 2" glass baking dish. Cover meat with onion slices. Sprinkle in the parsley and the rest of the seasonings. Pour tomatoes and water over the top. Bake covered for 30 min. A sheet of aluminum foil makes a good cover. Remove cover and bake another 1¼ hrs, or until the meat is very tender and the liquid is reduced to a gravy consistency. Serve with fluffy Boiled Rice. 4 servings.

Note: Large meaty shoulder chops may be used in place of the steaks.

BARBECUED LAMB RIBLETS

See Barbecued Spareribs, p 860. Substitute 3 lbs lamb riblets for 3 lbs spareribs. (Lamb riblets are lamb breast cut into serving portions.)

TABLE 33   TIME TABLE FOR BRAISING LAMB*

SUITABLE CUTS	AVERAGE WEIGHT OR THICKNESS	APPROXIMATE COOKING TIME
LAMB		
Breast—stuffed	2–3 pounds	1½–2 hours
Breast—rolled	1½–2 pounds	1½–2 hours
Neck slices	¾ inch	1 hour
Shanks	½ pound each	1–1½ hours
Shoulder—stew	1 inch	1–1½ hours
Chops	¾ inch	50–60 minutes
Patties	¾ inch	20 minutes

*Adapted from *Ten Lessons on Meat for Use in Schools,* Sixth Edition, published by National Live Stock and Meat Board, Chicago.

BRAISED LAMB WITH VEGETABLES

1 lb boneless lamb shoulder cut in 1-inch pieces
3 tbsp flour
1 tsp salt
3 tbsp drippings
1¼ cups water
1 medium sized eggplant, 1 lb
2 medium tomatoes
Salt and pepper

Dredge meat with the combined flour and salt and brown slowly in the hot drippings. Add ½ cup of the water, cover and simmer for one hr, adding more water as needed. Pare and slice the eggplant, arrange slices of eggplant over meat, then the thick tomato slices, and sprinkle with salt and ppper. Cover and simmer for about 20 min longer. When ready to serve, lift food carefully so as to keep the vegetables intact. 4 servings.

CREOLE LAMB SHOULDER CHOPS

2½ lbs lamb shoulder arm chops
1½ tbsp fat
2 tsp salt
⅓ cup sliced onion
1½ cups tomato juice
2 medium carrots, sliced
1 tsp chopped parsley

Wipe chops clean with a damp cloth and brown slowly on both sides in the fat. Add remaining ingredients; cover closely and simmer until tender (about 1½ hrs). 5 to 6 servings.

LAMB AND LIMA BEAN CASSEROLE

¼ lb dried lima beans, ⅝ cup
1½ lbs boneless lamb shoulder
2 tbsp shortening *or* bacon
   drippings

1 clove garlic, chopped
1½ tsp salt
Pepper, if desired
2 cups boiling water

Wash lima beans and drain. Wipe lamb clean with damp cloth; cut into 1-inch dice and brown in the shortening with the garlic. Add salt and pepper and turn into a 6-cup casserole. Add lima beans and boiling water, cover, and place in a slow oven (300° F) for 1 to 1½ hrs, or until meat and beans are both very tender. Add additional hot water as needed. 5 or 6 servings.

LAMB PAPRIKA

2 lbs lamb flank and boneless
   breast
2 tbsp flour
2 tsp salt
⅛ tsp pepper

4 tsp paprika
3 tbsp shortening
⅓ cup sour cream
1 large onion sliced
¼ cup water

Cut lamb across grain into narrow two-inch strips and dredge in flour seasoned with salt, pepper and paprika. Heat the shortening and brown the meat quickly. Reduce heat, blend in sour cream and add the onions. Cover and simmer for about 1½ hrs until meat is very tender. Add water as needed. 4 servings.

LAMB PILAF

1 lb lean boneless lamb breast
1¾ tsp salt
   Dash of pepper
2 tbsp shortening
1 medium onion, diced
½ cup raw rice

1 cup water
2½ cups peeled, diced fresh
   tomatoes *or* canned
⅛ tsp ground cloves
Dash of cinnamon
Parsley

Cut lamb into inch cubes, season with salt and pepper. Sauté in shortening in Dutch oven or deep skillet until delicately browned. Add onion and cook until soft and yellow. Add rice and water, tomatoes, cloves and cinnamon. Cover and cook slowly 1 to 1½ hrs. Add more water if necessary. Liquid should be absorbed by rice when done. Sprinkle with chopped parsley. 4 servings.

LAMB SAUSAGE CASSEROLE

5 shoulder arm *or* blade lamb
   chops, ¾ inch thick
2 tsp bacon drippings
5 pineapple slices, drained
5 medium sweet potatoes,
   pared and sliced ½ inch
   thick

5 pork sausage links
Butter, about 2 tbsp
¼ lb mushrooms, cleaned
3 tomatoes, peeled and cut in
   halves *or* 1½ cups canned
Salt and pepper
¾ cup pineapple juice

Brown chops on both sides in the drippings in a skillet; transfer to shallow casserole or ovenware platter, and lay a slice of drained pineapple on each chop. Lay sliced potatoes around the chops, and place sausages over the potatoes. Put a bit of butter in each mushroom cap and arrange tomatoes and mushrooms among the potatoes. Sprinkle salt and pepper over all, and pour pineapple juice into casserole. Cover and bake in a moderate oven (350° F) for 50 to 60 min, or until chops and potatoes are tender. 5 servings.

LAMB SHANKS WITH TOMATO PEPPER GRAVY

Attractive in appearance and flavor

3 lamb shanks	2 cups tomato juice
½ cup flour	1¼ cups hot water
2 tsp salt	1 tsp whole black peppers
½ tsp paprika	½ cup cold water
3 tbsp bacon fat	¾ tsp sugar
1 good sized clove garlic	

Ask butcher for the foreshanks which he usually cuts off and discards. Also have butcher cut shanks crosswise into 2 pieces. These add additional flavor to the dish. Wipe both shanks and foreshanks clean with damp cloth. Roll in 6 tbsp of the flour blended with the salt and paprika. Heat fat in Dutch oven or heavy skillet, brown meat, sliced garlic and bones slowly on all sides—20 min. Discard garlic. Add tomato juice, hot water and whole peppers. Cover closely, simmer until meat is very tender, 2 to 2½ hrs. Remove meat to hot platter; discard foreshanks; blend remaining flour with cold water and sugar. Gradually add to liquid in kettle or skillet. Cook until thickened, stir constantly about 5 min. Leave most of the peppers in for interest and bitey flavor. 4 to 5 servings.

Note: Water may be substituted for tomato juice for Danish Style Lamb Shanks.

LAMB SHANKS WITH VEGETABLES

4 small lamb shanks	1 cup water
2 tbsp flour	1 tbsp catchup
¼ tsp celery salt	1 cup fresh lima *or* green
1 tsp salt	beans
Pepper	1 cup fresh corn, cut from
2 tbsp shortening	cob

Dredge shanks thoroughly with the combined dry ingredients. Brown slowly on all sides in hot shortening in a heavy skillet or Dutch oven. Add a few tbsp of water, cover and simmer for 2 to 2¼ hrs, adding additional water as needed. Add any remaining water, the catchup and vegetables during the last 20 min of cooking. Cook until shanks are very tender. 4 servings.

LAMB SHOULDER CHOPS WITH DRESSING

5 shoulder arm *or* blade lamb
   chops
2 tsp bacon drippings
3 cups coarse dry bread
   crumbs
½ cup cold water

1 medium onion, grated
2 tbsp chopped parsley
½ to 1 tsp poultry seasoning
½ tsp salt
1 egg
5 slices bacon

Brown chops slowly in bacon drippings. Meanwhile soak crumbs in the water until they take it all up; squeeze out any excess. Sprinkle onion, parsley, and seasonings over crumbs, add beaten egg and mix very lightly to distribute well. Put dressing in bottom of a buttered baking dish; cover with the browned chops. Cover dish and bake in a moderate oven (325° F) about 1 hr. Remove cover, place a slice of bacon on each chop and bake 15 min longer to crisp bacon. 5 servings.

ROLLED STUFFED BREAST OF LAMB

1 lamb breast, 2 to 2½ lbs
2 tsp salt
Pepper
2 cups coarse, soft bread
   crumbs

½ cup diced celery
1 tbsp chopped onion
2 tbsp melted butter
¼ cup water *or* meat stock

Wipe lamb breast clean with damp cloth. Rub surface with half the salt, and pepper. Combine remaining ingredients and spread on the skin side of the breast. Roll up and tie securely. Place in baking pan, add water, cover, and bake in a moderately slow oven (325° F) until tender, allowing 45 min per lb of meat. Uncover during last ½ hr of cooking to brown. Make gravy from brown residue in pan, p 799, after draining off excess fat. 5 servings.

Note: If lamb breasts are trimmed so they will not roll up, make a pocket, fill with the dressing and skewer together.

STUFFED BREAST OF LAMB

3 lbs lamb breast
2 tbsp butter *or* margarine
3 tbsp chopped onion
¼ cup finely chopped celery
1 cup finely chopped carrots
¼ cup water
5 slices day-old bread, torn
   into coarse crumbs

1 tart apple, pared, chopped
1 egg, beaten
1 tsp salt
⅛ tsp pepper
2 tsp flour
Seasonings

Wipe off lamb breast with damp cloth. With a sharp knife, remove any tough skin from surface and slice a pocket in the lamb. If there is a solid piece of cartilage along the back, cut through in several places with kitchen or poultry scissors to make serving easier. Melt butter in skillet and sauté onion, celery, and carrots about 5 min. Pour water on bread crumbs and mix with cooked onion mixture in skillet. Add apple, egg, salt, pepper and mix well. Stuff firmly into pocket of lamb. Skewer and fasten opened end. Rub flour over top of lamb and sprinkle with additional salt, pepper and paprika. Roast covered in a moderately slow oven (325° F) for one hr. Add ½ cup water gradually as needed and continue cooking uncovered until tender, about 1½ hrs. 4 servings.

STUFFED LAMB BREAST WITH RICE

1 large lamb breast, 3 lbs
Salt and pepper
1½ tbsp chopped onion
1 tbsp butter
¾ cup uncooked rice

2 cups lamb broth* or chicken bouillon, 2 bouillon cubes to 2 cups hot water
1 tsp salt
½ tsp poultry seasoning
2 tbsp bacon drippings

Have pocket cut into lamb breast from large end. Wipe meat with damp cloth and sprinkle inside and out with salt and pepper. Cook onion in the butter until soft; add rice (see box directions), sauté until rice is golden; then add liquid and seasonings. Simmer 20 min, or until rice is soft. Stuff into pocket of breast, fold over once and tie with string to hold in shape. Brown breast on all sides in drippings in a heavy skillet or Dutch oven. Add ½ cup hot water, cover tightly and simmer gently for about 1½ hrs or until meat is perfectly tender. 5 servings.

SIMMERED LAMB

CURRIED LAMB

1½ lbs lamb shoulder
1½ tsp salt
3 tbsp butter or bacon drippings
1 cup diced celery
2 tart apples, pared and diced
½ cup sliced onions

2 cups lamb broth
1½ to 2 tsp curry powder
2 tbsp hot water
2 tbsp flour
3 or 4 cups cooked rice, 1 cup raw
Parsley

Wipe meat with damp cloth; fit snugly into kettle, barely cover with water, add salt and simmer until about tender. Drain, saving broth. Cut meat into 1-inch dice. Melt the butter or bacon drippings in a skillet, add celery, apples, and onions, and sauté until soft; then add lamb. Add lamb broth that has the excess fat skimmed from it, cover and simmer 20 to 30 min. Blend curry powder with hot water and let stand 5 min; then blend in the flour, adding cold water if necessary to

*When purchasing lamb, buy some extra bony pieces to prepare broth.

make a smooth paste. If lamb mixture is nearly dry, add about 1 cup boiling water and stir in the curry paste. Continue simmering for 5 min, stirring frequently. Serve on hot platter with border of fluffy boiled rice and garnish of parsley. 5 servings.

IRISH STEW

1½ lbs lamb shoulder cut in pieces for stew	2 tsp salt
Flour	Dash of pepper
2 tbsp butter *or* shortening	5 medium potatoes, pared
Water	5 carrots, scraped
	1 small onion, sliced

Wipe meat with damp cloth; dredge thoroughly with flour and brown slowly on all sides in a skillet or Dutch oven in which the butter or shortening has been melted. Add 1 cup water, cover and simmer 45 min; then add salt, pepper, diced potatoes, carrots cut crosswise in inch lengths, and onion, with 1½ cups more boiling water and continue simmering until all are tender, about 30 min. Serve piping hot. If desired, a little chopped parsley may be added just before serving. 5 servings.

GROUND LAMB

CHILI CON CARNE WITH LAMB

1 lb dried red chili beans	3 cups puréed cooked tomatoes
6 cups cold water	
1½ tsp salt	1 tbsp salt
1 large clove garlic	½ tsp sugar
1½ lbs ground lamb	1 tbsp chili powder
¾ cup coarsely chopped onion	⅛ tsp red pepper
¼ cup chopped suet, if needed	1½ tsp tarragon vinegar
3 tbsp flour	¼ tsp rosemary, if desired

Wash beans thoroughly; cover and simmer for 1½ to 2 hrs in water to which the 1½ tsp salt is added. Beans should be soft but not mushy. Do not drain. Allow to cool so they will absorb more of the liquid. When cool, drain and measure liquid. There should be 1 cup. If there is less, add water; if more, boil rapidly to concentrate to 1 cup. Slice garlic, keeping pieces large so that they may be easily removed from mixture. Combine with the meat and onion in a skillet and cook over medium heat until meat is lightly browned, about 10 min. (Suet should be used only if the meat is very lean.) Remove the garlic and discard. Drain all but 2 tbsp fat from the meat. Stir in the flour and add tomato purée gradually. Heat to boiling. Reduce heat, add remaining ingredients, the beans and the 1 cup of bean liquid and simmer for 10 min, stirring occasionally. Makes 8 or 9 cups of chili. 9 to 10 servings.

LAMB AND PORK LOAF

1 lb ground lamb	2 tbsp chopped onion
½ lb ground lean pork	2 eggs beaten
2 tsp salt	1 cup lamb broth* *or* milk
1½ cups coarse soft bread	Pepper
crumbs, firmly pkd	¼ cup melted butter
¼ cup finely chopped celery	

Combine all ingredients except ½ cup of the bread crumbs, and the butter. Mix thoroughly and press mixture into a loaf pan (8¼ x 4½ x 2¾ inches). Mix together melted butter and the ½ cup of bread crumbs, and pat over top of the loaf. Bake in a moderate oven (325° to 350° F) for 1½ hrs. Before turning out, let loaf stand 15 min to absorb meat juices. Garnish with parsley or mint. 5 servings.

LAMB LOAF WITH HARVEY SAUCE

1 small clove garlic	2 eggs, beaten
1 tbsp bacon drippings	½ tsp poultry seasoning
1½ lbs ground lean lamb	1¼ tsp salt
¼ cup chopped bacon	5 *or* 6 celery curls
1½ cups soft bread crumbs	½ cup currant jelly
2 tsp finely chopped parsley	¼ cup water
2 tbsp finely chopped onion	2 tsp prepared mustard

Sauté garlic slices in drippings for one min. Lift out garlic and discard. Add next 8 ingredients to drippings in pan and mix thoroughly. Press into a loaf pan (8¼ x 4½ x 2¾ inches). Then unmold onto a flat greased baking pan. Bake in a moderate oven (350° F) about 1½ hrs. Place on hot platter and garnish with celery curls. Serve with sauce made by heating the jelly, water, and mustard to the boiling point. 1 tbsp butter may be added for flavor. 4 to 5 servings.

SAVORY LAMBURGERS

A lamb hater's defeat

1 lb ground lamb, net wt	Pepper to taste
1 tsp salt	2 tsp lemon juice
1 tbsp water	Piece garlic size small pea
1 tsp monosodium glutamate	Chopped parsley *or* mint

Have butcher trim some of the fat off lamb shoulder before grinding. Turn meat into mixing bowl; add next 5 ingredients. Crush garlic to a fine paste with handle of a knife and add to lamb. Blend thoroughly. Form into 4 uniform patties about ½-inch thick. Heat skillet

*When purchasing meat buy some extra bony pieces of lamb to prepare the broth.

until hot, sift a little salt into skillet and lay in patties. Immediately lift patties up from skillet and move around to prevent sticking. Cook briskly until patties are nicely browned on underside, about 2 min. Turn over and brown on other side. Cover, reduce heat a little and cook 1 min longer. Turn patties again, cover, and cook another min, or about 6 min in all. Remove to a hot plate. Drain off all the fat collected in the skillet, add ¼ cup hot water to skillet and scrape loose the brown residue. Heat to boiling for very tasty pan gravy. Pour over patties and shower with a little freshly chopped parsley or mint. Serve very hot. Delicious served with Fried Eggplant, p 1348. 4 servings.

LAMB PATTIES

5 lamb patties *or* 1¼ lbs
   ground lamb and 5 strips
   bacon
2 tbsp shortening

½ tsp salt
1 chicken bouillon cube
½ cup hot water

If lamb patties are not already shaped and wrapped with bacon, form them 1 inch thick from the ground meat and surround each with strip of bacon, fastening with a toothpick. Brown patties in shortening on both sides, sprinkle with salt. Dissolve bouillon cube in hot water and pour around patties. Cover tightly and cook over moderate heat until thoroughly done (about 20 min). 5 servings.

Note: Lamb patties may also be broiled or pan-broiled, allowing 18 min altogether for 1-inch thick patties.

LAMB PATTY GRILL

1 lb ground lamb
2 chicken bouillon cubes
2 tbsp catchup
¼ tsp salt
⅛ tsp pepper
4 to 6 bacon slices

4 tomatoes
¾ cup whole kernel corn
4 medium-sized hot cooked
   potatoes
1 oz grated American cheese

Mix the ground lamb with the crushed bouillon cubes dissolved in the catchup. Season with salt and pepper. Shape in thick patties and wrap edge with bacon slices. Fasten ends of bacon with toothpicks or small skewers. Place lamb patties on broiler rack so there is a distance of 3 inches between top of meat and source of heat. When patties are browned on one side (about 9 min), turn. At this time, add to the grill the whole tomatoes, hollowed out and sprinkled generously inside with salt and pepper and then filled with corn and tomato pulp and seasoned with salt and pepper. Add potatoes, which have been cut in halves and sprinkled with dry grated cheese. Continue the broiling for another 7 to 9 min until patties are done and potatoes and tomatoes are lightly browned. 4 servings.

LEFTOVER LAMB

BAKED LAMB STUFFED TOMATOES

Lamb in a most appealing form

½ lb ground lamb, net wt
1 tbsp bacon fat
2 onions, egg size
¼ cup converted *or* enriched
    rice
½ cup tomato juice
1 cup water

¾ tsp salt
Pepper to suit taste
1 tsp monosodium glutamate
1 tbsp chopped parsley
2 lbs tomatoes, 4 large
½ tsp celery salt
Parsley *or* mint

Start oven 10 min before baking; set to moderate hot (400° F). Have butcher grind lamb from shoulder that has some of the fat trimmed off. Heat bacon fat in skillet. Add lamb, finely chopped onion and rice. Stir almost constantly until the meat particles are gray in color and the onion is soft. Add tomato juice, water, salt, pepper and monosodium glutamate. Cover, simmer 20 to 25 min or until rice is tender; stir frequently. Stir in parsley. Wash tomatoes, remove stem scar and a slice from the stem end. Hollow out tomatoes leaving a wall about ¼" thick. Chop the scooped out portion and add to lamb mixture and reheat. Sprinkle insides of tomatoes with celery salt, then stuff them with the hot lamb mixture and heap slightly. Put into a shallow pan and spoon any leftover filling around base of tomatoes. Bake until tomatoes are just cooked through. Remove to hot serving plate, garnish with parsley and serve steaming hot. 4 servings.

LAMB CURRY

3 tbsp butter *or* margarine
⅓ cup chopped onion
2 cups diced leftover cooked
    lamb, ½ lb
1 cup chopped celery cabbage
2 tbsp flour
1 cup water

1 chicken bouillon cube
¼ tsp curry
½ tsp salt
3 drops tabasco
½ tsp sugar
1 cup elbow macaroni, raw

Melt butter in heavy skillet. Sauté onion until transparent and golden yellow. Add diced lamb and cook to light appetizing brown. Add celery cabbage and sauté until soft. Push meat and vegetables to side of skillet, blend flour into melted butter until smooth. Add water gradually, stirring until it boils and thickens. Add bouillon cube and stir to dissolve. Add seasoning and stir all together. Cover and simmer over low heat for 30 min to blend and mellow flavors. Serve hot over hot, cooked, rinsed and drained macaroni. 4 servings.

Note: May be served over hot cooked rice or noodles with equal success.

LAMB HASH

2 tbsp fat
2 cups ground, leftover
  cooked lamb
3 cups mashed *or* chopped
  boiled potatoes

1 cup leftover lamb gravy
  or 1 chicken bouillon cube
  dissolved in 1 cup hot water
Salt and pepper to taste

Heat fat in a heavy skillet; add meat and potatoes, stirring to mix well. Add liquid and seasonings and stir again. Cover the skillet and heat thoroughly over low heat with occasional stirring to prevent sticking. 5 servings.

LAMB SCALLOP

3 cups diced, leftover
  cooked lamb
1 tbsp fat
1¼ tsp salt

No. 2 can tomatoes, 2½
  cups
1 cup fine dry bread crumbs
2 tbsp butter

Brown meat in a skillet in the 1 tbsp fat. Add salt. Arrange layers of browned meat, tomatoes and bread crumbs in a 6-cup casserole, topping with crumbs. Dot all over with butter and bake in a moderate oven (350° F) for ½ hr or until thoroughly heated through. 5 servings.

PORK*

CHART No. 34

Meat Cuts and How to Cook Them
PORK CHART

Retail Cuts

2 Sirloin Pork Roast — Roast —

1 Pork Tenderloin Frenched and Whole — Broil or Braise —

2 to 5 Canadian Style Bacon — Broil —

3 Loin Chop

4 Rib Pork Chop

Frenched Rib Chop

2 to 5 Butterfly Chop — Broil or Braise —

1. 2 Loin Roast Ham End

3. 4 Loin Roast Center Cut

5 Loin Roast Shoulder End

4 Crown Pork Roast — Roast —

Fat Back — Lard · Salt Pork

Lard — Shortening —

Blade Pork Steaks — Braise —

Smoked Cottage Roll — Bake or Panbroil —

Boston Style Butt

Rolled Boston Style Butt — Roast —

Wholesale Cuts

HAM

LOIN

SIDE

SPARE RIBS

BUTT

PICNIC

JOWL

Bacon Square — Seasoning · Panbroil —

Retail Cuts

Half Ham Butt End

Half Ham Shank End — Bake or Simmer —

Ham Butt Slice

Center Ham Slice — Broil or Panbroil —

Fresh Ham Roast

Rolled Fresh Ham Roast — Roast —

Bacon — Broil · Panbroil or Seasoning —

Salt Pork

Spareribs — Simmer · Braise or Roast —

Fresh Picnic Shoulder — Roast —

Smoked Picnic Shoulder — Bake or Simmer —

Cushion Style Picnic Shoulder

Rolled Picnic Shoulder — Roast —

Fresh Shoulder Hock — Simmer —

Arm Pork Steak — Braise —

*Ten Lessons on Meat for Use in Schools, Sixth Edition, published by National Live Stock and Meat Board, Chicago.

BACON AND SALT PORK

BAKED BACON

When baking a half or whole lb of bacon, lay unseparated slices flat on rack in a shallow baking pan. Bake in moderate oven (350° F) until golden and crisp. Bacon requires no turning and little attention until nearly done. It is an especially convenient method when cooking large amounts of bacon. When done, remove pan from oven. Lift bacon slices from rack to a hot platter. Drain into bacon fat container. If rack is not used, drain fat from bacon twice during cooking. When done, lift slices onto paper toweling to drain a min before placing on hot platter. One lb serves 6.

TABLE 35   TIME TABLE FOR BROILING BACON, HAM
AND SHOULDER BUTT SLICES

MEAT	WEIGHT	DONENESS	APPROXIMATE COOKING TIME — MINUTES
BACON (Ready Sliced)	....	Light Golden and Crisp	4 to 5
CANADIAN BACON ¼-Inch Slices	....	Fat Golden; Lean Reddish Brown	4 to 5
½-Inch Slices	....	Fat Golden; Lean Reddish Brown	6 to 8
HAM SLICE (Regular) ½-Inch Thick	¾ to 1 lb.	Fat Golden Brown; Lean Reddish Brown (Well Done)	20
1-Inch Thick	1½ to 2 lb.	Fat Golden Brown; Lean Reddish Brown (Well Done)	25 to 30
HAM SLICE (Tendered) ½-Inch Thick	¾ to 1 lb.	Fat Golden Brown; Lean Reddish Brown (Well Done)	10 to 12
1-Inch Thick	1½ to 2 lb.	Fat Golden Brown; Lean Reddish Brown (Well Done)	16 to 20
SHOULDER BUTT SLICE ½-Inch Thick	....	Fat Golden Brown; Lean Reddish Brown (Well Done)	10 to 12

Note: This time table is based on broiling at moderate temp (350°F). See special directions for regulating broiling heat, p 793. Ham is cooked well done. The time for broiling bacon is influenced by personal preference as to crispness.

BROILED BACON

Pre-heat broiler. If only a few slices of bacon are to be broiled, remove package from refrigerator to warm up a few min so whole slices may be removed easily. Separate slices, lay flat on broiler rack adjusted about 3 inches below source of heat. Broil slowly; watch carefully and turn once or twice during cooking. Broiling requires more care than baking, but broiled bacon has a particularly pleasing flavor and is free of greasiness. Remove fat collecting in broiler pan at once to a clean container with a tight cover.

PAN-BROILED BACON

Put slices of bacon in a cold skillet, laying them out flat. Cook over low heat, turning 2 or 3 times so bacon broils evenly. Drain off fat when bacon is about half done. When done, lift bacon onto paper toweling to drain a min before serving. Slow cooking gives the best flavor.

USES FOR BACON FAT

Store bacon fat in refrigerator

1. To make white sauce for creamed vegetables and creamed soups. 2. To season many vegetables. 3. To fry potatoes, onions, egg plant, parsnips, tomatoes, eggs, potato cakes, pancakes, liver, fish, etc. 4. To grease pans for muffins, biscuits and cornbread. 5. To brown meats for stews and pot roasts. 6. As a shortening in muffins, pancakes, waffles and corn bread.

SALT PORK AND CREAM GRAVY

¾ lb salt pork
Flour
1 tbsp bacon fat

3 cups milk
1 to 2 tsp finely chopped
    parsley

Cut salt pork into ⅛-inch thick slices. If salty, cover with hot water and let stand a few min, then drain well. Now dip slices in flour and fry in the hot bacon fat until brown and crisp, then remove to hot platter. Drain off all but ¼ cup of the fat, add 4 tbsp flour to fat left in skillet, blending until smooth; then add milk gradually and stir constantly until it boils and thickens. Simmer 5 min longer, stirring occasionally. If gravy becomes too thick, thin it with more milk. When ready to serve, stir in parsley and serve with the crisp salt pork. 5 servings.

Note: If preferred, the pork may be cut into ½-inch dice and cooked until crisp without dipping in flour and without the bacon fat. Then proceed as above. This gravy is excellent with mashed or baked potatoes.

CHOPS

BAKED PORK CHOPS WITH CARAWAY SEED

½ cup fine cracker crumbs   1 egg, slightly beaten
½ tsp caraway seed   1 tbsp water
⅛ tsp pepper   2 tbsp shortening
1¼ tsp salt   1 tbsp flour
    4 thick loin chops, 1¼ lbs 1 cup milk

Combine crumbs, caraway seed, pepper and 1 tsp of the salt. Dip chops into prepared crumbs, then into egg diluted with the water and again in crumbs, pressing crumbs firmly onto chops so they stay on while cooking. Brown slowly on each side in hot shortening in a heavy skillet. Remove from skillet. Blend flour and remaining salt into fat in skillet and add milk gradually, then 1 cup water. Stir until gravy boils, is smooth and thickened. Place chops in gravy, cover and bake in a moderate oven (350° F) 35 min. Remove cover and bake 10 to 15 min longer. 4 servings.

TABLE 36   TIME TABLE FOR BRAISING PORK*

SUITABLE CUTS	AVERAGE WEIGHT OR THICKNESS	APPROXIMATE COOKING TIME
PORK		
Chops	¾–1½ inches	45–60 minutes
Spareribs	2–3 pounds	1½ hours
Tenderloin		
Whole	¾–1 pound	45–60 minutes
Fillets	½ inch	30 minutes
Shoulder and leg steaks	¾ inch	45 to 60 minutes
Hocks	2½ pounds	2–3 hours

*Adapted from *Ten Lessons on Meat for Use in Schools*, Seventh Edition, published by National Live Stock and Meat Board, Chicago.

BRAISED PORK CHOPS

Have 5 pork chops cut at least 1 inch thick, weighing about 2 lbs. Wipe with a damp cloth. Hold chops together, fat-edge down in a heavy skillet or Dutch Oven over medium heat, until enough fat melts to grease skillet. Now lay chops down flat, increase heat slightly and brown on both sides. Sprinkle 1½ tsp salt over meat; cover tightly, reduce heat to simmering. Cook 30 to 40 min or until meat is tender, turning once or twice during cooking; add ¼ cup water after browning if chops seem tough. Remove chops to hot platter and keep warm. To make gravy, drain off all but 3 tbsp of the fat, blend in 3 tbsp of flour, add 1½ cups milk and cook with constant stirring until smooth and thickened, p 799. Serve gravy hot with chops. 5 servings.

Variation: Dredge chops with flour before browning.

BRAISED SPANISH PORK CHOPS

5 thick rib pork chops, 2 lbs	¼ tsp pepper
1 tbsp fat	3 tbsp flour
1 onion, sliced	3 to 4 cups hot Boiled Rice,
2 cups canned tomatoes	p 433, 1 cup raw
1½ tsp salt	

Brown chops slowly on both sides in the fat in a heavy skillet; remove chops from pan. Sauté onion in same pan; add chops, tomatoes and seasonings. Cover and simmer 45 to 60 min, or until tender. Remove meat and thicken the tomato mixture with the flour mixed to a smooth paste with ¼ cup cold water; boil 2 to 3 min, stirring constantly. Place rice in center of platter, arrange chops around rice and pour tomato sauce over the chops. 5 servings.

BRAISED PORK STEAK WITH SPANISH RICE

1½ lbs pork shoulder steak	1 cup water
½ cup chopped onion	2 tsp salt
½ cup chopped green pepper	⅛ tsp black pepper
½ cup chopped celery	1 tsp paprika
No. 2 can tomatoes,	2 tsp sugar
2½ cups	1 cup uncooked rice

Wipe meat with damp cloth; brown it slowly on both sides in heavy skillet. No added fat will be needed for browning if meat is well streaked with fat. Add all ingredients except rice, turn heat low, cover and simmer 30 min. Add rice (see box directions), and simmer 30 to 40 min longer, or until rice and meat are perfectly tender. Serve hot. 5 servings.

BRAISED STUFFED PORK CHOPS

5 double rib pork chops	½ cup finely diced celery
1½ cups soft, coarse bread crumbs	2 tsp melted butter
	Flour
¼ tsp poultry seasoning	Milk *or* water
1½ tsp salt	

Have butcher make a pocket for dressing on inside of each chop with opening between the two bones. Wipe chops with damp cloth. Lightly mix together the crumbs, seasonings, celery and melted butter, and stuff into chops. Lay in a baking dish or skillet (one with an oven-proof handle), and sprinkle with flour. Pour in milk to a depth of about

½ inch; do not cover the chops with it. Cover and bake in a moderately slow oven (325° F) for about 2 hrs or until chops are perfectly tender, removing cover for the last half hr. 5 servings.

Note: One cup chopped tart apple makes a fine addition to this dressing.

CASSEROLE PORK CHOPS

5 thick loin *or* rib pork chops
1½ tbsp fat
1½ tsp salt
Pepper

No. 2 can cream style corn
⅓ cup diced green pepper
2 tbsp hot water

Brown chops slowly in a skillet in the hot fat, and sprinkle with the salt and enough pepper to suit taste. Mix corn and green pepper, and arrange in buttered casserole in alternate layers with browned chops. Add the water, cover, and bake 45 min in a moderate oven (350° F); then remove cover and bake 15 min longer. 5 servings.

CASSEROLE OF CORNED PORK CHOPS

A one-dish meal you'll like and make time and again

6 loin *or* rib pork chops,
    inch-thick, 1¾ lbs
2¼ tsp salt
¹⁄₁₆ tsp pepper
¾ cup chopped onion
2 tbsp butter
1 cup finely chopped celery

⅓ cup finely chopped green
    pepper
1 egg
No. 2 can cream style corn
1 cup fine dry bread crumbs
1 tbsp flour
1½ cups milk

Start oven 10 min before baking; set to moderate (350° F). Lay chops out flat in a small roasting pan. Sprinkle 1¾ tsp salt and the pepper over chops. Cover and bake 25 min. Meanwhile sauté onion in 1½ tbsp of the butter until soft and yellow. Add the celery, green pepper and the remaining salt and stir thoroughly. Beat egg, stir in the corn and crumbs and add to the skillet. Stir and reheat thoroughly. Prepare white sauce of the remaining butter, flour and milk. Turn the hot corn mixture over the chops. Pour hot white sauce over the top and bake uncovered another 40 min. To serve, cut around the chops and lift them out with their topping of corn-custard intact and beautiful. 6 servings.

BRAISED PORK CHOPS WITH HOMINY, p 1350

BRAISED PORK CHOPS WITH SAUERKRAUT

5 pork shoulder chops,
    about 2 lbs
1½ tsp salt

No. 2½ can sauerkraut,
    3½ cups
2 tsp sugar

Wipe chops with damp cloth. Brown slowly on both sides in lightly greased heavy skillet; sprinkle with salt. Turn sauerkraut over chops, and sprinkle sugar over it if desired (sugar takes edge off sourness of kraut). Cover tightly and simmer gently for about 1 hr until chops are very tender. 5 servings.

Note: One-half cup of cider and 1 tsp caraway seed may be added with the kraut to make it juicy and mellow in flavor.

"PAN-BROILED" PORK CHOPS AND POTATOES

A super-duper, easy skillet meal

4 loin pork chops, inch-thick, 1½ lbs	2 tbsp water
2 baking potatoes, 1¼ lbs	1 tbsp flour
1¾ tsp salt	½ cup milk
	¼ cup water

It is important that the chops be thick and uniform in thickness. Heat skillet until hot, sprinkle a little salt over bottom, lay in chops. Lift chops up immediately, then let them drop back into place to keep them from sticking to the skillet. Cook moderately fast until chops are nicely browned on under side, turn and brown other side. Sprinkle with 1¼ tsp of the salt. Cover skillet, reduce heat and cook so that fat sizzles gently in skillet about 10 min. Meanwhile pare potatoes thinly, cut into 3 lengthwise, uniformly thick slices. Turn pork chops again and push together compactly. Lay potato slices flat around chops, sprinkle with remaining salt; cover and cook another 30 min; turn potatoes and chops once again. Add the 2 tbsp water last 15 min of cooking. When potatoes and chops are tender and a tempting brown, remove to a hot platter. Pour off all but 1 tbsp of fat from skillet. Add flour to skillet, then the milk and ¼ cup water. Boil gently and scrape all the brown residue from the bottom and sides of the skillet. Cook until smooth and thick. Serve with the chops. 4 servings.

HOCKS

"BOILED" DINNER WITH HAM HOCKS

2½ lbs ham hocks	5 medium onions
1 bunch carrots	1 medium head cabbage
5 medium potatoes	

Wipe ham hocks thoroughly with damp cloth. Fit them together snugly in a kettle. Barely cover with boiling water and simmer gently, covered, for 1½ to 2½ hrs or until meat is very tender. Time will depend on type of ham. Add salt if needed to season vegetables. Meanwhile, wash vegetables; scrape carrots and cut in halves lengthwise; pare potatoes and onions, and cut cabbage in wedges after removing soiled outer leaves. Add vegetables to kettle and increase heat so liquid boils gently; cook, uncovered, about 20 to 30 min longer until vegetables are tender. If preferred, cover the kettle and cook wedges of cabbage in a separate uncovered pan until just tender, and add to platter when ham hocks and other vegetables are served. 5 servings.

Note: The hocks may be browned slowly but thoroughly and the excess fat poured off before adding the water. This gives a more appetizingly colored meat.

FRESH PIG HOCKS

2½ lbs fresh pig hocks	Hot water
2 tsp salt	Parsley

Wipe meat with a damp cloth, place in kettle, sprinkle with salt and barely cover with boiling water. Cover the pan, heat until liquid boils, then reduce heat and simmer 2 to 3 hrs or until very tender. Remove hocks to baking pan, place in a hot oven (400° F) to brown and try out the excess fat. Serve on hot platter garnished with parsley. 5 servings.

Variation: One qt sauerkraut may be added the last half hr of cooking; reduce salt to 1 tsp.

SPARERIBS

BARBECUED SPARERIBS No. 1

3 lbs spareribs	½ tbsp prepared mustard
1 medium onion, chopped	½ cup water
1 tbsp butter *or*	½ cup chopped celery
bacon drippings	2 tsp salt
1 tbsp vinegar	Dash of cayenne
1 tbsp sugar	1 to 2 tbsp Worcestershire
3 tbsp lemon juice	sauce, if desired

Wipe spareribs with damp cloth; cut in serving-size pieces. Place in a shallow baking pan and bake uncovered in a moderate oven (350° F) for 30 min. Meanwhile, sauté onion in butter or bacon drippings for 5 min; then add remaining ingredients, mix well, and simmer 5 min. Pour over the spareribs and continue baking for an hr longer, basting the ribs from time to time with the sauce in the bottom of the pan. 5 servings.

BARBECUED SPARERIBS No. 2

2 to 3 lbs ribs	¼ tsp poultry seasoning
1½ tsp salt	1 small onion
¼ tsp pepper	1 can, 8 oz, tomato sauce
¼ tsp paprika	1½ cups water
¼ tsp chili powder	1 tsp sugar

Trim any excess fat from ribs. Place in large shallow baking pan so that ribs are in a single layer, if possible. For easier handling, measure seasonings and spices and mix together. Sprinkle generously over ribs on both sides. Slice onion over top and pour tomato sauce over all. Add water and sprinkle sugar over sauce. Bake in a moderate oven (325° F) from 2 to 2½ hrs or until very tender—baste often and turn ribs several times during cooking. Add more water if necessary, but sauce should be thick enough to cling to meat when done. 4 servings.

BRAISED SPARERIBS

Wipe 3 lbs of spareribs with a damp cloth, cut into serving portions, dip into flour seasoned with 1½ tsp salt and ⅛ tsp pepper and brown slowly in hot bacon drippings. Reduce heat, add water (about ¼ cup), cover and simmer until tender, from 1 to 1½ hrs. If preferred, place browned spareribs in baking pan, add water, cover and cook in a moderately slow oven (325° F), until tender. 5 servings.

Note: Spareribs may also be dipped in beaten egg and rolled in seasoned crumbs before browning in the hot bacon drippings. Continue to cook as directed in recipe.

CELERY STUFFED SPARERIBS

2 racks spareribs, 4 lbs	3 cups soft bread crumbs,
¼ cup bacon drippings	firmly pkd
1 medium onion, chopped	¾ tsp salt
1 cup celery, chopped	⅛ tsp pepper
	2 tbsp flour

Wipe ribs clean with a damp cloth. Heat the drippings in a heavy skillet, and sauté onion until soft, about 5 min. Add celery, bread and seasonings and continue to cook until heated through. Spread the dressing on one rack of ribs, cover with second rack and sew or tie in place. Sprinkle the outside generously with additional salt and pepper and rub flour into surface. Lay the stuffed ribs on a rack in a open roasting pan and bake uncovered in a moderate oven (350° F) for 2 to 3 hrs or until very tender. Baste several times during cooking with the liquid that accumulates in bottom of pan. Add ¼ cup of water if necessary to prevent pan from drying. 8 servings.

FRUITED SPARERIBS

1 lb dried prunes	1½ tsp salt
3 lbs spareribs	2 *or* 3 apples, sliced

Soak prunes in warm water for 1½ to 2 hrs; remove pits. Wipe spareribs clean with damp cloth. Cut in serving portions. Lay half in baking dish; add half the salt. Cover with soaked and pitted prunes. Put apples on top of the prunes. Cover fruit with the remainder of the spareribs and sprinkle on rest of salt. Cover, bake in a moderate oven (350° F) until meat is tender, from 1½ to 2 hrs. Cover may be removed for last half hr of baking to brown top. 5 servings.

Note: A No. 2 can of sliced pineapple may be used in place of the apples.

SPARERIBS AND SAUERKRAUT

Cut 3 lbs spareribs into serving-size portions. Wipe with damp cloth. Pack snugly into kettle and barely cover with water; add 1½ tsp salt and simmer until very tender, about 1 hr. Add a No. 2½ can sauerkraut, pushing kraut down into meat stock. Cook 30 min longer, or until most of liquid is evaporated. A tart apple sliced may be put in with the kraut. Some persons like the addition of a little sugar (about 1 tbsp) to take the edge off the sourness. A tsp of caraway seeds may be sprinkled over the kraut just before serving if desired. 5 servings.

Variation. Add 1 sliced apple, 2 tbsp sugar, 2 tbsp butter and 1 grated carrot with the kraut. Cover and cook 15 min. Drop in Potato Dumplings, p 245, cover and cook another 12 min. Serve immediately.

STUFFED SPARERIBS

3 lbs spareribs	1½ tbsp chopped onion
2 cups water	½ tsp celery salt
2 tsp salt	1 tsp sage
8 slices 3 day-old bread	1½ cups broth from spareribs
1 tbsp chopped parsley	

Wipe spareribs with damp cloth. Place in heavy saucepan or large skillet, add water and 1½ tsp of the salt, cover and simmer gently ½ hr or until bones can be slipped out. Remove from heat, and if desired, cool and remove the bones. If bones are pulled out carefully, rib meat will remain intact in one strip. Arrange a section of ribs in a casserole, and spread with half the dressing made by mixing remaining ingredients, and rest of salt. Add another layer of ribs, rest of dressing and top with remaining ribs. Bake in a moderately slow oven (325° F) 1 to 1½ hrs or until meat is tender and nicely browned. 5 servings.

ROAST PORK

ROAST FRESH BOSTON STYLE PORK BUTT

Wipe a 4 to 5-lb fresh pork butt with a damp cloth. Sprinkle the roast with salt and place on a rack in an open roasting pan with the fat side up. Roast in a moderate oven (350° F) until done, or from 3 to 4 hrs. Allow 45 to 50 min to the lb. The meat thermometer should register 185° F when meat is done. 10 servings.

Note: Roast pork is delicious with dressing or browned potatoes. Make Bread dressing (p 754 or 1072), reducing the butter half. When roasting pork butt, press dressing around meat on the rack when meat is three-fourths cooked. When roasting a loin, press dressing up under loosened backbone.

For browned potatoes, put even sized pared whole or halved potatoes around the roast 45 min before roast is done. Spoon some of fat from the pan over the potatoes, sprinkle with salt. Baste with fat once or twice during cooking.

TABLE 37   TIME TABLE FOR ROASTING PORK

SUITABLE CUTS	WEIGHT	OVEN TEMPERATURE CONSTANT	INTERIOR TEMPERATURE WHEN REMOVED FROM OVEN	APPROXIMATE TIME PER POUND
	Pounds	Degrees F.	Degrees F.	Minutes
PORK—FRESH				
Loin—Center	3-5	350	185	35-40
Half	5-7	350	185	40-45
Ends	2-3	350	185	45-50
Crown roast (2 centers)** . . .	5-7	350	185	30-35
Picnic Shoulder—Whole	4-6	350	185	30-35
Boned and rolled	3-5	350	185	40-45
Cushion	3-5	350	185	35-40
Boston butt	4-6	350	185	45-50
Fresh ham	10-12	350	185	30-35
PORK—SMOKED				
Ham—Whole, regular	10-12	300	170	25
Whole, tendered	10-12	300	160	15
Half, tendered	6	300	160	22-25
Butt or shank end	3-4	300	160	40-45
Smoked shoulder butt	2-4	300	170	35
Picnic	5-7	300	170	35

**CROWN ROAST OF PORK

A roast that adds a festive touch to any meal

Have butcher tie the rib sections of 2 pork loins together and shape them into a circle, and then French the ends of the bones. A crown roast prepared this way weighs from 5 to 7 lbs. Start oven 10 min before roasting; set to moderate (350° F). Sprinkle roast with salt and pepper as for Pork Loin Roast, p 864. Set crown upside down in a shallow roasting pan. Insert meat thermometer into center of meat so as not to touch fat or bone. Bake until done, 30 to 35 min to the lb, or until thermometer registers 185° F. When roast is two-thirds done, drain off some of the clear fat. Now turn roast right-side up and fill center with Bread Stuffing, p 1072, then finish roasting. When done, remove roast to hot platter and put frills on ends of bones for carver to take hold. Make gravy as for Roast Loin of Pork. 10 servings.

GOOD OLD-TIME ROAST PORK AND POTATOES

A little water in a covered roaster reduces shrinkage and keeps pork juicy and fine flavored. It does not interfere with attractive browning

3¾ lb pork loin, from	Pepper
ham-end	½ cup water
2¼ tsp salt	2½ lbs potatoes, pared, halved

Have ready a small roaster with trivet and cover. Start oven 10 min before roasting, set to moderate (350° F).

Have butcher saw backbone free from ribs but leave in place for roasting. Wipe meat with a damp cloth. If there is a thick layer of fat on top, slice some of it off, then crisscross the top into ¼ or ½-inch sqs so fat will cook out. Rub salt and pepper *well* into meat, under severed backbone as well as *all over* outside. Place meat fat-side up on trivet in roaster. Add water, cover and place in oven. Roast 2 hrs, then lay potatoes around roast, cover and continue roasting 1 hr longer, or until meat is tender and nicely browned and potatoes are done. Remove from oven. Loosen and remove backbone carefully. Lift roast and potatoes to platter, cover with roaster lid while making gravy. See p 765. 6 servings.

ROAST LOIN OF PORK

Have backbone sawed loose from ribs or cut through every 2nd rib so carving will be easy. Sprinkle with salt and pepper. Place in an open roasting pan, fat-side up to make roast self-basting. Insert meat thermometer into center of roast clear of bone or fat. Place uncovered in moderate oven (350° F). Bake 30 to 50 min per pound. See chart above. Pork must be well cooked. Thermometer should register 185° F. When done, turn roast over on side, loosen and remove backbone. Remove roast to hot platter; cover to keep hot. Drain off all the clear fat. Use rich, brown drippings in pan to make gravy, pp 765–766. Season gravy, add a pinch of sage, if desired. 4 to 6 servings.

HAM

BAKED GLAZED HAM

When buying a ham, be sure you know its weight. If it is to be glazed, be sure it is covered with an even layer of fat. Wipe the ham clean, using a dampened cloth. Carefully slit the skin the full length of the shank on the inside to prevent the skin and the fat on the top of the ham from bursting. This is important if a smooth, even layer of fat for scoring is desired. A meat thermometer is a great help in baking ham perfectly. To insert it properly, make a hole from the top side through to the center of ham using a large metal or wood skewer or an ice pick. Be sure bottom of hole is not on bone or in a pocket of fat. Push thermometer down into hole carefully. Place ham, fat side up, on rack in open roasting pan, and cover with a piece of clean brown wrapping paper, or a large paper sack torn open, tucking it well down at the sides. Place in an oven pre-heated to 300° F. to 325° F (moderately slow), and bake in an uncovered pan, allowing 15 to 25 min to the lb. Regular hams will require the full 25 min, but the new tender hams need 15 to 18 min to the lb. The internal temp registered by the meat thermometer should be 170° F for regular hams, 160° F for tender hams. (Tender hams differ in the degree of tenderness. Carefully study directions coming on tag with hams before cooking.)

To ascertain exact cooking time, multiply weight of ham by recommended number of min per lb. One half hr before ham is done, remove from oven, lift off paper covering. Cool enough to handle comfortably, carefully remove skin, if any. If no skin, shave off the paper-thin layer of browned fat to obtain a white surface. Keep fat smooth on surface and uniform in depth. Score neatly making sqs, diamonds, or triangles of a size to suit your fancy, but being cautious not to cut through to the lean. Stick cloves into centers or at corners of scored designs according to your whim. Put brown sugar into sifter, sift it evenly all over the fat, tilting ham sufficiently to obtain uniform coating of sugar. Lay ham on rack in roasting pan. Drizzle honey or corn syrup in a fine stream all over sugar. Return to moderate oven (375° F) to glaze and brown appetizingly, from 30 to 45 min. If ham is cold when returned to oven, it requires more time to glaze. For cooking half hams and shank or butt ends, see Table 37, p 863.

Variation I: Thin slices of pineapple, or peaches or nuts may be glazed on the ham. Apply these to fat before sticking with cloves, then proceed as usual. When using candied cherries, apply after ham is glazed by removing cloves, and using new cloves to attach cherries to ham.

Variation II: After sticking cloves into ham, pat slightly squeezed-out crushed pineapple in a uniform layer over ham. Sprinkle brown sugar over pineapple and glaze as described above.

BAKED PICNIC

Remove wrapping from picnic, noting exact weight. Calculate baking time, allowing 24 min to the lb if tenderized and 35 min per lb if not. Wipe with damp cloth and place the skin or fat side up in an open roaster; cover with brown wrapping paper or a brown paper sack torn open and tuck around sides. Place in a moderately slow oven (300°

F to 325° F) for the time calculated. When this time is up, remove from oven, discard paper wrapping and remove skin. Serve hot or cold.

If a glaze is desired, remove from oven half an hr before end of cooking time, take off skin, and score fat. Sprinkle generously with brown sugar and strained honey or corn syrup, stick with whole cloves, and return to moderately hot oven (375°–400° F) for at least half an hr or until surface is nicely glazed.

Note: If a meat thermometer is used, the internal temp should register at least 160° F for tender or 170° F for regular picnic when the meat is done.

BROILED HAM

Regulate heat for broiling (550° F). The best ham for broiling is the tenderized type. Have steaks cut 1-inch thick. Place steaks on broiler rack and place about 3 inches below heat. As soon as surface of ham appears dry (about 1 min), brush with melted butter, and continue brushing with butter frequently. When top side is well browned, turn, brush other side with butter and broil until done on that side. Allow 16 to 20 min for tenderized ham, 1-inch thick, and 25 to 30 min for regular ham. (See Table 35.) Remove ham to hot platter and pour brown drippings over it. Serve while piping hot. A 1½-lb ham steak will serve 5 generously.

Note: Instead of butter, the ham fat which collects in the drip pan may be used for brushing.

ESCALLOPED POTATOES AND HAM

¾ lb ham   2 cups milk
6 to 8 medium potatoes   1 tsp salt, if required

Cut ham in ½-inch cubes. Pare and slice potatoes. Heat milk to boiling, add ham and potatoes, and again heat to boiling; add salt if tenderized ham is used. Turn into a greased 6 or 8-cup baking dish; bake uncovered in a moderately slow oven (325° F) for 30 to 45 min, or until potatoes are tender. Ham cubes may be pan-fried before adding to potatoes, if desired. 5 servings.

Note: Leftover baked ham may be used in this way.

HAM AND POTATO CASSEROLE

1 lb ham, sliced ½ inch thick   Salt, if required
1 tbsp bacon *or* ham   Dash of pepper, if
   drippings   desired
2 tbsp butter   6 to 8 medium potatoes,
2 tbsp flour   sliced thin
1½ cups milk

Fry ham in drippings until browned on both sides. Place in bottom of well-greased casserole. Melt butter in same skillet used to fry ham and blend in flour. Add milk gradually, and stir over direct heat until sauce boils and thickens. Add salt, if tenderized ham is used, and pepper. Add sliced potatoes, reheat to boiling and pour over ham. Bake uncovered in a moderately slow oven (325° F) about 1 hr. Either raw or cooked ham may be used for this dish. 5 servings.

Note: Grated sharp cheese may be sprinkled over top for last 10 min of baking to give an attractive surface and add an interesting flavor.

HAM AND SWEET POTATO CASSEROLE

1½ cups diced cooked ham
1 tbsp butter *or* ham fat
6 cups hot, mashed sweet potatoes, 1½ lbs

2 eggs, beaten
½ cup milk
1½ tbsp lemon juice
½ tsp salt, *or* to taste

Brown ham slightly in 1 tbsp butter or ham fat. Whip potatoes until smooth and combine with beaten eggs, milk, lemon juice and salt; again whip thoroughly. Mix with the browned ham and drippings, and turn into an 8-cup greased casserole. Bake uncovered in a moderate oven (350° F) for 45 min. Serve hot. 5 servings.

HAM PATTIES ON YAM SLICES

½ lb ground fresh pork
½ lb ground smoked ham
⅓ cup dry bread crumbs
Dash of salt
Dash of pepper
1 egg

⅓ cup milk
1¼ lb yams
Salt
¼ cup brown sugar
1½ cups apple juice

Mix the 2 kinds of meat thoroughly with the next 5 ingredients. Shape into 8 patties. Wash, pare yams, and cut lengthwise into ½-inch thick slices. Place yam slices in a single layer in a flat greased baking dish, sprinkle lightly with salt, then with brown sugar. Lay patties over potatoes; pour on the apple juice and bake in a moderate oven (350° F) for 25 to 30 min or until yams are tender. Serve immediately. 4 servings.

HAM PUFFS WITH MUSHROOM SAUCE

½ lb ground ham
½ lb ground fresh pork
⅔ cup dry bread crumbs
2 eggs, beaten
2 cups grated raw potatoes, 1¾ lbs

2 cups grated raw carrots, 4 medium
½ tsp salt
2 tsp finely chopped onion
⅔ cup milk

Combine all ingredients thoroughly and fill 8 large, greased muffin cups. Bake in a moderate oven (325° to 350° F) for 40 min, or until baked through. Turn out and serve with hot fresh mushroom sauce. Cooked cabbage wedges are a suitable accompaniment.

Fresh Mushroom Sauce:

½ lb mushrooms	1½ cups milk
3 tbsp butter *or* margarine	½ tsp salt
3 tbsp flour	Dash of pepper

Wash and slice mushrooms and sauté in melted butter for five min. Blend in the flour until smooth and add milk gradually. Stir until sauce boils and thickens. Add seasonings and serve over Ham Puffs. 4 to 6 servings.

PAN-FRIED HAM

Cut ham in ¼-inch slices. Melt 1 tbsp ham or bacon drippings in a heavy skillet until sizzling hot, and lay in the ham slices. Cook quickly until fat on edge is browned, turning from time to time to cook evenly. Ham is done when fat is browned. Serve on hot platter. Any kind of ham—raw, baked, or boiled—may be cooked by this same method, and is delicious for hot sandwiches. Fry raw ham a little more slowly than cooked. Allow at least 5 min for each side.

SUGAR-CLOVE HAM LOAF WITH PLUM SAUCE

A Bohemian favorite good with or without sauce and makes delightful sandwiches

½ cup brown sugar, pkd	⅛ tsp pepper
1 tsp whole cloves, 24 to 30	3 tbsp green pepper, chopped
1 lb smoked ham, ground	2 eggs, beaten
1 lb lean pork, ground*	1 cup milk
½ tsp salt	4 cups corn flakes

Start oven 10 min before baking; set to moderate (350° F). Lightly grease loaf pan size 9½ x 5½ x 2¾ inches, and pat sugar evenly over bottom. Arrange cloves over the sugar. Combine meat, add seasonings and chopped pepper and mix thoroughly. Beat eggs, add milk and again beat lightly and add to meat mixture with the corn flakes. Mix until thoroughly blended and mixture is firm. Pack carefully over sugar mixture. Press down evenly and smooth top with spatula or knife. Bake 1 to 1¼ hrs or until nicely browned. Place on back of stove for 15 min to absorb juices and slice easier. To serve, invert on a hot platter and discard cloves. Serve with Plum Sauce or Mustard Sauce, p 1259. 8 servings.

Plum Sauce:

Juice from No. 2½ can of blue plums, about 1½ cups	3 tbsp water
Small piece of stick cinnamon, 1-inch	$\frac{1}{16}$ tsp allspice
	2 tbsp lemon juice
2 tbsp cornstarch	Blue plums, approximately 10, stoned and cut in half
¼ tsp salt	

*½ lb veal may be substituted for ½ the pork.

Heat juice to boiling with cinnamon. Mix cornstarch and salt with cold water and add to boiling juice. Stir constantly until mixture boils again and is thickened. Add remaining ingredients, simmer slowly 10 min. Serve hot over ham loaf, or the loaf slices.

TOP OF STOVE HAM LOAF

Tops for leftover ham and a Quick Boiled Dinner, good hot or cold and fine for company

1 lb ham, ground	½ tsp monosodium glutamate,
½ lb lean pork *or* veal, ground	optional
½ lb beef, ground	2 eggs, beaten
½ tsp salt	1 cup milk
⅛ tsp pepper	2 cups corn flakes
½ to ¾ tsp thyme	Parchment paper, cheese
	cloth *or* cloth bag

Combine meat in mixing bowl, add seasonings and mix thoroughly. Beat eggs, add milk, beat well and add to meat mixture with the corn flakes. Mix thoroughly until well blended and meat mixture thickens. Have parchment paper 15 to 20 inches wide, place meat mixture on it, shape into a 10 to 11-inch roll evenly, and quickly twist ends of paper in opposite directions, forcing meat into uniformly thick roll. Tie ends with string. Place in boiling water, cover and simmer 1 hr. Save liquid to cook vegetables such as potatoes, carrots, cabbage and other vegetables. Serves 6 to 8.

IDEAS FOR USING LEFTOVER HAM

Eggs Benedict, p 673; Spinach Scramble, p. 675; Soufflé, p 679; On platter of cold cuts and potato salad; Whole Meal Salad, p 1180; Sandwich Fillings, pp 1228, 1229; Asparagus Ham Luncheon Dish, p 1311; Lentil Stew, p 1356; Stuffed Onions, p 1363; Stuffed Green Peppers, p 1369.

MISCELLANEOUS PORK RECIPES

CHINESE PORK

2 cups chicken broth, *or*	1 tsp salt
2 chicken bouillon cubes	2 cups celery cut in 2 inch
and 2 cups boiling water	pieces
2 tbsp honey	1 cup celery cabbage sliced
2 tbsp soy sauce	across ½ inch thick
1½ lbs fresh pork shoulder,	8 green whole onions
sliced ½ inch thick	4 cups cooked white rice,
2 tbsp butter *or* margarine	1 cup raw, p 433
2 tbsp cornstarch	

Use chicken broth or dissolve cubes in water, add honey and soy sauce. Stir well, pour over meat (trimmed of excess fat) which has been placed in a shallow dish. Cover and let stand 4 or 5 hrs, or overnight in refrigerator. Turn over once or twice. Drain meat and save liquor. Brown meat slowly in butter. Add ¾ cup of the liquor in which meat has soaked. Cover and simmer about 45 min, adding ½ cup more liquor if necessary. Put meat to one side of pan. Blend cornstarch and salt with remaining liquor and add. Cook until thickened, stirring constantly to make a smooth gravy. Lay vegetables in this gravy, keep each separate. Cover and simmer just long enough to cook vegetables, about 10 min. Serve with hot rice. 4 servings.

MOCK CHICKEN LEGS

1 lb lean pork	¼ cup milk
1 lb boneless veal	½ cup fine dry bread crumbs
1½ tsp salt	¼ cup shortening
Pepper	½ cup meat stock *or* water
1 egg, beaten	

Trim off excess fat from pork and cut both kinds of meat into 1½-inch cubes. Stick skewers through the center of these cubes alternating pork and veal and using enough to fill skewers a little more than half full. Sprinkle salt and pepper over meat, then press into shape. Dip in egg diluted with milk. Then roll in crumbs until well coated. Brown slowly on all sides in the hot shortening in a heavy skillet. Add the stock, reduce heat, cover and simmer slowly over low heat about 1 hr or until very tender. Make gravy from drippings if desired, p 799, to serve with "legs." 5 to 6 servings.

PORK AND RICE CASSEROLE

2 eggs	1½ tsp salt
3 cups ground cooked pork	¼ tsp pepper
½ cup raw rice	½ tsp Worcestershire sauce
1 cup milk	

Beat eggs slightly and combine with remaining ingredients. Turn into a 6-cup casserole, cover and bake in a moderate oven (350° F) for 1½ hrs. Serve hot with Tomato Sauce, p 1261, if desired. 5 servings.

PORK CHOP SUEY

1 lb lean pork	1 tbsp soy sauce
1 tbsp bacon *or* pork fat	3 tbsp flour
2 cups diced celery	No. 2 can assorted chop
3 medium onions, sliced	suey vegetables
¾ tsp salt	4 to 5 cups Boiled Rice,
1 cup boiling water	p 433, *or* Chinese noodles
1 tbsp molasses	

Cut pork into thin strips and sauté for 5 min until delicately browned in the hot fat. Add celery and onions and cook 2 or 3 min longer until slightly softened. Add salt and the boiling water; cover, and simmer for 15 to 20 min. Add molasses, soy sauce, and flour which has been blended until smooth with ½ cup water. Cook until mixture boils, stirring constantly; then add drained chop suey vegetables and continue cooking until thoroughly heated. Serve with hot fluffy rice and additional soy sauce if desired. 5 servings.

Note: Pork must be cut no thicker than ¼-inch so it will be well-cooked; but do not cook longer than the time given in the recipe for the finest chop suey.

PORK SCRAPPLE

½ lb fresh lean pork	¼ tsp pepper
1 qt water	½ cup yellow corn meal
1½ tsp salt	

Simmer the pork in the water in a covered saucepan for about 1 hr or until very tender. Let cool. Skim off fat from surface of liquid. Remove meat and chop medium fine. Save broth. Combine 2½ cups strained broth with chopped meat, add seasonings and corn meal and cook over direct heat, stirring until thickened. Transfer to double boiler, cover and cook about 1 hr. Pour into a buttered bread pan, chill, and slice about ½ inch thick. Brown slices quickly on both sides in a hot skillet with butter or bacon fat and serve piping hot. 5 servings. If desired, a larger quantity may be made as it will keep in the refrigerator for a week or more.

SAUSAGE

BAKED ACORN SQUASH WITH LITTLE PIG SAUSAGES

3 medium-sized acorn squash	1 tbsp butter
	1 lb link pork sausages

Cut squash in halves and remove seeds and fibers. Butter cut surfaces and place cut side down on a baking sheet. Bake in a moderately hot oven (400° F) 30 to 40 min, or until squash is tender when pierced with fork. (If desired, squash halves may have a mixture of brown sugar and butter sprinkled over their rims; then returned to the oven to toast to a luscious brown.) Just before serving, broil the sausages, p 872, until nicely browned on both sides, but not dry or shriveled. Arrange sausages in cavities of squash halves, and serve. Sausage patties may be used instead of the links. 5 or 6 servings.

HOME-MADE PORK SAUSAGE

4 lbs ground fresh lean pork	1½ tsp black pepper
3 medium pods dry hot red	1 tbsp salt
pepper, crushed fine	2 tsp sage

Choose very fresh lean pork loin or pork shoulder. Put meat and red pepper through food chopper using medium knife. Add rest of seasonings, mix thoroughly. Pack firmly into clean bowls or loaf pans. Cover tightly and keep refrigerated until ready to fry. Measure out sausage meat by half cupfuls and shape into patties about 3 inches in diameter. If shaped in loaf pan, cut cold sausage meat into ½-inch slices. No shaping is required. Brown on both sides in a hot skillet, then reduce heat, cover and cook slowly until thoroughly done, about 20 min. When cut in half, thoroughly cooked patties are never pink in the center but a grayish white. 1 lb makes 4 to 5 servings.

PAN-BROILED LINK SAUSAGES

Separate 1 lb sausage links carefully so as not to break skin at each end. Put links in a cold heavy skillet, place over low heat and cook until well browned, turning frequently. It will take 12 to 15 min to cook well done. *Or* place links in skillet, add 2 tbsp of water for each half lb, cover and steam 5 min. Remove cover, drain off liquid that remains, then cook sausage slowly, turning frequently to brown evenly. *Do not prick.* Remove sausages to a hot platter. Drain off all fat. Add 3 tbsp water to skillet, reheat until brown residue dissolves. Pour pan-gravy over sausage and serve promptly. 4 servings.

PORK SAUSAGE PATTIES

Shape 1½ lbs pork sausage meat into 10 patties ½-inch thick and brown on both sides in a hot skillet. Cover closely and cook over low heat for 15 to 20 min, depending on thickness of patties. 5 servings. *Or* place patties in cold pan over slow heat. Cook until well browned on both sides and no longer pink in center. Pour off excess fat as it accumulates in pan.

SAUSAGE BACON AND TOMATO GRILL

1 lb pork sausage links	2 large tomatoes sliced
⅓ lb sliced bacon	thick

Place sausages on broiler rack and broil *slowly,* turning once or twice and watching carefully until sausages begin to brown. Be careful not to prick links when turning. Then place bacon on rack and cook about ½ done. Now place tomato slices on broiler rack and cook until just softened. All three foods should be done at the same time. When done, place on hot serving platter. If preferred, all three foods may be pan-fried on top of the stove. 5 servings.

Note: *Slow* cooking whether in the broiler or on top of the stove results in less shrinkage and better flavor and appearance in both sausage and bacon.

SPANISH SAUSAGE

1½ lbs pork sausage, country style	½ tsp salt
	Dash of pepper
No. 2 can tomato juice *or*	1½ tsp sugar
2½ cups strained tomatoes	2 tbsp flour
½ cup chopped onion	¼ cup water
½ cup chopped green pepper	Grated Parmesan cheese
½ cup finely chopped celery	

Shape sausage into 10 patties and brown slowly in moderately hot skillet. Drain off fat. Add tomato juice, onion, green pepper, celery and seasonings; cover and simmer 1 hr. Remove sausage to a hot platter. Blend flour and water and when smooth, add to tomato juice in which sausage was cooked. Stir until it boils and thickens. Pour sauce over meat, sprinkle with cheese and serve hot. 5 servings.

USES FOR SAUSAGE FAT

1. To season pea, bean or lentil soup. 2. Frying potatoes. 3. Seasoning stuffings for pork and veal.

VEAL*

CHART No. 38

Meat Cuts and How to Cook Them
VEAL CHART

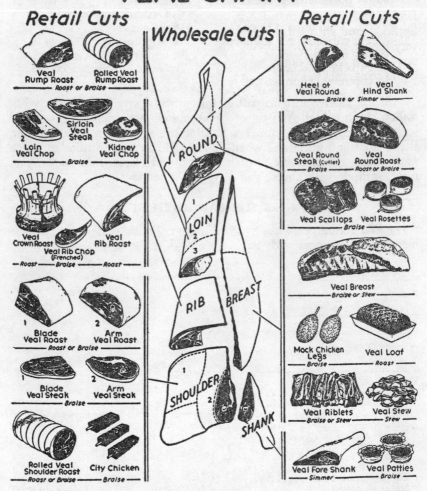

Retail Cuts

Veal Rump Roast
Rolled Veal Rump Roast
— Roast or Braise —

2 Loin Veal Chop
Sirloin Veal Steak
3 Kidney Veal Chop
— Braise —

Veal Crown Roast
Veal Rib Chop (Frenched)
Veal Rib Roast
— Roast — Braise — Roast —

1 Blade Veal Roast
2 Arm Veal Roast
— Roast or Braise —

1 Blade Veal Steak
2 Arm Veal Steak
— Braise —

Rolled Veal Shoulder Roast
— Roast or Braise —
City Chicken
— Braise —

Wholesale Cuts

ROUND

LOIN

RIB

BREAST

SHOULDER

SHANK

Retail Cuts

Heel of Veal Round
Veal Hind Shank
— Braise or Simmer —

Veal Round Steak (cutlet)
— Braise —
Veal Round Roast
— Roast or Braise —

Veal Scallops
Veal Rosettes
— Braise —

Veal Breast
— Braise or Stew —

Mock Chicken Legs
— Braise —
Veal Loaf
— Roast —

Veal Riblets
— Braise or Stew —
Veal Stew
— Stew —

Veal Fore Shank
— Simmer —
Veal Patties
— Braise —

*Adapted from *Ten Lessons on Meat for Use in Schools*, Sixth Edition, published by National Live Stock and Meat Board, Chicago.

BRAISED AND ROAST VEAL

BRAISED VEAL SHOULDER STEAK

2 lbs veal shoulder steak,	¼ cup butter *or* margarine
½ to ¾-inch thick	1½ tsp salt
Flour	¼ cup water

Wipe meat with a damp cloth and dredge thoroughly in flour. Brown slowly on both sides in the melted butter in a heavy skillet. Sprinkle meat with salt, add water, cover tightly and simmer gently until very tender, 45 to 60 min. Add more water from time to time if necessary. When meat is done, remove to a hot platter and make gravy from liquid remaining in skillet, p 799. 5 servings.

TABLE 39   TIME TABLE FOR ROASTING VEAL*

SUITABLE CUTS	WEIGHT	OVEN TEMPERATURE CONSTANT	INTERIOR TEMPERATURE WHEN REMOVED FROM OVEN	APPROXIMATE TIME PER POUND
	Pounds	*Degrees F.*	*Degrees F.*	*Minutes*
VEAL				
Leg roast	7-8	300	170	25
Loin.....................	4½-5	300	170	30-35
Rack—4-6 ribs	2½-3	300	170	30-35
Shoulder	7	300	170	25
Shoulder—Rolled	5	300	170	40-45

TABLE 40   TIME TABLE FOR BRAISING VEAL*

SUITABLE CUTS	AVERAGE WEIGHT OR THICKNESS	APPROXIMATE COOKING TIME
VEAL		
Shoulder—stew	2 inch cubes	1-1½ hours
Leg—steaks	½-¾ inch	45-60 minutes
Patties	¾-1 inch	30-45 minutes
Shoulder—pot roast	2-3 pounds	1½-2 hours
Breast—stuffed	3-4 pounds	1½-2 hours
Breast—rolled	2-3 pounds	1½-2 hours
Birds	½ in. x 2 in. x 4 in.	45-60 minutes
Chops—rib or loin..................	½-¾ inch	45-60 minutes
Chops—breaded	½-¾ inch	45-60 minutes
Steaks or cutlets.....................	½-¾ inch	45-60 minutes
Shoulder chops	½-¾ inch	45-60 minutes

Ten Lessons on Meat for Use in Schools, Sixth Edition, published by National Live Stock and Meat Board, Chicago.

BLANQUETTE OF VEAL

This French version of veal tastes like chicken—good over biscuits or mashed potatoes

1½ lbs boneless veal	1 tsp monosodium glutamate,
2½ cups water	optional but good
1½ tsp salt	3 tbsp butter
Pinch of thyme, optional	3 egg yolks
2 branches Pascal celery	2 tbsp water
8 onions, size small walnuts	1 tbsp flour
1 cup fresh mushrooms, 3 oz	Chopped parsley
⅛ tsp pepper	

Wipe veal with damp cloth. Cut into 1-inch cubes. Put meat, water and salt into Dutch oven or heavy saucepan; heat to boiling, reduce heat, cover and simmer 1 hr. Add thyme, washed celery cut in inch lengths, peeled whole onions pricked through twice with a skewer, and mushrooms wiped with a damp cloth and cut in half. Cover, simmer 20 min. Add the next 3 ingredients, then the egg yolks combined with the water and flour and beaten until smooth. Stir gently to blend, then heat to boiling and *simmer* 2 or 3 min to thicken to a smooth golden gravy. Serve hot with a generous sprinkling of parsley. 4 to 5 servings.

BREADED VEAL CHOPS

5 veal chops, about 2 lbs,	Pepper
½ to ¾-inch thick	¼ cup butter *or* margarine
1 egg, beaten	½ cup boiling water
¼ cup milk	2 tbsp chopped onion
Fine dry bread crumbs	2 tbsp chopped green pepper
1½ tsp salt	

Wipe chops with damp cloth. Dip first in beaten egg mixed with the milk, then in bread crumbs mixed with salt and pepper to coat well. Chops may be dipped twice if a thicker "breading" is desired. Brown chops slowly on both sides in hot fat in a heavy skillet. Add the water, onion, and green pepper if desired. Cover tightly and simmer gently for 1 hr, adding a little more water from time to time if needed. Serve chops with the liquid remaining in the pan. 5 servings.

POT ROAST OF VEAL

2½ lbs veal shoulder	⅓ cup chopped celery
3 tbsp bacon drippings	2 tsp salt
1 medium onion, chopped	

Wipe veal with a damp cloth. Brown slowly on one side in bacon drippings in heavy kettle or Dutch oven. Turn meat over, add onion and celery and stir occasionally until meat is well browned on other side. Sprinkle meat with salt. Add about ½ cup hot water, cover tightly and simmer until meat is tender, about 1½ hrs; add more water as needed. Serve with gravy which may be thickened if desired, p 799. 5 servings.

POT ROAST OF VEAL WITH APPLE DRESSING

2¾ lbs veal shoulder	1¼ cups hot water
¼ cup butter *or* bacon drip-	2 tart apples
pings	1 medium onion
2 tsp salt	2 tbsp sugar
Few grains of pepper	2 cups soft bread crumbs
1 bouillon cube	

Wipe veal clean with a damp cloth and cut it so the slices will about cover the bottom of the casserole or skillet being used. Melt half the fat in a heavy skillet and brown the veal slowly on all sides. Leave meat in the skillet or transfer to a baking casserole, as preferred. Add 1½ tsp salt, pepper, and the bouillon cube dissolved in the hot water. Pare and chop apples; also peel, chop, and slowly sauté onion in remaining fat. Add the apple, onion, sugar and rest of salt to bread crumbs and toss to mix ingredients well. Heap dressing on top of the veal which should be well above surface of the liquid or dressing will become soggy. Rub inside of lid of skillet or casserole with fat and cover the meat. Place in a moderately slow oven (325° F) for about 2½ hrs or until veal is very tender. Then remove cover and continue cooking for about 15 min to brown dressing slightly. Carefully remove veal and dressing, and thicken gravy as desired with a flour-water paste, p 163. 5 servings.

SAVORY VEAL STEAKS

1½ lbs veal shoulder steaks	2 tbsp shortening
2 tbsp flour	2 medium onions
1½ tsp salt	½ cup water
1½ tsp dry mustard	1 cup top milk

Buy 3 shoulder arm steaks. Wipe clean with a damp cloth. Mix dry ingredients and pound into meat with edge of a sturdy saucer or back of heavy knife blade. Brown slowly on one side in hot lard. Sprinkle with any remaining flour mixture. Turn and cover with sliced onions. When second side is brown, add water, cover and simmer gently for 45 min or until tender. Remove meat to platter. Blend milk with drippings, heat thoroughly and serve as sauce with meat. 5 or 6 servings.

Note: Gravies are useful even after the meat has been eaten. Read pages 797–800

STUFFED BREAST OF VEAL

Economical, good, easy oven meal

3 lb breast of veal	½ cup milk *or* chicken *or* veal
10 slices stale white bread	stock *or* canned chicken
from 1 lb loaf	soup
¼ tsp pepper	2 tbsp shortening
1 tsp powdered sage	2½ tsp salt
⅔ cup chopped celery	¾ cup water
⅔ cup chopped onion	

Start oven 10 min before baking; set to slow (300° F). Have butcher cut pocket in veal and cut bony edge every 2 or 3 inches to make serving easier. Tear bread into bite-size pieces, dropping into a mixing bowl. Sprinkle pepper and sage over bread. Toss to distribute seasoning. Sauté celery and onion in shortening until yellow. Add to stuffing; then add liquid and toss. Sprinkle half of salt on inside of veal pocket. Fill with stuffing. Skewer together with toothpicks or sew up with twine. Brush more shortening over surface of veal and sprinkle with rest of salt. Put into roasting pan, pour water around veal, cover roaster and bake 3 to 3½ hrs or until very tender. 4 to 5 servings.

STUFFED VEAL ROLLS

Veal birds

1½ lbs boneless veal steaks *or*	3 cups soft bread crumbs,
cutlets, sliced thin	firmly pkd
¼ cup flour	1 chicken bouillon cube
1 tsp salt	1 cup water
⅛ tsp pepper	½ tsp salt
1 cup diced celery	Dash of pepper
¼ cup butter	½ tsp sage

Wipe veal clean with damp cloth; cut into 5 pieces. Do not pound with edge of sturdy saucer or back of heavy knife blade, but dredge one side in flour mixed with salt and pepper. Sauté celery in 2 tbsp of the butter, add bread crumbs and toss together. Cool. Dissolve bouillon cube in water and add ½ cup to stuffing; add seasonings and mix well. Place a portion of stuffing on each piece of veal (unfloured side up), roll up with stuffing inside, and fasten securely with toothpicks. Brown rolls slowly in hot skillet with rest of butter. Add remaining bouillon liquid and ¼ cup water; cover tightly and simmer gently until meat is very tender, about 1 hr. Gravy may be thickened if desired, p 799. 5 servings.

Variation 1: Prepare veal cutlets as described above, using first four ingredients, but instead of the stuffing place a scraped carrot and small peeled onion on the unfloured side. Roll up, fasten with toothpicks and brown rolls in a hot skillet with 2 tbsp butter. Add 1 cup tomato juice; cover tightly and simmer until meat and vegetables are tender. 5 servings.

Variation 2: Use ½ cup evaporated milk and ½ cup water in place of tomato juice in Variation 1 and bake in slow oven (300° F) for about 1½ hrs. 5 servings.

STUFFED VEAL SHOULDER

3 lbs veal shoulder	1 egg
¼ cup shortening	½ cup meat stock *or* ½
1 tbsp chopped onion	bouillon cube in ½ cup
2 tsp chopped parsley	hot water
½ tsp celery salt	1¼ tsp salt
3 cups coarse soft bread crumbs	

Have pocket cut in meat to hold dressing. Wipe meat with a damp cloth. Melt half the shortening in a heavy skillet, add the onion and cook slowly until soft; then add parsley, celery salt, and bread crumbs. Toss about until well mixed. Cool. Add beaten egg and half the liquid and mix; stuff lightly into the pocket of the roast; tie or sew up with twine. Rub outside of roast with the salt; then brown it slowly on both sides in the remaining shortening in the same heavy skillet or in a Dutch oven. Pour in rest of liquid, cover tightly, bake in a moderately slow oven (325° F) until meat is tender, or for 1½ to 2 hrs, adding more boiling water if necessary. Liquid remaining in pan may be thickened or not, as desired, to use as gravy, p 799. 5 to 6 servings.

VEAL FRICASSEE

2 lbs boneless veal shoulder	4 carrots, diced
¼ cup butter *or* shortening	3 onions, sliced
1½ tsp salt	2 tbsp finely cut parsley
Water	4 potatoes, sliced

Wipe meat with damp cloth and cut in 1½-inch dice. Brown in butter in a heavy skillet. Sprinkle salt on meat and add water to just half cover meat. Cover skillet tightly and simmer slowly until meat is tender, or about 1 to 1½ hrs. Prepare vegetables and add them ½ hr before end of cooking time. Just before serving, thicken gravy if desired with flour and water paste, p 163, stirring over direct heat until it boils and thickens. 5 servings.

VEAL PAPRIKA

1½ lbs boneless veal shoulder	1 cup sour cream
1 clove garlic, sliced	1 tsp paprika, *or* to suit taste
¼ cup butter *or* shortening	2 tsp salt
¼ cup water	

Wipe meat with a damp cloth and cut in 1-inch dice. Sauté veal and garlic in butter until brown, about 10 min. Remove garlic and discard, if desired. Add water, cover tightly and simmer gently until veal is perfectly tender, about 1 to 1½ hrs. Add sour cream, paprika and salt, and reheat to boiling. Serve at once. 5 servings.

Variation. Buy veal steaks (4) about ½-inch thick. Leave whole and brown with the garlic. Proceed as directed in recipe. Serve a half steak to each person with a poached egg on top.

VEAL PARMIGIANO
Italian

1 lb veal steak ½-inch thick	3 tbsp grated Parmesan
1 egg	cheese
1 tbsp milk	⅓ cup olive oil
1 tsp salt	8-oz can tomato sauce, 1 cup
¹⁄₁₆ tsp pepper	1 cup water
1 tbsp fine-chopped onion	⅓ lb Scamorza cheese, sliced
⅔ cup fine dry bread crumbs	Parsley

Trim tough membrane from outer edge of veal, then put on cutting board and pound thoroughly with edge of saucer or a mallet to make thin, and to break tough fibers. Cut into serving portions or cutlets. Beat egg, stir in next 4 ingredients. Dip cutlets in egg mixture, then in blended crumb-cheese mixture, pressing firmly so crumbs adhere to meat. Heat oil in heavy 9-inch skillet, add cutlets and cook slowly to a golden brown on both sides, about 10 min. Now pour tomato sauce and water *around meat* and lay Scamorza *on* meat. Place skillet in a moderately slow oven (325° F). Bake 15 to 20 min or until meat is tender. Serve on hot platter with sauce poured around meat. Garnish with parsley. 4 servings.

VEAL SCALLOPINI
A popular Italian method of cooking veal

1½ lbs veal steak ½-inch thick	1 chicken bouillon cube in
½ tsp salt	3 tbsp water
⅓ cup flour	Pepper
⅓ cup butter *or* margarine	Juice of ½ lemon *or*
1 cup mushrooms sliced	2 tbsp sherry
¼-inch thick	Buttered toast

Remove bone neatly from steak, then cut meat into 5 uniform cutlets oval in shape if possible. Snip away tough membrane around edge of cutlets so meat will lie flat. Lay on a chopping board, sprinkle with salt and, with wooden potato masher or mallet, pound flour in lightly on both sides until cutlets are ¼-inch thick. Heat butter in heavy skillet until hot but not smoking. Lay in veal and brown richly on

both sides, from 6 to 8 min. Now remove to hot serving plate. Add
mushrooms to skillet, cover and cook 3 or 4 min, shaking pan several
times to prevent sticking. Now add bouillon cube and water, heat to
boiling, cover and simmer until cube is just dissolved. Add pepper and
more salt, if desired. Pour pan gravy and mushrooms around the veal.
Now use a fork and twist the juice from the half lemon all over veal.
Serve very hot with toast points. If sherry is used, add it with the pepper.
4 to 5 servings.

Variation: After veal is nicely browned, sprinkle with lemon juice
and add 2 tbsp melted butter and 1 tbsp chopped parsley before removing from skillet.

VEAL STEAK DELUXE

1 lb veal steak	Dash of pepper
¼ tsp dry mustard	2 tsp vinegar
⅛ tsp poultry seasoning	2 tbsp shortening
1 tbsp brown sugar	1 medium onion, sliced
¾ tsp salt	½ cup water
1 tbsp flour	

Wipe meat with a damp cloth. Combine next seven ingredients and
rub into the veal steak. Brown slowly on each side in the hot shortening.
Reduce heat to simmering temp. Arrange onion slices over meat, add
water, cover and simmer slowly for 1 to 1½ hrs, turning once during
cooking. Add additional water if needed. 4 servings.

VEAL SUB GUM

1 lb veal shoulder	1½ tbsp dark molasses
1 tbsp butter *or* margarine	1 tbsp bead molasses
2 cups shredded green	1 tsp vinegar
cabbage	1 tsp salt
1 cup diced green pepper	½ cup water
2 cups diced celery	2 large tomatoes, cubed
2 chicken bouillon cubes	Cooked rice, 3 to 4 cups
2 cups hot water	*or* Chinese noodles
2 tbsp cornstarch	¼ cup blanched almonds
2 tbsp soy sauce	

Wipe meat with a damp cloth. Cut into 1-inch cubes and sauté in
hot butter in a ten-inch heavy skillet for ten min. Add cabbage, green
pepper, celery, and the bouillon cubes dissolved in the hot water. Simmer slowly uncovered for fifteen min. Make a thin paste of the cornstarch and the next six ingredients and add it to meat mixture. Stir
gently until mixture boils and thickens. Add tomatoes and stir carefully
to mix them through the meat and vegetables without breaking them

up. Continue to cook for *one min* longer. Serve at once on hot rice or noodles and garnish with the almonds. 4 servings.

Note: Almonds may be omitted if desired, but they add greatly to the appeal of this very delicious Chinese dish.

VEAL BAKED IN MILK

2 lbs veal steak *or* cutlets
2 tsp salt
1 egg, beaten
Flour for dipping

¼ cup butter *or* bacon drippings
2 cups milk, *or* 1 cup milk and 1 cup cream

Wipe meat clean with a damp cloth and cut into serving-size pieces. Sprinkle with the salt; dip in beaten egg, and then in flour. Heat fat in a heavy skillet and brown the meat slowly on both sides. Transfer meat and fat to a glass baking casserole. Add milk. Cover, and bake in a slow oven (300° to 325° F) for 2 hrs or until very tender. 5 servings.

Note: Add ½ lb cleaned, sliced fresh or canned mushrooms on top of meat in casserole. Cover and bake as directed.

VEAL CHOPS IN SOUR CREAM

4 loin veal chops, ¾-inch thick
2 tbsp flour
2 tbsp lard *or* shortening

Paprika
Salt and pepper
½ cup water
1 cup sour cream

Wipe meat clean with a damp cloth. Dredge chops in flour and brown slowly on both sides in heated lard. When well browned, season with paprika, salt and pepper. Add water and sour cream, cover tightly and simmer very slowly until done, about 45 to 60 min. Remove to a hot platter and make gravy by thickening drippings and adding more milk as needed. 4 servings.

VEAL CHOP SUEY

¼ cup butter *or* shortening
1 lb veal round *or* shoulder, cut in ¼-inch strips
1 cup sliced onions
2 cups diced celery
1½ cups boiling water
1 tsp salt

1 tbsp molasses
2 tbsp chop suey sauce
2 tbsp cornstarch, mixed to paste with ¼ cup cold water
3 to 4 cups boiled rice, 1 cup raw

Melt butter in large skillet or Dutch oven. Add veal and cook, stirring occasionally, until nicely browned on all sides. Add onions, celery, boiling water, and salt; cover and simmer until veal is perfectly tender, about 25 to 30 min. Add remaining ingredients except rice and continue to cook with constant stirring until mixture comes to boil again, and is thickened. Serve at once with fluffy, hot Boiled Rice, p 433. 5 servings.

SIMMERED VEAL

JELLIED VEAL LOAF

2 lbs veal breast *or* shoulder　　6 tbsp mayonnaise
3 cups cold water　　　　　　　　Salt and pepper to taste
2 tsp salt　　　　　　　　　　　　1 to 2 tbsp gelatin
2 hard-cooked eggs　　　　　　　¼ cup cold water
2 tbsp chopped sweet pickle　　Lettuce
3 tbsp vinegar　　　　　　　　　Tomato wedges

Cut meat into 1-inch dice, removing fat and gristle. Simmer meat in a covered pan with water and salt for about 1 hr, or until very tender. Drain off broth and chill; there should be 2 cups—if not, add cold water. Combine meat with diced eggs, pickle, vinegar, mayonnaise and seasonings. If broth forms a stiff jelly when cold, use 1 tbsp gelatin, otherwise use 2 tbsp. Soften the gelatin 5 min in the ¼ cup cold water, then melt over hot water. Heat broth until just liquid, add melted gelatin, stir thoroughly into meat mixture. Pour into glass bread pan (8¼ x 4½ x 2½ inches) which has been rubbed with salad oil, and chill until firm. Turn out and slice. Garnish with lettuce and tomato wedges or radishes. 10 to 12 servings.

VEAL À LA KING

1 lb boneless veal　　　　　　1½ cups top milk *or* cream
¾ tsp salt　　　　　　　　　　1 cup veal stock
1 cup diced celery　　　　　　2 hard-cooked eggs, diced
2 tbsp chopped green pepper　1 tbsp chopped pimiento
¼ cup butter　　　　　　　　Salt and pepper to taste
⅓ cup flour　　　　　　　　Toast *or* noodles

Wipe meat clean with damp cloth; place in saucepan, add salt and barely cover with boiling water. Cover kettle and simmer gently from 1 to 1½ hrs, or until meat is just tender. Drain, saving broth. Cut meat in ½-inch dice. Sauté celery and green pepper in the butter for 5 min or until just soft; then blend in flour until smooth. Measure veal stock, adding water if necessary to make up 1 cup, and add with milk gradually to butter-flour mixture. Cook over moderate heat, stirring constantly until sauce boils and thickens. Add veal, eggs, pimiento and seasonings. Reheat thoroughly and serve on toast, in patty shells, or on Crisp Fried Noodles, p 431. 5 servings.

VEAL STEW

1½ lbs veal for stew　　　　5 small carrots
3 cups water　　　　　　　5 small onions
2 tsp salt　　　　　　　　3 medium potatoes
Dash of pepper　　　　　Flour

Wipe veal with damp cloth and cut in 1½-inch dice. Place in a 3-qt saucepan. Add water and salt. Cover, simmer gently for 45 min. Add pepper, carrots scraped and cut in thick crosswise slices, and peeled, whole onions; again cover and cook 10 min. Add pared, quartered potatoes and continue cooking until they are just tender, about 20 min longer. Thicken liquid with flour mixed to a smooth paste with cold water, using 2 tbsp flour to each cup of liquid and stirring until it boils. 5 servings.

Variation 1: Veal may be rolled in flour and browned in fat before adding the water to give a richer flavor and color to gravy.

Variation 2: Make up ½ recipe Baking Powder Biscuits, p 234. Turn hot veal stew into casserole. Lay unbaked small biscuits (cut around edge with a knife to give the effect of a flower) close together over the surface and bake in a moderately hot oven (425° F) for about 15 to 20 min, or until biscuits are well browned. This makes a delicious Veal and Vegetable Pie.

SAVORY VEAL STEW

Adding a little thyme to veal stew gives it a distinctive flavor

1 lb boneless veal cut for stew	Few dashes of pepper
3 tbsp margarine *or*	½ cup coarsely diced celery
shortening	¼ tsp thyme, optional
3 tbsp flour	1 cup water *or* more
½ egg-size onion	Fluffy hot rice
1 tsp salt	

Wipe veal pieces with a damp cloth and put on waxed paper. Sift flour over meat, then shift paper back and forth to coat all pieces evenly. Heat margarine in a 2-qt heavy saucepan until sizzling hot. Add veal with flour remaining on paper. Brown richly but slowly on all sides, about 20 min. Add sliced onion last 5 min of browning. Now add salt, pepper, celery and thyme, and enough water to almost cover meat. Cover pan and *simmer* until meat is tender, from 2 to 2½ hrs. Serve piping hot over rice, mashed or boiled potatoes. 3 to 4 servings.

Variations: Other seasonings pleasing in veal stew are:

1. Rub a cut clove of garlic over bottom and sides of saucepan in which stew is cooked, then discard garlic.

2. Add ¼ tsp marjoram or curry powder in place of the thyme.

3. Small potatoes may be added to stew the last half hour of cooking.

4. Or substitute green beans, fresh peas or diced carrots for the celery, but add the last half hour of cooking.

GROUND VEAL

BARBECUED VEAL BALLS

¾ lb ground veal shoulder
  or neck
¼ lb ground pork shoulder
1 tsp salt

1 tbsp finely chopped onion
½ cup fine dry bread crumbs
½ cup milk
1 egg, beaten

Mix all ingredients together and form into balls. Place in a shallow baking pan, cover with Barbecue Sauce and bake in moderate oven (350° F) for 45 min. Serve at once with Barbecue Sauce over all.

Barbecue Sauce:

⅓ cup dill pickle juice
⅓ cup chili sauce
1 tsp Worcestershire sauce

½ tsp salt
3 tbsp diced dill pickle
2 drops tabasco sauce

Combine all ingredients and pour over the meat balls before baking. 4 servings.

VEALBURGERS

1½ lbs lean veal
¼ lb salt pork
½ tsp salt
  Dash of black pepper
1 egg, beaten

2 tbsp shortening
¼ cup boiling water
1½ tbsp flour
1½ cups milk
Parsley

Mix meat (veal and salt pork that has been ground together once) with salt, pepper and egg. Divide into ¼-cup portions and shape neatly into flat patties. Brown slowly in heated shortening in a heavy skillet. Reduce heat, add boiling water, cover and simmer gently for 30 min. Remove patties to a hot platter and make gravy by blending the flour into the fat remaining in pan, then adding the milk gradually, stirring constantly until smooth and thickened. Pour gravy over patties, garnish with sprigs of parsley and serve at once. 4 servings.

VEAL LOAF

2 lbs ground veal
½ lb ground fresh fat pork
½ cup fine dry bread crumbs
2 tbsp top milk

1 tbsp melted butter
2 tbsp finely chopped onion
2 tsp salt
4 Hard-cooked Eggs, p 663

Combine meat thoroughly with other ingredients, except eggs. Pack ¾ of meat mixture into a buttered bread loaf pan (8¼ x 4½ x 2½ inches). Make a trench through center and place the shelled eggs in it, end to end; press rest of mixture over the eggs. Turn loaf out onto a greased shallow baking pan, brush surface with melted butter or bacon drippings and bake in a moderate oven (350° F) for about 1½ hrs, or until done through. Before slicing loaf, let it stand 15 min to absorb meat juices in bottom of pan. Serve either hot or cold. 8 to 10 servings.

VEAL PATTIES

1¼ lbs ground veal	1 egg, beaten
1 tsp salt	2 tbsp drippings
Few grains of pepper	1 chicken bouillon cube
1 tbsp chopped onion	1 cup water

Mix ground veal with seasonings, onion and beaten egg. Divide into ¼-cup portions and shape into patties ¾ to 1-inch thick. Brown slowly in hot drippings in a heavy skillet. Dissolve bouillon cube in 1 cup hot water. Pour bouillon around patties in skillet, cover and cook at simmering temp for 30 to 45 min or until well done. 5 servings.

Note: Pineapple slices browned in butter are a delicious accompaniment for these patties.

LUNCHEON MEATS
BOLOGNA

BOILED BOLOGNA

Purchase a one-lb piece of bologna with the casing on. Cover with boiling water and simmer 15 min in a covered kettle. Lift out, remove casing. Serve on hot platter, cutting in ¼-inch slices and overlapping. Garnish with parsley. 4 servings.

GRILLED BOLOGNA CUPS

Have ½ lb bologna sausage sliced thin with the casing left on the rims of the slices. Brown quickly on both sides in hot fat; the slices curl to form cups. Serve with five piping hot Poached, p 672, or Pan-Fried Eggs. Baking Powder Biscuits, p 234, and currant jelly are a pleasing accompaniment for breakfast or luncheon. 4 to 5 servings.

ROAST BOLOGNA

For an unusual buffet-picnic supper, buy a 2 to 3 lb large round bologna. Peel carefully to leave a smooth surface and score evenly in squares, oblongs or diamonds. Insert a whole clove in the center of each section on the top side. Place in a shallow roasting pan and bake in a moderate oven (350° F) for 45 min to 1 hr or until heated through and attractively browned on surface. Roll may be basted with 3 tbsp melted butter during baking if a browner surface is desired. Serve on hot platter, cutting in ¼-inch slices. Garnish with broiled tomato slices or pan-fried pineapple slices. 8 to 12 servings.

FRANKFURTERS

"BOILED" FRANKFURTERS

Drop 8 to 10 frankfurters into 1 qt actively boiling water, turn off heat, cover and let stand 5 min. Drain and serve immediately. 5 servings.

GRILLED FRANKFURTERS

Heat 2 tbsp fat in a heavy skillet and put in 8 to 10 frankfurters, whole or split in half lengthwise; brown moderately fast on all sides, cooking until heated through. Serve immediately. 5 servings.

BARBECUED FRANKFURTERS

1 lb frankfurters, 8 to 10	2 tbsp prepared mustard
1/3 cup finely chopped onion	1/2 tsp salt
1/4 cup bacon drippings	1 tsp sugar
2/3 cup catchup	1 beef bouillon cube *or* 1
2 tbsp Worcestershire sauce	tsp meat extract paste
1 tbsp vinegar	1/2 cup water

Sauté frankfurters and onions in hot drippings for 5 min, rolling the frankfurters over to lightly brown on all sides. Add the remaining ingredients, stir to blend, then reduce heat and simmer gently uncovered for 15 to 20 min. Turn sausages frequently and stir sauce as it thickens to keep it from sticking. Serve frankfurters piping hot with the sauce poured over them. 4 servings.

CREAMED FRANKFURTERS

8 frankfurters, about 1 lb, sliced about 1/4-inch thick	1/3 cup flour
3 tbsp chopped onion	2 1/2 cups milk
1/3 cup butter *or* bacon drippings	1 1/4 tsp prepared mustard
	1/4 tsp salt *or* to taste
	2 tsp chopped parsley

Sauté the sliced frankfurters and onion in the butter until onion is soft, about 5 min. Blend in flour; then add milk and cook with constant stirring until sauce boils and thickens. Stir in seasonings. Serve hot on hot toast or baked potatoes. Sprinkle with chopped parsley. 5 servings.

GRILLED CHEESE STUFFED FRANKFURTERS

6 slices bacon	3 oz tangy cheddar link
6 frankfurters	cheese

Pan-fry bacon very slowly until about half cooked. Lift out to drain and cool. Make lengthwise gash in each frankfurter for a deep pocket. Cut a 1/3-inch wedge of cheese to fit into pockets. Wrap bacon neatly around frankfurter to cover from end to end; secure each with 2 toothpicks. Lay franks cheese side down in shallow pan. Lining pan with sheet of aluminum foil reduces dishwashing and saves pan. This helps to keep cheese where it belongs. Place about 4 inches under broiler until bacon is crisp. Turn over carefully and broil until bacon is done on top side. Scrape any dripping cheese onto frankfurters; serve immediately. 4 to 5 servings.

ESCALLOPED POTATOES AND FRANKFURTERS

4 large potatoes, 2 lbs	2½ tbsp flour
½ lb frankfurters	2 tsp prepared mustard
1 cup diced celery	½ tsp salt
2 tbsp butter	2 cups milk

Pare and slice potatoes. Cut frankfurters in ½-inch slices. Arrange alternate layers of potatoes, frankfurters and celery in a greased 8-cup baking dish. Melt butter in a saucepan and blend in flour, mustard, and salt; add milk gradually and stir over direct heat until sauce boils. Pour over ingredients in casserole. Bake covered in a moderate oven (350° F) from 45 min to 1 hr until potatoes are tender. 5 servings.

FRANKFURTERS ON BUNS

1 lb frankfurters, 8 to 10	8 to 10 frankfurter buns
¾ cup grated sharp cheese	Mustard, sweet pickle
¼ cup grated onion	relish or catchup if desired

Split frankfurters lengthwise in half, but do not cut completely through. Combine cheese and onion thoroughly. Spread about 1½ tbsp of this mixture into the split frankfurters. Broil under medium heat with rack placed 3 inches below heat, until cheese is puffy and golden brown on surface and frankfurters are piping hot. Split buns about ⅞ of the way through lengthwise, spread with butter and place piping hot frankfurter inside. (Buns may be heated or toasted if desired before placing frankfurter inside.) Serve at once with mustard, relish or catchup. Serve these frankfurters immediately so they will be hot when eaten. 4 to 5 servings.

FRANKFURTERS IN BLANKETS

1 recipe Baking Powder Biscuits, p 234	10 frankfurters, about 1 lb

Roll dough into a rectangle 10 x 20 inches, then cut into ten 4 x 5 inch rectangles. Lay a frankfurter on each sq, roll up, and seal by moistening edges of dough and pinching together. Place on lightly greased baking sheet and bake in a moderately hot oven (425° F) 15 min, or until nicely browned. Serve with Mustard Sauce, p 1259. 5 servings.

Note: Link pork sausages may be browned slowly on all sides until half cooked, the fat drained off and used in place of the frankfurters.

SAUERKRAUT WITH FRANKFURTERS

No. 2½ can sauerkraut
1 tart apple, sliced
2 tbsp sugar
2 tbsp bacon *or* sausage drippings *or* butter

½ cup water
10 frankfurters *or* 16 half-cooked Pork Sausages, p 872

Turn sauerkraut into a 3 qt saucepan; add sliced apple, sugar, drippings, and water. Cover pan and simmer until apple is barely tender. Lay frankfurters or sausages on top of kraut; cover, and cook gently about 10 min longer until meat is heated through. 5 servings.

SAVORY FRANKFURTERS

8 to 10 frankfurters, 1 lb
¼ lb American cheese

½ cup sweet pickle relish
8 to 10 slices bacon

Make a lengthwise gash in the frankfurters to form a long pocket, being careful not to cut clear through. Grate cheese, mix it with the pickle relish and stuff into the frankfurter pockets. Wrap bacon around frankfurters and secure with toothpicks. Place in preheated broiler about 3 inches below source of heat, and broil until frankfurters are hot through, bacon is done and cheese is melted and slightly toasted. Serve hot. 5 servings.

LUNCHEON HAM

CREAMED LUNCHEON HAM OR CHICKEN IN BAKED HUBBARD SQUASH

½ Hubbard Squash, 2½ lbs
1 can spiced ham, 12 oz, *or*
1½ cups diced chicken
¼ cup butter

⅓ cup flour
2 cups milk
1 tsp salt
Dash of pepper

Scrape out seeds and fibrous material from cavity of squash. Rub the cut edges of the squash with butter and place upside down on a baking pan. Bake in a moderately hot oven (400° F) for 45 min to 1 hr, or until squash is very soft on inside when pricked with a fork. Meanwhile cut the spiced ham into ½-inch dice. Melt butter in saucepan; blend in flour, add milk gradually, and cook until mixture boils and thickens, stirring constantly to keep smooth. Add seasonings and spiced ham (or diced chicken) and place over very low heat or over boiling water until meat is hot through. Remove baked squash to platter, pour creamed mixture into cavity, serve immediately. In serving, scoop out the tender meat of the squash along with creamed mixture. 5 servings.

Variety Meats

Liver, heart, kidneys, sweetbreads, tripe, brains and tongue do not fit into the usual classifications of regular meat cuts, but are included in a group called Variety Meats *or* Meat Specialties *(or* Sundries*). All variety meats contribute the same essential food elements as are found in the muscle meat from the same animal and some of them, especially liver and kidney, are exceptionally outstanding sources of certain vitamins and minerals.[1] They are important in the diet nutritionally and for the variety and interest they introduce into the meat course.*

★ ★ ★ ★

THE days when one could buy "a pound of liver to feed the cat" for a nickel are gone forever; and liver, particularly veal liver, has graduated into the luxury class. It is probably the favorite of the variety meats and one of those meats that should appear at least once a week on the table of every well-fed family. Some of the other variety meats are less familiar and therefore less in demand than liver, but all have a definite place in the well-planned diet, and each can be cooked in a way that will make them delicious to eat and attractive in appearance.

The proper cooking methods for the variety meats are determined by their individual characteristics and cannot be easily classified into broiling, braising, stewing, etc. Some may be cooked by all methods and others need preliminary preparation or pre-cooking to make them most enjoyed. However, the same variety meat from the different animals, beef, lamb, veal or pork are cooked in much the same way and are best described under their separate classifications.

BRAINS AND SWEETBREADS

Brains and sweetbreads are soft, white, very delicate in flavor, and require special care in preparation. They are unusually perishable, and should never be stored without pre-cooking. To pre-cook sweetbreads or brains, soak them for 15 min in cold water; then remove the thin membranous covering carefully to retain the original form. Cover with cold water to which 1 tsp salt and 1 tbsp lemon juice or vinegar have

[1] See nutrition charts on pp 19 to 29.

890

been added for each qt of water, and *simmer* 15 min. Then drain and place into cold water just long enough to chill quickly. The acid helps to keep the meat white. The meat is now thoroughly cooked and may be used as it is in salad; any further cooking is simply to make it more attractive.

Sweetbreads are often creamed with chicken, mushrooms or veal, or they may be used in salads or browned in butter by broiling or pan-broiling. Pre-cooked brains are often broken into pieces and scrambled with eggs, or dipped in egg and crumbs and fried in deep or shallow fat until delicately browned, or dipped in melted butter and broiled. They may also be reheated in a well-seasoned cream sauce or tomato sauce, or used to make soup.

TABLE 41 VARIETY MEATS

Name	Characteristics	Cooking Methods

Brains
  Calf, Lamb,
  Pork, Beef
	Very tender, soft in consistency, delicate flavor.	Precook at once to make firm and keep fresh. Then cream, scramble, fry or make soup.

Hearts
  Calf, Lamb,
  Pork, Beef
	Muscular organ which has had continuous exercise. Beef heart largest and least tender. Little waste, high percentage of lean meat.	Stuff or slice and braise, or slice very thin and fry. Or cook in water.

Kidneys
  Calf, Lamb,
  Pork, Beef
	Veal kidneys sometimes cut with chops; lamb kidneys sometimes enclosed in English chops considered great delicacy; or all may be sold separately.	Braise or broil. Marinate in French dressing, if desired.

Liver
  Calf, Lamb,
  Pork, Beef
	Beef liver largest and less tender than others. All have same high food value, except pork highest in iron.	Braise, fry, or broil.

Sweetbreads
  Calf, Beef,
  Lamb
	Great delicacy. Tender, Thymus gland of calf, young beef and lamb. Divided into parts: heart and throat sweetbreads.	Precooked to make firm and keep fresh. Then cream, braise, fry or broil.

Tongue
  Calf, Lamb,
  Pork, Beef
	Beef and calf tongue are both a desirable size for household use. Pork and lamb tongues are usually sold in a ready-to-serve form. Tongue may be purchased fresh, pickled, corned or smoked. Little waste, high percentage of lean meat.	Cook in water until tender; remove skin and roots. May also then be pot-roasted or roasted to obtain an attractive browned surface.

Tripe Beef	First and second stomachs of beef. Smooth and honeycomb tripe, latter preferred. May be purchased fresh cooked, pickled or canned.	Pre-cook to make tender. Then broil, fry, or heat and serve in sauce.

*Adapted from *Ten Lessons on Meat for Use in Schools,* sixth edition, published by the National Live Stock and Meat Board, Chicago.

TABLE 42   TIME TABLE FOR VARIETY MEATS

Cuts	Average Weight or Thickness	Approximate Cooking Time
BEEF		*Braised*
Liver, large piece	1½ lb.	45 minutes to 1 hour
sliced or cubed	½-¾ inch	5 to 10 minutes
Heart, half or whole	1 to 1½ lb.	2 to 4 hours
slices or cubes	½ inch	1½ to 2½ hours
Kidney	1 inch dice	½ to 2 hours
Tongue	2½ to 3½ lb.	3 to 4 hours (simmered)
PORK		*Braised*
Heart, half or whole	¾-1 lb.	1 to 1½ hours
Kidneys	½ inch dice	30 minutes
Liver, sliced	½-¾ inch	5 to 10 minutes
Tongue	Usually sold ready-to-serve.	
LAMB		*Braised*
Heart, whole	½ lb.	1 hour
Kidney, halves	2 oz.	30 minutes
Liver, sliced	½ inch	5 to 7 minutes
Tongue	Usually sold ready-to-serve.	
VEAL		*Braised*
Heart, whole	½ lb.	1 hour
Kidney, halves	2 oz.	30 minutes
Liver, sliced	½ inch	5 to 7 minutes
Tongue		2 to 3 hours (simmered)

BRAINS À LA NEWBURG

1 lb calf brains
2 tbsp butter *or* margarine
1 tbsp flour
1½ cups cream, *or* ¾ cup cream and ¾ cup milk
2 egg yolks
½ tsp salt
Dash of cayenne
¼ cup dried mushrooms, soaked and cut fine, *or* ¾ cup sliced, fresh
1 tbsp sherry

Prepare and cook brains as directed, p 891. When cold, dice into 1-inch cubes. Melt butter in top of double boiler, blend in flour and stir until smooth. Stir in liquid gradually and cook until thickened. Blend a few tbsp of the hot mixture into the egg yolks, then return to mixture in double boiler. Cook 2 min longer with constant stirring. Add seasonings, mushrooms (sauté mushrooms in 1 tbsp of butter for 5 min if fresh are used), sherry and diced brains. Cook until thoroughly heated then serve at once on hot toast points, Patty Shells, pp 934, 612, or Baking Powder Biscuits, p 234. 4 servings.

BROILED SWEETBREADS

*As palatable as they are handsome—wonderful for sophisticated lunch-
eons*

1 lb sweetbreads	Parsley *or* parsley butter
Melted butter	Tartar Sauce
Salt and pepper to taste	

Prepare sweetbreads as described under Brain and Sweetbreads, p 891. Immediately after outer membrane is removed, separate into serving portions and lay on a waxed paper. Cover with another sheet of waxed paper and place a weight on each portion to make the top and bottom flat. A pint jar filled with water makes an excellent weight. Heat broiler, brush both sides of sweetbreads with butter and lay on a shallow pan or sheet of aluminum foil. Sprinkle top with salt and broil with heat adjusted to 550° F about 3 inches below source of heat. When browned on top, turn over, brush with butter, sprinkle lightly with salt and continue broiling until nicely browned. Broiling requires about 7 to 8 min on each side for sweetbreads about 1 inch thick. For quicker broiling and a crustier sweetbread, cut the flattened sweetbreads in ½-inch thick lengthwise slices. Serve with parsley butter or Tartar Sauce, p 1260. 4 servings.

CREAMED SWEETBREADS

2 pairs sweetbreads	Salt and pepper to taste
¼ cup butter	Toast *or* Crisp Noodles,
⅓ cup flour	p 431
2 cups milk	Parsley *or* paprika

Prepare sweetbreads as directed. When cool, cut into uniform 1-inch dice. Melt butter in top of a double boiler over direct heat. Blend in flour thoroughly then gradually add the milk, stirring constantly to keep smooth. Cook over boiling water, stirring constantly until thickened. Add seasonings. When ready to serve, add the sweetbreads and continue to cook over hot water until heated through. Serve at once over crisp toast or noodles. Garnish with chopped parsley or dash of paprika. 5 servings.

Note: One or two diced hard-cooked eggs or ½ lb sautéed sliced mushrooms may be added to the creamed mixture.

BRAIN FRITTERS

½ lb brains, precooked, p 891	1 recipe Batter for Meat
	Fritters, p 1349

Prepare brains. Chill. Cut into ½-inch dice and fold into batter. Fry at 360° F according to *General Directions for Frying,* pp 1349 and 739.

SCRAMBLED BRAINS No. 1

1 lb calf brains	Dash of pepper
¼ cup butter	1 tbsp Worcestershire sauce
5 eggs	2 tbsp tomato catchup
1 tsp salt	Parsley

Prepare and cook brains according to directions.* When cool, separate carefully into small pieces or cut into dice. Melt butter in a heavy skillet over moderate heat. Beat eggs slightly and combine with the remaining ingredients, except parsley. Add brains and turn into the skillet. Cook over low heat until eggs begin to coagulate on the bottom, then gently run a fork or spatula along the bottom to let the uncooked egg flow down. Cook slowly with occasional stirring until eggs are of the desired firmness. Serve on a hot platter with chopped parsley sprinkled over the top. 5 servings.

SCRAMBLED BRAINS No. 2

½ lb calf brains	3 tbsp butter
1 tbsp chopped onion	6 eggs
¼ lb mushrooms, 1 cup	1 tsp salt
sliced	Parsley

Prepare and cook brains according to directions. When cool, separate carefully into small pieces or cut into dice. Sauté onion and mushrooms in heated butter in a heavy skillet over low heat, stirring constantly. Add brains and allow to brown slightly. Beat eggs with a fork, add salt, then pour them over the ingredients in the skillet. Continue to cook over low heat until eggs begins to coagulate on bottom. Then gently run a spatula or fork along the bottom to allow the liquid portion to flow down. Cook with occasional stirring until eggs are of the desired firmness. Serve at once on a hot platter garnished with parsley. 4 servings.

SWEETBREADS À LA KING

1 lb sweetbreads	1¼ tsp salt
½ lb fresh mushrooms	Dash of pepper
½ green pepper, diced	1½ cups milk
3 tbsp butter	2 tbsp chopped pimiento
¼ cup flour	Toast

Prepare and cook sweetbreads according to directions. When cool, cut into ½-inch dice. Clean and slice mushrooms and sauté with the green pepper in heated butter in the top of a double boiler over direct heat for 5 to 6 min. Blend in flour, salt and pepper, then add milk gradually and stir constantly over direct heat until sauce boils and

Preparation of Brains and Sweetbreads, see p 891.

thickens. Add cooled diced sweetbreads and pimiento, place over boiling water and continue cooking until sweetbreads are heated through. Serve on hot, crisp toast or in Patty Shells, pp 934, 612. 4 generous servings.

SAUTÉED CRUMBED SWEETBREADS

These crunchy crusted sweetbreads will sell sweetbreads to everybody

1 lb sweetbreads	Salt and pepper
1 egg	¼ cup margarine *or* butter
2 tbsp milk	Parsley
⅔ cup fine dry bread crumbs	

Prepare sweetbreads as described.* After outer membrane is removed, slice thick sweetbreads neatly in half lengthwise. Beat egg, stir in milk. Dip sweetbreads in the egg mixture, then into crumbs to coat uniformly. Sprinkle with salt and pepper. Heat margarine in skillet until hot, lay in the crumbed sweetbreads and brown to a light golden brown on all sides. Remove to hot platter. Garnish and serve piping hot. 4 servings.

TARTAR SWEETBREADS

1 lb sweetbreads	¼ cup dry, fine bread crumbs
Salt	3 tbsp butter *or* margarine
Pepper	Toast
1 tbsp lemon juice	Parsley
¼ cup mayonnaise	

Prepare and cook sweetbreads according to directions. Drain and lay on waxed paper, cover with waxed paper and place a pan or board on top and weight down to press flat and to cool. When ready to cook, season with salt and pepper. Add lemon juice to mayonnaise and blend. Dip sweetbreads in mayonnaise, then in bread crumbs. Heat butter in skillet, add sweetbreads and fry on both sides over moderate heat until crispy and brown, 10 to 12 min. Serve hot on toast points with sprigs of parsley. 4 servings.

HEART

CLEANING AND COOKING HEART

Heart is the most exercised muscle in the animal body and therefore is the least tender of meats. It is best cooked by moist heat, simmered or braised. Veal, lamb and pork hearts are more tender than beef hearts. A beef heart weighing 3 lbs serves 5 to 6; a lamb heart weighing 4 to 6 oz, serves one; an average sized pork heart weighing 11 oz, serves two; an averaged sized veal heart weighing 12 oz, serves 2.

*Preparation of Brains and Sweetbreads, see p 891.

To clean a heart, use a sharp knife to split it open about half way down on one side. Cut away arteries and veins at top and the stringy fibers and dividing membranes on the inside to leave a clean, undivided cavity. Wash thoroughly in plenty of warm water. Drain well. An old-time method is to soak heart in buttermilk or a vinegar solution (half vinegar and half water) for several hrs, keeping it in a cold place. Heart is then drained and cooked in the preferred way. Results of experimental work done in different laboratories on the tenderizing effect of these acids on meat are not conclusive, but there is agreement that both acids impart a delicious flavor.

To simmer hearts, add just enough salted water to cover (1 tsp salt to each qt of water), heat to boiling, reduce to a simmer, cover and cook until tender. Beef hearts require about 3½ hrs, veal and pork hearts about 2½ hrs and lamb hearts about 2 hrs. To enhance the flavor, add an onion, a small carrot and a branch of celery when cooking beef heart or half this amount of vegetables for pork, veal or lamb hearts. Or add a few whole peppers and a pinch of marjoram to the water. When hearts are tender, strain remaining liquid, add a little kitchen bouquet or meat paste for coloring, thicken with a flour-water paste, p 163, to make gravy to serve with the sliced heart.

To braise, brown cleaned heart slowly on all sides in a small amount of fat in a heavy skillet or Dutch oven. Add seasonings and a small quantity of water, cover tightly and simmer until tender. Beef hearts require 2½ to 3½ hrs and lamb, veal and pork hearts 1½ to 2½ hrs. If desired, stuff hearts with a well-seasoned bread dressing and tie or sew together before browning.

DELICIOUS PAN-FRIED HEART

Clean 1 young beef or 2 small veal hearts. Cut heart crosswise in ½-inch thick slices. Dredge slices in flour; sprinkle with salt, pan-fry in butter or bacon fat about 10 min, or until well browned on both sides. Serve at once. 5 servings.

BRAISED STUFFED HEART NO. 1

1 beef heart about 3 lbs	Pepper to taste
2 tsp salt	1 egg, beaten
2 cups coarse, soft bread crumbs	¾ cup milk
½ tsp poultry seasoning, if desired	¼ cup chopped celery
	1 tsp chopped onion
	2 tbsp melted butter

Clean heart as described. Drain thoroughly, and sprinkle inside with half the salt. Combine bread crumbs with seasonings, then add beaten egg mixed with milk and remaining ingredients. Mix lightly and stuff into heart. Tie or sew up heart. Place in buttered casserole or Dutch oven. Add rest of salt and ½ cup water. Cover, bake in a moderate oven (350° F) 3 to 3½ hrs or until tender, adding more water if necessary. Make gravy, p 799, from liquid remaining. 5 servings.

BRAISED STUFFED HEART NO. 2

1 beef heart *or* 2 veal hearts	¼ tsp celery salt
2 tbsp chopped onion	¼ cup shortening
2 tbsp butter	2 whole cloves
1½ cups cracker crumbs	20 whole black peppers
¼ cup water	1 bay leaf
¾ tsp salt	10½ oz can consomme
¼ tsp pepper	

Clean heart as described. Drain. Sauté onions in butter; add cracker crumbs and mix well. Add water, salt, pepper and celery salt, stir to blend. Stuff into heart and tie around securely with twine. Brown slowly on all sides in hot shortening; add rest of ingredients, cover tightly and simmer gently 2 to 3 hrs, or until heart is perfectly tender. Lift out bay leaf and serve heart at once with the gravy. 4 or 5 servings.

HEART CHOP SUEY

1 small beef *or* 2 veal hearts	3 tbsp flour
¼ cup butter *or* bacon fat	½ cup cold water
4 medium onions, sliced	Salt and pepper to taste
1 small stalk celery, diced	2 tbsp soy sauce *or*
2 cups meat stock *or* 2	1 of Worcestershire
chicken bouillon cubes in	3 *or* 4 cups Boiled Rice,
2 cups hot water	p 433, 1 cup raw

Clean heart. Drain well. Cut into narrow strips and roll in flour. Brown lightly in melted butter in large heavy skillet or Dutch oven. Add onions and sauté lightly, about 5 min. Add celery and enough meat stock or bouillon to just barely cover. Cover tightly and simmer until meat is tender, about 1 hr. Blend flour and water to a smooth paste and stir into chop suey; if gravy is too thick, add a little boiling water. Add seasonings. A little dark molasses or caramel, p 165, may be added for color, if desired. Serve with hot boiled rice. 5 servings.

Note: Add a No. 2 can chop suey vegetables along with the flour-water paste for a pleasing variation.

HEART SAUERBRATEN

Veal hearts weighing	1 tsp salt
about 1½ lbs	3 tbsp vinegar
2 tbsp butter	1 bay leaf
1 tbsp flour	6 whole cloves
1½ cups meat stock *or* water	6 whole black peppers
1 onion, sliced	(peppercorns)

Clean heart. Drain dry. Melt butter in saucepan and brown heart slowly until golden. Push heart to one side. Blend flour into butter, add meat stock gradually and cook until thickened, stirring constantly. Add onion, salt, vinegar, and spices tied in a cheesecloth bag. Simmer on top of stove or in a moderate oven (350° F) for 2 hrs or until tender. Remove bag of spices before serving heart. 4 servings.

STEWED HEART

3 calf *or* 4 lamb *or* pork
hearts
2 tbsp finely chopped onion
¼ cup finely chopped celery
or carrot
1 tsp salt
Pepper to suit taste
2 tbsp flour

¼ cup cold water
Caramel, p 165, *or* brown
food coloring
Boiled Rice, p 433, *or*
Mashed Potatoes, p 1378
Parsley
Paprika

Wash hearts thoroughly in warm water, split, and remove veins and arteries. Drain. Cut in small dice and barely cover with boiling water. Add onion and celery, or carrot, cover and simmer for 2½ hrs; add water as needed. When heart is tender, add salt, pepper, and flour which has been blended to a smooth paste with the cold water. Boil 5 min, stirring until thickened. Add caramel or vegetable coloring to give the desired brown color. Turn out onto platter which has a border of hot boiled rice or mashed potatoes. Garnish with parsley and paprika. 5 servings.

Note: When using pork heart, add 1 tbsp of vinegar and/or a pinch of marjoram with the flour-water paste for a more interesting flavor.

KIDNEYS

Kidneys are a good source of vitamin A, B and especially G, and are also rich in iron. They are often left attached to the veal and lamb loin, and are included in the English lamb chop and in veal chops on request. They are considered a delicacy when cooked and served with the chop in this way. Beef and pork kidneys should either be braised or cooked in water, but the other two types, lamb and veal, are tender and mild enough to be broiled.

The proper preparation is essential to the enjoyment of kidneys. The thin tough membrane that covers the kidneys should be removed, as well as the fatty core and heavy tubes that can be seen when the kidney is split. They should always be washed thoroughly and many prefer to let them stand at least half an hr in salt water. Pre-cooking is not necessary, but if a more delicate flavor is preferred, the kidneys may be put into cold water, heated to boiling, and drained before using in a given recipe. Marinating in a well-seasoned French dressing also enhances the fine flavor.

Note: To clean Heart, see p 895.

Probably the most famous kidney dishes are beef-and-kidney pie, and the tiny lamb kidneys that are broiled and served with mixed grills.

BRAISED KIDNEYS AND SHORT RIBS

1 lb lamb *or* veal kidneys	1 tsp salt
1 lb beef short ribs	3 tbsp bacon drippings
½ cup flour	1½ cups boiling water

Remove membranes, split each kidney through center, and remove fat and tubes. Soak kidneys in cold water to cover with ½ tsp salt for 1 hr or more. Cut short ribs into serving portions and dredge thoroughly in flour which has been mixed with the salt. Melt fat in heavy iron or aluminum skillet and brown short ribs on all sides in the hot fat. Add water; cover and simmer for about two hrs or until tender. Cut kidneys in ½-inch dice and add the last half hr of cooking. Serve juices remaining in skillet as gravy. 5 servings.

DEVILED KIDNEYS

2 lbs beef kidneys	1 tbsp lemon juice
3 tsp salt	⅓ cup flour
¼ cup butter	¾ cup hot water
1½ tsp dry mustard	4 cups Boiled Rice, p 433
¼ tsp paprika	6 slices Broiled Bacon, p 855

Wash kidneys thoroughly, split and remove core and tubes; scissors are convenient for this purpose. Cover with cold water, add 1 tsp of the salt, and soak half an hr. Drain well. Cut each kidney into 6 pieces. Melt half the butter, blend with mustard, rest of salt, paprika, and lemon juice. Roll each piece of kidney in this sauce, then in the flour. Melt remaining butter in skillet, add kidneys and brown slowly on all sides. Add hot water, cover and simmer until kidneys are tender, about 20 to 30 min. If sauce becomes too thick, add a little more hot water. Serve kidneys hot in their own sauce with boiled rice and crisp broiled bacon. 5 servings.

KIDNEY AND SAUSAGE SQUARES

1 beef kidney, 1¼ lbs	2 eggs, slightly beaten
1 lb pork sausage, bulk	1 *or* 2 large tart apples,
2 small onions	6 to 8 slices
8 to 10 soda crackers	

Wash kidney in cold water. Split and remove fat, core and fibrous tubes. Place in cold water to cover and bring to boiling point. Reduce heat and simmer 5 min. Drain. Grind together kidney, sausage, onion and crackers and blend well. Mix with eggs and press firmly into a 10-inch sq pan. Arrange apple slices on top and bake in a moderate oven (350° F) for 30 min. Cut in sqs to serve. 6 to 8 servings.

KIDNEY HASH

1 beef kidney, 1¼ lbs	3 medium potatoes, diced
3 tbsp flour	1 tsp seasoning salt
1 small onion, finely chopped	1 tsp grated onion
3 tbsp butter	Few grains red pepper
1½ cups meat stock	2 tsp lemon juice

Wash kidneys thoroughly in cold water. Drain, split lengthwise and remove all fat, core and fibrous tubes using kitchen scissors and a sharp paring knife. Soak in cold water to cover for ½ hr. Drain. Cut kidney into ½-inch dice. Add flour and toss to dredge thoroughly. Brown kidney and chopped onion in hot melted butter in a skillet. Add stock and diced potato, cover and simmer gently from 20 to 30 min stirring occasionally. Stir in salt, grated onion, pepper and lemon juice and serve hot. If meat stock is not available, add 1 beef bouillon cube dissolved in 1½ cups hot water. 4 generous servings.

KIDNEY STEW

3 large *or* 4 medium pork	2 tbsp chopped onion
kidneys, about 1 lb	2 tbsp butter
½ tsp salt	3 tbsp bacon drippings
2 tsp lemon juice	1 tsp salt
⅓ cup flour	1 tbsp chopped parsley

Wash kidneys thoroughly and remove membranous coverings. Split kidneys through center and remove white fatty cores and large tubes. Cover with 2 cups cold water, add the ½ tsp salt and the lemon juice, and let soak at least half an hr. Drain and rinse well in cold water. Cut in ½-inch dice. Add 2 cups boiling water, cover and simmer 30 min; then drain, saving liquid. Dredge the partly cooked kidneys in flour. Brown kidneys and chopped onion in the heated, combined butter and bacon drippings. Blend in flour remaining from dredging kidney. Add salt and gradually stir in 2½ cups water, using half fresh water and half cooking water from kidneys. (For milder flavor, use all fresh water.) Stir constantly while cooking until gravy boils and thickens. Serve piping hot with a sprinkling of chopped parsley, over mashed potatoes, fluffy rice or toast. 5 servings.

LAMB AND KIDNEY KABOBS

8 lamb kidneys	½ lb medium sized mush-
1 lb boneless lamb shoulder	rooms
½ cup French Dressing	Salt and pepper
4 onions, walnut-size	Boiled brown rice

Remove cores from kidneys and wipe both kidneys and meat clean with a damp cloth. Cut the meat neatly into 1½-inch cubes, leave the small kidneys whole. Turn both kidneys and meat into a bowl and add the dressing. Toss with a fork to coat every piece well. Cover and let marinate at least an hr. Peel onions and clean mushrooms. Arrange all of the foods on skewers at least 8 inches long in the following way. Start with lamb cube, then kidney, then lamb cube. Next push the mushroom snugly against the meat, add onion, and a second mushroom. The mushroom and onions should be fitted closely together to prevent the mushroom from drying out during the length of broiling necessary to cook the meat. Finish the end of the skewer with another cube of lamb, a kidney and a cube of lamb. Sprinkle with salt and pepper. Broil this skewered arrangement on a preheated broiler with the rack placed 3 inches below the source of heat. Turn occasionally and broil for 10 to 12 min. Serve hot, skewer and all, with browned rice, p 433. 4 servings.

PORK KIDNEY SAUTÉ WITH SAVORY GRAVY

An inexpensive yet highly nutritive meat dish. Pleasing in flavor and appearance

3 pork kidneys, 1½ lbs	1½ chicken bouillon cubes
¼ cup butter *or* margarine	¾ cup hot water
¼ cup flour	Pepper to taste
½ tsp monosodium glutamate, optional	1 tbsp chopped chives *or* parsley
¼ cup finely chopped onion	

Wash kidneys well in cold water. Lay on cutting board and split lengthwise. Use kitchen scissors to cut all the white core out neatly. Lay kidney halves together and with a sharp knife cut into as thin slices as possible. Cut these slices into 3 or 4 pieces. Sprinkle flour on a sheet of waxed paper; turn kidneys into flour; holding paper by corners, shift kidneys back and forth until all slices are well coated. Heat butter until bubbling, add onion and kidneys. Cover and cook until both sides of kidney slices are a gray color, about 5 min. Stir frequently. Now add next 5 ingredients and stir thoroughly; reheat until sauce boils and thickens. Serve on toast or over mashed or boiled potatoes. Sprinkle with chopped chives. 4 to 5 servings.

STEAK AND KIDNEY PIE

1 beef kidney, 1 lb	1 lb ground steak *or* chuck
2 tbsp vinegar	1 lb diced pared potatoes
¼ cup bacon drippings	Plain pastry for single
2 tsp salt	crust, p 924
10 small white onions, about ¼ lb	

Split kidney and remove cores, tubes, and membranous covering. Soak 30 min in 1 qt cold water to which the vinegar has been added; then drain, dice and brown in 2 tbsp of fat. Barely cover with water, add 1 tsp salt, and simmer slowly until tender, about 30 to 45 min. Add water from time to time as needed to keep covered with liquid. Cut onions in halves or quarters and sauté in remaining fat until slightly browned; add ground meat and rest of salt, and continue cooking over moderate heat, stirring frequently, for 20 min or until meat is nicely browned. Meanwhile cook potatoes until tender in just enough boiling salted water to cover. Add the kidneys and potatoes with their cooking waters to the ground meat. Thicken gravy, p 799, if desired. Turn into an 8-inch casserole, cover with Plain Pastry, p 928, cut vents in several places to let steam escape, and bake in a moderately hot oven (425° F) about 20 min, or until crust is nicely browned. Serve piping hot. 5 servings.

LIVER

Liver is the richest of all food sources of iron, as well as a good source of several vitamins, see pp 19 to 29. Since its nutritional value was first discovered just over twenty years ago, it has become well established as a part of the meat diet in many American homes. Calf or veal liver is the most tender and delicate in flavor, and therefore the most popular. However, this popularity is reflected in its price which is much higher than that of pork, beef, or lamb liver. In food value, however, beef liver has one-third more iron per lb than that from calf or lamb, and pork liver is highest of all with three times as much iron as beef liver. Pork and beef liver are recommended therefore, both nutritionally and economically in preference to calf liver, and when carefully prepared they make just as good eating. Lamb liver, since it also comes from a very young animal is similar to calf liver, but it is only available in certain parts of the country.

Liver is a very tender meat except for the tough membranous covering or "skin" and the tubes (veins) which run through the whole organ. This skin is found only on the outside edge of sliced liver but the tubes (veins) may appear anywhere in the slice. Both of these parts appear as tough, stringy portions in cooked liver and should always be removed as directed in the following recipes. This requires some patience, but the housewife who persists will be rewarded by her family's increased enjoyment of this valuable meat.

Whatever cooking method is used, liver should always be cooked just long enough to lose the pink color at the center of the piece or slice. Overcooking makes it dry and hard. Caution the butcher to cut the slices of uniform-thickness throughout. If he is careless, his ½" slices of liver may be ¼-inch thick at one end and ½-inch or more at the other, and the thin end is sure to be overcooked before the thick end is done. Liver cooks quickly and requires only 2½ to 5 min on each side in a hot, well-greased skillet to pan-broil slices that are about ½-inch thick.

REMOVING SKIN AND TUBES (VEINS) FROM LIVER

The entire liver is covered with a membrane, so each slice cut from the liver has a strip of this membrane all around its edge. This is easily removed by inserting a sharp knife just under it at one point and pulling and scraping it from the meat. If the slice is floured first, this operation is easier as the liver is less slippery. The tubes may be cut out with sharp-pointed scissors. If liver is purchased in one piece, remove tubes by loosening at one end until the tube can be gripped with one hand, and scrape flesh away with the knife. This leaves liver looking somewhat torn, but the tears will not be seen after cooking, and the liver will be especially agreeable to eat. If liver is very slippery to handle, dip the hands occasionally into additional flour.

Note: Pork liver is very delicate and must be handled with particular care so it is not unnecessarily torn.

BAKED LIVER AND VEGETABLES

1½ lbs beef liver in 1 piece	1 cup strained tomatoes
¼ cup flour	1 tsp salt
5 slices bacon	2 lbs small new potatoes
1 large onion, sliced	⅛ tsp black pepper
2 cups diced celery	¾ cup hot water

Remove skin and tubes from liver and dredge liver in flour. Pan-broil bacon until just done in a heavy skillet. Lift bacon out and drain. Brown liver slowly in the bacon drippings on all sides and push to one side of pan. Sauté onion and celery in the drippings until soft and yellow. Add any remaining flour that did not cling to the liver, and stir until smooth. Then add strained tomatoes and salt, and continue stirring over moderate heat until sauce boils and thickens. Raise the browned liver so it lies on top of the gravy, and over it arrange the scraped, halved potatoes. Cover with a close-fitting lid and bake in a moderate oven (350° F) until potatoes are soft, about 45 min. Remove lid and place cooked bacon over the liver; replace in oven, uncovered, for about 5 min to reheat bacon. Remove liver and potatoes to a hot platter, arranging bacon over the liver. Pour gravy around liver or serve it in a separate bowl. 5 servings.

BRAISED LIVER

1½ lbs liver in one piece	Salt to suit taste
¼ lb salt pork	1 tsp poultry seasoning
1 large onion, chopped	Dash pepper
Hot stock *or* bouillon	Parsley

Wipe liver with a damp cloth; remove skin and tubes as directed. Lard rounded side with strips of salt pork (see directions for larding, p

164). Sauté the onion slowly until soft and yellow in salt pork fat; then add liver and brown it slowly on all sides. Half cover with hot stock or with bouillon made by dissolving 1 beef bouillon cube in each cup of hot water required. Add seasonings. Cover tightly and simmer about 45 min, or only until liver is no longer pink inside, basting frequently. Liquid may be made into gravy, or it may be flavored with lemon juice and served without thickening. Serve with a sprinkling of chopped parsley. 5 or 6 servings.

BRAISED LIVER WITH RICE AND TOMATOES

Substitute a No. 2½ can tomatoes for the hot stock or bouillon in the recipe for Braised Liver. After the liver has cooked 25 min, add ¾ cup uncooked rice. Add water to the tomatoes if necessary to prevent rice from becoming too dry. Simmer 20 min longer, or until rice is tender. 5 servings.

BROILED LIVER STEAK

1½ lbs beef liver sliced 1 inch thick	Pepper, if desired
3 tbsp butter, melted	2 tsp chopped chives *or* parsley
1 tsp salt	

Have liver sliced evenly, the same thickness all through for even cooking. Remove the skin and tubes as directed, p 903. Brush liver on both sides with melted butter, and place on the pre-heated broiler rack. Adjust broiler rack so surface of liver is 3 inches below the source of heat (electric heating element or tip of gas flame). Cook for 6 min on one side; then turn and cook about 6 min on other side, or until just cooked through. Remove to a hot platter. Brush with more butter, and sprinkle with salt, pepper and chopped chives or parsley. Garnish and serve immediately. A pleasing accompaniment is French-fried onions and Sour Cream Gravy, pp 1361 and 907. 5 servings.

FRENCH-FRIED LIVER

1½ lbs liver, cut ½-inch thick	1½ tsp salt
½ cup flour	Shortening for frying

These directions apply to liver sliced uniformly ½-inch thick. Liver sliced thicker or thinner requires proportionately more or less cooking.

Remove skin and veins from liver slices, p 903, and cut into neat strips ½-inch wide and about 4 inches long or longer. Mix flour and salt thoroughly, roll strips of liver in the mixture. Have fat heated to 360° F. Put 6 or 7 pieces of liver into frying basket, fry 1 to 2 min, not longer; they will be light brown in color. Drain quickly on absorbent paper or paper toweling, and serve hot. 5 to 6 servings.

Note: Directions for removing skin and tubes from liver, see p 903.

GRILLED LIVER SAUSAGE

Have liver sausage sliced about ½ inch thick. Remove casing and brush both sides with butter. Place on broiler rack about 3 inches below the source of heat and broil on one side only until hot through and slightly browned. Transfer to hot platter and serve with pan-fried tomatoes, onions or buttered cabbage. The slices may, if preferred, be pan-fried in butter or bacon drippings melted in a heavy skillet, turning to brown on both sides. 1¼ lbs liver sausage makes 5 servings.

ITALIAN STYLE LIVER MACARONI AND TOMATOES

2 cups macaroni, broken	¼ cup bacon drippings
1 lb beef *or* pork liver	1 tbsp chopped onion
¼ cup flour	¾ cup water
1 tsp salt	No. 2½ can tomatoes,
⅛ tsp pepper	3½ cups

Drop macaroni into rapidly boiling salted water (2 tsp salt to 2 qts water) and boil until just tender (about 20 min). Drain. Meanwhile remove skin and tubes from liver with a sharp knife, p 903. Cut liver in one-inch dice, roll in flour mixed with salt and pepper; brown in the bacon drippings in a large skillet along with the onion. Add water and tomatoes and heat to boiling. Add macaroni, cover, and simmer 10 min. Serve piping hot. 5 or 6 servings.

LIVER À LA GOURMET

2 tbsp salad oil	1¼ lbs beef liver, sliced
2 cloves garlic	3 tbsp flour
2 medium onions	½ tsp salt
½ lb mushrooms	Dash black pepper
No. 2 can tomatoes	2 tbsp butter

Heat oil in skillet; add peeled, sliced garlic and onions, and cook slowly until soft and yellow. Add cleaned sliced mushrooms; cover tightly and simmer 3 or 4 min. Put the tomatoes through a sieve to remove the seeds, and add to skillet; continue simmering gently. Meanwhile remove skin and tubes from liver, p 903, and dredge thoroughly in flour which has been mixed with salt and pepper. Brown liver slices in butter in another skillet until just lightly browned on both sides. Pour sauce over liver, cover, and simmer 5 min longer. 5 or 6 servings.

LIVER AND ONIONS

1½ lbs beef *or* pork liver	1 lb onions, peeled
2 tbsp bacon drippings *or*	½ tsp salt
shortening	Parsley *or* cress

For the best results, liver and onions should both be cooked at the same time so they can be served immediately when they are just done and at the peak of their high quality. If a 10 or 12 inch skillet is available, both liver and onions can be cooked in the same skillet; otherwise two skillets should be used. Remove skin and tubes from liver. Heat the bacon drippings in a heavy skillet and brown the liver quickly on both sides over moderate heat. Pile the slices on top of each other in one side of the pan, add sliced onions. Sprinkle with salt, cover and cook slowly until onions are tender, stirring occasionally to cook evenly, about 5 to 7 min. Lift liver slices out onto a hot platter, stir the onions quickly around in the drippings and serve on same platter with liver. If two skillets are used, the liver should be removed to a hot platter and the onions turned into the liver skillet for one min to be stirred quickly and mixed with the flavorful liver drippings. Garnish with parsley or cress and serve at once. 5 servings.

LIVERBURGERS

¾ lb ground beef *or* pork liver
¾ lb ground beef chuck
1 cup fine cracker crumbs
2 eggs
1 tsp salt
1 tsp celery salt
Few grains pepper
1 tbsp grated onion
3 tbsp bacon drippings
Tomatoes and parsley

Remove skin and tubes from liver, p 903; put liver through food chopper. Then combine with ground beef, add cracker crumbs to meat. Beat eggs and mix salt, celery salt, pepper, and onion with egg. Thoroughly mix seasoned egg mixture with meat and crumbs. Form into 10 medium-sized patties and fry about 4 min on each side in bacon drippings in a heavy skillet over low heat, turning only once. Serve hot with a garnish of pan-fried tomatoes and parsley. 5 servings.

LIVER LOAF

1¼ lbs beef *or* pork liver
1 cup milk
2 tbsp melted butter
3 eggs, beaten
2 tsp salt
¼ tsp pepper
1 tbsp grated onion
⅛ tsp nutmeg
1½ cups fine dry bread crumbs
1 tsp meat extract paste in ¼ cup water

Remove skin and tubes from liver; put liver through food chopper.* Add remaining ingredients and mix thoroughly. Turn into buttered bread-loaf pan (4½ x 8½ x 2¾ inches), and bake in a moderate oven (325° to 350° F) for 1 hr, or until a knife inserted in the center comes out clean. Unmold onto serving platter and garnish with parsley. Serve hot with Sautéed Mushrooms, p 1356, or cold with catchup or chili sauce. 10 servings.

*Liver may be simmered for 3 to 5 min in ¼ cup water before grinding for easier handling. Use cooking water to mix with meat extract paste.

LIVER SAUERBRATEN

1 lb beef liver in 2 thick
   slices
½ cup cider vinegar
1¼ cups water
1 tbsp sugar
¾ tsp salt
2 slices salt pork, ¼ lb

1 large onion cut into ¼″
   slices
3 tbsp shortening
1 medium bay leaf
6 whole cloves
½ tbsp flour

Remove tubes and skin from liver. Combine vinegar, water, sugar and salt and bring to a boil. Place liver in a glass or enamel dish and pour the partly cooled vinegar mixture over liver. Cover and set in refrigerator overnight. Drain the liver and "lard" with strips of salt pork, see p 164. Meanwhile sauté onion in the hot shortening, push onions to one side and brown the liver slowly in the remaining shortening. Add bay leaf and cloves and sprinkle flour on top. Concentrate the vinegar liquid by boiling down to ¾ cup and add gradually to liver as needed. Turn liver once during cooking. Simmer covered for 30 min. 4 servings.

LIVER SAUSAGE AND CREAMED CABBAGE

1 medium head green
   cabbage
2 tsp salt
¼ cup butter
¼ cup flour

2½ cups milk
1¼ lbs liver sausage sliced
   about ½-inch thick
1 hard-cooked egg
Paprika

Remove and discard soiled outer leaves of cabbage; cut head into thin wedges. Lay carefully in large saucepan; sprinkle with 1 tsp salt. In another saucepan, melt the butter, blend in flour, and add milk gradually and rest of salt; stir constantly over direct heat until sauce boils. Reduce heat as low as possible, cover and keep hot. Pour boiling water over the cabbage sufficient to cover it, and boil uncovered until tender, about 7 min. Meanwhile, remove casing from sausage slices and pan-broil in butter or bacon drippings until brown and hot through. Drain cabbage and transfer to hot platter or chop plate; pour white sauce around or over it, arrange hot sausage over the cabbage, and garnish with hard-cooked egg and sprinkling of paprika in center. 5 servings.

LIVER WITH SOUR CREAM GRAVY

1½ lbs sliced liver
   Flour for dredging
1½ tsp salt
¼ cup butter
2 tbsp flour

¾ cup hot water
¾ cup sour cream
Pepper to suit taste
Chopped chives

Remove skin and tubes from liver. Dredge liver well with flour and sprinkle with salt. Sauté in butter in a heavy skillet over moderate heat until browned on both sides, then continue cooking until no longer pink in center, 5 to 10 min. Remove to hot platter and cover to keep warm. Blend the 2 tbsp of flour into butter remaining in skillet, and add the hot water gradually stirring vigorously until gravy boils and thickens. Then add sour cream and reheat, stirring until smooth. Add additional salt if needed and pepper. Sprinkle liver with chopped chives and serve at once with the hot gravy. 5 servings.

PAN-FRIED LIVER

Have liver sliced uniformly ¼ to ½ inch thick. Remove skin and tubes and dredge with flour, p 903. Heat butter or bacon drippings in a skillet, and brown the liver first on one side and then on the other. Sprinkle with salt (¾ tsp to each lb of liver), and pepper if desired. Reduce heat and continue cooking slowly until liver is done, from 5 to 10 min, turning once or twice. Overcooking should be avoided as it makes the liver tough and dry. Serve with pan-broiled bacon, p 855, if desired. Garnish with parsley or watercress. 1½ lbs liver and ¼ lb bacon will make 5 servings.

Variation: Liver and Bacon with Fried Noodles: Pan-broil 5 slices of bacon until as crisp as desired; drain and place on hot platter. Add well-drained cooked noodles to bacon fat, turn carefully over and over to coat all noodles with fat without breaking them, and cook without further stirring until delicately browned. Turn and brown other side. While noodles are browning, pan-fry liver. Sprinkle noodles and liver with salt. Serve hot, surrounding noodles with liver and bacon. 5 servings.

POOR MAN'S GOOSE

1¼ lbs liver, sliced   5 medium onions, sliced
   2 tbsp bacon drippings   5 medium potatoes, sliced
   Salt and pepper   5 slices bacon

Remove skin and tubes from liver and cut liver in serving-size pieces. Brown slices slightly on both sides in hot drippings (about ½ min on each side). Sprinkle with salt and pepper. Put liver and drippings into bottom of large (10-cup) casserole. Add the onions, then the potatoes and sprinkle with more salt and pepper. Top with bacon slices. Cover casserole and bake in a moderate oven (350° F) for 1 hr. Remove cover and bake 15 min longer to crisp bacon. Serve piping hot. 5 servings.

Note: Directions for removing skin and tubes from liver, see p 903.

SPANISH LIVER

1 lb liver, sliced	2 large potatoes, 1½ lbs
½ medium size onion	½ bay leaf
¼ cup salad oil	1 tsp salt
3 tbsp lemon juice	1 tbsp catchup

Carefully remove skin and tubes from liver. Rub each slice with onion; then cover with oil and lemon juice mixed together, and let stand 1 hr. Pare and dice potatoes. Drain and dice liver (one-inch), combine with potatoes and cover with boiling water; add bay leaf and salt and simmer until potatoes are tender. When done, remove bay leaf, add catchup and reheat. Serve on a hot platter with a sprinkling of chopped parsley. 5 servings.

TONGUE

CLEANING AND COOKING TONGUE

Beef, Veal, Pork and Lamb

Tongue, like heart, is a much exercised muscle. Wash tongue in warm water, thoroughly scrubbing with a brush at root-end. Soak smoked or pickled tongue in water several hrs before cooking. Fit tongue into kettle, barely cover with water, add ¾ tsp salt per lb, a pinch of marjoram, small bay leaf and a tsp of whole peppers; cover, simmer until tender. An average beef tongue weighing 4 lb cooks tender in 3 to 4 hrs, and serves 8 to 11; a 1½ lb veal tongue in 1½ hrs and serves 3 to 4; a 12-oz pork tongue in 1½ hrs and serves 2 to 3; an 8-oz lamb tongue cooks in 1 hr, serves 1 to 2. Cooking time varies some with the quality. When tender, lift tongue from cooking liquid and dip quickly in cold water. This helps in stripping skin off easily and pulling out roots neatly. Return skinned tongue to cooking water; reheat to serve hot; if served cold, cool cooking water, add tongue, cover and refrigerate to keep juicy.

HOW TO SLICE BOILED TONGUE

Wash, cook and trim tongue as described above. Appetite and eye appeal depend on perfect cooking and slicing. Chilled tongue slices more easily than hot tongue. To slice attractively, place tongue on cutting board or platter with large end to your right, and rounded-side toward you; insert fork in center to hold firmly. Use a sharp knife, begin at large end; cut thin slices a little on the slant, which is exactly across grain of tongue. Near tip of tongue, slices are almost lengthwise. Slices cut across grain reveal interesting texture and variation in color of meat. The most desirable thickness for cold tongue slices is ⅛-inch or less, and for hot tongue ¼-inch.

SUGGESTIONS FOR SERVING TONGUE

1. Serve cold, thin-sliced tongue with mustard, horseradish sauce or currant jelly.
2. Heat sliced tongue in Barbecue Sauce, p 1250.
3. Heat slices in tongue liquid to cover with 2 tbsp vinegar for 4 servings. Drain, serve with hot spinach or other greens.
4. Brush cooked trimmed tongue with butter; roast in hot oven (450° F) until browned and hot. Remove to hot platter. Garnish root-end with bouquet of parsley. Good with baked apples.

COLD JELLIED TONGUE

1 medium beef tongue, about 3 lbs
2 tbsp plain gelatin
¼ cup cold water
2 cups boiled tongue stock
Cress, lettuce *or* parsley

Clean and cook tongue as described above. Press cooled tongue into mold, round or brick-shaped. Soften gelatin in the water 5 min; then stir in hot tongue stock. When dissolved, season with salt and pepper, and pour over tongue. Chill until firm. Slice tongue thin, leaving the gelatin adhering. Garnish with cress, lettuce or parsley. Serve cold. 10 servings.

OXTAILS

BRAISED OXTAILS

2 oxtails, about 4 lbs
⅓ cup flour
2 tbsp margarine *or* shortening
¾ cup chopped onion
1 tsp salt
2 cups boiling water
1 chicken bouillon cube
1 cup diced carrot
1 cup diced potato
1 cup sliced mushrooms, optional
⅛ tsp pepper
1 tbsp sherry, if desired

Have butcher cut oxtails at joints into 2 to 3 inch lengths. Wipe pieces clean with a damp cloth, then roll in the flour to coat well. Put oxtails onto a shallow pan and place under broiler or in a hot oven (450° F). Cook from 15 to 20 min or until uniformly browned on all sides, turning occasionally. Meanwhile heat margarine in a Dutch oven or heavy kettle with tight fitting cover. Add onion and sauté until soft and yellow. Add browned oxtails, salt, boiling water and bouillon cube. (If bouillon cube is not desired, add 1 tsp more salt.) Cover kettle, cook at simmering point, p 796, about 3½ hrs or until meat is very tender. Add a little boiling water every half hr or so if necessary. Add the vegetables and the sherry, cover and cook until tender or for about 15 min. Add more salt and pepper if necessary. 5 to 6 servings.

TRIPE

Whether fresh, pickled or canned, tripe is always pre-cooked when purchased. That is, the butcher cleans and parboils it. However, further cooking in water is necessary before the tripe is tender enough to eat.

Two varieties of tripe are sold, the plain or smooth type, and the more popular honey-comb tripe which is valued for its beautiful appearance. It is smooth on the outside, but the inside is deeply honey-combed. The method of preparation is the same for both kinds. They should be thoroughly washed and then simmered in salted water for at least 1 hr. After the tripe is tender, it may be served in a variety of ways: dipped in egg and crumbs and fried in deep fat, brushed with melted butter and broiled, creamed, spread with bread dressing and baked, served with tomato sauce, or combined with various ingredients in casserole dishes.

TRIPE À LA CREOLE

1 lb honey-comb tripe	1 tbsp Worcestershire sauce
⅓ cup drippings	2 tsp salt
3 tbsp chopped onion	½ tsp paprika
2½ cups canned tomatoes	3 tbsp chopped green pepper
1 tsp sugar	Flour
3 or 4 cups cooked rice	Parsley

Wash tripe thoroughly, cover with fresh cold water and simmer gently for 2 or 3 hrs or until very tender. Drain. Meanwhile melt half the drippings in a heavy skillet; add onions and cook until soft and yellow. Add tomatoes which have been rubbed through a sieve and the sugar. Simmer gently covered for 45 min to 1 hr. Add seasonings and green pepper and reheat to boiling. Dry the cooked tripe thoroughly, cut into 2½ inch sqs and dredge in flour. Brown on both sides in rest of hot drippings. Place on a hot platter and cover with the hot tomato sauce. Garnish with parsley and serve with fluffy Boiled Rice, P 433. 5 servings.

TRIPE DE LUXE

1½ lbs honey-comb tripe	2½ cups tomato juice,
3 cups chopped celery	No. 2 can
2 cups chopped onion	1 tsp salt
⅓ cup chopped parsley	Pepper
¼ cup olive oil or butter	¼ cup Parmesan cheese
	¼ cup fine dry bread crumbs

Wash tripe thoroughly and cut into 2½-inch sqs. Sauté next 3 ingredients in olive oil until lightly browned. Cover with the tripe. Add tomato juice, salt and pepper, cover closely, and bake in a moderately slow oven (325° F) about 3 hrs or until tender. Remove cover, sprinkle with Parmesan cheese mixed with the bread crumbs, and return to oven with temp increased to moderately hot (400° F) until nicely toasted, about ½ hr. 6 or 7 servings.

CARVING MEAT

It is a real achievement to learn how to roast or broil meat perfectly. But a perfectly cooked meat served in unattractive hunks or slabs cut in same direction of the fibers is not enjoyable. When carved in slices directly across the grain of the meat and of the right thickness, the goodness is greatly enhanced. Therefore, learning to carve all cuts of meat properly is a skill that every host and hostess should have an urge to learn. The following drawings should help one to learn how to carve with ease and confidence.

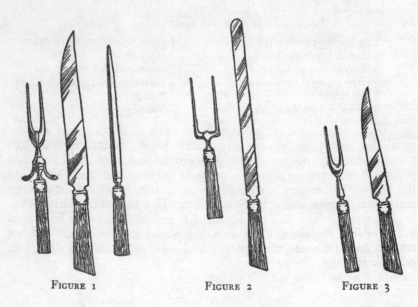

FIGURE 1　　　　　　　FIGURE 2　　　　　　　FIGURE 3

CARVING SET

The first requirement is the tools—a carving set, a steak set or a roast meat slicer and carver's helper. There are various sizes, shapes and kinds of handles. The most important feature about these sets is the quality of the steel. The blade needs to be the kind that will take and hold a keen edge.

Standard carving sets, Figure 1, which can be used to do all around carving consist of a knife, fork and steel. The knife has an 8 to 9-inch blade.

The fork has a guard to protect the hand when cutting toward the fork. *A steak set knife,* Figure 3, has a 6 to 7-inch blade. The fork may or may not have a guard. *The roast meat slicer,* Figure 2, is desirable for large roasts. It has a long flexible blade suitable for cutting large thin slices. The carver's helper has wide-spread tines and is helpful in holding the large roast steady.

THE STEEL AND HOW TO USE IT

The steel is used to keep the carving knife blade true and in perfect condition. To use the steel, hold firmly in left hand, thumb on top of handle with point slightly upward and away from the body. Now place the heel of knife blade against far side of tip of the steel. The steel and blade are at a slight angle, about 25 degrees.

(1st stroke) Draw knife blade down across steel toward left hand with a quick swinging motion of right wrist and forearm. The entire knife edge should pass lightly over the steel.

(2nd stroke) Bring knife into position again but with the blade against the near side of the steel. Repeat the same motion as in first, passing blade over steel. By alternating from side to side, 12 strokes should true the edge.

CARE OF CARVING SET

Always keep the carving set separated from other cutlery, so knife will not be nicked or dulled. When cared for properly, a good knife blade will need only occasional sharpening, but it should always be steeled before using. Good tools add to the carver's confidence.

1—*Standard carving set*
2—*Roast meat slicer and carver's helper*
3—*Steak set*

HOW TO CARVE A STANDING RIB ROAST

1. *This roast* is one that the butcher has removed shortribs and separated the backbone from the ribs. The backbone is left on roast while cooking but is removed before being placed on platter. Place roast on platter with the small cut surface up. With guard up on the fork, insert fork firmly between the 2 top ribs, Figure 1. From the far right, slice across grain toward ribs and close up to them make slice ⅛ to ⅜-inch thick.

FIGURE 1

FIGURE 2

2. Release each slice by cutting downward with tip of knife close to the bone, Figure 2.

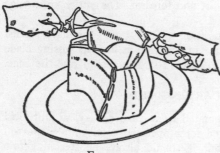

FIGURE 3

3. Lift slice onto blade, holding onto it with fork and lay on side of platter, Figure 3. If there is not room on platter, have another hot platter near on which to put slices. Cut enough slices to serve all before transferring slices to individual plates.

HOW TO CARVE A ROLLED RIB ROAST

1. Place on platter with large cut surface down, Figure 1. Use carving set or slicer and carver's helper. With guard up, push fork well into roast on left side an inch or more from top. Start from the far right side, slicing across grain toward fork to obtain slices from ⅛ to ⅜-inch thick.

2. When a slice is carved, lift to side of platter or to another hot platter, Figure 2. Remove the cords as you come to them in making slices. Sever cord with tip of blade, loosen it with fork and let it drop to platter.

FIGURE 1

FIGURE 2

HOW TO CARVE A CROWN ROAST
LAMB OR PORK

Lamb crown roasts are made from the rack or rib section of the lamb. A pork crown roast is made from rib sections of 2 or more loins. Both are carved in the same way. Use a standard carving set. Move garnish to side of platter where it will not interfere with the carving. Cut the stuffing and serve along with the meat slices.

1. *Hold the roast* steady by inserting the fork firmly between the ribs, Figure 1. Cut down between the ribs, allowing 1 rib to each slice.

2. *Lift the slice* with the knife blade, Figure 2, using fork to hold it steady.

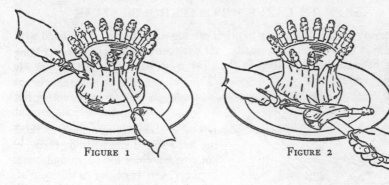

FIGURE 1   FIGURE 2

HOW TO CARVE A BLADE POT ROAST

This pot roast contains part of one rib and a portion of the blade-bone. Since this roast has had slow cooking in moist-heat, the tissues attached to the bone are softened enough for the bones to be slipped out easily before the roast is placed on the platter. Use the standard carving set or steak set.

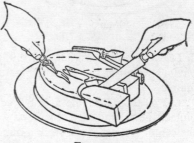

FIGURE 1

1. *Insert fork* at left of roast to hold firmly, then to remove a muscle section (white membrane separates sections), run the tip of the knife between the two muscles, then close to the bone if it has not been removed.

2. *Turn over* the section just separated so the grain of the meat is parallel with the platter. Then cut the slices across grain of the meat.

3. *Hold the section* firmly with the fork to cut slices ¼ to ⅜-inch thick. Separate remaining sections of roast, observe the direction of the fibers and slice across the grain. Serve 2 or 3 slices depending on size to each person.

FIGURE 2   FIGURE 3

HOW TO CARVE A PORTERHOUSE STEAK

The carving of steak is contrary to other carving rules, in that it is carved with the grain of the meat. This method is not only convenient, but it is very satisfactory because the meat fibers in the steak are relatively short and they are naturally tender.

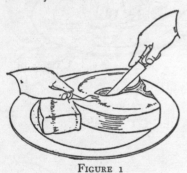

FIGURE 1

1. *Use a steak set* and insert fork at the left to hold steak firmly, then use knife to cut close to and around bone, Figure 1. Lift bone out to side of platter where it does not interfere with carving.

2. *Leave fork in* position and cut across the steak making wedge-shaped servings widest at the far side, Figure 2. Each serving is a piece of the large muscle.

3. *Cut flank end,* Figure 3, last if additional servings are wanted. *Note:* To protect the cutting edge of knife as well as platter, a board that will fit under the center section of the steak is almost a necessity.

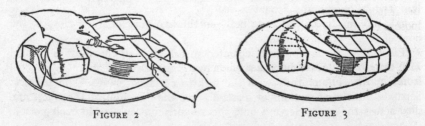

FIGURE 2   FIGURE 3

HOW TO CARVE A ROAST LEG OF LAMB

Place leg of lamb before carver so shank bone is to his right and the thick meaty section is on the far side of platter. Roasts will not always have the same surface uppermost because of the difference in the right and left legs. This, however, does not affect the method of carving. A right leg resting on the large smooth side is here illustrated. Use a standard carving set.

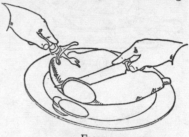

FIGURE 1

1. *Insert fork firmly* in large end of leg, Figure 1, and cut off 2 or 3 lengthwise slices from the near thin side.

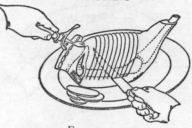

FIGURE 2

2. *Now turn the roast* so that it will rest on the just-cut flat surface, Figure 2. When in this position, the shank bone points up from platter. Insert fork into the left top side of roast. Start at shank end, cut a slice down to the leg bone. Make parallel slices until the aitch bone is reached. See dotted diagram of bone. Make slices from ¼ to ⅜-inch thick.

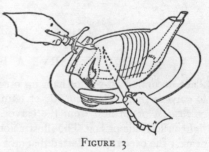

FIGURE 3

3. *Keep fork in* place and run the knife along the leg bone, Figure 3, to release all the slices.

HOW TO CARVE A PORK LOIN ROAST

The butcher separates the backbone from the ribs but leaves it attached and ties it in place to serve as a rack for roasting. As the loin roasts, the backbone loosens completely from the ribs.

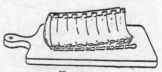

FIGURE 1

1. *Notice that* the backbone has fallen away from the ribs, Figure 1.

FIGURE 2

2. Remove the backbone by cutting between it and the rib ends, Figure 2.

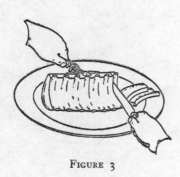

FIGURE 3

3. Place roast on platter so rib side faces carver to make it easier to follow rib bones which are the guides for slicing, Figure 3. Make sure of slant of ribs before carving, since all ribs are not perpendicular to platter. Insert fork firmly in top of roast, cut close against both sides of each rib. This makes one slice with bone and the next one without bone. Roast pork is most tempting when sliced fairly thin. In small loins, each slice may contain a rib; if loin is large, it is possible to cut 2 boneless slices between ribs. Two slices to each person is a usual serving.

HOW TO CARVE A BAKED WHOLE HAM

Place decorated fat-side of ham up on platter with shank end of ham always to carver's right. The thin side of ham from which first slices are made will be nearest or farthest from the carver, depending on whether ham is from right or left side of hog. The illustrations show a left ham with first slices cut nearest the carver. The dotted diagram shows bone structure and direction of slices. Use standard carving set or slicer and carver's helper.

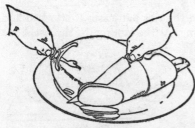

FIGURE 1

1. Insert fork as shown, Figure 1, and remove several slices parallel to length of ham on the nearest side. This makes a flat surface on which the ham can stand up firmly for carving.

2. *Turn ham up* so it rests on the just-cut flat surface, Figure 2. Hold it firmly with fork, and cut a small wedge from shank end. Remove this wedge for the succeeding slices to be more easily cut and released from the bone. Holding the fork firmly to steady the ham, cut thin slices all the way down to leg bone.

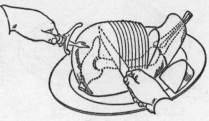

FIGURE 2

3. *Cut slices loose* from bone by running the knife along the bone at right angles to the slices, Figure 3.

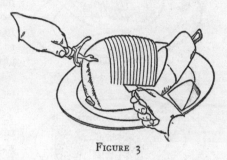

FIGURE 3

4. *To obtain more* servings, turn ham back to its original position and slice at right angles to the bone, Figure 4.

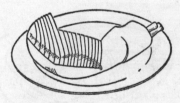

FIGURE 4

HOW TO CARVE

A CENTER HAM SLICE

1. *Cut the slice* into 3 pie-shaped sections, Figure 1. Turn one section on its side and cut slices of the desired thickness across the grain. Carve the other sections in same way, but the bone must be removed before slicing the end section.

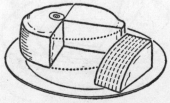

FIGURE 1

FIGURE 2

A CUSHION LAMB SHOULDER

2. This cut is easy to carve because it is boneless, Figure 2. Cut slices about ⅜-inch thick through meat and dressing.

FIGURE 3

A PICNIC HAM

3. Proceed in same way as in carving ham, Figure 3. Remove a few slices from the smaller meaty side; turn ham to stand on this flat surface. Slice down to bone, starting at shank end. Cut along bone to release slices.

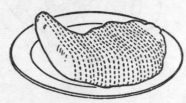

FIGURE 4

TONGUE

4. Slice off excess tissue and cartilage from large end of tongue. Continue making thin even and parallel slices, Figure 4. This gives lengthwise slices from tip end of tongue as shown in diagram.

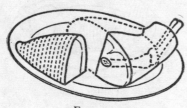

FIGURE 5

A HALF HAM

5. Slice off the cushion section and lay this section down on its cut side, Figure 5. Begin slicing at the large end. For additional servings, separate the remaining section by cutting through the joint and separating it from the shank bone. Remove bone, turn section and slice like first section.

FIGURE 6

BRISKET

6. Place on platter with round side away from carver, Figure 6. Trim off excess fat. Cut slices in rotation from 3 sides as shown in illustration. Make slices thin and at a slight angle. Carving in this way makes the cuts across the grain.

Carving Meat © National Live Stock and Meat Board, Chicago, Ill.

Pastry and Pies

If there is any Great American Dessert, one which more Americans like better than any other, it's probably pie. Fruit pies, cream pies, custard pies, chiffon pies—all have their backers for first place in this big league of favorite desserts. There is every reason why modern pies should be even better than those (of tender memory) which Grandma used to make; and there's no reason why YOURS shouldn't be better too, especially if you follow carefully the recipes in this chapter.

★ ★ ★ ★

FROM many historical accounts, we know that Americans started eating "pye" in early colonial days. These primitive "pyes" do not seem to have borne much resemblance to the dessert we know as pie today. But they must have been enjoyed, or homemakers would not have kept on making them generation after generation. As a result of this long pie-making experience by generations of good cooks, pie has improved considerably in form and quality, and the variety has increased tremendously.

Today, pie is one of the most popular of all desserts in this country. Excellent pie is served all over the land, from the smallest hamlet to the biggest city. And the variety is no longer dependent on the season. Now we eat pumpkin pie the year round, and with high-quality frozen and canned foods available everywhere, we can enjoy almost any kind of pie we please any day of the year. The type of pie obtainable, however, depends on the tastes of the eaters. Fruit pies, custard pies, cream pies, chiffon pies and angel pies all have their partisans.

Praise-winning pie may be of almost any variety, but one thing it always has is good pastry. Good pastry must be beautifully browned, tender, flaky and good in flavor. Equally important is the filling, which must be ample in quantity, delicious in flavor, true in color, and of the right consistency. The skill required to make such pies demands study, observation of other good pie makers at work, and much practice. Given these, in addition to the fine foods and excellent equipment that are available nowadays, there is no reason why today's cooks cannot make even better pie than their accomplished mothers and grandmothers.

WHAT MAKES GOOD PASTRY?

The ability to make good pastry every time, and not just now and then, is one of the severest tests of a good cook. To be able to do this, one of the first requirements is to learn to recognize what good pastry is.

Good baked pastry appears fragile, and has a blistery surface which indicates that it will be flaky when cut. It is tender and easily cut with a fork, but not so tender that pressure of the fork will crumble it into meal-like particles. Its color is a delicate, even golden-brown, which is slightly deeper at the edge. And it is as crisp and fragile on the bottom of the pie as at the rim.

The quality of pastry depends on the technique of the maker to the extent that two persons can work with exactly the same ingredients, the same recipe, and the same equipment, and obtain completely different products. One pastry may turn out perfect in shape, evenly browned, tender, flaky and crisp; the other may be irregular in shape, blotchy in color, compact, tough and hard. The only difference between the two crusts is the manner of handling the ingredients. Ingredients must be mixed just enough and no more. The pastry must be rolled with a light hand and with a minimum of handling. The technique of good pastry making, simple as it is, may be difficult for some people to learn; but once learned, it is like the techniques of swimming or knitting, almost impossible to forget.

Aside from the actual technique of handling, there are only two fundamental requirements for making good pastry: (1) Suitable ingredients accurately measured according to a good recipe; and (2) an understanding of the reason for each of the directions in the recipe, so that the proper methods of mixing, rolling and baking will be put into practice.

WHAT IS THE FUNCTION OF EACH PASTRY INGREDIENT?

Perhaps because pastry ingredients are so few—only four—it is especially important that each one be of the right type and accurately measured.

Flour forms the framework of pastry; it is the ingredient that makes up the bulk of the pastry. An all-purpose flour of good quality is best for pastry. Bread flour contains more gluten, and makes a heavier, tougher pastry than does all-purpose flour, unless the pastry is handled by an expert, and with extra care. Cake flour contains less gluten, and makes pastry which tends to be very tender and crumbly; in addition it costs more than all-purpose flour and is not practical for this reason.

An excess of flour, of whatever kind, makes pastry dry, hard and tough. Too little flour makes it sticky or greasy and difficult to handle. To be sure of getting exactly the same amount of flour every time pastry is made, *flour should always be sifted before measuring.* Flour packs during shipping and storing; its compactness depends on how long it has stood and how it has been handled. A cup of flour, unsifted, contains more or less flour depending on its compactness. Uniform products cannot be obtained from ingredients that vary in their measurements. Sifting before measuring, however, produces flour of uniform compactness and permits accurate measurement.

Salt is an essential ingredient in pastry because the other ingredients are all bland in flavor. Salt gives the "lift" that these ingredients need. A slightly salty flavor in plain pastry is pleasing with any type of pie filling. In addition, salt improves the color of pastry. If salt is accidentally left out, the pastry is not only flat in flavor but also pale.

Shortening is used to make pastry tender and flaky. Firm, bland-flavored shortening such as vegetable fat or hydrogenated lard is best for general pastry making, but other fats may be used for variation in flavor. Cold, rendered chicken fat, for example, makes delicious pastry for chicken pies or turnovers, or for fish or meat pies. Butter also gives a particularly pleasing flavor and a beautiful brown color to pastry; but butter contains water and milk solids in addition to fat, so butter pastry is never quite so tender as pastry made with shortening which is 100% fat. The same thing is true of pastry made with margarine. Oil is sometimes used, but it produces a different type of pastry than solid shortening. Oil pastry is very tender, but as a rule it is crumbly rather than flaky, though special handling can still produce flaky pastry when oil is used.

Too much shortening makes pastry greasy, crumbly and difficult to handle; too little makes it solid, hard and tough. Accurate measurement of shortening requires use of cups specially designed to measure dry ingredients. The shortening should be firmly pressed in, eliminating air pockets, and then leveled off with a straight-edged knife. Two-thirds to ¾ cup of shortening to each 2 cups of flour is a good proportion.

Water is used to bind and hold together the blended flour-shortening mixture. It should be ice-cold for the best results (although there is an excellent "hot water pastry" with which many beginners are able to obtain good results more easily than by using ice water). The exact amount of water required for a good pastry varies slightly with the season of the year, dryness of the flour, room temp, and humidity. Under normal atmospheric conditions, about ½ cup ice water is required for pastry made with 2 cups of flour. Too much water makes pastry wet and sticky, requiring use of extra flour for rolling, which in turn toughens the product. Too little water will not bind the flour-coated shortening particles enough to hold them together, so the pastry frays or cracks at the edges during rolling instead of rolling into a smooth, even-textured circle. An experienced pastry maker is able to judge when just enough water has been added.

Milk is sometimes used instead of water; it produces pastry that browns beautifully but tends to be less tender than that made with water. Chilled orange and lemon juice may also be used instead of water.

USE SIZE OF PAN THAT FITS BOTH CRUST AND FILLING

Almost all the following recipes are for 8 and 9-inch pies. An 8-inch pie is suitable to serve 4 or 5 people at one meal or 2 or 3 people at 2 meals. A

9-inch pie 6 or 8 people one meal or 3 or 4 people 2 meals. The longer wedges of a 9-inch pie look more attractive on the average size pie plate than the short wedges of an 8-inch pie. The pans used in our pie recipe development work were 1¼ inches deep, because these are the kind made nowadays by most manufacturers. Shallower pans made in aluminum or tin are often available in the dime stores. When using such pans remember that when they are lined with pastry, they will only take about ⅔ of the filling needed for a pan that is 1¼ inches deep.

THE IMPORTANCE OF PIE PAN MATERIAL

The material of which the pan is made also needs to be carefully considered. Glass, enamelware and aluminum pans with a dull finish brown pies on the bottom best. Pans that are very shiny do not bake pies well on the bottom because the shiny metal deflects the heat rays away from the pastry. Pans with black bottoms bake pies well and tin pans that have been used for some time or new empty tin pans that have been heated in a hot oven for a few hours until their shininess changes to a dull, frost-like pattern surface bake pies quite well.

WHY IS IT SO IMPORTANT TO *UNDERSTAND* DIRECTIONS FOR MAKING PASTRY?

Next to having good ingredients and a good recipe to follow, the technique of mixing the pastry is the most important part of pastry-making. Detailed and illustrated directions for making plain pastry are presented on the following pages. The method of combining the ingredients is based on the experience of successful pastry makers, and upon knowledge of the physical properties of the ingredients and their effect on each other. The directions are not arbitrary; there is a sound reason for each step, and understanding what the reasons are makes it easier to follow the directions so as to make good pastry every time.

Study carefully the detailed directions which follow the table of plain pastry ingredients below.

PLAIN PASTRY

PLAIN PASTRY INGREDIENTS FOR 2-CRUST PIE OF 3 DIFFERENT SIZES*

	For 9-inch pie	For 8-inch pie	For 6-inch pie
Flour	2 cups all-purpose	1½ cups all-purpose	1 cup all-purpose
Salt	1 tsp	¾ tsp	½ tsp
Shortening**	⅔ to ¾ cup	7 tbsp to ½ cup	⅓ cup to 6 tbsp
Ice water	½ cup	⅓ cup	¼ cup

*See p 928 for ingredients for single crust.
**If regular lard is the shortening, use the smaller amount; if a vegetable shortening, use the larger amount.

STEPS IN MAKING PLAIN PASTRY FOR A 2-CRUST PIE

Step 1. Assemble all ingredients. Assemble equipment: 3-qt mixing bowl, sifter, pastry blender, fork, measuring cups and spoons, paring knife, straight-edged knife or spatula, scissors, pastry cloth, rolling pin covered with stockinet, and pie plate. (Nested measuring cups—1 cup, ½, ⅓, and ¼ cup measures—should be used for measuring shortening and flour, filling them to the brim and leveling off with a straight-edged knife. The displacement method of obtaining, say, ⅓ cup of shortening by filling a graduated cup measure ⅔ full of water and then adding enough shortening to bring the water to the 1-cup mark, may be inaccurate because the shortening often encloses large air pockets which cause short-measuring.)

Step 2. Sift flour once onto waxed paper to eliminate packing and assure accurate measurements. Lift the sifted flour lightly into the cup with a spoon or wide spatula until it is heaped up; then level top with spatula or a straight-edged knife. Never shake the cup to level the flour, as this causes packing and inaccurate measurements. Turn flour immediately into mixing bowl.

Step 3. Dip measuring spoon into salt and level off with straight-edged knife; add to flour and stir it in thoroughly.

Step 4. Measure firm shortening by pressing it down well into cup of required size (use ⅓-cup measure when ⅔ cup shortening is required, or ¼-cup and ½-cup measure for ¾ cup shortening). Air pockets should be pressed out. Heap up slightly and level off with a straight-edged knife. Use a rubber scraper to remove the shortening cleanly from the cup; turn it into the flour.

Step 5. Cut shortening into the flour with a wire pastry blender or 2 knives, until the particles range in size from rice grains to navy beans. (Skilled pastry makers often rub it in with the fingers, but this may be difficult for beginners to do successfully.) The object is to divide the shortening into small particles, each coated with flour. It is these flour-coated particles of shortening which produce flakiness in the baked crust. The mixture should not appear oily or wet. If it does, the shortening has become too warm, perhaps through working too slowly, and has coated the flour instead of remaining in solid particles to be coated by it. When this occurs, a very small amount of water is required to bind the ingredients together, and a greasy, crumbly pastry will result. The wire blender is the quickest, easiest and most dependable tool to use to prevent warming of the ingredients.

Step 6. With the left hand, use a spoon or a clothes sprinkler to sprinkle over the flour-shortening mixture about a tbsp of ice water at a time. At the same time, toss the dampened particles together and to one side with a fork held in the other hand. Continue to sprinkle and toss until all the flour-shortening particles are uniformly moistened and will barely stick together. (Slightly more or less water may be needed, depending on atmospheric and other conditions.)

Step 7. Tip the bowl slightly and with the other hand gently press the pastry together into a ball; use this ball to clean the bowl of dry particles. Avoid overhandling the pastry after adding water. Let pastry ball stand 5 to 10 min for easy handling. In hot weather, wrap it in waxed paper and chill in the refrigerator for half an hr.

Step 8. While pastry rests or chills, prepare fruit filling as required. (For a fresh cherry pie, cherries should be pitted ahead of time.) The following amounts will be required:

For a 9-inch pie . . . . 4 cups prepared fruit
For an 8-inch pie . . . . 2⅔ cups prepared fruit
For a 6-inch pie . . . . 1⅔ cups prepared fruit

Step 9. Prepare pastry cloth and stockinet-covered rolling pin. Lay the cloth on a smooth-topped table or over a large dough board. Sift flour in a thin, uniform layer over the cloth and rub in well, using palm of hand. Sift on more flour and roll in with rolling pin. Enough flour should be worked in at the beginning to leave just a trace of flour on the surface after the rubbing and rolling-in process. The pastry cloth and stockinet are recommended for rolling pastry for several reasons:

1. They have rougher surfaces than a flour-dusted dough board, and these grip the pastry and hold it in position during rolling. This reduces the alternate stretching and shrinking which develops gluten, produce toughness and an irregular shaped crust.
2. They make it possible to roll pastry out more quickly, thus reducing risk of over-manipulation.
3. They reduce chance of sticking because they absorb and hold flour. (If sticking does occur, loosen the pastry gently with a spatula, lift it carefully, and rub in a little more flour where the sticking occurred before continuing the rolling.)

Step 10. Cut the ball of pastry into 2 portions, one slightly larger than the other. For the bottom crust, place larger piece cut side down on the floured pastry cloth. Gently press it out into a flat disc with hand or rolling pin. Place rolling pin in center of disc and roll *outward* with light even pressure. For each rolling stroke, start at the center and roll *outwards only.* Roll in *all* directions to produce a smooth-edged circle. Rolling pastry stretches the gluten, and if stretched more in one direction than another, it will tend to spring back, producing an irregularly shaped (and a less tender) crust. Rolling lightly from center to edge in all directions stretches it evenly. If edges of circle fray or crack, pull edges of cracks together overlapping them, or patch with pieces of pastry; then roll until repairs disappear. The pastry should be rolled into a smooth circle of even thickness (⅛ inch or a trifle less) in order to brown evenly; the diameter should be 1¼ inches greater than that of the pie pan. Hold the pie pan over the pastry to determine the right size.

Work quickly in rolling and do not add more flour unless absolutely necessary, because extra flour toughens pastry. In rolling, the flour-coated particles of shortening become flattened and form layers in the pastry; during baking these layers of fat melt and produce the puffs and flakes in the baked pastry which are the aim of every pastry maker.

Step 11. Now fold the pastry carefully through the center, and quickly lift it into the *ungreased* pie pan so the fold is across the center of the pan. The center fold makes it easy to center the pastry without pulling, and the double thickness of pastry is easier to move without cracking than the single circle.

Step 12. Unfold the pastry, being careful not to stretch it, and let it fall loosely into the pan's angles. Lift edges gently by slipping the hand underneath, and ease the pastry into the shape of the pan, fitting it down by running the bent forefinger of the other hand around the inside angle. Pastry should fit the pan snugly at all points. The angles where the sides of the pan meet the bottom are spots where pastry is likely not to fit, causing distortion of shape in baking.

Step 13. If bread crumbs are used (check the fruit or berry pie recipe you are using), sift them over the bottom of the pastry in the pan. Then cover with waxed paper and let pastry rest 5 to 10 min. This resting period allows gluten which was stretched in rolling to relax, and reduces shrinking greatly.

Step 14. Meanwhile, roll out remaining portion of pastry in the same way, to form a circle of uniform thickness, about ½ inch smaller in diameter than the first one. It should be no thinner, for a thin top crust soaks up the juice more readily and may take on the color of the juice, producing a wet-appearing and unsightly top crust.

Step 15. Gash the top crust to form an open design exactly in the center. Be sure the gashes open, for these are the steam vents; if they are not wide open, the boiling juice will close them before baking is finished, and the steam pressure that builds up will break the crust at its weakest point—usually around the edge. If the gashes are too close to the edge, juice is almost sure to run out over the rim. After gashing, leave the pastry on the pastry cloth, covering it with waxed paper or a slightly dampened towel to prevent drying out while finishing preparation of the filling. At this time adjust rack 4 or 5 inches above bottom of oven; start oven and set to hot (450° F).

Step 16. Finish preparation of fruit (check specific recipes for method and quantity needed). Measure and blend flour or cornstarch, sugar and salt. Sift ¼ of the mixture over crumbs in pastry-lined pan.

Step 17. Trim off pastry in pan flush with the pan rim, using a sharp paring knife to cut it cleanly.

Step 18. Turn fruit carefully into bottom crust, and spread out gently into a layer of even compactness, fairly smooth, and slightly rounded up. Dot with butter and sprinkle rest of flour and sugar mixture evenly over the top. (Some recipes call for folding this sugar-flour mixture gently through fruit before turning into the pan.)

Step 19. Moisten edge of lower pastry with cold water, using finger or pastry brush.

Step 20. Fold top pastry through center, lift carefully and place with fold across center of filling. Unfold gently and press down lightly at rim to seal. Use scissors to trim off edge of top crust ½ inch beyond pan rim.

Step 21. Fold the overhanging edge of top pastry under edge of bottom crust so fold is even with pan rim all around. Again press around rim to seal.

Step 22. Crimp edge with tines of fork, or flute with fingers for a stand-up edge. To keep rim from becoming browner than rest of pastry in baking, cover it with an inch-wide strip of moistened cloth before baking; remove when done.

PLAIN PASTRY INGREDIENTS FOR A SINGLE-CRUST PASTRY SHELL OF 3 DIFFERENT SIZES

For 9-inch pie	For 8-inch pie	For 6-inch pie
1 cup all-purpose flour	⅞ cup all-purpose flour	⅔ cup all-purpose flour
½ tsp salt	Scant ½ tsp salt	⅓ tsp salt
⅓ cup to 6 tbsp shortening*	4½ tbsp to ⅓ cup shortening	¼ cup to 5 tbsp shortening
¼ cup ice water	3⅓ tbsp ice water	3 tbsp ice water

For 2-crust pie recipe, see p 924.

*If regular lard is the shortening, use the smaller amount; if a vegetable shortening, use the larger amount.

STEPS IN MAKING PLAIN PASTRY FOR BAKED SINGLE-CRUST SHELLS

Step 1—To make a plain pastry shell follow steps 1 to 12 inclusive for making pastry for 2-crust pie, pp 924 to 928, but roll out all the pastry to make one single shell. After lining the pie pan carefully with pastry, let it rest 5 min to relax.

Step 2—Use scissors to trim off edge of pastry ½-inch beyond pan rim.

Step 3—Fold overhanging pastry under evenly so folded edge extends slightly beyond pan rim all around. A slight extension is desirable to compensate for a little shrinking in baking. This thicker edge makes a more attractive pie because it prevents the pastry from becoming too brown around the rim and facilitates cutting and serving of pie into neater wedges.

Step 4—Let pastry rest a few min, then flute edge by using *a plain handle of a metal knife* to make indentations on inside and two fingers of the hand to press pastry up around knife handle. The same kind of edge can be made by using a finger instead of a knife handle. Make sure that fluted edge when finished is even with pan rim.

Step 5—Prick bottom and sides of pastry shell thoroughly with a fork, wiggling fork tines back and forth to make wide-open holes. This keeps pastry from puffing up and warping during baking. Bake on center rack of a moderately hot oven (425° F) 15 to 18 min or until shell is a light golden color all over. After 5 min of baking look at pastry shell and quickly collapse any bubbles by pricking. Remove pastry shell to cake rack to cool thoroughly out of draft in pan. It is now ready for the cooked fillings made according to the recipes in this book.

HOW TO MAKE PASTRY SHELLS FOR CUSTARD, PUMPKIN, PECAN PIES, ETC.

Follow exactly the first 4 steps for a *plain* pastry *single-crust shell*. But *do not prick pastry*. If shell is pricked, the thin custard will run through the holes and spoil both crust and filling.

HOW TO MAKE CHEESE PASTRY FOR APPLE OR CHERRY PIE

Step 1—To ingredients in the *Plain Pastry Recipe* for a 9-inch pie, p 924, add 1 tbsp more of shortening.

Step 2—Combine flour, salt and shortening with a pastry blender, then stir in ⅓ cup grated sharp cheese. Now add the ice water and roll out dough in the same way as in plain pastry.

HOW TO MAKE CHEESE PASTRY FOR SOUP AND SALAD

Use leftover plain pastry scraps to make this pastry. Lay scraps out flat one on top of the other. Fold them together (no kneading) into a thick rectangular shape. Place on pastry cloth and roll into a rectangular shape about ⅛-inch thick. For enough pastry to line an 8-inch pie pan, have ready ⅓ cup grated sharp cheese. Sprinkle half the cheese over half the pastry evenly. Fold the other half of pastry over cheese and again roll out to ⅛-inch thick. Sprinkle on rest of cheese, and fold again, and again roll out into a rectangle about 7-inches wide. Cut into neat strips about ⅜-inch wide and 7-inches long. Lay strips flat on an un-greased baking sheet, or twist strips to put 2 or 3 waves in them, then press them down at both ends so they will stick to baking sheet and keep their shape. Bake on middle rack in a moderately hot oven (400° F) for 6 to 8 min or to a delicate golden brown, watching carefully to prevent scorching. Serve hot or cold, but if cold, serve while fresh and crisp.

CREAM CHEESE OR COTTAGE CHEESE PASTRY

1⅓ cups all-purpose flour   4½ oz soft cream cheese *or*
¼ tsp salt   creamed cottage cheese
½ cup butter

Sift flour, measure and resift with salt into a 2-qt mixing bowl. Add butter and cheese and with pastry blender cut together until well blended. Gather together and press into a ball. Wrap in waxed paper and chill over night. Roll and use like plain pastry. Bake in moderately hot oven (425° F).

CRUMB PASTRY SHELLS

These shells are easy to make, are attractive, interesting in texture, delicious and nutritious. They are especially appropriate for cream and chiffon pies to be stored for a few hrs in the refrigerator. For complete satisfaction, the flavor of filling should harmonize perfectly with that of the shell. A graham cracker shell, for example, is delicious with an eggnog, cream, lemon cream or lime chiffon filling. A vanilla wafer shell is good with lemon, coffee or chocolate chiffon filling. A gingersnap shell goes well with a cream or lemon filling. The flavor of these shells will be just as good as that of the ingredients used. So use only fresh, sweet-flavored butter and fresh crisp graham crackers, vanilla wafers, zwieback, rusks, gingersnaps or freshly dried bread.

BREAD CRUMB PASTRY SHELL

For 9-inch shell

⅓ cup soft butter *or* margarine
¼ cup light brown sugar, pkd

1⅓ cups fine dry bread crumbs, lightly pkd
1 tsp cinnamon
¼ cup finely chopped nuts

See steps below for making shell.

GINGER-SNAP PASTRY SHELL

For 9-inch shell

1⅓ cups ginger-snap crumbs, a little over ¼ lb

⅓ cup soft butter *or* margarine
Dash of salt

See steps below for making shell.

GRAHAM CRACKER PASTRY SHELL

For 9-inch shell

1⅓ cups graham cracker crumbs, 16 or 18 crackers

⅓ cup soft butter *or* margarine
3 tbsp sugar

See steps below for making shell.

VANILLA WAFER PASTRY SHELL

For 9-inch shell

1⅓ cups vanilla wafer crumbs,   ¼ cup soft butter *or*
   about 3 oz   margarine

See steps below for making shell.

CHOCOLATE COOKIE PASTRY SHELL

For 9-inch shell

1½ cups chocolate cookie   ⅓ cup soft butter *or*
   crumbs   margarine

See steps below for making shell.

STEPS IN MAKING CRUMB PASTRY SHELLS

Step 1—Be sure bread, snaps, crackers or cookies are crisp. Lay them in a clean brown paper bag of good size, close end and roll crumbs fine with a rolling pin. Or, lay between folds of heavy waxed or parchment paper and roll crumbs fine throughout. Or, best of all, put broken dried bread or whole crackers or cookies into a food mill and press them through into a bowl. This method we like best because it is quick, not messy and crumbs drop directly into a bowl. Measure crumbs, slightly pkd, and turn into a 2-qt glass or pottery mixing bowl.

Step 2—Stir in all dry ingredients called for, then add butter which has been softened to room temp.

Step 3—Mix thoroughly with hand until a little of the mixture squeezed firmly in the hand packs enough to hold together.

Step 4—Turn mixture into a pie pan, preferably glass or aluminum. Use back of a tbsp to spread crumbs out level over bottom and a little thicker up sides of pan. Use the flat bottom of a glass tumbler to smooth out the mixture over bottom, then press glass down firmly all over bottom to pack crumbs into a little more than ⅛-inch evenly thick crust. Use tbsp to pack crumbs firmly into angles of pan and up sides so crust will be about same thickness as on bottom. The sides of glass can now be used to roll carefully but firmly around sides of pan to further smooth and firm crust. Use hands to finish molding crust firmly around rim and make it slightly rounded and at least ¼ inch thick for easier cutting and serving of pie.

Step 5—Place shell in refrigerator to chill 4 or 5 hrs. This is a practical way to handle shell when a cold filling is poured into it, is chilled again then spread with whipped cream. Or, for a firmer crust, place freshly shaped crust into a preheated moderate oven (375° F) and bake 8 to 10 min. Or for a pie to be covered with meringue, pour cold filling into the freshly shaped crust, spread on meringue in usual way, then bake in a slow oven (300° F) for 20 min or in a moderate oven (350° F) 15 min to brown meringue. Remove to cake rack to cool to room temp before cutting pie. Do not place pie with meringue in refrigerator before the first serving. Meringue covered pie has its best appearance and eating quality when cooled at room temp. Leftover pie must of course be refrigerated for safe keeping.

Note: A little of the same crumb mixture used to make the crust sprinkled over the meringue before it is browned or over pie spread with whipped cream, adds a rich attractive touch. If this is desired, increase graham cracker crumbs in recipe to 1½ cups and butter to 6 tbsp, then reserve ½ cup of the crumb mixture to sprinkle over the meringue or cream.

HOT WATER PASTRY FOR A 9 OR 10-INCH 2-CRUST PIE

⅔ cup shortening   2½ cups all-purpose flour
7 tbsp boiling water   1 tsp salt

Step 1—Measure shortening into a 3-qt mixing bowl. Use measuring tbsp to dip water from kettle that is actually boiling onto shortening.

Step 2—With a fork beat together until mixture is smooth, creamy and cooled.

Step 3—Sift flour, measure, resift with salt into the shortening-water mixture and with a fork stir until well mixed.

Step 4—Shape into a ball and proceed as for *Plain Pastry for 2-Crust Pie,* dividing pastry into 2 portions, one a little larger than the other, or divide in half for 2 single-crust pastry shells then follow steps for making the 2-crust pie or single-crust shells.

MASHED POTATO PASTRY

Good for meat, chicken, fish pies or turnovers

½ cup unseasoned fresh-   ½ tsp salt
    mashed potatoes, no salt,   ½ tsp sugar
    pepper, butter *or* milk   ⅓ cup *plus* 1 tbsp shortening
1 cup all-purpose flour

Measure just-cooled potatoes—slightly pkd—and turn into a 3-qt mixing bowl. Sift flour, measure and resift with salt and sugar over potatoes. Use a fork to mix ingredients until consistency of corn meal. Add shortening and with pastry blender or 2 knives cut it into the potato-flour mixture until particles are size of rice grains. Gather together and press gently into a ball. Wrap in waxed paper and chill ½ hr. Then place pastry ball onto pastry cloth and shape into a flat disc or sq. Roll out into a circle or sq about ⅛-inch thick. Cut into circles of needed size to cover tops of individual casseroles (filled with hot chicken or meat mixture). Or make cardboard oval pattern 8 inches long and 4 inches wide and lay on pastry and cut out ovals to make meat or fish turnovers. Or roll into a 9 or 10 inch circle to cover a large round casserole. For either individual or large casserole, cut circle of pastry so it will extend ½ inch beyond rim. Then fold overhanging pastry under so fold is even with rim of dish. Flute edge of pastry or crimp with tines of a fork. Cut a few gashes in center of pastry on casserole or turnovers for steam vents. Bake in a moderate oven (400° F) 15 or 18 min, or until golden brown and the mixture bubbles up through vents.

PART WHOLE WHEAT PASTRY

For two 9-inch single pastry shells or one 9-inch double crust pie

1 cup whole wheat flour
1 cup all-purpose flour
1 tsp salt
½ cup *plus* 2 tbsp lard *or*

¾ cup hydrogenated vegetable shortening
About ⅓ cup ice water

Step 1—Spoon whole wheat flour lightly into cup to measure. Turn into 3-qt mixing bowl. Sift all-purpose flour, measure and turn into bowl. Stir in salt.

Step 2—Cut shortening into flour mixture, add ice water and mix and proceed as for Plain Pastry to make either a double-crust pie or 2 single-crust shells.

PASTRY FOR DESSERT DUMPLINGS

A special pastry recipe is required for apple, peach or berry dumplings as more pastry is needed than for a 9-inch double-crust pie

2½ cups all-purpose flour
½ tsp baking powder
½ tsp salt
1 tsp sugar

⅔ cup shortening
½ cup ice water *or* cold milk, about

Sift flour, measure and sift twice with next three ingredients, the last time into a 2-qt mixing bowl. Add shortening and cut in with pastry blender until particles are size of peas. Drizzle in water or milk and toss with fork to dampen in same manner as for pie pastry. Shape into a ball, then pat into a neat rectangular shape on a *well-floured* pastry cloth. Roll out carefully into a generous 14 x 21-inch rectangle. Trim off ragged edges. Cut rectangle in half lengthwise, then in thirds crosswise, making six 7-inch neat sqs. See special recipes for making fruit dumplings.

Note: For a fancy finish to dumplings, stack the trimmed-off pieces of pastry on top of each other and roll out. Cut out with a 1½ to 2-inch scalloped cookie cutter. Brush top of dumplings with Egg Yolk Wash, p 935, then lay cut-outs on top of dumplings. Prick or gash for steam vents.

PUFF PASTRY

This is the kind used for making those glamorous French pastries such as Patty Shells, Roses, Vol-au-vents, Cream Horns, Napoleon Slices and

Apple Turnovers described below. When baked, these pastries are fragile and feather-light and when broken apart, they show tissue-paper thin layers upon layers which are the result of rolling firm butter as thin as possible between many layers of dough. The flavor is rich yet delicate because of the butter. When filled or iced with some delicious mixture, these are superlative cookery creations.

PUFF PASTRY INGREDIENTS

1 cup butter	½ cup *plus* 2 tbsp ice water
1¾ cups all-purpose flour	

STEPS IN MAKING PUFF PASTRY

Step 1—Remove 1 tbsp of butter and chill in refrigerator. Put rest of butter in a 2-qt mixing bowl and work with hand until as pliable as putty. Should butter show signs of melting (beginning to look oily) rinse hand in very cold water from time to time. When butter is pliable, shape into a ½-inch thick sq. Wrap in waxed paper and chill until very firm in coldest place in refrigerator.

Step 2—Sift flour, measure and turn into the cleaned, dried 2-qt bowl.

Step 3—Add the 1 tbsp butter to flour and with pastry blender or finger tips, work it into flour until consistency is like corn meal.

Step 4—Add ice water gradually, mixing with fork to form a stiff dough.

Step 5—Turn dough onto a lightly floured board and knead hard for 5 min to obtain a very smooth, plastic ball. Grease ball of dough, then cut a deep cross in top of ball and place it on dough board, cover with a damp towel and let rest 30 min at room temp.

Step 6—Spread dough ball out by opening up the 4 points made by the cut and lay them out flat. This changes the shape of the dough ball to a rectangle.

Step 7—Next place the chilled sq of butter in center of rectangle and stretch and pat out dough keeping shape rectangular until it is large enough to fold over from both ends to completely cover and enclose the butter. The shape of this folded dough is still rectangular. Now roll this folded dough out on a slightly floured board to a rectangle about ¼-inch thick. Cover with a damp towel and let rest 10 min.

Step 8—Now (being sure to brush off any excess flour before folding) fold one short end of rectangle over one-third the length of the rectangle, then bring the other end up over the first fold to make 3 equal layers of dough. Now turn this folded dough ¼ the way around and fold the open ends over in the same way to make 9 layers. Wrap in waxed paper or damp cloth and chill 1 hr.

Step 9—Repeat three times, the process of rolling chilled dough out to the original rectangle size and ¼-inch thick, keeping corners sq and edges straight, each time folding into 9 layers as in Step 8 and chilling after each folding. If pastry is to be kept several days (and it can be), wrap well and snugly in waxed paper and store in the coldest place in refrigerator but never in contact with ice.

HINTS ON HANDLING PUFF PASTRY

Hint 1—Baking sheets on which puff pastries are baked should have a thin film of cold moisture all over them when the shaped raw pastries are placed on them. To obtain the cold moist film, run cold water on pans then shake off excess. In large sheets of pastry such as Napoleon Slices, the cold dampness prevents excessive shrinking.

Hint 2—To use scraps left over after cutting out the pastry shapes, lay one on top of the other and fold carefully into a ball rather than knead into ball. Wrap in waxed paper and chill. Roll and fold and chill again before shaping for baking. Puff pastry should always rest before rolling to make rolling easy, and it should also rest after it is shaped, before baking, to prevent shrinking. In hot weather, the resting should be done in the refrigerator. In cold weather it can be done at room temp.

EGG YOLK WASH FOR BRUSHING OVER
FRENCH PASTRIES

1 egg yolk   2 tbsp milk

Beat yolk well, stir in milk until thoroughly blended.

EGG WHITE WASH FOR BRUSHING OVER SOME
FRENCH PASTRIES

1 egg white   1 tsp water

Combine egg white and water and beat slightly.

APPLE TURNOVERS

Puff Pastry, p 934   Egg Yolk Wash, above
3 cups finely chopped tart   Egg White Wash, above
  apples*   xxxx sugar
½ to ⅔ cup sugar, depending
  on apple tartness

Start oven 10 min before baking; set to hot (450° F). Use about ¼ of the Puff Pastry at a time. Roll out on a pastry cloth ¼-inch thick. Cut into rounds with a 3-inch biscuit cutter. Let rounds rest 10 min. Meanwhile pare, core and chop apples. Mix with the sugar. Prepare egg

*Any other tart-flavored fruit may be used.

yolk and egg white wash. Now roll pastry rounds in center only enough to change the round to a 9-inch long oval shape. Heap on ½ of the oval the sweetened apples. Fold the other half of oval over the apples. Press gently to make sure of sealing all around the cut edges. Brush top with egg yolk wash. Place turnovers on a dampened baking sheet. Cover with damp towel and let rest 30 min. Bake 20 min, then remove from oven and quickly brush with egg white mixture and sprinkle with xxxx sugar. Quickly return to oven and bake 5 min longer or to a rich golden color.

CREAM HORNS

Puff Pastry, p 934　　　　　　Cream Filling for Cream
Egg Yolk Wash, p 935　　　　Puffs, p 397
Egg White Wash, p 935　　　 *or* whipping cream
Granulated sugar

Start oven 10 min before baking; set to hot (450° F). Use about ¼ of the Puff Pastry at a time. Roll it out on a pastry cloth ⅛-inch thick, keeping shape rectangular and about 8-inches wide. Brush dough with egg yolk wash. Now cut into strips ½-inch wide. Roll these strips around metal cream horn forms,* overlapping edges slightly. Lay on cold dampened sheet to rest 30 min. Then bake 20 min or until well puffed and lightly browned. Quickly remove from oven, quickly brush with egg white wash, sprinkle with sugar and return to oven to finish baking or about 5 min longer. Remove from oven, then remove horns from forms and cool on cake rack. When cool, fill with the cream filling or sweetened whipped cream flavored with vanilla if desired.

CREAM PUFFS

Chou Paste

½ cup butter, 1 stick　　　　　1 cup all-purpose flour
1 cup boiling water　　　　　　4 eggs, unbeaten

Grease a baking sheet 15½ x 11-inch; start oven 10 min before baking; set to hot (450° F).

Put butter in a 3-qt saucepan. Pour boiling water over butter; heat just to boiling stirring until butter melts. Sift flour, measure and add all at once to butter mixture. Stir constantly with a wooden spoon until mixture leaves sides of pan and forms a ball. Remove from heat. Immediately add eggs one at a time, beating to a smooth paste after each. Then beat mixture until smooth and velvety. Drop by heaping tbsp onto a baking sheet, keeping about 3 inches apart. Bake 15 min or until well

*If the metal forms are not available, a handy person can make good home-made ones by cutting triangles from bright, shiny tin cans with heavy metal shears and then carefully shaping them into cones which will serve the purpose nicely.

puffed and delicately browned. Then reduce heat to slow (300° F) and bake 30 or 40 min longer; this cooks centers thoroughly, but puffs become no browner. Remove to cake rack to cool. When cold, cut off tops with a sharp knife. Fill with Cream Filling, p 397, whipped cream into which is folded sweetened strawberries or raspberries and blueberries, or ice cream, hot creamed chicken or any creamed fish and replace tops. 12 to 14 cream puffs.

SWAN CREAM PUFFS

To make the swan neck and head, pipe the cream puff mixture through a large pastry tube, using a large star tip, onto the greased baking sheet in the shape of an S; for the tail, pipe a comma-shaped piece. Make a "tail" and a "head" for each puff and remove from oven after baking 15 min. After filling cream puffs, insert a head and a tail in each swan, cutting holes if necessary. The tops that have been cut off to admit filling may be cut in two and replaced to simulate lifted wings.

ÉCLAIRS

Make just like Cream Puffs above except draw out the heaping tbsp of dough dropped onto the baking sheet into finger shapes. Bake, cool and fill as for Cream Puffs. Frost tops of filled éclairs with Dark Chocolate Frosting, p 385.

NAPOLEON SLICES OR PETIT WEIVA

Puff Pastry, p 934   ½ cup xxxx sugar
Cream Filling, p 397   2 tbsp boiling water

Start oven 10 min before baking; set to moderately hot (425° F). Use about ¼ of the Puff Pastry at a time, leaving rest in refrigerator until needed. Roll dough out on pastry cloth that has practically no flour on its surface to a rectangular shape about ⅛-inch thick. Lift pastry onto a cookie sheet that has had cold water run over it and excess water shaken off. Prick the pastry well all over with a fork. Chill until dough is very stiff. Bake 12 to 15 min or to a delicate golden brown. Remove to a cake rack to cool on pan, then cut in 3 crosswise strips. Lay one of strips on a flat bottom platter. Spread Cream Filling generously on this strip, top with 2nd layer and spread with more Cream Filling. Top with 3rd layer. Now make a glaze by mixing the xxxx sugar and boiling water. Drizzle in a thin stream all over the top. Chill until filling is firm, then cut carefully into rectangular strips to serve.

PATTY SHELLS

Puff Pastry, p 934   **Egg Yolk Wash, p 935**

Use about ¼ of the Puff Pastry at a time, leaving rest in refrigerator until needed. Roll dough out on a pastry cloth that has practically no flour on its surface ¼-inch thick. Cut out rounds with a 3-inch biscuit cutter which is dipped each time before cutting into hot water. Use 2½-inch biscuit cutter to remove centers from half of the rounds, leaving rings of dough. Moisten edges of the solid rounds with cold water, then top with the rings of dough for walls of patty shells, pressing rings down lightly. Brush shells carefully with the egg wash and as you do this, place on baking sheet which has had cold water run over it and the excess shaken off. Cover with damp towel and let rest 30 min. Now cover shells with an unwrinkled sheet of greased brown paper to insure even rising and to prevent shells from tipping. Bake 25 min. Shells should rise to full height in 15 min and begin to brown. At this time, remove paper carefully and finish baking, turning the pan around frequently the last 10 min of baking to insure even browning of the delicate shells. Remove to cake rack to cool. While still hot, enlarge the shells for filling by lifting out the soft central portion of each with 2 forks.* Fill with any creamed or à la king mixture.

*Place these removed soft portions on baking sheet and finish baking to be used like crackers or toast.

PUFF PASTRY ROSES

Puff Pastry, p 934   xxxx sugar
Egg Yolk Wash, p 935   Jelly, jam *or* fruit preserves

Start oven 10 min before baking; set to hot (450° F). Use about ¼ of the Puff Pastry at a time, leaving rest in refrigerator until needed. Roll out dough on pastry cloth ⅛-inch thick. Cut out with a large star cookie cutter dipped in hot water before each cutting. Now brush stars with cold water then fold the points of the star over toward center of dough, pressing points down gently. Next brush with egg wash and carefully place on a baking sheet that has had cold water run over it and the excess shaken off. Let rest 30 min. Bake until a rich brown, 15 or 20 min. When nearly done, quickly remove from oven, dust with xxxx sugar and return to oven to finish baking. Fill roses with jam, jelly or preserves.

VOL-AU-VENTS

These are large patty shells to be filled with meat, poultry or game mixture

Puff Pastry, p 934   **Egg Yolk Wash, p 935**

Start oven 10 min before baking; set to hot (450° F). Use about ¼ of the Puff Pastry at a time, leaving rest in refrigerator until needed. Roll out dough on a very lightly floured pastry cloth ⅓-inch thick. Lay a cardboard oval pattern that is 4 inches long and 2 inches wide on the dough. With a sharp knife cut around the pattern for individual pastry cases or use larger pattern for family-sized shells. Now cut out centers from half the ovals leaving a rim about ¾-inch wide. Save cut-out centers to make covers for the vol-au-vents. Brush outside edge of the solid ovals all around with cold water. Then lay rims on solid ovals and press lightly around edges to seal. Prick bottoms of solid ovals several times with a fork. Brush all over with Egg Yolk Wash and place on a cookie sheet that has had cold water run over it and the excess shaken off. Let vol-au-vents rest 30 min. Now cover with an unwrinkled sheet of greased brown paper to insure even rising and to prevent shells from tipping. Bake for 25 min. Shells should rise to full height in 15 min, then remove paper so shells will brown. Turn pan around in oven frequently during last 10 min of baking to insure even browning. Remove shells from oven to cake rack and while still warm, lift out and remove the soft center portion* of each shell with 2 forks to enlarge hollows. Roll out the Puff Pastry that was cut from center of half the ovals ⅛-inch thick. Cut into ovals to fit the baked cases, chill 30 min, then bake until golden brown, about 15 min in the same hot oven. When cooled, fill vol-au-vents with any creamed meat mixture and place covers on top before serving.

QUICK "PUFF" PASTRY

When baked, this pastry has numerous fragile, flaky layers. It is wonderful for double- or single-crust pies, turnovers, or as a topping for meat pies

2 cups all-purpose flour	⅔ cup shortening
1 tsp salt	½ cup ice water
½ tsp baking powder	

Sift flour, measure and resift with salt and baking powder into a 3-qt mixing bowl. Cut in shortening with pastry blender or 2 knives until particles are about size of peas. Now remove and set aside ¼ cup of fat-flour mixture. To remainder, add ice water a few drops at a time, tossing with fork to dampen the particles evenly. Push aside the moistened part and continue until all particles are dampened. Add only enough water to press the dampened pastry gently into a ball that holds together. Cover and let stand about 15 min. Divide pastry in half. Roll each into a 10 x 14-inch rectangle. Sprinkle half of the reserved fat-flour particles over each sheet of dough. Roll up like jelly roll, then cut the

*Place these removed soft portions on baking sheet and finish baking to be used like crackers or toast.

roll into 3 even length pieces. Place one roll on top of the other (3 high), then press down with palm of hand to flatten. Roll out about ⅛-inch thick into about an 11-inch circle. Use for bottom of 9 or 10-inch double crust pie, or for a single crust pie. Or cut into 5 or 6-inch circles for turnovers, or to top individual meat pies. Finish according to your need, by pricking or cutting design for steam vents as in any other pastry. Bake double-crust or meat pies as described on p 925, or single-crust shells or turnovers as described on p 928. Enough for 1 double-crust pie, 2 single-crust shells, 6 or 8 meat pie tops or 10 to 15 turnovers.

Note: Use coffee can top to cut 5-inch rounds, and a bowl or pan lid to cut larger rounds.

CHIFFON PIES

BLACK BOTTOM PIE

We think it's tops, black bottom and all!

10-inch pastry shell, p 928
Filling—Dark Part:
    4 tsp cornstarch
    ½ cup sugar
    ¼ tsp salt
    2 cups milk
    4 egg yolks, well beaten
    1½ cups semi-sweet
      chocolate chips, 1½ pkgs
    ½ tsp vanilla
    Dash of salt

Filling—Light Part:
    2 tsp plain gelatin softened
      in ¼ cup cold water 5 min
    3 egg whites
    ⅓ cup sugar
    1 tsp rum flavoring
    ½ cup whipping cream
    1 tbsp sugar
    Sweet chocolate bar
      for shaving

Bake and cool pastry shell. *Filling Dark Part:* Blend first 3 ingredients in top of double boiler, using wooden spoon. Stir in milk. Cook and stir over medium direct heat until smooth and thick as whipping cream. Place over boiling water (top part should not touch water), cover and cook 10 min, stirring occasionally. Quickly stir about ⅓ cup of hot mixture into egg yolks; return to hot mixture and cook and stir 2 min longer. Remove from heat. Quickly measure 1¼ cups hot custard into bowl that held yolks. Stir softened gelatin into rest of custard and let stand. Stir chocolate into hot custard in bowl; let stand and stir until chocolate melts. Stir in vanilla and dash of salt. Spread smoothly in baked pastry shell. Cool at least 15 min. *Filling Light Part:* Beat egg whites to stiff foam, then beat in ⅓ cup sugar gradually to form a stiff shiny meringue. Stir rum flavoring into gelatin mixture; then lightly but thoroughly *fold* in meringue. Pour over chocolate filling, swirling out level. Chill until firm, 2 to 3 hrs. Then spread with the cream whipped until stiff and sweetened with the 1 tbsp sugar. Sprinkle with shaved chocolate. Again chill for an hr; serve same day. 8 servings.

To Make An 8-inch Pie: Use an 8-inch baked pastry shell, p 928 and just half the quantities of ingredients called for above.

Note: If a thinner layer of chocolate is desired, remove only 1 cup custard, add to it 1 cup (1 pkg) chocolate chips, and proceed as above.

COFFEE CHIFFON PIE No. 1

Endowed with delicious flavor

9-inch pastry shell, p 928
Filling:
¼ cup medium grind coffee
¾ cup boiling water
1½ to 1¾ tsp plain gelatin
¼ cup 12% cream,
   half-and-half *or* rich milk
3 egg yolks, beaten
¾ cup sugar

⅓ cup 12% cream
¼ tsp salt
1 tsp vanilla
2 tbsp sugar
Topping:
½ cup whipping cream
1 tsp sugar
Semi-sweet chocolate bar
for shaving

Bake and cool pastry shell. *Filling:* Add coffee to boiling water, stir, remove from heat, cover and let stand 5 min. Strain through 3 or 4 thicknesses of cheesecloth. There should be ½ cup strong coffee. Sprinkle gelatin over the ¼ cup cream, stir and let soften 5 min. Put the ½ cup coffee into top of double boiler; add next 4 ingredients, stirring well with wooden spoon. Place over gently boiling water and cook and stir until smooth and thick, about 5 min. Remove from heat. Stir in softened gelatine until dissolved. Cool in pan of cold (iced) water until like thick honey; then stir in vanilla. Beat whites to a stiff foam, add the 2 tbsp sugar gradually and beat to a stiff, shiny meringue. *Cut-and-fold* meringue lightly but thoroughly into coffee mixture with a rubber scraper. Turn into baked shell; spread lightly to level. Chill until set, 2 to 4 hrs, before cutting. Just before serving, spread thinly with sweetened whipped cream, then shave chocolate over the cream. (Store chocolate in refrigerator to shave easily.) 6 servings.

To Make An 8-inch Pie: Use baked 8-inch pastry shell; scant 3 tbsp coffee, ½ cup boiling water, 1¼ tsp gelatin, scant 3 tbsp 12% cream, 2 egg yolks, ½ cup sugar, ¼ cup 12% cream, ⅛ tsp salt, ¾ tsp vanilla, 1½ tbsp sugar; ⅓ cup whipping cream, ¾ tsp sugar, semi-sweet chocolate for shaving.

COFFEE CHIFFON PIE No. 2

Follow directions for Coffee Chiffon Pie No. 1, except use 2 tsp quality instant coffee dissolved in ½ cup boiling water in place of the ½ cup freshly brewed coffee.

CHOCOLATE CHIFFON PIE

Mmm! Here is good taste!

9-inch pastry shell, p 928
Filling:
1½ to 2 tsp plain gelatin*
¼ cup cold water
2 sqs, 2 oz unsweet chocolate
¼ tsp salt
½ cup 12% cream,
   half-and-half
¾ cup sugar

3 egg yolks
1 tsp vanilla
3 egg whites
¼ cup sugar
Topping:
½ cup whipping cream
1 tsp sugar
Bar sweet chocolate for
   shaving

Bake and cool pastry shell. *Filling:* Soften gelatin in water 5 min. Put chocolate, salt, half the cream, and the ¾ cup sugar into top of double boiler. Place over gently boiling water and cook and stir until chocolate melts and mixture is well blended. Beat yolks well, add rest of 12% cream, and quickly stir in about ⅓ cup of the hot mixture; return to double boiler and cook and stir 2 min longer or until thickened. Remove from heat. Stir in gelatin until dissolved, then the vanilla. Beat egg whites to a stiff foam; add the ¼ cup sugar gradually and beat until stiff and shiny. Use rubber scraper to *cut-and-fold* meringue into chocolate mixture lightly but thoroughly. Turn immediately into baked shell and spread out level. Chill until set, 2 to 3 hrs. When ready to serve, spread with sweetened whipped cream and shave chocolate over top. 6 servings.

To Make An 8-inch Pie: Use 8-inch baked pastry shell, p 928; 1¼ tsp gelatin, scant 3 tbsp water, 1⅓ sq unsweet chocolate, ⅛ tsp salt, ⅓ cup 12% cream, ½ cup sugar, 2 egg yolks, ¾ tsp vanilla, 2 egg whites; ⅓ cup whipping cream, ¾ tsp sugar, sweet chocolate.

Hint: Store chocolate bar in refrigerator; hold with waxed paper and with sharp knife shave directly onto top of pie.

EGGNOG CHIFFON PIE

Many rate this the best chiffon pie of all!

9-inch pastry shell, p 928
2 tsp plain gelatin
3 tbsp cold water
1 cup milk
3 egg yolks, beaten
½ cup sugar
½ tsp salt, scant

1 tbsp rum *or* 2 tsp rum
   flavoring
¾ cup whipping cream
3 egg whites
¼ cup *plus* 3 tbsp sugar
¼ tsp nutmeg *or*
2 tbsp chopped pecans *or*
   pistachios

Bake and cool pastry shell. Sprinkle gelatin over cold water to soften 5 min. Blend next 4 ingredients thoroughly in top of double

*Use 1½ tsp in cold weather, 2 tsp in hot.

boiler. Place over boiling water and cook and stir with wooden spoon until mixture just thickens. Remove from heat, stir in gelatin until dissolved; stir in rum. Chill until thick like syrup. Beat cream until thick but still smooth; remove mixture from refrigerator and fold in with rubber scraper. Quickly beat egg whites to stiff foam; gradually beat in remaining sugar until stiff and shiny. Fold meringue quickly but thoroughly into gelatin mixture; quickly pour into pastry shell. When filling settles, sprinkle with nutmeg or nuts; if both are desired, fold nutmeg into filling along with rum. Chill until set, 2 to 3 hrs.

To Make An 8-inch Pie: Use 8-inch baked pastry shell, p 928; 1½ tsp plain gelatin, 2 tbsp cold water, ⅔ cup milk, 2 egg yolks, ⅓ cup sugar, ⅓ tsp salt, 2 tsp rum or 1½ tsp rum flavoring, 2 egg whites, ⅓ cup sugar, ⅛ tsp nutmeg.

LEMON CHIFFON PIE

Made the day before the party, this pie will still be delicious

9-inch pastry shell, p 928
Filling:
  ½ tsp grated lemon rind, pkd
  ½ cup lemon juice
  2 tsp plain gelatin
  ⅓ cup cold water
  4 egg yolks
  ¾ cup sugar
  ¼ tsp salt

1 tbsp melted butter
4 egg whites
  Dash of salt
½ cup sugar
Topping:
  ½ cup whipping cream
  1 tsp sugar
  ½ cup fresh grated coconut

Bake and cool pastry shell. *Filling:* Wash lemons and grate off a little of the yellow rind onto waxed paper; measure and fold into paper to keep moist. Squeeze juice and remove seeds. Sprinkle gelatin over 2 tbsp of the cold water; let stand to soften. Beat egg yolks until thick, then beat in the ¾ cup sugar and ¼ tsp salt. Add lemon juice and rest of water and beat to mix well. Turn into top of double boiler. Place over gently boiling water and cook and stir with wooden spoon until thickened, about 5 min. Add butter last min of cooking. Remove from heat. Stir in rind and softened gelatin. Set in pan of cold (iced) water until mixture begins to thicken, stirring occasionally. Beat egg whites with dash of salt until almost stiff; then add the ½ cup sugar gradually, beating to a stiff, shiny meringue. *Cut-and-fold* meringue lightly but thoroughly into lemon mixture with rubber scraper until well blended. Turn into baked pastry shell; gently spread out level. Chill until set, about 3 hrs. *Topping:* Just before serving, spread with sweetened whipped cream and sprinkle with moist fine-cut coconut. 6 servings.

To Make An 8-inch Pie: Use an 8-inch pastry shell; ⅓ tsp grated lemon rind, pkd, ⅓ cup lemon juice, 1½ tsp gelatin, 3½ tbsp water, 3 small egg yolks, ½ cup sugar, scant ¼ tsp salt, 2 tsp melted butter, 3 small egg whites, ⅓ cup sugar; ⅓ cup whipping cream, ¾ tsp sugar, ⅓ cup fresh grated coconut.

Note: If canned coconut is used, cut fine with scissors.

LEMON AND ORANGE CHIFFON PIE

Cool, light as air, and smooth as velvet

9-inch pastry shell, p 928   3 egg yolks, beaten light
Filling: 1 cup minus 1 tbsp sugar
   ¼ tsp grated lemon   Dash of salt
      rind, pkd   3 egg whites
   ⅛ tsp grated orange   *Topping,* optional:
      rind, pkd   ½ cup whipping cream
   ⅓ cup strained lemon juice   1 tsp sugar
   ¾ cup strained orange juice   ½ cup moist shredded coconut
   1½ tsp plain gelatin

Bake and cool pastry shell. *Filling:* Wash fruit and grate off rinds onto waxed paper, keeping separate. Measure and fold into waxed paper to keep moist. Squeeze and measure juice. Sprinkle gelatin over ¼ cup of the orange juice to soften for 5 min. Turn rest of orange juice into top of double boiler; add rinds, lemon juice, egg yolks, ½ cup of the sugar, and salt. Stir with wooden spoon until blended; place over boiling water and cook and stir until thickened and smooth, about 5 min. Remove from heat. Stir in gelatin until dissolved. Cool until like thick honey. Beat egg whites to a stiff foam; add rest of sugar gradually and beat to a stiff, shiny meringue. Use a rubber scraper to *cut-and-fold* meringue into thickened gelatin mixture lightly but thoroughly. Turn into pie shell and quickly spread out lightly. Chill until set, 2 to 3 hrs, before cutting. *Topping:* Just before serving, spread thinly with sweetened whipped cream and sprinkle with coconut, or serve plain. 6 servings.

To Make An 8-inch Pie: Use 8-inch pastry shell, p 928; ¼ tsp grated lemon rind and ⅛ tsp grated orange rind *not* pkd, 3 tbsp plus 1 tsp strained lemon juice, ½ cup strained orange juice, 1 tsp gelatin, 2 egg yolks, ⅓ cup sugar, 2 egg whites, dash of salt, ⅓ cup sugar; ⅓ cup whipping cream, ¾ tsp sugar, ⅓ cup moist shredded coconut.

LIME CHIFFON PIE IN GRAHAM CRACKER CRUST

A pie with delicious zippy flavor and cheerful color

Crust: 3 egg yolks, beaten
   16 to 18 graham crackers,   ⅔ cup sugar
      1½ cups crumbs   ½ tsp salt
   ¼ cup sugar   2 tsp plain gelatin
   ⅓ cup butter, melted   ¼ cup cold water
Filling: 5 *or* 6 drops green food
   ½ tsp grated lime rind, pkd   coloring
   ½ cup lime juice, 4 medium   3 egg whites
      Persian limes   ⅓ cup sugar

Have ready a 9-inch glass pie pan. Start oven 10 min before baking; set to moderately hot (375° F).

Crust: Put crackers through food mill or crush fine with rolling pin. Combine with sugar, add butter gradually, and work with spoon until well blended; crumbs should pack slightly. Remove and set aside 2 tbsp of the mixture; turn rest into pie pan. Press crumb mixture into uniform layer with back of tbsp, using fingers to shape a low, firmly built-up edge around rim of pan. Bake 6 to 8 min. Remove to cake rack to cool.

Filling: Wash limes, grate rind onto waxed paper, measure and fold into paper to keep moist. Squeeze juice; measure into top of double boiler. Stir in next 3 ingredients with wooden spoon; place over boiling water and cook and stir until mixture thickens slightly, about 10 min. Remove from heat. Meanwhile sprinkle gelatin over cold water to soften 5 min. Stir softened gelatin into hot custard until thoroughly dissolved; then add food coloring. Set custard in cold (iced) water to cool until like thick honey, stirring frequently. Beat egg whites to stiff foam with washed beater, gradually beat in the ⅓ cup sugar until meringue forms soft peaks. Now *stir* ¼ of the meringue into the gelatin mixture. Return it to cold water until mixture thickens enough to hold ripples when dropped from spoon; then *fold in quickly* but thoroughly the remaining meringue. When mixture holds swirls, *pour quickly* into prepared crust. Sprinkle reserved crumb mixture over top. Chill until set, 2 to 3 hrs. 7 servings.

To Make An 8-inch Pie: Use 1 cup graham cracker crumbs (reserve 1 tbsp mixture to sprinkle on top), 2 tbsp plus 2 tsp sugar, 3½ tbsp melted butter. For filling, use ⅓ tsp grated lime rind, ⅓ cup lime juice, 2 egg yolks, ⅓ cup plus 2 tbsp sugar, ⅓ tsp salt, 1½ tsp gelatin, 3 tbsp cold water, 4 to 5 drops food coloring, 2 egg whites, ¼ cup sugar.

LIME CHIFFON PIE No. 2

This very delicious lime pie is different because it gets its color and part of its flavor from lime gelatin

9-inch pastry *or* graham
   cracker shell, pp 928, 930
½ tsp grated lime rind, pkd
5 tbsp lime juice, 2 medium
   limes
½ cup sugar
3 large egg yolks, beaten

½ tsp salt
½ cup boiling water
¼ cup lime-flavored gelatin
3 large egg whites
3 tbsp sugar
½ cup whipping cream,
   optional

Bake and cool pie shell. Wash limes and grate rind onto waxed paper; measure and fold into paper to keep moist. Squeeze juice; measure into top of double boiler. Stir in next 4 ingredients thoroughly. Place over boiling water and cook and stir with wooden spoon until slightly thickened, about 10 min. Remove from heat. Stir in rind, then gelatin until dissolved. Turn into 2-qt aluminum bowl or saucepan, set in cold (ice) water and stir often but lightly until mixture is like thick honey. Meanwhile, beat egg whites to a stiff foam with washed beater; then gradually beat in rest of sugar until stiff and glossy. Add about ¼ of meringue to lime mixture and stir in thoroughly. Again set in cold water until mixture will hold ripples when dropped from spoon; then *quickly fold in* remaining meringue. Pour *at once* into prepared shell. Chill 2 or 3 hrs. Just before serving, spread with slightly sweetened whipped cream. 5 to 6 servings.

To Make An 8-inch Pie: Use an 8-inch pastry or graham cracker shell, pp 928, 930; ⅓ tsp grated lime rind, 3 tbsp plus 1 tsp lime juice, ⅓ cup sugar, 2 large egg yolks, ⅓ tsp salt, ⅓ cup boiling water, 2 tbsp plus 2 tsp lime-flavored gelatin, 2 large egg whites, 2 tbsp sugar, ⅓ cup whipping cream.

ORANGE CHIFFON PIE

Creamy, smooth, tangy . . . delicious!

9-inch pastry shell, p 928
Filling:
    ½ tsp grated orange rind, pkd
    1¼ cups orange juice
    2¼ tsp plain gelatin
    ¾ cup sugar
    1 tbsp flour

¼ tsp salt
2 tbsp lime juice
1 cup whipping cream
Topping:
    1 tsp shredded orange rind
    mixed with 1 tsp sugar

Bake and cool pastry shell. *Filling:* Wash oranges and grate off some of the outer rind onto waxed paper; measure and fold into paper to keep moist. Squeeze juice and remove seeds. Soak gelatin in ¼ cup of the orange juice for 5 min to soften. Blend sugar, flour and salt in a 3 qt saucepan with wooden spoon; stir in ½ cup of orange juice. Place over heat and cook and stir until mixture is clear and thickened. Remove from heat. Stir in gelatin and rest of orange juice, lime juice and rind. Set in pan of cold (iced) water until consistency is like unbeaten egg white, stirring occasionally. Meanwhile beat cream until stiff. Then fold it into gelatin mixture lightly but thoroughly. Turn into pastry shell and chill until set, 2 to 3 hrs. Just before serving, freshly shred (do not grate) orange rind, mix with sugar, and sprinkle over top. 6 servings.

To Make An 8-inch Pie: Use 8-inch baked pastry shell, p 928; ⅓ tsp grated orange rind, pkd, ¾ cup plus 2 tbsp orange juice (3 tbsp to soak gelatin), 1½ tsp gelatin, ½ cup sugar, 2 tsp flour, ⅛ tsp salt, 1 tbsp plus 1 tsp lime juice, ⅔ cup whipping cream; ⅔ tsp shredded orange rind mixed with ⅔ tsp sugar.

Note: Orange rind tends to discolor if shredded too long before using. If shreds are long it can be mixed with sugar and stored in refrigerator for half an hr.

PUMPKIN CHIFFON PIE

A delicate, delectable and different pie

9-inch pastry shell, p 928

Filling:
2 tsp plain gelatin
¼ cup cold water
½ cup dark brown sugar, pkd
½ tsp salt
¼ tsp ginger
1 tsp cinnamon
Dash of cloves
⅛ tsp nutmeg, fresh
grated best
1 cup good quality canned
pumpkin

3 egg yolks, beaten
½ cup 12% cream,
half-and-half
4 drops orange extract *or* ⅛
tsp grated orange rind
3 egg whites
6 tbsp sugar

Topping, optional:
½ cup whipping cream
1 tsp sugar
8 pecan halves

Bake and cool pastry shell. *Filling:* Sprinkle gelatin over water to soften 5 min. Blend next 6 ingredients in top of double boiler; then stir in pumpkin, yolks and cream. Beat with rotary beater until thoroughly blended. Remove and wash beater. Place over boiling water and cook and stir with wooden spoon until thick and very smooth, about 5 min. Remove from heat. Stir in gelatin until dissolved; stir in extract or rind. Cool by setting in pan of cold (iced) water until like thick honey, but not congealed. Beat egg whites to a stiff foam, then add the 6 tbsp sugar gradually, beating to a stiff, glossy meringue. With a rubber scraper, *cut-and-fold* meringue into pumpkin mixture lightly but thoroughly. Turn mixture into baked pastry shell, quickly spreading out level. Chill until set, 2 to 3 hrs, before cutting. (This filling is soft, barely holding shape when cut.) *Topping:* Just before serving, spread with sweetened whipped cream and garnish with thinly cut nuts, or serve plain. 6 servings.

To Make An 8-inch Pie: Use 8-inch pastry shell, p 928; 1½ tsp plain gelatin, 3 tbsp water, ⅓ cup dark brown sugar, pkd, ⅓ tsp salt, ⅛ tsp ginger, ¾ tsp cinnamon, dash of cloves, ⅔ cup canned pumpkin, 2 egg yolks, ⅓ cup 12% cream, 3 drops orange extract or ⅛ tsp grated orange rind, 2 egg whites, ¼ cup sugar; ⅓ cup whipping cream, ¾ tsp sugar, 6 pecan halves.

STRAWBERRY CHIFFON PIE

A delicate, delicious pink-and-white beauty

9-inch pastry shell, p 928
1 qt fresh strawberries
⅔ cup whipping cream
3 large egg yolks, beaten
⅓ cup sugar
¼ tsp salt

¼ cup strawberry-flavored
gelatin
2 tsp lemon juice
3 large egg whites
⅓ cup *plus* 1½ tbsp sugar

Bake and cool pastry shell. Wash and hull berries. Save enough perfect ones for decorating. Blend next 4 ingredients thoroughly in top of double boiler; place over boiling water and cook and stir with wooden spoon until just thickened, about 10 min. Remove from heat and stir in gelatin until completely dissolved. Crush enough berries to make 1 cup, stir in lemon juice and add gradually to cooked mixture, folding in until thoroughly blended. Cool until like thick honey. Beat whites to stiff foam; beat in rest of sugar gradually until stiff and glossy. Fold meringue lightly but thoroughly into strawberry mixture and immediately pour into pastry shell. Chill until set, 2 to 3 hrs. Serve decorated with sliced perfect berries. 6 servings.

To Make An 8-inch Pie: Use 8-inch pastry shell, p 928; scant ½ cup whipping cream, 2 large egg yolks, 3½ tbsp sugar, 2 tbsp plus 2 tsp strawberry-flavored gelatin, ⅔ cup crushed strawberries, 1½ tsp lemon juice, 2 large egg whites, ¼ cup plus 2 tsp sugar.

RASPBERRY CHIFFON PIE

Make exactly like Strawberry Chiffon Pie, except substitute fresh red raspberries and raspberry-flavored gelatin for strawberries and strawberry-flavored gelatin.

CITRUS PIES

Almost any citrus fruit can be used to make excellent pie. Lemon is the best-known of the citrus pies, and lemon meringue is the most famous member of the Lemon Pie family. But all the other varieties are just as delicious as lemon meringue, and may be even more appealing because they are more unusual.

Orange pie is well worth eating, and so is lime, grapefruit and calamondin. If you are not acquainted with all the kinds of really exciting citrus pies, try the recipes in this section and be rewarded with some surprisingly delicious discoveries.

Note: A Minute Minder in the kitchen is an advantage—use it to time cooking of fillings for cream or citrus pies, when oven is used for baking.

CALAMONDIN PIE

The sprightly and refreshing flavor is reminiscent of lemon, yet it is distinctly different

9-inch pastry shell, p 928   Filling for Calamondin
                                          Tarts, p 1020

Bake pastry shell and cool. Then make filling and pour into the pastry shell. Let cool 10 to 15 min, then make meringue and spread over pie, being sure it touches crust all around. Bake on bottom rack in moderately hot oven (400° F) 8 to 10 min or until meringue is a luscious brown. Remove to cake rack for 2 or 3 hrs before cutting. 6 to 7 servings.

GRAPEFRUIT PIE

When grapefruit pie was first put on the menu of a big Chicago hospital a few years ago, it became the first choice of many patients. The reason—its flavor and sparkle tempts the appetite

9-inch pastry shell, p 928	2 tbsp butter
3 cups sectioned grapefruit	2 egg whites
½ cup sugar	Dash of salt
2 tsp cornstarch	¼ cup sugar
1 egg yolk, beaten	

Bake and cool pastry shell. Section grapefruit, turn into a bowl, sprinkle with the ½ cup sugar and let stand ½ hr. Drain off juice; there should be ½ cup. Put cornstarch into saucepan and slowly stir in grapefruit juice until smooth. Place over moderate heat and cook and stir until clear and thickened. Remove from heat and pour over egg yolk, stirring thoroughly; stir in butter, then carefully fold in grapefruit sections. Pour into pastry shell, spreading level. Beat egg whites and salt to a stiff foam, then add sugar in 3 portions, continuing to beat to a stiff, shiny meringue. Spread meringue over the pie, touching crust all around; swirl it over the top. Bake on top rack of a moderately hot oven (400° F) for 8 to 10 min or until golden brown. Remove to cake rack to cool an hr or two before cutting. 5 to 6 servings.

LEMON CAKE PIE

Easiest of all lemon pies and one of the best—delicate custard with a tender, spongy top

Pastry for 10-inch single crust, p 928	2 tbsp flour
	¼ tsp salt
1 tsp grated lemon rind, pkd	2 tbsp melted butter
⅓ cup unstrained lemon juice	3 eggs, separated
1 cup sugar	1 cup *plus* 2 tbsp milk

Bake on lowest rack in oven so crust will become crisp without overbrowning the surface. Start oven 10 min before baking; set to moderately hot (400° F). Make pastry; roll out and line 10-inch pie pan, fitting well into angles. Let rest 5 min, trim off pastry with scissors ½ inch beyond rim of pan; turn overhang under so fold is even with rim; crimp or flute to finish edge. Wash 2 lemons and grate some of the rind onto waxed paper; measure and fold paper over to keep rind moist. Squeeze lemon juice; remove seeds. Blend ¾ cup of the sugar, the flour and salt in a 2-qt mixing bowl, then stir in butter thoroughly. Beat in egg yolks with rotary beater until light, then lemon juice and milk. Wash beater and beat whites to a stiff foam; add remaining sugar gradually and beat to a stiff, shiny meringue. Fold meringue and rind thoroughly into yolk mixture with rubber scraper. Pour into prepared pan. Bake 35 min, or until crust and top is nicely browned. Remove to cake rack to cool at least 2 hrs before cutting. 6 to 8 servings.

To Make An 8-inch Pie: Use pastry for 8-inch single crust, p 928, ⅔ tsp grated lemon rind, 3½ tbsp lemon juice, ⅔ cup sugar, 1⅓ tbsp flour, ⅛ tsp salt, 1⅓ tbsp butter, 2 eggs, ⅔ cup plus 1⅓ tbsp milk.

LEMON CREAM PIE

An excellent, mellow lemon pie. Proportion of filling and meringue ideal

9-inch pastry shell, p 928   2 egg yolks
Filling: 1 tbsp butter
  ½ tsp grated lemon rind, pkd   *Meringue:*
  ⅓ cup lemon juice   Dash of salt
  1 cup sugar   2 egg whites
  ⅓ cup all-purpose flour   ¼ cup sugar
  ¼ tsp salt   1 tsp sugar
  1½ cups milk

Bake and cool pastry shell. *Filling:* Wash lemons, grate off some of the yellow rind onto waxed paper, measure and fold into paper to keep moist. Squeeze juice, remove seeds. Blend sugar, flour and salt in top of double boiler with wooden spoon, then gradually stir in milk so as to keep smooth. Place over direct heat and cook and stir until mixture is smooth, thickened and has boiled up. Now place over boiling water. Beat egg yolks, quickly stir in about ⅓ cup of the hot mixture; return to double boiler and cook and stir about 2 min longer. Stir in butter. Remove from heat and stir in rind, then lemon juice *gradually* in small portions, mixing well after each. Pour into pastry shell and *cool 15 to 20 min.* Meanwhile make *Meringue:* Add salt to egg whites and beat until stiff, then gradually beat in ¼ cup sugar until meringue is stiff and shiny. Spread lightly over pie so it touches crust all around; swirl, or spread smooth and mark into 6 serving pieces with long knife blade. Sprinkle with the tsp sugar. Bake in a moderate oven (350° F) for 12 to 15 min or until golden brown. Remove to cake rack, out of draft, to cool 2 or 3 hrs before cutting. 6 servings.

To Make An 8-inch Pie: Use 8-inch pastry shell, p 928, ⅓ tsp grated lemon rind, pkd, ¼ cup lemon juice, ¾ cup sugar, ¼ cup flour, scant ¼ tsp salt, 1 cup plus 2 tbsp milk, 2 small egg yolks, scant tbsp butter, 2 small egg whites, dash salt, 3 tbsp sugar, 1 tsp sugar.

Note: Cooling the filling before putting the meringue on prevents "weeping."

LEMON FLUFF PIE

Refreshing and zestful

9 *or* 10-inch pastry shell,
  p 928
1 tsp grated lemon rind, pkd
¼ cup lemon juice, 1½ lemons
4 eggs, separated
⅛ tsp salt

1 cup sugar
2 tbsp butter
½ cup whipping cream, optional
1 tsp sugar
½ cup moist coconut, optional

Bake and cool pastry shell. Wash lemons, grate rind onto waxed paper; measure and fold into paper to keep moist. Squeeze and measure juice after removing seeds. Beat egg yolks with rotary beater until very light; add salt and ¾ cup of the sugar gradually and continue beating until very thick. Remove beater and stir in lemon juice and rind. Turn into top of double boiler, scraping from bowl with rubber scraper. Add butter and cook over boiling water, stirring constantly with wooden spoon until very thick—10 to 12 min. Remove from heat, beat egg whites until stiff, add remaining sugar gradually and beat to a stiff, shiny meringue. *Cut-and-fold* into custard mixture, *lightly* but thoroughly. Pile *lightly* into pastry shell, swirling top. Place in hot oven (450° F) for 5 min, until meringue is a rich golden brown. Remove to cake rack to cool out of a draft to lukewarm before cutting. Serve plain, or when cold, spread with sweetened whipped cream and sprinkle with fine-cut coconut. 6 servings.

To Make An 8-inch Pie: Use 8-inch pastry shell, p 928, scant tsp grated lemon rind, 3 tbsp lemon juice, 3 eggs, scant ⅛ tsp salt, ¾ cup sugar, 1½ tbsp butter, ⅓ cup whipping cream, 1 tsp sugar, ⅓ cup coconut.

LEMON GLAMOUR PIE

Melt-in-the-mouth filling with the tantalizing flavor and fragrance of fresh lemons. The filling may seem scant, but its richness makes it ample, as the eater will see

9-inch pastry shell, p 928
Filling:
1 tsp grated lemon rind, pkd
6 tbsp lemon juice, 2
  medium lemons
½ cup butter, ¼ lb
1 cup sugar

2 whole eggs and 2 egg yolks
Meringue:
2 egg whites
¼ cup sugar
½ cup moist shredded coconut, lightly pkd, *or* fresh finely grated

Bake and cool pastry shell. *Filling:* Wash lemons and grate off yellow part of rind. Squeeze juice; put through coarse strainer. Put butter and sugar in top of double boiler and place over boiling water. Stir until butter melts; remove from heat. Beat eggs and yolks thoroughly, then stir into butter-sugar mixture. Add rind and lemon juice and beat thoroughly. Place over hot water and cook and stir just until mixture thickens, 4 to 5 min. Now remove from heat, cover to prevent formation of "skin," and cool about 5 min; or set in cold water to cool slightly. Turn into pastry shell, spreading well up sides. *Meringue:* Beat egg whites until stiff, add sugar gradually and continue beating to a stiff, shiny meringue. Spread over filling, touching crust all around. Sprinkle with coconut. Bake on bottom rack in moderately hot oven (400° F) for 8 to 10 min, or until golden brown, watching to avoid scorching coconut. Remove to cake rack to cool 2 to 3 hrs before cutting. Snip off any bits of over-browned coconut with scissors. 6 to 7 servings.

To Make An 8-inch Pie: Use an 8-inch pastry shell, p 928, ¾ tsp grated lemon rind, pkd, 4½ tbsp lemon juice, 6 tbsp butter, ¾ cup sugar, 2 small whole eggs and 2 small yolks, 2 small egg whites, 3 tbsp sugar, ⅓ cup coconut, pkd.

LEMON MERINGUE PIE

A perpetual favorite!

9-inch pastry shell, p 928   ¼ tsp salt
Filling: 1½ cups boiling water
  ½ to ¾ tsp grated lemon rind,   3 egg yolks
    pkd   3 tbsp firm butter
  ⅓ cup strained lemon juice,   *Meringue:*
    2 medium size lemons   Dash of salt
  ¼ cup cornstarch and   3 egg whites
    2 tbsp all-purpose flour   ⅓ cup sugar
  1⅓ cups sugar   1 tsp sugar

Bake and cool pastry shell. Wash lemons and grate off yellow part of rind. Squeeze juice; run through coarse strainer. Blend cornstarch, flour, sugar and salt in a 3-qt saucepan. Stir in boiling water. Place over direct heat, cook and stir constantly until thick and clear, about 3 min. Beat egg yolks, quickly stir in about ⅓ cup of hot mixture; return to double-boiler, cook and stir about 2 min longer. Remove from heat, stir in butter, then the rind, then the lemon juice gradually in small portions, mixing well after each. Pour into cooled pie shell. Meanwhile make *Meringue:* Add salt to egg whites and beat until just stiff, then gradually beat in ⅓ cup sugar until meringue is stiff and shiny. Spread lightly over pie so it touches crust all around; swirl or spread smooth and mark into 6 serving pieces with long knife blade. Sprinkle with the tsp of sugar. Bake at moderate (350° F) for 12 to 15 min or until golden brown. Remove to cake rack out of draft, to cool 2 or 3 hrs before cutting. 6 servings.

SLICED LEMON 2-CRUST PIE

Our forbears made this pie, it's unusual, rich and delicious. Today, it's a sure-fire conversation pie

Pastry for 9-inch double crust, p 924	1 cup sugar
	1 tsp cornstarch
½ cup sugar	¼ tsp salt
2 medium lemons	⅓ cup butter, melted
½ tsp grated lemon rind, pkd	1 tbsp cold water
2 eggs	

Place rack in center of oven. Start oven 10 min before baking; set to hot (450° F).

Make pastry and roll ½ of it out to line a 9-inch pie pan, fitting well into angles. Let rest 5 min; then trim off even with pan rim. Sprinkle bottom with the ½ cup sugar. Wash lemons; grate off yellow rind only onto waxed paper; measure and fold paper over it to keep moist. Peel lemons like an orange, cutting through rind and pulling peel away. Scrape off clinging fiber. Slice lemons on a cutting board *very* thin with a sharp knife. Cut slices into 6 sections with scissors, trimming out white fibrous centers. There should be about ½ cup prepared fruit; spread it evenly over sugar in pastry-lined pan. Roll out rest of pastry for top crust; cut design in center for wide-open steam vents. Beat eggs until thick with rotary beater; beat in the 1 cup sugar blended with cornstarch and salt, then butter and water. Remove beater and stir in rind. Pour mixture over lemon slices. *Do not stir.* Moisten edge of lower pastry, lay on top pastry, pressing gently around edge to seal. Trim off top pastry with scissors ½ inch beyond rim of pan; turn overhang under lower pastry so fold is even with pan rim. Again press gently to seal, then crimp with tines of fork to finish edge. Bake 15 min, then reduce heat to moderate (350° F) and bake 25 min longer, until crust is golden brown. Remove to cake rack, opening steam vents if closed, to cool 2 to 3 hrs before cutting. 8 servings.

To Make An 8-inch Pie: Use pastry for 8-inch double crust, p 924; 6 tbsp sugar, 2 small lemons, ⅓ tsp grated lemon rind, 2 small eggs, ¾ cup sugar blended with ¾ tsp cornstarch and scant ¼ tsp salt, ¼ cup butter melted, 2 tsp cold water.

KEY LIME PIE

A famous southern Florida favorite, but good wherever you eat it

8 *or* 9-inch pastry shell, p 928	3 eggs, separated
	14 *or* 15-oz can sweetened condensed milk
¼ tsp grated lime rind, pkd	
½ cup lime juice and pulp from either Key *or* Persian limes	½ cup xxxx sugar, pkd
	1 tsp granulated sugar

Bake and cool pastry shell. Wash limes and grate off a little of the rind onto waxed paper; measure and fold into paper to keep moist. Squeeze juice, remove seeds. Beat yolks with rotary beater until light colored. Remove beater and wash. Use wooden spoon to stir in lime juice and rind, then the condensed milk, until smooth and noticeably thickened. Pour into pastry shell, spreading to make filling a little higher at rim. Beat egg whites until stiff, then add xxxx sugar gradually, beating to a stiff, shiny meringue. Spoon meringue lightly over filling; swirl top or spread smoothly and mark into 6 serving pieces with a long knife blade. Sprinkle the tsp of sugar evenly over the top. Bake in moderate oven (350° F) 15 to 17 min or until golden brown. Remove to cake rack to cool 2 to 3 hrs before cutting. 6 servings.

LIME MERINGUE PIE

A refreshingly delicious pie

9-inch pastry shell, p 928
Filling:
 ¼ tsp grated lime rind, pkd
 ⅓ cup lime juice and pulp,
   about 2 Persian limes
 1¼ cups sugar
 3 tbsp cornstarch
 1 tbsp flour
 ¼ tsp salt

1½ cups boiling water
3 egg yolks
1 tbsp firm butter
Meringue:
 3 egg whites
 Dash of salt
 ⅓ cup sugar
 ⅛ tsp vanilla

Bake and cool pastry shell. *Filling:* Wash limes and grate required amount of rind onto waxed paper; fold paper to keep moist. Squeeze juice, remove seeds. Blend sugar, cornstarch, flour and salt with wooden spoon in heavy saucepan; add water gradually, stirring to keep smooth. Place over heat and cook and stir until thick and clear, 1 to 2 min after boiling starts. Remove from heat. Quickly beat yolks, stir in about ⅓ cup of hot mixture, then pour back into saucepan and cook and stir 2 min longer. Remove from heat. Stir in lime juice gradually in *small* portions; then rind and butter. Pour mixture into cooled pastry shell and cool 15 to 20 min. *Meringue:* Now beat whites with salt to a stiff foam; add sugar gradually, continuing to beat to a stiff, shiny meringue, adding vanilla with last few turns. Spread lightly over filling, touching crust all around. Smooth top and mark into 6 servings with long knife blade; or swirl top. Bake in moderate oven (350° F) for 15 min or until golden brown. Remove to cake rack to cool 2 or 3 hrs before cutting. 6 servings.

To Make An 8-inch Pie: Use 8-inch pastry shell, p 928, scant ¼ tsp grated lime rind, ¼ cup lime juice, scant cup sugar, 2¼ tbsp cornstarch, 2 tsp flour, scant ¼ tsp salt, 1 cup plus 1 tbsp boiling water, 2 large egg yolks, scant tbsp butter; 2 large egg whites, dash of salt, ¼ cup sugar, scant ⅛ tsp vanilla.

ORANGE MERINGUE PIE

Excellent color, delicious flavor

9-inch pastry shell, p 928
Filling:
- 1 cup sugar
- 3 tbsp cornstarch
- 3 tbsp flour
- ¼ tsp salt
- ¾ cup boiling water
- 1 cup fresh-squeezed orange juice

3 egg yolks
2 tbsp firm butter
½ tsp grated orange rind, pkd
1 tbsp lemon juice
Meringue:
3 egg whites
1 tbsp orange juice
6 tbsp sugar

Bake pastry shell and cool. *Filling:* Blend next 4 ingredients in top of double boiler. Slowly stir in boiling water, then ½ cup of the orange juice. Place over boiling water, cook and stir until clear and thickened. Cover and cook 10 min longer, stirring frequently. Beat yolks, then quickly stir in about ⅓ cup hot mixture, then pour back into double boiler and cook and stir 2 min longer. Remove from heat. Stir in butter, then rind, and *gradually* stir in remaining ½ cup orange juice in small portions, then lemon juice, stirring vigorously as you add the juices. Pour filling into cooled shell and cool 10 min. *Meringue:* Beat egg whites until barely stiff, add the tbsp orange juice and 6 tbsp sugar gradually, beating until thick and glossy. Pile quickly but lightly over filling, touching crust all around. Bake in a slow oven (300° F) 20 min. Remove to cake rack to cool 2 or 3 hrs before cutting. 6 servings.

To Make An 8-inch Pie: Use 8-inch pastry shell, p 928, ¾ cup sugar, 2¼ tbsp cornstarch, 2¼ tbsp flour, scant ¼ tsp salt, ½ cup plus 1 tbsp boiling water, 6 tbsp orange juice, 2 large egg yolks, 1½ tbsp firm butter, ⅓ tsp grated orange rind, 6 tbsp orange juice, 2 tsp lemon juice. For meringue 2 large egg whites, scant tbsp orange juice, 4½ tbsp sugar.

CREAM PIES

CREAM PIES ARE EASY TO MAKE AND EASY TO MAKE ELEGANT AND LUSCIOUS

The inexperienced cook as a rule starts off baking better *Cream Pies* than any other kind. *The Reason:* The 4 processes required in preparation —making the shell, the filling, the meringue and browning the meringue— are all of necessity done separately and may be done fairly leisurely without affecting the quality of the shell, filling or meringue.

How to Make a Tender, Crisp Pie Shell: Follow directions in *Plain Pastry* recipe, pp 924, 928, to the letter by using care in measuring the right kind of ingredients, and in the mixing and rolling.

How to Make a Beautifully Shaped Baked Shell: Fit rolled-out pastry loosely but well into angles of pie pan. Then let pastry relax 5 to 10 min before trimming off to turn under, and fluting or crimping edge. *Now with a fork, prick pastry all over bottom and up sides of pan, wiggling fork back and forth to make wide-open holes. This keeps air bubbles from forming under pastry and warping shape of shell.* Bake to a pale golden brown all over. If pastry is rolled to uniform thickness and it is baked in a well insulated, well regulated oven, it will bake to a beautiful, uniform brown. Remove baked shell (leave shell in pan) immediately to a cake rack to cool.

How to Make Velvet-Smooth Delicious Fillings of Right Consistency: As shell cools, make filling. As a rule these fillings should be cooked in a double boiler or at least in a heavy saucepan such as cast aluminum. Stir fillings during cooking with a wooden spoon. Measure ingredients accurately. The *Cream Pie* recipes in this book were developed to obtain fillings that would just bulge or sag a trifle when the pies are cut and giving the impression that if the piece of pie was shaken gently, the filling might flow slightly. This kind of filling is the only one that merits the name *Cream Pie.* Occasionally with the best recipe, a filling may turn out too stiff or too thin. The reason is that sometimes lemons, chocolate or brown sugar may have more than the normal amount of acid. This extra acid is just enough to break down the starch used for the thickening to the extent that the resulting filling is too thin. Also a variation in the heat used for cooking, or a variation in size and shape of the double boiler cooks the filling differently in a given length of time. Eggs may be very small and as a result do not add their necessary part of thickening. When a filling turns out stiffer or thinner than it should, remember the next time the filling is made to consider the possibilities listed above and correct the procedure by using a different kind of chocolate, lemons, brown sugar, etc., or larger eggs, a larger pan or lower heat or a longer cooking period, etc., rather than add more or less thickening. Of course, if the filling at hand is too thin to pour into a shell, it may be improved by making a thin, smooth paste of cold milk and cornstarch or flour and a little sugar, then very gradually stir it vigorously but very slowly into the filling which is cooking over slow heat. Use only enough of the paste to give desired consistency. A too-stiff filling may be improved by slowly stirring in a little thin cream or milk, a bit more butter and a little more sugar. Pour *hot* filling immediately into the *cooled* pie shell.

When Should Meringue Be Spread on Cream Pie? If you wish meringue to be free of those golden syrup-like drops one sees occasionally on these pies, then spread meringue on after filling in shell has been cooled to room temp. If those golden drops are wanted, then spread meringue over filling immediately after it is poured into shell and while still hot.

How to Make Meringue on Cream Pies Beautiful: Wait until just before or after pouring filling into shell to beat egg whites, depending on whether or not you want golden drops. Have egg whites warmed to room temperature. Follow directions in *Meringue* recipe below exactly. As soon as meringue is finished spread it on immediately with as *few* motions as possible to leave the surface in beautiful, bold, deep swirls. The spreading must be done quickly and spontaneously. When the job is labored over or there is indecision in the effort, the meringue is far less beautiful. Or the surface of the meringue may be left perfectly level and smooth. For an attractive surface of either swirled or smooth surfaced meringue, sift granulated sugar over top sparingly but evenly. Be sure meringue touches pie shell all around edge so it will not pull away from shell during baking or when pie is cut. Bake meringue to a point where it has its most appetizingly brown color and is cooked through to where it won't collapse when it is cooled. Use either temp for baking meringue and bake for time recommended in recipe below.

How to Finish Cream Pie Without Meringue: When using leftover egg yolks to make cream pie fillings, use *Whipped Cream* for a delectable topping. Spread it on *thinly* leaving the surface smooth or fluffy, or pipe the cream on in a fancy pattern. When spread smooth, the surface of the cream may be marked off in a "plaid" pattern with tines of a fork. The cream may also be sprinkled with grated or finely chopped nuts, such as pecans or pistachios. Grated semi-sweet chocolate or curls of shaved chocolate or chocolate decorettes may be sprinkled over the whipped cream to add an appealing touch and richness, provided the chocolate harmonizes with the flavor of the pie filling. Cream pies are best for eating and cut most attractively when they have just lost their oven heat. They are always best if eaten the day they are baked, but if any must be held over, be sure to keep it in the refrigerator.

MERINGUE FOR TOPPING CREAM PIE

For a 9-inch pie

3 egg whites, room temp   ⅓ cup sugar *plus* 2 tsp
¼ tsp cream of tartar,
   optional

Adjust top rack to center of oven. Start oven 10 min before baking; set to moderate (350° F).

Turn egg whites into a 2 or 3 qt mixing bowl. With a rotary beater, beat whites until frothy, then sprinkle in cream of tartar and beat until almost stiff. Now add sugar 1 tbsp at a time, beating well after each addition. Meringue should be stiff, glossy and stand in peaks that curve over slightly. Quickly pile it lightly onto filling that has had time to cool in the pastry shell. Then quickly swirl the meringue all over the filling lightly, leaving hills and valleys over the top, and touching the pastry all around. This prevents meringue from shrinking away from pastry during baking or serving. Make sure meringue is as deep at rim as in center. (Meringue may be spread perfectly smooth over top, but whether smooth or swirled, do it quickly and spontaneously for the most beautiful effect.) Now place pie on 2 baking sheets, one nested within the other. This serves as insulation to prevent overheating of lower pastry and filling. Bake 12 to 15 min or until meringue toasts to a luscious brown. Remove pie to cake rack to cool 2 or 3 hrs before cutting.

Meringue may be browned in a hot oven (450° F) for 4 or 5 min or in a slow oven (300° F) for 20 min.

Note: To make meringue for an 8-inch pie, use 2 egg whites, scant ¼ tsp cream of tartar and ¼ cup sugar.

BANANA CREAM PIE

An exciting climax to any meal

9-inch pastry shell, p 928
⅓ cup all-purpose flour
½ cup sugar
¼ tsp salt
2 cups milk
3 small egg yolks
1 tbsp firm butter

½ tsp vanilla
2 large *ripe* bananas
1 tsp xxxx sugar
½ cup whipping cream
1 tsp sugar
⅛ tsp vanilla

Bake and cool pastry shell. Blend flour, sugar and salt in heavy saucepan. Slowly stir in 1 cup of the milk until smooth; add rest of milk and cook and stir over direct heat until mixture boils and thickens, for 5 or 6 min. Remove from heat. Quickly stir about ½ cup of hot mixture into well-beaten yolks; pour back into saucepan and cook and stir 2 min longer. Remove from heat and stir in butter and vanilla. Cool about 5 min, then pour half the mixture into pastry-lined pan, spreading well up sides of shell. Peel and slice bananas and arrange over filling; sprinkle with xxxx sugar. Spread rest of filling over bananas. Cool. Whip cream until stiff but still smooth, adding the 1 tsp sugar and flavoring with last few turns. Spread smoothly over filling and mark criss-cross with tines of fork about an inch apart. Serve immediately, or place in refrigerator for not more than an hr or two. 6 servings.

To Make An 8-inch Pie: Use an 8-inch pastry shell; ¼ cup flour, 6 tbsp sugar, ⅛ tsp salt, 1½ cups milk, 2 egg yolks, 2 tsp butter, ½ tsp vanilla, 2 medium bananas, 1 tsp xxxx sugar, ⅓ cup whipping cream, ⅛ tsp vanilla, 1 tsp sugar.

Hint: Whipping the cream and folding into the cooled filling before spreading in the pie makes an extra rich, delicious pie.

STRAWBERRY OR PEACH CREAM PIE

Follow directions for Banana Cream Pie, using sliced strawberries or peaches in place of bananas (1½ cups fruit) and sprinkling with 2 or 3 tbsp xxxx sugar.

Note: Bringing filling up to ¼ inch below rim induces folks to eat *all* the crust. Adding firm butter to hot filling makes it extra shiny.
Putting bananas between two layers of filling keeps them from discoloring.

ABOVE: *The consistency of Chocolate Cream Pie filling, p 960, makes it superb, or "so-so." The proper, pourable, smooth quality of a perfect filling holds the pouring ripples, then levels out. It should always be poured while hot, to cut best after cooling.*

BELOW: *Chocolate Cream Pie is best when just cooled to room temp. Then the wedges will hold their shape. This meringue was swirled over the filling after it cooled, touching the pastry all around. To keep the filling from getting too hot while browning the meringue, the pie was set on two baking sheets with air space between.*

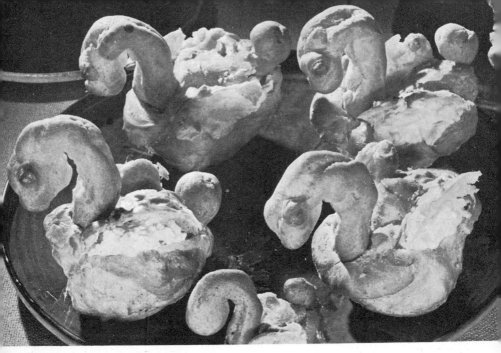

ABOVE: *Cream Puff Swans, p 937, are no trick to make and they are so fascinating when they are lined up on a very flat plate in a swimming pose and with a cygnet or two tagging along for the children's dessert.*

BELOW: *Peach Pie, p 1006, or any other fresh fruit pie takes kindly to a lattice crust, p 984, which is really just a simple problem in weaving strips of plain pastry together on top of the pie.*

1. Assemble all the ingredients needed for the pastry as well as all the equipment needed for measuring and mixing. Sift flour onto a sheet of waxed paper before measuring.

2. Lift the sifted flour lightly into a measuring cup with a spoon until it is heaping, then level the top evenly with a straight-edged knife or spatula. Add the salt to the flour in the bowl and stir to mix.

3. Measure the shortening by pressing it firmly into a cup so there will be no air pockets. Then level the surface with a spatula or straight-edged knife. See footnote on *p 924* for amount of shortening to use.

4. Cut fat into flour with a pastry blender or 2 knives, or rub in with finger tips until fat-flour particles range from the size of rice grains to the size of dried split peas.

5. The particles of fat-flour shown here are the correct size to produce a perfectly baked pastry. All of the methods for cutting in shortening can produce satisfactory results in the hands of an experienced pastry baker, but for the novice, the special wire blender used here is quickest, easiest, and most dependable.

6. Add water gradually from a tsp a few drops at a time and at the same time mix and toss very lightly with a fork to distribute the water evenly. Toss aside the part which has been moistened.

7. Add only enough water to make it possible to tip the bowl slightly to the side and press the mixture gently into a shape that can be picked up easily in the hands. Be particularly careful not to overhandle the dough after the water has been added.

8. Press the particles gently together into a ball. If the day is warm, it may be necessary to wrap the ball in waxed paper and chill for ½ hr. Cut the ball of dough into 2 portions, one slightly larger than the other. Use the larger portion for the bottom crust.

9. Place the larger portion of dough on a *lightly* floured board and shape it quickly into a thick, flat disc with the hands. This shaping forms a small circle of dough and then only the lightest touch is needed with a rolling pin to enlarge the circle to the desired size.

10. Roll the dough out for the lower crust, starting at center and rolling outward with *even light* pressure in all directions to obtain a circle about ⅛ inch thick around the rim but thinner at the center. If the edges fray, indicating that not enough water was added, pull the cracks together or patch them with pieces of pastry.

11. If there is any sticking, loosen the pastry with the edge of a spatula and lift it gently while spraying a small amount of flour under it. For successful rolling, lift the dough and turn it around (not over) several times during rolling. A pastry cloth and rolling pin cover are helpful to the inexperienced pastry maker.

12. Fold the sheet of pastry through the center and lift it carefully and quickly into an ungreased pie pan so the fold is across the center of the pan. The fold makes it easy to center the pastry and the folded sheet is easier to move without danger of cracking.

13. Unfold pastry without stretching and allow it to fall loosely into the angles of the pan. Lift crust gently with one hand and ease it without stretching into the shape of the pan, and at the same time run the finger of the other hand around the inside. Pastry must fit snugly into sides and bottom of pan, especially at angle where sides meet the bottom.

14. Leave the edge of the lower crust untrimmed and put in the filling. Roll out rest of pastry to same thickness as the outer edge of the lower crust and in a circle large enough to fit over top of pie, and make neat cuts in several places to allow steam to escape; it improves the appearance to make the cuts in some simple design. And this open design serves its purpose best as a steam vent when it is not too large and is exactly in the center. Trim off lower crust even with rim of pan, then moisten edges with water. Now lay top crust carefully over filling.

15. Press lower and upper crusts together gently to seal them well; them trim off top crust about ½ inch beyond the rim of the pan. Fold the edge under. See next page. Let rest, see *Step 8, p 926.* Then flute. Bake in a hot oven (450° F) for 12 to 15 minutes; then reduce heat to temp required for filling and continue baking until filling is done according to directions in recipe. The pie should be placed on the center of a rack slid into position in the middle of the oven.

HOW TO MAKE PIE SHELLS
Ingredients for Single Crust, see p 928

1. Follow Steps 1 to 13 for making pastry for double-crust pies on *pp 924–927* but do not divide dough. The ball of dough will be enough to make the single crust.

To make a *pre-baked crust,* fit dough loosely into pan and trim off edge with a scissors leaving ½ inch overhanging at edge of pan.

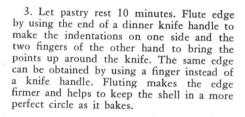

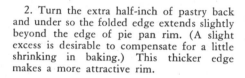

2. Turn the extra half-inch of pastry back and under so the folded edge extends slightly beyond the edge of pie pan rim. (A slight excess is desirable to compensate for a little shrinking in baking.) This thicker edge makes a more attractive rim.

3. Let pastry rest 10 minutes. Flute edge by using the end of a dinner knife handle to make the indentations on one side and the two fingers of the other hand to bring the points up around the knife. The same edge can be obtained by using a finger instead of a knife handle. Fluting makes the edge firmer and helps to keep the shell in a more perfect circle as it bakes.

4. Prick the pastry closely all over the bottom, in the angles, and up the sides with the tines of a fork to prevent puffing during baking. Bake on the center rack of a moderately hot oven (425° F.) for about 15 to 18 minutes, or until crust is a light golden color. After 5 minutes, look at the crust and collapse any bubble by pricking. Cool in the pan on a cake cooler. This crust is then ready to be filled with any one of numerous cold fillings that are placed in a "pre-baked crust."

ABOVE: *Your family's dessert will be apple pie, p 985, . . . in October. Then dress it up with cheese pumpkins or turkey or pumpkin cut-outs of sliced cheese to start getting into the Thanksgiving spirit.*

BELOW: *Pumpkin pie, p 978, the old-fashioned custard type like Mother used to make. How to make the little cheese pumpkins at bottom of picture, see p 436.*

BUTTERMILK RAISIN PIE

Don't let the buttermilk scare you. It gives the pie different texture and a tangy, unusual flavor.

9-inch pastry shell, p 928
Filling:
¼ tsp grated lemon rind, pkd
2 tbsp lemon juice
4 tbsp cornstarch
1 cup *plus* 2 tbsp sugar
¼ tsp salt

2 cups fresh buttermilk
½ cup seedless raisins
2 egg yolks
2 tbsp firm butter
Meringue:
2 egg whites
¼ cup sugar

Bake and cool pastry shell. *Filling:* Wash lemon; grate rind onto waxed paper, measure and fold into paper to keep moist. Squeeze and measure juice. Blend cornstarch, sugar and salt in top of double boiler; stir in buttermilk and raisins and cook and stir over direct heat until mixture boils and thickens. Remove from heat. Beat yolks until thick; quickly stir in about ⅓ cup of the hot mixture, then return to double boiler. Place over boiling water and cook and stir 2 min longer. Remove from heat and stir in lemon juice gradually, then butter until melted. Cool 10 min, stirring occasionally. Pour into pie shell. *Meringue:* Beat egg whites until stiff; gradually beat in the ¼ cup sugar to form a stiff, shiny meringue. Remove beater. Fold in grated lemon rind. Quickly swirl meringue over filling, touching crust all around. Bake in moderately hot oven (400° F) 8 min or until nicely browned. Cool on cake rack about 3 hrs before cutting. 5 or 6 servings.

To Make An 8-inch Pie: Use an 8-inch pastry shell, ¼ tsp grated lemon rind, not pkd, 1½ tbsp lemon juice, 3 tbsp cornstarch, ¾ cup plus 1½ tbsp sugar, ⅛ tsp salt, 1½ cups buttermilk, ⅓ cup raisins, 2 small egg yolks, 1½ tbsp butter; for meringue, 2 small egg whites, 3 tbsp sugar.

BUTTERSCOTCH PIE

Whether topped with meringue or whipped cream, it's rich and tasty . . . a delicious dessert

9-inch pastry shell, p 928
Filling:
¼ cup butter
1¼ cups dark brown
  sugar, pkd
⅛ tsp salt
⅓ cup all-purpose flour
1 tsp cornstarch

2 cups *plus* 2 tbsp milk
3 egg yolks
½ tsp vanilla
1 tbsp firm butter
Meringue:
3 egg whites
¼ tsp vanilla
3 tbsp sugar

Bake and cool pastry shell. *Filling:* Melt butter in heavy 2-qt saucepan; stir in ½ the brown sugar and heat with constant stirring until smooth, thick liquid forms; then boil 1 min. Remove from heat. Blend remaining sugar with next 3 ingredients and stir into hot liquid. Slowly stir in half the milk, so as to keep mixture smooth; then add rest of milk. Place over medium heat and cook and stir until thickened, 5 to 6 min. Remove from heat. Beat yolks well; quickly stir in about ½ cup of the hot mixture; then return to saucepan, cook and stir 2 min longer. Remove from heat; stir in ½ tsp vanilla, then butter until melted. Cool. *Meringue:* Beat egg whites until stiff, add sugar 1 tbsp at a time, beating well after each addition; add ¼ tsp vanilla and beat until stiff but still shiny. Turn filling into pastry shell, pushing well up around rim. Swirl meringue over filling so it touches crust all around. Bake in slow oven (300° F) 20 min, until golden. Remove to cake rack to cool before cutting. (Cool all Cream Pies about 2 hrs at room temp before serving.) 6 servings.

Variation: Cool filling thoroughly in the shell; then spread thinly with whipped, sweetened cream (½ cup whipping cream, 1 tsp sugar).

To Make An 8-inch Pie: Use an 8-inch pastry shell, 3 tbsp butter, 1 cup minus 1 tbsp dark brown sugar, pkd, ⅛ tsp salt, ¼ cup flour, ¾ tsp cornstarch, 1½ cups plus 1½ tbsp milk, 2 large egg yolks, ⅓ tsp vanilla, 1½ tbsp butter; for meringue, 2 large egg whites, ¼ tsp vanilla, 2¼ tbsp sugar.

Hint: Melting the butter with part of the sugar until a smooth liquid is formed is the trick that gives Butterscotch Pie that old-time flavor.

CHOCOLATE CREAM PIE No. 1

9-inch pastry shell, p 928

Filling:
2½ cups milk, scalded
2 tbsp *plus* 2 tsp cornstarch
1 cup sugar
¼ tsp salt
2 sqs unsweet chocolate
1 whole egg *plus* 2 egg yolks, beaten

2 tbsp firm butter
1 tsp vanilla

Meringue:
2 egg whites
Dash of salt
¼ cup sugar
¼ tsp vanilla

Bake pastry shell and cool. *Filling:* Scald milk in top of double boiler. Blend next 3 ingredients in bowl; stir in scalded milk until smooth. Pour back into double boiler; cook and stir over boiling water until smooth and thickened, about 10 min. Add chocolate cut into 8 to 10 pieces; continue to cook and stir until chocolate melts. Stir about ⅓ cup of hot mixture quickly into beaten egg and yolks. Return to double boiler and cook and stir 2 min longer. Remove from heat. Stir in butter until melted, then the vanilla. Cool 10 min stirring frequently; then turn into pie shell, spreading out evenly. *Meringue:* Beat egg whites until stiff, add sugar 1 tbsp at a time, and beat until stiff but still shiny. Beat in vanilla. Spread over filling, touching crust all around. Place in moderate oven (350° F) and bake 15 min. Remove to cake rack; cool 2 to 3 hrs before cutting. 6 servings.

To Make An 8-inch Pie: Use an 8-inch pastry shell, 1¾ cups plus 2 tbsp milk, 2 tbsp cornstarch, ¾ cup sugar, scant ¼ tsp salt, 1½ sqs chocolate, 1 small egg plus 2 small yolks, 1½ tbsp butter, ¾ tsp vanilla; for meringue, 2 small egg whites, dash of salt, 3 tbsp sugar, scant ¼ tsp vanilla.

CHOCOLATE CREAM PIE No. 2

9-inch pastry shell, p 928   2 tbsp firm butter
Filling: 1 tsp vanilla
  2½ cups milk   *Meringue:*
  ⅓ cup all-purpose flour   2 egg whites
  1 cup sugar   Dash of salt
  ¼ tsp salt   3½ tbsp sugar
  2 sqs unsweet chocolate   ¼ tsp vanilla
  4 egg yolks

Bake pie shell and cool. Follow directions for mixing and baking Chocolate Cream Pie No. 1.

Note: For a richer pie, instead of spreading with meringue, let pie cool, then spread with sweetened whipped cream (½ cup whipping cream, 1 tsp sugar).

FRESH COCONUT CREAM PIE

If you like coconut pie—this is the best

Fresh coconut   2 egg yolks
9-inch pastry shell, p 928   1 tbsp firm butter
Filling: ¾ tsp vanilla
  Coconut milk   1½ cups fresh grated coconut,
  ½ cup thin cream   lightly pkd
  Milk   *Meringue:*
  ⅔ cup sugar   2 egg whites
  ¼ tsp salt   Dash of salt
  1½ tbsp cornstarch   ¼ cup xxxx *or* granulated
  3 tbsp all-purpose flour   sugar

Prepare coconut, p 122, saving the milk, then grate, not shred. Cover and store in refrigerator while baking pie shell and making filling. Bake pastry shell and cool. *Filling:* Strain coconut milk, add the cream, then enough milk to make 2¼ cups, then heat to scalding over boiling water. Blend next 4 ingredients in top of double boiler, gradually add scalded milk, stirring to keep smooth. Now place over boiling water and cook and stir until smooth and thickened, about 10 min. Now quickly stir in about ⅓ cup of hot mixture into beaten egg yolks, then pour back into hot mixture and cook and stir 2 min longer. Remove from heat, stir in butter, then vanilla and 1 cup of the coconut. Turn into pie shell. *Meringue:* Beat egg whites until stiff, add salt, then xxxx sugar gradually, beating to a stiff shiny meringue. *Fold* in remaining coconut. Spread smoothly over pie, touching crust all around. A little more coconut may be sprinkled over meringue, then patted down slightly with knife blade. Bake in a moderate oven (350° F) 12 or 15 min or to a tempting brown. Remove to cake rack to cool 2 or 3 hrs before cutting. 5 to 6 servings.

To Make An 8-inch Pie: Use an 8-inch pastry shell, for filling use coconut milk, ⅓ cup cream and enough milk to make 1¾ cups, ½ cup sugar, scant ¼ tsp salt, 1 tbsp cornstarch, 2¼ tbsp flour, 2 small egg yolks, ½ tsp vanilla and 2 tsp butter, and for meringue, 2 small egg whites, dash of salt, and 3 tbsp xxxx sugar.

Note: Whipped cream may be spread over pie instead of meringue, then sprinkle with coconut.

CANNED OR PACKAGED COCONUT PIE

Prepare in same way as Fresh Coconut pie with following exceptions: (1) There will be less coconut milk in the can, so more milk will need to be added to supply the required amount of liquid for the cream filling. (2) When using packaged coconut, use all milk for the liquid, and if finer shreds of coconut are wanted for the cream pie filling, cut shreds with scissors to desired fineness.

DATE CREAM PIE

Different—extra good!

9-inch pastry shell, p 928	1 tbsp firm butter
½ lb pitted dates, 1 cup	¼ tsp lemon extract
2 cups milk	1 egg white
⅓ cup sugar	2 tbsp sugar
2 tbsp flour	½ cup whipping cream
¼ tsp salt	Chopped pecans, optional
2 egg yolks	

Bake and cool pastry shell. Put dates and 1 cup of the milk in top of double boiler. Place over boiling water and cook 25 min, stirring frequently. When dates are soft, beat vigorously with rotary beater. Blend sugar, flour, and salt in 3-qt saucepan; gradually stir in rest of milk. Place over heat and cook and stir until smooth and thickened, about 5 min. Beat yolks lightly; stir in about ¼ cup of the hot mixture, return to saucepan and cook and stir 2 to 3 min longer. Remove from heat. Stir in butter and lemon extract, then the date mixture. Quickly beat egg white to stiff foam, add sugar and beat until meringue stands in peaks. Then beat meringue thoroughly into hot date mixture. Pour into pie shell, spreading out. Cool, then store in refrigerator until ready to serve. Spread with whipped cream and sprinkle with a few chopped nuts just before serving. 6 servings.

To Make An 8-inch Pie: Use 8-inch pastry shell, ⅓ lb pitted dates (¾ cup pkd), ¾ cup milk, ¼ cup sugar, 1½ tbsp flour, scant ¼ tsp salt, ¾ cup milk, 2 small egg yolks, 2 tsp butter, scant ¼ tsp lemon extract; for meringue, 1 small egg white, 1½ tbsp sugar, ⅓ cup whipping cream, chopped pecans for garnish.

FRENCH CREAM PIE

The best of cream pies

9-inch pastry shell, p 928
Graham cracker crust, p 930

Filling:
2 cups milk
½ cup sugar
¼ tsp salt
2 tbsp cornstarch
3 egg yolks

1 tbsp firm butter
1 tsp rum *or* vanilla extract

Meringue:
3 egg whites
Dash of salt
⅓ cup sugar
½ cup fresh fine-grated *or* fine-cut canned coconut
1 tsp sugar

Bake pastry shell and cool or make graham cracker crust. *Filling:* Scald 1½ cups of the milk in top of double boiler over gently boiling water. Blend next 3 ingredients with remaining ½ cup milk until smooth, then stir gradually into scalded milk. Now cook and stir with a wooden spoon until mixture is smooth and thickened, from 10 to 12 min. Beat egg yolks, stir in about ⅓ cup of the hot mixture, then return to double boiler and cook and stir about 2 min longer. Remove from heat. Now stir in butter, then flavoring. *Meringue:* Beat egg whites with dash of salt, then gradually beat in ⅓ cup sugar until a stiff, shiny meringue forms. Fold about ⅓ of this meringue into the hot mixture lightly but thoroughly, then turn it into pie shell. Spread rest of meringue over pie filling being sure to touch crust all around. Smooth top with spatula or knife. Blend coconut and 1 tsp sugar and sprinkle evenly over meringue. Pat coconut *very slightly* into meringue with a knife blade. Bake in a moderate oven (350° F) 12 to 15 min or until attractively mottled. Cool on cake rack 2 or 3 hrs before cutting. 6 to 8 servings.

To Make An 8-inch Pie: Use an 8-inch pastry shell, 1½ cups milk, ⅓ cup plus 2 tsp sugar, scant ¼ tsp salt, 1½ tbsp cornstarch, 2 large egg yolks, 1½ tsp butter and ¾ tsp rum or vanilla extract, and for meringue, 2 large egg whites, dash of salt, ¼ cup sugar, ⅓ cup fresh grated coconut, and ¾ tsp sugar.

GRAHAM CRACKER CREAM PIE

Crust:
  1½ cups graham cracker
    crumbs, 16 to 18 crackers
  2 tbsp sugar
  ⅓ cup melted butter *or*
    margarine
  1 tbsp water
Filling:
  ¼ cup flour
  ½ tsp salt

⅔ cup sugar
2 cups milk
6 egg yolks, beaten
2 tbsp butter
1½ tsp vanilla
Meringue:
  2 egg whites
  ⅛ tsp salt
  ¼ cup sugar
  ½ tsp vanilla

Crust: Crush, grind or put crackers through food mill to make fine crumbs. Reserve 1 tbsp of crumbs for top of pie. Put crumbs and sugar into bowl, mix, then drizzle melted butter over mixture and toss with fork to distribute. Add water and mix until crumbs pack together. Turn mixture into 9-inch pie pan. Pat it firmly with palm of hand or spoon against the bottom and sides of the pan to form a pie shell uniform in thickness. Bake in moderate oven (350° F) 6 to 8 min. Remove to cake rack to cool. *Filling:* Measure flour, salt and sugar into top of double boiler and blend. Stir in 1 cup of the milk and when well blended stir in remaining milk. Place over gently boiling water and stir until smooth and slightly thickened. Beat yolks, stir in about ½ cup of the hot mixture, return to double boiler and cook and stir until thick and smooth, about 5 min longer. Remove from heat; stir in butter, then vanilla. Make *Meringue* by beating egg whites with the salt to a stiff foam, gradually beat in the sugar and vanilla until meringue is stiff, glossy and peaks bend over in soft curves. Fold 2 tbsp of meringue into filling and pour into crust. Pile rest of meringue onto pie; spread so that it touches crust all around. Sieve reserved crumbs evenly over top. Place pie on cookie sheet, bake in slow oven (300° F) 20 min or until meringue is lightly browned. Remove to cake rack to cool 2 or 3 hrs before cutting. Serve pie day it is baked. 6 servings.

REAL MAPLE CREAM PIE

It is just as logical and rewarding to put maple syrup into a pie as onto pancakes

  9-inch pastry shell, p 928
  ¼ cup all-purpose flour
1½ cups milk
  ¼ cup 12% cream, half-
    and-half
  ¾ cup maple syrup

¼ tsp salt
3 eggs, separated
⅛ tsp salt
2 tbsp chopped walnuts,
  optional

Start oven 10 min before baking; set to moderate (350° F). Bake pastry shell and cool. Measure flour into top of double boiler, slowly blend in milk, then add cream, ½ cup of the syrup and salt. Beat thoroughly with rotary beater. Place over hot water and cook and stir until mixture thickens. Beat egg yolks until thick, then stir in some of the hot mixture; return to double boiler and cook and stir 2 min longer. Remove from heat. Beat egg whites and salt with a *clean* rotary beater until soft peaks form. Then beat in rest of syrup, 1 tbsp at a time, beating between additions until stiff and glossy. Add about ¼ of meringue to hot custard, and quickly stir until just smooth. Turn into baked shell. Fold nuts into rest of meringue and spread evenly over pie touching crust all around. Bake in a moderate oven (350° F) 15 min or until meringue is nicely browned. Remove to cake rack to cool to lukewarm before cutting. 6 servings.

To Make An 8-inch Pie: Use an 8-inch pastry shell, 3 tbsp all-purpose flour, 1 cup plus 2 tbsp milk, 3 tbsp 12% cream, ⅓ cup maple syrup, scant ¼ tsp salt, 2 large egg yolks and for meringue, 2 large egg whites, ⅓ cup maple syrup, scant ⅛ tsp salt and 1½ tbsp chopped walnuts.

Note: Nuts may be sprinkled over filling before topping with meringue.

NESSELRODE PIE

Rich and a little costly, but befitting your most outstanding meal

9-inch pastry shell, p 928
Filling:
¼ cup all-purpose flour
½ tsp salt
½ cup sugar
1½ cups milk
1 cup whipping cream, chilled
¼ cup pineapple juice
5 egg yolks
¼ cup moist raisins, chopped
¼ cup blanched toasted almonds, chopped
1 tbsp butter
2 tbsp chopped maraschino cherries
1 tsp maraschino cherry juice
1 tsp rum flavoring
Topping:
1½ tbsp xxxx sugar, pkd
Sweet chocolate bar, chilled, shaved

Bake pastry shell and cool. *Filling:* Blend first 3 ingredients in top of double boiler. Gradually add milk, stirring well to keep smooth, then add ¼ cup of the cream and pineapple juice. Cook and stir over boiling water until smooth and thickened, about 10 min. Now stir some of the hot mixture into beaten egg yolks, then return to double boiler and stir thoroughly. Add raisins, almonds and butter, cover and cook 5 min longer with frequent stirring. Remove from heat. Stir in cherries and flavorings. Pour into cooled pie shell, spreading level. Cool to room temp. *Topping:* Whip remaining ¾ cup chilled cream until just thickened, then beat in xxxx sugar until stiff. Spread over pie. Scatter chocolate shavings over cream. Chill in refrigerator at least an hr before serving. 6 or 7 servings.

To Make An 8-inch Pie: Use an 8-inch pastry shell, 3 tbsp all-purpose flour, ⅓ tsp salt, ⅓ cup sugar, 1 cup plus 2 tbsp milk, ¼ cup whipping cream, 3 tbsp pineapple juice, 4 small egg yolks, 3 tbsp moist raisins, 3 tbsp blanched toasted almonds, 1½ tsp butter, 1½ tbsp chopped maraschino cherries, ¾ tsp maraschino cherry juice and ¾ tsp rum flavoring, and for topping use ½ cup whipping cream, 1 tbsp xxxx sugar and chocolate shavings.

Note: Commercial bottled Nesselrode Fruit may be used in place of the fruits and flavorings.

PINEAPPLE MERINGUE PIE

It's not an everyday meal when you serve this *pie!*

9-inch pastry shell, p 928

Filling:
9-oz can crushed
   pineapple, 1 cup
¼ cup water *or* canned
   peach syrup
1 cup sugar
2½ tbsp cornstarch
⅛ tsp salt

2 egg yolks
1 tbsp lemon juice
½ tsp grated lemon rind, pkd
1 tbsp firm butter

Meringue:
3 egg whites
Dash of salt
⅛ tsp vanilla
6 tbsp sugar

Bake and cool pastry shell. *Filling:* Heat pineapple and water or, yes, canned peach syrup just to boiling. With wooden spoon stir in sugar blended thoroughly with cornstarch and salt. Cook and stir only until clear and thickened. Remove from heat. Beat yolks with lemon juice, then quickly stir in about ⅓ cup of the hot mixture; pour back into rest of mixture. Return to heat and cook and stir 2 min. Remove from heat. Stir in lemon rind and butter. *Meringue:* Beat egg whites with salt until stiff, then beat in vanilla, then sugar gradually to form a stiff, shiny meringue. *Cut-and-fold* ⅓ of meringue lightly but thoroughly into pineapple mixture. Turn into pie shell, spreading level. Spread rest of meringue smoothly over top of pie, touching crust all around. With long knife blade, mark into 6 serving portions. Brown in moderately hot oven (350° F) 12 to 15 min. Remove to cake rack to cool, 2 to 3 hrs before cutting. 6 servings.

To Make An 8-inch Pie: Use an 8-inch baked pastry shell, ¾ cup crushed pineapple with juice, 3 tbsp water or *peach* syrup, ¾ cup sugar, scant 2 tbsp cornstarch, scant ⅛ tsp salt, 2 small egg yolks, 2 tsp lemon juice, 1 tbsp butter, ⅓ tsp grated lemon rind; for meringue: 2 egg whites, dash of salt, scant ⅛ tsp vanilla, 4½ tbsp sugar.

RHUBARB CREAM PIE

Attractive with lively good flavor

9-inch pastry shell, p 928	4 tbsp all-purpose flour
Rhubarb:	¼ tsp salt
¾ lb pink rhubarb	3 egg yolks
1 tbsp water	1 tbsp butter
½ cup sugar	*Meringue:*
Filling:	3 egg whites
2 cups milk	Dash of salt
½ cup sugar	⅓ cup sugar

Bake pastry shell and cool. *Rhubarb:* Trim leaves and ends from rhubarb; wash but *do not* peel as skin gives rhubarb its attractive color. Cut stalks with scissors into inch lengths, dropping into saucepan. Add water and the ½ cup sugar. Cover, place over heat and cook slowly until tender, about 5 min. Remove from heat. There should be 1 cup. Chill.

Filling: Scald 1½ cups of the milk in top of double boiler over gently boiling water. Blend the ½ cup sugar with flour and salt, using a wooden spoon, then stir in remaining ½ cup cold milk until smooth. Stir slowly into scalded milk. Cook and stir until smooth and thick, about 10 min. Beat yolks, then quickly stir in about ⅓ cup of the hot mixture and return to double boiler, add butter and cook and stir 2 min longer. Now pour into baked pie shell, spreading well up sides. Cool 15 or 20 min, then spread with cold rhubarb.

Meringue: Beat egg whites with dash of salt until stiff, then add the ⅓ cup sugar gradually and beat to a stiff, shiny meringue. Spread lightly over rhubarb, touching crust all around. Leave top level. Brown in a moderate oven (350° F) about 15 min. Remove to cake rack to cool 2 or 3 hrs, then serve *immediately* after cutting. 6 servings.

To Make An 8-inch Pie: Use an 8-inch pastry shell, ½ lb pink rhubarb, 2 tsp water and ⅓ cup sugar. *Filling:* 1½ cups milk, ⅓ cup plus 2 tsp sugar, 3 tbsp flour, scant ¼ tsp salt, 2 large egg yolks, 2 tsp butter. *Meringue:* 2 large egg whites, dash of salt, ¼ cup sugar.

SOUR CREAM PRUNE PIE

Compliments will fly when you serve this pie

9-inch pastry shell, p 928	1 tsp lemon juice, optional
Filling:	½ tsp vanilla
½ lb moist dried prunes	*Meringue:*
1 cup boiling water	2 egg whites
¾ cup sugar	Dash of salt
2 tbsp cornstarch	¼ cup sugar
⅛ tsp salt	1 tsp sugar mixed with
1 whole egg and 2 egg yolks	¼ tsp cinnamon
1 cup sour cream	

Bake and cool pastry shell. *Filling:* Cut dried prunes cleanly from pits with scissors in 4 or 5 pieces. Put fruit in top of double boiler, add boiling water. Place over direct heat, cover and *simmer* until prunes soften, 10 to 15 min. Remove from heat. Blend sugar, cornstarch and salt and stir into prunes, using wooden spoon. Place over boiling water and cook 10 to 15 min, stirring frequently. Beat whole egg and 2 yolks well, then beat in sour cream until just blended. Stir slowly into prune mixture, and cook and stir 5 or 6 min longer. Remove from heat. Stir in lemon juice and vanilla. Turn into pie shell, spreading level. Cool 15 min. *Meringue:* Beat egg whites with salt until stiff, then add the ¼ cup sugar gradually, beating to a stiff shiny meringue. Spread meringue over pie, touching crust all around. Leave top level. Mark meringue with long knife blade into 6 wedges; finish by leaving a little peak of meringue in the center. Sprinkle top evenly with sugar-cinnamon mixture. Brown on lower oven rack in moderate oven (350° F) for 15 min. Remove to cake rack and cool 2 to 3 hrs before cutting. 6 servings.

To Make An 8-inch Pie: Use an 8-inch baked pastry shell, 6 oz prunes, ¾ cup boiling water, ½ cup plus 1 tbsp sugar, 1½ tbsp cornstarch, scant ⅛ tsp salt, 1 small whole egg and 2 small egg yolks, ¾ cup sour cream, ¾ tsp lemon juice, ⅓ tsp vanilla; for meringue, 2 small egg whites, dash of salt, 3 tbsp sugar, ¾ tsp sugar and ⅛ tsp cinnamon.

DEEP SOUTH SUGAR PIE

This is a powerfully sweet but different cream pie. When served in modest portions, it is a delightful wind-up for a light meal. Golden drops—"honey dew"—appear on the meringue because it is put on the hot filling.

Pastry for 9-inch single crust, p 928

1½ cups moist brown sugar, pkd
1 whole egg and 2 egg yolks
1 tsp vanilla

Filling:
2 tbsp butter
1 tbsp flour
2 cups milk
¼ tsp salt

Meringue:
2 egg whites
⅛ tsp salt
¼ cup granulated sugar

Adjust rack 5 to 6 inches above bottom of oven. Start oven 10 min before baking; set to moderately hot (425° F).

Make pastry and roll out to line 9-inch glass pie pan. Trim pastry off ½ inch beyond rim of pan; turn overhang under so fold is even with pan rim. Flute with fingers or crimp with fork to finish edge. *Filling:* Melt butter in heavy 3-qt saucepan over moderate heat; stir in flour until smooth, then gradually add milk, stirring constantly. Cook and stir until mixture thickens, is smooth, and *just starts* to boil. Remove from heat. Stir in salt; then sugar *until dissolved.* Quickly beat egg and yolks well; stir in a little of the hot mixture, then return to saucepan, stirring thoroughly. Stir in vanilla. Pour at once into pastry-lined pan. Bake 10 min at 425° F; then reduce heat to moderately slow (325° F) and bake 15 min longer or until crust is browned and filling set *almost* to center. *Meringue:* Meanwhile beat egg whites until stiff with the salt, add sugar 1 tbsp at a time, and beat after each addition, until stiff but still shiny. Remove pie from oven to top of stove; immediately spoon meringue over pie, spread out with spatula to touch crust all around, and mark with spatula in 8 wedges. Return to oven for 15 to 17 min to brown to desired color. Remove to cake rack and cool 2 to 3 hrs before cutting. 8 servings.

To Make An 8-inch Pie: Use pastry for 8-inch single crust, p 928; 1½ tbsp butter, 2¼ tsp flour, 1½ cups milk, scant ¼ tsp salt, 1 cup plus 2 tbsp moist brown sugar, pkd, 1 small whole egg and 2 small yolks, ¾ tsp vanilla; for meringue, 2 small egg whites, ⅛ tsp salt, scant, 3 tbsp sugar.

"PEACHES-AND-CREAM" PIE

Swell eating, but watch out, it's loaded with calories

Pastry for 9-inch single crust, p 928	¼ cup flour
	¼ tsp salt
2 tbsp firm butter	⅛ tsp nutmeg *or*
1 cup 12% cream, half-and-half	¼ tsp cinnamon
	3 cups sliced fresh peaches
⅔ cup sugar	

Adjust rack 5 to 6 inches above bottom of oven. Start oven 10 min before baking; set to moderately hot (425° F). Make pastry and line a 9-inch pie pan, fitting well into angles. Let rest 5 min, then using scissors, trim pastry off ½-inch beyond pan rim. Fold pastry under so fold is even with pan rim, then finish edge in any way desired. Slice butter thinly over bottom of pastry. Measure sugar, flour, salt and nutmeg into small bowl and stir to blend well, then stir in cream until well mixed. Pare peaches, slice thinly, measure and turn into pastry-lined pan, spreading level. Then pour cream mixture over peaches, pressing slices down into cream with back of spoon. Bake 30 to 40 min or until pastry is nicely browned and peaches are tender. Remove to cake rack to cool to lukewarm before cutting. 6 servings.

"BERRY-AND-CREAM" PIE

Make exactly like "Peaches-and-Cream" Pie except substitute 2½ cups washed, well-drained berries for the sliced peaches. Blackberries, raspberries, loganberries or blueberries may be used. If well cooked berries are desired, cover pie with an inverted metal pie pan of same size for first 20 min of baking.

Note: Coffee cream may be used in place of the 12% cream and the butter in these peach and berry cream pies.

CUSTARD PIES

Plain custard pie is the favorite pie of millions. But the ability to bake it perfectly is possessed by too few cooks. The reason is that it combines 2 kinds of food that need to be baked at entirely different temps. Pastry bakes at hot (400° to 500° F) to be tender, flaky, golden brown and show little or no signs of soaking. Custard pie fillings consisting of eggs, milk and sugar bake most satisfactorily at slow (250° to 300° F) to be smooth and jelly-like, delicate in flavor, tender and free of any "weeping." The difficulty in bringing together these two opposing requirements causes many custard pies to fall far short of their possible goodness.

The problem is solvable, however. If the oven is not well insulated, chill the filling until very cold before pouring it into the crust which is at room temp. Bake in hot oven (500° F) for 15 to 18 min until crust begins to brown and the filling warms up. (A portable thermometer should be in such ovens). Then open the door 3 or 4 min for the temp to drop rapidly to slow (250° to 300° F). Then the custard can bake at this most desirable temp in about another 25 to 30 min. If the filling puffs up and acquires a skin over the top while baking, or if when cooled, it weeps or wheys when cut and is porous in texture, the oven temp has been too high. If the filling bakes too long even at the proper temp, the effect will be similar to baking it in too hot an oven.

One of the best ways to test for doneness is to shake the pie very gently. When the filling coagulates to within a half inch of the center, the pie is done. When pie is removed from the oven, this small area of uncooked custard will receive enough heat from rest of pie to cook it to desired firmness.

Custard pie should always be served the day it is baked, preferably just after it has lost its oven heat to be most enjoyable. If necessary to keep overnight, store in refrigerator.

Pumpkin, sweet potato, cottage cheese and some fruits can be added to the basic custard pie ingredients to make the many variations of custard pie. These added ingredients may slightly alter the baking procedure. If you have a modern, well-insulated stove use either the one or two-temp methods of baking described in Custard and Pumpkin Pie recipes.

CHESS PIE No. 1

Powerfully rich with tempting flavor

Pastry for 9-inch single
crust, p 928
1 cup butter, room temp
2 cups sugar
5 eggs, separated
⅛ tsp salt

½ tsp vanilla
½ cup chopped nuts, optional
½ cup seedless raisins,
chopped, optional
⅓ cup sugar

Adjust rack 5 to 6 inches above bottom of oven. Start oven 10 min before baking; set to hot (450° F).

Make pastry and line a 9-inch pie pan, fitting into angles. Trim pastry off with scissors ½-inch beyond pan rim, then fold overhang under even with pan rim; crimp with fork, leaving edge flat. Do not prick pastry. Cream butter until soft and smooth, add the 2 cups sugar gradually and blend thoroughly. Add egg yolks one at a time, beating in well. Beat two egg whites until just stiff, add them with the next four ingredients to creamed mixture and fold in thoroughly. Turn into pastry lined pan, spreading level. Bake for 12 min, then reduce heat to slow (300° F) and bake 20 min longer. Remove from oven and spread with meringue made by beating the remaining 3 egg whites until stiff, adding the ⅓ cup sugar gradually and beating until smooth and shiny. Be sure meringue touches crust all around and is spread smooth over top. Return to oven and bake 15 min longer or until meringue is delicately browned. Remove to cake rack to cool to room temp before cutting. Serve in small wedges. 8 to 10 servings.

To Make An 8-inch Pie: Use pastry for 8-inch single crust, ⅔ cup butter, 1⅓ cups sugar, 4 small eggs (use 2 of the whites for meringue), dash of salt, scant ½ tsp vanilla, ⅓ cup nuts, ⅓ cup raisins, ¼ cup sugar.

CHESS PIE No. 2

A famous Southern pie as delicious as pecan

Pastry for 9-inch Single Crust, p 928	2 tsp vanilla
	½ cup all-purpose flour
1 cup butter *or* margarine, room temp	¼ tsp salt
	4 egg yolks, beaten
2 cups granulated sugar	1 cup evaporated milk

Adjust rack 5 or 6 inches above bottom of oven. Start oven 10 min before baking; set to hot (450° F).

Make pastry and line 9-inch pie pan, fitting well into angles. Trim pastry off with scissors ½ inch beyond pan rim, then fold overhang under even with pan rim; crimp with fork, leaving edge flat. Cream butter with wooden spoon, gradually add sugar and cream well. Stir in vanilla, then flour and salt, and beat until well blended. Stir in egg yolks, then the milk gradually. Turn into pastry-lined pan. Bake 10 min, then reduce heat to moderately slow (325° F) and bake 25 to 30 min longer. Remove to cake rack to cool. Custard should be slightly soft in center when pie is removed from oven; it becomes firm as it cools. After cooling, pie may be placed in refrigerator. Fortunately this pie is just as delicious chilled as it is lukewarm and crust retains crispness remarkably well. So serve warm or cold. 7 or 8 servings.

CUSTARD PIE
—ONE TEMPERATURE METHOD

Pouring a little foamy custard over the top produces an attractive all-over brown top

Pastry for 9-inch single
crust, p 928
2½ cups milk, scalded
4 eggs
½ cup sugar

¼ tsp salt
½ tsp vanilla
Nutmeg, preferably whole,
freshly grated

Adjust rack 5 or 6 inches above bottom of oven. Start oven 10 min before baking; set to moderately hot (400° F).

Make pastry. Roll out and line a 9-inch pie pan, fitting well into angles. Trim pastry off with scissors ½-inch beyond pan rim; turn under overhang so fold is even with pan rim. Leave rim flat or imprint with tines of a fork. Do not prick. Place in refrigerator to chill at least 30 min. Scald milk in top of double boiler (milk is scalded when bubbles form around outer edge). Keep boiler covered to prevent skin from forming on top of milk. Beat eggs just enough to blend yolks and whites thoroughly, add sugar, salt and scalded milk, stirring constantly. Quickly strain custard mixture. Add flavoring and quickly pour all but ⅓ cup of mixture into pastry-lined pan. Beat remaining custard until very foamy and carefully flow it over top of custard. Place pie in center of oven rack and bake 25 to 30 min or until filling is all set with exception of about an inch circle in center. Make test for doneness, p 970. Remove to cake rack to cool 2 or 3 hrs before cutting. 5 or 6 servings.

CUSTARD PIE
—TWO TEMPERATURE METHOD

Follow directions for making *Custard Pie—One Temperature Method* above, except do not scald milk or chill the pastry. Bake pie first at hot (450° F) for 18 min, then reduce temp to slow (300° F) and bake about 30 min longer.

COCONUT CUSTARD PIE

Follow directions for making *Custard Pie—Two Temp Method,* except sprinkle ½ cup fine shredded coconut over top of pie before pouring in the last ⅓ cup of foamy custard. Bake the same way.

To Make An 8-inch Pie: Use pastry for an 8-inch single crust, p 928, 1⅔ cups milk, 3 small eggs, ⅓ cup sugar, ⅛ tsp salt, ½ tsp vanilla, nutmeg.

MARLBOROUGH PIE

A popular New England version of apple pie

Pastry for 9-inch single crust, p 928	½ tsp salt
1 tsp grated lemon rind, pkd	3 eggs
3 tbsp lemon juice	2 cups tart applesauce, freshly made *or* canned
1 cup sugar	3 tbsp melted butter *or* margarine
2 tsp flour	

Adjust rack 4 to 5 inches above bottom of oven. Start oven 10 min before baking; set to hot (450° F).

Make pastry. Roll out and line a 9-inch pie pan, fitting well into angles. Let rest 5 min. Trim off pastry with scissors ½ inch beyond rim of pan; turn overhang under so fold is even with pan rim. Crimp with fork. Do not prick. Wash lemon and grate yellow rind onto waxed paper; squeeze juice and remove seeds. Blend sugar, flour and salt in 2-qt mixing bowl with wooden spoon. Add eggs and beat thoroughly with rotary beater, then beat in applesauce. Remove beater and *stir* in lemon rind and juice with spoon, then melted butter. Pour mixture gently into pastry-lined pan. Bake 15 min at 450° F, then reduce heat to very slow (275° F) and bake 20 min longer. Remove to cake rack to cool 2 to 3 hrs before cutting. 6 servings.

To Make An 8-inch Pie: Use pastry for 8-inch single crust, ¾ tsp grated lemon rind, 2¼ tbsp lemon juice, ¾ cup sugar, 1½ tsp flour, ⅓ tsp salt, 2 large eggs, 1½ cups applesauce, 2¼ tbsp butter.

ORANGE COTTAGE CHEESE PIE

A rich orange layer topped with velvety custard. Here's a prize winner!

1 cup orange sections, drained	1 tsp lemon juice
¼ cup orange juice	1 tbsp butter
½ cup sugar	Pastry for 9-inch single crust, p 928
2 tbsp cornstarch	Cottage Cheese Filling, p 976
Dash of salt	
¼ cup water	

Adjust rack 5 to 6 inches above bottom of oven. Start oven 10 min before baking; set to hot (450° F).

Section oranges and place in strainer to drain, saving juice; there should be ¼ cup. Snip sections with scissors into 3 or 4 pieces. Blend sugar, cornstarch and salt in small saucepan, using wooden spoon; gradually stir in orange juice and water until smooth. Place over heat and cook and stir until clear and very thick, about 2 min. Remove from heat. Stir in lemon juice and butter, then gently stir in orange pieces. Chill until cold and thick. Make pastry and line 9-inch pie pan, fitting well into angles. Trim off with scissors ½ inch beyond rim of pan; turn overhang under so fold is even with rim, and crimp with fork or flute with fingers. Do not prick. Make Cottage Cheese Filling as for Pineapple Cottage Cheese Pie. Spread chilled orange filling over bottom of pastry-lined pan; place on stove. With cup dip up the Cottage Cheese Filling and pour *gently* over orange layer so as not to disturb the fruit. *Carefully* place in oven and bake 15 min at 450° F; then reduce heat to moderately slow (325° F) and bake 30 to 35 min longer. Remove to cake rack to cool for 2 to 3 hrs before cutting. 6 servings.

To Make An 8-inch Pie: Use ¾ cup orange sections, 3 tbsp orange juice, 3 tbsp water, 6 tbsp sugar, 1½ tbsp cornstarch, dash of salt, scant tsp lemon juice, scant tbsp butter, pastry for 8-inch single crust, Cottage Cheese Filling for 8-inch pie.

PAPAYA PIE

This tastes like delicately seasoned pumpkin pie

2½ lbs pared diced ripe papaya, about 2 qts
Pastry for 9-inch single crust, p 928
3 eggs
1 cup granulated sugar
¾ cup 12% cream, half-and-half
½ cup milk

3 tbsp melted butter
1 tsp lemon juice
¼ tsp orange extract
¼ tsp allspice
Dash of salt
Topping:
1 tbsp sugar mixed with
¼ tsp grated orange rind, pkd

Wash papaya and cut in half. Remove seed and fiber. Cut into 1-inch length-wise strips. Pare thinly, then dice, dropping into *heavy* 3-qt saucepan. Place over heat (no water) and cook and stir with wooden spoon 30 to 35 min, or until cooked down to thick pumpkin purée consistency. Remove from heat. Cool slightly and put through food mill or press through sieve. There should be 1½ cups purée.

Adjust rack 4 or 5 inches above bottom of oven. Start oven 10 min before baking; set to hot (450° F).

Make pastry. Roll out and line 9-inch pie pan fitting well into angles. Trim off with scissors ½ inch beyond rim. Turn overhang under so fold is even with rim of pan. Beat eggs with rotary beater; beat in papaya and sugar. Remove beater. Stir in remaining ingredients, except topping, in order listed. Turn into pastry-lined pan. Sprinkle top with sugar-orange mixture. Bake 15 min at 450° F, reduce heat to 325° F and bake 25 min longer or until crust is brown and custard set. Top does not brown. Remove to cake rack for 2 or 3 hrs before cutting. 6 servings.

PEACH BLOSSOM PIE

Attractive, colorful and good

Pastry for 9-inch Single
Crust, p 928
¾ to 1 lb ripe flavorful freestone peaches, 4 large
2 large eggs
1¼ cups milk

2 tbsp sugar
¾ cup sugar, blended with
1 tbsp flour and
Dash of salt
3 to 4 drops almond extract
1 tbsp melted butter

Adjust rack to 5 or 6 inches above bottom of oven. Start oven 10 min before baking; set to hot (450° F).

Make pastry. Roll out and line a 9-inch pie pan, fitting well into angles. Trim pastry off with scissors ½-inch beyond pan rim, then turn under overhang so fold is even with pan rim. Flute edge or imprint with tines of fork. Pare peaches thinly, halve and remove pits. Arrange peach halves, cut-side up, around outer edge of lined pan. Sprinkle peaches with 2 tbsp sugar. Beat eggs well; stir in milk, then sugar blended with flour and salt, then extract and butter. Carefully pour custard into pan. Bake 15 min, then reduce heat to moderately slow (325° F) and bake 40 min or until *only an inch-circle of custard* in the center remains liquid, when pan is slightly shaken. Remove to cake rack. Serve lukewarm or cold as is, or with whipped cream. 6 servings.

To Make An 8-inch Pie: Use pastry for 8-inch single crust, 3 large peaches, 2 small eggs, ⅞ cup milk, 1½ tbsp sugar, ½ cup sugar blended with 2 tbsp flour, dash of salt, 2 or 3 drops almond extract, 2 tsp melted butter.

Note: Instead of using peach halves, slice each half in fourths and arrange over bottom of pastry-lined pan. Sprinkle with sugar, then pour custard over peaches. Bake as above until custard is *just* set.

PECAN PIE—COLD FILLING METHOD

An excellent recipe for a favorite pie

Pastry for 9-inch Single
Crust, p 928
1 cup white corn syrup
½ cup brown sugar, pkd
¼ tsp salt

1 tsp vanilla
2 tsp lemon juice
3 eggs, *slightly* beaten
1 cup small pecans, *or*
large meats broken

Adjust rack 4 or 5 inches above bottom of oven. Start oven 10 min before baking; set to moderately hot (425° F).

Make pastry. Roll out and line 9-inch pie pan, fitting well into angles. Trim ½-inch from edge with scissors, turn overhang under so fold is even with pan rim. Flute or imprint with tines of fork. Do not prick. Combine next 6 ingredients and stir until well blended, then stir in nuts. Pour into pastry-lined pan. Bake 10 min, then reduce heat to moderately slow (325° F) and bake 35 to 40 min longer or until crust is golden brown and filling is set. Remove to cake rack to cool until just lukewarm. Serve plain or with whipped cream. 6 to 8 servings.

PECAN PIE—HOT FILLING METHOD

Heating the filling gives extra rich flavor

Pastry for 9-inch Single
Crust, p 928
1 cup dark corn syrup
½ cup granulated sugar
2 tbsp butter

¼ tsp salt
3 eggs
½ tsp vanilla
1 cup small pecans *or* large
meats broken

Adjust rack 4 or 5 inches above bottom of oven. Start oven 10 min before baking; set to hot (450° F).

Make pastry. Roll out and line a 9-inch pie pan, preferably glass, with pastry, fitting well into angles. Trim ½-inch from edge with scissors, then turn overhang under so fold is even with pan rim. Flute or imprint with fork tines at inch intervals. Measure next 4 ingredients into heavy aluminum saucepan and heat to boiling, stirring constantly with a wooden spoon. Break eggs into 2-qt bowl; remove 1 tsp white, beat slightly and use it to brush inside of pastry. Beat eggs with fork until well broken up but not until foamy—over-beaten eggs obscure nuts. Gradually stir in hot syrup, then vanilla and nuts. *Do not beat.* Pour into pastry lined pan. Bake 10 min, then reduce heat to moderately slow (325° F), and bake 25 or 30 min longer or until filling is set. Remove to cake rack to cool. Serve lukewarm or thoroughly cooled. 6 to 8 servings.

Hint: To avoid overbrowning, cover pie with aluminum pan of same size first 15 min of baking.

To Make An 8-inch Pie: Use pastry for an 8-inch single crust. ⅔ cup corn syrup, ⅓ cup sugar, 1½ tbsp butter, scant ¼ tsp salt, 2 eggs, ⅓ tsp vanilla, ⅔ cup pecans.

PINEAPPLE COTTAGE CHEESE PIE

An elegant two-layer custard pie

Pastry for 9-inch single
crust, p 928
Pineapple Filling:
  1½ cups crushed pineapple
  ½ cup sugar
  1 tbsp cornstarch
  1 tbsp water
Cottage Cheese Filling:
  ½ cup sugar

1 tbsp butter
¼ tsp salt
3 tbsp all-purpose flour
½ cup creamed cottage cheese
2 eggs
1 cup milk
½ tsp vanilla

Adjust rack 5 or 6 inches above bottom of oven. Start oven 10 min before baking; set to hot (450° F).

Make pastry. Roll out and line a 10-inch (not 9-inch) pie pan, fitting well into angles. Trim off with scissors ½-inch beyond pan rim; turn overhang under so fold is even with rim, then crimp with fork or flute with fingers.

Pineapple Filling: Measure pineapple and sugar into a 3-qt saucepan, and heat to boiling, stirring constantly. Remove from heat. Blend cornstarch and water to smooth paste and stir thoroughly into pineapple mixture. Again place over heat, cook and stir until thick and clear. Remove from heat and chill until cold.

Cottage Cheese Filling: Measure sugar and butter into mixing bowl. Mix thoroughly either with an electric mixer or rotary beater. Then add salt, flour and cottage cheese and beat until thick and smooth. Beat eggs with a fork and add them *very slowly* to cottage cheese mixture. Do not add any faster than the mixture will take up the eggs. In the same way add milk very slowly, turning mixer (if used) to lowest speed. Stir in vanilla. Spread pineapple mixture over bottom of pastry-lined pan; place on stove. With cup, dip up Cottage Cheese filling and pour *gently* over pineapple layer so as not to disturb the fruit. Carefully place in oven and bake 15 min at 450° F; reduce heat to moderately slow (325° F) and bake 30 to 35 min longer. Remove to cake rack to cool 2 or 3 hrs before cutting. 6 to 8 servings.

HONEY PUMPKIN PIE

Pumpkin, honey and orange juice combine well in this good pie

Pastry for 9-inch Single	¼ cup orange juice
Crust, p 928	¼ tsp grated orange rind, pkd
2 eggs	½ tsp salt
1½ cups pumpkin purée,	¼ tsp ginger
canned *or* home cooked,	1 tsp cinnamon
p 1390	¼ tsp mace *or* nutmeg
¾ cup evaporated milk	¼ tsp cloves
¾ cup mild flavored honey	1 tbsp boiling water

Adjust rack 4 or 5 inches above bottom of oven; set to hot (425° F).

Make pastry. Roll out and line a 9-inch pie pan, fitting well into angles. Trim off with scissors ½-inch beyond pan rim, turn overhang under so fold is even with pan rim. Crimp with fork, leaving edge flat. *Do not prick pastry.* Beat eggs in a 3-qt bowl until well mixed, stir in next 6 ingredients until well blended. Measure spices into a cup; add boiling water and stir to a smooth paste, then stir thoroughly into pumpkin mixture. Turn mixture into pastry-lined pan. Bake 15 min then reduce heat to slow (300° F), opening oven a min so heat drops rapidly to 300° F. Bake about 25 min longer or until custard tests done, p 970. Remove to cake rack to cool to lukewarm before cutting. 6 servings.

To Make An 8-inch Pie: Use pastry for an 8-inch single crust. 2 small eggs, 1 cup pumpkin, ½ cup evaporated milk, ½ cup honey, 3 tbsp orange juice, scant ¼ tsp orange rind, ⅓ tsp salt, ⅙ tsp ginger, ¾ tsp cinnamon, ⅙ tsp mace, ⅙ tsp cloves, 1 tbsp boiling water.

PUMPKIN PIE No. 1—BAKED AT TWO TEMPERATURES

A delicious mildly spiced pie. Scorching the pumpkin, as Grandma did, gives excellent flavor

Pastry for 9-inch Single Crust, p 928	¼ tsp ginger
1½ cups canned pumpkin purée *or* home cooked, p 1390	¾ tsp cinnamon
	⅛ tsp nutmeg
	2 tbsp boiling water
2 eggs	½ tsp salt
¾ cup brown sugar, pkd	¼ cup 12% cream, half-and-half
¾ cup evaporated milk	

Adjust rack 4 or 5 inches above bottom of oven. Start oven 10 min before baking; set to moderately hot (425° F).

Make pastry. Roll out and line a 9-inch pie pan, fitting well into angles. Trim off with scissors ½-inch beyond pan rim; turn overhang under so fold is even with pan rim. Crimp with fork leaving edge flat or flute with fingers. *Do not prick pastry.* Turn pumpkin into a 3-qt saucepan, place over direct heat, cook and stir until it is dried out and the natural sugar in it is slightly caramelized (scorched but not burned). This takes about 10 min. Remove from heat. Beat eggs until just mixed, stir in sugar, milk and spices that have been blended to a smooth paste with the hot water. Stir in pumpkin, salt and cream until thoroughly blended. Pour into pastry-lined pan. Bake 15 min; then reduce heat to slow (300° F), opening oven a min or so for heat to drop rapidly to 300° F. Bake about 25 min longer or until custard has coagulated all except a small circle in center. This will set later. Remove to cake rack to cool to lukewarm before cutting. 6 servings.

To Make An 8-inch Pie: Use pastry for an 8-inch single crust, 1 cup pumpkin purée, 2 small eggs, ½ cup brown sugar, pkd, ½ cup evaporated milk, ⅙ tsp ginger, ½ tsp cinnamon, ¹⁄₁₆ tsp nutmeg, 1½ tbsp boiling water, ⅓ tsp salt, 3 tbsp cream.

PUMPKIN PIE No. 2—BAKED AT ONE TEMPERATURE

Excellent pie. If pie cracks in baking the temp is too high. Pie puffs up near end of baking, but should not puff enough to crack

Pastry for 9-inch Single Crust, p 928	1 tsp cinnamon
1¾ cups canned pumpkin purée *or* home cooked, p 1390	½ tsp ginger
	2 eggs
	1 cup 12% cream, half-and-half
¾ cup sugar	½ cup milk
½ tsp salt	

Adjust rack 5 or 6 inches above bottom of oven. Start oven 10 min before baking; set to moderately hot (400° F).

Make pastry. Roll out and line a 9-inch pie pan, fitting well into angles. Trim off with scissors ½-inch beyond pan rim; turn overhang under so fold is even with pan rim. Crimp with fork or flute edge. *Do not prick pastry.* Chill in refrigerator for 30 min. Turn pumpkin into a 3-qt saucepan, place over direct heat and cook and stir until dried out and slightly caramelized. Remove from heat, but keep hot. Mix the sugar, salt and spices well, then stir into the hot pumpkin thoroughly. Beat eggs slightly, add cream and milk, then add to the pumpkin mixture and stir until thoroughly blended. Pour immediately into pastry-lined pan. Bake 25 to 30 min or until pastry is golden brown and only an inch circle in the middle of filling remains soft. It will set later. Remove to cake rack to cool to lukewarm before cutting.

Note: Perfectly baked pumpkin pie has neither wrinkles nor cracks on surface. Baking a hot filling in a chilled crust at 400° F for 25 to 30 min produces a smooth, shiny, good textured filling and a well baked crust free from soaking.

SHOO-FLY PIE

Pennsylvania Dutch made this pie famous. The following recipe has less molasses than old time recipes because present day palates don't approve of very potent molasses flavor. Made by this recipe the pie has engaging flavor

Pastry for 9-inch Single Crust, p 928	½ cup sorghum *or* dark corn syrup
1 cup all-purpose flour	1 cup water
¾ cup light brown sugar	½ tsp soda, generous
⅓ cup butter *or* margarine	1 tsp vinegar

Adjust rack 4 or 5 inches above bottom of oven. Start oven 10 min before baking; set to hot (450° F).

Make pastry. Roll out and line a 9-inch pie pan, fitting pastry well into angles. Trim off with scissors ½-inch from pan rim; turn overhang under so fold is even with pan rim. Flute with fingers or crimp with fork. Measure flour, sugar and butter into mixing bowl and use pastry blender or two knives to cut into a crumb-like texture. Sprinkle half the mixture into pastry-lined pan. Combine sorghum or corn syrup, water and soda thoroughly, then the vinegar. Pour mixture *onto spoon* so force of pouring will not displace crumb lining. Now sprinkle rest of crumbs over top of pie. Bake 15 min, reduce to moderately slow (325° F) and bake 25 to 30 min longer or until crust and top are well browned. Remove to cake rack to cool 2 or 3 hrs before cutting. 6 or 8 servings.

SLIP-SLIDE CUSTARD PIE

Has a crisp crust if served very shortly after assembling

9-inch pastry shell, p 928	1 tsp vanilla
4 medium eggs	½ tsp nutmeg, about, blended
½ cup sugar	with
¼ tsp salt	1 tsp sugar
2½ cups milk	

Bake pastry shell and cool. Do not build up a high fluted edge. Butter a pie pan, preferably glass, the same size as pan in which pastry shell was baked. Beat eggs *only enough* to blend yolks and whites. (Slightly beaten eggs produce a firmer custard than well beaten ones.) *Stir* in sugar and salt, then milk and vanilla. Remove ½ cup of mixture to small bowl. Set the buttered pie pan in a ¾-inch deep jelly-roll pan, then place on *top oven rack* which is slightly pulled out. Strain custard into buttered pan. Beat the ½ cup custard in bowl well with a rotary beater until very foamy. Pour carefully over top of custard in pie pan. Sprinkle with nutmeg and sugar. Pour enough hot water around custard to come half way up pie pan.* Push rack *gently* back in oven. Bake in a moderate oven (350° F) 30 min until custard is set, then increase temp to moderately hot (400° F) and bake 10 min longer or until lightly browned. Remove from oven. Cautiously remove custard immediately to cake rack to cool at least 3 hrs *at room temp.* Do not chill. Shortly before serving, loosen edge with pointed tip of paring knife, then shake gently to loosen custard in bottom. Hold custard over pie shell with both hands, tilt pan of custard and slide very carefully into shell. Shake gently into place. Let settle a few min before serving. 6 servings.

*Or place custard over an enamelware or glass baking dish of same size containing 1 cup hot water.

This Encyclopedia of Cooking is arranged for your convenience—completely alphabetical by chapter, by subject, and by recipe. Cross referenced, and indexed, with chapter and subject at top of every page.

SWEET POTATO PIE

*Evidently of plebeian origin, but now it's in high favor with folks of
all self-estimations*

Pastry for 9-inch Single	¼ tsp salt
Crust, p 928	¼ tsp nutmeg
3 medium sized sweet	1 tsp baking powder
potatoes	½ cup milk
¼ cup butter, room temp	½ tsp grated orange rind, pkd
2 eggs, separated	1 tsp brandy extract
½ cup strained honey	

Adjust rack 4 or 5 inches above bottom of oven. Start oven 10 min
before baking; set to hot (450° F).

Make pastry. Roll out and line a 9-inch pie pan, fitting well into
angles. Trim off with scissors ½-inch beyond pan rim; then turn overhang under so fold is even with pan rim. Crimp edge with fork or flute
with fingers. *Do not prick.* Cover pastry-lined pan with waxed paper.
Scrub potatoes thoroughly in cold water, place in a 3-qt saucepan, cover
with boiling water. Heat to boiling, then reduce heat to gentle boil,
cover pan and cook potatoes until soft, from 20 to 25 min. Drain potatoes, skin while hot and rub them through food mill or sieve to remove
fibers. Cool slightly. Beat in butter, then egg yolks and the next 4 ingredients and beat until smooth and creamy. Stir in last 3 ingredients. Pour
mixture into pastry-lined pan. Bake at 450° F for 15 min or until edge
of crust is lightly browned. Reduce heat to slow (300° F) and bake
25 to 30 min longer. Lift pie from oven to top of stove and quickly
spread with meringue made by beating the 2 egg whites until stiff, then
beating in the 3 tbsp sugar. Be sure meringue touches crust all around
and is smooth or swirled over top. Return to oven for 20 min longer to
brown meringue. Remove to cake rack to cool 2 or 3 hrs before cutting.
5 to 6 servings.

VINEGAR PIE

Oh so good pie! This flavorful dessert is an old-timer!

Pastry for 9-inch Single	½ tsp cinnamon
Crust, p 928	½ tsp allspice
1 cup seedless raisins,	¼ tsp cloves
chopped or cut	4 eggs, separated
¼ cup soft butter	2½ to 3 tbsp 5% cider vinegar
2 cups sugar	Dash of salt

Adjust rack 4 to 5 inches above bottom of oven. Start oven 10 min
before baking; set to moderately hot (425° F).

Make pastry. Roll out and line 9-inch pie pan, fitting pastry well
into angles. Trim off with scissors ½-inch from pan rim; turn overhang

under so fold is even with rim, then flute. *Do not prick pastry.* Wash raisins, drain and chop or snip each into 2 or 3 pieces with scissors. Cream butter and sugar thoroughly. Add spices and blend well. Beat in yolks with rotary beater until smooth and creamy. Add vinegar and again beat until smooth. Remove beater and wash. Stir in raisins with wooden spoon. Beat egg whites with dash of salt until stiff, then slide onto sugar mixture. *Cut and fold* in lightly but thoroughly. Turn into pastry-lined pan. Bake 15 min, then reduce heat to slow (300° F) and bake 20 min longer or until top is nicely browned and center of filling is jelly-like. Remove to cake rack to cool 2 or 3 hrs before cutting. 6 servings.

To Make An 8-inch Pie: Use pastry for an 8-inch single crust, ⅔ cup raisins, 3 tbsp butter (scant), 1⅓ cups sugar, ⅓ tsp cinnamon, ⅓ tsp allspice, ⅛ tsp cloves, 3 small eggs, 1⅔ tbsp vinegar, dash of salt.

FRUIT PIE TECHNIQUES

Past and Present

Modern standards for fruit pies require that the bottom as well as the top crust be flaky, tender and richly browned. The fruit should be cooked through while retaining its original form and natural lively flavor. The juice should be slightly thickened, with a clear fruit color and flavor. There should be enough juice to keep the fruit moist and to flow slightly when the pie is cut.

Old-time cooks rarely used any thickening in fruit or berry pies. They used a little baking powder in the pastry, which produced a thick, puffy, porous crust. The inside layers of the crust soaked up much of the fruit juice, and what remained was beautifully clear. When cut, wedges of these juicy pies were less neat than when thickening is used. But those who remember eating such pies have never found their equals.

Present-day standards require the good flavor of old-time unthickened fillings, but in addition they call for a crisp, flaky bottom crust instead of a juice-soaked one. Recipes in this chapter will produce juicy pies with the old-time flavor in a crisp bottom crust. A minimum of thickening, either cornstarch or flour or a combination of both, or sometimes dry bread crumbs, are used. A little butter is often added to enhance the flavor.

For fruit pies of the highest quality, use only highest-quality fruit. Barely ripe fruit is best. Then it has fine color and sprightly flavor, and is full of juice with high pectin content. When fresh fruit is not at its best, use high-quality frozen fruit. Mellow apples, dead-ripe cherries, soft plums and berries which have lost their bright color and juicy, firm texture never produce fine pies.

Be sure to seal the edges of top and bottom pastry together. Cut vents in the center of the top crust—not near the edges where they make it easy for juice to flow over. Both flavor and food value are lost with lost juice.

Most fruit pies require two-temp baking: first, in a *hot oven* (450° F) for 12 to 15 min, to bake the pastry before the juice cooks out of the fruit, thus reducing the tendency to soak the lower crust; second, in a *moderate* (350° F) to *moderately slow* (325° F) oven for the rest of the baking period. The moderate temp finishes baking the crust and cooks the fruit at *simmering*, so the juice is less likely to boil over. The fruit is usually done when juice flows up through the vents.

The old idea that inserting a piece of macaroni into the vent will prevent the loss of juice is a mistaken one. The macaroni end which is set into the filling cooks and expands to clog the vent. This creates enough steam pressure in the filling to break the seal around the edge of the pie and permit juice to flow out.

FRUIT PIE MAKING CAN BE FUN IF THESE TIME-SAVING, EASY STEPS ARE FOLLOWED IN ORDER GIVEN

Step 1—Assemble all ingredients, making sure everything is at hand. Assemble necessary equipment.

Step 2—Prepare fruit, if it does not discolor on standing.

Step 3—Make pastry, let stand 10 to 15 min. Roll out lower crust 1½-inch larger than pie pan, fit into pan, trim off flush with rim. Cover pastry-lined pan with waxed paper or slip into large plastic bag to keep moist in dry hot weather.

   a.—When making plain top crust, wrap remaining pastry in waxed paper, let stand at room temp while preparing filling.

   b.—If making lattice top, roll out remaining pastry and cut into strips for lattice, then cover closely with waxed paper (or in hot dry weather, with a moistened towel).

   c.—If top is to be Streusel, prepare mixture and set aside.

Step 4—Adjust oven racks to recommended position. Start oven, setting to initial baking temp, 10 min before putting in pie.

Step 5—Prepare sugar-flour mixture. Sprinkle crumbs, if used, over bottom pastry; then part of sugar-flour mixture. Add fruit, spreading into even and compact layer. Enough should be used to round up slightly, but not too much, because fruit pies can be too full to be appealing. Sprinkle with remaining sugar-flour mixture and dot with butter.

Step 6—Roll out top crust and cut vents in center. Cover pie with all-over crust, lattice top or streusel, first moistening edge of lower crust with cold water for the all-over or lattice top so it will seal well.

   a.—For all-over crust, trim dough to ½-inch beyond edge of rim. Turn the overhang under edge of lower crust so fold is even with rim; press down gently all around to seal, then crimp with tines of fork or flute with fingers.

   b.—For lattice top, arrange lattice strips over top, p 984. Trim ends of strips flush with pan rim. Moisten edge of bottom crust and press down gently. Now moisten again and cover ends of strips all around pan with long pastry strips, framing lattice; press to seal, then crimp or flute.

c.—For streusel top, sprinkle with streusel mixture.

Step 7—Place pie on oven rack, close door immediately. Set timer for baking at initial temp.

Step 8—When timer rings, readjust heat regulator and set timer for rest of baking. (This assumes that your oven regulator is accurate, in which case pie will bake in approximately the time recommended.)

Step 9—Remove baked pie to cake rack to cool away from drafts.

Step 10—Cool to suggested temp, for maximum palate appeal. Most fruit pies should be eaten lukewarm. Long standing encourages soaking of the bottom crust.

HOW TO MAKE A WOVEN LATTICE OR STRIPPED TOP FOR FRUIT PIE

For a 9-inch Lattice Top Pie: Make pastry for 8-inch double crust, p 924. A lattice top with spaces between strips does not require as much pastry as a fully covered pie.

Have Fruit and Filling Ingredients Ready before rolling pastry so pie can be assembled quickly. Have fruit washed, drained and prepared in a bowl. Have other ingredients *at hand* such as dry bread crumbs, if used, flour and sugar blended, etc. With filling almost ready, bottom pastry can be quickly rolled out, and lattice strips cut and laid over top of pie before they dry out. Pastry strips must be moist to fold back and weave together without breaking.

Preparation of Pastry: Make pastry. Roll out scant ⅔ of it for lower crust. Quickly fit into a 9-inch pie pan, then trim off flush with edge of pan. Roll out remaining pastry into a circle or egg-shape; egg-shape gives more long strips.

Cutting the Strips: Use a metal-edge ruler, a long bladed knife or a pastry jagger. When using knife or ruler, flour the edge well *before each cutting.* Press into rolled out pastry, cutting entire strip in one stroke. With a little care, this method insures even-width strips. Cut 14 to 16 strips scant ½-inch wide. Reserve 2 long strips to use to circle around edge of pie to cover ends of lattice strips.

Arrange Filling in Pastry: Fit fruit such as berries, cherries, sliced peaches, etc. *snugly and evenly* into pastry-lined pan to prevent depressions. Have filling slightly rounded and a little higher in center of pie; this holds the strips up so they can brown well before fruit shrinks down to level. Strips which sag or dip into the filling *do not brown well.* They are apt to soak and remain "raw looking," or take on the color of the fruit.

Laying Strips Over Filling for Woven Lattice: Lay strips *one way* about ¾-inch apart across top of pie. Start with a short strip at edge of pie, then increase lengths of strips up to center of pie. Decrease lengths toward opposite edge. Turn pie so that strips are vertical to you; *turn back* every other strip *onto itself* at middle of pie. Pick up a long strip and lay it perpendicular across the center, then *unfold strips over it.* Now fold back alternate strips; lay on another perpendicular one, etc. until half of pie is finished. Now turn the pie around and do same on opposite half to complete the lattice. The result is an interweaving of strips of pastry showing open sqs of filling. With a knife, trim off ends of strips flush with edge of pie. Moisten rim of pastry. Now lay on the 2 reserved long strips of pastry neatly over ends of lattice strips for pie rim; keep edge of strips flush with edge of pan. Press down gently to seal, or crimp strips and under-crust together with fingers or tines of fork. Bake as the individual recipe directs. For lattice that is not interlaced, see Dried Apricot Pie, p 990.

Note: Use only 10 pastry strips when making your first lattice-top pie for easier weaving. If smaller "windows" are desired (more pastry strips) cut extra pairs of strips to weave in. There must always be an equal number of strips both ways.

FINE DRY WHITE BREAD CRUMBS FOR JUICY FRUIT PIES

Using fine dry bread crumbs in these pies is a good trick. They absorb quite a little juice without thickening remaining juice. When pie is cut there is no evidence of their presence, and there is no difference in the flavor.

To prepare, use white bread. Dry it out thoroughly without toasting it. A good way is to put it onto a cake rack and place it into a warm oven with heat turned off, and leave until oven cools. Remove bread, if not dried, rewarm oven and return bread to oven until it is dry enough to break clean with a snap. Now use paring knife to shave off the thin brown crust. Then break up and place in food mill and rub through into bowl or leave slices whole and grate bread into fine crumbs. Turn crumbs into a clean, dry jar and cover with lid. Store in refrigerator. Will keep for several weeks.

APPLE PIE

The prince of pies!

Pastry for 9-inch double crust, p 924
7 to 8 medium-size tart, juicy apples, 2¼ lbs
1 tbsp flour
Dash of salt

⅔ to ¾ cup sugar, depending on tartness of apples
1 tbsp butter
1 tbsp lemon juice, optional
¼ tsp cinnamon, optional

Adjust rack to 5 to 6 inches above bottom of oven. Start oven 10 min before baking; set to hot (450° F).

Make pastry; roll out ½ of it to line 9-inch glass pie pan, fitting well into angles; trim off even with pan rim. Roll out remaining pastry for top crust. Cut design in center for wide-open steam vents. Cover pastry with waxed paper while preparing filling.

Wash apples, pare, quarter, remove cores and cut quarters lengthwise into 3 or 4 slices. There should be a full qt of sliced apples, firmly pkd. Blend flour, salt and sugar and sprinkle ¼ of mixture over bottom of pastry-lined pan. Stir rest of mixture lightly through apples and turn them into pan, arranging slices to fit shell compactly. Fruit should be slightly rounded up in center. Dot with butter and sprinkle with lemon juice, then with cinnamon. Moisten edge of lower pastry, lay on top pastry, and press down gently around edge to seal. Trim off pastry with scissors ½ inch beyond pan rim. Turn overhang under lower pastry so fold is even with pan rim. Again press down gently all around edge, and crimp with tines of fork or flute with fingers. Bake 15 min, then reduce heat to moderately slow (325° F) and bake 35 min longer or until apples are tender and juice bubbles out of vents. Remove to cake rack to cool 2 or 3 hrs. Serve lukewarm, plain, with cheese or ice cream. 5 to 6 servings.

To Make an 8-inch Pie: Use pastry for an 8-inch double crust, 1½ lbs medium-size tart juicy apples, 2 tsp flour, dash of salt, 7 tbsp to ½ cup sugar, 1 tsp butter, 2 tsp lemon juice, scant ¼ tsp cinnamon.

APPLE SOUFFLE PIE

A delicious pie—easy to mix, but baking temps must be heeded to keep the filling "fenced in."

Pastry for 9-inch Single Crust, p 928	2 eggs, separated
	Dash of salt
1 tbsp fine dry white bread crumbs, p 985	⅓ cup *plus* 1 tbsp sugar
	1 tbsp flour
2 cups cold tart applesauce*	

Bake on bottom oven rack. Start oven 10 min before baking; set to hot (450° F). Make pastry. Roll out to a 12-inch circle and fit snugly into angles of a *10-inch* pie pan. Yes, 10-inch pan. Let rest for 5 min; then use scissors to trim off pastry ½ inch beyond rim of pan. Turn overhang under so fold is even with pan rim. Flute with fingers to form high edge. Sprinkle crumbs over bottom of pastry. Measure applesauce into a 2-qt mixing bowl. Add egg yolks, salt and half the sugar blended with the flour. Beat with rotary beater until smooth. Scrape off,

*The applesauce recipe in this book makes a thick sauce. If a thin commercial applesauce is used, cook and stir contents of a No. 2 can (2½ cups) until amount is reduced to 2 cups.

remove and wash beater. Now beat egg whites until stiff, add remaining sugar in 2 or 3 portions, and beat to form stiff, shiny meringue. With rubber scraper, cut-and-fold meringue gently but thoroughly into apple-sauce mixture. Turn gently into pastry-lined pan, spreading level. Bake 10 min, then reduce heat to moderately slow (325° F) and bake 40 min longer, or until crust and top of pie are nicely browned. Remove to cake rack to cool 2 or 3 hrs before serving. 6 servings.

To Make a 9-inch Pie: Use pastry for an 8-inch single crust, to line a 9-inch pie pan. For filling, use 2 tsp fine bread crumbs, 1½ cups cold apple sauce, 2 small eggs, a dash of salt, ¼ cup plus 2 tsp sugar, 2 tsp flour.

CANNED APPLE PIE

With a good brand of tart and tasty canned apple slices, first-rate apple pie can be served all year 'round

Pastry for 9-inch double crust, p 924	1 tbsp flour
No. 2 can unsweet sliced apples	¾ tsp cinnamon
	⅛ tsp allspice
½ cup sugar	2 tsp lemon juice
¼ tsp salt	1 tbsp butter

Adjust rack 4 to 5 inches above bottom of oven. Start oven 10 min before baking; set to moderately hot (425° F).

Make pastry; roll out ½ of it and line 9-inch pie pan, fitting well into angles. Use scissors to trim off even with rim of pan. Roll out rest of pastry for top crust; cut design in center for wide-open steam vents. Turn apples into mixing bowl. Blend next 5 ingredients and sprinkle 2 tbsp of mixture over bottom of pastry-lined pan; add rest to apples and stir gently to mix. Stir in lemon juice. Turn into lined pan, spreading evenly. Dot with butter. Moisten edge of lower pastry. Lay on top pastry and press gently all around edge to seal. Trim top pastry off with scissors ½ inch beyond rim. Turn overhang under edge of lower crust so fold is even with pan rim; again press gently to seal. Crimp with tines of fork to finish edge flat. Bake 30 min or until golden brown. Remove to cake rack to cool to lukewarm. 5 servings.

FRENCH OR DUTCH APPLE PIE
Good-looking; good eating!

Streusel:
- ¾ cup all-purpose flour
- ½ tsp cinnamon
- ⅓ cup moist light brown sugar, pkd
- ⅓ cup firm butter *or* margarine

Pastry and Filling:
- Pastry for 9-inch Single Crust, p 928
- ¾ cup sugar
- 1 tbsp flour
- 1 lb 14 oz juicy tart cooking apples, 7 to 8 medium

Adjust rack 5 to 6 inches above bottom of oven. Start oven 10 min before baking; set to hot (450° F).

Streusel: Blend flour, cinnamon and sugar in a 2-qt mixing bowl. Add butter and cut in with pastry blender or 2 knives until particles are size of peas. Chill until needed.

Pastry and Filling: Make pastry; roll out and line 9-inch pie pan, fitting well into angles. Let rest 5 min; then trim off with scissors ½ inch beyond rim of pan. Turn overhang under so fold is even with pan rim and flute to make a stand-up edge. Blend ¼ cup of the sugar with the flour and sift over bottom of pastry. Wash apples, pare thinly, quarter and remove core; cut quarters into 4 lengthwise slices. Arrange slices compactly in pastry-lined pan; they should be heaped slightly in center. Sift remaining sugar over apples, then sprinkle evenly with Streusel. Bake 15 min, then reduce heat to moderate (350° F) and bake 30 to 35 min. (If apples are a slow-cooking variety, cover pie with a tin or aluminum pie pan of same size at the time heat is reduced, bake 15 min then remove cover and bake 15 to 20 min longer.) Remove to cake rack to cool 2 to 3 hrs before cutting. 6 servings.

To Make an 8-inch Pie: For Streusel, use ½ cup plus 1 tbsp all-purpose flour, ⅓ tsp cinnamon, ¼ cup brown sugar pkd, ¼ cup butter; for Pastry and Filling, use pastry for 8-inch single crust, 1 lb 6 oz apples, about 6 medium, ½ cup plus 1 tbsp sugar and 2 tsp flour.

FRIED PIES

An unforgettable old-time snack. Wonderful to eat right from the hand

Dried Apple Filling:
2 cups stewed dried apples, p 551
¼ cup sugar
2 tbsp melted butter
¼ tsp nutmeg *or* cloves *or* 1 tsp cinnamon

Pastry:
2 cups all-purpose flour
1 tsp salt
⅓ cup shortening
Ice water
3 cups shortening for frying

Filling: Cook apples, stir in sugar, butter and spices. Cool.

Pastry: Combine ingredients as for Plain Pastry, p 924. Roll out ⅛ inch thick on lightly floured pastry cloth. Cut into 5-inch rounds with top of 1-lb coffee can. Put spoonful of filling on ½ of each circle, keeping it ½ inch from the edge. Brush edge of pastry with water and fold the empty half of pastry round over the filling, make half-moons. Seal edges by pressing with tines of fork or thumb. Prick tops of pies 2 or 3 times with fork. Heat shortening in skillet or Dutch oven to 360° F. Slide 4 or 5 pies into hot fat, using pancake turner to lift them. Fry until golden-brown on underside, 2 to 3 min. Turn and fry other side. Lift out and drain on paper toweling. Serve warm or cold. These may be baked on a cookie sheet instead of fried; however, they then become Turnovers. 10 pies.

Note: Biscuit Dough, p 234, is excellent for Fried Pies when rolled thin.

APRICOT FILLING FOR FRIED PIES

1 cup apricot purée, p 551   1 tbsp melted butter
½ cup sugar

Prepare and use like Dried Apple Filling. 10 pies.

MINCE FRIED PIES

Prepare mince as for pie, p 1003. Makes excellent filling.

SOUR CREAM APPLE PIE

One bite calls for another!

Pastry for 9-inch double   ½ tsp cinnamon
crust, p 924 $\frac{1}{16}$ tsp nutmeg
2 lbs quick-cooking tart $\frac{1}{16}$ tsp salt
apples, 5 cups sliced   ½ cup sour cream
¾ cup sugar   1 tbsp sugar
2 tbsp flour

Adjust rack 4 to 5 inches from bottom of oven. Start oven 10 min before baking; set to moderately hot (425° F).

Make pastry; roll out ½ of it and line a *10-inch* pie pan, fitting well into angles. Trim off even with rim using paring knife. Roll out rest of pastry and cut 18 strips ⅜ to ½ inch wide for lattice top; lay aside 2 longest strips. Pare apples, quarter, core and cut in uniform ⅛-inch thick lengthwise slices. Blend next 5 ingredients thoroughly; sprinkle 2 tbsp of mixture over bottom of pastry in pan. Stir rest into sour cream and combine with apples. Turn mixture into pan; spread level. Moisten edge of pastry with water. Quickly lay 8 pastry strips each way across pie, without interlacing. Press ends gently down at rim to seal. Trim off ends of strips flush with pan rim. Again moisten edge and lay remaining long strips around the rim, covering ends of strips and joining neatly. Crimp gently at 1-inch intervals with tines of fork. Sprinkle the 1 tbsp sugar over top. Bake 15 min; then reduce heat to moderately slow (325° F) and bake about 45 min longer, or until apples are tender and crust is nicely browned. Remove to cake rack to cool 2 or 3 hrs before cutting. 6 servings.

To Make a 9-inch Pie: Use pastry for 8-inch double crust. Line 9-inch pie pan. Use 1½ lbs apples, 3¾ cups sliced, ½ cup plus 1 tbsp sugar, 1½ tbsp flour, ⅓ tsp cinnamon, 2 or 3 dashes of nutmeg, 2 or 3 dashes of salt, ⅓ cup sour cream, 2 tsp sugar.

CANNED APRICOT PIE

This tasty pie is good for you, because apricots contain the rare copper that good nutrition requires

Pastry for 8-inch double
crust, p 924
No. 2½ can apricot halves
in heavy syrup
⅔ cup sugar

⅛ tsp salt
3 tbsp flour
1 tbsp firm butter
Dash of nutmeg, optional

Adjust rack 4 to 5 inches above bottom of oven. Start oven 10 min before baking; set to moderately hot (425° F).

Make pastry; roll out a scant ⅔ of it and line a *9-inch* pie pan, fitting well into angles. Let rest 5 min, then trim off even with rim of pan. Roll out remaining pastry and cut 18 strips ⅜ to ½-inch wide for lattice top. Save 2 longest strips to finish edge of pie. Drain juice quickly from apricots and save. Turn fruit into mixing bowl. Blend sugar, salt and flour well; sprinkle 2 tbsp of mixture over bottom of pastry-lined pan and fold rest into apricots. Now gently stir in ½ cup of apricot juice. Turn fruit mixture into pastry-lined pan, spreading level. Dot with butter and sprinkle with nutmeg. Moisten edge of lower pastry. Quickly lay 8 strips of pastry each way without interlacing for lattice top, and press ends gently to edge of lower crust. Trim off even with rim of pan. Again moisten pastry around rim, and lay the 2 long strips of pastry around the edge, joining neatly. Crimp with tines of fork dipped in flour to finish the edge. Bake 30 min or until crust is nicely browned and juice bubbles up between lattice strips. Remove to cake rack to cool 2 to 3 hrs before cutting. 6 servings.

To Make an 8-inch Pie: Use pastry for 6-inch double crust, No. 2 can apricot halves, ½ cup sugar, dash of salt, 2¼ tbsp flour, 2 tsp butter and dash of nutmeg.

DRIED APRICOT PIE WITH LATTICE TOP

Tangy—reviving

½ lb good-quality dried
apricots
2 cups cold water
1 cup sugar
Water *or* canned peach
syrup

1 tbsp butter
1½ tbsp cornstarch
⅛ tsp salt
Pastry for 8-inch double
crust,* p 924

Wash apricots quickly but thoroughly through cold water. Put into saucepan, add the water, cover pan and let soak at least 2 hrs. Now add ½ the sugar, place over heat, cover and boil gently about 20 min or until fruit is about tender. Quickly drain off and measure juice; add enough water or peach syrup to make 1 cup.

*Pastry for an 8-inch double crust is enough for a 9-inch lattice top pie.

Start oven 10 min before baking; set to moderately hot (425° F). Make pastry; roll out a scant ⅔ of it and line a *9-inch* pie pan, fitting well into angles. Trim off even with rim of pan. Roll out rest of pastry and cut into 18 strips ⅜ to ½ inch wide for lattice top. Save aside 2 longest strips to finish edge. Now blend rest of sugar with cornstarch and salt; sprinkle 2 tbsp of mixture over bottom of pastry-lined pan. Stir remainder gently into apricots and turn into lined pan. Dot with butter. Moisten edge of lower pastry. Lay 8 strips across top each way to form lattice, without interlacing; press gently at rim to seal ends to bottom pastry. Trim off strips even with rim and again moisten edge. Lay the 2 longest strips around rim of pie and crimp with tines of fork to finish edge. Bake about 30 min, or until crust is nicely browned and juice bubbles up through lattice. Remove to cake rack to cool 2 or 3 hrs before cutting. 6 to 7 servings.

To Make an 8-inch Pie: Use 6 oz dried apricots, 1½ cups cold water, ¾ cup sugar, water or canned peach syrup to make ⅔ cup, 1 tbsp butter, 1⅛ tbsp cornstarch, scant ⅛ tsp salt, and pastry for 6-inch double crust.

CANNED BERRY PIES

Buy a brand of berries that has the can filled with large solid fruit and only enough juice to cover. (This can be determined by lightly shaking can.) Less canned berries are required for making pie than fresh berries because the cooked berries are fully shrunk. A No. 2 can holding 2½ cups for a 9-inch pie and a No. 303 can holding 2 cups makes an 8-inch pie. Be sure to look at the label to see if the berries are pkd in syrup or water. Syrup-pkd berries require less sugar than water-pkd. A No. 2 can syrup-pkd requires ⅔ cup sugar but if water-pkd requires about 1 cup. A No. 303 can will require a generous ½ cup sugar for syrup-pkd fruit, and a generous ⅔ cup sugar for water-pkd fruit. Drain off juice from berries, stir in from 2 to 3 tbsp flour mixed with the sugar and cook and stir until juice is thickened. A little lemon juice often points up the berry flavor. Now fold in the berries and cool. Then turn into pastry-lined pan. Lay on top pastry with design cut in center for steam vents, trim off, fold under, crimp, then bake.

FRESH BLACKBERRY PIE

Juicy, tangy and tops in eating pleasure

Pastry for 9-inch double
crust, p 924
5 cups blackberries, washed
and drained
½ to ⅔ cup sugar, depending
on ripeness of berries

Dash of salt
1½ to 2½ tbsp flour, depending
on juiciness of berries
1 tbsp butter

Adjust rack 4 to 5 inches above bottom of oven. Start oven 10 min before baking; set to hot (450° F).

Make pastry; roll out ½ of it and line 9-inch pie pan, fitting well into angles; trim off even with rim of pan. Roll out remaining pastry for top crust; cut design in center for wide-open steam vents. Prepare berries. Blend sugar, salt and flour; sprinkle 3 tbsp of mixture over bottom of lined pan. Turn in berries, spreading out compactly level; sprinkle rest of sugar mixture over them. Dot with butter. Moisten edge of lower pastry; then lay on top pastry. Press gently around edge to seal. Trim off top pastry with scissors ½ inch beyond pan rim. Fold overhang under bottom pastry so fold is even with rim of pan. Again press gently to seal, then crimp edge with tines of fork. Bake 12 to 15 min or until pastry begins to brown, then reduce heat to moderately slow (325° F) and bake 20 to 25 min longer, or until pastry is nicely browned and juice bubbles up through vents. Remove to cake rack to cool. 2 to 3 hrs. Serve lukewarm. 5 to 6 servings.

BLUEBERRY WHIPPED CREAM PIE

This delicious pie is in reverse. An attention getter!

9-inch pastry shell, p 928	⅔ cup boiling water
1 pt fresh blueberries	2 tbsp butter
⅔ to ¾ cup sugar	1½ tbsp lemon juice
¼ tsp salt	½ pt whipping cream
2 tbsp cornstarch	2 tbsp xxxx sugar

Bake and cool pastry shell. Pick over berries, wash and drain thoroughly. Blend sugar, salt and cornstarch; stir in water. Add 1 cup blueberries, place over heat, and cook with gentle stirring until mixture boils and becomes thick and clear, 3 to 4 min. Remove from heat; stir in butter and lemon juice. Cool until lukewarm, then gently fold in remaining berries. Cover and place in refrigerator until cold but not set. About 1 hr before serving, whip cream until thick, sift in xxxx sugar and continue beating until stiff. Spread quickly over bottom of pie shell, leaving cream layer a little higher around edge. Turn berry filling into pie, spreading it out gently over the cream. Return to refrigerator till serving time. No additional whipped cream is needed on the top. 6 servings.

DEEP DISH BLUEBERRY PIE

A luscious dinner climax!

1 qt canned blueberries in medium syrup	1 tsp lemon juice
3 tbsp flour	2 tbsp butter
⅛ tsp salt	Pastry for 8-inch double crust, p 924
1 cup sugar	

Adjust rack 5 to 6 inches below top of oven. Start oven 10 min before baking; set to moderately hot (425° F). Have ready a 12 x 7½ x 2-inch glass baking dish.

Drain blueberries; there should be 1½ to 2 cups juice. Blend flour, salt and sugar in saucepan with wooden spoon; then gradually blend in berry juice until smooth. Place over heat and cook and stir until it boils and is thickened. Remove from heat. Stir in lemon juice and butter, then fold in berries gently. Cool thoroughly. Roll pastry into rectangle ½-inch longer and wider than pan; cut steam vents in center. Pour cold berry mixture into baking pan. Fold pastry in half; lift onto filling and unfold carefully over filling. Now fold under overhang so fold is even with pan rim. Press edge of pastry gently against edge of pan. Bake 20 min; then reduce heat to moderately slow (325° F) and bake 10 min longer. Remove to cake rack and cool to lukewarm before serving. 6 servings.

FRESH BLUEBERRY PIE

Pastry for 9-inch double crust, p 924	3 tbsp flour
	1 cup sugar
1 tbsp fine dry white bread crumbs, p 985	Dash of salt
	2 tbsp lemon juice
1 qt blueberries	1 tbsp butter, optional

Adjust rack 4 or 5 inches above bottom of oven. Start oven 10 min before baking; set to hot (450° F).

Make pastry; roll out ½ of it and line a 9-inch pie pan, fitting well into angles; trim off even with pan rim. Sprinkle crumbs evenly over bottom of pastry-lined pan. Roll out remaining pastry for top crust; cut design in center for wide-open steam vents. Pick over berries, discarding damaged ones and wash thoroughly in cold water. Drain. Blend flour with sugar and salt and sprinkle ⅓ cup of it over crumbs, then turn in berries, spreading out compactly. Drizzle lemon juice over berries, then sprinkle rest of sugar mixture over top. Dot with butter, then moisten edge of lower pastry; lay on top pastry. Press gently around edge to seal. Trim off top pastry with scissors ½-inch beyond pan rim. Fold overhang under bottom pastry so fold is even with pan rim. Again press gently to seal, then crimp edge with tines of a fork. Bake 12 to 15 min or until pastry begins to brown, then reduce heat to moderately slow (325° F) and bake 20 to 25 min longer or until pastry is nicely browned and juice bubbles up through vents. Remove to cake rack to cool to lukewarm. 5 to 6 servings.

FROZEN BLUEBERRY PIE

An extra-good juicy pie to make any time of year

4 cups frozen blueberries,	1 tbsp flour
2 10-oz pkgs	2 tbsp cornstarch
Pastry for 9-inch double	1 cup sugar
crust, p 924	⅛ tsp salt
4 tsp lemon juice	1 tbsp butter

Adjust rack 4 to 5 inches from bottom of oven. Start oven 10 min before baking; set to hot (450° F).

Defrost berries 2 to 3 hrs at room temp; turn into 3-qt mixing bowl. Make pastry; roll out ½ of it and line 9-inch pie pan, fitting well into angles. Roll out rest of pastry for top crust and cut design in center for wide-open steam vents. Stir lemon juice into thawed berries. Blend flour, cornstarch, sugar and salt; sprinkle 2 tbsp of mixture over bottom of pastry in pan; stir rest thoroughly into berries. Turn berries into pastry-lined pan and spread out level. Dot with butter. Trim bottom pastry off even with rim of pan; moisten edge all around and lay on top pastry. Press down gently around edge to seal; then trim with scissors ½ inch beyond rim of pan. Fold overhang under edge of bottom pastry so fold is even with pan rim. Again press gently to seal, then flute with fingers or crimp with tines of fork. Bake 15 min, then reduce heat to moderate (350° F) and bake 30 min longer, or until crust is nicely browned and juice bubbles up through vents. Remove to cake rack to cool to lukewarm before cutting. Serve lukewarm. 6 servings.

To Make An 8-inch Pie: Use 3 cups frozen blueberries, pastry for 8-inch double crust, 3 tsp lemon juice, 2 tsp flour, 1½ tbsp cornstarch, ¾ cup sugar, scant ⅛ tsp salt, 1 tbsp butter.

FRESH BLUEBERRY AND RED RASPBERRY PIE

The keen flavor of the raspberries is an ideal complement for the mild blueberry flavor

1 pt fresh blueberries	⅓ cup *plus* 1 tbsp sugar
1 12-oz pkg frozen red	2 tbsp flour
raspberries	Dash of salt
Pastry for 8-inch double	1 tbsp lemon juice
crust, p 924, (top is lattice)	1 to 2 tbsp firm butter
1½ tbsp fine dry white bread	
crumbs, p 985	

Adjust rack 5 to 6 inches above bottom of oven. Start oven 10 min before baking; set to hot (450° F).

Pick over, wash and drain blueberries; turn into bowl with barely defrosted raspberries. Make pastry; roll out ½ of it and line a 9-inch glass pie pan, fitting well into angles. Trim pastry off ½ inch beyond rim. Roll out rest of pastry for top; cut into ½-inch strips with metal-edged ruler, knife or pastry jagger. Sprinkle crumbs evenly over bottom of pastry-lined pan. Blend sugar, flour and salt; sprinkle 2 tbsp of mixture over crumbs, then gently fold rest into berries. Turn berries into pastry-lined pan, spreading into even layer. Drizzle with lemon juice. Dot with butter. Moisten rim of bottom pastry and quickly lay pastry strips ½ inch apart across pie in 2 directions *without interlacing.* Trim strips even with edge of pan and gently press down against moistened lower pastry; moisten ends of strips and turn ½-inch overhang of bottom crust up, folding over ends of strips. Press down to seal, then flute edge; or crimp with fork. Bake 12 to 15 min; then reduce heat to moderate (350° F) and bake 20 to 23 min longer. Remove to cake rack to cool 2 to 3 hrs before cutting. 6 servings.

Note: A pt box of fresh red raspberries may be used, in which case the sugar should be increased.

CANNED CHERRY PIE WITH LATTICE TOP
Pie you'll be proud to serve!

Pastry for 8-inch double crust, p 924	⅛ tsp salt
No. 2 can sour red cherries, water-packed	2½ tbsp cornstarch
	3 to 4 drops almond extract
	1 tbsp butter
1 cup sugar	3 to 4 drops red food coloring

Adjust rack 4 to 5 inches from bottom of oven. Start oven 10 min before baking; set to moderately hot (425° F).

Make pastry. Drain juice from cherries; there should be ¾ to ⅞ cup juice. Blend sugar, salt and cornstarch in saucepan with wooden spoon. Stir in juice gradually until smooth. Place over heat and cook and stir until just clear and thickened. Remove from heat, stir in extract, butter and coloring, then the cherries. Set in pan of cold water to cool. Roll out a scant ⅔ of the pastry and line a *9-inch* pie pan, fitting well into angles. Roll out remaining pastry into an oval and cut into 18 strips ⅜ to ½ inch wide for lattice top. Save 2 longest strips to finish edge. Turn cooked cherries into lined pan, spreading level. Trim off pastry even with pan rim. Moisten edge. Lay 8 pastry strips each way across pie without interlacing, to form lattice; press ends of strips against edge of lower crust. Now trim off strips even with rim. Again moisten edge slightly, lay the 2 long strips around edge, joining neatly, and crimp with tines of fork. Bake about 30 min or until crust is nicely browned and juice bubbles up through lattice. Remove to cake rack to cool 2 or 3 hrs before cutting. 6 servings.

To Make An 8-inch Pie: Use only 2 cups of the canned sour red cherries and their juice, ¾ cup sugar, scant ⅛ tsp salt, 2 tbsp cornstarch, 2 to 3 drops almond extract, scant 1 tbsp butter, 2 or 3 drops red coloring, pastry for 6-inch double crust.

CHAMPION FRESH SOUR CHERRY PIE

The technique of pitting and sugaring keeps all the juice in this delicious pie

1 qt sour red cherries (*important:* see best way to wash and pit, p 573)
¾ to ⅞ cup sugar
2 tbsp cornstarch
2 tbsp water

1 tbsp butter
Red food coloring, optional
Pastry for 9-inch double crust, p 924
2 tsp thin cream
2 tsp sugar for sprinkling

Adjust rack about 5 inches above bottom of oven. Start oven 10 min before baking; set to hot (450° F).

Use fresh-picked sound cherries; wash, drain and pit, dropping into 2-qt bowl. There should be 3 cups. Add sugar and fold in gently with rubber scraper. Cover and chill overnight or for several hrs until sugar dissolves. Turn cherries into sieve placed over 1½-qt saucepan to drain. There should be ½ to ⅝ cup juice. Blend cornstarch and water until smooth, then stir into cherry juice. Place over heat, cook and stir until very thick and clear. Remove from heat, stir in few drops red coloring, and fold in cherries. Cool. Make pastry. Roll out ½ of it and line 9-inch pie pan, fitting well into angles. Roll out remaining pastry for top crust and cut design in center for wide-open steam vents. Turn cherries into pastry-lined pan, spreading level. Dot with butter. Trim off pastry even with rim. Moisten edge with water. Lay top pastry over pie and press down gently around edge to seal. Trim off top pastry with scissors ½ inch beyond rim of pan and turn overhang under bottom pastry so fold is even with rim. Again press down gently to seal, then crimp with fork. Brush top of pie lightly with cream and sprinkle with the 2 tsp sugar to give interesting surface to crust. Bake 15 min, then reduce heat to moderate (350° F) and bake 20 min longer. Remove to cake rack to cool 2 to 3 hrs before cutting. Serve lukewarm. 6 servings.

To Make An 8-inch Pie: Use 2⅓ cups pitted cherries, ½ cup plus 1 to 3 tbsp sugar, 1½ tbsp cornstarch, 1½ tbsp water, 2 tsp butter, red coloring, pastry for 8-inch double crust, 1½ tsp thin cream, 1½ tsp sugar.

FROZEN CHERRY PIE

By using frozen cherries you can extend the season for delicious "fresh cherry" pie through the whole year

1 qt frozen cherries
Plain *or* cheese pastry for 9-inch double crust, pp 924, 929
3 tbsp flour
4 tsp cornstarch
⅛ tsp salt

⅔ cup sugar
¾ cup cherry juice, drained from cherries
1 tbsp firm butter
Few drops red food coloring, optional

Adjust rack 4 to 5 inches above bottom of oven. Start oven 10 min before baking; set to hot (450° F).

Thaw cherries and drain; there should be 1¼ to 1⅓ cups juice and 3 cups drained cherries. Make pastry; roll out ½ of it and line 9-inch pie pan, fitting well into angles. Roll out rest of pastry for top crust; cut design in center for wide-open steam vents. Blend next 4 ingredients in 3-qt saucepan. Stir in cherry juice gradually until smooth. (Thicken leftover juice and serve over pie.) Cook and stir until thickened. Remove from heat, stir in butter, coloring and cherries. Cool thoroughly, then turn into pastry-lined pan, spreading level. Trim off lower pastry even with rim of pan. Moisten edge of lower pastry, lay top pastry on, and press down gently all around to seal. Trim off top pastry with scissors ½ inch beyond pan rim. Turn overhang under edge of lower pastry so fold is even with rim, and again press gently to seal. Crimp edge with tines of fork. Bake 15 min, then reduce heat to moderate (350° F) and bake 25 min longer or until nicely browned. Remove to cake rack to cool 2 to 3 hrs before cutting. 5 to 6 servings.

To Make An 8-inch Pie: Use 1½ pts frozen cherries, plain or cheese pastry for 8-inch double crust, p 924, 2¼ tbsp flour, 3 tsp cornstarch, scant ⅛ tsp salt, ½ cup sugar, ½ cup plus 1 tbsp cherry juice, 2 tsp firm butter, few drops red coloring.

FROZEN CHERRY PIE WITH LATTICE TOP

2 10-oz cans sweetened frozen sour red cherries
Pastry for 9-inch double crust, p 924

2½ tbsp cornstarch
½ cup sugar
⅛ tsp salt
1 tbsp butter

Adjust rack 4 to 5 inches from bottom of oven. Start oven 10 min before baking; set to moderately hot (425° F).

Have cherries just defrosted. Drain fruit and measure; there should be 1½ cups cherries and 1 cup juice. Make pastry; roll out ½ of it and line a 9-inch pie pan; roll out rest and cut in strips for lattice. Blend cornstarch, sugar and salt with wooden spoon in saucepan, add cherry juice and cook and stir until just thickened. Remove from heat. Stir in butter, then cherries very carefully. Set pan in cold water about 5 min to cool. Turn into pastry-lined pan; add lattice top and proceed as for Canned Cherry Pie, p 995. 6 servings.

OPEN-FACE CHERRY PIE

9-inch pastry shell, p 928
1 to 1¼ cups sugar
2 tbsp cornstarch
1 tbsp flour
3½ to 4 cups pitted sour red cherries

¼ cup water
1½ tbsp firm butter
2 *or* 3 drops almond extract
Whipped cream

Bake pastry shell and cool. Blend sugar, cornstarch and flour in 3-qt saucepan; stir in cherries, then water. Cook gently over moderate direct heat, stirring constantly but taking care not to break up fruit; then reduce heat and simmer until cherries are barely tender and juice is thickened and clear. Remove from heat. Stir in butter and extract. Cool slightly, then pour into pie shell. When cooled, set in refrigerator until filling thickens. Serve within a few hrs topped with whipped cream. 5 to 6 servings.

To Make An 8-inch Pie: Use an 8-inch pastry shell, ¾ to 1 cup sugar, 1½ tbsp cornstarch, 2 tsp flour, 2½ to 3 cups pitted sour cherries, 3 tbsp water, 1 tbsp butter, 2 or 3 drops almond extract, whipped cream.

CRANBERRY PIE

The brilliant color and lively flavor of cranberries is particularly appealing in a pie filling

Pastry for 9-inch double
crust, p 924
3¼ cups cranberries, about
1½ to 2 cups sugar
2 tbsp cornstarch
¼ tsp salt
½ cup water
¼ tsp almond extract
2 tbsp firm butter

Adjust rack 4 to 5 inches above bottom of oven. Start oven 10 min before baking; set to hot (425° F).

Make pastry. Pick over cranberries; wash and drain, then cut in halves. There should be 2⅔ cups halved berries. Turn into 3-qt saucepan, add sugar blended well with cornstarch and salt, and stir in water. Place over heat and bring slowly to boiling, then cook and stir for 5 min. Remove from heat, stir in extract, then butter until melted. Set aside to cool. Roll out ½ of pastry and line a 9-inch pie pan, fitting well into angles. Roll out remaining pastry for top crust and cut design in center for wide-open steam vents. Trim off pastry in pan even with pan rim. Turn cranberry mixture into pan, spreading level. Moisten edge of pastry all around. Lay on top pastry, press down gently all around edge to seal, and trim off with scissors ½ inch beyond pan rim. Turn overhang under edge of bottom pastry so fold is even with pan rim and again press gently to seal. Crimp with tines of fork or flute with fingers. Bake 30 to 35 min, or to a delicate golden brown. Remove to cake rack to cool 2 to 3 hrs before serving. 6 to 7 servings.

To Make An 8-inch Pie: Use pastry for 8-inch double crust, about 2½ cups cranberries (2 cups halved berries), 1⅛ to 1½ cups sugar, 1½ tbsp cornstarch, dash of salt, 6 tbsp water, ⅛ tsp almond extract, 1½ tbsp firm butter.

MOCK CHERRY PIE—CRANBERRY

Use pastry for 9-inch double crust, p 924. Combine 1½ cups halved cranberries, ⅔ cup seedless raisins, ¾ cup sugar and ⅔ cup water in 3-qt saucepan. Place over heat and cook and stir gently for 3 to 4 min. Remove from heat, add ¼ tsp salt blended with ¼ cup sugar and 1½ tbsp flour, stirring to mix well. Stir in 2 tbsp butter and ½ tsp vanilla. Bake as for Cranberry Pie between 2 crusts, or use a lattice top crust.

RED CURRANT PIE

As fine a pie as can be made

1 qt red currants	1 cup sugar
Pastry for 9-inch double	2 tbsp cornstarch
crust, p 924	1 tbsp butter, optional

Adjust rack 4 to 5 inches above bottom of oven. Start oven 10 min before baking; set to hot (450° F).

Wash currants carefully through 2 or 3 cold waters. Drain in colander, then strip fruit from stems. There should be about 3½ cups stemmed fruit. Chill thoroughly in refrigerator. Make pastry; roll out ½ of it and line 9-inch pie pan, fitting well into angles. Blend sugar and cornstarch; sprinkle 3 tbsp of mixture over bottom of pastry in pan. Turn in chilled currants, leveling surface. Sprinkle rest of sugar mixture over top. Dot with butter. Trim off lower pastry even with rim of pan. Roll out rest of pastry for top crust; it should be slightly thicker than bottom pastry. Cut design in center for wide-open steam vents. Moisten edge of lower pastry, lay on top pastry, and press gently around edge to seal. Trim off with scissors ½ inch beyond rim of pan and fold overhang under so fold is even with rim. Press down again gently to seal; then crimp edge with tines of fork. Bake 12 min; then reduce temp to moderate (350° F) and bake 25 to 30 min longer or until nicely browned and juice bubbles up through vents. Remove to cake rack to cool 2 to 3 hrs. Serve when just lukewarm. 5 to 6 servings.

To Make An 8-inch Pie: Use 3 cups currants, pkd, pastry for 8-inch double crust, ¾ cup sugar, 1½ tbsp cornstarch and 2½ tsp butter.

CANNED GOOSEBERRY PIE

Canned berries make it possible to serve excellent pie around the calendar

Pastry for 8-inch double	⅓ to ½ cup sugar
crust, p 924	1 tbsp all-purpose flour
No. 303 can gooseberries, in	1 tbsp butter
heavy syrup	

Adjust rack 4 to 5 inches above bottom of oven. Start oven 10 min before baking; set to hot (450° F).

Make pastry; roll out ½ of it and line an 8-inch pie pan, fitting well into angles. Let rest 5 min, then trim off pastry even with pan rim. Roll out remaining pastry for top; cut design in center for wide-open steam vents. Blend flour and sugar in a bowl, turn berries into bowl and stir gently to mix well. Turn berries into pastry-lined pan. Dot with butter. Moisten edge of lower pastry; lay on top pastry and press around edges to seal. Trim off pastry ½-inch beyond edge of pan rim; turn overhang under edge of lower pastry so fold is even with pan rim. Again press to seal, then crimp with tines of fork. Bake 15 min then reduce heat to moderate (350° F) and bake 25 to 30 min longer or until nicely browned. Remove to cake rack to cool to lukewarm before serving. 5 servings.

FRESH GOOSEBERRY PIE

One of the best pies ever invented! It has eye appeal and an irresistible fresh flavor. The quality depends largely on the quality of the berries. They must be not quite full grown. They should have a transparent green color and be almost hard. Full-grown berries have large dark seeds which make the filling unattractive; they are slightly mushy and whitish, so the juice of the pie has a murky color instead of the characteristic clear transparent greenness we expect in gooseberry pie

Pastry for 9-inch double crust, p 924	1 tbsp cornstarch *or* 2 tbsp flour
1 qt fresh green gooseberries	⅛ tsp salt
1¼ cups sugar	1 tbsp butter

Adjust rack 4 to 5 inches above bottom of oven. Start oven 10 min before baking; set to hot (450° F).

Remove stems and tails from berries, then wash through 2 cold waters, lifting into colander to drain after second washing. Make pastry; roll out ½ of it and line a 9-inch pie pan, fitting well into angles. Roll out remaining pastry for top crust and cut design in center for large steam vents. Blend sugar, cornstarch or flour and salt; sprinkle ⅓ of mixture over bottom of pastry-lined pan. Turn berries into pan, spreading compactly, and sprinkle with rest of sugar mixture. Dot with butter. Trim off lower pastry even with rim; moisten edge with water. Lay on top pastry, pressing down gently at rim to seal. Trim off top pastry with scissors ½ inch beyond rim of pan; fold overhang under edge of bottom pastry so fold is even with pan rim. Again press to seal, then crimp with tines of fork or flute with fingers. Bake 15 to 17 min, then reduce heat to moderately slow (325° F) and bake 25 to 30 min longer, or until crust is nicely browned and juice bubbles up through vents. Remove to cake rack to cool to lukewarm before serving. 6 servings.

FROZEN GOOSEBERRY PIE

Frozen gooseberries, barely defrosted, also make delicious pie and desserts. Use in same way as the fresh berries, except decrease the sugar; the amount needed will depend on the sweetness of the frozen berries.

CONCORD GRAPE PIE

This pie is as delicious as it is different. Try it and see!

2 lbs ripe Concord grapes	Pastry for 9-inch double
½ cup sugar	crust, p 924
2½ tbsp flour	2 tbsp fine dry white bread
⅛ tsp salt	crumbs, p 985
1 tbsp lemon juice	¼ cup sugar
	1 tbsp butter

Adjust rack 5 to 6 inches above bottom of oven. Start oven 10 min before baking; set to hot (450° F).

Wash grapes thoroughly, drain and stem. There should be 4½ cups. Press the clear green pulp from the skins, letting juice and pulp drop into a 1½-qt saucepan; put skins into a bowl, do not discard. Cook pulp and juice over low heat 5 min, stirring often. Turn into a sieve, and with a wooden spoon press all the pulp through into bowl containing skins. Discard seeds. Blend next 3 ingredients and stir into grape mixture; stir in lemon juice. Cool mixture by setting in cold water or refrigerator.

Make pastry; roll out ½ of it and line a 9-inch pie pan, fitting well into angles. Roll out remaining pastry for top crust; cut design in center for wide-open steam vents. Sprinkle ½ the crumbs over bottom of pastry-lined pan, then sprinkle in the ¼ cup sugar. Trim off bottom pastry even with pan rim. Turn in cooled grape mixture; sprinkle with rest of crumbs, dot with butter. Moisten edge of lower pastry; lay top pastry over pie. Press down gently around edge to seal. Trim off pastry with scissors ½ inch beyond rim of pan; turn overhang under edge of lower pastry so fold is even with pan rim. Again press down gently all around to seal. Crimp with tines of fork or flute with fingers. Bake 15 min, then reduce heat to moderately slow (325° F) and bake 25 to 30 min longer, or until well browned and juice bubbles up through vents. Remove to cake rack to cool 3 to 4 hrs. Serve lukewarm or cold. 6 servings.

To Make An 8-inch Pie: Use pastry for 8-inch double crust, 1½ lbs grapes, ⅓ cup sugar, scant 2 tbsp flour, dash of salt, 2 tsp lemon juice, 1½ tbsp fine bread crumbs, 3 tbsp sugar, 2 tsp butter.

GUAVA PIE

Many who dislike raw guavas enjoy this pie. We think it is wonderfully good!

Plain pastry for 9-inch	1 cup sugar, scant
double crust, p 924	1 tbsp butter
2¼ lbs ripe pink-fleshed guavas	Dash or more nutmeg

Adjust rack 4 or 5 inches above bottom of oven. Start oven 10 min before baking; set to hot (450° F).

Make pastry. Wash guavas, drain and pare thinly. Cut in half and use spoon to scoop out the seedy portion in center. Drop into food mill placed over a bowl or pan. Rub through food mill to obtain all purée. Discard seeds. Cut the fleshy guava shells into thin slices dropping them into purée. There should be 3 cups purée and slices. Stir sugar into fruit. Now roll out ½ the pastry and line a 9-inch pie pan, fitting well into angles. Roll out remaining pastry for top crust and cut design in center for wide-open vents. Trim off pastry in pan even with pan rim. Turn guava mixture into pan, spreading evenly. Dot with butter and dash with nutmeg. Moisten edge of pastry all around. Lay on top pastry, press down gently all around edge to seal, and trim off with scissors ½ inch beyond pan rim. Turn overhang under edge of bottom pastry so fold is even with rim. Press down again gently to seal; then crimp edge with tines of a fork. Bake 15 min, then reduce temp to moderately slow (325° F) and bake 30 min longer or until guavas are tender and pastry is a rich golden brown. Remove to cake rack to cool. Serve lukewarm, cold or chilled. 6 servings.

To Make An 8-inch Pie: Use pastry for an 8-inch double crust, 1½ lbs guavas (2 cups sliced guavas and purée), ⅔ cup sugar, 1 tbsp butter, dash or so of nutmeg.

LOQUAT PIE

This pie tastes like peach, but is less juicy. Loquats grow in southern U. S. and the sub-tropics

3½ cups skinned, pitted loquats, *or* about 2¼ qts whole fruit	4 tsp flour
	Dash of salt
Pastry for 9-inch double	2 to 3 tbsp water
crust, p 924	1 tbsp butter
⅔ cup sugar	

Remove stems from loquats, then wash thoroughly through 2 or 3 cold waters. Use sharp-pointed paring knife to strip off skins and remove seeds. Cover fruit and store in refrigerator while making pastry.

Adjust rack 4 to 5 inches above bottom of oven. Start oven 10 min before baking; set to hot (450° F).

Make pastry; roll out ½ of it and line 9-inch pie pan, fitting well into angles. Trim off even with rim of pan. Roll out rest of pastry for top crust and cut design in center for wide-open steam vents. Blend sugar, flour and salt. Sprinkle 2 tbsp of mixture over bottom of lined pan; add rest to loquats, stir in gently to mix, then stir in water. Turn into pastry-lined pan, spreading evenly. Dot with butter. Moisten edge of lower crust all around, then lay on top pastry. Press gently around edge to seal. Trim off pastry with scissors ½ inch beyond rim, then turn overhang under lower pastry so fold is even with pan rim. Again press gently to seal. Crimp with tines of fork or flute with fingers. Bake 15 min, then reduce heat to moderately slow (325° F) and bake 40 min longer or until nicely browned. Remove to cake rack to cool to lukewarm before cutting. 6 servings.

To Make An 8-inch Pie: Use pastry for an 8-inch double crust, 2½ cups skinned, pitted loquats, ½ cup sugar, 3 tsp flour, dash of salt, 1½ to 2¼ tbsp water, 2 tsp butter.

MINCE PIE

It takes mincemeat of high quality to make the very finest, most holiday-worthy mince pie

Pastry for 9-inch double 3 cups homemade or commer-
crust, p 924 cial mincemeat

Adjust rack 5 to 6 inches above bottom of oven. Start oven 10 min before baking; set to hot (425° F).

Make pastry; roll out ½ of it and line a 9-inch pie pan, fitting well into angles. Roll out rest of pastry for top crust and cut design in center for wide-open steam vents. Trim off lower crust even with pan rim. Turn mincemeat into pastry-lined pan and spread out level. Moisten edges of lower pastry and lay on top pastry, pressing down gently around edge to seal. Trim off top pastry with scissors ½ inch beyond pan rim, and fold overhang under edge of bottom pastry so fold is even with pan rim. Again press around rim to seal; then crimp with tines of fork or flute with fingers. Bake 30 to 35 min, or to delicate golden brown. Remove to cake rack to cool 2 to 3 hrs; serve lukewarm, plain or with Brandy Sauce, p 1238. 7 servings.

To Make An 8-inch Pie: Use pastry for 8-inch double crust, and 2¼ cups mincemeat.

Note: If mincemeat is so stiff that it does not spread out easily, add apple juice, cider, peach juice or juice from pickled peaches to give it the desired moistness. For a fruitier mincemeat, add 1 cup finely chopped tart apples to 3 cups mincemeat. Lattice top is also appropriate for mince pie.

MULBERRY PIE

Mulberries make a delicious pie. They need special preparation 2 or 3 hrs before using

1 qt mulberries, part under- ¾ cup sugar
ripe—dark red 3 tbsp flour
1½ tbsp salt Dash of salt
Pastry for 9-inch double 1 tbsp lemon juice
crust, p 924 1 tbsp butter

To remove insects from berries, place in 6 to 8 qt dishpan filled with cold water. Swish berries through water with hands; then lift into colander. Repeat through 2 to 4 fresh waters. Now put berries into enough cold water to cover; add 1½ tbsp salt and stir well. Let stand 30 min, stirring occasionally. Let cold water run to overflow pan, and remove berries to colander with hands. Repeat rinsing with fresh water 3 or 4 times. When thoroughly clean, lift out under running water to colander. With pointed scissors, snip stems from berries, cutting slightly into them.

Adjust rack 4 to 5 inches above bottom of oven. Start oven 10 min before baking; set to hot (450° F).

Make pastry; roll out ½ of it and line 9-inch glass pie pan, fitting well into angles; trim off even with rim of pan. Roll out pastry for top and cut design in center for steam vents. Blend sugar, flour and salt; sprinkle 3 tbsp over bottom of pastry-lined pan. Add rest to berries and mix gently; turn into pan and spread level. Drizzle with lemon juice and dot with butter. Moisten edge of lower pastry; lay top pastry over pie. Press gently around rim to seal; then trim off pastry ½ inch beyond rim with scissors and fold overhang under edge of bottom pastry so fold is even with pan rim. Crimp edge with tines of fork to seal and flatten. Bake 15 min, then reduce heat to moderate (350° F) and bake 40 min longer, or until nicely browned and juice bubbles through vents. Remove to cake rack to cool 2 to 3 hrs before cutting. 6 servings.

CANNED PEACH PIE

Good looking, good eating! Note "quick'n'easy" lattice

No. 2½ can peach halves in heavy syrup
Pastry for 9-inch double crust, p 924
½ cup sugar

3 tbsp flour
⅛ tsp salt
1 tbsp firm butter
Dash of nutmeg

Adjust rack 4 to 5 inches above bottom of oven. Start oven 10 min before baking; set to moderately hot (425° F).

Drain peaches, saving syrup. Slice halves neatly; there should be 2 cups sliced fruit. Make pastry; roll out ½ of it and line 9-inch pie pan, fitting well into angles. Roll out rest of pastry and cut into 18 strips ⅜ to ½ inch wide. Save the 2 longest strips to finish rim. Blend sugar, flour and salt well; sprinkle 2 tbsp over bottom of pastry-lined pan; stir remainder carefully into peaches. Gently fold in ½ cup of the drained-off syrup and turn into pastry-lined pan. Dot with butter and sprinkle *lightly* with nutmeg. Trim off pastry even with pan rim and moisten edge. Quickly, without interlacing, lay 8 strips of pastry across pie in 2 directions to form lattice. Press ends against bottom pastry to seal; trim off even with rim. Again moisten edge. Lay 2 remaining long strips around rim and crimp with tines of fork to seal and finish edge. Bake 30 to 35 min or until browned and juice bubbles up between lattice strips. Remove to cake rack to cool 2 to 3 hrs before cutting. 6 servings.

Variation: Substitute 3 or 4 drops of almond extract, stirred into peaches, for the nutmeg.

To Make An 8-inch Pie: Use a No. 2 can peaches, pastry for an 8-inch double crust, 6 tbsp sugar, 2¼ tbsp flour, scant ⅛ tsp salt, 1 tbsp butter, dash of nutmeg.

CANNED PEACH SOUR CREAM PIE

An extra-good year-round pie

Pastry for 9-inch single crust, p 928	½ tsp salt
	¼ tsp nutmeg
No. 2½ can sliced peaches in heavy syrup	¼ tsp cinnamon
	2 tbsp flour
⅓ cup sugar	½ pt sour cream, 1 cup

Adjust rack 4 to 5 inches above bottom of oven. Start oven 10 min before baking; set to moderately hot (425° F).

Make pastry; roll out and line a 9-inch pie pan, fitting well into angles. Let rest 5 min, then trim off with scissors ½ inch beyond pan rim. Turn overhang under so fold is even with rim and flute with fingers for stand-up edge. Drain peaches thoroughly; save syrup. Combine next 5 ingredients thoroughly; stir in ½ cup of the syrup and the sour cream, and fold gently into peaches. Turn into pan. Bake 30 min, or until pastry is browned and filling thickened. Remove to cake rack to cool 2 to 3 hrs before cutting. 5 to 6 servings.

To Make An 8-inch Pie: Use pastry for 8-inch single crust, No. 2 can sliced peaches, ¼ cup sugar, ⅓ tsp salt, scant ¼ tsp nutmeg, scant ¼ tsp cinnamon, 1½ tbsp flour, ⅓ cup peach syrup and ¾ cup sour cream.

Note: Leftover peach syrup may be reduced ½ by simmering, for an excellent pancake syrup.

FRESH PEACH PIE

In August or September, you can't make a more luscious pie than peach. For perfect eating, serve it just lukewarm

Pastry for 9-inch double crust, p 924	1 cup sugar
	Dash of salt
1 tbsp fine dry white bread crumbs, p 985	2 tbsp flour
	4 drops almond extract
2 to 2½ lbs juicy ripe peaches	2 tbsp butter

Adjust rack to 5 or 6 inches above bottom of oven. Start oven 10 min before baking; set to hot (450° F).

Make pastry; roll ½ of it out and line a 9-inch pie pan, fitting well into angles; trim off even with pan rim. Roll out remaining pastry for top and cut design in center for wide-open steam vents. Sprinkle bread crumbs over bottom of pastry-lined pan. Cover lined pan and top pastry with waxed paper. Wash peaches, pare, cut in halves and discard pits. Cut halves into 3 or 4 lengthwise slices, dropping into qt measure. There should be a full qt. Blend sugar, salt and flour and sprinkle ¼ cup of mixture over crumbs. Add rest to peaches turned into a bowl, sprinkle extract over, and mix gently. Turn into pastry-lined pan, spread to make them moderately compact. Fruit should be very slightly rounded up in center. Dot with butter. Moisten edge of lower pastry, lay on top pastry, and press down gently around rim to seal. Cut top pastry off with scissors ½ inch beyond pan rim, then turn overhang under edge of lower pastry so fold is even with rim of pan. Again press down gently around rim and crimp with tines of fork or flute with fingers. Bake 15 min, then reduce heat to moderately slow (325° F) and bake 25 min longer or until well browned and juice bubbles up thru vents. Remove to cake rack to cool 2 or 3 hrs. 5 to 6 servings.

To Make An 8-inch Pie: Use pastry for an 8-inch double crust, 2 tsp fine dry white bread crumbs, 1⅓ to 1¾ lbs peaches (3 cups sliced), ⅔ cup sugar, dash of salt, 1½ tbsp flour, 3 drops almond extract, 1½ tbsp butter.

FRESH PEACH PIE WITH LATTICE TOP

You'll have to go some to beat a peach pie!

Pastry for 9-inch double crust, p 924
2½ lbs ripe freestone peaches, about 10 medium
2 tbsp dry white bread crumbs, p 985

1 cup *plus* 2 tbsp sugar
1 tbsp cornstarch *or* 2 tbsp flour
Dash of salt
2 drops almond extract
1 tbsp butter

Adjust rack 5 to 6 inches from bottom of oven. Start oven 10 min before baking; set to hot (450° F).

Make pastry; roll out ½ of it and line a 9-inch pie pan, fitting well into angles. Sprinkle bread crumbs over bottom, then ¼ cup of the sugar over the crumbs. Pare peaches thinly; cut in half, remove pits and cut halves in 3 or 4 slices. There should be 4½ cups sliced fruit. Turn fruit into prepared pan, spreading evenly. Blend remaining sugar, cornstarch and salt; sprinkle over fruit. Add extract and dot with butter. Now trim pastry off even with rim of pan. Roll out remaining pastry to an 11-inch circle. Cut into 18 strips ⅜ to ½ inch wide. Save the 2 longest strips to finish edge. Moisten edge of lower crust and lay 8 strips across pie in 2 directions, without interlacing, to form lattice. Press ends gently against lower crust and trim off even with rim. Moisten edge again. Lay the 2 long strips around the edge, joining neatly, and crimp with tines of fork. Bake 15 to 17 min, then reduce heat to moderate (350° F) and bake 25 to 30 min longer, until pastry is well browned and juice bubbles up through lattice. Remove to cake rack to cool to lukewarm. 6 servings.

To Make An 8-inch Pie: Use pastry for an 8-inch double crust, 1¾ lbs peaches or scant 3½ cups sliced peaches, 1½ tbsp fine bread crumbs, ¾ cup plus 1½ tbsp sugar, 2 tsp cornstarch, dash of salt, 2 drops almond extract, 2 tsp butter.

FRESH PEACH SOUR CREAM PIE
An old-time farm favorite

Pastry for 9-inch single
    crust, p 928
1 cup sugar
2 tsp flour
1¼ lbs freestone peaches,
    6 size of large eggs

¼ tsp nutmeg, optional
2 egg yolks
½ pt sour cream, 1 cup
⅛ tsp salt

Adjust rack 5 to 6 inches above bottom of oven. Start oven 10 min before baking; set to moderately hot (425° F).

Make pastry; roll out and line a 9-inch pie pan, fitting well into angles. Let rest 5 min, then trim off with scissors ½ inch beyond rim of pan; turn overhang under so fold is even with pan rim. Flute with fingers or crimp with fork. Mix ¼ cup of the sugar with the flour and sift over bottom of pastry. Pare peaches thinly and cut away from pits in 6 or 8 lengthwise slices. Turn slices into pastry-lined pan, spreading level. Sprinkle ¼ cup of the sugar and the nutmeg over peaches. Quickly beat egg yolks with rotary beater, add cream, salt and remaining ½ cup sugar; beat until well blended. Pour over peaches, scraping out bowl with rubber scraper. Bake 15 min; reduce heat to moderately slow (325° F) and bake 18 to 20 min longer, or until filling is just set—no longer. Check by Custard Test, p 970. Remove to cake rack to cool to lukewarm before cutting. 6 servings.

To Make An 8-inch Pie: Use pastry for an 8-inch single crust, ¾ cup sugar, taking 3 tbsp of this sugar to mix with 1½ tsp flour to sprinkle inside of pastry and 3 tbsp to mix with 1 lb peaches, sliced, and 6 tbsp for the custard mixture made with 2 small egg yolks, ¾ cup sour cream, dash of salt and a few dashes nutmeg.

PEACH CRUMBLE PIE
Delicious-as-ever peach pie with a crunchy top that's different

Crumble:
    ¾ cup all-purpose flour
    ⅓ cup moist light brown
        sugar, pkd
    ⅓ cup firm butter *or*
        margarine
Pastry and Filling:
    Pastry for 9-inch single
        crust, p 928

¼ cup sugar
1 to 1½ tbsp flour, depend-
    ing on juiciness of peaches
1 lb 14 oz ripe freestone
    peaches, 8–9 medium, 4
    cups sliced
4 to 5 drops almond extract
½ cup sugar

Adjust rack 5 to 6 inches from bottom of oven. Start oven 10 min before baking; set to moderately hot (425° F).

Crumble: Blend flour and brown sugar in a 1½-qt bowl, add butter, and cut in with pastry blender or 2 knives until particles are size of peas. Chill until needed.

Pastry and Filling: Make pastry; roll out and line 9-inch pie pan, fitting well into angles. Let rest 5 min, then with scissors trim off ½ inch beyond pan rim. Fold overhang under so fold is even with pan rim. Flute edge with fingers or crimp with tines of fork. Sprinkle bottom of pastry with the ¼ cup sugar blended with flour. Pare peaches thinly; cut away from pits in 6 or 8 lengthwise slices. Turn fruit into pastry-lined pan, leveling evenly. Sprinkle with extract, then with the ½ cup sugar, then with the crumble. Bake 15 min, then reduce heat to moderate (350° F) and bake 20 min longer. Remove to cake rack and cool 2 to 3 hrs. Serve lukewarm or cold. 6 servings.

To Make An 8-inch Pie: For crumble topping use ½ cup plus 1 tbsp flour, ¼ cup brown sugar, pkd, ¼ cup firm butter. For pastry and filling, use pastry for 8-inch single crust, 3 tbsp sugar blended with ¾ to 1¼ tbsp flour, 1 lb 6 oz peaches (3 cups sliced), 3 to 4 drops almond extract, ⅓ cup sugar.

FRENCH PEAR PIE

Streusel-topped fresh pear pie is a real treat. Needs no adorning, but a little cream cheese whipped with cream is delectable

Streusel:
⅔ cup all-purpose flour
⅓ cup moist brown sugar, pkd
⅓ cup butter *or* margarine

Pastry and Filling:
Pastry for 9-inch single crust, p 928
1 tbsp fine dry white bread crumbs, p 985

1¾ lb Bartlett, Bosc, etc. ripe pears, 5 good-size, 4 cups sliced
¼ cup sugar
⅓ tsp ginger
1⅓ tbsp flour
4 tsp lemon juice
¼ cup white corn syrup

Adjust rack 5 to 6 inches above bottom of oven. Start oven 10 min before baking; set to hot (450° F).

Streusel: Blend flour and sugar in 2-qt bowl; add butter and cut in with pastry blender or 2 knives until particles are size of peas. Chill till needed.

Pastry and Filling: Make pastry; roll out and line 9-inch pie pan, fitting well into angles. Let rest 5 min; then trim off with scissors ½ inch beyond rim of pan. Fold overhang under even with pan rim, pressing down gently. Flute with fingers or crimp with fork. Sprinkle crumbs evenly over bottom. Wash pears, pare thinly; cut in half and remove cores with spoon or French ball cutter. Slice halves thinly crosswise; there should be 1 qt sliced, pkd. Blend sugar, ginger and flour; sprinkle ⅓ over crumbs. Turn pears into pastry-lined pan, spreading evenly. Drizzle with lemon juice and syrup; sprinkle with rest of flour mixture. Sprinkle Streusel evenly over top. Bake 15 min, then reduce heat to moderate (350° F) and bake 30 to 35 min longer. Remove to cake rack to cool to lukewarm before cutting. 6 servings.

To Make An 8-inch Pie: For Streusel, use ½ cup all-purpose flour, ¼ cup brown sugar pkd, ¼ cup butter; for pastry and filling, use pastry for an 8-inch single crust, 2½ tsp fine dry bread crumbs, 1 lb 5 oz pears (3 cups sliced), 3 tbsp sugar, ¼ tsp ginger, 1 tbsp flour, 3 tsp lemon juice and 3 tbsp corn syrup.

FRESH BLUE OR ITALIAN PLUM PIE

Don't fail to treat your family to this colorful, tangy, delicious pie

2 lbs blue plums, 23 *or* 24	¾ cup sugar
Pastry for 9-inch double	⅛ tsp salt
crust, p 924	2 tbsp flour
1 tbsp fine dry white bread	1 tbsp firm butter
crumbs, p 985	

Adjust rack 5 to 6 inches above bottom of oven. Start oven 10 min before baking; set to hot (450° F).

Wash plums; do not pare. Cut in halves, discard pits, cut in quarters. Make pastry; roll ½ of it out and line a 9-inch pie pan, fitting pastry well into angles; trim off even with pan rim. Roll out remaining pastry for top crust; cut design in center for steam vents. Sprinkle crumbs over bottom of pastry-lined pan. Blend sugar, salt and flour, sprinkle ¼ of mixture over crumbs; add rest to plums and mix gently, then turn into pastry-lined pan, spreading evenly. Dot with butter. Moisten edge of bottom pastry; lay top pastry over filling. Press down gently around edge to seal; cut off with scissors ½ inch beyond pan rim, and turn overhang under edge of lower pastry so fold is even with rim; now press gently all around edge to seal. Crimp with tines of fork to finish edge flat. Bake 15 min, then reduce heat to moderately slow (325° F) and bake 25 min longer, or until browned and juice bubbles up through vents. Remove to cake rack to cool to lukewarm. 5 to 6 servings.

To Make An 8-inch Pie: Use 1½ lbs blue plums, 17 or 18, pastry for 8-inch double crust, 2½ tsp fine bread crumbs, ½ cup plus 1 tbsp sugar, scant ⅛ tsp salt, 1½ tbsp flour, 2 tsp butter.

FRESH RED PLUM PIE

A delicious pie with bracing flavor and lively color

Pastry for 9-inch double crust, p 924	Dash of salt
1¼ lbs ripe red plums	2 tbsp flour
1⅓ to 1½ cups sugar, depending on tartness of fruit	1 tbsp butter

Adjust rack 4 to 5 inches above bottom of oven. Start oven 10 min before baking; set to hot (450° F).

Make pastry; roll out ½ of it and line a 9-inch pie pan fitting well into angles. Roll out remaining pastry for top and cut design in center for generous steam vents. Wash plums; do not peel, but cut cleanly from pits in 4 or 5 pieces, dropping into bowl. Blend sugar, salt and flour; sprinkle ⅓ over bottom of pastry-lined pan. Turn half the plums into pie pan, spread level and sprinkle with half of remaining sugar mixture. Add rest of plums, sprinkle with rest of sugar mixture, and dot with butter. Trim off lower pastry even with rim of pan and moisten edge. Lay on top pastry, pressing down gently at rim to seal. Trim off top pastry with scissors ½ inch beyond rim of pan; fold overhang under bottom pastry so fold is even with rim. Again press gently to seal; then crimp with fork or flute with fingers. Bake 15 to 17 min, then reduce heat to moderate (350° F) and bake 25 to 30 min longer or until nicely browned and juice bubbles up through vents. Remove to cake rack to cool to lukewarm before cutting. 6 servings.

To Make An 8-inch Pie: Use pastry for an 8-inch Double Crust, 1 lb red plums, 1 to 1⅛ cups sugar, dash of salt, 1½ tbsp flour, 2 tsp butter.

PRUNE PIE

An excellent wintertime choice

¾ lb moist prunes	2 tsp cornstarch
3 cups lukewarm water	⅛ tsp salt
Pastry for 9-inch double crust, p 924	1½ tbsp lemon juice
¾ cup sugar	1 tbsp butter

Adjust rack 4 to 5 inches above bottom of oven. Start oven 10 min before baking; set to moderately hot (425° F).

Wash prunes and place in saucepan. Add lukewarm water, cover and soak 2 to 3 hrs, then cook gently until barely tender, 10 to 15 min. Cool, then drain off juice and save. Remove pits and cut fruit in quarters. Make pastry; roll out ½ of it and line 9-inch pie pan, fitting well into angles. Trim off even with pan rim. Roll out rest of pastry for top and cut design in center for wide-open steam vents. Blend sugar, cornstarch and salt; sprinkle 2 tbsp over bottom of pastry in pan. Stir ⅔ cup drained-off prune juice into rest of mixture; then fold in prunes and lemon juice. Turn into pastry-lined pan; dot with butter. Moisten edge of lower pastry, lay on top pastry, and press down gently around rim to seal. Trim off with scissors ½ inch beyond rim of pan, then turn overhang under lower pastry so fold is even with rim. Again press gently to seal, then crimp with tines of fork. Bake 30 min or until nicely browned and juice bubbles up through vents. Remove to cake rack and cool 2 to 3 hrs before cutting. 6 servings.

To Make An 8-inch Pie: Use 9 oz prunes, 2¼ cups lukewarm water, pastry for 8-inch double crust, ½ cup plus 1 tbsp sugar, 1½ tbsp cornstarch, scant ⅛ tsp salt, 1⅛ tbsp lemon juice, 1 tbsp butter.

OLD-TIME RAISIN PIE

A fitting dessert to follow a light main course

Pastry for 9-inch double
  crust, p 924
2 cups seedless raisins
1⅓ cups warm water
¼ cup orange juice
2 tbsp lemon juice
3 tbsp cornstarch

¾ cup light brown sugar, pkd
¼ tsp grated orange rind, pkd
¼ tsp grated lemon rind, pkd
½ cup broken nut meats,
  optional
2 tbsp butter

Adjust rack to 5 to 6 inches above bottom of oven. Start oven 10 min before baking; set to hot (450° F).

Make pastry; roll ½ of it and line a 9-inch glass pie pan, fitting well into angles; trim off even with pan rim. Chill. Roll out remaining pastry for an all-over or lattice top, as desired. Cut wide-open steam vents in center for all-over pastry or cut into strips for lattice. Cover top pastry and pastry-lined pan with waxed paper.

Wash raisins quickly through cold water; then cover with warm water and cook slowly until fruit is plump. Drain off juice, and add enough of juice to the orange and lemon juice to make ¾ cup. Mix cornstarch and brown sugar; blend with the ¾ cup liquid until smooth, add rinds and nuts and stir into drained raisins. Pour filling into pastry-lined pan, spreading until level. Dot with butter. Moisten edge of bottom pastry and cover with all-over top or lattice strips. Press gently all around edge to seal. Cut all-over pastry off with scissors ½ inch beyond rim and turn overhang under edge of bottom pastry so fold is even with pan rim. Crimp with tines of fork to seal and flatten edge. Bake 10 min, then reduce heat to moderate (350° F) and bake 30 min longer or until well browned and juice bubbles up through vents. Remove to cake rack to cool 2 to 3 hrs before cutting. Serve lukewarm. 6 to 8 servings.

RAISIN PIE

Raisin pie made tangy with acid and mellow with butter and baked between two crisp, flaky crusts is something special in pies. An excellent wintertime dessert

Pastry for 9-inch double
crust, p 924
2 cups seedless raisins
Water
¼ tsp salt
½ cup sugar

1 tbsp cornstarch *or* 2 tbsp
flour
1½ tbsp cider vinegar *or* 2 tbsp
lemon juice
2 to 3 tbsp butter

Adjust rack 4 to 5 inches above bottom of oven. Start oven 10 min before baking; set to moderately hot (400° F).

Make pastry. Wash raisins and put into 3-qt saucepan with water to cover, about 1¾ cups. Place over moderate heat, cover, and boil gently 3 to 5 min, or until raisins are tender. Blend salt, sugar and cornstarch or flour. Sprinkle slowly into raisins, stirring constantly; then cook and stir until juice is thickened, 2 or 3 min. Remove from heat, add vinegar or lemon juice, and stir in butter until melted. Cool slightly. Roll out ½ of pastry and line a 9-inch pie pan, fitting well into angles. Roll out rest of pastry for top crust and cut design in center for wide-open steam vents. Trim off lower pastry even with pan rim. Turn raisin mixture into pan, spreading level. Moisten edge of lower pastry all around. Lay on top pastry and press down gently all around rim to seal. Trim off top pastry with scissors ½ inch beyond pan rim. Fold overhang under edge of lower pastry so fold is even with pan rim. Again press gently to seal, then crimp with tines of fork or flute with fingers. Bake 35 to 40 min, or until a delicate golden brown. Remove to cake rack to cool. Serve lukewarm. 6 to 7 servings.

To Make An 8-inch Pie: Use pastry for 8-inch double crust, 1½ cups seedless raisins, 1¼ cups water, scant ¼ tsp salt, 6 tbsp sugar, 2½ tsp cornstarch or 1½ tbsp flour, 1⅛ tbsp vinegar or 1½ tbsp lemon juice and 1½ to 2 tbsp butter.

Note: A lattice top is also appropriate for raisin pie.

FRESH RED RASPBERRY PIE

A luxury worth indulging in at least once a season

2 pts fresh red raspberries
½ cup *plus* 2 tbsp sugar
1 tbsp cornstarch *or* 2 tbsp
flour
1 tbsp water
Dash of salt

Pastry for 9-inch double
crust, p 924
2 tbsp fine dry white bread
crumbs, p 985
1 tbsp butter

Adjust rack about 5 inches above bottom of oven. Start oven 10 min before baking; set to hot (450° F).

Shake berries gently from box into hand, discarding hulls and imperfect berries; drop into cold water. Use hands to swish berries gently through the water, then lift berries with outstretched fingers into colander to drain well. Turn berries into bowl in 3 or 4 layers, sprinkling each layer with its part of the sugar. Cover and let stand several hrs for sugar to dissolve. Now turn berries into coarse-meshed sieve placed over 2-qt saucepan to drain. There should be at least ½ cup juice. Return berries to bowl. Blend cornstarch or flour with water; stir into berry juice. Place over heat and cook and stir until clear and thickened. Remove from heat, and with rubber scraper, scrape thickened juice over berries, using scraper to fold it in gently.

Make pastry and roll out ½ of it and line a 9-inch pie pan, fitting well into angles. Roll out rest of pastry for top. Cut design in center for generous steam vents. Sprinkle crumbs over bottom of pastry-lined pan and turn berry mixture over crumbs, spreading level. Dot with butter. Trim off pastry even with pan rim and moisten edge with water. Lay top pastry over pie, press down gently at edge to seal, and trim off ½-inch beyond rim of pan. Fold overhang under bottom pastry so fold is even with rim. Again press down gently to seal, then crimp with tines of fork. Bake 15 min, then reduce heat to moderate (350° F) and bake 20 min longer or until nicely browned and juice starts to bubble up through vents. Remove to cake rack to cool 2 or 3 hrs. Serve lukewarm. 6 servings.

To Make An 8-inch Pie: Use pastry for 8-inch double crust, 1½ pts raspberries, ⅓ cup plus 1 tbsp sugar, 2 tsp cornstarch or 1½ tbsp flour, 1 tbsp water, dash of salt, 1½ tbsp bread crumbs and 1 tbsp butter.

Note: For variation, cover this pie with lattice top, p 984.

RED RASPBERRY AND SEEDLESS GRAPE PIE

A surprising and surprisingly good combination fruit pie filling

2 cups stemmed white seedless grapes	Pastry for 9-inch double crust, p 924
1 pt red raspberries	2 tbsp fine white dry bread crumbs, p 985
⅔ cup sugar	1 tbsp butter
2 tbsp flour	
Dash of salt	

Adjust rack 5 to 6 inches above bottom of oven. Start oven 10 min before baking; set to hot (450° F).

Wash, drain and stem grapes. Wash and drain raspberries, then combine with grapes in bowl. Blend sugar, flour and salt. Make pastry; roll out ½ of it and line a 9-inch pan, fitting well into angles, and trim ½ inch beyond rim of pan. Roll out rest of pastry to 10-inch circle;

cut into ½-inch strips for lattice top. Sprinkle bread crumbs evenly over bottom of pastry-lined pan, then the ¼ cup of sugar mixture. Fold rest of sugar mixture carefully into fruit. Turn fruit into pastry-lined pan, spreading level. Dot with butter. Moisten rim of bottom pastry with water. Lay pastry strips across pie in 2 directions, ½ inch apart, *without interlacing;* trim edges of strips only even with pan rim and press gently to seal to lower crust. Moisten ends of strips. Fold overhang of lower pastry up and over ends of strips, and press down gently to seal. Flute with fork or fingers. Bake 15 min, then reduce heat to moderately slow (325° F) and bake 20 to 25 min longer, or until juice oozes through lattice over most of surface. Remove to cake rack to cool 2 to 3 hrs before cutting. Best served lukewarm. 6 servings.

RHUBARB PIE

Rhubarb is at its best in early spring—full of rousing flavor and glowing color. Fresh-pulled rhubarb from your own garden makes the most superb pie you ever served!

Pastry for 9-inch double crust, p 924	1 to 1¼ cups sugar
1½ lbs fresh juicy red rhubarb	1 to 2 tbsp flour
Water if needed	⅛ tsp salt
	1 tbsp butter

Adjust rack 4 to 5 inches above bottom of oven. Start oven 10 min before baking; set to hot (450° F).

Make pastry; roll out ½ of it and line a 9-inch pie pan, fitting well into angles. Roll out remaining pastry for top; cut design in center for wide-open steam vents. Cover with waxed paper.

Wash rhubarb thoroughly; trim off and discard leaves and root ends. Cut rhubarb into ¾-inch lengths. There should be 3½ to 4 cups. Add water if needed. (Early spring rhubarb is juicy and requires no water; late in season it may lack juice. Add 6 to 8 tbsp cold water to the late rhubarb and toss well.) Blend sugar, flour and salt (amount of flour needed depends on juiciness). Sprinkle ⅓ of this mixture over bottom of pastry-lined pan, and turn half of rhubarb over it; spread level and sprinkle with half of remaining sugar mixture. Add rest of rhubarb, level, and sprinkle with rest of sugar mixture. Dot with butter. Trim off bottom pastry even with rim of pan; moisten edge with water. Lay on top pastry, pressing gently at rim to seal. Trim off top pastry with scissors, ½ inch beyond rim of pan; turn overhang under edge of lower pastry so fold is even with rim of pan. Again press gently to seal, then crimp with tines of fork or make shallow fluting with fingers. Bake 15 to 17 min or until light brown; then reduce heat to moderate (350° F) and bake about 25 min longer, or until nicely browned and juice bubbles up through vents. Remove to cake rack to cool to lukewarm. 6 servings.

To Make An 8-inch Pie: Use pastry for 8-inch double crust, 1⅛ lb rhubarb or 3 cups cut, ¾ to scant 1 cup sugar, 2½ to 4½ tsp flour, dash salt, 2 tsp butter.

Note: Latice top is nice on rhubarb pie.

DIFFERENT STRAWBERRY PIE

This method produces a flaky bottom crust and a filling of whole, richly colored berries

Pastry for 9-inch double crust, p 924	¼ tsp salt
	½ cup water
1 qt sound ripe strawberries	2½ tbsp cornstarch
1 to 1⅛ cups sugar	2 tsp lemon juice

Adjust bottom rack in center of oven. Start oven 10 min before baking; set to moderately hot (425° F).

Make pastry; roll out ½ of it and line 9-inch glass pie pan, fitting well into angles. Trim pastry off with scissors about ⅛-inch beyond rim of pan. Leave edge plain. Prick bottom, into angle and up sides of pastry thoroughly with tines of fork. Bake 15 to 18 min or until light golden brown. Remove to cake rack to cool, and re-set oven to hot (475° F). While crust bakes, wash berries carefully; drain and hull. Chill all but 1 cup. Crush these in a saucepan; add sugar, salt and ½ the water. Heat to boiling; stir in cornstarch blended with rest of water. Cook and stir until thick and clear. Remove from heat; turn into sieve and press through with wood spoon, leaving only seeds in sieve. Chill sieved mixture. When cold, stir in lemon juice and fold in chilled berries. Turn into baked pie shell distributing fruit and juice evenly. Roll out pastry for top; cut design in center for steam vents. Moisten rim of lower crust; carefully lay top pastry over filling and press *gently* around edge to seal. Use paring knife to trim top pastry off even with pan rim, but *do not flute*. Place pie on tin or aluminum baking sheet (to prevent further baking of bottom crust). Bake on *top* oven rack 18 to 20 min, until upper pastry is golden brown. Watch carefully to avoid over-browning. Remove to cake rack and cool about 3 hrs before cutting. 6 servings.

FRESH STRAWBERRY PIE

A grand old-time favorite—double crust or lattice top

Pastry for 9-inch double crust, p 924	2½ tbsp cornstarch *or* 4 tbsp flour
1 qt sound ripe strawberries	Dash of salt
¾ to 1 cup sugar	1 tbsp butter

Adjust rack 4 to 5 inches above bottom of oven. Start oven 10 min before baking; set to hot (450° F).

Make pastry; roll out ½ of it and line a 9-inch pie pan, fitting pastry well into angles; trim off even with pan rim. Roll out remaining pastry for top and cut design in center for wide-open steam vents; or cut strips for lattice. Cover pastry-lined pan and top pastry with waxed paper or damp towel.

Wash berries, drain and hull, removing any bad spots. Cut large berries in half. Blend sugar, cornstarch or flour and salt; sprinkle 2 tbsp over bottom of pastry-lined pan. Turn remainder over berries and mix gently, then turn into pan and spread evenly. Dot with butter. Moisten edge of lower pastry; lay on top pastry (or lay lattice strips without interlacing) and press edge gently to seal. Trim off pastry ½-inch beyond edge of rim; turn overhang under edge of lower pastry so fold is even with pan rim. Again press to seal, then crimp with tines of fork. Bake 15 min then reduce heat to moderate (350° F) and bake 30 min longer, or until golden brown. Remove to cake rack to cool to lukewarm before serving. 6 to 7 servings.

To Make An 8-inch Pie: Use pastry for 8-inch double crust, 1½ pts sound ripe berries, ½ to ⅔ cup sugar, 1⅔ tbsp cornstarch or 2⅔ tbsp flour, dash of salt, 1 tbsp butter.

STRAWBERRIES IN WHIPPED CREAM

Sorry, but not for the calorie counters

1 pt sound ripe strawberries
9-inch pastry shell, p 928
1 cup whipping cream,
　chilled

1 tbsp lemon juice
½ cup sugar
Dash of salt

Bake and cool pastry shell. An hr before serving time wash berries, drain well, then hull. Save 5 perfect berries for garnish. Cut rest of berries in 4 lengthwise slices or in quarters, dropping into a bowl. Place in refrigerator. Just before serving, whip cream until thick, then add lemon juice gradually and beat until very stiff, then beat in the sugar. Now fold in cold berries lightly and turn into pie shell, gently spreading out to level. Garnish with saved whole berries and serve at once. 5 servings.

GREEN TOMATO PIE

Don't be prejudiced! It's amazingly rich and delicious—as good as Mince Pie!

Pastry for 9-inch double
　crust, p 924
1¼ lbs green tomatoes, 5
　medium, or 3½ cups sliced
¾ cup seedless raisins, washed
1½ tsp grated lemon rind, pkd
2 tbsp lemon juice
1 tbsp cider vinegar

½ tsp salt, scant
1⅓ to 1½ cups sugar
3 tbsp flour
½ tsp cinnamon
⅛ tsp ginger
1 tbsp fine dry white bread
　crumbs, p 985
2 tbsp butter *or* margarine

Adjust rack 5 to 6 inches above bottom of oven. Start oven 10 min before baking; set for hot (425° F). Make pastry. Wash tomatoes; remove stem and blossom ends; cut in quarters and slice *very* thin on cutting board. Put into 3-qt bowl and stir in next 5 ingredients. Blend sugar with flour and spices.

Roll out ½ of pastry and line a 9-inch pie pan, fitting well into angles; trim off even with pan rim. Roll out pastry for top; cut design for generous steam vents in center. Sprinkle crumbs evenly over bottom of pastry-lined pan, then 2 tbsp of the sugar mixture. Fold rest of sugar mixture into tomatoes, and turn into pastry-lined pan, spreading level. Dot with butter. Moisten pastry rim all around and lay on top pastry; press down gently all around edge to seal, and trim off with scissors ½ inch beyond pan rim. Fold the ½-inch overhang under lower pastry, so fold is even with rim, and crimp edge with fingers or fork. Bake 15 min; then reduce heat to moderately slow (325° F) and bake 50 min longer. Remove to cake rack; cool 2 to 3 hrs before serving. 5 to 6 servings.

To Make An 8-inch Pie: Use pastry for an 8-inch double crust, 2⅔ cups sliced green tomatoes, ½ cup plus 1 tbsp raisins, 1⅛ tsp grated lemon rind, 1½ tbsp lemon juice, 2½ tsp vinegar, ⅓ tsp salt, 1 to 1⅛ cups sugar, 2 tbsp flour, ⅓ tsp cinnamon, scant ⅛ tsp ginger, 2½ tsp bread crumbs and 1½ tbsp butter.

TARTS

Tarts—miniature pies—are as simple to make as full-sized pies, but require more time to prepare. They are appropriate for gala occasions, and whether they are served at tea, luncheon or dinner, they are interesting and irresistible. Tarts may be single or double crusted with a plain or lattice top. Any fruit, berry, cream or custard type filling may be used in making tarts.

TRICKS IN MAKING

1—Little tart pans are more tedious to line with pastry than a full-size pan. Therefore, cutting the rolled-out pastry first into circles of the right size does really speed up the work. Read carefully directions below for making the *Fluted* or the *Plain-Edge Tart Shells.*

2—The pastry-lined pans for empty tart shells or the pastry-lined pans containing filling are too difficult to place directly onto the oven rack and they are still more difficult to remove after baking. Several tart pans put onto a baking sheet are more easily placed into or removed from the oven but often do not bake satisfactorily. Usually the lower crust is imperfectly baked, especially if the tarts have custard or fruit filling. The reason is that the baking sheet deflects the heat away from the bottom of the tarts. Placing the filled or empty shells on an *inverted cake rack** permits enough heat circulation to bake the pastry on the

*Inverting the cake rack prevents the "feet" from catching onto oven rack.

bottom perfectly. Pastry that is shaped over the bottom of inverted tart pans, however, will bake well when the pans are grouped on a baking sheet.

FLUTED TART SHELLS

Have ready five or six 3½-inch fluted tart pans. Use an empty No. 3 can or cut a 4¼-inch cardboard circle to cut out circles from rolled pastry. Start oven 10 min before baking; set to moderately hot (425° F).

Make pastry for 9-inch single crust, p 928. Roll out into a circle ⅛-inch thick. Place can or cardboard pattern on pastry and cut around it with sharp-pointed knife. Line tart-pans with pastry circles, fitting in carefully; use metal knife with plain handle to press pastry into flutings on sides of pans. Press overhang of pastry against sharp pan edges to cut off neatly. *Prick pastry thoroughly all over,* wiggling fork tines back and forth. Place on *inverted* cake rack; slip into oven and bake 13 min at 425° F. Remove to another cake rack to cool before filling.

PLAIN-EDGE TART SHELLS

Have ready five or six 4-inch miniature pie pans. Use a 1-lb coffee can lid to cut out 5-inch pastry circles. Start oven 10 min before baking; set to moderately hot (425° F).

Make pastry for 9-inch single crust, p 928. Roll out pastry ⅛-inch thick and cut out 5-inch circles. Line pans, fitting well into angles. Trim off pastry with scissors ¼ inch beyond rim of pan. Fold overhang under so fold is even with pan rim. Flute edge with fingers or crimp with fork.

For Baked Tart Shells: Prick bottom and sides with fork, wiggling tines back and forth to make wide-open holes.

For Tarts Baked with Filling (such as pumpkin): *Do not prick* pastry. Pour filling into pastry-lined pans and place on *inverted cake rack* to bake. Follow individual recipe directions for baking.

For Double-Crust Tarts: Have ready for top crusts circles of pastry with carefully-cut fancy designs in center for steam vents. After filling pie, moisten edge of trimmed lower crust, lay on top crusts and press gently around edge to seal. Trim with scissors ¼ inch beyond rim of pan; turn overhang under lower crust so fold is even with edge of pan. Flute or crimp just as for a full-size double-crust pie. Fruit tarts may also be covered with lattice top if desired.

MUFFIN-PAN TART SHELLS

Baked on back of muffin pans

Have ready muffin pans with cups 3 to 3½ inches in diameter. Use 1-lb coffee can lid to cut out 5-inch circles of pastry. Turn muffin pan upside down. Center pastry circles exactly over backs of cups; let pastry drop down over sides of cups. Then, with hands on opposite sides of cups, pinch in 6 or 8 "tucks" so pastry fits snugly. Prick pastry thoroughly over "tops" of cups and halfway "down" sides, just to where tucks start. Bake in moderately hot oven (425° F) about 10 min or until delicately browned. Cool before removing tart shells from muffin cups.

APPLE SOUFFLÉ TARTS

Different and delicious

Pastry for 9-inch single
crust, p 928

Filling:
½ cup sugar
1½ tsp flour
¼ tsp salt
½ tsp grated lemon rind, pkd
1½ tbsp lemon juice

1 cup homemade or canned
apple sauce
2 egg yolks
2 tsp butter

Topping:
2 egg whites
2 tbsp sugar
1½ tbsp grated sharp cheese

Have ready 5 or 6 ½-cup capacity tart pans. Start oven 10 min before baking; set to hot (450° F).

Tart Shells: Make pastry. Roll out and cut into 4½-inch circles to line tart pans. Trim, fold under edge, crimp. Bake and cool, p 1018, leaving in pans. Leave oven on.

Filling: Blend sugar, flour and salt in a 2-qt saucepan. Stir in next 3 ingredients and heat to boiling, then cook and stir 5 min or until slightly thickened. Beat egg yolks; stir in a little of the hot mixture, then add to saucepan and cook and stir 2 min longer. Remove from heat. Stir in butter. *Topping:* Beat egg whites to a stiff foam using clean beater; add the 2 tbsp sugar gradually, beating until stiff, shiny peaks form that curve at tips when beater is raised. *Fold* meringue gently but thoroughly into hot mixture. Turn into tart shells, leaving tops rippled. Set tart pans on a baking sheet and brown lightly from 6 to 8 min. Remove from oven and *immediately* sprinkle with the cheese. Serve warm or cold.

Note: To make a 9-inch Apple Soufflé Pie, double filling ingredients.

APRICOT TARTS No. 1

5 or 6 baked fluted or plain-
edge tart shells, p 1018
1 cup sweetened apricot
purée, p 551

3 egg whites
¼ cup sugar
1 tbsp lemon juice

Bake and cool tart shells. Make and chill apricot purée. Beat egg whites to a stiff foam, then add sugar gradually, beating to a stiff, shiny meringue. Beat lemon juice into purée, then fold carefully but thoroughly into meringue. Heap into tart shells. Place on cookie sheet (not on cake rack) and bake in a moderate oven (375° F) 10 to 15 min or until top is delicately browned. Remove to cake rack to cool a few min; serve warm. 5 to 6 servings.

APRICOT TARTS No. 2

5 or 6 baked fluted or plain-edge tart shells, p 1018
1 cup sweetened apricot purée, p 551
$\frac{1}{16}$ tsp salt

1 cup whipping cream, chilled
Slivered pistachio nuts, optional

Bake and cool tart shells. Measure apricot purée into mixing bowl. Stir in salt. Whip cream until stiff but still smooth. Fold gently but thoroughly into purée. Mixture may be stored in refrigerator an hr or so. When ready to serve, heap lightly into the tart shells. Sprinkle with pistachios if desired. 5 to 6 servings.

BANBURY TARTS

Pastry for 9-inch single crust, p 928
$\frac{3}{4}$ cup sugar
1 tbsp cracker crumbs
$\frac{1}{16}$ tsp salt

1 small egg, beaten
3 tbsp lemon juice
$\frac{1}{2}$ tsp grated lemon rind, pkd
$\frac{3}{4}$ cup plumped, chopped raisins

Start oven 10 min before baking; set to moderately hot (400° F).

Make pastry. Shape into a rectangle and roll out carefully into a rectangle 8 x 16 inches. Cut into 2 lengthwise strips; then cut each strip across to make 4-inch sqs, 8 in all. Combine rest of ingredients in order given. Put 1½ tbsp filling onto ½ of each pastry sq, keeping it away from edges. Moisten edge of pastry half way around and fold over diagonally to make a triangle; press edges together with tines of fork. Prick top well for steam vents. Place on baking sheet and bake until browned to delicate golden color, 20 to 25 min. Remove to cake rack to cool. Serve lukewarm. 8 tarts.

CALAMONDIN GLAMOUR TARTS

The only complaint will be: "They're too small!"

Pastry for 7 to 8 tart shells, p 1018
½ tsp calamondin rind, pkd
6 tbsp calamondin juice

½ cup butter
1⅛ cups sugar
2 whole eggs and 2 yolks

Bake and cool 3½-inch tart shells. Wash calamondins and *carefully grate* off the *tender* rind. Squeeze juice, remove seeds and measure. Measure butter and sugar into top of double boiler and place over boiling water. Stir occasionally with wooden spoon until butter melts;

add beaten eggs and yolks, calamondin juice and rind. Cook and stir until smooth and like thick white sauce, 7 to 8 min. Remove from heat. Cool 5 min, then pour into tart shells. Serve plain, or when cool, top with sweetened whipped cream. 7 to 8 servings.

Note: Filling may be poured into 9-inch pie shell if desired.

CHERRY TARTS

A grand climax for a light meal

6 or 8 tart shells, p 1018	1 tbsp cold water
4 cups cherries, canned,	2 tbsp firm butter
frozen or fresh pitted	4 tbsp sugar
Sugar	¾ cup sour cream
1½ tbsp cornstarch	

Bake 3½-inch tart shells and cool. Heat cherries in their own juice just to the boiling point, if canned or fresh, or until heated through if frozen. Stir in sugar to suit taste. Remove from heat and drain off juice. There should be 1 cup. If not, add water to make 1 cup. Divide cooled cherries evenly between tart shells. Blend cornstarch and cold water in small saucepan to make smooth paste. Stir in cherry juice, place over low heat and cook and stir until thick and clear. Remove from heat and stir in butter. Pour over cherries and cool. Just before serving, stir sugar into sour cream and spread over top of tarts. 6 or 8 servings.

CHESS "PIELETS"

Once tasted, often wanted!

Pastry for 9-inch single	⅓ cup soft butter *or*
crust, p 928	margarine
½ cup brown sugar, pkd	½ tsp grated lemon rind, pkd
½ cup granulated sugar	4 egg yolks, medium
¼ tsp salt	

Have ready six to eight 3½-inch fluted tart pans. Start oven 10 min before baking; set to moderately hot (425° F).

Make pastry; roll into a rectangle about 8½ inches wide and slightly under ⅛-inch thick. Cut out 6 to 8 circles 4¼ inches in diameter, using bottom of No. 3 can or cardboard round cut to this measure. Fit pastry circles carefully into tart pans; press overhanging pastry down against sharp edges of tart pans to cut off evenly. With plain metal knife handle (not hollow handle) press pastry into flutings. Put remaining ingredients into bowl; use pastry blender or 2 knives to cut them together until thoroughly blended. Mixture is thick and resembles creamed butter-sugar-yolk mixture for cake. Spoon into lined tart pans. Place pans onto *inverted cake rack* and slide into oven; bake 25 to 27 min or until well browned. Remove to cake rack to cool. Serve lukewarm or cold. 6 to 8 "pielets."

GOOSEBERRY TARTS

Tart, sprightly flavored gooseberries make incomparable tarts

1 qt fresh green gooseberries, 1 cup sugar
  p 1000   1½ tbsp flour
Pastry for 8-inch double   ⅛ tsp salt
  crust, p 924   2 tbsp butter

Have ready six 4-inch plain-edge tart pans. Start oven 10 min before baking; set to hot (450° F). Look over berries, discarding soft or blemished ones, then stem and tail. Wash and drain well. Make pastry. Roll out slightly more than ½ of it about ⅛-inch thick. With top of a 1-lb coffee can, cut pastry out into six 5-inch circles, and line the tart pans. Trim pastry off even with pan rims. Roll out rest of pastry and cut six 4½-inch circles, using a number 3 tin can or its top as a guide. Cut design in centers for generous steam vents. Blend sugar, flour and salt and stir well into berries. Divide berries evenly between the tart pans. Dot tops with butter. Moisten edge of lower crusts and lay on the top pastry circles, pressing down gently at rims to seal. Pastry top circles should extend just ¼-inch beyond pan rims. Fold this overhang under so fold is even with pan rims. Again press gently around rims to seal, then flute or crimp edges with tines of a fork. Arrange on *inverted cake rack,* place in oven and bake 15 min, then reduce heat to moderately slow (325° F) and bake 20 or 30 min longer or until crust is nicely browned and berries are tender. Remove to another cake rack and cool to lukewarm. 6 servings.

JELLY CHEESE-FILLED TARTS

So easy and so good

Prepare pastry wafers exactly like those for *Jelly or Jam Filled Tarts,* p 1023, except spread all the pastry wafers generously with cream cheese softened to a good spreading consistency with cream. Leave the surface swirled and a slight depression in the center. Fill the center with currant or strawberry preserves or sweetened dried apricot purée, p 551. Serve soon after spreading.

LEMON TARTS

Little lemon pie cuties!

Pastry for 9-inch single   1¼ cups sugar
  crust, p 928   ½ cup cold water
1 tsp grated lemon rind, pkd   2 cups boiling water
⅓ cup *plus* 1 tbsp lemon juice, 3 egg yolks
  2 lemons   1 tbsp firm butter
3 tbsp cornstarch   ½ tsp salt
2 tbsp flour   Whipping cream

Make pastry; bake and cool eight to ten 3½-inch tart shells, p 1018. Wash lemons, grate rind, squeeze juice and remove seeds. Blend cornstarch, flour, sugar and cold water in 3-qt saucepan. Add boiling water slowly; blend well. Cook and stir over direct heat until mixture is thick and clear, about 3 min. Beat egg yolks; stir a little of hot mixture into them. Return to saucepan; cook and stir 2 min longer. Remove from heat. Add lemon juice slowly in small portions, mixing well after each. Stir in butter, lemon rind and salt. Pour into tart shells; cool. Spread with whipped cream just before serving. 8 to 10 tarts.

MINCE TARTS

Prepare and bake exactly like Gooseberry Tarts, p 1022, except substitute 1⅓ to 1½ cups mincemeat for the gooseberries and omit sugar, flour, salt and butter.

OLD TIME JELLY OR JAM FILLED TARTS

A child's favorite

Use leftover pastry from making pies or tarts, but use it while fresh. Pile trimmings on top of each other (do not knead or wad together) and roll out about ⅛-inch thick. Cut out with fancy scalloped round, oval or diamond-shaped cookie cutter. Place on baking sheet and prick well. Bake in hot oven (475° F) until delicately browned, 6 to 7 min. Remove to cake rack to cool. Spread half the pastry wafers with stiff jelly or thick jam and top with remaining wafers. Serve fresh.

ORANGE DATE TARTS

Appealing, rich and delicious

8 or 10 tart shells, p 1018	1 cup fresh orange juice
1 large seedless orange	1 tbsp lemon juice
1½ cups whole pitted dates	1 tsp grated lemon rind, pkd
¼ cup sugar	3 tbsp firm butter
2 tbsp cornstarch	⅔ cup whipping cream
¼ tsp salt	

Bake 3½-inch tart shells and cool. Wash orange and cut it unpeeled into 6 sections. Put it with the dates through a food chopper, using the fine blade. Turn into saucepan. Blend sugar with cornstarch and salt, stir in orange juice until smooth, then stir this into date mixture. Place over low heat and heat to simmering. Simmer and stir for 10 min. Remove from heat, stir in lemon juice, rind and butter until butter melts. Chill. Just before serving, spoon into tart shells. Top with whipped cream. 8 to 10 servings.

CANNED PEACH TARTS

A year-around favorite

Five 3½ to 4-inch tart
shells, p 1018
No. 2 can sliced peaches *or*
clingstone peach halves,
pkd in heavy syrup
1 tbsp cornstarch
Sugar

1 tbsp lemon juice
4 drops almond extract *or*
¼ tsp vanilla
1 tbsp firm butter
⅓ cup whipping cream,
optional

Bake tart shells and cool. Leave in pans. Drain juice from peaches
into a small saucepan. Blend 2 tbsp of this juice with cornstarch to a
smooth paste; stir well into rest of juice. Place over low heat and cook
and stir until juice boils, thickens and becomes clear. Add sugar if
needed. Remove from heat, stir in next 3 ingredients, then fold in
drained peaches. While warm, turn into tart shells still in the pans. Cool
to lukewarm. Remove tarts from pans to serving plates and garnish tops
with whipped cream just before serving. 5 servings.

PUMPKIN TARTS

Ideal for holiday meals

Pastry for 9-inch single
crust, p 928

Pumpkin Pie Filling, p 978
Whipped cream, optional

Start oven 10 min before baking; set to moderately hot (400° F).
Make pastry, roll out and cut 7 or 8 circles 4¼ inches in diameter
and line 3½-inch tart pans, p 1018. Make Pumpkin Pie Filling. Pour in
enough pumpkin filling to almost fill the tarts. Arrange on *inverted
cake rack,* then carefully place in oven and spoon in more filling to come
nearly to top edge of pastry. Bake about 20 min or until crust is beautifully browned and the filling is set except about ½-inch in the center,
shaking tarts to test for doneness, p 970. Remove to cake rack to cool
at least an hr before serving. Top with puff of whipped cream. 7 or 8
servings.

STRAWBERRY DEVONSHIRE TARTS

Elaborate in appearance, but simple to make and so easy to eat!

6 tart shells, p 1018
1 pt sound, well-ripened
strawberries

3 oz pkg Philadelphia cream
cheese
⅓ cup whipping cream
½ cup sugar

Bake 3½-inch tart shells and cool. Wash berries, drain well, then
hull. Reserve 6 small whole berries. Cut rest in half. Fold sugar carefully

into halved berries. Put cheese into mixing bowl, stir in cream, then beat until mixture looks like whipped cream. Spread about ⅔ of this mixture over bottoms and up sides of tart shells. Fill with sweetened berries. Garnish tops with puffs of the cheese mixture. Top each with a whole berry. May be stored in refrigerator for ½ hr before serving. 6 servings.

ANGEL PIES

An Angel pie is the dainty fragile member of the pie family. Its crust is a well baked thoroughly cooled large meringue shell. A thin layer of stiffly whipped cream is spread over the bottom and up the sides of the shell before adding the filling to prevent it from soaking into the shell. Whipped cream is then spread over the top like a meringue over a pie, or it is piped in lattice fashion or fancy designs over the top. These pies should be served immediately or stored not longer than one-half hr in refrigerator to be served at the peak of perfection.

ANGEL PIE WITH LEMON FILLING

An outstanding dessert with plenty of class

Meringue Shell:
  4 egg whites, room temp
  ¼ tsp salt
  ¼ tsp cream of tartar
  1 cup sugar
  ½ tsp vanilla
Filling:
  ¼ tsp grated lemon rind, pkd
  3 tbsp lemon juice

  4 egg yolks
  ⅔ cup sugar
  1 tsp flour
  Dash of salt
  3 tbsp water
  1 tsp butter
  1 cup whipping cream
  1 tbsp sugar

Meringue Shell: Bake on middle oven rack. Start oven 10 min before baking; set to very slow (225° F). Butter well a 9-inch glass pie pan, including rim. Beat whites with rotary beater or electric mixer until frothy in a 3-qt mixing bowl, add salt and cream of tartar and beat until stiff but not dry. Sprinkle sugar over whites in 5 portions, beating well after each, adding vanilla with last portion. Beat until *very stiff* and glossy. Thorough beating is most important. Turn lightly into prepared pan. Spread with rubber scraper or spoon pushing it around to shape shell with a rim ¾-inch thick and an inch high so center will hold filling. Rim should be evenly waved and center left smooth. Bake 20 min, then increase heat to slow (275° F to 300° F) and bake 1 hr longer or until outside is crisp. Then turn off oven heat; open door slightly and let meringue dry in oven 15 min longer. Remove to cake rack to cool, out of draft, to room temp.

Filling: Wash lemon; grate rind onto waxed paper; fold paper over to keep rind moist. Squeeze juice, do not strain but remove seeds. Beat yolks with rotary beater until light, then beat in sugar blended with flour and salt, add water and beat until thick. Turn into top of double-boiler, place over boiling water and cook, stirring constantly with wooden spoon 5 min or until smooth and thick. Remove from heat. Stir in rind and butter. Cover and cool to room temp. To finish pie, whip cream until almost stiff, then beat in sugar only until smooth and shiny. Do not over-beat. Spread about ½ of the cream over bottom and up sides of meringue shell. (Chill in refrigerator an hr if desired.) Then gently spoon filling over cream evenly. Now spoon or pipe rest of whipped cream evenly over filling. Chill in refrigerator or freezing compartment only a few min before serving. 7 to 8 servings.

Note: When these meringue shells were tested in Florida where atmosphere is moist, we found they became sticky after standing a short while. In such cases, reheat to crisp, then cool before filling. Store meringue shell in oven overnight if it has no pilot light.

ANGEL PIE—STRAWBERRY FILLING

A superb dessert

Meringue Shell:	Filling:
5 egg whites, room temp	½ pt whipping cream
¼ tsp salt	1 tbsp sugar
¼ tsp cream of tartar	1 pt strawberries, perfect
1 cup sugar	½ cup sugar
½ tsp vanilla	1 tbsp cornstarch

Bake on middle oven rack. Start oven 10 min before baking; set to very slow (225° F). Butter well a 10-inch glass pie plate, including rim.

Meringue Shell: Beat egg whites until foamy with rotary beater or electric mixer, sprinkle in salt and cream of tartar and beat until stiff. Add sugar, 2 tbsp at a time and beat thoroughly after each addition. Beat in vanilla with last few turns. Mixture should be satin-smooth and very stiff. Turn lightly into prepared pan, and using a spatula, shape as a shell so that when baked it will hold a filling. Bake 20 min at 225° F, then increase heat to slow (275° F), and bake 1 hr longer. Then turn off heat, open oven door and let cool in oven.

Filling: Whip cream until almost stiff, add sugar and beat until just stiff. Spread half of it carefully over bottom of meringue shell. Place in refrigerator to chill; also keep rest of whipped cream chilled. Wash strawberries, drain and hull, then slice lengthwise 2 or 3 times. Sprinkle with half the sugar and toss to distribute. Let stand 15 to 20 min, then drain off juice. There should be ¼ cup or more. Add ¼ cup water, the rest of sugar blended with cornstarch, then cook and stir until clear and thickened. Remove from heat and cool. Pour over strawberries, stir lightly, then spread evenly over cream in meringue shell. Spoon or pipe rest of whipped cream over strawberries. Chill about 30 min before serving. 5 or 6 servings.

INDIVIDUAL MERINGUE SHELLS

These pretty little "light-weights" add magic to your dessert

4 eggs whites, ½ cup, room temp
¼ tsp salt
½ tsp cream of tartar

1 tsp vinegar
1¼ cups granulated sugar
1 tsp vanilla

Start oven 10 min before baking; set to very slow (225° F).

Cut parchment or smooth unglazed brown paper to fit bottoms of baking sheets. Use cookie cutter or tin can to mark 3-inch circles 1-inch apart on paper as a guide for size of shells. If you have an electric mixer, use it because the beating is *very important* and becomes difficult at end of mixing. Turn whites into a 3-qt mixing bowl, sprinkle salt over them. Beat with rotary beater or electric mixer, until foamy, then sift in cream of tartar and drizzle in vinegar and beat until just stiff. Add sugar, 3 or 4 tbsp at a time and beat until so stiff that meringue crawls up on the beater and beater is difficult to turn. Beat in vanilla with last few turns. Clean off and remove beater. Now use a rubber scraper to remove meringue to an 11 or 12-inch pastry bag, fitted with a No. 4 star tube. Start at center of each circle; pipe meringue around and around to make bottom of shells 3 inches in diameter, then continue to pipe around edge 2 or 3 *rounds high* to make the shells. Or shape shells with the back of a spoon and spatula if a pastry bag is not used. Bake about 1 hr. Remove to cake rack, and with spatula slide meringue shells while hot onto cake rack to cool. Serve filled with ice cream or spread inside with whipped cream, then add sweetened fruit such as strawberries or peaches, then cover with more whipped cream to make individual Angel pies. 10 to 12 shells.

RE-CRISPING MERINGUE SHELLS

In damp weather meringue shells lose their crispness and become sticky. To restore them, place on cookie sheet or cake rack and place in a warmed oven (no turned on heat) until dry and crisp.

Poultry

Did you know there was a simple method of determining ahead of time how long it will take to cook a turkey? Just simmer the giblets the day before, note how long the gizzard takes to become tender, and add one hour—and that's the length of time your turkey should be roasted. This is only the first bit of helpful information to be found in this chapter that will make you feel as much at home with a chicken or a turkey as if you had spent your life on a poultry farm.

★　★　★　★

THE three-fold requirements for successful poultry cooking are: (1) Choosing a high quality bird for the method of cooking intended. (2) Careful and thorough cleaning and storage. (3) The correct cooking method and attractive service.

Choosing the poultry is of first importance, for the finished bird as it comes to the table can never be of any higher quality than the quality of the original poultry. It is essential that every homemaker know how to recognize prime quality so that she can avoid the disappointments which result from a poor or mistaken choice.

High quality poultry should be well-shaped, with a broad full-fleshed breast, and a creamy white or yellowish skin which is glossy, soft, and slightly waxy to the touch. There should be few if any bruises and abrasions, no tears in the skin of the breast, and none in the back that are not sewed up, no broken wings or legs, and practically no pinfeathers.

Both the skin quality and the presence of pinfeathers depend largely upon the manner of killing and dressing. The highest grade of poultry, U. S. Special or U. S. Grade AA, permits absolutely no pinfeathers or down to be left on the bird and no tears or bruises anywhere. If a bird falls short of these standards, it may still make good eating, but its quality is less dependable.

The quality of the dressed bird is the result of the breeding, the care and feeding of the live bird. To develop a tender, meaty, sweet-flavored bird, a good diet and regular feeding are important. Poultry raisers and packers are becoming more and more careful to feed their birds a diet which will insure good flavor in the meat. In addition, the practice of confining the birds a week before slaughter to finish-feed them is becoming common. The effect of this is the same as that of "finishing" steers and other meat animals by a similar method; it improves flavor and results in a "marbling" of fat through the lean meat of the poultry. Prime quality poultry is always fed in this manner. See Chart, No. 43, p 1035 for other specifications of quality for size, tenderness and age of chicken, and see description on p 1068 for quality in turkey.

POULTRY MAY BE PURCHASED IN 6 DIFFERENT STYLES

(1) *Dressed* poultry has the feathers removed, but *is not* drawn. It is then frozen and sent to the dealer in the frozen state. The dealer defrosts the bird under sanitary conditions, and he may or may not draw it before it is sold. Dressed poultry is satisfactory if held at sufficiently low temps, but if the temp of storage fluctuates, there is danger of spoilage. Then too, evisceration at the packing plant is one of the surest methods of detecting and eliminating unhealthy or diseased birds, and for this reason, drawn birds are usually most desirable.

(2) *Quick-frozen full drawn* poultry is fully drawn before freezing. It requires no further preparation by the dealer before selling it to the consumer, other than defrosting under sanitary conditions. This method is desirable because careful inspection of viscera is possible before freezing, but if the evisceration is carelessly done, there is danger of contamination.

(3) *Fresh-chilled drawn* poultry is one of the most recent and best forms to come to the market.

(4) *Live poultry* is also sold in many communities. The consumer may choose the live bird and have it killed, dressed and drawn, or not, according to the practice of the dealer or the preference of the consumer. It should be remembered that the finest flavor and tenderness are produced by holding the birds for 48 hrs after slaughter, including at least 36 hrs of chilling. If this length of time is not possible, a minimum of 8 hrs should elapse between killing and cooking. This will allow time for the poultry to pass through the rigor mortis stage with subsequent softening, see p 744.

(5) *Cut-up chicken and turkey* are now available quite generally. Instead of purchasing whole birds, one can buy whole legs, breasts, drumsticks, and wings, backs and necks from which to make soup, chicken livers for frying and gizzards for Gizzard Burgers. These pieces usually are from poultry of prime quality, but it is important to buy only from dependable and ethical dealers because cutting up the poultry could, in some cases, make it easier to disguise poor quality or careless handling and refrigeration. It is also possible that the cut pieces could have been repeatedly washed with a resultant loss of desirable flavor. The price per lb of cut-up poultry varies according to the pieces selected. Poultry in this form is not available everywhere, but the supply is growing rapidly with the increasing popular demand, and no doubt other kinds besides chicken and turkey will be sold in the near future. This makes it possible to serve just the parts of the birds the family prefers, with little waste and utmost convenience. It must be remembered, however, that delicate chicken or turkey flavor is lost rapidly with

the increasing number of cut surfaces, and if the cut pieces are allowed to stand, the meat may become dry and tasteless.

(6) *De luxe specialties such as Frozen Turkey Steaks* are new on the market. They are very perishable and are available only in certain localities.

There are many back-yard poultry raisers who do not depend on the markets for their poultry supply, and still many other consumers who prefer to buy live birds and prepare them carefully at home. These people should know how to kill and dress these birds in a professional way.

The birds should be separated from the flock a day before killing and no food, except water, given them. This allows the crop and intestines to become emptied and makes drawing easier. The fasting also improves the flavor and tenderness of the meat.

The best method of killing the bird is with a sharp, pointed, killing knife that has a blade about ¼-inch (or less) wide, and is 2 to 3 inches long. Hang the bird up securely by the feet, open the mouth, and insert

the knife, piercing the brain in the first motion, then pressing the knife firmly against the throat and making a single quick downward cut to sever both of the blood vessels. Bleeding will start through the mouth and should be quick and thorough. Adequate bleeding is essential for well-flavored and attractive meat that is free from dark bloody spots under the surface and in the joints. A bird killed in this way will be paralyzed immediately with all sensation destroyed. Its pinfeathers will be easily removed because the tiny muscles holding the feathers will be relaxed by piercing the brain.*

After the bird is killed, the feathers should be removed quickly and promptly by one of several methods. *Dry-picking* requires the most skill, is most tedious, and takes the longest, but a dry-picked bird has a finer flavor than a bird picked in any other way. The feathers must be pulled off with quick motions, that are strong enough to pull out the feathers, yet gentle enough so that the flesh is not torn. *Semi-scalding* is more easily done and can be successfully accomplished by any careful worker. The bird is dipped up and down quickly for 30 to 35 seconds in water heated to 128° to 132° F. *Scalding* differs from semi-scalding in that the water is *hotter,* 180° to 190° F, and the bird is dipped up and down quickly for *just a few* seconds. (For scalding temps most suited to ducks and geese and other types of poultry, see p 745.) With both scalding and semi-scalding, the container of hot water should be deep enough so that the bird is completely covered with water each time it is dipped. The best temp and the length of time

*Other methods of killing sometimes used are beheading and dislocating the neck. Commercially, birds are often paralyzed by electric shock before being bled.

varies with the age of the bird, the lower temp and shorter time applies to young birds around 2½ lbs. Each time or two that the bird is quickly dipped, test the looseness of the "tough-pulling" coarse tail and wing feathers. As soon as they seem loose, the bird is ready to be dressed.

Take a firm grip on a handful of feathers and rub against the lay of the feathers toward the front of the bird with a slight pulling, being careful not to break the skin. Continue pushing and rubbing toward the front of the bird until all of the feathers are removed. The bird may now be classified as a *dressed* bird. When the entrails are removed, it will be a *drawn* bird. After all the feathers are rubbed off, there may still be pinfeathers in the skin that should be removed with a strawberry huller, a small tweezers, or the fingers and a paring knife.

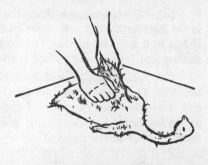

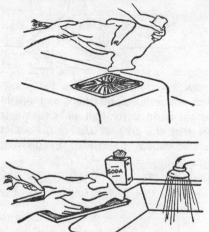

The bird is then singed to remove any hair. Singeing is done by holding the bird over a direct, smokeless flame, grasping the neck in one hand, the feet in the other and turning the bird quickly. Spread each wing to remove the hairs that are always present underneath, and be very careful to avoid scorching.

The bird is then ready for a thorough baking soda and water scrub to remove the surface oil and soil. Rub the soda well into the dampened skin, then thoroughly rinse with cold water. The bird should then be chilled to about 32° F to make drawing easier.

When ready to draw the poultry, place the bird on a large sheet of several thicknesses of clean paper. Remove the tendons connecting the muscles of the drumsticks with the toes. If these tendons are not removed, they may become dry and splinter-like within the drumstick, particularly if the bird is roasted. Make a cut about 2 inches long at the side of the shank just beyond the bone, and insert a nut pick or hook into this opening. Lift the tendons one at a time and pull them out; they will remain attached to the feet. Cut off the feet and use them for making excellent stock for soups and gravies. Remove the oil sac on the back at the base of the tail by cutting under the sac to the backbone and up toward the tail.

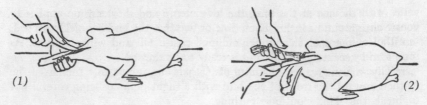

(1) *Slit the neck skin* down the back to the shoulder. Cutting the skin in the back rather than the front leaves the skin of the upper breast intact. If the bird is to be roasted, the neck skin may later be drawn back after stuffing and trussing and tucked firmly under the folded wing tips.

(2) *Pull the neck out* of the neck skin and cut off the neck close to the shoulder. The neck makes the cooked bird look less attractive if it is left on, and it usually becomes very hard and dry. By cutting it off, it may be simmered separately to make a richer stock to be used for gravy, and the bits of meat attached can be removed and also added to gravy, dressing or soup.

(3) *After the neck is removed, carefully loosen the crop,* gullet and windpipe from the binding membranes which surround them and gently pull them away from the skin and out of the body cavity. Cut off at the point where they enter the body. Remember that the *crop is always there and must be removed and discarded.* It may be collapsed and easily overlooked.

(4) *Make an incision* as small as possible along a line from ½ inch below the end of the breastbone to the vent. The cut must penetrate the body fat, but should be done very carefully so that it does not cut into the intestinal tract.

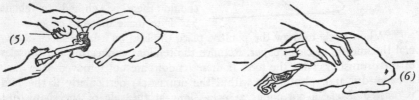

(5) *The forefinger may then be inserted* into the cut and circled around the intestine leading to the vent. The lower intestine can then be lifted up and a ¾-inch circle cut around the vent. Cutting off the gullet and windpipe from the neck end, and cutting around the vent loosens the entire intestinal tract so that it can be removed intact.

(6) *The next step* is to carefully work two fingers into the *body cavity,* locate the gizzard near the center right. Then grasp it firmly and pull steadily until all of the entrails come out in one piece. It is very important for the flavor and keeping quality of dressed poultry that the entrails be removed carefully without breaking into any of them.

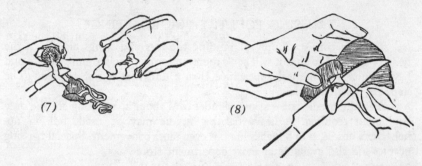

(7) *Cut the gizzard away* from its two attachments. Cut into one of the thick sides of the gizzard until the inner sac is reached, but do not cut into the sac. Place thumbs on either side of the incision made and peel the gizzard away from the inside sac. Discard the sac and remove any remaining intestinal attachment from the gizzard and place it on a sheet of waxed paper.

(8) *Cut the heart away* from the rest of the entrails and place it with the gizzard. Lift the liver away from the intestines and turn its under side up to find the gall sac. Slip the knife under this sac and cut it away removing any part of the liver stained by the gall. Take particular care to remove this sac without breaking it and to discard any part of the meat which may have been stained by its contents. Save the liver with the rest of the giblets.

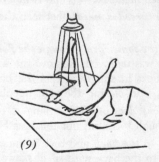

(9) *Rinse the giblets* and the inside of the body cavity with clear water to remove every bit of clinging viscera, the spongy lungs inside the thoracic cavity, and the kidneys that are inside the back cavities. Always wash inside and drain chicken thoroughly before cutting it for best flavor retention. Wrap loosely and store in a cold part of the refrigerator until ready to cook. Wrap giblets and neck separately and store carefully with the chicken.

Wrap up the waste in the paper on which the bird had been placed and discard. Once the process of dressing and drawing poultry has been mastered, many fastidious cooks will prefer to perform this task themselves rather than have it done carelessly. It can be quickly and neatly accomplished if the above directions are followed exactly.

TRUSSING POULTRY FOR ROASTING*

Trussing consists simply of binding the legs and wings closely to the body of the bird so that it will cook more uniformly, brown more evenly and have a more symmetrical appearance than a bird that is not trussed. (The steps are described below.)

A sturdy needle and a strong slender cord about a yard long are the only equipment required. A heavy darning needle may be used, but an upholsterer's needle, 6 to 8 inches long, is even more convenient. Special trussing needles are also available at most department stores.

1. *Lay the unstuffed bird on its back* with the tail to your right. Lift the legs so the drumsticks make right angles with the body, and insert the needle, guiding it to come out at the corresponding place on the opposite side. Leave an end of string several inches long.

2. *Fold the wings so the tips lie under the back,* turn the bird around. Insert the threaded needle down through the angle formed by the wing at your right; then across the back and up through the angle of the other wing. Cut the cord, leaving a long end.

3. *Tie to other end of string at the side of the bird;* draw cord up snugly so as to bring thighs close to the breast, and tie a secure knot. The body cavity may be stuffed at this point and opening laced together using strong toothpicks or small metal skewers and twine, if a stuffing is being used.

4. *Next insert the threaded needle* between the tendons at the ends of the drumsticks.

5. *Continue with the same cord through the flesh* behind the tail, at the point where the oil sac was removed. Remove the needle and draw the cord up tight so the drumsticks fit snugly against the body and the ends of the bones close to the tail, thus closing the vent opening.

6. *Now insert more dressing* (if stuffing is used) through the neck opening, using just enough to round out the breast nicely.

7. *Fold neck skin to the back* and tuck it under the cord and the wing tips. Fasten it securely to the back with small skewers.

8. *The stuffed and trussed bird,* ready for the oven, makes a neat, compact parcel with a minimum of protruding parts to become overbrowned.

For quick removal of the trussing cords before the bird is served, cut the cord opposite the knot and pull it out by the knot.

*By courtesy of Kathryn B. Niles, director of home economics, Poultry and Egg National Board, Chicago.

Table 43   Buying and Cooking Guide for Chicken*

Market Term Approximate Size—Sex	Characteristics	Quantity to Buy Per Person	Method of Cooking
Chicken—Under 1 Year Old—Tender Meat			
BROILER 1 to 2½ lb. (8 to 12 weeks old)	Smooth, thin skin; tender muscles with very thin connective tissue; small amount of fat under skin over the back; flexible tipped breastbone.	¼ to ½ bird	Broiling Roasting Frying
FRYER 2½ to 3½ lb. (14 to 20 weeks old)	Same as above except size and age, meaty enough to be disjointed and cut into serving pieces; noticeable layering (finish) of fat underneath the skin.	¾ to 1 lb.	Frying Roasting
ROASTER Over 3½ lb. (male) (5 to 9 months old)	Tender, soft-meated muscles; smooth skin; large enough in size and meaty enough to be roasted whole; excellent layering of fat underneath skin; flexible tipped breastbone; connective tissue only slightly more developed than in fryer but still thin.	½ to ¾ lb.	Roasting Frying (Older Roasters— 8 or 9 months may also be braised or steamed)
CAPON 4 lb. and over (unsexed male) (7 to 10 months old)	The deluxe in finish, flavor and tenderness brought about by caponizing; popular size 6 to 7 lb.; full-breasted, yielding a high proportion of white meat.	½ to ¾ lb.	Roasting
PULLET 2½ to 5½ lb. (young hen) (4 to 9 months old)	Similar to roaster except body is shorter and plumper; flexible tipped breastbone; smaller weights often marketed as fryers.	½ to ¾ lb. depending on method of cooking	Frying Roasting Braising
1 Year and Over—Less Tender Meat			
FOWL (Hen any weight and age over 1 year)	Thick, coarse skin; muscles well-developed with thick connective tissue; high proportion of fat underneath skin; breastbone no longer flexible.	¼ to ¾ lb.	Steaming Braising Stewing Soup making
COCK OR ROOSTER 3 to 6 lb. (Age over 1 year)	Thick coarse skin, dark tough meat. Muscles well-developed with thick connective tissue. Breastbone no longer flexible.	¼ to ¾ lb.	Simmering, chiefly soup

* Adapted from Poultry and Egg National Board, Chicago, Illinois.

CHICKEN

Chicken is sold at various ages, and each age is suitable for a particular type of cooking. It is important to choose the correct age because a high quality bird of a proper age to make a delicious fricassee would be very unsatisfactory if fried or roasted. The style of cooked chicken desired will determine the kind of bird to be purchased.

It is not wise to order a chicken by the common market term—"fryer," "roaster," etc.—and accept sight unseen any bird that a dealer supplies. For complete satisfaction, the homemaker should get the habit of picking out her bird according to the characteristics described in chart on p 1035.

The main requirement for successful poultry cookery is *low temp*. Regardless of the method of cooking or the age and size of the bird, a low temp cooks the bird more uniformly tender, and keeps the meat more juicy. A bird cooked at a low temp shrinks less, has better textured meat, and is more attractive when served. A high temp toughens and dries out the meat by any method of cooking.

Once the bird has been properly selected according to the Buying Guide, the success of the chicken dish desired depends on careful attention to the proper cooking method. Chicken cooked by all methods should be done to "fork tenderness" and may have the appearance of almost falling away from the bones. The proper cooking methods are described in detail in the recipes that follow.

MRS. DUKE'S CHICKEN BAKED IN STUFFING

3½ lbs roasting chicken, dressed wt
3 tbsp butter *or* chicken fat
⅔ cup finely chopped onion, 2 small
¾ cup fine cut celery
Stuffing:
1½ cups crumbled unsweetened corn bread, lightly pkd
3 cups crumbled baking powder biscuit, lightly pkd

1¾ tsp sage, finely crushed, pkd
¼ to ⅓ tsp pepper
¼ tsp salt
2 eggs
3 cups cooled chicken broth
Giblets
1 hard-cooked egg
2 tbsp flour
¼ cup cold water

Start oven 10 min before baking; set to moderate (350° F).

Singe chicken, remove pin feathers and wash thoroughly inside and out. Drain well. Cut chicken in serving pieces or leave whole. If left whole, tie legs closely to body to handle easily and keep good shape. Place in 4-qt saucepan; add 5 cups hot water and 1 tbsp salt. Cover, heat to boiling, lower heat and simmer until perfectly tender but not until chicken separates from bone, 1½ to 2 hrs depending on age of bird. Remove chicken to small roaster. Measure remaining broth. There should be 4½ cups.

Stuffing: Melt butter, add onions and celery and sauté until lightly browned—4 to 5 min. Place crumbled corn bread and biscuits in 3-qt mixing bowl. Sprinkle sage, pepper and salt over crumbs, and toss well to distribute. Add onion-celery mixture and toss together. Pour broth over crumbs, then well-beaten eggs; use 2 forks to mix stuffing lightly but thoroughly. This is a wet dressing. Pour stuffing around chicken. Place uncovered in oven and bake 30 min or until chicken and stuffing bake to an appetizing brown color. Have giblets and hard-cooked egg chopped medium fine. Blend flour to a smooth paste with water. Stir in remaining broth and boil gently until thickened and clear. Add giblets and egg last 5 min. Serve chicken on platter; spoon fluffy stuffing into separate dish. 5 to 6 servings.

BROILED CHICKEN

Choose chicken of the proper age and weight for broiling. See chart, p 1035. Prepare the cleaned, well-drained chicken for broiling by splitting directly in center of backbone to divide in half lengthwise. This is best done by making a clean cut through the flesh where the back-bone and the breastbone are to be split, then with a pair of poultry shears, a strong saw-tooth knife or a meat saw, cut through both back- and breastbone cleanly and evenly. It  is important that these bones be cut straight and through the center so that both halves are equal in size and will cook evenly and will be equally attractive. (Chicken may be cut into quarters, but halves are the usual form for broiled chicken.) Break each joint by snapping the cartilage so that chicken halves will not cup-up in broiling. Skewer halves into compact form with small metal or wooden skewers. Set range for broiling (550° F) and preheat according to directions that accompany range. Place broiling rack about 6 inches from source of heat, so that the top of the chicken will be about 4 inches from the heat. (This gives a temp of about 350° F at surface of chicken.) Brush cut side of chicken generously with ¾ cup thin cream blended smoothly with 1 tbsp flour, ½ tsp paprika and 1 tsp salt, and place cut-side up on broiler rack. Broil about 10 min. Turn chicken over, brush skin side with mixture and broil 10 min longer. Turn every 10 min, brush with mixture (the last time sprinkle with salt). Chicken should be well browned and perfectly tender in 35 to 60 min depending on the weight. Serve immediately with Pan Gravy, p 766, or Giblet Gravy, p 765. Allow ¼ to ½ bird for 1 serving.

Note: To test for doneness, press the joint between the drumstick and thigh with a fork. If the joint yields readily, the meat is well-cooked.

BARBECUED CHICKEN

3 broilers
Melted shortening
Barbecue Sauce:
  ½ cup cider vinegar
  1½ tsp salt
  1½ tsp Worcestershire sauce

⅛ tsp pepper
1 tsp freshly grated onion
¼ tsp paprika
1½ tbsp tomato paste
½ cup melted shortening

Clean broilers thoroughly and wash quickly inside and out in cold water. Drain well. Split broilers in half using poultry shears. Pat dry with a clean cloth inside and out. Brush with melted fat, place in a shallow roasting pan, skin side down, cover and place in a moderate oven (350° F). Bake for about 35 min or until half done, then turn over, brush with barbecue sauce. To make the barbecue sauce, combine the last 8 ingredients and blend well. Return to the oven to bake for 40 to 50 min longer or until the broilers are well cooked, basting the chicken every 5 min with the barbecue sauce. Serve the sauce which accumulates in the bottom of the pan with the chicken. 6 servings.

BRAISED CHICKEN—FRICASSEE

4 to 5 lb roasting chicken,
  pullet or young fowl
½ cup flour
2½ tsp salt

¼ tsp paprika
3 to 4 tbsp fat
About 1 cup water, broth
  or milk

Buy bird of the proper weight and age for braising. See Cooking Guide, p 1035. Clean, singe, draw and wash thoroughly according to directions. Cut into serving pieces, drain well. Dredge pieces of chicken in flour, seasoned with salt and paprika until each piece is well coated. See Fried Chicken. Brown pieces of chicken *slowly* on all sides in heated fat over medium heat, uncovered. Use a heavy iron or aluminum skillet or Dutch oven that can be tightly covered. The slow browning of all the pieces not only develops a rich brown color in the chicken and the gravy, but contributes a delicious flavor to the finished chicken; the browning should take about ½ hr. Add ¼ cup of the water or other liquid to the browned chicken, cover tightly and simmer gently over low heat until tender, from 1½ to 3 hrs, depending on age of bird. Or, cover and cook in a moderately slow oven (325° F) for the same length of time until tender. Add more liquid in small amounts during cooking if necessary. Remove chicken to a heated serving platter and cover to keep hot. Make gravy from the drippings, p 765, if desired, or add remaining liquid to drippings in pan, reheat to boiling and serve over the chicken or in a separate heated bowl. 5 generous servings.

Note: Chicken is done when a fork can be pierced easily to the bone through the thickest portion of the drumstick.

Note: Directions for Singeing, Drawing and Washing p 1031.

BRUNSWICK STEW

A famous 1-dish meal popular along the coast from Maine to Louisiana

1 dressed, drawn frying
chicken, 2 lbs
3 cups water
1½ tsp salt
3 medium potatoes, 1 lb
2 medium onions, egg-size
1 cup fresh *or* frozen lima
beans
1 cup fresh corn cut from
cob, *or*

1 cup canned whole kernel
corn
2 *or* 3 medium tomatoes,
peeled
Pinch of thyme
½ tsp salt
Few dashes of black pepper
Few dashes of red pepper

Clean and wash chicken; cut into quarters. Put into saucepan, add water and the 1½ tsp salt. Cover, heat to boiling, then reduce heat and simmer until tender, about 1 hr. Lift chicken from broth. Now add potatoes, pared and cut in half, onions, peeled and cut in quarters and limas. Again cover, boil gently 15 min or until about tender. Remove potatoes, mash and return to kettle with corn, quartered tomatoes and seasonings. Cover and simmer another 10 min. Meanwhile strip chicken from bones in large pieces and add to stew last 5 min of cooking. At this point the stew should be boiled down until only about a cup of broth remains. Serve piping hot in soup bowls. 4 to 5 servings.

Note: Brunswick stew may be made with an equal amount of squirrel, veal or lean pork instead of chicken. Different vegetables may also be added, such as 1 cup sliced okra, ½ cup diced sweet red pepper. In winter a pod of dry hot red pepper and frozen beans and corn may be used in place of fresh. The bones may also be left in the meat, if desired.

BREADED FRIED CHICKEN

Have ready about 1 cup or more of fine dry cracker or bread crumbs in a shallow pan. In another pan have ½ cup milk, or 1 beaten egg combined with ¼ cup milk. Sprinkle chicken with salt. Then dip in milk or milk-egg mixture, then in crumbs until well coated on all sides. Or put crumbs in a clean paper bag, add a few pieces of milk-dipped chicken at a time and shake thoroughly to coat well. Brown well on all sides and continue cooking either on top of stove or in oven as directed in either Fried Chicken or Oven Fried Chicken.

FRIED CHICKEN

2½ to 3½-lb frying chicken
1 tsp salt mixed with
each ⅓ cup flour

Shortening ¼-inch deep
in fryer
Clean paper bag

Clean and draw chicken, see p 1032. Wash and cut into serving pieces; dry well. See *Note,* p 1040. Roll pieces in salted flour to coat, or put flour-salt mixture into paper bag, adding a few pieces of chicken at a time and shake bag vigorously. Remove coated pieces to plate, keeping in a single layer, then flour remaining pieces. Heat shortening to moderately hot over medium heat in a heavy skillet or chicken fryer. If butter flavor is desired, use ⅓ butter and ⅔ shortening. Put in a single layer of the thick, meaty pieces first, then cover and fry slowly until delicately browned on all sides, turning frequently. Now pile browned pieces to one side to make room for browning other pieces. When all are browned, which takes about 30 min, reduce heat to *low,* cover and cook until done, about 15 min longer, turning occasionally. Add liver the last 10 min of cooking. Avoid piercing pieces when turning—use tongs or 2 spoons. Uncover last 10 min of cooking to crisp chicken. Make gravy from drippings, p 765. 4 servings.

Note: Frying chicken is usually cut into 11 pieces: 2 drumsticks, 2 thighs, 2 wings, 2 pieces of back—tail and rib pieces, 2 pieces of breast and neck, which should be cut off with skin attached. (If more pieces of breast meat are desired, cut the large breast pieces in two with kitchen scissors after frying.) In cutting up chicken, be sure the skin belonging to each piece is left attached for better appearance when fried and better flavor.

CRISP FRIED CHICKEN

3 lb frying chicken	⅔ cup lard
½ cup flour	2 cups milk *or* Chicken Consomme
1½ tsp salt	
¼ tsp pepper	Pinch of sage, optional

Clean chicken thoroughly, then wash quickly inside and out. Drain well, then pat dry with paper toweling. Cut into pieces. Break the rib piece and press it as well as all the other pieces so they will lie flat. Blend in half the flour, 1 tsp of the salt and pepper. Put into a paper bag and put in 2 or 3 pieces of chicken at a time and shake bag gently. Lay coated chicken on waxed paper and let stand 10 min to dry. If very crusty chicken is desired, shake chicken in flour a second time. Heat fat in a heavy 10-inch skillet. When fat is hot but not smoking, about 300° F, check temp if you have a thermometer, shake off excess flour from chicken, lay in the fat, the large pieces in center, small pieces at the edge. Wait to add liver the last 10 min of frying. See that there is enough fat in the skillet to make it about ⅓-inch deep around pieces of chicken. Add more if needed. Brown chicken slowly. The fat should never be hot enough to smoke or sputter. Do not cover skillet. This allows steam to escape and crust to develop. When underside of chicken browns to desired color, turn and brown on other side. When all sides of chicken are brown, turn heat very low, put lid only half way on skillet and continue cooking until chicken is tender. This requires about 45 min. Remove chicken to hot platter placed on back of stove. Drain off all but ¼ cup fat. Add rest of flour and salt, blend until smooth, scraping loose as much of the material adhering to bottom of skillet as possible. Slowly add milk, stirring constantly until smooth and thickened. Lower heat, add sage and simmer 10 min, stirring occasionally. Pour into hot gravy boat and serve immediately.

DEEP-FAT FRIED CHICKEN

2½ to 3½ lb frying chicken	1 egg
1 cup flour	½ cup milk
1 tbsp salt	2 to 3 lbs shortening

Clean and singe chicken, then wash well inside and out. Drain well, then pat dry with paper toweling. Cut into serving pieces and put into the top of a double boiler. Cover and place over gently boiling water to steam until tender. Meanwhile sift the flour and salt onto a sheet of waxed paper. Beat egg and stir in the milk. Put shortening into deep fat frying kettle and slowly heat to 350° F. Lift chicken out of double boiler, piece by piece and roll in flour mixture, then dip in egg mixture and again in flour. Place chicken piece by piece into hot fat. Since the fat drops to around 300° F when chicken is put into fat, increase heat so the temp is maintained around 350° F, but does not go above. Fry until crisp and brown, from 5 to 6 min. Lift chicken out, drain well over kettle and lay a min on piece of paper toweling. Then serve piping hot with gravy made by thickening the liquid left from steaming the chicken in top of double boiler. 4 to 5 servings.

OVEN-FRIED CHICKEN

Prepare and brown chicken as for Fried Chicken. When uniformly browned, transfer chicken and drippings to roasting pan with tight-fitting cover. Add 2 to 4 tbsp of water if chicken weighs over 3½ lbs dressed weight. Cover and bake in moderately slow oven (325° F) until tender, ½ to 1 hr. Uncover last 10 min to crisp. Make gravy from drippings left in roaster. Serve hot. 4 servings.

STEAMED CHICKEN

Choose a fowl or large roasting chicken for steaming according to chart. Singe, clean and wash according to directions, p 1031, and p 1032. Leave whole and place in the upper part of the steamer. Chicken may be wrapped first in 2 or 3 thicknesses of cheesecloth if desired; this will make the meat of thighs and drumsticks almost as white as breast meat. Have about 3 cups of water rapidly boiling in the bottom of the steamer, cover tightly and boil water gently until chicken is perfectly tender and meat begins to pull away from the bones. Add more water to bottom of steamer only if needed to prevent going dry so that the broth that collects on the bottom will have a concentrated chicken flavor. Steam for 2 to 4 hrs depending on the age and size of the bird. Cool, then cover and refrigerate promptly until ready to use. Store the chicken in the cooking liquid to keep the meat juicy. Use cooked meat for à la King, à la Newburg, chicken pie, escalloped dishes, salads, sandwiches, shortcake, etc. Use broth in aspic, sauces, gravy or soup.

STEWED CHICKEN

Choose a 3½ to 5 lb stewing or older roasting chicken or pullet according to chart on p 1035. Singe, clean and wash bird thoroughly, p 1031. Cut into serving pieces or leave whole according to manner of intended service. Fit pieces compactly into a kettle with a tight fitting cover. *Barely* cover with cold water and add 1½ to 2 tsp salt. For additional flavor, add one small carrot, one small onion, one branch of celery, and a few whole black peppers. Cover tightly, heat to boiling, then reduce heat and simmer gently until tender, 2 to 4 hrs depending on size and age of bird. Chicken is done when a fork can be pierced easily through the thickest portion of the drumstick to the bone. If the meat is to be served cold (as for salad or sandwiches), it should be removed from the broth, so both may cool quickly, and then returned to the cooled broth, covered and stored in the refrigerator until ready for use. Use cooked meat for à la King, à la Newburg, chicken pie, escalloped dishes, salad, sandwiches, shortcake, etc., or cook with noodles or dumplings and serve immediately as described in the separate recipes on p 1044. May also be cooked in pressure saucepan. 5 to 6 servings.

TASTY, CRUNCHY COATED PAN OR DEEP-FAT FRIED CHICKEN

½ cup fine, fluffy bread crumbs
½ cup all-purpose flour
1½ tsp paprika

2 tsp salt
½ cup milk
2½ to 3 lb fryer
Fat for frying

Let sliced bread dry in its cellophane bag (3 to 4 days) until it grates into fine, fluffy (not powdery) crumbs. Combine crumbs, flour, paprika. An hr and a half before frying time, dissolve salt in milk, dip chicken in milk, drain a min, toss in crumbs. Place coated chicken on cookie sheet or cake rack in refrigerator to dry for an hr. Remove 10 or 15 min before frying. Fry in deep fat heated to 350° F about 20 min or until golden and tender. Or fry in deep fat heated to 365° F to a golden brown, remove to cookie sheet, place in moderate oven (350° F), continue cooking until chicken is tender (30 to 45 min), time depending on size of chicken. Sprinkle with salt. 4 to 5 servings.

ROAST CHICKEN

Choose plump 4½ to 5½ lb chicken for roasting. Singe; thoroughly clean and wash the bird, p 1031 and p 1032. Drain, dry thoroughly; truss, stuff with any desired dressing, p 754 and p 1072. Place enough dressing in neck cavity to fill it out well. Place breast side down on trivet or wire rack in open roasting pan, brush with melted butter or tried-out chicken fat, p 166, or cover with several layers of cheese cloth dipped in melted fat. Roast in moderate oven (325–350° F) allowing 30 to 45 min to the lb (the larger the bird, the shorter is the time per lb). When cooking time is half over, turn chicken on its back, brush again with melted fat or replace cloth over breast. As breast, crop and thighs brown, cover with brown wrapping paper (fasten with a toothpick inserted into the crop stuffing), then with 2 or 3 layers of cheesecloth. Baste through paper and cheesecloth every 10 min with one part melted fat and 3 of hot water. Remove paper, cloth, trussing twine. Make gravy, p 765. Serves 5.

TEST FOR DONENESS OF ROAST POULTRY

Twist the leg and if the drumstick-thigh joint moves easily or breaks, the bird is done. The drumstick meat should be very soft when pressed between fingers. Do not pierce meat with a fork to test.

Cooking Hint: Use a roasting pan of smallest possible size to hold bird so drippings will not be spread in too thin a layer in pan to scorch. If pan is too large, to prevent drippings from scorching, add 1 to 2 tbsp chicken fat or shortening and a little water during first part of cooking. Leave pan uncovered for chicken to roast (not steam).

OLD-TIME ROAST CHICKEN

5 lb roasting chicken *or*	2 eggs, beaten
a young hen, see p 1031	6 cups coarse, stale bread
2 tsp salt	crumbs
1 branch celery	1 tsp poultry seasoning
1 slice onion	⅓ cup chopped celery
Dressing:	2 tbsp chopped onion
1½ cups cool chicken broth	3 tbsp butter

Clean chicken thoroughly. Wash quickly inside and out with cold water and drain thoroughly. Sprinkle half the salt on the inside of the chicken. Choose a kettle of a size into which the chicken will fit snugly. Keep shape uniform so that the bird will stand squarely on its back when put into the roasting pan. Add 2 cups water and the rest of the salt, the celery and onion. Cover tightly and heat to boiling, then reduce the heat and *simmer* for 30 min. To keep the top of the chicken moist, spoon some of the hot broth up over it from time to time during this parboiling. Remove chicken to roasting pan. Drain off the broth and measure. There should be about 2 cups. Cool quickly and add the 1½ cups to the beaten eggs. Then pour this over the other ingredients combined for the dressing and mix gently. Spoon the stuffing into the parboiled chicken. This chicken is not trussed in the usual way. Brush the outside of the chicken with melted butter or chicken fat. Place in roasting pan. Pour the remaining ½ cup broth around the chicken. Cover the roasting pan and place in a moderately hot oven (375° F) and bake until chicken is very tender and browned, or from 1½ to 2½ hrs, the time depending on the age of the chicken. 5 servings.

TABLE 44   TIME-TABLE FOR ROASTING CHICKEN

Market Dressed Weight*	Oven Temperature	Minutes per Pound	Total Roasting Time
3½ to 4 lb	350° F	40 to 45	2 to 2¾ hrs
4 to 5 lb	325° F	35 to 40	2½ to 3 hrs
5 to 6 lb	325° F	30 to 35	3 to 3½ hrs

*The oven weight of a stuffed bird approximates the market weight of a *Dressed* bird, p 1029. If a *Quick-frozen Full Drawn* bird is purchased, increase roasting time slightly to compensate for added stuffing weight.

STEWED CHICKEN AND DUMPLINGS

3½ to 4-lb stewing *or* roasting chicken
1½ cups all-purpose flour
3 tsp D.A. baking powder *or* 4 tsp tartrate *or* phosphate type
½ tsp salt
1 cup milk
1 tsp fine-chopped parsley, if desired

Stew chicken as described on p 1042. Fifteen min before chicken is done, add dumplings prepared as follows:

Sift flour, measure, and resift 3 times with baking powder and salt. Add milk all at once and stir until dry ingredients are just dampened; then add parsley and stir until parsley is distributed. Remove cover from stewing kettle. There should be enough liquid in kettle to barely cover the chicken. Dip a tsp first into the hot liquid, then dip up a heaping spoonful batter to drop onto the chicken. (Dipping the spoon in the hot liquid prevents batter from sticking to spoon). Drop all dumplings in quickly; then replace cover and cook 12 min. Remove dumplings to platter and arrange pieces of chicken around them. Pour the thickened liquid into hot gravy boat. 5 or 6 servings.

Variation: Noodles may be cooked in the chicken broth in place of the dumplings.

SPECIAL CHICKEN RECIPES

CHICKEN À LA KING

2 tbsp butter *or* chicken fat
⅓ green pepper, cut in strips
¼ lb fresh mushrooms, sliced
¼ cup flour
1⅓ cups cream *or* evaporated milk
1⅓ cups good strength Chicken Broth, p 1289
Salt and pepper to taste
2 cups cold diced steamed Chicken, p 1041, free of fat and skin
½ pimiento, cut in strips

Melt butter in top of double boiler over direct heat; add green pepper and mushrooms and simmer for 5 min, covered. Lift out pepper and mushrooms. Blend flour into the fat, add cream or milk, broth and seasonings and cook with constant stirring, still over direct heat, until sauce boils and thickens. Add chicken, pimiento, green pepper and mushrooms; place over boiling water, cover, and cook until chicken is heated through. Serve hot over toast. Baking Powder Biscuits, p 234, Crisp Noodles, p 431, or Boiled Rice, p 433. 5 servings.

CHICKEN AND OKRA GUMBO

4 lb stewing *or* older roasting chicken	5 cups peeled, chopped tomatoes
1/3 cup all-purpose flour	2 cups fresh corn, cut from the cob
1 1/2 tsp salt	
1/3 cup rendered chicken fat *or* other shortening	3 cups sliced okra
	1 1/2 tbsp salt
1 cup chopped onions	2 1/2 cups water
5 cups water	Dash pepper

Choose chicken for stewing according to chart. Singe, clean and wash, p 1031 and p 1032. Cut chicken into serving pieces. Dredge with flour and the 1 1/2 tsp salt mixed, and brown slowly in hot fat in a Dutch oven over moderate heat. Add onions and sauté for a few min until onions are soft. Add the 5 cups of water and simmer for 2 1/2 to 3 hrs until chicken is tender and about to fall from bones. Lift the chicken out onto a plate to cool. Add remaining ingredients to broth in Dutch oven. Simmer slowly for 20 min. Meanwhile remove meat from bones and cut chicken into neat cubes. Return chicken to broth mixture, heat through quickly and serve at once. 10 servings.

CHICKEN CACCIATORE

A popular Italian method of cooking chicken

4-lb young roasting chicken	2 tsp salt
1/2 cup olive *or* salad oil	1/8 tsp pepper
2/3 cup chopped onion	1/2 cup white wine, Chablis
1 to 2 small cloves garlic	Parsley
3 cups canned tomatoes, sieved	Cooked noodles

Clean chicken. Wash well inside and out; drain and cut into serving portions. Heat oil in Dutch oven or deep heavy skillet until hot, then add unfloured chicken and brown slowly on all sides, about 20 min. Remove chicken; add chopped onion and very finely chopped garlic to skillet, sauté 3 or 4 min, then stir in tomatoes and seasonings. Return chicken to skillet, cover and simmer 40 min or until chicken is tender and liquid is reduced to a sauce. Add wine the last 15 min of cooking.

Remove chicken to hot platter; pour sauce over it and sprinkle with chopped parsley. Serve immediately with noodles, mashed potatoes or fluffy rice. 4 to 5 servings.

CHICKEN CARUSO

5 to 6 lb roasting chicken, p 1035	¾ cup chopped celery (include leaves)
¼ cup flour	1 cup sliced carrots
1 tsp salt	1 small onion, cut fine
¹⁄₁₆ tsp pepper	1 tbsp chopped green pepper
¼ cup shortening	1 cup raw rice, not rinsed
1 qt tomato juice	1 tsp sugar
2 cups water	2 tsp salt

Cut the singed, cleaned chicken, p 1031 into serving pieces, dredge in the flour seasoned with salt and pepper and brown slowly on all sides in the hot shortening in a heavy skillet or Dutch oven that has a tight fitting cover. Add tomato juice and water and simmer covered for 1 to 1½ hrs, or until chicken is almost tender. Mix in remaining ingredients, cover and cook for 30 min longer or until rice and chicken are thoroughly tender. This will require frequent but careful stirring. This mixture becomes very thick and must be stirred gently; careless stirring will break the slices of chicken and cause the rice to be mushy. 6 servings.

CHICKEN CHOP SUEY

A welcome Chinese whole meal dish made with chicken

1 cup sliced Pascal celery	1 cup chicken broth *or* 1 cup water and 1 bouillon cube
5 water chestnuts, peeled	
2 tbsp diced green pepper	1 tbsp cornstarch
1 cup Chinese celery *or* Chinese cabbage	½ tsp salt
	1½ tsp soy sauce
⅓ cup sliced mushrooms	¾ tsp monosodium glutamate, optional
¼ cup green onions	
1 cup cooked sliced chicken *or* sautéed chicken strips	2 cups fresh *or* canned bean sprouts
2 tbsp chicken fat *or* butter	3 cups hot cooked rice

Clean all vegetables and prepare as follows: Cut celery diagonally in ½ inch lengths; the chestnuts into thin, crosswise slices; green pepper in ½-inch dice; the green onions in 1½-inch lengths, then into fourths lengthwise; the Chinese cabbage in 1 inch lengths; slice mushrooms vertically. Cut chicken in julienne strips. Heat chicken fat, add celery, cover and sauté 5 min. Add next 4 vegetables and sauté 3 or 4 min or until cooked through. Vegetables should remain slightly crisp. Add green onions, chicken and chicken broth in which cornstarch, salt, soy sauce and M S G have been stirred. Stir gently until mixture boils and thickens. Rinse bean sprouts, drain and add to skillet and cook about 2 min; toss until sprouts are thoroughly heated through but still remain crisp. Serve immediately with rice and additional soy sauce. 3 to 4 servings.

Variation: Pork Chop Suey may be made by substituting 1 cup thin lean pork slices for chicken.

Note: If thin strips of raw chicken are used, sauté in hot chicken fat first about 10 min; remove from pan and sauté celery.

CHICKEN OR TURKEY CROQUETTES

⅓ cup chicken fat *or* butter
½ cup flour
1¼ cups concentrated chicken
   broth, p 1289
2 egg yolks
¾ cup coffee cream

2 cups finely diced steamed
   chicken free of bone and
   skin, p 1041
Salt and pepper to taste
Fine dry bread crumbs
1 egg, slightly beaten
1 tbsp water
Fat for deep frying

Heat chicken fat in top of a double boiler over direct heat. Blend in flour until smooth. Add the chicken broth, slowly stirring constantly to keep smooth. Cook with constant stirring until sauce is smooth and thick. Beat egg yolks, add the cream, stir until smooth, then add to the chicken sauce. Add chicken and seasonings, stir thoroughly and place over hot water and cook for about 10 min, stirring occasionally. Turn out into a shallow dish to cool. Then cover with waxed paper and place in the refrigerator to chill very thoroughly. About 30 min before serving time, remove from refrigerator, quickly divide into ¼ cupfuls and form into cone or cylinder shapes. Roll in crumbs, then in the beaten egg diluted with the water, and again in crumbs. Fry in deep fat heated to 375° F to a golden brown and piping hot all through. Remove to a hot platter or keep hot in a slow oven until all are cooked. Garnish with parsley. A gravy made from extra chicken fat is delicious with these croquettes or serve with a creamed vegetable such as peas. 5 servings. Turkey croquettes may be made in the same way.

CHICKEN CURRY

An exotic Indian dish developed for American palates

½ cup flour
2 tbsp chicken fat *or* butter
½ cup onions, finely chopped
3 cups rich chicken broth
1 tsp lemon juice
1 tsp salt
2 tsp curry powder

2 cups cubed cooked chicken
3 to 4 cups hot cooked rice
Coconut
Chutney
Parsley
Salted peanuts, coarsely
   chopped

Brown flour very lightly by placing in saucepan over direct heat and stir until a very light tan. In another saucepan heat chicken fat or butter, add onions and sauté until cooked yellow and soft. Blend in flour, slowly add chicken broth, mixing constantly to keep smooth. After mixture is thickened, add lemon juice, simmer 5 min and stir occasionally. Add salt, curry powder and chicken. Heat thoroughly, stirring occasionally. Serve over hot fluffy rice. Freshly grated coconut, chutney, chopped salted peanuts and chopped parsley are the favored accompaniments. 4 servings.

Variation: Shrimp Curry may be made by following recipe for Chicken Curry, substituting 2 cups cleaned, cooked shrimp for the chicken. More lemon juice may be desired in the shrimp curry.

Note: An American made curry powder was used in this recipe. Other curries may be less or more potent in flavor. Therefore, add the amount of your curry that will suit your family's taste.

CHICKEN FRICASSEE

See recipe for Braised Chicken, p 1038.

ITALIAN CHICKEN FRICASSEE

Different but appealing

3 lb ready-to-cook chicken	1 cup chicken broth *or*
3 tbsp chicken fat *or*	1 chicken bouillon cube
margarine	dissolved in 1 cup hot water
¼ cup flour	¼ tsp rosemary
1¼ cups canned tomatoes	2 tsp sugar
2 tsp salt	⅓ cup water
½ cup sliced celery	Parsley

Buy a roaster or large fryer for fricasseeing. Clean and cut chicken into serving pieces. Remove excess fat if present and render in a heavy skillet over low heat. Roll chicken in flour. Heat chicken fat or margarine until hot, add chicken and brown slowly on all sides. This requires at least 20 min. Put tomatoes through a sieve to obtain purée. Add purée with remaining ingredients to chicken. Cover tightly and simmer until chicken is tender and sauce evaporates to a gravy-like consistency, about 2¼ hrs. Stir occasionally and add a little more water from time to time if necessary. Remove chicken to platter, pour gravy over chicken or into gravy boat. Garnish with parsley. 4 to 5 servings.

Note: *M S G is an abbreviation for monosodium glutamate, a salt which accentuates Chicken flavor.*

CHICKEN IN GRAVY

Easy to serve and a delight for everybody to eat. This chicken is tops in avoiding delay and confusion where children are served.

3½ lb moderately fat stewing
   chicken, drawn wt
5 cups water
2½ tsp salt
¾-inch piece dry red pepper
   pod

1 onion size small egg
2 branches celery
4 to 5 tbsp chicken fat
6 tbsp flour *or* 2½ tbsp
   cornstarch
¼ to ½ tsp salt

Leave chicken whole; singe and wash thoroughly inside and out. Place chicken in kettle with next 5 ingredients. Cover, heat to boiling, reduce heat to *simmer* and cook until tender, from 2½ to 3 hrs, time depending on age. When just tender, remove chicken from broth, then cool it and broth separately. When cooled, return chicken to *strained* broth, cover and place in refrigerator. To make gravy, skim off fat, measure 4 to 5 tbsp into top of double boiler, then blend in flour until smooth. Add the broth, about 3½ cups, slowly, stirring to keep smooth, then cook and stir until clear, thickened and smooth. Now place over hot water. Remove most of the skin from chicken, then remove meat from bones in as large pieces as possible. Cut meat neatly into inch dice and add to gravy. Cover and heat thoroughly. Taste and add salt if needed. If gravy is pale, beat an egg yolk, stir in some of the hot gravy, then stir into gravy before adding the chicken. Do not reheat after adding yolk. Serve with fluffy rice or mashed potatoes. 6 to 7 servings.

CHICKEN LOAF WITH MUSHROOM SAUCE

A worthy concoction from leftovers

2 cups chopped chicken, pkd
3 tbsp chicken fat
1 onion, size of egg, chopped
¾ cup chopped celery
6 slices day old bread, 1 qt
⅛ tsp pepper

½ tsp poultry seasoning
1 tsp salt
½ tsp M S G
1 egg
½ cup chicken broth

Start oven 10 min before baking; set to moderate (350° F).

Strip meat from chicken bones and chop medium fine. Turn into 3 qt mixing bowl. Put chicken fat into skillet, heat slowly until melted, then add onion and celery and sauté 4 or 5 min or until soft; stir occasionally. Tear bread into bite-size crumbs and add to chicken. Sprinkle

Note: If chicken broth is not available, use canned chicken bouillon or chicken bouillon cube dissolved in ½ cup milk instead and reduce salt to ¾ tsp.

next 4 ingredients over crumbs. Beat egg, stir in broth or milk and pour over bread. Mix with 2 forks very thoroughly. Turn mixture into greased 8¾ x 4¾ x 2½-inch pan, but don't pack down too firmly. Bake 30 to 35 min, or until nicely browned on top. Unmold onto hot platter. Serve with Mushroom Sauce, below. 4 to 5 servings.

MUSHROOM CREAM SAUCE

4 tsp margarine *or* butter	1½ cups milk
¾ cup sliced mushrooms, 4 medium size	½ tsp salt
2 tbsp flour	⅛ tsp pepper

Heat margarine or butter in saucepan, add mushrooms and toss in hot fat 1 min; cover and cook 2 or 3 min until mushrooms are juicy. Uncover, push mushrooms to one side, stir in flour, gradually add milk and cook and stir until thickened and smooth. Stir in seasonings. Serve hot over Chicken Loaf.

CHICKEN MARGUERITE

A top-notch way to serve stewed chicken

1½ cups chunks stewed chicken	¾ cup rich chicken broth
5 oz narrow noodles	8 ripe olives
1 qt boiling water	1 tbsp pimiento, cut in ½-inch pieces
¾ tsp salt	
4½ tbsp chicken fat	1 tsp sherry extract
¾ cup sliced mushrooms, 4 large	½ cup freshly grated Parmesan *or* aged American cheese
2½ tbsp flour	
¾ cup milk	

Remove meat from cold stewed chicken in as large pieces as possible. Strip off skin carefully and cut meat into neat inch-long chunks. Save skin to make Chicken Stretch, p 1055, or use in Chicken Soup, p 1289. Drop noodles into boiling water to which salt has been added. Cook until just tender, 6 to 8 min. Drain noodles and turn into a buttered 9-inch glass pie plate. Heat chicken fat in saucepan, add mushrooms, cover, sauté 2 or 3 min or until mushrooms are juicy. Push mushrooms to side, remove from heat and blend flour into fat and juice until smooth. Slowly stir in milk and chicken broth to keep smooth. Place over moderate heat and cook and stir until mixture boils and thickens. Add chicken, olives, cut away from seed in two pieces and pimiento. Reheat to boiling, remove from heat, stir in extract and pour over noodles. Sprinkle cheese uniformly over top. Broil with surface 3 inches below source of heat to a tempting brown—6 to 8 min. 4 to 5 servings.

CHICKEN MOUSSE WITH SUPREME SAUCE

High brow, chickeny flavored, economical

1 whole chicken breast,
  from a 4½ to 5 lb bird
2 eggs, separated
½ cup coffee cream
1 tsp salt
  Pepper
1 tbsp chicken fat

Supreme Sauce:
2 *or* 3 chicken backs *or* necks
  and bones from trimmed
  breast
2 cups water
½ tsp salt
2 egg yolks
4 tsp flour
  Salt and pepper
  Chopped parsley

Start oven 10 min before baking; set to moderate (350° F).

When cut-up chicken breasts are used, buy 1⅓ lbs. Be sure to buy enough chicken fat to make 1 tbsp when rendered. This is needed for fine flavored mousse. Wipe pieces of chicken clean. Cut and scrape meat away from breastbone as clean as possible and trim off any tough skin or fibers. Put chicken breast meat with attached skin through food chopper; use fine blade to obtain a fine ground meat. Stir in egg yolks, then cream, salt and pepper. Whip egg whites until stiff, then fold them carefully but thoroughly into chicken meat. Grease glass custard cups (⅔ cup capacity) with chicken fat; then pour in chicken mixture. Drop rest of chicken fat on top of chicken mixture. Set cups in pan containing enough hot water to come almost to top of cups. Bake 30 min, or until mousse is firm.

Sauce: Before making the mousse put bones and trimmings from breast with back pieces into a saucepan, add the water and salt and heat to boiling. Cover, reduce heat to simmering, and cook 1 to 1½ hrs to obtain good flavored broth. Strain off. There should be 1⅓ cups. Now blend flour and ¼ cup of the chicken broth to obtain a smooth paste; then stir in egg yolks and rest of the broth; stir constantly. Cook over low heat until sauce thickens and bubbles. Add salt and pepper to suit taste. Stand sauce over hot water to keep hot. Unmold mousse onto hot platter or individual serving plates and pour sauce over it. Sprinkle with chopped parsley. 6 servings.

CHICKEN MULLIGAN

4 lb stewing chicken
  Cold water to cover
  (about 5 cups)
1 tbsp salt
1 cup rice, unrinsed

1½ cups Pascal celery, cut
  into ½-inch lengths
1 cup carrots, cut into
  ½-inch dice

Clean chicken and disjoint. Add water and ½ of the salt to the chicken in a 4 qt kettle. Cover and *simmer* for 3 hrs or more until chicken is tender. Remove chicken and strain broth (should be about 5 cups). Remove chicken from bones, and cut julienne style including skin. Heat broth to boiling, add remaining salt, rice, celery and carrots. Cover and cook rapidly for 10 to 15 min or until rice and vegetables are tender. Add chicken and heat thoroughly. Serve immediately. 4 or 5 large servings.

CHICKEN FILLED PANCAKES WITH TOMATO SAUCE

½ cup fine-cut celery
3 tbsp fine-chopped onion
2 tsp chicken fat *or* butter
1 tbsp flour
¼ cup chicken gravy *or* rich broth
1½ cups fine-cut cooked chicken

Seasoning to taste
2 cups canned tomatoes
$\frac{1}{16}$ tsp chili powder
4 tsp sugar
¼ tsp salt
Dash of cayenne
4 freshly baked 6-inch pancakes

Sauté celery and onion in chicken fat 3 min or until half-cooked. Blend in flour, add gravy. Stir until mixture is smooth and thickened. Add chicken and seasoning if needed. Keep hot. Combine tomatoes with next 4 ingredients, cook rapidly until liquid is almost evaporated and tomatoes are thickened. Spoon hot chicken along center of each pancake and roll as for jelly roll. Pour piping hot tomato sauce over each roll and serve immediately. 4 servings.

CHICKEN PIE

½ cup cold Broth from Stewed Chicken, p 1042
⅓ cup all-purpose flour
1½ cups hot concentrated chicken broth
2½ cups stewed chicken, boned and cut in large dice
¾ cup fresh cooked, frozen *or* canned peas, drained

¾ cup diced celery
1 tsp salt
1 cup all-purpose flour
1½ tsp D.A. baking powder *or* 2 tsp tartrate *or* phosphate type
¼ tsp salt
3 tbsp butter
⅓ cup milk

Make a paste by blending cold chicken broth and ⅓ cup flour smooth. Add paste to the hot chicken broth and cook over direct heat, stirring constantly until sauce boils and thickens. Combine with chicken, peas, celery and 1 tsp salt, and pour into a 6-cup buttered casserole. Sift the 1 cup flour, measure, and resift 3 times with baking powder and ¼ tsp salt. Cut in butter with a pastry blender or 2 knives, and add milk all at once, stirring quickly with a fork until dough just stiffens. Turn dough out onto floured board, knead 8 times, and roll or pat out to make a circular sheet about 8½ inches in diameter, or to fit top of casserole, and about ¼-inch thick. Make several cuts for a design near the center to allow steam to escape, and place on top of hot filling in casserole.

Crimp edge of dough, pressing it firmly against edge of casserole. Bake in a moderately hot oven (425° F) for about 20 min or until nicely browned and the filling is boiling hot all the way through. 5 servings.

Variation: Omit peas and celery. *Or,* if desired, use instead of peas and celery, ½ lb mushrooms that have been sautéed in 2 tbsp of butter.

CHICKEN POT PIE

4 lb stewing chicken	3 sprigs parsley
2 tsp salt	1½ cups all-purpose flour
4 outer branches celery, optional	3 tsp D.A. baking powder *or* 4 tsp tartrate *or* phosphate type
2 carrots cut in pieces, optional	½ tsp salt
1 small onion, optional	¾ cup milk

Choose a chicken for stewing according to chart. Singe, clean and wash, p 1031 and p 1033. Cut up into serving pieces. Pack pieces compactly into cooking kettle. Sprinkle with the salt, add the celery, carrots, onion and parsley. *Barely cover* with cold water. Cover closely, heat to boiling, then reduce heat to *simmering* and cook until tender, 1½ to 2 hrs, depending on age of bird. Fifteen min before chicken is done, add dumplings prepared as follows. Sift flour, measure and resift 3 times with baking powder and salt. Add milk all at once and stir quickly with a fork until stiff. Roll or pat out to ¼-inch thickness. Cut in 1 x 2 inch strips and drop on top of stew. Cover and cook 15 min. Serve on large platter with the chicken. Serve gravy in a separate heated bowl. 6 to 7 servings.

POLLO CON ARROS OR CHICKEN WITH RICE

A complete meal and a favorite Spanish food

4-lb roasting chicken	½-inch thick slice ham, 1 lb
½ cup olive *or* salad oil	4 cups boiling water
1 medium-size green pepper	1½ tsp salt
2 medium onions, chopped, ½ lb	⅛ tsp pepper
1 small clove garlic	½ tsp saffron, optional
2 medium-size ripe tomatoes, ½ lb	1 cup converted rice
	½ cup pimiento, diced
	Stuffed olive slices

Clean chicken. Wash well inside and out, drain and cut into serving portions. Heat oil in Dutch oven or heavy skillet, add unfloured chicken, cover and brown slowly on all sides, turning frequently, about 20 min. Meanwhile wash pepper, remove seeds and dividing membrane; cut it and peeled onions into 8ths and chop garlic fine. Wash tomatoes; cut in 8ths. Remove chicken to plate, add green pepper, onion and garlic to skillet and sauté 5 min. Now push vegetables to one side; cut ham in serving portions, add to skillet and brown lightly, about 5 min, then add chicken. Lift the cooked vegetables carefully over the meat, then add tomatoes, boiling water, salt, pepper and saffron. Heat to simmering, cover and cook 30 min or until chicken is almost tender. Now add rice, cover and cook 30 min or until rice is tender, carefully stirring occasionally. Turn off heat. Gently fold in diced pimiento and let stand 5 to 10 min. Serve hot with garnish of olive slices. 6 to 7 servings.

RISOTTO MILANAISE

An Italian way of glorifying chicken leftovers

2 tbsp olive oil *or* butter	$\frac{1}{16}$ tsp pepper
½ cup chopped onion,	1 cup fresh mushrooms, 2 oz
2 egg-size	2 tbsp butter
1½ cups converted rice	¼ lb chicken livers *or*
3½ cups rich, tasty chicken *or*	1 cup diced leftover chicken
veal broth	2 cups fresh-grated
Pinch of saffron	Parmesan cheese
1 tsp salt	

Heat olive oil or butter in top of 2-qt double boiler over direct low heat, add onion, and sauté until yellow. Add unwashed rice, broth, saffron, salt and pepper and heat just to boiling, then place over gently boiling water, cover and cook 30 to 35 min. Meanwhile, cut cleaned mushrooms, p 1356, lengthwise. Heat 1 tbsp of the butter in saucepan, add mushrooms, cover and sauté 3 min or until very juicy, then fold into rice mixture. Now heat rest of butter in saucepan, add chicken livers cut medium-fine with kitchen scissors and sauté 2 min; fold gently into rice mixture. Cover and cook 15 to 20 min longer. Turn into heated serving dish and sprinkle with cheese. 4 to 5 servings.

Note: Chicken bouillon cubes may be used to make broth.

CHICKEN SHORTCAKE

4 to 5 lb fowl, p 1035, for	Salt and pepper
steaming, p 1041	½ lb mushrooms, if desired
⅓ cup flour	2 tbsp butter
¼ cup chicken fat	1 recipe Biscuit Dough, p 234
2 cups concentrated chicken	
broth	

Steam or stew chicken according to recipe. Meanwhile render out the excess fat that has been stripped from the chicken. Cool chicken, remove the skin, then the meat from the bones in as large pieces as possible. Then cut chicken into half-inch cubes. Blend the flour into the chicken fat in top of double boiler and add the broth slowly, stirring constantly to obtain a smooth thickened sauce. Add diced chicken, seasonings and the mushrooms which have been sautéed in the butter. Place over hot water and cook until chicken is thoroughly heated

Did you know that turkey is fast scrambling down out of the luxury class? Nowadays almost everyone can manage it for Thanksgiving, and if you want it for cold-slicing in the middle of summer, it's available then too. Here is the holiday bird, p 1071, with homemade frills made out of small paper doilies. Corn-on-the-cob, fresh or frozen, adds a glamour touch to the meal.

© Poultry and Egg National Board.

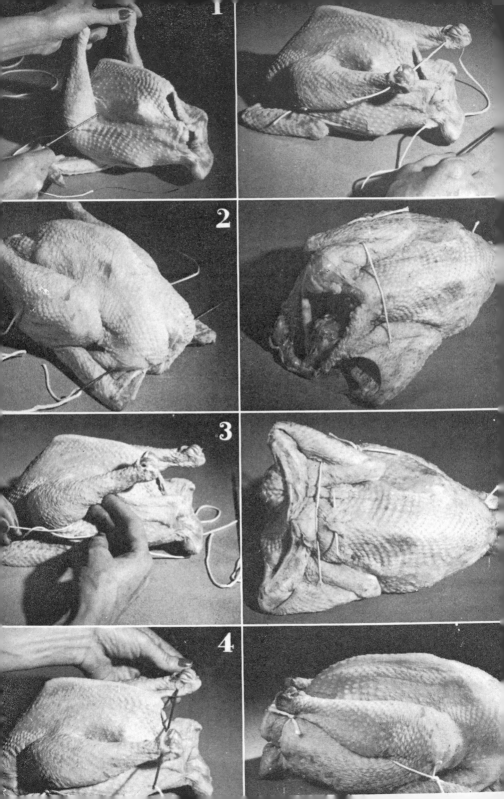

TRUSSING POULTRY FOR ROASTING

Trussing consists simply of binding the legs and wings closely to the body of the bird so that it will cook more uniformly, brown more evenly and have a more symmetrical appearance than a bird that is not trussed. (The steps are illustrated on the opposite page and are described below.)

A sturdy needle and a strong slender cord about a yard long are the only equipment required. A heavy darning needle may be used, but an upholsterer's needle, 6 to 8 inches long, is even more convenient. Special trussing needles are also available at most department stores.

1. Lay the unstuffed bird on its back with the tail to your right. Lift the legs so the drumsticks make right angles with the body, and insert the needle, guiding it to come out at the corresponding place on the opposite side. Leave an end of string several inches long.

2. Fold the wings so the tips lie under the back, turn the bird around. Insert the threaded needle down through the angle formed by the wing at your right; then across the back and up through the angle of the other wing. Cut the cord, leaving a long end.

3. Tie to other end of string at the side of the bird; draw cord up snugly so as to bring thighs close to the breast, and tie a secure knot. The body cavity may be stuffed at this point and opening laced together using strong toothpicks or small metal skewers and twine, if a stuffing is being used.

4. Next insert the threaded needle between the tendons at the ends of the drumsticks.

5. Continue with the same cord through the flesh behind the tail, at the point where the oil sac was removed. Remove the needle and draw the cord up tight so the drumsticks fit snugly against the body and the ends of the bones close to the tail, thus closing the vent opening.

6. Now insert more dressing (if stuffing is used) through the neck opening, using just enough to round out the breast nicely.

7. Fold neck skin to the back and tuck it under the cord and the wing tips. Fasten it securely to the back with small skewers.

8. The stuffed and trussed bird, ready for the oven, makes a neat, compact parcel with a minimum of protruding parts to become overbrowned.

For quick removal of the trussing cords before the bird is served, cut the cord opposite the knot and pull it out by the knot.

Photographs and directions by courtesy of Kathryn B. Niles, director of home economics, Poultry and Egg National Board, Chicago.

ABOVE: *Will your holiday fowl be a turkey? Prepare it handsomely, cook it with care, and garnish it simply but elegantly. The turkey illustrated here has a simple garnish of fresh grapes; its crisp brown doneness needs no further embellishment.*

BELOW: *This is the way the capable housewife puts Fluffy Dressing, p 1073, into the bird. An upholsterer's needle is threaded all ready to truss the bird when it is filled.*

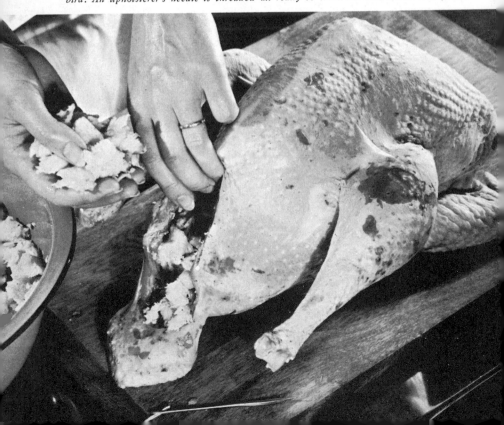

ABOVE: *This chicken is "fried" in the oven after first having a mixture of flour and fat spread over the entire surface of each half.*

BELOW: *Pan-fried Chicken, p 1039, Southern style served with fresh corn cut from the cob and buttered is just about the most delightful combination of protein and carbohydrates that can be found.*

ABOVE: *Potatoes boiled until almost done and then browned alongside the oven-fried chicken make a very impressive main-dish platter.*

BELOW: *Two big handsome roasted chickens, p 1043, on your big turkey platter and dressed up with frills, pickled peaches, p 1098, and parsley are elegant to behold and to eat.*

ABOVE: *When pheasant is properly cleaned, dressed and drawn, p 744, then roasted, p 772, you will be proud to serve it to your family and friends. They will enjoy it and look forward with pleasant anticipation to the next hunting season.*

BELOW: *If you have been of the opinion that wild fowl can never be as attractive as the domestic variety, this photograph of wild duck, p 758, roasted to a turn should convince you that it can be.*

ABOVE: *This melon mold has sections of grapefruit and avocado suspended in fruit-flavored gelatin. Keep the gelatin mixture liquid throughout the assembling process. Never stir or agitate it as it is put into the mold. Garnish with orange slices and spears of French endive or chicory.*

BELOW: *For an informal buffet supper, make and serve Hot Potato Salad, p 1130, in a shiny skillet to keep beautiful and hot to the last morsel. Garnish with other crisp salad greens and serve with cold meats, rye bread and crackers.*

through. Have biscuits freshly baked and hot. Break open. Cover the lower half with chicken in sauce, place on this the top of the biscuit and pour another spoonful of the chicken mixture over the top. 6 to 7 servings.

CHICKEN SOUR CREAM FRICASSEE

4 lb roasting chicken, pullet *or* young fowl	¼ cup shortening
¼ cup flour	1 large onion, sliced
1 tbsp paprika	2 cups hot water
1 tbsp salt	1 cup sour cream

Choose chicken according to chart. Singe, clean and wash, p 1031 and 1033. Cut in serving portions and dredge in the flour mixed with paprika and salt. Brown slowly on all sides in shortening; add onion during last stage of browning chicken and cook until soft. Add any flour mixture left from dredging, blend well with drippings, then add water all at once. Stir to blend flour with liquid, then cover and *simmer* 1½ hrs or until chicken is tender. Add sour cream and simmer 5 min. 5 to 6 servings.

CHICKEN STRETCH

Crunchy, chickeny flavored fried scrapple

3 cups boiling water	2 tbsp corn meal
1 tsp salt	3 tbsp chicken fat *or*
¾ cup yellow corn meal	shortening
½ cup chicken skin ground with medium cutter	

Heat water to boiling over direct heat in top of double boiler; add salt and corn meal and cook and stir until thickened, about 5 min. Add chicken skin. Place over boiling water and cook 45 min, stirring occasionally. Turn into 8 x 4 x 2½-inch loaf pan. Store in cold place over night. When ready to serve, unmold, slice ⅓-inch thick; dip in corn meal. Heat fat in heavy skillet, arrange slices in skillet and fry until crisp and nicely browned on both sides—from 15 to 18 min. Good for breakfast, luncheon or Sunday night suppers.

CHICKEN TERRAPIN

2 tbsp butter *or* margarine	1½ cups cubed moist cooked
2 tbsp flour	chicken *or* turkey
½ tsp salt	Dash of cayenne
2 cups milk	2 tsp sherry extract
	2 hard-cooked eggs

In top of double boiler make a thin white sauce of first 4 ingredients, p 1262. When thoroughly cooked and smooth, place over hot water. Add chicken and cayenne and heat thoroughly. Just before ready to serve, stir in the extract then fold in the sliced hard-cooked eggs. Serve very hot on hot toast triangles, hot fluffy rice, or riced potatoes. 4 servings.

CHICKEN WINCHELL

A pompous chicken specialty easy to make

1½ lbs chicken breast and thighs	4 tbsp flour
1½ tsp salt	½ cup cleaned sliced mushrooms
Dash of pepper	½ cup chicken broth
3 tbsp flour	¾ cup milk
2 tbsp chicken fat	¾ tsp salt
1 chicken back	Pepper, if desired
4 tsp chicken fat	

Use large pieces of tender chicken. Birds around 6 months are ideal. Remove meat by cutting and scraping it away from bone in whole pieces. Leave skin attached; trim away any tough skin or cartilage. Wrap meat in waxed paper and store in refrigerator while preparing the broth. Cover bones and the back with water, add ½ tsp of the salt, cover and simmer 1 hr for rich chicken broth. Strain off broth. There should be ½ cup. Cut the chicken meat into thin strips with kitchen scissors and put meat through food chopper fitted with medium blade. Stir remaining salt, and the pepper into meat and shape into 4 patties about 6 x 4 inches. Sprinkle both sides of patties with flour and lay in skillet containing the sizzling hot 2 tbsp chicken fat. Cover, cook briskly 2½ to 3 min or until underside is a luscious brown. Turn patties over, replace cover and cook another 3 or 4 min longer or until cooked through. Remove to hot platter. Make sauce by adding the 4 tsp chicken fat to that left in the skillet. Blend in the flour until smooth. Add sliced mushrooms and simmer 2 or 3 min. Stir in chicken broth and milk and seasonings. Cook and stir until sauce boils and thickens. Serve sauce over the patties. 4 servings.

CHICKEN WOR MEIN

A speedy tempting Chinese way to stretch chicken

¾ lb chicken breast *or* thighs	1 tbsp cornstarch
1 cup homemade *or* canned chicken broth	½ tsp monosodium glutamate
1 tsp salt	1½ tsp soy sauce
½ cup sliced Pascal celery	5 oz noodles
¼ cup sliced green onions	2 qts boiling water with
½ cup sliced mushrooms	2 tsp salt
1 tbsp chicken fat *or* butter	1 hard-cooked egg
Dash of pepper	Green onions

Remove meat in as whole pieces as possible by cutting and scraping it away from bones; leave skin attached, but trim off any tough membrane. There should be ½ lb meat. Wrap meat in waxed paper; store in refrigerator while making broth and preparing rest of ingredients. To make broth, cover bones with water, add half the salt and simmer 1 hr. Meanwhile prepare vegetables. Cut chicken into ¼-*inch wide* strips. Heat chicken fat until bubbly, add chicken, sprinkle with remaining salt and pepper and stir thoroughly. Cover and sauté 5 min, then add celery, onions, mushrooms and ½ cup of the broth; simmer 5 min. Blend remaining broth with cornstarch, monosodium glutamate and soy sauce; stir into chicken mixture and cook and stir about 5 min until thick and smooth. Meanwhile cook noodles about 8 min in the boiling salted water. Drain thoroughly and turn onto hot platter. Pour chicken mixture over noodles. Garnish with sliced egg and slivered white part of green onions. 4 servings.

CREAMED CHICKEN AND OYSTERS

2 tbsp chicken fat *or* butter	Salt and pepper to taste
⅓ cup flour	1 pt oysters
1 cup leftover chicken broth *or* milk	Biscuits, p 234, hot
1 cup cream	Corn bread, p 240 *or* hot toast
2 cups leftover roast *or* steamed chicken	

Heat chicken fat or butter in saucepan. Add flour and blend until smooth. Add the broth or milk slowly, stirring constantly. Cook with occasional stirring until sauce boils and thickens. Add the cream, chicken and seasonings and continue cooking until chicken is hot through. Look over oysters and remove any bits of shell. Add oysters to hot chicken mixture. Turn heat low and continue heating until edges of oysters curl. Serve over biscuits, corn bread or toast. 5 to 6 servings.

Note: The chicken and sauce may be heated in a covered casserole in the oven and when hot through, the oysters may be stirred in quickly, then the mixture covered with buttered crumbs and the baking continued in a moderately hot oven (400° F) until crumbs are golden brown and oysters are hot through, about ten min. 6 servings.

MORAVIAN CHICKEN

Whole Meal in One Kettle

3½ to 4 lb roasting chicken, pullet *or* young fowl, p 1035	1 medium carrot
1 tbsp salt	1 medium onion, cut in half
1 qt boiling water	1 small piece bay leaf
3 celery leaves	1 red pepper pod
	1 lb whole green beans
	4 oz noodles, 2 cups

Cut the singed, cleaned chicken into serving portions. Place in a 4-qt kettle that has a tightly fitting cover; add salt, then cover with water and add celery leaves, carrot, onion, bay leaf, and pepper. Cover and *simmer* 2 hrs or until almost tender, removing bay leaf after ½ hr. Add beans and cook 20 min, then add noodles. Continue cooking about 10 min longer. 4 to 6 servings.

OLD-FASHIONED CHICKEN SALAD

2 cups diced Stewed *or*
    Steamed Chicken, p 1041
¼ cup French Dressing,
    p 1200
1 cup thin-sliced celery

½ cup Mayonnaise, chilled
1 to 2 tbsp capers *or* sweet
    pickle, optional
Crisp lettuce *or* romaine
2 Hard-cooked Eggs, p 663

Chicken for salad should always be moist. It should be stored well-covered or in its own cooking liquid until ready to use so it will not dry out. Remove skin and fat and cut chicken neatly into cubes. Measure cubes firmly packed in a cup, turn into a flat bowl and drizzle on the French dressing so that all the pieces are well-coated with dressing. Cover tightly and place in refrigerator to marinate for 2 or 3 hrs. Just before serving time, drain off any excess French dressing, add the celery and the mayonnaise and capers and toss just enough to mix well. Arrange crisp greens on salad plates. Heap a half-cup of the salad mixture on each plate. If desired, a chilled slice of pineapple may be placed on lettuce first, and the salad heaped on this. Garnish salad with a few extra capers or thin slices of choice pickles and slices of egg. Serve immediately with additional mayonnaise, if desired. 5 servings.

SAUTÉED CHICKEN AND TOMATOES
WITH MUSHROOM SAUCE

A delicious dish using leftover chicken

2 oz pkg dehydrated
    mushroom soup
1 cup cold water
½ cup gravy, broth *or* milk
3 tbsp rendered chicken fat
1 tbsp chopped onion

8 thin slices left-over chicken
2 large tomatoes, peeled
    and sliced
Dash pepper
Dash celery salt

Pour contents of package of soup into the top of a double boiler and gradually add the cold water. Stir to make a thick smooth paste. Add the gravy and stir to keep smooth. Place over direct heat and heat to boiling, stirring constantly. Place over boiling water for 15 min. Meanwhile, heat chicken fat in a large skillet, add the onion, chicken and tomatoes. Dash lightly with celery salt and pepper and cook over low heat until heated through. Arrange chicken and tomatoes on a serving plate and pour the hot mushroom sauce over it. 4 servings.

Note: Canned cream of mushroom soup may be used in place of the dehydrated soup.

SOUTHERN CHICKEN STEW

4 lb stewing *or* older
    roasting chicken
⅓ cup flour
1 tsp salt
⅓ cup fat
3 cups water
1½ lb tomatoes, 4 medium

2 large onions
2¼ tsp salt
¼ tsp pepper
1 lb tender okra
1 tbsp flour
¼ cup water

Choose chicken for stewing according to chart. Singe, clean and wash, p 1031 and p 1033. Dredge with flour and the 1 tsp salt mixed. Brown slowly in hot fat in a large heavy skillet or Dutch oven. Add the 3 cups water, cover, reduce heat. Simmer gently for 1 hr. Add peeled, sliced tomatoes, sliced peeled onions and remaining salt and pepper. Continue to simmer until chicken is nearly tender enough to serve. Twenty min before chicken is to be served, add trimmed, sliced okra pods on top of stew and cook uncovered for remaining time. Add flour to the ¼ cup cold water and blend until smooth; stir gently into stew, stirring constantly and cook until stew thickens slightly. Serve at once. 6 servings.

CHICKEN LIVERS

BACON WRAPPED BROILED CHICKEN LIVERS

Appearance and flavor of these livers make them popular

¾ lb chicken livers, 12 livers
¾ tsp salt
Few dashes of pepper

Few drops of onion juice
6 10-inch strips bacon
1 tbsp fine-chopped parsley

Start broiler 10 min before broiling; set to hot (450° F). Use only carefully cleaned, whole livers for this preparation. Wash thoroughly in cold water, drain well and pat dry with paper toweling. Lay livers on waxed paper and sprinkle with next 3 ingredients. Cut bacon slices in half crosswise. Wrap each bacon slice snugly around each liver and fasten securely with a 4-inch skewer. Lay in shallow pan lined with sheet of aluminum foil if convenient. Place under broiler so that surface of livers is 3½ inches below source of heat. Broil 6 to 8 min or until top side of bacon is thoroughly cooked; turn over and brown until bacon is done on other side. Transfer to hot platter, drain off most of the clear bacon fat floating on top of juices left in pan and pour remaining rich brown pan gravy over livers. Sprinkle with parsley. 4 servings.

CHICKEN LIVER CURRY

Savory and appealing in flavor

3/4 lb chicken livers, 10
1/2 tsp salt
  Dash of pepper
2/3 cup dry, fine bread crumbs
2 eggs, slightly beaten
1/3 cup chicken fat *or*
  shortening

2 tbsp flour
1 1/2 cups rich chicken broth*
1/2 tsp grated onion
3/4 tsp curry powder
Parsley *or* cress

Wash livers carefully in cold water, drain and pat dry with paper toweling. Lay on sheet of waxed paper, sprinkle with salt and pepper, roll in crumbs, then dip in egg and again in the crumbs. Heat chicken fat in skillet over medium heat, add chicken livers, cover and sauté until nicely browned on all sides and just cooked through—8 to 10 min. Turn over 2 or 3 times to brown uniformly. Remove to hot plate and keep hot. Add flour to remaining fat in pan, blend till smooth, then stir in broth, onion and curry, cook and stir until sauce boils and thickens. Pour hot sauce over livers and garnish with parsley or cress. Serve immediately with rice. 4 servings.

FRIED CHICKEN LIVERS

After livers are washed and patted dry, sprinkle with salt and pepper, if desired. Then dip in flour until well coated. Use enough bacon fat or butter to well cover bottom of skillet when heated; heat over medium heat, add livers, cover and cook until lightly browned and crusty, turning frequently. Leave uncovered last few min of cooking, which takes from 10 to 12 min.

CHICKEN LIVER SAUTÉ WITH LEMON SAUCE

Rich, piquant—very tasty

3/4 lb chicken livers, 9 to 12
1 tsp salt
3 tbsp flour
1/3 cup butter *or* margarine
3 tbsp lemon juice

3 egg yolks
3/4 cup cold water
3/4 tsp sugar
Dash of red pepper
Fine-chopped parsley

Wash well-cleaned whole livers quickly in cold water; drain, pat dry with paper toweling and lay on waxed paper. Sprinkle with salt and flour and toss to coat. Heat butter in skillet until sizzling, add livers and sauté until delicately browned on all sides. Drizzle lemon juice

*Use canned consommé or 1/2 chicken bouillon cube in 1 1/2 cups water.

over livers and cook 2 to 3 min longer basting with the sauce. Draw skillet from heat and remove livers to hot serving dish; cover to keep hot. Beat egg yolks, water, sugar and pepper together thoroughly. Return skillet to heat, add egg mixture and cook and stir until sauce thickens and bubbles. Pour sauce around livers and sprinkle parsley over sauce. Serve with white or wild rice or potatoes. 4 servings.

Note: Buy whole chicken livers which usually means that gall sacs have been removed, but look livers over and cut away greenish stains from gall which give liver bitter flavor. If in doubt about flavor, soak in milk 15 min, then drain.

CHICKEN LIVERS WITH MUSHROOMS

Persuasive in appearance and flavor

¾ lb chicken livers, 9 to 12	1 cup rich chicken broth
1 tsp salt	1 cup milk
¼ cup flour	Dash of pepper
¼ cup butter *or* margarine	Toast triangles
1 onion walnut-size	Fine-chopped parsley
1½ cups sliced mushrooms, 8 medium	

Choose carefully cleaned whole livers for looks and flavor. Wash in cold water, drain and pat dry with paper toweling. Lay livers on waxed paper. Sprinkle with salt and half the flour to coat. Heat butter in 9-inch skillet, add peeled chopped onion and sauté 2 or 3 min, then add livers and cook until lightly browned on underside, turn, add mushrooms, lower heat, cover and sauté 5 to 6 min, turning occasionally. Push livers and mushrooms to one side of skillet, blend remaining flour into fat on other side until smooth, then gradually add broth, milk and pepper and cook gently 4 or 5 min, stirring to keep smooth. When thickened, stir livers into sauce. Serve on toast and sprinkle with parsley. 4 servings.

DUCK AND GOOSE

Duck and goose differ considerably from both turkey and chicken in shape, in proportions of dark and light meat and in fat content. Cleaning and drawing is similar to chicken, except that both goose and duck are covered with a coat of down that takes time and patience to remove, see p 745 for detailed instructions. Plain fruit stuffings, such as pared sliced apples, dried prunes (or a combination of the two), plain rice or mashed potatoes, celery or plain sauerkraut, in addition to the various bread stuffings are often used for duck and goose. They are also frequently roasted without stuffing.

Because the birds are very fat, they are efficient self-basters and no extra basting is necessary during roasting. Do not prick skin. Experiments show that fat does not ooze out any faster during roasting from pricked than from unpricked skin. Pricking may be deep enough to release meat juices leaving meat dry and skin a gray cast. Pour fat out of roasting pan once or twice as it collects to keep it clear and light-colored. Both goose and duck fat are very desirable for pan-frying or sautéing all kinds of foods such as potatoes and onions; goose fat is sometimes used for cookies, p 466, and can also be used to make pastry.

The oven temp for goose and duck, as for all poultry, should be moderate (325° to 350° F). Because of their fatness, it is not necessary to cook them breast side down, so the bird can be placed on a rack in open roaster, and cooked until tender, allowing 20 minutes per pound for duck and 25 to 30 minutes for goose.

Both duck and goose are occasionally cooked by fricasseeing or braising, but are seldom fried or stewed. Young ducklings are often fried or broiled. The technique used is similar to that used with chicken.

ROAST DUCK

Choose a young 4 to 6 lb duck for roasting. Clean thoroughly, singe, remove all down and pin feathers, and wash inside and out with cold water. Drain thoroughly. (See p 745 and 1030.) When ready to roast, sprinkle salt inside the cavity. Duck may be stuffed or not, as desired. When stuffing is not used, one or two cored and quartered apples may be placed inside to absorb any strong flavor. Chopped celery and onions add excellent flavor. Mashed potatoes and seasoned boiled rice are also popular stuffings for duck. Truss the duck like a chicken (see p 1034) or leave untrussed, sprinkle with salt and pepper, and place breast side up on a rack in an open roasting pan. Do not prick the skin (see explanation, above). Bake, uncovered, in a moderately slow oven (325° F) until tender, allowing 20 min to the lb. Once or twice during roasting take the duck from the oven and pour the fat into a container while it is bright and clear. No basting is required. Use brown residue and a small amount of fat to make gravy (p 765). Allow 1¼ to 1½ lbs dressed weight per serving.

Note: Many additional recipes for cooking duck may be found in the Game Chapter. All recipes for wild duck are also suitable for the domestic variety.

ROAST GOOSE

Have neck of the goose cut off close to the head. Clean goose, remove feathers and down, singe, then wash (p 745). Remove entrails (see p 1032). Wash thoroughly inside and out with clear water, and drain well for 2 or 3 hrs. Goose may or may not be stuffed. It will cook more quickly without stuffing. Sprinkle inside with 1½ tsp salt. If stuffing is desired, Fluffy Dressing (p 1073) may be used, but all the butter should be omitted because of fatness of goose. Truss by folding wings back and tying them so that cord is drawn tightly across the back;

tuck neck skin under cord; tie legs together. Rub 1 tsp salt over the skin. Lay breast side up in open roasting pan. Bake in moderate oven (325° to 350° F) for 1 hr. Do not prick skin with a fork. The fat under the skin drains out without pricking and the skin will be crisp, delicious and more beautiful in color. Pour off fat from time to time. (Goose fat makes excellent cookies and pie crust, see p 466 and 924.) Cook until very tender, 25 to 30 min per lb or 3 to 4 hrs for a 10 to 12-lb goose. Make gravy with juices and a little of the fat in the pan, using 1½ to 2 tbsp flour to each 2 tbsp fat and juice. Allow 1 to 1¼ lbs dressed weight per serving.

ROAST GOOSE WITH POTATO STUFFING

5 lbs potatoes	1 egg, beaten
¼ cup butter	¼ cup finely chopped
1½ cups milk	parsley, lightly pkd
2 tsp salt	12 lb goose
¼ tsp pepper	1 tbsp salt
½ tsp poultry seasoning	

Pare, boil and wash potatoes. Add next seven ingredients and beat until light and fluffy. Prepare goose for roasting as described in recipe above. Rub the tbsp of salt on inside. Fill goose with stuffing, skewer, lace together, see p 1034. Place breast-side up on rack in an open roasting pan, bake uncovered in moderately slow oven (325° F) 4½ to 5 hrs, or until tender. Do not prick skin to release excess fat during baking. Boil giblets in a small amount of salted water until tender. Chop and add giblets to drippings along with their cooking broth for gravy or reserve liver to make Pate de Foi Gras spread (p 190). 10 to 12 servings.

Note: Roast a young wild goose exactly like young domestic goose, but a different method is needed to roast an old wild one. Dress like domestic goose, then hang 2 or 3 days in a cold place. To cook, pare and quarter a large potato and onion; place inside goose. Arrange bird in kettle, barely cover with cold water; add 2 tsp salt; heat to boiling, cover, simmer until vegetables are tender. Drain goose; discard vegetables and water. Stuff with desired dressing. Roast like domestic goose until tender, 3 to 4 hrs.

SPECIAL RECIPES

SLICED GOOSE OR DUCK IN ORANGE SAUCE

2 seedless medium-size	2 tbsp sugar
oranges	Slices cold roast goose, ½ lb
1 tbsp lemon juice	

Slice ½ of an orange very thinly and cut into quarters; do not peel. Squeeze the juice from remaining 1½ oranges and strain into a small saucepan. Add lemon juice and sugar and heat to boiling. Add orange slices and simmer 15 min. Add sliced goose and simmer gently for 5 min longer, just enough to reheat. Serve at once. 4 servings.

Note: This sauce may also be served over freshly sliced roast duck.

PIGEON PIE

Although pigeons weigh only 12 to 14 oz, their tasty dark meat makes a pie filling as acceptable in flavor as chicken

4 dressed drawn pigeons, 2 lbs	2 tbsp flour
3 cups water	1 tbsp cornstarch
2 tsp salt	2 cups pigeon broth
½ tsp whole black peppers	1 cup milk
1 branch celery	½ tsp salt
1 small carrot	⅛ tsp celery salt, optional
1 egg-size onion	1 potato, ½ lb
1 tbsp lemon juice, optional	2 medium carrots
1 tbsp poultry fat *or* butter	Quick "Puff" Pastry, p 938

Start oven 10 min before baking; set to hot (450° F).

Dress pigeons as described under Potted Pigeons, p 1065. Singe; wash in water in which is dissolved 1 tbsp baking soda to each qt of water. Rinse thoroughly in clear water. Remove all pin feathers, then eviscerate, remove oil sac and with a crochet hook probe shot holes for shot and imbedded feathers. Wash these openings thoroughly as well as inside bird in cold water. Drain. Arrange birds in 4-qt kettle, add water, salt, peppers, the celery, carrot and onion, peeled and halved and lemon juice. Cover, heat to boiling, reduce heat and simmer until tender, from 2½ to 3 hrs. Cool in broth if desired. Strip meat from bones in as large pieces as possible, eliminating some of the skin if desired, and watch out for any broken bones. Strain remaining broth. There should be 2 cups.

Melt fat in saucepan, blend in flour and cornstarch, then stir in pigeon broth and milk gradually. Cook and stir over moderate heat until smooth and thickened. Remove from heat. Stir in seasonings and meat. Place in refrigerator to cool thoroughly. Make "Puff" Pastry. Now pare potato, cut into ¾-inch cubes, scrape carrot, cut into 1-inch lengths, add 1 cup water, cover and boil gently 5 to 6 min. Drain and add to meat mixture.

Roll pastry out into rectangle and cut out circles that just fit top of casseroles, using top of casserole to mark size of circles. Make open design in center for steam vents. Turn mixture into individual casseroles holding 1¼ cups. Place pastry rounds over filling in casseroles. Cold filling enables pastry to bake by the time filling heats up to boiling and prevents it from running over. Bake until brown and filling is boiling hot, about 20 min. Serve at once. 4 to 5 servings.

POTTED PIGEONS

4 dressed and drawn pigeons, 2 lbs
1½ tsp salt
1¼ cups water
1 tbsp butter

Stuffing:
4 slices 3-day old bread from 1 lb loaf
3 tbsp poultry fat *or* butter
1 egg-size onion, fine-cut
¼ cup fine-cut celery

1 tsp fine-cut parsley
¾ tsp leaf sage crumbled and put through sieve, pkd
⅛ tsp pepper
½ tsp salt
Dash of nutmeg

Gravy:
2 tbsp flour
¾ cup water
¾ cup milk
Parsley

Dress pigeons like chicken by wet-picking, p 1030. Singe, wash thoroughly in baking soda water (2 tbsp to 2 qts water). Then rinse well in clear water. Eviscerate and wash thoroughly on inside with cold water and drain well. Rub inside each bird with ¼ tsp salt.

Stuffing: Pull bread into bite-size pieces, dropping into a mixing bowl. Heat fat in skillet, add onion, celery and parsley, and sauté until onion is soft, about 5 min, stirring frequently. Sift sage, pepper, salt and nutmeg over bread and toss well; now add onion-celery mixture and again toss until well mixed. Put ¼ the stuffing into each bird. Pull long neck skin forward over breast down to tail and fasten with skewers to hold in the stuffing. Tuck giblets under wings close to body and tie firmly with twine, crisscrossing it 2 or 3 times around birds to obtain compact parcels. Place in Dutch oven without a rack, add 1 cup of water and rest of the salt; cover, heat to boiling, then reduce heat and *simmer* 2½ hrs, or until tender and birds have begun to brown. At this point the liquid is evaporated. If birds are not fat, add 1 tbsp butter and half the remaining water (2 tbsp), cover and cook to an appetizing brown, turning frequently and adding remaining 2 tbsp water. Browning takes about 30 min. Remove to serving platter; cover to keep warm.

Gravy: Blend flour into fat left in Dutch oven, add water gradually, then milk and cook and stir until gravy is smooth and thickened. Taste and add more seasonings if needed. Remove skewers and twine from pigeons, place on platter and pour gravy over birds. Garnish with parsley. 4 servings.

BROILED SQUAB

A rare food for special occasions—easy enough for an amateur to attempt

4 oven-ready squabs, 2 lbs
Melted margarine *or* butter
Salt to season

Pepper
Parsley

Look over squab for pin feathers etc, and clean as you would chicken, p 1031. Use kitchen scissors to cut birds open all the way down the back. Open up and flatten out. Pull the fatty ends of tail over the bony ends of the legs, and fasten with a small skewer to make birds as compact and uniform in thickness as possible. Lay on a shallow pan, lining pan with aluminum foil reduces dish washing, skin-side down. Brush top with melted margarine and sprinkle with salt. Broil with heat adjusted to 350° F about 2 inches from source of heat 15 min. Turn over again, brush with margarine and broil another 15 min or until a beautiful brown. Remove to hot platter and pour any juice collected in pan over birds. Garnish with parsley. 4 servings.

ROAST SQUAB

Nothing more delicious or more aristocratic in poultry

4 oven-ready squabs, 2 lbs
1½ tsp salt
Chestnut *or* Mushroom
Stuffing, pp 1072, 754

1½ tbsp melted butter in
¼ cup hot water
½ tsp salt

Look over squabs for pinfeathers, etc., and clean like chicken. Rub insides with the 1½ tsp salt. Pack stuffing lightly into birds. Close opening of body cavity with strong toothpicks, lace together with twine. Tie legs close to the body. Fold the wings under the back. Brush outside of the birds with melted butter and water. Bake uncovered, breast-down in a shallow pan lined with aluminum foil in a moderate oven (350° F) 20 min. Turn birds over, breast-up, baste again with butter-water mixture, sprinkle with ½ tsp salt, and bake 25 to 30 min longer or until plump and well browned. 4 servings.

GUINEAS

Guineas have been something of a rarity in the past, and breast of guinea hen is still a great delicacy. The distinctive dark color and wild flavor of this small, compact bird is becoming more popular and the supply is increasing. The breast is the meatiest part of the bird, and since the hen has the plumpest breast, the guinea hen is most prized for cooking.

Young guinea hen may be roasted like chicken. The cavity should be rubbed with butter, salt and pepper and filled with stuffing; or with one onion, one carrot and one branch of celery. Then the bird is trussed and placed breast down on a rack in an open roaster with strips of fat salt pork or bacon over the back. When half done, the bird is turned over and the salt pork transferred to the breast, then covered for the remainder of cooking. The oven temp is moderate (350° F) as for all poultry and 20 min per lb should be allowed if the bird has only the vegetable stuffing; if a bread stuffing is used, about 25 min per lb will be required. The guinea may be uncovered again during the last 10 to 15 min of cooking to recrisp skin.

The breast alone may be dipped in seasoned flour, pan-fried in chicken or bacon fat or butter and served with a cream gravy. The rest of the guinea hen then may be simmered in a small amount of water and served as stew with drop dumplings or noodles.

BAKED GUINEA

¼ lb butter
½ cup chopped onion
2 qt day-old bread crumbs
2 tbsp cut parsley
½ tsp salt
¼ tsp pepper
1½ tsp sage

½ tsp D.A. baking powder *or*
⅝ tsp tartrate *or* phosphate
type
2 eggs, beaten
Diced cooked giblets
¾ cup Giblet Broth, p 764
1 cup milk
2 2-lb guinea hens
⅓ lb salt pork

Melt butter in skillet, add onions and sauté until transparent. Add crumbs, parsley, salt, pepper and sage and toss until thoroughly heated. Mix in baking powder then lightly stir in next 4 ingredients. Rub 1 tbsp salt into cavities of singed, washed guineas, pp 1031 to 1033. Fill cavities loosely with prepared stuffing. Skewer and lace with cord. Lay thin slices of salt pork over back and wrap around legs of guinea. Place on rack, breast-side down. Bake uncovered in a moderate oven (350° F) 1 hr. Drain off excess fat, add ½ cup water. Turn guinea over, replace salt pork over breasts, cover and bake 1 hr or until tender. Remove cover and bake 15 min longer to crisp skin. Serve hot with gravy, p 765 made from drippings in pan. 5 to 6 servings.

ROAST GUINEA WITH VEGETABLE STUFFING

2-lb guinea hen, dressed
2 tbsp butter
2 medium branches celery, cut in inch pieces
1 walnut-size onion, quartered
1 medium carrot, halved lengthwise, cut twice crosswise

2-oz can sliced mushrooms *or*
½ cup sliced fresh
1¼ tsp salt
Dash of pepper
1 tbsp butter *or* margarine
1 tbsp flour
½ cup water

Clean guinea as you clean chicken, p 1031. Wash bird inside and out and pat dry with paper toweling or cloth. Heat butter in small skillet, add vegetables and sauté covered 4 or 5 min. Cool. Rub inside of bird with 1¼ tsp salt and sprinkle with pepper. Fill cavity with prepared vegetables. Truss as for Roasting Chicken, p 1034. Rub outside with butter or margarine and sprinkle with flour. Bake in casserole or 10¼ x 5¼ x 3-inch glass loaf pan in moderate oven (350° F) about 2 hrs or until tender and nicely browned. Add ¼ cup of water at end of 1 hr baking, and another ¼ cup after 1½ hrs. Cover, or place aluminum foil over baking pan after 1 hr and leave on until bird is done. Serve with pan-gravy. 3 to 4 servings.

TURKEY

FACTS YOU SHOULD KNOW ABOUT BUYING AND ROASTING TURKEY

Years ago turkey was available only during the holiday season and there was little or no demand for it at other times, and the cost was unusually high. Today turkey is available throughout the year, and costs no more than chicken. Very meaty turkeys are now produced so that a 10 to 12-lb bird generously serves 5 for two meals—roast turkey one day and turkey hash or turnovers the next, with the carcass still making a delicious soup.

In addition to developing smaller, meatier birds, turkey growers are marketing broiler-fryers, 12 to 14 weeks old, weighing from 4 to 8 lbs, for frying and broiling. Enormous mature Tom turkeys weighing 45 to 50 lbs are also being grown. These are sold in halves, quarters, turkey-burgers, steaks or any desired part. For years there have been dried and smoked turkeys available in some markets.

Whole turkey may be purchased ready-to-cook (eviscerated), frozen or unfrozen; or dressed with head and feet on, plucked but not drawn. A hen turkey has more meat in proportion to its weight than a Tom because of its thick, plump breast. Hen turkeys weigh from 13 to 15 lbs.

Estimating exact cooking time of a turkey has always been guesswork because the time depends on size and age, and age is not always easy to ascertain. However, a simple guide for roasting time can be found the day before the turkey is roasted. The gizzard holds the secret. Put gizzard, heart and neck in a saucepan, barely cover with cold water, heat to boiling, cover tightly, reduce heat and simmer until gizzard can be pierced with a fork as easily as cold mush—this may require 3 to 4 hrs. Now, add 1 hr to time it took to cook gizzard tender, and that will be the approximate time required to roast turkey. The liver cooks tender in about 10 min, so add it when gizzard is nearly done. Transfer cooled giblets, neck and cooking water to a bowl, cover; store in refrigerator. Use broth to make gravy or in dressing. Chop giblets to add to gravy or dressing.

For a smooth running turkey dinner, start roasting turkey 30 to 40 min ahead of schedule to avoid last min confusion. This gives ample time to make gravy, remove trussing cords, etc., and to serve dinner promptly on schedule.

Although turkey may be roasted without dressing, most folks anticipate the dressing as eagerly as the turkey. Allow 1 cup of dressing per lb of dressed weight, or 1½ cups per lb of ready-to-cook weight. Rub salt in cavity of bird 6 to 8 hrs before stuffing to give meat better flavor. Do not pack dressing in too tightly for it becomes firm and compact during baking and may burst skin as dressing expands. If outside of turkey is rubbed with fat, never sprinkle with salt as this causes skin to blister. When these blisters break, the exposed flesh loses juice.

After meal is served, remove dressing from inside bird and place in a separate bowl. If much meat is left on the bones, break carcass to make a compact parcel, then snugly wrap in waxed paper. Store dressing and carcass in refrigerator as soon as possible after the meal. If only a little meat clings to the carcass, strip it from bones and pack firmly in a bowl to eliminate as much air as possible, then cover and store in refrigerator until ready to use. Break carcass apart, fit pieces snugly together and wrap securely in waxed paper or aluminum foil until ready to make soup or broth.

ROAST TURKEY

The traditional holiday bird is so good and so costly that it should be cooked perfectly or not at all

Read preceding turkey material, then read this recipe carefully. Buy right sized turkey—1¼ to 1½ lbs per person if for one meal, 2 lbs per person if two leftover meals are the aim. Select turkey ahead of time, but don't bring it home until the day before. Clean immediately. Remove pinfeathers with care, singe, wash thoroughly, drain well. Remove turkey fat from gizzard; render. Cook giblets until tender; cool and store in refrigerator. Meanwhile, pull neck skin of turkey back as far as possible, rub ⅓ of the salt (a 14-lb bird requires 2 tbsp) into breast flesh, then rub remaining salt inside bird. Rub outside with turkey fat. Cover with waxed paper then with a cloth. Store in refrigerator.

The day before, prepare and combine all stuffing ingredients except onions, celery and liquids. See Stuffings, p 1072. Put dry stuffing ingredients in plastic bag, close and leave at room temp. When ready to stuff, prepare and add onion, celery and liquids to stuffing. Remove bird from refrigerator. Pack stuffing into neck and body cavities lightly, then truss. See p 1034. Start roasting immediately or place stuffed bird in refrigerator overnight. This chills stuffing as well as bird, so remove from refrigerator 2 hrs before roasting to warm to room temp. Fold enough cheesecloth 4 times to cover bird completely. Dip folded cloth into melted shortening and lay over bird. Place bird on rack, breast-side down in a pan large enough for bird to fit in comfortably; one too large lets juice spread out over exposed pan to burn and give gravy a scorched flavor; one too small, lets juice drip into oven to burn and "smell" up the house. Roast according to Chart, p 1070. Baste with ½ cup rendered turkey fat or butter and ½ cup hot water. When cooking time is half gone, turn bird on back, rearrange cheesecloth to cover well and baste again. To baste, remove turkey to top of stove, closing oven so it won't cool. Spoon basting liquid over cloth to coat skin of bird. Return to oven. Repeat basting every 20 min. Cover breast and thighs browning too fast, with brown paper or aluminum foil. To baste, lift paper or foil up, then replace. When done, lift bird to hot platter; cover to keep hot while making gravy, p 765. To serve, remove trussing cords neatly. Garnish platter simply with loose bouquets of crisp parsley leaving enough room for carver. A 10-lb turkey serves 6 to 7, a 14-lb 12.

Note: When the turkey is nearly done according to the time table, test for doneness by this method: Move leg by grasping the end bone; if the joint moves easily, the ligaments are tender and the meat is done.

TURKEY GRAVY

You can make only so much fine flavored gravy. The amount depends on the savory juices left in roasting pan. First, drain all fat and juice from pan into a glass measuring cup. Let stand for fat to float, then spoon off all but ⅓ cup of fat if turkey weighed 14 lbs, or correspondingly less amount for a smaller turkey. Return remaining fat and juice to roasting pan. Add ⅓ cup flour and stir and scrape until flour blends smoothly and residue in pan is loosened. Add 2½ cups giblet broth or 2½ cups of broth and milk. Place over low heat, stir constantly, shifting pan back-and-forth so gravy cooks evenly. Boil 5 min. If gravy is too thick, add more liquid to obtain right consistency. Season with salt and pepper. For pan-gravy, skim all but 2 tbsp of fat from pan juices, add 1 cup of broth, place over heat and stir and scrape until residue dissolves. Add ½ cup of cooked, mashed chestnuts for delicious variation. Serve in a very hot bowl. Makes 2½ cups thickened gravy or 1½ cups pan gravy.

For Giblet Gravy, add ground or finely chopped cooked giblets to thickened gravy and reheat.

TABLE 45   TIME-TABLE FOR ROASTING TURKEY

Weight ready for oven*	Oven temp	Cooking time min per lb	Total cooking time
8 to 10 lb	325° F	25 to 20	3 to 3½ hr
10 to 14 lb	325° F	20 to 18	3½ to 4 hr
14 to 18 lb	300° F	18 to 15	4 to 4½ hr
18 lb	300° F	15 to 13	4½ to 5 hr
20 lb	300° F	15 to 13	5 to 6 hr

*If stuffed weight cannot be ascertained, the dressed weight, p 1029 (feathers off, but not drawn) may be used to calculate roasting time.

Turkey roasted without stuffing requires less time than that suggested in above table.

OLD-TIME "ROAST" TURKEY

Prepare and cook like Old-Time "Roast" Chicken, see p 1043.

TURKEY À LA KING

¼ cup butter	1½ cups cubed cooked turkey
¼ cup flour	1 cup sliced mushrooms
1½ cups milk	½ cup sliced stuffed olives
½ tsp salt	

Melt butter in top of double boiler over direct heat. Blend in flour, add milk gradually, stirring constantly. Cook over boiling water until mixture thickens. Stir to keep smooth. Add next 3 ingredients, cover and cook 15 min. Add olives. Serve at once over toast, Chinese noodles or in Patty Shells, p 612. 4 to 5 servings.

TURKEY HASH

¼ cup chopped onion	1½ cups rich turkey broth
¼ cup chopped green pepper	made from bones
2 tbsp butter	Salt and pepper to taste
2 cups chopped leftover	1½ cups leftover dressing
turkey with some skin	3 cups cubed cooked potatoes

Sauté onion and green pepper in butter for 10 min until yellow and transparent. Add remaining ingredients and mix lightly. Heat thoroughly and serve immediately. 4 to 6 servings.

TURKEY TURNOVERS

Filling:

2 tbsp finely chopped onion	⅓ cup thin gravy *or* broth
¼ cup finely chopped celery	from bones
1 tbsp butter	½ cup grated carrot
½ tsp salt	1½ cups finely cut leftover
	turkey with some skin

Sauté onion and celery in butter until soft, about 5 min. Add remaining ingredients and stir lightly with a fork to mix well.

Biscuit Mix:

1 cup all-purpose flour	¼ tsp salt
2 tsp D.A. baking powder *or*	Pinch poultry seasoning
2½ tsp tartrate *or* phos-	⅓ cup shortening
phate type	About ⅓ cup milk

Sift flour, measure and resift 3 times with next 3 ingredients. Cut in shortening with pastry blender or two knives until consistency of rice. Add milk all at once and stir quickly with a fork until dough stiffens. Knead quickly on a lightly floured board 8 times. Roll out to a 12-inch sq, cut into 4 sqs. Place ¼ of filling in center of each sq, moisten edge of dough and fold over. Press edges together with fork, to seal. Prick tops for steam vents. Brush tops with melted butter. Bake on a cookie sheet in a moderately hot oven (425° F) 10 to 15 min, or until golden brown. Serve with hot Mushroom Sauce, p 1259. 4 servings.

DRESSINGS AND STUFFINGS*

BREAD STUFFING FOR ROAST TURKEY

1 large loaf stale white
  bread, 1½ lbs
1 cup diced celery
1 tbsp chopped onion
¼ cup butter *or* rendered
  turkey fat

2 tsp poultry seasoning
1½ tsp salt
⅛ tsp pepper
¾ cup cooled broth from
  cooking giblets, *or* milk

Remove crusts from bread and cut in 1-inch dice. Sauté celery and onion in butter until soft and yellow. Add bread and seasonings and toss together until well mixed. Cool. Add broth last and again toss until mixed. Stuff lightly into turkey. Makes enough for a 10-lb bird.

Note: Broth may be increased to 1¼ cups and 2 beaten eggs added, if desired. Beat eggs well and add with the cooled broth.

CELERY STUFFING

¾ lb loaf stale white bread
3 tbsp butter
1½ cups diced celery
1 tbsp chopped onion
½ tsp poultry seasoning

1 tsp salt
⅛ tsp pepper
½ cup broth from cooking
  giblets, *or* ½ cup milk

Pull bread into small pieces; use crumbs and crusts; there should be about 6 cups of coarse crumbs. Melt butter in large saucepan, add celery and onion, and cook with frequent stirring until soft and yellow. Add bread and seasonings and toss together until well mixed. Cool. Add the liquid, mix lightly with a fork and stuff lightly into the dressed chicken. Makes enough for a 4-lb chicken.

CHESTNUT STUFFING

1 cup shelled chestnuts,
  chopped
10 slices stale bread from
  1 lb loaf
½ cup chopped onion
1 cup sliced celery

3 tbsp margarine *or* chicken
  fat
1 tsp salt
¼ tsp pepper
1 to 2 tsp poultry seasoning
¾ cup chicken broth

*Other dressings suitable for poultry may be found in *Game Chapter*.

Prepare chestnuts as directed, p 122. Pull bread apart into bite-size pieces, dropping into a 3-qt bowl. Sauté onion and celery until transparent. Sift salt, pepper and seasoning over crumbs, toss to mix. Add broth, toss, then add vegetables and chestnuts, mix lightly again. Stuff lightly into chicken or turkey. Sufficient dressing for 4 lb roasting chicken. Double ingredients for 12 lb turkey.

CORN BREAD DRESSING*

½ cup butter *or* margarine
5 *or* 6 cups corn bread, crumbled
1½ qt (6 cups) soft bread crumbs
½ cup rendered turkey fat
1 cup chopped nutmeats, optional
1 cup diced celery

½ cup chopped onion
½ cup chopped green pepper
2 tsp salt
½ tsp pepper
1½ tsp poultry seasoning
2 beaten eggs
1 to 1½ cups broth from giblets

Cut butter into very small pieces and mix with corn bread and bread crumbs. Heat fat in a heavy skillet, add nutmeats, celery, onion and green pepper and sauté slowly for 5 min. Add to corn bread mixture. Add seasonings, mixing thoroughly. Add well-beaten eggs; sprinkle cooled broth over surface, stirring lightly until dressing is of desired moistness. Stuff lightly into breast region and body cavity of the bird. Makes enough for 12-lb turkey.

FLUFFY DRESSING FOR ROAST CHICKEN

6 cups white bread crumbs
6 tbsp butter
½ cup chopped celery

½ tsp salt
1¼ tsp poultry seasoning
⅛ tsp pepper

Use only crumbs from 3-day-old white bread. Crumble lightly between palms of hands. Crumbs should be fine but fluffy. Melt butter in large skillet; stir in the crumbs. Keep heat low, turning crumbs constantly until all are coated with butter and slightly brown. Remove from heat, add remaining ingredients, mixing thoroughly but lightly. Stuff lightly into chicken to keep fluffy. Enough for a 4 to 4½-lb chicken.

OLD-FASHIONED BREAD DRESSING

6 cups soft bread crumbs
1 tsp poultry seasoning
¼ cup butter
½ cup diced celery
⅓ cup diced onion

4 eggs
3 cups milk
1⁄16 tsp pepper
1 tsp salt

*Use yellow or white corn meal for corn bread.

Combine bread crumbs and poultry seasoning and toss. Melt butter in skillet, add celery and onion and sauté for 5 min. Beat eggs slightly, add milk, salt, pepper, then the sautéed onion, celery, and bread crumbs. Let stand 10 min. Stir well and pour (this is quite liquid in consistency) into thoroughly cleaned chicken. Do not close opening but have neck opening tightly closed to avoid loss of liquid at beginning of baking. If desired, liver and heart may be ground and added to the egg-milk mixture before adding crumbs, and 1 cup of rich chicken stock may be substituted for 1 cup of the milk. Dressing almost doubles in bulk in baking. Enough for a 5½ to 6½ lb roasting chicken.

OYSTER DRESSING

3½ qts coarse bread crumbs
1 tsp each salt and poultry
  seasoning
¼ tsp white pepper

¼ lb butter
¾ cup finely chopped celery
½ medium onion, chopped
1¼ cups chopped oysters

Measure crumbs. Add salt, poultry seasoning and pepper, and toss well. Melt butter in saucepan, add celery and onion and sauté until onions are softened, then stir in oysters. Pour over bread crumbs and mix lightly with a fork. Stuff lightly into turkey. Enough for a 12-lb bird.

HOW TO CARVE CHICKEN AND TURKEY

STANDARD STYLE

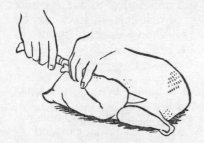
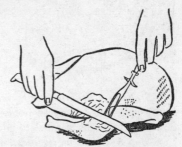

Step 1—To remove thigh and drumstick: Use the standard carving set for carving turkey or a steak set for carving chicken. Hold drumstick firmly with fingers, pull leg gently away from the bird's body and at the same time cut through the skin between the leg and body. Continue as follows:

Step 2—Press leg away from body with flat side of knife: Then insert fork near joint dividing thigh and backbone and with knife cut through this joint. If the "oyster" or "sweetmeat," a choice oval-shaped piece of meat lying in the spoon-shaped section of the backbone was not removed with the thigh, remove it at this point. Now insert fork near joint dividing thigh and drumstick. Holding the drumstick at a convenient angle to the plate, cut down through the joint to the plate to divide drumstick and thigh.

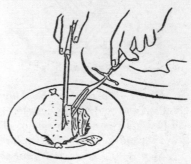

Step 3—Slice drumstick meat of turkey: Usually chicken drumsticks and thighs of average size are not sliced. Hold drumstick upright at a convenient angle to plate and cut down, turning drumstick to get uniform slices. Lay bone back on platter to be used later in making soup.

Step 4—Slice thigh meat of turkey: With the fork, hold thigh firmly on the plate. Cut off slices of meat parallel to the bone and place on plate with drumstick meat. Lay thigh bone on platter.

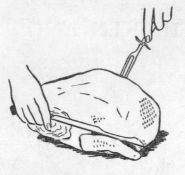
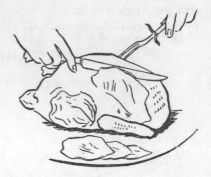

Step 5—Cut into white meat parallel to wing: With fork inserted firmly into bird's body to hold it steady, make a *deep* cut into the breast down to the bone, parallel to and as close to the wing as possible.

Step 6—Slice white meat: Begin at the front and starting halfway up the breast, cut thin slices of white meat down to the cut. The slices will fall away from the bird as they are cut to this line. Continue carving until enough meat has been carved for first servings. Carve additional meat as it is needed. Remove individual servings of stuffing from an opening cut into the side of bird where leg has been removed.

SIDE STYLE

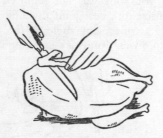
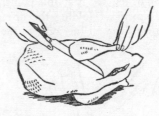

Step 1—To remove the wing: Grasp the wing tip firmly with fingers, lift it up and sever wing between the first and second joint. Place wing tip and first joint portion on side of platter. This part is not customarily served. Leave second joint attached to bird.

Step 2—To remove drumstick: Grasp end of drumstick, lift it up and away from body, severing it from the thigh or second joint of the leg. The thigh is left attached to the bird. Place drumstick on side of platter for slicing off the meat. To slice meat from drumstick hold it upright at a convenient angle and cut down toward the plate, parallel with the bone, turning the drumstick to make uniform slices.

(A variation not diagrammed is: Grasp end of drumstick to steady the leg, cut thin slices across the entire length of the leg until the bone of drumstick and thigh and the joint connecting them are exposed. Disjoint drumstick as suggested and finish slicing remaining meat. Proceed with step 3 "Run the point, etc.")

Step 3—To remove thigh bone: Insert fork where it is most convenient to steady the bird. Then cut slices of thigh meat parallel to the body until the bone is reached. Now run the point of the knife around the thigh bone, life bone up with fork, and use fork or fingers to remove the bone. Then slice remaining thigh meat. The choice dark meat above the thigh which lies in the spoon-shaped section of the backbone is called the "oyster." Use point of knife to lift it out.

Step 4—To slice the white meat: Insert fork into body to hold it steady. Beginning at front end of bird, slice upward until the wing socket is exposed. Now remove second joint of the wing. Continue making thin upward slices of white meat until enough has been made for first servings, or until the breastbone has been reached.

Step 5—To remove stuffing from hole cut into cavity under thigh: Slit the thin tissue in the thigh region with the tip of the knife and make an opening large enough to spoon out the stuffing. To serve stuffing in breast end, make an incision into breast skin and lay the skin back onto the platter.

Use this method also for carving *half* and *quarter* turkeys.

Preserves and Pickles

It's a proud moment when you open the first jar of your very own peaches, pickles, strawberry jam, or luscious red tomato juice! Even if you've never preserved or pickled before, it will be easy when you've read this chapter. These recipes for putting up your own jams, jellies, preserves, and pickles will help to assure you a maximum amount of applause from your family and friends.

★　　★　　★　　★

A supply of tomato and fruit juices can be a source of inspiration to a menu maker. They are ready at a moment's notice to serve the unexpected guest or the hungry child. Fruit juices may be canned unsweetened, then

Using Thermometer.　　　　　　　Draining Juice.

made into jelly when it is convenient. They can be used in unusual sauces and puddings, molded gelatin desserts, ice creams and ices. Use fruit juice for the liquid in spice or other cake batters or meat loaves for a delicate flavor. Turn to the chapters on molded desserts, beverages, and ice creams for other uses.

Most fruits are cut or crushed and then heated to break down the cell structures and extract the flavorful juices.

Since the delicate fruit flavor is impaired by boiling (212° F), it is advisable to use a thermometer to control temp accurately during the heating. If no thermometer is available, watch carefully to never let the fruit or juices heat above simmering, 185° F. At this temp bubbles appear in the liquid, but only occasionally break on the surface.

Strain the hot fruit through a pouch made of several thicknesses of cheesecloth or clean muslin bag. If juices are for jelly, do not squeeze the bag or jelly will be cloudy. If juices are for beverage use, squeeze bag to obtain the purée. The cloudiness will not detract from the appearance and purée will give juice richer flavor and color. The pulp left from jelly juice makes good jam if it is not completely drained of juice, or if some freshly cooked fruit is added. Press through sieve to obtain all purée.

If juices are extracted and canned to be used later for making jelly, no sugar is added. For beverage use, sugar is added to sweeten juices naturally low in sugar or high in acid, and to help preserve the natural color and flavor of the juice. Too much sugar, however, masks the delicate fruit flavor.

The fruits that are generally used for juices, and the method of extraction are included in table 46, next page.

CANNING THE EXTRACTED JUICES

To can fruit juices, reheat immediately after extraction to 170° F and pour into hot jars to within ⅛ inch of the top. If a thermometer is not available, regulate heat so juice barely simmers. Seal jars appropriately for the kind of lid used and process for 5 min in the boiling water bath. Or *pasteurize* by placing in a water bath heated *just to 165° F* for 15 mins. After processing, complete the seal if necessary and cool.

To can tomato juice, reheat immediately after extraction *just to boiling* and fill jars to within ¼ inch of the top. Seal according to the kind of lid used and process for 15 min in the boiling water bath. After processing complete the seal if necessary and cool.

Cooling the juice. A better product is obtained if the juice is cooled quickly after processing. A practical method of cooling for all jars, *except those sealed with a metal vacuum-seal lid,* is to put the sealed jars into a large container filled with water about 120° F (just too hot to hold the hand in comfortably). The jars should be completely covered with the water. This will cool jars quickly to 120° F. Later cool water can be run slowly into the container, or added from time to time until jars are cold. Do not allow the cool water to strike a hot jar.

JELLY

I think no one has improved on N. E. Goldthwaite's definition of an ideal jelly. "Ideal fruit-jelly is a beautifully colored, transparent, palatable product obtained by so treating fruit juice that the resulting mass will quiver, not flow when removed from its mold; a product with texture so tender that it cuts easily with a spoon, and yet so firm that the angles thus produced retain their shape; a clear product that is neither sirupy, gummy, nor tough;

TABLE 46   EXTRACTING FRUIT JUICES

| Kind of fruit | Preparation | Add Water Per Quart of Fruit | | Heat[1] | Strain[2] | Add sugar[3] |
		Jelly	Beverage			
Apples juicy, barely ripe, tart, fall varieties	Wash thoroughly to remove spray residue; grind as for cider for beverage. For jelly, quarter, remove seeds and slice.	Barely to cover apples fitted compactly in pan.	None	Do not heat for beverage. For jelly, simmer until soft.	Strain; press bag for beverage only.	None
Apricots Ripe, juicy, flavorsome.	Wash, cut in halves or leave whole.	Not generally used.	¾ cup	Simmer until soft.	Put through colander and discard skin and seeds.	Mix equal parts of pulp with thin syrup (1 cup sugar to 1 qt. water).
Berries Blackberry Boysenberry Loganberry Raspberry (red and black) Youngberry Well ripened, freshly gathered.	Sort, wash, stem or hull. Crush gently.	¼ cup in dry season. No water in a wet season.	½ cup	Heat at 175° F. until berries swim in juice.	Strain; press bag for beverage only.	Not necessary. If desired, 1 cup sugar to 1 gallon juice.

Currants Ripe, freshly picked.	Wash, pick off stems, crush gently.	1/4 cup	Heat at 160° F. until currants swim in juice.	Strain; press bag for beverage only.	To taste
Cherries Sweet or sour. Ripe, freshly picked.	Sort, wash, stem.	1/4 cup	Heat at 160° F. until cherries burst and swim in juice.	Strain; press bag for beverage only.	To taste
Grapes Concord Red	Wash and pick from stems. Crush gently.	1 tablespoon	Heat at 160° F. until grapes swim in juice.	Strain; press bag for beverage only.	Concord none Red—1 cup to 1 gallon of juice.
Grapefruit Fully tree-ripened. Use soon after picking.	Wash, extract juice as for table use. Do not use press type of reamer as oil from peel is undesirable.	Not generally used.	Do not heat.	Do not strain.	None
Guavas	Wash thoroughly, remove stem and blossom ends. Slice fruit thinly.	Barely to cover fruit fitted compactly in kettle.	For jelly or beverage, simmer 30 min.	Strain	1 cup sugar to 1 3/8 cup juice plus 2 tbsp. lime or lemon juice.
Plums Any variety.	Wash, stem, cut in halves.	1/4 cup	Heat at 180° F. until plums are soft and swim in juice.	Strain; press bag for beverage only.	To taste, about 1 cup to 1 quart of juice.
Tomatoes Well ripened, deep in color. Sound fruit only.	Wash, cut out core, quarter.	Not used	Boil briskly until soft, shaking pan to prevent sticking.	Rub through food mill to remove seeds and skins.	No sugar. Add 1 teaspoon salt to each quart of juice.

[1] Use a thermometer and never allow juice to exceed 185° F. If no thermometer is available, 185° F. can be described as that temperature at which bubbles appear in the liquid but break below the surface (simmering).

[2] Use a pouch made of several thicknesses of cheesecloth or clean muslin bags to strain the heated fruits.

[3] If juice is to be canned or frozen for jelly, do not add sugar. If for beverage use, sugar helps to preserve natural color and flavor.

neither is it brittle and yet it will break, and does this with distinct beautiful cleavage which leaves sparkling characteristic faces. This is that delicious appetizing substance, a good fruit jelly."

The general method for making jelly is the same for all kinds of fruits. There are three main constituents responsible for the jell formation: sugar, pectin, and acid. The acid is usually found in sufficient amounts in the

natural fruit, but if not present the addition of lemon juice or a combination of a low-acid and a high-acid fruit will make up the deficiency. The pectin is also found in the fruit, some fruits containing greater amounts than others. If there is not enough pectin in the fruit, it may be combined with a high-pectin fruit like apples, or additional commercial pectin may be used.

Jelly Test.

The sugar is added in proportion to the amount of juice used and then concentrated to the proper proportion by boiling. Boiling evaporates the water content of the juice and concentrates the sugar, acid and pectin to the stage where it will give the characteristic jelly test. When the jelly syrup cooks to the consistency where it will jell or "set" when poured into glasses, it will not flow in a stream from a spoon but will drip in two distinct drops that run together and fall from the edge of the spoon in a "sheet or flake."

When jelly "sheets" or tests done, stop the cooking at once. Then skim the jelly immediately and pour into hot sterilized glasses. Pour a thin coating of melted paraffin over the jelly immediately and allow to set. Add a second coating when the first has set, tipping the glass around gently so the edges are well sealed. It is important that glasses stand a day or two undisturbed so the pectin in the

Coat Jars with Paraffin.

jelly has time to mesh and set. Store in a cool dry place.

The recipes given for several jellies on the following pages fully describe the techniques. Table 47, p 1087 also lists ingredients for other jellies not included in the recipes.

Grapes, plums and apples are fruits which are especially good for the beginner to use for making jelly, because they contain enough pectin and acid for successful jelly and have good flavor besides.

WHAT EVERY EXPERIENCED JELLY-MAKER KNOWS

1. *Fruit that is slightly under-ripe jells best*—a combination of slightly under-ripe fruit for jell-formation and fully-ripened fruit for flavor is ideal.

2. *Fruits low in pectin* are raspberries, pineapple, cherries, pears,

peaches, strawberries, and huckleberries. Add a second fruit high in pectin or commercial pectin for a firm jelly.

3. *Fruits high in pectin* are apples, barely ripe blackberries, crabapples, currants, grapes, gooseberries, loganberries, plums, and cranberries.

4. *Water dilutes the flavor and color*—use only the required amount for hard fruits; soft juicy fruits will not need water to make juice for jelly.

5. *The best jelly* is made by cooking *small batches* at a time—no more than 4–6 cups.

6. *Begin to make jelly test* 5 min after sugar has been added. When the jelly test is obtained, stop cooking at once. (The average cooking time ranges between 12 and 20 min.)

7. *Do not boil unnecessarily*—quick, short cooking is best.

8. *Melt paraffin* over hot water to avoid the danger of catching fire. Paraffin that is too hot shrinks from sides of glass. A layer of paraffin ⅛-inch thick properly applied will protect jelly.

9. *Cover glasses* to keep clean. Label and date.

10. *Store* in cool, dark place.

APPLE JELLY

3 lbs firm tart apples	2 to 3 tbsp lemon juice,
3 to 5 cups water	if needed
Sugar	Rose geranium leaves, if
	desired

Apples that ripen in late summer or early fall are best for jelly. Choose tart, juicy apples which are barely ripe. Overripe fruit has insufficient pectin to jell perfectly.

Wash apples; remove and discard stem and blossom ends; cut in quarters, then slice quarters with skins and cores into a 4-qt kettle. Add cold water barely to cover, the amount depends on shape of pan. Cover pan, heat to boiling, then reduce heat and simmer without stirring until apples are soft, from 10 to 15 min. Crush apples with a potato masher and cook 5 min longer. Turn into a wet jelly bag, or into a bag made by gathering up several thicknesses of cheesecloth. Hang up to let juice drip into a bowl. Do not squeeze bag. There will be 3 to 3½ cups of clear juice, depending on juiciness of the apples and on amount of water used. Let drip at least 15 min. Measure juice into a 4-qt saucepan. Heat to boiling and boil rapidly 5 min. Taste juice and if flavor is not very tart, add lemon juice. Add ¾ cup sugar for each cup of measured juice and continue boiling rapidly until 2 drops sheet from edge of metal spoon simultaneously. See p 1082. Remove from heat, skim jelly and pour immediately into hot, sterilized glasses. If desired, place a washed rose geranium leaf into each jelly glass before pouring in jelly. Pour a thin layer of melted paraffin over top. When paraffin sets, add a second layer of paraffin and let stand undisturbed. 3 to 5 cups.

BLACK RASPBERRY JELLY

1 qt black raspberry juice,
  p 1080
½ cup lemon juice

7 cups sugar
1 cup liquid pectin

Combine raspberry juice, lemon juice and sugar in a 4 qt saucepan. Stir well to dissolve sugar. Heat to a full rolling boil. Add pectin slowly, stirring constantly. Boil for ½ min. Remove from heat, skim and pour into hot sterilized glasses. Pour a thin layer of paraffin over top. When paraffin sets, add a second layer. Let stand in same place undisturbed. It takes several days for this jelly to set. Twelve 6-oz glasses.

CRABAPPLE JELLY

5 lbs crabapples
About 6 cups water

About 5 cups sugar,
2½ lbs

Choose barely ripe, firm, crisp crabapples. Wash. Remove and discard stems and blossom ends. Cut apples into quarters and put in a 4-qt kettle with just enough water to cover, about 6 cups. Simmer covered until very soft, about 1 hr. Put in a jelly bag or into a pouch made of several thicknesses of cheesecloth and let drip 2 or 3 hrs. Do not squeeze bag. (See Crabapple Jam below). Measure juice and add an equal quantity of sugar. Stir well. Boil rapidly in a wide-4-qt kettle until 2 drops sheet simultaneously from edge of metal spoon. Cooking requires about 15 min. Skim and pour into hot sterilized jelly glasses. Cover with thin layer of hot melted paraffin; add a second layer of paraffin when first has set. About 8 cups.

CRABAPPLE JAM

Rub pulp left in jelly bag through a sieve. Measure and add an equal amount of sugar. Cook with occasional stirring to a thick jam-like consistency, about 10 min. Pour into glasses, seal and store like jelly. This is a pleasing jam, similar to apple butter.

GRAPE JUICE AND GRAPE JELLY*

Has the wonderful bouquet of ripe grapes

10 lbs ripe Concord grapes

Wash and stem grapes into 4 to 5-qt preserving kettle. *Add no water.* Set over very slow heat until juice is seen on bottom of kettle when grapes are lifted aside. Now turn up heat to medium and continue cooking until juice flows freely, about 20 min, shaking pan frequently to prevent scorching. Remove from heat and turn into jelly bag. Hang up to drip into large bowl until no more juice flows. Do not squeeze

*Grapes that are barely ripe jell more quickly than over-ripe ones.

bag. Juice is now ready for canning or jelly making. For canning, heat juice just to boiling, pour into hot sterilized glass jars. Seal with glass or enamel-lined lids. Process in boiling water bath for 5 min. Complete seal if necessary and cool. Makes about 3½ pt concentrated juice. For drinking, dilute and sweeten to suit taste. See recipe for making Grape Jam, p 1090.

To make jelly, measure juice, and to each cup allow ¾ cup sugar. If grapes were not fully ripe, use 1 cup sugar. Heat juice to rapid boil, add sugar all at once, and stir just until dissolved. Then boil rapidly without stirring until 2 drops sheet from edge of metal spoon simultaneously, p 1082. Pour into hot sterilized glasses, and cover with thin layer of melted paraffin. When the first layer sets, pour a second thin layer over top. Makes about the same amount of jelly as the sugar used. Jelly made from freshly extracted grape juice may crystallize after it stands several weeks. To be sure jelly will not contain crystals, can the extracted juice as described above. Let it stand a few weeks until the acid potassium tartrate forms deposits in the bottom of the jar. This is a purplish rock-like mass called "argol." (Cream of tartar is made from argol.) Pour juice off carefully from argol deposit. Make jelly in the usual way.

MINT JELLY

Prepare apple juice as for Apple Jelly, p 1080. Heat juice to boiling, add 4 to 5 drops green food coloring, and ¼ cup bruised, fresh mint leaves tied in 2 thicknesses of cheesecloth. Boil and add sugar and lemon juice as for apple jelly. Before pouring jelly in glasses, remove mint leaves. About 2 cups.

RED CURRANT JELLY

2 qts red currants   2½ cups sugar
1½ cups water

Wash currants in plenty of cold water, swishing them through water carefully so as not to break the fruit. Drain in colander, then strip currants from stems. There should be 6 to 7 cups of stemmed fruit. Turn into a 4 to 5-qt saucepan to permit rapid boiling. Add the water, heat to boiling and cook slowly about 15 min or until fruit has a whitish color. Turn into jelly bag to drip until there are 3 cups of juice; do not squeeze bag to hasten dripping or jelly will not be clear. See p 1078. Heat juice to boiling in a 4-qt saucepan. Add sugar and boil rapidly from 3 to 5 min, or until juice gives the jelly test, p 1082. Quickly skim and pour into hot sterilized jelly glasses. Cover immediately with a thin layer of melted paraffin; when set, add another layer of paraffin. 3 cups.

Note: For currant jam, press leftover juice and pulp through food mill. There should be 1¼ cups purée. Add 1 cup sugar and cook to thick jam stage. 1¼ cups.

STRAWBERRY JELLY

2½ qts strawberries	1 tbsp lemon juice
5¾ cups sugar	⅔ cup liquid pectin

Wash berries in 2 or 3 cold waters. Lift into a colander to drain, then hull and remove blemishes and soft spots. Place the berries in a 4-qt preserving kettle, crush slightly, and mix with ¼ cup of the sugar. Cover kettle and place over very low heat until juice begins to flow, then heat to simmering and remove from heat. Turn fruit into jelly bag. Let drip without squeezing or pressing until juice measures about 2¾ cups. (Save pulp and any juice left for jam.) Put measured juice, lemon juice and rest of sugar into the same kettle (washed) over moderate heat, stirring until sugar dissolves. Then heat to boiling and quickly stir in liquid pectin. Again heat to a full rapid boil, and boil hard without stirring for ½ min. Remove from heat and skim quickly. Pour into hot sterilized glasses, and cover with a thin layer of melted paraffin. Cool and add another layer of paraffin. About 5½ cups jelly.

SOUR CHERRY JELLY

4 lbs sour red cherries	About 7 cups sugar
½ cup water	1 bottle liquid pectin, 1 cup

Wash, stem and mash cherries without crushing pits. Add ½ cup water. Heat to boiling, cover and simmer 10 min. Turn fruit into jelly bag to drip into large bowl. There should be about 3½ cups juice. Squeezing bag extracts more juice, but jelly will be cloudy. Measure 2 cups of sugar for each cup of juice into large saucepan. Mix thoroughly. Heat to boiling quickly. Add liquid pectin, stirring constantly. Heat to full rolling boil and boil hard ½ min. Remove from fire, skim; pour quickly into hot sterilized glasses and cover with a thin layer of melted paraffin. Cool and add a second layer of paraffin. 7 to 8 cups jelly.

QUINCE JELLY

9 lbs quince	6 qts water
Peel from 2 lbs red apples	17 cups sugar

Wash quince thoroughly in warm water to remove dirt and waxy coating. Quarter and remove seeds and imperfections. Slice seeded quince into a 6-qt preserving kettle. Add 3¾ qts water and simmer covered for about 20 min or until nearly soft. Drain juice off into a cloth-covered colander set over a bowl. There should be about 8½ cups juice. Add apple peel and remaining 2¼ qts water to the drained quince and simmer again about 20 min. Drain in a jelly bag. There should be about 9 more cups of juice. Jelly may be made from the two lots of juice separately or the juice may be mixed.

Measure 4 or 5 cups of juice into a wide flat 4-qt pan. Add an equal amount of sugar; boil briskly for about 20 min or until 2 thick drops sheet from edge of metal spoon simultaneously. Remove from heat. Skim quickly and pour into hot sterilized glasses. Cover at once with a thin layer of melted paraffin. Cool and add a second layer of paraffin, tilting the glasses to be sure the edges are sealed. 25 glasses 1 cup-size.

TABLE 47 **OTHER JELLIES**

Make Juice According to Directions Page 1080 from Following Fruits	Mix Juices Together in the Following Proportions	Add Sugar for Each Cup of Juice
Apple and Blackberry	Equal parts of each	⅔ cup
Apple and Elderberry	Equal parts of each	1 cup
Apple, Quince, Cranberry*	Equal parts of each	¾ cup
Blackberry		¾–1 cup
Cranberry		¾ cup
Currant and Raspberry (black or red)	Equal parts of each OR 2 parts raspberries to 3 parts currants	1 cup
Gooseberries and Raspberries (black or red)	2 parts raspberries to 1 part gooseberries	¾–1 cup
Plum, red		¾–1 cup

*PARADISE JELLY. Use 25 large crabapples, 10 medium quinces, 1 quart cranberries. Cook apples and cranberries together barely covered with water. Cook quince separately covered with water. Combine cooked fruits and strain to extract juice. To make jelly, use 1 cup sugar for each cup juice.

JAMS—MARMALADES— PRESERVES, ETC.

Many other kinds of sweets besides jelly may be made from fruits and tomatoes. Among them are *butters, conserves, jams, marmalades* and *preserves.*

Butters are made from puréed fruits. They are cooked a long time to a very smooth consistency. They depend for their sweetness mostly on the sugars in the fruit rather than on added sugar.

Jam is made from both pulp and juice of the fruit or from the pulp only; or from pulp which has had part of the juice extracted. The fruit is never left whole in jam. It is most frequently made from berries with the seeds left in or with seeds removed, or from fruits such as peaches or plums with the seeds removed.

Marmalade is a special type of jam. Oranges, grapefruit, tangerines, calamondin and lemons are the fruits most frequently used. The seeds are discarded but all the rest of the fruit, including the finely cut rind, is used.

Preserves are made of whole fruit such as berries and cherries or pieces of larger fruits such as halves or slices of peaches or apricots. The shape of the fruit is preserved by cooking in a sugar syrup made either by sugaring the prepared fruit and letting it stand until sugar and fruit juice form a syrup, or by preparing a heavy sugar-water syrup. The former method gives a better flavor and a less intensely sweet product, but the latter is useful for fruits that are very ripe. By either method, this is one of the simplest ways of preserving fruit.

These sweets add interest to meals when served with bread or hot breads, and many of them serve as a delicious accompaniment for meat. They also make quick and attractive fillings for cake as well as delightful sauces for ice creams and puddings.

APPLE BUTTER

20 lbs apples	1 tbsp fresh ground cinnamon and ½ tsp ground
2 qts sweet cider	anise, *or* preferably 3 large
4 to 5 cups sugar	sticks cinnamon and 1 tsp
½ tsp salt	anise seeds

The best time for making Apple Butter is in Sept or Oct when the tart fall varieties still have a lively flavor and are firm, crisp and juicy. Jonathans, Northern Spys, Baldwins or Rhode Island Greenings are the best. Pare apples thinly, quarter, core and slice; there should be about 11 qts of sliced apples. Add cider and cook to a sauce; if a fine-textured butter is desired, rub through a food mill. Turn sauce into a large flat pan; an ordinary enamel-ware roasting pan is very satisfactory. Place in a moderately slow oven (325° F) and cook about 1 hr, or until sauce is reduced about half; stir occasionally. Add sugar and salt, stir thoroughly. Cook about 1½ hrs longer until butter is thick and a rich reddish amber color. If ground spices are used, stir them in when butter is removed from the oven; if whole cinnamon and anise seeds, tie them in a loose cheesecloth bag and add them about 30 min before the butter is done. Mixture should be stirred frequently after sugar is added to prevent sticking. When done, remove bag of spices and turn hot butter into hot sterilized jars; seal. Makes about 3 qts.

PEACH BUTTER

Long slow cooking is necessary to obtain that marvelous, completely cooked flavor and good color of a perfectly cooked butter

½ bushel perfect peaches, 12 qts sliced	4 cups water
	8 cups granulated sugar

Choose fully ripe, fine-flavored peaches, white or yellow, freestone or clingstone. Prepare freestone by scalding in boiling water for one min or until skins slip easily; strip off the skins. Other varieties will need to be thinly pared. Divide peaches among 3 pans holding 5 or 6 qts each. Put 1⅓ cups water into each pan and cook 20 min or until peaches are soft. Shake pans occasionally to prevent sticking. Peaches are less apt to stick if the pan is shaken rather than stirred. When fruit is tender, press through a sieve, food mill or potato ricer; the last two methods are easier. There should be 7 qts of purée. Turn purée into large enamel roasting pan and cook uncovered in a moderately slow oven (325° F) 1 hr, stirring frequently and thoroughly to prevent any sticking and scorching. Then add sugar, stirring in well, and reduce temp to 300° F (slow oven). Continue cooking, stirring thoroughly every 15 or 20 min until butter is thick, fine textured and a rich reddish amber color. This requires 3 to 3½ hrs of cooking. Pour into hot sterilized jars and seal. Makes about 9 pts.

PLUM BUTTER

3 qts red plums   9 cups sugar
½ cup water

Choose ripe but not overripe plums for the best butter. Wash plums carefully and put into a 5 to 6 qt preserving kettle with the water. Cover and cook over low heat at simmering point until plums burst and juice flows freely, shaking kettle frequently to prevent sticking. Rub plums and juice through a purée sieve. There will be about 9 cups purée. Return purée to preserving kettle, heat to simmering, and add sugar; stir until well mixed. Heat to boiling and boil vigorously, stirring almost continuously until mixture gives jelly test—2 drops sheet from edge of metal spoon. About 20 min cooking is required. Pour into hot sterilized glasses or ½ pt jars. Seal at once with melted parraffin. Makes about 2 qts.

PEACH CONSERVE

3 seedless oranges ✕200 size
3 tbsp lemon juice, 1 lemon
4½ to 4¾ lbs Elberta peaches,
   16 medium *or* 8 cups finely
   diced
8 cups sugar
½ cup golden raisins, washed

½ cup almonds sliced crosswise immediately after
blanching
3 peach pit kernels, peeled
and finely crushed before
adding

Pare oranges to remove all white skin. Cut out sections and press all juice from dividing membrane. Put orange sections, juice and lemon juice into a 5 or 6-qt enamelware or aluminum kettle. Scald and skin only a few peaches at a time. Remove pits and dice peaches into kettle, mixing with the juices to keep from discoloring. Stir in sugar and raisins, then heat to boiling, stirring to dissolve sugar. Cook over medium heat 1 hr after boiling starts, stirring frequently during last 15 min of cooking to prevent scorching. Add almonds and cook 15 min longer, stirring frequently. Remove from heat. Stir in peach kernels and continue stirring 5 min. Skim off foam. Pour into hot sterile jars and seal. Makes about 4½ pts.

DAMSON PLUM CONSERVE

Tart true plum flavor; rich purple color. Very delicious!

2 lbs Damson plums	¼ cup water
½ cup raisins, chopped	3½ cups sugar
⅔ cup walnuts	

Wash plums 2 or 3 times in lukewarm water and drain; cut in halves, discard pits. There should be 1 qt pitted plums, pressed down. Wash raisins, drain; place on cutting board, and with a knife, chop through a few times. Cover walnuts with briskly boiling water; let stand 2 min, then drain. Break nuts in medium pieces and remove loose skin which peels off easily. Skinned nuts are more tender and delicate in flavor. Combine plums, water and sugar in a 4-quart preserving kettle. Heat to boiling, stirring constantly with a wooden spoon, cook 10 min or until mixture barely gives jelly test. Add raisins, cook 2 or 3 min, then add nuts and cook 2 min longer. Pour immediately into hot sterilized glasses to within ¼-inch from top. Then pour melted paraffin over conserve. Cool and cover with lids. Makes about six 8-oz glasses.

GRAPE JAM

After extracting juice from grapes, put pulp and skins into a fine sieve, colander or food mill and rub as much through as possible. To each qt of purée add 3 cups granulated sugar and 2 tbsp lemon juice. Place in preserving kettle large enough to allow space for vigorous boiling. Cook rapidly with constant stirring for 20 min or until mixture gives the jelly test—2 drops sheet from edge of metal spoon. Pour into hot sterilized glasses and seal while hot with melted paraffin. Makes 1 qt jam from each qt of pulp. Use less sugar for very ripe grapes.

BAR LE DUC

Use 1 qt large, well ripened but not overripe red currants. Wash in cold water twice. Drain in colander, then stem. There should be about 3½ cups stemmed fruit. Put ½ cup mild flavored honey and ¾ cup plus 1 tbsp sugar into a 3-qt saucepan. Stir well, place over low heat to dissolve sugar. Heat to boiling, add currants, stir gently to distribute. Heat to boiling and boil gently 5 min. Strain out currants. Return syrup to heat and boil vigorously to jelly stage. This cooking requires 5 to 6 min. Skim jelly quickly; add drained currants. Let stand 10 to 15 min, stirring occasionally so fruit won't rise to top. Pour into hot, sterilized glasses. Cover with a thin layer of paraffin. When set, add a second layer of paraffin. Makes 3 cups or 4 glasses.

BLUE DAMSON PRESERVES

4 lbs plums, 3 qts   8 cups granulated sugar
½ cup water

Look over plums, discard imperfect ones; wash, cut plums in half and remove seeds or leave whole. Do not remove skin from Damson plums as they contribute much to flavor and color of preserves. Put plums and water into a heavy 8-qt preserving kettle, pour sugar on top. Heat slowly at first, stir gently every few min until sugar dissolves. Then increase heat, boiling briskly about 10 min. Reduce heat to simmering and cook until the syrup gives the jelly test—2 drops sheet from edge of metal spoon simultaneously. Preserves must be cooked from 40 to 50 min for juice to be thick enough when preserves are cold. Pour in hot sterilized pt or ½-pt jars, seal. 5 pts.

CHERRY PRESERVES

Delicious with hot breads or to make ice cream sundaes

2 qts sour red cherries,   6 cups sugar
3½ lbs, p 573   1 tbsp lemon juice

Choose well ripened firm fruit with stems left on. Cover with cold water, let stand 30 min for sprayed fruit, 5 min if not sprayed. Rinse in cold water twice. Drain well, pit fruit, keeping as whole as possible. There should be about 6 cups pitted fruit. Turn into 4-qt preserving kettle. Stir sugar into fruit. Cover, let stand 4 or 5 hrs or until sugar is almost dissolved. Place over low heat, stirring gently until all sugar dissolves. Heat to boiling, stir in lemon juice, boil rather rapidly 12 to 15 min, stirring occasionally, until fruit is clear and syrup is about consistency of corn syrup. Add *few* drops red food coloring if preserves are pale. Cover, let stand overnight for fruit to plump up. Next morning pack in hot sterile jars. Cover with hot paraffin, seal. In damp warm climate, omit paraffin, seal, process in boiling water bath 15 min. Store in cool dark place. Never attempt to make a larger quantity at one time. 2 pts preserves.

CITRON PRESERVES

Tedious to make but rare and delicious

1 large citron melon, 8-lb	6 cups sugar
2 tbsp salt	2 pieces ginger root,
5 cups cold water, about	1-inch long
3 cups water	2 large lemons

Cut citron in half, scoop out seedy portion being careful to keep flesh next to rind as thick as possible. A heavy tbsp or a metal sugar scoop is a good tool to remove the firm seedy center neatly. Cut hollowed melon into ¾ inch strips, pare strips, cut into cubes, dropping into glass or enamelware bowl. Sprinkle salt over citron, add just enough cold water to cover. Cover bowl and let stand at room temp overnight. Then turn into a colander to drain. Rinse in cold water and again drain. Turn into 4-qt preserving kettle, add the 3 cups water, cover, heat to boiling, then simmer until citron is almost tender, about 30 min. Add sugar and ginger root and cook at a moderate rolling boil (shaking pan occasionally or turning over carefully with a spoon), for at least an hr or until citron has a transparent appearance. Then drain off liquid and boil it rapidly for 30 to 40 min. Pour this syrup over citron. Cover and let stand about 4 hrs. Again drain off syrup. Have lemons sliced paper thin, flick seeds from slices, place in enamelware or aluminum pan, add 1 cup water, cover and cook five min until lemon is tender. Drain off liquid and add to citron syrup; add lemon slices to citron. Boil combined syrup for 30 min, pour over citron and let stand overnight. Again drain off syrup. Simmer 30 min and pour over citron. Again let stand overnight. Drain off syrup and reheat to boiling. Pack preserves in sterilized hot jars. Pour hot syrup over them and seal. Makes 3 pts.

KUMQUAT PRESERVES

A handsome, delicious meat or poultry garnish. Making the X-cut on both ends helps in absorption of syrup to make preserves plump, pretty

Fruit:	Syrup:
3 qts kumquats, pkd	3 cups sugar
3 tbsp soda	3 cups white corn syrup
Boiling water	3½ cups water
2 qts boiling water	1 cup sugar

Fruit: Use just-ripe kumquats full of juice and pectin. Wash fruit well in warm soapy water, then rinse well in cold water. Drain, put into *enamelware,* not aluminum, pan. Sprinkle with soda, pour on enough boiling water to cover. Let stand until water is lukewarm—25 to 30 min. Drain, cover with cold water and really *scrub* each fruit gently with vegetable brush to remove some of the oil from skin. Again rinse in cold water. Drain and make an X-cut on both blossom and stem end about ¼-inch deep to prevent bursting during cooking. Now drop fruit into the 2 qts boiling water, heat to boiling, then reduce heat and boil gently for 10 min or until tender. Then drain. *Syrup:* Meanwhile combine the 3 cups sugar, corn syrup and water in a 4-qt saucepan. Boil gently 10 min, removing any scum. Now add kumquats and boil *very gently* uncovered until fruit appears translucent and syrup is thickened, about 30 min. Remove to cake rack to cool to room temp, then cover and let stand overnight. Next morning, stir in rest of sugar and reheat just to simmering. Now use small sieve to lift out preserves and pack into sterilized pt jars. Now boil syrup about 5 min, then pour into jars to cover the preserves well. Seal, cool, then store in a cool dark place. About 2½ qts.

PEACH PRESERVES

8 qts pared, halved peaches   7 cups sugar

Choose just-ripe fine flavored freestone peaches. Discard peaches with soft bruised spots that would have to be cut out. White peaches produce a rich reddish preserve; yellow peaches make amber-colored preserves. Lay pared peach halves in layers in an enamel pan, sprinkling each layer with sugar. Cover pan; let stand overnight. Drain off syrup in morning, heat to boiling. Add peaches carefully. If they are soft, preserve shape by lifting with hands rather than with spoon. Boil rapidly about 30 min, shaking pan frequently to prevent sticking; stirring with a spoon spoils the shape. Reduce heat, simmer slowly until peaches are transparent and have rich, red color and the syrup is thick and waxy. Average-size peaches require about 2 hrs of cooking. Pack into hot sterilized jars, seal. About 8 pts.

STRAWBERRY ELECTRIC LIGHT PRESERVES

Wash, then hull 1 qt sound, ripe strawberries. Place in colander, stand it in bowl, and pour boiling water over berries; drain immediately. Turn into 3-qt saucepan, add 1 cup sugar, heat to boiling, and boil at a moderate rate for 2 min. Add 2 cups sugar, boil only 5 min longer. Skim. Pour into clean, shallow glass pan, 12 x 7½ x 2 inches. Place under 100-watt electric light—a goose-neck lamp is ideal. Cover lamp and preserves with a clean cloth. Let stand 36 to 48 hrs, turning berries over carefully every 6 or 8 hrs until they

Electric Light Preserves.

are translucent and syrup is waxy. Pack in hot sterilized jars. Seal with paraffin, then cover. About 1¼ pts.

Strawberry Sun Preserves—Follow above method. Place clean pane of glass over pan of preserves and place in the hot sunshine. Prop pane of glass up slightly on one end for evaporation. Immediately cover with a layer of cheesecloth to keep insects out. Bring preserves into house at sunset, return to sunshine the following day.

SEVEN-MINUTE STRAWBERRY PRESERVES

3 pts strawberries	3 tbsp lemon juice
⅓ cup sugar	2½ cups sugar

Use only perfect, firm, ripe, brilliant red strawberries. Wash. Hull and leave whole. Place in a 3-qt saucepan. Sift the ⅓ cup sugar over berries, add lemon juice and let stand overnight. Next morning, add the 2½ cups sugar. Heat to boiling; then boil 7 min, starting to count time when boiling starts. Shake pan occasionally during cooking. Pour into hot sterilized jars and seal. Makes about 1½ pts.

YELLOW TOMATO PRESERVES

3 qts yellow pear tomatoes, 4¾ lbs	2 pieces crushed ginger root, each 1 inch long
5½ cups sugar	8 lemons, sliced paper thin

Wash tomatoes, hold in boiling water ½ min or until the skin loosens easily. Cool and slip off skins. Place in bowl in alternate layers with sugar and let stand overnight or at least 4 hrs. Turn the tomatoes gently once in the juice which has formed. Drain off juice, about 3½ cups and boil until the syrup gives the jelly test. Simmer lemon slices in one cup of water for 5 min or until soft. Add lemon slices and water, ginger root and tomatoes to syrup and simmer until tomatoes are transparent, at least 15 min. Pour into hot sterilized jars. Seal. Makes 3½ pts.

RED TOMATO PRESERVES

2 lbs ripe red tomatoes	¼ cup lemon juice
4 cups sugar	1½ tbsp grated lemon rind, pkd
3 medium seedless oranges	
¼ tsp salt	

Choose firm, meaty tomatoes. Wash, dip quickly into hot water only long enough to slip skins. Remove core and skins and cut tomatoes in quarters. With a sharp pointed knife, carefully remove about half of the seeds, preserving the shape of the tomatoes as much as possible. Put tomatoes into a 4-qt preserving kettle, add sugar, then washed oranges, cut in quarters and sliced paper-thin. Add salt, lemon juice and rind; stir very carefully. Place over low heat and cook at a simmering temp 45 min to an hr, stirring occasionally until syrup is thick and tomatoes and orange slices are transparent. Pour into hot sterilized jars or jelly glasses. Cover wtih a thin layer of melted paraffin, then seal. Makes about 3 pts.

QUICK ORANGE MARMALADE

3 large oranges, about 1¾ lbs	5 cups water
2 lemons	6 cups granulated sugar
3 tbsp lemon juice	

Choose sound, juicy oranges, preferably seedless—they may be any size, but a large size is easier to prepare. If only a mild flavored product is desired, scrape the surface of the oranges with a sharp knife to open the cells. Boil for 3 min in 2 qts of water. Cool in cold water. Cut oranges and the 2 lemons into 8 sections each; scoop out pulp, discarding any seeds; cut it up and return to kettle. Then slice rind paper-thin and add to kettle. Add the additional lemon juice and water, heat to boiling, simmer 1 hr uncovered. Add sugar, stir until dissolved and return to heat; again heat to boiling and simmer about 50 min longer. Remove pan from heat. Test for doneness by dropping a tsp of the hot liquid onto a thoroughly chilled plate and place in refrigerator for 5 min; if jellied at end of this time, the marmalade is done; if not, continue cooking a few minutes longer, and again test for doneness. When done, pour into hot sterilized jelly glasses and cover immediately with melted paraffin. When set, add another thin layer of paraffin. Makes about 4 pts.

QUINCE HONEY

3 lbs sound quince	3 cups sugar
7½ cups water	

Select firm barely ripe quince. Wash thoroughly. If there are wormy portions, trim out and discard before weighing. Cut quince in quarters, flick out seeds and discard. Pare and remove cores and combine cores and parings in one saucepan. Cut quince in thin slices or grate on coarse grater. There should be about 2½ cups of quince slices and 2 cups combined cores and parings. Add 4½ cups water to quince slices, cover and boil gently 20 to 25 min or until tender. Add 3 cups water to the cores and parings, cover and cook rapidly for 20 min; strain through a clean muslin bag and add strained juice to the cooked quince slices. There should be about 6½ cups combined juice and quince. Add sugar and boil uncovered for 35 to 40 min until thick and a rich garnet colored honey is obtained. It may be necessary to add more water, ¼ cup at a time, if the syrup begins to get too thick before the rich color is obtained. Pour into hot sterilized jelly glasses. Cover with a thin layer of melted paraffin. Apply second thin layer paraffin when first has set. 2 pts.

PICKLES AND RELISHES

Pickles and relishes are easy to make, especially fruit, beet and cucumber pickles and piccalilli. The cost is rarely high, storage is no problem and no special equipment other than a preserving kettle and jars is required. The flavor of good home-made pickles lends an individuality to meals that is hard to match with the commercial variety.

Chilling pickles before serving improves their eating quality 100 per cent when they are served as a relish or as an accompaniment to meats, sandwiches, etc. As an ingredient, they can also be used to "pep-up" the flavor of salad dressings, meat loaves, sandwich fillings and canapés. Juice from pickles should never be discarded; it imparts a delightful flavor to roasts and braised meat. Salad dressings, vegetable sauces, and hot potato salad are only a few of the foods that can be made using pickle liquids of various types.

Crispness is a feature much prized in cucumber pickles. This is produced by soaking in ice-cold salt water then heating the vegetable for only a short time in the pickling solution. Alum also produces crispness. It is perfectly harmless and in the small quantity used it does not affect the flavor, but its use is not essential.

Care should be taken to avoid hollow, soft, or shriveled pickles. Hollow pickles are thought to be the result of faulty growth, of standing too long after harvesting (24 hrs is the longest time advisable), and of improper curing. Hollow raw cucumbers float in the water, therefore slice or grind them for relishes. Nature does not always produce perfect foods, so while we choose the best products available for canning and preserving, we must sometimes use inferior products and preserve by the method best suited to the quality.

Soft pickles are caused by bacterial action which results when the salt solution is too weak. One reason for a too weak solution is inaccurate measuring of salt. A second reason is using the wrong kind of salt. Use only pure granulated salt—never the free-flowing salt which contains other minerals. Another reason may be that too many cucumbers or beans are crowded into the jar and the strength of the brine is too low to provide the required amount of salt. Then there should be enough brine to cover the pickles well. *One pickle* sticking out of the brine can cause all the pickles under the brine to spoil. Also remove scum every day because the scum neutralizes the acidity in the brine and causes the pickles to spoil.

Pickles shrivel if the salt brine, the sugar syrup or the vinegar* is too strong. For very sweet or very sour pickles, start with a weak solution, then increase the sugar or vinegar every day or two until the desired sweetness or

How to reduce 5% vinegar to 4% acidity: Add ¼ cup water to each cup of 5% vinegar used.

sourness is reached. When curing pickles, start with a small amount of salt, and increase the amount after the fermentation is underway.

Because of the flavor it adds, cider vinegar (4 to 6% acetic acid) is used to make pickles. Distilled white vinegar is equally good and has the advantage of producing a clearer color in the finished pickle. Vinegar should be filtered if it contains any sediment. Only fresh mixed whole spices are satisfactory for pickling. Do not use spices left over from previous year because they do not give a clean, fresh tangy flavor. Soft water is recommended if it can be obtained clean and safe. A high proportion of mineral salts in water also prevents proper acid fermentation in brined pickles, and iron in the water may blacken them.

The preserving kettle should be aluminum or enamelware, never copper or iron. A copper kettle gives pickles a vivid green color indicating the presence of copper salts which are definitely harmful to the body. This vivid color should always be avoided. It is very essential that pickles be stored in a cool dark place to preserve crispness and good color.

FRUIT PICKLES

CRABAPPLE PICKLES OR SPICED CRABAPPLES

10 lbs Siberian *or* Dolgo crabapples	5 cups water
10 cups sugar	1 tbsp whole cloves
5 cups 5% cider vinegar	2 tsp cassia buds
	2 four-inch sticks cinnamon

Choose crisp, red, just ripened apples. Never use mellow fruit. Wash carefully in warm, soapy water, rubbing gently with the hands. Do not remove stems. Rinse well in cold water. Put next 3 ingredients into preserving kettle, stir well, heat to boiling. This makes about 14 cups syrup. Measure 2 cups syrup into a 3 or 4 qt saucepan. Add 15 to 16 apples pricked through several times with a skewer. Heat to boiling, add ¼ of the spices and boil gently, turning apples in syrup until they are thoroughly tender when pricked. Pack carefully into clean, hot qt jars. Cover well with syrup and seal. Repeat until all syrup, apples and spices are used. Strain syrup to remove spices, if desired. Store in cool, dark place. About 8 qts.

FROZEN CRABAPPLE PICKLES

Prepare the crabapple pickles as for canning, but pack in frozen food containers, lined with plastic or cellophane bags. Seal and freeze as any other food. These pickles keep their natural brilliant color beautifully.

PICKLED PEACHES OR SECKEL PEARS

1 cup 5% cider vinegar
1 cup water
4½ cups sugar
2 four-inch sticks cinnamon

1 tsp whole cloves
16 to 18 medium peaches,
4 lbs

Clingstone peaches make best pickles, but any fine-flavored tree-ripened peach free from blemishes is acceptable. Put vinegar, water and sugar into a 3-qt saucepan, simmer 5 min. Wash peaches, pare half of them neatly and thinly. Drop at once into the syrup, simmer until tender, about 12 min. Lift peaches out into bowl. Add rest of pared peaches, cook until tender. Remove from heat, add peaches in bowl, cover and let stand overnight. Next morning pack peaches into sterile, hot jars. Add spices to syrup and reheat to boiling. Pour syrup over pickles to cover fruit and come to within ¼-inch of jar top. Seal, cool and store in cool, dark place. 2 qts.

PICKLED PEACHES

6 lbs sugar
3 cups 5% cider vinegar
2½ cups water
1 tsp whole cloves

1 tsp cassia buds
2 four inch sticks cinnamon
10 lbs choice flavorful
    freestone peaches

Choose fully ripe well-developed peaches without bruises or soft spots. Put ⅓ of the sugar, vinegar and water into a 3 or 4-qt preserving kettle and heat to simmering, stirring occasionally until sugar dissolves. Add ⅓ the spices. Have ready enough boiling water to dip ⅙ of peaches in just long enough to cause skins to slip. Be careful not to leave peaches in long enough to soften the flesh and make it impossible to skin peaches smoothly. Drop skinned peaches into syrup; simmer until tender, about 6 min. Dip out peaches with slotted spoon into two jars. This fills jars only half full. Cover jars, let stand on back of stove. Now add another sixth of prepared peaches to syrup and again cook until tender. Finish filling the two jars with fruit and add syrup to fill up to ¼-inch of jar top. The amount of syrup should just fill the jars. Seal immediately with either glass lids or metal lids lined with enamel. Proceed in same manner with remaining peaches. Add any pickling syrup left from one batch to next. Cool pickles. Store in cool place. 6 qts.

AUNT PHOEBE'S PICKLED PEACHES

Excellent

11 lbs clingstone peaches
7 cups sugar
1 x ½ x ¼-inch piece dry
    gingerroot
4-inch stick cinnamon

1 tbsp whole allspice
1 tsp whole cloves
2 cups water
3 cups 5% cider vinegar

Use peaches free of blemishes and bruises and about size of a large egg. Wash in cold water, rubbing gently with hands. Drain. Measure sugar into 5-qt aluminum or enamelware kettle. Put gingerroot between 2 or 3 folds of waxed paper and pound with a hammer to crack root well. Put ginger with spices onto a 6 or 7-inch sq of cheesecloth and tie loosely making a spice bag. Put into pan with sugar, then add water and vinegar. Stir thoroughly to dissolve sugar, then place over moderate heat and boil gently 3 min, counting time after boiling actually begins. Meanwhile pare half the peaches thinly and neatly and drop into boiling syrup. Cook from 12 to 15 min, or until barely tender when tested with toothpick. Then lift peaches out of syrup with slotted spoon into a bowl. Cover to keep warm. Have rest of peaches pared and add to syrup and cook until just tender. Now remove kettle from heat and add first batch of peaches. Cover and let cool, then place in refrigerator for 24 hrs. Stir gently 3 or 4 times so that all peaches will have equal chance to absorb syrup and plump up. Now drain off syrup and heat to boiling. Pack peaches in sterile jars. Pour syrup into jars to come ¼-inch above peaches. Wipe jars clean and seal. 4 to 4½ qts depending on size of peaches.

WATERMELON PICKLES

This process is a little long, but draining off syrup, reheating and pouring on the rind pays off in a plump, clear pickle.

7 lbs prepared rind from a 25 to 30 lb melon	1 cup water
	1 tbsp whole cloves
2¼ qts water	1 stick cinnamon
⅓ cup salt	2 tsp cassia buds
6½ cups sugar	1 lemon, sliced paper thin
2 cups 5% cider vinegar	

Prepare rind by cutting into 1½" strips. Slice away pink flesh and pare off green rind. Now *cut strips neatly* into diamonds, sqs or triangles. Add salt to water, stir to dissolve, pour over the rind placed in an enamelware or glass bowl. Brine should barely cover rind. Cover bowl and let stand overnight. Next morning rinse in 3 or 4 changes of cold water. Drain, turn into 4-qt aluminum or enamelware preserving kettle. Barely cover rind with cold water, cover kettle, heat to boiling, reduce heat and simmer until rind is tender when pricked with a fork, from 40 to 60 min, time depending on thickness of rind. Drain in a colander. Make syrup in same kettle by heating 5½ cups of sugar, vinegar and 1 cup water to boiling, add drained hot rind, heat to boiling, reduce heat, and simmer uncovered about 1 hr or until rind begins to appear transparent. Add spices last 10 min of cooking. Remove from heat, cover and let stand overnight. Drain off syrup, add lemon slices and remaining cup sugar. Reheat to boiling, and again pour syrup over rind. Cover, let stand again overnight. Drain off syrup, heat to boiling. Pour over rind now packed in hot sterilized jars. Seal with glass or enamel-lined lids. Process 10 min in boiling water bath. Chill before serving, or reheat in syrup for delicious hot relish. 6 pts.

CANTALOUPE PICKLES

Cut 2 fine-flavored cantaloupe weighing about 3½ lbs into 12 lengthwise slices. Remove seeds, pare off skin. Put into enamel preserving kettle. Barely cover with water, stir in 1½ tsp powdered alum. Cover, soak overnight. Next morning, drain, rinse quickly in cold water. Cover with cold water, heat to simmering, cook until tender, about 20 min. Again drain, add to a syrup made of 4½ cups sugar, 2 cups 5% cider vinegar, ½ cup water and 1 lemon sliced thin. Boil gently until rind is beautifully transparent, about 1 hr. Add 1 tbsp pickling spices last 15 min. Pack in hot sterile jars. Seal. 2 pts.

VEGETABLE PICKLES

BEET PICKLES

Good as a vegetable or as relish with any meat or fish

6½ lbs beets   4 to 5 cups sugar
　3 cups 4% cider vinegar

Choose bright red tender young beets as nearly the same size as possible. If some are large, cut in halves or quarters after cooking and skinning. Cut off tops of beets leaving about 2 inches of stems. Wash carefully in 2 or 3 waters to remove all soil from beets and stems; rub with hands, never with a brush which breaks the skin and permits loss of color through "bleeding." The tap root should also be left unbroken. Place beets in a 4 to 5-qt kettle, cover with cold water, cover kettle, and boil slowly until tender, 35 min to 1 hr, depending on size and tenderness of the beets. When done, drain and cool just enough to handle comfortably. Slip off skins and stems. Return while still warm to the washed kettle, add vinegar and sugar. If vinegar is stronger than 4% acidity, more sugar may be added to give preferred flavor. Heat just to simmering. The pickling syrup barely covering the beets should have a thick, oily appearance. Pack the hot beets into hot sterilized jars, and pour the hot syrup over them so it just covers the beets in each jar. Seal immediately with glass or enamel-lined lids. Makes 6 pts. Chill before serving or reheat in syrup and serve hot.

BREAD AND BUTTER PICKLES

Green Tomato or Cucumber

3 lbs green tomatoes—10
   medium, *or* 3 lbs cucumbers 1½″ diam
⅓ cup salt*
5 cups cold water
½ lb onions, 3 med
2 cups vinegar

1⅔ cups sugar
1 tsp celery seed
2 tsp prepared mustard
1 tsp ginger
¼ tsp turmeric
⅛ tsp mace
Few dashes red pepper

Choose smooth, even-sized tomatoes that have acquired the whitish color which appears just before ripening, or use fresh crisp green cucumbers. Wash. Remove stem-end and blossom scar neatly from tomatoes, then cut into ¼-inch crosswise slices. Put into an enamelware or glass bowl. Sprinkle with the salt and add water. Cover and let stand 24 hrs. Turn into a colander to drain 10 to 15 min. Now put into a preserving kettle, add onions, peeled and sliced ⅛″ thick, then vinegar, sugar and spices. Heat to boiling, simmer only 3 or 4 min. Pack into hot sterilized jars with glass or enamel-lined lids. Seal. 3 pts.

CASSIA BUD PICKLES

4 pts water
1 cup salt*
3 doz 3-inch cucumbers
½ tsp powdered alum

3 cups vinegar
4 cups sugar
½ oz celery seed, 2 tbsp
½ oz cassia buds, 2 tbsp

Heat water and salt to boiling, cool and add to washed cucumbers, split lengthwise. Cover, let stand 1 week. Drain, cover with boiling water, add alum. Let stand 24 hrs. Drain, cover with hot syrup, made by heating vinegar and 2½ cups of the sugar and the celery seed and cassia buds tied in a bag. For 3 successive days drain off syrup, add ½ cup sugar, heat, pour over pickles. On third day, drain off syrup, heat to boiling. Pack pickles in hot sterilized jars, add boiling syrup to cover pickles. Seal with glass or enamel-lined lids. Makes 2 qts.

CELERY CUCUMBER PICKLES

20 cucumbers, about 3½ to 4
   inches long
⅓ cup salt*
   Ice water
3 cups cider vinegar

2 cups sugar
2 cups sliced celery
½ pod hot red pepper
½ pod sweet red pepper

Wash cucumbers thoroughly, split lengthwise and place in enamelware bowl; sprinkle with salt, add ice water to cover. Let stand over-

*Use cooking salt, not free-flowing table salt.

night. Drain. Put vinegar and sugar into enamelware kettle and heat to simmering; add celery and peppers, then put in cucumbers and simmer 3 or 4 min. Pack into hot sterilized jars, fill up with syrup and seal. Makes 4 to 5 pts. Chill before serving.

DILL BEAN PICKLES

4 lbs round-podded tender   ⅔ cup salt*
  green beans   12 large dill heads and stems
2 qts water   6 outer cabbage leaves
½ cup vinegar

Wash and remove tips from beans. Cook in boiling water 5 to 7 min or until half cooked; beans should still be slightly crisp. Drain. Make brine by boiling water, vinegar and salt together until salt dissolves. Cool slightly, remove any scum that forms. Place two heads and stems of dill in each pt jar. Pack beans lengthwise in jars; cover with brine, place 2 cabbage leaves on top. Screw glass or enamel lids on loosely. Store in cool place. If brine oozes out, add fresh brine to cover. Beans are ready to eat in 2 to 3 weeks. Serve chilled. Makes 6 pts.

DILL PICKLES

Keg Method

3 pecks cucumbers, 4 to 5   3½ cups salt *plus* 2 tbsp*
  inches long   6 gallons cold water
4 large bunches dill, 24   1 oz pickling spices
  heads and stems to bunch

Choose crisp straight fresh picked cucumbers and make pickles promptly. Fresh green dill with well developed seed heads is best. Do not wash dill, but remove damaged leaves, stems and roots. Add salt to water and stir thoroughly making sure all salt is dissolved. This produces a 29% brine tested by a saltmeter. Wash pickles lightly—just enough to remove soil and sand but not enough to remove the natural bloom on the pickles. This is important. Swishing them up and down in cold water is usually enough. Even the little black pricks at the top of the warts should not be rubbed off. This glaze or bloom left intact helps to ferment the pickles and keeps them firm. If there happens to be a little dirt left on the pickles, it sloughs off in the curing process. Drain well.

Have a clean 12-gallon crockery jar or wooden keg. Put a 1½ to 2 inch layer of dill in the bottom of the jar and press down firmly. Turn in about ⅓ of the cucumbers and shake container to shift them into a fairly compact position. Sprinkle ½ the spice over the cucumbers, add another ⅓ of the cucumbers and the rest of the spice. Shake the container again to shift the pickles, and if necessary use the hands to obtain

*Use cooking salt, not free-flowing table salt.

a compact arrangement. Add rest of the cucumbers and again shake and arrange. Add another 1½ to 2 inch layer of dill pressed down. Pour on the brine. It should come up over the dill. Lay a paraffined hard wood round cover cut to fit on inside of jar, or a heavy plate on top of pickles and over this put a scrubbed-clean flint rock heavy enough to keep board or plate not more than an inch below the surface of brine but not heavy enough to distort shape of pickles, about 3 or 4 lbs. Let container stand in a clean, moderately cool place, from 65 to 70° F. Cover top with clean cloth to keep out dust and insects. Do not move the keg for 15 to 18 days. In 3 or 4 days a scum will appear on top of brine. Skim off every 3 days.

If weather gets cold, brine may recede below surface of dill. If this happens, add cold water to come up to original height; dill should always be covered with brine. It takes from five to seven weeks for pickles to cure thoroughly or until they are firm and translucent all the way through. These pickles may be packed in sterilized jars. ¼ cup vinegar may be poured over each qt of pickles, then filled up with strained brine from jar or keg. Seal with glass or enamel-lined lids.

TO PREPARE KOSHER DILLS

When dill pickles made according to the preceding recipe have cured thoroughly, remove as many as desired and pack into wide mouth glass jars. Add ½ clove of garlic to each jar. Remove some of the brine from the original crockery jar of dills, strain through several folds of cheesecloth and pour over the pickles. If desired, pour 2 tbsp of vinegar into each jar before adding the brine. Wipe jars clean, seal and store in a cool place. In a few days sufficient garlic flavor will be imparted to the pickles. Then remove garlic.

TO PREPARE SWEET DILL PICKLES

Use dill pickles made according to recipe given above. When thoroughly cured, remove pickles and cut into crosswise slices about ⅛-inch thick. To each gallon of pickles, add 1 cup of vinegar, 2½ cups sugar and enough of the strained brine from the original dill pickles to cover the sliced pickles. Pack into clean sterilized jars and seal. In a few days the pickles will be ready for serving.

CUCUMBER OR GREEN TOMATO DILL PICKLES

8 to 9 lbs cucumbers *or* green tomatoes
16 to 20 stalks fresh dill
1 oz mixed pickling spices
1 cup cooking salt—not table salt

4 qts soft water
16 green grape *or* horseradish leaves rinsed well in cold water

Choose fresh-picked cucumbers 5 to 6 inches long, or green tomatoes size of golf ball. Wash vegetables well in cold water. Cover with cold water and let stand 1 hr. Wash a 3-gallon crockery jar clean; line bottom with half the dill and grape leaves. Drain vegetables; do not split, but pierce each with a knife or fork, then pack in the crock. Make a brine of the salt and water and pour it over vegetables. Cover with another layer of dill and grape leaves. Cover with a paraffined wooden lid that just fits within top of jar. Weight down with a glass jar filled with enough water to bring brine up to the cover, but not over it. None of the vegetables should be exposed to air. Cover jar with cloth. Let stand at room temp (65° to 70° F). Remove scum each day. Ready to use in 2 to 4 weeks, or when pickles are well flavored with dill and are clear with no white spots showing when cut.

To Store: Pack the cured, drained pickles in hot, sterilized qt or 2-qt jars. Strain pickle brine through 3 or 4 folds of cheesecloth into a saucepan. Heat to a rolling boil and pour over the pickles to fill jars to top. If a sour dill pickle is wanted, add 3 tbsp cider vinegar to each qt jar before adding the boiling brine. Seal with glass or enamel-lined lids. Store in a cool place. Makes 5 to 6 qts.

PICKLED ONIONS

As good as the most expensive store variety

2½ qts small white pickling
   onions, 2¼ lbs
Boiling water
1 cup pure coarse salt
1½ qts boiling water
Blade of mace,

whole cloves, white whole
peppers, bay leaves
1 cup 5% cider vinegar
   mixed with
⅓ cup water
½ cup sugar

To toughen onion skins for easier peeling, pour enough boiling water over them to cover; let stand 2 or 3 min, then peel carefully with a sharp-pointed paring knife. There should be 2 qts peeled onions. Turn onions into a glass or enamelware container. Make a brine of the salt and 1½ qts boiling water and pour over the onions. Cover, let stand 2 days, then drain off brine. Again make same amount of brine. Pour over onions placed in an enamelware saucepan; heat to boiling, then boil gently for 3 min. Again drain onions and pack them into clean hot jars. Add and distribute evenly through the jar, a dime-size blade of mace, 6 whole peppers, 2 cloves and ¼ of a bay leaf. Heat vinegar, water and sugar barely to boiling and fill jars to top. Seal with glass or enamel-lined lids. Ready to use in 3 or 4 weeks. Makes 5 half pts.

TEXAS SOUR PICKLES

Choose 25 shapely, fresh-picked, slender cucumbers 2½ to 4 inches long for each qt of pickles. Wash gently in cold water. Pack firmly in sterilized qt glass jars. Add salt water to cover (1½ tbsp salt* dissolved in 1¾ cups soft water). Cover, let stand overnight. Next morning, drain well. Cover with plain cold 4% cider vinegar. Add ¼ tsp green food coloring and ⅛ tsp powdered alum. Seal, store in cool dark place. Ready to eat in 3 or 4 weeks.

THUNDER AND LIGHTNING PICKLES OR SENF GURKEN
Attractive pickles with power!

6½ lbs ripe yellow cucumbers, 4 to 5 large
3 pts ice water
⅔ cup salt*
2 to 4 sprigs green dill blossoms, seeds well developed

1 tbsp white mustard seed
2 tsp fresh grated horseradish
2 pods hot red pepper, medium size
2½ cups 5% vinegar
⅔ cup water
¾ cup sugar

Wash and pare cucumbers thinly. Cut in half lengthwise and scrape out seedy portion. Cut halves in thirds lengthwise, then crosswise. Put into glass or enamelware bowl and cover with brine made with the ice water and salt. Cover and let stand overnight. Drain well. Divide next 4 ingredients between 2 sterilized qt jars. Heat rest of ingredients to boiling, add cucumbers and *simmer* only 5 min. Pack pickles in jars up to ¾-inch from top. Add boiling solution to ¼-inch from top. Seal with glass or enamel-lined lids. Makes 2 qts.

VAN'S TURN-ONCE-A-DAY PICKLES

2¾ lbs cucumbers, 2½ to 3 inches long
2½ cups 5% cider vinegar
½ cup water

3 tbsp prepared mustard
⅔ cup sugar
2 tsp salt
1½ tsp fresh grated horseradish

Wash cucumbers thoroughly. Cover with ice water to crisp 2 or 3 hrs. Drain. Pack in qt jars up to 1 inch from top. Blend remaining ingredients and pour over cucumbers. Remove air bubbles with spatula or knife, add more liquid to come up to ¼-inch of top. Seal loosely, let stand 24 hrs. Then tighten seal and turn jar upside-down to shake up the pickling solution. Loosen seal slightly. Repeat tightening seal, shaking, etc., each day for a week. 2 qts.

RELISHES
CATCHUP

7 lbs tomatoes
⅓ cup sugar
2½ tsp salt
1 cup cider vinegar

1 tsp dry mustard
2 tsp celery seed
½ stick cinnamon
1 tsp whole black peppers

*Use cooking salt, not free-flowing table salt.

Choose firm, red, ripe tomatoes to secure a good-colored catchup. Wash, core and cut tomatoes into quarters. Boil vigorously ½ hr in an uncovered kettle, stirring occasionally. Press through fine sieve or food mill, pushing all of pulp through. Return to kettle, add sugar, salt, vinegar and mustard; then celery seed, cinnamon and black peppers tied in a cheesecloth bag. Boil 45 to 60 min longer, or to thick catchup consistency, stirring frequently. Remove spice bag, squeezing thoroughly with two spoons. Pour hot catchup into clean, sterilized bottles and seal immediately. Makes about 1½ pts.

CHOW CHOW

1 qt chopped cabbage	2 cups 5% cider vinegar
3 cups cauliflowerets	1¼ cups sugar
2 cups sliced onions or	2 tsp dry mustard
small pickling onions	1 tsp turmeric
2 cups diced green pepper	½ tsp ginger
1 cup diced sweet red pepper	½ tsp white mustard seed
2 cups chopped green tomato	1 tsp mixed pickling spices
3 tbsp salt*	1 tsp celery seed

Wash, drain and prepare all vegetables. Sprinkle with salt, cover, let stand overnight. Then turn into a colander and drain well. Combine vinegar, sugar, and spices tied in a cheesecloth bag, and simmer 10 min. Add the drained vegetables; heat to boiling, decrease heat, simmer 10 min. Remove spice bag. Pack hot pickles into hot, sterilized jars and seal with glass or enamel-lined lids. Makes 3 pts.

CORN RELISH

5 or 6 fresh ears sweet corn	3 cups diced red tomatoes,
1½ cups chopped green	free of seeds
peppers, 3 peppers	1½ cups 5% cider vinegar
¾ cup chopped sweet red	1 cup sugar
pepper, 1 small	2½ tbsp salt
1 cup pared chopped ripe	1 tsp white mustard seed
cucumber	¾ tsp turmeric
½ cup diced celery	1 tsp celery seed
1 cup chopped onion	¼ tsp dry mustard

Wash and drain all vegetables. Cut corn from cob, scraping it to get all milk from kernels—there should be 1 qt. Combine all vegetables except tomatoes; turn into a colander to drain well. Then add tomatoes and remaining ingredients. Heat just to boiling, reduce heat and *simmer* 30 min or until vegetables are just tender. Pour at once into hot sterilized jars. Seal with glass or enamel-lined lids. Makes 4 pts.

*Use cooking salt, not free-flowing table salt.

GOOSEBERRY CHUTNEY

*Chutney like this is found in the most pretentious eating places—is
very good with curry as well as hot or cold roast meats and poultry*

5 cups stemmed gooseberries
1 cup water
3 cups sugar
1 cup fine-chopped onion,
 ⅓ lb
1 cup seedless raisins
1¼ tsp salt
 Piece candied ginger,
 1x1x¼", finely chopped
½ tsp ground ginger

½ tsp paprika
½ tsp dry mustard
¼ tsp white pepper
1-inch length dry hot red
 pepper
1 cup 5% cider vinegar
⅓ large lemon thinly sliced,
 slices cut in 8ths
¼ cup water

Stem gooseberries and wash in cold water. Put in saucepan, add
water, cover and boil gently until berries are soft, about 15 min. Put
berries through sieve; there should be 2¾ to 3 cups thick purée free
from seeds and skin. Turn purée into aluminum or enamelware 4-qt
kettle, add all but last 2 ingredients, and boil gently 15 minutes with
frequent stirring to prevent scorching; then add lemon slices simmered
until tender in the ¼ cup water. Continue cooking and stir until
chutney is thick and clear from 1 to 1½ hrs. Pour into hot sterile jars.
Seal with glass or enamel-lined lids. Store in cool dark place. 4 half pts.

HOT CHILI SAUCE

14 lbs tomatoes, 1 peck
2 hot red peppers, ½ cup
 chopped
3 cups finely chopped onions

2 tbsp salt
1 tbsp celery seed
¾ cup light brown sugar
1 qt cider vinegar

Choose firm, red, ripe tomatoes for bright colored chili sauce. Wash
tomatoes, dip in boiling water just long enough to loosen skins, cool,
and remove skins and cores. Cut up fine and place in a colander to drain;
save drained juice. Wash peppers, split lengthwise, remove and discard
seeds, then chop. Add peppers and chopped onions to the tomatoes.
Put drained juice in a 6-qt preserving kettle and boil rapidly about 30
min, or until reduced to half the quantity. Add tomato mixture and heat
to boiling; then add remaining ingredients and cook moderately fast,
stirring occasionally until of desired chili sauce consistency or about 2½
hrs. Pour into clean, sterilized ½ pt glass jars; seal immediately. This
sauce is good as a cocktail sauce for shrimp or oysters. Makes 5 pts.

MINT CHUTNEY

A tangy refreshing relish for lamb, pork or game

½ cup finely shredded mint
leaves, 1 large bunch
½ lb ripe red tomatoes, 3
small
5 onions size medium egg,
2 cups chopped
1 red hot pepper 6" to 7" long
2 sweet green peppers

2½ cups 5% cider vinegar
1½ cups brown sugar, pkd
2 tbsp lemon juice
2¼ tsp salt
1½ cups moist seedless raisins
1½ cups finely chopped tart
apples
2½ tsp dry mustard

Put washed jars on to sterilize. Swish mint clean through 2 or 3 cold waters; shake dry. Strip leaves from stems; cover with damp cloth. Skin tomatoes and remove cores. Peel onions and remove hard core at root-end. Wash peppers, cut in half lengthwise and remove dividing membranes and seeds. Put vinegar, sugar, lemon juice and salt into 6-qt preserving kettle and boil gently 10 min. Meanwhile chop raisins fine on a board, then chop tomatoes, onions and peppers very fine, and add them as you chop them to the vinegar mixture. Pare apples, quarter, core and chop fine; add to mixture. Now shear mint fine with scissors and add to mixture. Blend mustard to smooth paste with some of the hot liquid and add, then boil gently 45 to 60 min or until thick, stirring almost constantly as mixture scorches easily. Pour into hot sterile jars filling almost full. Seal with glass or enamel-lined lids. Store in a cool dark place. Makes 5 half pts.

PEPPY CHILI SAUCE

This sauce is what the name implies—it adds zest and color to the meal

7 lbs tomatoes
1 small bunch Pascal celery,
1 cup ground
½ lb hot green *or* red chili
peppers, 1 cup ground
1 large clove garlic

1 lb onions, 1 cup ground
1 cup 5% cider vinegar
1 tsp crushed whole peppers
1½ tsp dried orégano
⅓ cup sugar

Use very ripe solid tomatoes for best color and flavor. Wash, then dip in hot water a few seconds to loosen skins. Skin and remove all cores. Dice tomatoes and drop into a colander placed over a 6-qt enamelware or aluminum preserving kettle to drain 1 hr. There should be about 3 cups juice. Meanwhile, wash celery, break branches and strip off all strings possible; cut into ½-inch lengths. Wash peppers, cut in half lengthwise, remove seeds and dividing membranes. Peel garlic and onions. Put celery, peppers, garlic and onions through a food chopper, using coarse blade. Turn vegetables into a saucepan, add 2 cups of the tomato juice (use remaining juice for cocktail) and cook gently 15 to

20 min or until soft, stirring often. Turn drained tomatoes into preserving kettle, add cooked vegetables and sugar. Cook and stir about 45 min. Add peppers and orégano tied loosely in a cheesecloth bag, then stir, cook a min—yes, a min—lift out bag and taste to see if desired flavor is obtained. If not, return bag for another min and taste again. When desired flavor is obtained, remove bag and discard. Continue cooking until thick, about 15 min longer. Pour into hot sterilized ½ pt jars, filling almost full. Wipe necks of jars with a clean wet cloth. Seal with glass or enamel-lined lids. Store in a dark cool place. 3½ pts.

VEGETABLE CHILI SAUCE

7 lbs ripe red tomatoes	1 cup 5% cider vinegar
1 large clove garlic, peeled	⅓ cup sugar
1 lb onions, 1 cup ground	1½ tbsp salt
½ lb green chili peppers, 1 cup ground	1 tsp crushed whole white *or* black peppers
1 small bunch Pascal celery, 1 cup ground	1 tsp crushed dried orégano

Choose solid fine tomatoes. Wash, dip in boiling water just long enough to loosen skins. Remove skins and cores. Cut tomatoes into ½-inch dice, dropping into a colander placed over a 6-qt aluminum or enamelware preserving kettle. Drain 30 min. There should be about 3 cups juice. Meanwhile, peel garlic and onions. Wash peppers and remove stem and seed cores. Wash celery, trim off all blemishes, then break in 2 or 3 pieces to remove strings. Cut celery into half-inch lengths to eliminate stringiness in grinding. Put all vegetables except tomatoes through food chopper separately, using coarse blade. Measure each and add to tomato juice in kettle and boil gently until vegetables are tender—15 to 20 min. Now add drained tomatoes, vinegar, sugar and salt; boil moderately fast 30 to 40 min, stirring frequently. Now add crushed peppers and orégano tied loosely in a bag. In 2 or 3 min taste to determine when enough pepper and orégano flavor is extracted to suit taste. Remove bag, simmer, stir often until thick, about 45 min. Pour into hot sterile jars. Seal with glass or enamel-lined lids. 2½ pts.

HOT DOG RELISH

Don't serve this relish just with Hot Dogs—it will be just as welcome on Thanksgiving with turkey. An excellent all-purpose relish

1 bunch Pascal celery, 3 cups ground	1 qt water
3½ lbs cucumbers 1″ to 1½″ in diam, 5 cups ground	½ cup salt
	3 cups 5% cider vinegar
½ lb green sweet peppers	2 cups sugar
2 hot red peppers, 2 oz	2 tsp white mustard seed
2¼ lbs onions, 2¼ cups ground	2 tsp celery seed

Use tender celery. Wash clean and remove leaves; break into 2 or 3 pieces to strip off as many strings as possible, then cut into ½-inch slices. Wash cucumbers and cut in quarters. Wash peppers; cut in half, remove stems, seeds, cores and dividing membranes. Peel onions and cut in quarters. Put all vegetables separately through food chopper using coarse blade, then measure into a 6-qt glass or enamelware bowl. Add the water in which salt has been stirred; let stand 1 hr, then turn vegetables into a colander to drain thoroughly, 15 to 20 min, pressing gently with palm of hand to remove excess liquid. Turn drained vegetables into a 5 or 6-qt aluminum or enamelware preserving kettle. Stir in rest of ingredients and heat to simmering point; simmer only 2 or 3 min. Fill hot sterile jars almost to top. Seal with glass or enamel-lined lids. Makes 5 pts.

INDIA RELISH

2 lbs cucumbers	1½ cups sugar
2 lbs green tomatoes	2 cups 5% cider vinegar
4½ tsp salt	2¼ tsp salt
1 pt fine-cut celery	¼ cup white mustard seed
1 cup ground onion	2 tsp celery seed
1½ cups ground green *or* red	¼ tsp turmeric
sweet peppers	⅛ tsp each of ground
2 tbsp fine-chopped hot	mace and cloves
red pepper	

Choose firm, green cucumbers about 6 inches long and 1¼ inches in diameter, and tomatoes that have the whitish color acquired just before ripening. Wash vegetables, remove stems, cores and blem-

Press Out Liquid.

ishes. Put quartered tomatoes and cucumbers through a food chopper, using coarse blade. Put into a glass or enamel bowl, add salt, let stand overnight. Next morning turn into a colander, press out liquid and discard. Turn drained vegetables into a 4-qt aluminum or enamelware kettle, add remaining ingredients. Simmer 10 min, stirring often. Pour into sterilized jars and seal with glass or enamel-lined lids. Makes 4½ pts.

UNCOOKED TOMATO CATCHUP

½ peck ripe tomatoes	½ cup white mustard seed
1½ qts finely cut celery	1½ cups brown sugar, pkd
1 qt finely cut onion	1 tsp cloves
3 red apples, chopped fine	1 tsp mace
2 horseradish roots ground	½ tsp cayenne pepper
fine, 1¼ cups	2 tsp cinnamon
½ cup salt	1½ qts 5% cider vinegar

Choose meaty red tomatoes, remove skins and seeds. Chop tomatoes and add celery, onion and apples. Place in a colander and drain overnight. Next morning add remaining ingredients and stir to blend. Pack into hot sterilized jars without cooking. Seal with glass or enamel-lined lids. 4 qts.

PICCALILLI

2 qts chopped green tomatoes
2 tbsp pure, coarse salt
1 qt finely chopped cabbage
4 medium onions, chopped
1 qt finely diced celery
1 pt sliced green peppers

1 pt sliced sweet red peppers
2 hot peppers, chopped
1 tbsp white mustard seed
2½ cups 5% cider vinegar
1¼ cups sugar

Mix chopped tomatoes with salt and let stand 3 to 4 hrs. Turn into a colander and press out and discard liquid. Combine pulp with other vegetables; add mustard seed, vinegar and sugar. Heat just to boiling, then pack into hot sterilized jars. Seal with glass or enamel-lined lids. Makes 3½ to 4 qts.

MISCELLANEOUS

GREEN TOMATO MINCEMEAT

2 lbs green tomatoes
3 lbs tart cooking apples
1½ lbs seedless raisins
3¾ cups light brown sugar, pkd
3½ tsp salt
¾ cup 5% cider vinegar

¼ lb finely chopped suet
1½ tsp cinnamon
1 tsp nutmeg
1 tsp cloves
3 tbsp lemon juice
1 tsp grated lemon rind

Choose tomatoes that are whitish just before ripening. Wash well, remove core and blossom scar, cut into quarters and put into a chopping bowl. Chop medium fine, or if more convenient put through food chopper, using coarse blade. Turn tomatoes into a colander, press out the juice and discard. Turn tomatoes into a 5-qt kettle, add 1 cup of water, heat just to boiling, then drain off water. Again add 1 cup water, heat to boiling, and again drain. Now add 1 cup of water, the apples pared thinly, quartered, cored and chopped fine, or put through the food chopper. Then add raisins, sugar, salt, vinegar and suet, mix thoroughly and cook slowly until tomatoes and apples are transparent in appearance, or about 45 min. Stir often to prevent scorching. Add the spices, lemon juice and rind the last five min of cooking. Pack in hot sterile jars. Tap jar as it is filled to exclude air bubbles. Seal with glass or enamel-lined lids. 2½ qts.

MINCEMEAT

1 qt chopped cooked beef	4 lemons, juice and grated
1 cup chopped suet	rind
2 cups seedless raisins	4 cups brown sugar, pkd
2 cups dried currants, washed	4 tsp salt
2 cups cut candied citron	4 tsp cinnamon
2 qts chopped pared apples	4 tsp allspice
1 qt cider *or* apple juice	¼ cup brandy

Put all ingredients, except brandy, in saucepan. Cook slowly 1¼ hrs, stirring frequently. Stir in brandy. Pack in hot, sterilized qt jars. Seal. Makes 3 qts or 4 pies.

SAUERKRAUT

The characteristic flavor of sauerkraut is developed by the action of certain types of lactic acid bacteria found on raw cabbage. One type grows best at 65° F to 70° F, and as it grows and ferments the activity

raises the temp of the kraut and it becomes slightly acid. Other types of the lactic acid bacteria then develop which increase the acidity and complete the fermentation. If the temp rises much above 75° F at the beginning, the first type of bacteria will not thrive and the flavor of kraut will be disappointing. On the other hand, if the kraut is too cold, fermentation may not be complete.

Soft kraut may be due to the use of too little salt, failure to keep the cabbage covered with brine, or standing in too high a

Pressing Down Cabbage.

temp. If the shredded cabbage is crushed as it is being pkd, it will also tend to be soft. It is important that all equipment be clean as the introduction of undesirable bacteria may develop off flavors. A pink or red tinge is caused by the growth of a yeast. This may be prevented by mixing the salt well with the shredded cabbage and by keeping the kraut covered with the brine at all times.

5 lbs cleaned cabbage makes about ½ gallon kraut.
To each 5 lbs, use 3 tbsp pure coarse salt.

Select mature, sound, firm heads of cabbage. Green heads have more vitamins but the white cabbage makes a more attractive colored kraut. Trim off outer leaves and wash heads. Halve or quarter heads and cut out part of the core, leaving enough to hold the leaves together. The cores may be used if they are shredded fine. Weigh the cabbage in

5 lb lots and shred. Mix thoroughly with the salt. Pack in a clean stone jar, pressing down firmly but being careful not to bruise the cabbage. Brine should rise as the cabbage is pressed down. When the jar is filled to within 3 or 4 inches of the top, cover with trimmed and washed outer leaves. Place a piece of cheesecloth somewhat larger than the top of the jar over the leaves. Next put on a plate or paraffined wooden lid cut to fit inside the jar. On top place a qt jar filled with enough water just to hold the cabbage down under the brine. The brine should not cover the plate or lid, but should come just to the edge. As the brine evaporates, pour water into the jar used as a weight to cause the brine to rise. If the weather has been dry, the cabbage may be low in natural moisture and it may be necessary to add enough brine to cover the kraut. (1 tsp salt to 1 cup of water).

Once a day remove the scum which forms, or at least every other day. The yeasts which form the scum may also cause the kraut to spoil. Remove the cloth, wipe the side of the jar, and wash the plate or board. Replace, using a clean cloth. Wash and boil the one removed and use the next time. It takes 4 to 6 weeks to cure the kraut at a temp best for good flavor—65° to 70° F.

The kraut may be kept in the stone jar or it may be canned. If kept in the jar, remove the lid and cloth, clean off the scum and pour melted paraffin over the surface of the brine. Each time the seal is broken to take out some of the kraut, the paraffin should be reheated and the jar sealed again. Or the kraut may be canned. Heat to simmering —do not boil. Pack in clean hot jars, cover with hot kraut juice, leaving ¼ inch space at the top. Process in the boiling water bath, 25 min for pts, 30 min for qts.

GLASS JAR SAUERKRAUT

A good way to make delicious crisp sauerkraut in small quantities that will keep for months. An excellent appetizer.

Use tender firm sound cabbage heads. Let stand at room temp a day to wilt a little so cabbage will not break when shredded. Trim off outer leaves to obtain clean heads, then wash quickly in cold water. Cut heads in half, then shred on kraut cutting board. Pack shredded cabbage into clean glass jars, tamping down with a clean wooden spoon. Fill jar full so when lid is on there will be no air space at top of jar. Add 1 tsp pure coarse salt and 1 tsp sugar to each qt jar, then add boiling water to just cover cabbage. Jars should be only partially sealed for first 3 or 4 weeks. Set in a cool, dark place. Some juice flows out during fermentation. Refill jars after 2 weeks with brine made by adding 1 tbsp salt to 1 pt of water. Seal tight and let fermentation continue. The best kraut results when jars are kept at a temp of 70° F or a little lower for perfect fermentation. It takes 4 to 6 weeks for kraut to cure perfectly.

Salads

The idea of eating a salad every day is a modern nutritional concept, but history tells us that people have been enjoying the foods that go into salads for four or five thousand years. The Egyptians used cucumbers, garlic and onions with such success that their oppressed Hebrew slaves yearned for them even after they were free men in the wilderness. Farm families in this country have enjoyed cucumbers, onions, cabbage, lettuce, green onions, radishes, and raw turnips all summer long for generations, and even the early Americans learned to store cabbage and other root vegetables in cellars and pits in the earth to be eaten during the winter months. Raw vegetables were included in the menu for a number of reasons: their crispness was a pleasant contrast to the soft foods in the meal; their fresh flavor seemed to highlight the whole meal; they were usually slightly tart and peppy and perked up the appetite for the foods that were eaten with them, and they were beautiful in color and form and pleased the sight as well as the appetite.

★　★　★　★

FOR generations, Americans enjoyed eating green onions, radishes, sliced cucumbers, tomatoes and cole slaw . . . and then vitamins were discovered. And after that discovery followed the research that has shown vegetables and fruits to be highly important sources of many of the vitamins, and that they contribute their highest vitamin content when they are eaten raw. "Eat a salad every day" is a slogan that is now shouted by nutritionists all over the land. Starting with the original salad materials, new recipes were developed and perfected. Now almost all raw vegetables and fruits have been found to be delicious in flavor and interesting in texture when used as salad material and there are many other foods—meat, fish, poultry, cheese, nuts, eggs (and even some confections such as marshmallows and red hot candies) that are now being incorporated into delicious salads.

The tremendous expansion of types of salads have made various classifications necessary. One classification is based on the temp at which a salad is served: *Chilled* salads, *Frozen* salads, and *Hot* salads. Another classification is based on the method of serving the salad: *Bowl* salads, *Decorative* salads, *Platter* salads, and *Individual* salads. Another type of classification is based on a particular kind of ingredient that is added: *Molded* salads (gelatin

1114

added), *Whole Meal* salads (containing both meat and vegetables, or chicken and fruit in addition to the greens), *Fruit* salads, *Chicken* salads, etc.

No matter what kind of a salad is being made, it can never be any better than every particle of food and every spoonful of dressing that go into it. The salad material must be chosen for freshness and high quality and prepared with care. A salad is no place to sneak in the damaged leftover leaves of lettuce, the limp radishes or cucumbers, the bleached, wilted cress or parsley, the dried up pieces of cheese or meat, or a bit of rancid salad dressing. The selection of the foods, the care of these foods in the home, their preparation for the salad, the assembly of the ingredients and finally the immediate service, all influence the eye and appetite appeal as well as the vitamin content of salads that are served at your table.

SELECTION OF THE FOOD

In general, the food selected for salads must be of the highest quality possible and as fresh as practical. Vegetables should be gathered from the home garden or bought from the store the same day they are to be used, just long enough ahead of time so that they can be cleaned and stored properly to be crisp and cool. Since such a large variety of foods are used in salads, their selection has been discussed in the separate sections concerning the different foods, such as "Buying Fruits and Vegetables" in the *Homemaker's Handbook,* p 75, "The Answers to Your Questions about Nuts," p 120, about "Fats and Oils," p 106, etc.; the buying of Meats, p. 788, of Poultry, p 1028 and of Fish, p 687, and a discussion of canned foods on p 136. The three vinegars that lend the most character to salads are malt, cider and tarragon vinegar; these and other vinegars and their uses for unusual salad flavors are discussed on p 134.

CARE OF FOOD IN THE HOME

After the food is selected and brought into the home, it must be cared for immediately and stored so that all of its nutritional excellence as well as its fresh appeal will be at its highest point when the foods are served.

The care of food in the home is considered of such importance that a special chapter has been devoted to it starting on p 140.

PREPARATION OF FOOD FOR SALADS

The preparation of salad ingredients should be done just shortly before the salad is to be combined and served. Salad greens should be torn or cut into bite-size pieces and then dressed and served immediately, or stored *without dressing* the shortest time possible tightly covered in the refrigerator until ready to serve. Fruits that are to be pared and sectioned, sliced or diced should either be arranged directly on salad plates or in a bowl for immediate service, or arranged in one layer on a shallow tray lined with a sheet of waxed paper and a second sheet of paper over the fruit. They can then be stored for a short time in the refrigerator if necessary, and when ready to use can be picked up carefully with a spatula or the fingers without spoiling the shape and destroying the beauty. Chicken, veal, shrimps, lobsters, etc., should be stored in the refrigerator in their cooking liquid until assembly time to keep them juicy and plump. Bones, skin, gristle or excess fat should always be removed entirely from meat or fish, fresh or canned and the meat cut into neat cubes or julienne strips and the fish flaked. Canned foods should always be chilled in the can and opened and drained just before they are added to the salad. Foods like onions, cucumbers and tomatoes may be peeled ahead of time and wrapped in waxed paper but should be sliced or cut directly onto the serving plate or into the bowl. Foods that discolor rapidly such as apples, bananas, and avocado should be cut with a stainless steel knife, and always at the last possible moment. They should always be sprinkled with lemon or some other citrus juice, or combined quickly with some acid fruit. All foods that darken readily are usually mild or bland, and the flavor as well as the appearance is greatly improved by the addition of the tart fruit or juice. Sometimes it may seem impractical to delay so much of the salad preparation to the last min when there is gravy to be made, milk to pour, platters to serve and a number of other duties that precede a meal in the final stages, but it is always possible to prepare, cover with a damp cloth and store most of the ingredients *separately* ahead of time, and then to quickly combine or arrange the salad the last min, and finally add the dressing either at the table or just before it is brought in. The extra care will require a little planning but will be generously compensated for by your family's increased enthusiasm for salads and the knowledge that their health as well as their appetites are benefited.

ASSEMBLY OF INGREDIENTS

Arrangement of salad materials on a plate should be done with a sort of careful carelessness to avoid the appearance of having been handled or pushed and patted into place. Once a salad is on the plate, it should never be rearranged or it will look tired, overworked and unattractive. When arranging several salads, make use of the assembly-line technique and arrange one ingredient on all the plates before adding the next ingredient to any of them. Use a large enough plate so that the salad will not be overcrowded or difficult to eat. Apply the final touch of dressing or other bit of garnish with a spontaneous touch and bring them into the table to the seated diners. Special techniques that apply to the various classifications of salads are discussed separately preceding the recipes.

WHEN TO SERVE AND HOW TO EAT SALADS

At formal dinners, the salad is served alone following the main course and should always be very light, either crisp greens, or grapefruit and watercress, etc. Salad and dessert can sometimes be combined by serving a mixed fruit salad, or frozen fruit salad with toasted crackers and cheese.

More and more however, salads are served informally either at the beginning of the meal as an appetizer, or with the main course. In either case, it is desirable to supply an extra fork for the salad and preferably a salad fork. It is also perfectly proper and highly recommended that a knife be used to cut the lettuce. The use of a knife makes it easy and "safe" to eat every shred of lettuce on the plate and avoids the embarrassing accidents that occur so often trying to cut lettuce with a fork.

Hearty salads that are served as a main course of a luncheon or dinner are served like any other main course, after the soup or appetizer and before the dessert.

Young children are not capable of maneuvering a fork carefully enough to eat a salad gracefully and too often get weary of trying and declare "they don't want it" from discouragement. Cut their vegetables of a size and shape that can be easily picked up in their small hands and omit the dressing . . . they probably won't like it anyway . . . and watch them enjoy the crunchy "noise" that helps their new teeth and sound bodies to grow strong and healthy. It's one of the surest ways to instill a lifelong appreciation of vegetables of all kinds, and they'll do a neater job of picking it up in their fingers than they ever did with a fork.

BOWL SALADS

Bowl salads are usually a combination of vegetables, but they may also be made principally of fruits. The vegetables should be the type that do not easily mush up or wilt quickly such as head lettuce, romaine, French or curly endive, escarole, sliced radishes, sliced cucumbers, green peppers, and celery. Boston, Bibb Lettuce and leaf lettuce have such thin delicate leaves that they are not well adapted to this type of salad.

The ingredients should always be cleaned, crisped, and prepared just before the salad is to be served. Most discriminating salad eaters insist that they like the flavor of crisp greens that are broken rather than cut. Broken greens do not present as orderly appearance as those that are cut neatly, but since many of the other ingredients are sliced, the broken greens do not detract from the beauty if they are preferred. Special care should be taken not to chop up all the ingredients so they are no longer recognizable. Cucumbers may be sliced pared or unpared, green peppers should be cut in thin circles, radishes sliced thin, celery cut crosswise in at least quarter inch slices, and onions in thin rings. Very ripe tomatoes are objectionable because they mush up readily as the salad is tossed and make the dressing watery, but if firm red tomatoes with few seeds are used and cut in thick lengthwise wedges, there is nothing that adds more beauty and lift to the salad than these spots of brilliant red.

A bowl salad may be combined entirely in the kitchen or assembled at the table. Making and tossing a salad at the table is a ceremony that is enjoyed by many men and women. Those people who pride themselves on the art of salad making at the table like to have the lovely vegetables brought to the table on a tray with an empty bowl and the salad fork and spoon. They may use either a prepared French dressing, or vinegar, oil and seasonings to make the dressing at the table. The bowl may be rubbed first with a cut clove of garlic or a stale crust of bread may be added on which a cut clove of garlic was rubbed. Then in goes some dressing which has been prepared right in the bowl of the spoon. The lettuce is broken into the bowl followed by a layer of all the other vegetables. Then more dressing is concocted in the salad spoon and drizzled over the vegetables. The order is repeated until enough salad ingredients accumulate to serve the desired number and then the deft tossing begins. The vegetables are lifted and tossed until every piece is coated with a thin film of the dressing and then served onto individual plates or salad bowls. Anyone attempting this type of preparation must be experienced and have a keen sense of seasonings and proportions of ingredients that go into the dressing. A second system is to put the freshly prepared vegetables into the bowl, prepare the best possible dressing in the kitchen but leave out the salt and pepper. Then this lovely bowl arrangement and the salt and pepper in individual grinders can be brought to the table so that the master of the situation can grind first salt, then the pepper over the vegetables, then drizzles on just the amount of dressing needed and tosses to coat the vegetables. In either case, it is important that the bowl is not filled so full that there is danger of flipping the vegetables onto the table. A third method is to assemble the salad and toss with the dressing in the kitchen. Then the host or hostess can serve it at the table. This latter method permits the top to be garnished beautifully. In any instance, the salad should be served promptly after it is tossed.

A fruit salad bowl should be assembled in a way that will require no tossing. All the fruits should be prepared by peeling, paring, slicing, sectioning or dicing and arranged in one layer on a flat tray. Greens should be broken and placed in bottom of the bowl. Then alternate layers of fruit are carefully laid in the bowl. When one complete layer of all the food is in the bowl, it should be drizzled with the dressing so that every piece is coated. This alternate arrangement of greens and fruit drizzled with dressing is repeated until the bowl is filled. The top layer should be arranged as attractively as possible with the idea of assembling the colors to give the effect of a lovely garnish. Since the dressing is thinned by the fruit juices and is absorbed to some extent by the open texture of the fruit, it comes into contact with all the fruit without tossing. Attractively prepared fruit salad bowls are especially beautiful for buffet or holiday meals.

TOSSED OR FRENCH BOWL SALAD

1 solid head lettuce, 1 lb
1 small cucumber, pared
2 branches celery
3 tender green onions
6 crisp, red radishes

2 small firm tomatoes, peeled
1 clove garlic
1 slice very stale bread
⅓ cup French Dressing,
p 1200

Wash vegetables thoroughly, drain, and remove tops, stems, blemished parts, etc. Chill until just before serving time. Then cut clove of garlic in half and rub thoroughly over bread; drop bread into bottom of salad bowl. Pour in a third of the dressing. Break lettuce in chunks (flavor is better when broken than when separated leaf by leaf); slice cucumber and cut celery in ½-inch lengths, and green onion in ¼-inch lengths and add to the bowl. Drizzle the rest of the dressing over the top. Push salad fork and spoon under mixture on opposite sides, lift up, and turn over. Repeat this tossing motion until ingredients are well coated with dressing. Remove slice of bread, garnish bowl with sliced radishes, and wedges of tomato. Serve immediately on individual plates or in small salad bowls. 5 servings.

FRESH FRUIT SALAD BOWL No. 1

1 solid head lettuce, 1 lb
2 ripe avocados, peeled,
   sliced
4 tomatoes, quartered
4 oranges, peeled, sliced

1 medium cantaloupe, *or*
   honey-dew melon
½ cup pitted ripe olives
Celery Seed Dressing
Watercress

Line a salad bowl with crisp lettuce leaves or make a bed of broken pieces of lettuce. Arrange alternately slices of avocado, quarters of tomato, and slices of orange. Drizzle Celery Seed Dressing, p 1199 or Lime Honey Dressing, p 1202 over the layers. Continue until bowl is filled. Cut melon in cubes or balls and top with melon, ripe olives, and a few thin slices of orange. Drizzle remaining dressing over salad at the table. Be sure bowl and ingredients are chilled, and serve on chilled plates with sprigs of watercress or mint. 10 servings.

FRESH FRUIT SALAD BOWL No. 2

2 medium-size grapefruit
2 medium-size seedless
   oranges, sliced
3 sweet red plums
4 medium, juicy, firm freestone peaches

Lime Honey, p 1202, *or*
Celery Seed Dressing,
   p 1199
1 medium-size cantaloupe
1 pt choice blackberries
Leaf *or* head lettuce *or*
romaine

Wash all fruits, then chill thoroughly. An hour before serving, start preparing fruits. First, pare grapefruit, then oranges. Carefully section them, letting juice drip into a bowl. Spread sections out on a flat tray lined with waxed paper. Pour juice over fruit. Cut plums in half, remove seeds with care, lay plums on tray; return to refrigerator. Pare peaches with a stainless knife, then dip in dressing to prevent discoloring. Cut melon in half, remove seeds, cut in half-inch strips, then cut the strips crosswise into cubes. To assemble salad, line a large flat bowl with lettuce or romaine. Cut a pared peach in half, discard pit and then slice halves neatly in thirds, letting them drop directly into bowl. Use a pancake turner to put some grapefruit sections on top of peaches, then melon cubes and orange slices. Drizzle dressing over the fruit generously. Then start again by slicing another peach and repeat with layers of fruit and dressing until all the prepared fruit is used up. Last garnish with the plums arranged skin side up and a spontaneous heap of blackberries in the center. Drizzle dressing over the top and serve at once without tossing. 5 generous servings.

Note: Fresh julienned roast chicken or turkey breast may be heaped up in the center on top of the salad just before adding the blackberries.

KOHLRABI BOWL SALAD

2 large *or* 3 small kohlrabi
½ cup grated carrot
1 small green pepper,
   slivered

1 large tomato cut in wedges
¼ tsp salt
⅓ cup Tomato French
   Dressing, p 1202

Choose tender, fine textured kohlrabi. Strip off outer skin. Shred coarsely on sharp grater. Combine with rest of vegetables in a mixing bowl. Sprinkle with salt and toss lightly. Drizzle on French dressing, toss again and turn into individual salad bowls or on plates to serve immediately. 4 servings.

RAW SPINACH SALAD

½ lb tender spinach
2 firm, red tomatoes, diced
5 green onions, sliced
   (include half of tops)
½ cup diced celery

½ tsp salt
French dressing
Lettuce, if desired
1 hard-cooked egg, sliced

Have all ingredients chilled before starting salad. Carefully wash spinach leaves through 3 or 4 waters. Drain well and chill. Shred coarsely with kitchen scissors and combine with tomatoes, green onions, celery and salt. Drizzle dressing over the top and toss lightly until vegetables are well coated with dressing. Garnish with slices of hard-cooked egg. Serve immediately on individual plates. 5 servings.

Note: Recipe for French Dressing on p 1200.

WATERCRESS SALAD

1 bunch crisp watercress	2 slices crisp bacon crumbled
1 hard-cooked egg, chopped	5 red radishes
1 tsp chopped onion	½ cup French dressing, p 1200

Wash cress thoroughly, shake gently to remove excess water and separate sprigs. Discard any damaged leaves and heavy roots, and arrange loosely in a large salad bowl. Add the chopped egg, onion, bacon and sliced radishes; pour dressing over all, and toss lightly until cress is coated with dressing and ingredients are well mixed. Serve immediately. 5 servings.

DECORATIVE SALADS

Special occasions are highlighted by elaborate decorations and there are times when it is appropriate to serve a fancy salad that is decorated by using a pastry tube to pipe on cream cheese, etc., or that has the ingredients cut into fancy shapes. It is not the sort of thing that is done every day anymore than you would serve a wedding cake every time you baked a cake. However, even a fancy decorated salad *can* and *should* have the fresh unhandled look that is the goal of all salads. It is perhaps a little more difficult to learn to use your hand spontaneously and freely when making a hyacinth salad, for example, p 1122, than it is when making a bowl salad, but careful planning and a few rehearsals will convince you that it can be done. It is always a good plan to draw a rough sketch on paper and then practice with a salad or two long enough ahead of time to discover just how the work can be done with speed and ease to get the desired effect. Then the procedure is the same as for any arranged salad. The ingredients are all prepared and stored separately, the cheese colored if necessary, and the plates chosen. Then as short a time before serving as possible, spread out all the plates on an uncluttered table, and begin the "assembly-line" procedure of placing a lettuce cup or other base on each plate, then all the fruit that is to be the flower for example, all the stems, all the leaves, etc., then pipe on the cheese or apply whatever garnish is to be used and carry them to the table. After the salads are once assembled, never rearrange them or try to patch a decoration. It rarely improves the appearance and is more apt to make the salad appear messy. A slight variation from one salad to another adds a charm of imperfection like the beauty of a hand-turned dish over one that is machine made.

BUNNY SALAD

Lay canned or fresh pared pear halves rounded side up on a bed of finely shredded lettuce. (If fresh pears are used, sprinkle pared surface with lemon juice to prevent discoloration.) In the narrow end of the pear, insert two blanched almonds to simulate ears. Use pink jellied candy cut into shape for eyes and nose with a fluff of marshmallow for tail. Serve with mayonnaise blended with cream cheese or whipped cream.

CANDLE SALAD

Lay a slice of pineapple on a bed of lettuce for each salad. Remove skin from banana, cut in half crosswise and dip in lemon juice to preserve color. Insert banana in hole of pineapple to stand upright. Place blanched almond or half of maraschino cherry into tip of banana for candle flame. Stand on end a quarter slice of pineapple or clip a ring of green pepper over edge of pineapple to simulate a handle on candle holder. Note: If blanched almond is used, it may be lit before serving.

CHRISTMAS TREE SALAD

Spread rounded side of canned pear halves with softened cream cheese. Sprinkle generously with chopped parsley. Place green side up on an individual salad plate. Cut stars from maraschino cherries and place one at the tip of each pear. Place a whole pitted date at base to simulate the trunk. Dot "tree" with tiny bits of cherry, or pomegranate seeds, and silver "shot" for lights and decorations. Add finely shredded endive at base.

GIRLS' PARTY SALAD

Use recipe for Pineapple Lime Velvet, p 1166, and mold in individual dome-shaped custard cups or deep fancy individual molds. Unmold on bed of shredded crisp lettuce. Place a small china or glass doll (half-figure from waist up) on top of each mold. Doll will appear as though she were wearing an old-fashioned long bouffant skirt. Have cream cheese colored to harmonize with the other colors and pipe ribbons from waist to hem of the "skirt." (Use a No. 26 open star tube for piping.) Serve at once or keep chilled if necessary to hold for a short while. If weather is warm, add an additional tsp of plain gelatin for each pkg of flavored gelatin called for.

HYACINTH SALAD

Cut a stalk from a lengthwise slice of pared, fresh pineapple or use canned pineapple fingers and use an open star tube, No. 23 or 24. Pipe rosettes of softened cream cheese tinted delicately pink or blue all over the pineapple to resemble the hyacinth spike of flowers. Use half a thick slice from a large orange for each pot. Make leaves from French endive or romaine. See illustration.

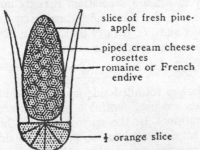

slice of fresh pineapple

piped cream cheese rosettes

romaine or French endive

½ orange slice

LILY OF THE VALLEY SALAD

Make leaves from romaine or French endive and lay long chives inside the leaves for stems. Pipe softened cream cheese along one side of each stem in dots for flowers. Use a single-hole pastry tube. Place a slice of congealed cherry, strawberry, or raspberry gelatin on bottom for the pot. See illustration.

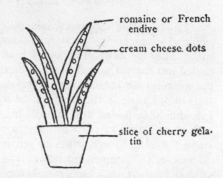

romaine or French endive

cream cheese. dots

slice of cherry gelatin

SANTA CLAUS SALAD

Choose large round apples that will stay firm when cooked (see chart 11). Pare and remove core very carefully making as small a hole as possible. Poach in sugar syrup tinted red, p 169, or cinnamon candy (red hots) syrup, p 559. Poach carefully just until tender. Apples must retain their plump round shape. Chill. Lightly shape cream cheese into balls for the head. Top with a half of maraschino cherry round-side up for the cap. Cut tiny rounds of ripe olives for eyes (or use appropriate sized hard candies) and a tiny piece of maraschino cherry or a cinnamon candy for the nose. Chill separately. When ready to serve, place a chilled apple on a bed of shredded lettuce on individual salad plates. Top with a cream cheese ball. Have softened cream cheese in a pastry tube and quickly pipe on "whiskers" and a band of "white fur" down the front and around the middle. Serve at once.

TULIP SALAD

Make flower stems from strips of green pepper, celery or romaine; and leaves (one on each side) of French endive or romaine. For the flower use one-half a peeled tomato sliced lengthwise and laid rounded side up, then cut in the shape of a tulip flower or profile. Pipe on cream cheese to outline petals. For the pot, use one-fourth of a peeled avocado laid rounded side up. (Dip avocado in lemon juice to preserve color.) See illustration.

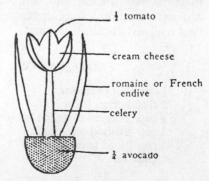

½ tomato

cream cheese

romaine or French endive

celery

¼ avocado

FROZEN SALADS

Frozen salads usually contain salad dressing or mayonnaise and often whipped cream, cream cheese or cottage cheese and whole, sliced, or puréed fruits. They are more often sweet than tart, and are either frozen solid or chilled just enough so that they can be cut into attractive thick slices. Usually the mixtures are turned into refrigerator trays that have been lined neatly with waxed paper so the salad can be unmolded smoothly. All solid ingredients should be folded into the soft blended mixture lightly but thoroughly, so that each slice of salad contains some of all kinds of fruit or nuts that are in the salad. Frozen salads are particularly suitable for buffet suppers and dinners, or for summer luncheons. They are often served as a combination salad and dessert; sometimes merely topping it with whipped cream or mayonnaise will determine whether it is eaten as a salad or as a dessert. Many people like to serve and eat it when it is frozen very solid and the pieces of fruit are icy, but it can also be cut and placed on the plates about 15 min before serving, so it will still retain its shape and be chilled but most of the iciness will be gone. Frozen salads may be held overnight successfully if they are made late in the day, but for the greatest appeal they should never be held longer.

FROZEN CHEESE AND DATE SALAD

½ cup evaporated milk
2 tbsp lemon juice
3 oz pkg cream cheese
¼ cup mayonnaise

½ cup sliced dates
½ cup crushed pineapple
Lettuce

Chill milk in refrigerator tray until ice crystals are formed. Remove to a chilled bowl and beat until smooth. Add lemon juice and continue beating until very stiff. Have cheese softened and blended with the mayonnaise until smooth. Fold thoroughly but lightly into whipped milk, then add dates and pineapple. Turn into waxed paper-lined refrigerator tray. Freeze until firm, at least 4 hrs. Cut in slices or sqs and serve plain on lettuce or top with mayonnaise that has been folded into whipped cream. 6 servings.

FROZEN FRUIT AND NUT SALAD

1 cup evaporated milk
2 tbsp lemon juice
1 cup creamed cottage cheese
1 cup crushed pineapple
¼ cup sliced maraschino
   cherries

½ cup diced peaches, canned
   or fresh
1 banana, mashed with 2 tsp
   lemon juice
¼ cup chopped nutmeats
2 to 3 tbsp sugar
Watercress

Chill milk in refrigerator tray until ice crystals are formed. Transfer to a cold bowl, add lemon juice and beat until very stiff. Combine cheese, fruit, nutmeats and sugar and then fold lightly but thoroughly into the stiffly beaten milk. Turn into a waxed paper-lined refrigerator tray and freeze until firm (at least 4 hrs). Cut into thick slices, remove paper, place on watercress. Serve as is, or with dressing made by combining ½ cup mayonnaise with ½ tsp grated lemon rind, a squeeze of lemon juice and ⅛ tsp paprika. 6 servings.

FROZEN FRUIT SALAD

3 oz pkg cream cheese	¹⁄₁₆ tsp salt
¼ cup mayonnaise	½ cup seedless raisins,
2 tbsp lemon juice	plumped, p 165
⅔ cup whipping cream, chilled	¼ cup sliced candied cherries
	¾ cup crushed pineapple
½ cup sugar	Endive or watercress

Soften cheese and blend thoroughly with mayonnaise and lemon juice. Turn cream into a cold bowl and beat until stiff. Fold in the salad dressing mixture but only until just mixed, then fold in the remaining ingredients except greens and mix lightly but thoroughly. Turn into a waxed paper-lined refrigerator tray and freeze until firm (at least 4 hrs). Cut into thick slices, remove paper, place on endive and serve plain or topped with additional mayonnaise. 6 to 8 servings.

FROZEN FRUIT SALAD SUPREME

4 canned pear halves	6 marshmallows, cut in
2 seedless oranges	quarters
1 cup whole strawberries	1 tsp lemon juice
½ cup crushed pineapple	1 cup whipping cream
¼ cup moist shredded coconut	½ cup mayonnaise

Cut pear halves to make quarters lengthwise. Pare and section oranges and if berries are very large, cut in half. Combine fruits, coconut, marshmallows, and lemon juice. Whip cream until stiff, add mayonnaise, continue beating until blended. Combine with fruits lightly but thoroughly. Turn into waxed paper-lined freezing tray (1 qt capacity). Freeze at least 4 hrs (until firm). Cut with a sharp knife into slices about 1¼ inches thick, remove paper and serve on lettuce. 8 servings.

Note: If small refrigerator trays are used, cut salad slices thicker. Excellent for party luncheon or dessert salad.

Some people prefer to cut this salad while frozen and arrange it on lettuce, then let stand at room temp for 10 to 15 min before serving if desired. It will still be cold, but the iciness will have disappeared from the fruit.

Note: Recipe for Mayonnaise on p 1202.

HOT SALADS

The three most famous hot salads are Potato, Celery Root, and the Endive and Potato Salad made famous by the Pennsylvania Dutch. Many new variations have been developed recently that are proving to be just as appreciated for cool weather meals as the three old-timers.

The hot salad dressing is usually made over a very low flame, and the salad ingredients added to the skillet. The ingredients are tossed carefully or the skillet rocked back and forth to coat each piece of food with dressing with as little manipulation as possible. The ingredients should be selected with every care and prepared with the idea of preserving the shape and beauty as much as possible. For example, a waxy type of potato should be chosen for hot potato salad and then cooked until just barely done so that it may be sliced neatly. The heat that is applied during marinating will finish cooking the slices. The potatoes may be cooked in the skins, then cooled before peeling and slicing, or pared first and then cooked. Some feel that pared potatoes absorb salt better and give a better seasoned salad, others believe potatoes cooked in jackets have better flavor. Bacon or ham is usually sautéed carefully to obtain the fat necessary for making the dressing and the meat is added to the salad. The addition of a crisp garnish at the last min gives these salads their greatest appeal. Sliced radishes are especially appropriate, also crisp greens such as fresh, thick, cut-up leaves of romaine, head lettuce, cucumber, green pepper, or the thick, juicy midribs of endive. The salad must be served promptly while texture and flavor are at their best. It is a good plan to make this salad in a skillet that is attractive enough to be brought to the table on a heavy platter. It not only helps to preserve the form of the vegetables if they do not have to be transferred, but it helps to keep the salad hot and palatable to the last bite.

HOT BAKED BEANS AND SAUERKRAUT SALAD

2½ cups sauerkraut, 1 lb
⅔ cup water
½ tsp caraway seed
1 tsp sugar

2 tbsp bacon drippings
2 cups baked beans, 1 lb 2 oz
2 tsp finely chopped parsley

Combine kraut, water, caraway, sugar and drippings preferably in a pottery skillet. Simmer over low heat 10 min tossing the kraut frequently. Add beans and mix lightly into kraut and continue to cook over low heat until beans are thoroughly heated through. Serve at once in the same skillet. Sprinkle the parsley over the salad the last min before serving. 4 servings.

HOT CAULIFLOWER SALAD

1 head cauliflower, 1½ lbs	½ tsp salt
2 oz bacon, 3 slices	1 tsp sugar
1 tsp flour	½ tsp caraway seed, crushed
2 tbsp vinegar	

Remove coarse leaves from cauliflower and trim stalk. Soak cauliflower 15 min in salted water (2 tsp salt to each qt of water). Drain, rinse thoroughly, split stalk so each portion is attached to each floweret with some tiny green leaves. Cover cauliflower with boiling water, add salt (1 tsp to pt of water) and cook uncovered 6 to 7 min. Drain and keep hot. Meanwhile, cut bacon into ½-inch lengths with kitchen scissors and sauté over low heat until done. Remove from fat onto absorbent paper to drain. Blend the flour into drippings, then add remaining ingredients. Simmer ½ min, stirring constantly. Pour over cauliflower turned into a warm salad bowl. Toss lightly but thoroughly. Sprinkle with bacon. Serve immediately. 4 servings.

HOT CELERY CABBAGE SALAD

1 small stalk celery cabbage, 1 lb	¼ tsp salt
4 slices bacon, 3½ oz	1 medium onion, sliced thin
1 tbsp flour	1 tbsp chopped pimiento
½ cup water	2 tbsp chopped green pepper
¼ cup vinegar	¼ cup mayonnaise
2 tsp sugar	½ cup ham, cut julienne style

Wash and drain celery cabbage and cut into thin crosswise slices; place in a large salad bowl. Pan-fry bacon in a small saucepan until done. Remove bacon, drain on absorbent paper and crumble coarsely when crisp. Sprinkle bacon bits over celery. Blend flour well into fat remaining (about 3 tbsp) in pan. Add liquid gradually and stir over medium heat until smooth and thickened. Add sugar and salt. Add remaining vegetables to celery cabbage and toss lightly to mix. Top with mayonnaise, pour hot vinegar mixture over salad. Toss lightly and quickly. Garnish with ham and serve immediately while still warm. 5 servings.

HOT CELERY ROOT SALAD

1 celery root, about 1⅓ lbs	1 tbsp flour
1½ cups boiling water	⅓ cup cooking liquid
2 tsp salt	2 tbsp vinegar
2 slices bacon, cut fine	2 tsp sugar
2 tbsp chopped onion	Chopped parsley

Wash and pare celery root. Cut julienne style and put in saucepan. Add boiling water and salt, and cook covered until just tender, about 10 to 12 min. Drain, saving ⅓ cup of the liquid. Sauté bacon until done and remove to absorbent paper to drain. Sauté onion in bacon drippings until soft, then blend in the flour and add the ⅓ cup of cooking liquid and vinegar. Cook with constant stirring until the sauce boils. Stir in sugar. Pour hot dressing over the drained celery root. Sprinkle with parsley and bacon bits. Serve at once while still warm. 4 servings.

HOT ENDIVE AND POTATO SALAD

1 medium bunch curly endive, about 1 lb	¼ tsp salt
	1 tsp sugar
2 slices bacon	½ tsp paprika
1 tbsp flour	2 tsp freshly grated onion
½ cup water	1 cup diced cooked potatoes, 2 medium
3 tbsp vinegar	

Wash and trim endive, shake free of excess water. Tear into bite-size pieces. Pan-fry bacon in a 9 or 10-inch skillet until done. Remove to absorbent paper to drain, then crumble into bits. Blend flour into drippings remaining in pan. Add liquids gradually and simmer until mixture is thick and smooth, stirring constantly. Add seasonings and onion; remove from heat, then add endive and potato. Toss lightly and quickly, then turn into a warm salad bowl (let hot water stand in it; pour out and wipe dry quickly) or serve directly from skillet. Sprinkle top with bacon. Serve immediately. 4 to 5 servings.

HOT MACARONI SALAD

4 slices bacon, 3½ oz	1 qt hot, cooked macaroni, 8 oz pkg
2 tbsp flour	
1 tbsp sugar	1 medium sized onion, sliced
1½ tsp salt	½ cup thinly sliced celery
⅔ cup vinegar	2 tbsp chopped parsley
¼ cup water	4 hard-cooked eggs, diced
	Romaine *or* watercress

Pan-fry bacon until delicately browned. Remove from fat onto absorbent paper to drain. Blend flour with drippings remaining in pan. Add sugar and salt, then gradually add liquids, stirring constantly until mixture boils and thickens. Crumble up bacon into small pieces and add with the next five ingredients. Toss lightly to mix. Serve hot directly from skillet. Garnish with crisp tips of romaine or sprigs of watercress. 4 generous servings.

HOT NAVY BEAN SALAD No. 1

½ lb navy beans	2 tbsp vinegar
5 cups cold water	1 medium onion, sliced
1 tsp salt	1 cup chopped celery
1 tbsp flour	¼ cup sliced radishes
½ tsp sugar	3 tbsp Mayonnaise, p 1202
½ tsp salt	Romaine *or* endive

Simmer beans in the 5 cups of water with 1 tsp salt for 2 or 2½ hrs or until tender, not mushy. Drain and reserve liquid. (There should be ½ cup). Meanwhile, combine flour, sugar and the ½ tsp salt in a saucepan; add the ½ cup reserved bean liquid and vinegar gradually, stirring to keep smooth. Cook until smooth and thickened. Combine beans, vegetables, mayonnaise in a warmed salad bowl. Pour the hot vinegar mixture over salad. Toss lightly and serve immediately while still warm. Garnish with crisp tips of romaine. 4 servings.

HOT NAVY BEAN SALAD No. 2

2 slices bacon	⅓ cup chopped celery and
¼ cup vinegar	tops
2 tsp sugar	¼ cup chopped green pepper
¼ tsp salt	2 cups curly endive, cut fine
2 cups cooked navy beans	
and their liquid, 1⅛ cups	
raw beans	

Cut bacon in ½-inch lengths with kitchen scissors and sauté in skillet until nearly done and delicately brown. Add vinegar, sugar, salt and beans and simmer for 5 min. Do not boil. Add remaining ingredients and toss together lightly. Remove from heat and serve immediately directly from skillet, if desired. 4 servings.

HOT MASHED POTATO SALAD No. 1

4 slices bacon	3 tbsp malt vinegar
2 tsp finely chopped onion	¼ cup mayonnaise
1 tsp celery salt	2½ cups hot mashed potatoes,
½ tsp salt	unseasoned
¼ tsp pepper	1 tbsp finely chopped parsley
1 tsp sugar	

Sauté bacon until done. Remove to absorbent paper to drain. Combine 2 tbsp of the bacon drippings drained from the skillet with the next seven ingredients and add to the potatoes and mix thoroughly. Fold the parsley in at the last. Serve in a heated salad bowl. Crumble the bacon over the top and serve at once. 4 servings.

HOT MASHED POTATO SALAD No. 2

3 cups unseasoned, riced, hot	1 tbsp chopped green pepper
potatoes	1 tbsp chopped radishes
¼ cup mayonnaise	½ cup finely cut celery
2 tsp vinegar	¼ cup finely cut green onion
¾ tsp salt	

Combine all ingredients. Stir lightly to mix. Serve warm or cold. May also be packed into molds, chilled and unmolded to serve. 4 servings.

HOT POTATO SALAD No. 1

¼ lb bacon, about 5 slices
3 tbsp flour
1½ cups water
⅓ to ½ cup vinegar
1½ tsp salt
4 tsp sugar
7 large potatoes, 2¼ lbs,
  cooked in skins in salted
  water

1 cup sliced celery
2 medium onions, sliced
1 small cucumber, 5½ inches,
  pared and sliced
Curly endive or romaine,
  about ¼ lb
4 or 5 radishes, sliced,
  ⅓ cup

Pan-fry bacon until done in a 10-inch skillet. Remove slices, drain on absorbent paper and crumble into small pieces when crisp. Measure drippings remaining in pan; there should be about 7 tbsp. To this, add flour and blend until smooth. Add water and vinegar gradually, and cook until mixture is thickened. Stir to keep smooth. Add seasonings. Pare and slice potatoes and add to sauce in pan alternately with celery, onions, cucumbers and greens that have been broken into bite-size pieces. Toss lightly or rock the skillet back and forth to bring the dressing in contact with all the vegetables. Keep skillet over very low heat during the mixing. Remove from heat, top with radishes and bacon bits and garnish with tips of greens. Serve immediately while still warm directly from skillet. 5 servings.

HOT POTATO SALAD No. 2

2 strips bacon
2 tbsp flour
¾ tsp salt
1½ tsp prepared mustard
1½ tsp sugar
¹⁄₁₆ tsp pepper
⅔ cup water
2 tbsp vinegar

1½ lbs freshly boiled potatoes,
  peeled and sliced, about
  6 medium
½ cup chopped celery
1 small onion, sliced
1 cup shredded endive
½ cup grated carrot

Cut bacon into ½-inch lengths with kitchen scissors and sauté for 10 min or until done. Remove pieces of bacon to absorbent paper to drain. Blend next 5 ingredients into drippings in pan, add liquids gradually and simmer until mixture is thickened and smooth. Stir constantly. Add potatoes, celery and onion and very carefully tilt pan back and forth to bring sauce over the vegetables. Heat through, then add remaining ingredients and mix carefully so that potato slices are not broken. Remove from heat immediately, top with crisp bacon pieces and serve immediately while still warm directly from skillet. 4 servings.

HOT POTATO SALAD No. 3

8 medium boiling potatoes,
2½ lbs
5 slices bacon, 4 oz
1 tbsp flour
½ cup water

½ cup vinegar
2 tsp salt
¾ tsp sugar
1 onion, sliced thin
2 tsp chopped parsley

Scrub potatoes but do not pare; cook until just tender in boiling salted water (1 tsp salt to 1 qt water). Meanwhile, pan-fry bacon until done; remove from the fat and drain on absorbent paper. Crumble into bits when crisp. To drippings remaining in pan, add the flour and blend well; then gradually stir in the water and vinegar, and cook over direct heat, stirring constantly until mixture boils and thickens. Add salt, sugar and thinly sliced onion. Peel and dice the hot potatoes, add bacon to them, and pour on the hot dressing. Mix lightly, add parsley and serve hot. 5 servings.

HOT RAINBOW SALAD

4 slices bacon
4 tsp flour
¼ cup vinegar
½ cup water *or* vegetable
liquor
1 tbsp sugar
¾ tsp salt

½ lb green beans cooked until
just tender
1 cup cooked sliced carrots
1 small onion, sliced
2 cups finely shredded
cabbage
2 tbsp pimiento, cut in
thin strips

Cut bacon in half-inch lengths with kitchen scissors and sauté in a 10-inch skillet until almost done. Blend in the flour thoroughly, then add the vinegar and water gradually. Stir constantly until mixture boils and thickens. Remove from heat and add sugar, salt, and vegetables. Toss lightly but thoroughly. Serve immediately while still warm directly from skillet if desired. 5 large servings.

HOT SLAW

½ medium head green
cabbage, about 1¼ lbs
thinly sliced
2 tsp sugar
½ tsp salt
½ tsp dry mustard

¼ cup vinegar
¼ cup cabbage liquid
1 strip bacon
1 tsp flour
1 egg
1 tbsp chopped pimiento

Parboil cabbage for about 2 min uncovered in barely enough boiling salted water to cover. Drain, save ¼ cup of the liquid. Mix sugar, salt, mustard, vinegar and cabbage liquid. Cut bacon in ½-inch lengths with scissors and pan-fry until done. Remove to absorbent paper to drain. Blend flour into drippings, then add vinegar mixture. Heat to boiling and cook until thickened, stirring constantly. Blend part of hot mixture with slightly beaten egg. Return to skillet and combine with remaining hot mixture and cook until just thickened. Do not over-cook or mixture will curdle. Pour over cabbage arranged in serving dish. Sprinkle with bacon and pimiento, toss lightly and serve immediately while warm. 4 servings.

HOT SPINACH SALAD

¾ lb tender, crisp spinach	1 tsp sugar
1 tsp salt	¼ tsp prepared mustard
1 tbsp chopped onion	¼ cup vinegar
2 strips bacon	¼ cup water
1 tsp flour	2 hard-cooked eggs

Wash spinach thoroughly, drain, and crisp in the refrigerator. Cut into fine shreds with kitchen scissors. Place in large bowl, sprinkling salt and chopped onion on the greens. Cut bacon into small pieces. Sauté until done; add flour and blend with the drippings. Add sugar, mustard, vinegar and water. Heat to boiling then simmer 2 min. Pour over the spinach and toss to coat well. Chop eggs very fine and sprinkle over top as garnish. 4 servings.

HOT SWEET POTATO SALAD

2½ lbs sweet potatoes	¼ cup lemon juice
4 slices bacon, 3½ oz	2 tsp sugar
¼ cup chopped onion	½ tsp salt
1 tbsp flour	¼ tsp grated orange rind
½ cup water	1 cup diced cucumber
½ cup orange juice	

Scrub potatoes and boil in jackets until just tender, then peel and cut into ¼-inch crosswise slices. Cut bacon into half-inch lengths with kitchen scissors and sauté with the onion until bacon is delicately browned. Blend in the flour thoroughly. Add the water and fruit juices gradually, then add sugar and salt. Heat to boiling, stirring constantly and cook for 2 min until smooth and thickened. Add the orange rind, cucumber and potatoes. Stir gently to coat with sauce. Heat thoroughly and serve at once while still warm directly from skillet. 4 servings.

HOT TURNIP CARROT SALAD

2 medium, white, tender turnips	5 strips bacon, about 4 oz
3 medium carrots, grated	3 tbsp vinegar
1 cup fresh cleaned tender spinach, pkd	¾ tsp salt
	1½ tsp sugar
	1 tbsp grated onion

Use a very sharp medium grater for turnips and carrots (there should be about 1 cup of each grated). Shred the spinach with sharp kitchen scissors. Heap lightly in salad bowl. Cover with waxed paper and a damp cloth or absorbent paper toweling while preparing dressing. Cut bacon with kitchen scissors in ½-inch lengths and pan-fry until done. Remove to absorbent paper to drain. Add vinegar, salt and sugar to drippings in pan. Heat to boiling, stirring constantly. Add onion, stir quickly to mix together. Pour over vegetables. Toss lightly to coat vegetables with dressing. Sprinkle bacon over top. Serve immediately while still warm. 4 servings.

WILTED LETTUCE

1 lb crisp leaf *or* head lettuce, washed	2 tbsp finely chopped onion
6 to 8 radishes, optional	1 tsp salt
5 slices bacon, 4 oz finely chopped	2 tsp sugar
	2 tbsp vinegar

Separate lettuce leaves and wash. To remove rinsing water roll up leaves in a towel and shake gently. Tear head lettuce into bite-size pieces and slice radishes. Pan-fry bacon in a skillet until half-done, add onion and continue cooking over low heat until bacon is done. Meanwhile warm a pottery or glass bowl by letting warm water stand in it. Pour out water, wipe dry quickly, turn lettuce, radishes and drained bacon and onion into it. To drippings remaining in pan (should not be more than 4 tbsp), add remaining ingredients. Stir to blend and heat to boiling, then pour over lettuce and radishes. Toss until thoroughly combined. Serve immediately while warm. 5 servings.

Variation: Add ½ cup sour cream to vinegar mixture when it begins to boil. Stir well, pour over lettuce and radishes. Toss, serve.

INDIVIDUAL AND DINNER SALADS

Individual Salads may be fruits or vegetables arranged on the individual plate on which they are to be served, and then drizzled with dressing either at the table or just before serving. The foods are handled as little as possible in this type of a salad and it therefore affords every opportunity for them to appear with all their fresh bloom intact. They may include such salads as stuffed tomatoes that are fairly hearty, but generally they are the type of salad that accompany or precede the main course. *Dinner Salads* may also be either fruit or vegetable mixtures, but they are mixed first in the kitchen in a larger bowl and served on individual plates for the meal, and they should always be of a size to be comfortably eaten along with a complete meal of potato, meat, and vegetable. Dinner salads are usually more enjoyed if they are light and slightly tart rather than sweet and heavy, and they should always be "fresh-as-a-daisy." Just remember that their purpose is to add beauty to the table, to whet the appetite for other foods, and to provide a contrast in texture and temp from other foods in the meal. If you keep these requirements in mind and choose your salads accordingly, then make them appear at their highest point of beauty, the individual or dinner salad will accomplish its intended purpose.

FRUIT SALADS

APPLE AND PEANUT SALAD

5 medium Jonathan *or*
Rome Beauty apples
Juice of 1 lemon, about
3 tbsp
5 medium branches celery

¼ cup Boiled Salad Dressing,
p 1198
¼ cup mayonnaise
½ cup coarsely chopped
peanuts
Lettuce

Pare, quarter and core apples. Cut into thin slices then cut slices into narrow strips and sprinkle with lemon juice to prevent discoloration. Thinly slice celery crosswise. Add the apples and combined dressings and toss lightly. Fold in peanuts and serve immediately on lettuce leaves, or as a stuffing for peeled whole tomatoes. 5 servings.

APPLE AND RAISIN SALAD

5 red, tart, juicy apples
½ cup raisins, plumped,
p 165

⅓ cup mayonnaise
Lettuce

Wash but do not pare apples; core, julienne or dice. Immediately toss with raisins and mayonnaise. Pile lightly into lettuce cups on individual salad plates. 5 servings.

Note: ¼ tsp cinnamon and 1 tbsp lemon juice are flavorful additions to the mayonnaise.

APPLE CHEESE SALAD

1 large, firm, juicy, red
apple, 1½ cups
2 tbsp lemon juice
½ cup diced celery
½ cup seedless raisins,
plumped
2 tbsp chopped walnuts

½ cup cubed American
cheese, 2 oz
¼ tsp sugar
⅛ tsp salt
¼ cup mayonnaise
Lettuce

Wash but do not pare apple. Cut in quarters, remove core, slice thinly, cut in thin strips. Mix with lemon juice immediately. Add next 7 ingredients. Toss thoroughly but lightly to coat all ingredients with the dressing. Serve at once by piling lightly on crisp lettuce leaves. 4 servings.

Note: Recipe for Mayonnaise on p 1202.

APPLE TURNIP AND PASCAL CELERY SALAD

2 large, tart, red apples
2 tsp lemon juice
1½ cups sliced Pascal celery,
  with some chopped tender
  leaves

1 cup shredded turnips,
  firmly pkd
½ cup mayonnaise blended
  with 2 tbsp cream
½ tsp salt

Cut apples crosswise in half. Remove cores with a spoon or an apple corer. Scoop out center portion of apple carefully in small pieces and let them drop directly into a bowl. There should be just a thin shell of apple left. Sprinkle inside of apple shells and apples in bowl with lemon juice to preserve color. Slice celery, shred tops. Pare and shred turnips on medium grater. Combine apple, celery, turnip and remaining ingredients. Toss lightly. Pile into apple cups. Garnish with leaves of celery. Serve immediately. 4 servings.

APRICOT COTTAGE CHEESE SALAD

No. 2 can apricots, or
1 lb fresh apricots
1 pt creamed cottage cheese

Lettuce
⅓ cup mayonnaise
Pecan halves

Drain canned apricots well, saving juice for beverage. If fresh apricots are used, wash, cut in half and remove pits. Put several apricot halves around a mound of cottage cheese on a bed of lettuce. Serve at once with mayonnaise thinned with 2 tbsp of apricot or orange juice. Garnish with nuts. 5 servings.

BANANA APPLE AND CRANBERRY SALAD

⅔ cup Cranberry Sauce,
  ¼ of recipe, p 563
¾ cup diced unpared apple,
  1 medium

¼ cup mayonnaise
1 large banana
Crisp lettuce

Chill cranberry sauce thoroughly and gently fold in the apples and mayonnaise. Slice banana directly into mixture and toss very carefully to mix. Serve immediately on lettuce leaves. 4 servings.

BANANA MARSHMALLOW AND NUT SALAD

5 bananas, well ripened
2 tbsp lemon juice
Lettuce
¼ lb marshmallows, quartered

¼ cup Boiled Salad Dressing,
  p 1198
2 tbsp whipping cream
½ cup chopped peanuts

Peel bananas and quarter, cutting once lengthwise and once crosswise. Dip quickly in lemon juice to prevent discoloration. Arrange on salad plates on lettuce leaves. Combine marshmallows with salad dressing and cream and pile lightly on top of banana quarters. Sprinkle peanuts on top. 5 servings.

BANANA SALAD

3 bananas, well ripened	Lettuce
¼ cup orange juice	Fruit Salad Dressing,
Chopped peanuts—*or*	p 1200, *or* mayonnaise
other nuts	

Peel bananas, cut lengthwise in half and then crosswise in half. To prevent them from discoloring, prepare salads just before serving and coat bananas at once with orange juice. Roll in chopped nuts, pressing slightly to partially imbed them. Arrange on lettuce and serve with preferred dressing. 4 servings.

CANTALOUPE AND BLACKBERRY SALAD

1 medium cantaloupe, chilled	Lettuce
1 pt fresh blackberries,	Lime Honey Dressing,
chilled	p 1202

Cut cantaloupe in wedges or rings, scoop out seeds and fiber from center and pare. Wash and drain blackberries. Arrange wedges or rings of melon on lettuce and fill center with berries. Serve with dressing. 5 servings.

Note: Bing cherries, raspberries or blueberries may be used with cantaloupe when in season.

CANTALOUPE BALLS AND CHERRY SALAD

With a French vegetable cutter, scoop out balls of cantaloupe. Combine with an equal quantity of pitted sweet black cherries, or of drained canned sweet cherries. Serve on crisp lettuce with Lemon French Dressing, p 1201, or Mayonnaise, p 1202.

CINNAMON APPLE SALAD

Prepare Cinnamon Apples, p 559, allowing 1 apple per serving. Chill, drain, and arrange on crisp lettuce. Fill hole with a mixture of finely chopped celery and cream cheese. Serve with Mayonnaise, p 1202.

CRANBERRY RELISH

See Recipe on page 1207.

DATE CREAM CHEESE AND LETTUCE SALAD

½ lb dates	3 tbsp mayonnaise
3 oz pkg cream cheese	1 solid head lettuce

Pit dates and cut into small pieces. Cream the cheese, then blend with mayonnaise and mix in dates. Shred outer leaves of lettuce and mix lightly with cheese and date mixture. Serve on remaining heart leaves of lettuce. 5 servings.

FRESH FRUIT AND DATE SALAD

1 small well-ripened pine- apple, chilled	¼ lb dates, pitted and chopped
2 well-ripened bananas	⅓ cup Fruit Salad Dressing,
2 oranges, chilled	chilled, p 1200
	Lettuce *or* romaine

Slice pineapple, pare slices, and cut in small wedges, discarding core of each slice. Peel and slice bananas and oranges; cut orange slices in quarters. Combine fruits quickly to prevent bananas from darkening, add dates and dressing. Mix gently with as little manipulation as possible. Drop lightly into lettuce cups on individual salad plates. 5 generous servings.

FRESH FRUIT SALAD

1 medium-sized cantaloupe	Lettuce
2 well-ripened bananas	Lime Honey, p 1202, *or*
Lemon juice	Celery Seed Dressing,
½ pt sweet pitted cherries	p 1199

Cut cantaloupe in quarters, remove seeds and pare. Peel and slice bananas crosswise, sprinkling with lemon juice to prevent discoloration. Place a cantaloupe wedge on each salad plate lined with lettuce. Lightly pile banana slices and cherries in hollow of cantaloupe. Serve with dressing. 4 servings.

FRUIT SALAD WITH MARSHMALLOWS

2 seedless oranges, chilled	⅓ cup Celery Seed Fruit
2 well-ripened bananas	Dressing, p 1199, *or* Lime
½ lb seedless *or* seeded grapes, chilled	Honey Dressing, p 1202
¼ lb marshmallows, quartered, 16	Lettuce *or* romaine

Pare and dice oranges, peel bananas and mix together to prevent bananas from darkening; add well washed grapes, quartered marshmallows, and dressing and mix gently. Drop lightly into lettuce cups on individual salad plates. 5 servings.

Note: Recipe for Mayonnaise on p 1202.

GRAPEFRUIT AVOCADO AND PERSIMMON SALAD

2 medium grapefruit
1 well-ripened avocado
½ cup French dressing

Lettuce
1 well-ripened persimmon

With a thin-bladed, very sharp knife, use a saw-like motion to pare the skin and membrane at the same time from the grapefruit. Keep the pared grapefruit smooth and round. Then remove sections carefully. Peel avocado, remove seed and slice thin. Marinate both fruits in the French dressing. Chill thoroughly. Just before serving, arrange drained fruits on lettuce leaves with a wedge of unpeeled seeded persimmon on the top of each salad. Serve at once. 5 servings.

Note: Pomegranate seeds may be substituted for persimmon.

GRAPEFRUIT SALAD

2 medium grapefruit
½ pt whole strawberries
Lettuce

⅓ cup Avocado Dressing,
p 1197

Pare grapefruit like an apple and remove the sections whole (see illus between pp 96–97). Wash berries, drain thoroughly, then hull. Chill. Arrange chilled sections of grapefruit and berries on lettuce leaves. Serve with dressing. 5 servings.

Variation: Slices of tomato or apple may be added to this salad in place of strawberries. Watercress or curly endive is a pleasant variation also.

ORANGE COCONUT SALAD

Ambrosia Salad

3 seedless oranges, pared
    and sliced
Lettuce *or* romaine

½ cup moist coconut
French Dressing, p 1200, *or*
Lime Honey, p 1202

Arrange a circle of thick overlapping orange slices on crisp lettuce with a light heap of coconut in the center. Serve with dressing. 5 servings.

Variation: A little grated or thinly sliced onion combined with the orange is a daring but pleasing addition.

ORANGE RAISIN SALAD

3 seedless oranges
½ cup raisins, plumped,
    p 165

⅓ cup mayonnaise
1 solid head lettuce, 1 lb

Note: Recipe for French Dressing on p 1200.

Pare oranges and dice or separate into sections. Combine with raisins and mix lightly with mayonnaise. Pile lightly on lettuce which has been cut into five crosswise slices and placed on individual salad plates. 5 servings.

ORANGE WALDORF SALAD

1 large seedless orange	Salt to suit taste
Lettuce *or* romaine	2 tbsp mayonnaise
1 cup pared and diced apples	2 tbsp Boiled Salad Dressing,
1 cup diced celery	p 1198
¼ cup chopped pecans	

Pare orange, cut into 5 slices and place in lettuce cups on individual plates. Combine other ingredients, tossing lightly together, and pile in light heaps on orange slices. Serve at once. 5 servings.

PAPAYA SALAD

½ cup lemon juice	1 large seedless orange
¼ cup honey	Watercress
Pinch of salt	Black olives, blackberries,
1 ripe medium papaya,	*or* blueberries
2½ to 3 lbs	

Combine lemon juice, honey and salt; chill in refrigerator. Pare and slice papaya; remove seeds. Pare orange and section. Arrange alternate slices of papaya and orange wedges in fan shape arrangement on a salad plate. Place a small bunch of crisp cress at the small end and garnish with black olives, blackberries or blueberries. Do not eat papaya seeds. Drizzle with chilled lemon-honey dressing and serve immediately. 4 to 5 servings.

PEACH PRUNE AND COTTAGE CHEESE SALAD

¼ lb large, moist prunes	Lettuce
No. 2 can peach halves	Dressing
½ lb creamed cottage cheese	

Soak prunes overnight in just enough water to cover. Drain (no cooking necessary), split on one side and remove pits. Drain peaches. (Save juice and use for beverage or as liquid in a molded salad.) Stuff pitted prunes with cottage cheese, and arrange in hollows of peach halves placed in lettuce cups on individual salad plates. Pile any excess cottage cheese in center of arrangement. Serve with French, p 1200, Lime Honey, p 1202, or Celery Seed Dressing, p 1199, as desired. 5 servings.

PEACH SALAD

5 freestone peaches, *or*
   No. 2 can peach halves
¼ cup chopped nuts
½ cup chopped celery

½ cup chopped dates
⅓ cup Celery Seed Dressing,
   p 1199*
Lettuce

Pare fresh peaches, cut in halves and remove stones. Sprinkle with 2 tbsp lemon juice to prevent discoloration.

If canned peaches are to be used, chill in the can, then drain. (Juice may be used in a fruit juice beverage or as part of the liquid in a fruit gelatin dessert.) Mix the chopped nuts, celery, and dates with about 2 tbsp of the dressing, and place a spoonful of this mixture in the center of each peach half. Serve on crisp lettuce with additional dressing in a separate bowl. 5 servings.

Variation: Centers of peach halves may be filled with cottage cheese, or cream cheese combined with mayonnaise, to which 1 tbsp finely cut chives have been added if desired. Ripe olives make a pleasing garnish.

PEAR SALAD

No. 2 can pear halves *or*
5 medium fresh pears,
   chilled
Lettuce *or* watercress

½ lb creamed cottage cheese
Mayonnaise, p 1202, *or*
French Dressing, p 1200

If canned pears are used, chill in the can, then drain. If fresh pears are used, pare, cut in halves lengthwise, remove cores and dip in lemon juice to prevent discoloration. Put pears on crisp lettuce leaves and fill hollows with cottage cheese, heaping up lightly. Serve with dressing. 5 servings.

Variation No. 1: Whip 2 tbsp currant jelly into ⅓ cup mayonnaise and serve over the pear and cottage cheese.

Variation No. 2: For cottage cheese, use ¼ lb American cheese coarsely grated and mixed with enough mayonnaise to hold together. Pile lightly into hollows of pear and top with mayonnaise to which ¼ cup very finely chopped celery has been added.

Variation No. 3: Substitute 6 oz (2 pkgs) cream cheese for the cottage cheese. Blend cream cheese with enough mayonnaise to soften, then add ¼ cup chopped celery and ¼ cup chopped nuts. Pile lightly into hollows of pear and serve with French dressing.

*2½ tbsp each of Mayonnaise (p 1202) and Boiled Salad Dressing (p 1198) may be substituted.

Definition: You PEEL with your fingers. You PARE with a knife.

PERSIMMON SALAD

4 large Japanese persimmons
No. 2½ can sliced pine-
apple, chilled

1 bunch watercress *or*
romaine
Tart French dressing

Choose well-ripened persimmons with wrinkled skins. Arrange pineapple slices on individual salad plates. Arrange ½ a persimmon cut petal fashion over each slice. Garnish one side of each plate with several sprigs of crisp watercress or romaine, serve with dressing at the table. 8 servings.

PINEAPPLE AND COTTAGE CHEESE SALAD

Lettuce *or* romaine
5 slices pineapple
½ lb creamed cottage cheese

Paprika
French Dressing, p 1200

Have all ingredients chilled. Arrange crisp lettuce leaves on salad plates. If using canned pineapple, drain pineapple slices (saving juice for beverage or gelatin dessert) and place a slice on each plate. If fresh pineapple is used, it is convenient to cut through the ring in several places, leaving shape of ring intact for easier eating. Place a mound of cottage cheese in the center of each slice of pineapple. Sprinkle with paprika. Serve with French dressing. 5 servings.

Variation: Drain pineapple thoroughly and cut slices in small wedges. Combine lightly with the cottage cheese. Arrange lettuce on individual salad plates and heap pineapple-cheese mixture lightly on lettuce. Top with mayonnaise.

PINEAPPLE DATE SALAD

½ cup finely chopped dates
½ cup finely diced celery
½ cup diced apple

4 slices pineapple, diced
¼ cup mayonnaise
Lettuce

Have all ingredients chilled. Combine dates, celery, apple, and pineapple and mix in enough mayonnaise to give a moist consistency. Heap on crisp lettuce on individual salad plates. 5 servings.

Note: Use 1½ cups fresh, sugared pineapple when in season in place of canned.

PINEAPPLE WALDORF SALAD

½ cup sugar
2 cups fresh pineapple
wedges
2 tbsp lemon juice
1 cup unpared, diced apple

1 cup sliced celery
⅛ tsp salt
Lettuce, romaine, *or*
escarole
Maraschino cherries

Note: Recipe for Mayonnaise on p 1202, and French Dressing, p 1200.

Blend the sugar with the pineapple and let stand in refrigerator 2 to 3 hrs. Drain and use juice to make salad dressing. When dressing is made and chilled, add the lemon juice to the apples and toss to coat them. Combine with the pineapple, celery and salt. Add salad dressing, toss lightly, and serve on crisp lettuce leaves. Garnish with maraschino cherries.

Salad Dressing:

½ cup pineapple juice, drained from fruit	½ tsp dry mustard
2 tbsp sugar	1 egg yolk, beaten
1 tbsp flour	1 tsp vinegar
½ tsp salt	3 oz pkg cream cheese

Pour pineapple juice in saucepan. Mix the sugar, flour, salt, mustard and add to the juice. Heat to boiling, stirring constantly; cook until thickened. Add part of hot mixture to egg yolk stirring well. Return to hot mixture, stir constantly, cook one min. Add vinegar. Remove from heat and chill. Add the chilled salad dressing to the softened cream cheese, a small amount at a time, whipping until smooth after each addition until all has been blended together. Chill and serve over the diced fruit. 4 servings.

PRUNE NUT SALAD

15 large moist prunes	Head Lettuce
1⅔ cups creamed cottage cheese	⅓ cup chopped walnuts
	French dressing

Wash prunes thoroughly, add water to barely cover, and soak 1 hr. Simmer gently 10 to 15 min, or until just tender. Remove prunes from liquid, saving juice to drink. Pit prunes, cover and chill. Place a mound of cheese and three pitted prunes in a lettuce cup or on a slice of lettuce on each plate, sprinkle with nuts and serve with French dressing. 5 servings.

Variation: Stuff prunes with cheese and nuts and serve on pineapple slices on lettuce.

STUFFED PRUNES

Very good and attractive

18 to 24 good size cooked prunes	1 tsp mayonnaise
3 oz pkg cream cheese	¼ cup chopped nuts

Drain prunes thoroughly and pit carefully to hold shape. Turn cheese into a 1-qt mixing bowl. Stir with spoon until creamy, then beat in mayonnaise. Now stir in nuts. Dip from ½ to ¾ tsp, depending upon size of prunes and fill cavities. Press cut edges of prunes gently up to only partly cover the stuffing. Place on a sheet of paper toweling to absorb excess moisture and place in refrigerator an hour before serving. Arrange attractively on serving plate around a dish of pickled peaches and serve as an appetizer, or arrange in crisp lettuce cups on a plate for salad. Serve plain or with French dressing. 5 to 6 servings.

STUFFED PRUNE SALAD

24 large *or* 36 medium prunes,   ½ tsp salt
   p 104   1½ tsp sugar
1½ cups grated carrots, pkd   2 tbsp mayonnaise
   lightly, 3 medium carrots   Lettuce
1 tsp lemon juice   French dressing

Cook prunes until barely tender. Drain well, chill, pit carefully for most attractive appearance. Combine carrots with next 4 ingredients, tossing lightly but until thoroughly blended. Dip out spoonfuls of carrot mixture and fill prunes neatly. Press cut edges of prunes up neatly but not to cover carrot. Arrange prunes on a sheet of paper toweling spread on a plate for excess moisture to be absorbed. Chill an hr before serving. Arrange in cups of lettuce placed on salad plates, or arrange on appetizer tray. Serve immediately, the salad with French dressing if desired. 8 to 10 servings.

RED RASPBERRY AND COTTAGE CHEESE SALAD

½ pt red raspberries   Sugar, if desired
1 lb creamed cottage cheese,   Lettuce
   chilled   5 tbsp mayonnaise

Wash raspberries; drain and chill. Fold berries very lightly into the cottage cheese, adding a little sugar if desired. Pile lightly in lettuce cups on individual salad plates, and serve immediately with a tbsp of mayonnaise to top each salad. 5 servings.

Note: Strawberries, cherries and most all berries in season combine well with cottage cheese in this way.

STRAWBERRY AVOCADO CUPS

Golden Fluff Dressing:
   ¼ cup salad oil
   2 tbsp white corn syrup
   2 tbsp lemon juice
   ⅛ tsp salt
   1 tsp sugar
   1 tsp flour
   1 egg, separated
Glaze:
   2 tsp gelatin

¼ cup lemon juice
1 tbsp corn syrup
Salad Ingredients:
2 avocados
½ cup grapefruit sections
1 cup small whole straw-
   berries
1 tbsp lemon juice
1 tbsp corn syrup

Dressing: Combine in top of double boiler the oil, syrup, lemon juice, salt, sugar, flour, and yolk of egg. Beat thoroughly. Cook until thick and fluffy, stirring constantly. Fold in stiffly beaten egg white, cook a min longer, stirring gently. Cool.

Glaze: Combine gelatin, lemon juice and syrup. Place over boiling water until gelatin is dissolved. Keep in warm water until ready to use.

Salad: Cut avocados in half lengthwise. Remove seed. Carefully scoop out each half in as large pieces as possible, preserving shape of shell. Dice avocado, combine with grapefruit and strawberries. Add lemon juice and syrup, which have been blended together. Fill shells with fruit mixture. Remove gelatin mixture from heat, cool slightly and spoon over fruit. Chill about ½ hr. Just before serving, top with a tbsp of the cooked dressing. 4 servings.

WALDORF SALAD

3 large Jonathan *or* Winesap apples
1 tbsp lemon juice
1 cup julienned celery, Pascal preferred

½ cup coarsely chopped walnuts
¼ cup mayonnaise
¼ cup Boiled Salad Dressing, p 1198
Lettuce *or* romaine

Pare apples, cut in quarters, and remove cores; cut quarters into thin slices, then into slender strips. Sprinkle with lemon juice. Cut celery in slender lengthwise strips; hold together and cut crosswise in ½-inch lengths. Add to apples and toss together. Cover and chill. Just before serving time, add nuts and combined mayonnaise and salad dressing to mixture, and toss lightly to distribute dressing. Pile lightly into crisp lettuce cups on individual salad plates. (If apples have red, tender skins, the skins may be left on for added color.) 5 or 6 servings.

Note: Celery Seed Dressing (p 1199) is an excellent variation for the dressing indicated.

VEGETABLE SALADS

FINGER SALADS

Many raw crisp vegetables alone or combined make glowing and delicious salads. Vegetables must be washed and chilled, then carefully cut just before serving. Here are a few suggestions:

1. Carrots: Scrape only enough to remove discolorations, then cut into ribbons with peeler, or into sticks with a knife. Serve plain or dip in orange or lemon juice.

2. *Celery:* Trim branches or the whole tender celery hearts. Split hearts lengthwise into quarters or stuff branches with cheese mixture, p 208.

3. *Cucumbers:* Use not overly developed ones. Pare thinly, then cut in thick crosswise slices. Or cut in half lengthwise, then the halves into quarters then these strips in half crosswise for sticks. Dip in French or Seasoned Vinegar, p 1177.

4. *Kohlrabi:* Peel young tender kohlrabi; cut in thick slices, sticks or wedges.

5. *Cabbage:* Cut tender cabbage into thin wedges. Drizzle with French dressing or serve with salt.

6. *Cauliflower:* Break into flowerets; if small, leave whole; if large, cut lengthwise into thick fan-shape slices. Dip in French dressing.

7. *Green Onions:* Leave on 3 or 4 inches of the green tops.

8. *Large Dry Onions:* Peel carefully. Slice crosswise ⅛ to ¼-inch thick. If very strong, soak in ice water 3 or 4 min.

9. *Red or Green Sweet Peppers:* Cut into sticks or rings. *Whole Hot Peppers:* Cut into ribbons or rings.

10. *Radishes:* Cut off roots. Leave on a few tender green sprigs.

11. *Cherry or Plum Tomatoes:* Leave whole with or without skins. Dip skinned tomatoes in fine chopped parsley or chives.

12. *Tomatoes:* Slice firm tomatoes thick. Or cut into wedges. Sprinkle with fine-chopped mint and drizzle with French dressing.

13. *Turnip or Rutabaga:* Pare and cut in slices, sticks or wedges.

14. *Raw Irish Potatoes:* Pare, cut in fingers and dip in lemon juice; sprinkle with chopped parsley or lightly with caraway seed.

15. *Apple:* Cut washed unpared crisp apple into wedges. Dip in lemon juice to prevent discoloration.

16. *Water Cress:* Trim white roots from crisp sprigs.

BEAN SPROUT SALAD

A salad treat that you can eat and eat

2 cups fresh *or* canned bean sprouts, mung	1 tbsp salad oil
	1 tbsp cider vinegar
⅓ cup sliced Pascal celery	1 tbsp soy sauce
2 green onions, sliced, some tops	¼ tsp salt
	Dash of pepper
1 tsp onion juice	1½ tsp sugar
1 good sized tomato cut in ¾" dice	Lettuce

Have all vegetables cleaned and chilled. Rinse bean sprouts in cold water, drain and shake as dry as possible in a clean cloth. Turn into mixing bowl. Add next 4 ingredients. Combine next 6 ingredients, shake or beat to mix thoroughly and pour over vegetables. Toss carefully but thoroughly. Serve in lettuce cups. 4 servings.

BEET CHEESE AND ONION SALAD

2 cups diced cooked beets, p 1324	⅓ cup Mayonnaise, p 1202, or French Dressing, p 1200
¾ cup diced Swiss cheese	Lettuce
1 tbsp chopped onion, or to suit taste	Chopped parsley

Combine beets with cheese, onion and dressing, tossing all together lightly. Serve on lettuce leaves, sprinkling with chopped parsley. For a more tart mixture, the beets may be marinated for an hr or two in diluted tarragon vinegar (⅓ cup vinegar and ⅓ cup water). 5 servings.

BEET AND GREEN ONION SALAD

2 cups cooked beets, p 1324	½ tsp salt
2 cups diced celery	⅓ cup French Dressing, p 1200
½ cup thinly sliced green onions	Crisp lettuce

Peel cooled beets, and cut into ¼-inch cubes. Combine all vegetables; sprinkle with salt and add dressing. Toss very lightly with a fork. Cover and chill thoroughly. Heap lightly on crisp lettuce leaves. 4 servings.

BEET AND PEA SALAD

2 cups diced or sliced cooked beets, p 1324	⅓ cup French dressing or mayonnaise
1 cup cooked fresh peas, p 1367	Lettuce

Combine chilled beets and peas with French dressing or mayonnaise and pile on lettuce leaves. Serve at once. If preferred, beets may be marinated in the French dressing for about 20 min before combining with peas. 5 servings.

Note: Sprinkle beets generously with chopped chives or parsley for a peppier salad.

Note: Recipe for Mayonnaise on p 1202, and French Dressing, p 1200.

Definition: You PEEL with your fingers. You PARE with a knife.

BIG WIG'S SALAD

Served in the most aristocratic restaurants

2 cups croutons, from French bread, see p 262

1 pt broken chunks head lettuce

1 cup broken crisp tender curly endive

1 cup shredded heart leaves of spinach

¾ cup thinly sliced crisp pared cucumber

6 small green onions with tops, finely sliced

½ cup coarsely torn parsley leaves

2 oz can of anchovies

1 large clove garlic, peeled, chopped fine

¼ cup wine vinegar

¼ cup olive oil

1 tbsp water

2 tsp Worcestershire sauce

2 coddled eggs

⅓ cup grated fresh Parmesan cheese

Prepare croutons. Clean, dry and chill greens. When ready to make salad, break up lettuce, tear endive, spinach and parsley into salad bowl, slice cucumber and onion into bowl. Drain anchovies, chop fine and add to salad bowl. Combine garlic, vinegar, oil, water and Worcestershire. Put eggs on to coddle, put them into enough boiling water to cover an inch deep, cover pan, remove from heat, let stand 5 min. Shake dressing thoroughly and pour on salad in bowl, toss well to distribute. Add croutons, break coddled eggs on top of salad, whites of egg should look like milk. Quickly toss to blend the egg all through dressing. Sprinkle cheese over top. Serve *immediately.* 5 to 6 servings.

CAULIFLOWER SALAD

1 small head cauliflower
½ cup French dressing

½ cup grated sharp American cheese
Lettuce

Soak cauliflower about 1 hr in cold water to which 1 tsp salt has been added. Rinse in cold water, then separate into flowerets. Cook in rapidly boiling salted water, uncovered, for 5 to 6 min or until about tender. Drain, cool and pour French dressing over cauliflower; allow to stand half an hr in refrigerator. Add cheese; toss together thoroughly. Serve chilled on crisp lettuce leaves. 5 servings.

Note: Raw cauliflower cut into bite-size pieces may be used in place of cooked to make this salad.

CELERY CABBAGE MEDLEY SALAD BOWL

A colorful, tasty winter salad

4 medium sized celery cabbage leaves

1 small bunch watercress

1½ tsp cut chives

1 cup sliced beets

½ cup Spanish Salad Dressing, p 1206, *or* other French dressing

2 hard-cooked eggs

Have first 3 vegetables crisp and fresh. Cut celery cabbage into ¼" crosswise slices, sprigs of watercress into inch-lengths and the chives in ¼" lengths. Cut beet slices into eighths, turn all vegetables into salad bowl. Drizzle all but 1 tbsp of the dressing over vegetables and toss lightly until every piece is coated with dressing. Slice eggs and arrange attractively at opposite sides of the salad bowl. Pour rest of dressing over eggs, serve. 4 to 5 servings.

CELERY STUFFED WITH CHEESE

6 oz, 2 pkgs, cream cheese	Mayonnaise
3 oz blue cheese *or*	1 medium stalk Pascal *or*
Roquefort	bleached celery

Blend the cheeses with just enough mayonnaise to make a stiff paste. Separate celery into individual branches, trimming off tough, coarse leaves. Scrape away all discolorations and wash thoroughly with cold water. Roll up in towel and shake to remove moisture. Stuff cheese mixture into branches and serve on relish dish, or pipe into celery grooves with a pastry tube. For more elaborate service, press stuffed branches together in original celery stalk form and chill in refrigerator until cheese is firm. Then slice crosswise about ½-inch thick. These slices make an attractive salad served on lettuce with French dressing. 5 servings.

CUCUMBER AND RADISH SALAD

Slice 1 bunch cleaned radishes and 1 medium pared or unpared cucumber quite thin, and arrange slices on lettuce. Serve with French dressing to which grated onion has been added in the proportion of 1 tbsp to ⅓ cup dressing. 5 servings.

FENNEL DINNER SALAD

Very edible

1½ cups sliced fennel	1 tbsp olive *or* other salad oil
½ cup water	1 tbsp wine *or* cider vinegar
¼ tsp salt	1 tsp sugar
2 onions, size of walnuts	Dash of pepper
1 medium sized tomato *or*	⅛ tsp salt
4 *or* 5 scarlet radishes	Small head lettuce
2 tsp parsley	

Prepare fennel as described under Fennel Waldorf Salad, p 1149. Cut into half-inch lengths. Put into saucepan with water and salt. Place over heat, cover and boil gently 3 or 4 min or until barely tender and still a little crisp. Drain off water, cool. Peel onions; slice onions and radishes thinly, cut tomato into thin wedges, cut parsley fine and add all to the fennel. Combine next 5 ingredients, beat until well mixed and pour over vegetables. Toss thoroughly. Serve in lettuce cups, or as a tossed salad. 4 servings.

FENNEL WALDORF SALAD

As delicious as Waldorf but different and new in flavor

1½ cups sliced fennel
1½ cups sliced tart apple
½ cup broken pecan, walnut
  or Brazil nuts
¼ tsp salt

¼ cup salad dressing or
  mayonnaise
1 tbsp thin cream
⅛ tsp finely grated or
  scraped onion
Small head lettuce

Choose crisp fennel with bright green feathery leaves. Clean like celery, slicing off any discolorations, removing coarse strings on branches, discard leaves. Wash clean in cold water. Cut fennel branches and pared, quartered cored apples into quarter-inch slices. Measure first 3 ingredients into mixing bowl. Blend next 4 ingredients and pour over vegetables. Toss carefully but thoroughly. Heap salad into crisp lettuce cups. 4 servings.

Note: A good sized bunch of fennel makes from 2¼ to 3 cups diced.

GREEN BEAN AND CELERY SALAD

½ lb green beans, cut in half
  lengthwise
1 cup boiling water
½ tsp salt
¼ cup sliced celery
1 tbsp chopped chives

2 tbsp chopped sweet pickles
1 hard-cooked egg, diced
2 tbsp slivered radishes
¼ cup mayonnaise
1 tsp lemon juice
Lettuce

Cook beans in water with salt until tender—about 7 min (most of the liquid will have boiled away). Chill in liquid, then drain. Add remaining ingredients and toss gently to coat with dressing. Serve immediately on a bed of crisp lettuce. 4 servings.

GREEN BEAN SALAD

½ lb green beans or No. 2
  can green beans
¼ cup sliced onion, dry or
  green
1 cup diced celery

½ cup sliced radishes
½ tsp salt
½ cup French dressing
Lettuce

If fresh beans are used, wash and cut in 1-inch lengths. Drop into boiling salted water and cook until tender, about 20 min. Drain beans, cook and chill. If canned beans are used, chill in the can and drain. When ready to serve, combine vegetables, sprinkle with salt, add French dressing and toss together gently until vegetables are well coated. Heap lightly on lettuce leaves and serve immediately. 5 servings.

GREEN PEPPER AND CHEESE RING SALAD

1 large green pepper	1/16 tsp salt
3 oz pkg cream cheese	1 seedless orange
1/4 cup raisins, plumped,	Lettuce
p 165	Salad Dressing
1/2 tsp grated orange rind	

Wash pepper. Cut a slice from the stem end and remove seeds and membrane. Work cheese until softened. Add the raisins, orange rind and salt and mix. Pack into the pepper shell and chill thoroughly. Pare orange and separate into sections over a bowl (reserve juice for dressing). When ready to serve, cut filled pepper into rings about 1/4 inch thick. For each serving place 2 or 3 rings on a bed of lettuce. Arrange 3 or 4 orange sections on each salad. Serve with the following salad dressing.

Salad Dressing:

1/4 cup mayonnaise	2 tbsp orange juice
2 tbsp tart jelly	Dash of salt

Combine all ingredients. Mix well, breaking up the jelly. 4 servings.

KIDNEY BEAN SALAD No. 1

No. 2 can red kidney beans	1/4 tsp chili powder
1 cup chopped celery	1/2 tsp prepared mustard
1 tbsp chopped onion	Lettuce
1/4 cup sweet pickle relish	Mayonnaise
1 tsp salt	

Drain kidney beans and discard liquid. Combine celery, onion and pickle relish. Stir in seasonings and mix thoroughly with beans, being careful not to mash them. Chill and serve on crisp lettuce with mayonnaise. This salad may also be used to stuff into tomatoes. 3 to 5 servings.

KIDNEY BEAN SALAD No. 2

No. 2 can kidney beans	1/4 cup French dressing
1 hard-cooked egg, chopped	1/2 tsp salt
2 tbsp sliced sweet pickle	1 tbsp vinegar
1/4 cup sliced celery	Head lettuce
2 tbsp chopped onion	

Note: Recipe for French Dressing, p 1200.

ABOVE: *Stuffed green, yellow, and red sweet peppers. The crisp, thick walled shells may be filled with combinations of seasoned shredded vegetables, fruits or vegetables in gelatin such as perfection salad, cottage or cream cheese mixtures, egg and fish salads. After chilling, the peppers can be sliced and arranged in alternating colors.*

BELOW: *Our grandmothers served this picturesque salad of thick meaty slices of tomatoes and mild sweet onions bathed with a simple dressing of flavored vinegar, p 135.*

ABOVE: *A dark glass chop plate is wonderful for making a spectacular display of fresh grapefruit sections and orange slices for salad. Add a touch of mint here and there for a dash of color, but it is more practical to have the greens on the side ready to place on the plates.*

BELOW: *Shredded salads do not mean mangled vegetables without beauty or form. Serve the dressing separately and the salad will be eaten while all of its freshness is still present.*

ABOVE: *A salad platter usually goes somewhat formal in arrangement. Even though it is "arranged," it must never look "handled" . . . it must be as fresh and crisp appearing as the Grapefruit and Apple Salad, p 1138, with curly endive and grapes shown here.*

Courtesy of Sunkist—California Fruit Growers Exchange.

BELOW: *Decorative "Horseshoe Salad." Cut "avocado horseshoes" with pieces of ripe olive for the "nails." Orange sections, strawberry slices, watercress and any desired salad dressing complete the picture that will decorate your midday meal.*

ABOVE: *Tossing a salad at the table adds a dramatic touch to any meal. It is practical to assemble the crisp chilled foods in the kitchen, then drizzle on the dressing at the table just before the tossing.*

BELOW: *Correctly cleaned, cooked, and marinated shrimp is combined here with sliced crisp tender celery and served with cucumber and pineapple aspic molds. Serve with a delicious combination of mayonnaise and boiled salad dressing into which is folded a wee bit of prepared horseradish.*

A satisfying luncheon or Sunday night supper may be arranged conveniently on a single big platter for buffet service. Whole tomato roses with whole hard-cooked egg centers, leaf lettuce and sliced cucumbers may be combined into a salad by each guest; there's the dressing in the center bowl. Everybody may carve his own portion of cream cheese from the big loaf which is helpfully scored into eighths and decorated with sliced ripe olives. Two-tone bread and butter sandwiches are provided, and so is a pitcher of iced tea.

ABOVE: *How those intriguing Mosaic sandwiches are made by using two colors of bread and various sizes of cutters to shape the sandwiches and to make the cut-outs and the inserts.*

BELOW: *The filling in these Ribbon and Checkerboard tea sandwiches may be be only simple mixtures such as cream cheese, parsley butter, or a peanut butter spread, but what added appeal a slightly different presentation will give!*

ABOVE: *Some ham sandwiches are just that, but these are four ham sandwiches, pp 1233–34 with imagination. Substantial and full of flavor, they combine ham with sliced bananas, big flakes of tuna, sliced cranberry jelly and cheese, and Swiss cheese, tomato and bacon.*

BELOW: *The Sandwich Bar, p 1217, provides everyone with an unusual opportunity to compose his own sandwich to suit his own taste and appetite.*

ABOVE: *A steaming hot tureen of unmashed, unsieved Split Pea Soup, p 1275, served with frankfurters rolled up in trimmed slices of buttered bread and grilled until the bread is golden and the sausage is hot through is a most appealing combination for flavor, color, and food value.*

BELOW: *A family-size bowlful of Cold Beet Borsch, p 1266, makes a pretty picture. Ice cubes serve not only to chill the soup but to dilute it to its most palatable concentration. Cool, thin cucumber slices add a finish to one of the most pleasant meal starters for hot days. The melba toast tied in bow knot shapes add both beauty and nourishment to the offering.*

Drain kidney beans and discard liquid. Combine all ingredients except lettuce, toss and chill in a covered bowl for an hr or more. Serve in lettuce cups placed in deep individual salad bowls. 4 servings.

KOHLRABI DATE SALAD

2 large *or* 3 small kohlrabi
½ tsp sugar
⅜ tsp salt
1½ tsp lemon juice

6 chopped dates *or* 2 tbsp raisins
2 marshmallows, cut up, optional
¼ cup mayonnaise

Only the tenderest of kohlrabi should be used for salad. Wash and strip peel from kohlrabi. Shred coarsely on a sharp grater into a salad bowl. Sprinkle with sugar, salt, and lemon juice. Add dates, marshmallows and mayonnaise. Toss lightly to thoroughly mix. Serve immediately on individual salad plates. 4 servings.

KOHLRABI WALDORF SALAD

1½ cups sliced kohlrabi,
    1 large *or* 2 medium
1 bright red apple
1½ tsp lemon juice

¼ tsp salt
1 tsp sugar
¼ cup mayonnaise
14 pecan halves, slivered

Use only very tender kohlrabi for salad. Wash and strip peel from kohlrabi, cut in thin slices, and then cut into ⅛-inch strips. Slice apple in ⅛-inch strips. Immediately combine kohlrabi and apples with lemon juice, salt and sugar in bowl. Add mayonnaise and pecans. Toss lightly and serve immediately on individual salad plates. 4 to 5 servings.

PARSLEY SALAD WITH CHIFFONADE DRESSING

A big shot of vitamin A

1 large bunch parsley
2 hard-cooked eggs, fine-
    chopped
3 medium tomatoes
½ cup salad oil
2½ tbsp cider vinegar
¼ tsp paprika

½ tsp salt
¼ tsp black pepper
2 tbsp fine-chopped onion
4 anchovies, fine-chopped
1 small clove garlic, fine-
    chopped

Clean parsley, wash, remove stems and crisp in hydrator, p 141. When ready to serve, cut parsley sprigs in 3 or 4 pieces, add tomatoes which have been cut into ¾-inch dice. Combine rest of ingredients in a small jar with a screw top; shake until dressing is a well-blended emulsion. Drizzle dressing over salad and toss until every ingredient is coated with a film of dressing. 4 to 6 servings.

PICKLED BEETS AND ONIONS

Cook beets as directed, p 1324. Peel and slice ⅛-inch thick, and measure. Add half this measure of Bermuda onions sliced very thinly to beets. Sprinkle lightly with salt. Heat to boiling enough sweetened cider or tarragon vinegar (half as much sugar as vinegar) to cover them; pour over beets and onions and let stand at least an hr or until cold, before serving. If a spicy pickle is desired, add any desired spices to the vinegar while heating (such as whole cloves, stick cinnamon, allspice, whole black peppers, etc.). One medium bunch of beets and 2 medium onions make 5 servings.

Note: The onions may be omitted and beets served as a salad with mayonnaise. Diced pickled beets with sliced chilled green pepper, or diced cucumbers or celery make a good salad combination.

PICKLED BEET SALAD

½ cup malt vinegar
¼ cup water
2 tsp dry mustard
½ tsp salt
⅓ cup sugar

½ tsp celery seed
2 cups sliced cooked beets, canned or p 1324
1 medium onion, sliced
2 tbsp finely chopped parsley

Heat vinegar and water to boiling. Add mustard, salt and sugar. Blend until mixed and heat again to boiling, then pour over the combined celery seed, beets and sliced onion. Cover and place in refrigerator or other cool place to marinate overnight or for several hrs before serving. Serve cold. Sprinkle parsley over beets just before serving. 4 servings.

RAW ASPARAGUS SALAD

2 cups thinly sliced, raw tender asparagus
2 tbsp finely sliced green onions, including tender tops
¼ cup sliced radishes

½ tsp salt
Lettuce
⅓ cup French dressing
1 tbsp catchup
⅛ tsp Worcestershire sauce

Lightly toss asparagus, onions and radishes together with salt. Divide the mixture lightly into four lettuce cups. Drizzle with French dressing to which the catchup and Worcestershire sauce have been added. Serve at once. 4 servings.

SLICED CUCUMBER SALAD

Wash, peel and slice 1 large cucumber. Sprinkle with salt and pepper; barely cover with vinegar diluted with half as much water, and chill at least an hr. Serve as is, or drain and serve on lettuce with mayonnaise or French dressing. Peeled, thinly sliced dry or green onions, radishes, or sliced tomatoes also combine well with cucumber in seasoned vinegar. 5 servings.

STUFFED CUCUMBER SALAD

2 medium-sized cucumbers	Lettuce
Pimiento Cheese, p 453	⅓ cup French dressing

Wash cucumbers. They may be pared or not, as desired. Cut in halves lengthwise, and scoop out center portion containing large seeds and discard. Fill centers with pimiento cheese, and press 2 halves together. Chill in refrigerator for an hr or more. To serve, slice cucumbers crosswise and arrange slices on lettuce leaves on individual salad plates. Serve with French dressing. 5 servings.

STUFFED TOMATO SALAD

5 good-sized tomatoes	1 tbsp finely chopped onion
1 cup diced celery	⅓ cup mayonnaise
1 cucumber, pared and diced	Lettuce

Wash tomatoes, cut out stem end, and scoop out centers. Dice centers and combine with celery, cucumber, onion and enough salt and pepper to suit taste. Then fold in the mayonnaise. Cover and chill filling and tomato shell separately. Stuff tomatoes with filling and serve at once on crisp lettuce. 5 servings.

TOMATO ANCHOVY SALAD

A particularly fine salad to serve as a first course

2 large tomatoes	1 hard-cooked egg, sliced in
¼ cup French Dressing,	4 crosswise slices
p 1200	4 tsp mayonnaise
¼ head lettuce, shredded	Sprigs parsley
1 tbsp anchovy paste	

Peel tomatoes and cut each in half crosswise. Dip in French dressing and place on bed of the shredded lettuce. Spread tomato slices with anchovy paste. Top with slice of egg. Drop a tsp of mayonnaise on each egg; then garnish with sprig of parsley. 4 servings.

TOMATO AND LETTUCE SALAD

4 medium tomatoes	1000 Island Dressing,
Head *or* leaf lettuce	p 1206

Scald, peel and chill tomatoes. Cut head lettuce into 4 thick crosswise slices or shred leaf lettuce and arrange on individual salad

Note: Recipe for French Dressing, p 1200, for Mayonnaise p 1202.

plates. Slice tomatoes, arrange overlapping slices over the lettuce. Pour dressing over the salad and serve at once. 4 servings.

OLD-TIME TOMATO AND ONION SALAD

4 large, meaty tomatoes, chilled	Blue Cheese Dressing, p 1197, *or* seasoned vinegar,
1 sweet onion, medium	p 1177

Choose red ripe tomatoes; wash. Peel and wash onion. Slice tomatoes in half crosswise and onion paper thin. Arrange slices alternately in a large bowl or on individual salad plates. Serve with dressing, or drizzle with seasoned vinegar. 5 servings.

Note: This type of salad with plain seasoned vinegar has been served for generations, but is still one of the most refreshing and beautiful of all salads. Pared sliced cucumber may be added or substituted for the onion.

TOMATO SALAD WITH CUCUMBER DRESSING

½ tsp salt	Dash of basil
1 tbsp vinegar	1 tsp grated onion
2 tbsp salad oil	½ medium cucumber, sliced
¼ tsp freshly ground black pepper	2 tbsp chopped green pepper
¼ tsp sugar	2 large tomatoes, peeled and chilled

Combine first 7 ingredients. Pour over cucumber and green pepper and let marinate 5 min. Slice tomatoes and serve with cucumber mixture poured over them. 4 servings.

SPLICED TOMATO SALAD

Choose brilliant colored meaty tomatoes just a trifle larger than an egg and have well chilled. Remove a thin slice from the stem end and use this for the bottom of the salad. Have a sharp knife to cut the tomato from the top downward into ¼-inch slices but leaving well intact at the bottom. Slide thin slices of pared cucumber or hard-cooked egg well down between the slices. Place carefully in crisp lettuce cups. Serve with Roquefort dressing or mayonnaise.

Spliced Cucumber. Two-inch lengths of pared cucumber may be used in place of the tomato. Use thin slices of radish or of small tomatoes to slide between the slices of cucumber. Serve as above.

MOLDED SALADS

Molded salads may be a spontaneous mixture of harmonious foods held together by a suitably flavored gelatin mixture, or may have the foods arranged in a pattern or design. The solid ingredients must be in neat attractive shapes and must complement each other in flavor and texture, and the gelatin mixture must blend in both color and flavor with the rest of the salad. A wide variety of fruits, vegetables, meat, fish, poultry and juices may be used in molded salads, but until the knack of making them is mastered, it is well to follow carefully the special recipes for the different types.

While the making of a fancy molded salad is not difficult, it does require a good deal of patience and will surely be imperfect if the procedure is rushed. When the mold is chosen, it will often suggest a type of arrangement, or the arrangement may be planned for a plain square or round pan. A thin layer of gelatin should be congealed first over the entire surface of the mold by holding it in a pan of ice water and tipping the mold from side to side to coat the entire surface in a uniform layer. This not only prevents any solid food from coming in contact with the mold, but adds a great deal of sparkling beauty. Then the food can be arranged in the bottom of the mold (which will be the top when it is unmolded) in a single layer in the desired pattern. Then a second thin layer of cooled gelatin is poured around the food to hold it in place, and allowed to set in the refrigerator until the gelatin has hardened completely and anchored the design securely. Then the entire mold can be filled in the same manner, layer after layer, or after the top is arranged the rest of the food may be added all at once. The mold must always be congealed between each layer and the gelatin that is added should be cool so it will not melt the previous layer and disturb the pattern.

After the salad is congealed, it should be covered with a waxed paper or an oil silk cover to prevent it from drying out on the surface. These salads will remain in excellent condition overnight, but it is never advisable to hold them any longer for the utmost in appetite appeal.

It is well to remember that in the summer a gelatin mold may require about 1 tsp more gelatin for each pt of liquid than in the winter to hold its shape at the table until the last morsel is consumed.

Unmolding the Salad: The molded salad must be unmolded carefully or all of the work that was put into it to make it beautiful will be lost. Many women have their pet theories about unmolding and some seem to have difficulty, but the process is very simple if care and patience direct the effort. The unmolding is like the making of the salad, if it is carelessly or hurriedly done, the results will surely be a failure. All that is needed is a thin, sharp-bladed knife, a pan of hot water that will be large enough for the mold to be dipped into it, and a flat plate of the appropriate size to hold the mold and any additional garnish without crowding. The knife should be run around the edge of the mold to a depth of about ½ inch only, and very close to the edge of the container to loosen the bottom edge. Then the mold is dipped quickly to within ½ inch of the top in hot water. By shaking the mold very gently, it can be quickly seen if the salad is loosened; if not, it should be dipped quickly again. It is much better to dip two or three times quickly and stop at just the right stage than to leave the mold in the hot water too long the first time and melt the gelatin. Then the plate should be centered over the top of the mold and both mold and plate inverted at the same time. Then the metal or glass mold can be lifted off carefully and the edges of the platter garnished with greens, fruits, or vegetables in a beautiful way. The salad can be put back in the refrigerator for a few min until ready to serve, but should be unmolded as near the time it is needed as practical.

MOLDED FISH AND MEAT SALADS

CHICKEN AND TONGUE IN ASPIC

2 envelopes, 2 tbsp plain gelatin
¼ cup cold water
4 cups cold concentrated chicken broth
½ to ¾ lb canned tongue, thinly sliced

4 lbs stewing chicken, simmered to make broth
2 hard-cooked eggs, sliced
2 tomatoes
Mayonnaise

Soften gelatin in cold water for 5 min. Skim off all fat from the cold broth. Heat broth to boiling, add softened gelatin and stir until dissolved. Pour about 1 cup of the gelatin mixture in a 6 to 7-cup ring mold. Set in a pan of ice water and tilt mold around until inside surface is covered with a thin layer of congealed aspic. Slice both the tongue and chicken thinly and neatly. Arrange shapeliest pieces of tongue and chicken alternately around the sides and bottom of mold. Place slices of egg near top all around mold. Combine remaining aspic with remaining chicken, tongue and egg and carefully spoon into mold. Press down gently to displace any air bubbles and make a smooth surface on top. Chill until firm. Unmold on a flat serving dish. Garnish with tomatoes cut in wedges and serve with mayonnaise blended with enough chili sauce or cream to give the desired consistency. 6 to 8 servings.

CHICKEN STEVENS

Handsome to see, delicious to eat

1 tbsp plain gelatin
½ cup cold water
2 cups rich chicken broth
¼ tsp salt
Dash of red pepper
¼ tsp onion juice
1 medium size ripe avocado

1 tbsp lemon juice
1½ cups thin-sliced breast of chicken
2 hard-cooked eggs
Cress *or* lettuce
Mayonnaise

Sprinkle gelatin over cold water, let stand 5 min. Chill chicken broth and remove all fat before measuring. Heat half of it to simmering, remove from heat, add gelatin and stir until dissolved. Add rest of broth and the next 3 ingredients. Cool until syrupy. Pour a half-inch layer of gelatin into a glass loaf pan 8¾ x 4½ x 2¾ inches. Congeal in refrigerator. Cut avocado in half, strip off peel and remove seed. Cut into ¼" thick lengthwise slices; arrange these in a pattern over the congealed gelatin. Drizzle half the lemon juice over slices to preserve color. Over avocado arrange neatly a layer of chicken slices which have been pricked with a fork. Cut eggs with an egg slicer and stand a row of slices up around the sides. Pour in enough of the syrupy gelatin to cover the chicken ¼" deep and to anchor the egg slices. Refrigerate to congeal. When firm, slice rest of avocado and arrange on gelatin, sprinkle with rest of lemon juice and add rest of chicken slices. Add remaining gelatin syrup. Use a paring knife to draw egg slices away from sides of pan just enough to allow a thin layer of gelatin to flow up against the pan. Cover, refrigerate 3 or 4 hrs until firm. Unmold onto a cold platter, p 1155. Garnish with cress. At the table cut slices 1¼ inches thick, garnish with cress and serve with chilled mayonnaise. A steak knife and cake server are ideal for serving this salad. 7 servings.

Note: Chicken should be moist and very tender. The slices are pricked to allow gelatin to run through them and make cutting the mold into whole slices easier. This salad may also be put into individual molds.

CHICKEN BROTH FOR ASPIC

The best flavored aspic for fish, chicken, or veal molds is a concentrated chicken broth. To prepare this broth, choose a fowl weighing 4 to 6 lbs. Clean chicken, cut into serving portions, and fit compactly into a kettle with a tight-fitting cover. Barely cover with water, add 1 tbsp salt, 1 small pod red pepper, 2 branches celery and 1 small onion. Cover tightly and heat to boiling, then reduce heat and simmer until fowl is tender. Strain off broth and reheat to boiling with 2 slightly beaten egg whites to make the stock sparkling clear. Cool, strain again and measure. For each quart of broth use 2 tbsp plain gelatin (2 envelopes) softened in ½ cup cold broth. Place softened gelatin over hot water until dissolved, then stir thoroughly into the chicken broth, or dissolve softened gelatin in the heated broth. This clear liquid is then ready to be used for aspic salads. Makes 1 qt. To make veal broth, use bony pieces of veal.

CHICKEN SALAD WITH CRANBERRY JELLY

Prepare Chicken Salad, p 1185. Prepare Cranberry Jelly, p 563, and chill in a ring mold. Heap chicken salad lightly into cranberry jelly ring unmolded on a flat serving dish. Garnish with watercress or endive.

JELLIED SALMON SALAD

¾ tsp salt	¼ cup cold water
½ tsp dry mustard	¼ cup vinegar
1 tbsp flour	1 tsp grated onion
1 tbsp sugar	1 lb can red salmon
½ cup milk	¾ cup finely diced celery
1 egg, beaten	2 hard-cooked eggs
1 envelope, 1 tbsp plain	Lettuce
gelatin	Mayonnaise

Combine first four ingredients in top of double boiler; add milk combined with beaten egg. Cook over boiling water until thickened, stirring constantly. Soften gelatin in cold water for 5 min, add to hot mixture and stir until dissolved and well blended. Add vinegar and onion. Cool until thick and syrupy. Flake salmon after removing skin and large bones; fold flaked salmon and celery into cooled mixture. Line a lightly oiled mold (3 to 4-cup) with egg, sliced or cut lengthwise into sixths, and turn salmon mixture into mold carefully. Press down gently to dislodge air pockets. Chill until firm. Unmold on chilled flat serving plate lined with crisp lettuce. Serve with mayonnaise. 5 servings.

Variation: Party Salmon Salad. For fancy party mold, use a fish mold (3-cup capacity) lined with a thin layer of plain gelatin over entire inner surface. Into partially congealed aspic, place slice of stuffed olive for eye of fish, slices of stuffed olives cut in half for scales, and strips of white of hard-cooked egg for tail and to simulate gills. Any egg left over may be chopped and mixed with salmon. Place salmon mixture into mold very carefully so as not to dislodge the pattern. Press down gently and flatten top. Chill until firm. Unmold on chilled flat serving dish. Garnish with watercress and cucumber slices marinated in tarragon vinegar. 5 servings.

MOLDED SALMON WITH CUCUMBER DRESSING

1 lb can red salmon	2 tsp flour
1 envelope plain gelatin,	1 tsp prepared mustard
1 tbsp	¾ cup milk
¼ cup cold water	2 egg yolks, slightly beaten
2 tsp butter	¼ cup vinegar
½ tsp salt	Lettuce
1 tsp sugar	

Remove skin from salmon and discard. Mash bones and add to coarsely flaked fish. Soften gelatin in the cold water. Melt the butter in a saucepan, add the dry ingredients and blend. Add combined milk and egg yolks and cook with constant stirring until mixture boils and thickens. Remove from heat, add the softened gelatin, and stir until dissolved. Add vinegar and salmon and mix very lightly. Turn into individual molds or into a small loaf pan brushed lightly with salad oil and chill until firm. Unmold, p 1155, on chilled flat serving plate. Surround with crisp lettuce leaves and serve with cucumber dressing. 4 to 6 servings.

Cucumber Dressing:

⅓ cup mayonnaise
2 tbsp sweet pickle relish
½ tsp celery salt

½ cup finely chopped pared cucumber

Mix thoroughly and serve over the molded salmon.

SALMON IN CUCUMBER ASPIC

1 envelope plain gelatin, 1 tbsp
¼ cup cold water
½ cup boiling water
1¼ tsp salt
1 tsp sugar
2 tbsp lemon juice
1 tbsp vinegar

Dash freshly ground black pepper
Large cucumber, pared and finely grated
1 lb can red salmon
Lettuce
Mayonnaise

Soften gelatin in cold water for 5 min. Add boiling water and stir until dissolved. Add salt, sugar, lemon juice, vinegar and pepper. Cool, then add cucumber with its juice. Chill until slightly congealed, stirring occasionally.

Remove and discard skin from salmon; crush the bones and flake the fish. Fold into gelatin mixture. Place in a lightly oiled mold (about 1 qt). Chill until firm, then unmold on flat serving dish lined with lettuce. Serve with mayonnaise. 4 servings.

SHRIMP AND LOBSTER MOUSSE

2 envelopes, 2 tbsp plain gelatin
½ cup cold water
1 cup concentrated chicken broth *or* bouillon
¼ cup mayonnaise
2 tbsp chili sauce
¼ tsp salt
1 tsp prepared horseradish

¼ cup finely cut celery
1 cup cooked, cleaned shrimp cut into small pieces
½ cup fresh *or* canned lobster *or* crab meat, stiff cartilage removed
½ cup heavy cream, whipped
Cucumber
Lettuce

Soften gelatin in cold water for 5 min. Heat broth to boiling, then add softened gelatin and stir until dissolved. Cool until thick and syrupy. Add next eight ingredients in order given. Place in a mold (3 to 4-cup) that has been brushed lightly with salad oil. Cover with waxed paper. Chill until firm. Unmold on chilled flat serving plate. Garnish with cucumber slices and crisp lettuce and serve with additional mayonnaise. 5 servings.

SHRIMP IN TOMATO ASPIC

Prepare Tomato Aspic as directed, p 1170. When aspic starts to congeal, fold in 1 cup cooked, cleaned shrimp, cut up or split in half lengthwise, 1 tbsp finely chopped green pepper and ½ cup finely diced celery. Turn into 4-cup mold that has been rinsed with cold water, chill until firm. Unmold, serve on crisp lettuce, garnish with ripe olives. Serve with mayonnaise thinned to desired consistency with cream, leftover pickle juice, lemon juice or vinegar. Serve at once. 5 to 6 servings.

CRAB STUFFED EGGS IN ASPIC JELLY

6 Hard-cooked Eggs, p. 663
⅓ cup mayonnaise
1 tbsp lemon juice
¾ tsp salt
⅛ tsp grated onion
1 tsp prepared mustard, optional
1 tsp finely chopped green pepper

1 tsp finely chopped pimiento
¼ cup finely chopped celery
1 cup crabmeat, boned and flaked, 6 oz
2 cups rich Chicken Broth, p 1289
1 tbsp plain gelatin
1 tbsp lemon juice
Salt to taste, about ½ tsp

Cut eggs in half lengthwise. Remove yolks carefully and drop into a bowl. Mash thoroughly, add mayonnaise, lemon juice, salt, onion, and mustard, and blend well. Mix in next four ingredients. Heap back into the halves of whites, garnish with bits of green pepper and pimiento. Place in a single layer in a shallow glass dish (about 6 x 10½ x 2 inches).

Have broth strained through double thickness of cheesecloth and chilled. Soften gelatin in ¼ cup of the broth. Let stand 5 min. Dissolve by adding ½ cup heated broth. Add lemon juice and salt and combine with remaining chilled broth. Pour around stuffed eggs, being careful not to dislodge fillings. Chill until set. Cut in sqs and place on lettuce. Serve with mayonnaise or Horseradish Dressing, p 1201. 6 servings.

MOLDED FRUIT SALADS

AVOCADO ASPIC RING

Smooth and has excellent flavor

1½ tbsp plain gelatin
¼ cup cold water
1 cup boiling water
2 tbsp lemon juice
1 tsp sugar
1½ cups puréed avocado, 1 good-size avocado that is just ripe
½ cup sour cream

½ cup mayonnaise
Scant ½ tsp salt
Pepper
Dash of cayenne
¼ tsp grated onion
1½ cups tomato wedges
¾ cup chopped watercress
Romaine, chicory *or* lettuce

Soften gelatin in the ¼ cup of water for 5 min, then stir in boiling water until gelatin dissolves, then 1 tbsp of the lemon juice and sugar. Cool until consistency of unbeaten egg whites. Cut avocado in half, carefully strip off peel, remove pit, then put through food mill or sieve to obtain purée. Stir in rest of lemon juice, then the next 6 ingredients. Now fold in the slightly thickened gelatin mixture until well blended. Pour at once into a 9-inch oiled ring mold or into 6 or 7 individual molds. Chill until firm or for about 2 hrs. When ready to serve, unmold onto a well chilled platter covered with crisp cress, romaine or curly endive or lettuce. Fill center with tomato combined with chopped cress. 6 to 7 servings.

Note: This aspic may be poured into a larger ring mold and tomato aspic poured over the top when it has congealed to obtain not only a beautiful but delicious salad ring.

AVOCADO MOUSSE

1 tbsp plain gelatin, 1 envelope	¾ tsp salt
	¾ cup mayonnaise
¼ cup cold water	¾ cup heavy cream, whipped
3 medium, fully ripened avocados, 1½ lbs	Watercress
	Sliced oranges *and* grape-
2 tbsp lemon juice	fruit sections
1½ tsp onion juice	

Don't attempt this mousse until you have high quality avocado with flesh ripened just to the right, soft, lovely green stage.

Soften gelatin in cold water for five min, then set over hot water until dissolved. Meanwhile purée the avocados. (There should be about 2 cups). Add next four ingredients. Add dissolved gelatin slowly, stirring constantly. Fold in cream thoroughly but lightly and pour into 6-cup mold or individual molds that have been rinsed with cold water. Chill until firm. Unmold on chilled flat platter and garnish with watercress, thick slices of orange and grapefruit sections. 6 to 8 servings.

Variation: Omit onion juice. Steep 1 tsp grated lime rind in 2 tbsp lime juice for a min. Press out juice, discard rind and substitute the lime juice for lemon juice in preceding recipe.

BING CHERRY JELLIED SALAD

Colorful, decorative and delicious

2 pkgs cherry-flavored gelatin	4 tsp lemon juice
2 cups boiling water	Dash of salt
2 No. 303 cans Bing cherries in heavy syrup	Lettuce
	Mayonnaise

Note: Recipe for Mayonnaise, p 1202.

Oil lightly an 8 x 8 x 2-inch pan. Drain cherries. Pit and cut fruit in half—there should be 2⅔ cups fruit and 1⅓ cups juice. Turn gelatin into 2-qt bowl; add boiling water and stir until gelatin dissolves, then cool slightly. Add cherry juice, lemon juice and salt. Cool until slightly syrupy. Now add cherries. Turn into prepared pan. Chill until firm. Cut into 2-inch sqs. Serve on lettuce, topped with plain mayonnaise, or mayonnaise into which a little sweetened whipped cream has been folded. 16 servings.

Note: For buffet service, congeal in a ring mold.

COOKED CRANBERRY APPLE SALAD

3 cups cranberries	¼ cup cold water
1¾ cups water	2 apples, pared
1½ cups sugar	1 cup diced celery
1 tbsp plain gelatin,	Lettuce
1 envelope	Mayonnaise

Wash and pick over cranberries, cook covered until soft in the 1¾ cups water, then add sugar. Strain and rub pulp through sieve. Soften gelatin in the ¼ cup cold water. Reheat cranberry purée to boiling and add the softened gelatin, stirring until gelatin is dissolved. Pour a thin layer of cranberry gelatin into individual molds which have been rinsed with cold water. Chill in refrigerator until set; then arrange apple cut in thin wedges in design and pour in a little more gelatin to hold them in place; chill until set. Add rest of apples and celery to rest of gelatin mixture, pour into molds, and chill until firm. Unmold on lettuce leaves and serve with mayonnaise. 5 servings.

CRANBERRY APPLE SALAD

2 cups cranberries	½ cup cold water
1 tsp orange rind	½ cup finely diced celery
1 cup sugar	1 apple, diced
1 pkg lemon-flavored gelatin	Lettuce
1 cup boiling water	Mayonnaise

Wash and grind the raw cranberries and combine with orange rind and sugar. Let stand 30 min. Meanwhile dissolve the gelatin in the boiling water, add the cold water and chill until slightly congealed and syrupy. Add the cranberries, celery, and apple. Turn into a mold that has been rinsed with cold water. Chill and serve on lettuce leaves and top with mayonnaise. 6 servings.

Note: Recipe for Mayonnaise, p 1202.

CRANBERRY SALAD MOLD

¾ cup ground raw cran-
berries, 2 cups whole
¼ cup orange juice, 1 small
orange
⅓ cup sugar

¼ tsp salt
5 tsp plain gelatin
1 cup apple juice
Lettuce
Mayonnaise

Wash, sort and grind cranberries. Add orange juice, sugar and salt and set in refrigerator to chill. Meanwhile soften gelatin in ¼ cup of the apple juice. Heat rest of juice to boiling. Pour over softened gelatin and stir to dissolve thoroughly. Combine all ingredients except lettuce and mayonnaise, pour into 3-cup mold that has been rinsed with cold water. Chill until firm. Unmold on flat serving dish. Surround with crisp lettuce and serve with mayonnaise. 4 to 6 servings.

GINGER ALE SALAD MOLD

2 tbsp gelatin, 2 envelopes
¼ cup cold water
1 tbsp lemon juice
No. 2 can crushed pine-
apple, 2¼ cups

1 seedless orange, pared and
diced, ⅓ cup
1 cup ginger ale
⅓ cup mayonnaise
Cream

Soften gelatin in cold water; then place over hot water until gelatin is dissolved. Add to lemon juice. Stir in the pineapple (with juice) and orange dice, then stir in ginger ale and turn into a 4-cup mold which has been rinsed with cold water; chill in refrigerator until firm. Unmold and serve with mayonnaise that has been thinned with 2 tbsp cream, or maraschino cherry juice. 5 servings.

Note: Ginger ale should be freshly opened, cold and sparkling to give the desired lively flavor.

GRAPEFRUIT ASPIC

Lively in flavor and a good summer pickup

No. 2 can grapefruit, 2½
cups
½ tsp sugar

⅛ tsp salt
1 tbsp plain gelatin
Dressing

Combine 2 cups of the grapefruit with sugar and salt. Soften gelatin in the remaining ½ cup grapefruit juice, then place over hot water to melt. Stir melted gelatin thoroughly into grapefruit mixture and turn into a mold rinsed in cold water. Place in refrigerator to congeal. Unmold onto plate and surround with crisp lettuce cups. Serve with Lime Honey or Celery Seed or any other sweet dressing. 2½ cups.

GRAPE THYME SALAD

1 tbsp plain gelatin	1 tbsp lemon juice
¼ cup cold water	1 cup white seedless grapes,
¼ tsp dried thyme	peeled, halved
¼ cup boiling water	½ cup celery, cut fine
1½ cups bottled *or* frozen	1 or 2 drops red food color-
grape juice	ing, optional

Soften gelatin in the cold water for 5 min. Combine thyme and boiling water in glass cup, cover and let stand 5 min; then strain through fine strainer or cheesecloth into a saucepan. Add gelatin, place over low heat and stir until gelatin dissolves. Remove from heat and stir in grape and lemon juices. Chill until thick and syrupy, then fold in grapes and celery. Add coloring if desired. Turn into individual molds first rinsed in cold water. Chill until firm. Garnish with avocado slices and frosted green grapes. 6 to 8 servings.

LIME OLIVE-NUT MOLDED SALAD

Beautiful and has most appealing flavor

1 pkg lime-flavored gelatin	½ cup coarsely chopped
1 cup boiling water	pecans
1 cup cold water	Lettuce
⅓ cup sliced stuffed olives	

Turn gelatin into mixing bowl. Add boiling water and stir until gelatin dissolves, then stir in cold water. Let cool to consistency of unbeaten egg white. Now fold in olives and nuts. Turn into a small glass loaf pan rubbed with salad oil. Place in refrigerator, until firm. Unmold just before serving and cut into ½ to ¾-inch thick slices. Use spatula or pancake turner to transfer to lettuce-lined salad plates. Serve plain or with mayonnaise. 6 to 9 servings.

PEACH FIG SALAD MOLD

No. 2 can large peach	1 pkg lemon-flavored gelatin
halves in heavy syrup	Lettuce
No. 2 can figs in heavy	Mayonnaise
syrup	

Drain peaches and measure peach syrup, add ½ cup fig syrup and enough water to make 1¾ cups of liquid. Heat liquid to boiling, and add gelatin, stirring until dissolved. Pour a layer of gelatin about ¼-inch thick in a pan about 9 x 5 inches. Chill until firm, then place drained figs at intervals down on firm gelatin. Over each fig, place a peach, hollow side down. Spoon in a little more gelatin and again chill until set to anchor the fruit. Then add the remaining gelatin and allow to set. To serve, cut the salad into sections, allowing one peach half to each serving. Serve on crisp lettuce, fig side up, with mayonnaise. 5 to 6 servings.

Variation: A few chopped toasted almonds make a tasty and attractive garnish.

PINEAPPLE COTTAGE CHEESE ASPIC

2½ cups unsweet pineapple juice, No. 2 can
1½ cups creamed cottage cheese
2 tsp sugar
2 tsp lemon juice
1/16 tsp grated onion
2 tbsp plain gelatin

Combine 2 cups of the pineapple juice with the next 4 ingredients. Soften gelatin in the remaining pineapple juice, then place over hot water until gelatin melts. Stir melted gelatin into Cottage Cheese mixture thoroughly. Turn into a 4-cup ring mold and place in refrigerator to congeal or put into loaf pan and cut in slices. Unmold on plate and fill center if desired with fresh halved apricots, peach halves or diced fresh peeled tomato. 4 cups.

PINEAPPLE GRAPE SALAD

Refreshing, velvety and pale green

1 pkg lime-flavored gelatin
1 cup boiling water
No. 2 can crushed pineapple
1 tbsp lemon juice
1 cup white seedless grapes
½ cup finely chopped celery
½ cup mild American cheese, cut in ¼″ cubes
½ pt whipping cream

Dissolve gelatin in water. Add juice drained from pineapple, about ¾ cup, and lemon juice. Chill until consistency of unbeaten egg white. Add pineapple, grapes, celery and cheese. Mix thoroughly, then fold in stiffly beaten cream. Turn into 4 to 6 cup mold rinsed in cold water. Chill until firm. Unmold on serving plate. Surround with curly endive. Garnish with sections of persimmon, small bunches of grapes and maraschino cherries. 6 to 8 servings.

MOLDED PRUNE SALAD

1 cup prunes
2 cups water
2 tbsp lemon juice
1 pkg orange-flavored gelatin
1½ cups creamed cottage cheese
¼ tsp salt
¼ cup chopped nuts
Lettuce
Lemon French Dressing

Simmer prunes in water from 20 to 25 min or until soft and puffy. Cool prunes, drain off and save juice. There should be 1⅓ cups juice.

Pit the prunes and chop. There should be 1½ cups. Heat prune juice to boiling. Remove from heat, add lemon juice and orange-flavored gelatin. Stir until thoroughly dissolved. Chill until gelatin is slightly congealed. Whip with a rotary beater until fluffy. Add remaining ingredients and fold in thoroughly but lightly. Turn into a 4-cup mold that has been rinsed quickly with cold water. Chill until firm. Serve on bed of lettuce with Lemon French Dressing, p 1201, or mayonnaise thinned to desired consistency with cream. 5 servings.

PINEAPPLE-LIME VELVET

1 pkg lime-flavored gelatin
1 cup boiling water
3 oz pkg cream cheese
⅔ cup crushed pineapple
  with its juice
½ cup finely cut celery
½ cup heavy cream, whipped
Watercress
Maraschino *or* fresh Bing
cherries

Add gelatin to water and stir until dissolved. Add cheese and beat with a rotary beater until cheese is well blended. Chill until slightly congealed, then add pineapple and celery. Fold in whipped cream lightly but thoroughly. Turn into 3 to 4-cup mold that has been rinsed with cold water. Chill until firm. Unmold. Serve on watercress. Garnish with cherries. 6 to 8 servings.

STUFFED PEAR SALAD

1¾ cups pear *or* raspberry and
  pear juice
1 pkg raspberry-flavored
  gelatin
6 pear halves, No. 2½ can
1 cup fresh, *or* frozen red
raspberries, half-thawed
Lettuce
⅓ cup mayonnaise
Cream

Heat juice and pour over gelatin in a bowl. Stir until gelatin is completely dissolved. Pour an eighth-inch layer into a glass baking dish 10 x 6 x 2 inches rinsed with cold water. Chill until gelatin layer is firm. Place pears, hollow-side-up on gelatin; fill hollows heaping with raspberries. Pour remaining gelatin over berries carefully so as not to displace them. Chill until firm. Unmold. Cut in sqs with stuffed pears in the center. Serve on crisp lettuce-lined individual salad plates, or arrange on a platter. Serve with mayonnaise, thinned to desired consistency with plain or whipped cream. 6 servings.

SUNSHINE SALAD

1 pkg lemon-flavored gelatin
1¼ cups hot water
1 tbsp cider vinegar
½ tsp salt
9-oz can crushed pineapple
1 cup grated raw carrot
Lettuce *or* romaine
Mayonnaise

Dissolve gelatin by stirring into the hot water. Add vinegar and salt, stirring to mix well, and chill until mixture becomes syrupy. Add the crushed pineapple (with its juice) and the raw carrot. Pour mixture into a 4-cup mold that has been rinsed with cold water, and chill until firm. Unmold onto chilled serving plate. Surround with lettuce and serve with mayonnaise. 5 servings.

TRI-COLOR FRUIT MOLD

First layer:

No. 2 can apricots, 2½ cups   1 pkg orange-flavored gelatin

Drain and save juice from apricots and purée fruit. Measure juice and add enough water to make 1¾ cups. Heat to boiling and add to gelatin. Stir until thoroughly dissolved, then chill until mixture is slightly congealed. Add purée and pour into round mold 8 or 9 inches in diameter and 2 inches deep or a deep layer cake tin that has been rinsed with cold water. Chill until firm.

Second layer:

1 cup boiling water   1 cup crushed pineapple
1 pkg lime-flavored gelatin   with juice
                                   ½ cup heavy cream, whipped

While the first layer is chilling, pour boiling water over lime-flavored gelatin and stir until dissolved. Chill until slightly congealed, add pineapple and fold in the cream. Pour over firm orange layer in mold. Chill second layer until firm.

Third layer:

1 cup boiling water   1 pt fresh, *or* frozen rasp-
1 pkg raspberry-flavored   berries, thawed
  gelatin   Mayonnaise

Pour boiling water over raspberry gelatin and stir until dissolved. Chill until slightly congealed. Pick out enough whole berries to fill ¾ cup. Purée remaining berries and measure pulp and juice (should be about ¾ cup). Add water if necessary to make ¾ cup. Combine with gelatin, fold in fruit and pour over two layers in the mold. Chill until top layer is firm. Unmold on chilled flat serving plate. Garnish with mayonnaise. To serve, cut into pie-shaped wedges. Lay flat side down on lettuce leaf. Serve with additional fresh fruits if desired. 12 to 14 servings.

Note: To unmold see directions, p 1155. Salad dressing section begins p 1197.

Definition: You PEEL with your fingers. You PARE with a knife.

MOLDED VEGETABLE SALADS

COTTAGE CHEESE IN TOMATO ASPIC

Prepare Tomato Aspic, p 1170. When partially congealed, fold in 8 oz (1 cup) creamed cottage cheese and 1 tbsp finely cut chives. Turn into mold that has been rinsed in cold water; chill until firm. Unmold and serve with mayonnaise if desired.

CREAMY TOMATO ASPIC

2 envelopes, 2 tbsp, plain gelatin
½ cup cold water
No. 2 can tomatoes, 2½ cups
1 tsp chopped onion
½ tsp salt
½ tsp celery salt
1 tsp sugar
2 tbsp vinegar
½ cup sour cream
Mayonnaise

Soften gelatin in cold water for 5 min. Heat all ingredients except sour cream to boiling. Add gelatin mixture and stir until dissolved. Rub mixture through sieve. Blend in sour cream. Cool slightly, then pour into a 2 to 3-cup mold of any desired shape that has been rinsed in cold water. Chill until firm. Unmold. Serve with mayonnaise mixed with chopped chives or with any fish, egg, or meat salad. 5 or 6 servings.

MOLDED BEET SALAD

1 lb partially cooked beets, 20 min
1 medium onion
¼ cup chopped parsley, lightly pkd
¼ cup vinegar
1½ tsp salt
1 tsp sugar
1 tbsp plain gelatin, 1 envelope
1½ cups cold water
1 small cucumber, sliced thin

Cook beets, cool in cold water, drain. Remove skins. Grate beets and onion on medium grater. Add parsley, vinegar, salt and sugar. Soften gelatin in ¼ cup of the cold water and dissolve over hot water. Add remaining water (1¼ cups) and pour a thin layer in bottom of a 9-inch ring mold that has been rinsed with cold water. Arrange cucumber slices in bottom of mold, and when partially set, pour in rest of gelatin combined with beet mixture. Chill until firm. Unmold on a chilled, flat serving dish. 4 generous servings.

Note: To unmold see directions, p 1155.

MOLDED CABBAGE AND PINEAPPLE SALAD

1½ cups boiling water
1 pkg lemon-flavored gelatin
3 tbsp lemon juice
1 tbsp sugar
½ tsp salt
9-oz can crushed pineapple

1½ cups shredded crisp
cabbage
Lettuce *or* endive
Mayonnaise
Paprika

Add boiling water to gelatin, stirring until dissolved. Add lemon juice, sugar, salt and juice drained from pineapple. Chill until gelatin begins to set. Combine cabbage with pineapple and fold into gelatin mixture. Turn into a 4-cup mold which has been rinsed in cold water. Chill until firm. When ready to serve, unmold on a chilled flat serving dish. Surround with lettuce or curly endive. Serve with mayonnaise and a dash of paprika on top. 5 to 6 servings.

MOLDED VEGETABLE SALAD

1 pkg lemon-flavored gelatin
2 cups boiling water
½ tsp salt
1 tsp grated onion

2 cups tender crisp
shredded cabbage
½ cup grated raw carrot
Lettuce
Mayonnaise

Dissolve gelatin in the boiling water, add salt, cool and chill until syrupy. Meanwhile prepare vegetables. When gelatin is slightly thickened, fold in onion, cabbage and carrot. Pour into a 4-cup mold or individual molds that have been rinsed with cold water and chill until firm. Unmold and serve on lettuce-lined individual salad plates. Serve with mayonnaise. 5 servings.

PERFECTION SALAD

1 tbsp plain gelatin,
1 envelope
¼ cup cold water
1 cup boiling water
2 tbsp lemon juice
2 tbsp vinegar
3 tbsp sugar
¼ tsp salt

½ cup grated carrot
½ cup shredded tender crisp
cabbage
½ cup crushed pineapple
2 tbsp chopped green pepper
2 tsp chopped pimiento
Endive
Mayonnaise

Soften gelatin in cold water for five min, then dissolve in boiling water. Add lemon juice, vinegar, sugar and salt; cool until mixture just starts to congeal, then fold in next five ingredients. Pour into a 4-cup mold that has been rinsed in cold water. Chill until set, unmold on chilled flat serving plate. Surround with crisp curly endive or lettuce. Serve with mayonnaise. 5 servings.

Note: A square eight-inch cake pan makes an ideal mold for this salad.

Note: Recipe for Mayonnaise, p 1202.

TOMATO ASPIC, No. 1

Spicy, tart, refreshing, good with sour cream or with mayonnaise into which is worked Cream Cheese or Cottage Cheese

2½ cups canned tomatoes, high quality	2 tbsp cider vinegar
	2 tsp lemon juice
¼-inch slice from a 2-inch onion	½ tsp Worcestershire
	2 tbsp plain gelatin softened in ½ cup cold water
2 tbsp sugar	
1 tsp salt	½ tsp celery salt

Put tomatoes and onion in a saucepan, and simmer for 5 min. Put through a sieve to remove seed and onion. Add rest of ingredients to hot purée, stir thoroughly until gelatin dissolves. Pour into a 3-cup mold rinsed with cold water and place in refrigerator to congeal. Unmold and serve with mayonnaise or sour cream and surround with watercress or curly endive. 3 cups.

TOMATO ASPIC, No. 2

Mild—good with Shrimp Salad

2 cups rich red tomato juice	2 tbsp plain gelatin softened in 1 cup cold water
2 whole cloves	2 tbsp sugar
1 sq inch of bayleaf	3 tbsp lemon juice
¼-inch slice from a 2-inch onion	4 drops tabasco
	⅛ tsp onion juice

Simmer tomato juice with next 3 ingredients in a covered saucepan for 3 or 4 min. Then strain to remove cloves, leaf and onion. Add rest of ingredients to the hot juice and stir until gelatin dissolves. Pour into a mold rinsed in cold water and place in refrigerator to congeal. Unmold and serve with mayonnaise. 2½ cups.

TOMATO ASPIC, No. 3

Before heating, this mixture makes a delicious cocktail. When it is congealed it is good with Cream Cheese whipped up with cream until fluffy

1 cup rich red tomato juice	½ tsp salt
1 cup unsweet grapefruit juice	⅟₁₆ tsp fresh grated onion
	2 tsp plain gelatin
3 tsp sugar	

Combine all ingredients, stir thoroughly and place over low heat stirring constantly until gelatin just dissolves. Pour into a mold and place in refrigerator to congeal. Serve with chicken or tuna salad. 2 cups.

TOMATO ASPIC SALAD

2 tbsp gelatin, 2 envelopes
½ cup cold water
No. 2 can tomatoes,
2½ cups
1 tsp chopped onion
½ tsp salt

½ tsp celery salt
2 to 3 tsp sugar
2 tbsp vinegar, cider,
tarragon *or* malt
Watercress *or* curly endive
Mayonnaise

Soften gelatin in cold water. Heat next six ingredients to boiling; add gelatin, stirring until dissolved, and rub mixture through sieve. Cool slightly, then pour into a 3-cup mold that was rinsed with cold water and chill in refrigerator until firm. Unmold on chilled flat serving dish. Garnish with greens. Serve with mayonnaise or sour cream. Makes about 2 cups. 5 or 6 servings.

SALAD PLATTERS

Salad platters are usually made from the same kinds of fruit that would be used in a fruit salad bowl, but by arranging the fruit on a large platter or tray there is a better opportunity to make the arrangement startlingly beautiful and to keep the pieces shapely. Any combination of fresh and firm canned fruits can be used as long as the colors and shapes are arranged in an artistic fashion. These platters are most picturesque for buffet or party luncheons where they can be eaten with the meal or served as dessert. They can also be served with a border of attractive slices of roast turkey, chicken or ham which can be taken on the plates along with the fruit salad. Generally any dressing that is to be used on this salad should be served in a separate cruet or bowl.

FALL SALAD PLATTER

Honey dew melon
Fresh peaches
Lime Honey Dressing,
p 1202

Blue plums
Red raspberries
Greens

Cut melon into wedges, remove seeds and fibers, then pare each wedge. Pare peaches thinly to preserve the shape, then cut in half, remove pits, then dip in dressing to prevent darkening. Cut plums in quarters and discard pits. Pick over berries, wash and drain. Arrange wedges of melon fan-shaped at the two ends of a platter large enough to hold all the fruits desired. Lay peach halves cut side up so the beautiful carmine will show in between melon along both edges of platter to complete the circle. Insert a quarter of plum between each wedge of melon, skin side up. Pile raspberries lightly in center of platter. Garnish with crisp greens and serve at once with lime honey dressing in a separate bowl.

SUMMER SALAD PLATTER

1 pt strawberries	2 tbsp lemon juice
1 tbsp sugar	1 small, very red apple
1 small cantaloupe	Leaf lettuce
1 small grapefruit	½ lb Bing cherries, pitted
1 large avocado	

Wash, hull and sort berries. Add the sugar to ½ cup of the strawberries. Crush and simmer a few min. Strain through cheese cloth. Chill and reserve juice for dressing. Cut cantaloupe in wedges, discard seeds and fibers and pare. Section grapefruit carefully. Cut avocado in half, discard pit, slice across, then dip in lemon juice. Peel off rind and dip again just before arranging on platter. Cut apple into thin wedges, remove core and dip in lemon juice to prevent discoloration. Arrange avocado and apple alternately on lettuce around outer edge of platter. In inner circle arrange cantaloupe and grapefruit alternately. Heap remaining strawberries in middle and drop cherries around for a dark accent. Serve with sour cream dressing made as follows: Blend 1 cup sour cream, ¼ cup strawberry juice made from the ½ cup of strawberries, 1 tbsp lemon juice, ½ tsp sugar, and ½ tsp salt. Chill. 6 servings.

"WHOLE MEAL" FRUIT PLATTER

Pare and separate the sections of each of 5 small oranges so as to form a cup. Place orange section cups in the center of salad plates and fill each with 3 or 4 avocado dice. Pare and section 5 large oranges, arranging the sections of each orange in 3 groups around each orange cup. Between the orange sections arrange: in one space, 3 walnut bonbons, made by pressing 2 walnut halves into opposite sides of balls of cream cheese; in second place, 3 pitted dates each stuffed with 3 blanched almonds; in third space, 3 cooked, pitted prunes stuffed with peanut butter. Garnish fruits with curly endive or crisp lettuce. Serve with a French dressing made by beating or shaking together thoroughly the following ingredients: ¼ cup lemon juice, ¼ cup salad oil, ½ tsp salt, ½ tsp paprika, and 1 tbsp honey or sugar. 5 servings.

WINTER SALAD PLATTER

2 medium grapefruit	½ medium, fresh pineapple,
3 medium seedless oranges	*or,* 5 slices canned
2 ripe avocados	2 pkgs, 6 oz cream cheese
½ Persian melon	1 medium pomegranate
	Salad greens

Pare and section grapefruit over a bowl to save juice. Pare oranges and cut in slices ¼-inch thick. Peel avocados and cut in half crosswise, remove stone and cut into rings ¼-inch thick. Marinate in grapefruit juice to prevent discoloration. Pare and cut melon in 1-inch cubes. Pare and cut pineapple in fingers about 3 to 4 inches long and 1-inch wide. Place avocado rings overlapping to form a circle in center of platter. Heap melon cubes in center of ring. Place fingers of pineapple at each end fan-fashion. Lay overlapping slices of oranges at base of fingers next to avocado rings following the line of avocados. Then arrange the grapefruit sections to complete the circle around the avocado. Chill cream cheese thoroughly and cut in ½-inch sqs. Open pomegranate and remove seeds. Roll cheese sqs in seeds just enough to pick up a few. Place these "burrs" in center of each avocado ring. Serve with French or Lime Honey Dressing, p 1200 or p 1202. Garnish salad platter with salad greens. 6 to 8 servings.

SHREDDED SALADS

There is no sorrier sight than a tired-looking, limp heap of mangled shreds of cabbage, carrot, turnip or kohlrabi; and no sight more fresh and beautiful than these same vegetables properly prepared and served. When vegetables are shredded, the area that is exposed is increased enormously and all of the destructive forces of air, heat, acid, liquid, etc., are able to accelerate their activity to a lightning speed. The appearance, flavor and nutritional value of the vegetables are seriously impaired by as little as 10 min of standing after the salad is mixed.

The means of prevention are so simple that there is no excuse for ever serving anything but the freshest appearing grated salad. The original vegetables should be the *most crisp* and solid available, then cleaned and stored to retain their quality until ready to use. Leafy vegetables like cabbage should be sliced with a very sharp, thin-bladed knife rather than grated; it is just as quick and easy to do and the cuts are clean and sharp rather than bruised. The shreds retain their crispness best if they are not sliced too fine. The solid vegetables like carrots should be grated on a *very sharp* grater that does not make ragged edges on each strip. Then the grated vegetables can be held a short time if necessary in a chilled bowl that is covered with a damp piece of paper toweling or damp cloth. This will retain the crispness as long as no dressing is added. Then after everyone is seated and just before the salad is carried into the table, or at the table if you prefer, sprinkle with salt and pepper and any other seasonings, tossing lightly with a fork to mix, then drizzle the dressing on top and continue to toss with the fork until the vegetables are well coated with a thin film of dressing. Then serve at once and the salad will be crisp, flavorful and interesting to eye and palate.

BEET RELISH

No. 2 can beets
1 cup finely diced, pared
   cucumber
1 small onion, finely diced
¼ cup vinegar
¼ cup juice drained from
   beets

1 tsp sugar
¼ tsp salt
Dash black pepper
1 tsp finely chopped parsley,
   or 2 tsp chopped fresh dill

Drain beets, saving juice. Shred beets coarsely on a sharp grater into
mixing bowl, and add remaining ingredients. Toss well. Cover tightly
and chill in the refrigerator for at least 1 hr before serving to blend
flavors. Serve instead of salad with cold meat or fish dishes. (Rest of beet
juice should be saved to combine with other vegetable juices and pot
liquors for vegetable cocktail.) 5 servings.

BERMUDA SALAD

1 bunch crisp watercress
1 large Bermuda onion,
   sliced very thin
1 cup shredded, cooked beets
¼ cup salad oil

2 tbsp vinegar
½ tsp salt
¼ tsp sugar
⅛ tsp freshly ground pepper
¼ tsp caraway seed, crushed

Arrange watercress on salad plate. In the center, overlap onion slices
to form a ring. Pile beets lightly in center of these. Have remaining ingredients beaten together and chilled. Serve immediately over salad.
4 servings.

CABBAGE AND APPLE SALAD

2 cups shredded, crisp tender
   cabbage, ⅓ lb
1 cup diced, tart apples

1 tsp sugar
¼ cup mayonnaise
Salt to suit taste

Slice cabbage with a sharp, thin-bladed knife. Combine cabbage,
diced apple (pared or not) and sugar; add mayonnaise and salt and toss
together until just mixed. A little lemon juice may be added if a more
tart dressing is desired. Serve immediately on individual salad plates. 5
servings.

CABBAGE CARROT AND RAISIN SALAD

2 cups shredded, crisp tender
   cabbage, about ⅓ lb
1 cup shredded carrots, 2
   large carrots
½ cup seedless raisins,
   plumped, p 165

½ cup mayonnaise
1 tsp salt
1 tsp sugar
2 tsp lemon juice

Slice cabbage with a sharp, thin-bladed knife. Shred carrots coarsely on a very sharp grater; always grate in one direction only. Chill plumped raisins before using. Blend mayonnaise well with remaining ingredients. Combine all ingredients and toss lightly but thoroughly to mix. Heap on individual salad plates and serve at once. 5 servings.

CABBAGE CELERY APPLE AND GRAPE SALAD

2 cups shredded, crisp, tender
  cabbage, about ⅓ lb
⅓ cup mayonnaise
1 tsp salt
2 tsp sugar
1 tsp lemon juice

4 tsp orange juice
1 cup diced celery
1 cup diced red apple, unpared
1 cup halved, white seed-
  less grapes

Slice cabbage with a sharp, thin-bladed knife. Blend mayonnaise and next four ingredients together well. Combine remaining ingredients with cabbage, add mayonnaise mixture all at once and toss lightly but thoroughly to coat well. Serve immediately on individual salad plates. 5 servings.

CABBAGE SALADS

2 cups shredded, crisp, tender
  cabbage, ⅓ lb
1 cup shredded lettuce
3 tbsp chopped onion

¼ tsp salt
½ tsp sugar
French dressing
Lettuce

Slice cabbage with a sharp, thin-bladed knife. Cut head lettuce the same way, cut leaf lettuce (if used) with a sharp scissors. Combine cabbage, lettuce and onion. Sprinkle with salt and sugar, add dressing slowly, tossing together until all ingredients are mixed and well coated with dressing. Serve immediately lightly piled in lettuce cups, or from salad bowl. 5 scrvings.

Variation No. 1. Add ½ cup sliced radishes and 2 tbsp chopped parsley.

Variation No. 2. Substitute ½ cup each thinly sliced red and green sweet peppers for the lettuce.

Variation No. 3. Substitute 1 cup sliced pared cucumbers for the lettuce, and add 2 medium tomatoes cut in wedges and 1 tbsp sweet pickle relish.

CABBAGE-PINEAPPLE-DATE SALAD

Tasty, and when this salad is served, only one vegetable is necessary

9-oz can crushed pineapple,
  drained
½ cup moist pitted dates
4 cups freshly sliced crisp
  tender cabbage, about ¾ lb

⅛ tsp salt
½ cup chilled salad dressing
  or mayonnaise

Have all ingredients chilled. Turn pineapple into coarse sieve to drain well. Cut dates with scissors into 4 or 5 pieces. Cut cabbage medium fine with sharp knife into a 2-qt bowl. Add rest of ingredients and toss with 2 forks to coat. Serve at once after assembling, but if it must stand 10 to 15 min, keep refrigerated. Serve in salad bowl or on plates in lettuce cups. 4 to 5 servings.

Note: Substitute washed moist raisins for the dates, and well-drained pineapple in chunks for the crushed.

CARROT AND CABBAGE SALAD

1 cup grated carrot, 2
   large carrots
1 cup shredded, crisp, tender
   cabbage, about 3 oz
½ green pepper, diced fine

¼ cup mayonnaise
1⅓ tbsp sweet pickle relish
¼ tsp grated onion
½ tsp salt
½ tsp sugar

Grate carrot coarsely on a very sharp grater; always grate in one direction only. Slice cabbage fine with a very sharp, thin-bladed knife. Combine with carrots and pepper. Mix mayonnaise with next four ingredients to blend. Pour over vegetables, and toss lightly to mix. Serve immediately on individual salad plates. 4 servings.

CARROT-COCONUT SALAD

Try this, it's an excellent combination of flavors

1½ cups fresh fine shredded
   carrot
½ cup fresh grated, *or* canned
   moist coconut, lightly pkd

⅓ cup mayonnaise blended
   with 2 tbsp sour cream
Dash *or* so of salt
Lettuce

Measure all ingredients except lettuce into a mixing bowl. Use 2 forks to toss together lightly but until dressing is well distributed. Arrange lettuce cups on salad plates and lift salad lightly into cups. 4 servings.

Note: A few plumped raisins and a spoonful or two of diced tender Pascal celery may be added to salad for color accent.

CARROT AND PEANUT SALAD

2 cups grated carrots, 4
   carrots
½ cup salted peanuts
⅓ cup mayonnaise

2 tsp lemon juice
1 tsp sugar
Lettuce

Grate carrots coarsely (using a sharp grater, and grating in one direction only) directly into mixing bowl. Add chopped nuts. Blend mayonnaise with lemon juice and sugar and pour over carrots and nuts.

Mix by tossing lightly. Serve immediately on a bed of shredded lettuce on individual salad plates. 4 to 5 servings.

Variation: Carrot and Raisin Salad. Substitute ½ cup raisins for the peanuts, and 1 tbsp of cream and ¼ cup mayonnaise for the mayonnaise.

COLE SLAW No. 1

Mayonnaise

¼ cup mayonnaise
¼ tsp salt
3 tsp sugar
2 tbsp cream

2 tsp prepared mustard
1 tsp vinegar
3 cups shredded crisp tender cabbage, ½ lb

Combine mayonnaise, salt, sugar, cream, mustard and vinegar. Blend well and chill. Slice cabbage fine with a sharp, thin-bladed knife. When ready to serve, pour dressing over cabbage and toss lightly but thoroughly. Serve immediately. 5 servings.

Variation: Add 1 tbsp thinly sliced fresh hot red or green chili pepper.

COLE SLAW No. 2

Sour Cream Dressing

Quick Sour Cream Dressing, p 1204
3 cups shredded crisp tender cabbage, ½ lb

¼ tsp caraway seed, crushed, optional
¼ tsp salt
1 tsp sugar

Prepare dressing and chill. Slice cabbage fine. When ready to serve, pour dressing over cabbage, sprinkle with caraway, salt and sugar, toss lightly but thoroughly. Serve immediately. 5 servings.

Variation: Substitute ⅛ tsp celery seed for caraway. Sprinkle ½ cup sliced radishes over top before tossing.

COLE SLAW No. 3

Seasoned vinegar

3 cups shredded crisp tender cabbage, ½ lb
3 tsp sugar
½ tsp salt

$\frac{1}{16}$ to ⅛ tsp black pepper, freshly ground
3½ tsp malt vinegar
½ tsp grated onion

Slice cabbage fine with a sharp, thin-bladed knife. When ready to serve, place cabbage in salad bowl. Sprinkle with remaining ingredients. Toss lightly but thoroughly to coat cabbage well with dressing. Serve immediately. 4 servings.

Variation 1: Mexican Slaw—Add ¼ cup finely sliced sweet green pepper and ¼ cup finely sliced sweet red pepper before tossing.

Variation 2: Carrot Slaw—Add ½ cup coarsely grated carrot before tossing.

Variation 3: Spring Slaw—Add ¼ cup sliced radishes and ¼ cup finely sliced green onion before tossing.

Variation 4: Cucumber Cress Slaw—Add ½ cup pared, julienned cucumber and ½ cup chopped watercress before tossing.

Variation 5: Tomato Slaw—Add 1 medium tomato, sliced; 1 medium onion, very thinly sliced.

Variation 6: Parsley Slaw—Add 2 tbsp finely chopped parsley before tossing.

DANDELION GREEN SALAD

1 cup finely shredded dandelion greens, very tender
2 cups shredded celery cabbage, ⅓ lb
¼ cup sliced radishes

1 hard-cooked egg, quartered and sliced
2 tbsp crumbled Blue Cheese Horseradish Dressing, p 1201

Use only the very tender heart leaves of either the wild or cultivated dandelions and shred by cutting with a very sharp scissors. Celery cabbage is best shredded by slicing with a sharp, thin-bladed knife. Combine all ingredients and toss lightly with horseradish dressing. Serve at once. 4 servings.

Note: If celery cabbage is not available, use crisp green cabbage.

MINTED COMPANY SLAW

So edible it will take place of a green vegetable

1½ cups fine-shredded cabbage, pkd
½ cup thinly sliced Pascal celery
¼ cup finely sheared fresh mint
⅜ tsp salt

1½ tsp sugar
1½ tsp 5% cider vinegar
Few drops of scraped onion
⅓ cup Sesame Seed Dressing, p 1205, *or* French Dressing, p 1200, chilled
Lettuce

Choose tender cabbage, celery and mint. Clean and chill. Prepare vegetables and turn into mixing bowl. Add remaining ingredients and toss gently but thoroughly. Serve in lettuce cups on individual salad plates or in a salad bowl "family style." 4 servings.

PINEAPPLE CABBAGE MARSHMALLOW SALAD

3 cups shredded crisp tender cabbage, ½ lb
1 cup crushed chilled pineapple, drained, 9-oz can

¾ cup diced marshmallows
½ cup chilled mayonnaise
⅛ tsp salt

Slice cabbage fine with a sharp, thin-bladed knife. Combine pine-apple, cabbage, marshmallows, mayonnaise and salt, and toss together lightly until mayonnaise coats all the ingredients. Then heap lightly on individual plates and serve immediately. 5 servings.

RAW BEET AND CUCUMBER SALAD

4 raw beets, 1 lb
3 tbsp chopped onion
Dash pepper
1 tsp salt

1½ tsp sugar
2 tbsp salad oil
2 tbsp vinegar
2 five-inch cucumbers, chilled

Wash beets thoroughly and pare. Grate coarsely into a bowl. Add onion, seasonings, sugar, oil, and vinegar; mix. Cover and chill until ready to serve. Cut the cucumbers in half lengthwise with a knife, cut around the edge of the cucumber, loosening the center part from the skin. Scoop out center, as close to the skin as possible, leaving a thin shell. Dice the fleshy portion and combine with the beet mixture. Blend quickly, then heap into the cucumber "boats." Serve immediately. These ingredients may be prepared ahead of time and then combined quickly just before serving. 4 servings.

Note: Cucumbers may be pared and diced instead of being made into "boats," combined quickly with beet mixture, then served at once in lettuce cups.

RED AND GREEN SALAD

1 cup cooked beets
1¼ cups shredded raw
    spinach, 2 oz

1 to 1½ tsp grated onion
3 tbsp French Dressing,
    p 1200

Chill drained, peeled beets and have spinach crisp and cold. Slice beets into narrow strips julienne style and cut spinach fine with sharp scissors. Combine all ingredients and mix lightly but thoroughly just before serving. 4 servings.

Note: Sprinkle vegetables lightly with salt and sugar if dressing is mildly seasoned.

RED CABBAGE SALAD

½ head crisp red cabbage,
    about ¾ lb
½ cup finely cut green pepper
½ to 1 tsp fresh grated onion
¼ cup cider vinegar
2 tbsp cold water

¼ cup corn syrup
¼ tsp paprika
¾ tsp salt
1 tbsp salad oil
1 tsp sugar

Slice the cabbage as fine as possible with a sharp, thin-bladed knife; add the green pepper and onion. Mix remaining ingredients thoroughly, pour over the vegetables, and toss lightly until well mixed. Serve immediately on individual salad plates. 4 servings.

SHREDDED CABBAGE AND CELERY SALAD

2 cups shredded, crisp, tender   ½ tsp grated onion
   cabbage, about ⅓ lb   ⅓ cup mayonnaise
1 cup diced celery   1½ tsp chili sauce
½ cup coarsely cut parsley   1 tsp salt

Slice cabbage finely with a sharp, thin-bladed knife. When ready to serve, add remaining ingredients and toss quickly but thoroughly to mix and coat vegetables with dressing. Pile on individual salad plates and serve at once. 5 servings.

SPINACH MEDLEY

½ lb clean, crisp, raw spinach   ¼ cup chopped green onions
1½ cups shredded lettuce, ¼ lb   ½ cup sliced radishes
1 cup grated raw carrots,   ½ cup French dressing
   2 large   ½ tsp salt

Have vegetables cold and crisp. Cut spinach into shreds with a sharp scissors. Cut head lettuce with a sharp knife. (If leaf lettuce is used, cut same as spinach.) Grate carrots on sharp, coarse grater. Combine all ingredients except carrots and mix very lightly but thoroughly using two forks. Do not stir. Then add the carrots and toss mixture two or three times only. Serve immediately. 4 servings.

VEGETABLE SLAW

½ cup mayonnaise   1 cup grated carrots, 2 large
1 tbsp prepared mustard   ½ cup finely diced celery
2 tsp peanut butter   2 tbsp finely chopped onion
3 cups shredded, crisp, tender
   cabbage, ½ lb

Thoroughly blend mayonnaise, mustard, and peanut butter. Slice cabbage with a sharp, thin-bladed knife. Grate carrots coarsely on a sharp grater. Turn vegetables into mixing bowl. Add dressing and toss lightly together until well mixed. Arrange lightly in heaps on individual salad plates and serve immediately. 5 servings.

WHOLE MEAL, MAIN DISH AND HEARTY SALADS

Whole meal salads are combinations of foods, potatoes-meat-vegetables, fish-eggs-vegetables, a mixture of greens and generous slices of meat, etc., that could be served with rolls and a beverage for a complete meal. *Main-dish salads* can be served as the main protein food in the meal and are made chiefly from such foods as chicken, fish, cottage cheese, cheddar cheese, eggs,

Note: Recipes for Mayonnaise p 1202, French Dressing p 1200.

and legumes. *Hearty salads* are not necessarily protein foods but they contain principally substantial ingredients such as potatoes, macaroni, etc., and are usually served in place of hot potatoes. The three types are somewhat similar and in many cases interchangeable. If your family has the impression that this type of salad is only a means to dispose of leftovers, your preparation and service is at fault. Resolve today that every ingredient for a hearty salad will be prepared so that it will be identifiable in both form and flavor and will come to the table with a just-prepared "intended-just-for-you" look. The seasoning of these salads is usually mild since a generous portion is intended. Fish salads will respond to piquant seasonings, but most of the others should be fairly bland. The flavor is greatly improved by allowing the meat, fish, chicken, beans, potatoes, etc., to marinate in French dressing or some other seasoned vinegar mixture in a covered container in the refrigerator for an hour or two before serving, or this part of the salad may be mixed with salad dressing and a little grated onion and salt and allowed to stand. The rest of the salad ingredients, however, should not be added until just before serving or they will become limp and unappetizing. Never use mayonnaise for this "ripening" period, since it breaks down and gets oily on standing; mayonnaise should always be added to any kind of a salad either just before serving or at the table.

CHEESE SALADS

CHEESE VEGETABLE STUFFED TOMATO SALAD

5 large, meaty tomatoes
  Salt
2 cups cooked fresh *or* frozen
  Green Beans, p 1314
¼ lb American cheese, diced
½ tsp salt

1 cup pared, diced, crisp
  cucumber
1 tsp grated onion
½ cup French dressing
  Lettuce

Have all ingredients chilled. Wash tomatoes, cut out cores, and carefully scoop out centers; dice the scooped-out pulp. Sprinkle inside of tomato with salt. Cover and return to refrigerator to keep chilled. Cut beans in short lengths and mix with tomato centers, cheese, cucumber, salt, and onion. Chill until ready to serve. Just before serving, add the French dressing to green bean mixture and toss together lightly. Heap this mixture into the tomato cups. Serve each stuffed tomato on lettuce with additional French dressing if desired or with mayonnaise. 5 servings.

COTTAGE CHEESE SALAD No. 1

1 lb creamed cottage cheese
1 tsp grated onion *or*
  1 tbsp chopped stuffed
  olives

Salt to taste
Lettuce
¼ cup mayonnaise *or* Lime
  Honey Dressing, p 1202

Combine cottage cheese with grated onion or olives and salt. Cover and let stand in refrigerator at least 30 min to blend flavors. Drop lightly into lettuce cups on individual salad plates, and serve with dressing if desired. 5 servings. (Onion may be omitted, and 2 tbsp chopped chives substituted, if preferred.)

Variation: Stuffed Tomato Salad—Chill 5 tomatoes and remove stem end. Cut into six sections leaving attached at bottom. Spread apart gently (petal-fashion) and pile cheese mixture lightly into hollow. Sprinkle with paprika.

COTTAGE CHEESE SALAD No. 2

1 cup dry cottage cheese	1 tbsp chopped parsley
1 tsp chopped chives	2 tbsp mayonnaise
2 tbsp cucumber cut in	1 tsp sweet *or* sour cream
thin strips	1/8 tsp salt
1/4 cup slivered radishes	1/2 tsp sugar, more if desired
2 tbsp shredded raw carrot	Lettuce
1/4 cup chopped celery	

Combine cottage cheese and vegetables. Blend mayonnaise, cream, salt and sugar, and add to vegetable mixture. Toss lightly. Serve at once in lettuce cups with more mayonnaise in a separate container if desired. 4 servings.

PEA CHEESE STUFFED TOMATO SALAD

2 cups fresh, cooked peas or	1/2 cup diced celery
No. 2 can peas, drained	1/3 cup mayonnaise
1/4 lb American *or* Swiss	5 medium, meaty tomatoes
cheese	Salt
3 tbsp chopped sweet pickles	Lettuce

Have the peas thoroughly chilled. Drain off liquid just before mixing salad. Dice cheese about the same size as the peas. Lightly combine cheese, peas, pickles, celery and mayonnaise. Cut tomatoes in six wedges leaving them attached at the bottom. Spread apart gently (petal-fashion) and sprinkle with salt. Place each tomato on lettuce-lined individual salad plate and heap cheese mixture into center. Serve at once. 5 servings.

EGG SALADS

EGG AND CUCUMBER SALAD

2/3 cup mayonnaise	2 cups diced, pared
2 tbsp lemon juice	cucumber
2 tsp vinegar	1 cup diced celery
1 tsp salt	2 tbsp finely cut chives
1/2 tsp paprika	Lettuce
6 hard-cooked eggs, diced	Paprika

Chill all ingredients. Blend the mayonnaise with the lemon juice, vinegar, salt and paprika. Add the eggs and vegetables, except the lettuce, and toss lightly. With a sharp knife or kitchen scissors, shred head or leaf lettuce to form a base for the mixed salad. Heap salad mixture lightly in center. Sprinkle top lightly with paprika and serve at once. 4 servings.

EGG AND SARDINE TOP TOMATO SALAD

5 hard-cooked eggs
1 can small sardines, 3¼ oz
½ cup chopped celery
¼ cup mayonnaise

Salt to suit taste
2 large, meaty tomatoes
Lettuce

Shell and dice the cooled eggs; drain sardines, remove tails, mash fish slightly and add celery, eggs, mayonnaise and salt to suit taste, mixing lightly. Heap on thick tomato slices placed on lettuce-lined individual salad plates. Serve at once. 5 servings.

EGG VEGETABLE SALAD

6 hard-cooked eggs
¼ cup diced sour pickle
½ cup finely diced celery
¼ tsp salt

⅓ cup Boiled Salad Dressing,
  p 1198
1 small, solid head lettuce

Dice eggs, add pickle, celery, salt and dressing. Toss lightly, cover, chill in refrigerator. When ready to serve, heap lightly in lettuce cups on salad plates. 4 servings.

SCRAMBLED EGG SALAD

4 medium, meaty tomatoes
¼ cup mayonnaise
⅛ tsp salt
1 tbsp chopped celery

1 tbsp chopped onion
3 tbsp butter
4 eggs (beaten just enough
  to break yolks)

Wash tomatoes, remove stem scar. Scoop out a tbsp of pulp from center of each, purée and combine with mayonnaise and salt. Sauté celery and onion in butter for 5 min. Then add the eggs and continue to cook over low heat, stirring the eggs very gently to obtain a yellow and white streaked effect, p 675, and the desired firmness. Add desired seasoning, cut tomatoes part way down into 5 sections leaving attached at bottom and separate slightly (petal-fashion). Place on individual plates and fill the center of each with the hot eggs, top with mayonnaise mixture and serve immediately. 4 servings.

VEGETABLE SALADS WITH MEAT, FISH, AND POULTRY

AVOCADO SHRIMP TOMATO SALAD

1 small, well-ripened avocado	½ cup diced celery
2 tbsp lemon juice	1 diced, hard-cooked egg
1 tsp salt	1 large tomato
⅓ cup mayonnaise	Lettuce
7 oz can shrimp, cleaned	Paprika

Have all ingredients chilled. Mash ¼ of the avocado. Blend with lemon juice, salt, and mayonnaise. Combine shrimp, celery and egg and mix with dressing. Serve on slices of tomato and avocado arranged on lettuce-lined individual salad plates. Sprinkle with paprika. 4 servings.

CAULIFLOWER LUNCHEON SALAD

3½-oz canned pork luncheon meat	¼ cup Boiled Salad Dressing, p 1198
1 cup cooked *or* raw cauliflowerets	2 tbsp cream
½ cup raisins, plumped, p 165	Lettuce
1 tbsp finely shredded, tender celery leaves	4 radishes, thinly slivered
Salt to taste	1 tbsp finely chopped green pepper

Cut luncheon meat into ¾-inch cubes. Add cauliflower cut into bite-size pieces, raisins, celery leaves and salt. Blend dressing with cream. Combine dressing with cauliflower mixture, toss lightly, cover and chill 30 min. Serve on crisp lettuce leaves. Sprinkle the radishes and green pepper over the top. 4 servings.

COLD MEAT SALAD

2 cups diced, cooked meat (leftover roast)	¼ cup mayonnaise
1 cup diced celery	1 tbsp prepared mustard
1 cup pared, diced, tart apple	½ tsp salt
	Lettuce

Combine meat, celery, and apple. Mix mayonnaise thoroughly with mustard and salt; add to meat mixture and toss lightly until all the pieces are well coated with dressing. Serve on crisp lettuce leaves. 5 servings.

CHICKEN SALAD

⅔ cup Boiled Salad Dressing,
   p 1198
1 to 2 tbsp prepared mustard
1 tsp sugar
2 tsp very finely diced onion
1 tsp salt
¼ cup chopped sweet pickle
1 to 2 tsp malt vinegar

4 cups diced, Steamed
   Chicken, 4 lbs, p 1041
⅔ cup mayonnaise
2 cups diced celery
¼ cup slivered, toasted
   almonds, if desired
Lettuce

Thoroughly blend the first seven ingredients in a large bowl. Add the chicken (no skin), toss lightly. Cover tightly, set in refrigerator 2 or 3 hrs to chill and marinate. Remove from refrigerator, add the mayonnaise, celery and almonds and toss very gently. Drop lightly into crisp lettuce cups and serve immediately. 4 servings.

CHICKEN AND SWEETBREAD SALAD

1½ cups diced, precooked
   Sweetbreads, p 890
1½ cups diced, Stewed
   Chicken, p 1042
1½ cups diced celery
1½ tsp salt

¾ cup mayonnaise
2 tbsp chopped stuffed olives
2 tbsp chili sauce
2 tsp lemon juice
Lettuce

Have all ingredients chilled. Combine sweetbreads and chicken, celery and salt. Mix mayonnaise with the olives, chili sauce and lemon juice, add to the meat mixture, and toss lightly. Serve on crisp lettuce on individual salad plates. 5 to 6 servings.

Note: ½ cup mayonnaise and ¼ cup French dressing may be substituted for the ¾ cup mayonnaise. Mix French dressing with sweetbreads and chicken, cover and let stand in refrigerator for 1 to 2 hrs to marinate before adding the remaining ingredients.

CORNED BEEF AND POTATO SALAD

4 medium potatoes, boiled,
   1 lb
12-oz can corned beef, chilled
2 tbsp chopped onion

2 tbsp chopped sweet pickle
¾ cup Sour Cream Salad
   Dressing, p 1203
Lettuce

Peel, cool and dice the potatoes. Trim fat from corned beef and discard. Dice beef. Combine potatoes, corned beef, onion, pickle and salad dressing, mixing together lightly. Cover and let stand at least 2 to 3 hrs in refrigerator to blend flavors. Serve on crisp lettuce leaves. 5 servings.

Note: Diced corned beef may be added to the regular Potato Salad (p 1188) if preferred. In either recipe, diced or chopped ham, tongue, bacon, frankfurters or other sausage may be substituted for the corned beef.

CRAB MEAT LOUIS

⅓ cup mayonnaise
1 tbsp chili sauce
1 tsp prepared horseradish
¼ cup finely cut celery
1 tsp finely chopped green
  pepper
⅛ tsp onion juice

1½ cups fresh *or* canned crabmeat, 9 oz, stiff cartilage
  removed
2 tbsp imported gray caviar
2 large, meaty tomatoes
1 medium avocado
Lettuce

Combine all ingredients in order given except tomatoes, avocado and lettuce. Place one thick slice tomato and 1 slice avocado on lettuce cup or bed of shredded lettuce. Heap salad mixture on top. Serve with French Dressing, p 1200. 4 servings.

CRABMEAT SALAD

A deluxe salad for any luncheon

1 cup crabmeat, 6½-oz can
1 tbsp French dressing
1 tbsp lemon juice
¼ tsp salt
¾ cup fine-diced celery
  Dash of cayenne
1 tsp cider vinegar

Few drops onion juice
Mayonnaise
4 medium *or* 2 large
  tomatoes, chilled
2 hard-cooked eggs
Lettuce

Use canned, frozen or freshly cooked crabmeat. Look over crabmeat and discard any cartilage. Do not flake fish too fine. Add French dressing and lemon juice and salt. Cover tightly and let marinate in refrigerator for an hr or so if possible as this standing improves flavor. Now add celery, cayenne, vinegar, onion juice, mayonnaise and toss with 2 forks just enough to blend. Wash tomatoes, remove stem and blossom scars. Cut medium tomatoes in petal shape or large tomatoes in halves crosswise. Arrange on lettuce. Heap salad lightly into cups or on slices. Garnish with hard-cooked egg slices. Serve with additional mayonnaise if desired. 4 servings.

DUBLIN SALAD

1 lb potatoes, 3 to 4 medium
1 cup cooked tongue, cut in
  julienne strips
¼ cup finely sliced green
  onion
¼ cup chopped sweet pickle

¼ cup Special Salad Dressing,
  p 1206
¼ cup sour cream
¾ tsp salt
1 tbsp vinegar
¼ cup mayonnaise
Lettuce

Cook potatoes in their jackets in boiling salted water until just barely done. Peel immediately and cut in small dice. Combine with the next three ingredients. Blend salad dressing and sour cream with the salt and vinegar. Pour over potato mixture; toss thoroughly. Chill for 30 min to 1 hr. Add mayonnaise, toss quickly and serve at once in lettuce cups if desired. 4 servings.

FISH SALAD

1½ cups cold halibut *or* pike,
  broiled *or* boiled
½ cup finely cut celery
2 Hard-cooked Eggs,
  p 663
3 tbsp Boiled Salad Dressing,
  p 1198

½ tsp celery seed
2 tbsp chili sauce
2 tbsp vinegar
¾ tsp seasoned salt
1 tbsp chopped parsley
1 tbsp chopped onion
Shredded lettuce

Flake the fish and dice celery and eggs. Blend the remaining ingredients, except the lettuce, and combine with fish mixture, mixing thoroughly but very lightly. Cover and chill for an hr to "ripen." Serve heaped on crisp lettuce. 4 servings.

HEAD CHEESE VINAIGRETTE

¼ lb head cheese
1 tsp grated onion
2 tbsp vinegar
¼ cup salad oil
1 tsp fine-chopped parsley

1 tbsp fine-chopped green
  pepper
1 tsp fine-chopped pimiento
⅛ tsp salt
Dash of pepper
½ tsp prepared mustard

Julienne head cheese fine. Add remaining ingredients, toss to distribute. Cover, place in refrigerator to marinate one hr. When ready to serve, lay crisp lettuce leaves on salad plates, heap ¼ cup cold slaw into cups, and top with a fluffy mixture of the head cheese mixture. 4 servings.

MACARONI ENDIVE SALAD

1 qt water
1½ tsp salt
1 small clove garlic
½ medium onion
½ pkg, 4 oz, elbow macaroni,
  3 cups cooked
¼ cup Tomato French
  Dressing, p 1202
1 cup sour cream

12 oz can luncheon meat, cut
  in julienne strips
2 cups chopped curly endive
  or broken into small pieces
1 cup thinly sliced celery
1 tbsp finely sliced green
  onion
¼ cup sliced radishes
2 medium tomatoes cut in
  eight wedges

Heat water to boiling. Add salt, garlic, onion, then add macaroni very slowly. Stir with a fork until water is boiling vigorously. Cook macaroni 12 to 15 min. Drain, but do not rinse. Remove garlic and onion and discard. Combine French dressing and sour cream and pour at once over hot macaroni and toss thoroughly. Chill. Combine remaining ingredients in large salad bowl, add chilled macaroni mixture and toss lightly but thoroughly. Serve at once. 5 servings.

MACARONI SALAD

7-oz pkg elbow macaroni	1 cup finely diced celery
¼ cup mayonnaise	½ cup pickle relish
¼ cup Boiled Salad Dressing,	2 tbsp chopped pimiento
p 1198	1 tbsp prepared mustard
2 tbsp chopped onion	1 tsp celery seed

Drop macaroni into 3 qts rapidly boiling salted water (about 1 tbsp salt), and boil until tender, from 15 to 20 min. Drain and rinse with cold water; chill thoroughly in refrigerator. Mix remaining ingredients. If dressing is too thick, thin it with 1 or 2 tbsp of juice from the pickles. Add dressing to chilled macaroni and toss together until each piece of macaroni is well coated with dressing. 5 servings.

OLD-FASHIONED CHICKEN SALAD

(See page 1058)

POTATO SALAD

2 lbs boiling potatoes, 6 to 8	1 to 2 tbsp chopped green
⅓ cup Boiled Salad Dressing,	pepper
p 1198	2 tsp grated onion
⅓ cup mayonnaise	¼ tsp dry mustard
2 tbsp chopped sweet pickle	½ tsp sugar
2 tbsp sweet pickle juice	1¼ tsp salt
1 tbsp vinegar	¼ tsp celery seed, if desired

Cook potatoes in their jackets in boiling salted water (1 tsp salt for each pt of water) until barely tender. Cool, peel, and cut in ¾-inch dice. Combine remaining ingredients thoroughly, pour over potatoes and mix together lightly. Cover bowl and let stand at room temp or chill in refrigerator several hrs (as preferred) to blend flavors. May be garnished with sliced radishes or sliced, diced or riced hard-cooked eggs, if desired. 5 servings.

Note: ½ cup coarsely grated raw carrot may be added just before serving if desired.

POTATO FRESH DILL SALAD

1 head fresh dill
¼ cup vinegar
1½ lbs boiled potatoes, 5 to
6 medium

1 cup chopped celery
1 small onion
1 cup Boiled Salad Dressing,
p 1198

Place whole head of dill in vinegar and let stand 1 hr. Remove dill. Peel and cube potatoes while warm. Add remaining ingredients and the dill-flavored vinegar. Toss lightly but thoroughly. A few fresh lacy leaves of dill may be sprinkled on salad as garnish. Serve at once. 4 servings.

POTATO PICNIC SALAD

With cream cheese

3 lbs boiling potatoes, 10
to 12 medium
3 tbsp vinegar
⅓ cup French dressing
1 tsp salt

2 tbsp grated onion
3 oz pkg cream cheese
½ cup mayonnaise
3 hard-cooked eggs, sliced

Boil scrubbed, unpared potatoes in enough water to cover, adding 1 tsp salt to each qt of water. Cook only until barely done. Drain, cool and peel, then slice ⅛-inch thick into large mixing bowl. Combine vinegar, French dressing and salt, pour over potatoes, toss lightly together, cover and marinate at least 30 min in refrigerator or at room temp as preferred. Blend onion with cream cheese, then gradually add mayonnaise, beating to a smooth consistency. Add to potato mixture with two of the eggs and toss gently but thoroughly. Cover and place in refrigerator to mellow and chill for at least 2 hrs. Garnish with slices of remaining egg and serve from bowl. 8 to 12 servings.

POTATO CARAWAY SOUR CREAM SALAD

2½ to 3 cups cubed freshly
boiled potatoes, 3 to 4
¼ cup thinly sliced green
onion
2 tbsp slivered radishes
2 hard-cooked eggs, diced

¼ cup mayonnaise
¼ cup sour cream
2 tbsp vinegar
¼ tsp sugar
1 tsp salt
⅛ tsp caraway seeds

Combine first four ingredients. Blend remaining ingredients and mix lightly but thoroughly with potato mixture. Cover and let stand at least half an hr at room temp or in refrigerator as preferred. Serve in lettuce-lined bowl. 4 servings.

Note: Recipes for Mayonnaise, p 1202, French Dressing, p 1200, Boiled Salad Dressing, p 1198.

POTATO SALAD WITH WHIPPED CREAM
SALAD DRESSING

English Potato Salad

1 lb boiling potatoes, 3 to
4 medium
¾ cup Boiled Salad Dressing,
p 1198
Salt if desired
1¼ cups Pascal celery, sliced

⅓ cup finely sliced green
onion
⅓ cup pared, diced cucumber
3 hard-cooked eggs, diced
3 tbsp coarsely chopped
pimiento
½ cup heavy cream, whipped

Wash potatoes, pare and cook in salted water until just done. Do not overcook. Cut into ½-inch cubes; there should be about 2½ to 3 cups. Add ¼ cup of the dressing and salt to taste. Mix well and let stand for 30 min at room temp or in the refrigerator as preferred. Add next five ingredients. Blend remaining dressing with the whipped cream and add to potato mixture. Toss lightly and serve at once. 4 servings.

SALMON SALAD

1-lb can red salmon
1 cup diced celery
½ cup Mayonnaise, p 1202
1 tsp chopped chives

1 tbsp chopped green pepper
2 tbsp chopped sweet pickle
2 tbsp lemon juice
Lettuce

Have all ingredients chilled. Drain salmon and flake after removing skin and bones. Crush bones and combine with fish if desired. Add next six ingredients and mix together lightly. Heap on lettuce-lined individual salad plates, and serve at once. 5 servings.

Variations 1: Diced cucumber may be substituted for the celery if desired. *2:* Two diced hard-cooked eggs may be added. *3:* ¼ lb cooked macaroni may be added.

SARDINE TOP TOMATO SALAD

2 cans sardines, 3¼ oz each
1½ cups diced celery
4 hard-cooked eggs
¼ cup diced sweet pickle
1 tsp vinegar

1 tbsp prepared mustard
¼ cup mayonnaise
3 large, meaty tomatoes
Lettuce *or* romaine

Have all ingredients chilled. Remove tails from sardines and discard. If fish are large, remove bones. Mash fish slightly and combine with celery, diced hard-cooked eggs and pickle. Sprinkle vinegar over mixture; let stand 5 min. Add mustard to mayonnaise and mix well with fish mixture. Heap on thick slices of tomato arranged on crisp lettuce leaves. 6 to 7 servings.

SHRIMP AND TOMATO SALAD

5¾ oz can wet-pack shrimps, cleaned
1 solid head lettuce, 1 lb
2 hard-cooked eggs, sliced
½ medium sized cucumber, pared and sliced

¼ cup finely chopped celery
or green pepper
2 large *or* 4 small tomatoes, quartered
French dressing

Drain shrimp and remove dark sand-veins down the backs. Wash quickly in cold water. Cut lettuce into four crosswise slices and arrange on salad plates. Combine shrimp, sliced eggs, sliced cucumber and celery and heap lightly on the lettuce, garnish with tomato wedges. Pour dressing over the salads and serve immediately. 4 large salads.

Note: ¾ lb fresh, cooked, cleaned shrimp may be used instead of canned.

SHRIMP SALAD No. 1

2 cups cleaned cooked Shrimp, p 726
½ cup diced celery
1 tsp finely chopped onion
⅓ cup mayonnaise

¼ cup Chili Sauce, p 1108
3 tbsp lemon juice
2 *or* 3 hard-cooked eggs
Lettuce

Let shrimp chill in its own cooking liquid until salad is ready to be mixed. Drain well. Have all remaining ingredients chilled. Combine first 6 ingredients lightly but thoroughly. Slice eggs and arrange in a ring on lettuce-lined individual salad plates. Pile salad mixture in the center of the ring. 5 servings.

SHRIMP SALAD No. 2

⅓ cup mayonnaise
¼ cup sour cream
1 tbsp Chili Sauce
¼ tsp sugar
1½ tsp salt
2 tbsp lemon juice
2 cups cooked, cleaned Shrimp, p 726

2 hard-cooked eggs, diced *or* sliced
1 cup celery, cut in thin strips
1 tbsp chopped chives
1 tbsp chopped green pepper
1 tbsp chopped pimiento
Salad greens

Have all ingredients chilled. Let shrimp chill in its own cooking liquid until ready to mix salad. Blend first six ingredients thoroughly. Drain shrimp and add to mayonnaise mixture. Add remaining ingredients except greens. Toss lightly but thoroughly. Heap lightly into lettuce cups, or on romaine or endive. Serve at once. 6 servings.

SHRIMP REMOULADE

¼ tsp salt
1 very small clove garlic,
  not more than ⅛ tsp
  chopped
1 raw egg yolk
½ tsp dry mustard
⅛ tsp cayenne
2 hard-cooked eggs, cut in
  half, yolks removed

Juice ½ lemon
1 tbsp tarragon vinegar
1 tbsp cider vinegar
3 tbsp salad oil
2 tbsp chopped anchovies
½ cup finely chopped celery
1 lb Shrimp, cooked, cleaned,
  chilled, p 726
Lettuce

Make a paste of the salt and garlic by crushing together with the tip of a knife. Blend raw egg yolk, mustard, cayenne, yolks of cooked eggs, and garlic paste. Add lemon juice, vinegars and oil. Beat until thick. Stir in chopped whites of eggs, anchovies and celery. Pour dressing over shrimp. Toss, cover with waxed paper and chill at least 1 hr. Heap lightly on bed of crisp lettuce. 4 servings.

Note: This salad is particularly suitable for a first course. May also be served in a stemmed glass as a cocktail if desired.

SPINACH LUNCHEON SALAD

2 cups shredded raw
  spinach, ¼ lb
2 hard-cooked eggs, cut in
  halves

1 large tomato, cut lengthwise in eighths
¼ lb cold, boiled, lean ham
1 small onion, chopped
French dressing

Wash spinach thoroughly in several waters. Allow to drain well; place in a hydrator to crisp. Cut spinach into fine strips with a sharp kitchen scissors and place on a platter. On the bed of shredded spinach, arrange the eggs, tomato and meat that is sliced and cut in julienne strips. Sprinkle onion over entire salad and lightly drizzle French dressing over all, toss and serve at once. 4 servings.

STUFFED LETTUCE

1 medium, solid head lettuce
3½ oz can tuna fish
1 cup chopped celery
¼ tsp salt
½ cup grated raw carrots

1 tbsp finely chopped onion
1 tbsp lemon juice
⅓ cup mayonnaise
2 hard-cooked eggs, diced

Wash lettuce in cold water run between the leaves to loosen them slightly. Drain thoroughly, wrap in waxed paper and damp cloth and place in refrigerator to chill and crisp for 1 to 2 hrs. Drain and flake the tuna fish rather fine and combine with remaining ingredients, mixing lightly but thoroughly. Just before serving time, loosen the leaves of the lettuce while still keeping the head together so the fish salad mixture may be stuffed between the leaves. Distribute it well around the whole head. Press the head firmly together again, cut in wedges and serve immediately. 4 servings.

SUNDAY SUPPER SALAD

¼ cup French dressing
2 tbsp prepared horseradish
1 cup diced celery
¾ cup cooked peas
¼ chopped green pepper

2 cups coarsely cut head lettuce
3 oz luncheon meat, cut into julienne strips
Crackers

Have all ingredients chilled. Mix the dressing and horseradish and pour over the combined vegetables and meat in a large bowl. Toss lightly until well coated with dressing. Serve at once with crisp, heated crackers. 4 to 5 servings.

SWEET POTATO SALAD

2 lbs sweet potatoes
⅔ cup mayonnaise
2 tbsp lemon juice
1 cup diced celery

2 tbsp diced sweet pickle
2 tbsp diced green pepper
2 tbsp diced onion
½ tsp salt

Boil potatoes in their skins until just barely tender. Cool, remove skins and dice. Combine remaining ingredients. Add the potatoes and toss to coat with dressing. Chill, or serve at once. 4 servings.

TOMATO STUFFED WITH KIDNEY BEANS

1½ cups canned *or* cooked Kidney Beans, p 1316
½ cup chopped dill pickles
2 hard-cooked eggs
1 tbsp vinegar
¼ cup mayonnaise

½ tsp salt
⅛ tsp pepper
½ tsp grated onion
Lettuce
4 large meaty tomatoes
Salt

Chill beans thoroughly, drain off all juice. (Juice might be used in soup if practical, otherwise discard.) Add chopped pickles and diced hard-cooked eggs to beans. Then add remaining ingredients except lettuce and tomatoes, chill. Peel chilled tomatoes, remove cores and place on bed of lettuce. Cut tomato almost to bottom in 6 even wedges and press apart like petals of flower. Sprinkle lightly with salt. Fill center with salad mixture. Half of one of the eggs may be retained and pressed through sieve over top of the salads. Serve at once. 4 servings.

TOMATO STUFFED WITH TUNA SALAD

5 medium, meaty tomatoes
7-oz can tuna fish
⅓ cup celery, thinly sliced
1 tbsp lime juice
¼ tsp grated lime rind
1 tbsp chopped sweet pickle
¼ tsp salt
¼ cup mayonnaise

1 hard-cooked egg, coarsely
chopped
Lettuce
Cucumber, about ½ medium, pared and cut into
⅛" slices
1 hard-cooked egg, sliced

Peel tomatoes, remove stem end and chill. Place drained tuna in bowl and flake. Mix celery, juice, rind, pickle, salt, and mayonnaise thoroughly. Combine with tuna and chopped egg, tossing lightly but thoroughly. Place each tomato in a lettuce cup or on a bed of shredded lettuce. Cut tomatoes petal-fashion into eighths or fifths, not severing the sections at the base. Sprinkle with salt. Heap tuna mixture in center of each tomato. Garnish with cucumber slices placed between tomato sections. Place slice of egg on top. 5 servings.

TUNA FISH SALAD No. 1

7-oz can tuna fish
½ cup chopped celery
1 tbsp lemon juice
1½ tsp capers, if desired

¼ cup chopped sweet pickles
⅓ cup Boiled Salad dressing
Lettuce

Drain tuna and flake. Add next five ingredients and toss lightly. Cover tightly and chill for 30 min before serving on crisp lettuce. 5 servings.

TUNA FISH SALAD No. 2

7-oz can tuna fish
1 cup finely sliced celery, including a few tender leaves
⅓ cup diced, pared cucumber
1 tbsp thinly sliced green onion
2 to 3 tbsp prepared brown mustard

⅓ cup Boiled Salad dressing
Curly endive
2 small tomatoes, sliced
2 hard-cooked eggs, sliced
Cucumber slices
Salt

Have all ingredients chilled. Drain oil from tuna, turn fish into a bowl and flake. Add celery, cucumber and onion. Add mustard to dressing, mix well and add to the vegetables. Toss thoroughly but lightly. Never stir. Arrange salad mixture on the crisp endive and garnish with slices of tomatoes, eggs and cucumber; sprinkle these lightly with salt. Serve immediately. 4 servings.

Note: Recipes for Mayonnaise p 1202, Boiled Salad Dressing p 1198.

TUNA FISH SALAD No. 3

As good as chicken salad but much more convenient to make

7-oz can tuna, solid pack *or*
  bite size, chilled
1 tbsp lemon juice
¼ tsp onion juice *or* scraped
  onion
Dash of tabasco

Dash of white pepper
¾ cup celery sliced ¼-inch
  thick
1 hard-cooked egg, coarsely
  diced
⅓ cup mayonnaise

Drain tuna, then turn into bowl. Break fish with fork into ½ to 1-inch size chunks. Drizzle with lemon juice. Add next 5 ingredients and toss lightly to mix. Now add mayonnaise all at once and toss with 2 forks or rubber spatula until pieces are well coated. Chill a few minutes if desired. Serve on thick big slices of tomato or on crisp lettuce. 3 servings.

Note: To stretch Tuna Salad to serve 4, add 1 to 2 hard-cooked eggs and ¼ cup sliced celery. Increase mayonnaise slightly.

TURKEY SALAD

2 tbsp vinegar
2 tsp water
½ tsp salt
¼ tsp sugar
2½ cups cold turkey cut into
  half-inch cubes
½ cup coarsely diced celery

½ cup Tokay grapes, halved
  and seeded
½ cup mayonnaise
Salad greens
Sliced, stuffed *or* ripe
  olives, 8 to 10
2 sliced, hard-cooked eggs

Combine vinegar, water, salt and sugar and drizzle over the turkey. Toss lightly. Cover and set in refrigerator to marinate for 2 or 3 hrs. Add chilled celery, grapes, and mayonnaise. Toss very lightly with a fork. Arrange on crisp greens and garnish with olives and eggs and serve immediately. 4 servings.

WHOLE MEAL TOSSED SALAD No. 1

½ large, solid head lettuce
1 cup diced cucumber
2 green onions, sliced, including tender part of
  green tops
1 small bunch radishes, sliced

3 tbsp chopped green pepper
¼ lb baked *or* boiled ham,
  julienned
1 large tomato, cut into
  wedges

Wash and clean all vegetables, chill thoroughly. Break lettuce into bite-sized pieces and prepare rest of ingredients as directed. Wait until the last minute to mix all ingredients. Toss lightly but thoroughly with the following dressing just before serving. Serve immediately.

Dressing:

¼ cup vinegar	¼ tsp sugar
2 tbsp oil	¼ tsp salt
3 tbsp prepared horseradish	2 tbsp mayonnaise

Combine all ingredients thoroughly and chill before adding to salad. 4 servings.

WHOLE MEAL TOSSED SALAD No. 2

2 cups shredded lettuce, ¾ lb	1 large tomato, peeled and cut in thin wedges
1 bunch crisp watercress	1½ cups leftover roast meat cut julienne style
½ cup sliced, cooked beets	
¼ cup sliced radishes	⅓ cup French dressing
¼ cup sliced cucumber	1 tsp grated onion
½ cup chopped celery	

Arrange vegetables and meat in salad bowl in order given. If necessary to hold for a short time, cover with a damp paper towel and keep refrigerated. When ready to serve, toss with French dressing to which grated onion has been added and serve immediately. 6 servings.

SALAD DRESSINGS

There are three types of salad dressing in common use: cooked or boiled salad dressing, mayonnaise, and French. Each of the three have innumerable variations such as Roquefort, Thousand Island, Russian, etc.

Boiled Salad Dressing: Boiled or cooked salad dressing has for a base a thickened sauce of flour, starch or eggs or a combination of these ingredients with a relatively large proportion of acid added. The ingredients may vary greatly—water or milk may be used for the liquid with either vinegar or an acid fruit juice added; seasonings may include sugar, salt, mustard, paprika, celery salt and others. A small amount of butter or bacon fat is often added for flavor and richness. This type of salad dressing is usually inexpensive, has a lively flavor, and is a very stable product. It is used particularly to bind ingredients together, as in chicken or potato salad, since it does not break down like mayonnaise. Salad dressing and mayonnaise are often mixed in equal proportion for all types of salads. Dressings on the market which do not meet the United States Department of Agriculture standards for mayonnaise are labeled "salad dressing" or "whips" but they are not always the same as the homemade type of salad dressing described above.

Mayonnaise: Mayonnaise is defined by the United States Department of Agriculture as a "clean, sound, semisolid emulsion of edible vegetable oil and egg yolk or whole egg, with vinegar and (or) lemon juice, and with one or more of the following: salt, spice, sugar. The finished product contains not less than 50 per cent of edible vegetable oil and the sum of the percentages of oil and egg yolk is not less than 78." Commercial mayonnaise is always more expensive than products labeled "salad dressing" since it is more costly to manufacture. It is easy to make mayonnaise at home if you have a good rotary beater and even easier with an electric mixer, and it is a convenient way to use up leftover egg yolks. Making mayonnaise that will stand up well and not separate into layers requires special techniques of combining ingredients and vigorous beating and is described in the recipe on p 1202.

French Dressing: French dressing is a combination of salad oil and lemon juice or vinegar (three parts of oil to one of acid are often used) with various seasonings added such as paprika, salt, pepper and herbs. The mixture is shaken or beaten to form a temporary emulsion. Beating must be repeated every time the dressing is used. However, a half tsp of egg white or yolk added to dressing helps it become a better emulsion when shaken. Variety is obtained by adding chili sauce, catchup, pickles, onions, capers, etc. French dressing is often used as a marinade; that is, certain foods are allowed to stand in the dressing for an hour or more to acquire peppier flavor; this is called marinating and is used for cooked potatoes and meat, etc.

For the average family, it is not practical to make or buy more than a qt of dressing at one time. It should be stored in an air-tight container in the refrigerator but should never freeze. If salad dressing is not chilled, it will cause the salad to be less fresh and crisp than it should be. Don't make the mistake of always serving the same kind of dressing . . . this section contains numerous variations of the three basic kinds of dressings with suggestions for the types of salads on which they will be most suitable.

AVOCADO SALAD DRESSING

1 medium-sized avocado,
  ripe but firm, about 8 oz
½ cup orange juice

1 tbsp lemon juice
½ tsp salt

Peel avocado, cut in half and discard pit. Press avocado through a fine sieve, add other ingredients, and beat with a rotary beater until perfectly smooth. Serve over fruit salad or head lettuce. Makes about 1 cup dressing.

BLUE OR ROQUEFORT CHEESE DRESSING No. 1

¼ cup Roquefort *or* blue
  cheese, 2 oz
⅓ cup cream
½ tsp dry mustard
¼ tsp salt

⅛ tsp pepper
1 tsp paprika
⅓ cup salad oil
3 tbsp lemon juice

Mash cheese with a silver fork; add cream, mustard, seasonings and blend well. Stir in salad oil 1 tbsp at a time. Add lemon juice and stir vigorously to blend. Serve on green vegetable salads. Makes about 1¼ cups dressing.

Variation: A simpler dressing may be made by beating ¼ cup of crumbled blue cheese into ⅓ cup of French dressing until creamy.

BLUE OR ROQUEFORT CHEESE DRESSING No. 2

Delicious on head lettuce or mixed green salad

1 cup salad oil	½ tsp paprika
¼ cup tarragon *or* wine	1 tsp sugar
vinegar	½ tsp dry mustard
1 tsp salt	¼ lb Roquefort *or* blue
Few dashes of white pepper	cheese, ⅔ cup

Combine first 7 ingredients and beat to a smooth emulsion. Crumble the cheese coarsely into mixture. Stir until just blended. Lumps of cheese should be present to make this dressing most interesting. 1½ cups.

BOILED SALAD DRESSING No. 1

2 eggs	½ cup cider vinegar
½ cup sugar	2 tbsp butter
2 tbsp flour	½ cup evaporated milk *or*
½ tsp salt	cream
¾ tsp dry mustard	Few grains red pepper

Beat eggs until light in top of double boiler. Mix dry ingredients together and blend thoroughly with eggs. Gradually add vinegar and cook over boiling water, stirring constantly until mixture thickens. Remove from heat and stir in butter, evaporated milk, and pepper. Cool; then store in covered jar in refrigerator. Makes about 1½ cups.

Note: Evaporated milk makes dressing smooth and velvety and less apt to curdle.

BOILED SALAD DRESSING No. 2

For fruit like pears, bananas, baked apples, etc.

½ cup egg yolks, 5 to 6	Dash black pepper
⅓ cup sugar	⅔ cup evaporated milk
2 tsp dry mustard	1 tbsp butter
1¾ tsp salt	¼ cup cider vinegar
2 tsp flour	3 tbsp lemon juice,
Dash red pepper	1 large lemon

Beat egg yolks thoroughly in top of double boiler. Thoroughly mix the sugar, mustard, salt, flour, and peppers and add to egg yolks. Beat until blended. Add evaporated milk and cook over hot water, stirring constantly until smooth and thickened (about five min). Remove from heat, add butter and cool. Then add vinegar and lemon juice and stir until mixed. Cool, then store in covered jar in refrigerator. Makes about 1¾ cups.

CELERY SEED FRUIT DRESSING

½ cup sugar	1 tsp salt
2 tbsp flour	¾ cup salad oil
1 tsp paprika	1 tsp celery seed
½ cup vinegar	Boiling water
½ tsp grated onion	

Mix sugar, flour and paprika thoroughly. Blend in vinegar. Place over low heat and cook until thick, stirring constantly to keep smooth. Add onion and salt. Cool. Gradually add the oil, beating with a rotary beater until all the oil is added and thoroughly blended in. Pour boiling water over the celery seed and let stand for ½ min. Thoroughly drain off water and add seed to salad dressing. Mix well. Chill and serve over fruit salad. Makes 1½ cupfuls.

CRANBERRY MAYONNAISE

Blend well ½ cup Mayonnaise, p 1202, and ½ cup Cranberry Jelly, p 563; fold in ¼ cup cream, stiffly whipped. Serve with Chicken or Banana Salad, pp 1185 and 1136. Makes about 1½ cups dressing.

CREAM CHEESE FRUIT DRESSING

3 oz pkg cream cheese	½ tsp sugar
¼ cup mayonnaise	Pinch salt
¼ tsp prepared mustard	

Soften cheese, then stir until smooth. Add remaining ingredients and beat until thoroughly blended. Chill. Serve with combination of fresh or cooked fruits. Makes about ¾ cup.

DILL SALAD DRESSING

½ cup vinegar	1 tbsp sugar
1 large head and stem of dill	1 tsp salt
1 lb ripe tomatoes	⅛ tsp pepper
1 cup salad oil	

Place vinegar and dill in closed jar overnight, may remain longer if desired. Cook tomatoes, rub through coarse sieve and continue cooking over low heat to form a thick paste (½ cup). Combine dill-seasoned vinegar, tomato paste, and remaining ingredients in a bowl. Beat with a rotary beater. Chill. Use in making fish or vegetable salad. Makes 1 pt.

Note: ¼ cup chili sauce may be substituted for the fresh tomato purée if desired.

FRENCH DRESSING No. 1

½ cup salad oil
⅓ cup cider, tarragon *or*
   malt vinegar
¾ tsp salt
4 tsp sugar *or* to suit taste

1⁄16 tsp dry mustard
1⁄16 tsp black pepper
1 tsp paprika
½ tsp onion juice (omit for
   fruit salad)

Combine all ingredients by beating thoroughly with rotary beater. Chill in a covered jar. Shake just before serving. Makes about ¾ cup.

FRENCH DRESSING No. 2

⅛ tsp dry mustard
¼ tsp celery salt
1⁄16 tsp black pepper
½ tsp paprika
¼ tsp salt
1¼ tsp sugar

Pinch of thyme
¼ tsp crushed caraway seed
⅓ cup vinegar
⅓ cup salad oil
3 tbsp water

Mix all dry ingredients in a bowl. Add remaining ingredients and beat well. Chill in a covered jar or wide-mouthed bottle. Shake well just before using. Makes about ¾ cup.

FRUIT JUICE SALAD DRESSING

⅓ cup sugar
3 tbsp flour
¼ tsp salt
½ cup orange juice
⅓ cup lemon juice

1 cup pineapple juice
2 eggs, beaten
6 oz, 2 pkgs cream cheese
½ pt whipping cream, if
   desired

Mix dry ingredients in top of double boiler. Add fruit juices and blend. Cook over boiling water for 20 min, stirring occasionally to keep smooth. Beat the eggs with a rotary beater, add a small amount of the hot mixture gradually stirring to keep smooth. Return to double boiler, cook for 5 min, stir constantly. Cool slightly, add slowly to softened cream cheese beating with a rotary beater until thoroughly blended and fluffy. Chill and store in a covered container. Makes 2 cups.

If desired, this dressing may be added to stiffly beaten whipped cream before serving.

FRUIT SALAD DRESSING

3 tbsp butter
2 tbsp flour
½ cup milk
¼ cup egg yolks, about
   3 yolks

¼ cup orange juice
1½ tbsp lemon juice
2 *or* 3 tbsp sugar
¼ tsp salt
¼ tsp prepared mustard

Melt butter, blend in flour, add milk gradually and cook over direct heat, stirring constantly until mixture boils and thickens. Gradually stir in beaten egg yolks and cook one min longer over low heat, stirring constantly. Remove from heat; stir in remaining ingredients. Chill thoroughly in a covered container before using. Makes about 1 cup.

CREAMY GOLDEN SALAD DRESSING

1 cup sugar
¼ cup flour
1 tsp dry mustard
Dash of red pepper
¼ tsp white pepper
1 tsp salt

1 cup egg yolks, 12
1 cup 5% cider vinegar, heated
½ cup thick cream, sweet *or* sour

Mix and thoroughly blend first 6 ingredients. Beat yolks with rotary beater, then beat in dry ingredients and hot vinegar. Turn into top of medium size double boiler—1½ qt preferably. Place over simmering water and stir and cook until thick and smooth. Now cover and cook 10 min, stirring frequently. Remove from heat and stir in cream. Pour into qt jar; cool and seal. When ready to use, stir in an equal portion whipped cream or soured commercial cream, commercial salad dressing or mayonnaise. Excellent for Waldorf or Potato Salad, and when combined with mayonnaise, makes wonderful Chicken Salad. Keeps 2 or 3 weeks refrigerated. 1 qt.

HORSERADISH DRESSING

⅓ cup prepared horseradish
¼ cup vinegar
1 cup salad oil
1½ tsp salt

½ tsp sugar
¼ tsp onion juice
1 tbsp ice water
⅛ tsp paprika

Soak horseradish in vinegar overnight. Drain in a sieve over a bowl, pressing horseradish until dry. Discard dry portion and to the strained liquid, add remaining ingredients. Beat well with a rotary beater. Excellent for salad containing ham, tongue, luncheon meat, or plain head lettuce. Makes about 1⅓ cups.

LEMON FRENCH DRESSING

⅓ cup lemon juice
½ cup salad oil
1 tsp salt
1 tsp paprika

2 tbsp sugar *or* honey
½ tsp celery seed, if desired
Clove of garlic, if desired
½ tsp egg white

Combine all ingredients and shake before serving. Makes 1 cup.

This dressing is an excellent marinade for cooked vegetables, meat and fish. Let them stand in the dressing until well seasoned. Drain, and serve with any additional dressing.

Variation: To make sweet French dressing for fruit salads, omit garlic, add ½ cup red jelly or ½ cup honey to the above ingredients.

LIME HONEY FRUIT SALAD DRESSING

⅓ cup lime juice	½ tsp paprika
⅓ cup strained honey	¾ tsp prepared mustard
¼ tsp salt	½ tsp seasoning salt
1 cup salad oil	¼ tsp grated lime rind

Combine all ingredients in a bowl or fruit jar; beat with a rotary beater or shake thoroughly. Chill before serving with any fresh or canned fruit salad. This mixture will remain emulsified much longer than many other dressings, but should be shaken up or beaten just before serving. Makes 1⅓ cups.

PINEAPPLE SALAD DRESSING

Excellent for slaw, delicious on fruit

2⅔ tbsp butter	2 eggs, separated
2 tbsp flour	1 cup pineapple juice
½ tsp salt	2 tsp lemon juice
10 tbsp sugar	

Melt butter in top of double boiler over hot water. Blend in flour, salt, 8 tbsp of the sugar and egg yolks, stirring vigorously. Beat egg whites to a stiff foam, then add remaining sugar and beat to a shiny meringue. Fold carefully into yolk mixture. Slowly stir in the pineapple juice. This mixture should be thick. Remove from heat, stir in lemon juice. Chill. Use as is for cole slaw but fold in ½ cup whipped cream for fruit salad. 2 cups.

Note: Keeps well refrigerated 4 or 5 days.

TOMATO FRENCH DRESSING

3 tbsp honey	2 tbsp vinegar
1 tbsp catchup	2½ tbsp lemon juice
½ tsp dry mustard	½ cup salad oil
1 tsp prepared horseradish	1 clove garlic, cut in half, if
1½ tsp salt	desired
½ tsp celery seed	½ tsp egg yolk

Combine all ingredients in a pt jar with tight fitting lid. Shake well and chill in refrigerator. Shake well before using. Makes 1¼ cups. Remove garlic after standing in dressing 12 hrs.

MAYONNAISE

1 tsp dry mustard	2 egg yolks
1 tsp salt	¼ cup cider vinegar *or*
2 tsp confectioners' sugar	lemon juice, chilled
Dash cayenne pepper	1½ cups salad oil, chilled

Blend dry ingredients in mixing bowl. Add unbeaten egg yolks and mix well; then add ½ tsp vinegar or lemon juice. Add a few drops of oil, beating in with a rotary beater or electric mixer. Continue adding oil by drops, beating thoroughly after each addition, until about 2 tbsp oil have been added and the mixture has thickened. Beat in a little vinegar, and then continue adding oil by tsp until 2 more tbsp have been used. As mixture thickens, oil may be added in larger quantities, beating well after each addition. Add vinegar to thin the mixture whenever it becomes very stiff. Continue adding oil and vinegar with continued beating until all has been used. Makes 1 pt.

Note: If oil is added too rapidly at first, mayonnaise will not thicken; but this thin mixture may be beaten into another egg yolk, a little at a time, and the rest of the oil and vinegar added when the new mixture has thickened up.

BEET MAYONNAISE

Fold ⅓ cup chilled salad dressing or mayonnaise lightly into ⅓ cup thick sour cream. Fold in 1 cup finely chopped or grated canned or fresh cooked beets chilled and patted between folds of paper toweling or paper napkin to absorb excess moisture. Serve over chilled, freshly cooked cauliflower or over lettuce wedges, thick slices of cucumber, tomatoes, or sliced green pepper. 4 servings.

GREEN MAYONNAISE

Blanch 1 pt chopped spinach in 2 tbsp boiling water for 1 min, chop fine and squeeze through double thickness of cheesecloth. Combine enough juice with mayonnaise to obtain desired shade of green. Green food coloring may be used for fruit salads.

RED MAYONNAISE

For fish salads, add tomato paste or lobster coral rubbed through a sieve, to mayonnaise and stir well. For fruit salads, add currant jelly, grenadine, or cherry juice to mayonnaise. Stiffened cherry or raspberry-flavored gelatin whipped into tiny particles and added to mayonnaise makes a pleasing, sparkling dressing for fruit salads.

OLD-FASHIONED SOUR CREAM DRESSING

Excellent to serve over sliced cucumbers and tomatoes or to combine with salted, sweetened shredded cabbage for cole slaw

1 tsp dry mustard	1 egg yolk
½ tsp salt	2 tbsp cider vinegar
1 tsp flour	1 tbsp salad oil
1 tbsp sugar	½ cup sour cream
Dash red pepper	

Blend all the dry ingredients in top of a double boiler. Beat egg yolk well, stir in the vinegar until well blended, then add to mixture in double boiler, stirring thoroughly. Place over boiling water and stir and cook for about 5 min, or until thick and smooth. Now remove from heat, cool then beat in oil and sour cream until velvety smooth. Scrape out immediately into a small container with cover. About ⅔ cup dressing.

PEANUT BUTTER DRESSING No. 1

¼ cup peanut butter	5 tsp sugar
⅓ cup salad oil	½ tsp prepared mustard
¼ cup cider vinegar	Dash paprika
½ tsp salt	Dash red pepper

Put all the ingredients into a small mixing bowl and beat until smooth with a rotary beater. Delicious on canned pears, peaches, bananas and apples. Makes about ¾ cup.

PEANUT BUTTER DRESSING No. 2

Add 1 tbsp peanut butter to ¼ cup mayonnaise. Blend thoroughly. This is popular with children and particularly good on apple salad.

PEPPER ONION MAYONNAISE

1 clove of garlic, cut	1 tbsp chopped pimiento
1 cup mayonnaise	2 tsp lemon juice
1 tbsp chopped parsley	⅛ tsp paprika
1 tbsp chopped green pepper	¼ tsp salt
1 tbsp chopped onion	⅛ tsp pepper

Rub bowl in which dressing is to be mixed with cut side of clove of garlic. Discard garlic. Combine mayonnaise with remaining ingredients and mix thoroughly. Serve with fish or meat salads or over cabbage to make cole slaw. Makes about 1¼ cups dressing.

QUICK SOUR CREAM DRESSING

Very tasty and easy and quick to make

1 cup sour cream	1 tsp salt
3 *or* 4 dashes black pepper,	2 tsp cider *or* wine vinegar
preferably fresh-ground	¼ tsp prepared mustard
4 tsp sugar	

Put all ingredients into a 1-qt mixing bowl and stir until well blended. Delicious on sliced cucumbers, or cucumbers and sliced onions and sliced tomatoes, or for making cole slaw. 1 cup.

ANOTHER QUICK SOUR CREAM DRESSING

To ½ cup mayonnaise or cooked salad dressing add ½ cup sour cream and stir well. Then stir in 1 tbsp very finely cut chives and a dash or so of coarse ground black pepper. 1 cup.

RANCHO DRESSING

2 green onions *or* scallions
1 cup sour cream, commer-
   cially processed type
2 tbsp mayonnaise

2 *or* 3 tbsp lemon juice
1¼ oz blue cheese
Salt and freshly ground
   pepper

Finely cut tops and all of the onions or scallions into sour cream. Add remaining ingredients and season to taste. Allow to "ripen" for several hrs before serving. Excellent on crisp wedges of lettuce or favorite combination vegetable salad. 4 servings.

RUSSIAN DRESSING

Combine 1 cup mayonnaise with ¼ cup chili sauce. Then add either 1 tbsp each of finely chopped celery and green pepper or add 1 tbsp imported gray caviar or chopped anchovies, 1 tbsp finely chopped cooked beets and 1 tsp chopped chives.

SESAME SALAD DRESSING

Toasted sesame seed add taste and eye appeal to this dressing

1 tbsp sesame seed
2 tbsp water
2 tbsp wine vinegar
1½ tsp lemon juice
1¼ tsp salt
½ cup salad oil

½ tsp sugar
1 medium clove garlic,
   peeled, sliced
Few dashes white *or* black
   pepper
1 to 2 tsp finely cut parsley

Spread sesame seed on a shallow pan and toast in a moderate oven (350° F) to a light tan color. Combine rest of ingredients in a pt jar. Add sesame seed. Close jar, shake vigorously. Let stand 30 min, remove garlic. Close and refrigerate. Shake thoroughly before serving on a green salad or over avocado. ¾ cup.

SOUR CREAM OLIVE FRUIT DRESSING

1 cup sour cream
1 cup finely chopped ripe
   olives
¼ tsp celery salt

2 tsp sugar
2 tsp lemon juice
Dash of salt

Combine all ingredients. Chill. Serve with any fresh or cooked fruit salad combination. Makes about 1½ cups.

SPANISH SALAD DRESSING

Excellent on salads made of mild flavored vegetables

1¼ cups coarsely sliced Pascal
  celery
½ large green pepper, ½ cup
  diced
1 medium onion, sliced
1 medium clove garlic
1 tbsp chopped parsley
½ tsp orégano
⅓ cup wine vinegar

⅔ cup salad oil
½ cup chili sauce
2 tbsp catchup
1⅓ tbsp salt
¼ cup sugar
Dash ground cloves *or* 2
  whole cloves
¹⁄₁₆ tsp pepper
¼ cup lime *or* lemon juice

Put first 5 ingredients through food chopper using fine blade. Add remaining ingredients and beat well. Store in tightly covered jar. 3 cups.

THOUSAND ISLAND DRESSING

1 cup mayonnaise
2 tbsp chili sauce

1 tbsp sweet pickle relish
1 tbsp chopped green pepper

Combine ingredients well. Serve over head lettuce wedges or mixed green salad.

Variation: 1 tbsp chopped stuffed olives and/or 1 hard-cooked egg, chopped fine may be added to Thousand Island Dressing.

SOUR CREAM SALAD DRESSING

1 egg yolk
2 tsp vinegar
½ tsp dry mustard
4 tsp sugar

¼ tsp salt
Pepper to suit taste
½ cup sour cream

Beat egg yolk in top of double boiler until thick, stir in the vinegar, mustard, sugar and seasonings. Place over simmering water and cook with constant stirring until slightly thickened. Cool and stir in sour cream. Chill thoroughly before serving. Serve with any shredded cabbage or other shredded vegetable salad mixtures. Makes ⅔ cup.

SPECIAL SALAD DRESSING

3 tbsp flour
3 tbsp sugar
1 tsp salt
¼ tsp dry mustard
½ tsp paprika

⅛ tsp black pepper
½ tsp celery seed, if desired
1 cup milk
1 egg
⅔ cup cider vinegar

Mix all dry ingredients and celery seed in a saucepan; add milk and heat to boiling; boil gently 3 min, stirring constantly. Remove from heat and stir hot mixture slowly into well-beaten egg which has been combined with vinegar. Chill in a covered container. This dressing is good for potato or macaroni salad, or wherever an oil dressing is not desired. Makes about 1½ cups.

WHIPPED CREAM SALAD DRESSING

½ cup vinegar
2 tbsp sugar
½ tsp dry mustard
¼ tsp salt

1 tbsp butter
2 tbsp lemon juice
6 egg yolks
Whipping cream

Combine all ingredients except yolks and cream, heat to boiling. Beat egg yolks in the top of a double boiler. Slowly stir in the hot vinegar mixture and cook over hot water until very thick. Beat constantly with a rotary beater. Cool. Cover and store in refrigerator. Makes about 1¼ cups. To serve, blend with an equal amount of whipped cream.

YOGURT SALAD DRESSING

3 tbsp flour
1¼ tsp salt
¼ tsp celery salt
1½ tsp dry mustard
Dash white pepper

1 egg, well beaten
⅓ cup milk
*¼ to ⅓ cup honey
1 tbsp vinegar
1 jar, 8 oz, Yogurt

Mix dry ingredients and combine with egg in the top of a double boiler. Add milk slowly, stir until smooth. Cook over hot water until mixture is very thick. Stir constantly to keep smooth. Then cook 5 min longer, stirring occasionally. Remove from heat, add honey and vinegar and stir to cool. Add Yogurt gradually, beating constantly to keep mixture smooth. Store in a covered container in the refrigerator.

*Use larger amount of honey for fruit salad dressing and smaller amount for vegetable dressing. This dressing is especially good on mixed fruit salad. Makes about 1¼ cups.

CRANBERRY RELISH

1 qt cranberries
1 large seedless orange

1 cup sugar

Pick over cranberries, discarding any soft ones, and wash in cold water. Peel orange with a knife and pull out the white inner portion of the skin. Separate the orange into sections, removing the membrane. Put cranberries, orange sections, and yellow part of orange peel through the food chopper, using the coarsest cutter. Stir in the sugar, turn mixture into a clean glass jar or bowl, cover tightly, and let stand overnight or longer in the refrigerator or any cool place, to blend the flavors. Serve as a relish with chicken, turkey, or roast meat. Makes about 2½ cups.

Sandwiches

Take women's funny hats and fussy party sandwiches out of this world, and what would men have to laugh about? But they have a secret admiration for that giddy hat after all; and there's nothing secret about the gusto with which they go for sandwiches, even the fancy ones. Men, children, and women too will find sandwiches they specially like in this varied collection of sandwich recipes for every occasion.

★ ★ ★ ★

PROBABLY there is not an American who does not know the story of how the Earl of Sandwich, nearly two hundred years ago, called for a piece of meat between two slices of bread so he could eat without leaving the gaming table. Pleased with his invention, he called it a "sandwich."

The inventive Earl would scarcely recognize his brain-child in the many sandwiches popular today, which have long ceased to conform to the pattern of a "piece of meat" between two slices of bread. Only the school child's or the working man's "lunch box" sandwich bears a marked resemblance to its first ancestor.

Here are the common types of sandwiches that are generally popular today:

1. *"Lunch box" sandwich:* 2 slices of any desired bread spread with butter and laid together with a filling; usually cut in half for convenience in eating from the hand.

2. *Hot sandwich:* slices of bread or toast placed on a plate, covered with hot sliced meat (sometimes fish), and then gravy or sauce poured over it. Eaten with fork and served for main dish.

3. *Grilled or toasted sandwich:* 2 slices of bread filled with any desired filling (cheese is often used); the whole sandwich toasted under the broiler, in a buttered skillet, or sandwich grill; served hot.

4. *Open-faced sandwich:* slices of bread spread with butter then topped with any desired sandwich spread, or covered with sliced meat, cheese, tomato, etc. Sometimes broiled or toasted, especially when cheese is used.

5. *Club sandwich:* 3 or more slices of bread or toast spread with butter and put together with a different filling in each layer, crusts usually trimmed off and sandwich cut in triangles.

6. *Canapés:* small open-faced sandwiches made of bread cut into fancy shapes, spread with butter and filling, p 187, and garnished attractively; usually served as appetizers.

7. Fancy sandwiches: rolled, ribbon, checkerboard, mosaic. Descriptions of some will be found in the following recipe section.

8. Sandwich loaf: slices of bread, cut either crosswise or lengthwise of a sandwich loaf of bread, spread with butter then laid together with a different filling in each layer; crusts are trimmed off and whole loaf "iced" with a cream cheese mixture. Crosswise slices of bread put together in groups of 3 or more make an individual loaf; lengthwise slices of an entire loaf make sandwich which is sliced like cake for individual servings.

SANDWICH FILLINGS

There are even more kinds of fillings than sandwiches, ranging from the famous Earl's simple slab of meat to the most elaborate combination of fancy ingredients. But they are still divided into 3 main classes:

1. "Main dish" fillings: include sliced meat and cheese, potted meat, fish, chopped meat, hard-cooked, scrambled and fried eggs, peanut butter, and any predominantly protein food mixture. May be combined with lettuce, sliced tomatoes, chopped pickles, chopped vegetables of various kinds.

2. Sweet fillings: include jams, jellies, preserves, honey, and spreads made by combining creamed butter or cream cheese with any of these ingredients, or with fruit, such as date paste, grated orange rind, or lemon juice.

3. Relish fillings: include chopped vegetables mixed with mayonnaise dressing.

Most of these fillings can be used in most types of sandwiches, and a good deal of overlapping is likely to occur. There is plenty of room for originality.

MAKING OF SANDWICHES

The best bread for sandwiches must be fresh enough to be palatable but not so fresh that it tears when spread (except for rolled sandwiches, which require very fresh bread). For thin, dainty sandwiches, buy bread unsliced and cut it just before making the sandwiches with a razor-sharp knife. The knife will need frequent sharpening if you have many sandwiches to make. Bread for dainty sandwiches should never be sliced more than ⅜-inch thick. Sliced bread is usually at least ½-inch thick, sometimes a little more, and a sandwich of these proportions is quite a mouthful, good for lunch boxes but not for teas.

The uncut loaf may be sliced either crosswise for regular sandwiches, or lengthwise for rolled sandwiches or a sandwich loaf, but in either case, it is important to slice it evenly. The crust can be cut from the loaf before slicing the bread if preferred, but though it means a little more work and also a little more waste, it is generally more satisfactory to trim the crusts off after the sandwich is made. It is easier to spread the bread before trimming, and the sandwich will look neater with filling that goes right to the edge of the bread, if trimming is done after applying the filling. The crusts will have a little butter and filling on them, but these make tasty after-school snacks for youngsters.

In making the sandwiches, be sure to spread the bread well with a uniform thin layer of softened butter (from 1½ to 2 tsp of creamed butter per slice) or mayonnaise, whichever you are using. This is especially important with a moist or soft filling, such as preserves, for it prevents excessive soaking of the bread. Of course each slice of bread must be buttered on the side next the filling.

Apply the filling generously, especially if it is mild-flavored. The thickness should vary according to the thickness of the bread; slices ⅝-inch thick will require more filling to be tasty than slices ⅜-inch thick.

If sandwiches are to be kept a while or carried in a lunch box, they should be wrapped in waxed paper as soon as they are made. If different fillings are used, each sandwich should be wrapped separately to prevent an interchange of flavors. Ribbon and checkerboard sandwiches, and others which need to be chilled or even frozen for a time, should always be snugly wrapped in waxed paper before storing in the refrigerator. It not only preserves flavor but prevents drying out.

SERVING OF SANDWICHES

Regular sandwiches for family luncheons or for lunch boxes present no particular problem of serving beyond that of making them as attractive and easy to eat as possible. This is done by cutting the whole sandwich neatly into halves or quarters so it can be handled conveniently. But if everyone is hungry and the sandwiches are good, no one will worry about a fancy arrangement.

Party sandwiches—finger, ribbon, rolled, checkerboard, mosaic—lend themselves to arrangement. Flat trays, platter and large chop plates are ideal. Sandwiches of the same kind should be grouped together. Several kinds may be put on the same plate, but may be separated by sprigs of parsley, olives, or small pickles, which make an edible garnish. Such a tray of carefully made sandwiches is appealing to the eye as well as to the palate, and most women enjoy the little stir of admiration which they are bound to create.

CHEESE SANDWICHES

CHEESE AND RAISIN SANDWICH FILLING

⅓ lb American cheese, grated
½ cup finely chopped celery
¾ cup chopped raisins
½ cup Mayonnaise, p 1202
1 tbsp milk

⅛ tsp salt
⅓ cup soft butter
100% whole wheat bread, sliced thin
Lettuce

Combine cheese and celery. Prepare raisins by placing in a sieve over boiling water, covering and steaming to soften and plump them.

Chop softened raisins and combine with cheese mixture. Add mayonnaise, milk and salt and mix well. Makes 1⅓ cups of filling. Butter slices of 100% whole wheat bread. Spread half the slices with 2 tbsp of the above mixture. Place a leaf of lettuce or other tender greens on top of filling and a second slice of bread over lettuce. Cut in any desired shape. Makes approximately 10 sandwiches.

COTTAGE CHEESE CARROT NUT DOUBLE DECKER SANDWICHES

12 slices whole wheat bread

Filling No. 1:
- 1 cup creamed cottage cheese
- 1 tbsp chives
- ½ tsp salt
- ⅓ cup butter, softened

Filling No. 2:
- 1 cup shredded carrots
- ¼ cup finely chopped nuts
- ¼ cup finely chopped celery
- ⅓ cup mayonnaise
- ⅛ tsp salt
- Radishes *or* olives

Combine ingredients for each filling thoroughly.

Butter all the slices of bread. Spread cottage cheese filling (No. 1) on 4 slices, and carrot-nut filling (No. 2) on 4 other slices. Place one slice with carrot-nut spread on top of the cottage cheese slice, and top this with remaining slices of buttered bread, butter side down. Cut across in fourths and serve with cut side facing up on sandwich plate. Garnish with radishes or olives. 4 sandwiches.

CREAM CHEESE CARROT FINGER SANDWICHES

- 3 oz pkg cream cheese
- 2 tbsp soft butter
- ¼ tsp onion juice
- ½ tsp salt
- ¼ tsp sugar
- 1 cup freshly grated raw carrot, 4 to 5 medium carrots

Blend first 5 ingredients thoroughly, then stir in carrots. Chill about an hr before making sandwiches. Spread 3 tbsp of the mixture between 2 slices of whole wheat bread. Trim off crusts neatly. Wrap in waxed paper and chill. Just before serving, cut slices into 3 or 4 finger sandwiches. About 1⅛ cups spread—enough for 6 full sized sandwiches.

DATE COTTAGE CHEESE SANDWICH

- 1½ cups creamed cottage cheese
- ¼ cup chopped dates, 6 large
- ¼ cup chopped salted nuts
- 2 tbsp apple *or* plum butter
- 10 slices bread
- ⅓ cup softened butter

Blend cottage cheese, dates, nuts and fruit butter. Spread bread with butter and spread half of the slices with cottage cheese mixture, then top with remaining slices. 5 sandwiches.

OLIVE CHEESE SANDWICHES

¼ cup chopped olives, 12
   large pitted
2 tbsp Mayonnaise, p 1202
3 tbsp pimiento, chopped fine
12 slices rye bread, sliced thin

¼ cup sharp-flavored cheese
   spread
¼ cup softened butter
Lettuce leaves

Combine olives, mayonnaise and pimiento. Spread 6 slices of bread with cheese and the other 6 with butter. Spread buttered bread with the olive mixture. Arrange leaves on top of this and top with bread spread with cheese. Cut each sandwich in half diagonally. 6 sandwiches.

SKILLET CHEESE SANDWICHES

½ lb American cheese
10 slices bread

⅓ cup softened butter

Lay slices of cheese on half the slices of bread; top with remaining slices, trim off crusts if desired. Spread *outside* of sandwiches lightly and evenly with butter. Place sandwiches in moderately hot skillet and brown both sides to the desired golden-brown color, watching carefully. When done, cheese will be slightly melted. Serve piping hot. 5 sandwiches.

WISCONSIN TOASTED CHEESE SANDWICH

For one sandwich, toast one side of 2 slices bread, butter untoasted side of one slice. Lay two ⅓-inch thick slices tomato on buttered side, spread with 1 tbsp each of finely chopped onion and green pepper. Sprinkle with salt, pepper and paprika, then sprinkle 3 tbsp of grated aged American Cheddar cheese over all. Place the cheese topped slice and the plain slice, untoasted side up, under broiler and broil until cheese is melted and toast is nicely browned. Remove from broiler and lay the toasted plain slice over the cheese topped slice and cut in half diagonally; serve immediately. For extra special sandwich, serve with 2 pieces of crisp bacon.

FANCY AND SPECIAL SANDWICHES

CHECKERBOARD SANDWICHES

Tongue Filling

12-oz can tongue
¼ cup mayonnaise

Salt, if needed
Dash of pepper

Put tongue through food chopper. Add remaining ingredients and mix well. Makes 1½ cups.

Peppy Cheese Spread

5 oz peppy cheese spread
1 tbsp cream

½ tsp prepared
mustard

Combine cheese, cream, and mustard and mix with a fork or spoon until smooth and easy to spread on bread.

Parsley Butter

¼ cup finely chopped
parsley

¼ cup soft butter
Dash of salt

Chop parsley by stripping leaves from stems, placing in a small glass. Snip very fine with a kitchen scissors. Combine with butter and salt and mix well.

Tuna Fish Filling

7-oz can of tuna
½ tsp freshly grated
onion

⅔ cup dill pickle, chopped
very fine
¼ cup Mayonnaise, p 1202

Drain oil from tuna and flake fish into a bowl. Add remaining ingredients and mix well. Makes about 1 cup, tightly pkd.

Prepare the sandwich spreads, cream the butter, and have enough mayonnaise available. Use whole wheat and white bread loaves of same size and sliced the same thickness. Lightly butter a slice of whole wheat bread, then spread it with a layer of tongue filling ⅛-inch thick. Spread this thinly with mayonnaise. Next spread a white slice of bread with a little parsley butter and a layer of peppy cheese ⅛-inch thick. Spread mayonnaise thinly over peppy cheese. Fit this slice of bread neatly over the top of slice spread with tongue and mayonnaise. Spread a whole wheat slice with tuna fish filling and place it on top of slice spread with cheese. Finally add a slice of white bread spread lightly with butter, buttered side down. Press together lightly but firmly. Wrap each sandwich in waxed paper. Place on a flat surfaced pan, and cover with a flat surfaced pan or light weight board and let chill for 2 hrs. Remove crusts and cut into slices a little thicker than the original bread slices. Re-stack 4 of these slices for each checkerboard loaf so that the brown and white breads alternate, one over the other. Spread mayonnaise between the slices as they are stacked to hold them together. A checkerboard surface appears on the two ends of the new stack. Press gently but firmly together. Wrap in waxed paper carefully so as not to distort shape. Place on a flat surfaced pan and chill for at least 2 hrs (these may be made the day before if desired; longer chilling makes them easier to cut). Cut slices from checkerboard end, any desired thickness. Each checkerboard loaf makes about 6 slices.

FANCY HOT CHICKEN SANDWICHES
Elegant

5 lb roasting *or* stewing
   chicken, boiled *or* steamed
   whole, p 1041
4½ cups rich chicken broth
4 tbsp flour

3 egg yolks
Large loaf white bread
Tomatoes, avocadoes *or*
   pimiento
Parsley

Cool cooked chicken in its broth to keep juicy. When ready to make sandwiches, lift out chicken, carefully remove skin. Cut thin slices as large as possible from breast and legs. Skim all fat possible from broth. Blend broth, flour and beaten yolks to a smooth paste. Cook with constant stirring until gravy boils and thickens. Add sliced chicken, cover and cook over low heat until chicken is hot. Cut loaf of bread into half-inch thick slices. Trim off crusts to obtain straight sides. Lift sliced chicken onto one slice of bread on serving plate, top with second slice. Place each sandwich on a small platter. Cut diagonally and slide the 2 triangular sandwiches together so as to make a diamond shape. Pour gravy all over sandwich to mask it and flow down a little into the platter. Lay thin slice of tomato, avocado or pimiento on top in center. Garnish center with parsley leaflets. 6 to 7 servings.

Note: If sandwiches are made of leftover roast chicken, buy extra bony pieces of chicken to make broth for gravy.

CLUB SANDWICHES

15 slices toasted bread,
   buttered
Lettuce
5 thin slices cheese

10 slices crisp, cooked bacon
¼ cup mayonnaise
2 medium tomatoes
1 small cucumber, sliced

On 5 slices of hot buttered toast, place lettuce leaves and over these arrange cheese and cooked bacon slices. Cover with 5 more slices of toast, buttered side down. Spread top of these toast slices with mayonnaise, and on them arrange slices of tomato and cucumber. Top with remaining slices of buttered toast. Stick toothpicks through opposite corners of each sandwich to prevent slipping. Trim off crusts if desired, and cut each sandwich in 2, 3, or 4 triangles or fingers before serving, using a very sharp knife. 5 sandwiches.

CRANBERRY CHICKEN SANDWICH LOAVES
So pretty, so good to eat

1½ lb loaf day-old white *or*
   whole wheat bread
1 cup softened butter *or*
   margarine

3 cups Cranberry Jelly, p 563
   molded in jelly roll pan to
   depth of ¼-inch thickness
2 cups Chicken Salad, p 1058
12 oz cream cheese
Milk

Make 5 stacks of bread slices of 4 slices each. Trim off crusts neatly to have perfectly straight sides. Butter one side of each slice. Cut cranberry squares the same size as the bread. Place cranberry slice on one slice bread. Lay on second slice of bread, butter side down. Spread top side of this second slice with butter, cover with ⅓ of the chicken salad. Lay on third slice bread, butter side down. Spread top side bread with butter, add another slice cranberry sauce. Top with fourth slice bread. Cut each sandwich stack in half with sharp knife. Have cream cheese blended until smooth and of good spreading consistency with milk. Quickly spread sides and tops of loaves smooth with cheese. Make quick swirls with knife across top and garnish with cutouts of cranberry sauce and tiny leaflets of parsley or cress. Repeat until 20 slices have been laid together enough to make 10 loaves. Cover, refrigerate until serving time. Sandwiches to be at their best should be served within an hr or so after making. 10 servings.

EGG SALAD AND SARDINE
DOUBLE DECKER SANDWICH

Filling No. 1:
3¼-oz can sardines
¾ tsp freshly grated onion

1 tbsp lemon juice
2 tbsp mayonnaise

Mash drained sardines thoroughly. Blend in remaining ingredients. Makes 9 tbsp.

Filling No. 2:
3 hard-cooked eggs, chopped
½ cup finely chopped celery
2 tbsp chopped green pepper

½ cup chopped sweet pickle
¼ cup mayonnaise
⅛ tsp freshly grated onion
½ tsp salt

Mix first four ingredients. Blend mayonnaise, onion and salt. Combine with first mixture. Makes 1 cup.

3 tbsp soft butter

9 slices white bread
Lettuce

Spread butter on one side of six slices of bread. Spread sardine mixture on 3 of the slices, 3 tbsp to each slice. Top with lettuce. Butter remaining 3 slices of bread on both sides and place on top of slices spread with sardine filling. Spread egg salad mixture over this using ⅓ cup of the mixture to each sandwich. Top with remaining slices of buttered bread, butter side down. Skewer with toothpicks to hold sandwich together. Cut diagonally into fourths. Lay cut side up on sandwich plate.

Note: Mayonnaise Recipe, p 1202.

FRIED TOMATO SANDWICH

4 medium tomatoes	2 eggs, beaten
1 cup creamed cottage cheese	1 tbsp milk
1 tbsp finely chopped chives	1 cup fine cracker crumbs
or tender green onion tops	¼ cup butter or margarine
¼ tsp salt	

Peel the tomatoes, slice each crosswise into 4 slices. Combine cottage cheese, chives, and salt. Spread cottage cheese mixture evenly over 8 of the tomato slices, top with remaining slices, sandwich fashion. Combine eggs and milk. Dip the tomato sandwiches into the egg mixture, then into the cracker crumbs. Fry in hot butter until golden brown on both sides and hot through (about 4 min). Turn with wide spatula or pancake turner to avoid breaking sandwiches. Serve hot. 4 servings.

HOT PRUNE SANDWICHES

2 eggs	2 tsp lemon juice
1 cup milk	8 slices day-old bread
½ tsp salt	2 tbsp shortening
¼ tsp cinnamon	¼ cup maple syrup
1 cup cooked prunes, pitted,	2 tsp lemon juice
chopped fine	

Beat eggs slightly. Add milk, salt and cinnamon and beat till well blended but not frothy. Mix prunes with lemon juice. Spread on four slices of bread. Lay remaining slices on top to make sandwiches. Cut in half. Dip halves in egg milk mixture and brown in the heated shortening over low heat. Serve with maple syrup mixed with lemon juice. 4 sandwiches.

ROLLED AND RIBBON SANDWICHES

Rolled—With very sharp knife, cut top crust evenly from an unsliced loaf of fresh white or whole wheat bread, lengthwise. Quickly spread cut surface thinly with creamed butter; then spread ⅓ of buttered surface with Ham and Cheese Spread, p 1228, next ⅓ with Carrot Butter, p 1222, and last ⅓ with Parsley Butter, p 1224. Cut off a thin slice, keeping it uniform in thickness the length of the loaf. Trim off edge crusts and roll up tightly like jelly roll. Wrap in waxed paper and store in refrigerator; repeat with rest of loaf. Chill several hrs and just before serving, slice like jelly roll about one-fourth inch thick.

Ribbon—Spread Ham and Cheese Spread, p 1228, on slice of buttered white bread; cover with slice of whole wheat bread, and spread this with Parsley Butter, p 1224. Top with another slice of white bread. Press together gently, wrap in waxed paper, and chill in refrigerator for several hrs. When ready to serve, trim off crusts neatly and slice loaf ¼-inch thick to make ribbon sandwiches.

PARTY ALMOND CHICKEN SANDWICH ROLLS

Delicious, dainty but substantial

6 slices very fresh bread from
1½ lb loaf
¼ cup softened butter
2 three oz pkg cream cheese

Milk
1½ cups chicken salad, p 1058
½ cup slivered, toasted
almonds, p 415

Cut crusts from bread, spread with the butter 2 tsp to each slice, then with the salad. Roll up each slice like jelly roll. Fasten with tooth picks. Cream the cheese and stir in enough milk to give a good spreading consistency. Spread neatly over rolls, roll in chopped almonds. Lay in wax paper lined shallow pan, refrigerate. Remove toothpicks just before serving. 6 servings.

SANDWICH BAR

Here is a new idea for summer refreshments or Sunday night supper: supply a plateful or a trayful of open-faced sandwiches with another plate or platter of buttered bread or toast on the side, and let your guests help themselves according to taste and appetite. Those with dainty appetites may cover the open-faced sandwich of their choice with a slice of plain buttered bread; heartier eaters may put two open-faced sandwiches together for an interesting flavor combination; and the hungriest of all may put a slice of buttered bread between two of the open-faced sandwiches, making a three-decker or club sandwich.

SANDWICH LOAF

Ham Salad Filling

1½ cups ground cooked ham
¼ cup finely chopped sweet
pickle

½ tsp prepared mustard
¼ cup Mayonnaise, p 1202

Combine all ingredients and mix well. If filling is too dry for spreading, add a small amount of cream or mayonnaise.

Parsley Butter

¼ cup finely chopped
parsley

¼ cup soft butter
Dash of salt

Chop parsley by stripping leaves from stems, placing in a small glass and snipping very fine with a kitchen scissors. Combine with butter and salt and blend well.

Egg Salad Filling

5 hard-cooked eggs	1 tsp prepared mustard
2 tbsp chopped pickle	½ tsp vinegar
¼ cup finely chopped celery	1 tsp salt
⅓ cup mayonnaise	⅛ tsp grated onion

Chop eggs very fine, or put through a sieve or ricer. Add remaining ingredients and mix well.

Have all fillings prepared and butter softened for easy spreading. Cut the crusts from a large unsliced loaf of bread (white or whole wheat) and cut into 4 uniform lengthwise slices.

Spread butter lightly on first slice of bread, then spread generously with ham filling. Spread second slice with butter and lay it, buttered side down, over ham filling.

Spread top of slice with a thin layer of parsley butter, then a layer of egg salad filling, same thickness as that of ham. Spread third slice of bread with a thin layer of parsley butter and place this side over the egg salad layer. Spread top lightly with butter and cover with overlapping thin slices of tomato (3 medium). Spread over tomatoes, chopped cucumber mixture made by combining ¾ cup finely chopped pared cucumber, ½ cup mayonnaise, ½ tsp salt, and a dash of pepper. Top with fourth unbuttered slice of bread. Wrap the loaf firmly in moist cheesecloth or towel, then in waxed paper. Place on a flat surfaced pan or board and chill thoroughly at least 3 hrs or longer. Unwrap and place on serving platter with layers of filling running horizontal or vertical as desired. Spread softened cream cheese (18 oz) over top and sides of sandwich loaf. Reserve a small amount of cheese. Tint any desired color and use to make a simple decoration on top of loaf. Make a border of crisp fresh watercress or parsley at base of loaf. Garnish with radish roses or stuffed olives. (Top of loaf may be garnished with hard-cooked eggs, pimiento, green pepper, stuffed olives, caviar, or watercress.)

SKILLET SANDWICHES

8 thin slices American *or* Swiss cheese, ½ lb	4 thin slices luncheon meat, ¼ lb
8 slices bread	⅓ cup shortening

Place a slice of cheese on each slice of bread, then meat on four of these slices. Form sandwiches and cut diagonally in half. Melt the shortening in a large skillet and sauté sandwiches. Turn once during cooking, and press each sandwich with a broad spatula to keep from separating. Cook covered until sandwiches are lightly browned on each side and cheese layer begins to melt. Serve immediately. 4 servings.

SQUARE-MEAL BISCUIT SANDWICHES

1 recipe Baking Powder
Biscuits, p 234
1 lb ground beef
1 tsp salt
3 tbsp butter *or* bacon
drippings

¼ lb mushrooms, cleaned
¼ cup flour
1½ cups milk
¾ tsp salt
¾ cup grated sharp cheese
2 cups cooked green beans

Turn biscuit dough onto floured board and roll ¼-inch thick and into a rectangle 12½ x 5 inches; cut into ten 2½-inch sqs. Transfer to slightly greased baking sheet and bake in a hot oven (425° F) for 8 to 10 min. Meanwhile, combine meat with the 1 tsp salt, shape in 5 thin patties, and pan-fry in a hot, slightly greased skillet until done. Melt butter in top of double boiler, add sliced mushrooms, cover and sauté just long enough for the mushrooms to be covered with their own juices, 2 or 3 min. Blend in flour, and add milk; stir constantly over direct heat until sauce boils and thickens. Add ¾ tsp salt and stir in cheese until melted. Add the green beans and keep hot over boiling water. To serve, place a meat patty between 2 biscuits and pour the hot sauce over all. Serve immediately. 5 servings.

FISH SANDWICHES

SALMON SALAD SANDWICH

7¾ oz can *or* 1 cup cold
boiled salmon
½ cup chopped celery
1 tsp fine-chopped onion
2 tbsp chopped sweet pickle,
optional
1 tsp lemon juice *or* vinegar

4 dashes cayenne
¼ cup mayonnaise *or* salad
dressing
¼ tsp salt
12 slices buttered bread *or*
toast
Lettuce

Drain chilled salmon. Turn out into small mixing bowl, remove and discard skin and firm bones. Break fish up slightly with a fork, then stir in next 5 ingredients. Add mayonnaise with the salt. Arrange lettuce on half the slices, spread filling on lettuce, cover with remaining slices. Cut diagonally. Serve at once with pickles and potato chips. 6 sandwiches.

BROILED SARDINE SANDWICHES

2 3¼-oz cans sardines
1½ tbsp catchup

1½ tbsp prepared mustard
10 slices buttered bread

Drain oil from sardines, remove tails and discard. Mash the fish fine and crush the bones. Add catchup and mustard, blending thoroughly. Spread on untoasted bread and place under broiler for 5 to 10 min or until hot and slightly browned. If desired, bread may be toasted on one side and sardine mixture spread on the untoasted side before broiling. 10 open-faced sandwiches.

LOBSTER AVOCADO SANDWICH

½ cup fresh cooked *or* canned
  lobster meat, 3 oz
2 tbsp finely chopped radishes
2 tbsp finely chopped celery
1 hard-cooked egg, chopped
¼ cup mayonnaise

2 tsp lemon juice
1 tsp salt
¼ cup diced well-ripened
  avocado
6 slices bread, buttered

Combine and blend first eight ingredients. Spread on three slices of bread. Top with remaining slices. Cut into triangles or fingers. Makes 1 cup filling or 3 sandwiches.

SARDINE SANDWICHES

3¼-oz can sardines
2 hard-cooked eggs, finely
  chopped
1 tsp lemon juice

½ tsp prepared mustard
Salt to taste
10 slices buttered bread

Drain oil from sardines thoroughly, and remove tails and discard. Mash sardines and crush the bones. Stir in eggs, lemon juice, mustard and salt. Spread between slices of buttered bread. A leaf of lettuce in each sandwich supplies crisp texture and a contrast in flavor. 5 sandwiches.

SHRIMP BUTTER

5¾-oz can moist pack shrimps
  or ¾ cup Cooked Fresh
  Shrimp, p 726

½ cup butter
2 tbsp lemon juice

Drain liquid from canned shrimp. Remove dark vein down back and rinse quickly with cold water. Pound to a paste in a wooden bowl. Cream butter until very soft and smooth, add shrimp paste and lemon juice and mix thoroughly. Makes 1¼ cups.

TUNA CUCUMBER SANDWICH

7-oz can tuna
2 tbsp lemon juice
¼ cup Mayonnaise, p 1202
¼ cup finely chopped celery
2 tsp chopped green pepper

¼ tsp salt
12 slices buttered rye bread
2 tbsp softened butter
1 large cucumber, pared
  and sliced ¼-inch thick

Drain oil from tuna and flake the fish. Add next five ingredients and blend well. Spread on 4 slices of the buttered bread, using ¼ cup of the tuna mixture to each slice. Top with buttered bread, butter side down, then spread the butter on top of bread, lay cucumber slices on top, sprinkle lightly with salt and top with remaining bread. Cut diagonally in quarters, place cut side up on serving plates. 4 sandwiches.

TUNA SPREAD FOR SANDWICHES

7-oz can tuna
½ tsp freshly grated onion

⅔ cup dill pickle, chopped
very fine
¼ cup mayonnaise

Drain oil from tuna. Turn fish into a bowl, flake and add remaining ingredients. Mix well. Makes about 1 cup, tightly packed.

FRUIT AND VEGETABLE SANDWICHES

EXCELLENT ASPARAGUS SANDWICHES

3 oz pkg cream cheese
2 tbsp milk
Few dashes of celery salt
8 slices hot, whole wheat
toast

1¼ lb bunch asparagus, freshly
cooked
Hot Egg Sauce
Parsley

Cream the cheese until smooth and soft, add the milk and celery salt, blend until smooth. Spread quickly on half the hot toast, lay additional toast slices on top. Lay one fourth of the hot asparagus neatly in bundle style on top of toast. Pour Hot Egg Sauce over top, garnish with parsley. 4 servings.

EGG SAUCE

3 tbsp butter
3 tbsp flour
2 cups milk
½ tsp salt
⅛ tsp pepper

Few drops Worcestershire
sauce
1 tsp lemon juice
4 hard-cooked eggs, diced

Melt butter, blend in flour and add milk gradually, stirring constantly over direct heat until sauce boils and thickens. Add seasoning, gently fold in eggs. Makes about 2½ cups.

Note: Mayonnaise Recipe, p 1202.

ASPIC SALAD SANDWICH FILLING

2 tbsp plain gelatin	¼ cup chopped celery
½ cup cold water	1 tbsp chopped green pepper
1 cup puréed tomatoes,	1 cup diced baked ham
fresh *or* canned	¼ cup coarsely grated carrots
½ tsp onion juice	½ tsp prepared horseradish
½ tsp salt	8 slices buttered bread
1 tsp sugar	3-oz pkg cream cheese
2 tsp cider vinegar	

Soften gelatin in the cold water. Heat tomato purée just to boiling.
Add gelatin and stir until it dissolves. Add the onion juice, salt, sugar
and vinegar and cool until partially congealed. Add all remaining ingredients except cream cheese. Mix and pour into shallow pans to a
depth of ¼ inch. Spread buttered bread with softened cream cheese.
Unmold aspic, cut pieces to fit bread and place on 4 slices of bread,
topping with the other 4 slices. Cut in fingers, triangles or any desired
shape. Serve at once. 4 sandwiches.

BAKED BEAN SANDWICHES

No. 1 can pork and beans	10 slices buttered bread
1 tbsp grated onion	Pickles *or* celery
Catchup *or* chili sauce	

Drain liquid from beans and discard. Mash beans and mix with
onion and a little catchup or chili sauce, if desired. Spread on half the
buttered bread. Top with remaining slices. Cut each sandwich in half
diagonally. Serve with sliced pickles or crisp celery. 5 sandwiches.

CARROT BUTTER

1 medium crisp carrot	¼ tsp sugar
½ cup soft butter	1 tbsp mayonnaise
⅛ tsp celery salt	

Scrape carrot and grate medium fine; mix to a spreading consistency
with the butter which has been creamed until smooth. Add celery salt,
sugar and mayonnaise. With this sandwich spread, the bread need not
be buttered. Enough for 5 sandwiches.

CARROT RAISIN SPREAD

2 medium carrots	¼ cup seedless raisins,
½ cup soft butter	chopped
	⅛ tsp salt

Scrape and grate carrots medium fine. Cream butter until smooth,
and blend with carrots, raisins and salt. A little mayonnaise may be
added if needed to produce a spreading consistency. Enough for 5 to 6
sandwiches.

CHOPPED CABBAGE AND BACON SANDWICHES

1 cup very finely chopped
    cabbage
3 slices crisply Broiled Bacon,
    chopped, p 855

¼ tsp salt
¼ cup mayonnaise
¼ tsp sugar
10 slices buttered bread

Crisp green cabbage is best for sandwich fillings; about ⅙ of a medium-sized head will be required to make 1 cup chopped. Chop, do not shred. Combine with the bacon, salt, mayonnaise and sugar, mixing thoroughly. Spread on half the slices of buttered bread. Top with remaining slices. Cut sandwiches in half diagonally. Serve immediately, or wrap securely in waxed paper if sandwiches must be prepared ahead of time. 5 sandwiches.

CUCUMBER ONION AND PICKLE SANDWICHES

1 small cucumber
1 small onion
¼ cup sweet pickles

¼ cup mayonnaise
10 slices buttered bread

Pare cucumber and peel onion, and chop together with the pickles. Mix with mayonnaise and spread on half the slices of buttered bread; top with remaining slices. Cut each sandwich in half diagonally. 5 sandwiches.

DATE NUT SPREAD

Mix ½ cup finely chopped walnuts, pecans or almonds with ¾ cup finely chopped pitted dates. Add a little lemon juice, if desired, and enough mayonnaise to give a spreading consistency. Add salt to taste. Makes about 1½ cups.

FRUIT AND CREAM CHEESE SPREAD

Cream a 3-oz pkg of cream cheese until soft and smooth; blend in 1 or 2 tbsp of orange marmalade, strawberry or raspberry jam, or use fresh strawberry or raspberry purée, adding sugar to suit taste. Spread on toast or crackers or use as sandwich filling. Makes about ½ cup.

KIDNEY BEAN SANDWICH FILLING

No. 2 can red kidney beans
½ cup finely chopped celery
¼ cup chopped sweet pickle
¼ tsp salt

2 tbsp pickle juice
Dash pepper
Tomatoes

Drain liquid from beans and discard. Mash beans thoroughly with potato masher; there will be about 1½ cups. Add remaining ingredients and mix thoroughly. Make sandwiches with buttered bread or toast, and serve with sliced tomatoes or pickled beets. Filling for 8 to 10 sandwiches.

LETTUCE BACON AND TOMATO SANDWICHES

Head *or* leaf lettuce	10 slices hot crisp Broiled
10 slices buttered bread	Bacon, p 855
2 medium tomatoes	3 tbsp mayonnaise

Wash lettuce, separate into leaves, drain well and chill thoroughly in hydrator to crisp. Arrange leaves of crisp lettuce on half the slices of buttered bread, over these lay thin slices of tomato and on top of tomato arrange the bacon. Top with rest of bread slices with under side spread with mayonnaise. If desired, both slices of bread may be spread with mayonnaise instead of butter. Cut in two diagonally. 5 sandwiches.

MIXED VEGETABLE SPREAD

Chop 1 medium pared cucumber fine; place in a piece of cheese-cloth and squeeze out the juice. (Juice may be combined with tomato juice for cocktail.) Combine cucumber with 1 cup of very finely chopped cabbage or lettuce, and mix with just enough mayonnaise to bind together. Add salt to taste. Enough filling for 5 sandwiches.

OLIVE AND TOMATO SANDWICH

8 slices whole wheat bread	Parsley
¼ cup mayonnaise	1 large tomato
⅓ cup stuffed olives	

Spread bread with mayonnaise. Slice olives in thin rings and press over entire surface of 4 slices of bread. Pat a layer of parsley leaves on remaining 4 slices. Top this with thin slices of tomato. Put bread slices together. Cut each sandwich in half diagonally. 4 sandwiches.

OLIVE NUT SPREAD

Combine ⅓ to 1 cup finely chopped walnuts or pecans and ½ cup finely chopped stuffed olives. Mix with just enough mayonnaise to bind together. Enough for 3 to 4 sandwiches.

PARSLEY BUTTER

Chop parsley in this way: strip leaves from stems, place them in a tall, slender glass and snip fine with kitchen scissors. Combine 3 tbsp of chopped parsley with ½ cup of creamed butter. Add salt to taste, and blend in a little mayonnaise if needed to give a spreading consistency. Filling for 5 sandwiches.

PEPPY BAKED BEAN FILLING

1 lb pkg frozen baked beans	2 tbsp mayonnaise
1½ tsp prepared horseradish	1 tbsp catchup
1½ tsp prepared mustard	1 cup finely chopped celery

Place frozen beans in a dish, cover and thaw at room temp. Mash and add the seasonings, mayonnaise and catchup and blend well. Stir in celery. Makes 2 cups.

VEGETABLE EGG SANDWICH

4 hard-cooked eggs	1 tsp vinegar
⅓ cup finely diced green peppers	½ tsp salt
	Dash pepper
⅓ cup finely grated carrots	8 slices white bread
3 tbsp finely diced radishes	3 tbsp softened butter
3 tbsp mayonnaise	1 tomato

Chop the eggs with 2 sharp knives until a coarse, crumbly mixture is obtained. Add next 7 ingredients, mix together carefully to avoid mashing eggs to a paste. Spread bread with softened butter, then spread 4 slices with egg salad mixture. Top with thin slices of tomato and remaining slices of bread. Cut in half diagonally. 4 sandwiches.

WATERCRESS AND BACON SANDWICHES

10 slices bacon	10 slices buttered bread
1 bunch watercress	

Pan-broil Bacon, p 855, until done; drain thoroughly. Wash watercress and shake water out; remove white roots and any discolored leaves. Arrange cress over 5 slices buttered bread, arrange bacon over cress, and cover with remaining bread slices. Cut sandwiches in two diagonally. 5 sandwiches.

WATERCRESS SANDWICHES

1 bunch watercress	10 slices buttered bread
Salt	

Wash cress thoroughly; discard damaged leaves and white roots. Shake water from cress. Arrange over 5 slices of buttered bread, sprinkling lightly with salt before covering with remaining bread slices. 5 sandwiches.

Note: Heart leaves of spinach may be used in place of watercress.

MEAT AND EGG SANDWICHES

BACON AND EGG SALAD SANDWICHES

3 slices bacon	3 tbsp mayonnaise
2 hard-cooked eggs	8 slices buttered whole
2 tbsp chopped chives	wheat bread

Note: Mayonnaise Recipe, p 1202.

Cut bacon in small pieces and pan-fry until delicately browned. Drain. Put the hard-cooked eggs through a sieve or mash very fine with a fork. Blend bacon, eggs, chives, and mayonnaise and spread on half the bread slices. Top with remaining slices. 4 sandwiches.

BOLOGNA FRENCH TOAST SANDWICHES

16 slices bread
8 slices large veal bologna
2 eggs

1 cup milk
½ tsp salt
Bacon drippings

Trim bread slices to fit bologna and make sandwiches, pressing them firmly together. Beat eggs and add milk and salt. Dip sandwiches into the mixture, being sure both sides are well coated. Pan-fry in bacon drippings or other fat until nicely browned on both sides. Serve hot. 4 servings. (For a pleasing luncheon menu, serve with a generous fresh vegetable salad and a fruit and milk beverage.)

BOLOGNA SANDWICH SPREAD

Good and inexpensive

6 oz bologna, ¾ cup ground
⅓ cup pimiento stuffed olives,
   ground

1 tsp Worcestershire sauce
3 tbsp salad dressing
2 tsp finely chopped parsley

Put bologna and olives through food chopper using medium blade. Measure all ingredients into a 1-qt mixing bowl. Blend well with fork. May be packed in a glass or plastic container with tight fitting cover and kept in refrigerator several hrs until ready to use. 1⅛ cups.

COLD ROAST MEAT SANDWICHES

10 slices bread
⅓ cup butter *or* ⅓ cup
   mayonnaise

Cold roast meat
Lettuce

Spread slices of bread with softened butter or mayonnaise. Slice meat thinly, trim off excess fat and any tough gristle just before serving sandwiches. Place slices of meat on half the slices of buttered bread; lay clean, dry, crisp lettuce on meat and top with another slice of buttered bread. Cut in desired shape and serve at once, or wrap lunch-box sandwiches in waxed paper. If the piece of cold roast is too small to slice, run meat through a food chopper or chop finely in a wooden bowl. Add mayonnaise to meat to obtain a spreading consistency. A little finely chopped celery or pickle may be added to the mixture to give a piquant flavor; then proceed as for sliced meat sandwiches. 5 servings.

CUCUMBER AND EGG SALAD SANDWICH FILLING

3 hard-cooked eggs, chopped
¾ cup diced cucumber
1 *or* 2 tsp finely chopped
   onion
½ tsp salt

Dash pepper
2 tbsp mayonnaise, mixed
   with ¼ tsp prepared
   mustard

Combine all ingredients lightly but thoroughly; use immediately as filling for sandwiches. Makes about 1 cup filling, sufficient for 5 sandwiches.

DENVER SANDWICHES

5 eggs
2 tbsp finely chopped onion
⅓ cup chopped green pepper

Salt and pepper to taste
10 slices buttered bread

Beat eggs slightly, add onion and green pepper, and pour into hot, buttered 9 or 10-inch skillet. Cook over low heat until eggs are just firm. Sprinkle with salt and pepper. Cut into five pieces and place between slices of bread or toast. (Two egg yolks may be substituted for one whole egg.) 5 sandwiches.

Note: If preferred, onion and celery may be sautéed lightly in butter for 3 min before adding egg. And ½ cup ground or finely chopped meat may be added to the raw egg mixture.

DEVILED EGG SANDWICHES

6 hard-cooked eggs
2 tbsp mayonnaise
   Salt to taste
   Prepared mustard, if
   desired

10 slices buttered bread,
⅓ cup butter
Crisp lettuce *or* watercress

Shell the eggs and put eggs through a ricer or sieve. Mix thoroughly with mayonnaise, salt and mustard, and spread on 5 of the bread slices. Cover with lettuce or cress and lay remaining slices of bread on top. Cut each sandwich in half diagonally. 5 sandwiches.

EGG AND BACON SANDWICHES

6 hard-cooked eggs
6 slices chopped Crisp
   Bacon, p 855

⅓ cup mayonnaise
10 slices bread, buttered
Lettuce

Shell the eggs and chop them rather fine; mix with the bacon and mayonnaise. Spread on half the slices of buttered bread; cover each with a leaf of lettuce, and place another slice of bread on top. Cut each sandwich in half. 5 sandwiches.

Note: Mayonnaise Recipe, p 1202.
Hard-cooked Eggs, p 663.

EGG SALAD SANDWICHES

6 hard-cooked eggs	1 tsp prepared mustard
Salt to taste	Mayonnaise
¼ cup chopped pickles	10 slices buttered bread

Shell the eggs and chop them rather fine. Mix salt, pickles, and mustard. Add just enough mayonnaise to give a good spreading consistency. Spread on half the slices of buttered bread; top with remaining slices. Cut sandwiches in thirds to obtain finger shapes. 5 sandwiches.

FRANKFURTER SANDWICHES

5 frankfurters	Lettuce
Mustard, sweet pickle	10 slices buttered bread
relish *or* catchup	

Split frankfurters lengthwise and grill, p 887, in a little butter or other fat. Place 2 halves on each of 5 slices of bread, and spread with mustard, relish or catchup, as desired. Cover with lettuce and other slices of buttered bread. 5 sandwiches.

HAM AND CHEESE SPREAD

2 cups baked *or* boiled ham, ground, about 1 lb	½ cup finely chopped pickles
2 cups grated American cheese, about ½ lb	Mayonnaise

Combine ham and cheese; blend with pickle and enough mayonnaise to give a spreading consistency. Enough filling for 10 to 15 sandwiches.

HAM AND EGG SANDWICH FILLING

4 hard-cooked eggs	¼ cup chopped sweet pickle
½ lb baked *or* boiled ham, ground	¼ tsp salt
½ cup mayonnaise	1 tsp vinegar
½ tsp prepared mustard	1 tsp finely chopped onion
1 tbsp finely chopped green pepper	Lettuce

Mash the eggs fine with a fork. Add the remaining ingredients except the lettuce. Mix well. Makes 2½ cups. Butter slices of bread. Spread half the slices using ¼ cup of the above mixture for each slice. Add a leaf of lettuce or other greens and top with another slice of bread. Cut in any desired shape. Enough filling for 10 sandwiches.

HAM SALAD SANDWICHES

1 cup baked *or* boiled ham,
    ground
¼ cup finely chopped sweet
    pickles

Mayonnaise
10 slices buttered bread

Combine ham and pickles thoroughly with enough mayonnaise to bind them together. Spread on half the slices of buttered bread. Top with remaining slices and cut in half diagonally. 5 sandwiches.

HOT ROAST MEAT SANDWICHES

For each sandwich, butter two slices of bread and place one of them in the center of the serving plate; cut the other slice into 2 triangles and place one on each side of the whole slice. Arrange thinly sliced roast meat, either hot or cold, on the whole slice, and pour hot meat gravy over the meat and the rest of the bread. For a full luncheon plate, serve mashed potato on the same plate, and a serving of jelly or fruit pickles either on the plate or in a side dish. Apple sauce is good with a hot pork sandwich, mint jelly with lamb, or apple jelly with roast beef.

LIVER SAUSAGE SANDWICHES

¾ lb liver sausage
10 slices buttered rye bread

Lettuce, if desired

Sausage should be sliced about ⅜-inch thick and casing removed. Arrange on half the slices of buttered bread, top with lettuce if desired and finally with remaining slices of bread. For hot sandwiches, sausage slices may be grilled, p 905, in a little butter or other fat, and bread may be toasted. 5 sandwiches.

LIVER SAUSAGE MUSHROOM SPREAD

1 cup liver sausage, ½ lb
½ cup finely chopped mush-
    rooms
1 tbsp butter

½ tsp Worcestershire sauce
Salt, if desired
Mayonnaise, p 1202

Combine liver sausage with the mushrooms which have been sautéed, p 1356, in the butter until tender (about 5 min). Add seasonings and mix in enough mayonnaise to bind the ingredients together. This mixture may be used for a sandwich spread. When spread on potato chips, it makes unusual hors d'oeuvres. Makes about 1½ cups.

LIVER SAUSAGE SPREAD

Mash ¾ lb liver sausage and mix with ⅓ cup chopped sweet pickles and a little mayonnaise to give a good spreading consistency. Grated sharp cheese makes a pleasing addition. After spreading on buttered bread, the sandwich may be left open-faced, or toasted under broiler, if desired. Enough for 5 open-faced sandwiches.

OLIVE AND EGG SANDWICHES

4 hard-cooked eggs	10 slices buttered bread
⅓ cup chopped stuffed olives	Lettuce
⅓ cup mayonnaise	

Shell the eggs and chop them quite fine. Combine with olives and mayonnaise. Spread on 5 of the bread slices, cover each with lettuce, and lay another slice of bread on top. Cut each sandwich in half diagonally. 5 sandwiches.

POTTED MEAT

1 lb beef for stew	¼ tsp mace
1 pt water	¼ tsp dry mustard
1 onion, sliced	½ tsp salt
1 tsp salt	Broth to moisten
Dash cayenne pepper	

Wipe meat with a damp cloth. Cut into inch dice; put into a 2 or 3 qt saucepan, add water, onion and the 1 tsp salt. Cover and simmer until meat is tender, about 1 hr. Lift meat out of broth and cool. Put through meat grinder and blend well with remaining ingredients, using just enough broth to moisten and hold meat together. Press firmly into cups or other molds; cover and store in refrigerator. When ready to serve, unmold and slice thin. Makes 4 cups. (Any remaining broth may be used in soup or gravy.)

SAUSAGE TOAST

¾ lb pork sausage meat	1 tbsp prepared mustard
2 tsp chopped parsley	10 slices hot buttered toast
⅓ cup grated American cheese	

Turn sausage into hot skillet and brown until well done. Drain off all the fat. Put meat into mixing bowl and add remaining ingredients, mixing thoroughly. Spread on hot buttered toast. 10 open-faced sandwiches.

SHRIMP SANDWICHES (See Shrimp Paste, p 1220)

SWEET SPREAD FOR SLICED DUCK SANDWICHES

1 cup seeded raisins, ground   Bread
¼ cup mayonnaise   Thinly sliced duck
1 tsp lemon juice

Combine first 3 ingredients and blend thoroughly. Spread on slices of bread and top with slices of duck. Cut into desired shapes and serve. Spread for 8 to 10 slices of bread.

Note: This spread may also be used for goose.

TONGUE SANDWICH FILLING

⅔ cup ground cooked tongue,   1 tsp grated horseradish
   pork or beef   ½ tsp salt
2 hard-cooked eggs, chopped   Few grains pepper
¼ cup salad dressing   8 slices bread

Mix first 6 ingredients until well blended, spread on half of bread slices and cover with remaining bread slices. 4 sandwiches.

MISCELLANEOUS

BREAD AND BUTTER SANDWICHES

For the best of sandwiches, use day-old unsliced bread, cut ¼-inch thick, and good fresh butter warmed to room temp so it can be thoroughly creamed for easy spreading. A generous amount of butter is required for high eating quality (1½ to 2 tsp creamed butter for each slice). Bread and butter sandwiches may have crusts left on but they are daintier if the crusts are trimmed off and the sq trimmed sandwiches cut into fingers (about 1 inch wide) for serving with tea. The bread should be buttered and the two slices pressed together before the crusts are removed in order to have the butter coming to the very edge.

Variation: Instead of plain butter, various seasonings may be added to the butter as it is being creamed. Lemon juice and a small amount of grated lemon rind, orange juice, onion juice, horseradish, mustard—these are all possibilities for butter seasoning. Butter seasoned in this manner is especially delicious with certain sandwich fillings; for example, lemon butter with a date-nut filling, or mustard butter with a ham filling. Instead of one kind of bread, a slice of each of two kinds may be used to give an attractive ribbon effect.

HONEY BUTTER

Cream ½ cup butter thoroughly and gradually beat in ½ cup of strained honey until mixture is light and fluffy. This spread is delicious on hot biscuits, toast, or crackers. Makes about ¾ cup.

JELLY SANDWICHES

Bread for jelly sandwiches should be generously buttered on the sides facing the jelly in order to prevent soaking as much as possible. Therefore the butter needs to be thoroughly creamed and softened for spreading. Jelly for sandwiches should be firm but it should be whipped up with a fork in order to spread smoothly. Cream cheese used instead of butter is especially delicious with a jelly filling.

PEANUT BUTTER AND BACON SPREAD

4 oz bacon (8 slices)	½ cup peanut butter
2 tbsp mayonnaise	¼ cup finely diced apples
2 tsp lemon juice	¼ cup finely diced celery

Pan-fry the bacon until done; drain on paper towel. Mix the mayonnaise and lemon juice. Add the peanut butter and blend. Fold in crumbled bacon, apples, and celery. Mix well. Makes 1 cup filling. Enough for 4 sandwiches.

PEANUT BUTTER AND WATERCRESS SANDWICHES

½ cup peanut butter	Salt to taste
1 bunch crisp watercress	10 slices buttered bread

Thin peanut butter with water, fruit juice, milk, cream or mayonnaise. Spread on half the buttered bread. Wash watercress, remove white roots and shake off the water. Place sprigs over peanut butter and sprinkle lightly with salt. Cover with rest of buttered bread slices. Cut each sandwich in half diagonally. 5 sandwiches.

PEANUT BUTTER BANANA AND JELLY SPREAD

¼ cup peanut butter	1 tbsp currant jelly
1 very ripe banana, mashed	

Mix all ingredients together just enough to blend. Use immediately. Makes about ¾ cup or enough for 5 sandwiches.

PEANUT BUTTER JELLY SANDWICHES

⅓ cup peanut butter	10 slices buttered bread
¼ cup tart jelly	

Mix peanut butter thoroughly with the jelly. If filling is too stiff to spread, it may be thinned with cream, milk or mayonnaise. Spread on half the slices of bread; top with remaining slices. Cut in half diagonally. 5 sandwiches.

PEANUT BUTTER SANDWICHES

Plain peanut butter is a sandwich spread in great favor with children and most grownups. To make it spread more easily, mix with milk, top milk, cream, mayonnaise, or water, as desired. Spread on half the buttered bread, top with remaining buttered bread. A leaf of lettuce in the sandwich adds fresh crispness.

Variation: Thin slices of banana may be arranged over the peanut butter spread on the bread. A blend of one-fourth cup of butter, one-fourth cup of peanut butter, and 2 to 3 tbsp strained honey is also a delicious spread.

OPEN-FACED SANDWICHES

BROILED AND SALAD STYLE

CHEESE AND TOMATO SANDWICHES

4 medium-sized tomatoes	10 thin slices American cheese
10 slices buttered toast	Parsley

Cut peeled tomatoes into thick slices and arrange on buttered toast. Lay slices of cheese over the tomatoes and place under broiler until cheese is lightly toasted and tomatoes hot. Transfer to hot serving plates, garnish with parsley and serve immediately. 10 open-faced sandwiches.

CHEESE PUFFS

1¼ cups grated sharp cheese, about ⅓ lb	3 tbsp thin cream
	Dash of salt
1 egg, beaten	10 slices bread

Thoroughly mix cheese, egg, cream and salt. Cut slices of bread in half and toast on one side. Spread untoasted side with the cheese mixture, and place under broiler until cheese is puffy and toasted. Serve immediately. 5 servings.

HAM AND BANANA SANDWICHES

3 cups boiled *or* baked ham, ground, about 1½ lbs	2 tbsp lemon juice
	Salt to taste
1 cup finely diced celery	10 slices buttered toast
1 tsp finely chopped onion	Lettuce
2 tbsp prepared mustard	2 ripe bananas, sliced
Mayonnaise to moisten	Maraschino cherries

Combine the first 6 ingredients, mixing thoroughly; season to taste. On each slice of buttered bread or toast, place a leaf of lettuce. On the lettuce spread a generous amount of the ham salad mixture. Garnish with slices of banana and with pieces of maraschino cherry. Serve at once. 10 to 12 open-faced sandwiches.

HAM AND CRANBERRY SANDWICHES

10 thin slices boiled *or* baked ham
1½ tbsp bacon drippings
10 slices buttered toast
No. 2 can cranberry jelly

½ lb sharp American cheese, grated
Parsley
Sweet pickles

Brown ham slightly in the bacon drippings in a skillet. Drain ham and place a slice on each slice of buttered toast. On top of ham, place an eight-inch slice of firm cranberry jelly, and top with a portion of the grated cheese. Place sandwiches under a broiler to melt and brown the cheese quickly. Serve immediately with a garnish of parsley and sweet pickles. 10 open-faced sandwiches.

HAM AND TOMATO SUPREME

4 slices bread
2 tbsp butter
2 large tomatoes

Dash of salt
4 thin slices boiled ham, ⅓ lb

Parsley Sauce:
3 tbsp butter *or* margarine
3 tbsp flour
1½ cups milk

1 tsp grated onion
½ tsp salt
½ cup chopped parsley

Toast the bread on both sides. Spread with butter. Cut four thick slices of tomato to cover each piece of toast. Sprinkle with salt. Top with a thin slice of ham. Dot with a bit of butter and place under the broiler. Broil until the ham slightly frizzles and the tomatoes are thoroughly hot. Serve hot with parsley sauce made as follows: Melt the butter in the top of a double boiler; add the flour and blend until smooth. Add milk, onion and salt and cook until smooth and thick, stirring frequently to keep smooth. Add parsley and serve immediately. 4 servings.

HAM AND TUNA FISH SANDWICHES

10 slices buttered toast
Lettuce
10 slices boiled ham
Prepared mustard

2 large tomatoes, peeled and sliced
1 lb can tuna fish
Mayonnaise
Parsley

On each slice of buttered toast, place a lettuce leaf, then a slice of ham. Spread ham very lightly with mustard. Top the ham with 1 or 2 slices of tomato. Drain oil from tuna and break fish into large flakes.

Divide it among the sandwiches. Garnish with a spoonful of mayonnaise and a tiny sprig of parsley. Serve immediately. 10 open-faced sandwiches.

LUNCHEON SANDWICHES

Broiled Cheese with Tomato Sauce

2 cups peeled, diced fresh tomatoes	2 tbsp chopped celery leaves
⅔ cup water	1 tsp sugar
¼ cup finely chopped onion	3 tbsp butter
1 tbsp chopped green pepper	4 slices bread
1 tsp salt	4 slices American cheese

Combine the first 7 ingredients, heat to boiling and simmer for 10 min. Add 1 tbsp of the butter and stir well. Meanwhile, toast the bread, spread with the remaining butter. Place a slice of cheese on each slice of bread and place under broiler until cheese bubbles and is partially melted. Pour the sauce over the toasted sandwiches and serve piping hot. 4 servings.

SOUFFLÉED SANDWICH SNACKS

6 slices bread	Few grains pepper
3 tbsp butter, softened	½ cup grated American cheese
½ tsp salt	3 egg whites
¼ tsp Worcestershire sauce	
3 egg yolks	

Spread bread with butter. Place under broiler, butter side up, and toast to a delicate gold brown. Add salt, Worcestershire sauce and pepper to the egg yolks, and beat until thick and lemon colored. Add cheese. Beat egg whites until stiff but not dry. Gently fold egg whites into yolk-cheese mixture. Heap on untoasted side of bread, place on baking sheet, and bake in a moderate oven (350° F) for about 15 min or until cheese topping is puffed and delicately browned. Pan-fried tomato slices make a delicious accompaniment. 6 sandwiches.

SPINACH SANDWICHES WITH CHEESE SAUCE

1 tsp prepared mustard	2 oz canned luncheon meat, chopped
¼ cup grated American cheese	Liquid from meat
1 cup hot Medium White Sauce, p 1262	½ tsp lemon juice
½ lb spinach, cooked, ¾ cup	½ tsp grated onion
	4 slices bread, toasted and buttered

Mix the mustard and the cheese into the hot white sauce. Keep hot over boiling water. Combine hot thoroughly drained, chopped spinach, meat, meat liquid, lemon juice and onion, and spread on buttered slices of toast. Pour hot sauce over the open sandwiches and serve immediately. Thick slices of tomato make ideal edible garnishes. 4 servings.

SWISS CHEESE HAM TOMATO SANDWICHES

10 slices buttered toast	10 slices Swiss cheese
Lettuce	10 slices crisp Broiled Bacon,
10 slices boiled *or* baked ham	p 855
3 medium tomatoes, peeled	¾ cup Thousand Island
and sliced	Dressing, p 1206

On each slice of buttered toast, place a crisp lettuce leaf; then a slice of ham, a slice of cheese, and one or two tomato slices (depending on size). Top with a slice of broiled bacon, and serve with dressing poured over sandwich or in little paper cups at the side. 10 open-faced sandwiches.

OPEN FACE TONGUE SANDWICHES

4 slices bread	1 tsp Worcestershire sauce
¼ cup ground cooked tongue,	2½ to 3 tbsp cream
pork or beef	¼ tsp salt
½ to ⅔ cup soft natural	¼ tsp onion juice
Cheddar cheese	Finely chopped onion

Toast bread on one side under broiler. Combine and blend well the next 6 ingredients. Spread untoasted side of bread with filling; keep it about ¼ inch from edge of bread; place under broiler and leave until filling bubbles and edge of bread is toasted. Sprinkle with a little chopped onion if desired; serve immediately. 4 sandwiches.

WHOLE MEAL SANDWICHES

¼ cup butter *or* margarine	½ tsp salt
¼ cup flour	4 slices bread
1½ cups milk	2 tbsp butter
1 cup fresh cooked *or*	3¼ oz can sardines
canned peas	2 tomatoes

Make a white sauce from the first 3 ingredients. Add drained peas, salt, and keep hot over boiling water. Toast the bread, butter the slices. Remove bones and any dark soft parts from sardines. Arrange on toast and top with tomato slices. Place under broiler long enough to heat tomatoes through. Serve hot with a generous helping of the creamed peas over the top. 4 servings.

Sauces

A perfect sauce can't hide poor food, but it can reveal and glamorize the simplest of food. In this chapter you will find recipes for many kinds of sauces to lend flavor and importance to many kinds of foods.

★　　★　　★　　★

SAUCES are of so many different kinds that it is difficult to lump them together under one heading. We have sauces for meat, for vegetables, for fish and for desserts of all kinds.

All types of sauce have the same fundamental purpose—to enhance the flavor and appearance and often the nutritive value of the foods they accompany. Therefore, the sauce should present a pleasing contrast in consistency, flavor and color with the food. It should in most cases be thin enough to flow readily, but thick enough not to soak into the food. There are, however, exceptions to this rule.

Hot sauces are usually more satisfactory if made just before they are to be used, although some may be made ahead of time and reheated. One of the most frequently used is white sauce; if this is properly cooked so as to be perfectly smooth, and if it is stirred as it cools and then stored in a tightly covered and thoroughly cleaned container to prevent formation of a skin and contamination, it can be kept and warmed up when needed. Mock Hollandaise sauce, which is of the white sauce type (though differing by the addition of eggs) can be treated in the same manner; but true Hollandaise sauce should not be reheated.

Cold sauces are always cooked ahead of time, then cooled, covered and placed in the refrigerator to chill. But there is a limit to the time during which they can be stored successfully because there is gradual deterioration.

The 4 basic sauces for meat, vegetable and fish are White, Velouté, and Hollandaise Sauces and Savory Butters. The numerous sauces by other names which are served on meat, fish and vegetables are derivatives of these 4 basic sauces. In *White Sauce* the basic ingredient is milk which is thickened with flour and is enriched with butter. In *Velouté Sauce* the chief ingredient is rich chicken broth thickened with flour and enriched with butter and seasonings and sometimes cream. The 3 basic ingredients in *Hollandaise* are butter, egg yolks and lemon juice with seasonings for accent. In *Savory Butters,* the basic ingredient is butter which is creamed and then blended with some other ingredient to give it individual flavor such as lemon for lemon butter, pounded lobster or shrimp to produce Lobster and Shrimp

Butter, etc. *The 2 basic classifications for dessert* sauces are *Hard Sauce* and *Liquid Sauce* such as Custard, Foamy, etc.

SWEET SAUCES

Butterscotch	Chocolate Peanut	Fresh Lime
Caramel	Butter	Guava Syrup
Caramel Syrup	Chocolate Peppermint	Honey Chocolate Dot
Chocolate	Coffee	Honey Nut
Chocolate Marsh-	Crispy Nut Topping	Lemon Orange
mallow	Fresh Fruit Sundae	Lemon Sundae
		Marshmallow Nut

This group of sweet sauce recipes appear in the dessert chapter under the ice cream section, p 642.

BRANDY SAUCE

½ cup butter
1 cup sugar
2 tbsp water
1 egg, beaten

2 tbsp lemon juice
½ tsp grated lemon rind
¼ cup apricot brandy
Dash of salt

Cream butter and sugar thoroughly until light and fluffy in the top of the double boiler. Add water and egg and beat well. Place over boiling water for about 15 min or until sugar is thoroughly melted and sauce is slightly thickened, stirring often to keep smooth. Add lemon juice and rind, brandy and salt. Continue cooking for 5 min, stirring to blend. Serve warm. Makes about 2 cups.

BRANDY CRÈME SAUCE

Delectable on any steamed or baked fruit pudding

2 egg yolks
1 cup xxxx sugar, pkd
⅛ tsp salt
¾ tsp vanilla

¾ tsp brandy extract
1 tsp hot milk
½ pt whipping cream, chilled

Beat egg yolks with rotary beater; add sugar, salt and flavorings and beat until light and fluffy. Add hot milk and beat until very light. Wash and dry beater. Whip cream stiff, then very gently *fold egg mixture into cream.* Keep in refrigerator until served, but serve within an hr or two after making. 8 servings.

BROWN SUGAR SYRUP

2 cups brown sugar,
firmly pkd
1 cup water

Dash salt
¼ cup white corn syrup,
if desired

Combine sugar, water and salt in a saucepan and heat to boiling. Cover and cook at a moderate rate for 10 min or until a thin syrup is formed. Keeping the pan covered prevents formation of crystals around sides of pan. Cool and put into covered jar. If more syrup is made than is needed immediately, the corn syrup may be cooked along with the sugar and water; this will prevent crystallization during the storage period. Keep in a tightly covered jar either in or out of refrigerator. Makes about 2 cups.

A maple-flavored syrup may be obtained by using white sugar instead of brown in the same proportion. When the syrup has cooked to the proper stage, add maple flavoring a little at a time until desired flavor is obtained.

CARAMEL SAUCE

A tempting sauce for Apple Dumplings; also appealing over a puff of whipped cream on Angel Food Cake

2 tbsp sugar
1 cup boiling water
1 cup sugar
¼ tsp salt
1 tbsp *plus* 1½ tsp cornstarch

¼ cup cold water
1 tbsp firm butter
½ tsp vanilla
½ tsp cider vinegar, optional

Measure the 2 tbsp sugar into 2-qt aluminum or stainless steel saucepan. Place over moderate heat and shake pan back and forth until sugar is melted to a liquid and turns rich amber in color; take care not to scorch. Remove from heat and add water cautiously. Return to heat and *stir* until caramel dissolves. Add the 1 cup sugar and salt, and the cornstarch blended smooth with the cold water. Cook and stir until thick and clear, about 5 min. Remove from heat. Stir in butter, then vanilla and vinegar if used. Serve warm or cold. 1⅓ cups.

CHOCOLATE SAUCE No. 1

5 sqs, 5 oz, unsweet chocolate
1½ cups water
1¾ cups sugar

½ tsp salt
¼ cup white corn syrup
2 tbsp butter

Add chocolate to water, heat to boiling and cook 4 min, stirring constantly. Add sugar, salt and corn syrup, and boil 4 min longer, continuing to stir. Add butter and beat until blended. Serve hot or cold as a sauce for ice cream, puddings or cake; or use as a base for hot or cold chocolate drinks, allowing 2 tbsp for each cup of hot or cold milk. Makes about 2¾ cups.

Note: See page 643 for other Chocolate Sauce recipes.

CHOCOLATE SAUCE No. 2

2 sqs unsweet chocolate	2 tbsp firm butter
1 cup water	2 tsp vanilla *or*
2 cups sugar	½ tsp mint extract
Dash of salt	½ cup sliced Brazil nuts

Cut chocolate into 5 or 6 pieces, dropping into a 3-qt saucepan. Add water, place over direct heat and cook and stir until smooth and thick. Stir in sugar until dissolved, then boil and stir for 3 min. Remove from heat, stir in butter, extract and nuts. Serve hot over ice cream or cottage pudding. 6 to 8 servings.

CINNAMON DIP

An old-fashioned, easy-to-prepare dessert sauce

1 cup coffee cream	Dash of salt
1 tbsp sugar	¼ tsp cinnamon

Have cream chilled, and stir in seasonings until very thoroughly blended. This is delicious on any sweet dumpling, on baked apples, stewed apples, etc. Serve promptly. Enough sauce for 4 servings.

Variation No. I: Almond Dip—Substitute for the cinnamon 2 drops of almond extract and 6 grated toasted almonds. Especially good on peach desserts either raw or cooked, also on apricot desserts.

Variation No. II: Nutmeg Dip—Substitute ¼ tsp nutmeg for the cinnamon.

Variation No. III: Lemon or Orange Dip—Substitute for the cinnamon ¼ tsp lemon or orange rind that has been rubbed in 1 tsp lemon juice for a min to extract the oils. This is good on fruit dumplings or puddings where a thickened sauce is not required.

CITRUS SAUCE

An appetite-tempting, easily-made sauce

1 cup sugar	4 tbsp firm butter, ½ stick
4 tbsp flour	1 tbsp lemon juice
1 cup boiling water	⅔ cup strained orange juice

Measure sugar and flour into a 2 or 3-qt saucepan and blend well with wooden spoon. Stir in boiling water, place over moderate heat and cook and stir until thickened, about 2 min after boiling starts. Remove from heat, beat in butter until it melts, then stir in juices. Serve lukewarm. Scant 2½ cups or 6 to 8 servings.

CITRUS MARSHMALLOW SAUCE

30 marshmallows, 10 oz pkg
½ cup boiling water
2 tbsp lemon juice

½ cup orange juice
1/16 tsp grated orange rind
Dash of salt

Put marshmallows and the water in top of double boiler, place over boiling water and cook for about 10 min. Cool, then beat with a rotary beater to a creamy consistency. Add the lemon and orange juice gradually, beating all the while. Add orange rind and salt and blend well. Chill and serve. 2 cups.

COCOA SAUCE No. 1

Smooth as satin. Delicious over ice cream or in milk drinks

1⅛ cups sugar
⅔ cup cocoa
¼ tsp salt
2 tbsp butter

1 cup hot water
1½ cups evap milk
1 tsp vanilla
4 marshmallows, quartered

Blend sugar, cocoa and salt in a 1½-qt saucepan. Add butter, then stir in water and milk. Place over moderate direct heat and gently cook and stir until smooth and thickened, about 8 min. Remove from heat; stir in vanilla, then marshmallows until melted. Pour into glass jar with tight fitting cover, rinsed in hot water then dried. Cover and cool, then store in refrigerator. Keeps a week or two. 2½ cups.

COCOA SAUCE No. 2

1 cup cocoa
1¼ cups sugar
½ cup white corn syrup
1½ cups water

¼ tsp salt
1 tsp vinegar
1 tsp vanilla

Combine all ingredients except the vanilla and mix thoroughly. Heat to boiling over direct heat, then simmer gently for 5 min, stirring occasionally. Remove from heat and stir in vanilla. Cool, and store in covered container in refrigerator. This sauce has a bitter-sweet flavor and is especially good on ice cream, cottage pudding or bananas; or 1 to 2 tbsp stirred into 1 cup of hot or cold milk makes a quick, delicious chocolate milk drink. Makes about 2½ cups.

COFFEE SAUCE No. 1

½ cup water
3 tbsp medium grind coffee
⅓ cup butter *or* margarine

1 cup xxxx sugar, firmly pkd
2 eggs

Use cold fresh water and add ground coffee. Heat just to boiling, remove from heat, stir quickly and let stand for 3 min. Strain, discard grounds and use infusion for strong coffee. Cream butter in top of double boiler, add sugar and eggs. Beat with a rotary beater until foamy over boiling water for 5 min; stir in 3 tbsp of the strong coffee infusion. Serve hot over warm pudding. (Leftover sauce may be reheated in the double boiler and beaten when hot for a few min until it is foamy.) 8 to 10 servings.

Note: Instant coffee may be used to make the coffee infusion.

COFFEE SAUCE No. 2

¾ cup boiling water	2 egg yolks, beaten
6 tbsp medium grind coffee	Dash of salt
1 tbsp butter	½ cup sugar
1½ tbsp flour	½ tsp vanilla
½ cup milk	½ cup whipping cream

Pour the boiling water over the coffee in a glass or enamelware saucepan, cover, heat just to the boiling point, and then remove it to a warm place to stand 5 min. Strain through four thicknesses of cheesecloth or through one thickness of firm muslin. Melt butter, blend in flour, and add milk slowly, stirring constantly over direct heat until sauce boils and thickens and is smooth. Stir some of the hot mixture into the beaten yolks; then stir the yolk mixture into the hot sauce. Place over boiling water and cook 2 min, stirring constantly. Remove from heat and add ¼ cup of the coffee infusion, salt and sugar; stir well. Chill, then stir in the vanilla and fold into the stiffly whipped cream. Serve immediately, or store in a tightly covered jar in the refrigerator; it may be kept 2 or 3 days. A delicious sauce for chocolate blanc mange, cornstarch pudding, ice cream or steamed fruit pudding. Makes about 2 cups.

CREAMY VANILLA SAUCE

¼ cup softened butter	3 to 4 tsp cream
1 cup confectioner's sugar	½ tsp vanilla extract

Combine ingredients in the order given and mix thoroughly.

CUSTARD SAUCE No. 1

1 cup cream	¼ cup sugar
1 cup milk	⅛ tsp salt
2 egg yolks and 2 whole eggs	½ tsp vanilla
_or_ 5 egg yolks	

Scald cream and milk in top of double boiler. Beat eggs slightly, add sugar and salt, and slowly stir in the scalded cream and milk. Return to double boiler and cook over boiling water until mixture just coats a metal spoon, stirring constantly. Remove from heat immediately, stir in vanilla and chill. (If overcooked, custard will curdle. Curdled custard may often be restored by placing the pan immediately in a bowl of cold water and beating with a rotary egg beater, but it will not be so thick.) Makes about 2¼ cups.

CUSTARD SAUCE No. 2

An excellent and pretty sauce for several desserts, such as Apple Snow, Baked Prune Whip, Chocolate Soufflé, etc

½ cup 12% cream, half and half
1½ cups milk
⅓ cup sugar

1½ tsp flour
⅛ tsp salt
4 egg yolks *or* 2 whole eggs
¾ to 1 tsp vanilla

Measure cream and milk into top of a 2-qt double boiler. Stir in sugar blended well with flour and salt. Cover and cook over boiling water with frequent stirring for about 5 min. Beat egg yolks well, then beat in a little of the hot mixture, then stir this into mixture in double boiler and continue cooking and stirring until custard coats a metal spoon. Remove from heat and stir in vanilla. Pour into a jar or other container. Cool, then cover and chill. 6 to 8 servings or about 2¼ cups.

FOAMY SAUCE

⅓ cup butter
1 cup xxxx sugar, firmly pkd
Dash of salt

1 egg, beaten
1 egg yolk, beaten
2 to 3 tsp brandy

Put butter into top of double boiler (do not place over heat) and cream until soft and smooth. Gradually blend in the sugar and salt. Add beaten egg and yolk, place over boiling water and continue beating with rotary beater until sauce is very foamy, about 3 to 4 min. Remove from heat, stir in brandy and serve warm or cold over steamed fruit puddings. (Other flavoring, such as vanilla or a combination of vanilla and lemon extract, may be substituted for the brandy.) Makes about 1 cup.

FUDGE SAUCE, HOT OR COLD

Thick enough for spoonfuls to hold shape. Creamy and delicious— makes ice cream extra imposing

¼ cup butter *or* margarine
2 sqs unsweet chocolate
⅛ tsp salt

1½ cups sugar
1 cup *less* 2 tbsp evap milk
1 tsp vanilla

Heat butter and chocolate in top of double boiler over *simmering water* until melted. Stir in salt, then the sugar in 4 or 5 portions, being sure to blend in sugar thoroughly after each portion. The mixture becomes very thick, dry and grainy. Now stir in milk *very slowly,* then cook 5 or 6 min longer or until slightly thickened, stirring frequently.

Remove from heat. Stir in vanilla. Pour into glass jar with tight fitting cover, first rinsed in hot water, then dried. Cover and cool, then store in refrigerator. To use as Hot Fudge Sauce for ice cream, set jar in warm water 30 min before dessert time, changing water once or twice. Ladle over ice cream and serve at once. Keeps well if tightly covered. 1 pt.

GRANDMA'S PUDDING SAUCE

Excellent for Cottage Pudding. Adding firm butter at end makes sauce shine

1 cup sugar	¼ cup firm butter
¼ cup all-purpose flour	2 tsp vanilla
2 cups boiling water	2 tsp lemon extract
1 tbsp cider vinegar	

Blend the sugar and flour in the top of a double boiler, or a *heavy* saucepan. Stir in boiling water. Place over boiling water, or saucepan directly over heat, and cook and stir until thickened, from 8 to 10 min. Remove from heat, add butter, vinegar and extracts and stir until butter melts. Serve warm over pudding. 6 to 8 servings.

GUAVA BUTTER

Exceptionally delicious for an Ice Cream Sauce or spread for hot breads

4½ lbs soft ripe guavas	3¼ cups sugar
2 cups boiling water	2 tsp lime juice
¼ tsp salt	

Sterilize jars. Wash fruit. Remove stem and blossom-ends and all discolorations. Slice guavas thin. Chop fine with heavy biscuit cutter. Rub through sieve or food mill—there should be 2 qts purée. Turn into 5-qt preserving kettle. Stir in water, salt, sugar and lime juice. Heat to boiling and cook moderately fast to a thick consistency, from 35 to 40 min. Stir constantly to prevent sticking. Pour into sterilized jars. While butter is hot, pour a thin layer of melted paraffin over top; when set, add second layer. Cool, cover and store. 6 half-pts.

GRAPE SAUCE

⅓ cup sugar	2 cups grape juice
Dash of salt	1 tbsp lemon juice
2 tbsp cornstarch	

Mix dry ingredients in saucepan; add grape juice and stir until blended. Cook over direct heat, stirring constantly until sauce boils and thickens. Remove from heat, add lemon juice and chill. Serve over ice cream. Also good over cottage pudding, leftover cake, baked custard, or sliced bananas. Makes 1½ cups.

HARD SAUCE

½ cup butter
1 tsp vanilla *or* ¼ tsp almond
extract *or* 1½ tbsp sherry,
rum or brandy

Dash of salt
1⅔ cups xxxx sugar, pkd

Cream butter until soft and smooth, add flavoring, then blend in salt and the sugar. Mixture should be fairly stiff when finished. Press into a shallow mold or a small 5-inch cake pan. Chill until hard. Serve in slices, or use a small fancy cutter to cut serving portions from the hard layer of sauce. Serve with any steamed fruit pudding. Use less sugar for a softer sauce. 5 servings.

LEMON HARD SAUCE

⅓ cup butter
½ tsp grated lemon rind, pkd
4 tsp lemon juice

1¼ cups xxxx sugar, pkd
Dash of salt

Cream butter until soft and smooth. Stir in the lemon rind and lemon juice, then blend in the sugar mixed with salt until smooth and stiff. Press into a mold or cup and chill in refrigerator until hardened. Unmold and cut into serving portions. Or serve without chilling in fluffy mounds. 5 servings.

LEMON SAUCE No. 1

A good inexpensive sauce that enhances many different desserts. Best when served the day it is made

½ tsp grated lemon rind, pkd
3 tbsp lemon juice
1 tbsp cornstarch
¾ cup sugar

⅛ tsp salt
¾ cup boiling water
1 egg yolk, beaten
1 tbsp firm butter

Wash lemon, grate rind onto waxed paper, squeeze juice. Measure juice and rind and mix. Blend next 3 ingredients in top of double boiler, then stir in boiling water. Place over direct heat and cook and stir until mixture boils, thickens and is clear. Remove from heat. Stir a little of the hot mixture into beaten yolk, then return to double boiler, stirring well. Place over boiling water and cook and stir 2 or 3 min. Remove from heat and stir in butter, lemon juice and rind. Serve warm over Cottage, Bread or Cornstarch Pudding, Gingerbread, Baked Apples, etc. 5 to 6 servings. 1 cup.

LEMON SAUCE No. 2

Delicious on Coconut Charlotte, Bread Pudding, Apple Dumplings, Ice Cream, etc.

½ tsp grated lemon rind, pkd
¼ cup lemon juice
¾ cup sugar
1 tbsp cornstarch
⅛ tsp salt

½ cup boiling water
2 egg yolks, beaten
¼ cup white corn syrup
2 tbsp firm butter

Wash lemon, grate rind onto waxed paper, squeeze juice; measure and mix. Measure next 3 ingredients into 2-qt saucepan; blend well, stir in boiling water. Place over direct heat and cook and stir until sauce boils and thickens. Stir a little of hot mixture into beaten yolks; return to mixture in saucepan, beating well. Add corn syrup and cook 5 min, stirring frequently. Remove from heat, stir in butter, then lemon juice and rind. Pour into clean jar, cool and seal. Chill until ready to use. Serve cold or reheat by placing jar in hot water. Sauce may be made a day or two before using. About ⅞ cup.

LEMON WHIPPED CREAM SAUCE

A superb sauce to serve over wedges of Angel Food, Date Pudding, etc. Omit lemon rind, and it becomes a wonderful Fruit Salad Dressing

1 tsp grated lemon rind, pkd
3 tbsp lemon juice, 1 lemon
2 egg yolks

⅓ cup *plus* 2 tsp sugar
¼ tsp salt
½ cup whipping cream

Wash lemon, grate rind onto waxed paper, squeeze juice. Measure and mix juice and rind. Put egg yolks in top of 1 or 2-qt double boiler. Beat yolks slightly, then stir in lemon juice and rind, sugar and salt to blend thoroughly. Place over gently boiling water and stir until very smooth and thickened. Remove from heat and scrape into small glass bowl. Cover and chill. Whip cream until just stiff, then with fork or rubber scraper, carefully fold chilled lemon mixture into it until smooth. Turn lightly into sauce boat. 3 to 4 servings, 1 cup.

LIME SUNDAE SAUCE

A glamorous and delicious sauce

1 cup sugar
⅓ cup water
3 tbsp white corn syrup
1 tbsp firm butter
2 tbsp lime juice

¼ tsp grated lime rind, pkd
2 drops green food coloring
Toasted shredded coconut
or coconut chips

Put sugar, water and corn syrup into 1-qt saucepan. Stir to mix and place over moderate direct heat. When mixture starts to boil, begin to

Swedish Tea Ring, p 294, is made from Sweet Roll Dough, p 279, rolled into a rectangle and sprinkled with cinnamon-sugar mixture, then rolled up jelly roll fashion. Ends are joined to make a ring, edges are sliced three fourths through and twisted to overlap. After baking drizzle with Confectioner's Icing, p 392, and shower with nuts.

Close-ups of interesting Yeast Dough Rolls, pp 273–277.

ABOVE: *These candied grapefruit shells, p 410, filled with fruit cake and garnished with glazed fruits and nuts are something to write home about.*

BELOW: *A simple Gold Cake, p 346, filled with strawberry pineapple filling and garnished with whipped cream is gorgeous and delicious.*

ABOVE: *Something new! A Ham or Chicken à la King, p 1044, Shortcake, p 1054. This leftover special always makes a hit.*

BELOW: *Meat Croquettes, p 505, with Mustard Sauce de Luxe, p 1259. Makes leftover meat fit for a king.*

ABOVE: *Thick Pork Chops, p 856, braised until tender and savory as chicken, with buttered corn and sliced green or red peppers make a perfect blend of color, flavor, and food value.*

BELOW: *Dill is the Scandinavian touch that makes this Tuna Fish Salad, p 1194, take the prize. Cucumbers supply the crispness, tomatoes the pep, and Melba Toast the crunch.*

Shredded cabbage in aspic, with a center of shredded beets, or if you prefer diced beets in aspic with a shredded cabbage center. Either way a healthful salad course.

ABOVE: *Macaroni Salad, p 1188, garnished with gherkins easy to make and a must when service is buffet.*

BELOW: *There are no complications in this pleasant luncheon dish. Just broiled tomatoes, English muffins, and a cheese sauce. Ready in a few minutes.*

ABOVE: *Old-Fashioned Marble Spice Cake*, *p* 354, *absolutely, and positively cannot be beaten for flavor.*

BELOW: *Gingerbread*, *p* 360, *with whipped cream and poached orange sections and walnuts is equally good as individual or family size cakes.*

count and cook just 2 min. Remove from heat, stir in butter, lime juice, rind and coloring. Serve over ice cream, then sprinkle with coconut. ⅞ cup.

NUTMEG SAUCE

An old-timer and a great favorite. Ideal with Apple or other Fruit Dumplings; delicious on Cottage Pudding or any dessert containing apples

¾ cup granulated sugar
1 tbsp *plus* 1½ tsp flour
¼ tsp salt
1 cup boiling water
1 tbsp cider vinegar

1½ tbsp brown sugar, optional
2 tbsp firm butter
Scant ½ tsp fresh-grated nutmeg

Blend first 3 ingredients in 1-qt saucepan. Stir boiling water in graduallly to keep smooth. Add vinegar and stir and cook over moderate direct heat until thick and clear, 4 to 5 min. Remove from heat. Stir in brown sugar, the butter 1 tbsp at a time, and the nutmeg. Serve warm or cold. 1⅓ cups.

ORANGE SAUCE No. 1

⅓ cup sugar
¼ cup cornstarch
⅛ tsp salt
1½ cups orange juice

¾ cup white corn syrup
3 tbsp butter
1 tsp grated lemon rind
¼ cup lemon juice

Mix sugar, cornstarch and salt together in a saucepan. Add orange juice and corn syrup, stir well and cook until the mixture boils and thickens, stirring constantly. Remove from heat and stir in butter, lemon rind and lemon juice. Serve cold on cottage pudding, cornstarch pudding, ice cream and similar desserts. Makes about 2½ cups.

ORANGE SAUCE No. 2

¾ cup sugar
2 tbsp cornstarch
¼ tsp salt
1⅓ cups water

⅓ cup orange juice
1 tsp grated orange rind
4 tsp lemon juice
1 tbsp firm butter

Combine sugar, cornstarch and salt in top of double boiler; add water and blend until smooth. Cook over direct heat, stirring constantly until mixture boils and thickens; then place over boiling water, cover, and cook 15 min with occasional stirring. Remove from heat and add remaining ingredients. Serve warm or cold as pudding sauce. Makes about 2 cups.

Note: Use only freshly squeezed orange and lemon juice and freshly grated orange rind.

CANNED PEACH JUICE PUDDING SAUCE

1 tbsp flour	2 tsp vinegar
¼ cup sugar	2 tbsp firm butter
1 cup thick juice from canned peaches	⅛ tsp nutmeg
	⅓ cup whipping cream

Blend flour and sugar in a 1-qt saucepan. Stir in juice gradually to keep smooth. Place over heat and cook and stir until sauce boils and thickens. Remove from heat, stir in butter, vinegar and nutmeg. Cool, then chill. Then fold in cream which has been whipped barely stiff until smooth and fluffy. 1¼ cups sauce.

PEANUT BUTTER SAUCE

For ice cream sundaes or to serve over sliced bananas

⅓ cup brown sugar, firmly pkd	1 tbsp butter
½ cup white corn syrup	2½ tbsp peanut butter
	¼ cup light cream

Measure sugar and syrup into 1-qt saucepan and simmer 5 min. Remove from heat, stir in butter, then peanut butter and finally cream. Continue stirring to obtain a velvety-smooth consistency. Store in covered jar. About 1 cup.

PINEAPPLE SAUCE

1 tbsp cornstarch	12-oz can pineapple juice
⅛ tsp cinnamon	2 tbsp firm butter
¼ cup sugar	1 tsp lemon juice

Combine the cornstarch, cinnamon and sugar in top of double boiler, add a little of the pineapple juice and stir until smooth. Add rest of juice and cook over direct heat until mixture boils and thickens, stirring constantly. Cover and cook over boiling water for 5 min, stirring occasionally. Remove from heat and add butter and lemon juice. Chill and serve over unfrosted plain cake or sponge cake, either fresh or stale. If stale cake is used, combine and allow to stand about 15 min before serving, so cake may become moist through. Makes about 1½ cups.

PUDDING SAUCE DELUXE

½ cup sugar	¼ cup soft butter
¼ cup cream	½ tsp vanilla

Heat sugar and cream over direct heat, stirring constantly until sugar thoroughly dissolves, but do not boil. Remove from heat. Place butter in small bowl over hot water until barely melted, add cream mixture and vanilla and beat with rotary beater 2 or 3 min. Serve hot or cold over steamed pudding. Store in refrigerator and reheat over hot water, if desired. ¾ cup.

1890 PUDDING SAUCE

Fine consistency—beautiful color—delicious flavor

1½ cups sugar	2 eggs
½ cup soft butter *or* margarine, 1 stick	2 tbsp cider vinegar
	1 tsp vanilla

Put sugar into a *heavy* 3-qt saucepan. Add butter and cream well, then add eggs and beat until smooth and fluffy. Stir in vinegar. Place over moderate heat and cook and stir constantly until mixture just reaches boiling. Remove from heat immediately and stir in vanilla. Serve warm over lukewarm pudding. (If heavy saucepan is not available, cook mixture about 10 min in double boiler, stirring constantly.) About 2 cups.

SABAYONE SAUCE

Excellent over Poached Pears, Apple Brown Betty, Baked Apples, Baked Bananas and Cranberries, Plum Pudding, etc.

6 tbsp sugar	¼ cup water blended with
⅛ tsp salt	2 tsp sherry extract
3 egg yolks	

Put sugar, salt and yolks into top of double boiler; place over *simmering water* and beat constantly with rotary beater until mixture is creamy. Add water blended with sherry extract, a little at a time and continue beating until sauce is thick and light. This takes from 5 to 8 min. Remove from heat. Serve warm over dessert. 3½ cups or 6 servings.

STERLING HARD SAUCE

A favorite for Steamed Puddings of most any kind including chocolate

½ cup butter, room temp	2 tbsp cream
1 cup sifted, moist light brown sugar, pkd	½ tsp brandy *or* sherry extract

Cream butter well, gradually beat in sugar, then beat in the cream and extract. Turn into a small shallow pan or a bowl with flat bottom. Spread top level. Cover and store in refrigerator until ready to serve. Cut in small, pie-shaped wedges. Lift out onto steamy hot pudding. 10 to 12 servings.

VANILLA SAUCE No. 1

⅔ cup sugar	⅔ cup white corn syrup
1½ tsp flour	1½ tsp vanilla
¼ tsp salt	¾ cup thin cream

Combine sugar, flour and the salt in top of a double boiler; add a little of the syrup and blend until smooth. Add rest of syrup and cook over direct heat, stirring constantly until sauce boils and clears up; then place over boiling water, cover, and cook 15 min with occasional stirring. Remove from heat and stir in vanilla and cream. Serve warm or cold as pudding sauce. Makes about 1¼ cups.

VANILLA SAUCE No. 2

Excellent over Apple or Peach Dumplings, Chocolate Pudding, etc.

½ cup sugar	3 tbsp firm butter
1 tbsp cornstarch	1 tsp vanilla
Dash of salt	¼ cup cream, optional
1 cup boiling water	

Blend sugar, cornstarch and salt in 1-qt saucepan. Stir in boiling water gradually to keep smooth. Cook and stir over direct heat until thick and clear, 3 to 4 min. Remove from heat. Beat in butter 1 tbsp at a time; then stir in vanilla and cream, if used. Serve warm. 5 or 6 servings, 1¼ to 1½ cups.

MEAT AND VEGETABLE SAUCES

ALLEMANDE SAUCE

3 tbsp butter	1 chicken-flavored bouillon
2 tbsp flour	cube
1¼ cups milk	2 egg yolks
¼ tsp salt	1 tbsp lemon juice

Make a white sauce of the butter, flour, milk, salt and bouillon cube, cooking it in the top of a double boiler over hot water until smooth and thick or for about 15 min. Add some of the hot sauce slowly to beaten egg yolks, stir thoroughly. Return to double boiler and continue cooking for 5 min, stirring often. Add lemon juice gradually, stirring constantly. This sauce is delicious served over broccoli, green beans, spinach and asparagus. 4 servings.

BARBECUE SAUCE

1 medium onion, chopped	½ cup catchup
1 green pepper, chopped	2 tbsp sugar
⅓ cup chopped sweet pickle	2 tsp prepared mustard
⅓ cup cider vinegar	

Combine all ingredients, heat to boiling, then simmer gently for 5 min. Serve with boiled tongue, pork chops or ham. Makes about 1¾ cups.

FINE HERBS BARBECUE SAUCE

Serve with any broiled or roasted meat, chicken or fish

2 cloves garlic
2 egg-size onions
1 cup tart catchup
1 cup tart chili sauce
1 cup India Relish
2 cups wine vinegar
1 bay leaf
1 tsp pepper
1 tsp coriander, crushed

½ tsp sweet basil
2 tsp orégano
4 tsp chili powder
1 tsp salt
2 cups boiling water
2 chicken bouillon cubes
2 tbsp prepared brown
    mustard
⅓ cup lemon juice

Peel garlic cloves and onions and chop fine. Put all ingredients into a 3-qt saucepan. Heat to boiling, reduce heat to simmering and cook slowly with frequent stirring for about 40 min. Strain sauce through a coarse sieve, using a wooden spoon to force most of the pulp through. For basting, use 1 cup sauce to each 2 lbs meat. Pour into heated bowl. About 4½ cups.

Note: Leftover sauce stored in a clean jar and covered tightly keeps well in refrigerator. Heat cold sauce over boiling water when ready to serve.

LIME BARBECUE SAUCE

So good it makes lamb delicious, and good cold for "dunking" boiled or French-fried shrimp

1 cup catchup—good commercial brand
1 onion, egg-size, chopped
½ clove garlic, cut fine
2 tsp pickled or fresh chili peppers, chopped
½ tsp dry mustard
½ small bay leaf

¼ tsp black pepper
1 tsp Worcestershire
⅓ cup fresh lime juice, 2
    medium
½ tsp salt
½ cup water
1 tsp sugar

Measure all ingredients into a 2-qt saucepan. Heat to boiling, cover, reduce heat and simmer 40 min, stirring frequently. Strain sauce through a coarse strainer using a wooden spoon to force pulp through. Turn into bowl and serve warm. Good on lamb, beef, pork, chicken or fish. 1½ cups.

Note: Cover and chill leftover sauce. Reheat for an excellent booster for chops or fish.

BÉCHAMEL SAUCE

1 cup good strength chicken
    or veal broth
1 slice onion
6 whole black peppers
1 slice carrot

3 tbsp butter
3 tbsp flour
1 cup milk
½ tsp salt
1 egg yolk

Put the chicken broth into a saucepan and add onion, the peppers and carrot. Cover and simmer for ten min. Strain off the broth, discarding pepper and vegetables. Blend butter and flour in the saucepan until smooth. Slowly add the broth, stirring to keep smooth, then add milk and salt and cook over medium heat until sauce boils and thickens, stirring constantly. Beat yolk, add a little of the hot sauce, stir thoroughly and return to sauce in pan, stirring vigorously. Continue cooking over low heat for a minute, but do not boil. Good over meat or vegetables. Makes about 1½ cups.

BROWN SAUCE

2 tbsp butter
¼ cup Browned Flour, p 161

1 cup milk, *or* well-flavored
meat broth
¼ tsp salt

Melt butter in saucepan, add flour and blend thoroughly. Add milk and cook over direct heat, stirring constantly until sauce boils and thickens; add salt, reduce heat and simmer about 5 min. Pour over plain boiled green beans or spinach and reheat. Makes about 1 cup.

CARROT SAUCE

1 tbsp butter *or* margarine,
   melted
1 tbsp flour
1 cup water
1 bouillon cube

1 cup grated raw carrots,
   firmly pkd, 4 medium
carrots
½ cup catchup

Blend butter and flour in a saucepan. Gradually add water, cook over low heat until mixture is smooth and thickened, stirring constantly. Heat to boiling, add remaining ingredients and simmer for 3 min, stirring occasionally. The carrots will retain their crispness in this time of cooking; if softer consistency is preferred, increase cooking time. Serve with meat loaf, pea loaf or pan-fried liver. Makes about 2 cups.

CELERY SAUCE

¼ cup butter
¾ cup finely diced celery
¼ cup flour

2 cups milk
1 tsp salt
Pepper to suit taste

Melt butter in saucepan and add celery; simmer over low heat, stirring occasionally for 5 min. Stir in flour until smooth; then add milk gradually and cook over direct heat, stirring constantly until sauce boils and thickens. Stir in salt and pepper. Makes about 2½ cups. This sauce is good as an accompaniment for fish, eggs, meat loaves or croquettes.

CHEESE SAUCE

To thin or medium White Sauce, p 1262, after it is thickened, add ¼ to 1 cup of grated sharp cheese, according to the flavor desired. Stir quickly until blended. If diced or sliced cheese is added to the sauce, it is advisable to place the sauce over boiling water while the cheese melts, stirring occasionally. One-fourth cup diced cheese is about equal to ½ cup grated.

CREAM CHEESE SAUCE FOR VEGETABLES

A creamy, striking white sauce of unusual flavor

2 tbsp margarine *or* butter	1½ cups milk
2 tbsp flour	3 oz pkg cream cheese
½ tsp salt	1 tbsp chopped chives,
Dash of pepper	parsley *or* pimiento

Melt margarine in a 3-qt saucepan, blend in flour, salt and pepper. Add milk gradually and cook and stir until smooth and thickened. Stir in cream cheese, beat until smooth with a rotary beater. Do not boil after cheese is added. Use immediately or keep warm over hot water. Serve over hot, boiled, well-drained potatoes, asparagus, onions, broccoli, green beans or peas, or hard-cooked eggs. 1½ cups sauce.

SMOKY CHEESE SAUCE

Smooth as satin, wonderful flavor, delicious on many foods

2 tbsp butter *or* margarine	Few grains red pepper
2 tbsp flour	2 oz smoked aged American
1 cup milk	cheese, 2¾ tbsp
⅛ tsp salt	2 tbsp cream

Melt butter in top of double boiler over direct heat. Blend in flour to form smooth paste. Add milk gradually stirring continuously until sauce boils and is very smooth and thickened. Stir in salt and pepper. Place over boiling water, add cheese and cream and stir until cheese melts, about 5 min. Serve hot on toast on a vegetable plate containing potatoes, onions, cauliflower etc., on poached eggs, warm hard-cooked egg slices, or anything else compatible with good smoky flavor. 1 cup.

CIDER RAISIN SAUCE

2 tbsp brown sugar	1 tsp butter *or* ham drippings
2 tbsp cornstarch	¼ cup seedless raisins
1½ cups sweet cider	

Combine sugar and cornstarch in a saucepan. Add cider and heat mixture to boiling, stirring constantly. Add butter or ham drippings and raisins and continue to simmer over low heat for 5 min, stirring occasionally. Serve with baked ham. (For baked or boiled ham, where no ham drippings are available, bacon drippings may be substituted.) Makes about 1¼ cups.

CURRY SAUCE

Good on fish or chicken

3 tbsp butter *or* rendered chicken fat
3 tbsp fine-chopped onion
3 tbsp flour
1 tbsp curry powder

3 cups well seasoned chicken broth *or* 3 chicken bouillon cubes dissolved in 3 cups boiling water
⅛ tsp ginger

Heat butter in a 3-qt saucepan, add onion and sauté until soft and yellow. Blend in flour and curry powder until smooth, then gradually add broth, stirring constantly to keep smooth. Add ginger and continue stirring until sauce boils, then simmer for 5 min. 2 to 2½ cups sauce. Add 1½ cups of any of the following cooked foods: cleaned shrimp, lobster meat, diced chicken or sweetbreads, then heat thoroughly. Serve with hot fluffy boiled rice.

DILL SAUCE No. 1

For fish or beans

2 tbsp butter
3 tbsp flour
1½ cups milk
1 egg yolk

½ tsp salt
Dash of pepper
1½ tsp finely chopped fresh dill leaves

Melt butter, blend in flour and add milk slowly, stirring constantly over low direct heat until sauce boils and thickens. Add a little of the hot sauce to the beaten egg yolk, beat thoroughly, then return to the hot sauce, stirring thoroughly. Add seasonings and dill, and place over boiling water for 2 or 3 min, stirring occasionally. Serve hot with cooked green beans or boiled fish. About 1¾ cups.

DILL SAUCE No. 2

For stew

2 tbsp butter
3 tbsp flour
2 cups meat broth, *or* broth and water
1 to 2 tbsp cider vinegar
1 tsp sugar

2 tsp finely chopped fresh dill leaves, or more
1 egg yolk, if desired
2 cups diced fresh boiled veal *or* lamb

Melt butter, blend in flour and slowly stir in the broth (from boiled veal or lamb, or from stew). Cook with constant stirring until sauce boils and thickens. Add vinegar, sugar and dill, and place over boiling water for 3 or 4 min, stirring occasionally. If egg yolk is used, beat and stir in a little of the hot sauce, then pour it into the rest of the sauce and stir about 2 min longer over the hot water. Pour over meat for stew. 5 servings.

DRAWN BUTTER SAUCE

¼ cup butter
2 tbsp flour
1 cup boiling water

¼ tsp salt
Dash pepper

Melt half the butter in a saucepan, blend in the flour and gradually add the boiling water, stirring constantly until smooth. Continue stirring until the sauce boils and thickens. Add salt and pepper and remove from heat. Add remaining butter by tsp, beating after each addition. Serve with boiled or baked fish. Makes about 1¼ cups.

EGG SAUCE

3 tbsp butter
3 tbsp flour
2 cups milk
½ tsp salt
⅛ tsp pepper

Few drops Worcestershire sauce
1 tsp lemon juice
4 hard-cooked eggs, diced *or* sieved

Melt butter, blend in flour and add milk gradually, stirring constantly over direct heat until sauce boils and thickens. Add seasonings, then gently fold in eggs. Serve with fish loaf or fish patties. Makes about 2½ cups.

GUACAMOLE

A popular Mexican concoction for dunking potato chips or tostadas

8 2-inch green chili peppers bottled in vinegar *or* fresh
⅔ cup canned *or* fresh tomato purée

8 to 10 oz thoroughly ripe avocado, chilled
½ tsp salt
⅛ tsp scraped *or* grated onion

Discard stems from peppers and pound to a smooth paste with potato masher. There should be 2 tsp purée. To make tomato purée, drain liquid from canned tomatoes and force them or fresh tomatoes through sieve to remove seeds. Cut avocado in half, strip off peel, discard seed and mash fine. Now stir in pepper and tomato purées and seasonings. Cover tightly and chill until serving time. The sooner Guacamole is served after mixing, the better and prettier it is. About 1⅓ cups.

HOLLANDAISE SAUCE (MOCK)

3 tbsp butter   ⅔ cup milk
2 tbsp flour   1 tbsp lemon juice
½ tsp salt   2 egg yolks, beaten

Melt butter in saucepan, blend in flour and salt and add milk; cook with constant stirring over direct heat until sauce boils and thickens. Remove from heat, add lemon juice and stir into beaten egg yolks. Place over boiling water and cook with constant stirring, about 2 min or until sauce is smooth and thick. Serve with cooked vegetables such as asparagus, broccoli, green beans or green onions which have been thoroughly drained. Makes about 1 cup.

HOLLANDAISE SAUCE (TRUE)

¼ cup butter   1 tbsp lemon juice
¼ cup cream, sweet *or* sour   Salt to taste
2 egg yolks   Dash of Cayenne

Melt butter in top of double boiler; add cream and beaten egg yolks, stirring well. Add lemon juice and salt and cook over boiling water, stirring constantly until thickened and smooth (about 2 min). Immediately remove from heat and beat until light. Stir in Cayenne. Serve hot with cauliflower, broccoli, spinach or asparagus. About ⅔ cup.

HORSERADISH SAUCE No. 1

To 1 cup of thin White Sauce, p 1262, add 4 tsp prepared horseradish, mixing well. Good with ham and other meat loaves, and with meat patties and croquettes.

HORSERADISH SAUCE No. 2

½ cup whipping cream   Dash of red pepper
¼ tsp salt   3 tbsp prepared horseradish

Prepare this sauce just before serving time. Have cream, bowl and beater chilled. Whip cream until stiff, then beat in salt and pepper. Fold in the horseradish. Good on beef or ham. 1 cup.

HORSERADISH SAUCE No. 3

½ cup sour cream   3 tbsp prepared horseradish
½ tsp salt

Whip cream until fluffy. Add salt and horseradish, fold in to blend. This sauce is delicious served over ham or ham loaves, tongue, and beef loaves. About ⅔ cup.

LEMON BUTTER SAUCE

For fish and vegetables such as cauliflower and broccoli

¼ cup butter   ⅛ tsp grated lemon rind
1 tbsp lemon juice

Let butter stand at room temp until soft. Grate lemon rind and squeeze juice. Combine, stir together until well blended. Have sauce at room temp when served.

Variation: To make *Almond Butter Sauce,* toast ⅓ cup slivered or chopped blanched almonds to a delicate brown, and either stir into lemon butter or sprinkle nuts over fish or vegetables after applying the *Lemon Butter Sauce.*

MAÎTRE d'HÔTEL SAUCE

¼ cup butter   ¼ tsp salt, *or* to taste
4 tsp finely chopped parsley   ⅛ tsp pepper
4 tsp lemon juice

Cream butter until soft and smooth, and add other ingredients in order named. Spread quickly over broiled fish, chops or steaks as soon as they are removed from the broiler or skillet and serve immediately. Do not return to the oven to keep hot after applying the sauce, or the parsley will lose its fresh green color. This sauce may be made ahead of time and stored in the refrigerator, but will have to be re-creamed to make it soft enough to spread. This sauce is an attractive garnish as well as a pleasing flavor accent. Enough for 5 servings.

MINT SAUCE No. 1

¼ cup chopped fresh mint   ¼ cup sugar
⅓ cup cider vinegar   Pinch of baking soda

Chop mint finely by putting leaves in glass and snipping with scissors. Heat vinegar and sugar to boiling and pour over the chopped mint. Mix in soda, let cool, and serve with any cut of lamb. 5 servings.

MINT SAUCE No. 2

Combine ½ cup very finely chopped mint with 1 tsp grated orange rind and ½ cup currant jelly. Mix thoroughly. Serve with roast lamb or lamb chops.

MINT SAUCE No. 3

Sauce for Roast Lamb with pleasing, pungent aroma and flavor of freshly bruised mint

1 cup sugar	2 tbsp finely chopped fresh
½ cup water	mint
⅛ tsp salt	4 drops green food coloring
2 tbsp 5% white vinegar	

Heat first 4 ingredients in a 1-qt saucepan to boiling, stirring constantly. Boil gently 5 min, remove syrup from heat and cool to lukewarm. Add mint and coloring. Stir occasionally until cold. Serve immediately or store in a clean jar with a tight fitting cover. About ¾ cup.

MORNAY SAUCE

Excellent French finishing touch for fish and eggs—toasts or bakes to a golden brown

¼ cup butter	½ cup grated cheese, Cheddar
¼ cup flour	or Swiss
2 cups milk	½ cup freshly grated
¼ cup thin cream	Parmesan cheese
½ tsp salt	2 egg yolks
$\frac{1}{16}$ tsp white pepper	

Melt butter in a 1-qt saucepan, blend in flour, then with constant stirring gradually add milk. Continue stirring until sauce boils and thickens. Add next 5 ingredients; stir until cheese melts. Beat egg yolks thoroughly, then stir in some of the hot mixture and return to saucepan; cook 2 or 3 min longer. 2 cups.

Note: May be prepared the day before needed—a great help to the busy hostess.

MOUSSELINE SAUCE

Serve with broccoli

½ cup butter *or* margarine	¼ tsp salt
4 egg yolks	2 tbsp strained lemon juice
¼ cup thin cream	

Place half the butter in top of double boiler, cream until soft, add yolks one at a time mixing well with the butter. Stir in cream and salt. Place over simmering water, stir constantly until sauce is just thick. Beat with a rotary beater until shiny. Add remaining butter, remove from heat, stir until butter is melted, then blend in lemon juice. 1 cup.

Variation: For fish, finely chopped capers or parsley may be added to the sauce.

MUSHROOM SAUCE

⅓ cup butter	1½ cups milk
2 cups sliced mushrooms,	½ cup cream
½ lb	1 tsp salt
¼ cup flour	

Melt butter in top of double boiler, add mushrooms, cover, and sauté directly over low heat for 5 min. Then sprinkle flour over buttered mushrooms, stirring thoroughly to blend. Add milk slowly, stirring thoroughly. Then add cream and salt. Place over boiling water and cook until mixture is thickened, stirring to keep smooth. Good to serve over Cheese Rice Loaf, p 444, meat croquettes and chicken and fish timbales. About 3 cups sauce.

MUSTARD SAUCE No. 1

To 1 cup of thin White Sauce, p 1262, add 1 tsp prepared mustard, mixing thoroughly. Excellent with ham or meat loaf.

MUSTARD SAUCE No. 2

Once you make this sauce, you'll be asked to make it time and again

2 hard-cooked egg yolks	Dash of pepper
1 raw egg yolk	1½ tbsp lemon juice, ½ lemon
¼ cup salad oil	1 tbsp prepared brown
1 tbsp sugar	Bahamian mustard
¼ tsp salt	1 tbsp thick cream

Hard cook eggs in the usual way. Shell immediately, remove whites. Use whites in sandwich filling or in 1000 Island Dressing. Rub yolks through a very fine sieve, then blend in raw yolk to a very smooth paste. Add oil, a few drops at a time, beating to a smooth emulsion. Stir in rest of ingredients in order given, beating thoroughly. Makes ¾ cup.

Excellent for ham loaf, frankfurters, tongue, corned beef, veal, pork, fish and for spreading on bread for sandwiches.

Note: Leftover whole egg yolks that are in good condition may be hard-cooked. Turn 2 into buttered custard cup, cover and place over, not in, boiling water and cook 20 to 25 min or until firm and mealy.

MUSTARD SAUCE DE LUXE

Good on ham, corn beef, fish or good cole slaw dressing

2 tbsp butter	¼ cup sugar
¼ cup flour	1 tsp salt
1¾ cups milk	3 tbsp vinegar
2 egg yolks, beaten	⅛ tsp paprika
1 tbsp dry mustard	

Melt butter in saucepan over low heat, blend in flour, then add milk slowly, stirring to keep smooth. Cook and stir until sauce boils and thickens. Remove from heat. Stir some of the hot sauce into yolks, then return to saucepan, stirring until smooth. Combine rest of ingredients, mix well and stir into sauce. Return to low heat and cook 2 min, stirring constantly. Remove from heat and beat with rotary beater until smooth. Serve warm or cold. Keep tightly covered in refrigerator. 1¾ cups.

ONION SAUCE

To 1 cup of thin White Sauce, p 1262, add 1 to 2 medium onions, finely chopped, and reheat just to boiling. Good with any meat loaf, also with salmon loaf or salmon croquettes.

REMOULADE SAUCE

Delicious French sauce for shrimp or lobster

3 small green onions
  trimmed to 6 inches
1 tsp capers
2 2-inch sour pickles
Yolk 1 hard-cooked egg

1 cup French Dressing,
  p 1200
2 tsp Bahamian *or* Creole
  mustard
1 tsp lemon juice

Chop cleaned onions, capers and pickles *very fine,* then put into a heavy bowl; add egg yolk and crush with wooden potato masher as fine as possible. Stir in dressing slowly with wooden spoon, then beat thoroughly. Beat in mustard and lemon juice last. Finished sauce consistency should be like that of thin mayonnaise. 1¼ cups.

SPANISH SAUCE

No. 2 can tomatoes
⅓ cup finely chopped onion
½ cup finely chopped celery

1 medium green pepper,
  finely chopped
Salt and pepper to taste

Combine tomatoes, onion, celery and green pepper in saucepan, heat to boiling, then cook slowly for 20 to 30 min or until somewhat thickened. Stir in salt and pepper to taste. About 2 cups.

If preferred, tomatoes may be rubbed through a sieve before combining with other ingredients; the sauce may then be thickened, if desired, by adding 1 tbsp flour blended to a smooth paste with 3 tbsp cold water, and again heating to boiling.

TARTAR SAUCE

⅔ cup Mayonnaise, p 1202
1 tsp grated onion
1 tsp chopped chives
1 tsp finely chopped parsley

2 drops tabasco, optional
1 tsp chopped sweet pickle
1 tsp capers, optional
1 tbsp finely chopped celery

Combine all ingredients and mix just enough to blend. Keep chilled until ready to serve. This is an excellent sauce for fish, and is also good on corned beef hash. Makes about ¾ cup sauce.

TOMATO SAUCE

Worth making!

3 tbsp salad oil	1 medium bay leaf
1 small clove garlic	Green celery leaves from
1 cup coarse-chopped onion	4 branches
½ cup chopped green pepper	½ tsp salt
½ small carrot, grated	Pepper to suit taste
1 qt canned tomatoes	1 tsp sugar

Heat oil in 3-qt saucepan, add next 4 ingredients and sauté until onion turns golden color, stirring constantly. Add next 5 ingredients, cover and cook slowly with occasionally stirring until sauce thickens— 40 to 45 min. Rub mixture through fine sieve. Stir in sugar, if desired. Excellent on spaghetti, ravioli or omelette. 2 to 2¼ cups.

VEGETABLE CREOLE SAUCE

3 slices bacon	1 bay leaf
1 medium onion, sliced	2 tbsp chopped parsley
3 tbsp flour	1 cup canned tomatoes
½ tsp salt	1 cup canned peas
1 cup finely chopped celery	

Pan-fry bacon until done in skillet; remove bacon and sauté onion in the fat until soft and yellow. Add flour and salt and blend until smooth, then add next 4 ingredients, stirring constantly until sauce boils and thickens. Reduce heat and simmer gently about 15 min. Remove bay leaf. Add peas and continue cooking until heated thoroughly, then stir in the chopped crisp bacon. Serve hot with Puffy Omelet, p 677, or Scrambled Eggs, p 675. 5 servings.

VELOUTÉ SAUCE

Pleasing on chicken, veal or sweetbread dishes

¼ cup rendered chicken fat *or* butter	Scant ½ tsp salt
	Little dash of cayenne
⅓ cup flour	½ cup thin cream
2 cups rich chicken broth	

Melt chicken fat in a 1-qt saucepan over low direct heat. Blend in the flour until very smooth. Add broth gradually, stirring constantly and cook and stir until very smooth and thickened. Stir in seasonings, remove from heat and stir in the cream. Serve in a heated sauce boat. 2 cups.

Variation: When 2 or 3 egg yolks are beaten into Velouté sauce, it becomes Supreme Sauce. When a few tbsp of grated Parmesan cheese are beaten into Supreme Sauce it becomes an Allemande Sauce. Sliced stuffed olives may be added to Velouté sauce to produce a delicious Olive Sauce. The addition of chopped chives produces another variation, toasted chopped almonds, still another, sliced sautéed mushrooms still another and on and on. All of these sauces are delicious on foods with which they harmonize.

VINAIGRETTE SAUCE

1 tsp grated onion
2 tbsp vinegar
⅓ cup olive *or* salad oil
1 tsp finely chopped parsley
1 tsp finely chopped green
pepper

1 tsp finely chopped pimiento
⅛ tsp salt
Dash of pepper
¼ tsp prepared mustard

Combine ingredients in order named and beat well. Excellent for asparagus, lettuce or any other vegetable salad. About ½ cup.

Note: Two hard-cooked egg yolks may be riced and added to this sauce for a delicious variation.

WHITE SAUCE

Thin:

1 tbsp butter
1 tbsp flour
½ tsp salt
1 cup milk, *or* ½ cup evaporated milk and ½ cup water

Medium:

2 tbsp butter
2 tbsp flour
½ tsp salt
1 cup milk, *or* ½ cup evaporated milk and ½ cup water

Thick:

3 *or* 4 tbsp butter
3 *or* 4 tbsp flour
½ tsp salt
1 cup milk, *or* ½ cup evaporated milk and ½ cup water

Melt butter in saucepan, add flour and salt and blend until smooth. Stir in cold milk gradually and cook over direct heat, stirring constantly until sauce boils and becomes thick and smooth. If stirring is done carefully, there will be no lumping, but white sauce that has lumped may often be smoothed by beating with a rotary beater. If it is necessary to keep white sauce more than a few min before using, place over boiling water and keep it covered, stirring occasionally. Makes about 1 cup sauce.

Soups

A thing of the past is the old-fashioned soup kettle which used to stand always on the back of the wood or coal kitchen range. Always ready to receive meat trimmings and bones, and broth left from cooking meats and vegetables, it simmered and seethed day and night and from it emerged the most savory of soups, "pot au feu."

★　★　★　★

MODERN kitchens have no room for such a "pot au feu," but it is possible to reproduce the old-fashioned soups without its help, and since soup can be such an important item in the diet, every housewife should develop her soup repertoire. One of the important functions of soup is as an appetizer, which is the reason it is served at the beginning of the meal. The hot, savory liquid puts the stomach in a good humor immediately. But the majority of soups are more than just appetizers; they are rich in food value.

Cream soups which contain both milk and butter in addition to the vegetable which usually gives them their flavor are one of the most nutritious soups. They are especially useful as a way of getting more milk into the diet, not only of children but of adults. Since most cream soups are easily and quickly made, they have become very popular for luncheons and are often carried in the thermos bottle of the lunch box.

Chowder is a special kind of cream soup containing a large proportion of solid food cut rather coarsely. Fish and clam chowders were the original members of this group, but modern chowders are often made with vegetables such as corn, potatoes, and even spinach. They are, as a rule, so substantial that a good-sized bowlful is a hearty luncheon main dish.

Clear soups are made with meat or vegetable broth for flavor, or with tomato juice. Vegetable soups often have a meat broth base, but their chief food value is derived from the vegetables they contain. Such soups closely resemble the old-time "pot au feu," and though the cooking time is longer than for cream soup, they are very simple to make. It is no chore for the homemaker to put a soup bone into the kettle and slowly simmer out the essences of bone and meat, perhaps using the water saved from yesterday's potatoes and other vegetables to add flavor and some vitamin and mineral value. After the soup bone is removed, the meat that remains on it may be chopped and returned to the soup along with the finely diced vegetables and seasonings.

For the housewife who likes to serve soup often for its warming, appetite-stimulating and nutritious qualities, but has no time to make even the quickest cream soup, there are the many varieties of canned soup. The quality of canned soups has improved so much in recent years that no one need hesitate to serve them whenever it is convenient. Both clear and cream soups are available in most of the leading brands. They may be the type which are ready to serve after heating just as they come from the can, or the condensed kind requiring the addition of water or milk before heating. And most of them are the type which will enable the home cook to elaborate to her heart's content. It is possible to combine two varieties of commercial soups and add a dash of this and a pinch of that and serve something that is really new and different. Each cook will want to develop her own specialties; we have included some in this chapter, which we call "soup blends."

ACCOMPANIMENTS AND GARNISHES

Most everyone likes some sort of crisp accompaniment with soup. This may be simply crisp toast in the form of Melba toast, croutons, fingers, rings. Cheese pastry sticks or bread sticks are especially dainty for a festive occasion. And the many kinds of crackers—plain salted soda crackers, oyster crackers, butter wafers, cheese crackers, and the various whole grain and shredded wafers—are always in favor. These are most attractive when they are freshened in the oven just before serving and served very hot, usually with butter.

If other relishes are being served, such as celery, radishes or olives, they should be served along with the soup because the contrast of their crisp, cool texture increases the enjoyment of both soup and relish.

Soups may be garnished in a variety of attractive ways; this possibility is too often neglected. The garnish may be just a few crisp croutons floating on top of the bowlful, a sprinkling of chopped parsley, a few kernels of puffy popcorn or one of the puffed cereals, some gratings of raw carrot, or a puff of whipped or thick sour cream. Whatever the garnish, it should be put on just before the soup is served in order to be its freshest and best when eaten.

CHOWDERS AND HEARTY SOUPS

BEET BORSCH

Hot or cold

No. 2 can sliced *or* diced beets	3 tbsp cider vinegar
½ cup meat broth *or* water	½ pt sour cream
2 tbsp grated onion	Chopped parsley, if desired

Drain off beet juice into saucepan and rice or grate beets into the juice. Add broth or water and onion, and heat to boiling. Remove from heat, add vinegar and serve at once with 3 tbsp sour cream floating on each serving and a sprinkling of chopped parsley, if desired. If preferred, the borsch may be served ice cold, adding cream and 1 tbsp chopped cucumber to each plate just before serving. 5 servings.

Note: One and one-half cups riced, fresh cooked beets and three-fourths cup of water may be used in place of the canned beets.

BOUILLABAISSE

A famous and delicious French chowder requiring at least 2 kinds of fish. A substantial 1-dish meal

1 large leek, sliced thin
2 onions size walnuts, chopped
1 small carrot, sliced thin
1 small clove garlic, cut fine
⅓ cup salad oil
1 lb fresh fillets (white fish, red fish, mullet, whiting, sole)
3 medium tomatoes *or* 1½ cups canned
2 branches celery, cut fine
1½ cups water
1 small bay leaf

1 cup cooked shrimp, crab *or* lobster meat
24 small oysters
Pinch of saffron
1 tbsp pimiento, chopped
2½ tsp salt
Several dashes pepper
Dash cayenne
½ tsp monosodium glutamate
2 tbsp lemon juice *or* vinegar
6 to 8 thin toast triangles
2 tbsp chopped parsley

Clean and prepare first 4 vegetables and add to salad oil heated in a 4-qt saucepan. Sauté 3 or 4 min, stirring occasionally. Add whole fish fillets skin-side up, peeled tomatoes cut in 4ths, celery, water and bay leaf; cover, simmer 20 min. Now carefully lift skin off fish and discard. Add shrimp cut in 3rds with next 8 ingredients. Stir very gently to distribute seasonings. Simmer 5 min. Place toast in a heated deep casserole or tureen, or in individual bowls. Turn hot chowder over toast. Sprinkle with parsley. Serve at once. 6 to 8 servings.

BOSTON CLAM CHOWDER

1 dozen fresh *or* 10½-oz can canned clams
1 carrot, diced, ½ cup
2 cups diced raw potatoes
⅓ cup diced celery
3 cups richly flavored Chicken Broth, p 1289

2 tbsp chopped onion
4 tsp chicken fat *or* butter
2 tbsp flour
½ cup cream
Salt and pepper

Steam clams and pry open, see p 712. Drain off and measure liquid; there should be 1 cup. Put the carrots, potatoes, and celery into the chicken broth, cover, and boil gently until tender. Then cut clams finely with sharp kitchen scissors, sauté the clams and onions in the chicken fat for 5 min. Blend flour evenly into this mixture. Add broth and vegetables gradually, stirring constantly to keep smooth. Add the clam broth, cream and seasonings. Reheat just to boiling and serve immediately. Makes about 8 cups.

CABBAGE AND DILL CHOWDER

3 tbsp butter	¼ tsp paprika
3 tbsp flour	2 large heads and stems of
2½ cups water	fresh dill
2 bay leaves	4 cups finely cut cabbage
1 medium onion, sliced	1½ cups milk
2 tsp salt	

Heat butter in a large saucepan, add flour and stir until evenly blended. Add water gradually, heat to the boiling point, stirring constantly. Add bay leaves, onion, salt, paprika and dill; cover and *simmer* 20 min. Remove bay leaves, dill, and onion with a slotted spoon. Some of the dill seeds will remain in the soup. Add cabbage and boil gently, uncovered for 7 min. Add milk and heat just to the boiling point. Serve at once. 4 generous servings.

COLD BEET BORSCH NO. 1

A delightfully refreshing soup for hot weather

No. 2 can beets *or* 2 cups grated fresh cooked beets and ¾ cup juice	1 tsp finely chopped green onion, optional
2 tsp vinegar	1 tsp salt
2 dashes red pepper	2 tbsp sugar
1⅓ cups cold water	¼ cup lemon juice
1 pt ice cubes	¼ cup very thinly sliced
½ cup very finely chopped cucumber	cucumbers
	½ cup sour cream
	Melba toast

Drain juice from the beets. There should be ¾ cup. (If fresh beets are used, add ¾ cup water for the canned beet juice.) Grate the beets and combine with the juice and the rest of the ingredients except sour cream and sliced cucumbers. Mix thoroughly and serve in individual soup dishes or from a tureen with the sliced cucumber disposed over the top for garnish. Serve with a spoonful of sour cream and melba toast, crisp crackers, or pumpernickel bread. 5 servings.

COLD BORSCH NO. 2

A delicious quickie

No. 2 can beets
1⅓ cups chicken broth, *or*
  1⅓ cubes chicken bouillon
  dissolved in 1⅓ cups cold
  water

1 cup sour cream
¾ tsp salt
⅛ tsp pepper
1½ tsp lemon juice
2 tbsp chopped chives

Use only half the beets and all juice in the can. Drain beets; save juice. Put drained beets through a food mill or potato ricer. Add beet juice and all ingredients except chives, stir thoroughly. Cover, chill thoroughly. Turn into individual soup dishes, sprinkle with chives. Serve with Melba rye toast. Serve remaining beets as a vegetable or in a salad. 4 servings.

CORN CHOWDER NO. 1

2 oz bacon *or* salt pork
2 slices onion
1½ cups diced raw potatoes
2 cups fresh corn, cut from
  cob, *or* No. 2 can cream
  style corn
3 cups hot water

3 tbsp butter
1 cup evaporated milk *or*
  coffee cream
2½ tsp salt
Dash pepper
2 tsp finely chopped parsley
or paprika

Chop bacon and onion coarsely and put into soup kettle; sauté until onion is soft and bacon done. Add potatoes, corn, and water, cover and *simmer* until potatoes are tender. Add butter, milk, and seasonings; reheat to boiling and serve piping hot with a little parsley sprinkled over the top, or a few dashes of paprika. 5 servings.

CORN CHOWDER NO. 2

2 cups diced raw potatoes
½ cup diced onion
1 cup diced celery
2 cups boiling water
¼ lb bacon
¼ lb mushrooms, sliced

¼ cup diced green pepper
No. 2 can cream style
  yellow corn
3 cups milk
2½ tsp salt
Dash of pepper

Pare and dice potatoes. Add to onions, celery and water in top of 2¼ qts double boiler. Heat to boiling over direct heat, cover, reduce heat and simmer for 10 min. Meanwhile pan-fry bacon. Drain on absorbent paper. Sauté the mushrooms and green pepper in ¼ cup of the bacon drippings for 5 min. Add this and remaining ingredients to the cooked vegetables and thin liquid. Reheat over boiling water. Stir gently to mix well. Serve piping hot garnished with the bacon, broken in bits. Makes 8 cups.

CRAB-SHRIMP GUMBO NO. 1

This famous Southern soup is a tasty nutritious main dish

2 lbs shank-end ham *or*
1 lb slice ham
6 cups water
4 tbsp butter, ½ stick
2 onions size large eggs
1 medium size green pepper,
chopped, 1 cup
1 large peeled clove garlic,
cut fine
2 10-oz pkgs frozen *or*
2 lbs fresh okra, washed,
trimmed

10-oz pkg frozen ready-cut
Alaska crab in shell *or*
1 lb fresh hard-shell blue
crabs, scalded, cleaned, cut
in 4ths, p 715
1 lb raw shrimp, cleaned,
cut, p 726
Pinch of thyme
4 to 6 drops tabasco
Fluffy cooked hot rice

Wash ham bone and trim off most all fat from shank or slice. (Use for other seasoning.) Put ham into a 4 or 5-qt saucepan, add the 6 cups water, heat to boiling, reduce heat to *simmer,* cover and *simmer,* don't boil, 2 hrs. Now lift out ham and use in some other way—ham was used to obtain broth with ham flavor. Heat butter to bubbling in heavy 9-inch skillet, add fine-chopped onion, green pepper, garlic and okra sliced ¾-inch thick. Cook until onion and garlic are soft, then turn mixture into ham broth. Add crab and shrimp, cover and continue simmering for another 2 hrs. Add tabasco. Ladle this hot thick soup into bowls and add 2 heaping tbsp rice to each. 6 to 8 servings.

Note: Store cooled leftover gumbo in tightly covered containers in refrigerator. When reheated, it is as good as when first cooked. No salt is added if ham has the usual saltiness. Fresh or frozen crab meat may be used to make this gumbo.

CRAB-SHRIMP GUMBO NO. 2

Flavorful but not heavy—yet most satisfying

6 cups chicken broth—not
greasy
3 cups chopped peeled fresh
tomatoes *or* 3 cups canned
2 tbsp chopped parsley
1 cup sliced celery
4 tbsp butter *or* margarine,
½ stick
1 cup chopped green pepper,
1 pepper
Pinch of thyme
3 onions, large egg size,
chopped

2 medium cloves garlic,
chopped fine
10-oz pkg frozen *or* 1 lb fresh
okra, washed, trimmed
1 lb raw shrimp, cleaned,
cut, p 726
10-oz pkg frozen ready-cut
Alaska crab in shell *or* 1 lb
fresh blue crab scalded,
cleaned, cut in 4ths, p 715
6 to 8 drops tabasco, optional
Cooked hot rice

Measure broth into a 5-qt kettle. Add tomatoes, parsley and celery. Heat butter to bubbling in heavy 9-inch skillet, add pepper, onion, garlic and okra cut in ¾-inch lengths. Cover and sauté without stirring until onion is soft but not browned, then turn mixture into broth. Add all remaining ingredients except tabasco. Heat to boiling, then reduce heat to *simmer,* cover and simmer from 2 to 2½ hrs or until gumbo is slightly thickened. Stir in tabasco. Serve in bowls with 2 or more heaping tbsp hot rice dropped into each serving. 6 to 8 servings.

CREOLE BEAN SOUP

2 oz diced salt pork	2 cups tomatoes, canned
¼ cup chopped onion	2 tsp salt
¼ cup flour	2 cups cooked navy beans
1 qt water	(1 cup raw yields 2 cups
2 cups diced raw potatoes	cooked)
1 cup chopped celery	1 tbsp chopped green pepper
½ cup sliced carrots	1 tbsp chopped parsley

Pan-fry pork in a saucepan until brown on all sides, then add onion and cook until soft. Blend in flour, add water slowly, stirring constantly to keep mixture smooth. Add potatoes, celery, carrots, tomatoes and salt. Cover and cook gently until vegetables are soft. Add beans, simmer about 10 min. Stir in the pepper and parsley and serve at once. 4 servings.

FRENCH ONION SOUP

2½ lbs veal knuckle	1 cup diced celery
1½ qts boiling water	Salt to taste
4 tsp salt	5 slices French bread
2 cups sliced onions	Parmesan cheese
2 tbsp fat	

Have knuckle cracked into several pieces. Wipe with a damp cloth. Put into soup kettle, add water and salt, cover and simmer for 1 hr. Sauté onions in fat until lightly browned. Add onions and celery to soup and simmer until both onions and celery are very soft, about 1 hr. Remove bone and season soup to taste. If desired, kitchen bouquet or a little Caramel, p 165, may be added for more color. Toast bread, leave crusts on, and float on top of bowlfuls of soup. Sprinkle grated cheese generously over toast. 5 servings.

Note: Slices of hard rolls may be used instead of French bread. The cooked meat may be stripped from the bone and used to make sandwich fillings. Rich chicken broth may be substituted for the veal broth.

FISH CHOWDER

2 slices bacon *or* 2 oz salt pork, cut in small cubes	½ cup water
⅓ cup sliced onions	1 lb boned halibut or pike
1½ cups sliced raw potatoes	3 cups milk *or* No. 2½ can tomatoes, sieved
½ tsp salt	1 tbsp finely chopped parsley
⅛ tsp pepper	Crackers

Place chopped bacon or diced pork in a heavy kettle or Dutch oven and fry slowly until golden brown. Add onions and cook until they are soft and light yellow in color, from 5 to 7 min. Add potatoes, sprinkle with salt and pepper, and add water; cover and cook at moderate rate until potatoes are half done, about 5 min. Then add the fish, placing in the kettle flesh side down. Again cover and continue cooking until potatoes are done and fish is tender enough to fall apart, from 10 to 12 min. Remove skin from fish and break fish into coarse flakes. For New England style chowder, add milk; for Manhattan style chowder, add tomatoes. Heat thoroughly but do not boil. Sprinkle parsley over each bowlful. Serve piping hot with crisp crackers. 4 to 5 servings.

LIMA BEAN CHOWDER

1 cup dried lima beans	1 cup diced carrot
3 cups cold water	1 cup water
½ tsp salt	¾ tsp salt
4 slices bacon	2 cups milk
¼ cup onion, finely chopped	2 tbsp finely chopped parsley
2 cups diced raw potatoes	

Wash beans thoroughly and put into soup kettle. Add water and salt, heat to boiling, reduce heat and *simmer* 45 min. Reserve ½ cup of whole limas; purée the remainder along with the liquid left from cooking. Pan-fry bacon until done. Remove and add the onion to the fat and sauté until soft. Add potatoes, carrots and 1 cup water and the ¾ tsp salt. Simmer for 15 min or until vegetables are tender. Add milk, the puréed and the whole beans. Heat to boiling. Serve immediately. Crumble bacon and sprinkle it and the parsley over the chowder. 4 generous servings.

MANHATTAN CLAM CHOWDER

1 dozen fresh *or* 10½ oz can clams	1 medium onion, chopped
	⅓ cup chopped celery
3 *or* 4 medium potatoes, cut into ½-inch cubes	2 tbsp flour
	1½ cups canned tomatoes
½ cup water	¼ tsp sugar
1½-inch cube of salt pork	Salt and pepper to taste

Steam clams and pry open, see p 712. Drain off liquid and measure; there should be about 1 cup. Cut clams finely with kitchen scissors. Cook potatoes (about 2 cups cubed) in water until just tender; do not drain. Cut salt pork into ⅜-inch cubes and render over low heat in a large saucepan. Add onion and celery and sauté 3 min. Blend flour evenly into this mixture. Add tomatoes gradually, stirring to keep smooth. Add potatoes and their liquid, clams, clam broth and seasonings. Heat quickly to boiling. Serve at once. Makes about 7 cups—6 to 8 servings.

BLACK BEAN SOUP

World renowned German soup made of simple ingredients, but served in many famous eating places

½ lb black beans	2 dashes cayenne
5 cups water	⅛ tsp white pepper
¼ cup chopped onion	⅛ tsp dry mustard
2 tbsp bacon *or*	1½ cups water
chicken fat	1 tbsp cornstarch
2 medium branches celery,	4 tsp sherry
some leaves	1 hard-cooked egg, sliced
1¾ tsp salt	Fine-cut chives *or* parsley

Pick over beans, discard imperfect ones, then wash well and drain; add cold water to come 1 inch over beans and let soak overnight. Next morning, drain, add the 5 cups water, the onion sautéed in the fat, and chopped celery. Heat to boiling, reduce heat, cover and simmer until beans are very tender, from 3 to 3½ hrs. Remove from heat and put beans through a sieve or food mill, rubbing through all pulp—there should be 1 qt purée. Return purée to kettle, add next 4 ingredients and 1¼ cups of remaining water; blend remaining ¼ cup water and cornstarch and stir into soup. Heat to boiling with constant stirring and simmer 2 min. Remove from heat and stir in sherry. Serve immediately in bowls or cups with slice of egg and sprinkling of chives floated on top. 5 servings.

NAVY BEAN SOUP NO. 1

2 slices bacon	¼ cup finely chopped celery
2 tbsp chopped onion	leaves
2 cups boiled Navy Beans	1½ cups milk
with liquid, p 1320	1¼ tsp salt
	1 tsp brown sugar

Cut bacon into small pieces and pan-fry with the onion until the bacon is slightly brown. Add the beans and liquid and mash. Add remaining ingredients, *simmer* 10 min. Serve at once. 4 servings.

NAVY BEAN SOUP NO. 2

½ lb dried navy beans
2 oz salt pork, sliced
1 qt water
1 medium onion, sliced

1½ cups hot water *or* scalded
milk
Salt and pepper to taste
Chopped chives *or* parsley

Wash beans thoroughly, cover with cold water, and let soak several hrs or overnight. Drain and put into kettle; add salt pork and water. Heat to boiling, reduce heat, cover tightly, *simmer* until beans are mushy, about 1½ hrs. Add onion the last half hr of cooking. Press soup through sieve, add water or milk and season. Reheat. Sprinkle chopped chives or parsley over each serving. 5 servings.

OYSTER STEW

3 cups milk
1 slice onion
2 branches celery
2 sprigs parsley
¼ bay leaf

⅔ cup coffee cream
¼ cup cracker crumbs
1 pt oysters
3 tbsp butter
Salt and pepper to taste

Heat milk, onion, celery, parsley and bay leaf over boiling water for 20 min. Remove vegetables and bay leaf and add cream and cracker crumbs. Meanwhile, heat oysters in their own liquor until edges curl. Combine with milk and cream mixture; add butter, salt and pepper and serve at once. 5 servings.

POTATO CARROT SOUP

4 medium potatoes, pared
3 medium carrots, scraped
2 medium onions
2 tsp salt
3 cups boiling water

1¾ cups cooking water from
vegetables
1⅔ cups cream *or* evaporated
milk
Dash cayenne
Dash celery salt

Dice potatoes, carrots, and onions, and turn into kettle. Add salt and the boiling water. Cover and cook gently until tender (about 15 min). There should be 1¾ cups liquid left. Mash the vegetables thoroughly in their liquid. Combine with cream, heat just to scalding. Add cayenne and celery salt, reheat and serve at once. Add a dash of paprika on top of each serving. 5 servings.

PRINTEMPS CHOWDER

1 cup shelled new peas, 1 lb
1/3 cup finely sliced green
  onions, including tender
  tops
1 cup water
1 cup raw potatoes, cut in
  1/4-inch cubes

1 tsp salt
2 tbsp butter
1 tbsp flour
2 1/2 cups milk
1/4 cup quartered, thinly
  sliced radishes
1 tbsp chopped parsley

Cook peas and onions in water uncovered for 10 min. Add potatoes and salt. Continue cooking 6 to 8 min. Blend butter and flour over low heat, add milk slowly, stirring constantly. Combine with peas, potatoes and their liquid. Simmer 10 min, stirring occasionally. Add radishes and parsley just before serving. 4 servings.

SALMON CHOWDER

2 large potatoes, 2 cups cut
  in 1/2-inch cubes
1/2 cup carrots, cut in 1/2-inch
  cubes
1 1/2 tsp salt
2 cups water
2 tbsp chopped onion
3 tbsp butter

2 tbsp flour
2 cups milk
1/2 lb can salmon
Small pinch marjoram
4 to 5 drops Worcestershire
  sauce
1/2 cup thinly sliced celery

Put potatoes and carrots in a saucepan, add salt and water, cover and cook gently until just tender. Remove from heat and do not drain. Meanwhile sauté onion in butter for 3 min. Blend in the flour until smooth, and add milk gradually, stirring over medium heat until mixture boils and thickens. Discard skin from salmon, crush the bones, and flake the fish. Combine fish, crushed bones, cooked vegetables and their liquid with the thickened milk sauce. Add remaining ingredients. Heat thoroughly and serve at once. Makes 6 cups.

SAVORY DINNER CHOWDER

With tiny meat balls

2 cups shredded lettuce
1 cup coarsely sliced celery
1 cup sliced carrots
  Small onion, sliced
3 cups cold water

No. 2 can tomatoes,
  2 1/2 cups
1/2 tsp sugar
1 1/2 tsp salt
Dash pepper
1/3 cup rice

Combine all ingredients except the rice. Heat to boiling; add rice and simmer for 20 min or until rice is tender. Stir frequently with a fork.

Meat Balls:

2 tbsp chopped onion
2 tbsp margarine *or*
  shortening
¾ cup water
Medium sized bay leaf

1 cup coarse cracker crumbs
½ lb ground lamb *or* beef
1 egg, slightly beaten
2 tbsp chopped parsley

Sauté onion in 1 tbsp of the margarine for 10 min, or until lightly browned. Add water and bay leaf and simmer for 3 min. Remove bay leaf and pour cracker crumbs into onion mixture and stir well; allow to cool. Add remaining ingredients and mix thoroughly. Allow to stand 10 or 15 min. Form into small balls and pan-fry over medium heat in the remaining margarine. Turn frequently to brown on all sides. Reduce heat, cover, and simmer for 5 min. Add meat balls to finished chowder and simmer 5 min. Do not add fat from lamb left in skillet. 4 servings.

SOY BEAN SOUP

½ lb dried soy beans
1 small onion, sliced
1 qt water
24-oz can tomato juice

1 tbsp sugar
2½ tsp salt, *or* to taste
Carrot

Wash soy beans thoroughly, cover with water, and let soak overnight. Drain beans and run through food chopper; put into saucepan with the onion and 1 qt water, cover, and simmer gently 1½ to 2 hrs or until soy beans are tender. Add remaining ingredients and reheat before serving. Shavings of grated carrot make an attractive garnish. 5 servings.

SPINACH CHOWDER

3 slices bacon
½ cup sliced onions
3 medium potatoes
½ tsp salt
¾ lb fresh *or* frozen spinach

3 tbsp flour
1 cup cream *or* evaporated
  milk
Salt
Pepper

Cut bacon into half-inch lengths with scissors and pan-fry in a saucepan until done. Remove bacon and save. Add onions to drippings and sauté until soft and yellow. Add the pared, diced potatoes, enough water to cover and the salt. Cover and cook until potatoes are just about tender. Now add the cleaned fresh spinach that has been coarsely shredded with scissors or the half-thawed frozen spinach and again heat to boiling, then simmer uncovered until spinach is tender, or from six to seven min. Blend the flour and one-fourth cup of the cream to a smooth paste, then add rest of cream and stir until thoroughly blended. Slowly pour this cream-mixture into the hot soup, stirring thoroughly to blend, then cook until soup boils and thickens, stirring constantly. Add more salt if needed, and pepper if desired. Serve immediately with the bacon dropped on top for garnish. 5 servings.

SPLIT PEA SOUP

2 tbsp butter *or* ham
   drippings
1 medium onion, sliced
2 qts water
1 lb split peas
1 carrot

1 branch celery
1 sprig parsley
4 tsp salt
1/16 tsp pepper
Hard-cooked egg
Paprika

Heat butter in soup kettle. Add onions and sauté until lightly browned. Then add boiling water, the washed peas, and all except last two ingredients. Cover kettle and reheat to boiling. Reduce heat and simmer for 1½ hrs or until peas are mushy. Stir occasionally to prevent sticking to the bottom. Serve piping hot with a garnish of puréed egg if desired, and a dash of paprika. Makes 8 cups.

Note: Grated cheese, sliced wieners, chopped parsley or grated carrot are other suggestions for garnishing.

TOMATO AND CABBAGE SOUP

1/4 cup butter
1/3 cup flour
1 cup tomato juice
1/2 bay leaf
1 tbsp chopped onion
1 tsp salt

1 tbsp sugar
1½ cups evaporated milk
2¼ cups finely chopped Cooked
   Cabbage, p 1329
1 cup water

Melt butter and blend in flour; add tomato juice and stir over low heat until mixture boils and thickens. Add bay leaf, onion, salt and sugar to evaporated milk, and heat separately in top of double boiler over hot water. Just before serving, lift out the bay leaf and add cabbage and water (may be cooking water from cabbage). Slowly stir the tomato mixture into the milk and cabbage. Serve immediately. 5 servings.

SUMMER VEGETABLE CHOWDER

As intriguing as it is delicious

1 cup shelled new peas, 1 lb
1/3 cup finely sliced green
   onions including tender
   tops
1 cup boiling water
1 cup whole kernel corn,
   fresh *or* canned
1 tsp salt

2 tbsp butter
1 tbsp flour
2½ cups milk
3-oz pkg cream cheese
4 slices pan-fried bacon *or*
   equal amount dried beef
1/2 cup coarsely grated carrots
1 tbsp chopped parsley

Turn peas and onions into a 3 qt saucepan. Add water and cook uncovered 10 min. Now add corn and salt and continue cooking 6 to 8 min. Meanwhile blend butter and flour in saucepan over low heat, add milk slowly with constant stirring and cook until thickened. Cut cream cheese into 12 cubes and shape into balls. Crumble pan-fried bacon or beef into bits and roll balls in it. Combine cream sauce with vegetables and their liquid, add carrots, simmer 10 min, stirring occasionally. Sprinkle with parsley and turn into hot tureen. Drop in bacon-cheese balls just before serving. 4 servings.

WATERCRESS OR SPINACH AND POTATO SOUP

3 cups Chicken *or* Beef Broth, p 1157 *or* 1286	¾ cup washed chopped watercress *or* raw spinach
4 medium potatoes, grated	1½ tsp salt
1 cup milk *or* cream	Dash pepper
	¼ cup grated cheese

Heat broth to boiling, add grated raw potato and simmer gently for 10 to 15 min, stirring occasionally. Just before serving, add milk, cress or spinach and seasonings. Serve hot with a sprinkling of grated cheese on each serving. 5 servings.

CREAM SOUPS

CREAM OF ALMOND SOUP

A delicious soup for unusual occasions

¼ cup butter	2 cups richly flavored Chicken Broth, p 1289
½ cup almonds, blanched	4 thin slices lemon
3 tbsp flour	Watercress
2 cups milk	

Heat butter in saucepan. Add almonds, toss to coat. Let almonds toast over very low heat, frequently tossing and stirring to brown evenly. When lightly browned (about 7 min) remove from butter, let cool, then put through a food chopper. Blend flour with butter left in pan. Gradually add the milk and chicken broth. Heat to boiling, stirring constantly. If broth is unsalted, add salt to taste. Add the ground almonds. Serve piping hot with a thin slice of lemon and a sprig of watercress floating on top. 4 servings.

CREAM OF ASPARAGUS SOUP

1 lb fresh asparagus	¼ tsp salt
2 cups boiling water	¼ tsp celery salt
1 tsp salt	1 tsp grated onion
¾ cup cream	1 tbsp butter
¾ cup milk	1 tsp finely chopped pimiento
3 tbsp flour	

Wash asparagus thoroughly, removing scales; swish heads vigorously about in cold water to loosen and remove any soil. Break off woody ends and discard. Cut stalks into ½-inch pieces. Drop into the boiling water, add the 1 tsp salt, and cook uncovered until very tender. Mash the cooked asparagus in its liquid. Combine cream and milk in a saucepan; mix flour to a paste with ¼ cup cold water, stir into milk mixture and heat until it boils and thickens, stirring constantly. Add salt, celery salt, onion and mashed asparagus with its liquid. Reheat and add butter. Serve with pimiento sprinkled over each serving. 4 servings.

CREAM OF BEET SOUP

3 tbsp butter	1½ tsp salt
3 tbsp flour	2 tsp grated onion
3 cups milk	1 tbsp pickle relish
No. 2 can sliced beets, 2½ cups	¼ cup cider vinegar or to taste

Heat butter in a saucepan, blend in flour, and gradually add milk; cook over direct heat, stirring constantly until sauce boils and thickens. Drain beets (save juice) and put through ricer or food mill; add to hot sauce. Add salt, onion, beet juice, and pickle relish and heat again to boiling point. Remove from heat, add vinegar and serve immediately. 5 servings.

CREAM OF BROCCOLI SOUP

1 bunch broccoli, 1 lb	14½ oz can evaporated milk
2 tsp salt	1 cup water
3 cups boiling water	1½ tsp salt
2 tbsp butter	1 tsp grated onion
3 tbsp flour	

Place broccoli, heads down, in 2 qts cold water to which the 2 tsp salt have been added and let soak for half an hr. Then drain and wash the broccoli in fresh cold water, swishing it back and forth to remove all soil. Drain. Strip off the small stem leaves and the fibrous outer peeling of the stalks. Cut broccoli into ½-inch pieces, saving a few of the choice flowerets for garnish. Put both cut broccoli and flowerets into a saucepan, add the boiling water, and cook 10 to 12 min at a rapid rate, uncovered. Remove the choice flowerets after 5 to 7 min of cooking. When tender, crush rest of broccoli with a potato masher; it should be well broken up, but not a purée. There should be 2½ cups of crushed broccoli and cooking water. In another saucepan heat the butter, blend in the flour and add the evaporated milk and the 1 cup water, stirring until sauce boils and thickens. Then add salt, onion, and crushed and whole broccoli. Reheat to boiling and serve piping hot with crisp whole wheat crackers. 4 servings.

Note: 3 cups milk may be used in place of evaporated milk and water.

CREAM OF CARROT SOUP

1 bunch carrots
2½ cups boiling water
2 tbsp butter
1 tbsp chopped onion
5 tbsp flour

1⅔ cups coffee cream *or* 1 tall
  can evaporated milk
1 tsp salt
Crackers

Scrape carrots, slice, add boiling water, cover and boil until tender; drain, saving water (there should be about 2¼ cups; if less, add additional fresh water). Put carrots through a ricer or food mill. (There should be 1¼ cups riced carrots.) Melt butter in a 3-qt saucepan, add onion and cook until soft; then blend in flour, and add water from carrots and cream; cook over direct heat, stirring constantly until mixture boils and thickens. Add riced carrots and salt, and reheat. Serve piping hot with crisp crackers or croutons. 5 servings.

CREAM OF CAULIFLOWER SOUP

1 small head cauliflower,
  3 cups broken into
  flowerets
1 cup boiling water
1 cup rich Chicken Broth,
  p 1289, *or* canned
  consommé
1 tsp salt

2 tbsp butter
3 tbsp flour
1 cup water
1 cup cream *or* evaporated
  milk
¼ tsp freshly grated onion
2 tbsp chopped parsley

Drop cauliflowerets into boiling water. Boil uncovered for 6 min. Remove from heat, break fine with a fork, but do not mash. Add chicken broth and salt to cauliflower and its cooking water and heat gently. In another saucepan melt the butter, blend in the flour thoroughly until smooth. Add water gradually and heat until mixture boils and thickens. Stir in the cream and add to cauliflower. Add onion, stir to blend, heat to boiling and serve garnished with parsley. 4 servings.

CREAM OF CELERY SOUP

2 cups diced celery
1 small onion, chopped
1½ cups boiling water
½ tsp salt
¼ cup butter

¼ cup flour
1 qt milk
1¼ tsp salt
1 tsp chopped parsley, if
  desired

Select crisp celery, wash thoroughly, trim off any discoloration on root and any damaged portions; chop both leaves and stems. Simmer celery and onion until tender (10 min) in the boiling water with the ½ tsp salt. Melt butter in saucepan, blend in flour, add milk gradually and cook with constant stirring until sauce boils and thickens. Add the 1¼ tsp salt and cooked vegetables and their liquid. Heat to boiling and garnish with chopped parsley. Chopped or riced hard-cooked egg is also an attractive and nutritious garnish. 5 servings.

CREAM OF CORN SOUP

¼ cup finely chopped celery	2 tbsp butter
2 cups boiling water	Salt and pepper to taste
No. 2 can cream style corn	Popped corn
1 cup evaporated milk *or* coffee cream	Chopped parsley

Cook celery in the boiling water until soft. Add next four ingredients and heat thoroughly. The soup may be rubbed through a food mill or sieve, or it may be served without straining. Garnish with a sprinkling of Popped Corn, p 429, if desired, or serve with Croutons, p 262, crackers, or crisp toast. Sprinkle each bowlful with parsley. 5 servings.

CREAM OF FRESH CORN AND TOMATO SOUP

4 to 5 ears corn	1½ tsp sugar
3 tbsp butter	¼ tsp celery salt
1¼ tsp grated onion	1¼ cups milk
3 good sized tomatoes, 1¼ lbs	½ cup thin cream *or* evaporated milk
1 tsp salt	
1⁄16 tsp pepper	

Use freshly gathered ears of sweet corn with kernels in their thin milk stage. Remove shucks, silks, and any blemishes. Grate ears on a coarse grater to obtain a cream-like purée. There should be 1¼ cups. Heat butter in 3-qt saucepan, add onion, cook a min or so; then add corn. Set aside. Wash tomatoes, remove core, and blossom end, cut fine into another saucepan. Place over heat and boil gently until soft—3 or 4 min. Rub tomatoes through a sieve or food mill. There should be 1¾ cups purée. Add this to corn with the seasonings, and boil gently with constant stirring for about 10 min or until corn has a cooked flavor. Heat milk and cream; then *stir corn-tomato mixture into milk.* Serve at once in heated bowls. 4 servings.

CREAM OF CUCUMBER SOUP

3 tbsp butter *or* margarine	2 medium cucumbers
3 tbsp flour	1 cup boiling water
3 cups milk	½ tsp grated onion
1½ tsp salt	

Melt butter in top of double boiler over direct heat. Add flour gradually and blend well. Add milk slowly, stirring constantly until mixture boils and thickens. Add salt. Place over boiling water and continue to cook. Meanwhile, pare and cut the cucumbers into small pieces. Cook in the boiling water until just tender, about 5 min. Add white sauce to cucumbers and their liquid, flavor with onion and serve at once. 4 servings.

Variation: A delicious version of this soup may be made by substituting 1½ cups of richly flavored chicken broth for 1½ cups of the milk.

CREAM OF LETTUCE SOUP

¼ cup butter
¼ cup flour
½ tsp salt
1 qt milk
2 bouillon cubes *or* 2 tsp
   meat extract paste

¼ tsp fresh onion juice
1 qt finely shredded lettuce,
   pkd slightly
¼ cup finely diced radishes

In the top of a double boiler, make a white sauce from the first four ingredients. Cook until thickened, stirring occasionally to keep smooth. Add the bouillon cubes and onion juice and stir well. Add the lettuce and let cook over boiling water for 10 min. Just before serving, sprinkle the radishes over each bowlful. Serve promptly. 4 servings.

CREAM OF LIMA BEAN AND CARROT SOUP

1 cup dried lima beans
1 qt cold water
1 medium carrot, sliced
2 slices medium onion
4 sprigs parsley
1⅔ cups evaporated milk

1 tsp Worcestershire sauce
Few drops of tabasco, if
   desired
2 tsp salt
¹⁄₁₆ tsp black pepper

Wash beans and soak overnight. Drain, discarding the water. Add the cold water, cover, heat to boiling, then reduce heat and simmer slowly until about tender, 30 min. Then add vegetables and cook until tender, about 20 min longer. Rub through a sieve or food mill; there should be 3 cups pulp and liquid. If not, add water to make that amount. Combine purée with milk and seasonings and reheat to the boiling point just before serving. 5 servings.

Note: One cup milk and ⅔ cup coffee cream may be used in place of the evaporated milk.

CREAM OF MUSHROOM SOUP

½ lb fresh mushrooms
2 small slices onion,
   chopped
1 qt milk

1 cup evaporated milk
1 tsp salt
2 tbsp butter

Wash mushrooms quickly in cold water. Drain, trim off ends of stems and any blemishes. Chop fine. Place mushrooms and onion in top of double boiler, add milk, and cook over boiling water, stirring occasionally until mushrooms are tender (about 45 min). Add evaporated milk and salt, and stir in butter. Serve piping hot. 5 servings.

CREAM OF NAVY BEAN SOUP

1 cup dried navy beans
1 qt cold water
2 tbsp diced onion
1 cup evaporated milk
1 tsp salt

½ tsp celery salt
Dash pepper
2 tbsp grated carrot
(may be omitted)

Wash beans, cover with water and let stand overnight. Drain off water and discard, add the 1 qt of cold water and onion, cover, simmer about 1½ to 2 hrs or until beans are soft. Put through food mill or sieve, return to cooking kettle, add milk, seasonings and carrot and reheat. Serve hot. 5 servings.

CREAM OF ONION SOUP

2 slices bacon
1 cup sliced onions
2 tbsp flour
3 cups water

1⅔ cups evaporated milk
1 tsp salt, *or* to taste
Pepper to taste
5 slices buttered crisp toast

Cut the bacon fine with kitchen scissors, place in the soup kettle and fry until just done, add onion and flour, and stir until the flour is blended with drippings. Add water gradually, and stir thoroughly until mixture is smooth. Cover, and simmer until onion is tender, about 15 min. Add milk, salt, and pepper, and reheat, uncovered, to boiling. Place a slice of toast in the bottom of each soup bowl and pour hot soup over it and serve immediately. 5 servings.

CREAM OF PEA SOUP

No. 2 can peas, *or* 2½ cups
fresh cooked peas and
their liquid
Cold water
1 slice onion

1½ tsp sugar
1 tsp salt
2 cups thin White Sauce,
p 1262
Croutons

Drain liquid from peas, measure and add cold water to make 2 cups liquid. Place liquid and peas in a saucepan; add onion, sugar, and salt. Place over heat and simmer 5 min, then rub through a food mill or sieve. There should be 2½ cups purée and liquid. Combine with hot white sauce, reheat and serve hot. Float 2 or 3 Croutons, p 262, on each portion just before serving. 5 servings.

CREAM OF POTATO AND MUSHROOM SOUP

4 chicken bouillon cubes
1 qt boiling water
2 cups diced raw potatoes
1 small pkg dried mush-
rooms, ½ oz
½ tsp salt

⅛ tsp marjoram
1 tbsp finely chopped onion
1 tbsp butter
1 tbsp flour
¼ cup cream

Dissolve bouillon cubes in boiling water. Add potatoes, mushrooms, salt and marjoram and simmer for 25 min. Sauté onion in butter, blend in flour and brown. Add soup slowly, stir until slightly thickened. Just before serving, stir in cream and reheat. 4 to 5 servings.

CREAM OF POTATO SOUP

5 cups sliced raw potatoes	3 tbsp butter
1 medium onion, sliced	2⅔ cups milk, about
2 tsp salt	1 tbsp finely chopped parsley

Put potatoes and onion into a 3-qt saucepan and barely cover with cold water. Add salt, cover tightly, and heat to boiling; reduce heat and simmer for 10 min or until potatoes are perfectly tender. Mash potatoes in their liquid. Add butter and enough milk to give the desired thickness. Reheat to scalding, remove from heat and add chopped parsley. Serve immediately. 5 servings.

CREAM OF SPINACH SOUP

1 medium onion, sliced	1½ tsp flour
2 tbsp butter	3 tbsp cold water
3 cups Chicken or Veal Broth, p 1157, or 3 bouillon cubes in 3 cups hot water	2 cups drained cooked spinach, 2 lbs raw
¾ tsp salt	1 cup cream or evaporated milk
Pepper	Croutons

Sauté onion slowly in butter until soft. Add broth, seasonings, and flour blended to a smooth paste with the cold water. Cook over direct heat, stirring constantly until mixture boils. Add spinach which has been finely chopped or rubbed through a sieve and cream. Reheat to scalding and serve piping hot with Croutons, p 262, or crisp crackers. 5 servings.

CREAM OF TOMATO SOUP

No. 2½ can tomatoes or 3½ cups peeled, diced fresh tomatoes	¾ tsp whole black peppers
	2 slices onion
3 sprigs parsley	2 tsp sugar
6 whole cloves	¾ tsp salt
½ bay leaf	2½ cups thin White Sauce, p 1262

Put all ingredients except white sauce into a saucepan; heat to boiling, reduce heat and simmer for 5 min. Rub through a food mill or sieve. There should be 2 cups purée; if not, add boiling water. Have white sauce thoroughly heated in another pan. When ready to serve, combine by stirring the hot tomato purée slowly *into* the hot white sauce. Serve immediately. 5 servings.

If the seasoned tomato purée and white sauce are heated to the same temp and the purée is added to the white sauce with no further heating, there should be no curdling. If re-heating is necessary, it should be done over boiling water with constant stirring.

Variation: An easy version is to combine 2 cans of condensed tomato soup (10½ oz each) with an equal amount of milk or one-half evaporated milk and one-half water.

CREAM OF VEGETABLE SOUP

1 small turnip	1 cup water
1 medium-sized potato	2 tbsp flour
1 small white onion	1 qt milk
2 medium-sized carrots	1½ tsp salt *or* to taste
3 tbsp butter *or* bacon fat	Dash pepper
¼ cup chopped celery leaves	

Pare vegetables and chop or dice fine. Melt butter in saucepan and stir in vegetables and celery leaves. Add water, cover, and simmer for 10 min, stirring occasionally. Add flour blended to a smooth paste with a little of the milk, stir well, add rest of milk and heat to boiling, stirring constantly. Add seasonings and serve at once. 5 servings.

GOLDEN POTATO SOUP

1 lb rutabaga	2 cups milk
1½ cups water	2 tbsp butter *or* margarine
2½ tsp salt	Few dashes pepper
1 lb potatoes	1 tbsp chopped parsley
¾ tsp sugar	

Pare rutabaga and slice crosswise in thin chips. Put into saucepan. Add water and half of salt. Cover tightly, heat to boiling, reduce heat and cook at a gentle simmer 20 to 25 min. Then add potato, pared and sliced thinly. Again cover and cook until both potato and rutabaga are tender, about 10 min. Mash with potato masher, add rest of salt, sugar, milk, butter and pepper. Reheat to boiling. Serve immediately with chopped parsley. 4 generous servings.

LEEK AND POTATO SOUP

4 medium potatoes, 2½ cups cut in ¼-inch dice	3½ cups milk
	1 tbsp flour
2 small leeks, trimmed, sliced thin	2 tsp salt
	½ cup milk
½ cup chopped celery	1 tbsp butter *or* margarine
2 cups water	

Put potatoes, leeks, celery and water into kettle. Cover and boil 8 to 10 min, or until about tender. Add the 3½ cups milk, then the flour and salt blended with the ½ cup milk to form a smooth paste. Stir thoroughly, reheat to the boiling point, stirring often, then simmer 2 or 3 min. 4 generous servings.

OYSTER BISQUE OR CHOWDER

½ pt oysters with liquor
2 tbsp butter
2 tbsp flour
2 cups cream *or* evaporated milk

2 cups water
⅛ tsp celery salt
¾ tsp salt
Crackers, heated

Drain oysters, saving the liquor. Cut oysters very fine in a chopping bowl or with kitchen scissors. Melt butter, blend in flour, add oysters and liquor, heat to boiling, stirring constantly. Add cream, water, seasonings; reheat. Serve immediately with crackers. 5 servings.

PEA AND RICE SOUP

¼ cup converted *or* enriched rice
3 cups boiling water
2 chicken bouillon cubes
1 cup cooked peas
1 tbsp chopped onion

2½ cups milk
1 tsp salt
1 tbsp parsley
½ tsp celery salt
1 tbsp butter

Put rice in top of double boiler, add water, cook according to directions on box until tender. Add remaining ingredients, stir thoroughly and place over boiling water to reheat thoroughly. Fresh celery tops or dried celery leaves may be used in place of the celery salt. 4 servings.

PUMPKIN SOUP No. 1

2 tbsp chopped onion
2 tsp chopped green pepper
2 tbsp margarine *or* butter
2 cups milk
1 cup cooked pumpkin

¾ tsp salt
Pepper
⅛ tsp Worcestershire sauce
Chopped parsley

Sauté onion and green pepper slowly in the margarine for 5 min. Add next five ingredients and cook over hot water until very hot. Add parsley just before serving. 4 servings.

PUMPKIN SOUP No. 2

1 tbsp finely chopped onion
½ tbsp butter
1½ cups cooked tomatoes
1 cup cooked pumpkin
1 cup cream

½ cup milk
¾ to 1 tsp salt
Pepper
1 tsp sugar

Sauté onion in butter for 2 min. Add tomatoes, pumpkin and heat thoroughly over low heat. Add remaining ingredients and reheat to simmering. Remove from heat and serve immediately. Makes about 2 cups. 4 servings.

RICE AND SPINACH SOUP

⅓ cup brown rice
1 qt boiling water
2 tsp salt
2 cups milk

2 tbsp finely chopped onion
¼ lb raw spinach, finely cut
2 tbsp margarine
Paprika

Add rice to boiling salted water and cook uncovered until rice is thoroughly tender (from 40 to 45 min). Add next four ingredients and simmer for 10 min. Serve at once with a sprinkling of paprika on each bowl for garnish. 4 servings.

SALMON BISQUE

¼ cup butter
¼ cup chopped onion
¼ cup finely chopped celery
¼ cup flour
3 cups milk

1½ tsp salt
1 cup tomato juice
1 lb can pink salmon
2 tbsp chopped parsley
Lemon wedges

Melt butter in top of double boiler over direct heat. Add onion and celery and sauté over low heat for 5 min. Add flour and blend thoroughly. Add the milk gradually and place over boiling water. Cook with occasional stirring until mixture is smooth and slightly thickened. Add salt and gradually add the tomato juice stirring constantly. Discard dark skin of salmon, flake the fish, crush the bones and add crushed bones and flaked fish to the cream sauce. Keep over boiling water just long enough to thoroughly heat. Add parsley and serve immediately. Serve with wedges of lemon, if desired. Makes 6 cups.

SOUPS CONTAINING MEAT, MEAT STOCK, BOUILLON OR TOMATO JUICE

AVOCADO CHICKEN SOUP

An unusual and delicious soup

2 cups Rich Chicken Broth, p 1289	2 tsp grated onion
1 cup milk	1 medium, well-ripened
2 tbsp flour	avocado, 1¼ cups
	Salt

Heat chicken broth to boiling. Make a thin paste with ¼ cup of the milk and the flour; stir this thoroughly into the rest of the milk. Add flour-milk mixture slowly to hot broth and again heat to boiling, stir occasionally and cook until the mixture boils and slightly thickens. Add onion and the avocado which has just been mashed or put through a sieve. Add salt to taste. Heat and serve immediately. 4 servings.

BEEF AND NOODLE SOUP

Have the butcher crack a 2½ to 3-lb soup bone in several places. Wipe thoroughly with a damp cloth and put compactly into a soup kettle; barely cover with cold water. Heat to boiling, cover tightly, reduce heat and simmer gently for at least 2 hrs. This will give concentrated beef broth. Drain off broth and skim off excess fat. Add enough water to make 6 cups. Season to suit taste with salt and pepper. Add noodles (about 4 oz) or ½ cup white, raw rice and cook briskly until tender, about 20 min. Add more salt if needed. 5 servings.

Variation: The meat on the bone may be removed, chopped and added to the soup.

BEEF BOUILLON

Place 1 bouillon cube or an equal quantity of bouillon powder or meat extract paste in each cup and pour boiling water over it, stirring until dissolved. Strength of bouillon will depend on size of cup and amount of water used. Canned beef bouillon requires only heating and, if condensed, the adddition of water to prepare for serving. A pleasing drink, which is not a true bouillon, is prepared by substituting hot milk for water with either the bouillon cube or canned bouillon.

BEEF VEGETABLE SOUP

2 to 3 lbs beef shank
7 cups cold water
2 tbsp salt
½ cup diced carrots
½ cup cut celery, outer
stalks and leaves
½ cup finely sliced cabbage

½ cup diced turnips
1 cup finely diced sweet
potatoes
1 cup cubed Irish potatoes
2 cups canned tomatoes
1 small onion

Select a meaty beef shank. Add an extra bone or knuckle if possible and have the bones sawed into several pieces. Add water and salt, place over low heat and slowly heat to boiling, then reduce heat, cover, and gently simmer for 3 hrs. Skim off excess fat. Strain off broth and add the vegetables and cook another 30 min or until vegetables are just tender. Serve piping hot. Remove meat from bones, chop and add to the soup or use for Potted Meat Sandwich Filling, p 1230. Approximately 2½ qts.

BOHEMIAN SPLIT PEA SOUP

1 cup split peas
1 qt water
¼ tsp dried dill seeds
or small spray of fresh dill
1½ tsp salt
¼ cup sliced green onion

½ cup chopped celery
2 tbsp butter
2 frankfurters cut crosswise
into ¼-inch pieces
Croutons

Pick over peas and wash thoroughly through two or three waters. Put water into soup kettle, heat to boiling, then add peas, dill seed and salt, cover and cook over low heat 1 hr, stirring from time to time with a fork to prevent sticking. Add green onion and celery and continue cooking until peas are soft, about ½ hr. Melt butter in saucepan, add frankfurters, brown slightly. Press vegetable mixture through a sieve or food mill over frankfurters in saucepan. Simmer 10 to 15 min longer. Serve with croutons or a few slices of toasted rye bread cooked in the soup the last ten min. 4 servings.

CABBAGE RICE SOUP

2 tbsp butter or margarine
¼ cup chopped onion
¼ cup raw rice
1 qt water
4 chicken bouillon cubes

½ tsp salt
2½ cups finely shredded tender
cabbage
¼ cup grated sharp cheese
Paprika

Melt butter in saucepan. Add onions and sauté for 5 min. Add rest of the ingredients except the cabbage and cheese, cover, and simmer for 15 min. Add the cabbage and cook uncovered another 5 min. Sprinkle 1 tbsp of grated cheese on top of each serving, then a dash of paprika. Serve immediately. 4 servings.

CHESTNUT SQUASH SOUP

Delicious, unusual in flavor and texture—ideal for between holiday meals

2 cups rich chicken *or* veal broth
1 acorn squash, 1¼ lbs, *or* an equal amount of Hubbard squash, 1 cup purée
½ lb chestnuts, 1 cup shelled
1 cup rich milk *or* ½ cup

evaporated milk and ½ cup water
1 tsp salt
¹⁄₁₆ tsp black pepper
¼ tsp onion juice
Few drops lemon juice, optional
Chopped parsley

Prepare broth by simmering 2 lbs bony pieces of chicken or veal, 1 small onion and 2 branches celery in 2½ cups water with 1 tsp salt until meat is tender, about 1½ hrs. Or dissolve 2 chicken bouillon cubes in 2 cups boiling water. Cut squash in half, remove seeds and grease cut surfaces with shortening. Turn upside down on baking sheet. Put chestnuts in shallow pan. Put squash and chestnuts in moderately hot oven (400° F). Bake chestnuts 15 to 20 min, shake pan once or twice. Bake squash 30 to 35 min, or until tender. Cool chestnuts slightly, and strip off shells and thin brown skin. Crush chestnuts fine with wooden potato masher or a wooden spoon. Add to broth. Scoop squash from shells, mash, add to soup; then add next 5 ingredients; heat just to boiling and stir occasionally. Pour into heated bowls; add a sprinkle of parsley. Serve with French bread or rye toast. 4 to 5 servings.

CHICKEN BROTH WITH RICE

Use at least 3 lbs of bony pieces of stewing chicken, such as wings, rib pieces and neck for making soup. Arrange compactly in the soup kettle. Barely cover with 2 qts cold water, heat to boiling, then reduce heat, remove any scum, cover, and simmer until meat slips easily from bones and broth has good, rich chicken flavor, about 1½ hrs. One onion, sliced, and 2 branches of celery may be added during the last half hr of cooking. Strain soup into another kettle. Skim off any excess fat. Return meat removed from the bones to soup. Season with salt and pepper to taste. Add 1½ cups Boiled Rice, p 434, and reheat to boiling. Serve piping hot with crackers. Chopped parsley may be sprinkled on top of each serving as a garnish. 5 servings.

CHICKEN BARLEY SOUP

From leftover chicken

Thoroughly broken up
carcasses of 2 roast chickens
1 small onion, sliced
3 tbsp butter *or* margarine
5 cups water
Small pod red pepper
¼ cup celery leaves

1½ tsp salt
4 tsp pearl barley
2½ cups boiling water
¼ tsp salt
¼ cup finely diced carrot
½ cup thinly sliced celery
2 tbsp parsley

Brown bones and onion lightly in heated fat in soup kettle. Add the next 4 ingredients, cover and heat to boiling, reduce heat, and gently simmer for 2 hrs. Strain. While the bones are being simmered, drop the pearl barley into the 2½ cups boiling water, add salt, cover and simmer for 1 hr 15 min. Then add the strained broth, carrots and celery and boil 10 additional min. Serve hot with a sprinkling of parsley on each serving. 4 servings.

RICH CHICKEN BROTH

An essential for many good dishes such as curries, chicken soup, chicken gravy, etc

2 lbs bony pieces chicken—
necks, backs, ribs, gizzards,
hearts, feet
3 cups cold water

2 tsp salt
1 branch celery
1 onion, size of egg
2 *or* 3 sprigs parsley

Put all the ingredients in a 3-qt saucepan. Cover, heat to boiling, reduce heat to simmering, and cook 2 or 3 hrs or until meat on bones is very tender. Strain off broth. Use immediately or cool. Cover tightly, and keep in refrigerator until ready for use. Chicken broth doesn't retain fine flavor very long, so plan to use it within a day or so for the desired results. 2 cups broth.

Note: Meat on bones may be chopped and used for sandwich filling.

COCKALEEKIE SOUP

6 leeks, cut into ⅛-inch
slices (about 4 cups)
3 cups water
1 tsp salt

2 tbps chicken fat
1½ cups rich, well seasoned
Chicken Broth, above
½ cup cream

Wash leeks and trim off roots and all but an inch of the coarse green tops, and discard. Cut leeks into ⅛-inch slices, place in a saucepan and add water and salt; simmer uncovered for 5 to 7 min or until leeks are tender but not mushy. Add remaining ingredients and heat just to boiling. Serve immediately. Makes 5 to 6 cups—4 to 6 servings.

COLD TOMATO SOUP

2⅔ cups fresh tomato purée,   2 tsp lemon juice
  6 to 8 fully ripe tomatoes   1 tbsp sugar
1 cup ice water   ½ cup sour cream
2 tsp salt   1 tbsp cut chives *or* green
¼ tsp onion juice   onions

Prepare purée by pressing washed, quartered, red, ripe tomatoes through a sieve or food mill. Chill purée thoroughly. When ready to serve, add water, salt, onion juice, lemon juice, sugar and mix. Add ¼ cup sour cream and beat with a rotary beater. Serve cold with a garnish of sour cream and a few cut chives or green onions sprinkled over the top. 4 generous servings.

DUCK SOUP

Use bones of 2 medium or 3 small roast ducks. Break into small pieces; arrange bones compactly in a soup kettle, cover with cold water, about 7 cups, and add 2 or 3 branches of celery and 1 carrot, sliced. Heat to boiling, reduce heat and remove scum; cover and simmer until a rich-flavored broth is obtained, about 2 hrs. Strain soup into another kettle. Skim off excess fat. Then add the meat left on bones to broth. Add 2 cups Boiled Rice, p 434. Reheat and season with salt and pepper. 5 servings.

HOT TOMATO BOUILLON

No. 2½ can tomatoes   Dash pepper
1 cup water   1 lemon
2 beef bouillon cubes   1 tsp chopped parsley
Salt to taste

Rub tomatoes through sieve or a food mill to remove seeds. Heat purée with water and bouillon cubes to the boiling point. Season and serve hot with a thin slice of lemon floating on the top and a sprinkling of parsley for each serving. 5 servings.

ITALIAN SOUP—MINESTRA

A delicious soup of two colors

3 tbsp butter   ⅛ tsp nutmeg
2 qts Beef Broth, p 1286   1 whole egg
1 cup boiling milk   1 egg yolk
1¾ cups cake flour   ½ cup grated **Parmesan** cheese
¼ tsp salt   ¼ cup cooked spinach

Dumplings:
Melt butter in saucepan, add 1 cup of the beef broth and boiling milk and heat to boiling. Add the flour all at once and blend, then

add salt and nutmeg and stir with a wooden spoon to smooth paste over a low flame. Remove from fire and stir in egg, egg yolk and cheese. Divide in 2 parts. Add well drained chopped spinach to one half and leave the other as is.

Soup:

Heat remaining broth to boiling. Quickly add dumplings by dipping the tsp first into the hot broth, then into the dumpling mixtures and drop into the boiling broth. When the desired number of the dumplings are in, cover and cook about 10 min. (The uncooked dumpling mixture may be held over for a day or two in the refrigerator.) Serve at once. 6 to 7 servings.

JELLIED TOMATO BOUILLON

To Hot Tomato Bouillon, p 1290, while boiling hot, add 1 tbsp plain gelatin which has been softened 5 min in ¼ cup cold water. Cool, place in refrigerator to congeal. Serve in cold dishes with a wedge of lemon or spoonful of sour cream. 5 servings.

KIDNEY BEAN SOUP

2½ slices bacon	1½ cups water
2½ tbsp bacon drippings	1 tsp salt
1 medium-sized onion chopped	2 cups Cooked, drained Kidney Beans, p 1316
¾ cup finely diced celery	1 cup canned tomatoes
1½ tbsp finely diced green pepper	1 tbsp fresh onion juice
3 small carrots, scraped	1 tbsp chopped parsley

Pan-fry bacon until delicately browned and remove from saucepan to crisp; there should be about 2½ tbsp bacon drippings in the pan. Sauté onion, celery and green pepper in the drippings for about 5 min. Add sliced carrots, water and salt to the saucepan; cover and simmer about 5 min. Meanwhile rub beans through a coarse sieve, gradually adding ½ cup water to the beans while pressing them through. There should be 1½ cups purée. Grate one medium onion, press out enough juice to make 1 tbsp and add it, the bean purée and the tomatoes to the hot vegetable mixture. Reheat to boiling and serve hot with crisp bacon and chopped parsley sprinkled over the top. 4 generous servings.

LAMB BROTH

2½ lbs lamb shoulder	1 green onion *or* 1 tbsp chopped onion
1½ tsp salt	¼ bay leaf
1 branch celery	Pinch of thyme

Have butcher cut meat in 4 to 6 pieces. Wipe with damp cloth. Fit compactly in a kettle and cover meat with cold water; add remaining ingredients and heat to boiling. Skim and reduce heat as low as possible; cover, simmer for 1 to 1½ hrs. Cool until fat on surface is congealed, then skim fat off. Strain if desired, reheat, and serve with crackers or Croutons, p 262. Meat may be removed from bone, chopped and added to broth for additional flavor and nutritive value. 5 servings.

LAMB BROTH WITH BARLEY

3 large lamb shanks	2 sprigs parsley
2 tbsp shortening	1 tsp sugar
1 qt cold water	½ cup uncooked barley
4 tsp salt	7 cups boiling water
1 cup coarsely cut celery	2 cups canned tomatoes
½ cup coarsely sliced carrot	

Trim only the largest muscles of meat from bones, grind and use for lamb patties. Discard fat. Saw bones in half and brown well on all sides in 2 tbsp shortening. Combine with the cold water and 2 tsp of the salt. Heat to boiling, cover, reduce heat and simmer for 2 to 2½ hrs, adding fresh vegetables and sugar the last hr. Remove bones and trim off bits of meat. Skim off fat and strain the broth. Purée the vegetables. Combine meat, puréed vegetables and broth. Meanwhile, cook barley for about 1½ hrs in the boiling water with the remaining salt. When barley is tender, add to broth without draining. Add tomatoes and simmer for 15 min. Serve hot. Makes 7 to 8 cups.

LIVER DUMPLING SOUP

A pleasant German way of eating liver

¼ lb calf *or* chicken liver	2 eggs, separated
⅓ cup fine dry bread crumbs	½ tsp salt
2 tsp flour	Dash or 2 of nutmeg
1 tsp soft butter	1 qt chicken *or* beef broth
½ tsp grated onion	Chopped parsley
1 tsp fine-cut parsley	

Remove skin and veins from liver, then put into bowl and chop fine with a biscuit cutter or kitchen scissors. Stir in crumbs mixed with the flour, and let stand 5 to 10 min. Add butter, onion, parsley, egg yolks, salt and nutmeg and mix well. Beat egg whites until stiff, then carefully fold into meat mixture. Dip a tsp into the gently boiling broth, then into meat mixture, turning spoon to shape round dumplings; drop into broth. Boil 15 min. Ladle balls and broth into heated bowls; sprinkle with parsley and serve with crisp crackers. 4 servings.

LIVER AND VEGETABLE SOUP

½ lb liver
1 tbsp butter *or* margarine
2 tbsp chopped onions
½ tsp seasoning salt

¼ tsp salt
1 can vegetable soup, 10½ oz
1½ cups hot water
Parsley

Remove skin and tubes from liver. Barely cover with water, heat to boiling, then simmer 5 min. Drain off liquid. Discard. Cool liver and put through a food chopper. Heat butter in a saucepan. Sauté onions in it for 5 min. Add liver and seasonings and sauté lightly for 3 min. Add soup and water and heat to boiling. Turn heat low and simmer for 3 min. Garnish each bowl with a tsp of chopped parsley. Serve immediately. 4 servings.

MINESTRONE

This hearty nutritious Italian soup with bread, salad and fruit dessert is a good meal

½ cup kidney *or* red beans
1½ lbs beef soup bone
½ lb lean beef
1½ qts water
2½ tsp salt
2 slices bacon, chopped
¼ lb ham, chopped
½ cup finely-chopped celery
1 cup chopped onion
¾ cup sliced leek, 1 large
1 medium clove garlic, crushed

1 zucchini, 4 x 1½ inches
No. 2 can tomatoes, 2½ cups
2 cups shredded cabbage
½ cup broken spaghetti *or* macaroni *or* rice
⅛ to ¼ tsp pepper
½ tsp dried basil
¼ tsp allspice
Grated fresh Parmesan cheese

Wash beans, cover with plenty of water and soak overnight. Have soup bone cracked. Wipe both bone and meat with damp cloth. Cut meat into small pieces. Place in soup kettle with bone, add water and salt. Cover tightly, heat to boiling, reduce heat and simmer 1½ hrs. Now add drained beans. Put bacon and ham in skillet with next 5 ingredients and sauté slowly, stirring almost constantly until fat tries out and vegetables are soft. Turn into soup kettle and simmer for another 1½ hrs or until beans are about tender. Now add tomatoes, cabbage, spaghetti and pepper; cook 20 min or until spaghetti is tender. Add basil and allspice the last 5 min of cooking. Remove soup bone; strip off clinging meat and add to soup. Ladle into hot bowls; sprinkle cheese over top. Serve with crisp crackers, Italian or French bread. 4 to 5 servings.

OXTAIL SOUP

2 oxtails, about 3½ lbs   ¼ tsp pepper
2½ qts cold water   1 cup diced potatoes
¼ cup barley   1 tbsp chopped parsley
½ cup chopped onion   1 tbsp Caramel, p 165,
½ cup diced carrot   kitchen bouquet, or other
1 tbsp salt   food coloring

Wipe oxtails with damp cloth. Chop at joints, making pieces 1 to 2 inches long. Put into soup kettle. Add water and barley, cover, and when water boils, reduce heat and simmer gently for 2 hrs. Skim off excess fat then add onion, carrot, salt and pepper, and continue cooking for 20 min. Add potatoes and cook until vegetables are tender. Remove oxtails, separate meat from bone and return meat to soup. Add parsley and caramel or other coloring. Serve hot. 5 or 6 servings.

CARRIE'S SPECIAL PEA SOUP

Delicious soup with golden ruffles and white dice. Green peas may be used instead of the yellow

2 qts rich beef broth   1 cup potatoes cut in ½-inch
1½ cups whole dried yellow   cubes
  peas   1 egg
1 branch celery   2 tsp flour
1 medium onion, chopped   Salt and pepper to taste

Start beef broth about 3 hrs before mealtime. Buy a 2½ lb meaty soup bone. Have butcher saw it in 4 or 5 pieces. Wipe pieces, put into soup kettle. Add 2 qts water and 4 tsp salt, cover, heat to boiling then reduce heat and *simmer* 1½ to 2 hrs, or until meat is tender and broth is rich in flavor. Lift out meat and bones. Add peas that have been washed and the sliced celery and chopped onion. Cover and simmer for about 45 min or until peas are about tender. Then add potatoes and simmer until barely tender, about 20 min. Do not cook potatoes until the cubes break. Season with salt and pepper. Now increase heat under soup. Beat egg, then beat in the flour until smooth and about 5 min before serving, drizzle this batter in a thin stream into the soup that is boiling very gently to cook into rippling thread-like noodles. Serve piping hot. Serves 6.

Note: Remove meat from soup bone, chop fine. To make sandwich filling, season with salt, pepper, add finely chopped celery and a few drops onion juice and enough salad dressing to give a spreading consistency. To make croquettes, add thick white sauce to the seasoned chopped meats. Shape croquettes, crumb and dip in egg and crumbs again. Fry in deep hot fat and serve with hot mushroom sauce (heated cream of mushroom soup).

PHILADELPHIA PEPPER POT

2½ lbs veal knuckle with
   some meat on it
5 cups cold water
2½ tsp salt
1 cup chopped celery
¾ cup chopped green pepper
¾ cup chopped onion
3 tbsp butter *or* margarine
2 tbsp flour
1 cup cooked tripe (cut into
   ½-inch sqs)*

2 cups diced raw potatoes
½ cup sliced leek
⅛ tsp marjoram
⅛ tsp thyme
½ of medium bay leaf
Dash of cayenne
1½ cups diced cooked veal
1 small hot red pepper pod,
   if desired for a hotter soup

Have the knuckle sawed through the center. Wipe clean with a damp cloth. Put the veal knuckle, water and 2 tsp of the salt into a soup kettle, cover and heat to boiling. Then reduce heat and simmer for 2 hrs. Remove meat and strain broth. There should be 3½ cups of broth. Sauté celery, green pepper and onion in butter for 10 min. Add flour and blend, then add veal broth gradually and stir over low heat until mixture is smooth. Add tripe, potatoes and leek and simmer covered for 10 min, or until potatoes are done. Do not over-cook vegetables. Add remaining ingredients and reheat. Remove bay leaf and pepper pod and serve immediately. 4 to 5 servings. Makes 6 cups.

QUICK RUTABAGA CHEESE SOUP

2 cups grated raw rutabaga
   firmly pkd, about 1 lb
2 cups boiling water
2 tbsp bacon drippings
3 tbsp flour
1¾ cups milk
1 chicken bouillon cube

⅓ lb sharp cheese, grated,
   1½ cups
½ tsp salt
¾ tsp seasoning salt
½ tsp sugar
1 tbsp chopped parsley

Cut rutabaga in 1-inch slices. Pare slices and grate on a medium coarse grater. Place in saucepan with the boiling water and cook, uncovered, until just tender, about 8 min. Heat bacon drippings in another saucepan, blend in flour, add milk and cook with constant stirring until the sauce boils and thickens. Then add rutabaga and cooking water, and stir in bouillon cube, cheese and seasonings. Stir while reheating to serving temp. Sprinkle each serving with parsley. 4 servings.

*Tripe should always be purchased cooked.

QUICK TOMATO OKRA SOUP

3 tbsp butter *or* margarine	2 cups Chicken *or* Veal
1 medium-sized onion	Broth,* p 1288
⅓ cup finely chopped celery	¼ tsp salt
¼ lb okra, 1 cup sliced	Dash of pepper
1 lb tomatoes, 2 cups	2 tbsp finely shredded ham
peeled, chopped	*or* grated cheese (sharp)

Melt butter in deep skillet or low heavy saucepan; add chopped onion and celery, then okra on top. Cover tightly and cook slowly five or six min, or until onion and celery are slightly soft. Push vegetables to one side of skillet, add tomatoes. Cover and cook 5 min. Add remaining ingredients except ham. Reheat, stir gently; add ham or cheese and serve immediately. 4 servings.

RUSSIAN RED CABBAGE SOUP

Goose and Cabbage Soup

Carcass of 10 to 12 lb goose	1 cup canned *or* fresh peeled
6 cups cold water	tomatoes
1½ tsp salt	⅔ cup leftover gravy
1 medium onion, sliced	2 to 3 cups finely shredded
3 tbsp vinegar	red cabbage
1½ to 2 tsp sugar	Bits of leftover goose

Break bones in small pieces and turn into a kettle. Add water, salt, and onion, cover and heat to boiling. Reduce heat and simmer for 2 hrs. Strain. Add remaining ingredients to the strained broth and boil gently, covered, for 15 min until heated through and cabbage is tender. Serve immediately. 4 servings.

SCOTCH BROTH

⅓ cup barley	½ cup diced carrot
1½ lbs lamb shoulder	½ cup diced celery
1½ qts water	½ cup diced turnip
1 tbsp salt	2 tbsp chopped parsley
¼ tsp pepper	

Add 1 pt of water to barley, cover and soak 2 hrs. Remove lamb meat from bones and cut into ½-inch cubes. Put meat and bones into kettle, add water, salt and pepper. Simmer gently, covered, until meat is tender, about 1½ hrs. Skim off excess fat. Drain barley and add to broth. Add carrot, celery and turnip and continue to simmer until vegetables and barley are done, from 30 to 40 min. Serve piping hot sprinkled with parsley. 4 servings.

*If broth is not available, use 2 chicken bouillon cubes and 2 cups of water.

SPLIT PEA SOUP

½ ham bone
1 qt boiling water
1 bay leaf
⅛ tsp celery seed

Pinch of thyme, if desired
1 cup green split peas
1 medium tomato, peeled,
  or ½ cup canned tomatoes

Use bone from which almost all meat is removed; crack bone, put into soup kettle, add remaining ingredients. Cover and simmer 1 to 1½ hrs or until peas are mushy. Remove bone, strain soup, pressing peas through sieve. Reheat to boiling. Serve hot. 5 servings.

TURKEY SOUP No. 1

Bones from 12 to 14 lb
  roast turkey
7 cups water
3 branches celery
2 carrots, diced

1 small onion, chopped
½ cup raw rice
1 tbsp salt
2 cups milk
2 sprigs parsley, chopped

Crack turkey bones, add water, chopped celery, carrots and onion. Cover, *simmer* 1½ hrs. Strain out bones and vegetables. There should be 1½ qts of broth. Reheat broth to boiling. Add rice and salt. Simmer 30 min longer or until rice is done. Add milk, reheat. Sprinkle freshly chopped parsley over each bowlful. 4 servings.

TURKEY SOUP No. 2

Bones from 10 to 12 lb
  roast turkey
6 cups cold water
2 tsp salt
2 cups coarsely cut celery,
  a few leaves

1 medium onion, coarsely
  chopped
2 carrots, coarsely chopped
1 cup leftover dressing
Parsley, finely chopped

Crack bones and place compactly in a kettle. Add the next 5 ingredients. Cover and heat to boiling, then reduce heat and simmer for 2 hrs. Strain. (There should be 5 cups broth.) Separate or cut dressing into small pieces and add. Heat thoroughly and serve with a sprinkling of parsley over each bowl. 4 to 5 servings.

VEGETABLE SOUP

2½ lb soup bone, meaty
  shank bone
½ lb heel of beef round
2 tbsp shortening
7 cups water
½ bay leaf, if desired
¼ tsp marjoram, if desired

3 whole black peppers
¼ cup sliced onions
1 tbsp salt
3 cups fresh vegetables,
  finely chopped
Crackers
1 tbsp parsley, finely chopped

Have soup bone cracked by butcher. Cut meat removed from bone and the round in small cubes and brown half of it in shortening. Add remaining meat, bone, water, spices tied in a cheesecloth bag, onion and salt; cover, simmer 2½ to 3 hrs. Strain through cheesecloth, reserving meat. Skim excess fat from broth, add remaining ingredients except parsley. Boil until vegetables are tender. Serve soup piping hot with crisp crackers. Carrots, celery, green beans, peas, lima beans and potatoes are all excellent soup vegetables. If desired, some of the meat may be chopped and served in the soup, or all of it may be saved for croquettes or hash at another meal. Sprinkle finely chopped parsley over each bowlful of soup. 5 servings.

PEPPY VEGETABLE SOUP

A well-made vegetable soup is the best there is

2 qts rich beef broth	1 pt canned tomatoes
1 medium onion, chopped	2 branches celery, sliced
2 medium carrots, cut in	¼-inch thick
½-inch cubes	3 *or* 4 sprigs parsley
1 cup coarsely chopped cabbage	

Prepare beef broth by *simmering* a 2½ lb meaty beef soup bone in 2 qts water with 4 tsp salt, for 1½ hrs in a tightly covered kettle. Lift out bones, add onion, carrots, cabbage and celery and simmer 30 min, then add tomatoes and parsley and continue simmering another 30 min. Remove beef from bones, cut into half-inch dice, add to soup and reheat. 5 to 6 servings.

SUMMER SOUPS

COLD BEET BORSCH, p 1266, COLD TOMATO SOUP, p 1290, JELLIED TOMATO BOUILLON, p 1291, VICHYSSOISE, p 1298

VICHYSSOISE

A fine French soup for company meals. Best when prepared well in advance. Serve cold in summer and hot in winter

3 small leeks, ½ cup	2 to 3 dashes nutmeg
½ egg-size onion	Dash of pepper
1 branch celery, ⅓ cup	¼ tsp salt
1 tbsp poultry fat *or* butter	½ cup cold thin cream
½ lb potatoes, 1 large	Chopped chives
2 cups rich chicken broth	

Clean vegetables and chop first 3 fine. Heat fat in saucepan, add chopped vegetables, cover and sauté until soft but not browned—about 5 min. Add potatoes cut in quarters and well-seasoned chicken broth; cover, heat to boiling, reduce heat and simmer 15 to 20 min or until vegetables are soft. Put mixture through a sieve or food mill. Add seasonings. Cover and chill in refrigerator. The flavor mellows on standing several hrs. To serve cold, stir in cream just before serving; reheat with cream to serve hot. Sprinkle each serving with chives. 3½ cups or 4 servings.

CURRIED VICHYSSOISE

Add 1 tsp or more curry powder to 2 tbsp boiling water, stir well and beat into Vichyssoise (above) before chilling.

SOUP BLENDS

CHICKEN NEWBURG SOUP

10½-oz can concentrated cream
  of mushroom soup
10½-oz can concentrated
  chicken noodle soup

1 cup water
2 tsp sherry extract
Paprika

Mix two soups and water well in a heavy saucepan. Cook over low heat until simmering but do not boil. Beat with a rotary beater to creamy smoothness. Ladle into 4 heated bowls and stir a tsp of sherry into each. Serve at once with a dash of paprika or a tiny sprig of parsley floated on top if desired. 4 servings.

SEA FOOD BISQUE

5-oz can moist-pack shrimp,
  cleaned, cut small
1 tsp finely chopped onion
2 tbsp butter or margarine
2 cups milk

10½-oz can concentrated cream
  of mushroom soup
10½-oz can concentrated cream
  of asparagus soup
1 tsp sherry extract

Sauté shrimp and onion in butter for 5 min. Add remaining ingredients gradually and stir until thoroughly blended. Heat to boiling. Serve at once. Makes 1 qt—4 servings.

Note: Crab meat or lobster may be substituted for shrimp.

SPINACH CONSOMMÉ

10½-oz can concentrated cream
  of spinach soup
10½-oz can concentrated
  consomme
1 cup water

¼ tsp salt
⅛ tsp sugar
⅛ tsp celery seed
Sour cream

Combine first 6 ingredients in a saucepan and heat to boiling. Serve immediately with a tsp of sour cream on each serving. 4 servings.

BEET TOMATO SOUP

1 tbsp butter	2 cups tomato juice *or*
1 tbsp finely chopped onion	canned tomatoes, sieved
2 cups diced, sliced *or*	1 bouillon cube
julienned canned beets	Half dozen rosemary
with juice	leaflets

Melt butter in saucepan, add onion and sauté until soft. Add rest of the ingredients, simmer gently 5 min. Serve in hot soup bowls. Cheese crackers are an excellent accompaniment. 4 to 5 servings.

CHICK PEA SOUP

Spanish Bean (garbanzos)

½ lb chick peas, *or* garbanzos	2 tbsp lard
1 beef soup bone, 2 lbs	Pinch of saffron
1 ham hock, 1 lb	3 medium potatoes
2 qts water	Salt and pepper
1 medium onion	Parsley

Pick over peas, wash thoroughly, add enough water to cover them 2 inches deep. Add 1 tbsp salt. Stir and let soak overnight. When ready to cook, drain off water, turn peas into soup kettle. Add beef bone that butcher has sawed in 3 or 4 pieces and ham hock that has been washed. Add 2 qts water. Cover, simmer 1½ hrs or until tender. Fry chopped onion in lard until soft and yellow, add onion, saffron, and pared potatoes to kettle, cook until peas and potatoes are tender. Add salt and pepper to taste. Lift out soup bone and ham hock. Remove any meat from bone, chop and return to soup. Serve very hot with sprinkling of parsley. Thick diagonal slices of reheated French bread make an attractive and palatable accompaniment. 4 servings.

Timbales

Timbales are of two types. The first, a custard or soufflé-like mixture is baked until firm in small molds such as custard cups, set in a pan of hot water. When baked, they are unmolded after standing 2 or 3 min and served warm as the main course, with or without an appropriate sauce.

The second type is a timbale or patty shell or case, plus creamed meat, fish, poultry or vegetable filling. Timbale or Patty Shells are made of Puff Pastry, p 937, Timbale Cases are made by dipping special Swedish rosette irons into batter and frying in deep fat, p 612, or Croustade Cases, p 263. The rich composition of timbales makes them the *main food* in the meal. Because they are dainty and reveal the touch of a fastidious cook (though easy to make) they are ideal for luncheon entrees.

CHEESE TIMBALES

1 cup milk
½ cup grated sharp cheddar cheese, pkd
½ tsp salt

Pepper
⅛ to ¼ tsp onion juice
3 eggs

Start oven 10 min before baking; set to moderate (350° F). Heat milk in top of double boiler until scalded. Add cheese, stir until almost melted, then stir in next 3 ingredients. Beat eggs until well blended, then add milk mixture, stir thoroughly. Pour into 4 well buttered custard cups holding from ⅞ to 1 cup. Set in a pan (preferably glass or enamelware), place in oven and pour in hot water to come up almost to top of cups. Bake 25 to 30 min. Cool 2 or 3 min. Run a thin-bladed knife around edge of timbales and unmold onto warm serving plates. Serve plain or with Tomato Sauce, p 1261. 4 servings.

CHICKEN TIMBALES

1 cup soft bread crumbs, pkd
1 cup 12% cream, half and half
2 eggs

1⅓ cups finely chopped moist cooked chicken, pkd, no skin
½ tsp salt
Pepper
2 tsp finely chopped parsley

Start oven 10 min before baking; set to moderate (350° F). Put crumbs into cream and let stand a few min to soften. Add eggs and beat thoroughly with rotary beater, then stir in chicken and seasonings. Pour into 4 well buttered custard cups holding from ⅞ to 1 cup. Set in a pan (preferably glass or enamelware), place in oven and pour in hot water to come up almost to top of cups. Bake 25 to 30 min. Cool 2 or 3 min. Run a thin-bladed knife around edge of timbales and unmold onto warm serving plates. Serve with thickened Rich Chicken Broth, p 1289, or Mushroom Sauce, p 1259. 4 servings.

EGG TIMBALES

2 cups milk
2 slices of medium onion,
  ¼-inch thick
2 sprigs parsley
¾ tsp salt

¼ tsp white pepper
½ cup soft white bread
  crumbs, pkd
6 eggs

Start oven 10 min before baking; set to moderate (350° F). Heat milk with onion and parsley in top of double boiler over boiling water until scalded. Remove from heat, lift out vegetables and discard. Add next 3 ingredients and let stand 5 min. Add eggs and beat with rotary beater to break up the crumbs. Pour into 4 well buttered custard cups holding from ⅞ to 1 cup. Set in pan (preferably glass or enamelware), place in oven and pour in hot water to come up almost to top of cups. Bake 25 to 30 min. Cool on cake rack 2 or 3 min. Run thin-blade knife around edge of timbales and unmold onto warm serving plates. Serve plain or with Tomato Sauce, p 1261, or chili sauce heated until warm. 4 servings.

HAM TIMBALES

1⅓ cups boiled or baked ham,
  ½ lb
1¼ cups soft white bread
  crumbs, pkd
1 cup milk
2 eggs, separated

½ tsp salt
Few dashes of pepper
¼ tsp dry or prepared Creole
  Mustard
2 tsp finely chopped parsley

Ham should be moist and lean. Chop fine on board. Measure crumbs into milk and let stand a few min to soften. Add egg yolks and beat with rotary beater to blend well. Stir in next 4 ingredients. Beat egg whites until stiff; fold lightly but thoroughly into ham mixture. Pour into 4 well buttered custard cups. Bake and serve as directed in Chicken Timbales. 4 servings.

SALMON TIMBALES

7¾ oz can salmon, 1 cup
1 cup salmon-milk liquid
⅓ cup soft white bread
   crumbs
2 eggs

1 tsp grated onion
2 tsp lemon juice
½ tsp salt
Few dashes of red pepper

Drain juice from salmon, save and add enough milk to make 1 cup. Add crumbs and let stand until soft, about 5 min. Discard skin from salmon, flake fish and crush bones and add to milk mixture with the eggs. Beat thoroughly with rotary beater. Stir in next 4 ingredients. Pour into 4 well buttered custard cups. Bake and unmold as directed under Chicken Timbales. Serve with Tartar Sauce, p 1260. 4 servings.

SWEETBREAD TIMBALES

½ lb sweetbreads, 1⅓ cups
2 tbsp butter
2 tbsp flour
1 cup milk
½ cup soft white bread
   crumbs, pkd

Few dashes of pepper
½ tsp salt
2 eggs
2 or 3 sliced ripe olives,
   optional

Precook sweetbreads according to directions p 890. Chop fine. There should be 1⅓ cups, pkd. Melt butter in saucepan, blend in flour, then add milk stirring to keep smooth. Add bread crumbs and cook with constant stirring until smooth and thickened. Remove from heat; stir in pepper, salt and egg yolks until well blended, then stir in sweetbreads. Beat egg whites until stiff, then fold them into sweetbread mixture. Lay a few slices of ripe olive in bottom of buttered custard cups, pour meat mixture in lightly. Bake and unmold as directed under Chicken Timbales. 4 servings.

Vegetables

Why should a few tart apples be cooked along with red cabbage? How can you preserve both the vitamin content and the color of green vegetables when they are cooked? Why does cabbage have stronger odor when you cook it covered? What is pot liquor and why is it important? These are just a few of the questions you will be able to answer to the benefit of your family's health and your own reputation as a cook when you have finished this chapter.

★　★　★　★

COOKING vegetables may be as dramatic as making the finest of angel food cake; it is just as rare an accomplishment, and much more practical. From a health standpoint, it is infinitely more important to your family that you be a good vegetable cook, since vegetables supply a large proportion of the vitamins and minerals needed for health. Well-cooked vegetables will be eaten and enjoyed where poorly cooked ones will be left on the plate doing no one any good.

Vegetable cookery is a matter of remembering a few simple facts about the nutritive elements in vegetables and about the preservation of the vegetable colors. The nutritive value and the means of its preservation is discussed in detail in the chapter on the "Diet Pattern." Note especially the charts on vitamins and minerals, pp 19 to 29.

GREEN VEGETABLES

The green color of vegetable leaves and stems is given by a substance called chlorophyll, the same substance that makes grass green. Chlorophyll is affected by acids, alkalies and certain minerals in the presence of heat. If acids or these minerals are present in the water in which green foods are cooked, the green gradually changes to an unattractive greenish brown. If alkali is present, the green gradually becomes more intense.

Both of these changes are undesirable, because the natural color of green vegetables is the most appetizing color they can have. To keep this natural color, green vegetables should be cooked quickly and for as short a time as possible. They should be cooked uncovered so the volatile part of the acids present in the vegetables themselves can pass off with the steam instead of remaining in contact with the chlorophyll. Vegetables cooked until just barely tender have a better flavor, better appearance, and retain more food value than when cooked longer.

The practice of adding a small amount of soda to the cooking water to intensify the green color is not recommended. Even a slight excess will make the vegetable slippery and unpleasant to eat. It destroys a considerable proportion of the vitamin content, and makes the color unnatural and unattractive.

This applies to all green vegetables, including spinach, chard, asparagus, Brussels sprouts, green cabbage, green beans, peas, and all leafy or stem vegetables which have a green color.

Fortunately, the same methods of cooking that are recommended for the greatest mineral and vitamin retention also preserve the color to the highest degree. It is reassuring to know that when vegetables are cooked so that they appear and taste best, they also contain the greatest amount of food value that cannot be seen or tasted.

RED VEGETABLES

In cooking red vegetables, the reactions are just the opposite of green ones. They turn redder and more attractive-looking when there is acid in the cooking water, while the presence of alkali causes them to turn bluish. The pigments which color red vegetables such as beets and red cabbage are called anthocyanins.

To give red vegetables the benefit of all their own acid, the kettle in which they are cooked should be tightly covered. Addition of a little vinegar or lemon juice, or of tart apples helps to keep the color brilliant. Vinegar or lemon juice is often added to beets toward the end of cooking, and it improves flavor as well as color. Red cabbage is also improved by cooking a few tart apples with it.

Red color in beets is also influenced greatly by care in preparation. About 3 inches of the stem should be left on, and care should be taken to avoid breaking the skin in washing and to keep the tap root intact. Any break in the skin or the tap root results in "bleeding" into the cooking water, and this makes the cooked beets pale in spite of an acid water.

YELLOW VEGETABLES

Yellow vegetables are the least susceptible to color changes of all the vegetables but careful cooking methods, nevertheless, are recommended to preserve food value and brilliant color. The yellow pigment, carotin, is not affected by either acid or alkali. Overcooking, however, often results in a gradual leaking of the pigment into the water, so the water becomes bright yellow and the food pale.

Yellow vegetables, which include carrots, yellow squash, sweet potatoes and yellow corn, may be steamed or boiled, either covered or uncovered.

Covering the kettle, if they are boiled, will hasten cooking and this is desirable to conserve the vitamin content.

WHITE VEGETABLES

Most white vegetables show no color, but they contain substances called flavones, which change to an unattractive brownish gray if there is an excess of iron in the water, or if the vegetable is overcooked. Therefore they should be cooked rapidly until just tender in order to expose them as briefly as possible to any iron that may be present in the water. Iron cooking utensils should be avoided.

Members of this group are white potatoes, white onions, white turnips and cauliflower. Potatoes may be cooked covered, but the others belong to the strong-juice class and should be cooked in an uncovered pan.

STRONG-JUICED VEGETABLES

The class of strong-juiced vegetables includes representatives of most of the color groups: broccoli, Brussels sprouts, cabbage, cauliflower, kohlrabi, onions and turnips. They all contain volatile substances which if retained in the kettle by covering it, react on the sulphur content of the vegetables to produce compounds that are not only disagreeable in odor and flavor, but difficult to digest. The unpleasant cabbage odor which permeates some houses when cabbage is cooked is caused not by the cabbage itself, but by these unsavory sulphur compounds resulting from prolonged cooking in a covered kettle.

Therefore it is desirable to cook strong-juiced vegetables quickly in slightly alkaline water until they are just tender and always in an open pan. A generous amount of water is *usually* recommended, too, for this dilutes the substances which cause the difficulty.

QUICK COOKING

Under several of the color classifications of vegetables, quick cooking has been specially advised. This is important enough to have a paragraph to itself. The briefer the cooking, the more of the food value of the raw food is retained in the cooked product, and the less will be lost to the cooking water or destroyed completely. Vitamins B_1 and C are readily destroyed at high temp, and the longer a vegetable is cooked, the greater the vitamin destruction. In order to get the fullest possible nutritive value out of foods, they should be cooked so as to lose a minimum of their vitamin content; and in the case of vegetables, this means quick cooking.

Use enough water to prevent the kettle from boiling dry, and heat to the boiling point before adding the vegetables. Then boil quickly until the vegetables are *just* tender, and serve at once.

POT LIQUOR

When a small enough amount of water is used so that all or most of it evaporates during cooking, there is danger of boiling dry. When a larger amount is used, there is danger of wasting some valuable minerals and vitamins which dissolve into the cooking water if the excess cooking water is discarded after the vegetable is done.

When more than the minimum amount of water is used for cooking, it should never be poured down the sink. This "pot liquor," as it is called, not only contains valuable food elements, but has a delicious flavor. It makes an unusual and very appealing broth while hot, or a good chilled cocktail. It may be added to tomato juice, or to any kind of soup to improve the flavor and increase the food value.

The water from potatoes cooked without their skins should also be saved. It may be used immediately or poured into a clean jar, tightly covered, and kept in the refrigerator and used within a short time for making meat gravy or to dilute evaporated milk in making white sauces for other creamed vegetables.

To avoid further loss of vitamins, the pot liquor should always be used as soon as possible after cooking.

TABLE 48

COOKING METHODS SUITABLE TO VARIOUS VEGETABLES

Boiling	Baking	Braising	Frying or Sautéing	Steaming
Asparagus	Eggplant	Celery	Eggplant	Beets
Beans, green and wax	Onions	Onions	Corn	Carrots
Beets	Potatoes, white and sweet	Lettuce	Onions	Corn
Broccoli		Squash	Parsnips (after boiling)	Parsnips
Cabbage	Squash		Potatoes, white and sweet	Potatoes, white and sweet
Carrots	Tomatoes		Tomatoes	Squash
Celery				
Corn				
Eggplant				
Kohlrabi				
Okra				
Onions				
Parsnips				
Peas				
Potatoes, white and sweet				
Spinach				
Squash				
Tomatoes				
Turnips				

OTHER METHODS OF COOKING VEGETABLES

The only cooking method which has been discussed so far is boiling, and this is the most common method of cooking all vegetables. However, baking, braising, frying and steaming are all used for various vegetables. Suitable methods for the different vegetables are shown on p 1307.

It will be noted that for green vegetables no other method than boiling is advised. All the other methods will bring about undesirable discoloration.

Some other methods, however, conserve the mineral content of the food better than boiling, and are highly desirable for vegetables to which they are suited. Baking whole in the skin is the best of these methods for conserving minerals, assuming that there is no overbaking or scorching to necessitate discarding part of the food itself. White and sweet potatoes, squash and onions are excellent cooked in this manner, and may be eaten to the thinnest layer of outer skin. Sometimes the skin may be eaten too, as with baked white potatoes.

Casserole dishes made with pared and sliced raw foods also come under this heading, for here the only loss of minerals occurs in the parings which can be reduced to a minimum by the homemaker who develops skill in paring thinly.

In braising, which is a method of cooking with very little water or with the steam formed from the vegetable's own juices, the liquid used becomes a part of the flavorful gravy which is always served with the vegetable. So any minerals and vitamins dissolved in the cooking water are still consumed along with the food itself. Here again, thin paring is important for the minerals are most abundant in the layers of tissue just under the thin skin. In frying and sautéing, there is no danger of mineral loss, but vitamins may be destroyed if the cooking temperature is too high, or if the cooking time is too long.

Steaming produces little loss in either minerals or vitamins A and B Complex, except in the juices that may leak out and drip down into the water in the bottom of the steamer. This is small compared with the loss that is possible in boiling.

It should also be pointed out that boiling produces a minimum loss if the vegetables are cooked without paring them, as may be done with new potatoes, sweet potatoes, beets, and onions. The skin is easily removed after cooking.

SERVING CANNED VEGETABLES

The quality of canned vegetables is improving steadily, and there are few homes where they are not served frequently. The vegetables are of high quality because they are picked at the peak of their goodness, and prepared and processed within a few hrs of harvesting. Therefore they are sometimes even fresher than the fresh vegetables which we buy at the grocery store, where they are seldom ever received in less than 12 hrs after gathering from the field or garden.

To serve canned vegetables with the utmost of flavor and food value, the liquid in which they are packed should not be discarded. Sometimes, as for whole kernel corn which has only a small amount of liquid, the vegetable may be heated and served in the juice. For some other vegetables, such as peas, which are packed with more liquid than it is desirable to serve on them, the liquid may be drained off and quickly boiled down to ⅓ the original quantity; then the peas may be put into the concentrated liquid to heat them, and served with whatever juices remain. Canned vegetables need only to be reheated; they are already cooked to doneness and should not be overcooked.

This liquid in which canned vegetables are packed consists of pure water, sometimes with a small amount of seasoning plus the vegetable juice which cooks out in processing. It therefore contains some of the flavor and food value of the canned product, and when concentrated by boiling down, adds to both the flavor and nutritive content of the food.

Butter and some additional salt are usually required to bring out the full flavor of any canned vegetable.

ARTICHOKES (FRENCH)

Choose fresh bright green artichokes with tight clinging fleshy petals. When tips of petals are hard, brown, and artichoke is open, the vegetable is overmature. Young artichokes are bright green, very tender and perishable. Cook within a short time after purchasing. To prepare, swish each vigorously upside down through plenty of warm water to rinse out the soil that is always found near the bottom of the outer petals. Cut off entire stem. Trim off any brown tips of the petals, using kitchen scissors. Wear a pair of gloves to protect hands from the sharp thornlike tips on the petals and gently press back the petals like opening a rose bud. This open arrangement allows the artichoke to cook more uniformly and quickly than if it is left closed. Cover with boiling salted water (1 tsp salt to each qt of water). Weight down with a heavy plate about 2 inches smaller in diameter than the saucepan to allow the escape of steam. Young tender artichokes cook in from 20 to 25 min, older ones in 35 to 40 min. When done, the petals will pull out easily. Then remove and turn the artichoke upside down to drain thoroughly. Place on hot serving plate. Serve with hot melted butter or Hollandaise Sauce, p 1256.

To eat the artichoke, pull the petals off one by one, dip the fleshy ends into butter or sauce, and slip the flesh off between the teeth, discarding the rest of the petals. When all the petals have been removed, only the hairy choke on top of the heart remains. Scrape the choke off neatly with a spoon or fork and discard. Eat the heart by cutting apart with a fork and dipping the pieces in butter or sauce. One medium artichoke weighing ¼ lb serves 1.

WHAT TO CONSIDER WHEN BUYING OR GATHERING JERUSALEM ARTICHOKES

Jerusalem artichokes are tubers resembling potatoes in color and form. They grow much more prolifically than potatoes and until recently were used chiefly as hog food in this country. When it was discovered their carbohy-drates are not in the form of starch, but inulin, their consumption as human food was increased considerably, especially by diabetics who can utilize this particular carbohydrate. Since these tubers are often irregular in shape, care should be used to select as smooth ones and as large ones as possible to avoid excessive waste in cleaning. These tubers are sold either by the quart or pound. Three to five medium ones weigh a pound.

BUTTERED JERUSALEM ARTICHOKES

1½ lbs artichokes
1 tsp salt
2 tbsp butter
1 tsp cider *or* tarragon
vinegar

2 *or* 3 drops of tabasco
sauce
1 to 2 tsp finely chopped
parsley

Wash artichokes and scrape them clean and again rinse quickly in cold water. Place in saucepan, barely cover with boiling water, add salt, cover and boil gently until tender, from 20 to 25 min. Drain thoroughly. Add butter, vinegar and tabasco and shake gently to coat the tubers, turn into a hot serving dish and sprinkle parsley over the top. Serve immediately. 5 servings.

WHAT TO CONSIDER WHEN BUYING OR GATHERING AND PREPARING ASPARAGUS

Asparagus is one vegetable that won't wait for harvesting. Once the spears push up through the earth and are three or four inches above the ground, they are ready to be cut down about two inches below the surface of the soil. If the weather is warm enough and the moisture is sufficient, this will be achieved easily in 24 hrs, and so it should be cut regularly every day. If asparagus grows taller, there may be considerable woodiness in the lower part of the spears, particularly in dry weather. For finest eating quality, full rich flavor, rich green color, and high vitamin value, the aspara-gus should be cooked as soon after it is cut as is feasible. The spears should be very tender and crisp and with as little woody fiber at the base of the stalk as possible. The finest asparagus procurable is from your own or local gardens or that shipped speedily by air. The best way to separate the woody fiber from the tender spears is to break the spears as low down the stalks as possible. The stalk will break with a snap where the woodiness begins. The lower woody part may be trimmed off and diced and cooked to make soup. Only enough water should be put on asparagus to cook it until tender which requires not more than 15 min for large tender spears and 20 min for trimmed off bottom stalks.

BUTTERED OR CREAMED ASPARAGUS

Clean asparagus by peeling off the paper-like scales on the sides and the woody fibers at the bottom of the stalks. Wash thoroughly in cold water and scrub gently with a vegetable brush. Break off the tough ends; these may be cooked separately for soup. The tender top of stalks may be left whole or cut in pieces 1 to 1½ inches in length. Barely cover with boiling salted water (1 tsp salt to each qt of water) and cook rapidly uncovered until tender. In general, asparagus will take about 15 min, but very tender asparagus may be done in less time. Test by piercing with metal skewer or tines of fork. Add more boiling water if liquid boils away during cooking; but at end of cooking period, water should be practically all evaporated. If any needs to be drained off, either boil it down to gravy-like consistency and serve over the asparagus or save it for soup or drink it as a beverage. Pour melted butter or a medium White Sauce, p 1262, or Cheese Sauce, p 1253, over the drained asparagus which may, if desired, be arranged on toast. Serve immediately. Allow 2 to 2½ lbs asparagus for 5 servings.

ASPARAGUS AND EGG CASSEROLE

1½ lbs asparagus   5 Hard-cooked Eggs, p 663
1½ cups thin white sauce   Buttered bread crumbs

Clean asparagus, cut in 1-inch pieces, and cook as described in preceding recipe for Buttered Asparagus. Drain, saving liquid. Make White Sauce, p 1262, using evaporated milk diluted with asparagus liquid. Fold in the cooked asparagus. Arrange layers of creamed asparagus in buttered casserole with shelled, sliced eggs between layers. Cover with Buttered Crumbs, p 162, and bake in a moderately hot oven (400° F) until thoroughly heated, about 20 min. 5 servings.

ASPARAGUS AND HAM LUNCHEON DISH

1½ lbs fresh asparagus   ½ tsp prepared mustard
2 tbsp butter   1 cup grated American
2 tbsp flour   cheese, ¼ lb
1 cup milk   ½ lb boiled *or* baked ham,
¼ tsp salt   lightly pan-fried
Pinch sugar

Wash, prepare and cook asparagus about 20 min as described in recipe for Buttered Asparagus. Meanwhile, make a white sauce by combining the melted butter and flour in the top of a double boiler and adding the milk gradually. Cook over hot water and stir until mixture is smooth and thickened. Blend in the salt, sugar and mustard, then add the cheese. Cook until cheese is melted. Arrange freshly cooked asparagus and ham attractively on a platter, then flow the sauce interestingly down through the center of the arrangement. Serve immediately. 4 servings.

Note: If there is a small amount of asparagus liquid remaining, it may be added to the white sauce (there should not be more than a couple of tbsp).

ASPARAGUS FONDUE

1 lb fresh asparagus
Milk *or* thin cream
1 tbsp finely chopped onion
2 eggs, well beaten

1 cup grated cheese, ¼ lb
2 cups fresh bread crumbs
⅟₁₆ tsp paprika

Wash, prepare and cook asparagus about 20 min as described in recipe for Buttered Asparagus, cutting the stalks into 1-inch lengths before cooking. When tender, drain off liquid, measure and add enough milk to make 2 cups. Beat the eggs and add to the milk. Add the onion, cheese, bread crumbs and paprika; heat over hot water until cheese is melted, add asparagus and pour into a greased glass loaf pan (8¼ x 4¼ x 2½ inches). Bake in a moderate oven (325° F) for 30 min or until a knife inserted in the center comes out clean. 4 servings.

ASPARAGUS IN EGG SAUCE

1½ lbs asparagus
3 tbsp butter
3 tbsp flour
1 tsp salt
2 cups milk

¼ tsp onion juice
Few drops Worcestershire sauce
1 tsp lemon juice, if desired
4 hard-cooked eggs

Prepare asparagus according to directions for cooking Buttered or Creamed Asparagus, p 1310. Meanwhile, melt butter, blend in flour and salt, and add milk; stir over direct heat until sauce boils and thickens. Add Worcestershire sauce, lemon juice and onion juice. Just before serving, fold in peeled and coarsely chopped eggs. Serve over the hot, freshly cooked drained asparagus. 5 servings.

ASPARAGUS NEWBURG

¾ lb fresh tender asparagus
1½ cups boiling water
1¼ tsp salt
9 almonds, blanched and sliced, ½ oz
3 tbsp butter *or* margarine

2 tbsp flour
½ cup milk
1 cup sliced fresh mushrooms
1 tsp cooking sherry
Toast

Clean asparagus for cooking (see Buttered Asparagus). Trim woody fiber from broken-off tough ends, cut in 1-inch lengths and place in a saucepan. Add water and salt and boil uncovered for 15 to 18 min. Add tips after the first 8 min of cooking. Meanwhile sauté almonds in heated butter for a few min until golden brown. Do not scorch. Stir in flour until well blended. Add milk gradually. Cook over medium heat until sauce boils and thickens, stirring to keep smooth. Add undrained asparagus, mushrooms and sherry. Blend carefully. Cover and simmer for 10 min. Stir occasionally. Serve over toast sqs. 4 servings.

ASPARAGUS POLONAISE

1 lb tender, fat asparagus
⅓ cup mayonnaise
4 tsp lemon juice
½ tsp salt

2 tbsp butter
⅓ cup fine, dry bread crumbs
2 tbsp finely chopped parsley
1 hard-cooked egg

Prepare asparagus for cooking as described in recipe for Buttered Asparagus, except do not cut or break the spears. Tie the cleaned bunch together with twine and stand it up in a tall saucepan. Add 1 cup boiling water, cover and boil vigorously until just tender, 10 to 15 min. Very little water will be left. Remove string from asparagus and lay on a hot plate. Add the combined mayonnaise, lemon juice and salt, and roll the asparagus around quickly to coat all over with the mixture. Meanwhile, melt the butter in a saucepan and brown very *lightly*, add the crumbs to the butter and toss about to heat thoroughly, then add the parsley, riced egg, and mix quickly. Arrange asparagus on the hot serving platter, and sprinkle the crumb mixture loosely and attractively over the tip ends. Serve immediately while piping hot. 4 servings.

ASPARAGUS ROYALE IN PUFF SHELLS

¼ lb mushrooms, washed and sliced
¼ cup butter *or* margarine
¼ cup flour
¾ tsp salt
Pinch sugar

1 cup milk (part asparagus liquid may be used)
1 egg, slightly beaten
¾ lb asparagus, cut into inch lengths, cooked
4 Cream Puff Shells, p 936

Sauté mushrooms for 5 min in butter. Blend in the flour and seasonings and add milk gradually. Stir until mixture is smooth and thickened; pour some of the mixture over the egg, mix and pour back. Add the asparagus and heat thoroughly, stirring carefully. Slice the top from each puff shell, fill with the hot mixture. Replace the top and serve immediately. If mushrooms are not available, use any dried mushroom soup mix or concentrated cream of mushroom soup (canned) as the cream sauce base. 4 servings.

ASPARAGUS TOAST ROLLS

Trim crusts from large slices of fresh white bread, curve opposite edges of the slice upward so as to come together, and fasten with toothpicks. Toast on all sides in broiler or hot oven, watching carefully. Fill toast rolls with drained hot asparagus (canned or fresh cooked) and arrange on platter. Serve with Cheese Sauce, p 1253, in which asparagus liquid or cooking water has been substituted for part of the milk. Garnish with crisp Broiled Bacon, p 855, and parsley. Two asparagus rolls make 1 serving.

WHAT TO CONSIDER WHEN BUYING OR GATHERING AND COOKING GREEN BEANS

As a rule, the round podded green beans are the best to buy or grow. But whether they have round fleshy pods or flat ones, the beans should be very green and crisp and tender enough to be easily pierced with the thumb nail. When bent sharply, the pod should break with a quick snap. Beans with pods that have begun to acquire yellow spots are too mature for green beans. Beans that are gathered while the dew is on, and are heaped up are sure to quickly acquire rusty spots all over the surface. These spots are only on the surface and there would be no harm in serving such beans cooked, but they make the vegetable unattractive, so fastidious housewives shave these spots off with a sharp knife and the result is increased labor and loss of food value. Beans that develop rapidly during a rainy season are liable to become covered with sand or a thin film of soil and should be gathered between rains when the surface of the beans is as dry as possible. And they should be spread in very thin layers to dry thoroughly before they are gathered into baskets or heaps to prevent rusting. For these reasons, if beans must be kept for a few hrs in the refrigerator before they are to be cooked, they should be stored dry. Because most varieties of beans have a delicate fuzz over their surface, they need to be washed most thoroughly in several waters, or a dark dirty scum is sure to collect on the top of the beans as they cook.

BUTTERED OR CREAMED GREEN BEANS

Choose fresh, crisp green beans, preferably the round podded variety. Wash (1½ lbs) beans thoroughly in cold water and snip off the ends. Leave whole or cut French style in thin lengthwise strips. Cover with boiling salted water. (Use 1 tsp salt to 1 qt water.) Cook uncovered until tender, 10 min for the French beans and from 20 to 30 min for the whole ones, the time depending on tenderness. Add more boiling water if needed. Drain, saving any liquid for vegetable juice cocktail; add 1 tsp sugar, pour melted butter, or a medium White or Brown Sauce, p 1262 or p 1252, over the hot beans, and reheat. Serve immediately. Allow 1½ to 2 lbs for 5 servings.

Variation: Beans and Potatoes. Half this amount of beans may be half-cooked, then combined with an equal quantity of diced potatoes and cooked until both are tender, then drained and buttered.

GREEN BEANS COOKED IN CREAM SAUCE

Beans stay green; retain all nutrients; taste good

1 lb tender green beans	1 tsp salt
3 tbsp butter	Pepper, optional
2 tbsp flour	1½ tsp very finely chopped
3 cups milk	onion, optional

Wash beans well through 2 or 3 waters. Snip ends from beans. Lay bundles of beans on board and cut into quarter-inch crosswise slices or use the special device on the end of many vegetable peelers to cut the beans French style. Heat butter in a 3-qt saucepan, blend in the flour, salt and pepper, then stir in the milk. Cook with constant stirring until sauce boils and thickens slightly. Add the beans, reheat to boiling, then reduce heat, boil gently with frequent stirring until beans are just tender, from 20 to 25 min. Stir in onion and serve piping hot. 4 servings.

GREEN BEANS au GRATIN

5 slices bacon
2 tbsp flour
2 cups cooked fresh *or* frozen
green beans with their
liquid
½ cup milk

¾ cup grated sharp cheese,
3 oz
½ cup rolled cornflakes *or*
bread crumbs mixed with
2 tbsp melted butter

Pan-broil the Bacon, p 855, until done; drain off fat, remove bacon to absorbent paper. Measure 3 tbsp of drippings and return to skillet. Add flour and stir until blended, then add liquid drained from beans (there should be about ⅞ cup) and the milk, and stir constantly over direct heat until sauce boils and thickens. Add beans and grated cheese, and turn into a buttered 6-cup casserole. Sprinkle with cornflake crumbs or bread crumbs and bake in a moderately slow oven (325° F) for about 20 min, or until browned and thoroughly heated through. Two min before removing from oven, sprinkle with the chopped crisp bacon. 5 servings.

GREEN BEAN PUFF

4 cups hot cooked Green
Beans, p 1314
½ cup finely diced celery
(outer stalks and leaves)
¾ cup mayonnaise
1 tsp prepared mustard

¼ tsp salt
1 tsp vinegar
¼ cup milk
1 egg white
¼ tsp paprika

Combine green beans and celery. Pile lightly into a 5-cup casserole. Mix together the mayonnaise, mustard, salt and vinegar. Gradually add the milk. Beat the egg white until stiff. Fold into the mayonnaise mixture and pile lightly on top of the beans. Sprinkle with paprika. Bake 15 min in a 400° F (moderately hot oven) until sauce puffs and browns and the beans are thoroughly heated. 4 servings.

SAVORY GREEN BEANS

1½ lbs green beans, 1½ qts
3 slices bacon, cut finely
1 cup chopped onion

½ tsp salt
Pepper
Paprika

Wash and string beans; cut lengthwise in three or four strips and then crosswise. Put into saucepan, add boiling water to cover and ½ tsp salt. Cook uncovered until tender—10 to 15 min. The liquid should be practically all evaporated by the time the beans are tender and will require no draining. Meanwhile pan-fry bacon over low heat, adding onions when bacon is half done. Heat together until bacon is done and the onions transparent. Stir in the beans, season with salt, pepper, and paprika and serve hot. 5 servings.

STRING BEANS IN EGG SAUCE

¾ lb tender string beans, 3 cups
2 tbsp margarine
2 tbsp flour
½ cup milk

⅛ tsp celery seed
¼ tsp salt
Dash pepper
3 Hard-cooked Eggs, p 663

Wash beans, clip off ends and cook in just enough boiling salted water to cover (½ tsp salt to each cup boiling water) for 20 to 30 min, or until just tender. Drain and reserve liquid; there should be about ½ cup. Melt margarine, blend in flour, then slowly add milk and bean liquid, stirring constantly. Cook until it bubbles and becomes thickened. Add celery seed, salt and pepper. Stir well, add sliced eggs and fold in gently. Reheat, pour over hot beans which have been placed in a hot serving dish. Serve immediately. 4 servings.

BUTTERED KIDNEY BEANS

Wash ½ lb small dried kidney beans thoroughly; add 3½ cups cold water and ½ tsp salt. Heat to boiling, cover and *simmer* gently 2 to 2½ hrs or until beans are very tender. There should be just enough water left so the beans will not be dry. Add butter to suit the taste. A garnish of chopped parsley or green pepper adds to the flavor as well as the appearance. Bacon drippings may be used in place of butter for seasoning. Makes 2 cups or 5 servings.

KIDNEY BEAN LOAF

No. 2 can red kidney beans
1 cup canned tomatoes
1 cup Boiled Rice, p 433
2 cups cornflakes
2 eggs, beaten
½ tsp salt

½ tsp sugar
¼ cup chopped onion
¼ lb bacon, diced, pan-broiled until crisp
2 tbsp chopped parsley, if desired

Drain liquid from beans and discard. Mash beans and mix well with all the other ingredients. Turn into buttered 4-cup loaf pan or casserole, bake in a moderate oven (350° F) 1 to 1½ hrs or until a sharp knife inserted in center of loaf comes out clean. Serve hot with Dill Sauce, p 1254. 5 servings.

KIDNEY BEANS WITH ONIONS

1 lb small dried kidney beans, 2 cups 1 cup sliced onions	3 tbsp butter Salt and pepper to taste 1 tbsp chopped parsley

Prepare kidney beans as described under Buttered Kidney Beans. Then sauté the sliced onions until soft and slightly browned in the butter. Drain the beans and add to the onions, tossing together until beans are coated with butter. Add seasonings and serve hot, garnished with chopped parsley. 5 servings.

KIDNEY BEANS WITH SALT PORK

3 oz salt pork 2 medium-sized onions, chopped No. 2 can red kidney beans	1 tbsp sherry extract 1 tbsp flour 1 green pepper

Cut salt pork into ½-inch dice; turn into skillet and pan-fry slowly until crisp and golden brown. Add finely chopped onion and cook slowly until onion is soft and yellow, stirring to prevent scorching. Add beans, blend sherry and flour to a smooth paste, and add. Stir thoroughly, and simmer gently for 10 min. Garnish with crisp green pepper cut into quarter-inch rings. 5 servings.

WHAT TO LOOK FOR WHEN BUYING OR GATHERING FRESH LIMAS

Since lima beans are one of the most expensive of all vegetables, it is well to know the earmarks of poor and good values. The pods should be a *bright, light* green and slightly rounded and full of beans from one end to the other. Many times big impressive-looking pods have only one bean in them. So it is a good plan to observe the pods closely to learn whether or not the price is not largely for pods rather than edible beans. One can easily see or feel the beans inside. Pods that have begun to take on a yellowish tinge are too old to contain beans that have the fine delicate flavor that fresh limas should have. Beans should not be hulled until they are ready to be cooked, so if they must be kept in the refrigerator a few hrs, they should be stored in the pods. The oft-seen shelled lima beans that are found in the best of groceries are the poorest of values, because it is the grocer's method of salvaging beans that could not be sold in the pod. And even if the beans were the best when he shelled them, much of their delicate flavor evaporates into thin air before the cook can get them into the kettle. So buying shelled beans may save the lazy one some energy, but she'll never be able to serve excellent limas. The best of fresh limas are one of the rarest and most delicious flavored of all vegetables, so they are always worth working for. The finest obtainable are from your own or local gardens or those shipped in rapidly from distant gardens by plane.

BAKED LIMA BEANS

2 cups dried limas   ¼ lb salt pork, sliced thin
3 cups water

Wash beans thoroughly, soak overnight in cold water to cover. Drain, turn into a 3-qt saucepan, add the 3 cups fresh water and sliced pork, cover, and *simmer* gently until soft (about 40 min). Remove the pork, add more salt if needed, and turn beans with remaining water into a buttered casserole. Arrange pork over top of beans and place in a moderately hot oven (425° F) until pork is browned. Serve hot. 5 servings.

BUTTERED DRIED LIMA BEANS

1½ cups dried limas   3 tbsp butter
3 cups water   Parsley *or* pimiento
1½ tsp salt

Wash beans thoroughly, cover well with cold water and soak overnight. Drain. Put into a 3-qt saucepan, add the 3 cups of water and 1½ tsp salt. Heat to boiling, reduce heat, cover and simmer gently until soft, from 30 to 40 min. If there is too much liquid, evaporate until liquid is a thin gravy-like consistency, and barely covers beans. Add butter to hot beans, and more salt, if desired. Serve hot. A sprinkling of chopped parsley, a few strips of pimiento, or a dash of paprika adds attractive color. 5 servings.

BUTTERED FROZEN LIMA BEANS

Frozen limas correctly cooked and seasoned are delicious and filling. Most directions call for too little water

2 cups boiling water   2 tbsp butter
10-oz pkg frozen large   ½ to 1 tsp sugar
     Fordhook limas   Pepper
¾ tsp salt

Measure water into a 1½ to 2-qt saucepan. Add solid-frozen beans and rest of ingredients. Heat to boiling, then boil gently uncovered 15 to 20 min, or until tender and liquid is reduced to where it barely covers the beans. The seasonings are put in at first to produce delicious flavor. Cooking should be done at a gentle rate to keep beans whole until tender. Limas taste their best when served with their rich juice. 3 servings.

BUTTERED NEW LIMA BEANS

3 cups shelled fresh limas   Salt and pepper to taste
2 cups boiling water   1 tbsp sliced pimiento,
3 tbsp butter   optional

Wash the beans thoroughly and drop into the boiling water. Cover and simmer until tender, about 20 to 30 min, depending on size of beans. Drain cooking liquid into saucepan and boil down until only ½ cup of liquid remains. Add butter and pour over beans. Season to suit taste. Reheat and fold the pimiento in gently. Serve immediately. 5 servings.

LIMA BEAN CASSEROLE

2 cups dried limas   3 tbsp molasses
1 medium onion, sliced very   3 tbsp granulated sugar
  thin   1 tsp salt
2 oz salt pork, sliced

Wash beans thoroughly and soak in cold water overnight. Next morning, drain. Put beans into a 3-qt saucepan, add 4 cups cold water and 1½ tsp salt, heat to boiling, then *simmer* gently until soft (about 40 min), being careful not to cook hard enough to break beans. Drain, saving cooking water, and pour half of beans into casserole or bean pot; lay onion slices over them. Add rest of beans and bury salt pork in them, leaving rind exposed. Combine molasses, sugar, salt, and 1½ cups cooking water and pour over beans; cover, bake in a moderately slow oven (325° F) 1½ hrs. Do not let beans get too dry, add boiling water to bring liquid almost to the top. Uncover and bake 2 to 2½ hrs longer, until a rich golden brown on top. (This dish may be reheated successfully, so it is practical to make twice the quantity, if desired.) 5 servings.

BAKED BEANS IN TOMATO CUPS

5 large tomatoes   No. 2 can baked beans
  Celery salt

Wash but do not peel tomatoes. Cut out stem end and scoop out center to form cups with walls at least ¼-inch thick. Sprinkle inside of tomatoes with celery salt and fill with baked beans. Butter a shallow baking pan and set the tomatoes in it. Bake in a moderate oven (350° F) until tomatoes are soft and beans are hot through, about 20 min. If desired, a slice of bacon may be laid across each filled tomato and baking continued until the bacon is crisp. The scooped-out centers of the tomatoes may be quickly stewed, seasoned with salt, prepared mustard, and a little sugar, and strained to serve as a sauce around the tomatoes. 5 servings.

BAKED BEANS WITH TOMATOES

1¼ lbs dried navy beans,   1 tsp salt
  2½ cups   ⅛ tsp dry mustard
5 cups cold water   Few grains of cayenne
1 medium onion, sliced   ⅓ cup dark brown sugar,
3 oz salt pork, sliced   firmly pkd *or* ⅓ cup
  No. 2 can tomatoes, sieved   molasses
2 cups water

Wash beans thoroughly, cover with the cold water. Add the next
8 ingredients, heat to boiling, reduce heat, cover, and *simmer* for 2 hrs,
or until beans are soft enough to break open. Turn into a buttered casserole or baking dish and add brown sugar or molasses. Pull slices of salt
pork to the top and bake, covered, in a very slow oven (250° F) for 2
hrs. Remove cover, and bake another hr. Serve hot. 5 servings.

BOILED NAVY OR SOY BEANS

1 lb dried navy beans   Small pod red pepper,
2 tsp sugar   optional
1 tsp salt   ¼ lb salt pork
7 cups cold water   1 small onion

Pick over and wash beans thoroughly in cold water. Place beans in
a 3 or 4-qt saucepan, add remaining ingredients, cover and *simmer* for
2½ to 3 hrs until beans are tender but not mushy. Shake the pan occasionally to prevent sticking. Edible cow peas and soy beans may be
cooked in the same manner. Makes about 6 cups.

These beans are delicious eaten as is or they may be used for making
soup or salad.

NAVY BEAN AND APPLE CASSEROLE

1 lb dried navy beans, 2 cups   ⅓ cup brown sugar, firmly
6 cups cold water   pkd
1 tsp salt   ¼ lb salt pork, sliced
3 large tart apples, pared
  and sliced

Wash beans and turn into a 3-qt saucepan. Add the water and salt,
heat to boiling, and *simmer* gently, covered, about 2 hrs. Drain, saving
cooking water. Arrange beans and apple slices in alternate layers in a
greased casserole, sprinkling sugar over each layer. Pour in 2 cups of the
cooking liquid and top with slices of salt pork. Bake, covered, in a very
slow oven (250° F) for about 2½ hrs, or until beans are light brown
and thoroughly cooked. If they become dry in cooking, add more cook-

ing liquid or hot water. There should be enough liquid on the beans to make a gravy-like sauce over them. 5 to 7 servings.

OLD-FASHIONED BAKED BEANS

2 lbs dried navy beans	2 tbsp brown sugar
2 qts cold water	½ cup molasses
1 medium onion, sliced	¼ cup tomato catchup
1 tbsp salt	⅟₁₆ tsp black pepper
4 tsp cider vinegar	Hot water, if needed
1 tsp prepared mustard	½ lb salt pork, sliced

Pick over and wash beans thoroughly. Add cold water, cover, heat to boiling and simmer for 30 min. Drain but do not discard the liquid. Place onion slices in bottom of a bean pot or a 10-cup casserole. Combine the next 7 ingredients and turn into the bean pot. Add the beans and enough hot drained liquid or water to cover (about 2½ cups). Arrange salt pork slices on top, cover and bake in very slow oven (250° F) 7 to 8 hrs. After 4 hrs, remove 2 cups of beans and mash. Then stir into the remaining beans carefully. Cover and continue to bake. Add additional hot bean liquid or water as needed. Beans should be just covered with thick, luscious liquid. Remove cover 1 hr before end of cooking time to allow salt pork to brown. 10 to 12 servings.

NAVY BEAN OR BLACK-EYED PEA STEW

1 lb dried navy beans *or* peas, 2 cups	4 oz salt pork, diced
6 cups cold water	1 pod dried hot red pepper
	Salt to taste

Wash beans thoroughly and turn into a 3 to 4-qt saucepan. Add the cold water. Heat to boiling and simmer for 15 min; then add diced salt pork, cover, and continue to *simmer* until beans and pork are both very tender, from 2½ to 3 hrs. About 15 min before they are done, add red pepper. Season to suit taste. 5 servings. Makes 5 cups.

CHILIED WAX BEANS

1 lb fresh wax beans	¾ cup bean liquid
⅔ cup finely diced celery	2 bouillon cubes
3 tbsp shortening, melted	¼ cup chili sauce

Wash beans thoroughly and snip off ends. Place in saucepan, cover with boiling water, cover and cook from 20 to 30 min or until tender. Drain and reserve liquid. If there is more than ¾ cup, concentrate the liquid by rapid boiling. If there is less, add enough water to make ¾ cup. Keep beans hot. Sauté celery in shortening for about 5 min. Add remaining ingredients and keep hot until bouillon cube is dissolved. Pour over the hot beans and serve. 4 or 5 servings.

CREOLE WAX BEANS

2 tbsp butter
1 medium onion, chopped
1 branch celery, chopped
1 small carrot, grated

1¼ cups fresh-cooked *or* canned tomatoes
No. 2 can wax beans
Salt and pepper to taste
2 tsp finely chopped parsley

Melt butter in saucepan. Add chopped onion and celery, and grated carrot. Cook slowly for about 5 min until vegetables are softened. Add tomatoes and cook rapidly for 10 min; add beans, reduce heat, and simmer until the sauce has the consistency of a thin gravy, about 10 min longer. Add seasonings. Shower with parsley and serve. 5 servings.

HARVARD GREEN OR WAX BEANS

3 to 4 cups water
¾ tsp salt
1½ lbs green *or* wax beans
3 to 4 tbsp sugar

3 tsp cornstarch
3 tbsp cider vinegar
Pimiento

Heat water to boiling, add salt and beans which have been washed, trimmed and cut into 1-inch lengths; cook, uncovered, in rapidly boiling water until tender, 20 to 30 min. Drain, saving the cooking water. Mix the sugar and cornstarch. Measure ¾ cup of cooking water, add to cornstarch mixture and cook, stirring constantly until sauce boils and becomes clear. Add vinegar. Pour over beans and let stand in warm place about 20 min to blend flavors. Add a few strips of pimiento and reheat before serving. 5 servings.

WAX OR GREEN BEANS WITH DILL SAUCE

2½ cups fresh cooked green
  or wax beans with their
  liquid
2 tbsp butter
2 tbsp flour

1½ tsp finely chopped fresh
  dill
Pepper
½ to 1 tbsp vinegar

Drain liquid from hot, fresh-cooked beans and measure it; add enough water to make 1⅓ cups of liquid. Melt butter, blend in flour, and add the liquid gradually, stirring constantly over direct heat until sauce boils and thickens. Add dill and beans, stirring just enough to distribute dill through sauce. Heat slowly to boiling point. Add pepper and vinegar to suit taste, and serve piping hot. If fresh dill is not available, substitute 1½ tbsp chopped stuffed olives or dill pickles for the dill, and omit the vinegar. 5 servings.

Note: An equal quantity of frozen or canned beans may be used in place of the fresh-cooked.

MRS. CRENSHAW'S PINTO BEANS

Mrs. Crenshaw, a Texan, prepared Pintos in our Chicago Test Kitchen to show us how Texans like them cooked. Served with Crisp Corn Cakes they are a hearty tasty meal for folks in any state

6 cups water, 1½ qts	1 tbsp sugar
½ lb salt pork	2½ tbsp maple-flavored syrup
2 cups pinto beans	½ tsp salt
2½ tbsp chili powder	1 onion size of egg

Heat water to boiling in a 4-qt saucepan. Add pork cut into ½-inch thick slices; cover and boil gently for 10 min. Meanwhile pick over beans, wash thoroughly through 3 or 4 waters, then add to saucepan. Cover and boil gently 1 hr. Then add chili powder, sugar and syrup. Cover and simmer 3 hrs longer, adding ½ cup more boiling water at end of 2 hrs. When beans are tender the thickened juice should just cover them. Now add salt and peeled chopped onion and continue simmering another half an hr. Most of the beans should be whole at finish and very tender. Serve with Crunchy Corn Cakes, p 242. About 1½ qts.

RED BEANS AND RICE

A lowly dish that New Orleans has made famous

1 lb small red beans	Few dashes pepper, black
6½ cups water	*or* red
2-lb shank-end ham bone	¼ tsp salt
split in half or 1-lb slice	5 drops tabasco, optional
ham	6 cups fluffy cooked hot rice,
2 onions large egg-size	1½ cups raw
1 medium clove garlic	Parsley

Pick over beans and wash well in 2 or 3 waters. Turn into 4-qt saucepan, add cold water to come 2 inches over beans and let soak overnight. Next morning, drain and add the 6½ cups cold water, ham shank or slice with most of fat trimmed off, chopped onion and finely cut garlic. Heat to boiling, reduce heat to simmer, cover and simmer about 3 hrs or until beans and ham are very tender. Lift out ham; remove bones, fat and skin and discard. Chop the lean ham and return to beans. Remove about ⅓ of the beans, mash fine and return to kettle to thicken the gravy. Add pepper, salt and tabasco and reheat. Serve beans over fluffy hot rice. Sprinkle with chopped parsley. 6 to 8 servings.

Note: No salt is needed if ham is salty.

SWEDISH BROWN BEANS

1 lb Swedish brown beans	⅓ cup maple *or* maple-
7 cups water	flavored syrup
½ tsp salt	¼ cup cider vinegar

Pick over beans and discard imperfect ones. Wash well in cold water, then add water to come *2 inches over beans,* and soak overnight. Next morning drain beans and put into a 3-qt saucepan, add the 7 cups water and salt. Heat to boiling, then reduce heat, cover and simmer until beans are tender, 2 to 3 hrs. Toward end of cooking, shake pan frequently and watch that beans do not burn. They should cook down until there is very little liquid. When beans are perfectly tender, stir in syrup and vinegar, then cook 5 to 10 min longer to give them the characteristic sweet-sour taste. 6 to 7 servings.

BUTTERED BEETS

Cut off beet tops leaving about 3 inches of the stems. If leaves and stems are tender, they may be cooked and served like Spinach (p 1394). Do not cut off the main or tap root. Wash beets thoroughly, especially around the top where soil is apt to cling. Do not scrub with brush, and take care not to break the skin or the tap root, as broken areas permit the beet to "bleed." Cover the beets well with water, either hot or cold and boil in covered kettle until tender—from 30 to 55 min, depending on size. Drain, cool quickly under cold water, drain again, slip off stems and skins. Slice, dice, or rice beets and reheat, adding melted butter. A little chopped chives or parsley or mint adds attractiveness to beets, and many persons prefer them served with vinegar or lemon juice. Allow 2 bunches of beets for 5 servings. Tender stems may be buttered and served with the beets, or served separately at another meal.

BEETS DE LUXE

2½ cups canned *or* fresh-
   cooked beets, sliced
1 tsp grated onion
¼ tsp salt
2 tsp cornstarch
2 tbsp cold water

¼ cup bread crumbs
2 tbsp butter, melted
1½-oz pkg grated Parmesan
   cheese
Chopped parsley

Heat beets in their own liquid, add onion and salt. Blend cornstarch to a smooth paste with cold water and add to beets, stirring well. Cook until mixture boils and thickens. Pour beets into a serving dish. Heat crumbs in butter until toasted. Sprinkle beets with hot buttered crumbs, then with cheese and parsley. Serve at once. 4 servings.

BEETS IN HORSERADISH SAUCE

1 tbsp butter
1 tsp sugar
2 tsp cornstarch
¾ cup water *or* liquid from
   canned beets
Dash of salt and pepper

1 tbsp vinegar
1 tsp fresh grated horseradish
2 cups fresh cooked *or*
   canned beets
Parsley

Melt butter in saucepan; blend in sugar and cornstarch. Add water if fresh cooked beets are used or beet liquid from canned. Stir constantly, cooking until sauce boils and thickens. Add next 3 ingredients, then sliced or quartered beets and continue cooking over low heat, turning beets over and over until they are hot through. Serve garnished with parsley. 4 to 5 servings.

BEETS IN ORANGE SAUCE

3 tbsp sugar	⅛ tsp orange rind
2 tbsp cornstarch	⅛ tsp lemon rind
¼ tsp salt	3 cups coarsely shredded,
½ cup orange juice	cooked fresh beets, *or*
¼ cup lemon juice	canned

Blend the first three ingredients together in the top of a double boiler. Add the orange and lemon juice and cook over boiling water until thick and transparent, stirring constantly. Add the orange and lemon rinds and the beets. Mix lightly. Cook over boiling water until thoroughly heated through. Serve at once. 4 servings.

BEETS WITH SOUR SAUCE

No. 2 can whole beets	2 tbsp vinegar
2 tbsp flour	½ tsp sugar
2 tbsp butter *or* margarine	¼ tsp salt
¾ cup milk	Pepper

Heat beets in their own liquid. Blend the flour and melted butter until smooth in a separate saucepan. Add the milk gradually. Cook and stir until mixture is smooth and thickened. Add remaining ingredients. Serve hot over hot drained beets. (Beet liquid may be used as a base for a salad dressing, or for a beet juice cocktail by adding a little lemon juice and a little chopped parsley.) 4 servings.

HARVARD BEETS

No. 2 can beets	2 tbsp cider vinegar
2 tbsp butter	¼ tsp salt
2 tbsp flour	Pepper
¼ tsp onion juice	1½ tsp sugar

Drain beets, saving liquid. Melt butter, blend in flour, slowly add beet liquid, and stir constantly over direct heat until sauce boils and thickens. Add remaining ingredients and the beets, and continue heating slowly until beets are hot through. Serve at once. 5 servings.

Note: Cooked fresh beets may be used, substituting water for the beet juice.

QUICK-COOKED CUBED BEETS

2 tbsp chopped onion   1¼ tsp salt
1 tbsp butter *or* margarine   2½ tsp sugar
1 bunch beets, 4 large   Dash pepper
1¼ cups boiling water   1 tbsp finely chopped parsley

Sauté onion in butter for 2 min. Pare uncooked beets thin and cut beets into ⅜-inch cubes (4 cups). Add beets and next four ingredients. Cover and *simmer* for about 25 min until tender. The liquid should be almost evaporated. Turn into hot serving dish, sprinkle with parsley. Serve immediately. 4 servings.

POLISH BEETS

Sparkling in color and flavor

2 bunches beets, size of golf   ½ cup water
   balls   1 to 2 tbsp sugar
2 tbsp butter   ¼ tsp grated onion
4 tbsp lemon juice   1 tbsp chopped parsley *or*
1½ tsp salt   mint
Dash of pepper

Wash beets, pare thinly and shred on medium coarse grater. There should be 4 cups. Melt butter in saucepan, add beets, lemon juice, salt and pepper. Cover tightly and cook over *very low heat* 30 min, lifting and turning over occasionally. Add next 3 ingredients. Cover and cook 10 or 15 min longer, or until beets are tender. Serve with chopped parsley or mint sprinkled over top. 4 to 5 servings.

RUBY RED BEETS

1 bunch beets, 4 large   ⅜ tsp salt
½ tsp onion juice   2 tsp sugar
2 tbsp lemon juice   ½ cup sour cream

Cook beets in skins as for Buttered Beets until just tender (30 to 55 min). Cool and slip off skins and stem ends. Grate beets into mixing bowl and add remaining ingredients except cream. Toss lightly to blend seasonings. Serve warm or chilled with a spoonful of sour cream on top. 4 servings.

BUTTERED BROCCOLI

Select compact heads of broccoli with tight, bright green buds that have not opened out or turned yellow. Place, heads down, into cold, salted water for about half an hr. (This is particularly necessary for home-grown broccoli.) Drain. Remove leaves and woody peeling from the stalks, stripping it off from the base of the stalk towards the head. Slash heavy stalks into halves or quarters lengthwise, but do not cut into head. Place in 3 to 4 qt kettle and barely cover with boiling salted water (1 tsp salt to 1 qt water). Boil quickly, uncovered, until just tender, from 10 to 15 min. Lift out with tongs or a slotted spoon to drain, and arrange on a hot serving dish. Pour melted butter or Cheese Sauce (p 1253) over it. Serve immediately. Broccoli is also good served with Hollandaise Sauce (p 1256). Allow 1½ lbs for 5 servings.

BROCCOLI NOODLE PLATTER

1½-lb bunch broccoli	¼ cup raisins
2 cups broad noodles, 4 oz	¼ tsp salt
2-oz pkg dehydrated mush-room soup	½ cup grated sharp American cheese, about 2 oz
1 cup milk	

Prepare broccoli as described in Buttered Broccoli and boil quickly uncovered 10 to 15 min. Meanwhile drop noodles into 2 qts boiling salted water in top of double boiler and boil 5 to 6 min over direct heat. Drain off all the water. Place over boiling water. Blend soup with milk and add to the noodles. Add the raisins and salt, and cook over boiling water for 15 min, stirring frequently to keep smooth. Heap lightly in the center of a warm platter, sprinkle with grated cheese. Drain broccoli and arrange around the hot, cheesy noodles. Serve piping hot. 4 servings.

BROCCOLI POLONAISE

1 lb broccoli	2 tbsp bread or cracker
2 tbsp butter or margarine	crumbs
Salt and pepper	1 hard-cooked egg
2 tsp lemon juice	

Prepare and cook broccoli as described in Buttered Broccoli until done (10 to 15 min). Meanwhile, put the butter in small skillet. Add salt and pepper, lemon juice and bread crumbs and brown slightly. Arrange drained, cooked hot broccoli on warm serving platter, sprinkle the flower-ends with sieved hard-cooked egg, then with browned buttered crumbs. Serve at once. 4 servings.

BROCCOLI WITH ALLEMANDE SAUCE

1½ lbs broccoli	1 chicken flavored bouillon
3 tbsp butter	cube
2 tbsp flour	2 egg yolks
1¼ cups milk	1 tbsp lemon juice
¼ tsp salt	

Prepare and cook broccoli until just tender as described in recipe for Buttered Broccoli. Keep hot. Meanwhile, make a white sauce of the butter, flour, milk, salt and bouillon cube, cooking it in the top of a double boiler over hot water until smooth and thick or for about 15 min. Add some of hot sauce slowly to beaten egg yolks, stir thoroughly. Return to double boiler and continue cooking for 5 min, stirring often. Add lemon juice gradually, stirring constantly. Serve over hot broccoli. 4 servings.

BUTTERED OR CREAMED BRUSSELS SPROUTS

1 qt box Brussels sprouts	3 tbsp butter, 1½ cups
2 tsp salt	medium white sauce, *or* ¾
1 tsp sugar	cup Hollandaise Sauce,
	p 1256

Choose crisp, solid, bright green sprouts, remove soiled outer leaves, and cut a thin slice from stem ends to remove all discoloration. Wash well and soak for 20 min in 1 qt cold water to which 1 tsp of the salt has been added. Drain. Add rest of salt, and sprouts to 1 qt boiling water and cook in an uncovered saucepan, boiling vigorously, until just tender, or from 12 to 15 min depending on size. Drain well and add sugar and butter and reheat just enough to melt the butter. Turn into a hot serving dish and serve immediately, plain with butter or with either white sauce or Hollandaise Sauce. 4 to 5 servings.

Note: Cooking time may be shortened to 8 min if quarter-inch crosswise slashes are made up through the stem end of each sprout.

RICH-TASTY BRUSSELS SPROUTS

Unusual and attractive

Cheese Sauce:	*Sprouts:*
2 tbsp butter *or* chicken fat	1 qt Brussels sprouts
2 tbsp flour	2 cups boiling water
1 cup milk	½ tsp salt
3 oz sharp cheddar cheese	3 tbsp fine dry bread crumbs
¼ tsp salt	3 slices bacon, pan-broiled
¹⁄₁₆ tsp chili powder	1 tbsp butter *or* chicken fat

Sauce: Melt butter in top of double boiler over direct heat. Blend in flour, add milk slowly and stir constantly until smooth and thick. Add grated cheese, ¾ cup, salt and chili powder, place over hot water and stir frequently until cheese melts. Cover to keep warm. *Sprouts:* Trim damaged leaves from sprouts, wash in cold water, drain. Make a ¼-inch-deep X-cut in stem-ends. Drop into boiling water, add salt and boil briskly uncovered until just tender when pricked with fork, about 10 min. Meanwhile pan-broil bacon. Brown crumbs lightly in butter until crisp. Drain sprouts, turn into hot dish. Pour hot cheese sauce over sprouts but not to completely cover; sprinkle with hot crumbs then with crumbled bacon. Serve at once. 4 to 5 servings.

Note: Recipe for Buttered Broccoli p 1326.

BUTTERED OR CREAMED CABBAGE

The green cabbage of spring and summer is the most attractive to the eye when cooked, but white winter cabbage though not so beautiful tastes just as good and has about the same food value when properly cooked. Trim off outer leaves from cabbage, remove a thin slice from the end of the stalk. If cabbage is old or poor in quality (due to drouth or other conditions), let the head soak at least 1 hr in ice water and drain. Cut either green or winter cabbage in quarters, and remove central stalk; slice or chop it coarsely. Drop into barely enough boiling water to cover, add ¾ tsp salt to each lb of cabbage and boil rapidly, uncovered, until just tender, 6 to 9 min. Drain thoroughly and pour melted butter, or medium White Sauce (p 1262) over hot cabbage. Serve immediately. Allow 1 small head (2 lbs) for 5 servings.

BRAISED CABBAGE

2 large onions, sliced	½ tsp salt
¼ cup shortening or bacon	½ tsp sugar
drippings	2 tbsp water
½ head of 2-lb cabbage, cut	⅓ cup dry bread crumbs
in 6ths	2 tbsp melted butter

Brown onion slices lightly in shortening. Push to one side of pan, then add the cabbage. Cook over low heat until cabbage is delicately browned. Turn carefully to preserve shape. Sprinkle both sides with salt and sugar during browning process. Add water, cover and simmer 7 to 10 min, turning once. Now toss onions over cabbage, then mix crumbs and butter together and sprinkle over vegetables. Serve immediately. 4 servings.

CABBAGE au GRATIN

1 medium head cabbage,	¾ cup evap milk
2 to 2½ lbs	Salt to taste
1 tsp salt	1½ cups grated cheese
3 tbsp butter	½ cup fine dry bread crumbs
3 tbsp flour	2 tbsp butter, melted

Discard soiled outside leaves of cabbage. Slice cabbage rather coarsely into saucepan. Add salt and barely enough boiling water to cover, boil uncovered until just tender (about 7 min). Drain, saving water. Melt butter, blend in flour, and add evaporated milk and ¾ cup of the water drained from cabbage; stir constantly until sauce boils and thickens. Add salt. Place a layer of cooked cabbage in bottom of a buttered casserole, pour part of the sauce over it, and sprinkle with part of the cheese. Repeat until all ingredients are used, ending with cheese on top. Sprinkle with crumbs which have been blended with the 2 tbsp butter. Bake in a moderate oven (350° F) for 20 min or until nicely browned. 5 servings.

CABBAGE IN RAISIN SAUCE

1 lb fresh green cabbage	⅛ tsp salt
¾ tsp salt	1 cup apple cider
2 tbsp butter *or* margarine	¼ cup raisins
1 tbsp brown sugar	Nutmeg
1 tbsp flour	

Trim cabbage and cut into thin serving wedges. Barely cover with boiling water. Add salt. Cook uncovered 7 to 9 min until cabbage is tender but not mushy. Drain, then add the butter. Meanwhile, mix sugar, flour and salt in a saucepan and gradually blend in the cider and cook over low heat. Stir until mixture boils and thickens, then add raisins and keep hot long enough to plump the raisins. Pour this hot sauce over the hot, freshly cooked cabbage. Sprinkle lightly with nutmeg and serve immediately. 4 servings.

CREAMED SAUSAGE MEAT WITH RED CABBAGE

1 lb sausage meat *or* links	1 small head red cabbage, 2
2 tbsp chopped onion	lbs, 3 cups of shredded
2 tbsp flour	½ cup water
Salt to taste	¼ tsp sugar
1¼ cups milk	2 tsp vinegar
	1 tsp caraway seed

Turn the sausage meat into a skillet and brown slowly over low heat for 20 min, stirring occasionally. Pour off the fat during the cooking, leaving only that which clings to the meat. Blend in the flour and salt and add milk gradually; cook until mixture boils and thickens. Meanwhile combine cabbage with remaining ingredients, cover, and simmer 20 to 45 min or until of desired tenderness. Serve the hot sauce over the cabbage. 4 servings.

ESCALLOPED CABBAGE

1 small head cabbage, 2 to	1 cup grated sharp cheese
2½ lbs	½ cup Buttered Bread
2 cups thin White Sauce,	Crumbs, p 162
p 1262	3 slices half-cooked bacon
½ green pepper, chopped	

Cut trimmed cabbage into eighths, remove core, and cook, uncovered, for 8 min in boiling salted water (1 tsp salt to 1 qt water). Drain. Place a layer of cabbage in a buttered baking dish or casserole, then a layer of white sauce, half the green pepper, and half the cheese. Repeat. Sprinkle top with buttered crumbs and chopped bacon, and bake in a moderate oven (375° F) until toasted, about 15 min. Serve immediately. 5 servings.

FRIED CABBAGE

Cabbage in one of its most appetizing cooked forms

1½ lbs green cabbage *or*   ½ tsp salt
  6 cups coarsely shredded   Pepper
2 tbsp bacon fat *or* butter

Prepare cabbage. Heat fat in a heavy skillet until barely sizzling. Add cabbage, spread out level and sprinkle with salt. Cover, reduce heat and cook gently, shaking skillet occasionally to prevent sticking. After 3 min cooking, turn cabbage over with a pancake turner. Replace cover and cook another 2 or 3 min or until cabbage is soft but still has a little crispness remaining, is a pale green color and has only a suspicion of brown on the bottom. Sprinkle with pepper and turn out into a hot dish and serve piping hot. 4 servings.

NEW CABBAGE WITH TOMATOES

2 tbsp chopped onion
2 tbsp bacon fat
¾ cup boiling water
1 tsp salt
½ tsp sugar
1 medium head cabbage, 2 lbs

2 cups canned tomatoes
2 tbsp flour
¼ cup fine dry bread crumbs
2 tbsp butter, melted
3 tbsp grated Parmesan
  cheese

Sauté onion in fat for 5 min. Add the water, salt, sugar, and the cabbage that has been trimmed and cut into thin wedges. Boil vigorously, uncovered, for about 8 min or until cabbage is tender, turning over once during the cooking. Add tomatoes, reserving some of the juice to combine with flour to make a paste. Add paste to the cabbage mixture, stirring thoroughly, and cook until liquid boils and thickens. Serve immediately topped with buttered crumbs combined with the cheese. 4 servings.

RED CABBAGE WITH APPLES

1 medium head red cabbage,
  2 to 3 lbs
3 tbsp butter *or* bacon
  drippings
1 small onion, chopped
½ tsp salt, *or* to taste

2 tart apples, quartered and
  cored
1 tbsp sugar
⅓ cup vinegar
½ tsp caraway seed, if desired

Trim off soiled outer leaves of cabbage; cut cabbage in quarters and remove the core. Slice rather coarsely. Melt butter or drippings in saucepan, add the onion and simmer 2 or 3 min; then add cabbage, apples and salt, and barely cover with boiling water. Cover pan and simmer gently for 45 min. Uncover pan, add sugar and stir. At this point, the water should be practically evaporated; if not, increase heat and continue to cook, watching carefully until water has evaporated.

No liquid should be drained off. Add vinegar, stir well, and continue heating until vinegar is well distributed. Stir in caraway seed and serve immediately. 5 servings.

Note: Do not substitute green or white cabbage for the red, as the vinegar which intensifies the red color will spoil the green.

HEARTS OF PALM OR SWAMP CABBAGE

Where cabbage palms grow, one can find them served in abundance as a cooked vegetable at fish frys and barbecues. In other parts of the country, only the expensive commercially canned are available which we use only on rare occasions in elegant salads

In central and southern Florida as well as in other subtropical areas, hearts of palm are common but highly prized food to many people. These hearts are the tender core found at the base of the cabbage palm. Harvesting them means sacrificing a palm tree for every heart that is obtained. Trees 8 to 10 feet high are cut and the upper part of the body that is 6 to 7 inches in diameter and 24 to 26 inches long contains the heart. Preparation for cooking consists in cutting through the thin strip of each layer of "bark" the entire 24 to 26-inch length. These layers called "boots" are pulled off one by one down to the heart. One knows when the heart is reached by the tenderness and flavor. The heart is as easily pierced with the thumbnail as the tenderest of celery, and it is without bitter flavor. It is cream colored and so delicate in texture that it can be used raw in salads with a French dressing. Or it may be cooked and served either as a salad or vegetable. Here are 2 favorite ways of serving.

BUTTERED HEARTS OF PALM

2 hearts of palm	Pepper
½ tsp salt	2 tbsp butter

Prepare hearts of palm as described above. Barely cover with boiling water, add salt, cover and boil gently until just tender—10 to 15 min. Drain off the water, add pepper and butter. Reheat, toss vegetable carefully to coat with butter and seasonings. 4 servings.

SWAMP CABBAGE WITH WHITE BACON

4 hearts of palm	Salt and pepper
Boiling water	½ cup evap milk
3 oz white bacon—salt pork	

Prepare hearts as described above. Rinse in cold water, and slice coarsely into a 4-qt kettle. Add enough boiling water to cover. Heat to boiling, reduce heat, cover, and boil gently 5 to 10 min. Taste of the cooking water; if it is bitter, drain off, and add fresh boiling water to cover. Cut pork in ¼-inch dice, and sauté in a skillet with frequent stirring until dice are crisp and golden brown. Drain off half the fat, and save for other cooking. Pour rest of fat and the bacon into the kettle, cover, and continue boiling gently until the vegetable and pork are meltingly tender, or for 1¼ hrs. Add salt and pepper to suit taste, and stir in the evaporated milk. Simmer another 10 min. Serve with fish or any other meat. In the southland, the vegetable is cooked much longer. The result is a mushy but tasty vegetable. 6 to 7 servings.

WHAT TO CONSIDER WHEN BUYING AND STORING CARROTS

Carrots of good quality are very firm and crisp, have smooth fresh appearing skin and are of a rich yellow color. Carrots of pale yellow color have grown in poor soil and are not as rich in vitamin content as the deep yellow ones. There should be very little or no green color around the top. The long slender-shaped root is usually of better flavor than the thick stubby-shaped one. Over-sized carrots are often strong-flavored and are coarse and woody in texture. Young carrots are always sold in the bunch with the green tops on. Mature carrots have the tops removed and are sold by the pound. When carrots are to be kept for several hrs or a day or so before cooking, they should be stored in the refrigerator. And the tops should always be removed to preserve both flavor, firmness and food value. Carrots that are shriveled and limp are not economical buys.

BUTTERED CARROTS

Scrub carrots thoroughly and scrape lightly to remove only the thin outer layer of skin. Tiny young carrots may be left whole for cooking, but older carrots should be split lengthwise in halves or quarters, or sliced crosswise. Barely cover with boiling salted water (¼ tsp salt to 1 cup water), cover and cook gently until tender, from 10 to 20 min, depending on size and age of carrots and how they are cut. Remove cover, evaporate remaining liquid, watching carefully to avoid scorching. Add 2 tbsp butter and sprinkle chopped parsley on top. Allow 1 large bunch carrots for 5 servings.

CARROT CUTLETS

2 eggs, beaten	2 cups grated raw carrots
2 cups day-old coarse bread crumbs	½ cup grated cheese, 2 oz
	¾ cup rolled corn flakes
½ tsp celery salt	¼ cup shortening
½ tsp salt	

Combine the first 6 ingredients and mix well. Divide mixture into cutlets by packing it firmly into a ¼-cup measure and dropping out onto the rolled flakes. Pat into a flat shape, lightly cover with the flakes. Pan fry over low heat to form a golden brown crust on each side of the cutlets. Turn once during the frying. Serve with 1½ cups medium White Sauce (p 1262), seasoned with 2 tbsp each finely sliced green onions and chopped parsley. 4 servings.

CARROT RING

1 large bunch carrots
3 eggs, separated
1 cup milk
1 tbsp melted butter
2 cups half-inch stale bread
  cubes

2 tbsp chopped celery
1 tsp finely chopped onion
2 tbsp chopped parsley
1 tsp salt

Clean and cook carrots until tender according to direction for Buttered Carrots. Drain if necessary, and mash. Add egg yolks to the milk, beat and add to the mashed carrots. Add remaining ingredients and fold in the stiffly beaten egg whites. Turn into a well-oiled 6-cup ring mold. (Waxed paper fitted into the bottom of the mold will aid in removing the ring, Note, p 445.) Place directly on the rack of moderate oven (350° F) and bake for 1 hr. Unmold and fill with hot creamed cauliflower, green beans or mushrooms. 6 servings.

CARROT SOUFFLÉ

2 tbsp butter
2 tbsp flour
½ cup milk
1 tsp salt

3 eggs, separated
2 cups raw grated carrots,
  5 medium carrots

Make a White Sauce (p 1262) of the butter, flour, milk, and salt. Pour hot sauce over the beaten egg yolks, stirring vigorously. Stir in carrots; then fold in stiffly beaten egg whites. Turn into ungreased 4-cup casserole and place (see method pp 678–9) in a moderate oven (350° F) and bake for 30 to 40 min or until a knife inserted in the center comes out clean. Serve with Buttered Peas (p 1367). 4 servings.

CREAMED CARROTS

To make creamed carrots, add to Cooked Carrots (p 1333) 2 cups medium White Sauce (p 1262) instead of melted butter.

CREAMED CARROTS AND CELERY

2 cups sliced carrots
1 cup diced celery
2 tbsp butter
3 tbsp flour
1 cup thin cream *or* evaporated milk

Cooking water from
vegetables, concentrated
to 1 cup
Salt to taste
Croutons, p 262

Cover carrots and celery with boiling salted water (1 tsp salt to 1 qt water), and cook until tender. Drain, saving water. Measure water and if necessary, boil rapidly to concentrate to 1 cup. Meanwhile melt butter in saucepan, blend in flour, and add cream and water drained from the vegetables, stirring constantly over low heat until sauce boils and thickens. Add salt and the cooked vegetables and reheat thoroughly. Serve the creamed vegetables poured over crisp croutons. 5 servings.

CREAMED CARROTS AND SPINACH

A fine combination of colors and flavors

1 lb fresh spinach	Cooking water from
1½ cups diced carrots	carrots concentrated
3 tbsp butter	to ½ cup
3 tbsp flour	½ to 1 tsp grated onion, if
1 cup cream or evaporated	desired
milk	Salt to taste

Pick over spinach carefully, discarding bad leaves and trimming off ends of stalks. Wash thoroughly through several cold waters. Place in a 2 to 3 qt saucepan, add 1 cup boiling water and ½ tsp salt, and cook until just tender (5 to 10 min), turning the spinach over two or three times. Drain well. Meanwhile, drop carrots into just enough boiling water to cover, add ½ tsp salt and cook until tender; drain, saving the water. If water measures more than ½ cup, boil rapidly to concentrate. Melt butter in saucepan, blend in flour, and add cream and the water from carrots; stir over direct heat until sauce boils. Stir in onion; add drained spinach and carrots, and stir just enough to mix. Add salt to suit taste. Reheat if necessary, and serve immediately. 5 servings.

ESCALLOPED CARROTS AND POTATOES

1 tbsp flour	1 small onion, sliced
2 cups milk	4 medium potatoes, pared
2 tsp salt	sliced
Pepper	2 tbsp butter
6 medium carrots, sliced	

Blend flour to a smooth paste with a little of the milk in a saucepan; add remaining milk, stir until smooth and cook, stirring constantly until sauce boils and thickens. Add seasonings and vegetables, and heat to boiling again. Turn into a buttered 8-cup casserole, dot with the butter, cover, and bake in a moderate oven (350° F) for 30 min. Uncover the last 10 min to brown surface. Serve at once directly from casserole. 5 servings.

GLAZED CARROTS

10 medium carrots   1 tbsp butter
½ cup brown sugar, firmly   ⅛ tsp salt
  pkd

Wash and scrape carrots and split in half, lengthwise; add just enough boiling water to cover and 1 tsp of salt, cover and boil 10 min. Drain carrots saving cooking water and transfer carrots to buttered baking dish. Concentrate water if necessary to measure ¼ cup by boiling rapidly. Add remaining ingredients and boil 5 min to make a syrup. Pour hot syrup over carrots, cover, and bake in a moderate oven (350° F) for 15 min, or until carrots are tender, occasionally dipping the syrup up over the carrots. 5 servings.

MINTED CARROTS

1 large bunch carrots   Pepper
½ tsp salt   2 tbsp sugar
⅓ cup butter   3 sprigs fresh tender mint

Choose medium size tender carrots. Wash, scrape, rinse and cut crosswise into quarter-inch thick slices. Barely cover with boiling water, add salt, cover tightly and boil at a moderate rate until carrots are about tender, from 4 to 6 min. Add next 3 ingredients, continue boiling until liquid is evaporated down to not more than a tbsp. Have mint leaves chopped medium fine. Remove carrots from heat, add mint and toss to distribute. 3 to 4 servings.

BUTTERED CAULIFLOWER

Select compact, curd-like flowers. Avoid those of loose formation and with discolored flowerets. Soak cauliflower in enough cold salt water to cover for half an hr. Drain. Wash head and trim by cutting off base of stalk and discarding all large leaves. The tiny leaves that cling to the outer flowerets may be left on. Break flowerets apart, removing large main stem. (The main stem is a delicious tidbit to eat raw.) Drop into a generous amount of boiling salted water (1 tsp salt to each qt of water), and cook rapidly in uncovered pan until tender, from 6 to 8 min. Test by piercing with fork. Do not overcook! Cooked cauliflower should be snow white and still slightly crisp. Drain thoroughly, turn into hot serving dish and drizzle with melted butter. (The cooking water makes good pot liquor.) Sprinkle with paprika. Serve immediately. Allow 1 large head (2 lbs) for 5 servings.

CAULIFLOWER IN DRIED BEEF CHEESE SAUCE

1 head cauliflower, 1½ to   1 cup grated sharp cheese,
2 lbs   4 oz
2 cups unseasoned medium   2 oz chipped beef
  White Sauce, p 1262   2 tbsp butter

Cook cauliflower as directed in recipe for Buttered Cauliflower until just tender, or from 6 to 8 min. Meanwhile make the white sauce and stir in the cheese until melted. Add chipped beef that has been snipped in small pieces and sautéed in the butter. Serve hot sauce over drained hot cauliflower. (If chipped beef is very salty, rinse it quickly in cold water; if not salty enough, add salt to sauce to suit taste.) Omit beef, if desired. 5 servings.

CAULIFLOWER WITH CORN FLAKE TOPPING

1 head cauliflower, 1½ lbs   ½ cup corn flakes, coarsely
1 tbsp very finely chopped   crushed
  onion   2 tbsp butter
                                       Dash of salt

Cook cauliflower as directed in recipe for Buttered Cauliflower until just tender, or from 6 to 8 min. Meanwhile combine remaining ingredients in a small skillet and brown slightly for 5 min. Drain cauliflower and arrange on a serving plate, then sprinkle with the hot crumb mixture. Serve at once. 4 servings.

CREAMED CAULIFLOWER

Cook cauliflower as directed in recipe for Buttered Cauliflower for 6 to 8 min. Drain thoroughly and pour hot White Sauce, p 1262, or Cheese Sauce, p 1253, over the hot vegetable. Serve at once.

FRENCH-FRIED CAULIFLOWER

Tempting in appearance and flavor

1 medium cauliflower, 2 lbs   2 tbsp cream *or* milk
1 qt boiling water   ⅔ cup fine dry cracker *or*
1 tsp salt   bread crumbs
1 egg, slightly beaten   1½ to 2 lbs shortening

Use a tight-flowered, curd-white cauliflower. Trim off leaves and stalk and save for making a boiled vegetable. Separate flowerets leaving stems attached. Wash in cold water and drop into the boiling water to which salt is added. Reheat to boiling and boil gently uncovered 2 or 3 min. Drain well. Beat egg, stir in cream. Dip flowerets in crumbs measured onto waxed paper, then into egg mixture and again in crumbs. Let stand in cool place or in refrigerator until about serving time. Place layer of cauliflower in frying basket and lower into shortening heated to

365° F. Keep heat constant and fry to a rich golden color. Drain quickly. Serve very hot. 5 servings.

French-frying Tip: Less shortening may be used without a frying basket, *but* a slotted or perforated spoon or food fork is needed to quickly "fish out" fried food so none of it overcooks.

BUTTERED CELERY

Outside branches of celery, left after hearts have been eaten raw, may be cooked very successfully. Scrub them, scrape away blemishes, and cut neatly into uniform lengthwise strips; then cut into ½-inch lengths. Barely cover with boiling salted water and cook at moderate rate until tender, about 10 or 15 min. Drain and add melted butter. (Celery cooking water should be saved for use in soup or vegetable juice cocktail.) Allow 2½ cups cut celery for 5 servings.

BRAISED CELERY

3 medium stalks celery	1½ cups meat broth *or* 1
¼ cup butter	chicken bouillon cube in
1 tsp cornstarch	1½ cups hot water
	Salt to taste

Trim off leaves and cut the top ends of branches squarely to leave stalk not more than 6 inches long. Then trim root ends of stalks, and wash thoroughly by swishing vigorously through cold water several times, but do not separate branches. Make sure all soil is removed. Cut stalk neatly in half lengthwise. Melt butter in large heavy skillet, lay celery cut-side down in it, cover, cook slowly until celery is delicately browned and is just soft. Lift celery out carefully, keep hot, blend cornstarch with the butter; add broth and stir briskly until sauce boils. Add salt to suit taste. Return celery to sauce, cover skillet, and simmer gently for 10 min longer. Serve at once with all remaining liquid poured over top. 5 servings.

CELERY au GRATIN

4 cups diced celery	1 cup grated sharp cheese
3 tbsp butter	Salt to taste
3 tbsp flour	¼ cup Buttered Bread
¾ cup evaporated milk	Crumbs, p 162
¾ cup cooking water from celery	

Cook celery until tender as directed in Buttered Celery. Drain, saving water. If water measures more than ¾ cup, boil rapidly to concentrate. Meanwhile, melt butter in saucepan, blend in flour, add milk and cooking water and stir until sauce boils and thickens. Remove from heat, add cheese and stir until smooth; add cooked celery and salt. Turn into buttered baking dish and sprinkle buttered crumbs over top. Bake uncovered in a moderate oven (375° F) for 15 to 20 min or until crumbs are toasted. 5 servings.

CELERY ROOT WITH HOLLANDAISE

A good pinch bitter for turnips or potatoes

2 celery roots, 12 oz   Mock *or* True Hollandaise
1½ cups milk, scalded   Sauce, p 1256
½ tsp salt

Pare celery roots, immediately slice ¼-inch thick and drop in hot milk. Cover and continue cooking over boiling water until just tender, from 30 to 35 min. Now drain off hot milk and serve hot vegetable with Mock or True Hollandaise Sauce. 4 servings.

Note: Use leftover flavorful milk for pork roast, pork chop or chicken cream gravy or in cream soups.

CELERY ROOT AND LEMON SAUTÉ

A pleasant vegetable especially good with fish

2 celery roots, 12 oz   Pepper, optional
3 strips bacon   1 tbsp lemon juice
¼ tsp salt

Wash and pare celery root. Allow to remain covered in cold water while preparing remaining ingredients. Do not slice as it discolors. Cook bacon until done, drain, set aside to keep warm. Slice celery root about ⅛ inch thick, then cut julienne style into bacon fat, sprinkle with salt, cover, cook over low heat until tender, from 20 to 25 min and turn occasionally. When just tender, add lemon juice and sauté a few min longer to allow lemon flavor to penetrate. Serve in hot dish with warm, crumbled bacon over top. 4 servings.

CHEESE-CRUSTED CELERY ROOT (CELERIAC)

A very good, very different German-style vegetable

1 cup milk   ¼ tsp salt
2 celery roots, ¾ lb   ⅛ tsp pepper
1 tsp flour   ¼ cup fresh-grated Parmesan
1 tbsp milk   cheese
1 tbsp butter

Heat milk over low heat in 3-qt saucepan. Scrub roots in cold water, pare quickly, cut into quarters and drop immediately into the hot milk to prevent discoloration. Heat to boiling, reduce heat to *simmer,* cover and cook 30 to 35 min or until just tender, stirring occasionally to prevent sticking. Mix flour with the tbsp of milk until smooth, then stir gently into the simmering milk. Add butter, salt and pepper and cook a min or two. Turn into a buttered glass 8 x 8 x 2-inch baking dish. Sprinkle with cheese. Place under broiler set at 450° F, or in oven of same temp until cheese melts and is nicely browned —10 to 15 min. 4 to 5 servings.

CREAMED CELERY

For creamed celery, substitute in Buttered Celery, p 1338, 2 cups thin or medium White Sauce, p 1262, for the butter.

BUTTERED SWISS CHARD

Allow 1½ to 2 lbs chard for 5 servings. Wash the leaves thoroughly, discarding any discolored tough leaves; then strip the green leafy part from the thick fleshy midrib, and cook like Spinach, p 1394. The midribs require longer cooking than the green leaves, and should be cooked separately in a small amount of salted water, like Asparagus, p 1310, either whole or cut in 1-inch lengths. Drain and add melted butter. Combine leafy part and midribs and serve hot.

BUTTERED CHAYOTE

Choose 2 medium-sized chayotes each weighing about ¾ lb, to serve 5. They should be tender enough to be easily punctured with the thumb nail; otherwise they must be thinly pared. Wash and remove any blemishes on the skin, and cut in quarters lengthwise, through flesh and seed; the seed is a special delicacy. Slice the quarters ⅛-inch thick. Put into a saucepan and add 1⅓ cups boiling water and ¾ tsp salt. Cover and boil briskly until tender, from 12 to 15 min; by this time most of the water should have evaporated. Add ¼ cup butter and pepper to suit taste. Reheat to melt butter and evaporate remaining liquid, watching carefully to prevent scorching. Serve immediately.

Variation: Sautéed Mushrooms, p 1356, combined with buttered chayote are delicious.

WHAT TO LOOK FOR WHEN GATHERING OR BUYING FRESH CORN

There is nothing more fleeting than the fine rare flavor of garden fresh corn gathered at the right stage of development and cooked promptly and properly. That old saying "twenty min from the stalk to the pot" puts all the precautions for gathering and buying into one short phrase. When corn develops to the point where the grains are of maximum size, filled out and bursting with sweet milky juice, it is just right for eating. When such corn is pierced with the thumbnail, the thin milky liquid spurts out with great force. Left on the stalk a few hrs more, the pierced grains would ooze juice so thick that it would have a soft cheesy-like consistency. At this point, the corn would not be worth eating as fresh corn. Once perfect corn is gathered, it cannot be cooked too quickly, because the enzymes work fast to turn the sugary liquid into a thick starchy one. Corn at the right stage of maturity has ears that have a well-filled-out feel, the shucks are a brilliant green from stalk to silk end. The silks are moist and creamy colored next to the ear with only the tips beginning to get brown and having a slightly dry feel. An amateur needs to double check the quality by stripping back the shuck and using the thumbnail test, but with a little practice this severe test is rarely ever necessary. Corn with shriveled, yellowish shucks and ears with silks and shucks cut off squarely at the tip are not ever good buys. The best corn is that from your own garden or close-by local gardens. Even that shipped in by airplane can never rate higher than second class.

BUTTERED CORN

Select corn that is at exactly the right stage for eating. Then husk and silk, see recipe for Corn on the Cob.

Fresh corn: Cut corn from 6 to 8 ears as directed for Fried Corn, P 1343, to make 3 cups. Barely cover with water, heat to the boiling point, reduce heat, then *simmer* 5 to 8 min. Add salt to suit taste, and 2 to 3 tbsp butter. Heat until butter is melted and most of water is evaporated. (2 tbsp diced green peppers may also be added.) 5 servings.

Canned creamed style corn: Put 2 tbsp butter into a saucepan and heat slowly until melted. Tilt the pan from side to side until about an inch of the sides is coated with butter. Turn the contents of a No. 2 can of corn into the pan, cover, and heat slowly to the boiling point. Serve immediately in small individual vegetable dishes with a sprinkling of paprika or finely chopped parsley, green pepper or pimiento on top. Ham or bacon drippings may be substituted for butter if desired. 5 servings.

Canned whole kernel corn: Use two 12-oz cans of whole kernel corn and proceed as for cream style corn, stirring occasionally while heating thoroughly. Turn hot corn into a hot serving dish, add a dash of paprika and serve immediately. 5 servings.

CORN ON THE COB

Choose the freshest corn possible. The sooner corn is cooked after it is pulled from the stalk, the better it will be. (To test for the freshness and tenderness of corn, break a kernel with your fingernail. If the milk spurts out, the ear is young, tender and at least fairly fresh.) Husk the corn and remove the silk, brushing back and forth with a soft cloth or a soft brush. Have plenty of boiling water ready. Drops the ears of corn into a kettle containing enough boiling water to cover. Boil 4 to 6 min, depending on age and tenderness of ears. Drain thoroughly and serve immediately with salt and plenty of butter. Allow at least 2 ears for each serving.

Note: Do not add salt or sugar to water in which corn is boiled because it shrivels the corn.

CREAMED CORN WITH GREEN PEPPER

6 ears fresh corn, 2½ cups   1 tsp salt
2 tbsp butter   ⅔ cup water
¼ cup finely chopped onion   ¼ cup chopped green pepper
1 tsp sugar   ½ cup milk

Cut corn from cob; be careful not to shave off any bits of cob. Melt butter in a saucepan; add corn, onion, sugar, salt and water. Cover, simmer about 6 min or until water is almost evaporated and the kernels are tender. Add green pepper and milk; cook just long enough to heat thoroughly. Serve at once. 4 servings.

ESCALLOPED CORN AND CHEESE

1 egg, beaten   1 cup coarse fresh bread
No. 2 can cream style corn   crumbs
1 cup milk   ¼ cup grated sharp American
¾ tsp salt   cheese, 1 oz

Beat egg in a 6-cup buttered casserole. Heat corn and milk and gradually stir into beaten egg. Add salt, bread crumbs, and cheese and mix thoroughly. Place directly on the rack of a moderately slow oven (325° F) and bake uncovered for 30 min or until custard tests done, p 526. 5 servings.

FRESH CORN AND TOMATO CASSEROLE

8 to 12 ears fresh corn   4 slices crisp bacon, crumbled
¼ cup butter or bacon   1 tsp salt or to taste
  drippings   2 large tomatoes, peeled and
2 cups water   sliced

Cut corn from cob as directed for Fried Corn. There should be 4 to 5 cups of cut corn. Melt butter or drippings in skillet, add corn, and sauté quickly for about 5 min. Add water, bacon and salt and pour in buttered casserole. Arrange sliced tomatoes on top. Place in a moderate oven (350° F) and bake uncovered about 30 min. Serve hot. 5 to 6 servings.

FRESH CORN RABBIT

2 cups peeled, diced   1 tsp salt
  tomatoes, 4 medium   ⅛ tsp pepper
1¼ cups fresh cut-off corn,   1 tsp sugar
  4 to 6 ears   ½ tsp Worcestershire sauce
¼ cup water   ½ lb American cheese cut in
3 tbsp butter   ¼-inch cubes
2 tbsp chopped onion   2 eggs, beaten
¼ cup chopped green pepper   Toast
1 tbsp flour

Vegetables have beauty that's more than skin deep. Vegetable Plates can be made beautiful and valuable—if the color, shape, fragrance and nutrients of the vegetables are preserved. Here are 2 examples: TOP PLATE is plain cooked buttered vegetable around a Tomato Cup of potato salad. LOWER PLATE adds Hollandaise Sauce to the broccoli with a center slice of Pan-broiled Tomato.

© Birds Eye Frosted Foods.

ABOVE: *Plain creamed peas plus plain (but well-seasoned) mashed potatoes equal a Pea and Potato Casserole which is anything but plain to look at, and as good to eat as it is beautiful. Cooked beets are put through a potato ricer, seasoned with salt and lemon juice or vinegar, packed into a ring mold and filled with marinated cucumbers to make the unusual vegetable dish in the background.*

BELOW: *Fat, tender spears of either fresh or frozen asparagus cooked to perfection, p 1310, and immediately transferred to a hot platter with Pan-broiled Tomatoes, p 1406, on the opposite side and a stream of luscious cheese sauce flowing between make a tempting luncheon or dinner main dish.*

ABOVE: *Another of those de luxe vegetable plates packed with vitamins and flavor. Steaming hot corn on the cob demands prompt attention. So do the Baked Stuffed Eggplant, ₱ 1346, and buttered little cauliflowers perched on pan-broiled tomato slices.*

BELOW: *When a famous opera star saw this attractive platter, she immediately wanted to know how the little Baked Acorn Squash, ₱ 1399, got their sugary brown crust and their moist sweet flesh underneath. The recipe tells you what we told her.*

ABOVE: *Whole translucent onions with delicate green stripes are combined here with bright colored whole green beans. A dill sauce adds the final exotic touch.*

BELOW: *The Texans use and enjoy okra, and have passed on to us one of the many ways to cook it . . . by dipping in cornmeal and frying. Try "Okra Texas Style" and we'll venture you'll have made a new friend.*

ABOVE: *Everybody who likes frankfurters will extend a warm welcome to this simple but very hearty Frankfurter and Lima Bean Casserole. Prepare Buttered Limas, p 1319, turn into casserole, lay frankfurters over the top and bake in a hot oven.*

BELOW: *Making stuffed cabbage rolls, p 832, violates one of the principles of vegetable cookery by cooking cabbage covered for 1 hr. It's the only way to acquire the characteristic flavor of this European favorite. It's one of those recipes in which it is commendable and desirable to let tradition step ahead of scientific practice.*

ABOVE: *It's really surprising what an imposing platter can be arranged with an assortment of vegetables, and no meat at all except a garnish of crisp broiled bacon. The cauliflower is split up from the bottom of the stalk into six sections to speed up the cooking. With cheese sauce poured over the top, it makes a handsome rallying point for any vegetable platter.*

BELOW: *These are homey foods—blackeyed peas cooked to mushy tenderness with sliced Boiled Tongue, p 909, and apples left with skins on stewed until translucent in a medium sugar syrup with green onions and bread sticks.*

Chilled flavorful Potato Salad, p 1188, tumbled into the center of an attractive platter, then flanked with equally chilled cold cuts such as liver sausage, veal loaf and salami. Dot with cold edible garnishes such as pickles, olives and hard-cooked eggs. Then tuck in some crisp lettuce here and there for a very tempting hot weather fare.

Red, yellow and green vegetables add beauty to the meal and elements essential in the diet for radiant good health. They are delicious plain-cooked and served with melted butter or variations of creamy white sauce. LOWER LEFT—*Parsley Sauce, which is plain white sauce with fine-chopped fresh parsley folded into it, p 1262. Or substitute sour cream for the milk to make Sour Cream Sauce, which is excellent on boiled cabbage.* LOWER RIGHT—*Catchup Sauce is made by folding ⅓ cup catchup into 2 cups of white sauce. Good on Fried Egg Plant, p 1348, or boiled cauliflower, p 1336.*

© Sealtest Laboratory Kitchens.

Combine tomatoes, uncooked corn cut from cob and water in top of double boiler. Heat to boiling over direct heat, then let simmer for 7 min. Meanwhile melt butter in a small skillet, add onions and green pepper and sauté until onions are slightly transparent. Add flour and blend. Combine with tomato mixture and heat just to boiling. Place over boiling water. Add seasonings and cheese and stir until cheese melts. Pour a small amount of hot mixture into the eggs, beat, return to double boiler and stir for 2 min. Serve piping hot on slices of lightly buttered toast. 4 servings.

FRIED CORN

Select corn at the perfect stage for eating. See recipe for Corn on the Cob. Husk and silk 8 to 12 ears of corn, and cut from the cob, using a very sharp knife and cutting off only about half the depth of the kernels. After cutting all around the ear, use the back of the knife to scrape out the remaining juice and pulp, scraping downward only, not back and forth. For 5 cups of corn, heat ⅓ cup butter (or half butter and half bacon fat) sizzling hot in skillet. Add corn and enough water to give consistency of thin gravy, season with salt, and cook with constant stirring for five min, then reduce heat to simmering, cover tightly, and cook about 20 min longer, stirring occasionally. The corn at this point should be quite thick. Good served either hot or cold. Fried chicken is a perfect accompaniment. 5 servings.

ROASTED CORN

No better way to retain fine fresh corn flavor

Dutch Oven Method—Strip back the shucks of *freshly picked corn*, remove silks, cut off tips of ears and dip ears quickly into cold water. Now pull shucks back into place. Trim off any brown tips of shucks with scissors. Fit ears snugly into a heated Dutch oven; cover tightly and cook over moderate heat without removing cover for 30 to 35 min, time depending on size of ears. Serve immediately with butter and salt.

Outdoor Grill Method—Use freshly picked ears with long stems, which aid in turning the hot corn on the grill. Strip back the shucks, remove silks, cut off tips of ears, dip corn in cold water; then pull shucks back into place. Lay ears close together on the grill that has a thick bed of glowing coals under it. As the shucks begin to turn tan on under side, begin turning the corn over to roast evenly until the outer layer of shucks becomes an even scorched brown-black all over. Roasting requires from 25 to 35 min, time depending on size of ears. Remove the outer layer of shucks and serve immediately.

STEWED CORN

Cut corn from cob as directed for Fried Corn. To 3 cups corn, add 1 cup water; cover and simmer gently for 10 min. Add 1 cup milk and 3 tbsp butter, and simmer 10 min longer. Season to suit taste with salt and pepper. Serve immediately with a sprinkling of chopped parsley or a dash of paprika. 5 servings.

SUCCOTASH No. 1

½ cup diced celery	2 tbsp chopped pimiento
2 tbsp chopped onion	½ cup milk
No. 2 can cut green beans	1 tbsp butter
No. 2 can cream style corn	¾ tsp salt *or* to taste

Simmer celery and chopped onion until tender in the liquid drained from beans. The liquid by this time should be almost evaporated. Add corn, drained beans, pimiento, milk, and butter, simmer until thoroughly heated. Salt to suit taste and serve at once. 5 servings.

SUCCOTASH No. 2

1 cup green lima beans	3 tbsp butter
10 ears corn	Salt and pepper to taste

Cook Lima Beans, p 1319. Drain, saving the liquid. Cut corn from the cob and combine with lima beans. Add enough of the bean liquid just to be seen through the mixture. Simmer until most of water is evaporated. Add butter, stir until melted, then add salt and pepper to suit taste. Serve immediately. 5 servings.

Dried limas cooked according to directions may be substituted for the green limas, and canned corn may be used instead of fresh. If dried limas are used, cooking a piece of salt pork and a little onion with them adds to the flavor.

BRAISED CUCUMBERS

2 large *or* 3 medium-sized cucumbers	1 tsp cornstarch
2 tbsp butter	¼ cup cold water
½ cup boiling water	¼ tsp salt
1 chicken bouillon cube	Dash black pepper
	Chopped parsley *or* chives

Pare cucumbers and slice crosswise about ½-inch thick. Melt butter in skillet, add cucumbers, and brown pieces delicately on both sides. Add the boiling water, cover tightly and simmer about 10 min until the cucumbers are transparent-looking and fairly tender. Add bouillon cube and cornstarch which has been blended until smooth with the cold water. Stir gently until sauce again boils. Continue simmering 5 min longer; then add salt and pepper and serve hot. A sprinkling of chopped parsley or chives makes an attractive, flavorful garnish. 5 servings.

Note: Use ¾ cup rich chicken broth instead of the boiling water and the bouillon cube if available. Omit browning and use milk instead of broth for Creamed Cucumbers.

CUCUMBERS au GRATIN

3 tbsp butter	1 cup grated sharp cheese,
3 tbsp flour	4 oz
1¼ cups milk	⅓ cup fine dry bread crumbs
1 beef bouillon cube	1½ tbsp butter, melted
Dash of pepper	2 medium cucumbers, pared
¼ tsp onion juice	

Blend the 3 tbsp butter and flour together well, add milk gradually and stir constantly over direct heat until sauce boils and thickens. Stir in bouillon cube, pepper, and onion juice and remove from heat. Add grated cheese, stirring until cheese is melted. Stir bread crumbs in the melted butter to coat them well. Slice pared cucumbers about ⅛-inch thick. Into a 6-cup buttered casserole, put alternate layers of cucumber slices and hot, seasoned cheese sauce. Top with buttered crumbs, cover and bake in a moderately slow oven (325° F) for about 30 min; then remove cover and continue baking about 10 min longer or until cucumbers are just tender and surface browned. Serve piping hot. 5 servings.

MINTED CUCUMBERS IN SOUR CREAM

Really good and so refreshing

2 cucumbers, 1¼ lbs	4 tsp sugar
1¾ tsp salt	Pepper, optional
1 hard-cooked egg yolk	Leaves from 3 *or* 4 sprigs
⅓ cup thick sour cream	fresh mint
2 tbsp 5% cider *or* tarragon vinegar	

Pare cucumbers thinly. Slice ⅛-inch thick into mixing bowl. Sift 1½ tsp of the salt over cucumbers, and toss gently to distribute. Cover, and refrigerate 20 to 30 min. Meanwhile mash hard-cooked egg yolk fine; add rest of salt and next 4 ingredients; blend well. Just before serving, turn cucumbers into a sieve to drain. Press gently to remove excess liquid. Return to mixing bowl, pour sour cream · dressing over cucumbers, and add mint sheared fine with kitchen scissors. Toss gently. Serve immediately or chill. 4 to 5 servings.

Note: Mint may be omitted but it is a delightful addition.

WHAT TO LOOK FOR WHEN BUYING EGGPLANT

Eggplant of high quality are heavy for their size, and are of a uniform purple color. They have a smooth glossy skin and are firm to the touch. Their shape ranges from a slender oval to pear shape. Fruit that is irregular in shape, wrinkled and wilted is not an economical buy. A medium size eggplant weighing 1½ lbs will yield when pared and cut into three-quarter inch cubes about five cups.

BAKED STUFFED EGGPLANT

1 large eggplant, 2 lbs	1 tsp sugar
2 cups chopped cooked meat	1 cup Cooked Rice, p 433
1 cup fresh *or* canned	2 tbsp butter
tomatoes	1 tsp salt
2 tbsp chopped onion	Paprika and black pepper
1 egg	½ cup Buttered Crumbs,
	p 162

Cut eggplant in halves lengthwise and scoop out pulp, leaving shells about ¼-inch thick. Place shells in cold water. Combine chopped eggplant pulp with meat, tomato, onion, egg, sugar, rice, butter and seasonings. Heat until boiling hot. Drain shells and fill with hot mixture. Sprinkle bread crumbs over top and bake 1 hr in a moderate oven (350° F). Serve on heated platter, cutting through eggplant, stuffing and all for each serving. 5 servings.

EGGPLANT AND ONION WITH CHEESE SAUCE

2 tbsp butter	¼ lb sharp cheese, diced
¼ cup flour	1 medium eggplant
1 cup evaporated milk	2 small onions
1 cup water	¼ cup butter *or* margarine
¼ tsp salt	Salt to taste

Melt butter in top of double boiler over direct heat. Blend in flour and add liquids, stirring constantly while heating until sauce thickens. Add the ¼ tsp salt and cheese, stir until cheese melts. Cover and keep hot over boiling water while preparing eggplant and onion. Slice eggplant ⅜-inch thick and thinly pare the slices. Peel onion and cut in about ¼-inch slices. Sauté eggplant and onion in butter, using moderately low heat. Sprinkle with salt and cook slices about 4 or 5 min on one side or until delicately browned, turn, sprinkle with salt and brown the other side. Arrange eggplant and onion slices overlapping on a hot platter and pour hot cheese sauce over vegetables. 5 servings.

Note: 2 cups milk may be substituted for the 1 cup evaporated milk and 1 cup water.

EGGPLANT EN CASSEROLE

1 medium-sized eggplant,
  1½ lbs
⅓ cup butter
2 onions, thinly sliced
3 medium tomatoes, peeled
  and sliced

1 cup grated cheese, 4 oz
1 tsp salt
Pepper
1 cup fine dry bread crumbs

Slice eggplant ½-inch thick, pare skin off thinly and cut eggplant into half-inch dice to make about 5 cupfuls. Melt 3 tbsp butter in a skillet and sauté the eggplant slowly for 5 min. Place in a buttered casserole with alternate layers of onions, tomatoes, and grated cheese (saving ¼ cup of cheese for top); season each layer with salt and pepper. Top with crumbs which have been mixed with remaining cheese and dot with remaining butter. Bake in a moderate oven (375° F) until vegetables are tender and surface nicely browned, about 35 min. 5 generous servings.

EGGPLANT SAUTÉ

¼ cup shortening
½ cup diced onion
⅓ cup chopped green pepper
1 cup diced celery
2½ cups tomatoes, No. 2 can
3 cups diced eggplant, 12 oz

1¼ tsp salt
⅛ tsp pepper
½ tsp sugar
1½ tbsp butter
¼ cup fine bread crumbs

Melt shortening, add onion, green pepper, celery and sauté until transparent. Then add next 5 ingredients, cover and cook for 15 min or until eggplant is tender. Meanwhile prepare buttered bread crumbs by melting butter and stirring in crumbs. Sprinkle hot buttered lightly toasted crumbs over eggplant as it is served. Serves 4 to 6.

EGGPLANT SUPREME

¼ cup butter *or* margarine
3 medium onions, sliced
1 small eggplant, 1 lb
  pared and sliced
2 eggs
1 tbsp cold water
½ cup fine dry bread crumbs

Sauce:

1 tsp paprika
1 tsp curry powder
1 tsp mustard
½ tsp grated horseradish
½ tsp celery seed
½ tsp salt
½ cup French Dressing, p 1200

Melt 2 tbsp of the butter in a skillet; add onions and sauté until soft (3 to 5 min). Remove onions. Add rest of butter, and the eggplant which has been dipped in *one* beaten egg diluted with the water and then in bread crumbs. Brown delicately on both sides. Add onions again and the thoroughly blended ingredients of the sauce combined with the other beaten egg. Cover and simmer slowly for 20 min. Arrange slices overlapping on a hot platter. 5 servings.

FRENCH-FRIED EGGPLANT

Prepare eggplant just as for pan-frying, below, except cut ¾-inch thick slices into strips like French-fried potatoes just before dipping in the egg mixture. Coat with egg and crumbs. Have deep fat heated to 375° F. Place a single layer of eggplant strips in a frying basket and lower into the hot fat; cook until golden brown, from 1⅓ to 3 min, according to color preferred. Drain on absorbent paper or paper toweling, sprinkle with salt, and serve piping hot.

FRIED EGGPLANT

A medium-sized eggplant (1½ lbs) will serve 5 persons. Wash and cut in slices about ¾-inch thick. Pare each slice and sprinkle with salt. Dip the slices into a mixture of 1 beaten egg and ¼ cup milk; then coat well with sifted dry bread crumbs, flour or corn meal. Melt ¼ cup fat (bacon drippings, or half butter and half shortening) in a large skillet; lay the eggplant slices in the melted fat, and cook over moderate heat until golden brown on both sides and thoroughly tender, about 4 to 6 min. When well done, eggplant should be very tender all through. Serve immediately either plain, or with Tomato, p 1261, or Onion Sauce, p 1260. 5 servings.

STUFFED EGGPLANT

1 large eggplant, 2 lbs	1 tsp salt
⅓ cup butter *or* margarine	Dash of pepper
¾ cup chopped onion	1 bouillon cube in 1 cup
2 tbsp parsley, chopped fine	of water
¾ lb ground beef	1 large tomato

Split eggplant neatly in half lengthwise, scoop out inside pulp leaving a shell ¼-inch thick. Chop pulp coarsely. Melt butter in skillet and add eggplant, onion, parsley, and meat and sauté for five min. Season with salt and pepper. Pack hot mixture into eggplant halves and pour half the bouillon over all. Bake at 375° F (moderate oven) 25 min. Now place thin slices of tomato all over top of stuffed eggplant halves. Baste with the rest of the bouillon and bake for 20 min longer. 4 to 5 servings.

FENNEL WITH CHEESE SAUCE

2 *or* 3 stalks fennel, about
1¼ lbs
1 cup water
½ tsp salt
3 tbsp flour
3 tbsp butter
¾ cup milk
½ cup liquid, drained from
fennel

½ cup grated sharp American
cheese, 2 oz
Pinch sugar
¼ tsp salt
Dash pepper
½ tsp lemon juice
4 *or* 5 drops Worcestershire
sauce

Separate stalks of fennel into branches. Wash thoroughly and trim off the feathery leaves. Cut branches into ¼-inch slices, add water and salt and simmer uncovered for 5 to 7 min until tender, but not mushy. Combine flour and melted butter in the top of a double boiler; add milk and liquid gradually and cook over hot water until mixture is smooth and thickened. Stir constantly; stir in remaining ingredients and continue to cook over hot water until cheese is melted. Drain the fennel, turn into a hot dish and pour the cheese sauce over it.

Note: The cooked drained fennel may also be served with melted butter. In this case, the liquid should be drained from fennel and cooked down to a minimum and served with the vegetable.

BATTER FOR VEGETABLES, MEAT AND SHELLFISH FRITTERS AND GENERAL DIRECTIONS FOR FRYING

1 cup all-purpose flour
1 tsp baking powder
½ tsp salt
1 to 2 tsp sugar for some
vegetables
1 egg

⅓ cup milk
1 tbsp melted shortening
1 cup diced cooked drained
vegetables *or* shellfish,
clams, oysters, etc.
Shortening for frying

Sift flour, measure and resift 3 times with baking powder, salt and sugar, if used. Beat egg, stir in milk and shortening. Add flour mixture all at once and beat until well blended. Fold in vegetables or fish.

General Directions for Frying: Heat fat in frying kettle to 360° F. No frying basket is needed. Dip spoon into hot fat then quickly dip a heaping tsp of batter and with a second spoon or a rubber scraper push batter into fat. Work fast so 6 or 7 fritters can fry at the same time. Do not dip rubber scraper into hot fat. Temp drops quite fast but try to adjust heat to maintain about 350° F throughout frying. When fritters brown on underside, turn over. Fritters of this size fry to perfect brownness and doneness in 4 to 5 min. Lift fritters out quickly with a food fork or slotted spoon onto absorbent paper to drain. Serve hot and crisp with desired meat or sauce. 16 to 20 fritters.

CORN FRITTERS

1 cup all-purpose flour	1 tbsp melted shortening
1 tsp baking powder	12-oz can drained whole
½ tsp salt	kernel corn, *or* 1⅔ cups
2 tbsp sugar	fresh-cut corn
1 egg	Shortening for frying
⅓ cup milk	

Sift flour, measure and resift with next 3 ingredients. Beat egg, add milk and shortening, then flour mixture and beat until just smooth. Fold in drained corn. Let stand 5 to 10 min while heating shortening. Fry at 360° F as described under *General Directions for Frying,* p 1349. Serve hot with fried chicken, roast ham or pork, or with syrup. 20 fritters.

HOMINY AND PORK CHOPS

4 medium pork chops,	Salt
1¼ lbs	Parsley
No. 2½ can hominy	

Cook pork chops according to directions described in recipe for Braised Pork Chops, p 856. Remove chops from skillet to a plate to keep warm. Turn the undrained hominy into the skillet containing the hot pan gravy from the chops. Cook the hominy over low heat, crushing it well with a potato masher, then stirring it occasionally until thoroughly heated through and the gravy has been absorbed. Add more salt if desired. Crushing the hominy permits it to acquire much more flavor than if the grains are left whole. Turn hominy into a heap in center of a hot platter and arrange hot chops around it. Garnish with parsley. 4 to 5 servings.

HOMINY POTATOES AND ONION SAUTÉ

¼ cup bacon drippings	2 cups diced cooked potatoes
⅓ cup coarsely chopped	No. 2½ can hominy,
dry *or* green onion	drained
	1 tsp salt

Heat drippings in a heavy skillet and cook onions slowly until transparent but not brown. Add potatoes and hominy, season with salt, and cook over moderate heat, stirring occasionally until vegetables are slightly brown, crusty and thoroughly heated through. 5 servings.

WHAT TO CONSIDER WHEN BUYING AND PREPARING GREENS

Greens of any kind—spinach, mustard, turnip or dandelion should be just what the name implies—the greenest and freshest possible in green color throughout leaves and stems. Fresh, tender juicy leaves are so crisp that you can hear that typical rustle when one is brushed against another. The leaves should not be torn or bruised because if they are, decomposition will soon set in if it already hasn't and there is sure to be excessive waste in the cleaning. Leaves should be very tender when torn and the stems should break with a sharp clean snap when bent. The best of greens develop when the weather is cool and moist, so they are rarely ever a good buy except early in the spring or late in the fall. During a very rainy season, in late spring, summer, or early fall when the leaves grow very rapidly, however, one can expect fine greens. In dry hot weather, they become tough and fibrous so quickly that they are practically worthless. Like green beans, any greens should be gathered dry if they must be stored for a few hours before using. If they are gathered directly from home gardens and are to be cooked promptly, then the presence of moisture on the leaves does not matter. Since the washing of any greens requires considerable time, it is practical to wash them an hr or so before they are required for cooking and in the meantime to store them in the refrigerator to keep them crisp. Home washing of greens continues to be advisable because most of the prewashed greens available in the stores are still not free from sand and most of them have been handled so roughly in the washing that they are badly mangled and so can be expected to be sources of rapidly growing colonies of organisms.

KALE AND OTHER GREENS

| ¼ lb salt pork | 2 lbs tender kale *or* |
| 1 qt water | dandelion greens |

Choose pork with strips of lean and cut into ¼-inch slices. Put into kettle and add water. Heat to boiling, cover, reduce heat and simmer for 30 min. Then add the well-washed greens. Cover and reheat to boiling. When greens have wilted down, turn over and press down until they are below the surface of the liquid. Continue cooking, uncovered, until they are very tender, 30 to 45 min, depending on age and tenderness. If more water is needed during cooking, add boiling water to keep the greens just covered. When done, drain off liquid and serve greens with pork laid over the top. If more salt is needed, add at end of cooking. 5 servings.

SOUTHERN STYLE KALE WITH BACON

One of the most delicious and nutritious of "greens"

1 lb kale	1 onion, size egg, chopped
5 cups boiling water	2 tsp flour, optional
1 tsp salt	1 tbsp vinegar, optional
2 to 3 slices bacon	

Wash kale in cold water, at least 4 or 5 times. Break off tough stem ends. Chop coarsely or cut with scissors. Place kale in 3-qt saucepan, pour in boiling water, add salt, cover, cook 1 hr or until tender. Stir occasionally as greens may mat and stick to bottom. Fry bacon until half cooked, add chopped onion and cook until onion is yellow and soft and bacon is crisp. Cut bacon in ½ inch pieces and add all ingredients in skillet to kale. Cover, cook 5 to 10 min longer to blend flavors. If desired, flour may be stirred to a smooth paste with 2 tbsp water and stirred into kale to thicken liquid slightly. Or instead of water 1 tbsp vinegar may be added. 4 servings.

MUSTARD GREENS

2 lbs mustard greens   ½ tsp salt
6 cups boiling water   ⅛ tsp sugar
¼ lb salt pork   ½ pod red pepper

Use a sharp knife to strip leaves from stems and to trim off damaged portions. Wash several times in warm water. Shake off excess water; place in kettle, cover with boiling water and slowly heat to boiling. Dice pork very fine; pan-fry until crisp and light brown. Skim off about 2 tbsp of the clear fat, then turn pork, remaining fat and residue into greens. Add salt, sugar and pepper and cook covered for 1¼ hrs, turning heat very low during last half of cooking period. Turn over occasionally while cooking. Serve with the pot liquor. 4 servings.

Note: The cooking time for greens is largely dependent on the growing conditions. In a rainy season, the cooking time may be as short as ½ hr to make the greens tender.

MUSTARD GREENS AND SPINACH WITH BACON

Southern style

2 lbs fresh, tender mustard   ½ tsp salt
  greens   Black pepper to suit taste
¼ lb bacon   ½ lb spinach
1 qt boiling water

Wash mustard greens very thoroughly, trimming off roots and tough stems; trim and wash spinach. Put mustard greens into kettle with bacon, add water, cover and boil gently for 45 min. Add salt and pepper, and put spinach into kettle, pressing down well. Again cover and cook until spinach is tender, from 10 to 15 min. More water may be added as needed, but amount of pot liquor should be just right to serve with greens when they are done. Serve piping hot. 4 servings.

Note: Dandelion or any of the other greens may be prepared in the same manner as the mustard greens.

TURNIP GREENS WITH BACON ONION SAUCE
Southern style

2 lbs fresh, tender greens	¾ tsp sugar
1 qt boiling water	1 tbsp flour
1 tsp salt	2 tbsp vinegar
2 oz bacon, about 3 slices	½ cup water
½ cup chopped onion	

Pick over the greens, wash leaf by leaf in several waters and let drain. Place in 3-qt kettle, add water, salt, cover and simmer for 1 hr, turning occasionally. Cut bacon in ¼-inch pieces; sauté about a min, then add onion and continue cooking until onion is limp and yellow, about 5 min, stirring frequently. Add flour, and sugar, then remaining ingredients, simmer 1 min or until mixture becomes smooth and thick. Turn into greens, mix well, simmer a few min. Serve immediately. There should not be more than one-half cup of pot liquor on the greens when the flour mixture is added. 6 servings.

WHAT TO LOOK FOR WHEN BUYING KOHLRABI

Kohlrabi is one of our most delightful vegetables if it is obtained from gardens where the growth has been rapid, the weather has not been too hot, and an abundance of moisture has been available. When grown under such ideal conditions, the ball is so tender that the skin is easily pierced with thumbnail and strips off like the skin from a tangerine. The flesh is very crisp and tender without the slightest indication of woody fibers either in the raw or cooked state. When grown in poor, dry soil during hot weather, it develops woody fiber all the way through and becomes worthless.

BUTTERED KOHLRABI

Choose young, tender kohlrabi; it should be sufficiently tender so the skin can be readily pierced with the thumbnail. Strip off stems and leaves and wash. Remove thin slice from root end. Then strip off the peeling, leaving the ball of flesh smooth. Cut in crosswise slices about ¼-inch thick. Drop into just enough boiling water to cover, and cook uncovered until just tender, from 6 to 10 min. Enough water should have evaporated so it will not be necessary to drain. Add 3 to 4 tbsp butter, reheat and add salt to suit taste. Allow 2 lbs for 5 servings.

KOHLRABI WITH CHEESE SAUCE

1½ lbs kohlrabi, 6 medium	¼ tsp prepared mustard
2 cups boiling water	1 cup milk
¾ tsp salt	¼ lb sharp cheese, grated
2 tbsp butter	½ tsp salt
1 tbsp flour	

Choose young tender kohlrabi. Wash, then strip off the peeling. Cut kohlrabi into ¼-inch slices directly into a saucepan. Add boiling water and salt and cook uncovered until tender, from 6 to 10 min. (See recipe for Buttered Kohlrabi.) Meanwhile melt butter in top of double boiler. Blend in flour and mustard. Add milk and cook over boiling water with occasional stirring until mixture thickens. Add cheese and salt and stir until cheese is just melted. Add the hot drained kohlrabi. Gently stir to coat with sauce. 4 servings.

KOHLRABI WITH PEANUT BUTTER SAUCE

1½ lbs tender kohlrabi,	2 tbsp butter
6 medium	2 tbsp peanut butter
2 cups boiling water	2 tbsp flour
¾ tsp salt	

Choose only tender kohlrabi (tender enough for the peeling to be easily pierced with the thumbnail). Strip off the peeling beginning at root end and pull upward toward stem end. Cut peeled kohlrabi into ⅛-inch thick slices directly into a saucepan. Add boiling water and salt and cook uncovered until tender, about 6 min. Drain, saving liquid. Melt butter, add peanut butter, blend in flour and add gradually 1¼ cups of the liquid drained from kohlrabi; if necessary, add water to make this amount. Stir constantly until sauce boils and thickens. Pour sauce over hot kohlrabi and serve immediately. 4 to 6 servings.

BRAISED LEEKS

A surprisingly attractive, sweet flavored tasty vegetable—too long neglected

8 to 10 small leeks, 1¼ to	⅔ cup chicken broth, fresh *or*
1½ lbs	canned
2 tbsp chicken fat *or* butter	Salt and pepper

Trim off root ends and tough green blades from leeks. Open blades up gently and wash well in cold running water until perfectly clean. Split lengthwise, then in half crosswise, keeping the shape perfect. Heat fat in skillet or saucepan, lay leeks in carefully. Cover and simmer about 5 min, then add broth, a dash of salt and pepper. Cover and simmer until tender, from 10 to 12 min, or until leeks are barely tender and liquid is almost evaporated. The leeks should be a lovely pale yellowish green color. Lift out with spatula to preserve shape. Serve like asparagus with fish, chicken, veal, steak or liver. Serves 4.

CREAMED LEEKS ON TOAST

2 large tender leeks
1½ cups water
1½ tsp salt
¼ cup butter *or* margarine

⅓ cup flour
2 cups milk
Toasted white bread
Paprika, if desired

Wash leeks thoroughly; trim off root and an inch or two of the coarse green tops. Slice ⅛-inch thick; add water and salt and simmer uncovered for 5 to 8 min until just tender but not mushy. Blend butter and flour in top of double boiler and add milk gradually. Cook over hot water until smooth and thickened. Stir constantly. Add the leeks and cooking liquid and heat thoroughly. Pour over toast, sprinkle with paprika and serve immediately. 4 servings.

LEEK AND POTATO CASSEROLE

4 cups sliced raw potatoes
1¾ cups milk
1¼ tsp salt
2 large leeks, sliced thin,
   about 1½ cups

¼ cup fresh dry bread
   crumbs
2 tbsp butter, melted

Turn potatoes into a saucepan, add milk and salt, cover and cook until slices are slightly tender, about 10 min. Shake the pan from time to time to prevent potatoes from scorching. Arrange layers of the partially cooked potatoes and the leeks in a 5-cup casserole; combine crumbs and butter and sprinkle over top. Bake, uncovered, in a moderate oven (350° F) for 30 min. 4 servings.

BRAISED LETTUCE

3 tbsp butter
1 large solid head lettuce

½ tsp salt

Melt butter in a ten-inch heavy skillet. Trim lettuce without removing core; cut in 5 neat wedges and cook with the cut surfaces down in the butter until delicately browned, turning gently so as not to spoil shape of wedges. Sprinkle lettuce with the salt, cover pan, and turn heat very low; let simmer until tender, about 15 min. Remove carefully to a hot serving platter, using a pancake turner or broad spatula. Serve immediately with the juice which collects in the pan. 5 servings.

BAKED LENTILS WITH BACON

1½ cups dried lentils
3 cups water
1 tsp salt
6 slices Pan-broiled Bacon,
   p 855

1½ tbsp bacon drippings
1 cup half-inch bread cubes
3 tbsp melted butter
1 tsp finely chopped parsley

Wash lentils thoroughly and soak overnight in cold water. Drain and rinse; then put into a saucepan with the 3 cups water and salt. Cover, heat to simmering and simmer until tender, about 15 min. Do not drain. Add chopped crisp bacon and melted bacon drippings, and mix well. Turn into a casserole, and sprinkle with the bread cubes which have been tossed in the melted butter. Bake, uncovered, in a moderate oven (350° F) until crumbs are nicely browned, about 20 min. Sprinkle with parsley. 5 to 6 servings.

LENTIL STEW WITH HAM

½ lb dried lentils
2 tsp salt
½ cup chopped onion
2 tbsp butter

2 cups cooked tomatoes
Dash pepper
½ lb boiled ham, sliced thin
3 tbsp chopped parsley

Wash lentils and soak overnight in cold water. Drain, cover with fresh cold water (about 2 cups), add salt, and boil gently for 15 min or until tender. Sauté onion in the butter in a large skillet. Add lentils with their cooking water, tomatoes and pepper; cook at moderate rate for 15 min. Turn into a heated serving dish. Arrange overlapping slices of delicately browned, pan-fried ham around edge and a sprinkling of chopped parsley in the center. 5 servings.

CREAMED MUSHROOMS

½ lb fresh mushrooms
¼ cup butter
¼ cup water
½ tsp salt

2 cups milk
3 tbsp flour
⅓ cup cold water
Toast

Prepare mushrooms as for Sautéed Mushrooms, and sauté in the butter for 5 min. Then add water and salt, cover, and simmer gently for 15 min. Just before serving, add milk, and again heat to simmering. Blend flour to a smooth runny paste with cold water and stir into the mushroom mixture, using just enough to produce the desired thickness. (Consistency preferred by most persons is that of thin white sauce.) Serve piping hot on crisp toast or in patty shells. Chopped parsley sprinkled over each serving makes an attractive garnish. 5 servings.

SAUTÉED MUSHROOMS

1 lb fresh mushrooms
⅓ cup butter

Salt, if desired

Clean the mushrooms by washing very quickly in cold water and trimming a slice from the stem end. Never allow mushrooms to stand in water because they quickly lose their delicate flavor and they also discolor. If skin is tough, caps may be quickly peeled by stripping off the skin. Slice mushrooms about ¼-inch thick, cutting vertically through stem and cap directly into the saucepan containing the melted butter. Cover tightly, shaking the pan every few seconds to prevent sticking. After 2 min, turn the mushrooms with a fork. Cover and cook 2 or 3 min longer, or until they are swimming in their own juice and have just started to boil. In this juice stage, they are most attractive in appearance and are best for eating. Add salt to suit taste. Serve immediately while juicy with broiled steak, chops or hamburger patties. 3 to 4 servings.

STUFFED MUSHROOMS IN CASSEROLE

A distinctive delicious vegetable combination

12 large mushrooms, 2 to 2½" in diam	1 cup fine cut boiled ham, 4 slices
1⅓ cups fine cut celery	Pepper to taste
¼ cup fine cut onion	1 tsp butter
2 tsp fine cut parsley	Salt

Start oven 10 min before baking; set to moderately hot (425° F). Wipe mushrooms clean with a damp cloth or paper towel. Carefully break stems away from caps of mushrooms. Discard thin slice from cut end of stems; chop stems coarsely and combine with next 5 ingredients. Drop ¼ tsp butter into each mushroom cap, sprinkle in salt, then heap filling into hollows of mushrooms. Place mushrooms, filling-side up, in a well greased casserole. Cover and bake 20 min. Should you have no cover to fit casserole, a sheet of aluminum foil makes a good cover. Serve piping hot. 4 servings.

Note: Chopped stewed chicken and 2 tbsp butter may be used in place of ham.

WHAT TO CONSIDER WHEN BUYING OR GATHERING AND COOKING OKRA

Okra is an excellent vegetable that has long been appreciated by people in the South but is not so favored in other parts of the country. It has a delicious individual flavor that blends exceedingly well with onions and tomatoes and in combinations with meat, poultry, or fish. The pods grow rapidly and in just a few hours after they reach their most edible state, they develop woody fiber that makes them tough. In fact, the okra pod is ready to eat in from two to four days after the blossom appears. The best okra obtainable is that from your own garden or nearby local gardens, or that shipped in by airplane.

The test for quality is an all-bright-green pod from stem to tip without any brownish discoloration or limpness whatever. The pods should pierce easily anywhere with the fingernail and they should be very crisp. They should be handled gently as rough handling will develop the sliminess which is so objectionable to most people. Once washed, the stem should be sliced off. The quickest method of cooking is to slice the pods into beautiful flower-like crosswise slices and they should be sliced directly into the cooking utensil so that they will have to be handled but once in the preparation. Then cook with a minimum of stirring and you will have okra without sliminess.

OKRA AND TOMATOES

A rare combination in color, form, and flavor

1½ pts of 3 to 4-inch okra pods	3 medium tomatoes *or* 1½
3 tbsp butter *or* bacon	cups cooked tomatoes
drippings	Salt and pepper to taste
2 medium onions, sliced	

Choose young tender bright-green okra pods. Pods should be easily pierced with thumbnail. Wash thoroughly, remove stems. Put butter or bacon drippings into skillet, add the sliced onions. Slice the okra ¼-inch thick directly into the skillet on top of the onions. Cover and simmer until onion is soft, or about 5 min. Slide okra and onion to one side of skillet (to preserve green color of okra); place the sliced raw or cooked tomatoes in other half of skillet and continue to simmer, covered, until okra is tender. Then fold tomatoes and okra together gently. Season to taste and serve immediately. 5 servings.

HOW TO SELECT AND PREPARE ONIONS

Onions, though counted among the plebeian foods, are the most useful of all the vegetables. We have only to do without them for a while or be forced to pay an unusually high price for them during scarcity to appreciate them for their own worth as a vegetable, or for their value to give numerous other foods delicious flavor. Onions vary greatly in sizes and flavor. They range all the way from the pearl white ones that are not any bigger than a hickory nut to the mammoth handsome ones that often weigh as much as a lb. The shape varies also from round as a globe to slender oval or bottle shaped ones and the color ranges from clear white through to pale yellow and red. Onions are bulbs and their flesh is arranged in concentric rings. When cut crosswise, the slices are most beautiful and interesting. Sometimes these rings are distorted in shape by dry or almost dry straw-like pieces of material slipped in between the rings. This is due to the fact that gardeners have allowed the seed stalk to develop during growth, but while this is undesirable, it in no way spoils the onion for use as a seasoning. But this dry stalk does spoil the shape and appearance of the onion when it is required for beautiful slices for broiling or sautéing to be served whole and for edible garnishes. To keep onions lovely in shape, they need to be peeled with care. Only the delicate paper-like covering should be removed. This requires the use of a sharp pointed knife as well as some patience to strip off the covering without digging into that first layer of flesh to mar its beauty. In peeling the small onions, it is a good plan to pour boiling water over them and let them stand just long enough to wet and toughen the skin, enabling it to be peeled off in much larger strips. To obtain sweet-flavored and clear-colored onions, they should always be boiled in an open pan in an abundance of water because they belong to the *strong-juiced* vegetables. The boiling should be gentle, and to keep them whole and prevent the concentric ring layers from pushing out in the center, the onions should be stuck through several times to the center with a large needle or a skewer. In frying, onions may be covered and cooked quickly to tenderness without any danger of acquiring a strong odor and flavor. When properly boiled or fried, onions are so pearly white and translucent in appearance that they are one of the most aristocratic appearing of vegetables.

BUTTERED ONIONS

Peel the outer skin from onions no larger than walnuts. Peel carefully to preserve natural shape. Wash. If left whole, pierce each onion through to the center several times using a large needle or small skewer. This helps to keep the onions whole. If onions are large, cooking time may be shortened by cutting them into quarters. Drop into three qts of boiling salted water and boil gently, uncovered, 20 min or until onions are barely tender when pierced with a fork. Drain and add 2 or 3 tbsp melted butter. Allow 10 medium onions (1¾ to 2 lbs) for 5 servings.

Note: The small white onions that are about the size of small hickory nuts are beautiful for serving buttered.

BAKED ONIONS AND APPLES

1 lb onions	3 tbsp flour
1 lb Jonathan *or* other tart	2 tbsp sugar
apples	2 tsp salt

Peel onions, wash and core apples. Slice onions and apples thinly. Apples need not be pared unless skin seems very tough. Toss apples in the flour combined with sugar and salt and arrange with onions in alternate layers in greased glass baking dish. Cover and bake at 350° F (moderate oven) for 30 min. Uncover and brown if desired. 4 to 5 servings.

BAKED ONION SLICES

5 large onions	1½ cups hot water
2 tbsp butter, melted	Salt
2 chicken bouillon cubes	

Start oven 10 min before baking; set to moderate (375° F).

See directions for selecting and peeling onions, p 1358. Slice onions one-fourth inch thick, arrange in baking dish containing the butter. Dissolve bouillon cubes in hot water and pour over onion slices. Bake, uncovered, 45 to 60 min or until tender. If they become dry before they are tender, add more hot water. 5 servings.

BOILED GREEN ONIONS IN CHEESE SAUCE

4 bunches green onions	1 cup water
3 tbsp butter	¾ tsp salt
¼ cup flour	1 cup grated cheese, 4 oz
1 cup evap milk	

Trim roots and ends of green stems from onions. Leave whole, wash through 2 or 3 waters to remove all soil. Place in 3-qt saucepan, barely cover with water, add 1 tsp salt. Boil uncovered until tender about 10 min. Meanwhile, melt butter, blend in flour, add milk and water and stir over direct heat until sauce boils and thickens. Add the ¾ tsp salt and cheese, stirring until cheese is thoroughly blended with sauce. Drain onions and pour sauce over them. Onions may be cut in 1-inch lengths, but there is less shrinkage if they are left whole. 5 servings.

For creamed green onions, omit cheese.

Note: 2 cups milk may be substituted for the evaporated milk and water.

BROILED ONIONS

Peel 2 large Spanish onions carefully and wash (see directions for selection and preparation, p 1358). Slice a little less than ½-inch thick. Brush both sides of slices with melted butter and place on heated broiler about 4 inches below heat. When onions begin to be tender, in 8 to 10 min, brush tops with butter and move nearer to heat so they brown nicely. It is not necessary to turn onions over. When done, sprinkle with salt and chopped parsley. 5 servings.

Note: Sliced onions are equally delicious pan-fried in butter. Cooking should be done slowly. Lift carefully from pan with pancake turner or large spatula to preserve shape.

CREAMED ONIONS

To make creamed onions, add to Buttered Onions, p 1359, 1 cup of hot coffee cream or substitute 2 cups thin or medium white sauce for the butter. The small white onions about the size of small walnuts make the most attractive Creamed Onions.

ESCALLOPED ONIONS

2 lbs medium-sized onions	⅓ cup buttered bread crumbs
2 cups thin White Sauce,	or ½ cup grated cheese
p 1262	

Start oven 10 min before baking; set to hot (425° F)

Peel onions carefully to preserve shape. Wash and slice about ¼-inch thick, cover with boiling salted water (1 tsp salt to 1 qt water) and boil gently, uncovered, until onions are tender, from 5 to 7 min. Drain, add white sauce and turn into buttered shallow casserole. Sprinkle with Buttered Bread Crumbs, p 162, or grated cheese, and place in a hot oven (425° F) until golden brown. Serve immediately. 5 servings.

FRENCH-FRIED ONIONS

1 cup all-purpose flour	6 tbsp water, about
¼ tsp salt	2 to 3 large onions, about
½ cup evaporated milk	1¼ lb, peeled and sliced
2 tbsp salad oil	about ¼-inch thick
1 egg white, unbeaten	Shortening for frying

Sift flour, measure and resift with salt into mixing bowl. Add milk, oil and egg white all at once and beat until smooth. Add just enough water to make a medium thin batter. Separate onion slices carefully into rings and dip into the batter so each ring is completely covered. Drop batter-covered rings a few at a time into deep fat heated to 375° F and fry until golden brown. Lift out with a two-tined fork, drain on absorbent paper; sprinkle with salt. Serve hot as a garnish and accompaniment for meat. These fried rings if kept in a warm oven should stay crisp from 15 to 20 min after frying. 5 servings.

PAN-FRIED ONIONS

1 to 1½ lbs onions	½ tsp salt
3 tbsp butter	

Either white or yellow onions may be used. Use mild, sweet-flavored ones. Peel carefully to preserve shape. Wash, remove thin slices from root and stem ends and slice onions ¼-inch thick. Have the fat heated to sizzling in a skillet; add the onions, then the salt; cover, reduce heat and cook slowly until they are soft and translucent, and very delicately browned on bottom, from 8 to 10 min. Shake skillet occasionally while cooking. Serve piping hot. These are delicious served with Pan-fried Liver, p 908, or hamburgers. 5 servings.

GLAZED ONIONS

1¼ lbs small white onions	3 tbsp sugar
¼ cup butter	¼ tsp salt

Use onions the size of hickory nuts. Cover with boiling water, drain and peel very carefully to preserve the shape. Pierce each onion with a needle several times to center to keep whole during boiling. Wash, cover with boiling salted water, boil gently, uncovered, until tender, about 15 min. Combine butter, sugar and salt in saucepan and heat slowly, stirring constantly until melted. Drain onions, place in syrup and cook a few min, turning frequently to glaze entire surface with syrup. 5 servings.

ONION AND APPLE FROMAGE

3 tbsp shortening
2 large sweet onions sliced
    medium thick
2 large Jonathan apples, cut
    in medium wedges

¾ to 1 tsp salt
4 tsp brown sugar
4 oz processed cheese, cubed

Melt shortening in a skillet, add the onion slices and then arrange the unpeeled apple wedges over the top. Cover the skillet and cook over low heat from 18 to 20 min, or until the onions and apples are tender but not mushy. Sprinkle with salt and sugar, then with cheese. Cover again and continue to cook for about 3 min longer or until cheese is just melted. 4 servings.

ONIONS au GRATIN

1½ lbs small white onions
2 tbsp butter
3 tbsp flour
1½ cups milk

¾ tsp salt
⅓ cup Buttered Bread
    Crumbs, p 162
½ cup grated sharp cheese

Start oven 10 min before baking; set to mod slow (325° F)

Peel onions carefully to preserve shape, wash and pierce each several times with a skewer. Turn into saucepan, cover with 3 pts of boiling water, add 1 tsp salt and boil gently uncovered until onions are almost tender. Drain and place onions in a buttered baking dish. Cover with white sauce made of butter, flour, milk, and salt, p 1262, sprinkle with buttered bread crumbs and top with the grated cheese. Bake until nicely toasted, about 25 min. For escalloped onions, omit the cheese. 5 servings.

SAUTÉED ONIONS AND PEPPER

A colorful, fine flavored, nutritious wintertime vegetable dish

1½ lbs medium-sized onions
1 large bell pepper
3 tbsp margarine

½ tsp salt
Paprika

Dip onions in boiling water and then into cold to toughen the thin, paper-like skin. Peel off skins carefully. Lay heavy waxed paper on cutting board, and hold onions by root end on paper firmly while cutting into uniform quarter-inch crosswise slices. Heat margarine in a 10-inch skillet. Slide onions into hot fat carefully. Remove stem end of pepper and the seed core. Cut pepper into rings or lengthwise strips and arrange over top of onions. Sprinkle with salt. Cover pan, reduce heat and cook slowly about 15 min or until onions and pepper are tender, but not brown. Turn vegetables into a hot dish, sprinkle with paprika and serve at once. 4 servings.

STUFFED ONIONS No. 1

5 large Spanish onions, 2 lbs
2 cups Cooked Rice, p 433
½ cup chili sauce

2 tbsp melted butter
¼ lb cheese, grated, 1 cup
Salt to suit taste

Start oven 10 min before baking; set to mod hot (425° F)

Peel onions carefully to preserve shape. Wash. Remove thick slice from stem end and scoop out ¼ cup pulp from center of each onion to reduce length of cooking time. Pierce each onion through to the center in several places to keep whole during the boiling. Drop onions into 4 qts boiling salted water, 1 tsp salt to each qt of water, and boil gently, uncovered, until just tender, 25 to 30 min. Drain, and remove more core from centers of onions to form cups. Centers may be cooked until done and served creamed. Combine hot rice with chili sauce, melted butter, and all but ¼ cup of grated cheese; salt to suit taste. Fill onion cups with this mixture and set into a buttered shallow pan. Sprinkle remainder of grated cheese over tops. Place in oven or under broiler, watching carefully until cheese is golden brown and stuffing is hot through. 5 servings.

Note: Baked Beans make an excellent stuffing for onions.

STUFFED ONIONS No. 2

5 medium onions, 1½ lbs
¾ cup chopped cooked ham
¼ cup chopped green pepper
1 cup soft bread crumbs
1 tbsp melted butter
½ tsp salt

Dash pepper
½ cup evap milk
⅔ cup water
½ cup Buttered Bread
Crumbs, p 162

Start oven 10 min before baking; set to mod (375°F)

Peel onions carefully to preserve shape. Wash and cut a slice from the top of each. Pierce each onion through to center in several places to keep whole during the boiling. Boil onions, p 1360, until almost tender; then drain and push out centers. Use centers and the raw slices for creamed onions. Combine the ham, green pepper, soft bread crumbs and melted butter. Add seasonings and stuff into onion cups. Place in a buttered baking dish. Mix milk and water and pour around onions. Cover top of onions with buttered crumbs. Bake until tender and the tops are a tempting brown, about 30 min. 5 servings.

HOW TO SELECT AND PREPARE PARSNIPS

One rarely finds parsnips prepared and served as attractively as they might be. As a result, many people strenuously object to both their flavor, color and appearance. Parsnips may be prepared to make a number of delicious dishes. Old-timers used to say that parsnips were only good to eat after they had remained in the ground long enough in the late fall to freeze thoroughly. Fortunately, this freezing does not harm the parsnip, but we know today that they are delicious whether they are frozen or not and may be served successfully from early fall until late spring. The parsnip root should be stored so that it is always crisp, firm and tender, never withered. It should be scraped rather than pared until all blemishes are removed and the natural form of the parsnip is retained and the flesh is a clean pale-yellow color. No matter how prepared, it is best to boil it first until just tender, and for quick cooking, it is advisable to split the parsnip lengthwise neatly in half. The parsnip has two kinds of flesh—the fine close-textured part on the outside and the coarser textured core in the center. Some people actually recommend removing this core before or after cooking. This is never necessary because under normal growing conditions, the core is perfectly edible and to remove it spoils the form, removes valuable food material, and prevents the cook from obtaining the most attractive vegetable. As soon as the parsnips are barely tender, they should be drained. Left in this state, the color is too pale to be attractive, so further treatment is necessary to bring out the beauty and flavor. Parsnips contain considerable sugar and for this reason, they may be sautéed in butter or shortening to the most tempting brown colors. When the cut side of the parsnip is browned, there is a gradation and distribution of color that makes them most beautiful. Parsnips are excellent served plain, or with some contrasting tart sauce.

BUTTER BROWN PARSNIPS

Choose firm parsnips, allowing one medium one per serving. Scrub and scrape to remove any blemishes or discolorations. Rinse in cold water, split lengthwise in halves. Add boiling water to cover, and 1 tsp salt for each qt of water. Heat to boiling, cover pan, then reduce heat and cook moderately fast until the parsnips are tender, from 20 to 25 min, depending on tenderness and size. Drain thoroughly. For 5 parsnips, melt ⅓ cup butter, margarine, or shortening in skillet. Lay cut side down, brown on all sides, watching *carefully* and turning *frequently*. Parsnips scorch easily because of their high sugar content. Serve hot. 5 servings.

FRENCH-FRIED PARSNIPS

3 medium-sized parsnips   Bread crumbs *or* salted
1 egg   flour
⅓ cup milk

Scrape parsnips, rinse in cold water and cut in quarters lengthwise, then cut quarters in half lengthwise and then once crosswise. Barely cover with boiling water, cover and cook until just tender or from 4 to 5 min. Avoid cooking so long that they get soft and mushy.

Drain. Beat egg, add the milk. Dip the strips in this mixture and then in either bread crumbs or flour. Fry in deep fat which has been heated to 375° F until golden brown. Drain on absorbent paper and serve hot. 5 servings.

PARSNIP FRITTERS

2 large parsnips, ¾ lb   1½ tsp sugar
Hot water   1 egg, beaten
1 tsp salt   ⅓ cup milk
¾ cup flour   ¼ cup shortening
1 tsp D.A. baking powder

Wash, scrape and dice parsnips. Add water to just barely cover and ½ tsp of the salt, cover and simmer for 5 min. Drain. Sift the flour, measure and resift three times with the baking powder, sugar and remaining ½ tsp salt. Combine the egg and milk and add the dry ingredients. Beat until smooth. Stir in the parsnips. Drop by spoonfuls into the hot fat and fry until delicately browned on both sides. 10 to 12 fritters.

PARSNIP PATTIES WITH GRAPEFRUIT SAUCE

3 medium cooked parsnips   1 tbsp flour
1 well-beaten egg   2 tbsp butter or margarine
¼ tsp salt

Chop parsnips fine or mash. There should be 2 cups. Combine mashed parsnips with egg, salt and flour. Stir to a smooth mixture. Use a ¼-cup measure for each patty, shape and place in hot butter; pan-fry over medium heat until a rich brown lower crust is formed, turn and finish cooking about 5 min on each side. Serve immediately with hot grapefruit sauce. Makes 8 patties.

Grapefruit Sauce:
½ of medium grapefruit   1 tsp cornstarch
2 tsp sugar   1 tbsp water
Dash of salt   1 tsp butter

Ream grapefruit and remove seeds. Pour juice and pulp, about ½ cup, into top of double boiler. Blend sugar, salt, cornstarch and water and stir into the grapefruit juice. Cook and stir over hot water until sauce is slightly thickened and clear. Stir occasionally; add butter. Remove from heat and serve.

PARSNIP STEW

2 lbs pork shanks   2½ cups diced potatoes
4 medium parsnips   1 tbsp salt

Wipe the pork shanks with a damp cloth. Simmer from 2 to 3 hrs in a qt of water, or until almost tender enough for meat to fall from bone. About 40 min before serving time, add parsnips prepared for Butter Brown Parsnips, p 1364, and more water if necessary to cover. Ten min later, add potatoes and salt. Continue cooking about 20 min. Remove bones and skin from shanks. Place meat on platter. For color, add a little caramel, p 165, a few drops of brown vegetable coloring or some kitchen bouquet to the parsnips. Pour vegetables around meat. 5 servings.

PARSNIPS AND TOMATOES

1 large *or* 2 medium parsnips, ½ lb	No. 2 can tomatoes
Hot water	1 medium onion, thinly sliced
¾ tsp salt	2 tbsp butter *or* margarine
Dash pepper	2 cups cubed bread, toasted

Wash, scrape and cut parsnips into crosswise slices ½-inch thick. Add hot water to just barely cover and salt. Cover and simmer for 15 to 20 min or until parsnips are tender. Add pepper and tomatoes and heat. Meanwhile sauté the onion in the hot butter for 5 min, mix in the bread cubes and add to the hot vegetables. Mix quickly and serve immediately. 4 servings.

PARSNIPS WITH SAVORY SAUCE

4 cooked parsnips, cut in half lengthwise	¼ tsp Worcestershire sauce
3 tbsp flour	⅛ tsp fresh onion juice
2 tbsp butter *or* margarine	¼ tsp prepared mustard
1 cup parsnip liquid	½ cup grated sharp American cheese
⅜ tsp salt	

Start oven 10 min before baking; set to mod (350° F)

Prepare parsnips as described on p 1363. Cut in half lengthwise, barely cover with water, cover and cook until just tender. Drain off liquid and save. Combine flour with melted butter or margarine in small skillet. Cook over medium heat until well browned but not scorched. Stir constantly. Add parsnip liquid gradually and stir until mixture boils and thickens. Add remaining ingredients except cheese. Arrange parsnips in an 8-inch glass pie plate; cover with hot sauce, sprinkle with cheese and bake 30 min or until top is slightly brown. Serve immediately. 4 servings.

WHAT TO LOOK FOR WHEN BUYING OR GATHERING PEAS

For the finest garden-fresh flavor, select only those peas with bright green, crisp and tender pods that are plumply filled out. The shortest possible time should elapse between pulling them from the vines and cooking. If peas must be stored a few hrs before cooking, they should be kept in the refrigerator. Shell them just before cooking. Shelled peas even though covered and kept cold allow more of their rare delicious flavor to escape than those kept in the pods.

BUTTERED OR CREAMED PEAS

Select peas and shell as described above. Wash in cold water and cook immediately. Barely cover with boiling water. Add ½ tsp salt for each pt shelled peas. Cook uncovered at a moderate rate until peas are tender, from 15 to 25 min, depending on age and size of peas. Add more boiling water if needed. When peas are done, the liquid should be nearly evaporated so that draining will be unnecessary. Pour melted butter or a thin White Sauce, p 1262, over them and serve immediately. Allow 2½ lbs unshelled peas for 5 servings.

Equal quantities of drained, fresh boiled peas and mushrooms, cauliflower or celery may be combined and buttered.

CREAMED PEAS AND NEW POTATOES

1 lb new potatoes	1 cup boiling water
2 lbs fresh peas, 1½ cups shelled	1¼ tsp salt
	½ cup evap milk
1 tbsp finely sliced green onion	2 tbsp butter
	2 red radishes, optional

Scrape potatoes and if they are larger than a good sized walnut, cut them in half or in quarters. Put the potatoes, shelled peas and onion into a saucepan, add the boiling water and salt. Cover and cook for 15 to 20 min or until vegetables are tender. Add milk and butter and simmer very slowly until liquid is somewhat thickened. Add the thinly sliced radishes just before serving. 4 servings.

PEA AND POTATO CASSEROLE

2 lbs boiling potatoes	3 tbsp butter
¼ cup butter	⅓ cup flour
1 cup hot milk	¼ tsp salt
¾ tsp salt	¼ lb sharp cheese, diced
No. 2 can or 2½ cups fresh cooked peas	1 egg yolk
	1 tbsp milk

Start oven 10 min before baking; set to mod hot (400° F)

Wash and pare potatoes thinly. Cook in boiling salted water in a covered pan. Drain, saving liquid. Mash. Add the ¼ cup butter, half the hot milk and the ¾ tsp salt and beat until potatoes are smooth, white and fluffy. Drain peas, and make a white sauce with the 3 tbsp butter, flour, ¼ tsp salt, the rest of the milk and liquid from peas and potatoes. There should be 1½ cups of this liquid. Stir in cheese until well blended. Add peas to sauce and heat. Spread two-thirds of the hot mashed potatoes over bottom and sides of a casserole, and pour the creamed peas into the center. Pipe remainder of potatoes over top of peas in a lattice, or drop in puffs from a tbsp, not covering the peas entirely. Use a pastry brush and pat the egg yolk beaten with the 1 tbsp milk all over the top of the potatoes. Brown and serve immediately. 5 servings.

PEA LOAF

No. 2 can *or* 2½ cups fresh
cooked peas
1 cup fine dry bread crumbs
1 egg, slightly beaten
1 tsp grated onion
½ tsp salt

Pepper
1 cup evap milk
1 cup finely chopped lettuce,
outer leaves, pressed down
firmly

Start oven 10 min before baking; set to mod slow (325° F)

Drain peas, saving liquid. Mash peas thoroughly. Add remaining ingredients and pea liquid, mixing just enough to blend well. Pour into well-buttered bread loaf pan, 6-cup size, and bake 50 to 60 min, or until a sharp knife inserted in center comes out clean. Unmold onto platter and serve with Mushroom Sauce, p 1259, Celery Sauce, p 1252, or Carrot Sauce, p 1252. 5 servings.

Note: A glass loaf pan bakes a browner crust than a metal one and its bottom crust which will be the top crust when unmolded will usually have a smoother surface than a loaf baked in a metal pan.

WHAT TO CONSIDER WHEN SELECTING AND PREPARING GREEN PEPPERS

Green peppers for stuffing should be uniform in height and shape and symmetrical enough to stand up straight. These features prevent tipping and spilling of stuffing during baking and assure even browning. For salad or seasoning, less shapely peppers are satisfactory. The best peppers are brilliant green, crisp and thick-walled. Ripe red or yellow ones are also delicious for stuffing and salads.

To prepare peppers for stuffing, cut a slice from stem-end to make them level on top. Discard stem from this slice, chop and add to pepper stuffing or use soon in salad or casserole mixtures. Use kitchen scissors to remove seed core and dividing membranes from pepper cups. Parboiling pepper cups is unnecessary. For years we parboiled to shrink the cups so they would hold more stuffing. Recently we learn that parboiling destroys part of the vitamin C. We now find that raw cups filled snugly finish baking sufficiently full and have better color and higher vitamin C content than parboiled cups. Heating the filling before stuffing peppers reduces the cooking time. This enables filling and peppers to cook to a palatable stage before peppers soften and slump. Cooked peppers are more attractive and appetizing if they retain some of their original crispness. Fit stuffed peppers snugly together in the pan for most perfect baking. One medium pepper serves 1, an unusually large one serves 2. Cut large peppers lengthwise in half for boat-shape. Almost any cooked meat, fish, poultry, rice, macaroni, mushroom or vegetable mixture makes good fillings for pepper shells.

BROILED GREEN PEPPERS
An appealing way to serve cooked peppers

4 medium-sized green
  peppers
1 tbsp olive oil *or* melted
  butter

Salt
Pepper

Choose thick-walled, crisp peppers. Wash, dry and brush with oil. Crumple sheet of aluminum foil into a shallow pan or broiler pan. Lay peppers on foil on their sides, press down so top surfaces will be parallel with broiler heat. Broil at 350° F about 3 inches from source of heat. Turn over 3 or 4 times and brush with oil. Broil about 8 min or until barely tender. Remove to hot plate, quickly cut in half lengthwise, remove seed cores and stems. Sprinkle insides with salt, pepper and olive oil. Serve immediately with steak, roast meats and fish. 4 servings.

FRIED GREEN PEPPERS
Beautifully green, sweet, nutritious

3 firm, thick-walled green
  peppers
2 to 3 tbsp olive oil, bacon
  fat *or* butter

Salt
Pepper, optional

Wash peppers, cut in half lengthwise, remove seeds, cores and stems and cut into ¾-inch wide strips. Heat oil or fat in skillet, keep at medium heat, add peppers and toss around until all of the pieces are coated with thin film of fat. Sprinkle with salt, cover and cook, stirring and tossing every min or two until barely tender, about 5 min in all. A good accompaniment to steak, veal, roast lamb. 4 servings.

STUFFED GREEN PEPPERS No. 1
Ground beef and bread

4 medium green peppers
2½ slices bread from 1-lb loaf
2 tbsp chopped onion
2 tbsp chopped celery
2 tbsp butter
½ lb ground beef

1 chicken bouillon cube
⅓ cup hot water
½ cup cooked tomatoes
⅓ cup buttered crumbs,
  p 162

Start oven 10 min before baking; set to mod (350° F)

Select and prepare peppers, as above. Cut bread into ½-inch cubes and toast. Sauté onion and celery in butter 2 min. Add beef and sauté with constant stirring until gray in color. Dissolve bouillon cube in hot water and add with tomatoes to meat. Heat well. Fold in bread cubes. Fill peppers with hot mixture. Top with buttered crumbs. Bake in a greased shallow baking dish 15 min; then 10 min at 400° F to brown tops. Serve at once. 4 servings.

STUFFED GREEN PEPPERS No. 2

Rice and Ham

1 tbsp chopped onion	1½ cups cooked rice
2 tbsp chopped celery	½ lb cooked ham, ground
2 tbsp bacon fat	Salt to taste
2 tsp flour	4 green peppers, large size
½ cup milk	¼ cup grated cheese, 1 oz

Start oven 10 min before baking; set to mod (350° F)

Sauté onion and celery in bacon fat 2 min. Blend in flour, add milk and stir constantly over medium heat until smooth and thickened. Fold in rice, ham and salt. Prepare peppers as described, p 1368. Fill with hot mixture. Top with grated cheese. Bake in greased shallow pan 15 min, then 5 min at 400° F to brown cheese. Serve at once. 4 servings.

STUFFED GREEN PEPPERS No. 3

Macaroni and Shrimp

1 egg yolk, slightly beaten	½ lb cooked shrimp, cleaned, cut in thirds
¼ cup French dressing	
1 cup cooked hot macaroni	4 green peppers, medium
Salt to taste	¼ cup grated cheese

Start oven 10 min before baking; set to mod (350° F)

Blend egg yolk and French dressing, fold in next 3 ingredients. Prepare peppers, p 1368. Fill snugly with hot mixture, sprinkle tops with cheese. Bake in greased shallow pan 15 min, then 5 to 10 min at 400° F to heat through and brown cheese. Serve at once. 4 servings.

STUFFED GREEN PEPPERS No. 4

Chicken, Veal or Ham

5 green peppers, medium	2 ripe tomatoes, medium
1 medium onion, chopped	2 tbsp butter
¼ cup finely chopped celery	½ tsp salt
1 cup chopped cooked chicken, veal *or* ham	2 slices stale bread
	⅓ cup buttered crumbs, p 162

Start oven 10 min before baking; set to mod (350° F)

Select and prepare peppers, p 1368. Sauté next 4 ingredients in butter until onion is slightly soft. Stir in salt and bread broken into coarse crumbs. Stuff hot mixture into pepper cases, top with buttered crumbs. Bake in a buttered shallow baking pan 15 min; then 5 min at 400° F or until crumbs toast and stuffing is hot. 5 servings.

STUFFED GREEN PEPPERS No. 5

Creamed Potatoes

Prepare Green Peppers, p 1368. Fill with hot Creamed Potatoes, p 1374. Bake in a moderate oven (350° F) 25 to 30 min, or until potatoes are brown and peppers are cooked. Sprinkle potatoes with grated sharp cheese, if desired.

PLANTAIN

Plantain is a variety of banana of Cariban origin; they look like huge bananas. The raw fruit is not edible. As a rule only the slightly underripe fruit is cooked; a favorite way of cooking is to fry the sliced fruit in shallow fat.

FRIED PLANTAIN FRITTERS

Interesting, attractive—flavor resembles that of sweet potato

2 plantain	¼ tsp salt
3 tbsp butter *or* margarine	1 tbsp sugar

Peel plantain just like bananas; save peelings. Cut peeled fruit crosswise into 1-inch thick slices. Heat butter in heavy skillet until it bubbles vigorously. Lay in plantain slices and sauté gently until golden brown on under side and soft all the way through. Remove skillet from heat. Lift out slices and place a row uncooked-side up 2-inches apart on a wide strip of the peeling. Lay a 2nd strip of peeling on top. With palm of hand press slices out to form thin cakes. Now remove top peeling and sprinkle uncooked side with salt and sugar. Lift slices from lower peeling and return uncooked side down to reheated skillet. Place over heat and brown the uncooked side. Serve these hot, thin fritters with ham or chicken. 4 servings.

WHAT TO LOOK FOR WHEN BUYING OR GATHERING POTATOES

Since potatoes are eaten regularly and in generous quantities, it is important that purchasers be able to recognize quality. Though nature does not always produce perfect products and sometimes only imperfect potatoes are available, it is well for any purchaser to be able to recognize the best values. For good keeping quality, any potato needs to be dug when mature and while the soil is dry enough to fall cleanly away from the tubers. If potatoes are dug before they are mature and the skins rub off or feather easily causing them to bruise deeply when roughly handled, such potatoes decay rapidly, they cannot be cooked satisfactorily and should always be bought in small quantities. If the trade demands that the potatoes be washed, this needs to be done in a manner to avoid bruising and to permit thorough drying before the potatoes are heaped or sacked. Otherwise the dampness is liable to cause spoilage. Potatoes that have deep cuts acquired in digging which have not been allowed to dry out and heal up will also spoil rapidly. Such potatoes even though sound are not worth as much as uncut potatoes because there is considerable waste in paring. Potatoes with very deep "eyes" and with little potatoes attached to the big one, which is a sign that the potato has remained in the ground too long after maturity and started a second growth, are also poor values because there is too much waste in the paring. Potatoes that have green areas due to growing too near the surface of the ground develop *solanin* which is bitter in flavor and is *poisonous* if consumed in sufficient amounts. These should also be avoided. It is well to become familiar with potato varieties and learn just how they respond to dry or moist heat. Boiling and mashing potatoes should be close textured, creamy in color, and should have a waxy consistency when cooked. Early Rose and Early Ohio potatoes are of this type. Potatoes for baking should be the kind that crumble easily into a white mealy mass when baked. And potatoes that are best for baking are also best for French fries, provided they are thoroughly matured. Immature potatoes that contain more or less sugar can never produce French fries of high quality. The western grown potatoes belonging to the Russet family are the best potatoes for both baking and frying.

AMERICAN-FRIED POTATOES

Pare 5 or 6 firm boiling potatoes thinly and cut into uniform thin slices. Melt 2 to 3 tbsp fat in a heavy skillet. When fat is hot, lay in the sliced potatoes, sprinkle with salt, cover skillet, and cook slowly. When underside is browned, in about 10 min, turn potatoes carefully with pancake turner; cover, and continue cooking 10 or 15 min longer, until potatoes are tender in center and crisp on bottom. Serve immediately while piping hot. 5 servings.

Note: Varieties of well-matured boiling potatoes best for American-fried are Triumph, Early Rose, Early Ohio, and Cobbler.

BAKED POTATOES

To obtain perfect, mealy baked potatoes, a baking type of potato, Russet, thoroughly matured is essential. Scrub the potato thoroughly and bake until soft. Fortunately, potatoes may be baked successfully in an oven ranging from 350° to 450° F., and can therefore be baked along with a wide variety of other foods that require various temps. An average-size potato, 10 oz, will require 40 to 55 min to become soft through in a moderately hot oven (400° F). Slightly more time will be required in a slower oven. Use potatoes of uniform size and shape so they will be done at the same time. Test for doneness by squeezing potato in hand through a pot holder or several thicknesses of a dry towel, or by piercing with a sharp-tined fork. To serve, split the potato across the top with two gashes at right angles, and press the sides so the baked contents are pushed up into a mealy mound. Top with a pat of butter and a dash of paprika, and serve promptly with additional butter and salt. Allow one average-size potato for each serving.

BAKED POTATOES WITH SALT PORK GRAVY

¼ lb salt pork
⅓ cup flour
Salt to taste
3 cups milk
2 tbsp chopped chives

Few drops Worcestershire
sauce, optional
4 medium-sized potatoes,
baked
Paprika

Cut salt pork into quarter-inch cubes. Pour hot water over cubes, let stand 1 min; then drain well. Pan-fry pork over low heat until brown and crispy. Pour off excess fat, leaving ⅓ cup in the pan. Blend in the flour and salt, add milk gradually, cook and stir until mixture is thickened and smooth. Add chives and Worcestershire sauce. Squeeze potatoes between thick folds of a cloth as soon as they are removed from the oven to crack them open and make them fluffy. Pour the hot salt pork gravy over the potatoes. Sprinkle with paprika and serve immediately. 4 servings.

BOILED POTATOES

When correctly done, boiled potatoes are most delicious and most attractive.

For boiling, select waxy potatoes which hold their shape well. Some good varieties are Rural, Early Rose and Early Ohio. Wash, scrape or pare thinly and cover with boiling salted water, 1 tsp salt to 1 qt water. Cover and cook at moderate rate until tender when pierced with a fork from 20 to 30 min, the time depending on the size and variety. Drain and save liquid. Return potatoes to heat for a min to evaporate excess moisture, shaking kettle gently to prevent scorching. This will give potatoes a mealy appearance on the outside. Transfer potatoes to a well-heated covered dish in which they will keep hot until served. Two or 3 tbsp of hot fat and brown residue left in skillet after frying ham or pork chops may be poured over the potatoes just after they are drained and just before they are shaken to give an appetizing brown-flecked surface and rich color.

Two lbs make 5 servings. Large potatoes may be cut in halves or quarters to hasten cooking. Small new potatoes are often boiled with their skins on; skins will slip off easily when done or may be eaten with the potato.

Note: Potato cooking water from pared potatoes contains valuable nutrients. Save it for making soup or gravy, or to boil other vegetables.

BROILED POTATOES

2 large baking potatoes,   Butter *or* margarine
¾ to 1 lb each   Salt

Parboil potatoes in jackets in salted water for 15 to 20 min or until not quite tender. Drain off water and cool. Do not peel. Cut into half-inch crosswise slices. Brush both sides of the hot slices with butter and place on a preheated broiler rack that is set about two inches from the heat. Broil under medium heat on each side to a golden brown. Remove to serving dish, sprinkle with salt and serve immediately. 4 servings.

CRUNCHY BROILED POTATOES

A quick, different, above par potato dish

2 lbs baking potatoes   2 tsp butter
½ cup cream   1 tsp salt

Pare potatoes, wash, dry and cut into shoestrings on a grater with large holes or by hand. Drizzle with the cream and toss to coat well. Rub butter over a shallow pan that fits under your broiler. Distribute potatoes in pan evenly. Sprinkle with salt and place about 3 inches from broiler heat adjusted to 500° F. Broil 12 to 15 min until top is brown and crunchy. Use pancake turner to remove potatoes crusty-side up to hot plates. Serve at once. 4 servings.

CREAMED POTATOES No. 1

6 medium boiling potatoes,   2 tbsp butter
2 lbs   Salt and pepper to taste
1 cup boiling water   Chopped parsley, if desired
1 cup cream *or* milk

Wash potatoes, pare thinly and cut into ½-inch dice. Add water, cover kettle, and cook moderately fast until half done, about 5 min; then add cream, butter and seasonings, again cover, and continue cooking *slowly* until potatoes are done and sauce is slightly thickened. Serve promptly with a sprinkle of chopped parsley. 5 servings.

Note: These potatoes are delicious stuffed into parboiled green peppers, then run under the broiler to brown tops.

CREAMED POTATOES No. 2

6 medium size boiling potatoes, 2 lbs	1½ cups thick White Sauce, p 1262

Wash potatoes, pare thinly, and cut into ½-inch dice. Barely cover with boiling salted water, 1 tsp salt to 1 qt water, cover and cook moderately fast until done, about 10 min. Drain thoroughly and add cooking water to hot white sauce to produce desired thin consistency. Combine hot sauce with hot potatoes. Serve immediately. 5 servings.

Variation: White sauce may be increased to 3 cups and 2½ cups hot fresh cooked peas may be added.

CREAMED POTATOES WITH CHEESE

6 medium potatoes, 2 lbs	2 cups thin White Sauce,
1 tsp salt	p 1262
¼ lb cheese, grated	

Wash potatoes, pare thinly. Cut neatly into half-inch cubes. Turn into a 3 qt saucepan, add barely enough water to cover, and salt. Cover and boil gently until tender, about 10 min. There should be only about ½ cup liquid left. Meanwhile stir cheese into hot white sauce until cheese is melted. Fold in undrained potatoes. Serve hot with sprinkling of chopped parsley or dash paprika. 5 servings.

DAKOTA POTATOES

4 slices bacon	2 tsp salt
4 cups pared, sliced raw potatoes	¼ tsp pepper
	½ tsp prepared mustard
1 onion, sliced	1 tsp sugar
2 cups cooked tomatoes	¼ tsp celery salt

Pan-fry bacon until done. Remove bacon and place on absorbent paper to drain. Add the potatoes and onion to the bacon fat and sauté for 10 min. Turn gently with a spatula to distribute the fat. Add remaining ingredients and simmer until potatoes are tender and tomato juice is slightly thickened, about 20 min. Break the crisp bacon into small pieces and sprinkle over top when ready to serve. 4 to 6 servings.

FRENCH-FRIED POTATOES, WHITE OR SWEET

Thoroughly matured baking potatoes are best for French-fries; sweet potatoes, not yams, are best for French-fried sweets. Wash and pare thinly, and cut into slices about ⅜-inch thick, lengthwise of the potato. Cut these slices into strips ⅜-inch wide, and dry thoroughly in a clean towel or with paper toweling. Place a handful of strips, about ⅓ lb, in a frying basket and lower carefully into deep fat heated to 385°

F. Make sure there is enough fat to cover the potatoes. Fry until they are cooked thoroughly through to the center and are a golden-brown. Lift out of the fat, drain thoroughly in the basket, and turn out onto paper toweling or other absorbent paper. Separate potato strips so they won't be piled on top of each other. Sprinkle with salt. Do not cook too many potatoes at one time; there should be only a single layer in the basket. 1 average-sized potato serves 1.

French-fried potatoes may be kept hot without losing their crisp freshness if they are spread out on flat baking pans after thorough draining on paper toweling and placed in a slow oven. Do not attempt to keep them more than half an hr.

Note: The reason matured baking potatoes are perfect for French Fries is because they hold their shape, have beautiful color and do not shrink or collapse.

OVEN FRENCH-FRIES

Easy to do, easy to eat

5 large baking potatoes, 3 lbs   1½ tsp salt
⅓ cup melted butter *or*
    margarine

Start oven 10 min before baking; set to hot (450° F)

Wash potatoes, pare and cut into 3 lengthwise slices (skins may be left on if desired); stack slices, then cut into half inch wide pieces. These pieces should be about ½ inch wide and ⅜ inch thick. Put potatoes into a bowl, drizzle melted fat over them and toss with hands until all pieces are coated. Arrange on a baking pan so that the strips do not lie parallel to allow the heat to circulate around them. Sprinkle salt over potatoes, place in oven and bake 30 min or until they are tender and top is delicately browned. Occasionally remove potatoes from oven, closing oven each time to retain heat and use pancake turner to turn potatoes. Serve very hot. 4 servings.

GNOCCHI

A famous Italian main dish—attractive color and texture and of good flavor. Made with potatoes

2 baking potatoes, 1 lb   1 tbsp salt
1⅓ cups all-purpose flour   1 cup coarsely grated
1 tsp salt   Parmesan cheese
3 qts boiling water *and*

Scrub potatoes; put in 3-qt saucepan, cover with cold water and heat to boiling, reduce heat to gentle boil, cover and cook until potatoes are tender—25 to 30 min. Meanwhile sift flour, measure and take out 2 tbsp for coating Gnocchi. Drain potatoes, quickly peel and put through ricer or food mill into mixing bowl. While warm, add salt and stir in flour gradually, then knead well to form a stiff dough. Divide dough in half. Shape into 2 rolls about ¾-inch in diameter. Cut rolls into inch-lengths. Toss pieces in reserved flour, then mark each with tines of a fork, making 4 distinct lines. Drop into boiling salted water and boil briskly about 8 min. As Gnocchi cook, they rise to surface. Drain quickly and arrange in a lightly buttered shallow pan, or line pan with greased aluminum foil. Sprinkle evenly with cheese. Place under 500° F broiler 3 inches below source of heat and broil until top is beautifully browned and crusty. Serve at once. 3 servings.

POTATO PANCAKES

A food made famous by Germans and Hebrews

1½ lbs potatoes, 3 large	1¼ tsp salt
⅓ cup all-purpose flour	⅛ tsp pepper
¾ tsp baking powder	4 tsp grated onion, optional
2 eggs	⅓ cup shortening

Pare potatoes and cover with water. Sift flour, measure and resift with baking powder. Beat eggs slightly with fork, add salt, pepper and onion. Drain potatoes, quickly grate them and pack into measuring cup; press out excess liquid. There should be 2½ cups drained grated potato. Stir potatoes into egg mixture and blend thoroughly. Heat shortening in skillet until medium hot, lift potato mixture into hot skillet by heaping tbsp, fry 3 or 4 cakes at a time to a crusty brown, 3 to 4 min. Turn and brown the other side. Drain on paper toweling. Serve hot with apple sauce. A good accompaniment with pot roast or Sauerbraten. 4 servings.

GRATED POTATO PATTIES

3 cups grated raw potatoes, about 2½ lbs boiling potatoes	2 tsp grated onion
	¼ cup bacon *or* ham fat
1½ tsp salt	¼ cup hot water

Thoroughly mix grated potato, salt and onion. Shape quickly into 5 patties, and place in hot fat in a large, heavy skillet. Brown well on both sides; then add water, cover, reduce the heat and cook 10 min longer, turning at end of 5 min. Serve hot. 5 servings.

HASHED BROWN POTATOES No. 1

Shred or dice fine 5 large cold boiled potatoes or hot, half-cooked boiled potatoes. Sauté in 4 tbsp butter or bacon fat in a skillet until hot through and browned on bottom side. Pour ¼ cup cream all over potatoes. Then turn over carefully with pancake turner. Drizzle another ¼ cup cream over potatoes. When done, potato should hold together like a cake and be richly browned on both sides and moist inside. 5 servings.

HASHED BROWNED POTATOES No. 2

Attractive, quick and tasty

2 lbs baking potatoes, 4   2 tsp grated onion, optional
1 tsp salt   ⅓ cup shortening *or* bacon fat

Scrub potatoes thoroughly and rinse well in cold water. Put into 3-qt saucepan, cover with cold water, heat to boiling, cover and boil very gently 12 to 15 min. The potatoes should be slightly underdone. Drain, cool and store in refrigerator, until needed. To hash brown, peel potatoes and shred on coarse part of shredder onto waxed paper. Shreds of underdone potato hold together. Sprinkle salt and grated onion over potatoes. Heat shortening in a 9-inch heavy skillet until just sizzling. Turn potatoes into skillet and pat down with spoon to uniform thickness. Cover and cook moderately fast until beautifully brown on bottom. Use pancake turners to flip potatoes over; brown on other side. Slide onto hot plate and cut into 4 pie-shape wedges to serve. 4 servings.

Note: Or divide potatoes into 4ths; shape into ovals and brown individual servings.

LYONNAISE POTATOES

1¾ lbs potatoes   Pepper
3 tbsp shortening   1 cup chopped onion
1 tsp salt   Vinegar

Wash potatoes, pare thinly and cut into ¾-inch cubes. Heat shortening in a heavy skillet. Add the potatoes, sprinkle with salt and pepper, cover and cook over medium heat for 20 min. Turn potatoes occasionally. Add onion and mix lightly. Cover and cook over low heat for about 15 min or until vegetables are done and have a crispy crust. A min before potatoes finish cooking, drizzle from 2 to 4 tbsp of vinegar over the top, if desired. 4 servings.

MASHED POTATOES

6 medium boiling potatoes,   About ½ cup hot milk
2 lbs   Salt to taste
2 tbsp butter

Wash and pare potatoes thinly, and cook as directed for Boiled Potatoes, p 1373, until soft when pierced with a fork. Drain thoroughly, saving the water. Mash potatoes or put them through a ricer or food mill, which has been heated by running hot water through it, forcing potatoes back into pan in which they were cooked. Add butter and hot milk, and beat vigorously over low heat, using a fork or wooden spoon until very light, fluffy and white. Add more salt if needed, and beat in. Pile immediately into a hot serving dish, leaving surface fluffy, and top with a pat of butter and a dash of paprika. Serve immediately. 4 to 5 servings.

Water drained from potatoes should not be discarded as it contains valuable minerals. Use it for making gravy or vegetable soup.

Note: Either baking or boiling potatoes, if thoroughly matured, may be used for mashed potatoes. Boiling potatoes, because of their waxy texture, whip into a fluffy and more cohesive mass that holds together slightly better than baking potatoes.

COMPANY OVEN-BROWNED MASHED POTATOES

A new twist that takes the last min rush out of mashing potatoes. Attractive, extra hot and delicious—and oh, so easy on the cook

2½ lbs boiling potatoes, mashed, make 5 to 6 servings	1¾ lbs potatoes, mashed, make 4 servings
Butter well 9″ glass pie pan	Butter well 8″ glass pie pan
Cream	Cream
Parmesan cheese, optional	Parmesan cheese, optional

Adjust oven rack to be in center of oven. Start oven 10 min before baking; set to moderate (375° F) or moderately hot (400° F).

Four to 6 hrs before mealtime, cook and mash potatoes in quantity required.

Plop the hot fluffy mashed potatoes by spoonfuls into prepared pan, leaving top fluffy, or gently spread smooth. Cool at room temp to lukewarm, then cover loosely with waxed paper and place in refrigerator. *20 to 25 min* before mealtime, brush top gently but generously with cream. Leave plain, or for extra glamour and flavor, sprinkle generously with *freshly grated* Parmesan cheese. Place immediately in oven and bake until both top and bottom are delicately browned and potatoes are puffy and hot through. Do not overbake. Serve at once from pie pan, placed on dinner plate or in a pie pan holder. When spooned into, bottom crust loosens from pan and potatoes lift out with a rich brown crust on bottom and top.

PIQUANT MASHED POTATOES
Irresistible

2 lbs boiling potatoes	Pepper to taste
2 cups water	1 tbsp fine cut tender green
1¾ tsp salt	onion tops *or* chives
¾ cup sour cream	

Pare potatoes thinly, wash. Cut in quarters if large; drop into saucepan, add water and salt; cover and boil gently until tender, about 20 min. Drain, save water. Put through ricer or food mill letting potatoes fall into pan in which they cooked. Push potatoes up around sides of pan, pour ½ cup water drained from potatoes and cream into center, place over heat until liquids almost boil. Remove from heat and beat vigorously. Add pepper and onion or chives. Serve hot. 4 servings.

POTATOES FOR BORDERING PLANKS
OR HEATPROOF PLATTER

Prepare *mashed potatoes,* then while hot beat in 2 egg yolks thoroughly. Now put potatoes into a pastry bag and pipe in any desired pattern around meat or fish on a plank or platter then around the spots where vegetables are to be arranged after browning the potatoes under broiler.

PARSLEY BUTTERED POTATOES

Choose small boiling potatoes of uniform size. Scrape and cook as for boiled potatoes. Drain thoroughly and immediately replace over heat for a min to evaporate excess moisture. Add butter and when melted, shake covered pan to distribute butter so each potato is coated all over. Sprinkle with finely chopped parsley and serve immediately. Ham or bacon fat may be used instead of butter.

Note: Any boiled potato that is not served promptly after it has finished cooking deteriorates in color and soon becomes soggy.

POTATO CHEESE PUFFS

4 large fresh boiled potatoes	1½ tsp salt
¼ cup top milk	1½ tsp fresh onion juice
2 eggs, separated	2 tbsp finely chopped parsley
¾ cup grated cheese	

Start oven 10 min before baking; set to moderately hot (425° F)

Drain off any liquid from hot potatoes. Rice potatoes while hot into a bowl. Add milk mixed with egg yolks and cheese, salt, onion and parsley and whip until fluffy. Beat egg whites until stiff. Fold into the potato mixture. Pile lightly into 8 mounds on a greased cookie sheet or shallow pan. Bake 15 to 20 min. Serve immediately while still puffy. 4 servings.

POTATO CROQUETTES, BAKED

Interesting, different, easy because they can be prepared ahead of time

2 lbs potatoes	1¼ tsp grated onion, optional
2½ cups water	1 cup fine dry crumbs, buttered, p 162
1 tsp salt	
⅓ cup milk, about	1 egg beaten with
⅓ cup butter *or* margarine	1 tbsp water
Pepper	

Start oven 10 min before baking; set to moderately hot (400° F)

Wash potatoes, pare thinly and if large, cut in half. Add water and salt, cover, boil gently until tender from 20 to 25 min. Only a tbsp or 2 of water should remain on potatoes, no more. Put potatoes through food mill or ricer. Return potatoes to liquid in saucepan. Add butter and most of the milk; beat until light and fluffy, adding rest of milk if needed. Potatoes for croquettes should be quite stiff and hold together well. Stir in pepper and onion. Cool to room temp. Measure ⅓ cup portions onto waxed paper spread with the buttered crumbs. Shape croquettes into cones, roll in crumbs, then in egg mixture and again in crumbs. Grease circles on a cookie sheet or shallow pan for croquettes to stand on. Store in refrigerator. About 20 min before serving time, place in oven and bake until golden brown and crusty, about 15 min. Serve on hot platter, garnish with parsley. 9 croquettes.

Hint: Potato croquettes bake more satisfactorily than they fry and are more economical of shortening. Cold mashed potatoes may be used to make these croquettes.

POTATO DUMPLINGS

2 cups riced boiled potatoes, about 3 potatoes
2 eggs, beaten
1 tsp salt
1 tsp grated onion
1 tbsp chopped parsley
½ cup toasted ¼-inch bread cubes
½ cup all-purpose flour, sifted with ½ tsp baking powder

Combine ingredients in order given, mixing thoroughly. Drop by tbsp on top of boiling Beef Stew, p 817, Sauerbraten, p 811, or sauerkraut about half an hr before serving; cover tightly and allow to steam for 25 min. Serve dumplings on or around the stew. 5 servings.

Note: These dumplings are also delicious baked and served with roast goose that is cooked without dressing. Drop the dumplings by tbsp around the goose in the pan gravy about 20 min before serving time.

POTATO PANCAKES

2 eggs, slightly beaten
1 cup milk
⅛ tsp fresh onion juice
¼ cup all-purpose flour
2 tsp D.A. baking powder *or* 2½ tsp tartrate *or* phosphate type
1 tsp salt
3 cups grated raw potatoes, 4 large
Shortening

Combine eggs, milk and onion juice and sift in the dry ingredients. Beat until smooth. Fold in the potatoes. Using a third or half-cup measure depending on desired thickness, pour mixture onto a griddle covered with about 1 tbsp hot shortening. Fry over medium heat until brown and crusty on the underside. Turn and finish cooking. Serve immediately. Apple Sauce is a favorite accompaniment. Makes about 8 eight-inch pancakes.

POTATO PATTIES

Homey, economical but appealing and good

2 cups stiff, leftover mashed potatoes	½ cup fine dry bread crumbs, p 162
1 tsp grated onion, optional	¼ cup shortening
1 egg beaten with	
1 tbsp water	

Blend potatoes with the onion and half of the egg mixture to a smooth uniform consistency. Divide into 4 portions. Shape into flat patties of uniform thickness. Dip both sides of patties into remaining egg mixture, then in the crumbs. Heat shortening until almost sizzling hot, then lay in the patties. Cook moderately fast until a beautiful brown on underside, turn carefully with pancake turner or spatula and brown other side. Serve very hot. 4 servings.

Note: Flour may be used instead of the crumbs, in which case omit eggs and water.

POTATOES au GRATIN

2 lbs boiling potatoes, 6 medium	2 cups thin White Sauce, p 1262
	¼ lb cheese, grated

Start oven 10 min before baking; set to moderate (375° F)

Wash potatoes, pare thinly and cut in uniform thin slices. Combine potatoes and white sauce in saucepan and heat gently until sauce bubbles. Arrange layers of the creamed potatoes in a buttered casserole with grated cheese between layers and on top. Cover casserole, and bake until potatoes are tender, about 25 min. Then remove cover and brown surface, either in oven with temp increased to 475° F or under broiler. 5 servings.

For variation in color and flavor, add diced green pepper or pimiento, or both to the creamed potatoes just before turning into the casserole.

Note: A speedy and highly satisfactory variation may be made by using 2 cups of hot milk in place of the white sauce.

POTATOES IN CARAWAY SAUCE

Delicious

6 small potatoes, 1¼ lbs	1¼ tsp salt
1½ cups water	½ tsp caraway seeds
1 cup sour cream	1 tbsp chopped parsley

Wash and pare potatoes. Turn into a saucepan, add water and ½ tsp salt, cover and boil gently for 20 to 25 min, or until done. No water should remain on the potatoes at the end of the cooking. Combine sour cream, remaining salt and caraway seeds. Pour the sour cream mixture over potatoes and heat for 2 min, turning the potatoes in the sauce as it heats. Transfer to a hot serving dish and garnish with the parsley. 4 servings.

POTATOES O'BRIEN

5 small baking potatoes, 2 lbs	1 pimiento, chopped
1 tbsp butter	½ tsp salt
1 medium onion, chopped	Pepper to suit taste
	1 tsp chopped parsley

Wash and pare potatoes thinly and cut into ¾-inch dice. Fry in deep fat heated to 360° F until golden brown; drain. Melt butter in a skillet and sauté the onion until soft and yellow. Add hot potatoes and pimiento and toss about until well mixed, and until hot through. Add seasonings, turn into a hot serving dish, and sprinkle with chopped parsley. 5 servings.

If preferred, the potatoes may be sliced and pan-fried rather than fried in deep fat, adding the onion and pimiento the last few min of cooking.

QUICK ESCALLOPED POTATOES

No curdling

2 tbsp butter	2 cups milk
2 tbsp flour	6 cups sliced potatoes, 2½ lbs
2 tsp salt	1 tbsp melted butter

Start oven 10 min before baking; set to moderate (350° F)

Melt butter in saucepan, stir in flour and salt and add milk slowly, stirring constantly until sauce boils and thickens. Add potatoes and heat with occasional stirring until the sauce boils again. Turn potatoes and sauce into a shallow, greased casserole, 6½ x 10 x 1¾ inches. Drizzle melted butter over top. Place on a rack a little above the middle of the oven and bake 35 min or until potatoes are tender, the creamy liquid bubbles up almost over them and the potatoes are a tempting brown on top. Serve hot. 5 servings.

Note: Flour may be omitted and the potatoes heated in the milk containing the butter and salt, provided the potatoes are thoroughly matured.

RICED POTATOES

Put hot, freshly boiled, peeled potatoes into a ricer that has been thoroughly heated by dipping it into boiling water. Rice the potatoes directly into a hot serving dish. (A good way to heat the dish is to pour boiling water into it and let stand a few min; drain and dry quickly.) Add a few shakes of paprika to the top, then drop on a pat or two of butter. Serve immediately with gravy in a separate bowl, if desired.

ROAST POTATOES

Pare thinly 6 to 8 medium-sized baking potatoes, 2½ lbs and place in roasting pan around the roast meat 1 to 1½ hrs depending on size of potatoes before the roast is to be done. When potatoes are browned on under side, turn over to brown other side and continue baking until tender when pierced with a fork. To shorten cooking time, parboil potatoes (cook until almost tender) and bake with roast for 30 min, or long enough to brown well.

Note: New potatoes may be used, but they take longer to cook and never become dry and mealy like old potatoes.

"FRIED" ROAST POTATOES

Potatoes boiled until barely tender make handsome potatoes similar to roast potatoes when fried in deep fat (360° F) until golden brown.

STUFFED BAKED POTATOES No. 1

5 large baking potatoes, 3 lbs   1 cup hot milk
⅓ cup butter   ½ cup grated American
1 tsp salt *or* to taste   cheese, 2 oz

Start oven 10 min before baking; set to moderately hot (400° F)

Use baking potatoes of uniform size and shape. Scrub thoroughly and bake until they are soft all through when pierced with a fork, from 50 to 60 min. Cut baked potatoes in half lengthwise, scoop out potato and put through a ricer or food mill or mash. Combine with butter, salt and hot milk, then whip with fork or wooden spoon until light and fluffy. Pile lightly into the potato shells, sprinkle with grated cheese and return to the oven (or to broiler), and toast until the surface is a tempting brown. If they are to be served with creamed or à la king meat, make a depression in the center when stuffing the potato into the shells and omit the cheese; after toasting, pour the meat mixture into and over the hot potato. 5 servings.

Note: Cheese may be omitted from this recipe if desired. Two tbsp finely chopped onion is a pleasant addition to the mashed potatoes.

STUFFED BAKED POTATOES No. 2

4 ten-oz baking potatoes	1 tsp salt
1 cup hot milk	Dash of black pepper
3 to 4 drops Worcestershire sauce	2 tbsp chopped parsley
	Parmesan cheese
½ tsp prepared mustard	Paprika

Start oven 10 min before baking; set to moderately hot (400° F)

Scrub potatoes and bake for 1 hr or until tender. See p 1372. Cut in half lengthwise. Scoop out potato and put through a ricer or mash. Add the milk and whip until fluffy and white. Fold in the next 5 ingredients thoroughly. Heap mixture into potato shells. Sprinkle top generously with cheese and paprika. Return to oven and bake from 10 to 15 min. Serve at once. 4 servings.

BAKED SWEET POTATOES

Start oven 10 min before baking; set to hot (450° F)

Use sweet potatoes (not yams) of uniform size and similar shape so the baking time will be the same for all of them. Allow 5 medium-sized potatoes for 5 servings. Scrub thoroughly, slice away any blemishes, and place in a shallow baking pan. Bake uncovered until soft when squeezed between the folds of a towel, from 20 to 30 min for medium-sized potatoes. Serve whole or remove from the shell and mash, seasoning with butter and salt.

BOILED SWEET POTATOES

Sweet potatoes are of two types; the long slender kind which is red or yellow in color, and has a firm, dry texture, and the yam, which is fatter, less tapering, much deeper in color, and is considerably more moist. If a mealy potato is preferred, the slender potatoes should be chosen. If a moist waxy one is desired, the yam should be selected. Either may be boiled, baked, or candied. The yam, however, is best when candied.

Use potatoes of uniform size, allowing 2 to 2½ lbs for 5 servings. Scrub potatoes very thoroughly and slice away any blemishes. Small slender sweet potatoes may be boiled whole. Paring is so difficult when raw that the skin is usually left on until they are cooked, when it comes off easily. However, the clearest, best color in sweet potatoes is obtained when they are pared before cooking. Paring should be done quickly and each potato as it is pared should be quickly rinsed and dropped into the hot water into which the potatoes are to be boiled to prevent discoloration. Large potatoes should be cut in half to hasten cooking. Boil either pared or unpared potatoes 15 to 25 min or until tender when pierced with a fork; drain. If skins have been left on, peel immediately. Serve promptly with plenty of butter and salt. 4 to 5 servings.

CANDIED SWEET POTATOES No. 1

5 medium sweet potatoes *or* yams	1 cup granulated sugar
	¼ tsp salt
½ cup water	2 tbsp butter

Scrub potatoes and pare thinly. Have the water, sugar and salt heated to boiling. As the potatoes are pared, leave whole or cut in half and drop into the hot syrup, turning to coat all over. Cover tightly, reduce heat and cook slowly, turning potatoes from time to time until potatoes are tender and translucent and syrup is cooked down to a thick candy-like consistency, or from 1 to 1½ hrs. Add butter, turning potatoes to mix well, and continue cooking 5 min longer. Serve hot with the syrup over them. Sweet potatoes may also be glazed by heating peeled, boiled potatoes and syrup in a covered pan in a moderate oven (375° F). Turn occasionally and add butter just before serving. 5 servings.

Variation: Hot boiled, well-drained sweet potatoes may be drizzled generously with melted butter, sprinkled with either brown or granulated sugar, and baked in a moderately hot oven (400° F), uncovered, until brown and sugar-crusted.

CANDIED SWEET POTATOES No. 2

2 lbs sweet potatoes	¼ tsp salt
⅓ cup butter	½ cup white corn syrup

Wash and pare potatoes; cut crosswise in ½-inch slices. Immediately put potato slices into melted butter in a skillet, cover, and cook over low heat for about 10 min, turning after about 5 min of cooking. When slices have browned delicately, add salt and pour corn syrup over them. Continue cooking slowly for 5 to 10 min longer until potatoes are tender and almost transparent in appearance. Serve hot with a light sprinkling of nutmeg or a squeeze of lemon juice if desired. 5 servings.

CANDIED COCONUT SWEET POTATOES

A surprise

4 medium size sweet potatoes, 2 lbs	½ tsp grated orange rind
	⅓ cup shredded coconut
⅓ cup margarine *or* butter	½ cup white corn syrup
¼ cup orange juice	

Wash potatoes, pare thinly, slice ¼-inch thick and lay immediately in the margarine heated in a heavy skillet. Cover, cook over low heat about 5 min or until delicately browned on underside. Turn over and brown on other side. Add remaining ingredients, continue cooking 10 min or until potatoes are tender and translucent in appearance. 4 to 5 servings.

CHEESE AND SWEET POTATO CASSEROLE

4 medium-sized sweet potatoes, about 2 lbs	1 tbsp sugar
1 cup boiling water	1 cup milk
1 tsp salt	¾ cup grated sharp cheese, 3 oz
Pepper to taste	1 tbsp butter

Start oven 10 min before baking; set to moderate (375° F)

Scrub potatoes; pare thinly, slice, and put into a 3-qt saucepan. Add boiling water and half the salt, cover, and boil 15 min. Turn into a 5-cup casserole in 2 or 3 layers, sprinkling each layer with some of the remaining salt, the pepper and the sugar. Pour milk over the top; sprinkle with the grated cheese and dot with butter. Bake uncovered for 30 min. 4 servings.

ESCALLOPED SWEET POTATOES AND APPLES

5 medium sweet potatoes *or* yams	½ cup brown sugar, firmly pkd
2 tart apples	3 tbsp butter
¾ tsp salt	

Start oven 10 min before baking; set to moderate (375° F)

Scrub potatoes, pare thinly and cut into ¼-inch slices. Core and cut apples into slices of the same thickness. Arrange in alternate layers in a buttered casserole, sprinkling each layer of potatoes with salt and each layer of apples with sugar. Dot with butter, cover casserole, and bake until both potatoes and apples are very tender and flavors are well blended, about 45 min. 5 servings.

Note: Red skinned apples add attractive color and this color is best retained if apple slices are sprinkled with lemon juice from ½ lemon.

HONEYED SWEET POTATOES

1½ lbs sweet potatoes	2 tbsp lemon juice
1 tsp salt	½ tsp grated lemon rind
3 tbsp butter *or* margarine	½ tsp salt
½ cup honey	1 tbsp maraschino cherries

Wash, pare and cut potatoes into crosswise slices ½-inch thick. Sprinkle with the salt and brown both sides of the slices carefully in the hot butter. Cover and cook for 8 to 10 min until potatoes are tender. Combine the next 4 ingredients and pour over the potatoes. Cover and simmer for 5 min. Garnish with cherries. Serve immediately. 4 servings.

MASHED SWEET POTATOES

A dressed-up, different, delicious way with sweet potatoes

2 lbs sweet potatoes, not yams	¾ to 1 cup hot, rich milk
2 cups boiling water	2 tsp brandy *or* sherry
4 tbsp butter *or* margarine	extract, *or* ½ tsp nutmeg
½ tsp salt	

Pare potatoes, cut in half lengthwise if large, add boiling water, cover and boil gently 20 min or until tender. The water should be practically evaporated. Drain off any remaining water. Mash or put hot potatoes through food mill or ricer, add butter, salt and milk; stir until smooth over heat. Remove from heat, quickly beat in desired flavoring and turn into hot serving dish. 4 or 5 servings.

SWEET POTATO APPLE CASSEROLE

1 lb sweet potatoes	¼ tsp salt
2 large tart apples, about 1 lb	2 tbsp butter *or* margarine
2 tbsp flour	½ cup cider
2 tbsp brown sugar	4 strips bacon

Start oven 10 min before baking; set to mod (350° F)

Scrub potatoes, pare thinly and cut into one-fourth-inch slices. Core and slice apples thinly but do not pare. Mix flour, sugar and salt and lightly dredge the potatoes and apples with the mixture. Arrange apples and potatoes in alternate layers in a buttered 5-cup casserole. Dot with butter, pour on the cider, and arrange bacon strips over top. Cover and bake 35 min or until potatoes and apples are tender. Uncover and bake for 5 or 10 min longer until bacon strips are crisp. Serve immediately. 4 or 5 servings.

SWEET POTATOES LYONNAISE

3 strips bacon	1 tsp salt
¾ cup chopped onion	From ¼ to 1 tsp sugar
1½ lbs sweet potatoes, cooked and peeled	

Cut bacon into half-inch pieces with kitchen scissors. Put into a skillet and sauté with the onion until done, or about 5 min. Add the diced sweet potatoes and seasonings and cook uncovered over medium heat until potatoes are hot through and acquire a golden crispy crust on underside. Serve immediately. 4 servings.

SWEET POTATOES WITH PINEAPPLE SAUCE

4 sweet potatoes, cooked, about 2 lbs	Dash of salt
3 tbsp butter *or* margarine	1 cup unsweetened pineapple juice
2 tbsp flour	Currant jelly

Peel sweet potatoes thinly and slice in half lengthwise. Pan-fry in butter over medium heat until lightly crusted on both sides and tender all the way through. Remove potatoes and keep hot. Blend flour and salt into butter remaining in pan; add pineapple juice gradually and cook until thick stirring constantly to keep smooth. Immediately pour hot sauce over potatoes and serve. Garnish with a few flecks of the red jelly. 4 servings.

VOLCANIC SWEET POTATOES

Appealing in appearance, texture, flavor

2 lbs sweet potatoes	6 marshmallows
¼ tsp salt	1½ cups cornflakes *or* corn
2 tbsp butter	and soya shreds
¼ cup broken pecans	

Start oven 10 min before baking; set to hot (450° F)

Heat 1 qt water in a 3-qt saucepan until boiling. Wash potatoes, pare thinly, quickly cut into halves and drop immediately into boiling water to prevent discoloration. Add salt, cover and boil gently until potatoes are just tender, about 20 min. Shake pan occasionally to prevent sticking. Practically all the water should be evaporated. Mash potatoes or put through a food mill. Add butter and beat hard. If potatoes are too moist to shape into balls, place over moderate heat and stir constantly until mixture is stiff enough to shape. Stir in pecans. Cool until mixture can be handled. Divide into 6 portions. Mold each portion around a marshmallow to form balls, but have layer of potato a little thinner on the top. Roll balls carefully in cornflakes to coat thickly. Lay on a greased shallow pan, keep thin side up, and bake until flakes are toasted and marshmallow melts and begins to flow out at the top. 4 to 5 servings.

YAM ORANGE CASSEROLE

Rich, sweet, translucent yams with tang that makes one come back for "seconds." Fine for company meals

2 lbs yams	½ cup white corn syrup
1 medium size orange	⅓ cup sugar
¼ tsp salt	¼ cup butter *or* margarine

Start oven 10 min before baking; set to moderately hot (400° F)

Scrub yams, and rinse well in cold water. Cut out neatly any discolored skin spots. Put into a 3-qt saucepan, add 1½ qts boiling water. Place over medium heat. Cover kettle, and boil briskly 10 min, or until skins will strip off. Yams will not be cooked through. Drain; rinse in cold water; peel off skins and any dark spots. Wash orange, preferably a seedless one. Remove slice of skin from both ends and discard. Cut orange into eighths lengthwise; then cut each slice into ½-inch lengths. Turn orange into a 6-cup casserole. Cut yams into 1½-inch crosswise slices, and arrange slices over the orange. Sprinkle in the salt; pour on the corn syrup; sprinkle on the sugar; dot top with butter. Cover casserole, bake 20 min; then uncover and baste potatoes with the syrup. Bake uncovered 40 min longer. Remove to a cake rack. The yams are so hot they can stand 10 min and still be hot, a quality that makes them ideal for meals calling for many last minute details. Serve from casserole. 4 to 5 servings.

COOKING FRESH PUMPKIN OR SQUASH FOR PURÉE

Start oven 10 min before baking; set to mod hot (400° F)

Select a mature pie pumpkin. A 5-lb pumpkin yields about the same amount of purée as does a No. 2 can, 2½ cups. To prepare the pumpkin, wash it and cut in halves. Do not scoop out seeds and fibers, but rub the cut surfaces with shortening, and place the halves cut side down on a baking sheet. Bake until tender when pierced with a sharp fork right through the skin. This will take from 45 to 60 min for a small pie pumpkin, longer for larger, thicker pumpkins. Then remove seeds and fibers and scoop out the flesh and press it through a potato ricer or a food mill. If the juice is pressed out first and kept separate from the pulp, it may conveniently be evaporated by boiling to almost nothing, and then mixed with the pulp. This gives a superior flavor and a good consistency for pie-making without further cooking of the purée itself. Hubbard Squash is best for purée.

BUTTERED RUTABAGAS OR WHITE TURNIPS

Wash rutabagas or turnips and cut in ½-inch crosswise slices. Pare each slice; cut into quarters, then into thinner slices or cut in dice if desired. Turn into saucepan, barely cover with boiling water, add salt, 1 tsp to 1 qt water, and boil vigorously, uncovered, for 15 min, then reduce heat, cover, and simmer until tender or 10 to 15 min longer, by which time very little liquid should remain. Serve the vegetable in remaining liquid, or thicken it with thin Flour-water Paste, p 163, or drain off, chill and use liquid in a vegetable cocktail. Add 3 tbsp butter, a dash of black pepper, and 1 tsp sugar to each pt of turnips with additional salt to suit taste. Instead of butter, the drained turnips may be combined with 1 cup thin White Sauce, p 1262, if preferred. 2 to 2½ lbs raw turnips make 5 servings.

Variation: Small white turnips may be cooked whole or may be scooped out to form cups for peas.

CREAMED RUTABAGAS

1 medium rutabaga,	3 tbsp butter
2 to 2½ lbs	3 tbsp flour
4 cups boiling water	¾ cup coffee cream
1 tsp salt	Salt to taste
2 tsp sugar	Chopped parsley

Wash rutabaga, cut into ½-inch thick crosswise slices. Pare and cut in ½-inch dice. Put into saucepan with water and salt and boil covered until just tender, 25 to 35 min. Drain, saving ¾ cup of the cooking water. Melt butter, blend in flour, add cooking water and cream, and stir over direct heat until sauce boils and thickens. Add sugar and more salt if needed. Turn hot rutabaga into hot platter or vegetable dish, pour cream sauce over it, and sprinkle finely chopped parsley over top for garnish. 5 servings.

MASHED RUTABAGA

1 small rutabaga, 1¼ lbs, sliced ¼-inch thick and pared	1½ tsp salt
	1 tsp sugar
	2 tbsp butter
3 medium potatoes, 1 lb, pared and cut in half	1 egg, beaten
	Salt and pepper to taste

Place rutabaga and potatoes in separate saucepans and add 3 cups boiling water and three-fourths tsp salt to each. Cook covered until tender, 20 to 25 min. Drain both vegetables, saving liquid. Rutabaga pot liquor makes a delicious vegetable cocktail; potato water should be used for gravy, soup or cooking other vegetables. Mash rutabaga and potato separately, then combine. Adding potato to rutabaga makes it mild in flavor and gives it a fluffy consistency. Add sugar, butter and beaten egg, and beat vigorously until mixture is smooth and fluffy. Add seasoning to taste. 5 servings.

RUTABAGA AND APPLE

1 small rutabaga, 1 lb	2 tbsp sugar
1 cup hot water	2 tsp lemon juice
1 tsp salt	2 tsp cornstarch
1 large tart apple, ½ lb	3 tbsp butter

Wash rutabaga, pare and cut into ¼-inch slices directly into the saucepan. Add water and salt, cover, heat to boiling, then reduce heat and simmer for fifteen min. Arrange unpared apple slices on top of rutabaga; add sugar and lemon juice. Cover and simmer for ten more min, or until vegetable and fruit slices are tender but not mushy. Thicken the sauce with the cornstarch mixed with 2 tbsp cold water. Add butter and reheat. 4 servings.

WHAT TO LOOK FOR WHEN BUYING SALSIFY

Salsify is always sold in bunches of from 10 to 12 long slender roots. Choose roots that are smooth to avoid waste in scraping. Many people think the flavor is similar to that of oysters and for this reason it is often called oyster plant. One bunch scraped and sliced makes about 3 cups.

CREAMED SALSIFY

3 cups sliced salisfy,　　　　2 tbsp flour
　　1 large bunch　　　　　　1 cup milk
1½ cups boiling water　　　　1 chicken bouillon cube
¼ cup finely cut celery　　　¾ tsp salt
3 tbsp butter　　　　　　　Dash pepper

Remove tops from salsify and discard. Scrub salsify roots and scrape off all blemishes. Rinse thoroughly in cold water. Slice about ⅛-inch thick directly into saucepan and barely cover with the boiling water. Add the celery, cover, and simmer until salsify is tender, or for about 15 min. Meanwhile make a White Sauce of the butter, flour and milk, p 1262. Drain liquid from salsify and measure; there should be ½ cup. If there is more, evaporate to ½ cup; if there is less, make up with water. Add salsify and liquid to the sauce. Reheat and stir in bouillon cube and seasonings. 5 servings.

SAUERKRAUT AND BEAN POT DINNER

2 cups navy beans　　　　　No. 2 can sauerkraut *or*
3 slices bacon　　　　　　2½ cups bulk kraut
2 tbsp flour　　　　　　　1 large apple, cored and
1 tbsp salt　　　　　　　　sliced but not pared
1 qt water

Pick over beans and wash thoroughly in cold water. Soak overnight in 2 qts water. Cut bacon with kitchen scissors into half-inch lengths and pan-fry until half done. Add flour and salt, blend well. Then add 1 qt water. Heat to boiling. Drain beans and add. Reduce heat, cover and *simmer* for two hrs. Stir in kraut easily so as not to break up beans. Slice apples on top, cover and continue simmering until beans are very tender, ½ to ¾ hr longer. 5 to 6 servings.

SAUERKRAUT AND FISH CASSEROLE

3 tbsp margarine　　　　　½ tsp dill seed
1½ tbsp flour　　　　　　1 pt sauerkraut
⅔ cup finely chopped onion　1 lb halibut
¼ tsp salt　　　　　　　　⅛ tsp salt
⅛ tsp pepper　　　　　　Dash of paprika
¼ tsp marjoram

Start oven 10 min before baking; set to mod (350° F)

Melt margarine, add flour and stir continuously until browned delicately. Add onion, salt, pepper, marjoram, dill seed and sauerkraut. Stir thoroughly and turn into baking dish, putting fish on top. Cover. Bake 40 to 45 min. Then sprinkle fish with salt and paprika and place under broiler for about 5 min to brown appetizingly on top. 4 servings.

SCHULTZIE'S SAUERKRAUT AND DUMPLINGS

Bohemian

1 tbsp lard
1 tbsp butter
2 onions, egg-size
1 qt sauerkraut rinsed
    quickly in cold water
2 tbsp sugar
1 tsp caraway seed

1 potato, size lemon, pared,
    grated on fine grater (not
    shredded) mixed with
2 tbsp flour and
½ cup water
Potato Dumplings, p 1381

Heat lard and butter in 3-qt saucepan, add thinly sliced onion and saute until yellow. Add sauerkraut, sugar and caraway, barely cover with water and heat to boiling. Reduce heat, cover and cook until tender—homemade sauerkraut 1 hr; canned about 45 min. About 10 min before sauerkraut is done, stir in potato-flour mixture and cook 10 min longer. Serve with Potato Dumplings and roast pork.

Note: Covering sauerkraut with water gives plenty of gravy to serve with dumplings and makes them good and tasty.

SAVORY SAUERKRAUT No. 1

3 *or* 4 tart cooking apples
No. 2½ can sauerkraut *or*
1 qt bulk sauerkraut

3 tbsp butter
3 to 4 tbsp sugar
1 tsp caraway seed

Pare apples, core and cut into eighths. Alternate layers of kraut and apples in a saucepan (2 or 3-qt capacity). Add water barely to cover, heat to boiling; add sugar and caraway, reduce heat, cover, and simmer until kraut is tender, or from 20 to 25 min. Most of liquid should be evaporated. Add butter, toss gently to blend, and watch carefully while cooking rapidly until all liquid has evaporated. Turn into a hot serving dish and serve immediately. 5 servings.

Note: If apples have tender red skins, leave skins on for beautiful color. Use sweet cider or apple juice instead of water to cook kraut but omit apple.

SAVORY SAUERKRAUT No. 2

1 small onion, sliced
⅓ cup bacon drippings
1 qt sauerkraut
4 bouillon cubes *or* 4 tsp
    meat extract paste

1½ cups water
1 tsp sugar *or* more
2 tbsp grated raw potato

Lightly sauté the onion in the bacon drippings. Add the sauerkraut. Dissolve the bouillon cubes in the water and add with the sugar. Gently simmer for 1 hr. Stir in the potato and cook another 30 min. 4 servings.

BUTTERED SPINACH

Use freshly cut, carefully boxed or basketed spinach with few torn or damaged leaves. Leaves should be thick and fleshy, bright green and very crisp. Stems should be tender enough to cook and eat with the leaves. Wash spinach very thoroughly through several cold waters if necessary, washing each leaf separately to remove all sand and grit. Discard bad leaves and any tough stems. *Lift* leaves out of water rather than *pouring* off water so that sand and grit that has fallen to bottom will not again mix with spinach. Put drained leaves into large saucepan, add 1⅓ cups boiling water and 1 tsp salt to each 2 lbs spinach, and boil gently until just tender, from 5 to 10 min, turning occasionally. Drain thoroughly (there should be about 2 cups) and pour melted butter over spinach. Serve immediately. Two lbs is sufficient for 4 to 5 servings.

CREAMED SPINACH DE LUXE

1½ lbs spinach	3 tbsp flour
1 tsp sugar	1½ tsp salt
3 tbsp butter	1 cup milk
½ clove garlic, chopped fine	1 cup cream

Clean and cook spinach as for Buttered Spinach, adding the sugar to the cooking water. Drain thoroughly. Meanwhile melt butter in a saucepan, add coarsely chopped garlic, and cook until soft; blend in the flour and salt, and add milk and cream. Stir constantly over direct heat until sauce boils and thickens; remove garlic if desired, then add the drained spinach which has been chopped, mix well, and reheat until the sauce bubbles up. Serve immediately. 5 or 6 servings.

CREAMED SPINACH ON NOODLES AND CHEESE

1 lb spinach	1⁄16 tsp pepper
3 slices bacon	1 tbsp finely chopped onion
3 tbsp flour	1 cup grated cheese, 4 oz
1½ cups milk	4 oz medium Noodles,
¾ tsp salt	cooked, p 430

Clean and cook spinach according to directions for Buttered Spinach. Cut bacon with scissors into small pieces and sauté until delicately browned, but not crisp. Remove bacon from fat and blend flour into the drippings. Add the milk gradually, cooking and stirring until the mixture is smooth and thickened. Add seasonings, spinach and onion. Heat thoroughly. Sprinkle the grated cheese over the hot noodles, then pour on the hot creamed spinach, add the sautéed bacon and serve. 4 servings.

GERMAN STYLE SPINACH

Spinach that is not a chore to eat

10 oz pkg washed, trimmed spinach	2 *or* 3 tbsp chopped onion
1 cup boiling water	1½ tbsp flour
½ tsp salt	Pepper to taste
4 slices bacon	2 tsp vinegar, optional

Look over spinach and rinse in cold water. Drain well, heap up on a cutting board and cut crosswise into half-inch strips with a sharp knife. Measure boiling water into a 3-qt saucepan. Add spinach and salt. Turn spinach over, cover and boil moderately fast until tender, about 6 min. Meanwhile pan-broil bacon until golden brown, remove from skillet and add chopped onion to the fat. Sauté until yellow, add flour and stir until thoroughly blended. Drain liquid from spinach into skillet; stir until well blended and smooth, then turn the onion mixture into the spinach. Continue cooking with constant stirring until the liquid is smooth and thickened. Add pepper and crumbled bacon and stir until well distributed. Or turn spinach into a hot dish and sprinkle the crumbled crisp bacon over the top. 4 servings.

Note: One pound of average spinach with most of stems left on will yield approximately 10 oz when trimmed and washed.

SAVORY CREAMED SPINACH

1½ lbs spinach	¾ tsp salt
3 tbsp butter	Pepper to taste
1 small onion, chopped fine	1½ cups milk
¼ cup flour	2 hard-cooked eggs, diced

Wash and cook spinach according to directions for Buttered Spinach. Drain, chop fine. There should be 1¼ to 1½ cups. Melt butter in saucepan, add chopped onion, and cook until soft; blend in flour, salt, and pepper. Add milk, and cook over direct heat, stirring constantly until sauce boils and thickens. Fold in chopped spinach and the eggs gently and reheat if necessary. Serve hot. 5 servings.

SPINACH COOKED IN BACON CREAM SAUCE

So creamy, so green, so good

10-oz pkg washed trimmed spinach	2 cups milk
¼ cup bacon fat	Pepper to taste
2 tbsp flour	1 tbsp coarsely grated onion
¾ tsp salt	Nutmeg, optional

Look over spinach and rinse in cold water. Drain; then lay on cutting board and with a sharp knife cut it crosswise into inch-wide strips. Put bacon fat into a 3-qt saucepan, add the onion and sauté for a min, then blend in flour and salt. Add the milk and cook and stir until sauce boils and thickens. Add the spinach and stir constantly for the first min or so; then stir frequently and boil gently 8 to 10 min longer or until the spinach is tender. Stir in pepper and a dash of nutmeg, if liked. 4 to 5 servings.

Note: A riced, hard-cooked egg or crumbled bacon bits may be sprinkled over the spinach in the serving dish.

SPINACH CHEESE CUSTARD

¾ lb raw spinach	1 cup milk
½ tsp salt	⅔ cup grated cheese, 2⅔ oz
2 tbsp butter	1 egg, slightly beaten
2 tbsp flour	Dash of red pepper

Start oven 10 min before baking; set to mod (350° F)

Pick over spinach, and discard any damaged leaves or stems. Wash carefully in cold water. Lift out onto clean cloth and shake to remove most moisture. Put into saucepan, sprinkle on salt, cover, and place over low heat for 10 min to steam until tender. Shake pan occasionally to prevent sticking. Drain juice from spinach, and save. Chop spinach fine. Melt butter in saucepan, and blend in flour to form smooth paste. Add milk gradually, and cook with continued stirring until sauce boils and thickens. Remove from heat, add half cup of the cheese, and stir until it melts. Beat egg, slowly stir in the hot cream sauce; add chopped spinach and 2 tbsp of the drained-off spinach juice; stir just enough to blend. Pour into 6 x 10 x 2-inch baking dish. Sprinkle top with remaining cheese, and bake 20 min, or until firm and delicately browned on top. Cut in sqs. 4 servings.

SPINACH SOUFFLÉ RING WITH CHEESE SAUCE

1½ lbs fresh spinach	3 eggs, separated
2 tbsp butter	¼ cup butter
2 tbsp flour	¼ cup flour
½ cup milk	2 cups milk
1 tsp onion juice	1 tsp salt
½ tsp salt	¼ lb cheese, diced *or* grated
Pepper	

Start oven 10 min before baking; set to mod hot (375° F)

Wash spinach thoroughly, drain and place in a 3-qt saucepan; add 1 cup boiling water and cook until just tender, 5 to 10 min. Drain, then chop; there should be about 1½ cups spinach. Make thick White Sauce, p 1262, of next 6 ingredients and cool slightly. Beat egg yolks slightly, add the white sauce slowly and stir until well blended. Add spinach and fold in the egg whites which have been beaten until stiff. Turn into a well-buttered 4-cup ring mold which has been lined in bottom with greased, plain paper; place directly on the oven rack and bake about 30 min or until a knife inserted in the center comes out clean. Meanwhile, make a white sauce with the remaining butter, flour and milk, adding salt and cheese at end and stirring until cheese is melted. Unmold spinach ring on hot serving plate, remove paper and serve soufflé immediately with the cheese sauce. 5 servings.

Note: The center of the ring may be filled with Buttered Onions (p 1359) if desired.

SPINACH RING

Vegetable Filled

1 lb spinach, cooked	⅟₁₆ tsp finely chopped
½ tsp salt	garlic, optional
1 tbsp butter *or* margarine	

Wash and cook spinach according to directions for Buttered Spinach. Drain. Melt butter, add garlic if used, simmer to a froth, remove garlic, then pour over spinach. Toss well and fill a 3-cup ring mold. Set in warm place while preparing rest of dish.

Creamed Vegetables:

½ cup diced potatoes	1 tbsp flour
½ cup sliced carrots	½ cup diced cheese
1¼ cups milk	1 tbsp chopped parsley
½ tsp salt	¼ cup fine dry bread crumbs
3 tbsp butter	

Put potatoes and carrots in milk. Add salt and cook slowly until vegetables are tender. Melt 2 tbsp of the butter, add flour and some of milk from the vegetables to make a smooth sauce. Combine with vegetables and simmer until mixture boils and thickens. Then fold in the cheese and parsley. Brown bread crumbs in remaining tbsp of melted butter. Turn out spinach mold on plate. Fill center with creamed vegetables and sprinkle browned bread crumbs around edge of creamed mixture. Serve immediately. 4 servings.

SPINACH WITH BACON AND EGG

1½ lbs spinach	Salt
8 slices bacon	3 Hard-cooked Eggs, p 663

Wash spinach thoroughly and cook as for Buttered Spinach. Meanwhile pan-fry bacon until done. Remove to absorbent paper to drain and crisp. Drain hot cooked spinach and combine and toss it with as much of the bacon fat as desired for seasoning. Season to taste and serve on a hot platter with bacon and the sliced, hot hard-cooked eggs. 5 servings.

SPINACH WITH BACON AND EGG SAUCE

1½ lbs spinach	4 tsp flour
2 cups boiling water	2 tsp sugar
½ tsp salt	1 tsp salt
4 slices bacon	½ cup water
⅓ cup bacon drippings	3 tbsp vinegar
2 tbsp finely chopped onion	2 hard-cooked eggs

Wash and cook spinach in boiling salted water as directed in Buttered Spinach. Drain well and serve with a sauce made by pan-frying the bacon until of desired doneness. Remove bacon and extra fat, if any. Lightly brown the onion in the drippings. Add the flour, sugar and salt. Add the water and vinegar and heat to boiling and simmer 2 min. Crumble the bacon into small pieces and add with the eggs, finely diced, to the sauce. Serve hot over the cooked spinach. 4 servings.

SPINACH WITH CHEESE SAUCE AND BACON

2 tbsp butter	1 cup grated sharp cheese,
3 tbsp flour	4 oz
2 cups milk	1½ lbs fresh spinach, cooked
Salt to taste	5 slices bacon

Start oven 10 min before baking; set to mod (350° F)

Make a white sauce of the butter, flour, milk, and salt. Add grated cheese and stir until thoroughly melted. Put drained spinach in a buttered baking dish and pour cheese sauce over it. Top with bacon slices which have been half cooked. Bake 15 to 20 min or until hot through and bacon is crisp. 5 servings.

WILTED SPINACH

3 slices bacon	1½ tsp sugar
3 tbsp chopped onion	Dash pepper
1½ tbsp flour	¾ lb shredded raw spinach,
½ cup water	3 cups, tightly pkd
¼ cup vinegar	½ cup chopped celery
¾ tsp salt	

Cut bacon in half-inch lengths with scissors and sauté with the onion for 10 min. Lift out bacon to crisp; blend flour into fat remaining in pan. Add liquids gradually and cook over low heat until thickened. Add seasonings, then the spinach and celery. Toss lightly until vegetables are coated with the dressing and stand over low heat until just warm. Sprinkle crumbled crisp bacon over the top. Serve immediately. 4 servings.

Note: Recipe for Hard-cooked Eggs p 663.

BAKED WINTER SQUASH

Start oven 10 min before baking; set to mod hot (400° F)

In general, the most satisfactory way of cooking the hard-skinned winter squashes (Hubbard, cushaw, etc.) is to bake them. Cut the squash lengthwise in half, using cleaver or a saw-tooth knife; remove seeds. Hubbard squash may be cut in serving size pieces, if desired. Butter cut surfaces of either the halves or pieces and place cut side down on a baking sheet, bake until tender when pricked with a fork. This will take about ½ hr for pieces of tender squash or 1 hr, or possibly longer for large halves of Hubbard squash. When tender (test with fork), remove from oven. Small squash may be served "on the half shell" with butter and salt. Larger squash should have the tender pulp scooped out and mashed with butter and salt, whipping up until smooth and fluffy. Three lbs squash will serve 5.

For a more elaborate dish, the mashed buttered squash may be placed in a buttered casserole and the top covered with marshmallows. Place in a hot oven (425° F) until the marshmallows are just toasted.

BAKED ACORN SQUASH

Start oven 10 min before baking; set to mod hot (400° F)

Scrub squash thoroughly; cut in half lengthwise and scrape out the seeds and the fibers, using a spoon. Butter cut surfaces, place cut side down on a baking sheet and bake 30 to 45 min, or until inside is very soft. Turn cut side up, place butter in the cavity of each half and on the rim, sprinkle with a little salt and brown sugar and replace in the oven until the sugar is melted and the rim of the squash is toasted to an appetizing brown. Serve in the shells while still hot. One good-sized squash serves 2 persons.

CRUSTY WINTER SQUASH WITH NUTS

3 lbs squash, ¼ medium large Hubbard *or* 1 butter-nut, cut in half lengthwise	¼ cup maple *or* maple-flavored syrup *or* honey
2 tbsp butter	¼ cup pecans *or* walnuts, half of them chopped
⅛ tsp salt	

Start oven 10 min before baking; set to mod hot (400° F)

Wash skin of squash. Butter cut edges and turn upside down on shallow baking pan with rim on all sides, to catch juice from squash. Bake until tender when pierced with fork, 35 to 40 min. Remove from oven, scoop out all squash down to thin skin using a heavy tbsp. There should be about 1⅞ cups. Add 1 tbsp of the butter, salt and 1 tbsp of the syrup or honey. Beat, then fold in the chopped nuts. Turn into buttered 2 cup casserole or glass pie dish. Smooth top and sides of squash using a knife. Combine rest of syrup with butter and drizzle over top of squash. Bake in a hot oven (450° F) until top is crusty and slightly browned and squash is hot all the way through. Remove from oven, garnish with whole pecan meats. Serve while hot. 4 servings.

FRENCH FRIED HUBBARD SQUASH

Cut Hubbard squash into quarters. Use only one quarter for this recipe. Remove seeds and fibers, then cut crosswise into ⅓-inch strips, or cut Acorn Squash into ½-inch wide circles. Pare thinly with a sharp knife. Fry in deep fat heated to 350° F. Remove strips or circles with fork as soon as they are a delicate brown and tender and drain on absorbent paper. Sprinkle with granulated sugar. 4 servings.

STUFFED SQUASH

2 acorn squash, ¾ lb each	2 tbsp bacon drippings
¾ cup finely diced celery	1 bouillon cube
¾ cup finely diced carrot	2 tbsp hot water
3 tbsp finely diced onion	4 strips bacon, pan-fried
¼ cup finely diced green pepper	

Bake squash as described in preceding recipe for Baked Acorn Squash. Cook until inside is very soft. In meantime, prepare vegetables, heat shortening in skillet, add vegetables and sauté for 10 min over low heat. Dissolve bouillon cube in water and pour over vegetables. Mix thoroughly and heap into centers of hot baked squash. Put 1 strip of bacon over heaped up vegetables on each squash. Serve immediately. 4 servings.

BUTTERED SUMMER SQUASH

Any variety of summer squash (Patty Pan, Yellow Crookneck, Zucchini, etc.) may be cooked by this method. Allow 2 lbs for 5 servings. Choose young, tender squash; it should be easy to pierce the skin with the thumbnail. Wash thoroughly and cut into half-inch crosswise or lengthwise slices, without removing skin. (If squash is mature and therefore tougher, it may be necessary to pare thinly and remove the large seeds.) Place in saucepan and add enough boiling water so it can just be seen through the top layer, not enough to cover. Add salt, allowing about ¼ tsp to each lb of squash. Cover pan and cook moderately fast until tender, about 6 min for young squash. Shake the pan from time to time to prevent sticking. Remove cover, add 3 tbsp butter and a dash of pepper if desired, and if water is not well evaporated, continue cooking uncovered until most of it has disappeared. Serve immediately.

PAN-FRIED SUMMER SQUASH

Choose young, tender squash as described in recipe for Buttered Summer Squash. Wash thoroughly and remove any blemishes. Slice crosswise ½-inch thick without removing skin or seeds. Dip slices in beaten egg diluted with ¼ cup milk and seasoned with salt and pepper; then dip in fine dry bread or cracker crumbs or flour. Pan-fry in butter or bacon fat until golden brown on both sides. Squash should be done through by this time; if not, reduce heat, cover skillet, and cook 2 or 3 min longer. 2 lb squash will serve 5.

STUFFED SUMMER SQUASH

5 small tender Patty Pan squash	¼ cup butter
	1 tsp salt
½ cup chopped green pepper	Pepper to taste
½ cup chopped celery	¼ cup cream
2 cups corn cut from cob	

Start oven 10 min before baking; set to mod (350° F)

Wash squash carefully, but do not pare. Place in large saucepan, cover with boiling water, cover and cook rapidly about 15 min, or until tender when pierced with fork; or place in covered casserole and bake 20 to 30 min or until tender. Meanwhile, sauté green pepper, celery, and corn in the butter until celery is soft. Drain squash, split crosswise, scoop out centers; combine centers with sautéed vegetables and seasonings. Heap mixture into squash shell, set in baking pan, and pour a little cream over the filling in each. Cover and bake for about 10 min. Serve hot. 5 servings.

Note: Use No. 2 can whole kernel corn in place of fresh.

TEN MINUTE CANDIED SQUASH

Select 2 lb acorn squash, ½ large butternut, or ½ small Hubbard squash. Remove seeds and fiber with a heavy tbsp. Cut halves into 4 strips, pare strips. Cut strips again into ¼-inch slices, then crosswise into 2 or 3 pieces. Melt 3 tbsp butter in skillet, add squash, sprinkle with ½ tsp salt. Cover tightly, cook moderately fast for 5 min. Use pancake turner to turn squash slices over carefully. Sprinkle 3 tbsp sugar over top. Again cover tightly, cook another 5 min or until squash is tender, translucent and browns appetizingly on bottom. Serve in hot serving dish garnished with chopped parsley. Add a squeeze of lemon if desired. 4 servings.

BRAISED ZUCCHINI

¼ cup butter	Few grains pepper
1 medium onion	½ cup water
8 small Zucchini squash	3 medium tomatoes
¾ tsp salt	2 tbsp shortening

Melt butter in a skillet and sauté thinly sliced onion until soft. Wash tender young squash, remove a small slice from stem and blossom end, and cut squash neatly in half lengthwise. Put squash cut-side down into butter, pushing the onions to one side. Heat slowly until delicately browned on underside, turn over, add salt, pepper and water. Cover tightly and continue cooking for 8 to 12 min, or until vegetable is tender and liquid is evaporated to about 1 tbsp. Carefully remove squash and onions to hot platter and garnish with Pan-broiled Tomato Slices, p 1406, or parsley. 5 servings.

WHAT TO LOOK FOR WHEN BUYING OR GATHERING TOMATOES

Tomatoes available on the market in winter and early spring are gathered green in distant gardens while still firm enough to be wrapped in paper and shipped without being damaged. In storage places near the distributing points, they are slowly ripened to the stage where their color appeals to the consumer. In recent years, there has been considerable improvement in the color of these ripened tomatoes so it is possible to serve in mid-winter salad almost as good in color as one made from mid-summer tomatoes. But the flavor of vine-ripened, sun-drenched tomatoes is not there. After either artificial or natural ripening, tomatoes are easily bruised and cracked, and because of their high water content, they spoil exceedingly fast. So in buying from the market or gathering from your own garden, it is wise not to select tomatoes with either bruises or cracks unless these are fresh ones and the fruit can be consumed immediately. Tomatoes that have cracks acquired during rapid growth and have healed up in the sunlight are just as sound as those without cracks. The only difference is that they are not so beautiful because when these cracks are cut out in the preparation, they will not be so handsome to serve. Tomatoes should be chosen not only for their brilliant color but also for the quality of their flesh. Those that are meaty and have few seeds are the ones that are weightiest for their size.

BAKED STUFFED TOMATOES No. 1

8 medium, firm, meaty tomatoes, 2½ lbs	1 lb hamburger
	2 tsp salt
½ cup chopped onion	⅔ cup dry coarse bread
1 cup chopped celery	crumbs
¼ cup shortening *or* bacon fat	2 tbsp butter *or* shortening

Start oven 10 min before baking; set to mod (350° F)

Wash tomatoes, remove a thin slice from the stem end, then scoop out pulp leaving cups with walls at least ¼-inch thick. Set cups in a shallow buttered baking dish, save the pulp. Sauté onion and celery in shortening about 2 min. Add meat, then salt and sauté 5 min, stirring frequently. Add tomato pulp; simmer a few minutes, then add half the bread crumbs. Fill tomato cups lightly, piling mixture high. Melt butter, add remaining crumbs, blend and sprinkle buttered crumbs over tomatoes. Bake 15 to 20 min. 4 to 8 servings.

BAKED STUFFED TOMATOES No. 2

5 large, firm, meaty
  tomatoes, 2½ lbs
5 slices white bread, cut in
  ½-inch dice and toasted

¼ lb sharp cheese, cut in
  ½-inch dice
Salt and pepper
¼ cup butter, melted

Start oven 10 min before baking; set to mod (350° F)

Wash tomatoes and cut a thin slice from the stem end of each. Scoop out center with a spoon, leaving walls at least ¼-inch thick. Chop tomato centers and combine with remaining ingredients, tossing lightly to mix well. Season with salt and pepper to taste. Stuff mixture into tomatoes, heaping up generously. Place tomatoes in a buttered shallow baking pan. Any leftover stuffing may be placed around the tomatoes. Bake 20 min. Serve immediately. 5 servings.

BAKED STUFFED TOMATOES No. 3

4 large solid tomatoes, 2 lbs
2 slices bacon, chopped
¼ cup chopped celery
2 tbsp chopped onion
¼ cup water

1 egg
½ tsp salt
Pepper
2 cups toasted bread crumbs

Start oven 10 min before baking; set to mod (350° F)

Wash tomatoes and remove a thin slice from stem end. Scoop out part of the tomato leaving wall of tomato cup at least ¼-inch thick; chop scooped out part of tomatoes and top slice. Sauté bacon, celery, and onion for about 10 min. Add remaining ingredients and tomato pulp. Sprinkle inside of tomato generously with salt; fill with stuffing and place in shallow greased baking dish. Bake 20 to 25 min or until tomatoes are soft but not mushy. Any extra stuffing may be placed around the tomato. 4 servings.

BAKED STUFFED TOMATOES No. 4

8 firm, meaty tomatoes,
  2½ lbs
½ cup chopped onion
1 cup chopped celery
¼ cup shortening *or* bacon fat

1 lb ground lean beef
2 tsp salt
⅔ cup coarse bread crumbs
2 tbsp butter *or* shortening

Start oven 10 min before baking; set to moderate (350° F)

Wash tomatoes, cut a thin slice from stem end, then scoop out and save pulp, leaving cups with walls at least ¼-inch thick. Set cups in a shallow buttered baking dish. Sauté onion and celery in shortening about 2 min. Add beef, then salt and sauté 5 min, stirring frequently. Add tomato pulp; simmer a few min; then add half the bread crumbs. Fill tomato cups lightly, piling mixture high. Melt butter, add remaining crumbs, blend and sprinkle buttered crumbs over tomatoes. Bake 15 to 20 min. 4 to 8 servings.

DELICIOUS BAKED TOMATOES

6 good-sized, ripe, firm tomatoes
1 tbsp finely chopped onion
½ cup finely chopped mushrooms
2 tbsp bacon fat *or* margarine

Salt and pepper
½ cup coarse bread crumbs
6 strips lean bacon
6 sqs of toast
Parsley

Start oven 10 min before baking; set to mod (350° F)

Choose even-sized tomatoes shaped to stand level in baking pan. Wash, but do not peel. Cut out a deep cone from stem ends. Cut core from removed cone and discard and chop the rest of the cone. Sprinkle salt and pepper into the hollowed out tomato. Heat fat in skillet, add onion and mushrooms and sauté 2 or 3 min, then add chopped tomatoes and bread crumbs. Toss just enough to mix. Add salt if needed. Heap this mixture into the tomato cups. Cut bacon strips into halves and cross the two halves over each tomato. Place tomatoes in shallow baking dish and bake 20 to 35 min or until bacon is crisp and tomatoes are just heated through. Remove tomatoes to hot toast. Arrange on a hot platter. Garnish with parsley and serve at once. 4 to 6 servings.

ESCALLOPED TOMATOES No. 1

2 tbsp butter *or* margarine
¼ cup chopped onion
4 slices day-old bread, cubed
3 large tomatoes, peeled and diced, 2 lbs

½ cup chopped parsley
½ cup grated carrots
1 tsp salt
⅛ tsp pepper
½ tsp dry mustard

Start oven 10 min before baking; set to mod (350° F)

Melt butter; add onions and bread. Sauté until light brown. Save out ½ cup of mixture for the top; combine remainder with all the other ingredients. Turn into a buttered 6-cup casserole and top with the ½ cup bread mixture. Bake 15 to 20 min. 4 to 6 servings.

ESCALLOPED TOMATOES No. 2

No. 2 can tomatoes *or* 4
large fresh tomatoes,
peeled and diced
2 cups soft bread crumbs

1 medium onion, chopped
¾ tsp salt
1 tbsp sugar
2 tbsp butter

Start oven 10 min before baking; set to mod (375° F)

Combine tomatoes with half the bread crumbs and stir in onion, salt and sugar. Turn into buttered 4-cup casserole. Brown rest of bread crumbs in the butter in a saucepan or skillet, and sprinkle over top of casserole. Bake 15 to 20 min, or until hot through. 5 servings.

FRIED GREEN TOMATOES

5 medium green tomatoes,
1½ lbs
⅓ cup flour

¾ tsp salt
Few dashes pepper
¼ cup shortening

Select firm tomatoes. Wash, remove the stem end and blossom scars and cut into half-inch, crosswise slices. Mix flour, salt and pepper, and dip both sides of tomato slices into the mixture. Heat shortening in a skillet until sizzling hot. Put in the tomatoes and cook rather quickly until browned on underside. Then turn tomatoes carefully, reduce heat and cook until thoroughly hot and soft through center. Remove to a hot platter and serve piping hot, either plain or with a Cheese, p 1253, or Onion Sauce, p 1260. 4 servings.

FRIED TOMATOES PENNSYLVANIA DUTCH STYLE

A deliciously sweet, crunchy crusted way with tomatoes

4 large firm tomatoes, 2 lbs
1 cup all-purpose flour
½ cup sugar

2 to 3 tsp salt
½ cup bacon drippings

Wash tomatoes, cut into slices ½-inch thick and discard stem-end slice. Mix flour and ½ of the sugar. Sprinkle tomato slices on both sides with remaining sugar and salt. Dip slices into flour-sugar mixture, coating both sides. Let stand about 5 min, then dip slices in mixture again. Most of the flour and sugar should be used up if slices are coated properly. Heat ½ the bacon fat in large skillet, then brown half the tomato slices on both sides over medium heat. Be sure to brown on one side thoroughly before turning. When thick crusts on tomatoes are brown, remove slices to hot platter, and keep warm while other half browns. Add rest of bacon fat, and fry rest of tomatoes. Serve hot. 4 to 5 servings.

Note: The trick in successful preparation is to let the tomatoes stand with their first coating until it melts before dipping again.

GREEN TOMATO AND ONION SLICES

¼ cup butter *or* margarine	2 medium onions
3 tbsp flour	¾ tsp salt
4 medium green tomatoes,	Pinch sugar
1¼ lbs	Dash pepper

Melt butter in a skillet and blend in the flour. Heat slowly until lightly browned, stirring frequently. Wash tomatoes, remove stem ends and blossom scars. Slice tomatoes and onions into pan and add seasonings. Cover and cook over medium heat for 10 to 15 min. Stir occasionally so that any liquid will blend with flour and fat and thicken. Vegetables should be tender but not mushy. Serve immediately. 4 servings.

BROILED STUFFED TOMATOES

Beautiful to see and eat

3 large, shapely tomatoes	*Celery salt *or* other season-
3 tbsp butter *or* margarine	ing salt and pepper
2½ slices of 2-day-old bread	Fresh grated Parmesan
from a lb loaf	cheese, optional
1¼ tsp grated onion	

Start oven 10 min before baking; set to hot (450° F).

Use ripe, firm tomatoes. Wash, remove core and blossom end neatly. Cut tomatoes in half crosswise. Remove seed clumps carefully leaving neat pockets. Save seed and juice. Sprinkle tomatoes with seasoning salt and let stand from 15 to 30 min for salt to penetrate. Pull bread apart into medium sized crumbs. Heat butter in small pan, add grated onion and tomato seeds with juice. Cook slowly 2 or 3 min. Toss with the crumbs. Just before broiling, stuff dressing into seed pockets. Sift ½ tsp of Parmesan cheese in center if desired. Arrange on shallow pan lined with sheet of aluminum foil. Broil 4 inches below surface of heat, or bake 10 min or until tomatoes are heated through, the stuffing is toasted and crisp on the surface and cheese is browned. 3 to 4 servings.

PAN-BROILED TOMATOES

5 large, meaty tomatoes,	1 tsp thyme
2½ lbs	¼ tsp salt
½ cup butter *or* half bacon	1½ tbsp finely chopped onion
drippings	Parsley

Wash tomatoes and cut out the core and the blossom end. Melt butter in a skillet, add the thyme, salt and onion and simmer gently until onion is soft, about 5 min. Slice tomatoes 1-inch thick or

*One may substitute ¼ tsp rosemary or orégano rubbed to a powder and blended with plain table salt for the seasoning salt.

cut them in half, crosswise. Lay them in the seasoned butter and simmer slowly, spooning the fat up over them from time to time. When tomatoes begin to soften on underside after cooking 1 or 2 min, turn carefully, using a pancake turner or large spatula and continue cooking about the same length of time on the other side, spooning fat over the top. They should not be cooked until mushy. Transfer to a hot platter and pour the savory butter over them. Garnish with parsley and serve immediately. 5 servings.

Variation: To the ½ cup butter melted in the skillet, add instead of thyme and onion, ⅓ cup grated raw carrot, 1 tsp celery salt, and a dash of pepper. Simmer 2 or 3 min or until carrot is soft; then add the sliced tomatoes and cook as described above.

HERB TOMATOES

3 cups canned tomatoes   ½ tsp rosemary
2 tbsp butter

Heat ingredients to simmering, cover and cook slowly 3 or 4 min or until enough of the butter and rosemary flavor have been absorbed by the tomatoes. 4 servings.

Note: A little chopped onion may be added to the butter and sautéed before tomatoes and rosemary are added for a different but equally delicious flavor.

NEW MEXICAN TOMATOES

Extraordinarily good cooked tomato dish

4 medium sized tomatoes   ⅓ cup bacon fat
6 to 8 slices streaked bacon   1 tbsp sugar
3 tsp grated onion   1 to 1½ tbsp cider vinegar
1 tsp salt   1 tbsp chopped parsley
Pepper to taste

Choose meaty, firm, ripe tomatoes. Wash, remove cores, cut in quarters. Pan-fry bacon until just done. Drain on paper toweling to crisp, keep warm. Pour off all but 2½ tbsp bacon fat. Add onion, cook a min or so, add tomatoes, salt and pepper. Cover and cook gently until soft but tomato is still in chunks. Lift out tomato skins with a fork and discard. Now sift sugar over tomatoes and sprinkle on the vinegar. Cover, cook another minute or so. Serve tomatoes sprinkled with hot crumbled bacon and parsley. 4 to 5 servings.

FRESH MINTED TOMATOES

Wonderful, refreshing

3 medium tomatoes, 1¼ lbs   Pepper
4½ tbsp 5% cider vinegar   1½ tbsp salad oil
1½ tbsp water   1½ tbsp sheared fresh mint,
1¼ tsp salt   4 to 5 sprigs
1½ tbsp sugar

Use firm, red-ripe tomatoes. Chill. Combine next 6 ingredients, cover and chill. Fifteen min before serving, wash, remove stem and blossom scars from tomatoes. Slice carefully into a shallow, flat serving dish. Drizzle dressing over tomatoes, sprinkle with mint, cover, and refrigerate 10 to 15 min. Spoon the dressing up over tomatoes 2 or 3 times. Excellent with any meat or fish course. 4 servings.

STEWED TOMATOES

1 small onion, finely chopped	5 large tomatoes, peeled
2 tbsp butter	1 tsp sugar
No. 2½ can tomatoes *or*	¾ tsp salt

Put onion and butter into saucepan, and simmer until onion is soft and yellow. Add tomatoes, sugar and salt, heat to boiling and simmer about 5 min. Serve immediately with a little more sugar, if desired. 5 servings.

Variation: Allow a No. 2 can of tomatoes for 5 servings, adding 1 cup freshly sautéed mushrooms just before serving.

MACARONI TOMATO AND GREEN PEPPER CASSEROLE

7 *or* 8 oz pkg macaroni	1 tsp salt
3 tbsp chopped onion	3 medium green peppers
2 tbsp butter	½ cup grated sharp cheese
No. 2 can *or* 2½ cups fresh cooked tomatoes	

Start oven 10 min before baking; set to mod hot (400° F)

Drop macaroni into 3 qts rapidly boiling water, add 2 tsp salt and boil, uncovered, for about 20 min or until tender. Turn into a colander to drain thoroughly. Sauté onion in butter until soft and yellow. Add tomatoes and simmer gently about 5 min. Add drained macaroni and salt, mix well and continue simmering about 10 min longer. Wash, quarter and remove seeds and membranes from peppers; boil for 5 min in 1 qt water with 1 tsp salt. Then drain and arrange in buttered casserole. Fill casserole with macaroni and tomato mixture; sprinkle cheese on top. Bake 15 min, or until cheese is golden brown. 5 or 6 servings.

POT DINNER

¼ lb salt pork	¾ tsp salt
3 cups cold water	¼ tsp sugar
1½ lbs green beans, julienned	Dash of pepper
4 small onions, halved	2 green peppers, halved and
3 small potatoes, pared and quartered	seeded
	¼ lb okra

Cut salt pork into 4 slices, put in kettle, add water and heat to boiling. Reduce heat, cover and simmer for 1 hr or until nearly tender. Add all the rest of ingredients except okra. Simmer for 10 min. Mix gently with a wooden spoon and slice the washed okra directly into the kettle on top of rest of ingredients. Do not stir after okra is added. Cover, simmer gently 15 min longer or until all vegetables are tender. 4 servings.

SKILLET DINNER

2 tbsp butter *or* margarine
12-oz can pork luncheon meat
2 tbsp coarsely diced onion
1½ lb head of cabbage, shredded

2 tbsp flour
¼ tsp salt
1 cup milk

Heat butter in a skillet. Add the luncheon meat cut into cubes and brown slowly for 5 min. Add onion and sauté for 2 min. Add cabbage and sauté for another 5 min. Sprinkle flour very lightly through cabbage, tossing and turning constantly. Add salt and milk and mix lightly but thoroughly. Heat the milk slowly to boiling, stirring carefully to thicken sauce. Turn heat low and cook for 5 more min. Serve at once directly from skillet. 4 servings.

SPANISH RICE

1 small onion, chopped
¼ cup chopped green pepper
3 tbsp butter
1¼ cups canned tomatoes

3 cups hot Boiled Rice, p 433, 1 cup raw
Salt and pepper to taste

Sauté onion and green pepper for 5 min in the butter. Add tomatoes and rice, heat to boiling, then reduce heat and simmer for 5 min more. Season to taste. 5 servings.

SPANISH VEGETABLES

½ lb tender green beans, cut into 1-inch lengths
2 slices bacon, cut into small pieces
2 tbsp chopped onion
1 tbsp flour
3 to 4 tomatoes, peeled and sliced, 2 cups

2 cups corn, cut from cob, 4 ears
2 tbsp chopped green pepper
1 tsp sugar
¾ tsp salt
Dash pepper

Cook green beans uncovered in just enough water to cover until barely tender, 15 to 25 min. Sauté bacon and onion 5 or 6 min. Blend flour into bacon fat in pan. Add the bean liquid (there should be only about ¼ cup of water left) and blend. Add beans and remaining ingredients and mix thoroughly. Cover and simmer for 7 to 8 min until corn is tender. Stir occasionally. 4 servings.

SPRING VEGETABLES WITH BUTTERMILK SAUCE

1 lb fresh peas, shelled	1 cup boiling water
1 bunch carrots, scraped and thickly sliced	½ cup thinly sliced green onions, including some green tops
½ tsp sugar	
½ tsp salt	

Add peas, carrots, sugar and salt to the boiling water; cook covered for 10 min or until vegetables are just done. Add the onions and cook for 2 min. The liquid should be just about evaporated. Serve with Buttermilk Sauce.

Buttermilk Sauce:

2 tbsp butter, melted	Generous dash of pepper
2 tbsp flour	¾ cup buttermilk
¼ tsp salt	¼ cup mayonnaise

Blend butter, flour, salt and pepper in top of double boiler. Add the buttermilk and cook over hot water, stirring constantly until mixture is smooth and thickened. Blend in the mayonnaise and continue cooking until hot through. Serve immediately over the hot vegetables. 4 servings.

VEGETABLE PLATES

Any desired combination of three or more vegetables, cooked separately according to the directions for each and combined with plenty of butter, makes a good vegetable plate dinner. One of the vegetables is usually potatoes, and the others should be chosen for contrast in color, flavor and texture. Suggested combinations are:

1. Cabbage wedges, sliced carrots, green beans, potatoes.

2. Spinach, sliced beets, small buttered onions, potatoes.

3. Braised celery, peas, carrots cut in quarters lengthwise, potatoes.

4. Cauliflower, broiled tomatoes, Zucchini squash or asparagus, parsley potatoes.

5. Baked acorn squash filled with creamed cauliflower and carrots, buttered asparagus, stuffed raw celery.

6. Broccoli, buttered corn, creamed sliced radishes, sweet potatoes.

7. New peas and mushrooms, buttered cauliflower, escalloped potatoes, sliced tomatoes.

8. Stuffed tomatoes, mashed rutabagas, spinach, French fried potatoes.

Broiled Bacon, p 855, or a Poached Egg, p 672, is an attractive garnish for any vegetable plate if desired. Cheese Sauce, p 1253, or White

Sauce, p 1262, served over one of the vegetables adds interest and appetite appeal.

TO PREPARE HOME-CANNED NON-ACID VEGETABLES

Turn the contents of the can or the jar into a saucepan. *Do not taste the unheated vegetable!* There should be almost enough liquid to cover the vegetables; if not, add some water. Heat to boiling, uncovered, and boil vigorously for ten min, counting the time accurately. If the odor is the good natural one at the end of this boiling, you can be sure the food is safe (if the food has an off-color, do not taste it, but burn it). If at the end of the boiling period, there is an excess of water, drain off the water into another saucepan and boil down until there is not more than a half cup of liquid remaining. Add the vegetables and seasonings such as butter, margarine, or cream sauce, reheat and serve. Tomatoes that have the natural odor, color and texture may be eaten without heating. If they are preferred hot, they need to be heated only to the boiling point and seasoning such as butter, a dash of pepper, sugar and onion juice need be added just before serving.

Kitchen Equipment

HOW TO JUDGE KITCHEN UTENSILS
TO GET YOUR MONEY'S WORTH

Kitchen utensils—egg beaters, measuring cups, pots, pans, skillets and spoons are not as spectacular as some of the other kitchen equipment, but they are so important in efficient cooking operations that they should be selected with the greatest of care.

The price of a kitchen utensil is based on the quality of the material from which it is made, the workmanship used in putting it together, and the kind of fittings involved. Special colors and trimmings require extra handling in manufacturing and add to the cost of the utensil, but they don't increase its efficiency or durability. They may actually add considerably to the care needed in cleaning and storing it. It's therefore wise economy to buy the best quality kitchen utensils that the family's budget will permit, but one needs to make sure not to pay a premium for nonessentials. Here are the basic characteristics of quality which you should consider before buying any kitchen utensil:

Durability. The material from which the utensil is made should be reasonably resistant to pitting, warping, bending, chipping, and breaking when used for the purpose for which it is intended. Rims and seams must be smooth and sturdy. Handles, knobs, and spouts must be securely attached. The material and finish should not be affected by grease, acids, or alkalis in foods.

Cooking Efficiency. The shape, size, and thickness of the utensil should be appropriate for its intended use, so that the kind of heat used (direct or oven heat) will be distributed evenly at the rate of speed desired.

Ease of Cleaning. Utensils which are smooth on the surface and at all the joints, that are stain resistant, and that have a minimum of parts are easiest to clean. Different materials are cleaned in different ways and must be cared for properly to be judged fairly.

Convenience. The type of utensil you find easiest to use is the one that's best for you. This may vary with the individual. The utensils should fit conveniently on the stove or in the oven, should be of a size to fit the varied needs of your family, and should be selected to serve more than one purpose as often as practical. In general, handles and knobs should be comfortable to grasp and shouldn't become heated. Utensils used both on top of the stove and in the oven should have handles that won't burn or that can be easily and safely removed. Covers should fit snugly. The utensil should be simple to put together or operate. Depending on your storage space, utensils should nest compactly or have eyebolts for hanging.

Safety. Utensils should be so well balanced that they won't tip whether they're empty or full, whether the lid is on or off. Vents, gauges, closures, and spouts should be reliably designed to assure safety to the user.

These basic characteristics are essential and are a more reliable guide to the justifiable cost of a utensil than are any supplementary gadgets or fancy designs. Of course you will also choose a utensil for its particular use. An iron coffee maker may fill all the basic requirements even better than a glass one, but this and some other metals unless specially treated tend to give a metallic taste to coffee. Also, utensils for certain purposes need not be as durable, etc. as other utensils. A fancy mold or pan that's used infrequently may safely be of a more inexpensive material and design than a saucepan intended for daily use. In the discussion that follows, there is described in more detail the basic characteristics as well as other important facts about kitchen utensils.

CHOOSING COOKING UTENSILS

MATERIALS

When you set out to buy a cooking utensil, it's important to have in mind the qualities of the various materials from which such utensils are manufactured today. Aluminum, enamel ware, copper, stainless steel, glass, pottery, tin, and iron are the materials commonly used, and no one material is superior in every respect, each having qualities to recommend it for certain purposes. For example, lightweight utensils that heat rapidly and lose heat quickly are best suited for baking sheets and muffin pans, while heavier utensils that heat less rapidly but hold heat well are desirable for long slow cooking on top of the stove. It's to your advantage to choose a utensil of the material that will best do the cooking job you want it to do.

Aluminum. There are two types of aluminum utensils on the market—cast aluminum ones which are made by pouring molten aluminum into castings or molds, and pressed aluminum ones which are made by pressing sheets of aluminum into the desired shape. The initial cost of cast aluminum utensils is comparatively high, but since they're strong and durable, they'll last a lifetime if given proper care. These utensils, heavy in appearance but light in actual weight, conduct heat quickly and evenly. For this reason, food isn't apt to scorch. As they hold heat, they're suitable for long, slow cooking, and for cooking foods with little or no added moisture.

Pressed aluminum utensils are available in different weights or gauges. The very light-weight utensils are low in cost, but warp and dent easily, and waste cooking fuel. For this reason, the slightly more expensive, heavier weight utensils are preferable. Light-weight utensils heat rapidly but lose heat quickly. They're best suited to quick cooking and oven baking.

Aluminum utensils are given different finishes. Those with the Alumilite finish won't smudge china, linen, or porcelain. Baking pans with this finish brown foods evenly. The spun aluminum finish given to pressed aluminum utensils by the circular motion of a steel brush is for appearance only, and is used mainly on serving pieces.

Cleaning and Care. Aluminum utensils become stained when used for boiling water or cooking foods containing iron, sulfur or alkalies. For this reason, dilute solutions of soap, soda or water softeners should not be allowed to stand in aluminum utensils. And eggs should never be cooked in them. This discoloration isn't harmful, but you'll want to remove it for the sake of appearance. It disappears quickly if an acid food, such as tomatoes or rhubarb, is cooked in the utensil, or if a weak solution of vinegar and water is boiled in it.

After each use, wash aluminum utensils with hot, soapy water, rinse with hot, clear water, and dry thoroughly. If a utensil is discolored, brighten it by rubbing with fine steel wool (size oo) and whiting paste or other fine abrasive.

Chromium. Chromium plating is a smooth, bright, attractive finish given to utensils made with a base of steel, copper, iron, or brass. This plating is durable and doesn't become tarnished or rusted. It's not affected by acids, alkalies, air, or water, and resists scratching. Its high luster, however, causes slow heat absorption.

Cleaning and Care. Wash chromium utensils with hot, soapy water, rinse with hot, clear water, and dry. If they become stained, rub with a soft cloth and whiting paste. Don't use steel wool or harsh abrasives which would scratch the plating. Chromium utensils may be replated when scratched or worn, but this is an expensive process.

Earthenware. Earthenware utensils are colorful and attractive, both for oven cooking and table service. Earthenware conducts heat slowly and evenly, and retains it for a long time.

In buying utensils of this material, watch for rough places, discoloration, and cracked or chipped spots, since earthenware is very porous underneath the outer glaze. Once the glaze is broken, the utensil will absorb moisture, grease, and dirt, and become useless as a cooking utensil. For this reason, guard earthenware utensils from sudden changes of temp and hard knocks. Earthenware utensils are cleaned just like glass ones.

Enamel Ware. Enamel ware utensils are made by dipping utensils made of a steel base into liquid porcelain enamel, then drying and firing them. There are three qualities of enamel utensils on the market—the inexpensive gray or dark blue graniteware utensils, which are dipped only once; the medium priced enamel ware, which is first dipped into the dark enamel and then in a second coat of the desired color; and the most expensive and durable triple-coated ware, called porcelain enamel, which has as its third coat an acid-resisting enamel.

Fancy colors and designs are often added in the process of manufacture to make the utensil more beautiful. These add to the cost of the utensil but not to its quality. A new process has recently been developed that will produce enamel with a narrow coefficiency of expansion so that the utensil is less apt to chip. This has increased the cost and also the efficiency. In selecting utensils of this ware, look for smooth surfaces free from tiny cracks or bubbles, since these flaws cause utensils to chip more easily.

Never use enamel utensils for waterless cookery, in which little or no water is used. They crack readily when brought in direct contact with heat. Any enamel utensil which is chipped where it touches the food should be discarded for cooking purposes, since slivers of the glasslike porcelain may break off into the food.

Cleaning and Care. In handling enamel utensils, guard carefully against dropping them, banging them against faucets or other equipment, or subjecting them to sudden changes of temp. Enamel ware shouldn't be scoured, as this will remove the surface glaze and the utensil will become darkened. Soak the utensil to loosen the foods which are stuck on. To remove hard water scale, fill the utensil with water to which a small amount of baking soda or lemon juice has been added. Boil for five to ten minutes. If the utensil is badly discolored, rub gently with a soft cloth and a paste of baking soda or whiting powder. Or treat with a good liquid cleaning solution that is not caustic. A sodium hypochlorite solution like chlorox is ideal for removing stains from tea kettles, coffee pots, saucepans, etc. You can prevent many dark marks by using a wooden spoon for stirring.

Glass. Glass utensils on the market are of two general types—oven ware, and flame ware or top-stove utensils. Oven ware mustn't be placed over direct heat. Glass utensils may be used for mixing, cooking, baking, serving, and storing foods. They heat slowly but transfer heat very readily, though somewhat unevenly. In top-stove cooking, therefore, it's necessary to use a fairly large amount of liquid. Glass retains heat for a long time, so foods continue to cook after the utensil is removed from the source of heat. Allow for this.

Glass is not affected by acid or alkali. It's easy to clean. It lets you watch your foods during the cooking process. It's a wise plan to use these glass utensils (or enamel or stainless steel ones) for cooking eggs and other foods that would darken and discolor aluminum.

Sudden changes in temp will crack glass utensils, so never set a hot utensil on a cold table, or pour boiling water into a cold utensil.

Remove stains from glass utensils with scouring powder and steel wool.

Iron. Most iron utensils are made of cast iron, but some lighter weight skillets are made of sheet iron, which tends to buckle and warp. Cast iron utensils are heavy and durable, and are good, even conductors of heat. For this reason, they're ideal for long, slow cooking. Iron utensils are comparatively inexpensive and will last a lifetime, actually, improving with use.

Most new iron utensils are lacquered to prevent rusting, and require conditioning before they're ready for use. Remove the lacquer by boiling the utensil in a solution of sal soda or salt and water. Then wash it thoroughly in soapy water, rinse, and dry.

Unless the manufacturer has labeled an iron utensil as already seasoned, it will need to be treated to make it resistant to rust. To treat it, rub the utensil and lid with unsalted cooking fat or oil and place for several hrs in a warm oven. Next let the utensil cool with the fat still on it, then wash again, and dry thoroughly. If the utensil shows any tendency to rust, repeat the seasoning process.

Iron utensils are also available on the market with a chromium plating, with an oxide finish (called Russian iron), and with a bright silver finish. These utensils should be seasoned or not, according to the recommendation of the manufacturer.

Cleaning and Care. Well-seasoned iron utensils don't become rusted easily. If rust does occur, remove it by scouring the spot with steel wool and kerosene. Then wash the utensil well, re-season, and store thoroughly dry. To remove a heavy coating of grease from an iron utensil, boil it in a strong solution of soda and water, scour with a good abrasive, then wash and dry thoroughly.

Stainless Steel. Stainless steel utensils are made of an alloy of steel, chromium, and nickel which doesn't become stained when acid or alkaline foods are cooked in them. They're more durable than aluminum utensils of the same weight. On the other hand, they heat slowly and conduct it un-evenly, so foods must be watched carefully to prevent sticking and scorching. Some of the newest stainless steel utensils are being made so that the bottom is 3 times as thick as the side walls to overcome sticking and scorching of foods. Stainless steel utensils, when overheated, grow dark and can't be brightened. It is safest to use any of them over a low flame to prevent hot spots and warping.

Stainless steel utensils with copper-clad bottoms are the most efficient steel utensils available. Copper is the best metal heat-conductor commonly used in the manufacture of cooking utensils, and is added to stainless steel to improve the speed and uniformity of heat transfer in cooking. The copper should never come in contact with the food.

Cleaning and Care. Clean stainless steel utensils with a mild abrasive such as whiting paste and fine steel wool (size oo). If the utensil is copper-clad, brighten the bottom by rubbing it with salt and a piece of lemon. Some of the newest copper-bottomed utensils have chromium plating over the copper so that they are easier to clean.

Tin. Tin utensils for baking are made from a base of steel or iron coated with tin. There are three methods of manufacturing tin utensils. The least expensive kind, the double seamed type, is made by bending a piece of sheet tin to form the bottom and two sides of a pan. The two end pieces are then cut separately and fastened in, leaving sharp corners and raw edges. This type of pan is difficult to clean, is apt to leak, and rusts easily.

A more expensive type of tin pan is made from one piece of sheet tin, with the edges bent up and the corners folded to make the pan waterproof and smooth.

Block tin utensils are made of a steel base and are dipped in molten tin after shaping. These utensils take more tin and so are more expensive to manufacture.

Tin utensils are desirable for quick baking, since they conduct heat well but don't hold it long. They become darkened with age, and bake foods to a richer and evener brown after they're darkened. For this reason, tin bread pans should be placed in a very slow oven (250° F) for several hrs to "cure" them before use. This is a practice of commercial bakers which the home-maker can also employ. If very light weight, they buckle and dent easily.

Cleaning and Care. Wash tin utensils in hot, soapy water, but don't scour them vigorously. Remove grease with whiting paste or other mild abrasive. Dry thoroughly. If the tin wears off or is scratched, the utensil will rust.

CONSTRUCTION

Now, keeping these characteristic qualities of the various utensil materials in mind, let's consider the matter of their construction. It's simple to choose attractive utensils, but you'll find cooking more enjoyable and dish washing much easier if you watch the following points:

Size and Shape. The capacity of the utensils you'll need will depend, of course, on the size of your family. For the most efficient use of fuel, choose top-stove utensils made with flat bottoms and of a size to cover the burner completely, but not to extend over onto the enamel surface of the stove. Too big a pan will cause the stove enamel to overheat and crack. Utensils with ridged bottoms that lift part of the pan above the source of the heat will waste fuel. If you have an electric range or grill, choose utensils with dull bottom surfaces to absorb rather than reflect heat.

Utensils with straight sides are more economical of heat and also of space (both on the stove and in storage) than those with rounded or flaring sides. However, the edge of the utensil, where the sides meet the bottom, should be shaped in a curve rather than a sharp angle for efficient stirring and easy cleaning.

Weight and Finish. The utensil should be heavy enough to be durable, but not so heavy as to be difficult to handle. Heavy utensils heat less rapidly but hold heat longer than do light weight ones, and so are desirable for long, slow simmering and "waterless" cooking. Light weight utensils heat rapidly but lose heat quickly, making them ideal for quick baking, cooking liquids, etc.

The surface of the utensil should be very smooth for easy cleaning, without cracks, ridges, riveting, or seams.

The finish given a material increases or decreases the amount of radiant heat absorbed. A polished surface reflects some of the heat that strikes it; a dull or dark surface absorbs it very rapidly. The cooking qualities of a utensil depend upon its ability to absorb, conduct, and retain heat.

Handles. If a utensil is well-balanced, it will stand steady whether empty or full. A handle which is too heavy or improperly placed disqualifies the whole utensil, since dangerous and wasteful spilling is unavoidable.

A handle should fit your hand comfortably. Metal handles frequently are flat and difficult to hold because of their sharp edges. Handles made of composition, hard rubber, or wood are easy to grip. However, composition

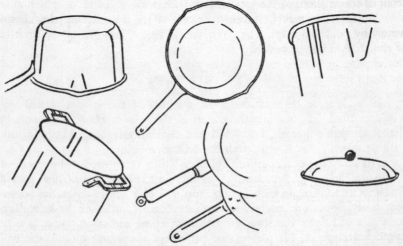

Some worthwhile features to look for when buying cooking utensils are illustrated above. Reading from left to right, top row:

1. Saucepan with sides meeting the bottom in a wide curve to provide for efficient stirring.

2. A double lipped saucepan is convenient for both right and left-handed persons.

3. A deep, sturdy rolled rim on a saucepan makes it more durable.

Reading from left to right, bottom row:

1. Metal handles should extend out far enough away from pan to permit firm grasp and they should be welded or riveted to the pan securely to make pan safe for handling.

2. Composition or wood handles are easy to grip. They should fit in the hand comfortably and be constructed so they will not loosen or twist after a few months use. Sturdy rings or eyes in the ends of the handle make it possible to hang the pans up.

3. Dome-shaped covers not only increase the cooking capacity of pans and kettles, but they aid in the condensation of steam.

handles may break and all three types may burn if placed too low on the utensil and not protected from the heat by metal. Wooden handles that are painted may flake, peel, and chip. *If* the utensil is to be used in the oven, the handle should either be easily removable or impervious to heat.

Handles must be joined securely to the utensil. Those welded to the body so that they're actually part of the pan itself are best, but a riveted handle is satisfactory if it's very secure and mounted at a wide angle for easy cleaning. Wooden or composition handles that can loosen and twist around are dangerous. The contents of the pan may spill out as the pan is lifted or tilted.

If you plan to hang your utensils, be sure the handles are equipped with sturdy rings.

Utensil Rims and Covers. For cooking with very little water or by steam, there must be close contact between the rim and cover of the utensil. This retained steam shortens the total cooking time.

The pan rim may be finished by rolling the edge, by beveling it, or merely by polishing it off. The cover should fit the utensil's particular style of rim. *1.* A rolled or beaded rim requires a beveled cover for steam retention. *2.* A beveled or steam-sealed edge needs a cover that will fit closely into the beveled groove. *3.* The polished-off rim found on cast aluminum and iron utensils takes a cover made flat to fit on the polished rim, but with a flange around the inside of the cover to provide a steam seal.

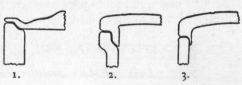

Dome-shaped covers increase the cooking capacity of a utensil and aid in condensing steam. However, being bulky, they require more space for storage. Flat lids with ring handles take little storage space, but are difficult to handle when hot. Small knob handles made of composition, hard rubber, or wood are comfortable to handle, and if such a handle is mounted in a depression in the lid, storage is simple.

If the lid is attached to the utensil, as it frequently is on a coffee pot, it should be so balanced that the empty utensil won't tip over when the lid is opened.

Lips and Spouts. Lips are usually formed as a part of the utensil, and should be fairly large and somewhat pointed for easy, safe pouring without spills and drips. Double-lipped utensils are convenient for use by either right or left-handed persons. Some utensils do not need lips such as a waterless cooker because there is no water to pour off.

Spouts may be welded or riveted to the utensil, or merely crimped at the side of the utensil itself. Welded spouts become part of the utensil, are as durable as it is, and are attractive and easy to clean. Riveted spouts are durable enough for general use and are less expensive to manufacture. They're not, of course, as smooth in appearance as a welded spout or as convenient to clean. Crimped spouts, found on inexpensive utensils, are less durable and a problem to keep clean.

Whether a spout pours satisfactorily or drips depends upon its design. A

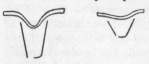

good pourer has high sides which direct the stream into the pointed center of the spout, preventing spilling. The edge of the spout should be thin and well-polished to cut the stream rapidly and eliminate dripping. Wide, short spouts are easy to clean, but don't pour as efficiently as longer ones.

A narrow pointed spout pours efficiently, a short wide one is apt to drip.

Once you've settled upon the material or materials you prefer for your cooking utensils and are clear on the points to watch for in the matter of construction, you're ready to decide just which utensils you actually need for your kitchen. If you're wise, you'll select comparatively few pieces but ones which have many uses, rather than a large assortment of one-job utensils.

The following list of utensils includes both the "must" items you'll need for pleasant and efficient work in your kitchen and many helpful-to-have pieces that may well fit into your own personal scheme of things. For each we suggest points to watch for in buying.

KITCHEN UTENSIL BUYING GUIDE

Look for these qualities when you shop.

Apple corer. Sharp cutting edge, comfortable handle, easy to clean and dry. Rust-proof, preferably stainless steel.

Bottle opener and tin can punch. Good grip and leverage, comfortable handle. Sharp blade to make clean puncture in can. Preferably chromium plated steel.

Bowl covers. Moisture-proof, washable, durably stitched, with strong elastic. Of good quality plastic or treated silk, nylon, rayon, or cotton.

Bread and pastry boards. Heavy, preferably seamless, of hard wood. Convenient to have both small and large boards.

Bread box. Well ventilated, of adequate size, easy to clean. Cake compartment, if included, should close separately. Enamel ware, aluminum, stainless steel or plastic.

Bread pans. Of one piece of material, without seams. Rounded corners, smoothly turned edges. Of glass, aluminum, heavy tin, or iron. Choose 2 or 3 sizes.

Broiler or sizzling platter. Easy to clean, with smooth grids rounded slightly to speed fat drainage. Oval shape saves oven space. Aluminum or chromium.

Cake cover with base. Base of hard wood, cover of glass, enamel ware or chromium plate, plastic or aluminum. Locking device is convenient for picnics.

Cake pan, tube. High tube and lugs for inverted cooling, loose bottoms. Sides slightly tapered. Of tin or aluminum. For angel and sponge cakes, gelatin rings, steamed puddings, vegetable molds.

Cake pan, square. Seamless, easy to clean, of tin, aluminum, or glass. Pans 8″ x 8″ x 2″ and 9″ x 9″ x 1¾″ bake small cakes, pan rolls, fondues, apples. Larger pan for roasting meats should have rounded corners.

Cake pans, layer. Round, with shallow, straight sides and flat bottom. Sturdy enough not to warp. Preferably of one piece of tin or aluminum. 8″ and 9″.

Cake pans, sheet. Shallow sides, about ¾ of an inch deep. Of tin or aluminum. Use for sheet cakes, jelly rolls, bar cookies, apple streudel, drop and roll cookies.

Cake rack. Of heavy parallel chrome wires, with short supporting legs. Must not sag under weight to permit good circulation of air to cool food quickly.

Cannister sets. Of heavy tin, enamel, plastic or quality glass. Wide openings with rust-proof lids tight-fitting yet readily removable.

Can openers.

Hand. Easy to operate, leaving smooth cut edge. Sharp blade, comfortable handle, preferably of stainless steel. Different types available for specialized jobs.

Screw lid. For opening screw-on jar and bottle lids. Adjustable for various sized lids. Rustproof, preferably of stainless steel.

Wall. Sturdy for long wear, easy to use, rust and acid proof. Should leave smooth cut edge with no metal shavings. May be left attached, folded back, or stored.

Casseroles, bean pots. Well glazed, with no cracks or flaws. Tight-fitting lid desirable. Glass or earthenware. For baking main dishes, puddings, deep dish pies, apples.

Chicken fryer or Dutch oven. Of heavy construction, with tight-fitting lid. Cast aluminum or iron. Heavy skillet with tight domed lid serves as small Dutch oven.

Coffee maker.

Dripolator. Coffee basket finely perforated, needing no filter paper. Well balanced, the bottom flame-resistant. Earthenware, glass, enamel ware, aluminum, stainless steel.

Percolator. Water should drip freely but not run through. Easy to clean, well balanced, cool handle, good pouring spout. Of glass, enamel ware, aluminum, stainless steel.

Steeped coffee. Handle protected from heat, balanced when open and empty, good pouring spout. Of glass, enamel ware, aluminum, or stainless steel.

Vacuum. Wide openings for easy cleaning. Cloth filter makes clearer coffee than plastic or glass filter but requires frequent replacement, is less sanitary. Glass, aluminum, chromium.

Colander, sink strainer, dish drain rack. Sturdy, rust-resistant, of aluminum or stainless steel. Sink strainers and dish racks may be rubber or plastic coated.

Cookie and doughnut cutters. Strong, easy to use and clean, with sharp edges and well defined shapes. Of stainless steel, tin, plastic. For biscuits, sandwiches, pastry, cookies.

Cookie jar. Easily lifted, washed and dried. Large opening. Cover easily lifted. Wide shallow jar better than high narrow one. Of earthenware or glass.

Cookie or baking sheets. Three sides open for easy removal of food with spatula. High sides retard browning. Of tin or aluminum. For cookies, biscuits, cooling candies, etc.

Custard cups, individual bean pots. See Casseroles. Use for baked or steamed puddings, gelatin molds, popovers, muffins, baked apples, individual pies and meat loaves.

Cutlery.

Bread knife and cake knife. Of high carbon steel, with keen cutting edge, wavy or saw tooth. The former is easier to wash. Forged blades excellent if well tempered. Stainless steel is rust-proof but dulls with use. Facts below apply to most cutlery pieces.

Carving set. Handles of hard rubber, fine grained hard wood, or composition, preferably with full tang construction (which means the end of the blade extends up through the handle). Metal collar over blade end of handle will loosen, harbor dirt. Forged blades have thick shoulders that strengthen and protect handles where they join blades. Test balance of blade and handle in your hand.

Paring knives—fruit, butcher, case, grapefruit. Handles of fine grained wood, composition, or metal of a size and length easy to grip. Blades should be of full tang construction made of high carbon steel that will hold a sharp edge. The saw toothed bent blade of grapefruit knives should be made of rust-proof stainless steel to prevent discoloration of fruit.

Peelers. Extremely sharp blade, rust-resistant, preferably metal throughout, with straight, comfortable handle. May have French bean cutter attached.

Deep fat fryer. Buy as a unit, or use saucepan with frying basket that fits deeply into it. Iron or aluminum. Use also for scalding foods to be frozen or canned.

Double boiler. Lower section—broad bottom for rapid heating. Upper section—curved bottom for efficient stirring, easy cleaning. Glass, enamel, aluminum, copper-clad stainless steel.

Egg beaters.

Dover or rotary. Most efficient have eight blades, cogs mesh smoothly, gears and handle are well above food, gears operate with ball bearings. Of stainless steel. False economy to buy anything but a very good one.

Turbine. Turns easily and rapidly for greatest efficiency. Excellent for beating small amount of food in small bowl such as whipping cream. Stainless steel.

Whisk. Of strong, medium fine stainless steel wire, firmly soldered at joinings. For whipping cream or eggs and folding ingredients into sponge and angel cakes.

Egg slicer. Wires firmly attached and set squarely into cutting sections. Of aluminum or stainless steel.

Electric mixer. Must have substantial motor and be guaranteed by reliable firm. Buy only attachments you're certain to use.

Flour sifter. Sturdy, shaker or crank type, at least 3 cup capacity. Cross wires or bars reinforce screen but are hard to clean. Of tin or stainless steel.

Food mill. Easy and efficient to operate. Attachment to scrape food off bottom as it's puréed. Of stainless steel, aluminum, or heavy tin.

Forks, long and short handled. Sharp, rigid, stainless steel tines, well tempered to prevent bending. Heat-proof handles strongly joined to shaft of tines. Two-tine for meat cookery.

Fruit juice extractors.

Press. Is very efficient and easy to clean, but tends to express skin oils along with juice, giving a tangy flavor. Of cast aluminum.

Reamer. Cone ridged deeply. May have strainer at bottom through which juice drips into sizable lower container. Of glass or stainless steel.

Funnels. One with lower opening that just fits into mason jar; another with pointed tip for small necked containers. Enamel ware, glass, aluminum, stainless steel, plastic.

Graters and Shredders. Rust-proof and rigid, in several sizes. Very sharp, to make smooth cuts with minimum pressure. Some of wire or plastic won't knick hands. Drilled holes better than punched ones. Aluminum, stainless steel, plastic, or wire.

Griddle. Groove for draining off surplus grease. Heavy in construction for slow, even heating. Of aluminum, iron, or soapstone. For pancakes, bacon, French toast, hamburgers.

Ice cream freezer. Large enough for "company" desserts. Drainage holes in outer container for melted ice. Mechanism easy to operate and clean.

Ice crusher. Should crush efficiently without too much effort.

Kettles. Bail handle with support to keep it away from source of heat. Hand grip cool and impervious to heat. Of stainless steel, aluminum, enamel ware.

Knife sharpeners. Sharpening stones or hones of medium fine texture are best. Either carborundum or alundum is a good stone. See illustration.

 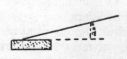 

Knife grinding is practically a polishing operation, therefore the best kind of a sharpener is a stone or hone. The stone should be fine grained but soft enough to crumble ever so slightly in the sharpening process. One of the best known stones is carborundum. Very little pressure on the knife blade is needed to sharpen it. The stone should be moistened a little with either water or oil and if not clean, should be cleaned thoroughly with kerosene or a soap and water bath before using to remove grit and dirt. Movement of the blade on the stone should be either a push or pull in a straight line direction as though one were shaving the sharpening surface of the stone. Short strokes should always be taken and the blade should be held at a 20 degree angle. See illustration. A greater angle dulls the edge, and a smaller one will not sharpen the knife. Never touch the surface of the blade to the stone for to do so grinds off the chrome or other finish of the blade and the fine steel will be exposed to rusting. Very few strokes should reset the edge. If the cutting edge of a really sharp knife is observed under a microscope, the edge would look as though it had the tiniest of saw-teeth all slanting straight in the same direction toward the point of the knife. A dull knife appears rippled with the tiny sawteeth often broken off and some slanting in one direction and the rest in the opposite direction.

Ladle. Good lip for easy pouring without dripping, adequate size bowl, handle long enough for use in deep kettle. Of aluminum, stainless steel, or enamel ware.

Measures.

Cup, pint, quart, and graduated set. For liquids, rust-proof measures, marked in ozs and in multiples of ⅛ and ⅓ cup, U. S. Standard, markings visible inside and out, no deep markings to clean. Good pouring lip. Space above cup mark to prevent spilling. For dry ingredients—graduated 1-cup measure that measures brimful, can be leveled with spatula and set of four measures—¼, ⅓, ½, and 1 cup. Of sturdy aluminum, heat-proof glass, or tin. Plastic measure may warp and become less accurate.

Spoons. Set of four—¼, ½, 1 tsp and 1 tbsp of sturdy aluminum. Plastic spoons may warp and lose accuracy.

Meat grinder. Heavily plated with tin, or of stainless steel. Assorted cutters. Easiest to wash if it opens.

Mixing bowls. Nested set of three or more, heavy enough to remain steady during stirring process. Sloping sides rounding gradually into bottom. Bent-over edge make holding and pouring easier. Glass, earthenware or plastic.

Molds.

Butter. Presses and paddles of smooth, close-grained hard wood; stainless steel for shell and patty cutters.

Gelatin. Heavy enough to hold shape, family size or individual, bold and simple in design. Of aluminum, glass, or heavy tin. For desserts, salads, cakes, steamed puddings.

Ring. Large or individual, sturdily constructed, the hole properly proportioned. Aluminum, stainless steel, glass, heavy tin.

Muffin pans. Few or no seams or ridges for easy cleaning. Of tin, iron, or aluminum. For cup cakes, muffins, tarts, popovers, gelatin molds.

Pancake turner. Flexible stainless blade for easy turning of food. If slotted, can be used to lift and drain bacon, vegetables, etc. A bent-in shaft makes it convenient to use in removing food from a skillet or pan.

Pastry blender. Wires heavy enough not to bend with reasonable use, rigidly attached to handle. Stainless steel.

Pastry cloth. Of firm, closely woven material. Buy or make. Heavy duck, canvas, or linen.

Pastry crimper. Rotates easily with sharp cutting edge. Of wood or stainless steel. For cutting pastry, noodles, and rolled cookie dough into fancy strips and shapes.

Pie pans, tart pans. Deep rather than shallow pans. Those 3, 4, 6, 8, and 9 inches across make useful assortment. Tin, aluminum, enamel ware, glass, earthenware.

Potato masher. Smooth, with stainless steel wires set close together and secure in handle; or of very hard, close-grained wood.

Pots. Handle on each side should be unharmed by heat and cool to grasp when pan is hot. Stainless steel, aluminum, enamel ware or iron.

Pressure saucepan. Easy to seal, operate, and clean, with over-pressure safety device. Of stainless steel or aluminum. For speedier cooking, better appearing foods, higher food values. (See p 1426.)

Refrigerator dishes. Durable enamel, glass ware, aluminum or plastic, with tight-fitting, flat covers. Square or oblong for economy of storage space. If metal, food can be reheated without transfer.

Roasting pans. Heavy enough to prevent warping in oven. May have tight-fitting lid, and rack. Folding handles for space economy, rounded corners for easy cleaning. Allow 1 to 2 inches clearance around meat; more permits burning of fat and juice. Of iron, enamel ware, aluminum, stainless steel, glass, heavy tin. For moist or dry meat cookery, baking sheet cakes or double or triple loaves of bread, storing bread, sterilizing jars, steaming puddings.

Rolling pin. Very hard smooth wood, or durable glass. Roller spins easily on handle. Comfortable grips, high enough so fingers won't touch board.

Rubber scraper. Good quality flexible rubber sealed firmly into handle. For removing batter, cleaning plates before washing, cutting and folding.

Sandwich grill. Guaranteed by reliable manufacturer. Of chromium plate. For toasting sandwiches, grilling meats and vegetables.

Saucepans. Well balanced, with little or no slope to sides. Bottom with wide, rounded angles. Secure, heat-proof handle, comfortable to hold. Of aluminum, stainless steel, enamel ware, or fireproof glass.

Scissors, kitchen and poultry shears. Sturdy, with long-lasting edges, comfortable handles. All metal best. Of high carbon steel, well tempered.

Scoops. Simple construction for easy washing. Handle rigidly attached and sanitary, or of extended metal. Stainless steel, aluminum, heavy tin, chromium plate, plastic.

Sieves. Supports under mesh desirable if sieve is removable. Otherwise they catch food, are hard to clean. Assorted sizes and meshes.

Skewers. Smooth wood or stainless steel with sharp tapered point. Flat head or bend on handle for easy removal. For meats "en brochette," veal birds, stuffed meats and poultry.

Skillets. Lipped for easy pouring. If heavy and tightly dome-covered, becomes small Dutch oven. Glass, aluminum, iron, stainless steel. Sizes to fit your needs.

Spatulas. Flexible enough to bend safely almost at right angles, handle rigidly attached. Levels measuring cups and spoons, frosts cakes, removes hot cookies from sheet, etc.

Spoons.

Short and long. Rust-proof, heavy enough not to bend easily. Wood or composition handles cool and comfortable to use. Stainless steel, aluminum, chromium, enamel ware.

Slotted. Same qualities as unslotted spoons. Handy for lifting poached eggs, fried doughnuts and croquettes, or blanched foods from scalding water.

Wooden. Best with very shallow bowl. Shorten handle if too long. Of very hard wood with smooth finish. Bowl should be rounded smoothly with no angles.

Steamed pudding pans. Flat bottom and slightly rounded corners for easy removal of pudding. Aluminum, stainless steel, heavy tin. For steaming or baking or as large casserole.

Steamer. Generous size most useful. Steams vegetables and puddings, warms over foods, keeps foods hot. Sterilize jars in lower part. Use upper as colander. Stainless steel, aluminum, enamel.

Strawberry huller. Rust-proof if possible, easy to grip, with sturdy "spring." Stainless steel or heavy tin. For hulling strawberries, picking pin feathers from poultry.

Tea kettle. Broad flat bottom, good pouring spout, wide top for easy cleaning. Of aluminum, glass, copper, stainless steel, enamel ware.

Thermometer. Reliable, sturdy, easy to use and read. For candy, jelly, frying. Has clip to hold it to pan. Special type for meat. Of glass or metal.

Timing device. Made by reliable manufacturer. Alarm clock type or part of stove. Accurate, loud clear alarm. Enamel shell.

Toaster. Guaranteed by reliable manufacturer. Browns evenly. If automatic, best if degree of browness can be regulated. Chromium plate.

Tongs. Sturdy and easy to operate with one hand. Grip foods better if toothed. Stainless steel or heavy tin.

Waffle iron. Product of reliable manufacturer. Dependable heat indicator. Available in square or round shape. Chromium plate.

PRESSURE SAUCEPANS

One of the most modern and efficient of cooking utensils is the pressure saucepan. Any food that cooks successfully in a covered saucepan or kettle will cook faster and more beautifully in the pressure saucepan. Fast cooking in a little water conserves both flavor and food value and it also saves fuel and time. While every household could use a pressure saucepan with benefit, it is of special advantage to those who have little time for cooking and who must always cook in a hurry. With these people, there is danger of having too little variety in meals. For example, they are forced to buy the tender, expensive cuts of meat that may be successfully pan-fried or broiled. But if they had a pressure saucepan, they could purchase a wide variety of inexpensive cuts for pot roasts and stews, and the less tender variety meats such as tongue and heart. It would also make possible the purchase of less expensive poultry such as hens for a stewed chicken and dumpling dinner. Legumes such as dried beans and peas could also be cooked, even luscious steamed fruit puddings could easily and quickly be cooked in this utensil.

It is also possible to cook whole meals of meat and vegetables if the meat is cut in thin enough slices and the vegetables are left a size where both meat and vegetables will cook equally well done in a reasonably short time. With a little practice, it is possible to work out several interesting meals and include a variety of meats and vegetables.

The manufacturers include recipe booklets with timetables for cooking all kinds of individual foods as well as combinations of meats and vegetables.

The best of pressure saucepans are always made of light weight material that heats up rapidly and cools very quickly. Their construction should be such as to make them perfectly safe. They should be shaped so as to be easily handled.

There are two types of cookers on the market differing in the type of seal. The first has a lid which flexes sufficiently to slip inside the top of the cooker and snaps tightly into position against the rim of the pan as soon as the handles are pressed together. The second is the one with a rigid lid which has a rubber sealing ring. All pressure saucepans have a pressure control of the spring or weight type, an opening for air exhaust, a gasket, a safety device, a seal band, and a signal. Some have audible signals on them and some have not and have to be watched. It is desirable to have a signal. This does not eliminate, however, careful watching during the cooking process.

PLANKS FOR PREPARING PLANKED MEALS

Foods cooked or partially cooked and served on a plank are so elegant that many people imagine they are too difficult for the average homemaker to prepare. When one has the right kind of plank, a planked meal is as easy as any other style of preparation and service. One can buy good hardwood planks from any well stocked housewares department and they usually come fitted into a metal holder. However, a handy husband or son with a drawing knife and a gouge can make a good looking, inexpensive plank provided he can secure the right length and width of inch-thick, well-cured white oak lumber. A good plank lasts for years if given the right care. A plank needs special treatment to prevent the wood from burning or scorching when it is exposed to oven or broiler heat. A practical way to treat planks is to soak them in cold water 3 or 4 hrs before using. Then they are wiped dry, rubbed well with oil on the side to be used and then put in a slow oven to heat through thoroughly. This preheating does not scorch the wood but it does absorb enough heat to speed up cooking and to keep the food hot through the meal. As soon as food on the plank browns appetizingly and is cooked through, the plank is transferred to its holder, or to a hot platter of ample size. Garnish, serve at once.

Oiling the plank before preheating and brushing it with melted butter before the food is placed on it keeps the food from sticking and makes it easier to serve. After use, scrape plank, scrub with coarse bristled brush, wipe thoroughly with cloth wrung from hot water. Wrap in waxed paper, store in cool, moderately dry place. Foods most commonly planked are steaks, chops, boned chicken and fish. Often these foods are partially cooked on both sides, then are removed to the plank and bordered with mashed potatoes blended with beaten egg. Plank is then placed in hot oven or under broiler to finish cooking meat and to brown potatoes. Other freshly cooked vegetables are slid into spaces allotted them, and a garnish of parsley or cress added.

Glossary

If you were going to have a mousse for dinner, would you marinate, freeze, or julienne it? Would you frizzle, fricassee or fry a sausage? Is pot liquor intoxicating? What's the difference between cutting, and cutting and folding? Can you poach other foods than eggs? This chapter defines dozens of the terms constantly heard in modern cooking. Study them and you won't need to look puzzled when your neighbor uses them so glibly.

★　★　★　★

After-dinner coffee . . . strong coffee served at the end of a meal, usually without sugar or cream.

Aigre-doux . . . . sour-sweet.

À la, à le, au, aux . . . . . in the manner or fashion of.

À la carte . . . . meal planned by diner. Individual food items priced separately.

À la mode . . . . literally, in the fashion; in common usage (1) of beef, prepared by marinating and braising in the marinade; (2) of pie, served with a scoop of ice cream.

Allemande . . . . German—a smooth sauce made of white sauce and added butter, egg, catchup, etc.

Americaine . . . . American.

Andalouse . . . . the name of a section of Southern Spain often given to sauces, soups, and garnishes containing tomatoes, ham, rice and seasonings.

Angelica . . . . an aromatic plant grown in the Alps, the young leaf stalks and midribs of which are candied.

Antipasto . . . . an Italian appetizer course, usually consisting of salad greens, tomatoes, pickled hot peppers, anchovies, salami and olives.

Aspic . . . . Originally a savory meat jelly often containing diced meat and other foods; now used for many gelatin, fruit and vegetable combinations.

Au gratin . . . . literally, with a crust; usually of cheese or fine bread crumbs or both.

Bake . . . . to cook by dry heat in an oven.

Barbecue . . . . to roast slowly on a spit or over coals in a specially prepared trench, usually basting with a highly seasoned sauce; used loosely of any meat served in such a sauce.

Bar-le-duc . . . . a fruit preserve originally made of white currants but frequently made of gooseberries and other berries.

Baste . . . . to pour liquid over a food while cooking to prevent drying out. The liquid is usually meat drippings, melted butter or shortening, or a mixture of these with water; or the juice of the food itself may be used.

Béarnaise . . . . Hollandaise sauce with added tarragon, chervil, shallot, parsley, etc.

Beat . . . . to manipulate a food mixture, usually a batter, with a brisk regular circular and lifting motion which incorporates air; also to use a mechanical egg beater.

Béchamel . . . . a cream sauce made of chicken broth, cream and milk seasoned with onion.

Beef à la mode . . . . . . marinated beef, well larded, braised with vegetables.

Beurre . . . . butter.

Bisque . . . . a thick soup made of seafood; a frozen cream dessert containing nuts.

Blanch . . . . to pour boiling water over a food, drain and rinse immediately in cold water. Used to loosen the skins of nuts and fruits, such as almonds and tomatoes; also to destroy enzymes and set color.

Blanc Mange . . . . a white cornstarch pudding made without eggs but containing milk.

Bland . . . . having a very mild, pleasant flavor.

Blanquette . . . . a meat stew made with a white sauce.

Blend . . . . to mix two or more ingredients thoroughly.

Bleu . . . . blue.

Bombe . . . . unstirred frozen molded dessert, usually consisting of two layers of contrasting color and flavor, packed into a round or melon-shaped mold.

Borsch . . . . a tart Russian soup made of vegetables, sometimes with meat broth, usually served with sour cream.

Bouillabaisse . . . . a French soup made of fish, highly seasoned, and served in plates with dry toast.

Bouillon . . . . a clear meat broth delicately seasoned.

Braise . . . . to cook by browning in a small amount of fat, adding a small amount of water at a time and simmering gently, covered, until tender.

Bread . . . . to roll in bread crumbs.

Brine .... a solution of salt in water with or without other preservatives, used for preserving meats, vegetables, etc.

Brochette .... a small spit or skewer used for roasting or broiling meats.

Broth ....?...... a thin soup; also the liquid in which meat, fish and vegetables have cooked; contains bits of solid material and sometimes fat. See Stock.

Brown .... to cause a food to become brown by sautéing, frying, toasting, broiling or baking.

Canapé .... a type of appetizer made by topping small pieces of plain or toasted bread with well-seasoned spreads and fancy garnishes.

Carafe .... a decanter or water bottle.

Caramelize .... to melt sugar and cook it until golden brown.

Carte .... menu card or bill of fare.

Casserole .... (1) an earthenware, glass or metal dish for baking; (2) a combination of foods, usually with cream sauce, baked in such a dish.

Caviar .... the roe of sturgeon or other large fish, eaten as a relish, fresh or salted, usually on toast with oil and lemon juice.

Charlotte .... a mold lined with cake, cookies, or lady fingers, and filled with fruit and whipped cream; also called Charlotte Russe.

Chaud-froid .... literally, hot-cold; a molded gelatin sauce containing game or meat.

Chicory .... the root of a plant which is roasted, ground, and added to coffee to make it blacker and stronger. This addition, enjoyed by some, is considered an adulteration unless noted on the label. Also a plant used as a salad green, also known as French endive.

Chop .... to cut into irregular small pieces.

Chou paste .... the paste used in making cream puffs and éclairs.

Chowder .... a kind of stew, originally applied only to fish or clam stews, now also applied to many mixed vegetable stews, usually without meat other than chopped bacon or salt pork.

Chutney .... a relish of Oriental origin containing fruits and vegetables highly seasoned; a sweet pickle relish.

Citron .... a sub-tropical fruit which is candied and used in fruit cakes, cookies, and candies.

Clotted cream .... Devonshire cream; an English dish made from rich milk allowed to separate and then scalded. The thickened cream is then skimmed off and served for dessert as an accompaniment to strawberries or eaten on bread.

Coca Cola .... a sweet, carbonated beverage containing caffeine and flavorings.

Cocktail .... an appetizer, either a beverage or a light, highly seasoned food, served before a meal.

Cocotte .... a small individual casserole of saucepan shape, made of French china or earthenware.

Compote .... fruits cooked in a heavy syrup so as to retain their shape; also a serving dish used for candies, fruits, and preserves, etc.

Condiment .... a seasoning or flavoring added to, or served with a food to improve its flavor, such as salt, pepper, vinegar, herbs and spices.

Confectioners' sugar .. a very finely pulverized sugar combined with cornstarch, used for cake icings, etc., also identified by XXXX to XXXXXX.

Confectionery ...... ordinarily candy; sometimes other sweet foods such as pastry.

Conserve .... a fruit preserve made of several fruits, often with added nuts and raisins.

Consommé .... a clear broth made from 2 or 3 kinds of meat and highly seasoned.

Cos lettuce .... a salad green belonging to the lettuce family; also called romaine.

Coupe .... a cup; also a frozen dessert served in a cup.

Course .... a portion of a meal served at one time, as a cocktail, soup, entrée, dessert, etc.

Court-bouillon ..... a highly seasoned broth made from fish and one in which fish is cooked.

Cream .... to soften a fat with a spoon or beater; also to combine the softened fat with sugar.

Cream of tartar ..... acid potassium tartrate, used in angel food cake to keep it white and tender; also to acidulate other foods.

Creole .... a well-seasoned tomato sauce containing green pepper and chopped onion.

Crêpe .... a very thin, crisp pancake.

Croquettes .... finely chopped foods such as meat, poultry, fish, or vegetables and usually combined with thick white sauce and shaped into small molds, coated with egg and crumbs, and fried until crisp in deep fat.

Croustade .... a crisp toasted basket or box cut from bread and used as a container for serving creamed foods.

Croûtons .... small cubes of toast used as a garnish for soups.

Crown roast .... a roast shaped like a crown, made by Frenching ribs of pork or lamb and sewing or skewering them to form a crown.

Cruller .... a doughnut of twisted shape, very light in texture.

Crumb .... to coat a food with crumbs, as a croquette before frying or a casserole dish before baking.

Crumpet .... an English bread similar to an English muffin.

Curry .... an East-Indian dish similar to a stew, but characterized by the pungent flavor of curry powder.

Cut and fold .... to blend a mixture by using two motions; (1) cutting down through the mixture with the edge of a spoon or other implement; (2) sliding the implement along the bottom of the bowl and bringing it up at the side so as to lift the lower portion of the mixture and fold it over the upper portion; these motions are repeated until blending is complete. The object is to mix without loss of air, as when blending stiffly beaten egg whites into a cake batter.

Cut into .... to incorporate fat into a flour mixture by dividing it finely with knives or pastry blender.

Cutlet .... a croquette mixture shaped in flat form; a piece of veal or beef round steak cut in round shape, coated with egg and crumbs and braised.

Dariole .... a small tart filled with custard or cream; also an appetizer containing caviar.

Daube .... a spicy stew; a larded piece of meat, or one cooked covered with slices of bacon or salt pork.

Demi-tasse .... literally, a half cup; a small after-dinner cup of black coffee.

Devil .... to season a food in such a way as to make it hot; as deviled eggs, ham, crab, etc.

Dextrin .... a carbohydrate obtained by partially hydrolyzing starch, which does not have the thickening properties of starch, but which is used in cooking for its rich brown color and flavor.

Diastase .... an enzyme which hydrolyzes starch.

Dice .... to cut into small pieces of uniform size and shape, approximately cubical.

Dissolve .... to pass into solution in water or other liquid; also to cause to pass into solution.

Drain .... to free from liquid.

Dredge .... to coat with flour or fine bread crumbs by sprinkling or by rolling the food in them.

Éclair .... an oblong, hollow pastry made of cream puff paste; usually filled with cream filling and covered with icing; sometimes served as an entrée filled with creamed foods.

Emulsion . . . . the combination of two immiscible liquids such as water and oil, in such foods as homogenized milk, mayonnaise and French dressing.

Entrée . . . . a subordinate dish served between the main courses at a formal dinner which is pleasing but not satisfying to the appetite; also the main dish at a luncheon.

Escallop . . . . to bake food, usually a mixture with white sauce and topping of crumbs or crumbs and cheese in a baking dish or casserole; originally, to bake in a scallop shell. Same as Scallop.

Farce . . . . forcemeat; stuffing.

Filet, Fillet . . . . a boneless piece of fish or lean meat.

Filet mignon . . . . a slice of beef tenderloin, sometimes wrapped in bacon; cooked by broiling.

Foie . . . . liver, usually goose.

Fondue . . . . a fluffy preparation of eggs and milk, usually containing bread crumbs and flavored with cheese; similar to an omelet.

Forcemeat . . . . a stuffing or dressing made of fine-chopped foods, the ingredients differing with the type of poultry, fish or meat being stuffed.

Four . . . . literally, an oven; small cakes or pastries baked in an oven.

Frappé . . . . a liquid mixture frozen to a mush.

French . . . . (1) to trim meat away from the end of a bone, as a lamb chop;
(2) to flatten boneless meat with a cleaver, as a slice of beef tenderloin;
(3) to cut into thin slivers, as green beans.

French fry . . . . to fry in deep fat.

Fricassee . . . . to cook meat, usually cut in pieces, by braising; the meat is most commonly fowl, rabbit or veal.

Fritter . . . . a fried cake similar to a doughnut containing fruit or vegetables.

Frizzle . . . . to sauté until the edges become curly, sometimes crisp, as chipped beef or thinly sliced ham.

Fromage . . . . cheese.

Frost . . . . to cover a cake with icing or frosting.

Gâteau . . . . cake.

Glace . . . . ice.

Glacé . . . . crystallized; frosted; frozen.

Glaze . . . . as a noun—a shiny coating applied to certain foods, such as baked ham, fruit cake, rolls, etc.; may be a mixture of sugar and fat, sugar and water, egg white, cornstarch, etc.

as a verb—to apply such glaze, either with or without heat.

Glucose .... a slightly sweet, simple sugar which is readily utilized by the body.

Gnocchi .... an Italian dish made of starch, milk, eggs, butter, and cheese served as a main dish.

Goulash .... a highly seasoned stew, often containing vegetables, popular in Hungary.

Gourmet .... an epicure.

Grate .... to obtain small particles of a food by rubbing it on a grater.

Gravy .... a sauce similar to cream sauce, made with meat drippings, flour and milk, water, cream, sour cream, or broth, etc.

Grenadine .... pomegranate syrup; also larded meat or fish.

Grill .... to broil; to cook by direct contact with heat.

Gumbo .... okra; a thick, rich Creole soup containing okra.

Haggis .... a Scotch dish made by stuffing a sheep stomach with a seasoned mixture of ground meat, oatmeal, onions, suet, and herbs, and cooking it in water.

Haricots .... kidney beans; haricots verts—green beans.

Herb .... a wide variety of aromatic plants used for seasoning and garnishing foods; also used medicinally.

Hollandaise .... literally, Dutch; a sauce made of egg yolks and butter with seasonings, served hot with vegetables or fish.

Hors d'oeuvre .... a side dish or relish used as an appetizer, made of salty, tart, or crisp foods, as canapés, etc.

Ice .... as a noun—a liquid mixture frozen until firm but smooth;

as a verb—(1) to chill by addition of chopped or crushed ice, as a beverage;

(2) to cover a cake with icing or frosting; same as Frost.

Irish moss .... a form of seaweed used as a thickening agent in puddings.

Irradiate .... to enrich with added "sunshine" vitamin D, by exposure to ultraviolet light.

Jambalaya .... meat or lobster served with a Creole sauce.

Jardinière .... a dish of mixed vegetables.

Julienne .... to cut into long slender pieces, as vegetables and sometimes cooked meats.

Jus .... juice or gravy.

Kedgeree .... a combination of rice and smoked fish.

Kippered .... lightly salted and smoked fish.

Kitchen bouquet ..... a mixture of herbs used for seasoning soup, sauces, stews, etc.; also a dark liquid flavoring used to season and darken gravies.

Kosher .... meat slaughtered and prepared in accordance with the Jewish custom.

Koumiss .... a fermented milk beverage.

Lactose .... a sugar found in milk.

Lady apples .... bright-colored, small-sized apples used for decorative purposes.

Lard .... to introduce fat into a lean meat by threading slivers of fat salt pork or bacon through it.

Lardoon .... a long, narrow strip of salt pork, bacon, or suet used in larding lean meat.

Leavening agent ..... an ingredient used in baked products to make them light and porous by releasing or forming gas during baking; typical ones used are liquid which forms steam; baking powders and soda which form carbon dioxide; and yeast with sugar which forms carbon dioxide.

Legumes .... the seeds of certain plants, as peas, beans, peanuts, and lentils.

Liquor .... the liquid in which a food is packed, as oysters or canned foods. See also Pot liquor.

Lukewarm .... of a temp about blood heat, or 100–110° F.

Macédoine .... a mixture of cut vegetables or fruits.

Maître d'hôtel sauce .. a sauce containing chopped parsley, lemon juice, and melted butter, which is served on potatoes and fish.

Maraschino .... a famous liqueur of Italian origin, containing honey, clear syrup, and the marasca cherry, used as a flavoring.

Marinade .... a mixture, usually of vinegar or lemon juice and water, or a well-seasoned oil and vinegar dressing in which certain foods are seasoned.

Marinate .... to let stand in a marinade.

Marrons .... chestnuts; often preserved chestnuts.

Marzipan .... a paste of sweet almonds and sugar, used in confections.

Melt .... to become liquefied, usually through the application of heat.

Meringue .... a stiffly beaten mixture of egg white and sugar; may be cooked or uncooked.

Mignon .... dainty, pretty; small, choice foods.

Minestrone .... a thick Italian soup containing meat, vegetables, and legumes, and usually served with Parmesan cheese.

Mixed grill ....a combination of meats, vegetables, and fruits broiled and served together.

Mode ....custom, fashion.

Mornay ....a white sauce containing cheese.

Mousse ....a type of still-frozen dessert consisting chiefly of flavored and sweetened whipped cream.

Mulligatawny ....a highly seasoned, thick soup containing vegetables, mango chutney, coconut, rice, curry powder and other seasonings.

Muscovite ....fruit pulp and sugar frozen without stirring.

Napoléon ....a French pastry made of sheets of puff paste put together with cream filling, and topped with jam or icing, nuts, and whipped cream.

Neapolitan ....a dessert made of layers of ice cream and ices, frozen, and sliced for serving.

Nesselrode ....a frozen pudding made of a custard foundation with added fruit and puréed chestnuts.

Newburg ....a cream sauce with egg yolks added, usually flavored with lime or sherry, and frequently served with lobster.

Nougat ....a chewy type confection containing egg whites, frequently made with added fruit and nuts.

Oeuf ....egg.

Olla podrida ....a rich Spanish stew containing foods such as sausage, poultry, beef, bacon, cabbage, legumes, etc., which is baked slowly until tender.

Pain ....bread.

Panada ....a paste of bread and milk; sometimes a bread sauce made of milk and meat broth thickened with bread crumbs.

Pan-broil ....to cook in a skillet with just enough fat cooked out of the meat to prevent sticking. Excess fat is drained off at intervals.

Pan-fry ....to cook in a skillet with shallow fat.

Papillote ....a paper frill used for food decoration.

Parboil ....to cook partially in boiilng water; cooking is usually completed by some other method.

Parfait ....a frozen dessert containing egg and syrup; also a frozen dessert such as ice cream served in a parfait glass in combination with a sweet sauce and whipped cream.

Parmentière ....potato.

Pasteurize ....to apply heat below the boiling point to a food for the purpose of destroying certain organisms, especially those which cause fermentation. Applied commercially to milk; in the home principally to fruit juices which are being preserved.

Pâté .... pastry, patty-shell, piecrust, or tart.

Pâtisserie .... pastry.

Paysanne .... peasant style; country style.

Pemmican .... dry, lean venison or other meat, first preserved by American Indians; sometimes pulverized and mixed with fat to form cakes; used by exploring expeditions to Arctic regions because it keeps indefinitely.

Peppercorn .... the whole pepper berry, before grinding.

Pepper pot .... a thick, rich soup made very spicy with pepper.

Périgord .... with truffles.

Petit .... small, new.

Petite marmite ..... literally, little pot; unstrained brown stock.

Petits fours .... small, fancy cakes for tea, usually iced by dipping the small cakes individually in icing so as to coat them completely.

Pfefferneusse .... pepper nuts; small, spicy, German cookies.

Pièce de résistance .... the main dish of a meal, such as a roast.

Pilau also pilaf ...... a Turkish dish consisting of rice, seasonings, and meat, fish, or poultry.

Pimiento .... a large, sweet, red pepper, available fresh, canned, or dried, much valued for its flavor and color.

Pipe .... to force through a pastry tube, as cake icing.

Plank .... a heavy, flat piece of hard wood designed for the cooking and serving of foods. Usually a piece of broiled steak garnished with mashed potatoes and other vegetables.

Plat .... dish.

Plombières .... a frozen dessert made of ice cream, candied fruits, and whipped cream, served in paper cups.

Poach .... to cook food in a hot liquid in such a manner that it retains its original shape.

Poivrade .... pepper sauce.

Polenta .... an Italian dish made of cereal mush and cheese.

Pomme .... apple; pomme de terre—apple of the earth; potato.

Pot liquor .... the liquid in which vegetables have been boiled.

Pot roast .... a large piece of meat, usually a less tender cut, cooked by braising rather than by baking or roasting.

Powdered sugar ...... white sugar partially reduced to powder.

Punch .... any beverage composed chiefly of mixed fruit juices.

Purée .... as a noun—the smooth sauce so obtained originally, a thickened soup; as a verb—to rub through a sieve or colander, obtaining a thick smooth sauce.

PRESSURE COOKING

Pressure cooking is the modern kitchen's greatest time saver. It also has the advantage of using less liquid and thus preserving many of the vitamins and minerals essential to health. Many of the basic recipes in this book can be adapted to pressure cooking, particularly soups, stews, cereals, dried fruits and all vegetables.

Pressure saucepans come in different styles from different manufacturers, you will note from the five leaders illustrated. When buying be sure to get one that has adequate safety features, that closes easily, but cannot be opened until the pressure has been entirely released or subsided. Check the number of parts that can wear out or get lost, the service, the weight, rapidity of heating, ease of cleaning and durability.

Through the courtesy of the manufacturers of the stainless steel Flex-Seal pressure cookers (upper right), which we are told meet all the U.S. military requirements, we are including facts from their latest recommended cooking time table and guide.

Note the Following: Under Flex-Seal techniques pressure is allowed to drop naturally. Just move off the burner. *Do not* reduce pressure with cold water. Other cookers may require chilling. Follow manufacturer's directions.

It is *important* that cooker be level on stove so vent weight is free to oscillate, or jiggle to release excess pressure. When pressure is reached turn down heat so vent weight barely moves, especially with cereals, soups or other foods which ordinarily froth while cooking. *Never* fill cooker more than ⅔ full (legal limit).

Frozen Vegetables should be partially thawed or broken apart and cooked like fresh vegetables. The *exception* is corn-on-the-cob which should be completely thawed, and cooked half the time of fresh corn.

Cereals: Bring water to boil in open cooker, salt, and sprinkle in cereal. Close cooker, and bring to pressure on slow heat to prevent sticking on bottom. Stir well before serving for smooth texture.

Soups and Stews: Use slightly less water than our regular recipe calls for, as there is no evaporation in pressure cooking. *Never* fill cooker more than ⅔ full.

Meats, Poultry, Fish: (except stews and fricassees) Brown in open cooker with minimum fat; then add ¼ to ½ cup of water depending on size of piece and cooking time. For crisp outside, cook first, then dip in batter, flour or crumbs and brown quickly in shallow skillet.

Flex-Seal Cooking Time Tables

FRESH VEGETABLES	Amount of Water	Minutes at 15 lbs	COMMENTS
Asparagus		0	Break off tough ends. Lay stalks criss-cross.
Artichoke		10	
Beans, wax and green		1½	
Beans, Lima		1	Remove tops only. Peel after cooking. Time depends on size and age.
Beets		15	
Broccoli		0	Slice stems.
Brussels Sprouts		0	
Cabbage		1	Remove core. Cut in eighths.
Carrots, Whole		3	
Sliced		1	
Cauliflower		½	Break into flowerets. Slice stems.
Celery		2	
Whole kernel corn		1	
Corn on cob		5	
Egg plant, ¼″ slices		0	
Kohlrabi, ⅛″ slices		2½	
Mushrooms, ⅛″ slices		0	
Okra		2	
Onions		8	Whole, medium sized.
Parsnips		10	Peeled, cut in half lengthwise.
Peas		0	Add a few pods for flavor.
Potatoes, Sweet, halved		8	Depending on size and age.
Potatoes, halved		8	
Pumpkin		10	Cut in small pieces.
Rutabaga		15	Peeled. Cut in eighths.
Spinach		0	
Squash, Summer		2	Peeled. Cut in fourths.
Winter		15	Cut in small pieces.
Turnips, White, quartered		10	15 min whole: 12 min halved.

Amount of Water column notes:
Use ¼ cup of water for 1 qt and 2 qt Flex-Seal.
Use ⅓ cup of water for 3 qt and 4 qt Flex-Seal.
Use ½ cup of water for 7, 9 and 12 qt Flex-Seal.

DRIED VEGETABLES Cook covered with water	Minutes to cook at 15 lbs Pressure	
	Soaked 1 hr	Soaked Overnight
Kidney Beans	50	15
Lentils	25	10
Lima Beans (large)	30	20
Lima Beans (small)	25	15
Navy Beans (large)	50	40
Navy Beans (small)	45	30
Peas, Split (unsoaked 10 min)	..	..
Peas, Black Eye	40	30
Pinto Beans	50	45

SOUPS	Minutes at 15 lbs			Minutes at 15 lbs
Chicken	30	Pea		25
Navy Bean	50	Soup Stock		45
Beef of Tomato	1	Vegetable		3
(With Bouillon Cubes)		(First make soup stock)		

MEATS

MEATS	Minutes per lb of Meat at 15 lbs Pressure	Cooking Time in Minutes at 15 lbs Pressure		Cooking Time in Minutes at 15 lbs Pressure
Beef, Braised Ribs		30	Lamb, Chops	10
Beef, Corned, (Brisket)		60	Lamb, Roast breast, with dressing	30
Beef, Hamburg Cakes, brown one side and turn		5	Lamb Stew	20
Beef Heart		50	Meat Loaf	45
Beef Loaf		45	Pork, Chops	10
Beef, Pot or Rump Roast	18		Pork, Spareribs	20
Beef, Rib Roast (Rolled) Well done	16		Pork, Ham shank or butt ..	40
Medium	14		Pork, Ham slices (½-inch thick)	15
Rare	12		Veal Birds	15
Beef, Swiss Steak (cut ½-inch thick)		20	Veal Cutlets	10
Beef Stew		20	Veal Fricassee (see recipe)	7
Beef Tongue		60	Chicken, Fricassee	25
Lamb, Roast boned Shoulder	15		Chicken, Fried	12
Pork, Roast Loin	18		Chicken, Stew	25
Pork, Roast Shoulder .	20			
Veal Roast	15			

FISH

FISH	Minutes at 15 lbs		Minutes at 15 lbs
Baked Fish, minutes per lb	6	Fried Fish	5–7
Fillet of fish, stuffed, minutes per lb	7	Halibut Steak	5–7
Finnan Haddie Savory, minutes per lb	6	Halibut Steamed	15
		Fish Steak	5

DRIED FRUITS

DRIED FRUITS	Am't of Water	Minutes at 15 lbs	Comment
Apples		5	Soak overnight
Apricots		4	No soaking
Figs { Sun Dried	Cook covered with water	40	No soaking
Figs { Dehydrated		10	No soaking
Peaches		5	Soak overnight
Prunes { Large		10	No soaking
Prunes { Small		8	No soaking

CEREALS

CEREALS	Cups of Cereal	Cups of Water	Teaspoon of Salt	Minutes at 15 lbs
Cornmeal	1	4	1	8
Cracked Wheat	1	4½	1	25
Hominy grits	½	3	1	25
Macaroni	4 oz.	3½	1	5
Spaghetti	4 oz.	3½	1	8
Barley (for soups)	⅓	2½	½	10
Scotch Style Oatmeal	1	4½	1	10
Quick Cooking Rolled Oats	1	2½	1	2
Rice	1	2½	½	5

One fruit which both the city and country woman can store away to advantage is the juicy Concord grape. The most practical way to prepare it is to make Juice and Purée, p 1078, to be canned for later use—the juice for jelly and as a beverage or dessert, and the purée for jam.

Modern refrigeration helps.

An important part of making good doughnuts, *pp 288–290*, is the frying of them. A deep fat frying thermometer is a sound investment, because the temp of the fat must be just right for good flavor, crispness, and freedom from soaking. Thorough draining on absorbent paper or paper toweling is necessary, too. Try French-fried potatoes and pan-broiled steak. **Read Frying with Deep Fat, *p* 738.**

ABOVE: *This electric range has two sizable ovens. Right one bakes up to a 35 lb turkey. When done, cloth is lifted from turkey, see p 1069, to add final brown touch. Marshmallow sweet potatoes toast on upper rack. While turkey bakes, so can two pies in left oven.*
Photograph, Courtesy Hotpoint, Inc., Chicago

BELOW: *Steaks broil perfectly in this electric oven. Tongs help keep steaks juicy because they don't pierce meat. Surface units of this range are efficient, too. The New Calrod has lightweight, ample surfaces and starts cooking at "black heat."*

The efficient mechanism and design of this gas range enables one to bake, broil, braise, roast, steam and stew foods perfectly and with ease. Note the oven and broiler space which permits the cooking of several foods at the same time. The staggered burners are an advantage too, because they allow the safe removal of any pan on whatever burner it is placed without interfering with other pans.

Quenelle ....a type of forcemeat; a dumpling made of forcemeat and poached before serving.

Ragout ....a thick, well-seasoned meat stew.

Ramekin ....a small individual casserole dish.

Ravigote ....a sauce made of tarragon vinegar, seasoned with chives, shallots, etc.

Ravioli ....small pieces of Italian noodle paste rolled thin, filled with chopped meat or vegetables, folded together, sealed, and poached in broth.

Rémoulade ....a pungent sauce made of vinegar, oil, mustard, hard-cooked eggs and seasonings, served with cold dishes.

Rice ....to press through a potato ricer.

Risotto ....an Itailan dish of rice and cheese; also a stew of chicken, rice, and olive oil, etc.

Rissole ....a small fried pie with a filling of chopped meat or fish.

Roast ....to cook by dry heat. See Bake.

Rosette ....a thin batter fried in fancy shapes by means of a special iron, and served with creamed foods as an entrée, or with fruit or ice cream as a dessert.

Roulade ....rolled; usually rolled meat.

Roux ....the paste of melted fat and flour which is the basis of all cream sauces and gravies.

Sabayon ....a sweet dessert, sauce, or punch made with eggs and flavored with wine.

Saccharine ....chemical used as a substitute for sugar in special diets; has no food value nor any of the physical properties of sugar.

Salmagundi ....a mixture; especially a mixture of chopped fish, meat, onions, etc., seasoned with oil, vinegar and herbs.

Samovar ....a Russian urn of copper or other metal constructed with a chamber for boiling water surrounding an internal stove heated by charcoal; used for serving tea.

Sauerbraten ....a pot roast of beef or pork, or a combination of the two, acidulated before cooking by soaking the meat in seasoned vinegar: marinating.

Sauté ....to toss a food in a pan by moving the pan quickly back and forth over a fire; to cook in a small amount of fat.

Savarin ....a French bread; a brioche dough shaped into a loaf, with a topping of almonds and candied fruits and sugar.

Scald ....(1) to bring just to the simmering point, as milk; (2) to pour boiling water over, as in cleaning a pan.

Scallion ....an onion which has not developed a bulb.

Scallop . . . . see Escallop.

Score . . . . to cut part way through, as through the fatty covering of a ham and around the fatty edge of steak.

Sear . . . . to brown the surface of meat quickly by exposing it to a high temp during the first few min of cooking. This has recently been discarded as a practice of meat cookery because it increases weight loss and loss of juices.

Season . . . . to add salt, pepper, spices, herbs, etc. for purpose of improving the flavor.

Simmer . . . . to cook very gently in water just below the boiling point.

Sherbet . . . . see Ice—as noun. Sometimes made with milk rather than water.

Skewer . . . . as a noun—a long metal or wooden pin for fastening meat;
as a verb—to fasten meat with such a pin.

Smorgasbord . . . . a Swedish appetizer course consisting of a wide variety of foods from which each person selects the foods he prefers.

Sorbet . . . . a sherbet made of several kinds of fruit.

Soubise . . . . a white sauce containing onions and sometimes parsley.

Soufflé . . . . a baked dish made basically of milk and eggs, to which separately beaten egg whites give an airy lightness; means literally, "puffed up."

Soya . . . . a salty brown sauce served with Chinese foods, made by fermenting soybeans, roasted wheat, water, salt, etc.

Spatula . . . . a sort of flexible knife with rounded end and without sharp edges, available in many sizes.

Spun egg . . . . beaten egg dropped from a colander into hot soup and thereby formed into vermicelli shapes.

Spun sugar . . . . sugar syrup cooked to the thread stage, and then drawn out into long strands and shaped into nests and baskets, etc.

Steam . . . . to cook by steam rather than in boiling water; usually without pressure.

Steep . . . . to allow a substance to stand in liquid below the boiling point for extraction of flavor, color or other qualities, as tea.

Stir . . . . to mix food materials with a circular motion in order to blend them or produce a uniform consistency.

Stock . . . . liquid in which meat, fish and sometimes vegetables have been cooked.

Suet .... the firm, white fat of the loin and kidney regions of beef, highly prized for cooking.

Sundae .... ice cream served with a sweet sauce or fruit over it.

Tabasco .... a long, red, very hot pepper, used chiefly in sauces.

Table d'hôte .... a meal planned by the establishment and served for a set price. Frequently considerable choice is permitted.

Tamale .... a Mexican dish made of cornmeal, ground meat, chili, onions, garlic, etc., and cooked in oiled corn husks.

Tartar .... a sauce made of a base of mayonnaise with various additions, such as pickle relish, finely chopped onion, parsley, chives, capers, etc., and served with fish.

Timbale .... a delicate creamed or custard mixture baked in individual molds, usually containing fish, poultry or meat.

Toast .... to brown by means of direct heat or oven heat.

Torte .... strictly, a hard meringue baked in the form of a cake; loosely, any cake baked in a torte pan, especially one with a meringue topping baked on.

Tortilla .... a large, thin bread popular in Mexico, made of a corn meal paste shaped and baked on iron or earthenware plates; eaten alone and also used as the base of many Mexican dishes.

Tortoni .... a frozen dessert containing macaroon crumbs and chopped, blanched almonds; also called biscuit tortoni.

Toss .... to mix by lifting lightly and repeatedly, usually with a fork, or a fork and spoon.

Truffle .... a species of fungi similar to mushrooms which grow below the ground, chiefly in France; used principally for garnish and flavor.

Truss .... to fasten into position with skewers and twine, as a fowl.

Turbans .... fillets, usually of fish, rolled and skewered.

Turkish paste .... a confection made of a sweetened fruit juice stiffened with gelatin to a consistency that permits cutting it into squares for serving.

Velouté .... a rich white sauce made with chicken or veal broth.

Vinaigrette .... a sauce made of oil and vinegar and pickle relish.

Vol-au-vent .... large patties of puff paste made without a mold, and filled with meat, fish, poultry, preserves, etc.

Whip .... to beat vigorously with a rotary beater or wire whip so as to incorporate air.

XXXX sugar .... see Confectioners' sugar.

Zabaglione .... a delicate dessert consisting of beaten eggs sweetened and flavored with wine.

Casserole Suggestions

In today's modern living, "Casseroles" have taken on importance as BUDGET STRETCHERS, using left overs or inexpensive ingredients; as TIME SAVERS, the whole meal in the oven at one time; as CONVENIENCES, for many can be prepared in advance to feed the family or guests when mother is tired or busy or not at home. Even father can put a "Casserole" in the oven to get boiling hot through and toasty brown on top.

Cheese and Egg

Baked Macaroni and Cheese, 441, 442
Cheese and Shrimp Custard, 437
Cheese Egg Float, 437
Cheese Fondue, 437
Cheese Ham Bake, 445
Cheese Pudding Spanish Sauce, 438
Cheese Ring, 439
Cheese Souffle, 439
Egg and Asparagus au Gratin, 668
Egg Casserole, 683
Lasagne, 443
Quick Baked Macaroni and Cheese, 442
Souffles—celery, chicken, dried beef, mushroom, tuna, 679 to 681
Tomato Cheese Fondue, 441

Fish

Codfish Casserole, 714
Crabmeat Mornay, 717
Escalloped Oysters, 723
Fish Cobbler, 732
Fish Pudding, 711
Salmon and Macaroni Casserole, 730
Salmon and Rice Casserole, 731
Tuna and Noodle Casserole, 733, 734

Meat

Beef and Kidney Casserole, 820
Beef and Vegetable Pie, 816
Casserole Corned Pork Chops, 858
Dried Beef and Noodle Casserole, 834
Escalloped Potatoes and Frankfurters, 888
Fruited Spareribs, 861
Ham and Potato Casserole, 866
Ham and Sweet Potato Casserole, 867
Lamb Sausage Casserole, 844
Lamp Scallop, 852
Oven Braised Brisket of Beef, 809

Poor Man's Goose, 908
Pork and Rice Casserole, 870
Stuffed Spareribs, 862
Tamale Pie, 833
Veal Baked in Milk, 882

Poultry

Chicken Pie, 1052
Pigeon Pie, 1064

Vegetable

Asparagus and Egg Casserole, 1311
Baked Beans with Tomatoes, 1320
Baked Lima Beans, 1318
Baked Onions and Apples, 1359
Cabbage au Gratin, 1329
Carrot Souffle, 1334
Celery au Gratin, 1338
Cheese and Sweet Potato Casserole, 1387
Cucumbers au Gratin, 1345
Eggplant en Casserole, 1347
Escalloped Cabbage, 1330
Escalloped Carrots and Potatoes, 1335
Escalloped Corn and Cheese, 1342
Escalloped Onions, 1360
Escalloped Sweet Potatoes and Apples, 1387
Escalloped Tomatoes, 1404
Leek and Potato Casserole, 1355
Lima Bean Casserole, 1319
Navy Bean and Apple Casserole, 1320
Old Fashioned Baked Beans, 1321
Onions au Gratin, 1362
Pea and Potato Casserole, 1367
Quick Escalloped Potatoes, 1383
Sauer Kraut and Fish Casserole, 1392
Spinach Cheese Custard, 1396
Stuffed Mushrooms in Casserole, 1357
Stuffed Onions, 1363
Sweet Potato Apple Casserole, 1388
Yam Orange Casserole, 1389

Note: For Dessert Casseroles see Baked Puddings 617-624, Cobblers, 518-524, etc.

Index

Bold face page references will be found in **Volume I**
Light face page references will be found in this book, Volume II

A

À la King
  Chicken 1044
  Eggs 667
  Shrimp 728
  Turkey 1071
Acid-Alkaline effect of foods 6
Acidophilus milk 117
Air as a leavening agent 112
Alaska, Baked 610
Alewife, *cooking methods for* 691
Allegretti Frosting 383
Allemande Sauce 1250
Allemande Sauce, Broccoli with 1327
Alligator pears, *buying and care of* 86
Allspice, *description and uses* 128
Almond extract 133
  paste, *how made* 121
  Bacon Cheese Dip 199
  Chicken Sandwich Rolls 1217
  Crescents 473
  Soup, Cream of 1276
  Spritz Cookies 477
Almonds
  cups per pound 159, *how to blanch* 121
  Glazed 414
  Toasted 415
Ambrosia 571
American cheese 437
Anchovy Canapé Butter 187
Anemia 5, 31
Angel, *Standard method* 313
  Food Cake 315
  Pie 1025
Anise, *description, uses* 128
  extract 134
  Milk 223
Antelope 747
APPETIZERS 173–211
  easy to make 173, *how to garnish* 175–180, 191, *organize preparation* 174
  Canapés 181–186
    Avocado 181
    Baked Bean 181
    Caviar 182
    Caviar Biscuits 182
    Cheese Cone or Roll 182
    Cheese Trays 185
    Chicken Brazilian 182
    Crabmeat-Onion 183

    Cream Cheese Appetizer Roll 183
    Diplomat 183
    Nutty 184
    Poppy Seed Cheese Strips 184
    Roquefort 184
    Sardine 184
    Shrimp 184
    Smoked Turkey or Capon 185
    Tangy Chips 185
    Tomato-Cheese 185
    Tuna-Olive 185
  Canapé Butters or Spreads 186–188
    How to prepare 186
    Anchovy 187
    Cheese 187
    Chili 187
    Chives, Parsley or Mint 187
    Egg Yolk 187
    Garlic 187
    Horseradish 187
    Lemon 188
    Mustard 188
    Olive 188
    Piquant 188
    Shrimp, Lobster, or Crabmeat 188
  Canapé Fillings or Spreads 188–191
    Avocado 190
    Chicken or Calves' Liver 189
    Crabmeat Caper 189
    Crabmeat, Tuna or Lobster 189
    Cream Cheese Anchovy 188
    Cream Cheese Caviar 188
    Cream Cheese Tomato Nut 189
    Egg Salad 189
    Ham Chutney 189
    Ham-Olive 189
    Olive-Celery 190
    Pâté de Foie Gras 190
    Peanut Butter-Bacon 190
    Peanut Butter-India Relish 191
    Sardine 189
  Cocktails 191–198
    Beet 197
    Beet Juice 197
    Canned Juices and Nectars 192
    Clam Juice 195
    Clam and Tomato Juice 195
    Clams on Half Shell 194
    Cocktail Sauce 195
    Crabmeat 195
    Crabmeat Avocado 195

Appetizers: Cocktails—(Cont'd)
  Crabmeat-Grapefruit 196
  Cucumber 197
  Fresh Fruit Juices 192
  Fresh Winter Fruit 192
  Grapefruit Brazilian 193
  Grapefruit-Grape 193
  Grapefruit-Grape Juice 193
  Jiffy Fruit Cup 193
  Lobster 196
  Melon 193
  Melon-Plum 194
  Oysters on Half Shell 196
  Papaya 194
  Peach and Orange 194
  Pot Liquor 198
  Raspberry-Currant 194
  Sauerkraut Juice 198
  Shrimp 197
  Tomato Juice 198
  Yogurt-Tomato 198
Dips or Dunks 199–200
  Almond Bacon Cheese 199
  Clam Cheese 200
  Cream Cheese 200
  Deviled Ham 200
  Green Cream 200
Hors d'Oeuvres 201–211
  Apple Celery Kabobs 207
  Bacon 201
  Beets, Baby, Stuffed 208
  Blinis 205
  Braunschweiger Balls 211
  Caviar and how to serve 204
  Celery, Stuffed 208
    with Avocado 208
    with Cream Cheese 208
    with Roquefort or Blue 208
  Celery Root, Marinated 209
  Cervelat Dumbbells 211
  Cheese Balls, Fried 202
  Chicken Livers Broiled in Bacon 201
  Cottage Cheese Blends 203
    Blushing Lady 203
    Green Cheese 203
    Intrigue 203
    Spring Song 203
    Waldorf 204
  Croquettes, Cocktail 206
  Cucumbers, Stuffed 209
  Deviled Eggs 204
  Dills, Stuffed 209
  Dried Beef Whorls 202
  Egg Salad in Chips 204
  Grapes, Stuffed 207
  Herring, Pickled, De Luxe 206
  Leek-Cheese Appetizer Pie 209
  Lobster 206
  Mushrooms, Stuffed, Broiled 210
  Olives Broiled in Bacon 201
  Olives, Garlic 208

  Oysters Broiled in Bacon 202
  Oysters, Smoked 207
  Pecans or Walnut Cheese Stuffed 203
  Prunes Broiled in Bacon 202
  Radishes, Caviar Stuffed 210
  Salami, Tasty Sticks 211
  Sardine Spirals 207
  Sardine Surprises 207
  Shrimp Broiled in Bacon 202
  Tomatoes, Plum Stuffed 211
Shrubs, 198–199
  Cranberry 199
  Grape 199
  Orange 199
  Raspberry 199
Apple
  Corer 1420, nuggets, buying of 102, pie
    and Henry Ward Beecher 77, powder,
    quarters and rings 102
  and Blackberry Jelly 1087
  and Cranberry Salad, Banana 1135
  and Cranberry Sauce 557
  Betty, Brown 510
  Butter 1088
  Cake, Dutch 514, 515
  Casserole, Navy Bean and 1320
  Casserole, Sweet Potato 1388
  Celery Kabobs 207
  Charlotte 615
  Cheese Salad 1134
  Cinnamon, Salad 1136
  Coffee Cake, Hasty 290
  Crunch 512
  Dressing, Pot Roast of Veal 877
  Dumplings 540, 541
  Elderberry Jelly 1087
  Fritters 549
  Fromage, Onion and 1362
  Grape Salad, Cabbage, Celery 1175
  Grunt 513
  Jelly 1083
  Juice, canning 1080
  Milk Sherbet, Cranberry 605
  Pandowdy 513
  Peanut Salad 1134
  Pie 985
  Pie, Canned 987
  Pie, Dutch, or French 987
  Pie, Sour Cream 989
  Quince and Cranberry Jelly 1087
  Raisin Salad 1134
  Rutabaga and 1391
  Salad, Cabbage and 1174
  Salad, Cooked Cranberry 1162
  Salad, Cranberry 1162
  Sauce 556
  Sauce Cake 331
  Sauce Cookies 462
  Sauce, "Dressing Up" Canned 556
  Snow 649
  Soufflé Pie 986

Apple—(Cont'd)
  Soufflé Tarts 1019
  Streusel Coffee Cake, Quick 238
  Tapioca 638
  Turnip and Pascal Celery Salad 1135
  Turnovers 935
Applecot Sauce 557
Apples
  Ascorbic acid (vit. C), value 19, caloric
    value 11, care 89, definition of "quality"
    77, dried, buying 102, dried, cups per
    pound 157, for pie 97, buying 77, 89,
    97, in diet 5, serving 571, storage of 89
  Baked, No. 1, 2, 3 557, 558
  Chocolate Caramel 411
  Cinnamon 559
  Fried 559
  Honeyed, and Cranberries 563
  Onions and Baked 1359
  Pheasant with Sauerkraut and 771
  Poached 560
  Red Cabbage with 1331
  Sauerkraut with (Savory) 1393
  Scalloped 560
  Stewed 560
  Stewed, Dried 551
  Stuffed 559
  Sweet Potatoes and Scalloped 1387
Apricot juice, canning, freezing 1080
  Bavarian 577
  Canned, Pie 990
  Cottage Cheese Salad 1135
  Dried, Pie 990
  Dried, Purée 551
  Filling, for Bride's Cake 344
    for Fried Pies 989
    for Kolachy 284
  Fritters 549
  Glaze, for Fruit Cake 368
  Ice Cream 592
  Nectar 218
  Nut Bread 250
  Tarts 1019, 1020
  Upside Down Cake 362
  Whip 655
  Whip, Baked 652
Apricots
  Buying, care 89, 144, caloric value 11,
    dried, buying 102, dried, cups per pound
    157, in diet 5, vitamin, values 24, 26,
    28
  Dried Stewed 551
  Red Plums and Sugared Fresh 571
Arrowroot, 424
Artichokes
  Buying, care 79, in diet 4, as food for
    diabetics 1310
  French 1309
  Jerusalem, Buttered 1310
Ascorbic acid
  Daily allowance 8, 19, 20, effects of

cooking on, and story on 19, 20, values
    of foods (Table) 19, 20
Asparagus
  Buying, care 79, 142, caloric value of 11,
    cooking methods 1310, in diet 4, select-
    ing of 1310, vit. values of 20, 24, 26, 27
  au Gratin, Eggs and 668
  Buttered 1310
  Creamed 1310
  Egg Casserole 1311
  Fondue 1312
  Ham Luncheon Dish 1311
  in Egg Sauce 1312
  Newburg 1312
  on Toast, Creamed Eggs and 665
  Polonaise 1313
  Raw, Salad 1152
  Royale in Puff Shell 1313
  Sandwich, with Egg Sauce 1221
  Soup, Cream of 1276
  Toast Rolls 1313
  Vegetable Plate 1410
Aspic
  Avocado Ring 1160
  Chicken and Tongue in 1156
  Chicken Broth for 1157
  Cucumber, Salmon in 1159
  Grapefruit 1163
  Jelly, Stuffed Eggs in 1160
  Pineapple Cottage Cheese 1165
  Salad Sandwich Filling 1222
  Salad, Tomato 1171
  Tomato, Cottage Cheese in 1168
  Tomato, Creamy 1168
  Tomato, No. 1, 2 and 3 1170
  Tomato, Shrimp in 1160
Au Gratin Eggs and Asparagus 668
Avocado Aspic Ring 1160
  and Persimmon Salad, Grapefruit 1138
  Canapé Filling 190
  Canapés 181
  Chicken Soup 1286
  Cups, Strawberry 1143
  Ice Cream 593
  Mousse, 1161
  Salad Dressing 1197
  Sandwich, Lobster 1220
  Shrimp Tomato Salad 1184
Avocados
  Buying, care 89, caloric value 11, in diet
    5, niacin (nicotinic acid) value 26

                    B

Bacon
  Broiling 854, 201, caloric value of 11,
    in children's diet 36, slices per pound
    158
  and Egg Salad Sandwiches 1225
  and Egg Sauce, Spinach with 1398
  and Egg, Spinach with 1397

Bacon—(Cont'd)
  and Olives, for Appetizers 201
  and Tomato Grill, Sausage 872
  and Tomato Sandwiches, Lettuce 1224
  Baked and Broiled 854, 855
  Chicken Livers, Wrapped Broiled 1059
  Corn Meal Muffins 241
  for Vegetable Plate 1410
  Hors d'oeuvres 201
  Kale with 1351
  Lentils, with, Baked 1355
  Muffins 254
  Mustard Greens and Spinach 1352
  Omelet 676
  Onion Sauce, Turnip Greens with 1353
  Pan-Broiled 855
  Rings, Eggs, Baked in 664
  Sandwiches, Chopped Cabbage and 1223
  Sandwiches, Egg and 1227
  Sandwiches, Watercress and 1225
  Spinach with Cheese Sauce and 1398
  Spread, Peanut Butter and 1232
Baked Alaska 610
Baking Powder
  Action of 112, Biscuits, steps in making
    234, cake using different types 326,
    double-action 112, how to measure 160,
    measurement of 113, types of 112
Baking Soda, use 114
Balls, Fish 711
Balm, description, uses 128
Baltimore (see Lady, Lord)
Banana
  flakes, powder, buying 102
  and Cream 572
  and Jelly Spread, Peanut Butter 1232
  Apple and Cranberry Salad 1135
  Bread, 250
  Coconut Cream for 572
  Cream Pie 958
  Doughnuts 288
  Fritters 549
  Fruit Cake 369
  Grape Mold 588
  Marshmallow and Nut Salad 1135
  Nut Cake 332
  Salad 1136
  Sandwiches, Ham and 1233
  Shake 220
  Waffles 260
Bananas
  Ascorbic acid (vit. C) value of 20, buying
    and care of 90, 143, caloric value of 11,
    in diet 5
  Baked 561
  Baked in Cranberry Sauce 561
  Sauté 561
Banbury Tarts 1020
Barbecue Sauce 1250
  Fine Herbs 1251

Lime 1251
  Mint, for Lamb 841
Barbecued
  Chicken 1038
  Frankfurters 887
  Lamb Riblets 843
  Spareribs 860
  Veal Balls 885
  Venison Tenderloin 750
Bar le duc 1090
Barley
  Care of 152, flour 109
  Lamb Broth, with 1292
Barracuda, cooking methods 691
Basil, sweet 128
Bass, cooking methods 692, 693
Bavarian 577–583
Bay Leaves 128
Bean, Black, Soup 1271
  Navy Soup 1271, 1272
Bean pots, casseroles 1421
Bean Sprout Salad 1145
Beans, Baked
  and Sauerkraut Salad Hot 1126
  Canapés 181
  in Tomato Cups 1319
  Old-Fashioned 1321
  Peppy Sandwiches 1224
  Sandwiches 1222
  Swedish Brown 1323
  with Tomatoes 1320
Beans, Dried
  Caloric value of 11, cups per pound 158,
    protein value of 15, vit. values of 24, 26
Beans, Green (String or Snap)
  Buying 80, caloric value 11, care 142,
    cooking method 1307, in diet 4, selecting
    and storing 1314, vitamin values 1314
  and Celery Salad 1148
  au Gratin 1315
  Buttered 1314
  Cooked in cream sauce 1314
  Creamed 1314
  for Vegetable Plate 1410
  Harvard 1322
  in Egg Sauce 1316
  Pickles, Dill 1102
  Puff 1315
  Salad 1149
  Savory 1315
  with Dill Sauce 1322
Beans, Kidney
  Vitamin values 22, 24, 26
  Buttered 1316
  Casserole, Beef and 820
  Loaf 1316
  Pot, Beef 820
  Salad, No. 1, No. 2 1150
  Sandwich Filling 1223
  Soup 1291
  Tomato stuffed with 1193

Beans, Kidney—(Cont'd)
  with Onions 1317
  with Salt Pork 1317
Beans, Lima
  Buying, care 79, in diet 79, selecting
    1317
  and Carrot Soup, Cream of 1280
  Baked 1318
  Buttered Dried 1318
  Buttered Frozen 1318
  Buttered New 1319
  Casserole 1319
  Chowder 1270
Beans, Miscellaneous
  and Rice, red 1323
  Pinto 1323
Beans, Navy
  Thiamine (vit. B₁) value 22
  and Apple Casserole 1320
  Boiled 1320
  Pot Dinner Sauerkraut and 1392
  Salad, hot 1128, 1129
  Soup, No. 1 and 2 1271, 1272
  Soup, Cream of 1281
  Soup, Creole 1269
  Stew 1321
Beans, Soy
  Vitamin value 24
  Soup 1274
Beans, Wax
  Cooking methods 1307
  Chilied 1321
  Creole 1322
  Harvard 1322
  with Dill Sauce 1322
Bear
  Removing glands 747, 748
  Bear Loin Steaks 747
Beaver Meat
  Qualities of 748, removing glands 747
  Roast 748, 749
Bechamel Sauce 1251
Beef 800–838
  General directions 791–796, buying hints
    Rib Roast 805, Pot Roast 807, ground
    820, simmered 816, caloric value 11,
    cooking of 801, cuts 801, 806, servings
    per pound 158, U.S. government grades
    790, time table for braising 806, broiling
    800, ground 800, roasting 804, vitamin
    values 21, 23, 25
  and Green Pepper Tomato 816
  and Kidney Bean Casserole 820
  Bean Pot 820
  "Boiled" and Noodles 818
  Bouillon 1286
  Braised Beef Balls 821
  Braised Brisket with Sweet-Sour Gravy
    809
  Braised Flank Steak with Vegetables 813
  Bubble and Squeak 835

Cantonese (note) 816
Cheese Meat Loaf 830
Cheeseburgers, Piquant 821
Chili Con Carne Western Style 822
Chili Con Carne with 822
Chili Mac 823
Chili Sauce-Meringue Meat Loaf 823
Corned and Cabbage 819
Corned Beef, "Boiled" Dinner 819
Creamed Eggs and Dried, on Toast 834
Diced Meat Roast 805
Dried 834
Dried, and Noodle Casserole 834
Dried, Creamed 834
Dried, Pinwheels 202
Frizzled Dried 835
Goulash 837
Green Tomato Stew 819
Ground in Gravy 823
Hamburger and Corn Pie 826
Hamburger, Broiled on a Bun 823
Hamburger, Noodle Casserole 825
Hamburger Patties 825
Hamburger Picnic 826
Hamburger Rolls with Tomatoes 826
Hamburger with varied flavors 825
Hamburgers Barbecued 824
Hamburgers Big and Half Size 825
Hash No. 1 and 2 835, 836
Italian Rice 827
Italian Spaghetti with Meat Balls 828
Jambalaya 828
Leftovers 835
Lemon Tanged Meat Balls or Patties 829
Meat Balls with Sauerkraut 838
Meat Loaf 829, 830
Noodle Soup 1286
Odds and Ends Spaghetti Sauce 832
Old-Fashioned Hash 836
Oven Braised Brisket of Beef 809
Pan-Fried Ground Beef Patties 831
Pepper Steak 813
Pinwheels with Mushroom Sauce 836
Pot Roast 806
Pot Roast, Spanish Style 807
Pot Roast with Macédoine of Vegetables
  807
Pot Roast with Vegetables, 807
Quick Spaghetti 831
Rib Roasts of 803 804
Rich Brown Beef Stew 818
Rolled Steak 809
Roulades—(Stuffed Beef Rolls) 810
Round Steak Birds 810
Salisbury Steak 832
Sauerbraten, No. 1 and 2 811
Short Ribs and Yorkshire Pudding 812
Short Ribs Pot Roast 812
Slices in Onion Sauce 808
Steak Short Cake 833
Steak with Spanish Sauce 814

Beef—(Cont'd)
  Stew 817
  Stroganoff 808
  Stuffed Cabbage Roll 832
  Stuffed Flank Steak Roll 814
  Swiss Steak, No. 1 and 2 815
  Tamale Pie 833
  Tomato-Macaroni Medley 821
  Turnovers 837
  Upside-down Meat Loaves 829
  Vegetable Pie 816
  Vegetable Soup 1287
Beet, and beet greens
  and Green Onion Salad 1146
  and Pea Salad 1146
  Borsch 1264
  Borsch, Cold 1266, 1267
  Cheese and Onion Salad 1146
  Cocktail 197
  Juice Cocktail 197
  Mayonnaise 1203
  Pickled, Salad 1152
  Pickles 1100
  Raw, and Cucumber Salad 1179
  Relish 1174
  Salad, Molded 1168
  Soup, Cream of 1277
  Tomato Soup 1300
Beets
  *Buying and care 77, 143, caloric value
  of 11, cooking methods 1307, tops 143,
  stems 1324, in diet 4*
  Buttered 1324
  de Luxe 1324
  Harvard 1325
  in Horseradish Sauce 1324
  in Orange Sauce 1325
  Pickled and Onions 1152
  Polish 1326
  Quick Cooked, Cubed 1326
  Ruby Red 1326
  Stuffed, baby 208
  Vegetable Plate 1410
  with Sour Sauce 1325
Benedictine, Eggs 673
Beriberi 22
Bermuda Salad 1174
Berries
  Care and washing of 143, serving of 570
  and Cream Pie 969
  Canned, Pie 991
  Jelly 1080
  Sugared 572
Betty, Brown
  Discussion of 510
  Apple 510
  Plum 511
  Rhubarb Fig Bar 511
BEVERAGES 212–231
Beverage juices 1078
Big Wig's Salad 1147

Binding, eggs for 661
Biscuit Tortoni 601
Biscuits, Biscuit Dough 234–239
  Reheating 235
  Baking Powder, *steps in making* 234
  Buttermilk 236
  Butterscotch Pinwheels 237
  Cheese 236
  Drop 236
  Orange Pinwheels 237
  Sandwich, Square Meal 1219
  Turnovers, Turkey 1071
  Whole Wheat 237
Bismarcks 289
Bisque
  Oyster 1284
  Salmon 1285
  Sea Food 1299
Black Bean Soup 1271
Black Bottom Pie 940
Black Crow Ice Cream Soda 221
Blackberries
  *Buying and care 90, 143, caloric value
  11, in diet 5*
  Cobbler 519
  Dumplings 543
  Jelly 1087
  Jelly, Apple and 1087
  Juice 1080
  Pie 991
  Salad, Cantaloupe and 1136
  Sally Lunn 515
  Stewed 562
Blanc Mange 625
  Caramel 625
  Chocolate 626
  Cinnamon 626
  Puddings and 625, 628
Blanquette of Veal 876
Blinis 205
Blitz Torte 375
Blueberries
  Buying and care 90
  Buckle 517
  Ice-Box Pudding 630
  Muffins, or Other Fruit 254
  Pie 992, 993, 994
Blue Cheese 448
Blue Cheese Dressing 1197, 1198
Bluefish, *baking* 698, *cooking methods* 691
Blue runner, *cooking methods* 691
Blue vein cheese 448
Bohemian
  Rye Bread 301
  Split Pea Soup 1287
Boiled Dinner with Ham Hocks 859
Boiled Salad Dressing No. 1 and 2 1198
Bologna
  *Caloric value 11, care 146, vitamin values
  21, 23, 25*
  Boiled 886

Bologna—(*Cont'd*)
Cups, Grilled 886
French Toast Sandwiches 1226
Roast 886
Sandwich Spread 1226
Bon Bon Centers 404
Borage, *description, uses* 128
Borsch, Beet 1264, Cold 1266, 1267
Boston
Brown Bread 253
Cream Pie 322, 332
Bouillabaisse 1265
Bouillon, *caloric value of* 11
Beef 1286
Hot Tomato 1290
Jellied Tomato 1291
Boys, *dietary needs* 8
Boysenberries, *buying, care* 90
Jelly, Juice 1080
Braided Rolls 274
Brain Fritters 893
Brains
Discussion, cooking methods 890, 891,
refrigeration 153
A la Newburg 892
Scrambled No. 1 and 2 894
Braised Oxtails 911
Braising
Beef 805, 806
Vegetables 1308
Bran
Thiamine (vit. B₁), value of 22
Muffins 255
Brandy Sauce 1238
Crème Sauce 1238
Snaps 487
Braunschweiger Balls 211
Brazil nuts
Caloric value 12, *cups per pound* 159
BREAD 212–231
Boards 1420, *box* 1420, *caloric value* 11,
care 150, *crumbs, buttering* 162, *care*
151, *enriched* 233, *flour and corn meal*
233, *in children's diet* 36, *in diet* 3
and 5, *knife* 1422, *pans* 1420, *reheating*
166, 235, *shaping loaves* 271, *vitamin*
values 22, 24, 25, *stale, use of* 168,
yeast, steps in making 270
and Butter Pickles 1101
and Butter Sandwiches 1231
Apricot Nut 250
Banana 250
Basic White 269
Boston Brown 253
Cases 263
Cinnamon Whirl 295
Crumb Griddle Cakes 246
Crumb Pie Pastry 930
Crusty French 267
Currant Oatmeal 298
Date-Nut 250

Dressing 753, 1073
Garlic 295
Herb 296
Nut 251, 296
Oatmeal 297
Old-Time Molasses 251
Orange Nut 252
Peanut Butter (Buttermilk) 252
Prune or Raisin 298
Prune Nut 252
Pudding, Cocoa 538
Pudding, Lemon Grape-Nut 539
Pudding, Orange Marmalade 539
Puddings 536
Pumpernickel 299
Pumpkin or Squash 298
Quick Yeast 300
Rye 301
Squash 298
Sticks 268
Stuffing, for Turkey 1072
Swedish Limpa 300
Whole Wheat Bread, 50% 302
Whole Wheat Bread, 100% 302
Breads, Quick and Yeast 232
Breakfast *of school child* 34
Rice Cakes 247
Brick cheese 448
Bride's Cake 341
Brie cheese 448
Brioche 303, 304
Brisket, Braised, Sweet-Sour Gravy 809
Brittle, Peanut 413
Broccoli
Buying care 80, *caloric value* 12, *cooking*
methods 1307, *in diet* 4, *vitamin values*
20, 24, 26, 27
Buttered 1326
Noodle Platter 1327
Polonaise 1327
Soup, Cream of 1277
Vegetable Plate 1410
with Allemande Sauce 1327
Broiler 1420
Broiling 800, 840, 854
Broth
Chicken with Rice 1288
for Aspic 1157
Lamb 1291
Rich Chicken 1289
Scotch 1296
Brown Sauce 1252
Sugar Custard 527
Sugar Syrup 1238
Brownies 457
Butterscotch or Blond 457
Cocoa 457
Peppermint Cream 460
Brulée, Crème 530, 531
Brunswick Stew 1039

Brussels Sprouts
Ascorbic acid (vit. C) value 20, *buying,
care* 80, *caloric value* 12, *in diet* 4
Buttered 1328
Creamed 1328
Rich-Tasty 1328
Buckle, Blueberry 517
Buckwheat flour 110
Cakes, Grandma's Yeast 305
Budget, *for food* 72
Buffalofish, *cooking methods* 693
Buffet meals, *discussion, service, vol. 1, xxv
menu, No. 1 and 2, vol. 1, xxvii*
Bulk foods, *use in body* 6
Bullhead, *cooking methods* 693
Bunny Salad 1121
Buns
Hot Cross 283
Pineapple Butter 286
Burnet, *description, uses* 128
Burnt Sugar
Cake 333
French Butter Cream Frosting 391
Syrup or Caramel 643
Butter
Alternate for 5, *caloric value* 12, *care*
106, 148, *cream* 119, *cups per pound*
157, *elaborations* 161, *federal standard*
106, *how made* 106, *how to measure*
160, *in diet* 3, 5, 36, *"sweet"* 107, *vita-
min A value* 28
Apple 1088
Cakes 322
Cookies, Delicate 488
Cream, Peppermint 461
Frosting 380
Frostings, *how to make shiny* 381
Icing, Thin 395
Lemon Sauce 1257
Nut Frosting 383
Peach 1088
Plum 1089
Sponge Layer Cake 316
Butterfish, *cooking methods* 691
Butterfly Rolls 274
Orange 285
Butterhorn Rolls 274
Buttermilk
Caloric value 12, *types* 116
Biscuits 236
Cake 353
Corn Bread 240
Doughnuts 288
Dumplings, Rolled 245
Fruit 224
Grape 225
Griddle Cakes 247
Jelly, Orange 590
Peppermint 226
Pineapple 226
Raisin Pie 959

Rolls 277
Sauce for Spring Vegetables 1410
Sherbert, Pineapple 606
Tomato 227
Waffles 260
White Cupcakes 359
Butter Nutties 474
Butters 1087
Butterscotch
Brownies 457
Cream, Tapioca 639
Custard 527
Ice Cream 594
Patties 412
Pic 959
Pinwheels 237
Sauce 642
Sugar Cookies 486
Buying 70–139

C

Cabbage
Ascorbic acid (vit. C) value 20, *buying,
care* 78, 141, *caloric value* 12, *celery,
buying, care* 79, *Chinese, buying, care*
79, *cooking methods* 1307, *in diet* 4
and Apple Salad 1174
and Celery Salad, Shredded 1180
and Dill Chowder 1266
and Pineapple Molded Salad 1169
au Gratin 1329
Braised 1329
Buttered 1329
Carrot and Raisin Salad 1174
Celery, Apple and Grape Salad 1175
Chopped, and Bacon Sandwiches 1223
Corned Beef and 819
Creamed 1329
Creamed, Liver Sausage and 907
Creamed Sausage Meat with 1330
for Vegetable Plate 1410
Fried 1329, 1331
in Raisin Sauce 1330
New, with Tomatoes 1331
Pineapple and Marshmallow Salad 1175
Red, Salad 1179
Red, with Apples 1331
Red, with Braised Wild Duck 756
Rice Soup 1287
Salad, Carrot and 1176
Salad, Variations 1175
Scalloped 1330
Soup, Russian Red 1296
Soup, Tomato and 1275
Stuffed Roll 832
Cacciatore, Chicken 1045
Cacio Cavallo Cheese 450
CAKE 308–399
Causes for angel or sponge failure 315,
baking at high altitude 309, *how to use*

Cake—(Cont'd)
baking powder 326, caloric value of 12, care, freezing and storing 329, causes of butter type failure 324, 325, cooling 328, covers 1420, factors of success 308, flour 110, 310, flour sifting 313, facts on making and serving, decorating, storing and glazing of fruit cakes 364–368, knife and rack 1422, 1421, leavenings 311, liquids in baking 311, preparing pans 312, placing in oven 315, 328, shortening and sugar 310, why function and quality ingredients, equipment at hand, and accurate measurement are important 310–312
Angel and Sponge Cakes, True 313, 314
Angel Food 315
Apple Sauce 331
Apricot Glaze for Fruit 368
Apricot Upside-Down 362
Banana Fruit 369
Banana-Nut Layer 332
Banana-Vanilla Wafer Refrigerator 372
Blitz Torte 375
Blue Ribbon Fruit 369
Boston Cream Pie 322, 332
Bride's—4 Tier 341
Burnt Sugar 333
Butter 322
    Old-time creaming and electric mixer methods 322, 323, making and baking 326–329
Buttermilk 353
Butter Sponge Layer 316
Cheese 378–380
Cheese Refrigerator, No. 1, No. 2 373
Cherry Chocolate 349
Chocolate 338–340
Chocolate Cream Sponge Roll 317
Chocolate, extra special dark 339
Chocolate Loaf 352
Chocolate Marble 349
Chocolate Refrigerator 374
Cocoa 338
Corn Syrup for Fruit Cake 368
Cottage Cheese 378
Cream Cheese 379
Crumb 334
Cupcakes 356–360
Currant Loaf 352
Cutting the Bride's Cake 343
Daffodil 318
Dark Chocolate 339
Dark Fruit 371
Devil's Food 339, 350
Dobos Torte 376
Dolly Varden 334
Double Orange 335
Egg Yolk 346–351
Fillings 397

Fresh Coconut 350
Frostings 380–391
Fruit 364–371
Fruit Refrigerator 374
Gingerbread 360, 361
Gingerbread-Pear Upside-Down 362
Gold Loaf 346
Gold Spot Angel Food 318
Golden Gate 347, 348
Graham Cracker 336
Graham Cracker Torte 377
Groom's 370
Hickorynut 344
Holiday Light Fruit 370
Honey 330
Icings 392
Jelly Roll 319
Lady Baltimore 344
Lemon Ice Box 375
Lemon Jelly Roll 319
Loaf 352–356
Lord Baltimore 348
Maraschino Cherry 336
Marble Spice 354
Moss Rose 319
No-Bake Fruit 371
Peanut Butter 337
Petits Fours, No. 1 and No. 2 344, 345
Pineapple Crush Upside-Down 363
Pineapple Wheel Upside-Down 363
Pound 355
Quick-Mix—One Bowl 348
Quick-Mix Sponge 320
Red Devil's Food 339
Refrigerator or Icebox 372–375
Schaum Torte 378
Silver White 351
Silver White Loaf 355
Sour Cream 337
Sour Cream Cheese 380
Spicy Splendor 338
Sponge-type 315–322
Standard Sponge 321
Stuffed Angel Food—Chocolate 372
Sunshine 321
Toppings 380–397
Tortes 375–378
Upside-Down 362–364
Washington Pic 322, 332
Whipped Cream 346
Whipped Cream Sponge Loaf 322
White Cakes 340–346
    3 or 4 Egg with Buttermilk 341
    3 or 4 Egg with Sweet Milk 340
Yellow Cakes 326, 338
    2 or 3 Egg with Buttermilk 330
    2 or 3 Egg with Sweet Milk 326, 329
Cakes, Miscellaneous
Fish 709, 710
Griddle or Pancakes 246

Calamondin
　Glamour Tarts 1020
　Pie 948
Calcium and iron
　Values of foods, Table 29–30, *daily allowance* 29–30, *grams, daily allowances* 8, *in enriched bread and flour* 233, *in fish* 687, *other sources* 30, *functions of phosphorus, iron, copper, iodine* 31, *use in body* 16–18, *value of milk and milk products* 29
Caloric Table 11–14
　Calories, daily allowances 8, *in diet* 10
Cambric Tea 230
Camembert Cheese 448
Camomile Tea 230
Canapes (see Appetizers) 181–186
　Butters and Spreads for 186, 187, 188
　Fillings for 188–191
Candied
　Coconut Sweet Potatoes 1386
　Squash, Ten Minute 1401
　Sweet Potatoes 1386
Candle Salad 1122
CANDY 400–419
　Cooking temperatures, table 402, *Hints on making* 401, *in the diet* 400, *nutritive values of* 400, *storage of* 402, *tests, cold water* 402, *thermometer* 402
　Beaten 403–409
　Butterscotch Patties 412
　Candied Apples 409
　Candied Puff Balls 412
　Caramel Popcorn 413
　Chocolate Caramels 416
　Chocolate Clusters 414
　Chocolate Creams, Quick 419
　Chocolate Dipping 408
　Chocolate Fudge 403
　Coconut Kisses, baked 418
　Cream Mints, Uncooked 419
　Creamy Caramels 415
　Divinity 403
　Fondant 404
　Fruit 409–411
　Fruit Nut Caramels 416
　Fruit Roll, Candied 411
　Glazed Almonds 414
　Hard and Brittles 412–415
　Honey Taffy 416
　Mexican Orange 405
　Nougat 406
　Nut 414–415
　Nut Caramels 416
　Oatmeal Toffee 412
　Old English Nut Toffee 413
　Orange-Coconut Creams 406
　Orange or Grapefruit Peel, Candied 410
　Panocha 407
　Peanut Brittle 413
　Peanut Butter Pinwheels 418

Popcorn Balls 414
Potato Kisses 418
Poured 415, 416
Pulled 416–418
Pralines 407
Quick and Uncooked 418
Salt Water Taffy 417
Sea Foam 407
Taffy (Swedish style) 417
Toasted Almonds 415
Toasting Coconut 415
Canning, *extracted juices* 1079
Cans
　Contents and sizes 137, *openers* 1421, *tin, kinds of* 136, *various foods and weights* 137
Cantaloupe
　Caloric value 12, *care, buying* 93, 573, *in diet* 5, *vitamin values* 20, 22, 28
　and Blackberry Salad 1136
　Balls and Cherry Salad 1136
　for Dessert 573
　Pickles 1100
Capers 128
Capon 1035
Caramel
　Apples, Chocolate 411
　Blanc Mange 625
　Chocolate 416
　Creamy 415
　Custard 528
　Eggnog 227
　Fruit Nut 416
　Hot, Milk Shake 225
　Mousse 608
　Nut 416
　Popcorn 413
　Sauce 642, 1239
　Syrup 643
Caraway 128
　Potato Salad with Sour Cream 1189
　Sauce, Potatoes in 1382
　Seed, Baked Pork Chops with, 856
Carbohydrates, *use of in body* 5
Cardamon seed 128
　Coffee cake, Sweet Roll Dough 279
Carp 693, 697, 698
Carrot
　Nut Sandwiches, Cottage Cheese and, 1211
　Peanut Salad, 1176
　Pudding, Baked 616
　Raisin Salad, Cabbage 1174
　Raisin Spread 1222
　Ring, 1334
　Salad, Turnip, Hot 1132
　Sauce, 1252
　Soufflé 1334
　Soup, Cream of 1278
　Soup, Lima Bean and Cream of 1280

Carrot (*Cont'd*)
  Soup, Potato 1272
  Sticks 162
Carrots
  Buying, storage 81, 1333, *caloric value
  12, care* 81, 143, *cooking methods* 1307,
  in diet 4, *vitamin A, value* 27
  and Cabbage Salad 1176
  and Celery, Creamed 1334
  and Spinach, Creamed 1335
  Buttered 1333
Carrot Butter 1222
  Coconut Salad 1176
  Cream Cheese Finger Sandwiches 1211
  Creamed 1334
  Cutlets 1333
  for Vegetable Plate 1410
  Glazed 1336
  Minted 1336
  Potatoes, Escalloped 1335
Carving
  Care of Carving Set 913, *set* 912, *steel
  and how to use it* 913
  Directions for Carving:
    Baked Whole Ham 918
    Brisket 920
    Crown Roast 915
    Ham, half 920
    Ham Slice, center 919
    Lamb, Roast Leg of 917
    Lamb Shoulder 920
    Picnic Ham 920
    Pork Loin Roast 917
    Porterhouse Steak 916
    Pot Roast, blade 915
    Rib Roast, rolled 914
    Rib Roast, standing 913
    Tongue 920
    Turkey and Chicken 1075, 1076, 1077
Cash and carry service 71
Cashew nuts
  Caloric value, weight 12, 159
CASSEROLE SUGGESTIONS 1442
Casseroles 1421
Cassia, *uses*, 128, 129
  Bud Pickles 1101
Catchup 1105
  Uncooked Tomato 1110
Catfish, *cleaning and cooking* 696
Cauliflower
  Buying and care of 81, *caloric value of*
  12, *in diet* 4, *vitamin values* 20, 22, 24
  Buttered 1336
  Creamed 1337
  for Vegetable Plate 1410
  French-Fried 1337
  in Dried Beef Cheese Sauce 1337
  Luncheon Salad 1184
  Salad 1147
  Salad, Hot 1127

Soup, Cream of 1278
  with Corn Flake Topping 1337
Caviar, *how to serve* 204
  Biscuits 182
  Canapés 182
  Stuffed Radishes 210
Cayenne pepper, *uses* 129
Celeriac, *buying, care* 81
  Cheese-Crusted 1339
  Marinated 209
Celery
  Buying, care 81, 141, *caloric value* 12,
  cooking methods 1307, *in diet* 4, *salt,
  seed, description, uses* 129
  Apple and Grape Salad, Cabbage 1175
  au Gratin 1338
  Braised 1338
  Buttered 1338
  Cabbage Salad 1147
  Cabbage Salad, Hot 1127
  Carrots and Creamed 1334
  Creamed 1340
  Cucumber Pickles 1101
  for Vegetable Plate 1410
  Pascal Salad, Apple Turnip and 1135
  Root and Lemon Sauté 1339
  Root, Cheese-Crusted 1339
  Root, Marinated 209
  Root Salad, Hot 1127
  Root with Hollandaise 1339
  Salad, Cabbage, Shredded 1180
  Salad, Green Bean and 1148
  Sauce 1252
  Seed Fruit Dressing 1199
  Soufflé 679
  Soup, Cream of 1278
  Stuffed 208
  Stuffed Spareribs 861
  Stuffed with Cheese 1148
  Stuffing 1072
Cereal, in children's diet 34
CEREALS 420–434
  Caloric value 12, *care* 152, "*enriched*"
  420, *General methods and direction for
  cooking* 426, 427, "*restored*" 420, *serv-
  ing suggestions* 428, *units per pound*
  157, *vitamin, values* 22, 24, 25
Cereals, breakfast 424
  How made 420, *in diet* 3, 5, *nutritive
  values* 420, *ready-to-eat* 421, 425, *served
  with fruit* 425, *uncooked* 421
Chard
  Ascorbic acid (*vit. C*) *value* 20, *buying,
  care* 83, *in diet* 4
  Swiss, Buttered 1340
Charlotte Russe 578
Charts, See List Page v Vol. 1
Chayote, Buttered 1340
Checkerboard or Ribbon Cookies
  Checkerboard Cookies 480
  Cherry Chews 481

Checkerboard or Ribbon Cookies—(Cont'd)
  Orange Cookies made with poultry fat
  483, 487
Checkerboard Sandwiches 1212
CHEESE 435–453
  *As an alternate 4, answers to questions
  about 448, 453, caloric value 12, care
  148, cheddar 449, cooking of 436, cups
  per pound 157, equivalent of milk 4,
  history of 435, in diet pattern 3, in-
  formation on 47 varieties 448, 453,
  nutritive value 435, protein value 14,
  scientific making 436, sources 435, vita-
  min values 23, 28*
Cheese Cake
  Cottage 378
  Cream 379
  Refrigerator No. 1 and No. 2 373
  Sour Cream 380
Cheese, Cottage
  and Carrot Nut Sandwiches 1211
  and Honey 610
  Blends—Appetizers 203, 204
  Cookies 488
  Filling 285
  in Tomato Aspic 1168
  Kuchen 291
  Orange Custard Pie 973
  Peach Prune Salad 1139
  Pie, Pineapple 976
  Rennet Custard 612
  Salad, Apricot 1135
  Salad No. 1 and No. 2 1181, 1182
  Salad, Pineapple and 1141
  Salad, Red Raspberry and 1143
  Sandwich, Date 1211
Cheese, Cream
  Anchovy fillings—Canapés 188
  and Lettuce Salad, Date 1136
  Appetizer Roll 183
  Carrot Finger Sandwiches 1211
  Caviar Filling—Canapés 188
  Date Salad, Frozen 1124
  Dip 200
  Frosting, Chocolate 384
  Fruit Dressing 1199
  Sauce for Vegetables 1253
  Tarts, Vienna 494
  Tomato-Nut Filling—Canapés 189
Cheese Dishes, Baked
  and Shrimp Custard 437
  Biscuits 236
  Corn and Escalloped 1342
  Egg Float 437
  Fondue 437
  Ham Bake 445
  Lasagne 443
  Macaroni, Baked 441, 442
  Macaroni Loaf 442
  Pizza 440
  Pudding Spanish Sauce 438

Puffs, Potato 1380
  Quick Baked Macaroni with 442
  Rice Loaf Mushroom Sauce 438
  Ring 439
  Soufflé 439
  Timbales 1301
  Tomato Fondue 441
Cheese, Miscellaneous
  Butter—Canapés 187
  Celery Stuffed with 1148
  Chicken de Luxe 445
  Cone or roll—Canapés 182
  Creamed Potatoes with 1375
  Croquettes, Hominy 502
  Croquettes, Rice and 503
  Jiffy Noodles 443
  Noodles and Creamed Spinach on 1394
  Omelet 676
  Onion Salad, Beet 1146
  Pastry 929
  Pimiento 447
  Puffs 1233
  Pumpkins 436
  Quick Macaroni Meal 444
  Rabbit, Corn and 446
  Raisin Sandwich Filling 1210
  Ring Salad, Green Pepper and 1150
  Salad, Apple 1134
  Salad, Pea and, Stuffed Tomato 1182
  Sandwiches 1210
  Sandwiches, Olive 1212
  Sandwiches, Skillet 1212
  Sandwiches, Toasted 1212
  Soup, Quick Rutabaga 1295
  Spoon Bread with 243
  Spread, Ham and 1228
  Sweet Potato Casserole 1387
  Toasties 446
  Tomato Rabbit 447
  Tomato Sandwich Spread 446
  Tomato Sandwiches 1233
  Tomato Vegetable Stuffed Salad 1181
  Trays 185
  Welsh Rabbit 447
Cheese Sauce and variations 444, 1253
  Basic 444
  Boiled Green Onions in 1360
  Dried Beef, Cauliflower in 1337
  Egg Plant and Onion with 1346
  Fennel with 1349
  for Vegetable Plate 1410
  Kohlrabi with 1353
  Smoky 1253
Cheeseburgers Piquant 821
Cherries, Cherry
  *Caloric value 12, care, buying 91, in diet
  5, vitamin values 20, 28*
  Citron Cookies 479
  Cobbler 520
  Coffee Cake, Hasty 291
  Dumplings 543

Cherries, Cherry—(Cont'd)
Jelly and Juice 1081
Maraschino, Soda 222
Marlow 606
Pie, Mock—Cranberry 998
Pies 995, 996, 997
Preserves 1091
Pudding, Upside-Down 616
Salad, Cantaloupe Balls and 1136
Salad, Jellied 1161
Sauce, Egg Pancakes with 563
Sour, Jelly 1086
Stewed 562
Sugared Fresh 573
Tarts 1021
Chervil 129
Cheshire cheese 449
Chess Pie 970, 971
Pielets 1021
Chestnut Squash Soup 1288
Chestnut Stuffing 1072
Chestnuts
Cups per pound 159, to prepare 122
Chick Pea Soup 1300
Chicken (also see Poultry)
Buying guide 1035, caloric value 12,
characteristics and cooking of broilers,
capons, fowl, fryers, pullets, roasters
1035, pieces for frying 1040, fryers and
Dutch ovens 1421, how to carve 1075,
1076, 1077, time table for roasting 1044,
roasting pan 1043, servings per bird 159,
vitamin values 21, 23
à la King 1044
Almond, Sandwich Rolls 1217
Aspic 1156
Aspic, Chicken Broth for 1157
Baked in Stuffing 1036
Barbecued 1038
Barley Soup 1289
Braised 1038
Brazilian Pinwheel Canapés 182
Broiled 1037
Broth
with Rice 1288
for Aspic Salads 1157
Brunswick Stew 1039
Cacciatore 1045
Caruso 1046
Chop Suey 1046
Cranberry Sandwich Loaf 1214
Creamed, in Baked Squash 889
Croquettes 507, 1047
Crunchy Coated 1042
Curry 1047
De-Luxe, Cheese 445
Dressing with Old-Time Roast 1043
Filled Pancakes with Tomato Sauce 1052
Fluffy Dressing for 1073
Fricassee 1038, 1048
Fried 1039, 1040, 1041

in Gravy 1049
Legs, Mock 870
Loaf with Mushroom Sauce 1049, 1050
Marguerite 1050
Moravian 1057
Mousse with Supreme Sauce 1051
Mulligan 1051
Newburg Soup 1299
Okra Gumbo 1045
Oysters, Creamed 1057
Pie and Pot Pie 1052, 1053
Pollo Con Arros 1053
Risotto Milanaise 1054
Roast, and Old-Time 1042, 1043
Salad 1185
Salad, Molded with Cranberry Jelly 1157
Salad, Old-Fashioned 1058
Sandwich, Fancy Hot 1214
Shortcake 1054
Soup 1289
Soup, Avocado 1286
Sour Cream Fricassee 1055
Steamed and Stewed 1041, 1042
Stew, Southern 1059
Stewed, and Dumplings 1044
Stretch 1055
Sweetbread Salad 1185
Terrapin 1055
Timbales 1301
Tomatoes, Sautéed, with Mushroom
Sauce 1058
Tongue and, in Aspic 1156
Winchell 1056
Chicken Livers
Bacon Wrapped Broiled 201, 1059
Canapé filling 189
Curry 1060
Fried 1060
Mushrooms 1061
Sauté with Lemon Sauce 1060
Chicory in Coffee 213
Chiffon Pie 940–948
Children
Dietary needs 8, breakfast 34, food for
feeding of school and pre-school 33,
food prejudices of 33, meals to fit needs
of 36, salads for 1117
Chile Butter Canapés 187
Chile peppers, uses 129
Chile Tepines, uses 129
Chili Con Carne
with Beef 822
with Lamb 848
Chili Powder, uses 129
Chili Sauce
Hot 1107
Peppy 1108
Vegetable 1109
Chinese
Cabbage, buying and care 79
Chicken Wor Mein 1056

Chinese—(Cont'd)
  Egg Foo Yeung 684, 685
  Egg Rolls 683
  Pork 869
Chives
  Buying, care 84, *uses* 129
  Butter Canapés 187
  Dressing for Pheasant 772
Chocolate
  Cooking with 106, *dipping* 408, *grated, melted, units per pound* 156, *how made, kinds, storage* 105, 106, *unsweetened, caloric value* 12
  Angel Food, Stuffed 372
  Bavarian 578
  Blanc Mange 626
  Butter Frosting 384
  Cakes 338
    Cherry 349
  Caramel Apples 411
  Caramels 416
  Chiffon Pie 942
  Clusters 414
  Chip Cookies 463
  Chip Cupcakes 357
  Cookie Pastry Shell 931
  Cream Cheese Frosting 384
  Cream Pie, No. 1 and No. 2 960, 961
  Cream Sponge Roll 317
  Creams, Quick 419
  Crusted Bavarian 579
  Cupcakes 356
  Drop Cookies 463, 464
  Frosting, Creamy 385
  Frosting, Dark 385
  Fudge 403
  Hobnail Frosting 384
  Hot 223
  Ice Cream 594
  Malted Milk 224
  Malted Milk Shake 220
  Marshmallow Pudding 627
  Marshmallow Sundae 643
  Mexican 226
  Milk 117
  Mousse 608
  Nut Cookies 479
  Peanut Butter Sauce 644
  Peppermint Sauce 644
  Pots de Crème 528
  Pudding, Steamed 632
  Refrigerator Cake 374
  Rice Pudding 636
  Sauce 643, 1239, 1240
  Soda 221
  Soufflé 650
  Sour Cream Cookies 464
  Syrup 223
  Syrup, Bitter-Sweet 223
  Upside-Down Dessert 617

Chop Suey
  Chicken 1046
  Heart 897
  Pork 870
  Veal 882
Chops, *broiling of* 793
Chou Paste 936
Chow Chow 1106
Chowder 1263
  Boston Clam 1265
  Cabbage and Dill 1266
  Corn No. 1 and No. 2 1267
  Fish 1270
  Lima Bean 1270
  Manhattan Clam 1270
  Printemps 1273
  Salmon 1273
  Savory Dinner 1273
  Spinach 1274
  Summer Vegetable 1275
Christmas dinners, 1 and 2, Vol. 1—xxx
Christmas Tree Salad 1122
Cider
  Cooler 219
  Mulled (Spiced) Apple 218
  Punch, Grapefruit 216
  Raisin Sauce 1253
Chutney
  Gooseberry 1107
  Mint 1108
Cinnamon, *uses,* 129
  extract 134
  Apple Salad 1136
  Apples 559
  Blanc Mange 626
  Coffee Cake 290
  Dip 1240
  Rolls 275
  Stars 495
  Toast 262
  Whirl Bread 295
Citron Preserves 1092
Citrus
  Pies 948
  Marshmallow Sauce 1241
  Sauce 1240
Clam
  and Tomato Juice 195
  Bake, Wash Boiler 713
  Cheese Dip 200
  Chowder, Boston and Manhattan 1265, 1270
  Fritters 712
  Juice 195
  on the Half Shell 194
Clams
  Buying and cleaning of 712, *cooking methods* 694, 712, *species of* 711, *steaming and roasting of* 712, 713, *yield from* 690
Clarifying, eggs for 661

Cloth, pastry 926
Clothespin Rolls 275
Clove extract 134
Cloverleaf or Shamrock Rolls 275
Cloves, *uses* 129
Club Sandwiches 1214
Clusters, Chocolate 414
Cobblers 517
  Apple 518
  Black Raspberry 524
  Blackberry 519
  Cherry 520
  Fish 732
  Fresh Apricot 518
  Gooseberry 521
  Guava 521
  Peach 522
  Plum 523
  Raisin 523
  Yam, Texas 524
Cockaleekie Soup 1289
Cocktails 191–198 (*see Appetizers*)
Cocoa
  Making, storage, cooking 106, *cups per pound* 156, *substitute for Chocolate* 106
  Bread Pudding 538
  Brownies 457
  Cocoa, Hot and Chilled 224
  Custard with Meringue 651
  Filling 397
  Indians 458
  Layer Cake 338
  Macaroons 470
  Sauce, No. 1 and No. 2 1241
  Whipped Cream Topping 396
Coconut
  Cups per pound 159, *getting ready to use* 123
  Carrot Salad 1176
  Charlotte 579
  Cookies, Lemon 486
  Cream for Bananas 572
  Cream Pie 961, 962
  Creams, Orange 406
  Custard Pie 972
  Fingers 458
  Fresh Cake 350
  Icing 392
  Kisses, Baked 418
  Macaroons 471
  Salad, Orange 1138
  Toasting 415
Codfish
  Baking, boiling and broiling 698, 702, 704, *liver oil, vitamin A, values* 28, *information on* 691, 713
  au Gratin 714
  Balls 714
  Casserole 714
  Creamed 713
  Fried with Mayonnaise Sauce 715

Coffee
  Care of and making 150, 212, *cups per pound, servings per pound* 156, *decaffeined instant, substitutes* 213, *different strengths* 214, *coffeemakers* 1421
  Boiled, Drip, Vacuum 213, 214
  Butter Frosting 385
  Cherry-Nut Frosting 385
  Chiffon Pies 941
  Cooler 219
  Demitasse 215
  Ice Cream 594
  Iced 214
  Percolator 213
  Pots de Crème 529
  Sauce 644, 1241, 1242
Coffee Cake, *Quick Bread Type* 238
  Apple, Streusel Topping 238
  Blueberry Buckle 517
  Plum Kuchen 239
  Sally Lunn 239
Coffee Cake, *Yeast Bread Type* 290
  Cinnamon Twist 290
  Cottage Cheese Kuchen 291
  Danish Pastry 305
  Hasty Apple 290
  Hasty Cherry, Plum or Peach 291
  Jule Kake 291
  Laced-Up Apple-Raisin 292
  Laced-Up Apricot 293
  Laced-Up Prune 293
  Old-Fashioned Streusel Nut 295
  Plum Kuchen, No. 1 and 2 292
  Quick Old-Time Streusel 293
  Swedish Tea Ring 294
Cola drinks, *caloric value* 12
Cold cuts, *care of* 146
Cole Slaw, No. 1, 2 and 3 1177
Collards, *buying and care* 83
Coloring, *food buying, forms, use* 134
Compote
  Dried Fruit 553
  Fruit Honey 554
  Nectarine-Raspberry 565
  Winter Fruit 554
Condensed Milk 118
Confectioners' Icing 392, 393
Confections, Nut 414
Conserve
  Damson Plum 1090
  Peach 1089
Conserving food values, 31–32
Consommé, Spinach 1299
Container sizes 137
Cookie cutters, jars, sheets 1422
COOKIES 454–500
  Baking 456, *bought* 423, *care of* 150, *cutting out rolled* 484, 485, *in children's diet* 36, *mixing* 455, *press dough* 477, 478, *quality of, depends* 455, *re-rolling*

Cookies—(Cont'd)
cookie dough 485, storing and re-storing 456
Almond Crescents 473
Almond Spritz 477
Apple Sauce 462
Bar 456–462
Basic Spritz 478
Basic Sugar 486
Brandy Snaps 487
Brownies 457
Blond or Butterscotch Brownies 457
Butter 488
Butter Nutties 474
Butterscotch 486
Checkerboard 480
Cherry Chews 481
Cherry-Citron Nut Refrigerator 479
Chocolate Chip 463
Chocolate-Nut Refrigerator 479
Chocolate Pinwheels 482
Chocolate Sour Cream Drop 464
Chocolate Spritz 478
Cinnamon Stars 495
Cocoa Brownies 457
Cocoa Indians 458
Cocoa Macaroons 470
Coconut Fingers 458
Coconut Macaroons with Condensed Milk 471
Corn Flake Kisses 471
Cottage Cheese 488
Cream Cheese Tarts, Vienna 494
Creole Maple Kisses 471
Date-Nut Refrigerator 479
Date Oatmeal Squares 459
Date Pinwheels 483
Double Chocolate Drop 463
Drop 462–470
Easy Sugar 474
Fork-Print 459
Fruit Bars 460
Fruit Filled 489
Ginger Crisps 489
Ginger, 3-way 476
Gingerbread Men 496
Ground Oatmeal 490
Gumdrop 464
Hermits 465
Holiday 495–500
Jelly-Filled Crescents 490
Lebkuchen, dark 497
Lebkuchen, light 497
Lemon-Coconut 486
Lemon-Coconut Refrigerator 479
Lemon Cream Cheese 491
Lemon Sugar 475
Macaroons, Almond 472
Mandel Kakas 499
Maple-Pecan 487
Meringue 470–473

Meringue Kisses 473
Mincemeat 465
Molasses Drops 466
Molasses, Rolled 493
Molded and Stamped 473–477
Nut Refrigerator 478
Oatmeal Drops 467
Old-Fashioned Lace 468
Orange 487
  made with poultry fat 487
Orange Cream Kisses 473
Orange Pecan Refrigerator 484
Peanut Butter 475
Peppermint Cream Brownies 460
Pfefferneusse, Dark 498
Pfefferneusse, Light 499
Praline 476
Refrigerator 478–479
Ribbon 480
Rocks 468, 469
Rolled 484–495
Sand Tarts 487
Scotch Shortbread 492
Shortbread Fans 493
Soft Chocolate Drop 464
Soft Ginger, Rolled 491
Soft Sugar 494
Sour Cream 469
Sour Cream, Rolled 492
Spice 487
Springerlie 500
Vanilla Crisps 470
Walnut Sticks 461
Coolers, Ice Cream 218–220
"Coon-Cured" Cheese 448
Copper
  Amounts needed 9, in fish 687, use of in body 17, 31
Coriander, uses 129
Corn
  Buying, care 82, caloric value 12, cooking methods 1307, flour 110, in diet 4, selecting 1340, care of syrup 151, niacin (nicotinic acid) in yellow corn 26
  and Cheese, escalloped 1342
  and Cheese Rabbit 446
  and Tomato Soup, Cream of 1279
  Buttered 1341
  Cereals 421
  Chowder, No. 1 and 2 1267
  Creamed, with Green Pepper 1342
  Flake Topping, Cauliflower with 1337
  for Vegetable Plate 1410
  Fresh, and Tomato Casserole 1342
  Fresh, Rabbit 1342
  Fried 1343
  Fritters 1350
  Muffins 241
  on the Cob 1341
  Popped 429
  Relish 1106

Corn—(Cont'd)
Roasted 1343
Soup, Cream of 1279
Stewed 1344
Sticks 241
Corn Bread and Spoon Bread
Description of 240
Bacon-Corn Meal Muffins 241
Buttermilk 240
Corn Bread, Sweet Milk 240
Corn Sticks or Muffins 241
Cracklin', 241
Crunchy Fried Cakes 242
Dressing (or Stuffing) 1073
Hush Puppies 242
Sour Cream 241
Southern 242
Spoon 243
Spoon with Cheese 243
Corned Beef, care of 146
and Cabbage 819
and Potato Salad 1185
"Boiled" Dinner 819
Corn Meal 421
Caloric value of 12, enriched 233
Griddle Cakes 247
Muffins 241
Muffins, Bacon 241
Mush 427, 428
Rolls (Yeast) 278
Waffles 260
Corn Flake Kisses 471
Cornflakes, caloric value 12
Cornstarch, how to measure 160
Pudding 625, 628
Corn Syrup
Definition 125, glazing 368, storage 151
Cottage Cheese. (See Cheese—Cottage)
Cottage Pudding 618
Country Fried Steak 803
Crabapple
Frozen pickles 1097
Jam 1084
Jelly 1084
Pickles or Spiced 1097
Crab Meat
Avocado Cocktail or Salad 195
Butter—Canapés 188
Cakes 717
Caper Filling Canapés 189
Cocktail 195
Croquettes 504
Filling—Canapés 189
Grapefruit Cocktail No. 1 and 2 196
Louis 1186
Mornay 717
Onion Canapés 183
Salad 1186
Shrimp Gumbo Soup 1268
Crabs 690
Buying 715, cooking methods 694, 715,

716, information 694, cups of meat per
pound 159
Deviled 717
French-fried Soft Shell 716
Crackers
Caloric value 12, units per pound 156
Cracklin' Corn Bread 241
Cracklings 109
Cranberry, cranberries
Buying, care 90, Caloric value 12, diet 5
Apple Milk Sherbet 605
Apple Salad 1162
Chicken Sandwich Loaf 1214
Cooked Apple Salad 1162
Honeyed Apples and 563
Jelly 563, 1087
Jelly, Apple, Quince and 1087
Jelly, Chicken Salad with 1157
Mayonnaise 1199
Mock Cherry Pie 998
Muffins 255
Old-time 564
Pie 998
Punch 215
Relish 1207
Salad, Banana, Apple and 1135
Salad Mold 1163
Sandwiches, Ham and 1234
Sauce 563
Sauce, Apple and 557
Cream
Caloric value 12, care 147, how to whip
169, in diet 5, pasteurized 116, sweet,
kinds sold 119, sour or soured 119,
vitamin A, value of 28
Cheese 449
Cheese and Lettuce Salad, Date 1136
Cheese Cake 379
Gravy, Salt Pork and 855
Horns 936
Maple Butter 472
Pie 955
Puffs 936
Puffs, Cream Filling for 397
Puffs, Swan 937
Sour, Cake 337
Sour, Cheese Cake with 380
Sour, Corn Bread 241
Whipped, Topping, Cocoa 396
Cream of Tartar, use 114
Creamed
Eggs and Asparagus on Toast 665
Eggs and Deviled Ham 666
Luncheon Meat or Chicken in Squash 889
Mushrooms and Eggs 666
Creams
Orange-Coconut 406
Quick Chocolate 419
Creamy Caramels 415
Crème Brulée 530, 531

Creole
  Bean Soup 1269
  Eggs 682
  Fish 710
  Kisses 471
  Lamb Shoulder Chops 843
  Sauce, Vegetable 1261
  Tripe 910
  Wax Beans 1322
Crêpes Suzette 610
Crescents
  Almond 473
  Hungarian Filled 490
Cress, care of 141
Crisps, Ginger 489
Croaker, cooking methods 691
Crooked Miles 276
CROQUETTES 501–508
  General directions for making 501
Croustades 263
Croutons 262
Crumb Cake 334
Crumbles, discussion of 510
Crunch, Apple 512
Crusty French Bread 267
Crusty Water Rolls 268
Cucumbers
  Buying, care 82, 142, in diet 4
  and Egg Salad Sandwich 1227
  and Radish Salad 1148
  au Gratin 1345
  Aspic, Salmon in 1159
  Braised 1344
  Cocktail 197
  Creamed 1345
  Dill, Pickles 1103
  Dressing for Salmon Salad 1158
  Dressing for Tomato Salad 1154
  for Pickles 124
  Minted in Sour Cream 1345
  Pickles, Celery 1101
  Salad, Egg and 1182
  Salad, Raw Beet and 1179
  Salad, Sliced 1152
  Sandwich, Tuna 1220
  Soup, Cream of 1279
  Spliced Salad 1154
  Stuffed 209
  Stuffed, Salad 1153
Cumin or Cumino, description, uses 129
Cupcakes 356–360
  Baking in muffin pans 312
Currants, Currant
  Buying, care 91, dried, cups per pound
    157
  and Raspberry Jelly 1087
  Gravy for Wild Duck 765
  Jelly 1085
  Oatmeal Bread 298
  Sugared Fresh 573

Curried
  Eggs 666
  Lamb 847
  Vichyssoise 1299
Curry
  Powder, description, uses 129
  Lamb 851
Cusk 691
Custard
  Cups 1422, ice cream discussion 591,
    in children's diet 36, care of 149
  Baked 526
  Bread Puddings 536
    Lemon Cake 532
    Lime Cake 535
    Orange Cake 533
    Pineapple Cake 533
  Brown Sugar 527
  Butterscotch 527
  Cake Crumb, Lemon Ginger Sauce 537
  Caramel 528
  Cocoa Meringue 651
  Cottage Cheese Rennet 612
  Floating Island 531
  French 532
  Jam Meringue Puff 535
  Lemon 527
  Mincemeat 527
  Orange Cake Bread Pudding 533
  Peanut Butter 533
  Peppermint Rennet 612
  Pies 972
  Pumpkin 534
  Sauce 1242, 1243
  Soft or Stirred 534, 535
  Steamed 535, 536
Custard Pies 970
Cutlets, Egg 668

D

Daffodil Cake 318
Dakota Potatoes 1375
Damson
  Blue Preserves 1091
  Plum Conserve 1090
Dandelion Greens 1350, 1352
  Buying, care 83, in diet, 4
  Salad, 1178
Danish Pastry 305
Date, Dates
  Caloric value 12, care, buying 91, cups
    per pound 157, dried varieties 103, in
    diet 5
  Cake Pudding 618
  Cookies, Nut 479
  Cottage Cheese Sandwich 1211
  Cream Cheese and Lettuce Salad 1136
  Cream Pie 962
  Fig Pudding 633
  Filling 398

Date, Dates—(Cont'd)
  Graham Cracker Torte 619
  Nut Bread 250
  Nut Spread 1223
  Oatmeal Squares 459
  Orange Tarts 1023
  Pinwheel Cookies 483
  Pudding
    with Brandy Cream Sauce 619
    Saucy 620
  Salad, Cheese and Frozen 1124
  Salad, Fresh Fruit 1137
  Salad, Kohlrabi 1151
  Salad, Pineapple 1141
  Salad, Pineapple, Cabbage 1178
  Whip, Pineapple 654
Decorating
  Eggs for 661
  Fruit Cake 367
Decorative Frosting 386
Deep fat fryer 1422
Deep fat frying 738
Deep South Sugar Pie 968
Deer Meat 749–753
  Qualities of 749, removal of glands 746
  Gravy for 765
Dehydrated foods, nutritive values 100
Demitasse 215
Denver Sandwiches 1227
Dessert, Waffles 260
DESSERTS, 509–655
  Ambrosia 571
  Apple and Cranberry Sauce 557
  Apple Brown Betty 510
  Apple Cobbler 518
  Apple Crunch 512
  Apple Dumplings 540, 541
  Apple Grunt 513
  Apple Pandowdy 513
  Apple Rings, Poached 560
  Apple Sauce 556, 557
  Apple Snow 649
  Applecot Sauce 557
  Apples, Baked 557, 558
  Apples, Fried 559
  Apples, Mincemeat, Stuffed 559
  Apples, Pineapple, Stuffed 559
  Apples, Scalloped 560
  Apples, Stewed 560
  Apples, Stewed Dried 551
  Apricot, Bavarian, Dried 577
  Apricot Cobbler, Fresh 518
  Apricot Ice Cream, Refrigerator 592
  Apricot Whip 655
  Apricot Whip, Baked 652
  Apricots and Red Plums, Sugared Fresh 571
  Apricots, Stewed Dried 551
  Avocado Ice Cream 593
  Baked Alaska 610
  Baked Custards 526

  Baked Raisin Dumplings 548
  Banana Crescents 542
  Banana Grape Mold 588
  Banana Ice Cream 593
  Banana Sauté 561
  Bananas and Cream 572
  Bananas, Baked 561
  Bananas, Baked in Cranberry Sauce 561
  Berries, Sugared 572
  Biscuit Tortoni 601
  Blackberries, Stewed 562
  Blackberry Cobbler 519
  Blackberry Dumplings 543
  Blackberry Sally Lunn, Fresh 515
  Blueberry Buckle, Fresh 517
  Blueberry Fritters 550
  Blueberry Roly Poly 543, 544
  Boysenberry Pandowdy, Canned 516
  Butter Pecan Ice Cream 597
  Butterscotch Ice Cream 594
  Cantaloupe 573
  Caramel Mousse 608
  Caramel Peach Crème 529
  Charlotte Russe 578
  Cherries, Stewed Sour Red 562
  Cherries, Sugared Sour Red 573
  Cherry Cobbler, Fresh Red 520
  Cherry Dumplings 543
  Cherry Marlow 606
  Cherry, Stewed Sour Red, Pancake or Pudding Sauce 563
  Chocolate Bavarian 578
  Chocolate Ice Cream 594
  Chocolate Mousse 608
  Chocolate Pots de Crème 528
  Chocolate Soufflé 650
  Cinnamon Apples 559
  Coconut Charlotte 579
  Coconut Cream for Bananas 572
  Coffee Ice Cream, Refrigerator 594
  Coffee Pots de Crème 529
  Cottage Cheese and Honey 610
  Cranberries, Old-Time 564
  Cranberry Fritters 550
  Cranberry Jelly 563
  Cranberry Sauce 563
  Creamed Rice, Fluffy 637
  Crème Brulée 530, 531
  Crêpes Suzette 610
  Currants, Sugared 573
  Dried Fruit Compote 553
  Dried Fruit, Stewed 552
  Dutch Apple Cake 514, 515
  Floating Island 531
  French Custard 532
  Fruit Combinations 574
  Fruit Cups 574
  Fruit-Nut Jelly 588
  Golden Mousse 608
  Golden Sapote 577
  Gooseberry Cobbler 521

Desserts—(Cont'd)
Gooseberry Dumplings 544
Gooseberry Fool 653
Grape Bavarian 580
Grape Ice 603
Grapefruit, Broiled 564
Grapefruit Shortcake 647
Guava Cobbler 521
Guava Ice Cream 595
Guavas, Baked 564
Guavas, Sugared 575
Honeyed Apples and Cranberries 563
Jellied Fruit Delight 589
Lemon Cake Custard 532
Lemon Cream Freeze 601
Lemon Fluff 584
Lemon Ice Cream 595
Lemon Sherbet 606
Lime Cake Custard 533
Lime Ice 604
Mangoes 575
Marshmallow Pudding 584
Melon Mold 589
Meringue Glacé 611
Meringue Shells 611
Mincemeat Custard 527
Mincemeat Ice Cream, Refrigerator 595
Mocha Whip 585
Nesselrode Ice Cream 596
Nesselrode Pudding 580
Orange Bavarian, Fresh 581
Orange Buttermilk Jelly 590
Orange Fritters 550
Orange Ice 604
Orance Ice Cream 596
Orange Jelly 590
Orange Marmalade Soufflé 650
Orange Shortcake 648
Orange Slices Poached 560
Orange Spanish Cream 585
Patty Shell Cases 612
Peach Dumplings 545
Peach Fritters 551
Peach Ice Cream, Refrigerator 596
Peach Meringues with Orange Sauce 652
Peaches, Fresh Baked 565
Peaches, Stewed Fresh 565
Peaches, Stewed in Red Plum Purée 566
Peaches, Sugared Fresh 575
Peanut Brittle Ice Cream 597
Peanut Brittle Whip 653
Peanut Butter Custard 533
Pears, Baked 566
Pears, Baked, Gingered 566
Pears, Cranberry Glazed 567
Pears, Poached 567
Pears, Poached Gingered 568
Pears, Stewed 568
Peppermint Candy Ice Cream, Refrigerator 598
Peppermint Stick Ice Cream 597, 598

Persimmon Bavarian 581
Pineapple Bavarian 582
Pineapple Cake Custard 533
Pineapple Cones 576
Pineapple, Fresh in the Shell 576
Pineapple Ice 604
Pineapple Mousse 609
Pineapple Snow 586
Pineapple, Sugared, Fresh 576
Plum Brown Betty 511
Plum Fritters 550
Plum Pudding, Molded 589
Plums, Stewed Red 568
Prune Ice Cream 598
Prune Marlow 607
Prune Whip 655
Prune Whip, Baked 654
Prunes, Soaked 552
Prunes, Stewed Dried 552
Prunes with Lemon Slices 552
Prunes with Orange 552
Pumpkin Custard 534
Purée of Dried Fruit 553
Quinces, Baked 569
Quinces, Stewed 569
Raisins, Stewed 553
Raspberry Bavarian, Fresh Red 582
Raspberry Fluff, Fresh Red 586
Raspberry Freeze 601
Raspberry Ice, Black 605
Raspberry Ice Cream 598
Raspberry Mallow Cream 587
Rhubarb 569, 570
Rhubarb Marlow 607
Rhubarb Shortcake 648
Russian Cream 583
Shortcake 648
Snow Pudding 587
Soft or Stirred Custard 535
Spanish Cream 587
Steamed Custard 536
Strawberry Bavarian 583
Strawberry Ice Cream 599
Strawberry Mousse 609
Strudel 613
Swedish Rosettes 612
Texas Yam Cobbler 524
Three-Fruit Ice, 605
Vanilla Bavarian or Crème Vanilla 583
Vanilla Ice Cream 599, 600
Velva Fruit 602
Winter Fruit Compote 554
Deviled
Crabs 717
Egg Sandwich 1227
Eggs, Hot 670
Eggs No. 1 and 2 667
Ham Dip 200
Kidneys 899
Devil's Food Cake, Red 339, 350
Dewberries, care, buying 90, 143

Diabetics, Jerusalem Artichokes, for 1310
Diet
  Elements of 5, general discussion of 7, 8, 9, pattern 3
Dill, use of 130
  Bean Pickles 1102
  Chowder, Cabbage and 1266
  Cucumber Pickles 1103
  Fish with, and Tomatoes 709
  Pickles, Keg Method 1102
  Pickles, Sweet 1103
  Potato Salad, with Fresh 1189
  Salad Dressing 1199
  Sauce, Green or Wax Beans with 1322
  Sauce, No. 1 and 2 1254
Dills, Kosher 1103
  Stuffed 209
Dinner, Boiled, Fish 702, with Ham Hocks 859
Diplomat Canapés 183
Dipping, with Chocolate 408
Dips or Dunks (Appetizers) 199
Dishes
  Discussion of Vol. 1, xx, "fishy," how to wash 698, what to buy Vol 1, xxi
Divinity 403
Dobos Torte 376
Dolly Varden Cake 334
"Double Action" baking powders 112
Dough
  Plain Roll 273
  Rich and Sweet Roll 279
  Water Yeast 267
  Yeast, types and elaboration 265
Doughtnut Cutters 1422
Doughnuts 288–290
  Caloric value 12
Drawn Butter Sauce 1255
Dressings for Game, Meat, Poultry, Fish. (Also see Stuffings)
  Apple for Veal Pot Roast 877
  Bread 753, 771, 1072
  Bread Stuffing for Fish 700
  Chives for Pheasant 772
  Corn Bread 1073
  Fluffy for Chicken 1073
  Mushroom 754
  Noodle 754
  Old-Fashioned Bread 1073
  Oyster 1074
  Relish for Fish 704
  Sage 754
Dressings for Salad. (See Salad Dressing)
Dried
  Eggs 659
  Foods 100, 101, 102
  Fruit. (See Fruit, Dried)
Dried Beef 834
  and Cheese Sauce, Cauliflower in 1337
  and Noodle Casserole 834
  Creamed 834

Creamed Eggs on Toast 834
Frizzled 835
Soufflé 680
Drippings, Meat, uses for 109
Drop Cookies 462
Drumfish 691
Dry milk 118
Dry-picking poultry 1030
Dublin Salad 1186
Duck
  Discussion of cookery 1061, wild, picking, preparation of 745, 755, vitamin values 21, 23
  Baked, Wild Rice Stuffing 755
  Roast 1062
  Sandwiches, Sweet Spread for 1231
  Soup 1290
  Soup, Wild 757
  Wild, Baked with Sauerkraut 755
  Wild, Braised with Red Cabbage 756
  Wild, Currant Gravy for 765
  Wild, Dinner, Braised 756
  Wild, Gravy, Giblets for 765
  Wild, King 757
  Wild, Quick Roast 758
  Wild, Roast, Wild Rice, Liver Stuffing 759
    with Mashed Potatoes 759
    without Dressing 758
Duckling, Braised Dinner 756
  Broiled Wild, 757
Dumplings 244
Dumplings, discussion of 539
  and Sauerkraut, Schultzie's 1393
  Apple 541
  Blackberry, Mohawk 543
  Cherry 543
  Drop 244
  Egg Drop 244
  Gooseberry 544
  Marrow Ball 244
  Peach Skillet 545
  Plum 546, 547
  Potato 245, 1381
  Raisin, Baked 548
  Rolled, Buttermilk 245
  Stewed Chicken and 1044
Durum Wheat 422
Dutch or Cottage Cheese 449
  Oven or skillet 1421, 1426
  Apple Cake 514, 515
  Apple Pie 987

E

Eating pears 95
Éclairs 937
Economy, through use of menus 37
Edam cheese 449
Eel 691, 693, 696
Egg beaters, slicers 1422, 1423

Egg dishes, *Baked*
  Baked Eggs 664
  Casserole, Asparagus and 1311
  in Bacon Rings 664
  in Potato Nests 665
  in Tomato Cups 664
  Shirred 664
  Timbales 1302
Egg Dishes, *Fried*
  Fried Eggs 671
  Lyonnaise 672
Egg Dishes, *Hard Cooked*
  and Dried Beef Creamed on Toast 834
  and Mushrooms Creamed on Toast 666
  and Tuna Fish à la King 733
  Crab Stuffed in Aspic Jelly 1160
  Creamed Eggs 665
  Creamed Eggs and Asparagus on Toast 665
  Creamed Eggs and Mushrooms on Toast 666
  Curried Eggs 666
  Deviled Eggs, No. 1 and 2 667
  Deviled Eggs as Hors d'Oeuvres 204
  Egg Cutlets 668
  Eggs à la Goldenrod 667
  Eggs à la King 667
  Eggs and Asparagus, au Gratin 668
  Eggs in Mustard Sauce 669
  Eggs Tetrazzini 669
  Eggs with Watercress Sauce 669
  for Stuffing 663
  Hard Cooked Eggs 663
  Hot Deviled Eggs 670
  Hot Stuffed Eggs Supreme 670
  Lobster Stuffed Eggs in Tomato Sauce 670
  Spanish Eggs on Toast 671
Egg Dishes, *Miscellaneous*
  Chinese Egg Rolls 683
  Creole Eggs 682
  Drop Dumplings 244
  Egg and Fish Loaf 682
  Egg and Rice Surprise 682
  Egg Casserole 683
  Egg Foo Yeung 685
  Egg for Vegetable Plate 1410
  Egg Pancakes with Cherry Sauce 685
  Float, Cheese 437
  Old Time Egg Pancake 686
  Punch, Pineapple 228
Egg Dishes, *Omelets*
  American Type 676
  Bacon Omelet 676
  Cheese Omelet 676
  French Omelet 676
  Green 678
  Mushroom Omelet 677
  Parsley Omelet 677
  Puffy Omelet 677
  Sta-Puff Omelet 678

Egg Dishes, *Poached*
  Eggs à la Rockefeller 673
  Eggs Benedictine 673
  Eggs in Potato Nests 674
  Eggs Poached in Milk 674
  Eggs Poached in Tomatoes 674
  Poached Eggs, Method 1 and 2 672, 673
  Tasty Sauced Eggs 674
Egg Dishes, *Scrambled*
  Egg Spinach Scramble 675
  Hearty Scrambled Eggs 675
  Kippered Herring with 711
  Parsley Egg Scramble 675
  Scrambled Eggs 675
  Tomato Scramble 676
Egg Dishes, *Soufflés*
  Discussion of 678
  Celery Soufflé 679
  Cheese Soufflé 439
  Chicken or Meat 679
  Dried Beef Soufflé 680
  Mushroom Soufflé 680
  Oatmeal Soufflé 680
  Spaghetti Ring Soufflé with Creamed Ham 681
  Tuna Soufflé 681
Egg Dishes, *Soft Cooked* 662
Egg Salad
  and Cucumber 1182
  and Sardine, Top Tomato Salad 1183
  Canapé Filling 189
  for Sandwich Loaf 1218
  in Chips 204
  Scrambled 1183
  Vegetable 1183
Egg Sandwiches
  Bacon and 1227
  Bacon and Egg Salad 1225
  Cucumber and Egg Salad 1227
  Deviled Egg 1227
  Egg Salad 1228
  Egg Salad and Sardine Double Decker 1215
  Ham and 1228
  Olive and 1230
  Vegetable 1225
Egg Sauce 700, 1255
  Asparagus in 1312
  Spinach with Bacon and 1398
  String Beans in 1316
Egg Yolk Butter for canapés 187
Eggnog 1, and 2 228
  Caramel 227
  Lemon 228
  Pie 942
  Shake 220
EGGS 656–686
  Alternates for 5, *as a binder* 661, *as adhesive agents* 661, *as clarifying agents* 661, *as decoration* 661, *as emulsifiers* 661, *caloric value* 12, *care* 148, 657,

Eggs—(Cont'd)
   danger of eating raw whites 659, dried
   659, for cake 310, for garnish 661, 663,
   for leavening 660, for pleasing texture
   661, for thickening 661, freezing and
   yield of 660, grading of 656, in children's diet 36, how reconstituted 659,
   how used 659, peeling of 662, protein
   value 15, vitamin values of 22, 23, 28,
   wash for French Pastries 935, ways to
   use whites 658
Eggplant
   Buying, care 83, cooking methods 1307,
   in diet 4, selecting 1346
   and Onion with Cheese Sauce 1346
   Baked Stuffed 1346
   en Casserole 1347
   French-Fried 1348
   Fried 1348
   Sauté 1347
   Stuffed 1348
   Supreme 1347
Elderberry Jelly, Apple and 1087
Electric Light Preserves, Strawberry 1093
Elk cookery 760
   Chops in Mushroom Gravy 749
   Sandwich Spreads 760
   Soup 760
   Steak, Pan-Fried 761
   Steak, Smothered in Onions 760
   Steak, Swissed Round 761
Emmenthaler cheese 449
Emulsification, eggs for 661
Endive
   Buying, care 86, 141, in diet 4, vitamin
   values 20, 27
   and Potato Salad, Hot 1128
   Salad, Macaroni 1187
English dairy cheese 449
English Muffins 306
Enriched
   Bread 233
   corn meal 233
   flour 110, 233
Entire wheat flour 110
Escarole
   Buying and care of 86, in diet 4
Evaporated milk 118
   Griddle Cakes, Pancakes 248
Extracts 126
   Care of 151, flavoring, combining of 134,
   how to buy and use 133, sources of 127

F

Fad, the vitamin 29
Fall Salad Platters 1171
Fan Tan Rolls 276
Fans, Short Bread 493
Farina 421, 427
Farina (dark) thiamine (vit. B_1) value 22

Fatigue 5
Fats
   Care of 106, importance in cooking 106,
   rendering poultry 166, use in body 5
Feathery Waffle 260
Fennel
   Seed, uses 130
   Dinner Salad 1149
   Waldorf Salad 1149
   with Cheese Sauce 1349
Fig-Bar Betty, Rhubarb 511
Figs
   Care of 88, dried, buying of 88, 103, in
   diet 5
   Fig Date Puddding 633
Filberts, cups per pound 159
File, description, uses 130
Fillets, Fish 698
   of Sole and Oyster Parmesan 706
Fillings 381, 382
   Apricot, Kolachy, Cake 284
   Canapé 188, 189, 190
   Chocolate Cream, Cake 397
   Chocolate Torte 377
   Cocoa for Cake 397
   Cottage Cheese for Kolachy 285
   Cream, for Cake 397
   Date, for Cake 398
   for Bride's Cake and Petits Fours 344
   for Cake 397
   Fruit, for Cookies 489
   Lemon Butter Jelly Cake, Tarts 398
   Lemon, for Cake 398
   Maple Butter Cream 472
   Marshmallow, for Cake 399
   Orange, for Cake, No. 1 and 2 399
   Orange Cream 473
   Peppermint Butter Cream 461
   Prune, for Kolachy 285
   Sour Cream, for Blitz Torte 376
Finnan Haddie 691
   and Potato Casserole 718
   Creamed 718
   Supreme 718
FISH 687–736
   Alternates for 4, buying, care 695, caloric values 12, 691, skinning carp to
   improve flavor 697, cleaning cat fish and
   eel 696, description, weights, cooking
   methods 691, fillets 689, 690, fresh
   water 693, frozen 695, how to buy, cook,
   handle 695, 697, how to clean, prepare,
   store 696, in diet pattern 3, kinds 691,
   694, liver oil in children's diet 36, market forms of 688, nutritive value 15,
   687, pan-dressed 689, producing areas
   691, protein value 15, round or whole
   688, salt water 691, servings, weight
   159, 690, steaks and sticks 689, 690,
   vitamin values 21, 23, 25
   Aspic, Chicken Stock for 1157

Fish—(Cont'd)
Baked in Parchment 701
Baked, Spencer Method 701
Baked, Whole, with and without Stuffing 698, 699
Balls 711
Birds, Baked 699
Boiled 701, 102, 703
Broiled
Brown Butter Sauce for 707
Cakes 709
Carp 697
Chowder 710, 1270
Cobbler 732
Cold Boiled 703
Creole 710
Croquettes 504
Delicious Boiled 704
Dill, and Tomatoes 709
Dinner, Boiled 702
Egg Sauce for Baked 700
French-Fried 736
Fried and Pan-Fried 707
Halibut Steaks, Savory Baked 700
Loaf, Egg and 682
Planked 735
Pudding 711
Relish Dressing for 704
Roe, Broiled 706
Salad 1187
Salmon, Ways to Serve Cold 735
Sandwiches 1219
Sauces and Stuffings 700
Sauerkraut and, Casserole 1392
Shape—Pastry Shell 729
Smoked 710
Flavoring in cake 311
Floating Island 531
Flounders, *blackback, dab, fluke, sole* 691
Flour, all-purpose
Barley, bread 109, *browning* 161, *buck-wheat, cake, corn* 110, *caloric value of* 12, *care of* 152, *cups per pound* 157, *enriched* 110, *enrichment standards for, table* 233, *entire wheat, gluten graham* 110, *for cake* 310, *for pie crust, 922, how to measure* 160, *how to sift* 313, *oat, potato, pumpernickel* 110, *rice, rye, self-rising* 111, 422, *semolina, soft wheat, soy* 110, 111, *sifter* 1423, *stone-ground, whole wheat* 111, *water paste for thickening gravy* 163
Fluff, Lemon 584
Tapioca Lime 639
Fluke, *cooking of* 691
Foamy Sauce 1243
Fondant 404
for Bon Bon Centers 404
for Dipping 405
Frosting 389

Fondue
Asparagus 1312
Cheese 437
Tomato Cheese 441
Tuna and Celery 733
Foo Yeung, Egg 684, 685
Food
Buying, care 140, *canned* 136, *coloring* 134, *dollar, stretching of* 70, *for children* 33, *mill* 1423, *minimum for health* 7, *purchasing and storage space* 140, *servings, caloric value* 11, *storage of canned, unopened* 136, *values, conserving* 31, *varieties of* 136
Foods
Alternate for menus 4, *cooked, care of* 149, *graded* 71, *in refrigerator* 140, *ready-to-eat, cost of* 70, *units per pound of* 156
FOREIGN FOODS 737
Fork Print Cookies 459
Forks, for cooking 1423
Fowl, *protein value* 15
Wild, Gravy for 765
Frankfurters 887
Units per pound 158
Barbecued 887
Boiled 887
Creamed 887
Grilled 887
Grilled Cheese Stuffed 887
in Blankets 888
on Buns 888
Sandwiches 1228
Sauerkraut with 889
Savory 889
Scalloped Potatoes and 888
Frappés 591
Freezes 601
Freezing Cakes 329
French
Apple Pie 987
Artichokes 1309
Bread, Crusty 267
Cream Pie 963
Custard 532
Ice cream 591
Omelet 676
Onion Soup 1269
Pancakes 248
Toast 263
Toast, Puffy 264
Toast Sandwiches, Bologna 1226
French dressing. See *Salad Dressing*
Caloric value of 12, *care of* 151, *discussion of* 1197
French-Fried. (See *Frying with Deep Fat* 738)
Fricassee
Beef, Table 29 806
Chicken 1038, 1048

Fricassee—(Cont'd)
  Chicken, Sour Cream 1055
  Muskrat 766
  Pheasant 771
  Rabbit 774
  Squirrel 779
  Veal 879
Fritters, Dessert 548–551
  General directions for frying 548, 1349
  Batter for fruit 548
Fritters, Vegetable
  Batter for 1349
  Corn 1350
  Parsnip 1365
  Plantain 1371
Frog Legs 719
Fromage, Onion and Apple 1362
Frostings. (See Icings, Fillings and Toppings
  380, 381, decorating bride's and party
  cakes 386, frost or ice cake promptly
  381, getting cake ready for filling and
  frosting 381, preparing plate 381, spread
  frosting or icing, how to 382, storing
  cake to keep fresh 382)
Frostings, Cooked 388
  Caramel (Quick), for Applesauce Cake
    390
  Chocolate Fudge 389
  Cocoa, 3-Minute 388
  Fondant or Petits Fours 389
  Penuche 389
  French Butter Cream 391
  French Butter Cream Burnt Sugar or
    Caramel 391
Frostings, Uncooked 383
  Allegretti 383
  Anise Butter 383
  Basic Butter 383
  Browned Butter 384
  Butter Frosting Made Shiny 381
  Butternut 383
  Chocolate Butter 384
  Chocolate Cream Cheese 384
  Chocolate Hobnail 384
  Coffee or Mocha Butter 385
  Coffee-Cherry-Nut 385
  Creamy Chocolate 385
  Dark Chocolate 385
  Decorative 386
  Fool-Proof Chocolate 387
  Glossy Cream Cheese 387
  Lemon Butter 387
  Orange Butter 387
  Rum-Nut Butter 388
  Strawberry 388
Frozen foods, care of 145
  Desserts 590
  Eggs 660
  Fish 695
  thawing of 145, 146
Frozen salads 1124

Fruit. (Also see Dried Fruit)
  Alternates for vitamin C 5, alternates
  in (other than citrus) 5, baked and
  broiled, poached and stewed 554, canned
  and fresh, care of 144, dehydrated and
  dried 100, raw 570, effects of storage
  on vitamins 31–33, Federal grades 89–
  95, for dessert 554, 570, fresh, hints on
  buying 101, fresh, raw 570, frozen, care
  of 145, guide for buying 86, juice in
  children's diet 36, canning juices 1079,
  canned uses 168, peeling of 555, percentage of waste 89, storage 89
  and Cream Cheese Spread 1223
  and Date Salad 1137
  and Nut Breads 249, 253. (See Recipes
    under Nut Breads)
  and Nut Breads, how to prepare, bake,
    and slice 249
  Bars 460
  Buttermilk 224
  Cooked Fruit 554
  Cocktail, Fresh Winter 192
  Combination Desserts 574
  Cups 193, 574
  Juice
    Cocktail 192
    Mergers 216
    Salad Dressing 1200
  Muffins 254
  Nut Jelly 588
  Nut Pudding, Steamed 633
  Nut Salad, Frozen 1124
  Pickles 1097
  Pies 982
  Platter, "Whole Meal" 1172
  Punch, Hot 216
  Roll, Old-Fashioned Candied 411
  Salad Bowl, No. 1 and 2 1119
  Salad Dressing 1200
  Salad, Fresh 1137
  Salad, Frozen 1125
  Salad, Frozen, Supreme 1125
  Salad with Marshmallows 1137
  Sandwiches 1221
  Tapioca 639
Fruit Cake, decorating, glazing, storing
  367, 368, facts you should know about
  364–368
  Banana 369
  Blue Ribbon 369
  Groom's Cake 370
  Light, Holiday 370
  No-Bake 371
  Old-Fashioned Dark 371
Fruit Candies 409
Fruit Dressing. (See Salad Dressing)
Fruit, Dried 551
  Care and storage 100, 144, general in-
    formation 100
  Applecot Sauce 557

Fruit, Dried—(Cont'd)
  Apples, Stewed 551
  Apricot Purée 551
  Apricots, Stewed 551
  Compote 553
  Honey Compote 554
  Prunes, Stewed 552
  Purée 553
  Raisins, Stewed 553
  Stewed 552
  Winter Fruit Compote 554
Fruit Drinks 215–218
Fruit Fizz 215
Fruit Juice Medley 215
Fruit Juice Mergers 216
  Spiced or mulled Apple Cider 218
Fryers, *weight per person* 159
FRYING WITH DEEP FAT 738–740
Fudge, *caloric value of* 12
  Balls 403
  Chocolate 403
  Frosting 389
  Marshmallow 403
  Sauce, Hot or Cold 1243
Functions of minerals, calcium, phosphorus,
  iron, copper, iodine 31

G

GAME 741–782
  Bleeding, evisceration, health of 742–
  744, *cooking and storage* 746, *for food*
  741, *preparation, cooking* 743–747
Game birds
  Bleeding and drawing of 742, 743, "*high
  flavor*" *in* 744, *removal of feathers, shot
  areas* 744, 745, *rigor mortis in* 744
  Dressing and Stuffing for 753
Garden, vegetable, advantages of 72
Garlic, *buying, care, use* 84, 130
  Bread 295
  Butter Canapés 187
  Olives 208
Garnish, eggs for 661, 663
  how, what, where 783–787
GARNISHING 783–787
  for soups 1264
Gas, as a leavening agent 112
Geese, wild, picking of 745
Gelatin Desserts 577–590
  Care of 149, 152, *to elaborate and con-
  geal* 577
Giblet Gravy 765
Giblets, cooking for gravy 764
Ginger, *uses* 130
  Cookies, Soft Rolled 491
  Cookies, Three-Way 476
  Crisps 489
  Sauce, Lemon, with Custard 537
  Tea 230
  Tea Cooler 219

Ginger Ale Salad Mold 1163
Gingerbread
  Buttermilk 360
  Cupcakes 357
  George Washington 360
  Honey Ginger Cake 361
  Men 496
  Pear Upside-Down Cake 362
Gingersnap Pastry Shell 930
Girls, dietary needs 8
Gizzard test for cooking turkey 1068
Glassware Vol. 1, page xxii
Glaze, Apricot
  for Fruit Cake 368
  for Ham 865
Glorified Rice 637
Glossary 1429
Glossy White Icing 393
Gluten flour 110
Glycerine in icing 381
Gnocchi 1376
Goiter and iodine 687, 688
Gold Cake 346
Golden
  Cupcakes 357
  Fluff Salad Dressing 1143
  Gate Cake 347, 348
  Mousse 608
  Salad Dressing 1201
  Sapote 577
Goldenrod, à la, Eggs 667
Goose, *cookery* 1061
  Roast 1062
  Roast, Wild 1062
  Roast, with Potato Stuffing 1063
  Sliced, in Orange Sauce 1063
Gooseberry
  Care, buying 87, *in diet* 5
  and Raspberry Jelly 1087
  Chutney 1107
  Dumplings 544
  Fool 653
  Pie 999, 1000
  Tarts 1022
Gorganzola cheese 449
Gouda cheese 449
Goulash 837
Grade, labeling 136
Graham Cracker
  Cake 336
  Cream Pie 964
  Pastry Shell 930
Graham flour 110
Grape Juice
  Caloric value of 12
  Juice 1081, 1084
  Juice, Hot Spiced 217
  Lemonade 216
  Mold, Banana 588
  Sauce 1244
  Soda 222

Grapes
   Caloric value 12, *buying, care* 92, *in diet* 5, *serving of* 571
   Bavarian 580
   Buttermilk 225
   Cooler 219
   Ice, No. 1 and 2 603
   Jam 1090
   Jelly 1084
   Pie 1001
   Red Raspberry Pie 1013
   Salad, Cabbage, Celery, Apple and 1175
   Stuffed 207
   Thyme Salad 1164
Grapefruit
   Caloric value 12, *care, buying* 76, 91, *in diet* 5, *serving of* 571, *vitamin values* 19, 22
   Aspic 1163
   Avocado and Persimmon Salad 1138
   Brazilian Cocktail 193
   Broiled 564
   Cider Punch 216
   Grape Cocktail 193
   Grape Juice Cocktail 193
   Peel, Candied 410
   Pie 949
   Salad 1138
   Sauce, Parsnip Patties with 1365
   Shortcake 647
   Tangerine Juice 216
Grapefruit Juice 1081
   Ascorbic acid (vit. C) value 19, *caloric value of* 12, *in diet* 5
Grapenut Pudding, Lemon 539
Grapenuts, *caloric value* 12
Graters, Shredders 1423
Grating food 163
Gravy
   Cooking giblets for 764, *flour-water paste for thickening* 163, *liquids for* 798, *making of meat* 797, *meat elaborations—sauces* 799, *nutritive values of* 797, *on braised meats* 795, *serving of* 799, *and pre-school child* 33
   Braised Meat or Pot Roast 799
   Brown Thickened 799
   Currant, for Wild Duck 765
   Giblet 765
   Milk or Thickened 799
   Onion, for Venison 752
   Pan 766, 800
   Sour Cream, Liver with 907
Green Cream Dip 200
Green Peppers 1368
   Broiled 1369
   Casserole, Macaroni, Tomato and 1408
   Creamed Corn with 1342
   Fried 1369
   Stuffed, No. 1, 2, 3, 4, 5 1369, 1370, 1371

Green Tomato
   Pickles 1103
   Pie 1016
   Stew 819
Greens 1350
   Buying, care 83, 141, *in diet* 4, *pre-washed* 1350, 1351, *selecting* 1350, *vitamin values* 20, 24, 27, *washing* 1351
   Mustard 1352
   Mustard, Spinach with Bacon 1352
   Turnip, with Bacon-Onion Sauce 1353
Griddle Cakes, Pancakes, Flapjacks 246–249
   Temperature 246
Grill
   Lamb Patty 850
   Sausage, Bacon and Tomato 872
Grinding food 163
Grits, Hominy 421, 427
Groom's Cake 370
Groupers 691
Grouse, *cooking* 761–762
Gruyère cheese 450
Guacamole 1255
Guava
   In diet 5
   Baked 564
   Butter 1244
   Jelly 1081
   Pie 1001
   Sugared 575
Guide for Buying Apples 97
   for Buying Fruits 89
   for Buying Vegetables 79
Guinea, *cookery* 1066–1067
Gum Drop Cookies 464
Gumbo
   Chicken and Okra 1045
   Crab Shrimp 1268

H

Haddock
   Cooking methods 691
   Broiling of 704
Hake 691
Halibut
   Cooking methods 691, *liver oil, vitamin A value* 28
   Baked, Savory 700
Ham 864
   Caloric value 13, *care* 146, *time tables, broiling* 854, *roasting* 863, *vitamin values* 21, 23, 25
   and Banana Sandwiches 1233
   and Cheese Spread 1228
   and Cranberry Sandwiches 1234
   and Sweet Potato Casserole 867
   and Tomato Sandwiches, Swiss 1236
   and Tomato Supreme 1234
   and Tuna Fish Sandwiches 1234

Ham—(Cont'd)
Baked and Broiled 864, 866
Baked Picnic 865
Chutney Cheese Canapé Filling 189
Creamed Luncheon Meat, in Baked Hubbard Squash 889
Deviled, Creamed Eggs and 666
Egg Sandwiches 1228
Hocks, "Boiled" Dinner with 859
Ideas for Leftover 869
Lentil Stew with 1356
Loaf, Top of Stove 869
Loaf, with Plum Sauce 868
Luncheon Dish, Asparagus and 1311
Olive Canapé Filling 189
Pan-Fried 868
Patties on Yam Slices 867
Potato Casserole 866
Puffs with Mushroom Sauce 867, 868
Salad, for Sandwich Loaf 1217
Salad Sandwiches 1229
Scalloped Potatoes and 866
Spaghetti Ring Soufflé, with Creamed 681
Timbales 1302
Hamburger
Broiled on a Bun 823
Noodle Casserole 825
Pan-Broiled 825
Picnic 826
Rolls with Tomatoes 826
with varied flavor 825
Handbook, homemaker's 69–170
Hand cheese 450
Hard Sauce 1245
Lemon 1245
Sterling 1249
Harvard Beets 1325
Green or Wax Beans 1322
Harvey Sauce, Lamb Loaf, with 849
Hasenpfeffer 774
Hash, Beef, No. 1 and 2 835, 836
Kidney 900
Lamb 852
Rabbit 775
Turkey 1071
Hashed Brown Potatoes 1377, 1378
Head Cheese Vinaigrette 1187
Heart
Cooking time of 892, cleaning and cooking 891, 895, refrigeration of 153, vitamin values of 21, 23, 25
Beef, Braised Stuffed 897
Braised Stuffed 896
Chop Suey 897
Pan-Fried 896
Sauerbraten 897
Stewed 898
Hearts of Palm 1332
Heating oven to bake 313
Hens, weight per person 159

Herb Bread 296
Herbs
Guide to uses 126, 133, care and how to dry 133, sources and uses of 128, 133
Herkimer County cheese 448
Hermits 465
Herring
Broiling of 704, cooking methods for lake 693, for sea 691
Kippered, with Scrambled Eggs 711
Pickled 206
Three-Way 710
Hickory Nut Cake 344
Hocks
Fresh Pig 860
Ham, "Boiled" Dinner with 859
Holiday Cookies 495
Hollandaise Sauce
Celery Root with 1339
Mock 1256
True 1256
Homemaker's Handbook 69–170
Hominy, how made 421
Braised Pork Chops with 1350
Cheese Croquettes 502
Lye 429
Potatoes with Onion Sauté 1350
Homogenized Milk 116
Honey
Caloric value 13, care, varieties, weight 126, 151, 159
Butter, 1231
Compote, Fruit 554
Cottage Cheese and 610
Lime Fruit Salad Dressing 1202
Milk, Lemon 226
Nut Sundae 645
Pumpkin Pie 977
Quince 1095
Spice Sour Cream Cupcakes 358
Taffy 416
Honey Ball Melon, care, buying 93
Honeydew Melon
Ascorbic acid (vit. C) value 20, care, buying 93
Honeyed Sweet Potatoes 1387
Horns, Cream 936
Hors d'oeuvres 201–211, See Appetizers
Horse Mackerel 692
Horseradish
Grinding of 164
Butter Canapés 187
Salad Dressing 1201
Sauce, Beets in 1324
Sauce, No. 1, 2, 3 1256
Hot Dog Relish 1109
Huckleberries, buying, care 90
Hungarian Filled Crescents 490
Hunger, hidden 5
Hush Puppies 242
Hvid Gjedeost cheese 450

Hyacinth Salad 1122
Hydrogenated vegetable shortenings 108

I

Ice Cream 592–599
    Caloric value 13, *care* 153, *commercial, elaboration of* 218, 641, *freezing* 592, *in children's diet* 36, *kinds of* 591, *packing of* 592, *vitamin A, value* 28
    Apricot 592
    Avocado 593
    Banana 593
    Biscuit Tortoni 601
    Butter Pecan 597
    Butterscotch 594
    Chocolate 594
    Coffee 594
    Coolers 218
    Fresh Peach 596
    Guava 595
    Mincemeat 595
    Lemon 595
    Nesselrode 596
    Old-Fashioned Vanilla 600
    Orange 596
    Peanut Brittle 597
    Peppermint Stick, No. 1 and 2 597, 598
    Prune 598
    Raspberry 598
    Refrigerator Peppermint Candy 598
    Shakes 220
    Sodas 221
    Strawberry 599
    Sundaes 641–647
    Vanilla, American Style 600
    Vanilla, French Style 600
    Vanilla, No. 1 and 2 599
Ices 603–606
    Caloric value 13, *discussion of* 591
    Black Raspberry 605
    Grape, No. 1 and 2 603
    Lime 604
    Orange 604
    Pineapple 604
    Three-Fruit 605
Icings, Cake
    Definition of 380
    Basic 7-Minute 392
    Brown Mountain 392
    Coconut 392
    Confectioners' 392, 393
    Egg Yolk Icing 393
    Glossy White 393
    Lady Baltimore 394
    Lemon Confectioners' 394
    Lord Baltimore 394
    Moss Rose 393
    Strawberry 7-Minute 394
    Thin Butter, for Coffee Cakes 395
    White Mountain 395
Income, budget of 72

India Relish 1110
Indian Pudding 620
Indians, Cocoa 458
Iodine
    And goiter 687, 688, *in diet* 9, *in fish and vegetables* 687, *use of in body* 16, *iodized salt* 687
Irish Stew 848
Iron
    Daily allowance 8, 29–30, *in enriched bread and flour* 233, *in fish* 687, *use of in body* 16, *value of, other foods* 30, *value of, whole grain, enriched cereals* 30
Italian
    Cheese 450
    Rice 827
    Soup, Minestra 1290
    Spaghetti, with Meat Balls 828
    Style Liver, Macaroni and Tomatoes 905

J

Jack Cheese 450
Jam 1087
    Care of 151
    Crabapple 1084
    Grape 1090
    Meringue Puff 535
Jambalaya 828
Jellied
    Fruit Delight 589
    Veal Loaf 883
Jelly
    Description of 1079, *care of* 151, *general method for making* 1082, 1083, *storage* 1083, *test* 1082
    Apple 1083
    Apple and Blackberry 1087
    Apple and Elderberry 1087
    Apple, Quince and Cranberry 1087
    Berry 1080
    Black Raspberry 1084
    Blackberry 1087
    Cheese-filled Tarts 1022
    Crabapple 1084
    Cranberry 1087
    Currant and Raspberry 1087
    Doughnuts 289
    Gooseberry and Raspberry 1087
    Grape 1084
    Guava 1081
    Juices 1079
    Mint 1085
    Paradise 1087
    Plum, Red 1087
    Quince 1086
    Red Currant 1085
    Roll 319
    Sandwiches 1232
    Sandwiches, Peanut Butter 1232
    Sour Cherry 1086

Jelly—(Cont'd)
  Spread, Peanut Butter, Banana and 1232
  Strawberry 1086
  Tarts 1023
Jerusalem Artichokes 1309
  As food for diabetics 1310
  Buttered 1310
Jiffy Noodles 449
Juice, fruit extractors 1423
Juices
  Making and uses of 1078, 1079
  for Beverages 1079
  for Jelly 1078, 1079
Jule Kake 291
Juniper Berries 130

K

Kabobs, Lamb and Kidney 900
Kale 1351
  Ascorbic acid (vit. C) value 20, buying,
    care 83, in diet 4
  Southern Style, with Bacon 1351
Keg Method Dill Pickles 1102
Kidney
  and Sausage Squares 899
  Hash 900
  Kabobs, Lamb and 900
  Pie, Steak and 901
  Pork, Sauté with Savory Gravy 901
  Stew 900
Kidney beans, See Beans
Kidneys
  Cooking methods 898, cooking time 892,
    characteristics of 891, 898, refrigeration
    153, vitamin values of 21, 23, 25, 28
  and Sausage Squares 899
  and Shortribs, Braised 899
  Deviled 899
King Fish 692
King Mackerel 692
Kippered Herring 711
Kisses, Baked Coconut 418
  Cornflake 471
  Creole 471
  Meringue 473
  Orange Cream 473
  Potato 418
Kitchen and poultry scissors 1425
Kitchen utensils
  Buying guide 1420, cleaning and care of
    1412–1417, construction and economy
    of 1417, materials 1413
Knife sharpeners 1423
Knives 1422
Knots (a Yeast Roll) 276
Kohlrabi
  Ascorbic acid (vit. C) under 20, buying,
    care 83, cooking methods 1307, in diet
    4, selecting 1353
  Buttered 1353
  Date Salad 1151

Salad Bowl 1120
  Waldorf Salad 1151
  with Cheese Sauce 1353
  with Peanut Butter Sauce 1354
Kolachy 283
  Bohemian 284
  3 Fillings for 284, 285
Kosher Dills 1103
Kuchen
  Cottage Cheese 291
  Plum 292
Kumquat Preserves 1092
Kumquats, care, buying 92

L

Lace Cookies, Old-Fashioned 468
Laced-Up Apple Raisin Coffee Cake 292
  Apricot Coffee Cake 293
  Prune Coffee Cake 293
Lady Baltimore Cake 344
Lamb 839–852
  Caloric value 13, cuts 839, servings per
    pound 158, protein value 15, time-tables
    for broiling, roasting 840, U. S. Govern-
    ment grades 791, vitamin values 21, 23,
    25
  Braised with Vegetables 843
  Breast with Rice, Stuffed 847
  Breast, Stuffed 846
  Breast, Stuffed Rolled 846
  Broth 1291
  Broth with Barley 1292
  Chili Con Carne with 848
  Chops, Broiled 840
  Chops, Pan-Broiled 841
  Curried 847
  Curry 851
  Hash 852
  Irish Stew 848
  Kidney Kabobs 900
  Lamburgers 849
  Leftover 851
  Lima Bean Casserole 844
  Loaf with Harvey Sauce 849
  Paprika 844
  Patties 850
  Patty Grill 850
  Pilaf 844
  Pork Loaf 849
  Riblets, Barbecued 843
  Roast Leg of 842
  Roast Shoulder Mint Barbecue Sauce 841
  Roast Shoulder with Dressing 841
  Sausage Casserole 844, Scallop 852
  Shanks with Tomato Pepper Gravy 845
  Shanks with Vegetables 845
  Shoulder Chops, Creole 843
  Shoulder Chops with Dressing 846
  Steaks, Baked 842
  Stuffed Tomatoes, Baked 851

Lard
  Care 151, *cups per pound* 157, *how made and stored* 107, *how to measure* 160, *nutritional and shortening value* 108
Larding meat 164
Lasagne 449
Leavening
  Agents 111, *by eggs* 660, *baking powder in cake* 311, 326, *effect of altitude* 114, 309
Lebkuchen
  Dark 497
  Light 497
Leek
  Buying, care 84
  and Potato Casserole 1355
  and Potato Soup 1283
  Braised 1354
  Cheese Appetizer Pie 209
  Creamed, on Toast 1355
Leftovers
  Use of 73, *care of meats* 146, 147
  Ham ideas 869
  Lamb 851
Lemon extract 133
Lemon juice
  Vitamin C, value 19, *caloric value* 13, *in diet* 5
  and Orange Chiffon Pie 944
  Angel Pie 1025
  Butter—Canapés 188
  Butter Jelly 398
  Butter Sauce 1257
  Cake Custard 532
  Cake Pie 949
  Celery Root, Sauté 1339
  Chiffon Pie 943
  Coconut Sugar Cookies 486
  Confectioners' Icing 394
  Cooler 219
  Cracker Pudding 538
  Cream Cheese Cookies 491
  Cream Freeze 601
  Cream Pie 950
  Cream Pudding 629
  Custard 527
  Eggnog 228
  Fluff 584
  Fluff Pie 951
  French Dressing 1201
  Frosting, Butter 387
  Ginger Sauce, with Custard 537
  Glamour Pie 951
  Grape-Nut Pudding 539
  Hard Sauce 1245
  Honey Milk 226
  Jelly Roll 319
  Meringue Pie 952
  Orange Sauce 646
  Pie, Sliced, 2 Crust 953
  Sauce 542, 1245, 1246

  Sauce with Chicken Livers 1060
  Shake 220
  Sherbert, Creamy 606
  Sugar Cookies 475
  Sundae, Syrup 645
  Syrup 217
  Tarts 1022
  Whipped Cream Sauce 1246
Lemonade 217
  Grape 216
Lemons
  Buying, care 92, 96, *in diet* 5
Lentils
  Cups per pound 158, *dried, protein value* 15
  with Bacon, Baked 1355
  Stew with Ham 1356
Lettuce
  Buying, care 83, 141, *caloric value* 13, *cooking methods* 1307, *in diet* 4, *vitamin values* 20, 27
  Bacon and Tomato Sandwiches 1224
  Braised 1355
  Salad, Date, Cream Cheese and 1136
  Salad, Tomato and 1153
  Soup, Cream of 1280
  Stuffed 1192
  Wilted 1133
Leyden, special cheese 451
Liederkranz cheese 450
Lily of the Valley Salad 1123
Lima beans
  Buying, care 79, *selecting* 1317, *vitamin values* 20, 22, 24, 26
  and Carrot Soup, Cream of 1280
  Baked 1318
  Buttered
    Dried 1318
    Frozen 1318
    New 1319
  Casserole 1319
  Casserole, Lamb and 844
  Chowder 1270
Limburg cheese 451
Lime juice
  Ascorbic acid (vit. C) value 19, *in diet* 5
  Barbecue Sauce 1251
  Cake Custard 533
  Chiffon Pie 945
  Chiffon Pie, Graham Cracker Crust 944
  Fluff Tapioca 639
  Honey Fruit Salad Dressing 1202
  Ice 604
  Key Pie 953
  Meringue Pie 954
  Olive-Nut Molded Salad 1164
  Sauce, Fresh 646
  Velvet, Pineapple 1166
Limeade 217
Limes, *Buying, care* 92
Lincod 692
Linens, table, Vol. I, xix

Liquids in Baking Cake 311
Liver 902
    Caloric value of 13, *characteristics and
    cooking of* 891, *in diet pattern* 3, *protein
    value* 15, *refrigeration* 153, *removing
    skin, tubes or veins* 903, *sliced, cooking
    time of* 892, *vit. values* 21, 23, 25, 28
    à la Gourmet 905
    and Onions 905
    and Vegetables, Baked 903
    and Vegetable Soup 1293
    Braised 903
    Dumpling Soup 1292
    French-Fried 904
    Loaf 906
    Macaroni and Tomatoes, Italian Style 905
    Pan-Fried 908
    Poor Man's Goose 908
    Rice and Tomatoes, Braised 904
    Sauerbraten 907
    Spanish 909
    Steak, Broiled 904
    Stuffing, Wild Rice and 759
    with Sour Cream Gravy 907
Liver Sausage
    and Creamed Cabbage 907
    Grilled 905
    Mushroom Spread 1229
    Sandwiches 1229
    Spread 1230
Liverburgers 906
Loaf
    Baked Macaroni 442
    Breads, Quick Fruit Nut 249
    Cheese Rice, with Mushroom Sauce 438
    Cinnamon Whirl 295
    Egg and Fish 682
Loaf cheese 451
Loaves, bread, *shaping* 271
Lobster 694
    Units per pound 159, *yield from* 690,
    buying of 719
    Avocado sandwich 1220
    Boiled 720
    Broiled 720
    Canapé Butter 188
    Canapé Filling 189
    Cocktail 196
    Dunk—Appetizers 206
    Filling, Salmon, Fish Pastry Shell with
    729
    Mousse, Shrimp and 1159
    Newburg 721
    Stuffed Eggs in Tomato Sauce 670
    Tails, Broiled 721
    Thermidor 721
Loganberry
    Buying, care 90, *in diet* 5
    Juice 1080
    Tapioca 640
Loin of Pork, Roast 864
Longhorn Cheese 448

Loquat Pie 1002
Lot-ju-kair-ngow 816
Lovage, *uses* 130
Lunch of school child 35
Luncheon Meats 886
    Sandwiches 1235
Lye Hominy 429
Lyonnaise
    Eggs 672
    Potatoes 1378
    Sweet Potatoes 1388

M

Macaroni
    As substitute for potato 3, *caloric value*
    13, *care* 152, *cooking* 430, *cups per
    pound* 157, *in pie vents* 983, *types and
    ingredients in* 422
    and Cheese, Baked 441, 442
    Casserole, Salmon and 730
    Endive Salad 1187
    Loaf, Baked 442
    Medley, Beef-Tomato 821
    Quick Baked 442
    Quick-Meal 444
    Salad 1188
    Salad, Hot 1128
    Tomato, Green Pepper Casserole 1408
    Tomatoes, Liver, Italian Style 905
Macaroons 470–472
Mace, *uses* 130
Macedoine of Vegetables, Beef Pot Roast
    with 807
Mackerel
    Baking and broiling 699, 705
Magnesium, in Fish 687
Maître d'Hôtel Sauce 1257
Malted Milk
    Chocolate 224
    Powder 118
    Shake, Chocolate 220
Man, *dietary needs* 8
Mandel Kakas 499
Mangoes
    In diet 5, *serving of* 575
Manhattan Clam Chowder 1270
Maple
    Butter Cream 472
    Cream Pie 964
    extract 134
    Pecan Sugar Cookies 487
    sugar 126
    syrup, *care of* 151
Maraschino
    Cherry Cake 336
    Cherry Soda 222
Marble Chocolate Cake 349
    Old-Fashioned 354
Margarine
    Care 148, *coloring* 107, *cups per*

Margarine—(Cont'd)
  pound 157, how made 107, in diet 3, 5,
  nutritive value 107, vitamin A, value 28
Marjoram, use 130
Market, dependable, choose 70, dressed
  poultry 1029
Marlborough Pie 973
Marlows 606–607
Marmalade 1088
  Quick Orange 1095
Marrow Ball Dumplings 244
Marsh Hare or Muskrat 766
  removing glands from 766
Marshmallow
  Caloric value 13, no. per pound 159
  and Pineapple Cabbage Salad 1178
  and Nut Salad, Banana 1135
  Filling 399
  Fudge 403
  Nut Sundae 646
  Pudding 584
  Salad, Fruit 1137
  Salad, Pineapple Cabbage 1175
  Sundae, Chocolate 643
Mashed Potato Salad No. 1 1129
Mayonnaise 1202. (See Salad Dressing)
  Care 151, discussion of 1196, caloric
  value 13
Meal time for pre-school child 33
Meals, special, Vol I, page xxviii
Measurements 154
  Substitutions and equivalents, table 155,
  units per pound of foods 156
Measurements and Equivalents 155
Measures 1424
MEAT 788–890
  Alternatives for 4, bones for extra gravy
  798, braising 794, 805, broiling of 793,
  care of canned and cured 146, carving
  912, classes and grades of 790, cooked,
  care of 147, cooking 791, cooking in
  water and for soup 795, cooking method
  and cuts 788, deep-fat frying 738, federal grading and inspection of 788, 789,
  fish, poultry and eggs, iron value of 29,
  fresh, care of 145, fritter batter 1349,
  frying of 794, grade stamps on 789,
  gravy, serving of 799, ground, buying
  hints 820, in diet 3, 33, larding 164,
  lean, protein value of 15, leftover, care
  of 147, pan-broiling of 793, pan gravy
  for 800, place in menu 788, protein value
  of glandular 15, salting of roast 792,
  roasting and searing of 792, shrinkage in
  cooking 792, simmering 796, skewers
  1426, stewing of 795, thermometer 792
Balls, Savory Dinner Chowder 1273
Balls, Swedish 827
Balls with Sauerkraut 838
Braised or Pot Roast Gravy 799
Cold Salad 1184
Croquettes 505

Meat Gravy 797
  Brown, Thickened 799
  Milk or Thickened 799
  Pan 800
Meat Loaf 829, 830
  Chili Sauce-Meringue 823
  Upside-Down 829
Meat Roast, Diced 805
Meats, luncheon 886
MEATS, VARIETY 890
  Cooking methods table 41, 891, and time
  table 892
Melba Bow Knots 264
  Cheese Toast 264
  Toast 264
Melons
  Ascorbic acid (vit. C) value 20, care
  144, in diet 5, serving 144, 570
  Cocktail 193
  Mold 589
  Plum Cocktail 194
MENUS
  Adjusting quantities 41, adjusting to can-
  ning program 43, family cooperation 43,
  basic plan 40, contrasts and economy in
  4, for new ideas and recipes 39, for sea-
  sonable foods and variety 39, for showers,
  weddings, Vol I, pages xxvii–xxxi, how to
  use 39, monthly menus 44, planning
  ahead 42, special days, Vol. I, page xxx,
  switching 42, table of alternate foods for
  4, why use 37
Meringues 610
  for Cream Pie 952
  Glacé 611
  Kisses 473
  Peach, with Orange Sauce 652
  Re-crisping shells 1027
  Rhubarb Strawberry 624
  Shells 611, 1027
  with Cocoa Custard 651
Mexican Chocolate 226
  Orange Candy 405
Milk
  Acidophilous 117, and acid foods at
  same meal 120, and fish at same meal
  120, and milk products, calcium value
  29, as fattening food 120, buttermilk
  116, caloric value 13, care of fresh milk
  and dairy products 147, certified 116,
  chocolate 117, concentrated fresh, or
  frozen 116, condensed 118, descriptions
  115, milk drinks 222, dry, how made,
  kind, uses 118, fallacies 120, flavored
  117, governmental control 115, graded
  117, hints 119, homogenized 116, how
  to measure 160, in children's diets 34,
  in diet pattern 3, malted, powder 118,
  pasteurized and cream 116, plain, un-
  treated 115, products, alternates in 4,
  protein value 14, skim, nutritive value
  117, skim, precautions in using 120, soft

Milk—(Cont'd)
  curd 117, sources of contamination 115,
    souring 167, vitamin values 22, 23, 28,
    vitamin D 116, yogurt 117
  Toast 264
Milk Drinks 222–227
Milk-Egg Drinks 227–228
Milk, evaporated 118
  Equivalent of fresh 4, souring 167, sub-
    stituting for fresh 167, whipping 168
Milks, cultured 116
Mince Pie 1003
Mincemeat 1112
  Custard 527
  Fried Pies 989
  Green Tomato 1111
  Ice Cream 595
  Pudding 629
  Tarts 1023
Minerals In fish 687, in diet 16
Minestra, Italian Soup 1290
Minestrone 1293
Mint, care, uses 130, 133, 142
Mint
  Barbecue Sauce, for Lamb 841
  Chutney 1108
  Jelly 1085
  Sauce 1257, 1258
  Tea 231
Mints, Uncooked Cream 419
Mocha Butter Frosting 385
Mocha Whip 585
Molasses, black strap cane
  How made 125, care 151, weight per
    cup 159
  Cookies, Drop 466
  Cookies, Soft, Rolled 493
  Nog 226
  Shake 221
Molds, assorted 1424
Mono Sodium Glutamate 131
Moravian Chicken 1057
Mornay Sauce 1258
Moss Rose Cake 319
Mousse 591
  Avocado 1161
  Caramel 608
  Chicken, with Supreme Sauce 1051
  Chocolate 608
  Golden 608
  Pineapple 609
  Shrimp and Lobster 1159
  Strawberry 609
Mousseline Sauce 1258
Muenster cheese 451
Muffins 253
  Cup sizes 254
  In diet 5
  Bacon 254
  Bacon, Corn Meal 241
  Banana 255
  Basic or Plain 254

Blueberry 254
Bran 255
Corn Meal 241
Cranberry 255
English 306
Fruit 254
Graham Gems 256
Plain 254
Potato Flour 256
Rice 257
Rolled Oat 257
Soy 257
Twin Mountain 258
Whole Wheat or Graham 256
Mulberry Pie 1003
Mullet, cooking methods 692
Mulligan, Chicken 1051
Mush, Fried Corn Meal 428
Mushrooms
  Buying, care 84, in diet 4
  and Eggs, Creamed 666
  Chicken Livers with 1061
  Creamed 1356
  Dressing 754
  for Vegetable Plate 1410
  Omelet 677
  Sauce 1259
  Sauce, Beef Pinwheels with 836
  Sauce, Cheese Rice Loaf with 438
  Sauce, Chicken Loaf with 1049
  Sauce, for Broiled Hamburger 824
  Sauce, Fresh, Ham Puffs with 867
  Sautéed 1356
  Soufflé 680
  Soup, Cream of 1280
  Soup, Potato and Cream of 1281
  Spread, Liver Sausage 1229
  Stuffed, Broiled 210
  Stuffed, in Casserole 1357
Muskmelon
  Buying, care 93, in diet 5, vitamin A and
    C, value 20, 28
Muskrat
  Removing glands from 766
  Fricassee 766
  Maryland 767
Mustard
  Seed and uses 131
  Butter—Canapés 188
  Sauce 1259
  Sauce De Luxe 1259
  Sauce, Eggs in 669
Mustard Greens
  Buying, care 83, in diet 4
  and Spinach with Bacon 1352
Mutton, U. S. Government grades 791
Mysost cheese 451

N

Napoleon Slices 937
Nasturtium, uses 131

National Research, *dietary allowances* 8
Navy Beans. (*See Beans, Navy*)
Nectarine-Raspberry Compote 565
Nectarines, *buying, care* 93
Nesselrode Pie 965
Nesselrode Pudding 580
Neufchatel cheese 451
Newburg
    Asparagus 1312
    Lobster 721
    Soup, Chicken 1299
New Year's Day Dinners, Vol 1, page xxx
New York ice cream 591
Niacin (nicotinic acid)
    Daily allowances 8, 25, *effects of cooking on* 25, *functions of in body* 26, *in enriched bread and flour* 233, *in fish* 687, *table sources of* 25
No-Bake Fruit Cake 371
Nokkelost cheese 451
Noodles
    As substitute for potato 3, *cooking of* 430, *cups per pound* 157, *how made, kinds* 422
    and Cheese, Creamed Spinach on 1394
    "Boiled" Beef and 818
    Casserole, Dried Beef and 834
    Dressing 754
    Fried, Crisp 431
    Golden 430
    Homemade 431
    Jiffy 443
    Platter, Broccoli 1327
    Poppy Seed 431
    Sautéed 431
    Soup, Beef and 1286
    Stuffed 432
    Supreme Tuna and 734
    Tuna and 733
Nougat 406
Nut and Fruit Breads 249–253
Nut Butters, *how made* 121
Nuts
    Blanching 121, *Brazil, caloric value* 12, *butters and pastes* 121, *buying and care* 122, *cashew, caloric value* 12, *nutritional value* 121, *peanuts, caloric value* 13, *rancidity* 121, *roasting* 121, *varieties* 120, *where grown* 121, *why they turn purple* 121
    Breads 296
    Caramels 416
    Caramels, Fruit 416
    Confections 414
    Date Bread 250
    Rolls, Poppy Seed or 296
    Salad, Banana, Marshmallow and 1135
    Salad, Fruit and, Frozen 1124
    Salad, Lime Olive, Molded 1164
    Salad, Prune 1142
    Spread, Date 1223
    Sundae, Honey 645

Sundae, Marshmallow 646
Tangy Cheese 203
Topping, Crispy, for Sundaes 646
Nutmeg, *uses* 131
    Sauce 1247
Nutrition, improved by menus 37, 39
Nutty Canapés 184

O

Oat flour 110
Oats
    Caloric value 13, *rolled, kinds* 421
Oatmeal
    Thiamine (vit. B₁) value 22
    Bread 297
    Bread, Currant 298
    Drop Cookies, No. 1 and 2 467
    Rolled Cookies, Ground 490
    Soufflé 680
    Toffee 412
Oil
    How to measure 160, *mineral, use in cooking* 109, *salad, cups per pound* 157, *kinds, uses of* 109, 1081, *care of* 151
Okra
    Buying, care 84, *cooking methods* 1307, *in diet* 4, *selecting* 1357, *vitamin A, value* 27
    and Tomatoes 1358
    Gumbo, Chicken and 1045
    Soup, Quick Tomato 1296
Old English Nut Toffee 413
Old-Fashioned
    "Boiled Coffee" 213
    Bread Dressing 1073
    Candied Fruit Roll 411
    Chicken Salad 1058
    Lace Cookies 468
    Marble Cake 354
    Sour Cream Salad Dressing 1203
Old-Time
    Egg Pancakes 686
    Streusel Coffee Cake 293
Oleomargarine, substitute for 5
Olives
    Caloric value 13, *care and sizes* 123, 124, *green or Spanish, how produced* 123, *queen* 123, *sizes, illustrated* 124
    and Egg Sandwiches 1230
    and Tomato Sandwich 1224
    Butter—Canapés 188
    Celery Filling—Canapés, 190
    Cheese Sandwiches 1212
    Nut Spread 1224
    Nut Molded Salad, Lime 1164
Omelets 676–678. (*See Egg Dishes*)
Onion
    and Apple Fromage 1362
    Eggplant with Cheese Sauce 1346
    Gravy for Hamburger 824
    Gravy for Venison 752

Onion—(Cont'd)
Green, Salad, Beet and 1146
Juice, *how to make* 164, 165
Salad, Best Cheese and 1146
Salad, Tomato and 1154
Sauce 1260
Sauce, Beef Slices in 808
Sauté, Hominy Potatoes 1350
Slices, Baked 1359
Slices and Green Tomato 1406
Soup, Cream of 1281
Soup, French 1269
Onion flakes, dried 101
Onions
Buying and care of 84, *caloric value* 13, *cooking methods* 1307, *green, care of* 142, *in diet* 4, *preparing, selecting* 1358
and Apples, Baked 1359
au Gratin 1362
Boiled Green, in Cheese Sauce 1360
Broiled 1360
Buttered 1359
Creamed 1360
Escalloped 1360
for Vegetable Plate 1410
French-Fried 1361
Glazed 1361
Kidney Beans with 1317
Liver and 905
Pan-Fried 1361
Pickled 1104
Pickled Beets and 1152
Sautéed and Pepper 1362
Stuffed, No. 1 and 2 1363
Opossum. (*See* Possum)
Oranges
Buying, care 76, 93, *in diet* 5, *serving of* 571, *sizes* 96, *varieties* 76, *vitamin values* 22, 24, *caloric value* 13, *extract* 133, *ascorbic acid (vit. C) value of juice* 19, *caloric value of juice* 13, *juice in diet* 5
Bavarian, Fresh 581
Butter Sauce 611
Buttermilk Jelly 590
Cake Custard 533
Cake, Double Orange 335
Candy, Mexican 405
Chiffon Pie 946
Coconut Creams 406
Coconut Salad 1138
Cookies with Poultry Fat, 483
Cookies, Sugar 487
Cottage Cheese Custard Pie 973
Cream Kisses 473
Cup Cakes 358
Date Tarts 1023
Filling, No. 1 and 2 399
Float 629
Frosting, Butter 387
Glazed Butterfly Rolls 285
Ice 604
Jelly 590

Juice 218
Marmalade Bread Pudding 539
Marmalade, Quick 1095
Marmalade Soufflé 650
Meringue Pie 955
Meringue Pudding 621
Nut Bread 252
Pecan Cookies 484
Peel, Candied 410
Pinwheel Biscuits 237
Pinwheels, Marmalade 286
Pocketbook Rolls 286
Raisin Cupcakes 359
Raisin Salad 1138
Sauce, No. 1 and 2 1247
Sauce, Beets in 1325
Sauce, Lemon 646
Sauce, Sliced Goose in 1063
Shortcake 648
Slices, Poached 560
Soda 222
Spanish Cream 585
Sugar Cookies 487
Tapioca 640
Waldorf Salad 1139
Yam Casserole 1389
Order of Table Service, Vol 1, page xxiv
Orégano, *uses* 131
Overweight 10
Oxtail Soup 1294
Oxtails, Braised 911
Oyster Plant, *buying of* 87
Oysters
Buying 722, *cooking methods* 694, *how to open and clean* 722, 723, *serving per quart* 159, *yield from* 690
au Gratin 723
Bisque or Chowder 1284
Broiled in Bacon 202
Creamed Chicken and 1057
Dressing 1074
Escalloped 723
Fillets of Sole and, Parmesan 706
French-Fried 724
Fried 724
Fritters 723
on the Half Shell 196, 724
Pan-Fried 724
Rockefeller Moderne 725
Sandwiches 724
Smoked 207
Stew 724, 1272

P

Package sizes, yeast 267
Palm, Hearts of, Buttered 1332
Pan
Gravy 766, 800
Rolls 276
Pancakes
Chicken Filled, Tomato Sauce 1052

Pancakes—(Cont'd)
  Egg, with Cherry Sauce 685
  French 248
  Grandma's Buckwheat, Yeast 305
  Griddle Cakes 246, 248
  Old-Time Egg 686
  Potato 1377, 1381
Pandowdies, discussion of 512
Pandowdy, Apple 513
  Canned Boysenberry 516
Panocha 407
Pan-Fried Fish 707
Papaya
  In diet 5
  Pie 974
  Salad 1139
Paprika, description and uses 131
Paradise Jelly 1087
Paraffin, to cover jelly 1082, 1083
Parboiling 165
Parchment, Fish Baked in 701
Parkerhouse Rolls 277
Parmesan cheese 451
Parmesan, Fillet of Sole and Oysters 706
Parmigiano, Veal 880
Parsley
  Buying, care 86, chopping 162, dried 101, in diet 4, use of 131, vitamin A, value 27
  Butter 1224
  Butter for Sandwich Loaf 1217
  Buttered Potatoes 1380
  Omelet 677
  Salad with Chiffonade Dressing 1151
  Sauce, for Ham and Tomato Supreme Sandwich 1234
Parsnips
  Buying, care 85, cooking methods 1307, in diet 4, preparing and selecting 1363
  and Tomatoes 1366
  Butter, Brown 1364
  French-Fried 1364
  Fritters 1365
  Patties with Grapefruit Sauce 1365
  Stew 1365
  with Savory Sauce 1366
Partridge, cookery 761
  Broiled 762
  Roast 763
Party Salad, Girls' 1122
Pascal Celery Salad, Apple-Turnip 1135
Pasteurization 116
PASTRY 921–1027
  Advantages of cloth 926, baking of 929, blender 1425, cloth 1425, crimper 1425, discussion of 921, flour 110, function of each ingredient 922, pan size 923
  Cheese 929
  Danish 305
  Egg White Wash 935
  Egg Yolk Wash 935
  Hot Water 932

  Mashed Potato 932
  Plain, ingredients and directions for making 2-Crust pies 924, 925
  Puff 933, 939
  Steps in Making Single-Crust Shells 928
  Whole Wheat 933
Pastries and the pre-school child 34
Pastry Shells
  Pan size 923, pie pan 924, steps in making Crumb Crust, 931
  Chocolate cookies 931
  for Dessert Dumplings 933
  Vanilla Wafer 931
Pate De Foie Gras 190
Patties, Butterscotch 412
Patty Shell Cases 612, 938
Pea, Peas
  Ascorbic acid (vit. C) value 20, buying, care 82, 142, caloric value 13, cooking methods 1307, dried, protein value 15, in diet 4, selecting 1366, split, cups per pound 158, vitamin values of 22, 24, 26, 27
  and Cheese Stuffed Tomato Salad 1182
  and Potato Casserole 1367
  and Rice Soup 1284
  Buttered 1367
  Creamed 1367
  Creamed, and New Potatoes 1367
  for Vegetable Plate 1410
  Loaf 1368
  Salad, Beet and 1146
  Soup, Cream of 1281
  Soup, Special 1294
  Split, Soup 1275, 1297
  Split, Soup, Bohemian 1287
Peaches
  Ascorbic acid (vit. C), value 20, 26, buying, care 93, caloric value 13, in diet 5, niacin (nicotinic acid) value 26, serving 570, dried, buying of 103, cups per pound 157, vitamin value of 97
  and Cream Pie 969
  and Orange Cup 194
  Baked 565
  Blossom Pie 975
  Butter 1088
  Canned, Tarts 1024
  Cobbler 522
  Conserve 1089
  Cream Pie 958
  Crumble Pie 1007
  Dumplings, Skillet 545
  Ice Cream 596
  Juice Pudding Sauce 1248
  Meringues with Orange Sauce 652
  Pickled 1098
  Pie, 1004, 1005, 1006
  Preserves 1093
  Prune and Cottage Cheese Salad 1139
  Pudding, Fresh 621
  Salad 1140

Peaches—(Cont'd)
Salad Fig Mold 1164
Shake 221
Sour Cream Pie 1005, 1007
Stewed 565
Stewed, in Red Plum Purée 566
Sugared 575
Shortcake 648
Tapioca Pudding, Baked 640
Peanut Brittle
Ice Cream 597
Salad, Apple and 1134
Salad, Carrot and 1176
Whip 653
Peanut Butter
Caloric value 13, how made 121, vitamin
values 22, 24, 26
and Bacon Spread 1232
and Watercress Sandwiches 1232
Bacon filling, Canapés 190
Banana and Jelly Spread 1232
Bread (Buttermilk) 252
Cake 337
Cookies 475
Custard 533
Dressing, No. 1 and 2 1204
India Relish Filling—Canapés 191
Jelly Sandwiches 1232
Pinwheels 418
Sandwiches 1233
Sauce, Chocolate 644
Sauce, Kohlrabi with 1354
Peanuts
Caloric value 13, vit. values 22, 24, 26
Pear, Cheese 452
Salad 1140
Salad, Stuffed 1166
Pears
Caloric value 13, dried, buying 103,
dried, cups per pound 157, fall and
winter for eating 95, guide for buying
94, in diet 5, serving of 570
Baked 566
Cranberry Glazed 567
French, Pie 1008
Gingered, Baked 566
Gingered, Poached 568
Pickled 1098
Poached 567
Sabayone, Poached 568
Stewed 568
Pecans
Caloric value 13, cups per pound 159
Pie 975, 976
Rolls or Schnecken 287
Pellagra 5, 26
Pepper, black, white
Description, uses 131
Green, and Cheese Ring Salad 1150
Onion Mayonnaise 1204
Peppers
Ascorbic acid (vit. C) value 20, buying,

care 85, caloric value 13, green 1368, in
diet 4
Stuffed Green, No. 1, 2, 3, 4, 5 1369,
1370, 1371
Peppermint
Extract 134
Butter Cream 461
Buttermilk 226
Candy Refrigerator Ice Cream 598
Cream Brownies 460
Rennet-Custard 612
Sauce, Chocolate 644
Stick Ice Cream, No. 1 and 2 597, 598
Perch 693, 694
Perfection Salad 1169
Persimmon, Bavarian 581
Pudding, Wild 622
Salad 1141
Salad, Grapefruit and Avocado 1138
Persimmons, buying, care 94
Petits Fours 344, 345
Fondant for 405
Weiva 937
Pfefferneusse, Dark 498, Light 499
Pheasant 769, 772
Gravy for 765
Gravy, Cooking Giblets for 764
Philadelphia
ice cream 591
Pepper Pot 1295
Phosphate baking powders 112
Phosphorus
In fish 687, use of in body 17, 31
Piccalilli 1111
Pickerel 693
Pickle Sandwiches, Cucumber, Onion and
1223
Pickled Onions 1104
Peaches 1098
Pears 1098
PICKLES 1096–1113
Amount of brine for 1096, care of 151,
crispness in 1096, elaboration of brine
pickles 123, hollow, shriveled, soft 1096,
kettle and salt for 1096, "salt stock,"
how made 123, serving of 1096, vinegar
and water for 1096
Beet 1100
Bread and Butter 1101
Cantaloupe 1100
Cassia Bud 1101
Celery Cucumber 1101
Crabapple 1097
Dill 1102
Dill Bean 1102
Dill Cucumber 1103
Fruit 1097
Green Tomato 1103
Kosher Dill 1103
Sweet Dill 1103
Texas Sour 1104
Thunder and Lightning 1105

Pickles—(Cont'd)
  Van's 1105
  Vegetable 1100
  Watermelon 1099
Picnic Ham, Baked 865
Picnic menu, *prepared, No. 1, prepared, No. 2 and 3, quit-and-go, No. 1, 2, 3, Vol. 1, xxix*
Picnics, Vol. 1, xxviii
PIES 921–1027
  Pie apples 97–99, *care* 150, *bread crumbs for juicy pies* 985, *Chiffon* 939, *Cream, consistency of* 956, *Cream, discussion of* 955, *Custard, baking hints* 970, *Custard, discussion of* 970, *Fruit, reheating of* 150, *function of each ingredient* 922, *how to make best fruit* 983, *meringue topping* 957, *woven lattice or stripped top* 984
  Angel 1025–1027
  Angel, Lemon Filling 1025
  Angel, Strawberry Filling 1026
  Apple 985
  Apple, Canned 987
  Apple, French or Dutch 987
  Apple Soufflé 986
  Apple, Sour Cream 989
  Apricot, Canned 990
  Apricot, Dried 990
  Banana Cream 958
  Berry and Cream 969
  Berry, Canned 991
  Black Bottom 940
  Blackberry 991
  Blueberry 993, 994
  Blueberry and Red Raspberry 994
  Blueberry, Deep Dish 992
  Blueberry Whipped Cream 992
  Buttermilk Raisin 959
  Butterscotch 959
  Calamondin 948
  Cherry 995, 996, 997
  Chess 970, 971
  Chocolate Chiffon 942
  Chocolate Cream 960, 961
  Chiffon 940–948
  Citrus 948–955
  Coconut, Canned or Packaged 962
  Coconut Cream 961, 962
  Coffee Chiffon 941
  Cranberry 998
  Cream 955–969
  Currant, Red 999
  Custard 970–982
  Crusts, Pie. *See Pastry Shells*
  Date Cream 962
  Deep South Sugar 968
  Eggnog Chiffon 942
  French Cream 963
  Fried and variations 988, 989
  Fruit 982–1017

  Gooseberry 999, 1000
  Graham Cracker 964
  Grape, Concord 1001
  Grapefruit 949
  Green Tomato 1016
  Guava 1001
  Honey Pumpkin 977
  Key Lime 953
  Lemon and Orange Chiffon 944
  Lemon Cake 949
  Lemon Chiffon 943
  Lemon Cream 950
  Lemon Fluff 951
  Lemon Glamour 951
  Lemon Meringue 952
  Lime Chiffon 945
  Lime Chiffon, Graham Cracker Crust 944
  Lime Meringue 954
  Loquat 1002
  Maple 964
  Marlborough 973
  Mince 1003
  Mock Cherry—Cranberry 998
  Mulberry 1003
  Nesselrode 965
  Orange Chiffon 946
  Orange Cottage Cheese 973
  Orange Meringue 955
  Papaya 974
  Peach 1004, 1005, 1006
  Peach Blossom 975
  Peach Cream 958
  Peach Crumble 1007
  Peach Sour Cream 1005, 1007
  Peaches and Cream 969
  Pear, Fresh 1008
  Pecan 975, 976
  Pineapple Cottage Cheese 976
  Pineapple Meringue 966
  Plum, Blue or Italian 1009
  Plum, Red 1010
  Prune 1010
  Pumpkin 978, 979
  Pumpkin Chiffon 947
  Raisin 1011, 1012
  Raspberry Chiffon 948
  Raspberry, Red 1012
  Red Raspberry and Grape 1013
  Rhubarb 1014
  Rhubarb Cream 967
  Shoo-fly 979
  Sliced Lemon, 2-Crust 953
  Slip-Slide Custard 980
  Sour Cream Prune 967
  Strawberries in Whipped Cream 1016
  Strawberry 1015
  Strawberry Chiffon 947
  Strawberry Cream 958
  Sweet Potato 981
  Tarts 1017–1025
  Vinegar 981

Pigeon
  Pie 1064
  Potted 1065
Pike, *cooking methods for* 693, 694, 699
Pilaf, Lamb 844
Pimiento, *description, uses* 131
Pimiento cheese 447
Pineapple
  Ascorbic acid (vit. C) value 20, *buying, care* 94, *caloric value* 13, *cheese* 452, *how to select and prepare* 576, *in diet* 5, *thiamine (vit. B₁) value of* 22
  Bavarian 582
  Butter Buns 286
  Buttermilk 226
  Buttermilk Sherbert 606
  Cabbage and Date Salad 1175
  Cabbage and Marshmallow Salad 1178
  Cake Custard 533
  Cones 576
  Cooler 219
  Cottage Cheese Aspic 1165
  Cottage Cheese Pie 976
  Cottage Cheese Salad 1141
  Cottage Pudding 623
  Date Salad 1141
  Date Whip 654
  Egg Punch 228
  Fresh, in the Shell 576
  Fresh Sugared 576
  Grape Salad 1165
  Ice 604
  Lime Velvet 1166
  Meringue Cream Pie 966
  Mousse 609
  Salad, Cabbage and, Molded 1169
  Salad Dressing 1202
  Sauce 1248
  Sauce, Sweet Potatoes with 1388
  Snow 586
  Soda 222
  Tapioca 641
  Upside-Down Crush Cake 363
  Upside-Down Wheel Cake 363
  Waldorf Salad 1141
Pinto Beans 1323
Pinwheels, *miscellaneous*
  Butterscotch Biscuit 237
  Chocolate Cookies 482
  Orange Biscuit 237
  Orange Marmalade Roll 286
  Peanut Butter Candy 418
Piquant Butter—Canapés 188
Pizza 440
Plain Muffins 254
Planked Fish 735
Planked Steak 838
Planks, *preparation* 1427
Plantain, *description of* 1371
  Fried Fritters 1371
Plate, beef, *braising time* 806
Plates, Vegetable 1410

Plum
  Betty 511
  Butter 1089
  Cobbler 523
  Dumplings 546, 547
  Jelly 1081
  Juice 1081
  Kuchen 239, 292
  Pie 1009, 1010
  Pudding, Molded 589
  Red, Jelly 1087
  Sauce with Ham Loaf 868
  Sugared Fresh Apricots and Red 571
Plum Pudding 634
Plum Tomatoes, Stuffed 211
Plums
  Caloric value 13, *buying, care* 94, *in diet* 5
  Stewed 568
Poached Eggs 672–674
Polenta 440
Polish Beets 1326
Pollo Con Arros or Chicken with Rice 1053
Pollock 692
Polonaise Asparagus 1313
  Broccoli 1327
Pomegranates, *buying and care of* 95
Pompano 692
Poor Man's Goose 908
Pop Corn, *cups per pound* 157
Pop Corn Balls 414
Popovers 261
  Basic 261
  Cheese 262
Popped Corn 429
Poppy Seed, *uses* 131
  Cheese Strips 184
Poppy Seed or Nut Rolls 296
Porgy 692
Pork 854–873
  Broiling 793, *caloric value* 13, *cuts* 853, *servings per pound* 158, *protein value* 15, *time table for braising, broiling chops, hocks, spareribs, steaks, tenderloins* 854, *time table for roasting* 863, *U. S. Government grades* 790, *vitamin values of* 21, 23, 25
  and Rice Casserole 870
  Barbecued Spareribs, No. 1 and 2 860
  Braised Spareribs 861
  Butt, Roast Fresh Boston-Style 862
  Casserole of Corned Chops 858
  Chinese 869
  Chop Suey 870
  Chops, Baked, with Caraway Seed 856
  Chops, Braised 856
  Chops, Braised, with Sauerkraut 858
  Chops, Casserole 858
  Chops, Hominy and 1350
  Chops, Pan-Broiled, and Potatoes 859
  Chops, Spanish 857
  Chops, Stuffed 857

Pork—(Cont'd)
Crown Roast 863
Fresh Pig Hocks 860
Gravy 864
Link Sausages, Pan-Broiled 872
Loaf, Lamb and 849
Mock Chicken Legs 870
Roast Crown of 864
Roast Fresh 862
Roast, Good Old-Time, and Potatoes 864
Salt, Kidney Beans with 1317
Salt Pork and Cream Gravy 855
Scrapple 871
Spareribs
    and Sauerkraut 862
    Barbecued No. 1 and 2 860
    Celery Stuffed 861
    Fruited 861
    Stuffed 862
Steak, Braised with Spanish Rice 857
Sausage
    Bacon and Tomato Grill 872
    Baked Squash with 871
    Home-Made 872
    Patties 872
Spanish Sausage 873
Possum
Removing glands from 746
and Sweet Potatoes 768
Casserole of 768
Potato, Potatoes
White: planks or platters 1380, *alternates
for* 5, *buying* 82, *cooking methods* 1307,
in children's diet 36, *selecting and varie-
ties* 1371, *flour* 110, *in diet pattern* 3,
in diet 5, *substitutes for* 3, *caloric value*
13, *vitamin values* 20, 24, 26, *sweet:
buying and care* 83, *in diet* 5, *vitamin
values* 20, 27, *caloric values* 13
American Fried 1372
and Mushrom Soup, Cream of 1281
and Onion Sauté, Hominy 1350
au Gratin 1382
Baked 1372
Baked, with Salt Pork Gravy 1373
Boiled 1373
Caraway Salad with Sour Cream 1189
Casserole
    Finnan Haddie and 718
    Ham and 866
    Leek and 1355
    Pea and 1367
Carrot Soup 1272
Cheese Puffs 1380
Creamed No. 1 and 2 1374, 1375
Creamed with Cheese 1375
Croquettes, Baked 1380
Crunchy Broiled 1374
Dakota 1375
Dumplings 245, 1381
Escalloped
    and Frankfurters 888

and Ham 866
Carrots, and 1335
Quick 1383
Flour Muffins 256
French-Fried 1375
"Fried" Roast 1384
Gnocchi 1376
Grated, Patties 1377
Hashed Brown 1377, 1378
in Caraway Sauce 1382
Kisses 418
Lyonnaise 1378
Mashed 1378, 1379
Mashed, Pastry 932
Nests, Poached Eggs in 674
New, Creamed Peas and 1367
O'Brien 1383
Oven French Fries 1376
Pancakes 1377, 1381
Parsley Buttered 1380
Patties 1382
Pie Crust 932
Riced 1383
Roast 1384
Salad
    Potato 1188
    Corned Beef and 1185
    Endive and, Hot 1128
    English 1190
    Mashed, Salad No. 1 and 2 1129
    No. 1, 2, 3, Hot 1130, 1131
    Picnic 1189
    with Fresh Dill 1189
    with Whipped Cream Dressing 1190
Soup
    Cream of 1282
    Golden 1283
    Leek and 1283
    Watercress or Spinach and 1276
Stuffed, Baked, No. 1 and 2 1384, 1385
Stuffing, Mashed
    for Wild Duck 759
    Roast Goose with 1063
Vegetable Plate
"Pot au feu" 1263
Pot Liquor 1307
Cocktails 198
Pot, Dinner 1408
Pot Roast
Cuts for 807, *braising time* 806
Beef 806
Beef, Spanish Style 807
Beef, with Macedoine of Vegetables 807
Beef, with Vegetables 807
of Veal 876
of Veal with Apple Dressing 877
Shortribs 812
Potted Meat for Sandwiches 1230
POULTRY 1028–1077
Care of 147, *cookery* 1028, *cut-up, con-
venience of* 1029, *drawing of, illustrated*
1032, *drawn, fresh-chilled* 1029, *dressing*

Poultry—(Cont'd)
  for market 1029, *U. S. Government grades*
  1028, *in diet pattern* 3, *judging for qual-*
  ity 1028, *live and dressed* 1029, *methods*
  of killing and dressing 1030, *niacin*
  (nicotinic acid) value 25, *preparing of*
  (killing and cleaning) illustrated 1030,
  quick frozen, full drawn 1029, *removing*
  tendons 1031, *scalding* 1030, *seasoning,*
  description and uses 131, *semi-scalding*
  1030, *shears* 1425, *singeing* 1031, *tem-*
  perature for cooking 1036, *trussing* 1034,
  weight to allow per person 159
  Croquettes 507
  Stuffings 1072
Poultry Fat
  Orange Cookies with 483
Pound Cake 355
Praline Cookies 476
Pralines 407
Preparing Ingredients and Pans for Cake
  Baking 312
Pre-School Child, *feeding of* 33
PRESERVES 1078–1095
  Definition of 1088
  Bar le Duc 1090
  Blue Damson 1091
  Cherry 1091
  Citron 1092
  Kumquat 1092
  Peach 1093
  Seven-Minute Strawberry 1094
  Strawberry Electric-Light 1093
  Strawberry Sun 1094
  Tomato, Yellow and Red 1094
Pressure saucepans, *discussion of* 1425, 1426
Primost cheese 452
Printemps Chowder 1273
Processed cheese, how made 451
Protein, *body needs for* 14, *grams, daily*
  allowances 8, *how used in body and*
  sources 14, 15, *in fish* 687, *use of in*
  body 5, *values of foods, Table* 14
Provolette cheese 450
Provoloncinni cheese 450
Provoloni cheese 450
Prune, Prunes
  Buying 104, *caloric value* 13, *dried, cups*
  per pound 157, *in diet* 5, *vitamin values*
  of 24, 26, 28
  and Cottage Cheese Salad, Peach 1139
  Bread 252
  Broiled in Bacon 202
  Filling for Kolachy 285
  Ice Cream 598
  Marlow 607
  Milk 227
  Nut Bread 252
  Nut Salad 1142
  or Raisin Bread 298
  Pie 1010
  Pie, Sour Cream 967

Pudding, Baked 623
  Salad, Molded 1165
  Salad, Stuffed 1142, 1143
  Sandwiches, Hot 1216
  Shake 221
  Stewed 552
  Whip 655
  Whip, Baked 654
Pudding Sauces
  Caramel 1239
  Chocolate 1239, 1240
  Chocolate Peppermint 644
  Cinnamon Dip 1240
  Coffee Sauce 1241, 1242
  Creamy Vanilla 1242
  Grandma's 1244
  Lemon Orange 646
  Peach, Canned 1248
  1890 Sauce 1249
Puddings, *in children's diets* 33, *pans* 1425
  Apple Charlotte 615
  Baked 614–625
  Blueberry Refrigerator, Fresh 630
  Bread 536, 539
  Caramel Blanc-Mange 625
  Carrot 616
  Cheese with Spanish Sauce 438
  Cherry, Upside-Down 616
  Chocolate 632
  Chocolate Blanc-Mange 626
  Chocolate Custard 627
  Chocolate Marshmallow 627
  Chocolate, Upside-Down 617
  Cinnamon Blanc-Mange 626
  Cocoa Bread 538
  Cornstarch 628
  Cottage 618
  Date Cake 618
  Date-Fig 633
  Date Graham Cracker Torte 619
  Date, Saucy 620
  Date, with Brandy Crème Sauce 619
  Fish 711
  Fruit Cream, Fresh 628
  Fruit-Nut 633
  Indian 620
  Lemon Cracker Meringue 538
  Lemon Cream 629
  Lemon Grape-Nut 539
  Mincemeat 629
  Orange Float 629
  Orange Marmalade Bread 539
  Orange Meringue 621
  Peach, Fresh 621
  Persimmon, Wild 622
  Pineapple Cottage 623
  Plum 634
  Prune, Baked 623
  Raisin, Crumb 635
  Raisin, Everyday 624
  Rice 636, 637
  Rod Grod or Danish Red 630

Puddings—(Cont'd)
  Steamed 631–636
  Sweet Potato 624
  Tapioca 638–641
  Vanilla, with Crispy Topping 631
  Yorkshire and Shortribs 812
Puff
  Jam Meringue 535
  Pastry 933
  Pastry, Hints on Handling 935
  Pastry, Ingredients, Steps in Making 934
  Pastry Patty Shells 938
  Pastry, Quick 939
  Pastry Roses 938
  Shell, Asparagus in 1313
Puff Balls, Candied 412
  Yeast Rolls 277
Puffs, Cream 936
  Swan Cream 937
Puffy French Toast 264
  Omelet 677
Pumpernickel
  Flour 110
  Bread 299
Pumpkin
  *Buying, care 86, fresh, cooking of 1390,
    in diet 4, vitamin A value 27*
  Bread 298
  Chiffon Pie 947
  Custard 534
  Honey Pie 977
  Pie, No. 1 and 2 978, 979
  Purée 1390
  Soup, No. 1 and 2 1284, 1285
  Tarts 1024
Punch
  Cooler 220
  Cranberry 215
  Grapefruit Cider 216
  Hot Fruit 216
  Hot Tea 230
  Pineapple Egg 228
Purchasing 70–135
  Fruits and Vegetables 75–104
  Staples 105–135
Purée
  Freezing, storage, use 602, 603
  Apricot 551
  Berries 602
  Cantaloupe, Cranberry 602
  Dried Fruit 553
  Grape, Nectarine, Peach 602
  Pumpkin or Squash 1390
  Rhubarb, Strawberry 602, 603

Q

Quahaug Clams, *how cooked* 711
Quail 761–764
Quantity Buying 71
Quick Breads 232
  Bread (Yeast) 265, 300

Quinces
  Buying, care 92
  and Cranberry Jelly, Apple 1087
  Baked 569
  Honey 1095
  Jelly 1086
  Stewed 569

R

Rabbit 772
  Fever 742, removing glands 772
  Broiler Barbecued 773
  Corn and Cheese 446
  Fresh Corn 1342
  Fricassee 774
  Fried 773
  Hasen Pfeffer 774
  Hash 775
  Jugged 775
  Roast, with Dressing 776
  Soup 776
  Tomato 447
  Welsh 447
Raccoon 777, 778
  Removing glands of 777
  Baked, with Southern Dressing 777
  Barbecued 778
  Dressing for 778
Radishes
  *Buying, care 83, 142, cooking leaves of
    142, caloric value 13, in diet 4*
  for Vegetable Plate 1410
  "Roses" 165
  Salad, Cucumber and 1148
Rainbow Salad, Hot 1131
Raisins
  *Buying of 104, caloric value 13, cups
    per pound 157, in diet 5, vitamin value
    104, Plumping 165*
  Cobbler 523
  Crumb Pudding 635
  Pie 1011, 1012
  Pie, Buttermilk 959
  Pudding 624
  Salad
    Apple and 1134
    Cabbage, Carrot and 1174
    Orange 1138
  Sandwich Filling, Cheese and 1210
  Sauce, Cabbage in 1330
  Spread, Carrot 1222
  Stewed 553
Raspberry
  *Ascorbic acid (vit. C) value 20, buying,
    care 90, 143, caloric value 13, in diet 5*
  Black, Cobbler 524
  Black, Ice 605
  Black, Jelly 1084
  Black, Shake 220
  Black, Soda 221
  Chiffon Pie 948

Raspberry—(Cont'd)
 Currant Cocktail 94
 Extract 134
 Freeze 601
 Ice Cream 598
 Mallow Cream 587
 Nectarine Compote 565
 Pie 1012
 Red, and Blueberry Pie 994
 Red, and Cottage Cheese Salad 1143
 Red, and Grape Pie 1013
 Red, Bavarian 582
 Red, Fluff 586
Ravioli with Tomato Sauce 432
Red and Green Salad 1179
Red Beans and Rice 1323
Red Snapper, *cooking methods for* 692
Refrigerator
 Cleaning and defrosting of 153, *dishes* 1425, *management of* 152
 Cookies, Basic Dough 478
 Rolls, Plain 280, 281
Refrigerator Cakes 372
 Banana Vanilla Wafer 372
 Cheese 373
 Chocolate 374
 Fruit 374
 Lemon 375
 Stuffed Angel Food—Chocolate 372
Relishes 1105
 Beet 1174
 Corn 1106
 Cranberry 1207
 Dressing, for Fish 704
 Hot Dog 1109
 India 1110
 Sauce for Tuna Turnovers 735
Remoulade Sauce 1260
Rennet-Custard, Cottage Cheese 612
 Peppermint 612
Rhubarb
 Buying, care 92, *caloric value* 13, *in diet* 5
 Cream Pie 967
 Fig-Bar Betty 511
 Marlow 607
 Pie 1014
 Shortcake 648
 Stewed 570
 Strawberry Meringues 624
Rib, beef
 Braising time 806, *roast buying hints* 805
 Roast of beef 803
Ribbon Cookies 480
Ribbon Sandwiches 1216
Riboflavin
 Mg., daily allowances 8, *effects on in cooking* 23, 24, *functions of* 24, *in enriched bread and flour* 233, *in fish* 687
Rice 433–434
 As substitute for potato 3, *brown coated, converted* 423, *caloric value* 13, *care*

152, *cooking of* 423, 433, *cups per pound* 158, *flour* 111, *white or polished* 423, *wild* 424, *cooking wild*, Vol. 1, xxx
 Broiled, Modern and Old Methods 433
 Cakes, Breakfast 247
 Casserole, Pork and 870
 Casserole, Salmon and 731
 Cheese Croquettes 503
 Cooked in Milk 434
 Glorified 637
 Italian 827
 Loaf Cheese with Mushroom Sauce 438
 Muffins 257
 Red Beans and 1323
 Soup, Cabbage 1287
 Soup, Pea and 1284
 Spanish 1409
 Spanish, Braised Pork Shoulder Steak with 857
 Spanish Vegetables 1409
 Spinach Soup 1285
 Stuffed Lamb Breast with 847
 Stuffing, Wild, for Brazilian Duck 755
 Surprise, Egg and 682
 Toasted 434
 Tomatoes, with Braised Liver 904
 Wild and Liver Stuffing 759
Rice Pudding 636–638
Ricotta cheese 452
Rigor Mortis 744, 1029
Ring, Cheese 439
Risotto Milanaise 1054
Roast Meat Sandwiches 1226, 1229
Roast Squab 1066
Roaster (chicken), *per person* 159
Roasting of Meat 791
 pan size 1043
Rocks 468, 469
Rockfish 692
Rod Grod or Danish Red Pudding 630
Roe, Fried 708
Roe, Shad, Broiled 706
Roll, Chocolate Cream Sponge 317
Roll, Stuffed Cabbage 832
Rolls, from Plain Yeast Dough 273
 How to divide dough to make rolls 273, *why brush rolls* 273
 Braided 274
 Butterfly 274
 Butterhorns 274
 Cinnamon 275
 Clothespin 275
 Cloverleaf or Shamrock 275
 Crooked Miles 276
 Fan Tan 276
 Kneadless Drop 279
 Knots 276
 Nut 296
 Pan 276
 Parker House 277
 Poppy Seed or Nut 296
 Puff Balls 277

Rolls, etc., from Sweet Roll Dough 279
  Bismarcks or Jelly Doughnuts 289
  Butterscotch 282
  Cinnamon Crown Roll 282
  Glazed Orange Butterfly 285
  Hot Cross Buns, and Icing for 283
  Kolachy 284
  Orange Marmalade Pinwheels 286
  Orange Pocketbook 286
  Pineapple Butter Buns 286
  Raised Doughnuts 290
  Royal Rusks 287
  Schnecken or Pecan Rolls 287
Rolls, Special
  Buttermilk 277
  Corn Meal 278
  Kneadless Drop 279
  Potato Refrigerator 281
  Refrigerator, Plain 281
Rolls, Water Dough 268
  Crusty 268
  Dumbbells 269
  Twin 269
  Vienna 269
Rolled
  Buttermilk Dumplings 245
  Oat Muffins 257
  Oats, *how to cook* 427
  Rib Roast of Beef 804
  Sandwiches 1216
  Wheat, *how to cook* 427
Rolls, Chinese Egg 683
Roly Poly, Blueberry 543, 544
Romaine, *buying, care* 86
Romano Cheese 452
Roquefort
  Canapés 184
  Cheese 452
  Dressing 1197, 1198
Rose extract 134
Rosefish, *cooking methods* 692, 704
Rosemary, *description, uses* 132
Roses, Puff Paste 938
Rosettes, Swedish 612
Round Steak, Beef, Birds 810
Rubber scraper 1425
Rue, *description, uses* 132
Rum-Nut Frosting 388
Rump, Beef, *braising time* 806
  for Pot Roast 806, 807
Russian
  Cream 583
  Red Cabbage Soup 1296
  Salad Dressing 1205
  Tea 231
Rutabaga
  Ascorbic acid (vit. C) value 20, *caloric value* 13
  and Apple 1391
  Cheese Soup, Quick 1295
  Creamed 1391

  for Vegetable Plate 1410
  Mashed 1391
Rutabagas
  Buying, care 88, *in diet* 4
  Buttered 1390
Rye
  flour 111
  Bread 301

S

Sablefish, *cooking methods* 692
Sabayone Sauce 1249
Saffron, *uses* 132
Sage, *uses* 132
  cheese 453
  Dressing 754
  Milk 227
Sago, *how produced* 424
SALAD DRESSING 1114–1195
  Caloric value 12, 13, *amounts to make* 1197, *boiled, discussion of* 1196, *French, discussion of* 1197, *mayonnaise, discussion of* 1196
  Avocado 1197
  Beet Mayonnaise 1203
  Blue Cheese 1197, 1198
  Boiled, No. 1 and 2 1198
  Celery Seed for Fruit 1199
  Cranberry Mayonnaise 1199
  Cream Cheese 1199
  Dill 1199
  for Cheese Ring 1150
  for Pineapple Waldorf Salad 1142
  for Whole Meal Salad 1196
  French, No. 1 and 2 1200
  Fruit 1200
  Fruit Juice 1200
  Golden, Creamy 1201
  Golden Fluff 1143
  Green Mayonnaise 1203
  Horseradish 1201
  Lemon French 1201
  Lime-Honey Fruit 1202
  Mayonnaise 1202
  Old-Fashioned Sour Cream 1203
  Peanut Butter, No. 1 and 2 1204
  Pepper-Onion, Mayonnaise 1204
  Pineapple 1202
  Quick Sour Cream 1204, 1205
  Rancho 1205
  Red Mayonnaise 1203
  Roquefort 1197, 1198
  Russian 1205
  Sesame 1205
  Sour Cream 1206
  Sour Cream-Olive Fruit 1205
  Spanish 1206
  Special 1206
  Thousand Island 1206
  Tomato French 1202

Salad Dressing—(Cont'd)
Whipped Cream 1207
Yogurt 1207
Salad Sandwiches
See Sandwich Spreads and Fillings
Bacon and Egg 1225
Cucumber and Egg 1227
Egg 1228
Ham 1229
SALADS 1104–1207
Assembling ingredients for 1116, Bowl, ingredients and preparation 1117, greens, care of 141, vegetables, care of 1115, Dinner, discussion of 1133, Frozen, discussion of 1124, Hearty, discussion of 1180, 1181, Hot, discussion of 1126, Individual, discussion of 1133, ingredients for 1114, Main Dish, discussion of 1180, Molded, discussion of 1154, Molded, making of 1154, nutritive values from 1114, preparation of for children 1117, preparation of food for 1115, service of 1117, Shredded, discussion of 1173, unmolding of 1155, vinegars for 1115
Apple and Peanut 1134
Apple and Raisin 1134
Apple Cheese 1134
Apple, Turnip and Pascal Celery 1135
Apricot Cottage Cheese 1135
Asparagus, Raw 1152
Aspic, Sandwich Filling 1222
Avocado Aspic Ring 1160
Avocado Mousse 1161
Avocado Shrimp Tomato 1184
Baked Bean and Sauerkraut, Hot 1126
Banana 1136
Banana Apple and Cranberry 1135
Banana Marshmallow and Nut 1135
Bean Sprout 1145
Beet and Cucumber, Raw 1179
Beet and Green Onion 1146
Beet and Pea 1146
Beet Cheese and Onion 1146
Beet, Molded 1168
Beet, Pickled 1152
Beet Relish 1174
Beets and Onion, Pickled 1152
Bermuda 1174
Big Wig's 1147
Bing Cherry Jellied 1161
Bunny 1121
Cabbage 1175
Cabbage and Apple 1174
Cabbage and Celery 1180
Cabbage and Pineapple, Molded 1169
Cabbage Carrot and Raisin 1174
Cabbage Celery Apple and Grape 1175
Cabbage Pineapple Marshmallow 1175
Cabbage, Red 1179
Candle 1122
Cantaloupe and Blackberry 1136
Cantaloupe Balls and Cherry 1136

Carrot and Cabbage 1176
Carrot and Peanut 1176
Carrot-Coconut 1176
Cauliflower 1147
Cauliflower, Hot 1127
Cauliflower Luncheon 1184
Celery Cabbage, Hot 1127
Celery Cabbage Medley 1147
Celery Root, Hot 1127
Celery Stuffed with Cheese 1148
Cheese 1181
Cheese and Date, Frozen 1124
Cheese Vegetable Stuffed Tomato 1181
Chicken 1185
Chicken and Sweetbread 1185
Chicken and Tongue in Aspic 1156
Chicken Stevens 1156
Chicken, with Cranberry Jelly 1157
Christmas Tree 1122
Cinnamon Apple 1136
Cold Meat 1184
Cole Slaw 1177
Corned Beef and Potato 1185
Cottage Cheese 1181, 1182
Cottage Cheese in Tomato Aspic 1168
Crab Meat Louis 1186
Crab Stuffed Eggs in Aspic Jelly 1160
Crabmeat 1186
Cranberry Apple 1162
Cranberry, Mold 1163
Cucumber and Radish 1148
Cucumber, Sliced 1152
Cucumber, Spliced 1154
Cucumber, Stuffed 1153
Dandelion Green 1178
Date Cream Cheese and Lettuce 1136
Decorative 1121
Dublin 1186
Egg 1186
Egg and Cucumber 1182
Egg and Sardine Top Tomato 1183
Egg Vegetable 1183
Endive and Potato, Hot 1128
Fall, Platter 1171
Fennel Dinner 1149
Fennel Waldorf 1149
Finger, Vegetable 1144, 1145
Fish 1187
French Bowl 1119
Fruit 1134
Fruit and Date, Fresh 1137
Fruit and Nut, Frozen 1124
Fruit Bowl, Fresh 1119
Fruit, Fresh 1137
Fruit, Frozen 1125
Fruit Platter, Whole Meal 1172
Fruit, with Marshmallows 1137
Ginger Ale, Mold 1163
Girl's Party 1122
Grape Thyme 1164
Grapefruit 1138
Grapefruit Aspic 1163

Salads—(Cont'd)
Grapefruit Avocado and Persimmon 1138
Green Bean 1149
Green Bean and Celery 1148
Green Pepper and Cheese Ring 1150
Head Cheese Vinaigrette 1187
Hyacinth 1122
Kidney Bean 1150
Kohlrabi Bowl 1120
Kohlrabi Date 1151
Kohlrabi Waldorf 1151
Lettuce, Stuffed 1192
Lily of the Valley 1123
Lime, Olive, Nut, Molded 1164
Macaroni 1188
Macaroni Endive 1187
Macaroni, Hot 1128
Mashed Potato, Hot 1129
Minted Company Slaw 1178
Molded, Fish and Meat 1156
Navy Bean, Hot 1128, 1129
Orange Coconut 1138
Orange Raisin 1138
Orange Waldorf 1139
Papaya 1139
Parsley with Chiffonade Dressing 1151
Pea Cheese Stuffed Tomato 1182
Peach 1140
Peach Fig, Mold 1164
Peach Prune and Cottage Cheese 1139
Pear 1140
Pear, Stuffed 1166
Perfection 1169
Persimmon 1141
Pineaple and Cottage Cheese 1141
Pineapple Cabbage and Marshmallow 1178
Pineapple Cottage Cheese Aspic 1165
Pineapple Date 1141
Pineapple Grape 1165
Pineapple-Lime Velvet 1166
Pineapple Waldorf 1141
Potato 1188
Potato Caraway Sour Cream 1189
Potato Fresh Dill 1189
Potato, Hot 1130, 1131
Potato Picnic 1189
Potato with Whipped Cream Dressing 1190
Prune, Molded 1165
Prune Nut 1142
Prunes, Stuffed 1142
Rainbow, Hot 1131
Raspberry and Cottage Cheese, Red 1143
Red and Green 1179
Salmon 1190
Salmon in Cucumber Aspic 1159
Salmon, Jellied 1158
Salmon, with Cucumber Dressing, Molded 1158
Santa Claus 1123
Sardine Top Tomato 1190

Scrambled Egg 1183
Shrimp 1191
Shrimp and Lobster Mousse 1159
Shrimp and Tomato 1191
Shrimp in Tomato Aspic 1160
Shrimp Remoulade 1192
Slaw, Hot 1131
Spinach, Hot 1132
Spinach Luncheon 1192
Spinach Medley 1180
Spinach, Raw 1120
Strawberry Avocado Cups 1143
Stuffed Prune 1143
Summer, Platter 1172
Sunday Supper 1193
Sunshine 1166
Sweet Potato 1193
Sweet Potato, Hot 1132
Tomato Anchovy 1153
Tomato Aspic 1170, 1171
Tomato Aspic, Creamy 1168
Tomato and Onion 1154
Tomato, Spliced 1154
Tomato, Stuffed 1153
Tomato Stuffed with Kidney Beans 1193
Tomato Stuffed with Tuna 1194
Tomato with Cucumber Dressing 1154
Tri-Color Fruit Mold 1167
Tulip 1123
Tuna Fish 1194, 1195
Turkey 1195
Turnip Carrot, Hot 1132
Vegetable 1144
Vegetable, Molded 1169
Vegetable Slaw 1180
Waldorf 1144
Watercress 1121
Whole Meal Tossed 1195, 1196
Wilted Lettuce 1133
Winter, Platter 1172
Salame Cheese 450
Salami, care of 146
Salami Tasty Sticks 211
Salisbury Steak 832
Sally Lunn 239
Salmon
Caloric value 13, cooking methods 692, 699, information on 692, niacin (nicotinic acid) value 25
au Gratin 730
Bisque 1285
Boiled with Egg Caper Sauce 703
Canapé Filling 189
Chowder 1273
Creamed 729
Croquettes 504
in Cucumber Aspic 1159
Loaf 731
Lobster Filling, Fish Pastry Shell with 729
Macaroni Casserole 730
Patties 731

Salmon—(Cont'd)
  Rice Casserole 731
  Salad 1190
  Salad, Jellied 1158
  Salad Sandwich 1219
  Salad, with Cucumber Dressing 1158
  Soufflé 732
  Timbales 1303
  Ways to Serve Cold, Red 735
Salsify
  Buying, care 87, selecting 1392
  Creamed 1392
Salt
  For pie crust 923, how to measure 160,
  iodized 688
  Mackerel, Broiled 705
Salt Pork
  and Cream Gravy 855
  Gravy, Baked Potato with 1373
Salt Water Taffy 417
Sandwich Spreads and Fillings
  Aspic Salad 1222
  Baked Bean 1222
  Bologna 1226
  Carrot Butter 1222
  Carrot Raisin 1222
  Cheese 1213
  Cheese-Raisin 1210
  Cucumber and Egg Salad 1227
  Date Nut 1223
  Egg Salad 1218
  Elk 760
  Fruit and Cream Cheese 1223
  Ham and Egg 1228
  Ham Salad 1217
  Honey Butter 1231
  Kidney Bean 1223
  Liver Sausage 1230
  Liver Sausage Mushroom 1229
  Main Dish 1209
  Olive Nut 1224
  Parsley Butter 1213, 1224
  Peanut Butter Banana and Jelly 1232
  Potted Meat 1230
  Relish 1209
  Shrimp Butter 1220
  Sweet 1209
  Sweet, for Sliced Duck 1231
  Tongue 1212, 1231
  Tuna Fish 1213, 1221
  Vegetable, Mixed 1224
SANDWICHES 1208–1236
  Types 1208, 1209, Grills 1425, canapés
  1208, club 1208, fancy 1209, grilled or
  toasted 1208, hot 1208, "lunchbox" 1208,
  making of 1209, serving of 1210
  Almond Chicken Rolls 1217
  Asparagus 1221
  Bacon and Egg Salad 1225
  Baked Bean 1222
  Bar 1217
  Bologna French Toast 1226

  Bread and Butter 1231
  Cabbage and Bacon, Chopped 1223
  Checker Board 1212
  Cheese and Tomato 1233
  Cheese Puffs 1233
  Cheese, Skillet 1212
  Cheese, Toasted 1212
  Cheese Tomato 446
  Club 1214
  Cottage Cheese, Carrot, Nut Double
  Decker 1211
  Cranberry Chicken Loaves 1214
  Cream Cheese Carrot Finger 1211
  Cucumber, Onion and Pickle 1223
  Date, Cottage Cheese 1211
  Denver 1227
  Deviled Egg 1227
  Egg and Bacon 1227
  Egg Salad 1228
  Egg Salad and Sardine Double Decker
  1215
  Elk 760
  Frankfurter 1228
  Ham and Banana 1233
  Ham and Cheese 1228
  Ham and Cranberry 1234
  Ham and Tomato 1234
  Ham and Tuna Fish 1234
  Ham Salad 1229
  Hot Chicken 1214
  Jelly 1232
  Lettuce, Bacon and Tomato 1224
  Liver Sausage 1229
  Loaf 1217
  Lobster Avocado 1220
  Luncheon 1235
  Meat, Cold Roast 1226
  Meat, Hot Roast 1229
  Olive and Egg 1230
  Olive and Tomato 1224
  Olive Cheese 1212
  Peanut Butter 1233
  Peanut Butter and Bacon 1232
  Peanut Butter and Watercress 1232
  Peanut Butter Jelly 1232
  Prune, Hot 1216
  Rolled and Ribbon 1216
  Salmon Salad 1219
  Sardine 1220
  Sardine, Broiled 1219
  Sausage, Toast 1230
  Skillet 1218
  Souffléed, Snacks 1235
  Spinach, with Cheese Sauce 1235
  Square-Meal Biscuit 1219
  Swiss Cheese, Ham, Tomato 1236
  Tomato, Fried 1216
  Tongue, Open Face 1236
  Tuna Cucumber 1220
  Vegetable Egg 1225
  Watercress 1225

Sandwiches—(Cont'd)
  Watercress and Bacon 1225
  Whole Meal 1236
Santa Claus Salad 1123
Sapote, Golden 577
Sap Sago Cheese 453
Sardines
  Caloric value of 13
  Canapé filling 189
  Canapés 184
  Double Decker Sandwich, Egg Salad and 1215
  Salad, Egg, Top Tomato 1183
  Sandwiches 1220
  Sandwiches, Broiled 1219
  Spirals 207
  Surprises 207
  Top Tomato Salad 1190
Sassafras Tea 231
Sauce
  Allemande, Broccoli with 1327
  Basic Cheese 450
  Brown Butter, for Broiled Fish 707
  Buttermilk, for Vegetables 1410
  Cheese, Variations 444, 1253
  Cherry, Egg Pancakes with 563
  Cocktail, for Seafood 195
  Fresh Mushroom Ham Puffs 867
  Guacamole 1255
  Harvey, Lamb Loaf with 849
  Lemon Butter 1257
  Lemon Ginger, with Custard 537
  Mornay 1258
  Mushroom, Cheese-Rice Loaf with 438
  Mushroom, for Broiled Hamburger 824
  Mustard, Eggs in 669
  Onion Gravy for Broiled Hamburger 824
  Orange 1247
  Parsley, for Ham and Tomato Sandwich 1234
  Plum, with Ham Loaf 868
  Relish, for Tuna Turnovers 735
  Remoulade 1260
  Sour Cream for Fish 704
  Soy, thickened, for Egg Foo Yeung 685
  Spanish, Cheese Pudding with 438
  Supreme with Chicken Mousse 1051
  Tomato, Lobster Stuffed Eggs in 670
  Watercress, Hard-Cooked Eggs 669
  White 1262
SAUCES 1237–1262
  Discussion of 1237, *for meat and vege-tables* 1250, *sweet* 1238, *care of white* 149
Sauces, Fish
  Barbecue, Fine Herbs 1251
  Barbecue, Lime 1251
  Celery 1252
  Curry 1254
  Dill No. 1 1254
  Drawn Butter 1255
  Egg 1255

  Lemon Butter 1257
  Mornay 1258
  Mousseline 1258
  Mushroom 1259
  Mustard 1259
  Onion 1260
  Remoulade 1260
  Tartar 1260
Sauces, Meat
  Barbecue 1250
  Barbecue, Fine Herbs 1251
  Barbecue, Lime 1251
  Béchamel 1251
  Carrot 1252
  Celery 1252
  Curry 1254
  Dill No. 2 1254
  Horseradish 1256
  Maître d'Hôtel 1257
  Mint 1258
  Mushroom 1259
  Mustard No. 1 and 2 1259
  Mustard De Luxe 1259
  Onion 1260
  Spanish 1260
  Tartar 1260
  Tomato 1261
  Velouté 1261
Sauces, Sweet for Dessert
  Brandy Crème 1238
  Butterscotch 642
  Caramel 642, 1239
  Chocolate 643, 1239, 1240
  Chocolate Peanut Butter 644
  Chocolate Peppermint 644
  Cinnamon Dip 1240
  Citrus 1240
  Citrus Marshmallow 1241
  Cocoa 1241
  Coffee 644, 1241, 1242
  Creamy Vanilla 1242
  Custard 1242, 1243
  1890 Pudding 1249
  Foamy 1243
  Fresh Lime 646
  Fudge, Hot or Cold 1243
  Grandma's Pudding 1244
  Grape 1244
  Hard 1245
  Hard, Sterling 1249
  Lemon 1245, 1246
  Lemon, Hard 1245
  Lemon, Orange 646
  Lemon Sundae 645
  Lemon Whipped Cream 1246
  Lime Sundae 1246
  Nutmeg 1247
  Orange 1247
  Peach Juice Pudding, Canned 1248
  Peanut Butter 1248
  Pineapple 1248
  Pudding, De Luxe 1248

Sauces, Sweet for Dessert—(Cont'd)
  Sabayone 1249
  Vanilla 1249, 1250
Sauces, Vegetable
  Allemande 1250
  Béchamel 1251
  Brown 1252
  Carrot 1252
  Cheese 1253
  Cheese, Smoky 1253
  Cream Cheese 1253
  Dill No. 1 1254
  Guacamole 1255
  Hollandaise (Mock) 1256
  Hollandaise (True) 1256
  Maître d'Hôtel 1257
  Mousseline 1258
  Mustard De Luxe 1259
  Spanish 1260
  Tomato 1261
  Vegetable Creole 1261
  Vinaigrette 1262
  White 1262
Saucepans, selecting 1417
Sauerbraten
  Beef 811
  Heart 897
  Liver 907
Sauerkraut 1112, 1113
  Caloric value 13, in diet 4
  and Apples, Pheasant with 771
  and Bean Pot Dinner 1392
  and Dumplings, Schultzies 1393
  and Fish Casserole 1392
  Baked Wild Duck with 755
  Juice Cocktail 198
  Meat Balls with 838
  Pork Chops with 858
  Salad, Baked Beans and, Hot 1126
  Savory No. 1 and 2 1393
  Spareribs and 862
  with Frankfurters 889
Sauger Pike, cooking methods 693
Sausage, Liver
  Vitamin values 21, 23, 25, 28, season-
    ing, description, uses 132
  Grilled Liver 905
  Liver and Creamed Cabbage 907
Sausage, Meat
  Bacon and Tomato Grill 872
  Casserole, Lamb 844
  Creamed with Red Cabbage 1330
  Fat, uses of 873
  Link Pan Broiled 872
  Little Pig, Baked Squash with 871
  Patties, Pork 872
  Pork, Home-Made 872
  Spanish 873
  Squares, Kidney and 899
  Toast 1230
Savory
  Description and uses 132

Dinner Chowder 1273
Green Beans 1315
Veal Steaks 877
Scallop Lamb 852
Scallopini, Veal 880
Scallops
  Cooking methods 694, how to buy 725,
    information 694
  French-Fried 725
  Pan-Fried 726
Scarmorze or Pear Cheese 452
Schaum Torte 378
Schmeerkaase 449
Schnecken 287
Scones 238
Scotch
  Broth 1296
  Shortbread 492
Scrambled Eggs 675
  Eggs, Hearty 675
  Salad 1183
Scrapple, Pork 871
Scup or Porgy, cooking methods 692, 704
Scurvy 5, 20
Sea Bass, 692
  Trout, cooking methods for 692
  Foam 407
  Food Bisque 1299
Seasoning salt, description, uses 132
Self-rising flour 111
Semolina flour 422
Senf Gurken 1105
Service, cash-and-carry 71
Serving the meal, Vol. 1, xxiii
  order of, table, Vol. 1, xxiv
Sesame seed, uses 132
  Salad Dressing 1205
Seven-Minute Icing 392
Shad, cooking methods 692
Shad Roe, Broiled 706
Shakes, Ice Cream 220–222
Shallots
  Buying, care 84, use of 132
Sheepshead, cooking methods 692
Shellfish
  Cooking methods, market forms of 715,
    719, 726
  Fritter Batter 1349
Shells, Patty 612, 938
Sherbets and Ices 603–606
  Caloric value 13, in children's diet 33
Shirred Eggs 664
Shoo-Fly Pie 979
Short Bread
  Fans 493
  Scotch 492
Shortcake
  splitting of 649
  Chicken 1054
  Grapefruit 647
  Orange 648
  Peach 648

Shortcake—(Cont'd)
  Rhubarb 648
  Strawberry 648
Shortenings 107
  Care of 151, cups per pound 157, for
  cake 310, for pie crust 923, how to
  measure 160, importance in cooking 106,
  shortening compounds, how made and
  used 107, 108, storage of 107, advan-
  tages of hydrogenated vegetable 107,
  108, how made and stored 107, 108,
  emulsified 108, non-emulsified 108
Short Ribs
  and Yorkshire Pudding 812
  Kidney and Braised 899
  Pot Roast 812
Shower Menus, Vol. 1 xxxi
Shredded Wheat
  Thiamine (vit. B₁) value 22
Shrimp
  Cooking methods 694, fresh, preparing
  of 726, how to buy 726, servings per
  pound 159, yield from 690
  à la King 728
  and Lobster Mousse 1159
  and Tomato Salad 1191
  Broiled in Bacon 202
  Butter 1220
  Butter, Canapés 188
  Canapés 184
  Cocktail 197, 728
  Creamed 727
  Creamed, with Omelet 678
  Curry 727
  Custard, Cheese and 437
  French-Fried 727
  Gumbo, Crab 1268
  in Tomato Aspic 1160
  Jambalaya 728
  Paste 728
  Remoulade 1192
  Salad, Avocado, Tomato 1184
  Salad, No. 1 and 2 1191
Shrubs 198, 199 (See Appetizers)
Silver White Cake 351, 355
Silverware, discussion of, Vol. 1 xxii
Skillet
  Cheese Sandwiches 1212
  Dinner 1409
  Peach Dumplings 545
  Sandwiches 1218
Slaw
  Carrot 1178
  Cole, No. 1, 2 and 3 1177
  Cucumber-Cress 1178
  Hot 1131
  Mexican 1177
  Minted Company 1178
  Parsley 1178
  Spring 1178
  Tomato 1178
  Vegetable 1180

Slip-Slide Custard Pie 980
Smelt, cooking methods 692, 694
Smoke Salt, description, uses 132
Smoked Turkey or Capon Canapés 185
Snaps, Brandy 487
Snow Pudding 587
Social use of food, Vol. 1 xvii
Soda and vitamin C 19
  Baking 114, how to measure 160
Soda, Ice Cream 221–222
Sole, cooking methods 691
  Fillet of, and Oysters Parmesan 706
Sorghum, how made and uses 126
Sorrel, use of 132
Soufflé
  Carrot 1334
  Celery 679
  Cheese 438
  Chicken or Meat 679
  Chocolate 650
  Dried Beef 680
  Mushroom 680
  Oatmeal 680
  Orange Marmalade 650
  Salmon 732
  Sandwich Snacks 1235
  Spaghetti Ring, with Creamed Ham 681
  Spinach 1396
  Tuna 681
SOUPS 1263–1300
  In children's diet 33, broth, making of
  796, 797, garnish accompaniments for
  1264, blends 1299, 1300, discussion of
  canned 1263, 1264, chowder 1263, clear
  1263, cream 1263, meat cuts for making
  797, meat stock, bouillon or tomato juice
  1286–1297
  Almond, Cream of 1276
  Asparagus, Cream of 1276
  Avocado Chicken 1286
  Beef and Noodle 1286
  Beef Bouillon 1286
  Beef Vegetable 1287
  Beet Borsch 1264
  Beet Borsch, Cold 1266, 1267
  Beet, Cream of 1277
  Beet Tomato 1300
  Black Bean 1271
  Bouillabaisse 1265
  Broccoli, Cream of 1277
  Cabbage and Dill Chowder 1266
  Cabbage Rice 1287
  Cabbage, Russian Red 1296
  Carrot, Cream of 1278
  Cauliflower, Cream of 1278
  Celery, Cream of 1278
  Chestnut Squash 1288
  Chick Pea 1300
  Chicken Barley 1289
  Chicken Broth with Rice 1288
  Chicken Broth, Rich, 1289
  Chicken Newburg 1299

Soups—(Cont'd)
Chowders and Hearty 1264–1276
Clam Chowder, Boston 1265
Clam Chowder, Manhattan 1270
Cockaleekie 1289
Corn and Tomato, Cream of 1279
Corn Chowder 1267
Corn, Cream of 1279
Crab-Shrimp Gumbo 1268
Cream 1276–1285
Creole Bean 1269
Cucumber, Cream of 1279
Duck 757, 1290
Elk 760
Fish Chowder 1270
Kidney Bean 1291
Lamb Broth 1291
Lamb Broth with Barley 1292
Leek and Potato 1283
Lettuce, Cream of 1280
Lima Bean and Carrot, Cream of 1280
Lima Bean Chowder 1270
Liver and Vegetable 1293
Liver Dumpling 1292
Minestra, Italian 1290
Minestrone 1293
Mushroom, Cream of 1280
Navy Bean 1271, 1272
Navy Bean, Cream of 1281
Onion, Cream of 1281
Onion, French 1269
Oxtail 1294
Oyster Bisque or Chowder 1284
Oyster Stew 1272
Pea and Rice 1284
Pea, Cream of 1281
Pea, Special 1294
Philadelphia Pepper Pot 1295
Potato and Mushroom, Cream of 1281
Potato Carrot 1272
Potato, Cream of 1282
Potato, Golden 1283
Printemps Chowder 1273
Pumpkin 1284, 1285
Rabbit 776
Rice and Spinach 1285
Rutabaga Cheese, Quick 1295
Salmon Bisque 1285
Salmon Chowder 1273
Savory Dinner Chowder 1273
Scotch Broth 1296
Sea Food Bisque 1299
Soy Bean 1274
Spinach Chowder 1274
Spinach Consomme 1299
Spinach, Cream of 1282
Split Pea 1275, 1297
Split Pea, Bohemian 1287
Summer 1297–1299
Summer Vegetable Chowder 1275
Tomato and Cabbage 1275
Tomato Bouillon, Hot 1290

Tomato Bouillon, Jellied 1291
Tomato, Cold 1290
Tomato, Cream of 1282
Tomato Okra, Quick 1296
Turkey 1297
Turtle 781, 782
Vegetable 1298
Vegetable, Cream of 1283
Vegetable Peppy 1298
Vichyssoise 1298
Vichyssoise, Curried 1299
Watercress or Spinach and Potato 1276
Sour Cream
Apple Pie 989
Cake 337
Cookies, Chocolate 464
Cookies, Plain 469
Cookies, Rolled 492
Corn Bread 241
Cucumbers Minted in 1345
Doughnuts 289
Dressing, Quick 1204, 1205
Gravy, Liver with 907
Old-Fashioned Salad Dressing 1203
Olive Fruit Dressing 1205
Peach Pie 1005, 1007
Prune Pie 967
Salad Dressing 1206
Sauce, for Fish 704
Southern
Corn bread 242
Style, Mustard Greens 1352
Style, Turnip Greens 1353
Soy
Flour 111, protein content 111, sauce, description, uses 132
Sauce for Egg Foo Yeung 685
Soya products
Niacin (Nicotinic acid) value 25
Soy Bean Soup 1274
Soy Beans
In diet 4, vitamin values of 22, 24, 26
Spaghetti
As substitute for potato 3, care of 152, cooking of 430, cups per pound 157, forms and ingredients of 422
Italian, with Meat Balls 828
Quick 831
Spanish
Cream 587
Eggs on Toast 671
Liver 909
Mackerel, cooking, method 692, 704
Olives, discussion 123
Orange Cream 585
Pork Chops 857
Rice 1409
Rice, Pork Steak with 857
Sauce 1260
Sauce, Cheese Pudding with 438
Sauce, Steak with 814
Sausage 873

Spanish—(Cont'd)
  Style Beef Pot Roast 807
  Vegetables 1409
Spareribs
  Time for braising 856
  and Sauerkraut 862
  Barbecued, No. 1 and 2 860
  Braised 861
  Celery Stuffed 861
  Fruited 861
  Stuffed 862
Spatulas 1426
Special Bread Recipes 295
Special Salad Dressing 1206
Spencer Method of Baking Fish 701
Spice
  Buying, care, uses of 127, *sources of* 126
  Cake 338
  Honey, Sour Cream Cupcakes 358
  Sugar Cookies 487
Spicy Splendor Cake 338
Spinach
  Buying, care 83, 141, *caloric value* 13, *cooking methods* 1307, *in diet* 4, *vitamin values* 20, 27
  Buttered 1394
  Carrots and, Creamed 1335
  Cheese Custard 1396
  Chowder 1274
  Consomme 1299
  Creamed, on Noodles and Cheese 1394
  De Luxe, Creamed 1394
  Egg, Scramble 675
  for Vegetable Plate 1410
  German Style 1395
  in Bacon Cream Sauce 1395
  Luncheon Salad 1192
  Medley 1180
  Mustard Greens and, with Bacon 1352
  Potato Soup 1276
  Ring, Vegetable Filled 1397
  Salad, Hot 1132
  Salad, Raw 1120
  Sandwiches with Cheese Sauce 1235
  Savory Creamed 1395
  Soufflé Ring with Cheese Sauce 1396
  Soup, Cream of 1282
  Soup, Rice and 1285
  Wilted 1398
  with Bacon and Egg 1397
  with Bacon and Egg Sauce 1398
  with Cheese Sauce and Bacon 1398
Split Pea Soup 1275, 1297
  Bohemian 1287
Sponge Cake 315–322
  Causes of failure 315, *cooling of* 314, *electric mixer mixing* 314, *standard method of mixing* 313
Spoon
  Bread 243
  Bread with Cheese 243
Spoons, cooking 1426

Spot, *cooking methods* (fish) 692
Spreads (sandwich)
  Bologna 1226
  Carrot Raisin 1222
  Date Nut 1223
  Fruit and Cream Cheese 1223
  Ham and Cheese 1228
  Liver Sausage 1230
  Liver Sausage, Mushroom 1229
  Mixed Vegetable 1224
  Olive Nut 1224
  Peanut Butter and Bacon 1232
  Peanut Butter, Banana and Jelly 1232
  Sweet, for Duck Sandwiches 1231
Springerlie 500
Spritz Cookies
  Almond 477
  Basic 478
  Chocolate 478
Squab
  Broiled 1065
  Roast 1066
Square-Meal Biscuit Sandwiches 1219
Squash
  Buying, care 87, *caloric value* 13, *cooking methods* 1307, *in diet* 4, *vitamin A, value* 27
  Acorn, Baked 1399
  Baked Acorn, with Sausages 871
  Baked Winter 1399
  Bread 298
  Buttered, Summer 1400
  Candied, Ten Minute 1401
  for Vegetable Plate 1410
  French-Fried Hubbard 1400
  Hubbard, Creamed Chicken or Ham in 889
  Pan-Fried 1401
  Purée 1390
  Soup, Chestnut 1288
  Stuffed 1400, 1401
  with Nuts, Crusty Winter 1399
  Zucchini, Braised 1402
Squirrel
  Removing glands from 778
  Fricassee 779
  Pot Pie 779
Sta-Puff Omelet 678
Stars, Cinnamon 495
Starches, *edible, kinds of* 423, 424
Steak
  and Kidney Pie 901
  Beef, braising time 806
  Broiled 802
  Broiling of 793
  Broiling time table for 800
  Country Fried 803
  "Cubed" 803
  "Minute" 803
  Rolled 809
  Short Cake 833
  with Spanish Sauce 814

Steam, as a leavening agent 111
Steamer 1426
Steaming 167
Stew
  Beef 817
  Black-eyed Pea, Navy Bean 1321
  Brunswick 1039
  Chicken, Southern 1059
  De Luxe, Venison 753
  Green Tomato 819
  Irish 848
  Kidney 900
  Lentil, Ham with 1356
  Navy Bean 1321
  Oyster 724, 1272
  Parsnip 1365
  Veal 883
Sticks, Bread 268
  Corn 241
Stilton cheese 453
Stirred Custard 534, 535
Stock, fish 711, see Fish Balls
Stollen 307
Strawberry
  Ascorbic acid (vit. C) value 20, buying,
    care 90, 143, caloric value 13, in diet 5
    extract 134, huller 1426
  Angel Pie Filling 1026
  Avocado Cups 1143
  Bavarian 583
  Chiffon Pie 947
  Cream Pie 958
  Different Pie 1015
  Electric Light Preserves 1093
  Filling for Cream Puffs 936, 937
  Frosting 388
  Ice Cream 599
  Jelly 1086
  Meringue Pudding 624
  Meringues, Rhubarb 624
  Mousse 609
  Pie 1015
  Preserves, Seven-Minute 1094
  Seven-Minute Icing 394
  Shortcake 648
  Tarts 1024
  Whipped in Cream Pie 1016
Stretching the Food Dollar 73
Streusel
  Coffee Cake, Apple 238
  Coffee Cake, Old-Time 295
  Confectioners' Sugar 294
  Old-Fashioned Nut Coffee Cake 295
  Topping for Dutch Apple Pie 988
Striped Bass, cooking methods 693
Stroganoff, Beef 808
Strudel 613
Stuffed
  Apples 559
  Cabbage Roll 832
  Noodles 432
  Tomato, Cheese Salad 1181

Tomato Pea, Cheese Salad 1182
Tomato, with Kidney Beans 1193
Tomato, with Tuna Salad 1194
Stuffings, for poultry, meat, fish
  Bread for Chicken and Turkey 1072
  Celery 1072
  Chestnut 1072
  Fish 700
  Mashed Potato for Wild Duck 759
  Poultry 1072
  Wild Rice and Liver 759
Sturgeon, cooking methods 693
Sub Gum, Veal 881
Succotash, No. 1 and 2 1344
Suckers, cooking methods 694
Suet 1441
Sugar
  Beet 125, caloric value of 14, cane, how
    made 124, confectioners' uses for 126,
    corn 125, cube 125, cups per pound
    159, dark and light brown 125, domino
    125, for cake 310, how to caramelize
    165, how to measure 160, loaf and cubes,
    per pound 159, maple, how made 126,
    pulverized 126
  Cookie, Basic 486
Sugar Cookies
  Easy 474
  Lemon 475
  Soft Rolled 494
Sulfate-phosphate baking powders 112
Summer Salad Platter 1172
Sundaes, Ice Cream 642–646
Sunday Supper Salad 1193
Sunshine Cake 321
Sunshine Salad 1166
Surprise, Egg and Rice 682
Swamp Cabbage 1332
  with White Bacon 1332
Swan Cream Puffs 937
Swedish
  Brown Beans 1323
  Limpa Bread 300
  Meat Balls 827
  Rosettes 612
  Taffy 417
  Tea Ring 294
Sweet basil, use of 128
Sweet Dill Pickles 1103
Sweet Potatoes, also yams
  Buying, care 86, cooking methods 1307,
    vitamin values 20, 27
  Apple Casserole 1388
  Apple and Escalloped 1387
  Baked 1385
  Boiled 1385
  Candied Coconut 1386
  Candied No. 1 and 2 1386
  Casserole, Cheese and 1387
  Casserole, Ham and 867
  for Vegetable Plate 1410
  French-Fried 1375

Sweet Potatoes—(Cont'd)
Honeyed 1387
Lyonnaise 1388
Mashed 1388
Pie 981
Possum, and 768
Pudding 624
Salad 1193
Salad, Hot 1132
Slices, Ham Patties on Yam 867
with Pineapple Sauce 1388
Volcanic 1389
Sweet Roll Dough 279
Sweetbreads
Cooking methods 891, discussion of 890,
891
à la King 894
Broiled 893
Creamed 893
Salad, Chicken and 1185
Sautéed Crumbed 895
Tartar 895
Timbales 1303
Swiss
Cheese 453
Cheese Ham and Tomato Sandwiches
1236
Steak 815
steak, braising time 806
Swiss chard
Buttered 1340
Swordfish, cooking methods 693
Broiled 706
Syrup
Caloric value of 13, corn 125, how to
measure 160, care of 151
Brown Sugar 1238
Burnt Sugar for Cake 333, 643
Caramel 643
Chocolate Beverage 223
Chocolate Bitter-Sweet 223
Guava 645
Lemon for Lemonade 217

T

Tabasco, description, uses 132
Tables. See list of charts and tables Vol. 1, v
Taffy
Honey 416
Salt Water 417
Swedish Style 417
Tamale Pie 833
Tangerine Grapefruit Juice 216
Tangerine juice, in diet 5
Tangerines
Ascorbic acid (vit. C), value 19, in diet 5
Tangy Chips 185
Tapioca
Cups per pound 157, how produced and
used 424
Apple 638

Butterscotch Cream 639
Cream 639
Fresh Fruit 639
Lime Fluff 639
Loganberry 640
Orange 640
Peach 640
Pineapple or Fruited 641
Tarragon, use of 133
Tarts
Pans 1425, shells, tricks in making 1017,
definition of 1017, tricks in making 1017,
1018
Apple Soufflé 1019
Apricot 1019, 1020
Banbury 1020
Calamondin Glamour 1020
Canned Peach 1024
Cherry 1021
Chess Pielets 1021
Cream Cheese or Vienna 494
Gooseberry 1022
Jam 1023
Jelly Cheese Filled 1022
Lemon 1022
Mincemeat 1023
Old-Time Jelly 1023
Orange Date 1023
Pumpkin 1024
Sand 487
Strawberry Devonshire 1024
Vienna 494
Tartar
Sauce 1260
Sweetbreads 895
Tartrate baking powders 112
Tautog, cooking methods for 693
Tea
And the pre-school child 34, cups per
lb., servings per lb. 156, general direc-
tions on making 229
Cambric 230
Camomile 230
Ginger 230
Hot, and Iced 229
Hot, Punch 230
Instant 230
Mint 231
Russian 231
Sassafras 231
Tea Ring, Swedish 294
Test for Jelly 1082
Tetrazzini Eggs 669
Texas Sour Pickles 1104
Thanksgiving Dinner Menus, Vol. I, xxx
Thawing fruits 145
Thawing meat 146
Thawing vegetables 145
Thermometer 1426
Candy 402, for griddle cakes 246, meat
792
Thermos, in school lunch 35

Thiamine
  Daily allowance 8, 21, *effects on of cooking* 21, *functions of in body* 22, *in enriched bread and flour* 233, *in fish* 687, *table sources of* 21
Thousand Island Dressing 1206
Three-Fruit Ice 605
Three-Way Ginger Cookies 476
Thunder and Lightning Pickles 1105
Thyme, *description and uses* 133
Tilefish, *cooking methods* 693
TIMBALES 1301–1303
Timing device 1426
Tin Can and Glass Jar Sizes 137
Tin Cans and Their Contents 136, 139
Toast, kinds 262
  Cinnamon 262
  Croustades or Bread Cases 263
  Croutons 262
  Cups or Patty Shells 265
  French 263
  Melba 264
  Melba Bowknots 264
  Melba Cheese 264
  Milk 264
  Puffy French 264
  Rolls, Asparagus 1313
  Sausage 1230
  Skillet, John Bixby 265
Toasted Almonds 415
Toaster 1426
Toasties, Cheese 446
Toffee
  Oatmeal 412
  Old English Nut 413
Tomato
  Anchovy Salad 1153
  and Cabbage Soup 1275
  and Lettuce Salad 1153
  and Onion Salad 1154
  Avocado Shrimp Salad 1184
  Bouillon, Hot 1290
  Bouillon, Jellied 1291
  Buttermilk 227
  Casserole, French Corn and 1342
  Catchup, Uncooked 1110
  Cheese Canapés 185
  Cheese Fondue 437
  Cups, Baked Beans in 1319
  Cups, Baked Eggs in 664
  Egg and Sardine Salad 1183
  French Dressing 1202
  Fried, Sandwich 1216
  Green and Onion Slices 1406
  Green, Pie 1016
  Green, Stew 819
  Grill, Sausage Bacon and 872
  Juice Cocktail 198
  Juice Cocktail Yogurt 198
  Macaroni, Green Pepper Casserole 1408
  Macaroni Medley Beef 821
  Milk 227

Okra Soup, Quick 1296
Preserves, Red and Yellow 1094
Rabbit 447
Salad, Stuffed 1153
Salad, Shrimp and 1191
Salad with Cucumber Dressing 1154
Sandwich, Olive and 1224
Sandwich Spread, Cheese 446
Sandwiches, Cheese and 1233
Sandwiches, Lettuce, Bacon and 1224
Sandwiches, Swiss Cheese, Ham 1236
Sardine Top Salad 1183
Sauce 1261
Sauce, Chicken Filled Pancakes 1052
Sauce, Lobster, Stuffed Eggs in 670
Scramble 676
Soup, Cold 1290
Soup, Cream of 1282
Soup, Cream of Corn 1279
Spliced, Salad 1154
Stuffed Cheese Vegetable Salad 1181
Stuffed Kidney Bean Salad 1193
Stuffed Pea, Cheese Salad 1182
Stuffed with Tuna Salad 1194
Supreme, Sandwich, Ham and 1234
Tomato Aspics 1170
  Cottage Cheese in 1168
  Creamy 1168
  Salad 1171
  Shrimp in 1160
Tomato juice 1081. *See Tomatoes*
Tomatoes
  Ascorbic acid (vit. C) value 19, *buying, care* 88, 142, *caloric value* 14, *canning of juice* 1079, *cooking methods* 1307, *in diet* 3, 5, *selecting* 1402, *vitamin values* 22, 26, 27
  Baked 1404
  Baked Beans with 1320
  Baked Stuffed 1402, 1403
  Braised Liver with Rice and 904
  Broiled Stuffed 1406
  Chicken and, Sautéed with Mushroom Sauce 1058
  Eggs poached in 674
  Escalloped, No. 1 and 2 1404, 1405
  for Vegetable Plate 1410
  Fried Pennsylvania Dutch Style 1405
  Green Fried 1405
  Hamburger Rolls with 826
  Herb 1407
  Minted 1407
  New Cabbage with 1331
  New Mexican 1407
  Okra and 1358
  Pan-Broiled 1406
  Parsnips and 1366
  Stewed 1408
Tomcod, *cooking methods* 693
Tongs 1426
Tongue
  Characteristics 891, *cooking methods,*

Tongue—(Cont'd)
   time 891, 892, *cleaning, cooking tongue* 409, *vitamin values* 21, 23, 25, *Boiled and How to Slice It* 909, *Suggestions for Serving* 910
   Cold Jellied 910
   Filling for Sandwiches 1212, 1231
   in Aspic, Chicken and 1156
   Sandwich, open face 1236
Toppings, Cake 381
   Baked 395
   Broiled 396
   Cocoa Whipped Cream 396
   Crispy for Vanilla Pudding 631
   Gelatin Whipped Cream 396
   Nut, Crispy for Sundaes 646
   Plain Whipped Cream 397
Torte
   Blitz 375
   Dobos 376
   Graham Cracker 377
   Schaum 378
Tri-Color Fruit Mold 1167
Tripe 910
   Cooking methods 891, *discussion, varieties* 910
   à la Creole 910
   De Luxe 911
Trout
   Lake, Sea, *cooking methods* 692, 693
Tularemia 742
Tulip Salad 1123
Tuna
   Cooking methods 693, *information on* 693, *niacin (nicotinic acid) value* 25
   and Celery Fondue 733
   and Egg à la King 733
   and Noodle Casserole 733
   and Noodle Casserole Supreme 734
   Canapé Filling 189
   Creamed 732
   Cucumber Sandwich 1220
   Filling, for Sandwich 1213
   Olive Canapés 185
   Salad 1194, 1195
   Salad, Tomato Stuffed with 1194
   Sandwiches, Ham and 1234
   Soufflé 681
   Spread for Sandwiches 1221
   Turnovers 734
Turkey 1068
   Facts you should know 1068, *gizzard test for cooking time* 1068, *how to carve* 1075, 1076, 1077, *storage of leftover* 1069, *market forms of* 1068, *tests for doneness* 1070, *time table for roasting* 1070, *vitamin values of* 21, 23
   à la King 1071
   Bread Stuffing for 1072
   Croquettes 1047
   Gravy 1070
   Hash 1071

   Roast 1069
   "Roast" Old Time 1071
   Salad 1195
   Soup, No. 1 and 2 1297
   Turnovers 1071
Turmeric, *description and uses* 133
Turn-Once-A-Day Pickles 1105
Turnip Greens
   Ascorbic acid (vit. C) value 20, *buying, care* 83, *cooking methods* 1307 (*see Spinach*), *in diet* 4
   with Bacon-Onion Sauce 1353
Turnips (*see Rutabagas*)
   Ascorbic acid, value 20, *buying, care* 88, *cooking methods* 1307, *in diet* 4
   and Pascal Celery Salad, Apple 1135
   Carrot Salad, Hot 1132
   white, buttered 1390
Turnovers
   Apple 935
   Beef or Chicken 837
   Tuna 734
   Turkey 1071
Turtle
   How to dress 781, *food species of* 781,
   Soup, No. 1 and 2 781, 782
Twin Mountain Muffins 258
Two Egg Cake, Basic 326–329

U

Uncooked Cream Mints 419
Upside-Down Cake 362–363
Upside-Down Puddings 616–617
U. S. Government grades of meat 790, 791
   grades for poultry 1028
   inspection of meat 789

V

Vanilla
   Extract 133
   Bavarian 583
   Crisps 470
   Sauce 1249, 1250
   Sauce, Creamy 1242
   Wafer Pastry Shell 931
Vanilla Ice Cream, No. 1 and 2 599
   Old-Fashioned 600
Vanilla Pudding with Crispy Topping 631
Van's Pickles 1105
VARIETY MEATS 890–911
   Brains, Heads, Kidneys, Liver, Sweetbreads, Tongue, Tripe, characteristics 891, *cooking methods* 891, *cooking time of* 892
Variety, through use of menus 37
Veal 875–886
   Time tables for braising and roasting 875, *do not broil* 793, *caloric value* 14, *cuts* 874, *servings per pound* 158, *protein*

Veal—(Cont'd)
  value 15, U. S. Government grades 791,
  vitamin values 21, 23, 25
  à la King 883
  Baked in Milk 882
  Balls, Barbecued 885
  Birds or Stuffed Rolls 878
  Blanquette of 876
  Braised Shoulder Steak 875
  Breaded Chops 876
  Breast of, Stuffed 878
  Burgers 885
  Chop Suey 882
  Chops in Sour Cream 882
  Fricassee 879
  Loaf 885
  Loaf, Jellied 883
  Mock Chicken Legs 870
  Paprika 879
  Parmigiano 880
  Patties 886
  Pot Roast of 876
  Pot Roast with Apple Dressing 877
  Scallopini 880
  Steak, De Luxe 881
  Steaks, Savory 877
  Stew 883
  Stew, Savory 884
  Stuffed Rolls 878
  Stuffed Shoulder 879
  Sub Gum 881
Vegetable
  Cheese, Stuffed Tomato Salad 1181
  Chili Sauce 1109
  Chowder, Summer 1275
  Creole Sauce 1261
  Egg Salad 1183
  Egg Sandwich 1225
  Finger Salads 1144
  Pickles 1100
  Pie, Beef and 816
  Plates 1410
  Salad, molded 1169
  Salads 1144
  Sandwiches 1221
  Slaw 1180
  Soup 1298
    Beef 1287
    Cream of 1283
    Liver and, soup 1293
  Spread, mixed 1224
VEGETABLES 1304–1411
  Boiling of, green 1304, quick cooking
  1306, red 1305, strong-juiced 1306, white
  1306, yellow 1305, braising of 1308,
  canned, care of 144, preparing 1308,
  serving of 1308, cooking of 1304, to pre-
  serve minerals 1308, to preserve vitamins
  1306, dehydrated and dried 78, 100,
  dried, storage of 101, federal grades of
  79, fresh, care of 140, fresh, hints on

buying 101, frozen, care of 145, green
and yellow, alternates in 4, guide for
buying 79, in children's diet 34, in diet
pattern 3, iodine in 687, 688, market
season of 79, methods of cooking 1307,
"non-acid", preparing home canned 1411,
other than green and yellow alternates
in 4, per cent waste 79, pot liquor from
1307, purchase unit of 79, quality stand-
ards 79, references on buying 75, root,
care of 143, steaming of, discussion 1308,
storage of, and yield per unit 79
  Beef Pot Roast with 807
  Braised Lamb, with 843
  Creamed 1397
  Fritter Batter 1349
  Lamb Shanks with 845
  Liver and Baked 903
  Macedoine of, Beef Pot Roast with 807
  Spanish 1409
  Spring with Buttermilk Sauce 1410
Velouté Sauce 1261
Velva Fruit 602
Venison
  Qualities of 749
  Braised, in Mushroom Gravy 749
  Broiled Tenderloin of 750
  Chops, Pan-Broiled 750
  Gravy for 752, 765
  Loaf 751
  Loin Roast 751
  Patties in Onion Gravy 751
  Pot Pie 752
  Steak, Swissed Round 761
  Stew, De Luxe 753
  Tenderloin, Barbecued 750
Vermicelli
  form and ingredients 422
Vichyssoise
  Curried 1299
  Soup 1298
Vienna
  Bread 267
  Rolls 268
  Tarts 494
Vinaigrette Sauce 1262
Vinegar
  Flavored, how made, how used 135,
  strengths of 135
  Cider, Malt, Wine 135
  Pie 981
Vitamin A
  Daily allowances 8, 27, daily allowances
  for 27, effects of cooking on 27, effects
  of lack of 28, functions in body 28, in
  fish 687, sources of 27
Vitamin B-complex
  Biotin, effect of raw egg white on 659,
  in fish 687
Vitamin B1
  Daily allowance 21, effects on of cooking

Vitamin B₁—(Cont'd)
21, *functions of in body* 22, *mg., daily allowances* 8, *table, sources of* 21
Vitamin B₂
Effects on in cooking 23, *functions of* 24
Vitamin C
Daily allowance 19, *effects of cooking, storage on* 19, *function of* 20, *values of foods (Table)* 19
Vitamin concentrates 29
Vitamin D
Daily allowance 8, *(sunshine vitamin) importance to children, adults* 28, *in fish* 687
Vitamin fad, harmful practice 29
Vitamin G, *functions of* 24
Vitamin K, *how supplied* 9
Vitamins
Adequate amounts of 16–18, *children's need for* 16–18, *food sources of* 17, *in pot liquor* 1307, *kinds of* 16–18, *sensitivity to alkalies* 32, *solubility in water* 32, *use of in body* 6, *variations in amounts in foods* 17–18, *ways to preserve in foods* 32
Vol-au-Vents 938

W

Waffle iron, cleaning, treatment 259, 1426
Waffles 258–261
Characteristics and rules for baking 258, *irons for* 259
Waldorf
Fennel Salad 1149
Kohlrabi 1151
Pineapple 1141
Salad 1144
Walnut
Black, extract 134, *cups per pound* 159, *thiamine (vit. B₁), value* 22
Sticks, Cookies 461
Washington Pie 322, 332
Waste, avoidance of 73
Water
For pastry 923, *use of in body* 6
Yeast Dough 267
Watercress
Buying, care 83, *caloric value* 14, *in diet* 4
and Bacon Sandwiches 1225
and Potato Soup 1276
Salad 1121
Sandwiches 1225
Sandwiches, Peanut Butter and 1232
Sauce, Hard Cooked Eggs with 699
Watermelon
Caloric value of 14, *vitamin A value of* 28, *buying and care of* 89
Pickles 1099

Weakfish, *cooking methods* 693
Wedding Menus, Vol. I, xxvii
Weight, table of children's growth 10
Weights and measurements, equivalent, table of 154
Welsh Rabbit 453
Wheat
Niacin *(nicotinic acid) value* 25, *shredded, thiamine (vit. B₁), value* 22, *whole or cracked, thiamine (vit. B₁) value* 22
Cereals 421
Whole Biscuits 237
Wheel, diet 7
Whipped Cream Salad Dressing 1207
Whips
Apple Snow 649
Apricot or Prune 655
Baked Apricot 652
Mocha 585
Peanut Brittle 653
Pineapple Date 654
Prune 655
Prune, Baked 654
White
Buttermilk cupcakes 359
Cupcakes 359
Perch, *cooking methods* 693
Sauces 1262
White Layer Cake
Bride's—4 Tier 341
Buttermilk, 3 and 4 Egg Whites 341
Sweet Milk, 3 and 4 Egg Whites 340
Whipped Cream 346
Whitefish
Cooking methods for 694, 698, 701
Baked Stuffed 698, 702
Whiting, *cooking methods* 693
Whole
Meal Fruit Platter 1172
Meal Sandwiches 1236
Meal Tossed Salad No. 1 and 2 1195, 1196
Whole grain, enriched cereals, iron value of 30
Whole Wheat
Biscuits 237
Bread, 100% 302
Bread, 50% 302
Muffins or Graham Gems 256
Pastry 933
Wilted Lettuce 1133
Winter Salad Platter 1172
Wintergreen extract 134
Wolfish, *cooking methods for* 693
Woman
Dietary needs 8, *lactating, dietary needs* 8, *pregnant, dietary needs* 8
Woodchuck, *cookery* 780
Woodchuck Pie 780
Wor Mein, chicken 1056

Y

Yams, *in diet* 5
 Orange Casserole 1389
Yeast
 Compressed 114, *dry granular* 115,
 Package sizes 267
Yeast Bread Doughs, *see Bread
 Chart for elaboration* 266, *ingredients*
 232, *steps in making* 270, *types* 265,
 water 267
Yeast Doughs—Special Recipes
 Buckwheat cakes, Grandma's 305
 English muffins 306
 Stollen 307
Yeast Roll Doughs 273

Yellow Cupcakes 360
Yellowtail, *cooking methods* 693
Yogurt 117
 Salad Dressing 1207
 Tomato Juice Cocktail 198
Yorkshire Pudding, Short Ribs and 812
Youngberries
 Buying and care of 90
 Jelly 1080
 Juice 1080

Z

Zucchini for Vegetable Plate 1410
Zucchini Squash, Braised 1402